Jane Austen

A Literary Reference to Her Life and Work

WILLIAM BAKER

Facts On File

An imprint of Infobase Publishing

Critical Companion to Jane Austen

Facts On File, Inc.
An imprint of Infobase Publishing
132 West 31st Street
New York NY 10001

Library of Congress Cataloging-in-Publication Data
Baker, William, 1944–
Critical companion to Jane Austen: a literary reference to her life and work / William Baker.
p. cm.
Includes bibliographical references and index.
ISBN-13: 978-0-8160-6416-8 (acid-free paper)
1. Austen, Jane, 1775–1817. I. Title.
PR4036.B255 2007
823'.7—dc22   2006102848

Facts On File books are available at special discounts when purchased in bulk quantities for businesses, associations, institutions, or sales promotions. Please call our Special Sales Department in New York at (212) 967-8800 or (800) 322-8755.

You can find Facts On File on the World Wide Web at http://www.factsonfile.com

Text design by Erika K. Arroyo
Cover design by Salvatore Luongo

Printed in the United States of America

VB Hermitage 10 9 8 7 6 5 4 3 2 1

This book is printed on acid-free paper.

To the memory of my beloved mother,
Mabel (Woolf) Baker (1908–1992),
who introduced me to Jane Austen and great literature.
Her price is far above rubies.

CONTENTS

ACKNOWLEDGMENTS

Special thanks are due to Jeff Soloway, my superb editor, who encouraged this book from its very beginnings and has been a source of eminently sensible advice and suggestions throughout. The copy editor at Facts On File is blessed with an eagle eye. Professor Donald Hawes read most of the book in its various stages and supplied many wise suggestions.

Thanks are also due to the staff at the wonderful Information Delivery Services (IDS) at Northern Illinois University Founders Memorial Library. They kept me supplied with books and articles, as did Professor John Peters of the University of North Texas, book review editor of *Studies in the Novel*; Tony Chalcraft, editor of *Reference Reviews*; and Rebecca Bartlett and Carolyn Wilcox at *Choice*. Successive deans of the Northern Illinois University Libraries, Dr. Arthur Young and Mary Munroe, proved most sympathetic to this project, as did Charles Larry, head of the Department of Social Sciences and Humanities, and Professor Deborah Holdstein, then chair of the Department of English at Northern Illinois University. The graduate director of the Department of English, Professor Philip E. Eubanks, provided the opportunity in spring of 2006 to teach a graduate course on Jane Austen. My graduate students in English 607 taught me much about differing perspectives on Jane Austen.

Special thanks must also go to Professor Joseph Wiesenfarth. I have always gained much from his encouragement, wisdom, and work. Special thanks are also due to Jayne Crosby-Lindner, who, with patience and good humor, word processed my chicken scratch. Most illustrations in the text are in the public domain; or, where they are not, specific acknowledgment is given. In the writing of this book, I am deeply indebted for the work of many scholars and critics who have written about Jane Austen. From them, indeed, much has been learned, and I am honored to join their august company. Last but by no means least, my indebtedness to my wife, Rivka, is beyond words: Without her, this work would not have been written.

INTRODUCTION

This *Critical Companion* represents a personal odyssey. Since childhood, I have had an abiding interest in, and enthusiasm for, the work of Jane Austen. Her writing still speaks to me and to countless others of all ages and nationalities, as she is concerned with universal themes, such as love, marriage, property, relationships, human survival, the place of the individual in the wider community, growing up, and so much more.

There is no doubt that Jane Austen's work appeals to something deep in us all. For some, her novels conjure a world now gone forever, a universe of stately homes, gardens, and ways of appropriate and inappropriate behavior—a world of order and stability. For others, her novels represent technical innovation, stylistic brilliance, and a wonderful way with words. Still others see Austen as a radical among her contemporaries, attacking chauvinistic attitudes toward women and exposing colonial exploitation and sexual immorality. Her characters have enraged and engaged: Houses and pets have been named after them. For the English poet and critic, W. H. Auden (1907–73), Jane Austen was not simply a stuffy intellectual. Indeed, he wrote about her in a poem:

> You could not shock her more than she shocks
>   me . . .
> It makes me most uncomfortable to see
> An English spinster of the middle class
> Describe the amorous effects of "brass,"
> Reveal so frankly and with such sobriety
> The economic basis of society.

At the start of the 21st century, Jane Austen is still a hot commodity. In the United Kingdom and Commonwealth countries such as Australia, New Zealand, and Canada, the 2005 book *So You Think You Know Jane Austen? A Literary Handbook* was a best seller. This book was presided over by, according to its blurb, "Ace literary detective turned quizmaster John Sutherland and Austen buff Deirdre Le Faye." (The former, an eminent scholar critic, is Chair of Judges for the Booker Prize and the latter a renowned Austen scholar.) Austen is also a perennial favorite for film adaptations. The "Internet Movie Database" (IMDb) records that between the years 1940 and 2007 there have been 34 adaptations of Jane Austen.

How to Use This Book

The aim of this book is to help readers and students of Jane Austen in their endeavor to enjoy and understand her work and to make sense of the vast amount of literature on her. The book also provides scholars and advanced students with a convenient, accessible reference source.

The essays in the book supply critical information on a diverse range of topics directly related to the study of Jane Austen's life and work, including the publication and critical history of her novels, as well as her characters, family, friends, themes, ideas, influence, and much more. Further, this book combines plot synopses with accessible, yet detailed, critical analysis and commentary. *Critical Companion to Jane Austen* provides a research companion to enrich a reader's experience and to encourage users to revisit Jane Austen's wonderful writing.

Part I of the book contains a biographical essay covering Jane Austen's life and career from birth to death, as well as her family and other people associated with her. Part II contains detailed essays on all of Jane Austen's writings, including her six novels, her other posthumously published prose, letters, juvenilia, poetry, and more. Entries on important works cover the origins of the work, the publication history, initial and later reactions to the work, and afterlife. Detailed, critical synopses examine each chapter of the work, and a critical essay discusses central critical concerns, crucial historical and thematic information, and relevant scholarship. Subentries on characters in each work appear in a section at the end of each entry. A further reading list is also provided.

Part III of the book contains essays on people, places, themes, topics, and other information important to an understanding of Austen's life and work. Part IV contains appendixes, including a chronology of key events of Jane Austen's life and work, an up-to-date bibliography of the most useful primary texts, and secondary sources, including books and articles.

To indicate a cross-reference, any name or term that appears as an entry in Part III is printed on first appearance as an entry in SMALL CAPITAL LETTERS.

Note that the standard scholarly edition of Jane Austen's writings was prepared in the period following World War I and was edited by the Oxford scholar R. W. Chapman and largely published in the 1920s. *The Cambridge Edition of the Works of Jane Austen* will replace this: The first of its projected nine volumes appeared in 2005.

A NOTE ON TEXTS, ABBREVIATIONS, AND ONLINE RESOURCES

References to Jane Austen's writings are from R. W. Chapman's Oxford University Press edition of *The Novels of Jane Austen* (vols. 1–5, 3rd edition, 1933 and subsequent revisions and reprints) and *Minor Works* (vol. 6, 1954 and subsequent revisions and reprints). *The Cambridge Edition of the Works of Jane Austen* (9 vols., 2005–) appeared too late to be included as the base text in *Critical Companion to Jane Austen*. Citations to the "Juvenilia" are from *Minor Works*. Other textual references are clearly indicated in the reading lists following each entry. Page numbers are inserted directly into the text, and the following abbreviations are used if necessary:

Emma (E)
Mansfield Park (MP)
Minor Works (MW)
Northanger Abbey (NA)
Persuasion (P)
Pride and Prejudice (P&P)
Sense and Sensibility (SS)

Readers with other editions of Jane Austen may locate quotations easily electronically by using only online texts, such as those found at the following links: http://www.pemberley.com/janeinfor/novlsrch.html.

References to *Jane Austen's Letters* are indicated as *Letters* and are from the third edition of Deirdre Le Faye's *Jane Austen's Letters* (Oxford: Oxford University Press, 1995), J. E. Austen-Leigh's *A Memoir of Jane Austen and Other Family Recollections* (Kathryn Sutherland, ed. Oxford: Oxford University Press, 2002) is referred to as *Memoir* (M).

The following abbreviations refer to works about Jane Austen: again, they and other references are clearly indicated in the reading lists following each entry.

Gilson: Gilson, David. *A Bibliography of Jane Austen*. Winchester and New Castle, Del.: St. Paul's Bibliographies, Oak Knoll Press, 1997.

Hardy: Hardy, Barbara. *A Reading of Jane Austen*. London: Peter Owen, 1975.

Family Record (FR): Le Faye, Deirdre. *Jane Austen: A Family Record*. Second Edition. Cambridge: Cambridge University Press, 2004.

Jane Austen: Le Faye, Deirdre. *Jane Austen: The World of Her Novels*. New York: Harry N. Abrams, 2002.

Page: Page, Norman. *The Language of Jane Austen*. Oxford: Basil Blackwell, 1972.

Phillipps: Phillipps, K. C. *Jane Austen's English*. London: Andre Deutsch, 1970.

Critical Heritage, I, II: Southam, Brian C., ed. *Jane Austen: The Critical Heritage*. 2 vols. London: Routledge & Keegan Paul, 1979, 1987.

Literary Manuscripts: Southern, Brian C., ed. *Jane Austen's Literary Manuscripts: A Study of the Novelist's Development through the Surviving Papers*. 1964; rev. edn., London: Athlone Press, 2001.

Textual Lives: Sutherland, Kathryn. *Jane Austen's Textual Lives from Aeschylus to Bollywood*. Oxford: Oxford University Press, 2005.

These and other references found at the conclusion of entries in a *Critical Companion to Jane Austen* are also included in the bibliography at the conlusion of this book.

Austen Internet Resources

Two Internet sites devoted to Jane Austen seem to be stable (as of 2007) and are very helpful. The Republic of Pemberley (www.pemberley.com) provides a "discussion group and information on the works, life and culture of Jane Austen" and much more, including an index to where words and phrases may be found in her work, and a guide to Jane Austen locations.

The Jane Austen Society of North America (www.jasna.org) maintains a Web site "devoted to the appreciation and study of Jane Austen and her writing." Its "publications section offers dozens of articles and book reviews on her writing, life and times, all of which can be searched on line." The society also publishes *Persuasions,* an excellent source for "Austen studies, featuring essays about Jane Austen's work and world." *Persuasions On-Line* is the Internet version of the journal.

General Internet Resources

The following Internet resources, although general, are very helpful for students of Jane Austen. Access to them may require a subscription.

The Modern Language Association (MLA) International Bibliography (http://www.mla.org) Web site "offers a detailed bibliography of journal articles, books and dissertations." Produced by the Modern Language Association, "the electronic version of the bibliography dates back to the 1920s." Clicking onto "Austen, Jane," as a subject or author, provides many books and articles on or by Jane Austen. On the whole, this site is enumerative; it lists items, provides their publication details, and sometimes full text coverage: It is not evaluative.

The Annual Bibliography of English Language and Literature (ABELL) (http://collections. chadwyck.com) Web site is essentially the British equivalent of the MLA Bibliography and also is not evaluative; however, it is more comprehensive in its review coverage.

Years Work in English Studies (YWES) (http://www.ywes.oupjournals.org) provides evaluative assessments of criticism and scholarship. The coverage is annual and comprehensive.

Internet Movie Database (IMDb) (http://www.imdb.com) is an excellent resource for movies of Jane Austen's work and other movies based on the life of Jane Austen. Searches are by title, person, character, key word, and plot summary. Entries vary in content; some are fuller than others. It also includes some reviews of movies.

PART I

Biography

Jane Austen

(1775–1817)

Jane Austen's afterlife is easier to document than her actual life. The paucity of biographical information on her is limited and largely dependent on family records. As the author of NORTHANGER ABBEY (written 1798–99), SENSE AND SENSIBILITY (written 1795, 1797–98, 1809–10), PRIDE AND PREJUDICE (written 1796–97, 1811–12), EMMA (written 1814–15), and PERSUASION (written 1815–16), she has a secure reputation within the literary pantheon. In the 19th century, her novels were translated into various European languages, including French, German, Danish, Russian, and Swedish. In the following century, there was an avalanche of translations into many languages. These parallel the more than 100 books and stories serving as sequels, prequels, retellings, and spin-offs existing by the mid-1990s, a period that witnessed innumerable films, television and, also in the early years of the 21st century, video adaptations (see FILMS AND ADAPTATIONS).

Born Jane Austen at the parsonage in the tiny Hampshire village of Steventon on December 16, 1775, she was the seventh child in a family of eight. Her father, the Reverend GEORGE AUSTEN (1731–1805), was the local rector. From a prosperous and well-educated Kent family, he went to St. John's College, Oxford, graduating in 1760 with a degree in divinity. Family connections secured him the Steventon living. He married CASSANDRA AUSTEN (1739–1827, née Leigh) on April 26, 1764. She was from a distinguished lineage: One of her ancestors founded St. John's College, Oxford. Jane Austen's brothers were able to attend this college on scholarships because of the family connection. Between 1765 and 1779, the Reverend George and his wife Cassandra produced eight children—seven of these were born at Steventon parsonage, family home for 33 years until the Reverend Austen retired and in 1801 moved to Bath, a traumatic move for Jane Austen.

Family records and Jane Austen's surviving letters suggest that the family was closely knit. Jane was very close to her only sister, Cassandra, three

Engraving of Jane Austen modeled after the frontispiece to J. E. Austen-Leigh's *A Memoir of Jane Austen,* 1870

years older than herself. In spring 1783, when she was seven years old, Jane and Cassandra, with Jane Cooper, their cousin, were sent to away to a school in Oxford run by a Mrs. Cawley, Jane Cooper's aunt. Following a typhus fever outbreak at the school during the summer of 1783, Mrs. Cawley moved her school to Southampton, on the Hampshire coast, and after falling seriously ill, the girls returned home. Jane Cooper's mother, Jane and Cassandra's maternal aunt, died from typhus fever in October 1783. Two years later, in spring 1785, Jane and Cassandra were sent to a school in Reading that they attended until the end of 1786.

Jane, as James Edward Austen-Leigh's (1798–1874) *Memoir* of her and her letters provide witness, was also close to her fourth brother, HENRY THOMAS AUSTEN. In common with the eldest brother, James, he went to St. John's College, Oxford. James and Henry, with her father, continued Jane's education at home. Two of her brothers, FRANCIS (1774–1865) and CHARLES (1779–1852),

Map of Hampshire, from *The English Atlas by Laurie & Whittle,* 1807

her fifth and her youngest brothers, joined the navy and both reached the rank of admiral. Jane read voraciously at home in Shakespeare, English history and fiction, contemporary fiction, and the 18th-century philosophers, moralists, and poets. Although the family was far from wealthy, her father being a rector, she was surrounded by books and by intellectual and cultural conversation. Family favorites included the fiction of SAMUEL RICHARDSON and HENRY FIELDING, LAURENCE STERNE, Tobias Smollett, and OLIVER GOLDSMITH's four-volume *The History of England, from the Earliest Times to the Death of George II* (1771), among other works readily available to the young Jane Austen.

According to family tradition, her elder brother James shaped and directed his sister's reading. Her father had accumulated by 1801 a library of approximately 500 volumes to which his children had access. Her brother Henry is quoted in the *Memoir* as remembering that "at a very early age [Jane Austen] was enamoured of Gilpin (1724–1804) on the Picturesque. . . . Her reading was very extensive in history and belles lettres; her memory extremely tenacious. Her favorite moral writers were SAMUEL JOHNSON in prose and WILLIAM COWPER in verse (140–141). Jane Austen's own copy of the second volume of Johnson's *Rasselas* survives and demonstrates that she knew the work from an early age. Richardson's *SIR CHARLES GRANDISON* she continuously reread; consequently "all that was ever said or done in the cedar parlour, was familiar to her; and the wedding days of Lady L. and Lady G. were as well remembered as if they had been living friends" (71).

In addition to reading, she and Cassandra would have learned to sew and embroider, and Jane became very adept at satin stitching. A family passion was theatrical performance. Neighbors were recruited into Steventon dramatic performances. The rectory barn became a small theater during the summers, and over Christmas and the New Year plays were performed in the Rectory itself—in addition to innumerable card games and charades. The theatricals started in 1784 with R. B. SHERIDAN's *The Rivals* and Thomas Francklin's *Matilda*. On March 22, 1788, Henry Fielding's parody of the contemporary theater, *The Tragedy of Tragedies, or The Life and Death of Tom Thumb the Great*, initially written in 1731, was performed before a small group of selected friends. "Cassandra and Jane might then have been Queen Dollalolla and Princess Huncamunca respectively" (*FR*, 63). The final performance appears to have taken place in January 1790 when Jane was just 14. Some biographers have speculated that Jane may have helped James, who was 10 years older than she, and Henry Austen with a humorous weekly newspaper they founded and largely contributed to during their Oxford days, *The Loiterer*. The paper ran for 60 issues from January 31, 1789, to March 20, 1790—Jane being about 15 at the time (M: 16, 204 n 16).

Jane Austen appears to have written from a very young age, and the earliest writings to survive, her Juvenilia begin in 1787, when she was 11. For the following six years until June 1793, she wrote sketches and over 20 pieces, many of them parodies of her reading, which are transcribed into her three manuscript notebooks, referred to as *Volume the First, Volume the Second,* and *Volume the Third*. In July and August 1788, her parents visited relations in Kent, taking Jane and Cassandra with them, returning via London. This probably was the source for "The BEAUTIFULL CASSANDRA," set in London and found in *Volume the First*. In the same collection the short play "The MYSTERY" is dedicated to her father and perhaps may have been part of a 1788 family theatrical exhibition. "SIR WILLIAM MOUNTAGUE," dedicated to her younger brother CHARLES as "an unfinished performance," refers to "Monday, which was the first of September" (MW: 40–41). This date is correct for 1788. Her fifth brother, FRANCIS WILLIAM (b. 1774), had left home in April 1786 to join the Royal Naval Academy in Portsmouth. From December 22, 1789, to November 5, 1791, he served as a midshipman aboard HMS *Perseverance*. The very short tale "The ADVENTURES OF MR HARLEY" and the parody "JACK & ALICE, A NOVEL" are dedicated to Francis "on board . . . the Perseverance" (MW: 40) and far away at sea.

In 1790, Jane was in her 15th year. The first item in *Volume the Second,* her burlesque of fiction, "LOVE

AND FREINDSHIP," is dated at its conclusion Sunday June 13, 1790. It is dedicated to her cousin ELIZABETH ("ELIZA") HANCOCK MADAME LA CONTESSE DE FEUILLIDE (1761–1813), who in 1781 married Jean Capot de Feuillide, destined to be guillotined in February 1794. Jane's burlesques of the themes of love and friendship are placed on firmer foundations in 1791. Her third brother, EDWARD (1767–1852), became the first of the Austen sons to marry, becoming engaged on March 1, 1791, to Elizabeth Bridges (1773–1808). Since 1783 he had lived with distant wealthy relatives at Godmersham Park in Kent, subsequently frequently visited by Jane Austen. During 1791 two of Elizabeth's sister, Fanny and Sophia, married. On December 27, 1791, at Goodnestone near Godmersham, Elizabeth married Jane's brother Edward, and Elizabeth's sister Sophia married William Deedes. *The THREE SISTERS*, an unfinished novel in letters focusing on three squabbling sisters lacking in manners or social graces, is dedicated to "Edward Austen" and usually attributed to a 1792 date—it is included in her *Volume the First*. In 1791, Jane's eldest brother, James, who in the spring of the previous year had moved back to the Steventon area from Oxford to become a curate, became the vicar of Sherborne St. John near Basingstoke. In 1792, he married the older Anne Mathew (1759–95), daughter of a general who had returned from service in the West Indies. Also in 1791, in July, the youngest of the boys, Charles, left home at age 12 to follow his brother Francis to the Portsmouth Royal Naval Academy and a life at sea.

From 1791 to 1796, Jane and Cassandra had the Rectory to themselves, although their father continued to take in boy boarders whom he tutored. On November 26, 1791, Jane completed her parody of Goldsmith's *History of England*. She dedicated to Cassandra "The HISTORY OF ENGLAND FROM THE REIGN OF HENRY THE 4TH TO THE DEATH OF CHARLES THE 1ST," found in *Volume the Second*. Her close friend Mary Lloyd (1771–1843), who subsequently became the second wife of Jane's brother James, lived near the Austens at Deane parsonage, rented from Jane's father in spring 1789. Mary, her sister, and her mother moved near Andover in Hampshire in January 1792. Jane presented Mary with a needlework bag and accompanying verse

dated "January 1792." Jane's unfinished fantasy fiction *EVELYN* is dedicated to "Miss Mary Lloyd" and found in *Volume the Third* given to Jane by her father on May 6, 1792. It is followed by CATHARINE, OR THE BOWER, dedicated to her sister Cassandra, dated August 1792, and considered to be the most mature example of her "Juvenilia."

On February 26, 1792, her father's younger sister PHILADELPHIA HANCOCK (1730–92) died after a serious illness, probably breast cancer. She had an adventurous life, being sent to India to be married off (rather in the manner of Cecilia Wynne in Jane Austen's *Catharine*), where she married Tysoe Saul Hancock (1711–75), an East India Company surgeon. They moved to Calcutta, where she became friendly with Warren Hastings (1732–1818), subsequently the governor-general of India (1773–85). He became the subject of an impeachment trial in England (1788–95). There was a rumor that Philadelphia's daughter Elizabeth Hancock, Jane's first cousin, was Hastings's illegitimate daughter. He was her godfather and in 1775 settled a large sum of money on her. In June 1765, the Hancocks returned to London. From 1777 to 1779, Philadelphia and her daughter visited Germany and Belgium. They settled in Paris, and in 1781 Elizabeth married Jean Capot de Feuillide (1750–94), a soldier and self-styled comte. In 1786, Elizabeth gave birth to her only child, Hastings, in London. She participated in the Steventon Christmas theatricals, nursed her mother, and cared for her disabled son. She was in Paris when the French Revolution broke out in 1789, and from 1792 until her death became associated with the Austen family circle. Her husband was guillotined in Paris by the revolutionaries on February 22, 1794. From around 1795, a relationship between her and Jane's fourth and favorite brother, Henry, developed or was renewed as Henry stayed with her in London when he was 15. They married in London on December 31, 1797.

Also in late August 1792, another death occurred, that of Dr. Edward Cooper. His daughter Jane (1771–98) came to stay at Steventon rectory until her marriage in December 1792. Jane Austen dedicated her parody of sentiment fiction *HENRY AND ELIZA, A NOVEL* to Jane Cooper. Appearing in

Volume the First, this piece of juvenilia is attributed to the beginning of 1789. She also dedicated the "Collection of Letters" in *Volume the Second* to Jane Cooper, probably during the autumn of 1792 when she was staying at Steventon.

In the late summer of 1792, Jane visited her friends the Lloyds at their new home. The same autumn, not yet 17, she made her debut dancing at Enham, near Andover, and at Hurstbourne Park nearby. Writing to her sister Cassandra eight years later on Thursday and Friday November 20 and 21, 1800, she recognized "the two Miss Coxes . . . I traced in one the remains of the vulgar, broad featured girl who danced at Enham eight years ago." Further, she "had the comfort of finding out the other evening who all the fat girls with short noses were that disturbed me at the 1st H. Ball" (*L,* 61, 63).

Jane herself between 1792 and 1795 was described by a Mrs. Mitford as "the prettiest, silliest, most affected, husband-hunting butterfly she ever remembered" (*FR,* 81). In 1792 Cassandra became engaged to a former pupil of her father, TOM FOWLE. The marriage was delayed owing to financial reasons, and he died in 1797. On January 23, 1793, Jane became an aunt for the first time. Her brother Edward's daughter FRANCES (FANNY) CATHERINE (d. 1882) was born. Fanny became the dedicatee of Jane Austen's five pieces on nonsense known as "Scraps" and included in *Volume the Second* of her Juvenilia. Also early in 1793, on April 15 to be precise, her brother James's wife, Anne, gave birth to JUNE ANNA ELIZABETH—she recorded her memories of the Austen family many years later.

In winter 1793, Francis (Frank) returned to Steventon from the Far East. He left home at the age of 12, became at the age of 18 a naval lieutenant, and returned home briefly after a seven-year absence. Probably Francis escorted his sisters Cassandra and Jane to Southampton in December 1793, where they danced at the Assembly Ball. Jane remembered 15 years later with pleasure the ball (letter to Cassandra, December 9, 1808: *L,* 156). In addition to visiting cousins in Southampton, the sisters during 1793 and 1794 made other visits, including, for instance, to Adlestrop in Gloucestershire, where her mother's brother James Leigh-Perrot (d. 1817)

lived. Jane wrote letters to her brothers Frank and Charles, both of whom were at sea. On June 3, 1793, she dedicated her "Ode to Pity" to Cassandra, included in *Volume the First.* There appears to be a consensus that after she completed *Volume the Third* of the Juvenilia, there is a transition from her youthful writing to the more mature style found in the epistolary novel *Lady Susan,* the first drafts of which are attributed to the 1794 period.

There is evidence that Jane Austen's family at this time took her writing seriously. Her father purchased at a Basingstoke auctioneer's "a Small Mahogany Writing Desk with 1 Long Drawer and Glass Ink Stand Compleat" for which he paid 12 shillings. Such a description coincides with that of Jane Austen's writing desk, which remained in her family's possession until presented to the British Library in 2000 (*FR,* 89, 298 n 44). She probably used the desk for the writing in 1795 of *Elinor and Marianne,* her first full-length projected novel, which eventually and certainly by its 1811 publication, was transformed into SENSE AND SENSIBILITY.

For the Austen family, the winter of 1794–95 proved difficult. In common with the rest of the country, they experienced severe weather with a thaw that brought in its wake flooding to Steventon and the surrounding area. The weather may have contributed to the sudden death on May 3, 1795, of Anne, the first wife of James, Jane Austen's eldest brother, at the age of 36. She left an infant daughter, Anna (Jane Anna Elizabeth Lefroy [1793–1872]), who spent two years at Steventon until her father remarried in 1797—to Mary Lloyd—who was particularly close to Jane Austen

Cassandra was spending more time with her fiancé, Tom Fowle, and his family at Kintbury, Berkshire. In autumn 1795, he accepted an offer from his patron Lord Craven to accompany him to the West Indies as his personal chaplain—he sailed in mid-January 1796. Jane wrote to Cassandra on Thursday January 14: "By this time therefore they are at Barbadoes I suppose" (*L,* 4). During this time, she was meeting young men. These included Tom Fowle's youngest brother, Charles Fowle (1770–1806), who became a lawyer. Her letters, however, show that she was more interested in Tom Lefroy

Thomas Lefroy (1776–1869), miniature by G. Engleheart, 1799

(1776–1869), whose uncle the Reverend George Lefroy (1745–1806) held a living at Ashe, a parish near Steventon, and was in addition vicar of Compton, near Guildford in Surrey. His wife, Anne (née Brydges [1749–1804]), known as "Madam Lefroy," befriended the young Jane Austen. In the earliest extant Jane Austen letter, she refers several times to Tom. The second sentence of the letter written to Cassandra on Saturday, January 9, 1796, might be read as suggestive. "Mr Tom Lefroy's birthday was yesterday, so that you are very near of an age." It is worth remembering that Jane was born on December 16, 1775, so when she wrote that she had just turned 21, her sister, Cassandra, born January 9, 1773, was two years older, about the same age as the eligible Tom Lefroy. Cassandra apparently objected to her younger sister's overfamiliarity with Tom. Jane replies in her January 9 letter: "You scold me so much in the nice long letter I have received from you" and "Imagine to yourself everything most profligate and shocking in the way of dancing and sitting down together. . . . He is a

very gentlemanlike, good-looking, pleasant young man, I assure you." Jane adds: "But as to our having ever met, except at the three last balls, I cannot say much" (*L*, 1).

Tom Lefroy left the area soon afterward to resume his legal studies at Lincoln's Inn. Called to the Irish bar in 1797, he practiced law in Dublin and in 1852 became lord chief justice of Ireland. He married the sister of a college friend, Mary Paul, in 1797, and they had nine children. Jane wrote to Cassandra on Friday, January 15, 1796: "At length the Day is come on which I am to flirt my last with Tom Lefroy & when you receive this it will be over—My tears flow as I write, at the melancholy idea" (*L*, 4). Whether she was serious or not is open to question; however, Tom Lefroy and Jane were in no economic position to marry. There was family disapproval of his actions, the opinion being that "he had behaved so ill to Jane Austen." The two did not apparently meet during autumn 1798, when he revisited the Steventon area. Tom seems not to have forgotten Jane Austen, and "to the last years of his life she was remembered as the object of his youthful admiration." He is reported as having had a "boyish love" for Jane (*FR*, 94). A highly imaginative account of the relationship formed the foundation for the 2007 film *Becoming Jane*. This starred Anne Hathaway as Jane and James McAvoy as Tom Lefroy. Julian Jarrod directed.

It is just after this that Jane Austen according to Cassandra wrote "First Impressions" between October 1796 and August 1797, subsequently transformed into PRIDE AND PREJUDICE, eventually published in 1813. In April 1796, Jane and Cassandra stayed with their cousins the Coopers at Harpsden in Oxfordshire just outside of Henley-on-Thames. In June 1796, her brother Charles was involved in a naval engagement following which his captain, Williams (1761–1841), married to her cousin Jane Cooper (1771–98), received a knighthood and became Sir Thomas. In August, Jane was once again on her travels, this time to relatives at Rowling in Kent and to attend dances at the neighboring Goodnestone. Jane's letters of description reveal acute character insight. She writes to Cassandra on Thursday, September 1, 1796: "Lady Hales, with her two youngest daughters, have been to see us. Caroline is not grown at all coarser than she was, nor Harriet at all more delicate" (*L,* 7). On Thursday, September 15, she writes, "Miss Fletcher and I were very thick, but I am the thinnest of the two—She wore her purple Muslin, which is pretty enough, tho' it does not become her complexion." Jane adds in her letter an allusion to FANNY BURNEY's (Madame d'Arblay's) novel *Camilla,* published in 1795: "There are two Traits in her Character which are pleasing; namely she admires Camilla, & drinks no cream in her Tea" (*L,* 9).

James, Jane's widowed brother, married on January 17, 1797, Jane's friend Mary Lloyd following her autumn 1796 stay at Steventon parsonage. Jane was working on her first full-length novel, which, as with her other novels, she read aloud to her family as she was writing it. In Spring 1797, news came that Tom Fowle was a victim of yellow fever contracted at sea near St. Domingo in the West Indies. He was buried at sea in February 1797, and left his fiancée, Cassandra, his savings of £1,000, providing her with enough income not to make her totally dependent on her family. Although she continued to go to balls and other social activities with Jane, with whom she became even closer, Cassandra remained a spinster. As Mrs. Austen aged, she took over family duties. According to Fanny-Caroline Lefroy's unpublished history of the Austen family, Jane and Cassandra "seemed to lead a life to themselves within the general family life, which was shared only by each other. I will not say their *full* feelings and opinions were known only to themselves. They alone fully understood what each had suffered and felt and thought."

Jane completed her "First Impressions" in August 1797. She would be 22 in December 1797. Her father thought that it should be published and wrote on November 1, 1797, a brief letter to the leading London publisher of fiction, Thomas Cadell of CADDELL AND DAVIES. The Reverend Austen told Cadell, "I have in my possession a Manuscript Novel, comprised in three Vols. about the length of Miss Burney's Evelina." He asks Cadell, "What will be the expence of publishing at the Author's risk; & what will you venture to advance for the Property of it, if on a perusal, it is approved of? Should your answer give me encouragement I will send you

the Work." It is hardly surprising that Cadell's clerk scrawled across the top of such a letter "declined by Return of Post" (*FR,* 104).

Such a response apparently did not discourage Jane, and in November 1797, she began to transform *Elinor and Marianne* into what became *Sense and Sensibility.* In the meantime, she, Cassandra, and her mother went to visit relatives in Bath, where Jane remained for around a month. Christmas 1797 brought the news that her brother Henry and Eliza(beth) de Feuillide were engaged, and they married on the final day of 1797. At this time, Jane became acquainted with the Reverend Samuel Blackall (1771–1842), a fellow of a Cambridge college visiting the Steventon area as a guest of "Madam Lefroy." Remarks in a letter of Jane to Cassandra written on Saturday November 17 [1798] relating to a possible subsequent Samuel Blackall visit reveal that she was not sympathetic toward him: "There seems no likelihood of his coming into Hampshire this Christmas, and it is therefore most probably that our indifference will soon be mutual, unless his regard, which appeared to spring from knowing nothing of me at first, is best supported by never seeing me" (*L,* 19). On July 3, 1813, 15 years later, she wrote to her brother Frank (Francis), after hearing of Blackall's marriage: "I should very much like to know what sort of a Woman she is. He was a peice [*sic*] of Perfection, noisy Perfection himself which I always recollect with regard." She hopes that his wife to be will "be of a silent turn & rather ignorant . . . fond of cold veal pies, green tea in the afternoon, & green window blind at night" (*L,* 216).

Jane Austen was working on what became *Sense and Sensibility* during the period in which the threat of a French invasion became serious. In April 1798, the Defence of the Realm Act was passed, putting the country on a war footing; it strengthened local militias to protect the local population. During Easter 1798, her father's elder half brother William-Hampson Walter (b. 1721) died in Kent, and on August 9 Jane Cooper (now Lady Williams), a close friend of Jane and Cassandra, was the victim of a carriage accident—a runaway horse running into her horse-driven carriage—while she was visiting the Isle of Wight.

In August 1798, Jane Austen and her family made their first visit to Godmersham Park, where her brother Edward and his wife, Elizabeth (née Bridges), had moved. Godmersham Park was an impressive mansion eight miles from Canterbury, surrounded by a landscaped park and woodlands. During her stay at Godmersham Park, Jane went to balls in Ashford in Kent but found them crowded and hot. Probably during this visit, she completed *Sense and Sensibility* and began *Northanger Abbey*. In her memorandum, Cassandra remembered that "North-hanger Abbey [*sic*] was written about the years 98 & 99" (*MW*, facing, 242). In a letter to Cassandra dated Wednesday October 24, 1798, from Dartford in Kent, where she was staying with her parents on the way to visit Godmersham, Jane told her sister: "My father is now reading the 'Midnight Bell,' which he has got from the library,

and mother sitting by the fire." Francis Lathom's (1777–1832) gothic novel published in 1798 is one of those recommended by Isabella Thorpe to Catherine Morland in the sixth chapter of *Northanger Abbey* (*L*, 15).

On October 10, 1798, Edward and Elizabeth's fifth child was born—William (d. 1873), the first at Godmersham. Jane and her family started their journey home on the day she wrote her letter to Cassandra, who remained at Godmersham until March 1799 helping with the new baby and running the household. During the six months of their separation, 10 letters survive written by Jane to her sister. Many of these letters are preoccupied with the health of their mother, who until the end of November 1798 was ill, partly a result of the three-day homeward journey from Godmersham. Another birth took place at the time. On November 18,

Godmersham Park, from Volume 2 of John P. Neale's *Views of the Seats of Nobleman and Gentleman in England, Wales, Scotland and Ireland*, 1825

Mary Lloyd's son appeared. This was James Edward Austen-Leigh (1798–1874), whose 1870 *Memoir* provides the foundation for much of our knowledge of Jane Austen's life. Jane Austen and Mary Lloyd had been friendly before she became her brother Edward's second wife. He had also wanted to marry Eliza de Feuillide, and Jane's letters to Cassandra reveal that she became less sympathetic toward Mary as the years went by. Jane seems to have protected the six-year-old Anna, James's first child, who since the death of her mother had lived at Steventon parsonage, returning to her father after his remarriage. Anna recalled that her Aunt Jane was "especially kind, writing for her the stories she invented for herself long ere she could write and telling her others of endless adventures and fun which were carried on from day to day or from visit to visit" (*FR*, 112).

Jane and Cassandra's brother Charles had been promoted to lieutenant, and the letters toward the end of 1798 are replete with information concerning the ambitions of both her sailor brothers. Excitedly, Jane begins her Friday December 28 letter, "My dear Cassandra Frank is made.—He was yesterday raised to the Rank of Commander, & appointed to the Petterel Sloop, now at Gibraltar." Charles also got his wish to be transferred to a large ship (*L*, 32). In January 1799, Charles managed to get some shore leave and briefly visited Steventon. In March 1799, Edward and his wife, Elizabeth, with two of their eldest children, journeyed to Steventon from Godmersham—perhaps because Edward felt ill and was fearful of developing gout. Although Cassandra remained at home with her father, Jane and her mother accompanied Edward and Elizabeth to Bath, where Edward rented rooms. They arrived on Friday, May 17, 1799, on a wet afternoon. The visit may have cured Edward as there is no further mention of his illness in Jane's letters.

While in Bath, Jane met her uncle and aunt the Leigh-Perrots. Earlier in a letter to Cassandra, on Tuesday January 8, 1798, written from Steventon, Jane made one of her first references to her own serious work. She tells Cassandra, "I do not wonder at your wanting to read *first impressions* again, so seldom as you have gone through it, & that so long ago" (*L*, 35). Writing from Bath on Tuesday June

11, she tells Cassandra, "I would not let Martha [Lloyd—Jane's close friend] read First Impressions again upon any account, & am very glad that I did not leave it in your power.—She is very cunning, but I see through her design;—she means to publish it from Memory, & one more perusal must enable her to do it" (*L*, 44).

The winter of 1799–1800 was spent largely at Steventon. Jane attended social gatherings and the Basingstoke assembly ball on Thursday November 7, 1799. However, she was probably aware of a disturbing turn of events concerning her mother's brother and sister-in-law, the Leigh-Perrots. On August 14, 1794, Mrs. Leigh-Perrot (Jane Cholmeley, 1744–1836), was apprehended as she left a Bath shop after purchasing some black lace and accused of stealing some white lace found wrapped up in her parcel. Apparently a victim of a setup and blackmail, Mrs. Leigh-Perrot was charged with theft and sent to Ilchester prison to await trial. If found guilty, she might have been hung or sent to an Australian penal colony for 14 years. Her trial took place at Taunton, the county town of Somerset, on March 29, 1800, following a confinement of seven months. The trial lasted seven hours, and the jury, after retiring to consider their verdict, returned in under 15 minutes to find Mrs. Leigh-Perrot not guilty.

The winter had not been an easy one at Steventon. In addition to their anxiety concerning the upcoming trial, the Austen family learned that James, Jane's brother, fell from his horse and broke his leg. Further, the health of Jane's mother remained fragile. It is probable that following the trial and acquittal, Mrs. Leigh-Perrot came to stay at Steventon to recuperate. Overseas both Frank and Charles were involved in naval warfare against the French fleet and France's allies in the Mediterranean. In September 1800, both Jane and Cassandra attended at least one ball. Jane observed in a letter to Cassandra of Thursday November 20 that she saw once again a Mrs. Blount "with the same broad face, diamond bandeau, white shoes, pink husband, & fat neck" (*L*, 61), and she reveals her acumen in character delineation. In October, Edward, this time with his six-year-old son, Edward (1794–1879), paid yet another visit to Steventon. They returned to Godmersham in Kent by way of London, taking Cassandra with them. She did not return to Steventon until the end of February 1801. At the end of November Jane went to visit the Lloyds at Ibthorpe, in Hampshire. She returned to Steventon after seeing Martha and her mother just before Christmas 1800. At Ibthorpe, she and Martha, in spite of the inclement weather, spent a good deal of time outdoors and walking.

Her return home coincided with traumatic news. Her father announced that he had decided to leave Steventon to retire, and that the family would move to Bath. Jane was very distressed and, according to family reminiscences, fainted at the news. The reasons for the move were probably her father's age; on May 1, 1801, he would turn 70, and her mother's health—she was eight years younger than her husband and had borne eight children. Early 1801 was spent in making arrangements for the move and deciding where they should live in Bath. Also in January 1801, Jane's favorite brother, Henry Thomas, decided to resign his commission in the Oxford militia and become banker and army agent in London, living in the fashionable Upper Berkeley Street area. At the end of January, Jane stayed with the Bigg-Wither family at Manydown, in Hampshire, six miles from Steventon. Jane and Cassandra had been close to three of the Bigg-Wither children, Elizabeth (b. 1773), Catherine (b. 1775), and Althea (b. 1777) since childhood and also to their brother Harris (b. 1781).

In February 1801, Cassandra returned home. Edward and Elizabeth came from Godmersham to visit in April, Jane helped her father with parish affairs, and Frank too managed to secure shore leave at Steventon before the family left for Bath. The contents of the rectory, including Jane's Ganer pianoforte and her large collection of music, were auctioned at a three-day sale. Monday May 4, 1802, saw Jane and her mother travel to Ibthorpe and then to Bath, where they stayed with the Leigh-Perrots.

The move from Steventon, where Jane Austen lived for the first 25 years of her life, to Bath was difficult, and the period following it was an unsettled one. Jane wrote to Cassandra on Saturday January 3, 1801, "I get more & more reconciled to the idea of our removal. We have lived long enough

in this Neighbourhood, the Basingstoke Balls are certainly on the decline, there is something interesting in the bustle of going away & the prospect of spending future summers by the sea or in Wales is very delightful" (*L*, 68). Perhaps she was looking on the bright side when she wrote these words. She lived in rented accommodation with her parents while they looked for a permanent home in Bath. She attended a ball on Monday May 11 at the Bath Upper Rooms, and flirted with the aging, horse-loving Mr. Evelyn, who took her for some fast drives in his four-horse phaeton.

At the end of May, the Austens took a three-and-a-quarter-year lease on a house at 4, Sydney Place, Bath, and spent a good deal of the summer at Sidmouth, in Devon. They returned at the end of September 1801 to stay with James and Mary, who had moved into the Steventon rectory, and following a day spent with Madam Lefroy at Ashe, and dining at Steventon, Jane and Cassandra returned to Bath on October 5, 1801—a Monday. There is a gap in Jane Austen's correspondence until at least September 14, 1804. However, rumor circulated in the family that she was involved in a romance during this period, that is, between 1801 and 1804 in the West Country. On October 9, 1801, the young, disabled Hastings de Feuillide died in London. In April 1802, James and Mary, with young Anna, now nine years of age, visited the Austens in Bath. The Treaty of Amiens, which produced a respite in the Napoleonic Wars, was signed on March 27, 1802. Consequently, Charles Austen was able to leave his ship and spent the summer with the Austens. They visited Dawlish and probably Teignmouth in Devon. In the late summer they also probably went to South Wales. Frank Austen, now captain of HMS *Neptune*, was at Portsmouth, and his parents, with James and Mary, visited him on August 23, 1802. Cassandra and Jane were elsewhere and returned to visit Steventon on September 1, 1802. Two days later, they and Charles went to Godmersham, with Charles bringing them back to Steventon on October 28, whence Cassandra and Jane went to Manydown to visit their friends Catherine and Althea Bigg.

Cassandra and Jane were back at Steventon rectory on Friday December 3, 1802. Mary Lloyd recalled that a tearful Jane and Cassandra insisted on returning to Bath on Saturday—the reason being that on the evening of December 2, Harris Bigg-Wither had proposed to Jane. She accepted and then the following morning changed her mind. Mary Lloyd wrote that "Mr. Wither was very plain in person—awkward, & even uncouth in manner—nothing but his size to recommended—he was a fine big man." She added, "He had sense in plenty & went through life very respectably, as a country gentleman" (*FR*, 137). He married in 1804, lived until February 1813 near Cosham, in Hampshire, where seven of his 10 children were born and then at Manydown, the family estate in Hampshire, until his death in 1833.

Jane spent the winter of 1802–03 revising *Susan*, or what became *Northanger Abbey*. In spring 1803, her brother Henry arranged for his lawyer William Seymour to sell the manuscript to a London publisher of fiction, Benjamin Crosby & Co, for 10 pounds provided there was an early publication date. The first volume was advertised as being in the press, but *Susan* was never published. According to family tradition, Jane was not discouraged by this but began a new novel, known as *The WATSONS*, and before the end of 1804 she had completed about 17,500 words. In the meantime, the war with France resumed and her brothers Frank and Charles returned to sea and to active duty. Frank became engaged, and September to October 1803 was probably spent by Jane and Cassandra at Godmersham and October at Ashe to visit "Madam Lefroy." In November 1803, the family went to Lyme Regis—the setting for an important part of *Persuasion*—for an autumn holiday.

Jane's mother was seriously ill during spring 1804, but she was fit enough to travel with the family to the Devon and Dorset coast including another Lyme Regis visit, and walk on the Cobb, where Jane remained until returning to Bath on October 25, 1804, with her parents. They moved to 3 Green Park Building East. On December 16, 1804, Jane's 29th birthday spent in Bath, Madame Lefroy, while out riding, was thrown from her horse and died. Four years later, Jane wrote a moving 13-verse tribute to her friend, "To the Memory of Mrs. Lefroy, who died Decr 16.—my Birthday.—written 1808."

If the first four years of the 19th century were not kind to Jane Austen, the new year did not see an improvement. On January 21, 1805, her father died following a short illness. He would have turned 74 on May 1, 1805. Jane's task was to inform her brothers: James at Steventon, Henry and Edward at Godmersham. Charles, however, was onboard ship at Halifax, Nova Scotia, and Frank off Dungeness, Kent—the ship already set sail for Portsmouth when Jane wrote to him. The Reverend Austen was buried on January 26 in the St. Swithin's, Walcot, Bath church, where he had been married on April 26, 1764, to Jane's mother, Cassandra.

Mrs. Austen and her daughters were now left in financial difficulties. The sons joined together to help the mother, and Cassandra retained some financial independence as she had an annual income from the £1,000 Tom Fowle left her. Jane, however, had nothing and was now financially and socially dependent on her brothers. Being single, she could not undertake any long journey unaccompanied. At the end of March 1805, Mrs. Austen with her daughters moved into lodgings at 25 Gay Street, Bath. Cassandra around this time went to Ibthorpe to nurse Mrs. Lloyd and help Martha Lloyd. On April 16, 1805, Mrs. Lloyd died. To cheer Martha up, Jane sent her the poem "Lines *supposed* to have been sent to an uncivil Dressmaker." Shortly after, Martha went to live with Mrs. Austen, Cassandra, and Jane—a relationship broken only in 1827 by Mrs. Austen's death, and Jane's death 10 years earlier.

Family tradition has it that, owing to the death of her father and the subsequent unsettled condition of her life, Jane failed to finish *The Watsons*. In June 1805, Mrs. Austen, Jane, and Cassandra traveled to Steventon, collected Anna, then went on to Godmersham. Cassandra and Jane remained at Godmersham after the others departed, and they attended balls in Canterbury, which took place during the Race Week of Middle August. Living at Godmersham was the still single Edward Bridges (1779–1825). Jane wrote to Cassandra on Tuesday August 27, 1805: "It is impossible to do justice to the hospitality of his attentions towards me; he made a point of ordering toasted cheese for supper entirely on my account" (*L*, 110): Whether she received a proposal of marriage from Edward remains open to speculation. At any rate, on September 18, Cassandra and Jane joined their mother and Martha Lloyd at Worthing on the Sussex coast west of Brighton, where they remained until early November 1805.

Frank in the meantime was serving as flag captain to Admiral Louis, the second in command to Admiral Nelson. Frank had taken part in the blockade of Cádiz but was sent to Gibraltar to replenish supplies and then to Malta; consequently he missed the battle of Trafalgar, fought on October 21, 1805. In May 1806, Frank returned from the West Indies, and on July 24, 1806, at Ramsgate, he married Mary Gibson. It was hoped in the Austen family that Frank would marry Martha Lloyd. He did so in 1828, five years after the death of his first wife.

The year 1806 was also unsettled for Jane. Most of January was spent at Steventon. Cassandra and Jane then went to Manydown for three weeks in the company of Elizabeth and Catherine Bigg-Wither, returning to Bath via Steventon in mid-March. Mrs. Austen was still looking for somewhere suitable to live on her reduced income with her daughters in Bath. They with Martha Lloyd left Bath finally on July 2, 1806; even two years later, Jane remembered their "happy feelings of Escape!" (letter to Cassandra, Friday July 1, 1806: L, 138). The Austens then went to Clifton near Bristol, then to Adlestrop, Gloucestershire, the home of the Leigh family, where Mrs. Austen (née Leigh) had grown up, and at the beginning of August to Stoneleigh Abbey in Warwickshire concerning a family inheritance and succession matter—the Leighs and Leigh-Perrots having a distant claim to the Stoneleigh estates. From Stoneleigh the nomadic existence continued, for they traveled to the Staffordshire border, staying about five weeks well into September, visiting Edward Cooper (1770–1835), another relative and his family at their house in the village of Hamstall Ridware. In early October, Jane, Cassandra, and their mother returned to Steventon. Jane meanwhile had picked up whooping cough from Edward's eight children. On October 10, they left Steventon with the newlyweds Frank and Mary to lodgings in Southampton before moving into the house they were to share.

Christmas and New Year 1806–07 were also difficult for Jane in her new surroundings. Cassandra left for her annual Godmersham visit, the weather was bad, Martha Lloyd was elsewhere, James and Mary with their very young daughter Caroline appeared for the New Year, Mary Gibson (Frank's wife) was experiencing a difficult pregnancy, and Jane was more or less in charge. No letters to Cassandra survive from this period—the next letter is from February 8, 1807. It seems that Jane went through a time of gloom and depression. This may account for her negative depiction of Bath, Portsmouth, and Southampton in her work—Southampton being where Fanny Price grows to maturity and realizes how good her life was previously. In March, the Austens moved out of their lodgings into a large house near the old city walls, with views from the walls to the sea, and they had a garden in which Jane and her mother could cultivate plants: "We talk also of a Laburnam.—The Border under the Terrace Wall, is clearing away to receive Currents & Gooseberry Bushes, & a spot is found very proper for Raspberries" (letter to Cassandra, February 8, 1807: L, 119).

The corner of Castle Square, Southampton, was to remain home until July 7, 1809. Little information has come to light concerning the period between March 1807 and July 1809. Frank returned to his ship and the sea. Cassandra returned from Godmersham in April 1807 to Southampton. Frank attended the christening of his baby daughter at All Saints Southampton on May 31, 1807. Following a difficult pregnancy, Mary gave birth on April 27 to Mary Jane (1807–36). News was also received from Jane Austen's brother Charles. Since 1804, he had been on convoy duty along the American Atlantic seaboard ensuring that American neutrality was maintained by ensuring that America and other neutral countries were not trading with France. Based in Bermuda, he met and married on May 19, 1807, Fanny Palmer (1790–1814), the just 17-year-old daughter of a former attorney-general of Bermuda, John Grove Palmer (d. 1832), who retired to a fashionable Bloomsbury London address. Charles did not return to England until August 1811, by which time he already had two daughters. In August, Edward Cooper stayed with Jane, Cassandra, and their mother, bringing his three eldest children. At the end of August, Edward visited his Hampshire estate at Chawton, and there was a family reunion at Chawton Great House followed by family gatherings in Southampton. At the end of December 1807, Jane noted at the end of her diary that she began the year with £50.15s6d and finished it with £6.4s6d. The largest amount she spent was £13.19s3d on "Cloathes & Pocket." She spend over £9 on "Washing" and had hired a piano for more than £2 (FR, 163).

The first part of 1808 seems to have been occupied in visiting various family members and friends—no letters survive from the period. The period of January to March was spent by Jane and Cassandra at Steventon, Manydown, with the Bigg-Withers, then at Kintbury, Berkshire, where the Fowle family lived—Cassandra was engaged to young Tom, who died in February 1797. Jane and her brother Henry spent the night of May 15, 1808, at Steventon before leaving for London. She stayed with Henry at his London house until mid-June. On June 14, Jane, Mary Lloyd, and Jane's brother James set off for Godmersham. Jane returned to Southampton on July 8, 1808. Meanwhile, her brother Frank was involved in naval engagements during the Peninsular Wars when the Portuguese and Spanish rebelled against the French.

In autumn 1808, Elizabeth at Godmersham was expecting her 11th child, and Cassandra arrived on September 28, a few hours after the birth of Edward Austen's sixth son, Brook John (d. 1878). In letters to Cassandra written on October 1 and 7, there is first mention of the Austens' plan to leave Southampton for Alton in Hampshire and settle next to Edward's estate at Chawton. Rents had rapidly risen in Southampton, and given her son Frank's family commitments, Mrs. Austen felt that she could no longer accept an annual gift of £50 from him. However, death in the family occurred yet again. Elizabeth, who had 10 days previously given birth to Brook John, died suddenly on October 10. Jane's thoughts were much with her eldest daughter—"My dear, dear Fanny!"—then aged 16, upon whom so much depended once Cassandra left (L, 146). Fanny married Sir Edward Knatchbull and had nine children; she died in 1882. Her

eldest son, Edward, first Lord Brabourne [1829–93], edited the Letters of Jane Austen [1884]). The two eldest boys, Edward and George, both were at school at Winchester and were taken to stay at Steventon with James. Jane helped, and they then came to be with her at Southampton during the difficult time following their mother's death.

Around mid-October 1808, Edward presented Mrs. Austen with the choice between a house at Wye in Kent or one at Chawton; they chose the latter. By November, plans were already being made by Edward for the move. Cassandra remained at Godmersham until February 1809, assisting Fanny and her father, Edward, with the running of a big house and caring for the 10 younger brothers and sisters. Jane, meanwhile back in Southampton, went with Martha Lloyd on December 6 to an Assembly Ball and participated fully in royal celebrations for Queen Charlotte's 65th birthday in January 1809. On December 16, she composed her melancholy verses recalling her friendship with Madam Lefroy, who had died four years previously. Probably in January 1809, Jane also wrote her "Evening Prayers" for her mother, who due to wet and windy weather was unable to attend church.

Mrs. Austen, Cassandra, and Jane planned to leave Southampton on April 3, 1809, but Mrs. Austen became unwell during March and did not arrive as planned at Godmersham until May 15, where they would stay until the Chawton cottage was made ready for them. Interestingly, on April 5, before departing from Southampton, Jane using the assumed name of "Mrs. Ashton Davis," contacted Crosby and Co. in an attempt to publish Susan. The reply was curt. Jane offered to supply them another copy of the manuscript if they had lost the copy sold to them for £10 in 1803. Crosby replied that no specific publishing time had been stipulated. In June 1809, another publisher, John Booth, published a two-volume novel entitled Susan. Clearly, if Jane's novel was ever to be published, the title needed changing—it subsequently became Northanger Abbey.

On June 30, 1809, Mrs. Austen and Jane left Godmersham. On July 7, with Cassandra they entered the house by a pond on Edward's Chawton estate—this was to be their final home. Chawton village was approximately a mile southwest of Alton, a town on the coach road from London to either Winchester or Southampton (today the A31) or to Fareham or Gosport (the A32). Around 400 people then lived in Chawton and its surroundings, in other words, 60 families, and the majority of the rest worked for Edward or other local landowners. The house was more than sufficient for the nearly 70-year-old Mrs. Austen, Cassandra, Jane, and Martha Lloyd, who lived with them.

CAROLINE (1805–80), James Austen's youngest daughter, frequently visited her aunts and grandmother at Chawton. She recorded in 1867 her memories of Jane Austen, and these were drawn upon by J. E. Austen-Leigh in his *Memoir*. Caroline's is probably the best description of her aunt's physical appearance at this time. She wrote, "Her face was rather *round* than long—she had a *bright*, but not a pink color—a clear brown complexion and a very good hazle [*sic*] eyes." Caroline adds, "She was not, I beleive [*sic*], an absolute beauty, but before she left Steventon she was established as a very pretty girl." She continues, "Her hair, a darkish brown, curled naturally—it was in short curls round her face." In addition, "She always wore a cap—Such was the custom of ladies who were not quite young" (*M*, 169). Prior to departing from Southampton, Jane intended to purchase a pianoforte when she settled at Chawton. She wrote to Cassandra on Wednesday, December 28, 1808: "Yes, yes, we *will* have a Pianoforte, as good a one as can be got for 30 Guineas—& I will practise country dances, that we may have some amusement for our nephews & nieces, when we have the pleasure of their company" (*L*, 161). She began at Chawton most days with the piano out in the evenings and occasionally would "sing, to her own accompaniment, some simple old songs" (*FR*, 179).

The Chawton period witnessed Jane Austen's creativity coming to fruition and the publication of her work. Jane was nearly 34 years old when she went to live at Chawton. The eight years left to her were spent in family visits and writing: Her health began to be fragile during the last two years of her life. She was surrounded by her mother, Cassandra, and dear friend for life Martha. Caroline recalled that "it was a cheerful house—my Uncles, one or another, frequently coming for a few days; and they were all pleasant in their own family." Caroline adds, "there was a firm family union, never broken but by death" (*M*, 170).

July to August 1810 witnessed Jane and Cassandra visiting Manydown and Steventon. In November, Edward came to visit Chawton with his daughter Fanny—they had visited the previous October, too. There are no letters from Jane to Cassandra between July 1809 and April 1811. Between these dates, Jane returned to *Sense and Sensibility*, which she updated by referring to a new postal service and rate within London, and adding SIR WALTER SCOTT's name to Cowper and Thomson as popular poets. Her brother Henry Austen remembered, "It was with extreme difficulty that her friends, whose partiality she suspected whilst she honoured their judgement, could prevail on her to publish her first work." Yet during the winter of 1810–11, THOMAS EGERTON, the London publishers, accepted *Sense and Sensibility*. They would publish it at the author's expense. Henry, her brother, recalled, "so persuaded was she that its sale would not repay the expense of publication, that she actually made a reserve from her very moderate income to meet the expected loss." Henry notes, "She could scarcely believe what she termed her great good fortune when 'Sense and Sensibility' produced a clear profit of about £150." He movingly adds, "Few so gifted were so truly unpretending" (*M*, 140).

In February 1811, Jane Austen began to plan what eventually became MANSFIELD PARK. Toward the end of the next month, when Cassandra went to Godmersham, Jane went to stay with her brother Henry and his wife, Eliza, in the fashionable Sloane Street area of London. In addition to correcting the proofs for *Sense and Sensibility*, published in three volumes on October 30, 1811, she led an active social life at Henry and Eliza's. On April 23, for instance, Eliza threw an evening party engaging professional musicians, and Jane "was quite surrounded by acquaintance, especially Gentleman," old friends and family. Jane wrote to Cassandra, "No indeed, I am never too busy to think of S & S. I can no more forget it, than a mother can forget her sucking child" (*L*, 183, 182; Thursday April 25, 1811).

During this London visit, Jane had some interesting encounters. In a letter to Cassandra, written on April 25, she describes meeting an émigré French family. This was the comte d'Antraigues and his wife, an opera singer, who had a son, Julien, who was also musical. Jane writes, "Monsieur the old Count, is a very fine looking man, with quiet manners, good enough for an Englishman—& I beleive is a Man of great information & Taste" (*L*, 185). Le Faye indicates in her "Biographical Index" to the *Letters* that the Comte Emmanuel-Louis d'Antraigues (1756–July 22, 1812) was "an accomplished scholar who was also a professional spy, forger, and double agent." This suitable subject for fictional transformation "and his wife were both murdered in their Barnes house one evening by their Italian servant, possibly on account of a personal grievance or possibly for political reasons" (*L*, 514–515).

Although Jane Austen was now in her 36th year, she was not without male admirers. Jane reported to Cassandra that a Wyndham Knatchbull (1750–1833, a wealthy London merchant) referred to her as "A pleasing looking young woman" (*L*, 186, Tuesday April 30, 1811). Her brother Henry's lawyer William Seymour contemplated proposing to her (*FR*, 186). Jane left London in early May, and on the way home to Chawton called on her old friend Catherine Bigg (Mrs. Hill, 1775–1848). She had married the Reverend Herbert Hill (1749–1828), uncle of the poet Robert Southey, and had six children. Jane returned to her mother at Chawton in May, where, apart from a visit to Steventon in November 1811, she was to spend the rest of the year. In the meantime, her brother Charles returned to England with his wife and two daughters, Cassandra (1808–97) and Harriet-Jane (1810–65). A third daughter, Frances Palmer, was born December 1, 1812 (d. 1882), and a fourth, Elizabeth, born on August 31, 1814, died on September 20 of the same year.

Perhaps it was the worry caused by the delay in the publication of *Sense and Sensibility*, and the anxiety over financial loss, that formed the foundation for Jane's verses beginning "When stretch'd on one's bed / with a fierce-throbbing head," written on October 27, 1811. Three days later the novel

was published, priced at 15 shillings in a probable print run of 750 or 1,000 copies. The sales were steady and the first review, a favorable one, appeared in the *Critical Review* for February 1812. By July 1813, the first edition was sold out, and Jane made a reasonable £140 profit. Her contemporary, the novelist Susan Ferrier (1782–1854), for instance, received £150 for her novel *Marriage*, published in 1818.

Such encouragement probably led to the attempt to publish *Pride and Prejudice*. As Cassandra notes, giving its dates of composition: "First Impressions begun in Oct. 1796. Finished in Augt. 1797. Publish'd afterwards, with alterations & contractions, under the Title of Pride & Prejudice" (*MW*, plate facing, 242). Probably most of 1812 was spent writing at Chawton. Edward and his daughter Fanny visited in April. From June 9 to June 25 Jane accompanied her mother on what was to be Mrs. Austen's final visit to Steventon. During this period, Cassandra once again went to Godmersham. The declaration of war by America on Great Britain on June 17, 1812, affected her brothers serving in the navy. On October 14, 1812, Mrs. Thomas Knight II (née Knatchbull, b. 1753), who had more or less adopted Edward many years previously, died. As a consequence, Edward and his family took on the name Knight and came into the Knight inheritance. The name change annoyed Fanny, who wrote in her diary, "Papa changed his name about this time in compliance with the will of the late Mr. Knight and we are therefore all *Knights* instead of dear old *Austens*. How I hate it"—this is followed by not one but six exclamation marks (*FR*, 192–193).

Jane wrote to her friend Martha Lloyd, who was staying away from Chawton at a friend's, on Sunday, November 29, 1812, as an incidental mention interposed among chatter on domestic trivia: "P & P is sold—Egerton gives £110 for it." Jane "would rather have had £150, but we could not both be pleased, & I am not at all surprised that he should not chuse to hazard so much." In addition, "Its' being sold will I hope be a great saving of Trouble to Henry," her brother who advised her as a kind of literary agent, "& therefore must be welcome to me—The Money is to be paid at the end of the twelvemonth" (*L*, 197).

On January 28, 1813, *Pride and Prejudice* was published by Thomas Egerton in three volumes priced 18 shillings in a print run of probably no more than 1,500 copies. By this time, Jane was well into *Mansfield Park*. Cassandra was at Steventon until late February or early March, so there are more letters to her from Jane and more information concerning Jane's activities. Cassandra wrote in her memorandum that *Mansfield Park* was "begun sometime about Feby.1811—Finished soon after June 1813" (*MW*, facing, 242). Jane's letters contain little mention of the most favorable reception *Pride and Prejudice* was receiving—it was *the* novel to read during spring 1813! For *Mansfield Park* she drew on her personal experiences of Portsmouth and Southampton. She also used her mother's cousin, the Reverend Thomas Leigh's (1734–1813) Adlestrop architectural improvements based on HUMPHRY REPTON (1752–1818), which form the backdrop to the discussion in the novel relating to improvements at the fictional Sotherton and Thornton Lacey. Other personal matters that found their way into fictional form include her brother Charles's gift of a topaz cross to Jane and Cassandra in 1801. Writing to Cassandra on January 24, 1813, Jane mentions that she was reading Sir John Carr's *Travels in Spain*, published in 1811. Details from Carr, such as that "there is no Government House at Gibraltar—I must alter it to the Commissioner's," also are written up in *Mansfield Park* (see book 2, chapter 6: *L*, 198).

On April 21, Edward Austen, now Knight, and his extensive family, came to stay for four months at the Great House, Chawton. The very next day Jane heard that her brother Henry's wife, Eliza de Feuillide, was very ill, and Jane went immediately to London to see her. She arrived shortly before Eliza's death on April 25, and returned to Chawton on May 1, 1813. However, Henry, now a prosperous banker, needed Jane to help him, and on May 19, he collected Jane once again for London, where she stayed for an additional two weeks.

Probably some time in July 1813, Jane completed *Mansfield Park*. Not everything around her was doom and gloom. Frank, who since July 1811 had been commanding the 74-gun HMS *Elephant*, was engaged in the war against Napoleon and was

the sole member of Jane Austen's family who did not visit Chawton during the summer of 1813. In addition, the secret Jane Austen wished to keep, of her authorship of *Pride and Prejudice,* was no longer a secret in the family. In a letter to Francis Austen dated July 3, 1813, at sea, Jane added as a postscript, "I have now . . . written myself into £250.—which only makes me long for more.—I have something in hand" (*L*, 217)—*Mansfield Park.*

On August 17, 1813, the formal announcement was made of the engagement of ANNA, James's first daughter (1793–1872) and Ben (1791–1829) the youngest son of Rev. Isaac George Lefroy and James's friend from childhood, Madam Lefroy. They married at Steventon on November 8, 1814, and had seven children—six of them daughters. As Ben lacked a profession and prospects, Jane was not too happy about the engagement. In September, Edward and James traveled to Godmersham, stopping off in London on the way. They reached Godmersham on September 17, 1813 and this was to be Jane's final visit there. Charles and his family managed a flying visit to Godmersham during October. Charles had told Jane that it would be unwise to use the names of actual ships in *Mansfield Park* as it would be evident that a member of the Austen family had written it. In the same letter, Jane told Frank that "There is to be a 2d. Edition of S. & S. Egerton advises it" (see Jane Austen to Francis Austen, September 25, 1813: *L*, 223).

While still at Godmersham, Jane Austen made some textual changes to *Sense and Sensibility*, which Egerton published at the end of October with a second edition of *Pride and Prejudice*. Now nearly 38, Jane faced the future with humor. During November she attended dinner parties at Chilham Castle, and a concert and ball at Canterbury. She writes to Cassandra in her final letter from Godmersham Park on Saturday November 6, 1813: "By the bye, as I must leave off being young, I find many Douceurs in being a sort of Chaperon for I am put on the Sofa near the Fire & can drink as much wine as I like" (*L*, 251). She returned to London with Edward on November 13, and stayed with Henry for a fortnight. During this period she received an invitation from "a nobleman, personally unknown to her" to join "a literary circle at his house." Henry

Austen, the source of the information, adds that she "declined the invitation. To her truly delicate mind such a display would have given pain instead of pleasure" (*M*, 149–150). Probably at this time Henry negotiated with Egerton for the publication of *Mansfield Park*. Egerton felt it would not be as popular as *Pride and Prejudice,* only agreeing to publish it on a commission basis with Jane retaining the copyright.

Jane returned to Chawton before the intense frost of December 27, 1813, began with an accompanying fog in London lasting for eight days. More or less forced to remain indoors, she began a new book, Cassandra recording that *Emma* was begun on January 21, 1814 (*MW*, facing 242). Jane Austen is recorded as observing, "I am going to take a heroine whom no one but myself will much like" (*M*, 119). It was completed on "March 29, 1815" (*MW*, facing 242). Jane spent the early part of 1814 writing *Emma*. Caroline Mary Craven Austen recalled, "My aunt must have spent much time in writing—her desk lived in the drawing room. I often saw her writing letters on it, and I believe she wrote much of her Novels in the same way—sitting with her family, when they were quite alone; but *I* never saw any manuscript of *that* sort, in progress" (*M*, 173).

On March 1, 1814, Henry took Jane to London, where she remained for at least a month. She spent time with the proofs of the as yet unpublished *Mansfield Park,* which Henry was reading as Jane reports in three letters to Cassandra written from London, Wednesday March 2–Thursday March 3, Saturday March 5–Tuesday March 8, and Wednesday March 9, 1814. There is also a fragment of a letter dated Monday, March 21, probably to her brother Frank: "Perhaps before the end of April, *Mansfield Park* by the author of S & S—P. & P maybe in the World—Keep the *name* to yourself" (*L*, 262). Edward and Fanny came to stay with Henry and Jane in London during the period March 5–9. They went to the theater, Jane being very impressed with Edmund Kean's performance as Shylock at Drury Lane. Cassandra joined them later in March, and she and Jane probably returned to Chawton early in April following a visit to their old friend Catharine Bigg Hill in Streatham, Surrey, south of London and on the road to Brighton.

On May 9, Thomas Egerton at last published *Mansfield Park*. Edward and his family returned in April to stay at Chawton Great House for two months, interacting with Jane and Cassandra. The new novel in three volumes cost 18 shillings, and it appears not to have been reviewed. By November 1814, the probably 1,250 copies produced were sold out and Jane made a £350 profit. Meanwhile in the wider world, hostilities with Napoleon appeared to be winding down. On April 5, 1814, he abdicated as emperor of France and was exiled to Elba. Frank, in May 1814, left his ship, and Charles, in command of HMS *Namur,* was hoping for shore leave soon. Jane went to stay for a fortnight in midsummer 1814 with the Cooke family, cousins on her mother's side, who lived at Great Bookham near Leatherhead in Surrey. She uses this area and the neighboring Box Hill in *Emma,* the composition of which she was well into at the time. Jane returned home in July for a month and then in August returned to London to stay with Henry, who had moved back to Chelsea. She attended a few small dinner parties, went for drives in Henry's curricle, drank tea and visited 125 Pall Mall to see the artist Benjamin West's (1738–1820) latest painting, *Christ Rejected by the Elders.* In March 1811, during a previous London visit, she saw West's *Christ Healing the Sick.*

On August 31, 1814, Charles's wife, Fanny Palmer, gave birth to their fourth daughter. Complications set in, Fanny died on September 6, and the baby Elizabeth died two weeks later. At the end of September, Charles resigned his command of HMS *Namur* and moved to HMS *Phoenix,* which was sent into the Mediterranean. His three small girls went to live with Fanny's parents in Bloomsbury, from where they could easily be sent to Chawton. September 3 saw Henry accompany Jane home to Chawton. Frank in the meantime moved into the Chawton Great House, where he remained with his family for about two years. The remainder of 1814 was clouded by a lawsuit brought by Chawton neighbors against Edward's claiming possession of the Hampshire estates. The lawsuit dragged on until April 1818, when a costly settlement was reached. Edward had to cut down a great deal of timber on his estate to raise the £15,000 needed to buy his opponents off and to ensure that their claims were relinquished.

Ben Lefroy agreed to take Holy Orders and married Anna Austen at Steventon on November 8, 1814. So not all was sad. On November 25, Jane was back at Henry's again in London to negotiate with Egerton over the publication of a second edition of *Mansfield Park*. She and Henry saw Egerton November 30, 1814; he refused to bring out another edition, and this may have been why Jane's later works were not published by him but by JOHN MURRAY. Jane returned to Chawton on December 5. The day after Christmas, she and Cassandra traveled to Winchester to stay with old friends, Elizabeth Bigg-Wither, now the widowed Mrs. Heathcote (1773–1855), her son, and her sister the unmarried Althea (1777–1847). They remained until January 2, 1815, before moving on to Steventon and visiting old friends and family before returning to Chawton on January 16, 1815.

In March 1815, Napoleon escaped from the island of Elba and war broke out again, to be finally settled on June 18, 1815, at the Battle of Waterloo. On March 29, Jane Austen concluded *Emma* and on August 8 began *Persuasion*. It is probable that in March or April, she and Cassandra visited Henry in London. In July, Mary Lloyd and the 10-year-old Caroline came to stay at Chawton, leaving only on August 4. Caroline remembered that her Aunt Jane "was the one to whom we always looked for help . . . *she* would often be the entertaining visitor in our make believe house—She amused us in various ways" (*M*, 174). Probably during August, Jane went to London to stay with Henry and to negotiate the publication of *Emma*. She and Henry were back in Chawton by Sunday September 3, 1815. Meanwhile by September 29, Murray's reader William Gifford, who edited the *Quarterly Review*, gave *Emma* a highly laudatory review. Henry returned to Chawton once again to collect Jane, and on October 4, they traveled to London. On October 17, Jane wrote to Cassandra: "Mr. Murray's Letter is come; he is a Rogue of course, but a civil one. He offers £450—but wants to have the Copyright of MP. & S & S included." Her letter also contained information unrelated to business: "Henry is not quite well—a bilious attack with fever. . . . the

comical consequence of which was that Mr Seymour & I dined together tête a tète [*sic*]" (*L*, 291). William Seymour was the friend of Henry and his lawyer. Appearances to the contrary, he never got around to proposing to Jane Austen.

In spite of his illness, which took a serious turn, followed by a full recovery, Henry tried to negotiate with Murray on his sister's behalf. Murray did not offer more money but agreed to publish 2,000 copies of *Emma* on a commission basis and a second edition of *Mansfield Park*. During Henry's illness, he consulted one of the prince regent's physicians, who told Jane "that the Prince was a great admirer of her Novels: that he often read them, and had a set in each of his residences" (*M*, 176). On November 13, 1815, Jane was shown over Carlton House, the prince's residence. She understood from the Reverend JAMES-STANIER CLARKE (1767–1834), the royal librarian, that the prince more or less expected a forthcoming novel to be dedicated to him. A few days prior to the publication of the three-volume *Emma*, a specially bound set, including the dedication to the prince regent, was sent to the official royal residence at Carlton House. The meeting with Clarke led to a correspondence between Jane Austen and the royal librarian. Jane returned to Chawton on December 16, her 40th birthday, in time to spend Christmas and the New Year at home.

Emma was published on Saturday December 23, 1815, with the date 1816 on the title pages. Murray published the second edition of *Mansfield Park* on February 19, 1816—it did not sell well. *Emma*, on the other hand, did well, sales no doubt boosted by a laudatory review by the great SIR WALTER SCOTT in the *Quarterly Review*, in the March 1816 issue. The encouragement led her and Henry to negotiate with Crosby and Co. in the spring of 1816 to get back the manuscript of *Susan*. The heroine's name was changed to Catharine, and plans were made for publication. Unfortunately, personal matters intervened. Perhaps as a consequence of attendance at her brother's sick bed, and the excitement over the publication of *Emma*, and the seal of royal approval, early in 1816 as Caroline Austen recorded, "I believe Aunt Jane's health began to fail some time before she knew she was really ill" (M, 177). Further, her brother Charles's ship ran aground near Smyrna, Turkey. He was not to blame but was aware that this might adversely affect his naval career. Also the immediate postwar period was difficult economically and on March 15, 1816, Henry's banking business and army agency collapsed. Resilient Henry left London and his extravagant lifestyle, lived either at Steventon, Chawton, or Godmersham, in December 1816 took Holy Orders, and became a curate in Chawton. In 1818 he became chaplain to the British embassy in Berlin, remarried in 1820, and was both a schoolmaster and a curate before dying in 1850!

Jane managed to come through the banking collapse relatively unscathed. She had made £600 profit from her novels and safely invested this in naval stock. The financial losses do not seem to have resulted in family bitterness. Edward and Fanny came to stay at Chawton on May 2, 1816, for three weeks. Jane's health was already suffering, and this was the final time Jane saw Fanny. Jane had what became known as Addison's disease: she lost weight rapidly, and suffered pain and other physical problems. On May 22, 1816, the day after Edward and Fanny left, she and Cassandra went to Cheltenham and to the spa waters for a cure. They stopped at Steventon on the way, and remained at Cheltenham until June 15. Caroline noted that she was told "that Aunt Jane" while in Cheltenham "went over the old places, and recalled old recollections associated with them, in a very particular manner—looked at them, my cousin [Mary Jane] thought, as if she never expected to see them again" (M, 178).

Back at Chawton the by now ill and weak Jane continued working on *Persuasion*, noting on July 8, 1816, that she was writing the first draft of the 10th chapter of volume 2. At the conclusion of this initial draft she wrote "Finis July 18. 1816." She was dissatisfied: "She thought it tame and flat, and was desirous of producing something better. This weighed upon her mind, the more so probably on account of the weak state of her health" (M, 125). Cassandra notes in her Memorandum that "Persuasion begun Augt 8th 1815 finished Aug 6th 1816" (MW, facing, 242). In the meantime, Mary Lloyd was unwell, and in August 1816, accompanied by

Cassandra, she too went to Cheltenham for the spa waters. In a letter dated September 8 to Cassandra at Cheltenham, Jane observes, "my Back has given me scarcely any pain for many days.—I have an idea that agitation does it as much harm as fatigue, & that I was ill at the time of your going, from the very circumstances of your going."

In August and early September, Jane's nephew James Edward Austen-Leigh, then 18 years old, in his last year at Winchester, prior to going to Exeter College, Oxford, stayed at Chawton and gave his aunt a good deal of pleasure. He became a curate, then a vicar, producing 10 children in addition to the celebrated *Memoir* of his aunt written in 1869. There were other family developments around this time. Frank and his wife moved with their six children from Chawton Great House to Alton, a town approximately a mile away. On September 21, 1816, Cassandra returned from Cheltenham. The sisters were not separated again until Jane's death, and there appear to be no more letters from Jane to Cassandra. Jane was busy with family matters. She wrote on Sunday September 8, 1816, in her last surviving letter to Cassandra: "I wanted a few days quiet, & exemption from the Thought & contrivances which any sort of company gives." She added, "Composition seems to me Impossible, with a head full of Joints of Mutton & doses of Rhubarb" (L, 320–321).

Toward the end of 1816, she found it increasingly difficult to accept invitations to dine with family away from Chawton Cottage. The new year saw a temporary recovery in Jane's health, and on January 27, 1817, she began a new novel known as SANDITON, which she worked on during spring, completing 12 chapters by March 18, 1817. However, her illness returned and the novel remained unfinished. On April 27, she made her will, giving almost everything to "my dearest sister," and a few weeks previously on March 28 an aged relative Leigh-Perrot died. Expectations to the contrary, the Austens did not really benefit from the terms of his will. This hit hard as their income had been seriously depleted. Jane, in spite of profits from the sales of *Emma*, was earning small amounts from her literary property—her books. She wrote on April 6 to Charles, "I am ashamed to say that the shock of my

Uncle's Will brought on a relapse," adding, "I live upstairs however for the present & am coddled . . . a weak Body must excuse weak Nerves" (*L,* 338). This was her final letter to her brother Charles.

On May 24, 1817, Cassandra accompanied her on the 16-mile journey to Winchester so that she could consult a highly respected surgeon at the county hospital. They lodged at 8 College Street, where she died on the morning of Friday July 18, 1817. Cassandra on July 20 wrote Fanny Knight a detailed account of her sister's last few hours. Jane's last words were that "she wanted nothing but death & some of her words were 'God grant me patience, Pray for me, O Pray for me'" (*L,* 344). She was buried on the morning of Thursday July 24 in the north aisle of the nave of Winchester Cathedral. It was not then customary for women to be at a funeral, and only three of her brothers, Edward, Henry, and Frank, were able to attend. At the end of December, Murray posthumously published *Northanger Abbey* and *Persuasion* with Henry's "Biographical Note."

Cassandra and Martha remained at Chawton Cottage until 1827 looking after Mrs. Austen. She died at the ripe old age of 87 on January 18, 1827. Her will left Cassandra a legacy of £600 per annum. Cassandra lived until March 1845, preserving her sister's beloved memory. Mary Lloyd and Martha had died two years previously. Jane's

posthumous literary reputation in her own century waned, although her novels were reprinted and she was praised by admirers and reviewers. By 1870, the time was appropriate for the publication of J. E. Austen-Leigh's *Memoir* based on family recollections, and in 1884, Edward Brabourne's two-volume edition of the *Letters of Jane Austen* appeared. Jane Austen's life was encompassed by the archetypes of birth, death, and family. She lived in interesting, turbulent times with the Napoleonic Wars and their naval conflicts, and economic instability directly affecting her and her family.

FURTHER READING

Austen, Jane. *Jane Austen's Letters.* 3rd ed. Collected and edited by Deirdre le Faye. Oxford: Oxford University Press, 1995.

Austen-Leigh, J. E., *A Memoir of Jane Austen and Other Family Recollections.* Edited by Kathryn Sutherland. Oxford: Oxford University Press, 2002.

Gilson, David. *A Bibliography of Jane Austen.* Winchester and New Castle, Del.: St. Paul's Bibliographies, Oak Knoll, 1997.

Le Faye, Deirdre. *A Chronology of Jane Austen and Her Family.* Cambridge: Cambridge University Press, 2006.

———. *Jane Austen: A Family Record.* 2d ed. Cambridge: Cambridge University Press, 2004.

PART II

Works A to Z

Adventures of Mr. Harley, The (1933)

COMPOSITION AND PUBLICATION

The fifth in order of appearance in Jane Austen's juvenilia *Volume the First*, probably written early during the 1787–90 period and transcribed from a lost original early in 1790. *The Adventures (MH)* "a short, but interesting Tale, is with all imaginable Respect inscribed to Mr. Francis William Austen Midshipman on board his Majesty's ship the Perseverance by his Obedient Servant" by Jane Austen. The author's fifth brother, FRANCIS WILLIAM AUSTEN, became a midshipman on the *Perseverance* in December 1789. Consisting of three brief paragraphs and the dedication, *MH* is included in the sixth volume of R. W. Chapman's edition of Jane Austen's *The Works. MH* is published in Margaret Anne Doody's and Douglas Murray's 1993 edition of *Catharine and Other Writings* (37). To date, no Juvenilia Press edition exists. The manuscript is in the Bodleian Library.

SYNOPSIS

The first paragraph of three sentences presents Mr. Harley, who becomes a ship's chaplain. The second paragraph of two sentences tells of Mr. Harley's return with "his fellow travellers." The third and final single sentence paragraph recounts his recollection that he is sitting next to Emma, the 17-year-old whom he married just before he went to sea (40).

CRITICAL COMMENTARY

According to Poplawski, "the essential joke of the 'tale' is that it compresses an eventful plot—a mini-parody of conventional novel plots—into only three very short paragraphs" (51). Ellen F. Martin views the paragraphs as symbolic: "the juvenilia's textures is a float of . . . fetishes, of misdirected details ripe for the interpreter's obsessing." These include Harley's haircutting, his lack of a hat, and his loss of memory, his "*head* has forgotten that he had married" (85).

CHARACTERS

Harley, Emma (40) Described as "about 17 with fine dark Eyes & an elegant Shape" (40). Harley married her before going to sea on his adventures.

Harley, Mr. (40) The forgetful hero of *MH*, "one of many Children" and "Destined by his father for the Church & by his Mother for the Sea"—he chooses to become a Chaplain "on board a Man of War" (40).

Sir John (40) Harley prevails upon "Sir John to obtain for him a chaplaincy" (40).

BIBLIOGRAPHY

Primary Texts

Austen, Jane. "The Adventures of Mr. Harley." In *The Jane Austen Library. Volume the First*, edited by R. W. Chapman with a foreword by Lord David Cecil, a preface by Brian Southam, and a preface by R. W. Chapman; 73. London: Athlone Press, 1984.

———. "The Adventures of Mr. Harley." In *The Works of Jane Austen*. Vol. 6, *Minor Works*, edited by R. W. Chapman. Oxford: Oxford University Press, 1986. [All textual references are to this edition.]

———. "The Adventures of Mr. Harley." In *Jane Austen's* Catharine and *Other Writings*, edited by Margaret Anne Doody and Douglas Murray, 37. Oxford: Oxford University Press, 1993.

Secondary Texts

Martin, Ellen E. "The Madness of Jane Austen: Metonymic Style and Literature's Resistance to Interpretation." In *Jane Austen's Beginnings: The Juvenilia and Lady Susan*, edited by J. David Grey, [83]–94. Ann Arbor and London: UMI: Research Press, 1989.

Poplawski, Paul. *A Jane Austen Encyclopedia*. Westport, Conn.: Greenwood Press, 1998, [51].

Amelia Webster (1933)

COMPOSITION AND PUBLICATION

The 10th of Jane Austen's youthful tales is found in her *Volume the First* and probably recopied by the author from a previous original between 1787 and 1790. Subtitled "an interesting & well written Tale," it "is dedicated by Permission to Mrs. Austen," the author's mother, CASSANDRA (née Leigh) AUSTEN, "by Her humble Servant" her daughter (47). Consisting of seven letters, it is included in the sixth volume of R. W. Chapman's edition of Jane Austen's *The Works. Amelia Webster* (AW) is also found in Margaret Anne Doody's and Douglas Murray's 1993 edition of *Catharine and Other Writings* (45–47). Juliet McMaster, with her students, prepared an illustrated Juvenilia Press edition published in 1993 and reissued in 1995. The manuscript copy is in the Bodleian Library, Oxford.

SYNOPSIS

A takeoff on the epistolary fiction popular at the end of the 18th century, AW consists of seven short letters usually no longer than one or two short sentences each. In these letters, three courtships take place, and at least three marriages are constructed. The correspondents are Matilda Hervey to Amelia Webster; George Hervey, Matilda's brother, to Henry Beverley; Amelia to Maud Hervey, George's sister; Benjamin Bar to Sally Hervey (possibly a relative of George, Matilda, and Maud); Amelia to Maud; and George to Amelia. In the final letter, newspaper announcements of three marriages are conveyed by Tom to Jack—whoever they may be. The three marriages are George Hervey to Amelia Webster, Henry to Miss Hervey, and Benjamin to Sarah Hervey.

CRITICAL COMMENTARY

In addition to the probability that AW was written by Jane Austen between the ages of 12 and 15, critical interest has indicated its use of contemporary letter writing, its use of newspaper announcements of marriage to replace courtship accounts, and its brevity. Deborah J. Knuth comments that the "three-page bagatelle introduces six characters—to the reader, hardly to one another. One eventual bridal couple 'meets' only because George Hervey has seen the heroine through a telescope" (97–98). Michael Londry, in his note on AW in the Juvenilia Press edition, draws attention to its reversals of contemporary fictional conventions. For instance, "the convention of the title sets up the character of Amelia as the protagonist, yet the young Austen makes her the least active, least enthusiastic and least communicative of the characters." The letters

she writes consist "of unconvincing assurances that she would like to say more but cannot just now." She indeed does appear "ever in retreat from the narrative" (4).

Londry also draws attention to Benjamin's treatment of Sarah. He requests that she go out of her way by walking seven miles along a route she does not usually take, and in a "weak uncertain state of Health" (48). The fourth letter, in which he makes his invitation, "calls up an absurd image of the pale, sickly Sarah staggering along the seven-mile journey to Benjamin's love-notes—perhaps only to collapse in a heap of bad health when she arrives." The sixth letter burlesques "the conventional motif of falling in love." In short, AW "is a rambunctious little fiction, whose verve springs largely from its playfulness, from conventions" (5-4).

CHARACTERS

Bar, Benjamin (48) The secret correspondent of Sally Hervey.

Beverly, Henry (47) George Hervey's friend who marries Maud Hervey.

Hervey, George (48) He marries Amelia Webster.

Hervey, Matilda (Maud) (48) A correspondent of Amelia Webster, she marries Henry Beverley.

Hervey, Sarah (Sally) (48) She corresponds secretly with Benjamin Bar, whom she then marries.

Webster, Amelia (47–49) The "heroine," a correspondent who marries George Hervey.

BIBLIOGRAPHY

Primary Texts

Austen, Jane. "Amelia Webster." In *The Works of Jane Austen.* Vol. 6, *Minor Works,* edited by R. W. Chapman, 47–49. Oxford: Oxford University Press, 1986. [All textual references are to this edition].

———. "Amelia Webster." In *Jane Austen's Catharine and Other Writings.* Edited by Margaret Anne Doody and Douglas Murray, 45–47. Oxford: Oxford University Press, 1993.

———. "Amelia Webster." In *The Jane Austen Library. Volume the First*, edited by R. W. Chapman with a foreword by Lord David Cecil, a preface by Brian Southam, and a preface by R. W. Chapman, 86–89. London: Athlone Press, 1984.

———. *Amelia Webster and The Three Sisters Epistolary "novels" by Jane Austen*. Edited by Juliet McMaster and others. Edmonton, Alberta, Canada: Juvenilia Press [Department of English, University of Alberta], 1993, reissued 1995.

Secondary Texts

Knuth, Deborah J. "'You, Who I Know will enter into all my feelings': Friendship in Jane Austen's Juvenilia and *Lady Susan*." In *Jane Austen's Beginnings: The Juvenilia and Lady Susan*, edited by J. David Grey, 95–106. Ann Arbor and London: UMI Research Press, 1989.

Londry, Michael. "Amelia Webster." In Amelia Webster *and* The Three Sisters *epistolary "novels" by Jane Austen*. Edited by Juliet McMaster and others, 4–6. Edmonton, Alberta, Canada: Juvenilia Press [Department of English, University of Alberta], 1993.

The Beautifull Cassandra, A Novel in Twelve Chapters (1933)

COMPOSITION AND PUBLICATION

The eighth in order of appearance in Jane Austen's juvenilia *Volume the First*, written between 1787 and 1790, and probably between 1787 and 1788. The setting is London, which the Austen family visited in August 1788. The 12 short chapters contain a five-sentence dedication, longer than any of the chapters. The dedication is to the author's elder sister, CASSANDRA AUSTEN, after whom the "novel" is titled. *The Beautifull Cassandra (BC)* is included in the sixth volume of R. W. Chapman's edition of Jane Austen's *The Works* and in Margaret Anne Doody and Douglas Murray's 1993 edition of *Catharine and Other Writings* (41–47). Juliet McMaster edited an edition first published by the Sono Nis Press, in Victoria, B.C., Canada, in 1993. The manuscript is in the Bodleian Library, Oxford.

SYNOPSIS

The 12 chapters rarely exceed more than a brief sentence each. The main protagonist is the 16-year-old "Daughter of a celebrated Millener in Bond Street" named Cassandra. The only daughter, she ventures out alone into London "to make her Fortune," taking with her "an elegant Bonnet her Mother" had just made for a Countess. She is away from home for "nearly 7 hours," and the chapters describe her adventures. These include a curtsy to a young viscount whom she otherwise ignores, and the eating of six ices, which she refuses to pay for. She takes a hackney coach she cannot pay for as she has no money, has a silent nonencounter with a Maria, a brief meeting with a friend, a widow. She then in the final chapter returns to the family shop, "to her Mother's bosom" and "whispered to herself, 'This is a day well spent'" (44–47).

CRITICAL COMMENTARY

BC serves as another illustration of its author's use in her juvenilia of truncated form to parody literary styles, in this instance, the picaresque tale in which the hero or heroine goes on a journey usually to London, where they encounter many dangers of a physical and moral kind (HENRY FIELDING's *Tom Jones* [1749] is perhaps the best-known example).

BC has not gone critically unnoticed with its autobiographical elements, treatment of class pretensions, parody, symbolism, and noncompelling plot (nothing really happens to the 16-year-old Cassandra except that she steals!) being among the areas of interest. The fact that in her dedication Jane Austen refers to her sister, Cassandra, as "a Phoenix" is puzzling. It could simply mean that Cassandra reappears "phoenix-like" in fictional form in "a novel in twelve chapters" (44). The fictional Cassandra removes a Bonnet meant for a countess and treats the Viscount with disdain. A shopkeeper's daughter taking on airs and graces, pretending to be what she is not. The bonnet has been read symbolically: She falls "in love with a Bonnet rather than a Man" (Martin, 86). Martin also draws attention to Cassandra's "empty-pockets"—Cassandra, unable to pay the Coachman, "placed her bonnet on his head & ran away" (46)—which invites "psychoanalytic readings" (Martin, 94).

MAIN CHARACTER

Cassandra (44–47) The "heroine" is the "Daughter of a celebrated Millener in Bond Street." An "only Daughter" (44), just 16, obsessed with a Bonnet not belonging to her, she steals it and wanders alone for seven hours in London. Her encounters and actions form the narrative of BC.

BIBLIOGRAPHY

Primary Texts

Austen, Jane. "The Beautifull Cassandra." In *The Jane Austen Library. Volume the First*, edited by R. W. Chapman, with a foreword by Lord David Cecil, a preface by Brian Southam, and a preface by R. W. Chapman, 81–85. London: Athlone Press, 1984.

———. "The Beautifull Cassandra A Novel in Twelve Chapters." In *The Works of Jane Austen*, Vol. 6, *Minor Works*, edited by R. W. Chapman, 44–47. Oxford: Oxford University Press, 1986. [All textual references are to this edition.]

———. "The Beautifull Cassandra." In *Jane Austen's Catharine and other Writings*, edited by Margaret Anne Doody and Douglas Murray, 41–47. Oxford: Oxford University Press, 1993.

———. *The Beautifull Cassandra*. Edited by Juliet McMaster. Victoria, B.C., Canada: Sono Nis Press, 1993.

Secondary Texts

Martin, Ellen E. "The Madness of Jane Austen: Metonymic Style and Literature's Resistance to Interpretation." In *Jane Austen's Beginnings: the Juvenilia and Lady Susan*, edited by David Grey, [83]–94. Ann Arbor and London: UMI Research Press, 1989.

Catharine or the Bower (1951)

COMPOSITION AND PUBLICATION

A fair copy with the title changed from "Kitty," and a dedication to her sister, CASSANDRA AUSTEN, dated "Steventon August 1792" is found in *Volume the Third*. The concluding three and a half pages of the text are "evidently not of Jane Austen's composition and transcribed in an unidentified family hand, possibly that of one of her nieces or nephews." Scholarly consensus agrees that the copy was transcribed around 1796, with some additions dated 1809 (Rosenblum, 27).

The manuscript of *Volume the Third* remained in the Austen-Leigh family until 1963. After a period at the British Library it was sold at Sotheby's London auction rooms on December 14, 1976, and returned to the British Library, where it was catalogued early in 1991. The text was first published in R. W. Chapman's 1951 Oxford edition of *Volume the Third* by Jane Austen. Three years later, "Catharine" [C] appeared in the sixth volume of R. W. Chapman's Oxford edition of *The Works of Jane Austen*, revised by B. C. Southam in 1969. In addition to its publication in Margaret Anne Doody and Douglas Murray's 1993 edition of *Catharine and Other Writings* ([186]-229), a Juvenilia Press edition edited by Juliet McMaster and others was published in 1996 and reissued in 2005.

SYNOPSIS

The incomplete narrative centers on the heroine Catharine (or Kitty), an orphan brought up by her wealthy, unmarried aunt Mrs. Percival at Chetwynde in Devon. The prudent Mrs. Percival is overprotective and secludes her charge from company; but Catharine takes refuge in her cheerful disposition and spending much time in "a fine shady Bower, the work of her own infantine Labours." In such an environment she is able to relax.

Catharine built the bower with the help of Cecilia and Mary Wynne when their father served as the clergyman at Chetwynde. Following the death of their parents, Cecilia was financed by a cousin to India, and in Bengal soon after she arrived, she married "Splendidly, yet unhappily" a man twice her age. Mary, her younger sister, took up a situation with a relative in Scotland, "the Dowager Lady Halifax as a companion to her Daughters."

The Wynnes were followed at the parsonage by the Reverend and Mrs. Dudley and their daughter, "whose Family unlike the Wynnes were productive only of vexation trouble to Mrs. Percival and her Neice." They envy Mrs. Percival's fortune and aim to improve their own by a "Splendid Marriage" for their beautiful, "unreasonably vain" daughter (193–196).

Catharine, or Kitty, looks forward to the visit of her aunt's cousin, the rich and fashionable Member of Parliament, Mr. Stanley, his wife, and daughter Camilla. The family spends six months of the year in London and the remainder in the country. In London, they devote much time and money to Camilla, who is concerned with appearance rather than substance. Catharine attaches herself to Camilla in spite of having little in common with her and asks her for information relating to the Halifax family, where her childhood friend Mary is employed. Camilla perceives both the Wynne girls to be very "lucky," as the eldest "they say she is most nobly married and the happiest Creature in the World—Lady Halifax you see has taken care of the youngest and treats her as if she were her Daughter" (203).

Catharine/Kitty and Camilla are invited to a ball at the Dudleys. Catharine develops a "violent" (208) toothache the day of the ball. Mrs. Percival attributes this to Catharine's "sitting so much in that Arbour, for it is always damp." Camilla, on the other hand, does not help the situation by commenting, "I had rather undergo the greatest Tortures in the World than have a tooth drawn" (210–211). Catharine, after writing a letter to Mary Wynne, feels much better and decides to follow the others to the ball by taking her aunt's carriage. Just as she is about to leave, the elegant, high-spirited Edward Stanley arrives and insists on taking her to the ball. He enters the ballroom without explanation. This offends the Dudleys, and Catharine's aunt is annoyed by Catharine's lack of propriety in accompanying Edward. In the meantime, Camilla has learned that her brother Edward has returned home suddenly from France as the life of his favorite horse—a hunter—is in danger.

Camilla is also annoyed at Edward's dancing with Catharine more than anybody else, but once Catharine explains, they are reconciled. Mrs. Percival, on the other hand, regards Edward Stanley as a nuisance and danger to Catharine and believes that he should leave her house as soon as pos-

sible. Edward takes delight in annoying the aunt and spends most of the following day in Catharine's company discussing books and history. Together in the bower, "conversing . . . on the character of Richard the 3rd, which he was warmly defending [Edward] suddenly seized hold of [Catharine's] hand." This is witnessed by Mrs. Percival, who overreacts and harangues Catharine for behaving in a "Profligate" manner, adding "Such Impudence, I never witnessed before in such a Girl!" For Mrs. Percival (sometimes referred to as "Mrs. Peterson" in the manuscript) "every thing is going to sixes and sevens and all order will soon be at an end throughout the Kingdom" (231–232).

Catharine's responses to Edward's solicitations are confused; there are occasions when she perceives that he is in love with her. Camilla is more convinced and tells Catharine that Edward's father has insisted that he leave the house immediately. On his departure, Edward, in addition to expressing his regrets that he has to leave Catharine, hopes that she will not be married when he returns. (At this point in the manuscript, there is a change to italicized type handwriting. There has been speculation that "this is the work of" the author's "nephew, James Edward Austen-Leigh, writing as a child under Jane Austen's supervision" [McMaster, 48]). The Stanleys leave and hope that Catharine will visit them in London. For her aunt, London is "the hot house of Vice where virtue had long been banished from Society & wickedness of every description was daily gaining ground"; consequently, her niece Catharine was "the last girl in the world to be trusted in London, as she would be totally unable to withstand temptation."

With the "departure of the Stanleys Kitty [Catharine] returned to her usual occupations," but the "bower alone retained its interest in her feelings." The summer passes, but she receives a letter from her "friend Cecilia, now Mrs. Lascelles, announcing the speedy return of herself & her Husband to England" from India. Camilla has written that her brother Edward has gone abroad, to Lyon, without mentioning her name. Catharine does persuade her aunt to accompany her to the performance "of strolling players" in the Exeter neighborhood on condition that Miss Dudley join them. There is also the problem of finding "some Gentleman" to come with them. The manuscript breaks off, to be followed by "a contribution to *Evelyn* by Jane Austen's niece Anna Lefroy" (239–240).

CRITICAL COMMENTARY

There has been considerable critical interest in C. Areas of note include its autobiographical features; depiction of bitterness; use of dialogue; treatment of the themes of education, the family, contemporary reading habits, and friendship; characterization; style; and its role as a precursor of Austen's subsequent work. In his *Jane Austen and the Body*, John Wiltshire indicates the significance of Catharine's being "prevented from going to the ball by an arbitrary, unmotivated interruption, a sudden and violent toothache" (7). The emphasis is on Camilla's reaction; ironically, she adds to Catharine's pain by her far from sympathetic observation: "Lord, if I were in your place I should make such a fuss, there would be no bearing me. I should torment you to Death" (210). So there is at work, according to Wiltshire "the contrast between a character's experience of the body and others' readings of it"—in this instance Camilla's: So the latter's reaction creates an "ironic incongruity" also found in later work such as in *Emma* (Wiltshire, 7–8).

Catharine's retreat to her bower "gives it an almost symbolic significance." For Catharine, it is associated with memories of her childhood, innocence, hopes, and thoughts. For her aunt Percival, on the other hand, the bower is associated with damp, with colds and rheumatism. At one instance in the narrative, she goes so far as to say that if it isn't chopped down, it will result in her death. So on the one hand, it represents youthful innocence, and on the other neurotic anxiety (Pinion, 67). Further, it has been suggested that "the Bower has a subtextual, sexual significance." Edward's kissing of Catharine's hand representing her growth to sexual maturity. Indeed, "the Bower *is*, in a sense Catharine. It is an external symbol of her past and constitutes a crucial part of her psychological makeup" (Herrle, ix–x).

C exhibits the influence of FANNY BURNEY's *Evelina: The History of a Young Lady's Entrance into the World* (1778) and her *Cecilia* (1782). The themes are similar and Catharine has affinities with Burney's heroine Evelina in her lack of social experience. Parallels have also been noted between contemporary conduct books and C. Advice in Dr. John Gregory's A *Father's Legacy to Daughters* (1790) finds verbal parallels in Mrs. Percival's strictures to Catharine concerning her behavior. Other verbal parallels are noted between passages in Edmund Burke's *Reflections on the Revolution in France* (1790) and Mrs. Percival's fear of chaos and social disorder (Waldron, 19–21).

In C, B. C. Southam believes "for the first time, in attempt if not in achievement, we see the mark of an ambitious novelist. In scope and proportion, the fragment is suited to the opening of a full-scale work." He adds, "the range and depth of the characterization, and the fullness of dialogue and action, are far in advance of anything she had attempted before." He speculates that Jane Austen may have left C unfinished because she was dissatisfied with "her drawing of the heroine" and the narrative style. While "much of the dialogue [occupying] nearly half of the work, is crisply handled," some of "the prose often lapses into an elegant and formal periodic manner." For instance, "the account of Cecilia Wynne's Indian marriage" is heavy and unsatisfactory (Southam, 38, 42–43).

CHARACTERS

Amyatt, Lord and Lady (204)   The Reverend Dudley's brother and sister-in-law.

Anne, or Nanny (213–217)   The impressionable young maid who informs her mistress, Catharine, of the arrival of Edward Stanley, whom she describes as "vastly handsome" (213). He refers to her as "the prettiest little waiting maid in the world" (217).

Barlow, Augusta (also called Barker) (204)   A correspondent of Camilla Stanley, she has sisters too, and Camilla describes them to Catharine as "just such other sweet Girls" comparable to the Wynne sisters (204), Catharine's dearest friends.

Barlow, Sir Peter (204)   The father of Augusta Barlow and her sisters. Camilla tells Catharine, "I

Catharine or the Bower **31**

cannot bear Sir Peter—Horrid wretch! He is *always* laid up with the Gout" (204).

Devereux, Sir Henry (199) An acquaintance of Camilla Stanley, he is supposed to go with her and her family to the Lake District.

Dudley, Rev. and Family (195, 204) The Reverend Mr. Dudley replaced Mr. Wynne at Chetwynde. He and his wife and daughter, from Catharine's perception, are unable to replace the Wynnes. The Dudleys are vain and conceited. They come from distinguished families (the Reverend Mr. Dudley is the younger brother of Lord Amyatt), and they resent what they perceive to be a lack of deference and respect to them in the community. Their daughter has inherited many of her parents' disagreeable qualities.

Fitzgibbon, Sir George (203) A well-connected and wealthy cousin of the Wynnes who "sent the eldest girl [Cecilia] to India entirely at his own Expence" (203) to find a husband.

Halifax, Lady Dowager, Miss Caroline, and Miss Maria (195, 202–203) Following the Reverend Wynne's death, the Lady Dowager, "a very distant relation," takes in Mary Wynne as a companion for her daughters Caroline and Maria. They go to Scotland; however, Mary's letters to Catharine suggest that she is not being treated too well. Lady Halifax and her daughters are also known to Camilla (202–203).

Hutchinson, Sarah (233) Mrs. Percival's friend whose death she claims "was occasioned by nothing more—She staid out late one Evening in April, and got wet through . . . and never changed her Cloathes when she came home" (233).

John (210) A servant of Mrs. Percival's whom she wishes to "pull . . . down" Catharine's bower.

Lascelles, Mr. (194, 239) Catharine's friend Cecilia soon after arriving at Bengal finds a husband. She is "Splendidly, yet unhappily married. United to a Man of double her own age, whose disposition was not amiable, and whose Manners were unpleasing, though his Character was respectable" (194).

Lascelles, Mrs. *See* Wynne, Cecilia

M—The Bishop of (203, 206) According to Camilla, "The Bishop of M—has got into the Army" ["sent to Sea" erased in the manuscript] Charles Wynne (203). There is some ambiguity here, as later we are told that he is sent "to sea" (206).

Percival, Catharine (or Kitty) (192 and throughout) The heroine of C, orphaned early in childhood and adopted by her overprotective aunt, Mrs. Percival. Catharine's, or Kitty's, "Spirits were naturally good, and not easily depressed, and she possessed such a fund of vivacity and good humour as could only be damped by some serious vexation" (193). The first sentence of the story places her in relation to her fictional counterparts, to "many heroines," also to "many people" and to herself. Not only has she lost her parents, she is lonely, wanting in love, and socially deprived (a Fanny Price antecedent). So she is related to other fictional selves and to those around her. There is a distinction between what others think of her and what she herself thinks. As a character, Catharine contrasts with the older, more experienced, and repressive "Maiden Aunt" [192]—Mrs. Percival—and the intelligent, snobbish Camilla Stanley. In the company of Camilla, Catharine seems to be responsible and sensible. From Mrs. Percival's perspective, she is foolish. She is somewhat of a paradox represented by her bower—her retreat from the world yet the place in which she experiences male contact—the hand of Edward Stanley, to whom she behaves inappropriately.

Percival, Mrs. (192 and throughout) She behaves as a "Maiden Aunt" although she is referred to as "Mrs.": "while she tenderly loved [Catharine], watched over her conduct with so scrutinizing a severity, as to make it very doubtful to many people . . . whether she loved her not." She brings up Catharine with "jealous Caution" [192] and overprotects her to the point of socially isolating her, especially from meeting young men. She harks back to an older set of values, believing "that every thing is going to sixes & sevens and all order will soon be at an end throughout the Kingdom" (232), and that London is "the hot house of Vice" (239). A hypochondriac, she has a special phobia of dampness and of catching cold (shades of Mr. Woodhouse). For Mrs. Percival, "the whole race of Mankind were degenerating" (200).

Stanley, Mr. and Mrs. (197 and elsewhere) Relatives of Mrs. Percival who stay at Chetwynde, "Mr. and Mrs. Stanley were people of Large Fortune & high Fashion. He was a Member of the house of Commons, and they were therefore most agreeably necessitated to reside half the Year in Town" (197). Mr. Stanley discusses politics with the much more Conservative (Tory) Mrs. Percival.

Stanley, Camilla (197 and following) The 18-year-old daughter of the Stanleys, socially adept with extensive contacts, and not unintelligent, a gossip. Catharine, partly due to the lack of other company of a similar age, is drawn to Camilla, who spent "twelve Years . . . dedicated to the acquirement of Accomplishments which were now to be displayed and in a few Years entirely neglected. . . . And she now united to these Accomplishments, an Understanding unimproved by reading and a Mind totally devoid either of Taste or Judgment" (198).

Stanley, Edward (213 and following) Camilla's brother, "one of the handsomest young Men you would wish to see" (213). Returning from France after he has learned that his favorite horse is sick, he decides unannounced to call at Chetwynde. He enjoys flouting convention, revels in inappropriate behavior, and deliberately annoys Mrs. Percival. Without formally introducing himself to Catharine, yet familiar with her, he whisks her off to the ball, to which he has not been invited, dances, flirts with her, and subsequently kisses her hand. All seems part of an elaborate game (shades of Frank Churchill) before departing to France, whence he came. He is the representative of the Byronic hero/antihero, ignoring convention and rules: the Lord of Chaos or Misrule—exactly what Mrs. Percival fears.

Susan, Lady (211) In a letter to Camilla, Augusta Barlow "sends . . . a long account of the new Regency walking dress Lady Susan has given her" (211).

Tom (213) Servant to Mrs. Percival who, according to Anne, "looks so awkward . . . now his hair is just done up" (213).

Wynne, Rev. and Mrs. (193–194) "The Clergyman of the Parish" (193) of Chetwynde, both close friends of Catharine and Mrs. Percival, they died about two years before the narrative starts.

Wynne, Cecilia (193–195, 239) The close childhood friend of Catharine. Following her father's death, she is dependent upon her relative Sir George Fitzgibbon. He pays for her trip to India, where she married a wealthy older man, Mr. Lascelles, whom she does not love. At the conclusion of the narrative, Catharine receives a letter from her "announcing the speedy return of herself & Husband to England" (239). According to Jane Austen's family tradition, Cecilia is based upon Jane Austen's aunt PHILADELPHIA. Shipped to Madras in 1752, within seven months she became Mrs. Hancock.

Wynne, Charles (203, 206) The eldest of the Wynne sons, intended for the church, "the profession that Charles liked best" (206), is curiously sent by Mr. Bishop to "the Army as a Lieutenant" (Camilla supposes) (203), although subsequently the reader is told that he is sent "to Sea" (206).

Wynne, Mary (193–195, 202–203) The younger of the Wynne girls. Following her father's death, a relative, Lady Halifax, takes her to Scotland as a companion to her daughters. Mary's letters to Catharine suggest that she is unhappy and not well treated by the Halifaxes.

BIBLIOGRAPHY

Primary Texts
Austen, Jane. "[Catharine] Kitty, or the Bower" in *Volume the Third, by Jane Austen.* [Edited by R. W. Chapman]. Oxford, U.K.: Clarendon Press, 1951, pp. [29]–128.

————. "Catharine or the Bower." In *The Works of Jane Austen,* Vol. 6, *Minor Works,* edited by R. W. Chapman. Oxford: Oxford University Press, 1986. [All textual references are to this edition.]

————. "Catharine or the Bower." In *Jane Austen's Catharine and other Writings.* Edited by Margaret Anne Doody and Douglas Murray, [186]–229. Oxford: Oxford University Press, 1993.

————. *Jane Austen's Catharine or the Bower.* Edited by Juliet McMaster and others. Edmonton, Alberta, Canada: Juvenilia Press [Department of English, University of Alberta], 1999, reissued 2005.

Secondary Texts

Herrle, Jeffrey, "Introduction." In *Jane Austen's Catharine or the Bower,* edited by Juliet McMaster and others. Edmonton, Alberta, Canada: Juvenilia Press [Department of English, University of Alberta], 1999, reissued 2005.

Pinion, F. B. *A Jane Austen Companion.* London: Macmillan, 1973.

Rosenblum, Barbara, and Pamela White. *Index of English Literary Manuscripts. Volume IV 1800–1900. Part I. Arnold-Gissing.* London and New York: Mansell, 1982.

Southam, Brian C. *Jane Austen's Literary Manuscripts. New Edition.* London: Athlone Press, 2001.

Waldron, Mary. *Jane Austen and the Fiction of Her Time.* Cambridge: Cambridge University Press, 1999.

Wiltshire, John. *Jane Austen and the Body: "The picture of health."* Cambridge: Cambridge University Press, 1992.

A Collection of Letters (1922)

COMPOSITION AND PUBLICATION

A Collection of Letters (CL) follows *The History of England* in the second of the three notebooks in Jane Austen's handwriting into which she copied her childhood compositions. Dedicated to her cousin Jane Cooper, the undated collection of five unrelated letters, each containing differing styles and perspectives, are assigned to the late 1791 period, that is, when Jane Austen was 16. Following the author's death, the manuscript went to her sister, CASSANDRA, and remained in family hands until being sold at Sotheby's on July 6, 1977. It is now in the British Library.

CL was first published in 1922 in an edition containing a preface by G. K. Chesterton. Subsequently, it appeared in the sixth volume of R. W. Chapman's Oxford edition of *The Works of Jane Austen,* revised by B. C. Southam in 1969. Southam also published them in his edition of Jane Austen's *Volume the Second,* and they appear in Margaret Anne Doody and Douglas Murray's 1993 edition of *Catharine and Other Writings* ([145]–164). Juliet McMaster with students produced an illustrated annotated edition in the Juvenilia Press series published in 1998 and reissued in 2005.

SYNOPSIS

The five letters are described in the dedication as a "Clever Collection of Curious Comments, which have been Carefully Culled, Collected & Classed by your Comical Cousin." The first, "From A Mother to her Friend" (150), according to Southam in *Jane Austen's Literary Manuscripts,* "mocks the tradition of the moral and didactic epistle, perfected by Richardson and subsequently used as an editorial device in the periodicals" (31). In the letter, two young sisters are initiated into the "wonderfull Things," including "Follies & Vices" of the world. For "their first *entrée* into life," they are taken by their doting Mother to tea with her friend Mrs. Cope and her daughter. The actual events, the tea, are so "mighty" that they are hardly mentioned. The Mother and her daughter return home happy (150–151).

The second letter, "From a Young Lady crossed in Love to her freind," attempts to burlesque sentimental fiction. The young lady is so inflicted with the pangs of love that her communication with her friend, the "more than Mortal" Miss Jane, becomes meaningless: "Oh! Miss Jane (said I)—and stopped from inability at the moment of expressing myself as I could wish. . . . I was confused—distressed—my thoughts were bewildered" (153). The third letter, "From A Young Lady in distressed Circumstances to her freind," presents three sketches of a much older woman, Lady Greville, insulting Maria, a much younger one. She is accused of being a "Fortune-hunter" (156–157) and continually humiliated. The fourth letter, "From a Young Lady rather impertinent to her freind" (160), consists of an inquisitive girl questioning her friend who is withdrawing from social activity. The fifth and final letter is similar to the second in that it is essentially a burlesque of sentimental fiction. The longest of the letters, "From a Young Lady very much in love to her Freind" (163), is in some sense a continuation of the third letter, focusing on snobbery and lack of money. Lady Scudamore's cousin, Thomas Musgrove, in spite of his lack of wealth, gains the love of the rich Henrietta Halton. He is assisted by two things. First, according to Lady Scudamore, his ability to write "the best Love-letters I have read" (165). Second, by Lady Scudamore's willingness to assist him in his pursuit of Henrietta.

CRITICAL COMMENTARY

CL prefigures much of Jane Austen's later fiction. An outline of the names used in the letters includes, for instance, the names of Willoughby, Dashwood, and Crawford, which subsequently occur in the novels.

> *Letter One:* A. F., Augusta, Mrs. Cope and daughter, Margaret, the Misses Phillips, Mr. Stanley, Sir John Wynne.
> *Letter Two:* Belle, the two Mr. Crawfords, Lady Bridget Dashwood, Captain Henry Dashwood, Admiral Annesley (deceased), Miss Jane Annesley, Fitzowen, Colonel Seaton, Edward Willoughby, Sophie.
> *Letter Three:* Mr. Asburnham, Mr. Bernard, Lord and Lady Clermont, Lady Greville, Ellen and Miss Greville, Miss Mason, Mrs. Williams, Maria Williams, Sir Thomas Stanley.
> *Letter Four:* Miss Dawson, Dr. Drayton, Mr. and Mrs. Evelyn, Miss Greville.
> *Letter Five:* Henrietta Halton, Matilda, Thomas Musgrove, Lady Scudamore.

Lady Greville in the third letter is "a very recognizable forerunner of Lady Catharine de Bourgh" (McMaster, "Juvenilia," 183). This last letter with the name Musgrove suggests *Persuasion*, although in the later work, the reverse of what happens in *CL* occurs: The now wealthy hero marries the impoverished heroine Anne Elliot. Other elements

stimulating critical attention include the stylistic experimentation in five letters that move from sentimental burlesque to dialogue. The realism of the third letter, with its conflict between a young woman of spirit but no money or connections, and a snobbish, aristocratic, well-connected older woman, has been noted.

The "Introduction" by Heather Harper to the Juvenilia Press edition extends A. Walton Litz's remark that "Where a serious concern for manners is dominant we are entering a world alive with suggestions of the later fiction" (253). Harper finds in *CL* "the foundations for" Jane Austen's "later themes: false values, vanity, superficiality, self-indulgence, pomposity and insincerity" (xi–xii). In addition to the parody of work being read by her friends and family circle, *CL* "is a literary experiment in meta-textuality: a work that calls attention to its own operations and literary traditions" (xi–xiii). For instance, in the second letter, Miss Jane and Lady Bridget "loved each other in idea" although they never met: "We wrote to one another on the same subject by the same post, so exactly did our feelings & our Actions coincide" (155). Textual references are annotated in Doody and Murray's "Explanatory Notes" (332–339).

BIBLIOGRAPHY

Primary Texts

Austen, Jane. "A Collection of Letters." In *Love & Freindship and other early works, now printed from the original Ms. by Jane Austen, with a preface by G. K. Chesterton.* New York: Frederick A. Stokes, 1922, 127–157.

———. "A Collection of Letters." In *The Works of Jane Austen,* Vol. 6, *Minor Works,* edited by R. W. Chapman. Oxford: Oxford University Press, 1986. [All textual references are to this edition.]

———. "A Collection of Letters." In *Volume the Second, by Jane Austen,* edited by B. C. Southam. Oxford: Clarendon Press, 1963, [152]–192.

———. "A Collection of Letters." In *Jane Austen's Catharine and other Writings,* edited by Margaret Anne Doody and Douglas Murray. Oxford: Oxford University Press, 1993, [145]–164.

———. *A Collection of Letters.* Edited by Juliet McMaster and others. Edmonton, Alberta, Canada: Juvenilia Press [Department of English, University of Alberta], 1998, reissued 2005.

Secondary Texts

Harper, Heather. "Introduction." In *A Collection of Letters,* edited by Juliet McMaster and others. Edmonton, Alberta, Canada: Juvenilia Press [Department of English, University of Alberta], 1998, ix–xviii.

Litz, A. Walton. "*The Loiterer*; A Reflection on Jane Austen's Early Environment." *Review of English Studies* N.S. 12 (1961): 251–261.

McMaster, Juliet. *A Companion to Jane Austen Studies.* Edited by Laura Cooner Lambdin and Robert Thomas Lambdin. Westport, Conn.: Greenwood Press, 2000, [173]–189.

Southam, Brian C. *Jane Austen's Literary Manuscripts: A Study of the Novelist's Development through the Surviving Papers.* New Edition. London: Athlone Press, 2001.

"Detached Pieces" (1933)

COMPOSITION AND PUBLICATION

The 13th and penultimate in order of appearance in Jane Austen's juvenilia *Volume the First,* the three pieces were dedicated on June 2, 1793, by the author to her second niece, ANNA. In her "Dedication," the 18-year-old Jane Austen refers to "the following Miscellaneous Morsels, convinced that if you seriously attend to them, You will derive from them very important Instructions with regard to your Conduct in Life" (71). Possibly the pieces were copied from earlier originals. They are included under the general title "Detached Pieces" on the contents page of *Volume the First* and in the sixth volume of R. W. Chapman's edition of Jane Austen's *The Works,* and Margaret Anne Doody and Douglas Murray's 1993 edition of *Catharine and Other Writings* (67–70). Other editions do not appear, but "Detached Pieces" are published in the 1984 reprint of *Volume the First,* edited by Chapman with a preface by Brian Southam.

SYNOPSIS

The first of the three short pieces is "A Fragment written to inculcate the practise of Virtue" and is erased in the manuscript copy now in the Bodleian Library at Oxford. It consists of a sermon of four sentences seeming to attack those who "perspire away their Evenings in crouded assemblies" and with no thought for those who "sweat under the fatigue of their daily Labour" (71).

The second piece has an elaborate title, "A Beautiful Description of the Different Effects of Sensibility on Different Minds," and a send-up, or burlesque, of a sentimental scene by a sickbed as appeared in fashionable contemporary fiction. There are nine characters in the paragraph: the personal "I" or first-person narrator; the apparently unwell Melissa; her family, consisting of Sir William, Mrs. Burnaby, Julia, Maria, and Anna. Then there is the "melancholy" Charles, who may be Melissa's lover. In addition, there is Dr. Dowkins, who enjoys puns. Upon hearing that Melissa is "very weak," he comments, "aye indeed it is more than a very *week* since you have taken to your bed" (72).

The third piece has the title "The Generous Curate, a moral Tale, setting forth the Advantages of being Generous and a Curate." It also has a single paragraph and is the account of a Mr. Williams from "the County of Warwick," who has a family of six. His eldest son, in a similar manner to Jane Austen's two brothers FRANK and CHARLES, goes to the naval academy at Portsmouth. Posted to Newfoundland, the elder son "regularly sent home a large Newfoundland Dog every Month to his family" (73).

Very little has been written critically on these three youthful pieces.

BIBLIOGRAPHY

Primary Texts

Austen, Jane. "Detached Pieces." In *The Jane Austen Library. Volume the First,* edited by R. W. Chapman, with a foreword by Lord David Cecil, a preface by Brian Southam, and a preface by R. W. Chapman, 131–136. London: Athlone Press, 1984.

———. "Detached Pieces." In *The Works of Jane Austen,* Vol. 6, *Minor Works,* edited by R. W. Chapman. Oxford: Oxford University Press, 1986. [All textual references are to this edition.]

———. "Detached Pieces." In *Jane Austen's Catharine and other Writings,* edited by Margaret Anne Doody and Douglas Murray, 67–70. Oxford: Oxford University Press, 1993.

Secondary Reading

Poplawski, Paul. *A Jane Austen Encyclopedia*. Westport, Conn.: Greenwood Press, 1998, 121–122.

Edgar & Emma: A Tale (1933)

COMPOSITION AND PUBLICATION

The third in order of appearance in Jane Austen's juvenilia in *Volume the First, Edgar & Emma, A Tale (EE)* is dated by Southam to the early 1787–90 period and believed to be a copy from a lost original. Consisting of three very brief chapters, it is included in the sixth volume of R. W. Chapman's edition of Jane Austen's *The Works. EE* is also included in Doody and Murray's 1993 edition of *Catharine and Other Writings* (27–30). To date, no Juvenilia Press edition exits. The manuscript is in the Bodleian Library, Oxford.

SYNOPSIS

A satire on contemporary sentimental fiction. In the first of the three short chapters, Sir Godfrey Marlow remonstrates with his wife why they are living in "such deplorable Lodgings" when they possess "3 good Houses of our own." With their two daughters they return to "their seat in Sussex." The second chapter deals with the consequences of their arrival upon local society and focuses on the visit to the Marlows of Mr. and Mrs. Willmot with their sons and daughters. In the shortest and final chapter, Emma Marlow hopes for a visit from Edgar Willmot, whom she loves. He, however, is away from home. The ending is replete with mock solemnity. Emma retires "to her own room" and "continued in tears the remainder of her Life" (29, 30, 33).

CRITICAL COMMENTARY

Critics have found little to interest them in this example of Jane Austen's juvenilia. The parents Godfrey and Lady Marlow are "guided by Prudence & regulated by discretion" (30). They serve as examples of parents in Jane Austen's early work who represent stable values and families. John Halperin has noted "the hero never appears, while the heroine does little but cry" (32). Textual references are thoroughly explicated in Doody and Murray's 1993 edition (296–297).

CHARACTERS

Marlow, Emma (31–33) The youngest of the two daughters of Sir Godfrey and Lady Marlow. When she fails to get what she wants, a re-meeting with Edward, whom she loves, she is overcome with grief, retires to her own room, and cries for "the remainder of her Life" (33).

Marlow, Sir Godfrey and Lady (29–31) Described as "very sensible people" who "sometimes did a foolish thing, yet in general their actions were guided by Prudence & regulated by discretion." Initially living in rental accommodations even though they "have 3 good Houses . . . situated in some of the finest parts of England," they return to Marlhurst with their two daughters, "their seat in Sussex" (30).

Willmot, Edgar (32–33) The hero who does not appear, beloved by Emma.

Willmot, Mr. and Mrs., with at least 11 (?) children (31–33) Mr. Willmot is the "representative of a very ancient Family & possessed besides his paternal Estate, a considerable share in a Lead mine & a ticket in the Lottery. His Lady was an agreable Woman. Their Children were too numerous to be particularly described" (31).

BIBLIOGRAPHY

Primary Texts

Austen, Jane. "Edgar & Emma." In *The Jane Austen Library. Volume the First*, edited by R. W. Chapman, with a foreword by Lord David Cecil, a preface by Brian Southam, and a preface by R. W. Chapman, 54–60. London: Athlone Press, 1984.

———. "Edgar & Emma." In *The Works of Jane Austen*, Vol. 6, *Minor Works*, edited by R. W. Chapman. Oxford: Oxford University Press, 1986. [All textual references are to this edition.]

———. "Edgar and Emma." In *Jane Austen's Catharine and other Writings,* edited by Margaret Anne Doody and Douglas Murray, 27–30. Oxford: Oxford University Press, 1993.

Secondary Texts

Halperin, John. "Unengaged Laughter: Jane Austen's Juvenilia." In *Jane Austen's Beginnings: The Juvenilia and* Lady Susan, edited by J. David Grey, [29]–44. Ann Arbor, Mich., and London: UMI Research Press, 1989.

Southam, Brian C. *Jane Austen's Literary Manuscripts.* Revised Edition. London: Athlone Press, 2001.

Emma (1815)

COMPOSITION AND PUBLICATION

Jane Austen began *Emma* on January 21, 1814, and finished the novel on March 29, 1815. It was written at the same time her niece Anna asked Jane Austen for criticism of her novel *Which Is the Heroine?* Her aunt responded to Anna on September 9, 1814, "3 or 4 families in a Country Village is the very thing to work on" (*Letters,* 275). The manuscript was probably submitted to the London publisher John Murray in late summer or early autumn 1815. Murray, after receiving a very favorable reader's report from William Gifford, offered Jane Austen £450 for her copy of *Emma* plus the copyrights of *Mansfield Park* and *Sense and Sensibility.* Jane Austen did not approve of the suggestion, and *Emma* was published at her expense with profits to her after payment of 10 percent commission to Murray the publisher. The copyright remained with Jane Austen. She was staying with her brother Henry in London when proofs were received in November 1815. The book was advertised on December 2.

Publication, again anonymous, did not take place until December 23, with the title pages of the three volumes dated 1816. Two thousand copies were printed. The selling price was £1.1s for the three volumes. By October 1816, 248 copies were sold. Jane Austen gained a profit of more than £221; but Murray placed his considerable losses on the second edition of *Mansfield Park* against this. Consequently,

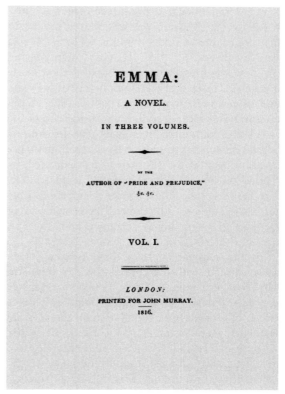

Title page of the first edition of *Emma*

when Jane Austen received her first payment for *Emma,* it was only for just over £38. Two years later, in December 1818, 565 copies were unsold. In 1820, 539 copies of *Emma* were remaindered at two shillings each. Had she lived, and before deductions for the losses incurred by the second edition of *Mansfield Park,* Jane Austen would have made £372.12.11 from *Emma.* The novel went to America. The Philadelphia publisher Mathew Carey in 1818 sold copies of the Murray edition for $4, and his Philadelphia edition was priced at $2.50. A Swedish translation was published in 1857–58. Since the publication of a 10-volume *The Novels of Jane Austen* by R. Brimley Johnson in 1892, *Emma* has frequently been republished (see Gilson, E 75).

Jane Austen visited Carlton House, the home of the prince regent, to whom the novel was dedicated, in autumn 1815. She corresponded with the prince regent's librarian, Mr. Clarke, who must have informed her that the prince regent admired her work. Jane Austen was irritated by the delays in the printing of *Emma*, writing to John Murray on November 23, 1815, "I cannot help begging to know whether there is no hope of their being quickened. Instead of the Work being ready by the end of the present month, it will hardly, at the rate we now proceed, be finished by the end of the next." She continued, "It is likely that the Printers will be influenced to greater Dispatch Punctuality by knowing that the Work is to be dedicated, by Permission, to the Prince Regent?" (*Letters*, 297). The next day Jane Austen wrote to her sister, Cassandra, telling her, "The Printers have been waiting for the Paper—the blame is thrown upon the Stationer" (*Letters*, 298).

In the summer of 1814, Jane Austen stayed for a fortnight with her cousins the Reverend and Mrs. Samuel Cooke of Great Bookham, a village near Leatherhead. Austen family tradition believes that Leatherhead is the foundation for the fictional Highbury. Jane Austen probably, during one of her visits, visited Box Hill, which is more than 600 feet in height and afforded magnificent views of the neighboring surroundings. Kingston-upon-Thames, 10 miles west of London, was at the time a leading county town. According to another Austen family tradition, the author said that in *Emma* she intended to create a heroine "whom no one but myself will much like" (Le Faye, 255).

According to Edward Copeland, the plot of the novel "is in fact, preempted by a tale published in the *Lady's Magazine* (November 1802), a popular monthly compendium of fiction and fashion." A tale featured a "Mr. Knightley" and "a deserted orphan." "Mr. Knightley, a country-gentleman of not very large fortune . . . had married from the purest affection . . . a deserted orphan [left] at a boarding school." As a consequence of "this union he made no addition to his property, nor formed any advantageous connexion, he was by some blamed, and by others ridiculed. He however found himself amply compensated . . . by the amiable qualities and virtues of his wife." Of course, Knightley in Jane Austen's *Emma* does not marry Harriet (E. Copeland and J. McMaster, 142). Another probable source was August von Kotzebue's *Die Versöhnung*, a drama that Jane Austen saw in

Bath on June 22, 1799. The version she witnessed was Thomas Dibdin's *The Birth-Day*, which glamorized "filial love by showing a faultless Emma Bertram whose almost slavish devotion to her invalid father has kept her from marrying" (Honan, 361). At the end of Jane Austen's *Emma*, Emma's father is unable to prevent her marrying Knightley.

In chapter 17 of the final volume of *Emma*, Knightley is told by Emma that Mrs. Weston "practised on" her "like La Baronne d'Almane or La Contesse d'Ostalis, in Madame de Genlis' *Adelaide and Theodore*" (2, 461). The French author on education, Mme de Genlis's (1746–1830), novel (its English subtitle being *Letters on Education*), appeared in English translation in 1783. According to Park Honan, from the novel Jane Austen "borrows the technique of the concise, seemingly full opening description of a heroine's traits and by failing to complete the list and not mentioning Emma's failure in self-knowledge she makes the reader into a moral searcher" (Honan, 361).

SYNOPSIS

Volume 1

Emma is the story of the wealthy, beautiful, spoiled only daughter of an aging widowed hypochondriac, Mr. Woodhouse. Nearly 21, she runs their large house, Hartfield, in Highbury, Surrey. The novel opens with the marriage of her former governess and close companion, Miss Anne Taylor, to Mr. Weston, a neighbor and local gentleman. Feeling alone and bored, Emma will have to struggle through many winter evenings before her elder sister, Isabella, comes to visit with her family at Christmas time. Isabella married John Knightley, a London lawyer and brother to Mr. George Knightley, the neighbor of the Woodhouses at Donwell Abbey. Emma is under the impression that she arranged the match between Miss Taylor and Mr. Weston. George Knightley arrives and challenges her on this belief and the idea that she can arrange other people's lives. This makes Emma determined to find a bride for Mr. Elton, the newly arrived vicar of Highbury.

Mr. Woodhouse holds regular card evenings at Hartfield. At one of these, the headmistress of the local school is accompanied by a young boarder. Harriet Smith is 17, her parents are not known, and Emma decides to take her on, to introduce her socially, and to educate her. Emma decides that Harriet will be a good match for Mr. Elton. Harriet has a suitor in Robert Martin, one of Knightley's tenant farmers at the prosperous Abbey Mill Farm on his estate. Emma attempts to lessen Martin in the eyes of Harriet and leads her, without any evidence, to perceive that her father is a gentleman and that it is inappropriate to mix too closely with Martin and his family, as they are of a lower social status. Knightley tells Mrs. Weston that he strongly disapproves of Emma's conduct toward Harriet. Knightly believes that Emma is using Harriet to satisfy her own vanity and that she is creating in Harriet false expectations.

Emma manipulates Harriet into believing that she loves Elton. She also tries similar tactics on Elton, who evidently is much more interested in Emma than in Harriet Smith. Emma draws Harriet; Elton enthusiastically admires the portrait and goes to London to have it framed. Emma perceives this to show that her matchmaking is working successfully and that Elton is attracted to Harriet. Elton thinks that he will gain Emma's favor by framing her picture of Harriet.

In a very well-written letter that surprises Emma, as she thought incorrectly that Robert Martin was illiterate—a major concern of the novel is Emma's own education—Martin proposes to Harriet. Emma, through the use of emotional blackmail, persuades the pliable, weak-willed Harriet to reject the proposal. After learning of this, Knightley is very angry and tells Emma that by interfering, she has ruined Harriet's chances of a respectable marriage. It emerges that before sending the letter, Martin had asked for Knightley's advice, and he had told Martin that Harriet would look favorably upon the proposal. Knightley and Emma argue, and Emma is surprised by Knightley's strength of feeling and conviction that she has acted inappropriately.

As a pastime, Emma and Harriet play riddles and charades. Emma invites Elton to participate and he seizes upon the opportunity to ask Emma to agree to his courtship of her. Emma again misreads Elton's actions and perceives that his attentions are focused on Harriet. Following a charity visit to the poor of the neighborhood, Emma and

Harriet encounter Elton. Emma falls behind in the walk, leaving Elton and Harriet together. She is surprised that Elton does not take the opportunity to propose.

Christmastime arrives and Isabella with her husband and five children come to visit. Weston arranges a Christmas eve party for the Woodhouses and others at his house, Randalls. Emma thinks that as Harriet has caught a cold and is unable to attend, Elton will not go either. He accepts readily the invitation and uses the opportunity to court Emma. A light snowfall that unsettles the nervous Mr. Woodhouse curtails the party. Emma, much to her annoyance, finds herself alone in a carriage with an inebriated Elton, who proceeds to seize her hand, declares his love for her, and proposes. Emma rejects him and gathers that he has no interest whatsoever in Harriet, especially given her lowly social status. The journey ends in a hostile silence between them.

Emma realizes how seriously her misperceptions have been. She is annoyed at herself and Elton, but resolves to finish with matchmaking. Emma is fortunate in that the weather is bad, keeping people indoors for the next few days, so she does not have to face anyone but her immediate family. The Knightleys leave for London, Elton departs for Bath, and Emma tells Harriet what has happened. Harriet is very upset but does not blame Emma, believing that she did not deserve Elton. Her response makes Emma feel even more ashamed and humble.

New characters appear and the narrative focus moves from Harriet and Emma. Discussion takes place of Frank Churchill, the 23-year-old son of Mr. Weston from his first marriage. Following the death of his mother when he was very young, Frank was adopted by his wealthy aunt and uncle, the Churchills of Enscombe in Yorkshire, whose heir he has become. He has been expected to visit his father and new wife for some time but keeps delaying his visit. The reason is that his aunt is unwell. Emma has imagined a match between herself and the elusive Churchill. Emma discusses Frank Churchill with Knightley and they argue again. Knightley criticizes Frank Churchill for his attitude toward his father, and Emma defends Churchill and is surprised by Knightley's strength of feeling on the matter.

Volume 2

Emma and Harriet visit Mrs. and Miss Bates, the aging widow of the former vicar of Highbury and her middle-aged, well-meaning, garrulous unmarried daughter. They learn of the impending visit of Jane Fairfax, Miss Bates's niece, an orphan, brought up by her aunt and grandmother. At the age of nine she went to live with her late father's former commanding officer in the army, Colonel Campbell and his wife. A companion to their daughter, who had recently married and gone to live with her husband, Mr. Dixon, in Ireland, she is coming to stay for three months. Emma's age but without money, she is going to prepare to find a position as a governess. Emma is surprised to hear that she has not gone to Ireland too, and her active imagination begins to fantasize a relationship between Mr. Dixon and Jane. Emma has previously met her and dislikes her, due to what she considers to be a coldness and reserve. Jane is praised in Highbury generally; people perceive that she and Emma are friends. Jane, of course, provides competition for Emma, who regards herself as the prominent young lady in the area.

Following Jane's arrival, Emma finds her to be more beautiful and poised than ever, and reflects upon Jane's unhappy fate as a prospective governess. Emma's attempt to be more friendly does not outlast their second meeting, at which she objects to what she regards as Jane's excessive reserve concerning Dixon and Frank Churchill, although Emma does learn that Jane and Frank did meet at Weymouth.

Elton has been gone a month to Bath. News reaches Highbury that he is shortly to marry the independently wealthy Augusta Hawkins, the daughter of a Bristol merchant. The information reinforces Emma's view that Elton was more interested in her status and fortune than any genuine affection for her and leads her to be more hopeful considering Harriet's future prospects. Frank Churchill finally arrives and Emma finds him to be charming. Mr. Weston hopes that there will be a match between the two. Frank pays a courtesy visit

upon Jane Fairfax and he appears to share Emma's critical perception of Jane. Emma finds Churchill's sudden disappearance to London in order apparently to receive a haircut to smack of "foppery and nonsense" (205). Frank has told Emma that he is resolved not to marry. That does not diminish the admiration for him. Only Knightley remains with reservations.

A neighboring family, the Coles, holds a dinner party attended by Emma, Mr. and Mrs. Weston, Frank Churchill, Knightly, the Cox males, and later on, Miss Bates, Jane Fairfax, and Harriet Smith. At the party, Frank pays particular attentions to Emma, Jane Fairfax has received from an unknown source a piano, and speculation is rife as to the sender. Jane arrives after dinner and is asked to her obvious embarrassment about the piano. Emma believes that she has a personal understanding with Frank. Mrs. Weston informs Emma that Knightley specially sent his carriage to take Jane and Miss Bates to the party. She suggests that Knightley is romantically interested in Jane. Emma is shocked by such a thought.

The following day, Emma and Harriet are at the Fords' Highbury shop. Miss Bates and Mrs. Weston invite them to hear Jane's new piano, where they find Frank with Jane mending Mrs. Bates's spectacles. While Jane plays, Frank and Emma make comments about Ireland and Mr. Dixon. Jane blushes at this. Knightley passes in the street. Miss Bates thanks him for the large basket full of apples he has given the Bateses. He agrees to come in when he learns that Emma is visiting but changes his mind once he discovers that Frank is also present. Meanwhile, Frank and Emma plan a ball at the Crown Inn. Frank is suddenly called back to Enscombe as his aunt has become ill. Emma thinks that she is falling in love with Frank, but she decides that she is flirting rather than being seriously engaged.

Emma, once again bored, focuses on Harriet and the Eltons. Mrs. Elton emerges as arrogant, vulgar, and conceited, and she starts to compete with Emma for the position of leading Highbury lady. Her first wish is to use supposed contacts to find Jane a suitable governess position. Emma is surprised at Jane's reactions in accepting Mrs. Elton's concerns for her future welfare. Knightley suggests to Emma that this is because no one else seems interested in her. He also tells Emma that he has no intention of proposing to or even courting Jane.

Emma organizes a dinner party at Hartfield in honor of Mrs. Elton. Present in addition to Emma and her father and the Eltons are Knightley, his brother John, Jane Fairfax, and later Mr. Weston. Harriet Smith has declined the invitation. Before the formal dinner, in conversation it is learned that Jane has walked in the morning in the rain to the post office. Mrs. Elton insists that she not do this and says that a servant can take her mail. Jane refuses and Emma's imagination works once again, speculating that Jane is receiving letters from Mr. Dixon. Following the meal, Mrs. Elton again pursues the matter of Jane's application for positions. Jane firmly says that she will wait until later on in the summer. It is now April, and Mr. Weston arrives with a letter from Frank. In this letter, Frank says that the Churchills are moving to London because of Mrs. Churchill's illness and that he will be able to visit Highbury more frequently.

Volume 3

The third volume begins with Frank's reappearance after a two-month absence. He spends little time with Emma and goes to visit others instead. He will spend even more time locally, as the Churchills have taken a house at Richmond for the months of May and June. The Crown Inn ball is now arranged. One of the set pieces of the novel, the ball is attended by most of its characters. The scene is set by Miss Bates in a lengthy verbal account of the participants. Before the dancing, Mrs. Elton speaks, much to Frank Churchill's annoyance, in an overly familiar manner to Jane. Frank is not at ease, and even though dancing with Emma, keeps looking at Knightley. Emma notices that Harriet is without a partner and sees that Mr. Elton is deliberately snubbing her when he publicly refuses to dance with her. Knightley comes to the rescue and dances with Harriet, who enthusiastically dances with him. Emma smiles at Knightley, and Elton retreats into the card room. Over supper, Knightley and Emma are reconciled concerning Emma's behavior with Harriet and Elton. Following supper, Knightley and Emma dance.

The following day, Emma having settled one matchmaking error, commits another. She assumes that Frank Churchill and Harriet Smith are forming a relationship following their appearing arm in arm together. Frank has rescued Harriet from some Gypsy children demanding money from her. Emma resolves not to interfere; however, Harriet burns anything that she has kept concerning Elton and confesses to admiring someone far superior to him, but out of her reach. Emma assumes she means Frank.

Jane Fairfax remains at Highbury until at least August. It is now June and Knightley is beginning to suspect a relationship between Frank Churchill and Jane, especially following a remark by Frank about the local apothecary Mr. Perry's plan concerning a carriage. Only Miss Bates and Jane were privy to the information. Knightley is unable to decide how to interpret this and other signs of a relationship. He discusses the matter with Emma, who assures him that there is nothing between Frank and Jane. This certainty leaves Knightley puzzled, thinking that Churchill may well be playing games with both Jane and Emma.

A planned visit to a nearby beauty spot has to be delayed and is replaced by a mid-June strawberry picking outing at Donwell Abbey attended by Knightley, Emma and her father, the Westons, Harriet, the Eltons, Miss Bates, and Jane, with Frank arriving late. Mrs. Elton tells Jane that she has found her a governess position, which she urges her to accept, upsetting Jane in the process. Emma, seeing Knightley and Harriet walking together, jumps to conclusions about their relationship but is upset when she sees Robert Martin's farm nearby. Emma goes into the hall of Knightley's house to find a very distressed Jane Fairfax, who insists on walking home alone in the heat and confesses to being tired and unhappy. Frank Churchill then arrives tired, late, and out of sorts. He mentions encountering Jane on the way and observes that she is out of her mind to walk in the heat. Emma persuades him to stay for the Box Hill party to take place the following day, June 24, midsummer's day.

Emma, Frank Churchill, Knightley, Mr. Weston, Harriet Smith, the Eltons, Jane, and Miss Bates participate in the outing to Box Hill. The ill will among them and Frank Churchill's defiance of propriety cause Emma to make a singularly inappropriate remark to Miss Bates. Frank makes obvious remarks regarding the Eltons and challenges Emma to find him a suitable wife. Jane takes Miss Bates and leaves the main party. Knightley takes Emma aside and tells her frankly that she deeply hurt Miss Bates by her cruel, arrogant, and insolent remarks. Emma is silent, recognizing the truth of Knightley's reprimand. Knightley takes her to her carriage and leaves her without saying anything. All Emma can do is cry alone.

The next morning, Emma goes to Miss Bates's to apologize. There she finds that Jane has suddenly accepted the governess position and will leave in a fortnight. Jane avoids Emma. She spent the previous evening at the Eltons, where she accepted the position. During the evening the hostler at the Crown Inn arrives to tell Mr. Elton that Frank Churchill left for Richmond after Box Hill earlier than expected.

Back at home, Emma finds Knightley and Harriet. The former is very pleased that she has been to visit Miss Bates. He is going to London to stay for a few days with his brother and upon leaving almost kisses her hand.

Frank's aunt Mrs. Churchill has died. Emma concludes that there is nothing between Frank and Harriet, who appears full of hope. Emma reflects on Jane's situation, offers her friendship, and sends a present. All her offers are rejected by Jane. Emma believes that her own intentions are altruistic.

Ten days after Mrs. Churchill's death, early in July, Frank visits Randalls, the home of the Westons. Emma is called to Randalls after Frank has left. The Westons tell her the news they have only just heard from Frank. He and Jane have secretly been engaged for eight months, since Weymouth. He dared not make the engagement public while his aunt was alive as she would have refused her consent. In a subsequent lengthy letter to Mrs. Weston, Frank explains his previous behavior. The strain of keeping the engagement secret explains his flirtation with Emma and results in an argument with Jane, whom he met on her walk back to Highbury from the strawberry picking. At Box Hill, they had argued even more. At a very low ebb under Mrs.

Elton's pressure, Jane had accepted the governess position. Following his aunt's death and this decision, Frank decided to tell his uncle, who was far more sympathetic than his aunt would have been. Frank then went to see Jane and they were reconciled. He then came to the Westons to tell them.

Emma thinks immediately of what has transpired between her and Frank and the silly things she said about Jane. She also considers the situation of Harriet, whom she believes to be in love with Frank. Emma is critical of Frank for his deception and toying with others' emotions. Mrs. Weston agrees but believes that judgment should be delayed until they hear more from the letter he has promised to write explaining his actions. Emma is once again full of self-recrimination. Harriet appears and exhibits no sign of being upset, revealing that Knightley and not Frank is the object of her affections. Emma is shocked, asks herself why, and the answer comes to her "with the speed of an arrow, that Mr. Knightley must marry no one but herself" (408). Yet another period of doubt takes place. Emma is fearful that Knightley has fallen for Harriet mainly through Emma's own actions. She wishes she had not taken Harriet on, and had not prevented the marriage to Robert Martin. Intense self-criticism and self-examination results in her fully admitting and taking responsibility for "the blunders, the blindness of her own head and heart" (411).

Mrs. Weston calls at Hartfield to tell Emma that she has visited Jane Fairfax, who is ashamed of her deception and rejection of Emma's kindness. Emma understands Jane's situation and does not blame her. Subsequently, Emma, Jane, and Frank are reconciled. Knightley still has reservations concerning his character. After their marriage, Jane and Frank go to live with Mr. Churchill at Enscombe in Yorkshire.

Rainy July weather reflects Emma's glum mood facing a future without Knightley. Brighter weather accompanies Knightley's return from London, and he joins her walking in the Hartfield Garden. He is relieved to learn that Frank Churchill does not mean anything to her, and rather than, as Emma expected, speaking of his love for Harriet, Knightley declares his love for Emma. She accepts his marriage proposal.

Two problems remain. Both are solved by Knightley. Harriet goes to stay with Emma's sister, Isabella, in London. Knightley arranges for Robert Martin to call at his brother's house to deliver some papers and he is invited to dinner. This rekindles the relationship with Harriet. He proposes a second time and she accepts. At the end of September, Emma is very happy to accompany Harriet to church for her marriage with Robert Martin.

The other problem is how to reconcile Mr. Woodhouse to his daughter's marriage. Knightley agrees to live at Hartfield after the marriage and Isabella Knightley, Mrs. Weston, Emma, and Knightley join forces to win Mr. Woodhouse over to the idea of the marriage. Just before the wedding, a sequence of poultry thefts takes place locally and Mr. Woodhouse realizes that it is safer to have Knightley under the Hartfield roof to protect him and Emma. A wedding date is arranged and they marry in October, just over a year after the novel opened with Miss Taylor and Mr. Weston's marriage.

CRITICAL SYNOPSIS AND COMMENTARY

Chapter 1

The opening paragraph of the novel gives its readers specific data concerning the character, personality, intelligence, and economic disposition of Emma, the heroine. The reader is told that she is "handsome" and "clever" and has a "happy disposition." She is also "rich, with a comfortable home." We are not told the source of this wealth. A note of ambiguity is struck with the use of the word "seemed" before "to unite some of the best blessings of existence." In other words, all may appear fine in her existence but not everything is as it seems. The reader in this way is invited to question and to scrutinize Emma Woodhouse. Apparently she "had lived nearly twenty-one years in the world with very little to distress or vex her." Whether or not this pattern of existence will continue is questioned and placed in doubt by the use of the word "seemed." We as readers are not explicitly told that she is selfish, egocentric, vain, or spoiled.

The second paragraph supplies some details of her family background. Emma is "the youngest [sic]" of two daughters. Her father, we are told, was

"most affectionate [and] indulgent." As a "consequence of her sister's marriage" Emma obtained power and authority, a situation of authority and control "from a very early period," as she had "been mistress of his [her father's] house." Emma's mother "had died too long ago for her to have more than an indistinct remembrance of her caresses." The place of Emma's mother "had been supplied by an excellent woman as governess." She "had fallen little short of a mother in affection," a somewhat ambiguous statement.

The governess, the surrogate mother, becomes the subject of the third paragraph. The reader learns that the governess's name is "Miss Taylor," that she had served in the Woodhouse family for 16 years, and that she was "very fond of both daughters, but particularly of Emma." The second short sentence reveals that "Between *them*," Emma and Miss Taylor, "it was more the intimacy of sisters" and the next sentence that "the mildness of" Miss Taylor's "temper had hardly allowed her to impose any restraint." Also that "the shadow of authority" had "passed away." Consequently, Emma and Miss Taylor "had been living together as friend and friend very mutually attached." The same lengthy sentence adds as a matter of fact without passing judgment that "Emma [was] doing just what she liked." This is elaborated. She, Emma, was "highly esteeming Miss Taylor's judgment, but directed chiefly by her own."

In the fourth paragraph, some kind of criticism or reservation concerning the character of Emma is conveyed. The omniscient narrator observes: "The real evils indeed of Emma's situation were the power of having rather too much her own way, and a disposition to think a little too well of herself." In the language of a Jane Austen novel, "evils" is a very strong, but not uncommonly used, word in either its singular or plural forms, being used in its plural form on 33 occasions. The negative connotation is reinforced in the clause at the end of the first sentence of the fourth paragraph: "these were the disadvantages which threatened alloy to her many enjoyments." In other words, no one had disciplined Emma or told her that there were other points of view and perspectives. At the start of the novel, however, "the danger . . . was . . . so unperceived, that they," the limitations, the fact that she had her own way, "did not by any means rank as misfortunes with her."

As in life, so in the world of a Jane Austen novel, and in Emma Woodhouse's world, change occurs. "Sorrow came," though even this sorrow is described as "a gentle sorrow." The reason is "that Miss Taylor married." There is something of an irony that marriage, a wedding day, something to celebrate, should result in "sorrow" and "loss," rather than happiness and celebration. The four relatively short sentences of the fifth paragraph well convey the sense of loss and transition in Emma's life produced by the marriage of her governess. "It was on the wedding-day of this beloved friend that Emma first sat in mournful thought of any continuance." She is left alone with her father. "The wedding day over and the bride-people gone, her father and herself were left to dine together, with no prospect of a third to cheer a long evening." Emma is left to her own devices: "Her father composed himself to sleep after dinner as usual, and she had then only to sit and think of what she had lost." Without conversation and company, the sense of loneliness and loss is accentuated.

The narrative focus then shifts in the next paragraph, the sixth and longest so far in the novel with five sentences, some of which have lengthy cumulative compound clauses, to Miss Taylor, the governess. The narrator weaves into Emma's consciousness as she contemplates the complication of marriage for her friend and for herself. Her governess has married a Mr. Weston, "a man of unexceptionable character, easy fortune, suitable age and pleasant manners." The use of the word "easy" to convey wealth and richness does not mean to imply that these have come improperly, but is used rather as in the sense of abundance. From Emma's point of view "there was some satisfaction in considering with what self-denying, generous friendship she had always wished and promoted the match." However, the final part of the second sentence of this paragraph conveys a negative sense: "but it was a black morning's work for her." The reason is succinctly given in the second-shortest sentence of the paragraph, the third one. "The want of Miss Taylor would be felt every hour of every day." The

first sentence of the paragraph is the shortest one. "The event had every promise of happiness for her friend." Alone with her thoughts, Emma reflects on the 16 years she had been with the former governess, a period in effect since Emma was five years old. Emma reflects upon her "kindness" and her "affection" reflected in teaching, play, "and how [she had] nursed her through the various illnesses of childhood." However, since she was 14, for "the last seven years" the relationship has been "of equal footing and perfect unreserve." This followed the marriage of Emma's older sister, Isabella, whose name is suddenly dropped into the narrative as Emma recalls the period of closeness and relationship with Miss Taylor, now Mrs. Weston, although she has not yet been referred to in that way. Following the departure from the home of Isabella, her sister, Emma and her governess had grown closer together. Miss Taylor "had been a friend and companion" and also "intelligent, well-informed, useful, gentle, knowing all the ways of the family, interested in all its concerns, and peculiarly interested in herself"—that is, in Emma. Miss Taylor's interests were "in every pleasure, every scheme" of Emma's. She also was "one to whom she," Emma, "could speak every thought as it arose, and who had such an affection for her as could never find fault." Again, this is not at this point of the novel condemned by the author but simply stated through Emma's perspective.

The next paragraph opens with a question Emma addresses to herself. "How was she to bear the change?" The use of questions addressed to the self is common to *erlebte Rede,* or inner thought process conveyance. The facts relating to the change are then specified. The geographical difference between Emma and her former governess is that of half a mile. For the first time Miss Taylor is referred to as "Mrs. Weston": this name change from the unmarried one of the governess to her married name denotes the change in Emma's and her situations and is used to convey the effect on Emma. The "difference between a Mrs. Weston—only half a mile from them, and a Miss Taylor in the house" is that "she was now in great danger of suffering from intellectual solitude." Although Emma "clearly loved her father . . . he was no companion for her. He could not meet her in conversation, rational or playful." An interesting feature of this paragraph is that it begins with the first sentence in the *erlebte Rede* mode, and by the last sentence of four, the second of which is a lengthy cumulative one, has moved into omniscient narration, with the author telling the reader about the deficiencies in the relationship of Emma and Mr. Woodhouse.

These differences form the focus of the next single-sentence paragraph. The omniscient narrator tells the reader that there is a tremendous difference in age between father and daughter. Indeed, the word "evil" is used once again, on this occasion to describe "the actual disparity of their ages," although the difference is not specifically given. The author states that "Mr. Woodhouse had not married early" and that the "disparity" is "much increased by his constitution [physical makeup] and habits." The reason being that he "having been a valetudinarian all his life, without activity of mind or body, he was a much older man in ways than in years" (5–6: [5]–7). These ailments can, of course, be primarily psychological rather than actually physical. In Mr. Woodhouse's case, Jane Austen explicitly does not say which. Interestingly, an examination of Peter L. De Rose and S. W. McGuire's *A Concordance to the Works of Jane Austen* (1982) reveals that this is the only use of the word "valetudinarian" in Jane Austen. The first instance of its usage is dated by the *OED* (*Oxford English Dictionary*) in 1703. The rest of the sentence is condemning hardly mitigated by the comment that Mr. Woodhouse was "everywhere beloved for the friendliness of his heart and his amiable temper." These positive attributes are followed by the authorial comment "his talents could not have recommended him at any time." In other words, he has no abilities whatsoever apart from "the friendliness of his heart," whatever that means, "and his amiable temper." The author does not specifiy what is meant by the expression "friendliness of his heart."

The next paragraph, also a single sentence, conveys some information of a basic nature about Emma's sister. She lives in London "only sixteen miles" from where Emma and her father live, but in Jane Austen's time "much beyond [Emma's] daily reach." We also learn for the first time the name of the place where Emma lives: Hartfield. Her sister, Isabella, has a husband and small children and visits Hartfield with them "before Christmas." So Emma is left to her own devices.

The succeeding paragraph places Hartfield, the house where Emma lives, within a social context. Hartfield is part of "Highbury, the large and populous village almost amounting to a town." Hartfield has a "separate lawn and shrubberies" and the "Woodhouses were first in consequences" in Hartfield; whether they are the wealthiest family in the neighborhood is not stated. Certainly "all looked up to them." Although Emma "had many acquaintance[s]," none can replace her former governess. "It was a melancholy change" ([5]-7)—the action has moved again from omniscient third person into *erlebte Rede,* to Emma's thoughts, which are interrupted when her father wakes up. Emma is then forced to think of someone apart from herself.

Mr. Woodhouse, Emma's aging father, is as preoccupied with himself as his daughter is with herself. Their mutual self-absorption mirrors each other's. As Norman Page in *The Language of Jane Austen* appositely indicates, Mr. Woodhouse has "fourteen speeches in" this opening chapter. His representative manner of speaking is evident from "Poor Miss Taylor," his opening words, an expression repeated three times, to "poor James," a reference to his servant, to "What a pity" and "a sad business." Page observes "what superficially appears to be kindness and sympathy for others is soon seen as a self-indulgent sensibility and a somewhat factitious melancholy" (142). Mr. Woodhouse's second utterance wishes for the impossible, "I wish she were here again." The concern is not for Miss Taylor, who is no longer unmarried, but for his own welfare. A similar vein of self-pity is found in his third sentence, "What a pity it is that Mr. Weston ever thought of her!" Emma's reply is meant to appeal to his sense of propriety, possession, and also her sense of herself, not her father's concerns: "you would not have had Miss Taylor live with us forever and bear all my odd humours." Emma adds "when she might have a house of her own?" To which her father replies that there is no advantage to possessing her own house; his, at any rate, is three times larger and his daughter does not suffer at any time from "any odd humours." His is indeed a world of self-denial.

Mr. Woodhouse creates difficulties. When Emma suggests that they both should pay a "wedding-visit very soon," her father responds that Randalls, where the Westons live, is too far away to walk. To her counterproposal that they take their carriage, her father finds a problem. The servant "will not like to put the horses to for such a little way," and also "where are the poor horses to be while we are paying our visit?" This elicits the lengthiest reply from Emma so far in the chapter, one that counteracts his negatives by turning them into positives. He suggests that their servant James's daughter Hannah become a housemaid at the Westons' at Randalls, their home. As Emma points out, "Nobody thought of Hannah till you mentioned her." Mr. Woodhouse's response reveals that his motives in placing Hannah at the Westons' are a combination of selfish ones. She, Hannah, was always deferential to him, and she will "be a great comfort to poor Miss Taylor to have somebody about her that she is used to see," and also whenever James goes to see her, "he will be able to tell her how we all are" (7–9). Emma's reaction is to keep her father in a positive mood, "his habitual mode of expression is in the negative form (there are 10 negatives in his speeches in this opening chapter)," which provides "a linguistic clue to his character . . . the implication is of a timidity in the face of experience, a shrinking from positive commitment to life" (Page, 142). She, Emma, must keep him preoccupied. She "hoped, by the help of backgammon, to get her father tolerably through the evening, and be attacked by no regrets but her own."

The third character to make an appearance in the world of *Emma,* is "Mr. Knightley, a sensible man about seven or eight-and-thirty." Being "sensible" with the meaning of being reasonable, judicious, and wise is an epithet of high commendation in Jane Austen's world. Emma is nearly 21. Mr. Knightley is nearly old enough to be her father. Indeed, if a dominant theme of *Emma* is marriage, then another is father-daughter relationships, or daughter relationships with surrogate fathers. Knightley is also connected with the family as "a very old and intimate friend" and "as the elder brother of Isabella's [Emma's older sister] husband." The omniscient narrator, Jane Austen, conveys a good deal of specific information about Knightley in this chapter. He lives "about a mile from" the Woodhouses, frequently visits, and on this occasion comes "directly from their mutual connections in London." So he can convey family news, information, and gossip. The ostensible reason for his visit is "to say that all were well in Brunswick-square," the fashionable address in what is now the Bloomsbury area of London near the British Museum, where his brother and Emma's sister live. This news "animated Mr. Woodhouse for some time." Mr. Knightley's approach to Mr. Woodhouse's negativism is different from Emma's. When Mr. Woodhouse observes that Knightley "must have had a shocking walk," the reply is not one of assent, of pandering to Mr. Woodhouse, but of contradiction. It "is courteously laconic." Knightley "states his conviction," to use the words of J. F. Burrows in his *Jane Austen's Emma,* "supplies his evidence, and has done" (17), telling Mr. Woodhouse "Not at all, sir. It is a beautiful, moonlight night; and so mild that I must draw back from your great fire." In response to the reply, "But you must have found it very damp and dirty. I wish you may not catch cold," Knightley quips, "Dirty, sir! Look at my shoes. Not a speck on them."

Mr. Woodhouse is concerned with irrelevances. He wanted the wedding to be "put off," it is unclear whether delayed or canceled, because "it rained dreadfully hard for half an hour." Mr. Knightley ignores such a comment, congratulating instead father and daughter on the wedding and on their "joy," asking them how they behaved and "who cried most?" To which the response is, "Ah! poor Miss Taylor! 'tis a sad business." The self-pitying remark is turned against Mr. Woodhouse. Knightley cannot agree with the sentiments and even feels sorry for "Poor Mr. and Miss Woodhouse," he raises "the question of dependence or independence," and pragmatically states that "it must be better to have only one to please, than two." It is Emma, rather than her father, who responds, drawing attention to herself. "Especially when *one* of those two is such a fanciful, troublesome creature." Of course, her father believes that the reference is to himself. The response from Emma reveals that she has insight as to what others think of her, at least where Knightley is concerned. As she tells her father and Knightley, the latter "loves to find fault with me you know—in a joke—it is all a joke. We always say what we like to one another."

Another dimension of this novel is that the "joke" becomes deadly serious, and Emma and Knightley, in spite of the disparity in their ages and misunderstandings during the course of the novel, are able eventually to unite. The following paragraph of omniscient narration concurs with Emma's comment to Knightley. He was "in fact, . . . one of the few people who could see faults in Emma Woodhouse, and the only one who ever told her of them." Of course "this was not particularly agreeable to Emma" personally and even "so much less so to her father," who regarded everybody as thinking his daughter the paragon of perfection. Dialogue plays a crucial role in this chapter and in the novel. The three-way exchange among Emma, her father, and Knightley occupies the remainder of the chapter. There is almost no remaining authorial interference, and as the chapter progresses the speeches, especially those of Emma and Knightley, increase in length. The dialogue reveals character, values, and attitudes. Knightley reassures them that practically, materially, Miss Taylor, as she is still being called, even by him, has made a very successful marriage. At her "time of life," she has her own home, she is comfortable, provided for and consequently "cannot allow herself to feel so much pain as pleasure."

There is little here of feeling but of material convenience and practicality. Emma's response to this pragmatism is to remind Knightley of her own role in bringing about the marriage. "I made the match, you know, four years ago; and to have it take place, and be proved in the right, when so many people said Mr. Weston would never marry again, may comfort me for any thing." Her exaggeration, sense of her own righteousness, and crucial matchmaking role is further fueled by a disapproving shake of the head from Mr. Knight-

ley and her father's praise of her abilities. He tells Emma, "whatever you say always comes to pass," and implores her using religious language, "Pray do not make any more matches." This provokes Emma to a lengthy reply in which she first promises her father not to make a match for herself. This remark by the end of the novel is viewed in an ironic perspective. She then repeats herself about perceptions that Mr. Weston would never remarry, having "been a widower so long" and how she believed none of the rumors about him, that he had made "a promise to his wife on her deathbed" and so on. By the end of her response, she tells him "dear papa, you cannot think that I shall leave off match-making."

Mr. Knightley questions Emma's perceptions of her "success," mediating it, and reducing her achievement to "a lucky guess; and *that* is all that can be said." Knightley, in his version of what occurred, views Emma's efforts from two perspectives, either: "endeavoring for the last four years to bring about this marriage;" or "saying to yourself one idle day" that it would be a good idea. Emma's reply moves from the sarcastic to thoughtfulness, revealing high intelligence and an ability to think things through. She begins by castigating Knightley. She pities him for not knowing "the pleasure and triumph of a lucky guess," and for that he has her "pity." Emma then expostulates upon Knightley's explanation of the word "success," which ignores a third possibility, "a something between the do-nothing and the do-all." She had, given her father's fussiness, his absorption with the trivial, to "promote Mr. Weston's visits here," to give "many little encouragements," also she "smoothed many little matters." She respects Knightley enough by adding, "I think you must know Hartfield enough to comprehend that."

Knightley's reply ignores the sophistication of Emma's. He refers to the necessity of people to be left to manage their own activities and condemns Emma for unnecessary "interference," which may "likely" do "harm to" herself "than good" to others (9–13). These words prove to be somewhat ironic in the plot of the novel when Knightley does exactly what he at this initial chapter condemns Emma for. He will send Robert Smith on a business transaction to his brother's London home knowing that Harriet Smith is staying there. However, he does to Emma confess his "interference" (462).

Mr. Woodhouse interrupts the verbal dueling between Emma and Knightley over conduct, values, and attitudes to others. He naturally defends his daughter, believing that she behaves altruistically. He tells Knightley, "Emma never thinks of herself, if she can do good to others." Yet Mr. Woodhouse reiterates his dislike for marriage, "matches . . . are silly things," and "break up one's family circle grievously." They change the status quo, which for the egocentric Mr. Woodhouse is almost the one thing to be avoided.

Emma brushes aside her father's reservations. She will make one more attempt at matchmaking. This time it will be for a Mr. Elton, about whom the adjective "poor" is used. He has a settled house, has been in the neighborhood for a year, and a position—that of a clergyman. In this way, through dialogue and assertion of intentions, the author adds to the canvas of the novel yet another character. The introductory chapter has already given the reader a glimpse of Emma, her father, Mr. Knightley, and mention of Emma's older sister, Isabella, her husband, the servant James, and his daughter Hannah, Mr. Weston, his new wife Miss Taylor (that was), and now Mr. Elton, Isabella's children, Farmer Mitchell, and the inhabitants of Highbury.

Mr. Woodhouse's reply placates Emma by agreeing with his daughter's sentiments concerning Mr. Elton's positive qualities (ironically the novel's plot will expose these as negative). Mr. Woodhouse reveals his preference for the status quo and for Knightley, requesting that Knightley be present when the newcomer arrives to dine. Knightley has the last word in this opening chapter. He advises Emma to invite Elton "to dinner . . . and help him to the best of the fish and the chicken, but leave him to chuse his own wife." The reason for this conveys through direct speech more information, on this occasion concerning Elton's age. Knightley tells Emma, "Depend upon it, a man of six or seven-and-twenty can take care of himself" (13–14).

In the closing dialogue of the first chapter, one of the most significant features of *Emma* emerges. "Among Jane Austen's novels," writes Maggie

Lane, in *Jane Austen and Food*, "*Emma* is uniquely laden with references to food. Food anchors the fictive to the real world, contributing to that powerful sense of fidelity to life which so many readers have testified to feeling most especially with this book." Lane adds that "more profoundly, the giving and sharing of food becomes a symbol or extended metaphor for human interdependence, resonating through the entire text" (153). At the conclusion of the first chapter, the invitation to dinner helps to reinforce the clash of personalities between the two major figures: the heroine and Mr. Knightley. For the latter, Elton can share a meal with them. For Emma the meal is an excuse for something else, the choice of a wife.

Chapter 1 then of *Emma* interweaves omniscient narration with free, indirect discourse, *erlebte Rede,* dialogue, and an abundance of adjectival description. These are the means by which three main characters and a myriad of others, places, situations, and intentions are conveyed to the reader. Through them the major themes of the novel emerge: a clash of wills, selfishness, the concern for others, marriage, change, the sense that what may appear to one may not be the same for another. The quality of irony, of another possible perspective, of disguise and revelation pervades *Emma*.

Chapter 2

The second chapter opens from another perspective. Not that of Emma, Mr. Woodhouse, or Mr. Knightley but of Mr. Weston. His marriage to Miss Taylor has been a primary topic of conversation in the first chapter. Omniscient conventional narration is the order of the day. The reader is told about Mr. Weston's origins, family, social and class status, education, financial situation, and "social temper." A word most frequently used, in fact 157 times, in Jane Austen's work, "temper" is used in this instance as a noun to convey social status, temperament (in a positive manner), and inclination in addition to duly duty. In other words, Mr. Weston is a concerned citizen who does the right thing. It also means that he has a sociable disposition—Jane Austen has told us that he was not very homely and that he had an "active cheerful mind." We are told that he "had become indisposed for any of the more homely pursuits in which his brothers were engaged" and consequently "had satisfied an active cheerful mind and a social temper by entering into the militia of his county, then embodied." The first chapter informs us that he married Miss Taylor. We subsequently learn that he had a son Frank by his first wife, the wealthy Miss Churchill, who died three years after the marriage. His brothers are "already established in a good way in London," enough to help Mr. Weston in business, but they disappear from the novel. The use of the noun refers to brethren, neighbors rather than to Mr. Weston's blood relatives. So Jane Austen, at the opening of her novel, is creating somewhat misleading signals to an attentive reader who may be expecting a "brother[s]" of Mr. Weston to reappear somewhere in the plot.

Mr. Weston's commitment to the "militia" enlarges the fabric of the fiction, which so far has been confined to a very small world. To all intents and purposes, the war against Napoleon had concluded by the December 1815 publication of *Emma.* Inevitably it haunted contemporary readers' imaginations. The "militia" reference is an initial evocation of the presence of traumatic political and social events lurking in the background while the events of *Emma* unfold. Following the declaration of war in 1793 by England on Revolutionary France, the historical period probably coinciding with Weston's militia service, the militia was revived to supplement regular military forces. Raising numbers in the volunteer forces strengthened national defenses. So Mr. Weston "by entering into the militia of his county" remains near home, demonstrates his patriotism by defending his country, and behaves as a good citizen should. The use of the noun "brothers" has an echo of that "band of brothers" evoked by Henry V before the Battle of Agincourt to stimulate his soldiers to fight and die: "We few, we happy few, we band of brothers" (*Henry V*: 4.3.60). Those not in the militia are engaged in "the more homely pursuits" to which Weston is "indisposed." This indisposition is the reason why Weston has joined the militia. Somewhat curiously, given that Jane Austen's life and writing career coincided with the Napoleonic Wars, there are but eight references to the militia in her work. Six of these are in *Pride and Prejudice* and two in *Emma.*

The single sentence second paragraph of the second chapter states one of the important consequences of Weston's joining the service and being a "Captain." It leads to his meeting "Miss Churchill of a great Yorkshire family." The word "great" meaning wealthy and important, "and Miss Churchill fell in love with him." It is not said that Weston fell in love with her, but rather the reverse. Her brother and his wife were "surprized" because they "were full of pride and importance, which the connection would offend." In other words, Weston was socially and economically not of the same status. The sense of money and status, family disagreement, disapproval, and personal independence are enlarged upon. Miss Churchill, the reader is told, was "of age," in other words, over 21, "and with the full command of her fortune . . . was not to be dissuaded from the marriage, and it took place to the infinite mortification of Mr. and Mrs. Churchill, who threw her off with due decorum" (15). Willful personal decisions, ignoring social propriety and family considerations, are not very favored in Jane Austen's world, as may be seen from Lydia's behavior and Darcy's reactions to Elizabeth and the Bennets in *Pride and Prejudice*. The assumption in *Emma* is that Miss Churchill's deceased parents "specifically willed a significant fortune to their daughter, rather than leaving it in trust to her brother, who has inherited the 'family-estate'" (Pinch, 393).

Miss Churchill on marrying Weston has acted from her feelings rather than sense, regrets her decision, and dies after a marriage of three years. "It was an unsuitable connection, and did not produce much happiness," the reader is told. This is not the perspective of the disapproving brother and his wife, but of the author Jane Austen. The reasons are clearly expressed and the fault is Miss Churchill's—Mrs. Weston's, not her husband's. She "ought to have found more in it, for she had a husband whose warm heart and sweet temper made him think every thing due to her in return for the great goodness of being in love with him." However, his wife "had not the best" kind of "spirit," temperament, will power. She egotistically pursued her preference against family wishes but selfishly lacks the "resolution . . . to refrain from unreasonable regrets at that brother's unreasonable anger, nor from missing the luxuries of her former home." Consequently, she and her husband "lived beyond their income," which was unable to compare with what Mrs. Weston had been used to as Miss Churchill at Enscombe: "she did not cease to love her husband, but she wanted at once to be the wife of Captain Weston and Miss Churchill of Enscombe." In other words, material considerations override "love," and personal choice is more complicated than it seems. It does not fully consider consequences, especially material and social ones.

The fourth paragraph of this second chapter presents Weston's perspective rather than that of his wife. Perceived "especially by the Churchills, as making such an amazing match," appearances, in Jane Austen's world, are not what they appear. "Captain" Weston, as he is called by the narrator in this paragraph, is a reflection of Miss Churchill's attraction to him—his militia rank and standing being one of the features that attracted her to him. He "was proved to have much the worst of the bargain; for when his wife died after a three years' marriage," owing to their overexpenditure, "he was rather a poorer man than at first, and with a child to maintain." This child, to play an important role in the plot of the novel, is "the means of a sort of reconciliation" between him and his deceased wife's brother and wife. "The child was given up to the care and the wealth of the Churchills," and Weston has only his own welfare to concern him.

Subsequently, the course of his life changes totally. He leaves the militia, engages in trade, having connections, "brothers already established in a good way in London." Weston maintains "a small house in Highbury, where most of his leisure days were spent; and," the narrator informs her readers, "between useful occupation and the pleasures of society, the next eighteen or twenty years of his life passed cheerfully away." Further, having "realized an easy competence," Weston acquired more property, purchasing "a little estate adjoining Highbury," and "enough to marry a woman as portionless even as Miss Taylor" (16). So Mr. Woodhouse's exclamation in the first chapter of "poor Miss Taylor" (9) is literally true, a reflection of her economic state and dependency upon oth-

ers. Weston is able, because of his success in trade, "to live according to the wishes of his own friendly and social disposition" (16), and to marry "poor Miss Taylor."

The focus of the narrative then switches from Weston alone, to his relationship with his new wife, referred to still, by the narrator, as "Miss Taylor" (9). She literally was that at the period described—before the wedding to Weston. His perspective, attitude to his future bride, purchase of "Randalls," his property near Highbury, acquisition of fortune, and state of mind in terms of happiness or unhappiness are presented through financial metaphors. "He had made his fortune, bought his house, and obtained his wife." The operative word here is "obtained" in the sense of purchasing, acquiring a possession or goods. His "second" wife "must shew him how delightful a well-judging and truly amiable woman could be." There is no sense here of a romantic passion. She "must give him the pleasantest proof of its being a great deal better to chuse than to be chosen, to excite gratitude than to feel it." Weston's first marriage was one in which he was selected by someone with financial power and social status greater than his own. The second marriage demonstrates the reverse of this. He does the selecting and the controlling of power.

Weston's relationship with his son and his deceased wife's relations becomes the subject of the next paragraph. Independently wealthy, Weston "had only himself to please in his choice." His son Frank had assumed the name "Churchill" rather than "Weston" when he was 21. The assumption is consequently that "it was most unlikely . . . that he should ever want his father's assistance." Weston sees "his son every year in London, and was proud of him." His perception of his son is a highly positive one, and the positive image spreads to Highbury. A note of discord is spread by the narrative observation that "the aunt was a capricious woman, and governed her husband entirely." The effect of this upon the adopted son, whom Weston sees but once a year, is left up in the air at this point in the novel. A short two-sentence paragraph informs readers that while Frank Churchill "was one of the boasts of Highbury, and a lively curiosity to see him prevailed . . . he had never been there in his life." In short, he failed to visit his father's home (16–18).

In this manner the author introduces her readers to other perspectives in the novel. She has moved from the lenses of Mr. Woodhouse, his daughter Emma, and Mr. Knightley to Weston, and now some of the other members of the local Highbury community, not necessarily belonging to its upper echelons. The reader is introduced to other characters who will play various roles. One of these characters is immediately associated with a domestic beverage, "tea." This drink is frequently referred to in Jane Austen's letters, and is liable to scarcity. It becomes a means of social interaction between people in her novels. There are more than a hundred references to "tea" in them. In this instance it is the excuse that Mrs. Perry, Mrs. Bates, and Miss Bates use to converse with one another. These characters are not without interest and play a part in the novel. Mrs. Perry plays a lesser role than Miss Bates. The wife of the Highbury apothecary who accommodates Mr. Woodhouse, Mrs. Perry and her small children appear in two other chapters (2:17 and 19). Miss Bates, on the other hand, plays a much more prominent role in the novel. Middle-aged and unmarried, socially dependent on others' "favours" and good will, far from wealthy, she cares for her aging mother. Emma's rudeness to her will become a way of exposing the heroine's deficiencies. Miss Bates, as the author indicates ironically in the next chapter, enjoys an "uncommon degree of popularity" though she is "neither young, handsome, rich or married" (21).

This is to anticipate. At this early stage of the novel, Miss Bates and Mrs. Perry enlarge the fabric of characters and convey opinion. In this instance, they serve as a chorus, as representatives of local gossip and opinion relating to Frank Churchill and his long anticipated, long awaited rumored visit to Highbury upon his father's marriage. Their conversation "I suppose you have heard of the handsome letter Mr. Frank Churchill had written to Mrs. Weston?" is prefaced by omniscient narrator reference to "the handsome letter Mrs. Weston had received." The word "handsome" is reiterated in the subsequent elaboration following the question: "I understand it was a very handsome letter, indeed. Mr. Woodhouse told me of it. Mr. Woodhouse saw the letter and he says he never saw such a handsome letter in his life." The chorus of Highbury public opinion, represented by Mrs. Perry and Miss Bates, already associates Frank Churchill with the word "handsome" (18). This epithet conveying positive qualities has already been used as the third word of the first chapter. "Emma Woodhouse, *handsome* [my emphasis], clever, rich" (5). These are opposite qualities the reader learns attributed to the likes of Miss Bates by Emma. Such use four times of the epithet "handsome" in relation to Frank Churchill ought to raise eyebrows and questions. Is he physically "handsome," and what lies beneath the surface: Are appearances indeed deceptive?

The next paragraph focuses not on the contents of the letter but on the reaction of Mrs. Weston to the "highly-prized letter." Mrs. Weston is separated from the chorus, the Mrs. Perrys and Miss Bates of the novel. Mrs. Weston's reactions allow the narration to return to Emma, Mr. Woodhouse, and Hartfield. Mrs. Weston is prejudiced in Churchill's favor. She "had, of course, formed a very favourable idea of the young man." His writing to Mrs. Weston must put a seal of approval upon the marriage. Consequently, "she felt herself a most fortunate woman." The word "fortunate" is repeated, on the second occasion relating to what others "might" think of her. In the first instance it relates to her perception of herself. Her "only regret was for a partial separation from friends, whose friendship for her had never cooled, and who would ill bear to part with her!" So Mr. Woodhouse's sentiments are repeated.

The sense of her loss from Hartfield dominates the succeeding paragraph. This consists of two sentences. The first is of a four-part structure: "She knew . . . be missed"; "and could not think . . . her companionableness"; "but dear Emma of no feeble character;" "she was more . . . privations." The second sentence begins with "And." The paragraph from its opening moves into free indirect discourse. Mrs. Weston's thoughts on Emma's reactions, take over: "dear Emma was of no feeble character"; "And then there was such comfort in the very easy distance of Randalls from Hartfield," with the social detail thrown in "so convenient for even solitary female walking." A malevolent world lurking beyond Randalls and Hartfield is not far away from the perceived idyllic existence of Hartfield, marriages, Emma, her father, and the impending visit of Frank Churchill.

The narrative then moves from various perceptions and voices. From that of Mrs. Weston, to Emma, and then to Mr. Woodhouse's giving a gentle sigh and saying: "Ah! poor Miss Taylor. She would be very glad to stay." However, time brings "some alleviation to Mr. Woodhouse." The relief follows a disquisition on the adverse effect food, specifically the wedding cake, has upon him. The return in the narrative at the close of chapter 2, to Mr. Woodhouse and his reactions to change (17–19) reinforce "one of the motifs of the novel: weddings, the match-making that leads up to them, and the changes that come in their wake." The "wedding-cake is . . . the ultimate in a foodstuff designed to be handed round among friends and eaten not for its own sake only but in celebration of a joyful development in the life of a community (Lane, 154–155). There is an irony implied in Mr. Woodhouse's adverse reaction to "the wedding-cake which had been a great distress to him, was all eaten up." Not by him but by everybody else. To obtain confirmation of his dislike, Mr. Woodhouse consults the local apothecary Mr. Perry "on the subject."

The report of the apothecary's reaction mediates between conveying Mr. Woodhouse's internal thoughts and omniscient narration. The latter tells the reader that "Mr. Perry was an intelligent, gentlemanlike man, whose frequent visits were one of the comforts of Mr. Woodhouse's life." The former is indicated in Perry's opinion "that wedding cake might certainly disagree with many—perhaps with most people, unless taken moderately." Perry's use of "might," his correction of "many" to the more general "most," and qualification "unless taken moderate," convey the apothecary's attempts not to offend Mr. Woodhouse. Mr. Woodhouse, after all, helps to pay his bills, to feed his wife and children, so that they can also enjoy slices of the wedding cake. They also reflect Perry's effort to be truthful. The emphasis

is on moderation, an ideal that runs throughout Jane Austen's writing.

The second chapter has moved in perspective from Mr. Weston, his career, first marriage, thoughts on his son Frank, back to Highbury, then to members of the Highbury community and its chorus of commentators, Mrs. Perry, Mrs. Bates, and Miss Bates. A transition is made back to a subject of concern in the first chapter, Mrs. Weston, or "poor Miss Taylor." This takes the reader to Emma and Mr. Woodhouse. The chapter ends ironically with a short double-sentence structure. "There was a strange rumour in Highbury of all the little Perrys being seen with a slice of Mrs. Weston's wedding-cake in their hands: but Mr. Woodhouse would never believe it" (19). This refusal to "believe," to enjoy food, the wedding cake, places Mr. Woodhouse outside the social norm. "Despite his preeminent position in the community, despite the fact that everybody defers to him, Mr. Woodhouse cannot prevent people doing what they like and eating what they like; he cannot prevent their marrying, and, happily, he cannot prevent other people sharing their joy" (Lane, 155).

Chapter 3

Chapter 3 opens with Mr. Woodhouse's preoccupations. These are a narrative device to introduce other characters and settings in the novel. Mr. Woodhouse possesses authority measured by social position and wealth largely to control his own world: "from his long residence at Hartfield, and his good nature, from his fortune, his house, and his daughter, he could command the visits of his own little circle, in a great measure as he liked." He has power, but is possessed with "good nature." His control of "his own little circle" is the reason why he dislikes change. Mr. Woodhouse's world is a very restricted one. He has a "horror of late hours and large dinner-parties." Thus those who visit him do so "on his terms." Mr. Woodhouse's world, that of Highbury, includes Randalls, the home of the Westons, and Donwell Abbey, "the seat of Mr. Knightley." His routine is somewhat controlled by his daughter Emma, who chooses "the best to dine with him," in spite of his preference for evening parties. Additionally, "there was scarcely an evening in the week in which that Emma could not make up a card table for him."

A short single paragraph, structurally consisting of a double sentence, using a separation into two parts through a semicolon, divides the visitors. In the first, "the Westons and Mr. Knightley" visit out of motives of "real, long-standing regard." The other visitor, Mr. Elton, has other motives. He lives alone "without liking it," so he can exchange "his own bleak solitude for the elegancies and society of Mr. Woodhouse's drawing room." Further, "the smiles of" Emma, Mr. Woodhouse's "lovely daughter," provide an incentive. Following these, three of whom are males, Mr. Weston, Mr. Knightley, and Mr. Elton, in the third paragraph come "three ladies" from a different social stratification of Highbury: "Mrs. and Miss Bates and Mrs. Goddard." The first two already have been briefly introduced in the novel. The third, a member of this "second set" of the society frequenting Mr. Woodhouse's evening drawing room, we as readers shall learn, is a respected head of a local girls school. The three, "almost always at the service of an invitation from Hartfield," function at the behest of Mr. Woodhouse. They are willing to be at his service, "fetched and carried home so often that Mr. Woodhouse thought it no hardship for either James or the horses." If their attendance was irregular, taking "place only once a year, it would have been a grievance."

Neither Miss Bates nor her mother actually appears in the novel until the opening of the second book, but readers are informed about them at an earlier stage of the narrative. They belong to "the second set" frequenting Highbury. Mrs. Bates is "the widow of a former vicar of Highbury"; she is "a very old lady" and "almost past every thing but tea and quadrille." In other words, the drink "tea" and a card game for four players played with 40 cards are the routine of her existence. She lives with her unmarried daughter "in a very small way, and was considered with all the regard and respect which a harmless old lady, under such untoward circumstances, can excite." Miss Bates, her daughter, is the opposite of Emma in appearance, social class, and status, economic well being, and living situation. However, in spite of their differences,

they communicate through card games, and the attentions of Emma's father. One, Miss Bates, the poor one, is "a happy woman, and a woman whom no one named without good-will." She loves "every body, was interested in every body's happiness, quick-sighted to every body's merits." Miss Bates considers "herself a most fortunate creature." In short, she is "surrounded with blessings in such an excellent mother and so many good neighbors and friends, and a home that wanted for nothing" (except largeness, servants, economic security). Miss Bates has deficiencies. "She had never boasted either beauty or cleverness. Her youth had passed without distinction, and her middle of life was devoted to the care of a failing mother, and the endeavour to make a small income go as far as possible." These are balanced by positive qualities such as "good-will," "temper," "simplicity," and "cheerfulness." She is an example of fortitude and endurance, making the best of what she has. She is content with her lot in life—unlike the much more complex heroine, Emma. The contrast between the two—between the wealthy and the impoverished, the well connected and the socially dependent—is not explicit at this stage in the novel. Further, Miss Bates is useful for Mr. Woodhouse, being "a great talker upon little matters" and in addition, "full of trivial communications and harmless gossip."

The introduction of the schoolmistress, Mrs. Goddard, provides the opportunity to enlarge the portrait of Highbury society and its activities. Mrs. Goddard's only real appearance in *Emma* is in this third chapter: She is a device for the author to make observations on the local early educational system, and introduce Harriet Smith, who will play a more important role in the novel. The first sentence of the fifth paragragh describes the kind of school Mrs. Goddard runs. It is not a "seminary, or an establishment, or any thing which professed in long sentences of refined nonsense, to combine liberal acquirements with elegant morality upon new principles and new systems—and where young ladies for enormous pay might be screwed out of health and into vanity." The use of "screwed" (20–21) is particularly interesting. It is used only on one other occasion in Jane Austen's fiction. In *Mansfield Park*, the heroine Fanny Price is reported to have "screwed up her mouth" (50), implying some kind of physical contortion perhaps reflecting nervousness or social discomfort. In *Emma* the sense is a modern one of upset, trouble, neurosis, and contortion with an implication of *taken* or *removed*. Mrs. Goddard's school is "a real, honest, old-fashioned Boarding-school, where at a reasonable quantity of accomplishments were sold at a reasonable price." Noticeable are repetition of "reasonable" and the repeated emphasis upon economic considerations. At her education establishment, "girls might be sent out of the way and scramble themselves into a little education, without any of the danger of coming back prodigies" (21–22).

Jane Austen in this lengthy sentence indulges in parody and conveys the attributes her contemporary readers would expect from a young lady's education. "The intellectual education of women in Austen's day was generally considered unnecessary or extravagant, even detrimental." On the whole, "it was thought that the knowledge a girl needed was available in her home." The education at a girls' boarding school such as Mrs. Goddard's would probably concentrate "on etiquette and artistic accomplishments such as drawing, painting, or musical performance," to impress a future husband, than "academic learning" (Pinch, 393). The special features of Mrs. Goddard's school are enumerated. Explanation is given for its high reputation: "Highbury was reckoned a particularly healthy spot." Mrs. Goddard had "an ample house and garden." She fed her pupils well, she "gave the children plenty of wholesome food," let them exercise, and tended to them. Her educational system is a reflection of her character. Mrs. Goddard "was a plain, motherly, kind woman, who had worked hard in her youth." She is without artifice. Her indulgences are a "tea-visit," and she indulges Mr. Woodhouse by leaving "her neat parlour hung round with fancy-work whenever she could, and win or lose a few sixpences by his fireside." The "fancy-work" contrasts with her "plain" character. It is ornamental needlework, crochet, knitting, or similar nonplain work probably done by her pupils.

These three women, Mrs. and Miss Bates and Mrs. Goddard, are the women Emma "collect[s]," now that Miss Taylor has left the fold, to entertain her father. Emma herself, though, is not entertained. A note from Mrs. Goddard alleviates her boredom. She requests to bring a "Miss Smith . . . a girl of seventeen whom Emma knew very well by sight and had long felt an interest in, on account of her beauty." The word "interest" (21–22) has more than one meaning. It means in this context, concern with. In Jane Austen's fiction, "interest" frequently refers to "position in the higher ranks of society, whether in the services or professions, depend[ent] on birth, money and influence" (Phillips, 96). These are attributes, as the reader will learn, Harriet Smith lacks. It is in Emma's "interest" to promote her. The activity gives Emma an illusion of power as "the fair mistress of the mansion."

The description of Harriet Smith has not gone critically unnoticed. Wiesenfarth remarks in *The Errand of Form* that "the first volume of the novel (Chapters 1–18) dramatizes Emma's attempt to dominate by making Harriet Smith into a suitable wife for Mr. Elton. . . . Emma understands her father completely and has fitted herself into his system." However, as Wiesenfarth indicates, Emma "turns to creativity precisely because her relation to her father allows her none." Consequently, "when Harriet Smith arrives on the scene," (116–117)—she is "the natural daughter of somebody" (22)—she "almost immediately turns her into the daughter of a gentleman" (117).

Nicholas Marsh in his *Jane Austen: The Novels* contrasts the two initial paragraphs describing Harriet Smith. The first begins with two sentences, "She was a very pretty girl." The second is a lengthy cumulative one with a semicolon and conjunction linking the two sections. The vocabulary of the first is brief and to the point. Harriet is "short," "plump," "fair," with "blue eyes, light hair," and her features are "regular." (23) Marsh writes, "Not only does this give a simple and vivid impression of Miss Smith, but also the language is simple enough to suit Harriet's mind." The second paragraph is a complete antithesis. Constructions in this second paragraph are more "elaborate and several of them are negative" (29). For instance, Emma was "not struck by any thing remarkably clever in Miss Smith's conversation." Miss Smith is "far from pushing," she is "not inconveniently shy, not unwilling to talk." The vocabulary is now Emma's, her viewpoint, perspective has taken over. Her free indirect discourse takes over. Harriet, Emma finds, demonstrates "so proper and becoming a deference." She, Harriet, is "pleasantly grateful for being admitted to Hartfield." Emma believes that Harriet is "so artlessly impressed by the appearances of every thing in so superior a style to what she had been used to." In short, Emma is attributing qualities to Harriet she wishes her to have.

The ironies in Emma's perception of Harriet become clear when she thinks that Harriet's "soft blue eyes and all those natural graces should not be wasted on the inferior society of Highbury and its connections." According to the snobbish Emma, Harriet's "acquaintance[s]," these "she had already formed were unworthy of her." Harriet is of a much lower social status than Emma, she lacks family and connections. Consequently, the "inferior society" of the local town is "unworthy of her." Emma will take her in hand: "*She* [the emphasis is Jane Austen's] would notice her." The bored Emma has found a means to fill the vacuum created by Miss Taylor's marriage. She will direct her energies to improving Harriet Smith. The narrative repeats the pronoun "she" 11 times in the paragraph beginning "She was not struck," in addition to emphasizing it through the use of a typographical stress. Such repetition occurs in the following paragraph to a lesser extent. Emma, the "she," has taken over, as it were, Harriet's identity and role. Her thoughts have moved away from her social duties, her role as a hostess, to her personal feelings and ambitions. She, Emma, is going to exercise power, while carrying out her social role as hostess.

She is able to do so because Harriet Smith is defenseless. She "was the natural daughter of somebody," in other words, the illegitimate daughter Harriet is a "parlour-boarder" and lives with Mrs. Goddard's, the principal's, family. She has a privilege that the other boarders do not share. She has a backer, as "somebody" (repeated three times) "had placed her . . . at Mrs. Goddard's school, and somebody had lately raised her from the condition of scholar to that of parlour-boarder." Otherwise, her "history" is a mystery, and "she had no visible friends." The use of the adjective "visible" indicates once again that distinction between what appears to be so and what is, appearance and reality, at the heart of Jane Austen's work and the foundation for her irony.

Harriet Smith, the reader learns from Emma's thoughts, "had just departed" from friends, who, "though very good sort of people, must be doing her harm," the reason being that they rent "a large farm off Mr. Knightley, and residing in the parish of Donwell—very creditably she believed." In other words, they, the Martins, have money but are socially unworthy. Emma knows that "Mr. Knightley thought highly of them." In spite of his judgment, she believes that they must be "coarse and unpolished, and very unfit to be the intimate of a girl who," Emma assumes, "wanted only a little more knowledge and elegance to be quite perfect." This conflict between what Emma believes to be Mr. Knightley's judgment and her own belief forms an important part of the plot of *Emma,* as does the theme of the conflict between private and public worlds. Emma, bored, fantasizes that she will "notice her [Harriet]: she would improve her; she would detach her from bad acquaintance, and introduce her into good society; she would form her opinions and her manners." The "she" is Emma, the pejorative "her," Harriet. The final sentence of the paragraph almost gives away Emma's motives: "it would be an interesting, and certainly a very kind, undertaking," to take the socially inferior Harriet under her wing. It is "highly becoming her own situation in life, her leisure and powers." Emma has the time, the inclination, and the social power to form another life and to direct it in the way she thinks fit.

While she is indulging in these fantasies, she does not neglect her function as a hostess. She did "all the honours of the meal," at the dinner party at the Woodhouse residence. She helped and was able to "recommend the minced chicken and scalloped oysters." Their description, "minced" and "scalloped," has an implication of not being direct, of being interfered with. Harriet Smith is to become Emma's "minced chicken" and "scalloped oysters." Narrative attention moves away from Emma to her "poor" father. For him "suppers" are "very unwholesome," and his care for the health of his visitors gains priority over their eating habits. So he, too, has to accommodate his private desires, an extreme concern with health, to his public role of providing "suppers." During the supper he addresses Mrs. Bates, her daughter Miss Bates, and Mrs. Goddard, offering each advice on what to eat. Mrs. Bates is recommended boiled egg, which his cook "Serle understands . . . better than any body." For Miss Bates, Emma will assist with "a *little* bit of tart—a *very* little bit." His are "apple tarts" with no "unwholesome preserves." And for Mrs. Goddard, "*half* a glass of wine" will suffice provided it is "put into a tumbler of water?" This is of course comic, especially in the concern Mr. Woodhouse displays for the smallest needs of his guests. But underlying the incongruity is a serious side. Like his daughter Emma, Mr. Woodhouse attempts to manipulate others' lives, in this case what they eat and drink. Mrs. Bates, her daughter, and Mrs. Goddard are his guests. They will not disobey Mr. Woodhouse, whose desires as to what he thinks they should consume will not be thwarted.

In the final paragraph of three sentences of this third chapter, Emma Woodhouse again takes control. She "allowed her father to talk—but supplied her visitors in a much more satisfactory style." In other words, the guests may not be able to refuse her father's wishes, but she ignores them. She is made "happy" by the evening. The second and shortest sentence tells readers that "the happiness of Miss Smith was quite equal to her intentions." The final sentence weaves in and out of various perspectives moving from Emma's to that of Harriet Smith's. "Miss Woodhouse was so great a personage in Highbury, that the prospect of the introduction had given as much panic as pleasure" to her. The author tells us that "the humble, grateful, little girl went off with highly gratified feelings." She is "delighted with the affability with which Miss Woodhouse had treated her all the evening, and" has received what is a high accolade in this social world, "actually shaken hands with her at last!" In Jane Austen's time, shaking hands was a sign of affection and intimacy and not simply a gesture of formal greeting. So the signal has been given to Harriet Smith that she has "socially" transcended

her limitations, to be highly regarded by "so great a personage in Highbury" as Miss Emma Woodhouse (22–25).

Chapter 4

The consequences of the intimacy become the focal point of the fourth chapter. In the first paragraph the reader learns that Harriet Smith has replaced Mrs. Weston (no longer "Miss Taylor") as Emma's "walking companion." Emma's father's physical activities are confined to the immediate vicinity of his house. "Her father never went beyond the shrubbery, where two divisions of the grounds sufficed him for his long walk, or his short, as the year varied." Emma, on the other hand, since the marriage, has had to curtail her walks. "She had ventured once alone to Randalls," where the Westons live, "but it was not pleasant." There is the unstated threat of something dangerous lurking outside Emma's home for unaccompanied young ladies. Consequently, "a Harriet Smith . . . one whom she could summon at any time to a walk, would be a valuable addition to her privileges." In addition to Emma's being able to exercise power, to manipulate Harriet, the young Harriet Smith is useful to Emma. The final sentence of the paragraph confirms this: "in every respect as she saw more of her, she approved her, and was confirmed in all her kind designs." The last word takes on the meaning of plans and schemes.

The second paragraph follows the mode of the initial paragraph in being direct discourse. Emma specifically appears in the "she" of the third sentence: "Altogether she [Emma] was quite convinced of Harriet Smith's being exactly the young friend she wanted." In the previous two sentences authorial direction and opinion appears to coincide with Emma's thinking. "Harriet certainly was not clever, but she had a sweet, docile, grateful disposition." Further, she "was totally free from conceit; and only desiring to be guided by any one she looked up to," in other words, qualities not conflicting with Emma's and ones Emma can manipulate. This sense of Harriet's usefulness to Emma is reinforced by a contrast with Mrs. Weston. "Such a friend as Mrs. Weston was out of the question." The reason is succinctly conveyed in a short sentence of free indirect discourse, "For Mrs. Weston there was nothing to be done; for Harriet everything." In other words, Mrs. Weston, when Miss Taylor, was useful to Emma (and her father); no longer useful, she is replaced by Harriet.

Emma's interference in all aspects of Harriet's life becomes evident. She attempts unsuccessfully "to find out who were [Harriet's] parents" and is "obliged to fancy what she liked," to imagine ancestry, origins, and parents. Harriet's experience beyond the world of Mrs. Goddard's school, "the teachers and the girls, and the affairs of the school in general," seems to be confined to the world of "the Martins of Abbey-Mill-Farm." Harriet's way of speaking about the Martins and how they live is conveyed through Emma's perception and her reporting of Harriet's speech patterns. The vocabulary is simplistic, the word choice repetitive. Harriet is fascinated by Mrs. Martin's space and possessions. She has "*two* parlours, two very good parlours indeed." Her "upper maid"—Mrs. Martin has more than one maid—has "lived five-and-twenty years with her." The family has "eight cows, two of them Aldeneys, and one a little Welch cow, a very pretty little Welch cow" of which Mrs. Martin is particularly fond. They have "a very handsome summerhouse," this being repeated twice, which is "large enough to hold a dozen people" and "where some day next year they were all to drink tea."

Emma's reaction to this is one of amusement until she realizes that something in the Martin family structure may well prove to be a threat to her plans. Emma discovers "that there was no young Mrs. Martin, no wife in the case." Consequently, "she did suspect danger to her poor little friend from all this hospitality and kindness—and that if she were not taken care of, she might be required to sink herself for ever." Here, Emma's snobbery is evident. She elicits more information from her protégée Harriet about the young Mr. Martin. Emma learns about Harriet and her admirer Martin. They experienced "moonlight walks and merry evening games." Martin was "so very good-humoured and obliging," going for instance three miles "in order to bring [Harriet] some walnuts, because she had said how fond she was of them." Owing to her being "very fond of singing," he invited his "shepherd's

son into the parlour one night on purpose to sing to her." Harriet believes him to be "very clever, and understood every thing." The wool from his flock fetches the highest price at auction than anybody else's. Martin is highly spoken of, "his mother and sisters were very fond of him." She, Harriet, had been told by his mother "that it was impossible for any body to be a better son, and therefore she was sure whenever he married he would make a good husband."

The passage of reported speech is followed by a dialogue initially in Emma's thought and then transferred into an actual conversation between Emma and Harriet. The latter continues to repeat what she has said, for instance, that Mrs. Goddard was kindly sent by Mrs. Martin "a beautiful goose," which becomes "the finest goose Mrs. Goddard had ever seen." Emma, however, is not as interested in this goodwill gesture toward Harriet's educators, as she is in eliciting further information about the person who may well prove to be a stumbling block to her plans. She asks Harriet, "Mr. Martin, I suppose, is not a man of information beyond the line of his own business. He does not read?" The response reveals much about Martin and Harriet. "He reads the Agricultural Reports and some other books, that lay in one of the window seats—but he reads all *them* to himself." This implies a separation of professional work and other reading on Martin's part. Occasionally, "before we went to cards, he would read something aloud out of the Elegant Extracts—very entertaining. And I know he has read the Vicar of Wakefield." Neither of these demonstrates that Martin is a voracious and discerning reader. Both *Elegant Extracts; or Useful and Entertaining Passages in Prose* and *Elegant Extracts: or Useful and Entertaining Pieces of Poetry* were widely available anthologies specifically aimed at the market for younger readers. Initially published in the 1780s, they were frequently reprinted in the early 19th century. Oliver Goldsmith's *The Vicar of Wakefield* (1766) was a very popular sentimental novel. Harriet indicates to Emma that Martin "had never heard," prior to her mentioning them, of "the Romance of the Forest, nor the Children of the Abbey." Neither reveals that her reading tastes are in any way superior to Martin's. Ann Radcliffe's

The Romance of the Forest (1791) and Regina Maria Roche's *The Children of the Abbey* (1798) are both gothic novels commonly found in lending libraries of the period.

Having ascertained to her satisfaction her apparent rival's intellectual and educational tastes, Emma must establish his physical appearance. Emma asks Harriet, "What sort of looking man is Mr. Martin?" To which she receives a response replete with repetition and qualifications representative of Harriet Smith's personality: "Oh! not handsome—not at all handsome. I thought him very plain at first, but I do not think him so plain now." Harriet is without guile and seems genuinely unaware that the new world that she has entered, that of Emma, the world outside the apparently safe confines of Mrs. Goddard's educational establishment, is pervaded by a sense of social hierarchy. She tells Emma that Martin rides frequently into Highbury on a weekly basis and must have frequently "passed" Emma. Martin is on his way to Kingston, the nearest market town to Hartfield. Information of this kind leads to an outburst from Emma. "A young farmer, whether on a horseback or on foot, is the very last sort of person to raise my curiosity." She adds that "the yeomanry are precisely the order of people with whom I feel I can have nothing to do." The yeoman are the small landowners, or in the Martins' case, renters who work the land and gather together in voluntary forces to ensure peace and order and maintain the status quo. They operate and work the land owned by the Knightleys and presumably by the Woodhouses of the world. They, as Emma recognizes, as farmers "can need none of my help," and are "therefore in one sense as much above [her] notice as in every other he [Martin] is below it." He is too independent for Emma. Those who are "a degree or two lower, and a creditable appearance, might interest" her, to the extent to which she can exercise power over them and make them dependent and grateful.

Implicitly, Emma is attempting to turn Harriet's attentions away from Martin. She reinforces this effort to prejudice Harriet by indicating the disadvantage of Martin's age and prospects. Upon learning that he is "Only four-and-twenty," she comments, "that is too young to settle" and that "six years hence, if he could meet with a good sort of young woman in the same rank as his own, with a little money, it might be very desirable." This observation lends to despair on Harriet's part. "Six years hence! Dear Miss Woodhouse, he would be thirty years old!" Emma assumes that Martin is "not born to an independence"; she "imagine[s]" that he "has his fortune entirely to make" and will inherit little, assumptions based on little evidence. Harriet tries to correct her: "they live very comfortably. They have no in-doors man—else they do not want for any thing. And Mrs. Martin talks of taking a boy another year."

Emma is replete with pointers to status and class. The Martins lack an "in-doors man" (26–30). In other words, they are without a "male servant whose responsibilities were restricted to the house, rather than to work around the farm." However, during the late 18th century and early 19th century, "the social and economic threshold for employing domestic help was relatively low." The Martins as prosperous farmers would probably have "female servants, but employing an adult male indoor servant, such as a butler or footman, implied a significantly higher degree of social and economic distinction." In addition, "Hiring a 'boy' . . . represents both aspiration and compromise" (Pinch, 394).

Emma's failure to discover Harriet's parentage results in the creation of a lineage. She tells Harriet, "There can be no doubts of your being a gentleman's daughter," and she must act appropriately according to the fantasy status Emma has created for her. Martin, to Emma's way of thinking, is clearly unsuited for Harriet. Harriet, in an amusing and deliberately grammatically incorrect reply, assures Emma: "Not that I think Mr. Martin would ever marry any body but what had had some education." Both encounter him "as they were walking on the Donwell road." He is accorded a high compliment in Jane Austen's vocabulary: "he looked like a sensible young man." Here, the author's and her character Emma's judgment coincide, only to depart in the rest of the sentence "but his person had no other advantage . . . in Harriet's inclination," when Emma's thought process takes over. As Emma observes Harriet and him talking, she thinks, "Mr. Martin looked as if he did not know what manner was." Harriet reports the conversation to the observer and judge Emma: Martin's words, his speech patterns are conveyed through Harriet's lenses.

The meeting and reactions to it provide Emma with the opportunity to point out Martin's deficiencies to Harriet. Emma compares him with "very real gentlemen" Harriet has been introduced to at Hartfield, where she has seen "very good specimens of well educated, well bred men." These men appear to Emma as "specimens" to be cultivated and eventually captured. Emma asks Harriet: "Were you not struck? I am sure you must have been struck by his [Martin's] awkward look and abrupt manner—and the uncouthness of voice . . . wholly unmodulated." The response is not what Emma expects. Harriet replies, "Certainly, he is not like Mr. Knightley," a reply that helps Emma to appreciate Knightley's qualities, which she appears to take for granted. It is not Knightley on whom Emma has set her designs as a suitable partner for Harriet, but Mr. Elton.

Elton is indirectly introduced to Harriet. Emma begins by contrasting Elton's behavior with that of the older Mr. Weston. She tells Harriet, "Compare Mr. Martin with either of *them* [Emma's emphasis]. Compare their manner of carrying themselves; of walking; of speaking; of being silent. You must see the difference." As he grows older, to be Mr. Weston's age, Mr. Martin "will be a completely gross, vulgar farmer—totally inattentive to appearances, and thinking of nothing but profit and loss." Exhibiting Martin's deficiencies to Harriet is a part of Emma's stratagem to make Harriet into an appropriate wife for Mr. Elton. The pursuit of this aim, hatched in Emma's "brain during the very first evening of Harriet's coming to Hartfield," is to preoccupy the rest of the first of the three books of *Emma*. The heroine, Emma, has not consulted Elton or Harriet, or even considered their wishes. She makes assumptions about both. She believes, for instance; that Elton is "without low connections, at the same time not of any family that could fairly object to the doubtful birth of Harriet." The novel as it unfolds will reveal just how incorrect Emma is in her judgment of Elton, whom she "imagined [had] a very sufficient income." Although Emma does recognize that in Elton there was "a want of

elegance of feature." The rest of the last sentence of chapter 4 takes on a comic and not unironic note. For Emma, Harriet, "who could be gratified by a Robert Martin's riding about the country to get walnuts for her, might very well be conquered by Mr. Elton's admiration" (30–33, 35). Earlier in this chapter, Harriet told Emma that Martin "had gone three miles round one day, in order to bring her some walnuts because she had said how fond she was of them" (28). Martin's kindness, his offerings of walnuts, will ultimately triumph over Emma's stratagems. The comic element at the end of the chapter lies in the fact that Martin and Elton are at cross-purposes. Elton's actions are make-believe, products of Emma's imagination.

Chapter 5

The fifth chapter highlights the differences between Emma and Knightley over her scheming. It centers on conversations between Mrs. Weston and Knightley over the matter and conveys the first lengthy speech in the novel by Mrs. Weston and Knightley's clear-sighted, levelheaded awareness of Emma's deficiencies. Emma is the focus of attention but does not appear directly in the chapter. Mrs. Weston's conversation reveals her to be sensible, dependent on her husband's opinion, and also demonstrating a willingness to consider others. Above all, she wishes to see the positives in Emma and ignore the negatives. "Harriet must do Emma good." Harriet and Emma are mutually beneficial for each other. Knightley, according to Mrs. Weston, is unable "to be a fair judge in this case." He is too "used to live alone," no longer appreciates "the value of a companion," and moreover "no man can be a good judge of the comfort a woman feels in the society of one of her own sex, after being used to it all her life." Mrs. Weston sees Knightley's objection to Harriet as "not the superior young woman . . . Emma's friend ought to be." However, they will mutually "read together."

Knightley, on the other hand, is much more skeptical and sees Emma's faults. She is full of good intentions but "will never submit to any thing requiring industry and patience, and a subjection of the fancy," a combination of getting her own way, and imagination, "to the understanding." It is this process of learning common sense and rationality, seeing the implications of "fancy" upon others, that Emma learns as the novel develops. This learning process, from the subjugation of the "fancy" to that of "understanding," is one of the central concerns of the novel and a lesson its heroine must learn, sometimes painfully. At this early stage in the plot development, Knightley "may safely affirm that Harriet Smith will do nothing" for Emma. From the overall shaping of the novel, Emma does eventually learn something from her abortive attempts to marry Harriet to Mr. Elton, Mr. Elton to Harriet, and separate Harriet from Martin.

Knightley reminds Mrs. Weston that Emma has been spoiled. "At ten years old, she had the misfortune of being able to answer questions which puzzled her sister at seventeen." Emma's sister, Isabella, was "slow and diffident." Emma, on the other hand, "was always quick and assured." Furthermore, "ever since she was twelve, Emma has been mistress of the house and of you all." According to Knightley, "In her mother she lost the only person able to cope with her. She inherits her mother's talents, and must have been under subjection to her." Knightley turns Mrs. Weston's response, that he is always negative, into a positive. Mrs. Weston's new situation as a married woman is a better situation than her previous one for which she at Hartfield had been preparing herself. She might not have given "Emma such a complete education as [her] powers might seem to promise" but received "a very good education from *her,* on the very material matrimonial point of submitting your own will, and doing as you were bid." Knightley's response reveals a perception of marriage as that of submission of the "will" to that of another. The narrative as it unfolds reveals just this clash of "wills" between him and Emma before they can reach a balance, a compromise.

Knightley has a considerable degree of foresight perceiving that Weston's son "may plague him," although it is not Weston or his new wife for whom Frank Churchill is to make life difficult, but Emma. Somewhat ironically in view of the unfolding of narrative events, Knightley tells Mrs. Weston that he does "not pretend to Emma's genius for foretelling and guessing." Somewhat as a warning to the reader, Knightley adds that "the young man may be a Weston in merit, and a Churchill in fortune." Knightley's insights are presented in terms of antithesis: "merit" and "fortune." Harriet "knows nothing herself, and looks upon Emma as knowing every thing." He comprehends that Harriet "is a flatterer in all her ways; and so much the worse, because undesigned." Such distinctions are sophisticated ones in terms of character analysis and may easily be overlooked in reading. For Knightley, "Harriet is presenting such a delightful inferiority" that can only flatter Emma.

Knightley's assessment of the Emma and Harriet friendship is founded on a scrutiny of the choices and differences between them. He too is not unaware that Harriet's social status is different from Emma's, but he fears that Harriet's introduction to the lifestyle of a wealthier class will make her unhappy. Harriet "will grow just refined enough to be uncomfortable with those among whom birth and circumstances have placed her home." She will be given expectations that must remain unfulfilled. Emma's assumption that, while pleasing herself, she will be helping Harriet may have the opposite consequence. Harriet may well prove to be very unhappy. Emma may afford Harriet "a little polish," but not "strength of mind," or how to behave "rationally." When Mrs. Weston commends Emma's physical appearance, her "face and figure,"—"she is loveliness itself"—Knightley's response is to differentiate between Emma's "person," on the one hand and her "vanity." Knightley also admits bias; he is, after all, a "partial old friend."

In these judgments of Emma, omniscient narrator and character, Jane Austen and Knightley, are in accord. The chapter concludes with Mrs. Weston reminding Knightley that "it cannot be expected that Emma [is] accountable to nobody but her father." In a way, Mrs. Weston is a memory bank for what has occurred in Emma's life. She reminds Knightley that his brother's wife, Emma's sister, Mrs. John Knightley, who "is easily alarmed," should not be by the relationship. Knightley then reveals that his affection, his friendship, for Emma is more complex for he brings up the subject of her observations about marriage, and ironically comments, "I have no idea that she has yet ever seen a man she cared for." He is indeed that very man. Knightley "should like to see Emma in love, and in some doubt of return; it would do her good. But there is nobody hereabouts to attach her." Here he forgets himself. The rest of the chapter hints at possibilities formed in Mr. and Mrs. Weston's minds concerning a suitable match for a heroine who is very much home based ([36]–41).

Chapter 6

Chapter 6 focuses on Emma's stratagems to unite Harriet with Mr. Elton. It opens with a lengthy sentence relating to Emma's reaction to Harriet. The author emphasizes that Emma's manipulation of Harriet appeals to "her young vanity," although it is unclear whose vanity is being referred to in this opening sentence—it could be Emma's, Harriet's, or both. Emma's assessment of Elton, "she was quite convinced of Mr. Elton's being in the fairest way of falling in love, if not in love already," is ironic. Emma perceives Elton to be "falling in love" with Harriet, whereas, as she discovers, he is "falling in love" with Emma herself. Emma "had no scruple with regard to him." In other words, Emma has no hesitation in her behavior toward Elton, although his continual use of personal pronouns in addressing Emma and stressing her role in transforming Miss Smith should have set up warning signs. Elton tells Emma, "*You* [my emphasis] have given Miss Smith all that she required . . . *you* [my emphasis] have made her graceful and easy. She was a beautiful creature when she came to *you* [my emphasis], but, in my opinion, the attractions *you* [my emphasis] have added are infinitely superior to what she received from nature." The overflattering tone of Elton's comments should be obvious to Emma, but they are not, and she takes them at face value. Emma's attentions are directed at persuading Elton that Harriet is a worthy future bride.

The dialogue between Emma and Elton regarding Harriet's attributes at the beginning of chapter 6 is notable for an obvious example of free indirect speech. Elton's reply to Emma, "I have no doubt of it," is followed by the sentence "And it was spoken with a sort of sighing animation which had a vast deal of the lover," clearly represent Emma's inner thoughts. These are immediately followed by

a sentence of authorial narration: "She was not less pleased another day with the manner in which he seconded a sudden wish of hers to have Harriet's picture" ([42]–43). Of course, Elton is flattering Emma in order, he thinks, to ingratiate himself with her. Emma, on the other hand, misreads his actions as displays of affection toward Harriet. Elton encourages Emma to draw, something she has given up, confirming Knightley's opinion in chapter 5 that "she will never submit to anything requiring industry and patience" (37). Emma almost sees through Elton's flattery. "Yes, good man!—thought Emma—but what has all that to do with taking likenesses? You know nothing of drawing. Don't pretend to be in raptures about mine. Keep your raptures for Harriet's face."

A good deal of the remainder of the chapter is preoccupied with Emma's attempt to draw Harriet's portrait in an endeavor to attract Elton's interest in Harriet. A lengthy description of Emma's previous attempts draws attention to her failure to finish what she has started: "Her many beginnings were displayed." The descriptions of her subjects provide the narrator with the opportunity to convey additional information concerning Emma's elder sister, Isabella, who married Knightley's brother. They have four children, Henry, John, Bella, and "little George," all of whom Emma has attempted to sketch. Following Harriet's initial sitting, Emma is satisfied with the result: "as she meant to throw in a little improvement to the figure, to give a little more height, and considerably more elegance, she had great confidence in its being in every way a pretty drawing at last, and of its filling its destined place with credit to them both." In other words, to attract Elton's attentions, she has, as it were, "touched up" the portrait, given it "a little improvement to the figure." Emma's is not a precise likeness; she has "improved" Harriet. So Emma's motives are clarified. She was not interested intrinsically in Harriet but in what she can gain from her to satisfy her own wishes and desires. Mrs. Weston sees that Emma has created an artificial Harriet: "Miss Smith has not those eye-brows and eye-lashes," she tells Elton. Knightley tells Emma, "You have made her too tall," to which the narrator adds, "Emma knew that she had, but would not own it." Elton wishes to flatter Emma by minimizing the differences. Mr. Woodhouse, while praising Emma's drawing, is concerned with the possibilities of Harriet's catching cold: "she seems to be sitting out of doors with only a little shawl over her shoulders—and it makes one think she must be cold" (43–45, 47–48). As Joseph Wiesenfarth judiciously observes in *The Errand of Form*, "Knightley appears . . . to judge the reality and predict the course of action and its conclusion. He is the choric voice of reality that sounds on deaf ears. He comes and judges persons while Emma ignores individuals and tries to make and match social entities" (121).

Through the reactions of her character to a drawing, Jane Austen brilliantly conveys character, artifice, deception, and honesty. Emma, by adding to Harriet's eyebrows and eyelashes, and giving her height, implicitly acknowledges that Harriet lacks these qualities. She attempts to improve her subject, Harriet, to give her additional features, physical and social stature. Elton is only too willing "to take the drawing to London, chuse the frame, and give the directions." The drawing, being Emma's, is from his point of view "precious deposit!" His feelings are genuine and "tender." As Emma recognizes, "This man [Elton] is almost too gallant to be in love" (49). She sees things through her own lenses, and the course of the novel shows her growing awareness of her own limitations. Her growth to recognition of others' viewpoints occurs after she has hurt both Harriet and herself and demonstrated Knightley's acuteness when he told Mrs. Weston at the start of chapter 5: "they will neither of them do the other any good" (36).

Chapter 7

Chapter 7 contains a description of the first letter in the novel. This letter is Robert Martin's proposal of marriage to Harriet Smith, from which readers learn much. First, it provides a guide to the criterion for a good letter held by Emma and those of her social rank and background. "The style of the letter was much above [Emma's] expectation." The reasons why are succinctly given: "There were not merely no grammatical errors, but as a composition it would not have disgraced a gentleman; the language, though plain, was strong and unaffected, and

the sentiments it conveyed very much to the credit of the writer." So Robert Martin can write a grammatically correct letter, and one of which a gentleman (let alone a farmer) would have been proud. His language is unadorned or "unaffected" and to the point, containing genuine feelings, not artificial ones. Second, Harriet's reaction to the letter, her reluctance to reject it, reveals her true feelings too.

The letter is presented, indirectly framed by Emma's reactions to it. She finds Martin's letter "above her expectation," and "She paused over it." The letter gains Emma's approval, and is "A better written letter Harriet . . . than I had expected." J. F. Burrows perceptively notes in his *Jane Austen's Emma* that the hesitation here on Emma's part, indicated by the parenthetical pauses following "Harriet" and before "than I had expected" ([50]–51) has its very origins in the difference between Emma, Robert Martin, and the quality of the letter he has written. Fact has intruded into Emma's self-contained world. Emma "can tell Harriet anything she pleases, but she cannot disguise from herself the merits of the letter or persist in telling herself that it is his sister's work. For a moment [Emma] is genuinely puzzled—but she soon persuades herself that she can" (Burrows, 30) comprehend the kind of mind that composed the letter and she returns to the easier assignment of manipulating Harriet.

Among the reasons Emma uses to persuade Harriet to reject the proposal is a snobbish one. She, Emma, "could not have visited Mrs. Robert Martin, of Abbey-Mill Farm. Now I am secure of you for ever." By marrying Martin, Harriet, according to Emma, would be "confined to the society of the illiterate and vulgar all [her] life!" This is an observation that once again leads Harriet Smith to defend Martin, although she admits that since visiting Hartfield she has encountered others but she does "really think Mr. Martin a very amiable young man, and have a great opinion of him." Persuaded by Emma to reject the proposal, Emma assists Harriet in writing the negative reply. Again, the author does not give her readers the text, merely a summary of the content and a statement of fact: "This letter . . . was written, and sealed, and sent. The business was finished, and Harriet safe," from Emma's viewpoint. Interestingly, chapter 7 provides very useful illustrations of Jane Austen's narrative techniques. First, she uses omniscient narration: "The letter . . . was written, and sealed, and sent." Second, she allows her characters' words and their actions to reveal themselves. Consequently, this same sentence could well also be Emma's inner thoughts at work. The words "and Harriet safe" clearly represent Emma's thoughts and not the omniscient narration.

The last section of this chapter returns to the everyday domestic world of trivial conversation but one revealing social hierarchy. We are reintroduced to another inhabitant of Highbury, a Miss Nash, the head teacher at Mrs. Goddard's school who influenced Harriet. According to Harriet, who tells Emma that she is "never happy but at Hartfield," her former head teacher "thinks her own sister very well married, and it is only a linen draper." Harriet is a good pupil, adopting the attitudes and prejudices of her mentor, Emma. Harriet's teacher Emma returns to her object, to unite Harriet with Mr. Elton, although Harriet's thoughts are with Robert Martin and his sisters and their reaction to the rejection. In the final speech of the chapter, Emma speculates on Elton's reactions to her picture: Her last words undercut what she has just said. She comments, "How cheerful, how animated, how suspicious, how busy their imaginations all are!" She seems to refer to Elton's family but is also commenting on human speculation, especially her own. She, Emma, has not the final words of the chapter. These are left to the omniscient narrator with the ambiguous "Harriet smiled again, and her smiles grew stronger." Why she is smiling is deliberately unclear—perhaps she is still thinking of Robert Martin and his declaration of love (53–56).

Chapter 8

Chapters 8 and 9 focus on Harriet and Emma's plans for her. The main interest in chapter 8 resides in the reaction of Knightley to Emma's persuading Harriet to reject Robert Martin's proposal. Knightley directly tells Emma, "Better be without sense, than misapply it as you do" and spells out the harmful effects of her actions upon Harriet: "Vanity working on a weak head, produces every sort of mischief." Emma in her response to Knightley is disingenuous. "I will not pretend to say that I might not influence her a little, but I assure you there was very little for me or for anybody to do"—this is patently untrue as is her further observation, "I have done with match-making indeed" (64–66). Knightley acts openly and honestly, Emma dishonestly. In chapter 8, Knightley attempts to teach Emma common sense. Emma, on the other hand, tries to justify her actions and denies interference in Harriet's decisions. Knightley's tone can be perceived as patronizing. Emma is "uncomfortable," dislikes the fact that she feels "very disagreeable," and creates an "unpleasant silence." Her negative feelings seem unconnected to her disagreement with Knightley, "she still thought herself a better judge"; however, Emma has "a sort of habitual respect for his [Knightley's] judgment in general" (65).

Emma's argument with Knightley in this chapter is conveyed in generalized gender parameters. She tells Knightley, "It is always incomprehensible to a man that a woman should ever refuse an offer of marriage. A man always imagines a woman to be ready for anybody who asks." To which Knightley responds, "Nonsense! a man does not imagine any such thing." Knightley also speaks to Emma in general terms of "men of sense," "men of family," and "prudent men." He tells Emma that "Men of sense, whatever you [Emma] may chuse to say, do not want silly wives. Men of family would not be very fond of connecting themselves with a girl of such obscurity." This is not only gender-based language but also a reflection of the harsh realities of existence in Jane Austen's world and her fictional canvas. According to Knightley's perceptions, "men of sense," men of "prudence," (60, 64) when marrying, carefully assess whom they are to marry, with materialistic considerations being primary ones. For Emma, there is "passion" allied with attractiveness possessed by Harriet Smith, which will allow her to "pick and choose" the right partner (63–64). Emma is using Harriet; however, there are essential differences between them in social status and wealth. Emma has all of these; Harriet has none. The latter will have to marry a wealthy man; the former, Emma, who is independently wealthy, an heiress, can bring other considerations into play when making a decision.

In chapter 8, following Knightley's departure, "Emma remained in a state of vexation." Further, "she did not always feel so absolutely satisfied with herself, so entirely convinced that her opinions were right and her adversary's wrong, as Mr. Knightley." The confrontation with Knightley reveals a feeling of unhappiness and an alternative explanation for her involvement with Harriet. She, Emma, is not merely using Harriet to alleviate her boredom as a result of Miss Taylor/Mrs. Weston's wedding. Emma uses Harriet to sublimate her own problems. She, Emma, will have to confront the matter of her own marriage. Why does she wish to evade the matter? This may have something to do with her relationship with her father, who is totally dependent on her. Further, her own sense of marriage is not a simple one. Although financially independent, she is aware that marriage in the world she inhabits is necessary; she also feels that "Knightley did not make due allowance for the influence of a strong passion, at war with all interested motives." Harriet, in the previous chapter, by returning to her concern for the feelings of Robert Martin and his family, exhibits feelings, "a strong passion." Emma, after Knightley has left her, also exhibits such "passion"—for Knightley.

The final paragraph of chapter 8 returns to Harriet, who "came back, not to think of Mr. Martin, but to talk of Mr. Elton," to the world of local gossip and rumor, to Miss Nash, Harriet's former head teacher, to Perry the apothecary. It is Perry who is the source of information concerning Elton's activities. Perry "found to his great surprise that Mr. Elton was actually on his road to London," that Elton would not return until the next day, which meant that he would miss "the whist-club night, which he had never known to miss before." Both Perry and Miss Nash are sure that "there must be a *lady* in the case" (67–68). Emma, as readers have seen, assumes that Elton's concern is for Harriet. Her misreading of Elton preoccupies the next chapters.

Chapter 9

The opening paragraph of chapter 9 tells readers that Knightley has "not forgiven" Emma and

that "She was sorry, but could not repent." Emma believes that "her plans and proceedings were more and more justified." The rest of the final sentence of the four-sentence paragraph is ironic: "justified" is followed by "and endeared to her by the general appearances of the next few days." The key words are "general appearances." Earlier, Knightley had told Mrs. Weston that Emma rarely if ever completed what she started out. His analysis is confirmed. Emma's intention "of improving her little friend's mind, by a great deal of useful reading and conversation, had never yet led to more than a few first chapters, and the intention of going on tomorrow." Emma finds chatting easier than studying and "much pleasanter to let her imagination range and work at Harriet's fortune, than to be labouring to enlarge her comprehension or exercise it on sober facts."

In chapter 9, Emma and Harriet have started a collection of riddles and Elton has been "invited to contribute any really good enigmas, charades, or conundrums that he might recollect." These were domestic games exercising the mind and did not necessarily encourage conversation. In *Emma* they play charades, which are riddles conforming to a certain regulated pattern. Mr. Woodhouse half-remembers a riddle that "always ended in 'Kitty, a fair but frozen maid'" (69–70). This in fact is a riddle by the great actor David Garrick (1717–79). The final verse of the poem reads

> Say, by what title, or what name,
> Must I the youth address?
> Cupid and he are not the same,
> Tho' both can raise, or quench a flame—
> I'll kiss you if you guess

The answer to the question of the second line is "a chimney sweeper." Adela Pinch notes that "The sexual innuendo of this riddle marks it as belonging to the taste of the earlier parts of the" 18th century. Consequently, Mr. Woodhouse's decision to choose this riddle, plus the fact that he cannot remember it, show that he is aging (395).

> Mr. Elton's first charade
> My first doth affliction denote,
> Which my second is destin'd to feel

And my whole is the best antidote
That affliction to soften and heal

The solutions "woe" and "man," hence "woman," are suggestive. Elton delivers another charade the following day directed to Emma more than Harriet. Emma finds the solution to the three-verse charade. The answer being "court," "ship" making "courtship." Again, Emma misperceives Elton's intentions. She speaks to herself with Knightley rarely from her thoughts. "Ah! Mr. Knightley, I wish you had the benefit of this; I think this would convince you." She adds, "For once in your life you would be obliged to own yourself mistaken." Her following four words are ironic in view of Emma's misreading of Elton, whose verses are not directed, as she thinks, to Harriet but to Emma herself. She muses, "An excellent charade indeed!" The word "charade" has the meanings of a mental game played in verse riddle and a performance, an act where appearances are deceptive.

Emma has to explain to Harriet the solution to the charade. Emma tells Harriet, "That I [she] cannot have a moment's doubt as to Mr. Elton's intentions. You are his object." Her words, of course, her perceptions of "Elton's intentions" are totally incorrect. Again, in Jane Austen's work appearances and perceptions are deceptive. What appears to be so is not so, in spite of Emma's "I thought it must be so." She has falsely anticipated, telling Harriet, "I could never tell whether an attachment between you and Mr. Elton were most desirable or most natural. Its probability and its eligibility have really so equalled each other! I am so very happy. I congratulate you, my dear Harriet, with all my heart." Emma then specifically reveals the foundations for marriage, what she perceives it offers Harriet: "It will give you every thing that you want—consideration, independence, a proper home—it will fix you in the centre of all your real friends, close to Hartfield and to me, and confirm our intimacy for ever." Personal affection between the two people getting married does not enter into Emma's selfish, self-interested considerations. She adds, again ironically in view of her total misreading of the situation, "This, Harriet, is an alliance which can never raise a blush in either of us." The opposite is in fact the case.

Emma must learn, by the resolution of the novel, to become aware of others' thoughts and feelings. She must learn to interpret more perceptively others' intentions and behavior.

Harriet is a victim of Emma's misjudgments. She tells Emma, "Whatever you say is always right." This may appear to be stupid, and too trusting, yet is also flattering to someone who has so much social power over her, Emma. Emma tells her charge Harriet: "It is a certainty. Receive it on my judgment. It is a sort of prologue to the play, a motto to the chapter; and will be soon followed by matter-of-fact prose." The threefold repetition of the neuter pronoun "it," for marriage and Elton, reinforces the sense of marriage as a business contract, and as something inevitable in the life of young women such as Emma and Harriet. The theatrical metaphors are just one example of many from a novel replete with references to the theater. The sequel will indeed be "matter-of-fact prose," more so for the victim Harriet than Emma, who is cosseted by her social position and status (70, 72–74).

Lines from Shakespeare's *A Midsummer Night's Dream*, "The course of true love never did run smooth" (I.i.123), are cited by Emma as an observation upon her reading of "something in the air of Hartfield [giving] love exactly the right direction." Again, her words have multiple meanings placed in the context of the rest of the novel and the unfolding of its plot. Shakespeare's line does provide a commentary on the surface and underlying meanings. Emma believes that Elton will propose to Harriet, whose feelings, if any for him, are created by Emma. Elton has intentions not toward Harriet but Emma. Unconsciously, Emma has deep feelings for Knightley as he has for her. Thus indeed "the course of true love never did run smooth."

Lengthy conversation between Harriet and Emma dwells on the misperceptions of Elton's behavior and misreading of his charade verses. Harriet's true feelings are revealed by her reaction to the letter received from Martin and Elton's verses. Emma controls the situation even to the point of restricting the number of lines from the verses Harriet is permitted to write down. She even tells Harriet not to "be over-powered by such a little tribute of admiration"; she is only too aware of the elaborate social games, or charades, played by people. Harriet, from another world, is not. Mr. Woodhouse appears and breaks up their revelries and fantasies concerning Elton. He, too, reflects upon the significance of the words used in the charade, evoking for one of the few occasions in the novel memories of Emma's late mother: "Your dear mother was so clever at all those things! If I had but her memory! But I can remember nothing, not even that particular riddle which you have heard me mention." He then quotes lines from Garrick that he heard Emma "copied from the Elegant Extracts," which make him think of Emma's sister, Isabella, who is due to visit shortly. His rambling reflections based on disconnected memory recall (Mr. Woodhouse has the symptoms of being in the earlier stages of Alzheimer's) are a means to review plot development: Miss Taylor has become Mrs. Weston and left Emma and Mr. Woodhouse; Emma's sister, Isabella, her husband, and children will stay for a short period over Christmas. In one of his longest speeches so far in the novel, Mr. Woodhouse muses on his grandchildren Henry and John, complaining that "their father is too rough with them very often." Emma, in company with Mr. Knightley, is one of the few who can disagree with her father to make him see other viewpoints. She praises Knightley's behavior as an uncle and concludes "one half of the world cannot understand the pleasures of the other," words that will shortly rebound at her own expense, given the certainty of her belief that Elton's verse charades are directed at Harriet.

The end of chapter 9 focuses on a visit from Elton. Emma tells him that she and Harriet "admired . . . so much" his charade and that she, Emma, has "ventured to write it into Miss Smith's collection" and she has "not transcribed beyond the eight first lines." The last two lines with their ambiguity are omitted. Elton considers Emma's reply "as the proudest moment of his life." Such hyperbole, such exaggeration, leads even Emma to have doubts about Elton's sincerity. "There was a sort of parade in his speeches which was very apt to incline her to laugh" (75, 77–78, 81–82). It is Harriet who must suffer the consequences of Emma's misperceptions.

Chapter 10

Chapter 10 focuses on a visit by Emma accompanied by Harriet to the neighborhood poor and what happens subsequently. Another perspective of Highbury and the surroundings is displayed. So far the narrative has been placed in the setting of Hartfield, with excursions to Weston's wealthy residence and indirect accounts of events at John and Isabella Knightley's in London, Knightley's residence on the outskirts of Highbury, the Martins' farm, and Mrs. Goddard's school. Now Emma is shown displaying her social responsibilities as the daughter of the wealthiest and well-established member of the community by dispensing charity and visiting "a poor sick family" living "a little way out of Highbury." On their way to visit and passing the Vicarage inhabited by Elton, a most revealing conversation takes place between the two. In this Emma reveals her attitudes to marriage. Her response contains insights into her personal viewpoint and those of young women of similar wealth and status in early 19th-century provincial England. She tells Harriet first that she has "none of the usual inducements to marry." Second, that if she "were . . . to fall in love . . . it would be a different thing!" However, Emma feels that to "fall in love . . . is not my way, or my nature; and I do not think I ever shall." Emma adds, "without love, I am sure I should be a fool to change such a situation as mine." She tells Harriet that she does not need money, employment, or social position—what she calls "consequence." She has more control at Hartfield than married women have "of their husband's house." Emma also reveals a deep relationship with her father and love for him. She tells Harriet, "never, never could I expect to be so truly beloved and important, so always first and always right in any man's eyes as I am in my father's."

This reintroduces a reference to a character, Miss Bates, who is to play an important role in the novel and especially regarding Emma and her process of education. Harriet's response to Emma's strictures on marriage is, "But then, to be an old maid at last, like Miss Bates!" Emma's objections to Miss Bates are not those of Harriet, that she has aged and remained a virgin, poor and without social status. Her objections are that Miss Bates *is* (my emphasis), to use Emma's words "so silly—so satisfied—so smiling—so prosing—so undistinguishing and unfastidious." She, Emma, objects and resents Miss Bates's contentment. Emma is aware of general perceptions of those who remain single. She tells Harriet that "it is poverty only which makes celibacy contemptible to a generous public!" Emma in this way becomes the voice for many of Jane Austen's contemporary readers when she informs Harriet that "A single woman, with a very narrow income, must be a ridiculous, disagreeable, old maid! the proper sport of boys and girls." On the other hand, in the balance and antithesis so common to Jane Austen and her sentence structures, Emma tells Harriet, "but a single woman of good fortune, is always respectable, and may be as sensible and pleasant as anybody else."

Here is contained a remarkable insight into values permeating the world of Jane Austen's novels and the judgments upon human activity contained within them. As long as the "single woman" possesses "good fortune," has more than sufficient wealth, she is fine in the eyes of others. Not only that, a "very narrow income," Emma tells Harriet, "has a tendency to contract the mind, and sour the temper." She elaborates, "Those who can barely live" survive economically "and who live perforce in a very small, and generally inferior society, may well be illiberal and cross." Economic conditions and situation influence human behavior and psychology. Yet what is even more annoying to Emma is her perception that Miss Bates is an exception to this rule. Miss Bates is poor and unmarried yet still "very much to the taste of everybody." In fact, according to Emma, "Poverty certainly has not contracted her [Miss Bates's] mind" and Emma adds, "I really believe, if she has only a shilling in the world, she [Miss Bates] would be very likely to give away a sixpence of it." In addition, "nobody is afraid of her: that is a great charm."

Harriet reveals in her questions to Emma in this chapter that she is not as simple as she appears. Aware of aging, that her youth will not endure forever, she asks Emma directly and pointedly what she, Emma, will do when she "grow[s] old?" The answer reveals much about Emma and her sense of what women of her wealth and background

can and cannot do, given the social constraints under which they live. Her mind, she believes, is "an active, busy" one. She has "a great many independent resources." Also open to her are what she refers to as "Woman's usual occupations of eye and hand and mind." If she will "draw less," she, Emma, will "read more," "carpet-work" can replace "music." She recognizes that by "*not* marrying," she may lack "objects for the affections." However, she will have "all the children of a sister I love so much, to care about." Attachment to her nephews and nieces cannot "equal that of a parent," yet they can provide comfort in her declining age. This introduces the subject of Miss Bates and Jane Fairfax, who will subsequently play an important role in the novel and of whom Emma is already "sick of the very name," as she is spoken about so much.

At this juncture in the novel, Emma and Harriet reach the cottage she is visiting. Her charitable work, as the omniscient narrator comments, Emma's being "very compassionate," has a reason. This is because "the distresses of the poor were as sure of relief from her personal attention and kindness, her counsel and her patience, as from her purse." In this way she is able to forget herself and her own problems, however briefly. As she says, "These are the sights, Harriet, to do one good." The noun "good" here refers to moral values and worth contrasted with its previous adjectival meaning of "good fortune" relating to the way others value worth and behavior based on economic considerations. The conditions in which the poor live reinforce Emma's reflections that poverty is related to narrowness of mind. Leaving the home of the "poor creatures," they cross "the low hedge, and tottering footstep which ended the narrow, slippery path through the cottage garden, and brought them into the lane again."

Following the visit they accidentally meet Elton. Emma cleverly manages to distance herself from Harriet and Elton to create the opportunity for Elton to propose to Harriet. The fact that she is able to separate herself from them is due to an illustration of the important welfare role her Hartfield home plays in the surrounding area. She is "overtaken by a child from the cottage" they have just visited "setting out, according to orders, with her pitcher, to fetch broth from Hartfield." This stratagem of helping the child not having worked, she then finds an excuse to stop at the Vicarage to have some of her clothing, her lace, attended to. Even this plan fails ([83]–88).

Chapter 11

The next two chapters, 11 and 12, may be seen as containing one of the major scenes of the novel. The chapters are concerned with the visit of the John Knightleys to Hartfield, and their initial Hartfield dinner. Emma has other things to attend to than manipulating the affections of Harriet and Elton. In the last sentence of the first paragraph of chapter 11, Jane Austen uses inner thought processes to convey Emma's summation of the situation between Harriet and Elton: "There are people, who the more you do for them, the less they will do for themselves."

The activities of Mr. and Mrs. John Knightley with their five children are described. They divide their leisure time "between Hartfield and Donwell Abbey"—the home of Mr. Knightley. Mr. Woodhouse "could not be induced to get so far as London, even for poor Isabella's sake." His anxieties concerning the journey from London to Hartfield are allayed. In a paragraph, the narrator in three lengthy sentences describes Mrs. John Knightley's physical appearance, her behavior, whom she takes after, and her character. She is, the reader is told, "a pretty, elegant little woman, of gentle, quiet manners." She is "amiable and affectionate" and "wrapt up in her family." She takes after her father, Mr. Woodhouse, "She was not a woman of strong understanding or any quickness," who has also inherited her father's "constitution." In other words, she is "delicate in her own health, overcareful of that of her children, had many fears and many nerves." Her father at Hartfield has Mr. Perry at his beck and call. In London she has found a surrogate for Perry in "her own Mr. Wingfield."

Mr. John Knightley, on the other hand, is a more complicated figure than his wife. The narrator tells her readers that he "was a tall, gentleman-like, and very clever man" who is advancing professionally. He however has "reserved manners which prevented his being generally pleasing" (touches of Darcy in *Pride and Prejudice*). Also he is "capable

of being sometimes out of humour." He has "a worshipping wife" who remains blind to his tantrums. Emma, on the other hand, is not so sympathetically disposed toward him. Her adverse judgment toward him and the narrator's are in accord. Emma "was quick in feeling the little injuries to Isabella," her sister, "which Isabella never felt herself." The fact that judgment of a narrator and a character, such as Emma whose misperceptions of people's actions and motives, such as those of Elton, have been continually exposed in the narrative, is revealing. The omniscient narrator's attitude to the flawed heroine Emma is indeed complex throughout the novel. In this instance specifically, what Emma finds wanting is "the want of respectful forbearance towards her father" on the part of her brother-in-law, John Knightley.

The remainder of chapter 11 serves little to advance the plot, although there are pointers to what is to come. Conversation between John Knightley, his wife Isabella, Emma, and Mr. Woodhouse focuses on "Miss Taylor," now Mrs. Weston, Mr. Weston, and Weston's mysterious son. The son, readers as well as characters are reminded, was supposed to have visited "soon after the marriage, but it ended in nothing." A letter he wrote congratulating Mrs. Weston on the marriage is brought up, as is "Frank C. Weston Churchill's" age, which is 23. Chapter 11 concludes with Isabella reflecting "there is something so shocking in a child's being taken from his parents and natural home." In this instance her husband is less distressed, arguing that Weston "takes things as he finds them, and makes enjoyment of them somehow or other" as he is an outgoing social being. This is an attitude to which Emma is not too sympathetic but does not argue the case. She reflects on "the all-sufficiency of home to" her brother-in-law, and by implication to herself (91–93, 95–97).

Chapter 12

In chapter 12, Knightley joins the family gathering at Hartfield. There are several matters of interest in the chapter. Emma and Knightley affect some kind of reconciliation, although Knightley bluntly tells Emma, "I have still the advantage of you by sixteen years' experience, and by not being a pretty young woman and a spoiled child." He adds, "Come, my dear Emma, let us be friends and say no more about it." The characters in this family party at Hartfield are divided into two groups, with Emma hovering between them. There are Mr. Woodhouse, his daughter Isabella, and the two Knightley brothers. Each of them is playing a role. Mr. Woodhouse is trying unsuccessfully to recover for himself his married daughter, Isabella. John Knightley as son-in-law resents his father-in-law's possessiveness toward a daughter and his wife, both of whom possess similar qualities: selfishness and hypochondria. Emma and Knightley both play similar roles in diverting attention from sensitive subjects. For instance, Emma switches the subject away from her father's dwelling on the dangers and perils of the Knightley journey to Hartfield and the fact that her father claims to have been "almost killed . . . once" by the sea, exclaiming, "I must beg you not to talk of the sea." In spite of her efforts, her father's dwelling on health leads his son-in-law to react in a "voice of very strong displeasure." This forces his brother Knightley to change totally the subject away from an obsession with health to the subject of a diverted local footpath.

During the conversations much is learned about Knightley's social responsibilities as a magistrate and as a landowner. Mr. Woodhouse, again in conversation, frequently refers to the advice and role of Perry the apothecary. Much of the conversation in the chapter turns on the subject of health and the obsession with it. There is also discussion of Jane Fairfax, an orphan (as Harriet Smith), brought up by her grandmother and aunt since the age of three and then at the age of nine informally adopted by Colonel and Mrs. Campbell. She is "exactly Emma's age" (99, 101, 106, 104). So in addition to conveying the intricacies of social relationship, Jane Austen as narrator also lays the groundwork for subsequent character introduction. The chapter exhibits its author's "sense of a balance, loss and recovery of power, dependent on kinship, marriage, congeniality, complicity, intelligence and imagination. Personal powers are exhibited in personal relations and in public life" (Hardy, 118).

Chapter 13

Chapter 13 centers on the family dining at Randalls, the home of the Westons, on Christmas eve. Harriet spoils Emma's plans by catching a cold and being unable to attend. Again, as in the previous chapter, health, the lack of it becomes a topic, with Perry the apothecary once again becoming a subject: "Why does not Perry see her?" as if Perry has a magic cure to all physical ailments. Emma is surprised that in spite of Harriet's illness, and her giving Elton every opportunity not to attend, he is eager also to go to the Westons' dinner party. As the omniscient narrator observes, Emma was "too eager and busy in her own previous conceptions and views to hear [Elton] impartially, or see him with clear vision." When John Knightley offers Elton a seat in his carriage, Elton is only too eager to accept the offer. This leads to an *erlebte Rede* passage conveying Emma's inner reactions to what she regards as "strange" behavior. She explains it to herself by generalizing about the habits of "single men," rather than focusing on Elton. In an ensuing conversation, her brother-in-law, John Knightley, makes Emma aware of Elton's attentions toward her and warns her. Emma's response is to amuse "herself in the consideration of the blunders which often arise from a partial knowledge of circumstances, of the mistakes which people of high pretensions to judgment are ever falling into." She is directing her response to her brother-in-law's strictures. Soon in the narrative, these words are to rebound upon her.

An additional example of Jane Austen's irony pervading her work should not go unnoted. Mr. Woodhouse, who is constantly concerned about the weather and its effects on others, is oblivious to "the increasing coldness" and "seemed to have no idea of shrinking from it." He "set forward at last most punctually with his eldest daughter in his own carriage, with less apparent consciousness of the weather than either of the others." Mr. Woodhouse is "too full of the wonder of his own going, and the pleasure it was to afford at Randalls to see that it was cold, and too well wrapt up to feel it." However, during the evening, a snow flurry occurs, provoking Mr. Woodhouse to insist that the dinner party be curtailed, the carriages recalled, and that they return from Randalls to Hartfield. This return to social form, to obsession with the weather, results in the collapse of Emma's illusions about Elton.

To return to chapter 13, the visit leads to a lengthy outburst of "discontent" from John Knightley. His wife "could not be complying, she dreaded being quarrelsome; her heroism reached only to silence." Austen uses short clauses: "They arrived, the carriage turned, the step was let down, and Mr. Elton, spruce, black, and smiling, was with them instantly." The remainder of the journey to Randalls is largely taken up with Elton's ingratiating remarks directed toward Emma, with John Knightley replying in short, sharp sentences when questions are directed to him. Elton, Emma perceives, seems a little too uninterested in Harriet's illness. He, as others, defers to Perry, the apothecary and seeming miracle worker with all who are ill. Elton is enthusiastic about what he perceives to be the latest developments in carriage comforts, with "the use of a sheep-skin for carriages." There is an indirect topical allusion to "slavery" when replying to John Knightley's observation "I never dine with any body." Elton responds, "I had no idea that the law had been so great a slavery. Well, sir, the time must come when you will be paid for all this, when you will have little labour and great enjoyment." These observations are made just before "they passed through the sweep-gate" in the carriage. These allusions to slavery, payment, labor, living with enjoyment, and the work of chimney-sweepers (109–116), are indirect and not developed in *Emma.* Yet they underline the wealth and leisure enjoyed by many in the real rather than fictional world in which Jane Austen's readers lived.

Chapter 14

Randalls, the dinner party, the return to Hartfield provide the setting for chapters 14 and 15. Chapter 14 contains much of interest. There is Elton's persistent attempt to gain Emma's attention, and Emma's quarrels with Mrs. Weston. The subject of disagreement concerns Frank Churchill, Mr. Weston's son, and his apparent impending visit to the area. This perspective in the chapter, as in a good deal of the novel, is Emma's. She sees Elton's attentions as "terribly like a would-be lover," although "for her own sake she could not be rude." At the dinner table she is "happily released from Mr. Elton," as if he is attempting to entrap

or to imprison her. Mrs. Weston, Emma is told by Mr. Weston, believes that Frank Churchill will yet again "put-off" his visit to them. Mrs Weston is reserved about Frank Churchill, publicly ascribing the difficulties of his visit to "Mrs. Churchill [who] rules at Enscombe," where he lives. Weston, in common with John Knightley and Elton, following these chapters, all but disappears from direct participation in the narrative, having but three or four speeches in the remainder of the novel. They are replaced in the focus of attention by other characters: Jane Fairfax, Frank Churchill, and Miss Bates. At this juncture, Mr. Weston tells Emma, "there are secrets in all families, you know." These words will reverberate throughout *Emma* and Jane Austen's other novels. Indeed, her plots may be viewed as ones that unravel family secrets.

Often Jane Austen's irony depends on the perceiver. Early in the narrative, illustrations were provided of John Knightley's ill temper. His wife, Isabella, replies to Mrs. Weston that she, Isabella, "never think[s] of that poor young man [Frank Churchill] without the greatest compassion." She adds, "To be constantly living with an ill-tempered person must be dreadful. It is what we happily have never known anything of; but it must be a life of misery," words demonstrating that she is seemingly oblivious to what others regard as her husband's choler and her father's oddities. Two other observations in chapter 14 should not go unnoticed. Emma has a tendency to gender generalization. For instance, she tells Mrs. Weston, "A young *woman,* if she falls into bad hands, may be teazed, and kept at a distance from those she wants to be with; but one cannot comprehend a young *man's* being under such restraint." Mrs. Weston tries to reason with Emma but to no avail (110–122).

Chapter 15

Chapter 15 brings resolution to one strand in the plot: Elton's intentions and Emma's misreading of them until this point in the story. There are two parts to the chapter: the remaining time at Randalls and Emma's ride home with Elton. Focus on the encounter between them results in insufficient attention being paid to elements earlier on in chapter 15. Emma at last, it may be felt, begins to discern Elton's true intentions. She does so through reacting to Elton's attitude toward Harriet's condition, being more concerned that Harriet's "bad sore throat" should not affect either him or Emma, rather than Harriet. Once again, he is dependant on the opinion of Mr. Perry. His overprotectiveness leads Emma, in a passage conveying her inner thought processes, to be "vexed. It did appear— there was no concealing it—exactly like the pretence of being in love with her [Emma], instead of Harriet."

In the second half of the chapter, Emma finds herself alone in a carriage with Elton, who reveals his true intentions toward her. Elton had drunk "too much of Mr. Weston's good wine." His inhibitions are released in the coach. His overtures and declaration of love are conveyed in a paragraph combining omniscient narration and *erlebte Rede,* or free indirect discourse, followed by dialogue. Thus, "to restrain him [Elton] as much as might be, by her own manners, she was . . ." the author tells her readers. Further, "she [Emma] found her subject cut up—her hands seized . . . and Mr. Elton actually making violent love to her." Then we enter into her direct thoughts, her immediate reaction. "Mr. Elton, the lover of Harriet, was professing himself *her* lover." Emma "felt that half this folly must be drunkenness," but Elton repeats himself. Stylistically Jane Austen depicts Emma's total amazement at what is taking place on the journey home from Randalls. Jane Austen achieves this by a lengthy sentence of 125 words.

The omniscient narrator observes, "But Mr. Elton had only drunk wine enough to elevate his spirits, not at all to confuse his intellects. He perfectly knew his own meaning." Elton's and Emma's misreadings of each other's intentions are now made apparent to both. Emma refuses Elton unambiguously and he denies displaying any interest in Harriet whatsoever, especially in view of her lowly social status. The remainder of the journey is passed in hostile silence between the two: "their straightforward emotions left no room for the little zig zags of embarrassment." Both must deal with the consequences of their mutual misreadings of each other. In the last paragraph of chapter 15 Emma is welcomed home "with the utmost delight, by her father who had been trembling for the dangers of a solitary drive from Vicarage-lane." His anxiety is genuine. Even "Mr. John Knightley, ashamed of his ill humour was now all kindness and attention" toward Emma, whose "mind had never been in such perturbation" (125, 129–130, 132–133).

Chapter 16

Chapter 16 focuses on Emma's "mind . . . in such perturbation" (133). The narrative is straightforward. Emma is shocked when she discovers just how inadequate her perception, her judgment of Elton has been and is most concerned regarding the consequences of her stupidity on Harriet. A restless night of self-recrimination, and wishing she had acted differently, combine with anger at what she perceives to be Elton's arrogance in proposing marriage: "He only wanted to aggrandize and enrich himself." She comes to the conclusion that she should not in the first place have started matchmaking, and she resolves not to do so anymore. For the next few days, the weather is on her side. The rain, snow, and slush prevent her even from going to church on Christmas Day. She does not have to encounter Harriet, and there is "no need to find excuses for Mr. Elton's absenting himself."

There are several areas of interest in chapter 16. The opening three paragraphs provide interesting illustrations of Jane Austen's style. Free indirect discourse is combined with the use of the past tense. Sentences and paragraphs vary greatly in length. Narrators' and characters' voices become indistinguishable. Jane Austen's style, her choice of words, of punctuation, of tenses, of mode of stylistic address, interweaving between indirect free discourse conveying Emma's thoughts and omniscient direction, are important. They provide a guide to an understanding of her techniques and narrative development. How genuine is Emma's remorse is left somewhat ambiguous. The narrator notes that "the return of day will hardly fail to bring return of spirits." Emma concludes "that there could be no necessity for any body's knowing what had passed except the three principals," herself, Elton, and Harriet. Her father is rarely out of her mind and she is "especially [concerned] for her father's being given a moment's uneasiness about it" (133, 135, 137–138).

Chapter 17

Chapter 17 is relatively brief. Several important narrative transitions occur. Mr. and Mrs. John Knightley and their three children leave Hartfield for London. Elton leaves Highbury for the fashionable spa town of Bath. Emma tells Harriet what has occurred between her and Elton. Harriet, while upset, does not blame Emma. For Harriet, "she never could have deserved him," Elton. Whether or not Harriet would have felt like that before being taken up by Emma and made aware of differences in social status is left unclear. In reaction to Harriet's genuine distress and humility—"Her tears fell abundantly—but her grief was so truly artless that no dignity could have made it more respectable in Emma's eyes"—Emma feels even more ashamed. She determines from now on to "being humble and discreet." Also, she will be "repressing imagination all the rest of her life." This is a hyperbolic resolution that leaves Emma's intentions open to considerable doubt. The final paragraph of the chapter draws out the pressures involved in the world of Jane Austen's fiction. There is not only Harriet herself to consider but also the world in which she lives. Elton was "the adoration of all the teachers and great girls" at Mrs. Goddard's educational establishment. Therefore, "it must be at Hartfield only that she could have any chance of hearing him spoken of with cooling moderation or repellant truth." However, to use a medical metaphor, Emma unlike her father or others in the novel, does not run for advice at every opportunity to Perry, "where the wound had been given, there must the cure be found if anywhere." Emma felt this particularly, as "till she saw her in the way of cure, there could be no true peace for herself." The use of the pronoun "her" is somewhat ambiguous as it may relate both to Emma and to Harriet (141–143).

Chapter 18

Chapter 18 is the final one of the first volume of *Emma*. Mrs. Weston proves to be correct in her doubts about Frank Churchill's imminent appearance. His visit to his father at Randalls has once again been delayed. The reasons this time provoke yet another disagreement between Emma and Knightley, who chastised Churchill for his apparent neglect of his father. Emma tells Knightley, "You are the worst judge in the world . . . of the difficulties of dependence. You do not know what it is to have tempers to manage." Her dogmatic tone is ironic in view of her total misjudgment of Elton and reveals that in spite of her resolution of good intentions, Emma still has much to learn. Perhaps Emma is speaking from recent experiences when she tells Knightley, "It is very unfair to judge of any body's conduct, without an intimate knowledge of their situation." She adds, "Nobody, who has not been in the interior of a family, can say what the difficulties of any individual of that family may be." Knightley's reply is placed in general gender terms: "There is one thing, Emma, which a man can always do, if he chuses, and that is, his duty," as if "duty" does not also apply to women. He goes on at some length, unlike his previous short sentences, about Churchill's lack of responsibility and family duty. He even makes a distinction between the French and English usage of the word "amiable." Knightley tells "Emma, your amiable young man can be amiable only in French, not in English. He may be very 'amiable,' have very good manners, and be very agreeable; but he can have no English delicacy towards the feelings of other people; nothing really amiable about him" (146, 149). Knightley is making a distinction between the French *aimable*—which he construes as mere politeness—and its English cognate, "amiable," which in Austen's era belonged in "'a much more serious register:' an innate, fundamental warmth of temper or disposition" (Pinch, 395–396, citing M. Stokes, 162–165).

It is Emma who brings the argument to an end. She is surprised by the strength of Knightley's feeling on the matter and takes his role as mediator. Emma is the voice of moderation, telling Knightley, "I will say no more about him . . . you turn everything to evil. We are both prejudiced; you against, I for him; and we have no chance of agreeing till he is really here." This leads to yet another outburst from the usually even-tempered Knightley. In the last paragraph of the chapter consisting of a single lengthy sentence, dialogue is replaced by omniscient narration, with elements of inner thought processes. Knightley's reaction, she thinks, "was unworthy [of] the real liberality of mind which she was always used to acknowledge in him." Further, "she had never before for a moment supposed it could make him unjust to the merit of another." The pronoun "it" refers to their disagreement and to what Emma perceives to be Knightley's prejudice against Frank Churchill. The remainder of the novel will reveal why he reacts so strongly in this way (146, 149–151).

Volume 2, Chapter 1 (Chapter 19)

The second volume focuses on Emma and her social position in Highbury society. It opens with Emma and Harriet walking together. To divert Harriet's attention from continuously dwelling on Elton, Emma does something she does not like doing, calling on Mrs. and Miss Bates. The visit, seen largely from Emma's perspective, introduces other characters who will play a prominent role in the narrative. It also reveals a good deal about Emma and the role Miss Bates plays in the novel. In the third paragraph of the first chapter of the second volume, Emma remembers hints from Knightley concerning her negative attitudes to Mrs. and Miss Bates. She finds them "a waste of time—tiresome women." Her visits to their rented accommodation in a house belonging "to people in business" may well result in "all the horror of being in danger of falling in with the second rate and third rate of Highbury, who were calling on them for ever, and therefore she seldom went near them." In this instance, to divert Harriet from thoughts of Elton, Emma conquers her snobbery.

On one level the visit is dominated by health concerns and Mrs. Bates's deafness, as well as the illness of Jane Fairfax: Again Perry apparently will prove to be her salvation. Miss Bates believes that though Perry "would not mean to charge anything for attendance, we could not suffer it to be so, you know. He has a wife and family to maintain, and is not to be giving away his time" ([155], 162). On another level, the visit is replete with information conveyed in a special way by Miss Bates. These data are important for the plot, as viewed through Emma's lenses, and are misinterpreted by her. Miss Bates's manner of conveying information has special characteristics. First, her sentences are rarely

completed. Second, "each sentence flies off at a tangent from the last, but so characteristic are the trains of thought that, when need is, every sentence elucidates its curtailed predecessor." In other words, Miss Bates uses "fragmentary speech" (Lascelles, 94–95). What she says consists of very detailed accounts of daily events and the conversations she has had, interladen with positive valuations concerning the kindness of her neighbors. She shuffles from each point by way of elementary chronology, and regularly goes off her subject into something else. Her speeches are marked by an abundance of dashes, or parentheses and digressions.

Initially Miss Bates mentions her friends the Coles, Highbury citizens who watch over her and Mrs. Bates, then she moves to Elton, to social activities in Bath, and then to a letter from her niece Jane Fairfax she has just received. Her speech is full of detail, repetition, the necessities of daily living, not among the rich like Emma, but those like Miss Bates existing on the breadline and the charity of others in rented accommodation. She is unable initially to find Jane's letter as "I had put my huswife upon it, you see, without being aware, and so it was quite hid but I had it in my hand so very lately that I was almost sure it must be on the table." She relates how much Jane writes. She "in general . . . fills the whole paper and crosses half" (157). According to Pinch, "that Jane Fairfax crosses her letters is in part an indication of her frugality, as paper and postage could be quite costly" (396).

After dwelling for some time on the consequences of her mother's apparent deafness and its effects upon herself and Jane Fairfax, Miss Bates conveys the actual content of the letter. In it, she informs Emma that Jane was due to visit Ireland to visit Miss Campbell, who readers are subsequently told is the daughter of Colonel and Mrs. Campbell, with whom Jane went to live when she was nine years old. Miss Campbell recently had married a Mr. Dixon and gone to live in Ireland. Emma, on hearing this, does what she had promised earlier not to do, lets her imagination wonder. "At this moment, an ingenious and animating suspicion entering Emma's brain with regard to Jane Fairfax, this charming Mr. Dixon, and the not going to Ireland." She speculates why Jane prefers to spend three months with Mrs. and Miss Bates. In the rambling answer related by Miss Bates, Emma learns that Mr. Dixon saved "Jane at Weymouth," a popular West Country seaside resort, "when they were out in that party on the water, and she, by the sudden whirling round of something or other among the sails, would have been dashed into the sea at once, and actually was all but gone." She continues, "if he had not, with the greatest presence of mind, caught hold of her habit. . . ."

Emma continues to ask Miss Bates, "Miss Fairfax prefers devoting time to you and Mrs. Bates?" She is fishing for further information, even going so far as eliciting data from Miss Bates on the relative physical attractiveness of Jane and Miss Campbell, now Mrs. Dixon. Miss Bates's concern is with Jane's health. She "caught a bad cold, poor thing!" She even gives the date on which it was caught, "so long ago as the 7th of November (as I am going to read to you,) and has never been well since." Subsequently, readers will learn that Emma has only too quickly forgotten her mistake with Harriet. Her imagination is running away with her concerning an assumed illicit relationship between Jane and Mr. Dixon. So the first chapter of the second book of *Emma* introduces new characters, presents the realities of everyday Highbury existence, and shows that Emma has learned little. Mention should also be made of the fact that Miss Bates introduces a world beyond Hartfield, Highbury, and Weymouth, and even England. She mentions that Jane, in her letter, mentions Dublin and a "country-seat, Balycraig, a beautiful place that I [Miss Bates] fancy." Earlier, Miss Bates refers to "different kingdoms, I was going to say, but however different countries" (160–161, 159). In this way, through the seemingly most innocuous, less political of all characters (although one loved by her neighbors and content with her life), Jane Austen is able to convey a political reality and allusion to a recent political event. Following the abortive 1798 Irish uprising against British rule, the 1800 Act of Union "abolished Ireland's state as a separate kingdom, dismantling the Irish parliament and the Irish church" (Pinch, 396).

Volume 2, Chapter 2 (Chapter 20)

The first half of the second chapter supplements through omniscient narration biographical information about Jane Fairfax gleaned from Miss Bates's reportage. The second half of the chapter then moves to Emma's perspective. Jane Fairfax is an orphan. In common with Frank Churchill, she has been adopted. Both have lost mothers when young, and in Jane's case, she has lost both parents rather than one. Another character, Harriet Smith's parentage is unknown. The author as narrator relates that Jane "by birth . . . belonged to Highbury." She lost her mother when she was three years old, her father being an army lieutenant from an infantry regiment. The second paragraph consists of a single sentence in which the transition from happiness to sorrow is movingly conveyed: "The marriage of Liet. Fairfax, of the — Regiment of infantry, and Miss Jane Bates, had had its day of fame and pleasure, hope and interest; but nothing now remained of it, save the melancholy remembrance of him dying in action abroad—of his widow sinking under consumption and grief soon afterwards—and this girl." Such a paragraph moves from the microcosm of a wedding day to the macrocosm of war. The army was on active duty. Mr. Weston as a member of the locally raised militia served at home. Members of the regular army served also overseas, for instance, in Ireland, in the West Indies, the Indian subcontinent, or in the Peninsula Wars fought in Spain and Portugal during the first decade of the 19th century. Jane herself seems to suffer from fragile health: A severe cold in the previous chapter is given as part of the reason why she did not go to Ireland.

The third paragraph is also a single sentence. It relates what happened to young Jane, "this girl." The vocabulary used is interesting: "she became the property, the charge, the consolation, the fondling of her grandmother and aunt." The language is stark, apart from "consolation," unemotional and factual. The young girl becomes "property." The rest of the paragraph emphasizes that she grew up "with no advantages of connections or improvement to be engrafted on what nature had given her." Her only "advantages" consist of "a pleasing person, good understanding, and warm-hearted, well meaning relations." Jane Austen as narrator does not evade the harsh realities of existence in her world. Life for the Jane Fairfaxes of the world is going to be harsh. She is fortunate: "the compassionate feelings of a friend of her father gave a change to her destiny." The friend, her father's commanding officer, Colonel Campbell, is "indebted to him for such attentions, during a severe camp-fever, as he believed had saved his life." The realities of army life are made evident. Camp fever, or typhus epidemics, were frequent occurrences in the confined restricted quarters of many camps during the 19th century. Jane is brought up from before she was nine by Colonel Campbell and his wife. "The plan was that she should be brought up for educating others."

Work opportunities for women such as Jane were severely limited in early and mid-19th-century England. Without husbands, families, or an inheritance to sustain them, the outlook was bleak. One possibility was to work as a governess in a private home. Governesses were badly paid, had almost no privacy, and were dependant on their employers and the whims of their children. Such is the situation in Charlotte Brontë's *Jane Eyre,* written during the 1840s. Jane Fairfax knew this would be her fate but it is made even harsher by the kindness of the Campbells. Colonel Campbell's "income, by pay and appointments, was handsome, his fortune was moderate and must be all his daughter's." On his military income he can live and support his family in some style but is unable to leave anything to his widow and daughter or to Jane. Jane, however, has been fortunate, "She had fallen into good hands, known nothing but kindness from the Campbell's and been given an excellent education." The possibilities of having "fallen into" bad or indifferent "hands" are left open to the reader's fears and imagination.

Jane's adopted sister, Miss Campbell, too, has been fortunate in the game of life presented by Jane Austen in which a fortuitous marriage plays such an important part. The narrator writes "that luck which so often defies anticipation in matrimonial affairs, giving attraction to what is moderate rather than to what is superior, engaged" her to "a young man, rich and agreeable, almost as soon as they

were acquainted." She, Miss Campbell "was eligibly and happily settled, while Jane Fairfax had yet her bread to earn" in the harsh real world of survival. Jane has similarities with Harriet Smith: Both are alone in the world. Harriet has also been given "a taste of such enjoyments of ease and leisure" that must make a return to the harsh realities even more difficult. Jane, subsequent to the marriage of her stepsister, has been physically unwell. The narrator reveals that "with regard to her [Jane] not accompanying" the Campbells "to Ireland, her account to her aunt contained nothing but the truth." She adds "though there might be some truths not told," and refers to "motive or motives, whether single, or double, or treble." These ought to serve as warning signs to readers that there is much more to Jane's decision to visit Highbury, and not go to Ireland, than is evident. Her absence and return is contrasted with Frank Churchill's—he still remains away from Highbury.

At this point in chapter 20, the viewpoint changes to that of Emma. For the rest of the chapter, Jane is seen through her lenses in a mixture of omniscient narration and inner thought processes. "Why she did not like Jane Fairfax might be a difficult question to answer." Knightley has supplied an answer: "it was because she saw in her the really accomplished young woman, which she wanted to be thought herself." Regarding Jane, Emma's "fancy," or imagination, which earlier she had promised to suppress, interferes. She is fascinated by Jane's physical appearance, especially by Jane's "eyes, a deep grey, with dark eye-lashes and eye-brows," and indeed her whole appearance. Emma is aware "what all this elegance was destined to, what she was going to sink from, how she was going to live." Already Emma is wishing she could "scheme" to find Jane a suitable husband. However, her sympathetic feelings toward Jane do not last long. In the presence of Mrs. and Miss Bates, Jane's "grandmother and aunt," Jane's superior ability at the piano, and her "reserve," Emma's reservations and animosity toward Jane resurface. Emma "saw . . . artifice, and returned to her first surmises" concerning a supposed relationship between Jane and Mr. Dixon, the latter having neglected Jane "for the sake of the future twelve thousand pounds."

This is all supposition, however. "Emma could not forgive" Jane for revealing so little, especially on the topic of Frank Churchill (163–169).

Volume 2, Chapter 3 (Chapter 21)

Chapter 3 uses Hartfield as a stage for various visitors to Emma and her father. First of all there is Knightley. Then Miss Bates and Jane Fairfax join them. Knightley and the two ladies leave, and Emma is left alone with her father. Outside there is a short but heavy shower, "and it had not been over five minutes, when in came Harriet." The main topic of conversation among Emma, her father, and Knightley is the previous night, and Jane Fairfax with Knightley trying to get Emma's opinion of Jane sensing that she has reservations. There is in addition discussion of food, which moves from the muffins handed around to guests, to "Hartfield pork." Emma "sent the whole hind-quarter" on her father's behalf to the Bateses: His generosity is repeatedly dwelled upon by Miss Bates, who appears with Jane Fairfax. Miss Bates has come to impart the news that "Mr. Elton is going to be married" to a Miss Hawkins. Miss Bates's dialogue is punctuated by parentheses and moves from the height of Miss Hawkins, to a comparison with the height of the apothecary Perry, Elton's attention to the needs of her mother, the deafness of her mother, and Jane saying "that Colonel Campbell is a little deaf." She then moves to a remedy for deafness, bathing, then to Colonel Campbell being "quite our angel," then to the positive characteristics of Mr. Dixon. Miss Bates's world is inhabited by the worthy: "It is such a happiness when good people get together—and they always do." There are permanent silver linings in her vision. Further, "there never was a happier or a better couple than Mr. and Mrs. Perry," and addressing Mr. Woodhouse, she says, "we are quite blessed in our neighbours," before returning to the pork.

Miss Bates's circular reasoning, her garrulousness is stopped by Emma trying to discover "As to who, or what Miss Hawkins is." Emma is surprised at Jane Fairfax's apparent disinterest in the subject. She learns, however, from Miss Bates that Elton and Miss Hawkins met within the four weeks that Mr. Elton was away from Highbury. However, as Miss Bates confesses, "I do not think that I am particularly quick at these sorts of discoveries. I do not pretend to it. What is before me, I see." She is an empiricist knowing realistically that Emma "lets [her] chatter on, so good-humouredly." Miss Bates adds, "she knows I would not offend for the world," which makes Emma's behavior toward her subsequently even more painful. Miss Bates then directs her attention and questions to concern for others such as Mrs. John Knightley's children.

Miss Bates and her niece briefly discuss the grounds for making judgments of others. Jane freely confesses that "Where I have a regard, I always think a person well-looking." Miss Bates then leaves with Knightley and Jane, but not before once again mentioning such members of local society as Mrs. Cole and Mrs. Goddard, and pork. Emma, left alone with her father, feels now, "Sorry for Harriet." Following a shower Harriet appears and, in a lengthy passage using simplistic vocabulary and excessive use of the personal pronoun "I," tells Emma of an encounter in Ford's—"the principal woollen-draper, linen draper, and haberdasher's shop united; the shop first in size and fashion in the place"—with Elizabeth and Robert Martin. She needs Emma to talk to her "and make me comfortable again." This is a task Emma is not good at, and she tells Harriet about Elton's forthcoming marriage. However, Harriet seems more preoccupied with the meeting with the Martins. At the end of the chapter, Emma reflects on how rarely Harriet would in future encounter them (172–180).

Volume 2, Chapter 4 (Chapter 22)

Chapter 4 conveys more information about Miss Hawkins. The youngest daughter of a Bristol merchant, her fortune is considerable; she "was in possession of an independent fortune, of so many thousands as would always be called ten." Miss Hawkins is exceedingly wealthy. Such information is conveyed by the omniscient narration in the fourth paragraph of the chapter. This consists of a single sentence, 163 words in length containing the total narrative of Elton's capture of his bride (181–182). It contains their first initial meeting to her acceptance of his proposal. Page comments that "the compression of the material within a single sentence constitutes an ironic comment on the haste and determination with which the business was, on both sides, pushed to a conclusion" (Page, 107).

The vocabulary provides a commentary on the underlying meaning of the paragraph and a reflection on the cynical contract made in it. "The charming Augusta Hawkins" has "all the usual advantages." These are "perfect beauty and merit." The words are appropriately vague but explained more specifically in term of "an independent fortune." The phrase "the story told well" appeals to public perceptions of a romantic alliance in which an impoverished young man captures through a whirlwind courtship a wealthy, beautiful bride. The "delightful rapidity" of the proceedings is preceded by the word "gained" repeated twice and associated with a business transaction. Augusta, the reader is told, is "so sweetly disposed." This raises the question whether she may have favored or been attracted to Elton her suitor, or been under other pressures to accept him. There is a nice ambiguity reinforcing the mercenary nature of the quick events, in the final words of the sentence. She had "been so very ready to have him, that vanity and prudence were equally contented." She will possess Elton. She and his "vanity" are satisfied; they act out of mutual self-interest dictated by "prudence," the necessity for Elton to marry for money and for "the lady" to marry.

Augusta Hawkins has entered into a necessary transaction. The reader learns from Emma's free indirect discourse that "She brought no name, no blood, no alliance. Miss Hawkins was the youngest of the two daughters of a Bristol merchant" (181–183). She has just purchased Mr. Elton for "so many thousands as would always be called ten" (181). It is appropriate that she is from Bristol, a leading slave-trading port "inferior to none, except London, for wealth, trade, and number of inhabitants" (*Encyclopaedia Britannica*: cited Pinch, 397). Bristol was the central port for the slave trade until it was abolished in 1807 and especially for the transportation of slaves to and form North America, the West Indies, and Africa. Probably the daughter of a merchant engaged in such trade, she, Augusta Hawkins, is prepared, too, to sell herself and what she offers.

The rest of the chapter moves to Emma's thoughts concerning the effects of Elton's forthcoming marriage on Harriet, and Emma's reactions to the visit of Robert Martin's sister to see Harriet. At the end of the chapter, Emma decides to take Harriet to visit the Martins. Her final rhetorical question of the chapter, "what would become of Harriet?" (185), contains the implication that Emma is willing to reconsider the connection and possible alliance of Harriet with Robert Martin.

Volume 2, Chapter 5 (Chapter 23)

Chapter 5 moves from Emma collecting Harriet and conducting other local social responsibilities such as visiting "an old servant who was married," to her initial meeting with Frank Churchill. The chapter is pervaded by time. The precise minutes, "fourteen," are given to Harriet's first visit to the Martins; Frank Churchill arrives a day earlier than expected and is anxious to renew an old acquaintance, Jane Fairfax. This chapter is replete with deception and deliberate false hopes and perceptions. The eagerly anticipated arrival of Frank Churchill changes Emma's perspective on life: "every thing wore a different air; James and his horses seemed not half so sluggish as before. When she looked at the hedges, she thought the elder at least must soon be coming out."

Emma is immediately attracted to Frank Churchill on their first meeting. Jane Austen uses dialogue between characters and direct authorial narration to convey many strands of meaning. Both Frank Churchill and Emma, for instance, compliment Mrs. Weston on her appearance and youthfulness. Emma is also flattered by Frank Churchill, for "Miss Taylor had formed Miss Woodhouse's character," and also the reverse, "Miss Woodhouse Miss Taylor's." On one level this is a mutual superficial flattery and social conversation. Emma then tells Frank "were you to guess her to be *eighteen,* I should listen with pleasure; but *she* would be ready to quarrel with you for using such words." In other words, Emma is saying to Frank, "Look, you are a flatterer, however, the truth is different." Frank's reply reveals that he is aware of this: "I hope I should know better." but then he adds that Mrs. Weston will understand that he is merely indulging in complimentary banter.

So Emma and Frank are playing games of deception with each other. Emma is concerned by "what might be expected from their knowing each other." The hint of their falling in love is reinforced by a shifting away of the narrative focus from Emma's thoughts of Frank to her thoughts of her father, who "Happily . . . was not farther from approving matrimony than foreseeing it." Frank, on the other hand, as the plot will reveal, is engaged in an elaborate covering up of his attachment to Jane Fairfax. In this chapter, Frank introduces her name and wishes to know where she lives. The last section of the chapter is concerned with Mr. Woodhouse's insistence that one of his servants accompany him on his visit and Frank's and Mr. Weston's refusal to accept such an offer. Frank learns that Jane "is with a poor old grandmother, who has barely enough to live on," but according to Mr. Woodhouse she is with "very worthy people." In this sense as used by Mr. Woodhouse, "worthy" refers not to financial, economic worth but moral stature.

The chapter ends with Emma's perspective: She is "very well pleased with this beginning of the acquaintance" (186, 189, 192, 194–195). It has proceeded through dialogue and narration revealing, first, the superficial words and utterances on a surface playful level of social interaction. Second, there is the implication of what has been said between them, concerning, for instance, their perceptions of each other. On a third level there is the unspoken, what Emma and Frank are really thinking as they speak to each other. Finally, there is at work our perceptions as readers, given what we know from other parts of the novel that relate to them as they speak to each other.

Volume 2, Chapter 6 (Chapter 24)

The next chapter is also replete with dialogue between Emma and Frank. The surface meanings disguise different agendas. In the company of Mrs. Weston, they spend the following morning walking around Highbury. Emma asks Frank about his relationship with Jane Fairfax. Frank initially evades her question by going into Ford's which sells "gloves and every thing." Following some reflection and after ascertaining that Jane has not revealed anything, Frank says that he "met her frequently at Weymouth." He does not expand on this. Previously during the morning walk, they enter the Crown Inn, where Frank praises dancing, and then they go to Elton's vicarage. Here Frank "could not believe it a bad house; not such a house as a man was to be pitied for having. If it were to be shared with a woman he loved, he could not think any man to be pitied for having that house." This observation makes Emma think that Frank "did perfectly feel that Enscombe could not make him happy." Placed in the context of the total novel and of what Frank is concealing, his praise of the vicarage takes on a different meaning. Similarly, the discussion between Emma and Frank of the merits of Jane Fairfax and her piano playing is seen from a different perspective. Emma is totally deceived: "after walking together so long, and thinking so much alike, Emma felt herself so well acquainted with him, that she could hardly believe it to be only their second meeting."

"Thinking so much alike" and "Emma felt" (200–204), clearly are Emma's thoughts and assumptions. These are undercut in the opening sentence of the next chapter: "Emma's very good opinion of Frank Churchill was a little shaken the following day, by hearing that he was gone off to London, merely to have his haircut." The next sentence introduces an element of doubt concerning Frank's intentions, for he "seemed to have [been] seized" by "a sudden freak . . . at breakfast" resulting in his decision to go to London; also his visit "appeared" to have no other intent than "merely to have his haircut" (205). The words "seemed" and "appeared" suggest that his visit to London may well have other motives and reasons. However, Frank's 16-mile journey from Highbury to London to have a haircut is not as curious as it may appear. Wigs, dominant among male fashion in the 18th century, were increasingly going out of fashion, and by the second decade of the 19th century, short hairstyles for men were becoming fashionable.

Volume 2, Chapter 7 (Chapter 25)

The seventh chapter of the second book of *Emma* serves as a prelude for the Coles' dinner party. Apart from the apparent "foppery and nonsense" of Frank's sudden decision to go to London, there are other elements to notice in the chapter. Knightley is one of the few "throughout the parishes of Donwell and Highbury" who has a negative opinion of Frank, regarding him as a "trifling, silly fellow." The Coles have been neighbors of the Woodhouses for 10 years. Emma and the narrator regard them "of low origin, in trade, and only moderately genteel." A social pecking order is revealed in the area through Emma's attitude to the Coles. The "best families" live at "Donwell," the home of Knightley; "Hartfield," her own home; and "Randalls," where the Westons live. For Emma, "the Coles were very respectable in their way, but they ought to be taught that it was not for them to arrange the terms on which the superior families would visit them." She is persuaded to attend a dinner party with the Coles by their thoughtfulness in specially ordering "a folded-screen from London, which they hoped might keep Mr. Woodhouse from any draught of air" and the fact that all her other friends are attending. Mr. Woodhouse will not go and encourages his daughter to go, telling the Westons "as you will both be there, and Mr. Knightley too, to care of her"—an insight that proves only too true placed in the context of the total novel.

After Emma agrees to attend, the remainder of the chapter is taken up with arrangements for her and her father's welfare during her absence at the Coles. A seemingly trivial dialogue among Mr. Woodhouse, Mr. Weston, and Emma reintroduces themes of the novel never far from the surface: concern for others' feelings, especially in this instance on the part of Mr. Woodhouse, health, and comfort. Nobody seems to be concerned for Frank Churchill's welfare when he announces that he will ride 16 miles to London and back for a haircut. A visit by Emma to the Coles' for an evening out raises all sorts of issues concerning Mr. Woodhouse's comfort, such as who will look after him, and the health of Mr. Cole, the host. Once again, the name of the apparent health miracle worker is introduced by Mr. Woodhouse, Perry. Questions are raised as to transportation, the use of servants, how late Emma will stay out, and the problem of accommodating her "if she came home cold" and hungry (205–211). The basic realities of life such as health, comfort, and not becoming ill are never far

away or forgotten in a narrative often focusing on illusions people have of each other.

Volume 2, Chapter 8 (Chapter 26)

The Coles' dinner party is an important one and one of the longest chapters in the novel. It is divided into two main sections, an introduction and a conclusion. The prelude, or introduction, focuses on Frank's return from London with his hair cut short. As is revealed much later in the narrative, his real purpose in visiting London is to buy a piano, a Broadwood, the best kind of piano that money can buy, for Jane Fairfax. Who bought the piano for Jane is the subject of intense speculation at the Cole house. This is the setting, the venue, for the introduction to the chapter consisting of Emma and Frank discussing Jane's piano. They are agreeing to some extent that it is a love token, and there is an apparent mutual agreement that Mr. Dixon, the admirer or lover, must have sent the piano to the Bateses', where Jane is living. The second section of the chapter is largely preoccupied with Emma's conversation with Mrs. Weston. The discussion again centers on the issue of who purchased the expensive piano for Jane. Mrs. Weston, much to Emma's annoyance, believes that Knightley is in love with Jane and is the source of the gift. In this way, Mrs. Weston reflects Emma's belief that she too discerns others' motives and arranges marriages. The conclusion of the chapter focuses not on Jane's Broadwood piano but on the Coles' new piano, on which Emma plays and sings less favorably than Jane does. Their performances are followed by Mrs. Weston, who plays country dances for the others to dance to. Frank compares Emma's dancing to Jane's, regarding Emma's as superior. This contrasts with Knightley's consideration for Jane. He sends her home in his carriage. Emma correctly observes that Knightley "is not a gallant man, but he is a very humane one" (223).

There is much detail and plotting in the chapter, which moves almost in a musical structure. Its prelude is the discussion of Frank's haircut and results in Emma's inner thoughts on how people should behave. Emma then views Knightley arriving in a carriage at the Coles'. This is unusual for him, as he does not usually use one, and they discuss his actions as a "gentleman" and hers as a "nonsensical girl" after she has praised him for being without artifice. Emma tells him, "You are not striving to look taller than any body else. *Now* I shall really be very happy to walk into the same room with you" (214). The lack of artifice and pretense highlights the role-playing and performance, which then unfolds at their destination, the Coles'. There is then a lengthy conversation between Frank and Emma, as has been indicated, of the person most likely to have given the piano. Frank is, of course, as the narrative reveals, covering up for himself and misleading Emma in suggesting that his preference is for her. Then after a break, "in the awkwardness of a rather long interval between the courses" (218), which suggests that the Coles' servants are not up to the task of behaving as servants of the upper class rather than of tradespeople, "the less worthy females," such as "Miss Bates, Miss Fairfax, and Miss Smith" (214) arrive. The larger assembly of men and women then mingle with a focus on who is sitting next to whom and opposite whom. At the conclusion of the chapter, Frank talks to Emma. Both are the focus of attention at the start of the chapter.

Four motifs emerge in the plethora of detail contained in this chapter depicted against the backdrop of an evening out at the Coles'. First, there is the perpetual concern running through the novel with food. Interestingly, the specific details of the meal, what was actually eaten, are not given. Second, there is the concern with property. The Coles are rising in the world; they wish to rise to the same social standing as the Woodhouses, the Knightleys, and the Westons. Property is also commented upon in the gift of the best piano that money can buy, the Broadwood, and the Coles' own acquisition of a grand piano. Third, the piano is central to this chapter. H. R. Haweis observed in *Music and Morals* (1876), "a good play on the piano has not infrequently taken the place of a good cry upstairs." Earlier in 1798, Maria Edgeworth noted in her *Practical Education* "that musical skill improves 'a young lady's' chance of a prize in the matrimonial lottery." Further, the piano "offered opportunities for representation of women's active sexual desire" (Vorachek, 38:22,37). A fourth motif is seen in the constant comings and goings during the dinner

party: As characters in the novel, they also have their exits, and their entrances, their eventual reconciliations, unions, and separations.

This chapter has an enormous amount of revealing detail. Frank's deception will rebound upon him. Emma's emotional overreaction to Mrs. Weston's near certainty that Knightley is in love and will marry Jane Fairfax bring to the surface Emma's hitherto more or less repressed feelings for Knightley and her jealousy of Jane Fairfax. Further, Emma's meanness of spirit toward Miss Bates, for which she is rightly chastised by Mrs. Weston, "For shame, Emma! Do not mimic her" (225), prefigures Emma's disgraceful behavior toward Miss Bates at Box Hill. It prepares the reader for what is to come, as does so much else in the chapter.

Volume 2, Chapter 9 (Chapter 27)

The morning following the Coles' dinner party, Emma considers her "suspicions of Jane Fairfax's feelings to Frank Churchill"; she also acknowledges to herself, and then to Harriet, that Jane is the superior musician. Emma "did most heartily grieve over the idleness of her childhood": Her self-education is beginning. Harriet, however, as Knightley earlier feared, has through her friendship with Emma become aware of social differences. She tells Emma that Jane, "will have to teach" and expresses concern that Robert Martin will be attracted by one of the daughters of Cox the lawyer. Emma regards them as "the most vulgar girls in Highbury." Emma then accompanies Harriet to Ford's. From the door of the shop she can observe the world of Highbury carrying on its daily round of activity with people passing to and fro. She then views Frank Churchill and Mrs. Weston in the distance and learns that they are stopping off at Mrs. Bates's before visiting Hartfield. Harriet reminded Mrs. Weston that she promised Miss Bates last night "that I would come this morning. I was not aware of it myself . . . but as he says I did, I am going now." Following a bit of fortuitous luck, Frank Churchill goes alone to Miss Bates's. After Harriet has deferred to Emma as to where the ribbon she has purchased should be sent, to Mrs. Goddard's, the school, or to Hartfield, where she spends most of her time, they are met at the shop by Mrs. Weston and Miss Bates. The latter, in her garrulous, disconnected way, manages to convey a good deal of information. First, that Frank Churchill has been "so very obliging" and fastened a "rivet" in her mother's spectacles. Second, that Knightley has been exceedingly generous and benevolent by sending a "most liberal supply" (231–233, 237–238) of apples so that they and especially Jane can eat them.

Volume 2, Chapter 10 (Chapter 28)
The party—Emma, Harriet, Mrs. Weston, and Miss Bates—then proceed to Mrs. Bates's home. Mrs. Bates is found, at the start of the next chapter, "slumbering on one side of the fire." Frank Churchill is "most deedily occupied about her spectacles, and Jane Fairfax, standing with her back to them, intent on the pianoforte" (240). In her *Our Village: Sketches of Rural Character and Scenery* (1824), Mary Russell Mitford comments on the use of "deedily," or actively, busily. She writes, "I am not quite sure that this word is good English, but is genuine Hampshire ... It means ... any thing done with a profound and plodding attention, an action which engrosses all the powers of mind and body" (cited Pinch, 399). The word is used ironically. Frank uses the spectacles and Mrs. Bates's lack of vision to spend time with Jane Fairfax. His motivation and actions are almost discerned by Mrs. Weston, who remarks on the amount of time he has taken to fix the spectacles. Emma notices that Jane's "state of nerves" are not what they should be so that she is not "quite ready to sit down at the pianoforté again" (240). Frank insists on duplicity and encouraging "conjecture" in making comments about Ireland and Colonel Campbell directly to Jane. However, as noted by the rest of the company, he speaks truthfully to Jane, asking her to play "one of the waltzes we danced last night; let me live them over again." He is concerned about her health and tells Jane, "I believe you were glad we danced no longer; but I would have given worlds—all the worlds one ever has to give—for another half hour." Unbeknown to all but Jane, he has even supplied her with sheet music, with "Cramer," the popular music of the London-based composer and pianist Johann Baptist Cramer. Also he has provided Jane with "a new set

of Irish melodies" by Thomas Moore. Perceptively Emma notices a "deep blush of consciousness" and "a smile of secret delight" on Jane's face. Emma thinks correctly, "This amiable, upright, perfect Jane Fairfax was apparently cherishing very reprehensible feelings."

The subtext of intense feeling between Jane and Frank is further suggested by the popular song from Moore's Irish melodies, which Jane plays. It is supposed to be Colonel Campbell or Dixon's favorite. "Robin Adair," the lyrics of which concern a young woman's secret love for the young man she eventually marries, exactly describes the situation between Jane and Frank. The chapter ends with Knightley being spotted by Miss Bates riding on horseback. The others overhear their conversation. Knightley's negative feelings for Frank Churchill are revealed. At first he agrees to Miss Bates's invitation to come in. As soon as he hears that Frank is present, Knightley makes an excuse: "No, no, your room is full enough. I will call another day, and hear the pianoforté" (242–244).

Volume 2, Chapter 11 (Chapter 29)
Emma and Frank plan another ball initially to be held at Randalls, but the venue is transferred to the Crown Inn, which has more room. Mr. Woodhouse, in chapter 11 of the second book, makes two remarks both related to Frank, which are worthy of notice. In the first he tells Mrs. Weston that Frank "is very thoughtless ... I do not mean to set you against him, but indeed he is not quite the thing!" (249). This reveals that Mr. Woodhouse, in spite of his fussiness and obsession with health, is not as stupid as he may appear. In the second, he tells Frank, "I live out of the world, and am often astonished at what I hear." His world is circumscribed by what he knows, the health and welfare of those he loves and knows. He remembers when his daughter, his "little Emma! ... were very bad with the measles; that is, you would have been very bad, but for Perry's great attention" (252–253). He disagrees with Frank when he implies that Perry "might have reason to regret" that they might not catch cold so that he could charge more for his services. Mr. Woodhouse tells Frank "rather warmly, 'You are very much mistaken if you suppose Mr. Perry to be

that sort of character. Mr. Perry is extremely concerned when any of us are ill" (251).

Other points of interest are Emma's reiterated hostility to Miss Bates. Emma tells Mrs. Weston that she will gain nothing in consulting Miss Bates, who "will be all delight and gratitude, but she will tell you nothing" (255). Not for the first time, Jane Austen in her narrative refers pointedly and humorously to the controversial political discourse of her contemporaries. Thomas Paine's *The Rights of Man*, published in 1791, Mary Wollstonecraft's *A Vindication of the Rights of Men*, published the previous year, and her *A Vindication of the Rights of Women* (1792) emphasize gender rights. During the discussion of arrangements of the hall at the Crown Inn: "A private dance, without sitting down to supper, was pronounced an infamous fraud upon the rights of men and women" (254). Jane Austen's microcosm of English life, Hartfield and its activities, is placed somewhat incongruously through the author's choice of language in the macrocosm of English life and radical ideas.

Volume 2, Chapter 12 (Chapter 30)
Somewhat surprisingly given what has taken place in the narrative in the last 11 chapters or so, Frank Churchill has been in Hartfield only for two weeks. Once again he is to disappoint others' expectations. He is recalled to Enscombe, where apparently "Mrs. Churchill was unwell," although "he knew her illnesses; they never occurred but for her own convenience" (258). His parting from Emma gives her misleading signals, although Frank seems to be on the point of confession. She misreads his protestations as directed at her. "Such a fortnight as it has been! . . . every day more precious and more delightful than the day before! . . . Happy those, who can remain at Highbury!" He does not say Hartfield. Frank does confess to calling at Miss Bates's, "It was a right thing to do. I went in for three minutes, and was detained by Miss Bates's being absent" (260). He does not add how long he stayed. In the final paragraph of this 12th chapter of the second volume, the narrator tells her reader that Jane subsequently "has been particularly unwell . . . suffering from headache to a degree" (263). As so often in this novel and in the world of Jane Austen's fic-

tion, physical health is determined by psychological well-being.

Volume 2, Chapter 13 (Chapter 31)
Emma considers her feelings toward Frank. She has "no doubt of her being in love. Her ideas only varied as to how much." However, after reflection in a passage combining inner thought processes with authorial direct narration, she decides that she would "refuse" Frank Churchill: "in spite of her previous and fixed determination never to quit her father, never to marry, a strong attachment certainly must produce more of a struggle than she could foresee in her own feelings." She misperceives whom Frank is in love with: "*He* is undoubtedly very much in love—every thing denotes it—very much in love indeed," assuming it is with her. There are fewer letters in *Emma* than in some of Jane Austen's other novels, such as for instance *Pride and Prejudice* and *Mansfield Park*. In this chapter, Emma reads a lengthy letter Frank has sent to Mrs. Weston. The contents are summarized through her reading rather than being quoted directly. She finds that the letter "had not added any lasting warmth, and that she could still do without the writer, and that he must learn to do without her" (264–266).

Attention is now turned to the wedding day of Mr. Elton, and Emma transfers her focus once again to Harriet and her feelings. She admits yet again to Harriet, "[I] deceived myself, I did very miserably deceive you"—she is again mistaken in believing that Frank Churchill is in love with her. Emma manages apparently to persuade Harriet that her continually speaking of Elton reflects "wanting gratitude and consideration" for herself, Emma. Harriet bursts out in response that "Nobody is equal" to Emma and that she cares "for nobody as [she]" does for Emma. This leads Emma to reflect, in the last paragraph of chapter 13 of the second volume, that the virtues of "warmth and tenderness of heart, with an affectionate, open manner, will beat all the clearness of head in the world, for attraction." These are qualities Harriet, her "superior" in these attributes, shares with her father and her sister, Isabella. She reflects on "the coldness of a Jane Fairfax!" and thinks little of herself, "happy the man who changes Emma for Harriet!" (268–269).

Volume 2, Chapter 14 (Chapter 32)

Chapter 14 of the second book continues the shift in narrative focus away from Frank Churchill. One world of deception is now replaced by another. Personal deception on the part of Frank and Jane, their effort to disguise their relationship, is replaced by the artifice of social pretense and snobbery represented by Elton's bride. The Eltons' pretensions dominate the closing five chapters of the second book of *Emma*. Mrs. Elton immediately is revealed in chapter 14 as arrogant, vulgar, and full of herself. She reveals her pretensions in her initial meeting with Emma. Continually boasting about her exceedingly wealthy sister and brother-in-law who live on the outskirts of Bristol at "Maple Grove," she expects a visit from them in "their barouche-landau" (274). This is equivalent to saying in modern parlance that they will visit in the latest Porsche or bring their own private plane, since it was a luxurious carriage. As she continually plays a game of one-upmanship on Emma, Mrs. Elton's solecisms are reflected in her calling her husband "caro sposo," the Italian for "dear husband." Of this Emma comments to herself, "A little upstart, vulgar being, with her Mr. E., and her *caro sposo*, and her resources, and all her airs of pert pretension and under-bred finery." Emma's anger has its genesis in her snobbery. Emma is also offended by Mrs. Elton's affronting of accepted social modes of address: "Knightley!—I could not have believed it. Knightley!—never seen him in her life before, and call him Knightley!" (278–279). Page writes that "one is reminded . . . forcibly that forms of address . . . were regarded in this period as very important and very revealing; the code determining which forms might and might not be used in the context of different relationships was, in well-bred society, a strict one" (152).

At the conclusion of the chapter, Emma's father observes that Mrs. Elton "speaks a little too quick. A little quickness of voice there is which rather hurts the ear." He does "not like strange voices," and these are increasingly entering into Highbury and its surroundings. In the final sentence of the paragraph, Emma's "mind returned to Mrs. Elton's offences, and long, very long, did they occupy her" (279–280), the omniscient narrator relates. The

similarities and differences between Emma and Mrs. Elton, who has pretensions to control the social activities of Highbury, are the prime subject of the next few chapters.

Volume 2, Chapter 15 (Chapter 33)

Chapter 15 opens with the narrator affirming Emma's harsh judgment of Mrs. Elton: "Her observation had been pretty correct." On their second encounter, Mrs. Elton "appeared to her [Emma] . . . self-important, presuming, familiar, ignorant, and ill-bred." In addition, "she had a little beauty and a little accomplishment, but so little judgment." Mrs. Elton exhibits "ill-will" toward Emma and she and Elton "were unpleasant towards Harriet."

Jane Fairfax becomes the focus for the rivalry between Mrs. Elton and Emma. The latter seems alone in her dislike of Mrs. Elton, who locally is praised by Highbury society. The rivalry is referred to as "a state of warfare." Mrs. Elton's solecisms are shown in her inaccurate quoting from Thomas Gray's "Elegy in a Country Churchyard" when she mistakes "fragrance" for "sweetness" (281–282). Her language is full of personal pronouns such as "I" and "me" intermixed with "we" directed at Emma. Mrs. Elton assumes that she and Emma will cooperate in directing Jane Fairfax's future and finding a suitable position for her. Emma, Mrs. Weston, and Knightley unite in their reactions to Mrs. Elton's pretensions and are surprised to see Jane Fairfax accepting Mrs. Elton's company and assistance. Knightley tries to find a rationale for Jane's actions. He too is disturbed by Mrs. Elton's violation of recognized codes. He tells Emma and Mrs. Weston, "We all know the difference between the pronouns he or she and thou, the plainest-spoken amongst us." Knightley, though, tells Emma and Mrs. Weston that Mrs. Elton is the only person of any social consequence in the neighborhood who has taken notice of Jane. "Could she have chosen with whom to associate, she would not have chosen her. But (with a reproachful smile at Emma) she receives attentions from Mrs. Elton, which nobody else pays her" (286). Emma is provoked into asking Knightley what his intentions are toward Jane. He praises Jane but finds that she "wants openness. She is reserved, more reserved, I think, than she used to be." He "love[s] an open temper" but has no intentions of proposing to her (289).

Volume 2, Chapter 16 (Chapter 34)
The dinner party organized by Emma at Hartfield for the Eltons occupies chapters 16 and 17 of the second book. Emma invites Jane, too, after Harriet has declined to attend. Emma "was more conscience-stricken about Jane Fairfax than she had often been—Mr. Knightley's words dwelt with her. He had said that Jane Fairfax received attentions from Mrs. Elton which nobody else paid her" (291). John Knightley reappears on the scene for a brief visit accompanied by two of his young children. During his conversation with Jane while they are waiting for dinner, it is revealed that Jane went to the post office in the rain to collect the post: "I always fetch the letters when I am here." There follows a subsequent discussion between them about the future and Mr. Woodhouse's comment that "Young ladies are delicate plants. They should take care of their health and their complexion." Mr. Woodhouse adds the incongruous and hence comic observation and question, "My dear, did you change your stockings?" (293–294).

Mrs. Elton displays much concern for Jane's welfare. Her "effusive and officious anxieties" (Page, 122) are expressed in direct speech. "My dear Jane, what is this I hear?—Going to the post-office in the rain:—This must not be, I assure you.—You sad girl, how could you do such a thing?—It is a sign I was not there to take care of you." This receives a put-down comment expressed not in direct speech but in indirect speech form: "Jane very patiently assured her that she had not caught any cold." Jane resists Mrs. Elton's commands that she be allowed to arrange for a servant to collect the mail for her. A discussion on the lack of "negligence or blunders" (295–296) gives way to reflections on handwriting. Before they go into dinner, Emma reflects on the reasons why Jane insists on going to collect letters in all weathers, suspecting that the letters are coming from Ireland. She even "thought there was an air of greater happiness than usual—a glow both of complexion and spirits." But she refrains from raising the subject with Jane, showing at least that she, Emma, has learned something: "She was

quite determined not to utter a word that should hurt Jane Fairfax's feelings" (298).

Volume 2, Chapter 17 (Chapter 35)
The actual dinner and what is eaten are not described. The next chapter, 17, focuses on what happens after the dinner. Several matters of interest are found in the chapter. On the narrative level, Mrs. Elton draws Jane Fairfax away from the others and insists on her finding an appropriate position as a governess. Jane again resists her interference and insists on not making any move in that direction until late in the summer. Mr. Weston makes an appearance with a letter from his son, saying that the Churchills are relocating to London. Frank will be spending half his time at Highbury and the other half in London. The conversation between Mrs. Elton and Jane contains a sustained analogy between being a governess and the slave trade (the source of Mrs. Elton's family wealth being centered in Bristol, with its slave-exporting and -importing activities). Jane speaks of being "glad to dispose of herself." She tells Mrs. Elton that if she intended to seek employment as a governess, "There are places in town, offices, where inquiry would soon produce something—Offices for the sale—not quite of human flesh—but of human intellect." This remark Mrs. Elton takes personally as a reflection upon her friends and family, her brother in Bristol: "Oh! my dear, human flesh! You quite shock me; if you mean a fling at the slave-trade, I assure you Mr. Suckling was always rather a friend to the abolition." Jane replies, "I did not mean, I was not thinking of the slave-trade . . . governess-trade, I assure you, was all that I had in view" (300). Mrs. Elton's allusion to abolition refers to the 1807 outlawing by a Parliamentary Act of participation in the slave trade. However, it was not until 1833 that slavery was abolished in British colonial possessions. Up till 1833, the issue was a leading political one and the comparison was frequently made between the situation of women as governesses and the lot of slaves.

Volume 2, Chapter 18 (Chapter 36)
The final chapter of book 2, chapter 18, concentrates on a lengthy conversation between Mrs. Weston and Mrs. Elton ranging over various sub-

jects. These include Frank Churchill, Weston's son, and further evidence of Mrs. Elton's snobbery is provided. In the course of the dialogue information is offered about geographical location, health resorts, and other provincial cities. Enscombe in Yorkshire is "about 190 miles from London. A considerable journey," or 65 miles farther than Bristol from London. Mrs. Elton recommends Bath or Clifton, near Bristol, as the best spas for those who are "really ill" (306–307). Mrs. Elton's wealthy Bristol relatives have been joined by wealthy companions: "how they got their fortune nobody knows. They came from Birmingham" in the Midlands "which is not a place to promise much. . . . One has not great hopes from Birmingham." In addition, Mrs. Elton has "quite a horror of upstarts," which is ironic in view of the fact that Emma, Mrs. Weston, and Knightley regard her as an "upstart." At the end of the chapter and of book 2, John Knightley "proved more talkative than his brother," who is silent after learning of Frank Churchill's imminent appearance. John Knightley's remark to Emma, "Your neighborhood is increasing, and you mix more with it," adequately sums up what has taken place in the second book of *Emma*. She laughs at this for literally all that has taken place is "dining once with the Coles—and having a ball talked of, which never took place." But John Knightley has correctly sensed that she has become more socially engaged and committed—the chapter and book ends appropriately with Knightley "trying not to smile" (310–312) at Emma's protestations that she rarely leaves Hartfield.

Volume 3, Chapter 1 (Chapter 37)
The first chapter of the third and final book opens appropriately with Emma's reflection on the "news of Frank Churchill." Events in this chapter move quickly from February to May, winter to spring. Frank appears once again briefly in Highbury two months after his previous visit. Emma is somewhat relieved to find that his ardor for her has cooled. Apparently nervous, Frank spends little time with her, "only a quarter of an hour," before "hurrying away to make other calls in Highbury." Following only 10 days in London, Mrs. Churchill decides "to move immediately to Richmond," a fashionable

town on the river Thames, eight miles southwest of London, "an hour's ride" and nine miles away from Highbury. This information is conveyed in letters Frank sends to the Westons. The information means that the projected ball at the Crown Inn can now go ahead.

Two interesting sentences from this chapter should be noted. One is indirect narration conveying Emma's thoughts. The other is direct authorial comment. In the first, Emma "felt as if the spring would not pass without bringing a crisis, an event, a something to alter her present composed and tranquil state." Her sense of foreboding, of foreshadowing, is apposite and serves as a signpost of transformation for Emma and the reader. Second, at the end of the chapter, the narrator directly states, "Mr. Weston's ball was to be a real thing" and adds, "A very few to-morrows stood between the young people of Highbury and happiness" ([315]–318). The elegiac note is a preparation by the author for the resolution of her narrative: the beginning of the end.

Volume 3, Chapter 2 (Chapter 38)
The relatively lengthy second chapter of the final book begins the resolution of problems in the narrative. Its focus is the ball at the Crown Inn. Much occurs in this chapter on various levels. It opens with a prelude to the ball, focusing on the arrivals at the inn, where "Frank Churchill seemed to have been on the watch." Emma begins to have reservations concerning her judgment of Mr. Weston: "a little less of open-heartedness would have made him a higher character—General benevolence, but not general friendship, made a man what he ought to be." The chapter will reveal Emma's development into much more mature judgment of others. She notices that Frank has "a restlessness, which showed a mind not at ease." The Eltons then appear, there is a misunderstanding concerning who is to send a carriage for Miss Bates and Jane, Frank telling his father, "Miss Bates must not be forgotten." Emma overhears Mrs. Elton giving Mr. Weston her opinion of Frank Churchill, his son. There follows an "incessant flow" (319–322) of speech from Miss Bates. This is characterized by dashes, parentheses, short sentences, a lack of

direction, a continual going off into tangents. Miss Bates also has another lengthy speech toward the end of the chapter (328–330). In the words of J. F. Burrows, "By virtue of her incessant talk of everything about her, she becomes an unofficial assistant to the narrator" (101). Her perceptions are acute. She, for instance, notes Mrs. Elton's obsessive wish to be "the queen of the evening" (329). Miss Bates is aware that Jane Fairfax is distracted during the dancing. She praises Frank Churchill's kindnesses to her and her mother, rhetorically asking Jane: "Do not we often talk of Mr. Frank Churchill?" (323). She also tells us about other inhabitants of Highbury, of Dr. Hughes and his family, and the Otway family. She provides information on dresses and hairstyles, on the heating, lighting, and kind of food eaten. Miss Bates comments on behavior, on character, and on atmosphere.

Emma is another observer of behavior at the Crown Inn. She overhears Mrs. Elton speaking to Jane Fairfax about her gown and looking for compliments from Jane. She observes Frank Churchill's objection to Mrs. Elton's over-familiarity when she refers to "Jane" by her first name, thus breaking social convention yet again in referring to people in this way. She asks Frank, "How do you like Mrs. Elton?" and receives the direct reply, "Not at all." Emma notes that Frank "seemed in an odd humour." The narrator notes that she "must submit to stand second to Mrs. Elton, though she had always considered the ball as peculiarly for her." This is followed by what appears to be Emma's curious thought, "It was almost enough to make her think of marrying," implying that with her husband, she, Emma, would regain social pre-eminence and position. Emma is attracted to Knightley, who is not dancing: "She was more disturbed by Mr. Knightley's not dancing, than by anything else." Emma is attracted to him, "so young as he looked!" She notes "his tall, firm, upright figure, among the bulky forms and stooping shoulders of the elderly men" (324–326). She also notices that nobody is dancing with Harriet Smith and observes Elton rudely, deliberately, and openly snubbing Harriet. Emma finds it difficult to control her anger and then sees "Mr. Knightley leading Harriet to the set!—Never had she been more surprised, seldom

more delighted" (328). After supper Emma's "eyes invited [Knightley] irresistibly to come to her and be thanked." He roundly condemns the Eltons, and she asks Knightley, "Does my vain spirit ever tell me I am wrong?" She admits "to have been completely mistaken in Mr. Elton." They then discuss Harriet Smith, and the chapter ends with them dancing. Knightley asks Emma, "Whom are you going to dance with?" She replies, "With you, if you will ask me," which of course he does. The last line of the chapter is her somewhat ambiguous reply to Knightley's "We are not really so much brother and sister as to make it at all improper." She responds, "Brother and sister! no, indeed" (330–331).

The chapter contains much of interest. The metaphor of "eyes" and seeing runs as a motif through it. At first Frank Churchill "seemed to have been on watch" with "his eyes" (319). Then the perspective moves to Emma's overhearing conversations, then to Miss Bates as commentator on the proceedings. Then the perspective shifts back to Emma as observer: "she saw it all" (327), then once again to Miss Bates for a more overall, wider perspective on proceedings in general. At the conclusion of the chapter, the omniscient narrator controls the dialogue between Knightley and Emma. There is much else at work in the chapter. The Eltons, especially Mrs. Elton, are trying socially to dominate Highbury society and gain revenge upon Emma for attempting to arrange a marriage between Elton and what they perceive as the socially inferior Harriet. Mrs. Weston tries to create a superficial harmony. Mr. Knightley again comes to the rescue and does the decent thing by dancing with Harriet. Emma is realizing that on a personal level she is more and more attracted to him and is beginning to become aware of her previous errors of perception.

Volume 3, Chapter 3 (Chapter 39)

Chapter 3 opens the next morning, and Emma reviews what took place at the ball. Emma has Knightley's behavior utmost in her mind and remembers their "understanding respecting the Eltons . . . his praise of Harriet, his concession in her favor." She also has "strong hopes" that Harriet's "eyes were suddenly opened, and she were enabled to see that Mr. Elton was not the superior creature she had believed him." However, an external event intrudes upon Emma's thoughts, demonstrating that there are less fortunate people in society and there is a world beyond Hartfield, its "great iron sweepgate," and Highbury. In the previous chapter, the Eltons' behavior threatened to challenge the status quo, the stability of Highbury proceedings. In this chapter, the very fabric of a stable, prosperous, structured society is threatened by the perception of threat posed by "a party of gipsies." Frank Churchill appears at Emma's "with Harriet leaning on his arm." She "looked white and frightened, and he was trying to cheer her." He relates how "she had suffered very much from cramp after dancing" and had been unable to run away from "a party of gipsies" who had come "to beg" (332–333). The fear of the gypsies, the wanderers, is clearly depicted by Frank Churchill in his description of how Harriet and her party run from them in panic: "There was a clearly delineated picture in the English mind of Gypsies as thieves, fortune-tellers, and tricksters" (Olsen, *All Things Austen*, I:341).

In the previous chapter, Knightley rescued Harriet from being snubbed by the predatory Eltons. In this chapter, Frank rescues her from other perceived predators, the Gypsies. The news of the episode with the Gypsies spreads quickly throughout Highbury; in spite of Emma's efforts, even her father cannot be protected from it, "last night's ball seemed lost in the gipsies." The Gypsies, fearful for themselves, "did not wait for the operation of justice; they took themselves off in a hurry." The "whole history dwindled soon into a matter of little importance." They are only remembered by Emma's "imagination" and ironically by her young nephews, who insist on "the story of Harriet and the gipsies" being repeated every day accurately (336). In this way legends are preserved, stereotypes reinforced, and fears of the outside are perpetuated. The Gypsies represent the world outside the comfortable surrounds of Highbury and its environs. In the outer world, an "era of social upheaval for the poor, due to the wars and to economic changes in the countryside, fears" (Pinch, 401) lay not far from the seemingly tranquil surface of society and its social structures.

Emma, "an imaginist," seeing Harriet on Churchill's arm was led to "speculation and foresight"

concerning a romantic entanglement. But this time she proceeds cautiously, her scheming has to be "a mere passive" one, for she is learning from experience (335).

Volume 3, Chapter 4 (Chapter 40)

In the next chapter (4), Harriet confesses to Emma her stupidity and foolishness over Mr. Elton and brings mementos of Elton, "a small piece of court plaister," or adhesive plaster made of silk, and "the end of an old pencil,—the part without any lead," to throw on the fire. Emma too is full of remorse, exclaiming to Harriet in a melodramatic fashion "Oh! my sins, my sins! . . . my senseless tricks!" (338–339). Harriet tells Emma that she now admires someone who has an "infinite superiority to all the rest of the world" (341), whom she cannot hope to marry. Emma again misjudging believes that the person is Frank Churchill—it is in fact Knightley, who is now the object of Harriet's obsessions. Emma and Harriet share in common delusions.

Volume 3, Chapter 5 (Chapter 41)

The theme of "appearances," (351), of mistaken judgments, underlies chapter 5. In a real sense this chapter brings to the fore a basic motif for the total novel: dreams and reality; the creation of illusions by the imagination; the need for hard evidence to corroborate what is imagined. Seeing provides such evidence. The chapter opens with the movement of the seasons, of time to June and early summer. Knightley, who "for some reason best known to himself, had certainly taken an early dislike to Frank Churchill" (343), looks for reasons why he is suspicious of Frank's relationship with Jane Fairfax. Instead of jumping to conclusions not based on evidence, Knightley tries to find reasons for his judgment. He quotes William Cowper's (1731–1800) lines from "The Winter Evening" in his poem *The Task* (1785): "Myself creating what I saw" (344). The poet imagines seeing "a waking dream of houses, towers / Trees, churches, and strange visages," the fireplace and its dying flames (cited Pinch, 401). So Knightley is not only commenting on his own fantasies but on those of Harriet and Emma in the previous chapter.

To corroborate his fancies, Knightley uses his perceptions as observer, a spectator. He watches closely the behavior of Jane and Frank at an informal after-dinner evening at Hartfield. Frank makes a tactless error when he speaks of Perry's plans to set up or maintain a carriage. Only Miss Bates and Jane knew about this. Frank attempts to change the subject and say that he was dreaming, leading his father, ironically, to comment to his son and to the others, "What an air of probability sometimes runs through a dream! And at others, what a heap of absurdities it is!" Mr. Weston then adds, "Well, Frank, your dream certainly shows that Highbury is in your thoughts when you are absent," which is indeed the case. Weston then tells Emma that "you are a great dreamer, I think?" (345). Frank, unbeknown to his father, is dreaming, thinking of Jane. Emma, as the reader has seen, has various dreams and imaginings that are not grounded in reality: she is "[herself] creating what I saw"—to misquote Cowper. Knightley also observes that Frank causes Jane to "blush" by using the words "blunder" and "*Dixon*" during a word game played with a child's alphabet. He observes and notes but is unable to interpret or provide a satisfactory explanation except that "Disingenuousness and double-dealing seemed to meet him at every turn" (348).

Hints of Knightley's isolation are dropped in the chapter. He is used to dining at Hartfield "round the large modern circular table which Emma had introduced" rather than "the small-sized Pembroke" ("a small, drop-leaf table" (Pinch, 401) "on which two of his daily meals had, for forty years, been crowded" (347). At the end of the chapter, "irritated" by the fire and Emma's reaction to his sharing of his observations and suspicions concerning Frank and Jane, Knightley "took a hasty leave, and walked home to the coolness and solitude of Donwell Abbey." As "an anxious friend," Knightley feels it "his duty" to share his feelings with Emma. On the other hand, in spite of what she may feel, "interference—fruitless interference . . . he would speak. He owed it to her, to risk any thing that might be involved in an unwelcome interference." He seeks corroboration and support from Emma, recognizing the negative aspects of interference and that Emma has opinions of her own, and perceptions that are as valid as Knightley's in terms of belonging to her as an independent

being. It is Emma who chastises Knightley for letting his "imagination wander" and being influenced by "appearances" (349–351).

Volume 3, Chapter 6 (Chapter 42)

Chapter six of the final book centers upon Donwell Abbey. The chapter operates on several levels. There is knowledge that is concealed from the other characters to be subsequently revealed in the novel. Emma does not know that Jane Fairfax's distress evident in the chapter is due to an argument she has had with Frank Churchill. He has arrived late. The reason is that he has been quarreling with Jane: one of the main reasons for the argument is his flirting with Emma. He is using this as a cover, it later emerges, but Jane resents it. Second, the landscape, the setting, and the weather should not be ignored. The environs of Knightley's estate at Donwell Abbey play a similar role in making Emma aware of his virtues, as the environs of Pemberley in *Pride and Prejudice* play in reflecting Darcy's strengths. Emma "felt an increasing respect for" Knightley's house, its grounds, and the views of a river, woods, meadows, and even Abbey Mill Farm. They represent "the residence of a family of such true gentility, untainted in blood and understanding" (358).

Knightley plays along with the strawberry-picking idea of Mrs. Elton's, made as the Box Hill expedition suggestion, as part of her social war with Emma. The food Knightley offers his guests is symptomatic of his common sense. He tells Mrs. Elton, "When you are tired of eating strawberries in the garden, there shall be cold meat in the house" (355). As Maggie Lane indicates, "Strawberries here represent the more superficial things of life, which can be safely compromised on in the interest of social harmony, while cold meat stands in for the fundamentals of human conduct." Further, as is reflected in the next chapter set at Box Hill, on the Surrey Downs near Dorking, a popular picnicking and sightseeing site, "the cold meat part of life cannot be tampered with, as Mr. Knightley knows, without dangerous consequences" (161).

Hints and clues that Knightley and Emma will join together are scattered throughout the chapter. Emma "felt all the honest pride and complacency which her alliance with the present and future proprietor could fairly warrant." Knightley goes out of his way to accommodate her father, Mr. Wood-house. Knightley becomes associated with England and its positive qualities. Emma views his estate: "It was a sweet view—sweet to the eye and the mind. English verdure, English culture, English comfort, seen under a sun bright, without being oppressive" (358, 360). The negative qualities of Frank Churchill are brought to the foreground in a conversation between Emma and him. He tells her, "I am sick of England—and would leave it to-morrow if I could." To which she replies, "You are sick of prosperity and indulgence!" (365). He denies possessing either.

Volume 3, Chapter 7 (Chapter 43)

The inner tensions between the characters simmer in the Donwell Abbey chapter and come fully to the surface in the next chapter, the Box Hill adventure. In the summer heat Emma and Har-

riet, Weston, Knightley, and Frank Churchill, Miss Bates and Jane Fairfax, the Eltons, Mrs. Weston, and Mr. Woodhouse gather on Box Hill. Frank and Emma attempt to make playful and witty conversation, leading Emma to be very rude to Miss Bates. Frank, in addition to pointed observations about the apparent success of Elton's marriage after "they only knew each other, I think, a few weeks in Bath!" (372), half-seriously asks Emma to seek out a suitable wife for him. She takes this at face value and thinks of Harriet. Jane takes her aunt Miss Bates and leaves them. Before leaving for home, Knightley chastises Emma for her disgraceful rudeness to Miss Bates. Emma returns home in tears, realizing the truth of what Knightley has said.

There are many points of interest in this chapter to attract attention. "The beauties of Box Hill and

View of Box Hill, Surrey, from F. Shoberl, *Topography of Surrey,* 1868

all the pleasures of the picnic are wasted. There is division instead of unity: Jane Fairfax avoids Frank Churchill, and takes away her aunt with her, to find refuge in the Eltons' company" (Hardy, 114). The strain of the secret engagement between the two, an engagement unknown to others, is showing in the tensions between them and the consequences of their disguise on others. Frank's flirtation with Emma is misperceived by her and by Knightley. It leads Jane Fairfax to tell Frank openly, "A hasty and imprudent attachment may arise—but there is generally time to recover from it afterwards." Mrs. Elton patronizes the others, Emma's exasperation with Miss Bates finally boils over and she insults her publicly. After Knightley's frank chastisement of her behavior, she has spoken "in thoughtless spirits, and the pride of her moment" made worse being directed at somebody of Miss Bates's "character, age, and situation," Emma's feelings are "only of anger against herself, mortification, and deep concern" (373–376). The reactions and remorse are expressed in what C. S. Lewis refers to as "the great abstract nouns of the classical English moralists . . . unblushingly and uncompromisingly used" (*Essays in Criticism*, 4[1954]: 363).

Previously in the novel, Emma has been a successful hostess. At Box Hill the several groupings disintegrate, people go off alone, and she leaves the party in tears of self-recrimination. In the next chapter following an evening of disquiet, only relieved by an escape into a game of backgammon with her father, the next morning Emma visits Miss Bates "in the warmth of true contrition" (377).

Volume 3, Chapter 8 (Chapter 44)

To describe Emma's feelings, the author in an *erlebte Rede* passage, in the opening paragraph of the eighth chapter of the final book, uses a word that does not occur elsewhere in *Emma*. The transitive verb "abhorred" is found only twice elsewhere in Jane Austen's works—in both cases in *Sense and Sensibility*. In this instance in *Emma*, the Box Hill morning was "a morning more completely misspent, more totally bare of rational satisfaction at the time, and more to be abhorred in recollection, than any she had ever passed" (377). At Miss Bates's, Emma finds that Jane is ill and unable to see her. Jane's

illness is yet another example in the novel of psychological distress and anxiety displayed physically. When Miss Bates does appear, as usual her lengthy speeches are replete with information. Among the information conveyed by Miss Bates, Emma and the readers learn that Jane Fairfax, following the Box Hill incident, has reversed her previous stance and accepted a governess's position arranged by Mrs. Elton. She is due to leave the Bateses within a fortnight. Mrs. Bates, Miss Bates, and Jane spent the previous evening with the Eltons, Mrs. Elton playing the role of hostess. During the evening, Miss Bates relates, the local rumor mill confirmed that Frank Churchill departed for Richmond and the Churchill family as soon as he returned from Box Hill.

Apart from learning of Elton's parish duties as the local clergyman, the interrelationship of Highbury society emerges. Frank's departure is conveyed through information received from Mr. Elton. His source is John the hostler, and "the chaise having been sent to Randalls to take Mr. Frank Churchill to Richmond. That was what happened before tea. It was after tea that Jane spoke to Mrs. Elton" (383) to accept the governess position. None of the characters at this stage in the narrative makes a connection between the sequence of events so precisely conveyed by Miss Bates: the events of the morning at Box Hill, Jane's outspokenness, Frank's leaving for Richmond, Jane's acceptance of the position and imminent departure from Highbury. Also of interest are examples of unconscious irony from Miss Bates. She, no doubt sincerely, tells Emma, "you are always kind." Shortly after, she tells Emma concerning Box Hill, "I shall always think it a very pleasant party, and feel extremely obliged at the kind friends who included me in it!" (380–381). Coming after Emma's cruelty and unkindness to her at Box Hill, these comments are especially ambiguous, yet given Miss Bates's lack of guile, not overtly deliberately so. At the end of the chapter Emma movingly compares "the contrast between Mrs. Churchill's importance in the world, and Jane Fairfax's . . . ; one was every thing, the other nothing—and she sat musing on the difference of woman's destiny" (384). To Emma, this may well appear to be the case. As the narrative shortly will reveal, with Mrs. Churchill's death, the situation reverses, and Jane's destiny is transformed.

Volume 3, Chapter 9 (Chapter 45)

Chapter 9 moves from Knightley and Harriet awaiting Emma's return from the Bateses', news of the death of Mrs. Churchill, the immediate reaction to it, to Jane's illness and rejections of Emma's offers of friendship. Knightley praises Emma for her visit to the Bateses', eye contact and physical contact is made between them. Without giving reasons, Knightley tells Emma that he is "going to London, to spend a few days with John and Isabella" (385). Following the announcement of the death of Mrs. Churchill, Emma speculates on the effect it might have for Harriet Smith's future—of course, she has once again misread the situation as the unfolding of the narrative will reveal. In a lengthy paragraph interweaving omniscient narration and *erlebte Rede*, Jane Fairfax's condition is described partly through the viewpoint of Perry the apothecary. Jane's "health seemed for the moment completely deranged." The adjective "deranged" is infrequently used in Jane Austen's novels. There are three other instances, and the word has the meaning of unhinged with physical and mental implications as if Jane is totally disoriented. She steadfastly and pointedly, however, rejects Emma's attempts at reconciliation and her offers of assistance. Jane's short note to Emma saying that she "is quite unequal to any exercise" is subsequently revealed to be an excuse "when Emma afterwards heard that Jane Fairfax had been seen wandering about the meadows, at some distance from Highbury." Jane has seen "the Mrs. Eltons, the Mrs. Perrys, and the Mrs. Coles," but not Emma. She, Emma, "did not want to be classed with" them. At the end of the chapter she consoles herself by thinking that Mr. Knightley would have not "found any thing to reprove" (389–391) concerning her actions.

Volume 3, Chapter 10 (Chapter 46)

Chapter 10 is important for the unraveling of the plot. Ten days after Mrs. Churchill's death, Mr. Weston calls Emma to Randalls, where his wife will impart important news to her. On the way, Emma's immediate thoughts are that something has occurred

at Brunswick Square to the Knightley family. She exclaims with reference to them "Good God!" and charges Weston "by all that is sacred" not to conceal anything relating to them. The word "sacred" is used very sparingly in Jane Austen's work, in fact only on three other occasions. Its use here (393) reveals the depth of Emma's feelings toward Knightley and his family. Mrs. Weston reveals Frank Churchill's secret engagement since October to Jane Fairfax. One reason for the revelation of the news now is the death of Mrs. Churchill. Mrs. Weston tells Emma that "while poor Mrs. Churchill lived . . . there could not have been a hope, a chance, a possibility;—but scarcely are her remains at rest in the family vault, than her husband is persuaded to act exactly opposite to what she would have required." Mrs. Weston adds, "What a blessing it is, when undue influence does not survive the grave!" The other reason for the revelation of the engagement is due to Frank's chance hearing of Jane's intention to become a governess.

Emma, after reassuring Mrs. Weston that she has no emotional attachment to Frank Churchill, becomes aware of the errors she has been making. She condemns: "What has it been but a system of hypocrisy and deceit,—espionage and treachery?—To come among us with professions of openness and simplicity; and such a league in secret to judge us all!" She excuses Jane Fairfax's behavior by misquoting lines from Shakespeare's *Romeo and Juliet* V.i.72. Emma tells Mrs. Weston, "If a woman can ever be excused for thinking only of herself, it is in a situation like Jane Fairfax's—Of such, one may almost say, that 'the world is not theirs, nor the world's law'" (398–400). The line citing Romeo's words to the poor apothecary, "the world is not thy friend, nor the world's law," Jane Austen's *Emma* misquotes to transform Romeo's words "into a sympathetic comment on the outcast lot of women constrained by circumstance" (Pinch, 402).

Volume 3, Chapter 11 (Chapter 47)

The next chapter deals with Emma's thoughts on the engagement, and from Emma's point of view, surprising developments relating to Harriet Smith. It also contains Emma's realization "that Mr. Knightley must marry no one but herself!" (408). The insight, a moment of self-awareness of previous misreadings and misperceptions, is induced by Harriet's further blunder, that Knightley shows her personal preference. Emma is full of self-recrimination. Harriet has indeed been "the dupe of her misconceptions and flattery" (402). Harriet still idealizes Emma, telling her that she is "too good" (407). Harriet tells Emma her perception of Knightley's changed attitude to her from the time of the dances at the ball at the Crown Inn. Harriet's account is corroborated by Emma's observation of Knightley's behavior toward her. He had walked with Harriet "apart from the others, in the limewalk at Donwell." Second, Emma reflects that Knightley had "sat talking with [Harriet] nearly half an hour before Emma came back from her visit, the very last morning of his being at Hartfield." On this occasion Knightley had told Emma "that he could not stay five minutes" as he had to go to London but then he remained with Harriet.

Their conversation is cut short by Mr. Woodhouse's appearance. Once more he acts as a saving relief for his daughter in times of trouble and distress. Emma wishes she "had never seen" Harriet. She goes through acute recrimination once again: "She was bewildered amidst the confusion of all that had rushed on her within the last hours . . . the deceptions she had been then practicing on herself, and living under!—The blunders, the blindness of her own head and heart!" She examines her own past thoughts and actions. The positive that emerges is "her affection for Mr. Knightley.—Every other part of her mind was disgusting" in the sense of offensive as opposed to the modern one of revolting or nauseating. The word "disgusting" (410–412) is used only on nine other occasions in Jane Austen's work. She "intends only the comparatively mild etymological force of 'distastefully,' not the stronger modern connotation of 'nauseatingly'" (Phillipps, 22). Emma thinks initially of herself and Knightley before turning to the impact of her misperceptions on others: "she was proved to have been universally mistaken . . . she had done mischief."

Emma reflects on the mismatch between Knightley and Harriet Smith and how others would perceive it. She asks herself whether it was anything new "for a man of first-rate abilities to be captivated by very inferior powers?" Philosophically she sees that "in this world" it is not new for the "unequal, inconsistent, incongruous—or for chance and circumstance (as second causes)," as distinct from God or Providence, "to direct the human fate?" She wishes that "she had never brought Harriet forward!" Emma realizes "how much of her happiness depended on being *first* with Mr. Knightley" (413–415). She has obtained self-knowledge, knowledge of herself and what she feels and desires. She, however, misjudges Knightley.

Volume 3, Chapter 12 (Chapter 48)

The 12th chapter of this final book opens with Emma's continual self-reflection, focusing on her past relationship with Knightley and hoping that he will remain a bachelor. "Marriage, in fact, would not do for her. It would be incompatible with what she owed to her father, and with what she felt for him" (416). Mrs. Weston calls on Emma and tells her that Jane has also been indulging in self-recrimination. Emma's recall of how badly she treated Jane is accompanied by gloomy July weather: "A cold stormy rain set in" (421) paralleling Emma's state of mind. In the penultimate paragraph of the chapter, we learn that Mrs. Weston is expecting a baby, hence she too will no longer be at Hartfield. The future for Emma does indeed appear as the "winter of her life" (423).

Volume 3, Chapter 13 (Chapter 49)

The opening of chapter 13 of the final book reinforces the emotional, mental, and social isolation of Emma. Once the dominating, initiating influence in Highbury and Hartfield affairs, she is now dejected and alone: "The weather continued much the same the following morning; and the same loneliness, and the same melancholy, seemed to reign at Hartfield." The afternoon brings a transformation in the weather and Emma's mood: "in the afternoon it cleared; the wind changed into a softer quarter; the clouds were carried off; the sun appeared; it was summer again" (424). Perry comes to be with her father and Knightley appears. This important chapter resolves perhaps the most important unresolved issues in the novel: the nature of the relationship between Emma and Knightley. Mutual misperceptions are cleared up. Knightley assumed that Emma had feelings for Frank Churchill; Emma perceived that Knightley, similarly, was attached to Harriet. The chapter is dominated by the imagery of "eyes" being opened, "a blind to conceal his real situation" (427), in the case of Frank Churchill, and awareness of the limitations of individual perceptions. At the start of the meeting between Emma and Knightley, Jane Austen conveys both physical and emotional attraction: "She found her arm drawn within his, and pressed against his heart, and heard him thus saying, in a tone of great sensibility"—mutual confessions then follow (425).

Knightley has heard the news of Jane and Frank's engagement and information that they will live in Yorkshire. He learns from Emma that she has no emotional attachment to Frank and he condemns Frank, trumpeting Jane's virtues. Fearing that Knightley will now raise the issue of Harriet and his assumed feelings for her, Emma attempts to quiet him. However, when the question of Harriet seems to come into the conversation, it is Emma who is the object of his love and proposal of marriage. Jane Austen does not use *erlebte Rede* in this chapter but dialogue and omniscient narration, conveying and relating the way in which Knightley surprisingly and unplanned makes his proposal. She comments, "Seldom, very seldom, does complete truth belong to any human disclosure; seldom can it happen that something is not a little disguised, or a little mistaken," adding "but where, as in this case, though the conduct is mistaken, the feelings are not, it may not be very material." The immediate context is Knightley's "anxiety to see how she [Emma] bore Frank Churchill's engagement" (431–432). Her words as narrator provide a commentary on the whole novel where different perspectives, especially those of Emma, the central protagonist, are revealed to be limited. Vision is restricted with fuller sight demonstrated as the narrative unfolds and draws to a conclusion.

There are, at the end of chapter 13 of this final book and Emma's acceptance of Knightley's proposal, still issues to be resolved. The transformation of Emma's fortunes, from despair, reflected by the summer weather, to happiness, is reflected in the appearance of the sun and the lifting of the clouds,

Emma and Mr. Knightley, illustration used as the frontispiece to *Emma (London: Routledge, 1870s)*

within the course of a chapter. There are, however, still some problems to be dealt with. Her father has to be won over to the marriage; he detests change, and Harriet has to be dealt with. The novel has a remaining six chapters and 50 pages to go.

Volume 3, Chapter 14 (Chapter 50)

The next chapter, 14, focuses on Emma's feelings—"What totally different feelings did Emma take back into the house from what she had brought out!" and a very lengthy letter addressed to Mrs. Weston from Frank Churchill. Her father is "totally unsuspicious of what" Emma and Knightley, who stayed with Emma following the proposal, "could have told him in return": again another illustration of limited perspective and vision. Emma decides during "the course of the sleepless night" that follows (434) to have a prolonged engagement while her father lives. She decides to arrange to send Harriet to London for a visit to her sister, Isabella, and her family.

Emma has fewer letters than Jane Austen's earlier novels. "The secretive Jane Fairfax is evidently an industrious correspondent as well as a talented stylist, but none of her letters is actually quoted" (Page, 182). Frank Churchill's lengthy letter written to Mrs. Weston is, however, cited in its entirety (436–443). It explains events from his perspective and provides a review, from Frank's point of view, of what previously has taken place in the narrative of the novel, filling in missing pieces in the jigsaw puzzle of *Emma*. He describes the situation with Jane Fairfax. Frank admits: "My behaviour to Miss Woodhouse indicated, I believe, more than it ought" and explains why it was necessary for him to act in that way—"concealment" being "essential to me." Frank wishes Mrs. Weston to show Emma his explanation of his actions. He explains the gift of the piano: "its being ordered was absolutely unknown to Miss F." He had "to blind the world to our engagement," whereas even before "the morning spent at Donwell," Jane "disapproved" of his behavior to Emma. Frank explains from his point of view why Jane accepted "the offer of that officious Mrs. Elton." He still smarts from Mrs. Elton's familiarity at addressing Jane by her first name. Jane meanwhile "dissolved" their engagement. Following the death of his aunt, he spoke to his uncle again about his marriage to Jane: he was "wholly reconciled and complying" (438–443).

Volume 3, Chapter 15 (Chapter 51)

Chapter 15 opens with Emma's reactions to Frank Churchill's letter. She shares it with Knightley, who reads it aloud to her, providing a running commentary as he does so. Knightley agrees with Frank's self-assessment, "You did behave very shamefully," and comments, "You never wrote a truer line" (446). Tactfully, he glosses over Emma's conduct at Box Hill. Knightley then turns to his marriage to Emma and how they will win over her father.

He agrees to come to live at Hartfield rather than remaining at Donwell. For Emma, "this proposal of his, this plan of marrying and continuing at Hartfield—the more she contemplated it, the more pleasing it became" (450). Consequently, Emma remains a "dutiful daughter" and gains "a loving husband." Knightley's solution, the move to Hartfield, is an incredible one in that he leaves his seat of power at Donwell. However, his move "permits the hero and heroine to be husband and wife, yet live and rule together" over Hartfield and its surroundings (Johnson, 142–143). A problem remaining is Harriet, and the chapter ends on an ironic note of inner thought process, of exaggeration: "it really was too much to hope even of Harriet, that she could be in love with more than *three* men in one year" (450).

Volume 3, Chapter 16 (Chapter 52)

The next chapter, 16, begins the resolution of the Harriet problem troubling Emma. They communicate through letters that are briefly related by Emma. She uses Harriet's need "to consult a dentist"—such basics are not ignored in Jane Austen's fictional world—to engineer for Harriet a stay for a fortnight at least with Isabella and her family in London. Emma then can "enjoy Mr. Knightley's visits . . . unchecked by that sense of injustice, of guilt, of something most painful" that she feels in Harriet's actual company (451). Emma also feels a "sense of past injustice towards Jane Fairfax" (421). She visits her, only to find Mrs. Elton with her, and consequently neither Emma nor Jane can openly speak of the new situation. Jane has made a remarkable recovery in terms of health and state of mind: "There was consciousness, animation and warmth." Mrs. Elton largely attributes this transformation to Perry, who she believes "has restored her in a wonderful short time!" (453–454). Mrs. Elton tries to annoy Emma, recalling that not everybody was allowed to see Jane when she was sick, and she alludes to events at Box Hill. On this occasion, Emma chooses not to be provoked. Elton appears, having gone on a fruitless quest searching for Knightley, thus confirming Emma's account of where Knightley may well be and exposing Mrs. Elton's inaccuracies. She maintained formerly that they had agreed to meet at the Crown Inn. Jane accompanies Emma downstairs when she leaves, apologizing to her. Emma compliments Jane on her frankness: "if you knew how much I love every thing that is decided and open!" (460). This represents a reversal from the previous misunderstandings reverberating through the novel.

Volume 3, Chapter 17 (Chapter 53)

The next chapter focuses on two main concerns. First, Mrs. Weston has moved from "Poor Miss Taylor" of the first chapter of the novel (8) and her wedding day, to giving birth, to being "the mother of a little girl." So the narrative has moved forward nine months from her wedding day and its opening chapter. Almost nothing is related of the labor or childbirth and its dangers, or even of Perry's role in it. Focus rather is on Emma's and Knightley's reactions to the birth of "poor little Anna Weston." Both reinforce the advantages to be gained from having a daughter: having the "fireside enlivened by the sports and nonsense, the freaks and the fancies of a child never banished from home" or being sent away from home to school as boys are. Knightley is provided with the opportunity to reflect on "spoilt children" like Emma. In their witty and affectionate conversation on Mrs. Weston's giving birth, Emma refers to Knightley's first name "George." This gives them both the opportunity to comment upon "the elegant terseness of Mrs. Elton" (461–463).

The second major focus of the chapter is their conveying news of the engagement to Mr. Woodhouse, Isabella, and John Knightley. Jane Austen uses omniscient narration, rather than dialogue or inner thought processes, to convey Emma's telling her father the news. She then moves into a combination of omniscient narration and *erlebte Rede* to convey her father's and Emma's reactions: "Did not he love Mr. Knightley very much?" and "Why could not they go on as they had done?" (466). The news of the engagement also spreads through Highbury with different reactions conveyed especially to the news that Knightley is leaving Donwell for Hartfield. The only dissenting voice is that of the "very much discomposed" Mrs. Elton, who reflects, "How could he be so taken in?" by Emma (469).

Volume 3, Chapter 18 (Chapter 54)

The penultimate chapter of the novel returns to the unresolved problem Emma has to face—Harriet. It opens on an elegiac note, "Time passed on. A few more to-morrows, and the party from London would be arriving" (470). Knightley, called still "Mr. Knightley" by Emma rather than "George" (473), tells Emma that Robert Martin and Harriet Smith are engaged. Knightley wishes that their "opinions were the same" on the matter "but in time they will. Time, you may be sure," he tells her, "will make one or the other of us think differently." He relates how he sent Martin to London, to deliver papers to his brother, John, thus affecting a reconciliation and remeeting between Martin and Harriet. Knightley speaks of Martin's "good sense and good principles." Emma, after gaining verification from Knightley that Harriet has actually accepted Martin, confesses to having behaved foolishly. "I was a fool." Knightley responds by saying, "I am changed also" (471–472, 474).

Not for the first time, they are interrupted by Mr. Woodhouse. Plans have been made to drive to Randalls. At Randalls, Emma encounters unexpectedly Frank and Jane in addition to Mrs. Weston. Emma and Frank review the misunderstandings between them and in this manner revisit from a different perspective key narrative events, such as her perception of Dixon and his imagined liaison with Jane. Emma compares her situation to Frank's, confessing "there is a likeness in our destiny; the destiny which bids fair to connect us with two characters so much superior to our own." Toward the end of the chapter the focus moves away from Frank and Emma to Mrs. Weston and a mistaken fear that her little girl might be unwell. Once again, Perry is reintroduced into the narrative, Mr. Woodhouse assuring her that "though the child seemed well now . . . it would probably have been better if Perry had seen it" (478–479). Mention of Perry leads Emma to recollect the incident earlier in the narrative concerning the carriage. Perry yet again then plays the role of linking characters and situations to one another and to reinforcing a central motif in the novel: its fascination with health and illness, "issues of physical, psychological, even moral health that are vital to life itself" (Wiltshire, "Health, Comfort, and Creativity," 178).

At the end of the penultimate chapter, Emma "had never been more sensible of Mr. Knightley's high superiority of character" (480).

Volume 3, Chapter 19 (Chapter 55)

In the final chapter, Mr. Woodhouse, somewhat reluctantly, accepts that Emma is getting married. Harriet's parentage is revealed: "She proved to be the daughter of a tradesman, rich enough to afford her the comfortable maintenance which had ever been hers." So Emma's inference concerning Harriet's origins, "the blood of gentility," proves not to be totally inaccurate. But as Jane Austen, in an *erlebte Rede* observation, satirically comments "The stain of illegitimacy, unbleached by nobility or wealth, would have been a stain indeed." Money or birth in her world covers a multitude of "sins." Increasingly Harriet disappears from Hartfield to the Martins, "but Emma attended Harriet to church" for her wedding. In the November Jane and Frank are to be married, both have left Highbury. The date is settled for Emma's wedding, a month following the Martins' marriage, that is, before the end of October. An external event finally persuades Mr. Woodhouse that he needs "his son-in-law's protection" owing to the fact that "Mrs. Weston's poultry-house was robbed one night of all her turkeys—evidently by the ingenuity of man." The security and seeming placid surface of Highbury is yet again threatened. There is both a comic and a serious element to the poultry-house robbery. Mr. Knightley's "strength, resolution and presence of mind" allows Mr. Woodhouse to give "cheerful consent" to his daughter's marriage.

The final paragraph of the novel briefly relates the wedding, "where the parties had no taste for finery or parade." The dissenting voice being that of Mrs. Elton, whose husband conveyed the details leading her to consider "it all extremely shabby, and very inferior to her own." In the final sentence of the novel, "the wishes, the hopes the confidence, the predictions of the small band of true friends who witnessed the ceremony, were fully answered in the perfect happiness of the union." Taken at face value, "the perfect happiness of the union"

(481–484), would mean closure on the novel and its characters' lives. Perhaps this final sentence is not without its ironies and ambiguities always present in Jane Austen's writing. In an earlier chapter, Knightley had paradoxically observed that Emma is "faultless, in spite of all her faults" (433). Whether or not marriage and the lessons she has learned, or not learned in the course of the novel, will dampen Emma's ardor to interfere in the lives of others is open to question. Also, as the stealing of Mrs. Weston's turkeys demonstrates, there are always unforeseen dangers lurking around the corner of the world of Hartfield and Highbury.

CRITICAL COMMENTARY

Immediate reactions of readers of *Emma* reflect subsequent ones indicating the novel's qualities. John Murray, Jane Austen's publisher, sent the manuscript of *Emma* to William Gifford (1756–1826) for a report. Gifford, who edited Murray's prestigious journal the *Quarterly Review*, responded that he had "nothing but good to say. I was sure of the writer before you mentioned her" (*Letter*, September 29, 1815). On December 25, 1815, Murray wrote to his most eminent contributor, Sir Walter Scott, asking if he had "any fancy to dash off an article on *Emma?*" Scott's review, extending to about 5,000 words, published anonymously as was the custom, constitutes the initial significant assessment of Jane Austen as a novelist. The review goes beyond *Emma*, drawing attention to the writer's use of detail, fineness of prose style, and depth of characterization. These elements of technique Scott relates to Jane Austen's creation of a universe of fiction that retains fidelity to everyday life. This is placed in historical perspective: In Jane Austen there is "the modern novel" in contrast to "sentimental romance, in which the nature imitated is *la belle nature*" or "an imitation of nature." Scott writes that he "bestow[s] no mean compliment upon the author of *Emma*, when we say, that keeping close to common incidents, and to such characters as occupy the ordinary walks of life, she has produced sketches of such spirit and originality." Jane Austen "confines herself chiefly to the middling classes of society: her most distinguished characters do not rise greatly above well-bred country gentlemen and ladies; and those which are sketched with most originality and precision, belong to a class rather below that standard" found in other contemporary writers. Scott compares Jane Austen's art with "the Flemish school of painting. The subjects are not often elegant, and certainly never grand; but they are finished up to nature, and with a precision which delights the reader" (Southam, *Critical Heritage:* I, 13, 61, 63–64, 67).

Private comments responding to the initial publication of *Emma* were not so favorable. Jane Austen sent Maria Edgeworth (1767–1849), a fellow writer and rival novelist, complimentary copies of *Emma*. She wrote in 1816 to her half brother Charles Sneyd Edgeworth that "There was no story in [*Emma*], except that Miss Emma found that the man whom she designed for Harriet's lover was an admirer of her own—& he was affronted at being refused by Emma & Harriet wore the willow—and *smooth, thin water-gruel* is according to Emma's father's opinion a very good thing & it is very difficult to make a cook understand what you mean by *smooth, thin water-gruel*!!" However, another contemporary novelist, Susan Ferrier (1782–1854), praised *Emma* highly. She wrote to a friend, also in 1816, "I have been reading 'Emma,' which is excellent; there is no story whatever, and the heroine is not better than other people; but the characters are all so true to life, and the style so piquant, that it does not require the adventitious aids of mystery and adventure" (Gilson, 71).

The author herself collected opinions of *Emma*, mostly by members of her family or family friends. One preferred it to *Pride and Prejudice* and *Mansfield Park*. "There might be more Wit" in the former, "and an higher Morality" in the latter. But "on account of it's peculiar air of Nature throughout," it was preferable to either. Another was "dissatisfied with Jane Fairfax" and for Jane Austen's friend Miss Bigg the "language [was] superior to the others." Jane Austen's mother "thought it more entertaining than MP.—but not so interesting as" *Pride and Prejudice*. "No characters in it equal to [Lizzy], Catharine, & Mr. Collins." Jane Austen also notes that Judge Francis Jeffrey (1773–1850), the influential editor of the *Edinburgh Review*, and a stern critic, "was kept up by it three nights" (Southam, I, 55–57).

An unsigned notice in the *Literary Panorama*, June 1816, commented, "The story is not ill conceived; it is not romantic but domestic." For the *Monthly Review*, July 1816, "the character of Mr. Woodhouse, with his 'habits of gentle selfishness,' is admirable drawn, and the dialogue is easy and lively." In general, published reviews found *Emma* "amusing, if not instructive" (*Gentleman's Magazine*, September 1816). Richard Whately's (1787–1863) influential unsigned review of *Northanger Abbey* and *Persuasion* published in the *Quarterly Review* in January 1821, apart from a mention of Miss Bates and Knightley in the context of a comparison with Shakespearean characters, pays little attention to *Emma*. For Whately, "Jane Austen is fundamentally a serious writer whose morality and values are communicated implicitly, wholly in terms of her fiction," unlike a contemporary such as Maria Edgeworth (Southam, I, 70, 70, 72, 19). Writing in 1837, John Henry Newman (1801–90), the distinguished theologian, observed in a letter following a reading of *Emma*, "Everything Miss Austen writes is clever, but I desiderate something. There is a want of *body* to the story. The action is frittered away in over-little things. There are some beautiful things in it. Emma herself is the most interesting to me of all her heroines. I feel kind to her whenever I think of her. But," Newman adds, "Miss Austen has no romance—none at all. What vile creatures her persons are! . . . That other woman, Fairfax, is a dolt—but I like Emma." The distinguished actor-manager William Charles Macready (1793–1873) wrote in his diary, February 15, 1834, after finishing *Emma* that Jane Austen "is successful in painting the ridiculous to the life."

The great essayist and historian Thomas Babington Macaulay (1800–59) considered Jane Austen a "Prose Shakespeare" (Southam, I, 117–118, 130), a judgment also of George Henry Lewes (1819–1878). Writing in *Blackwood's Edinburgh Magazine* in July 1859, he notes, "Mrs. Elton . . . is the very best portrait of a vulgar woman we ever saw: she is vulgar in soul, and the vulgarity is indicated by subtle yet unmistakable touches, never by coarse language, or by caricature of any kind" (Southam, I, 165). Sir William Frederick Pollock (1815–88), a distinguished lawyer, writing in *Fraser's Magazine* in January 1860, in an essay on Samuel Richardson, Scott, and Jane Austen, believes that *Emma* "will generally be recognized by the admirers of Miss Austen as the best of her works." For Pollock, Mr. Woodhouse is "as finely drawn as one of Shakespeare's fools," and "No other novels but Miss Austen's have ever excited so much minute as well as general interest." The novelist Margaret Oliphant (1828–97), in an assessment of "Miss Austen and Miss Mitford" published in *Blackwood's Edinburgh Magazine* in March 1870, prefers *Emma* to the author's other work, believing it to be "the work of her mature mind" (Southam, I, 172–173, 222). In the same year, Richard Simpson's (1820–76) unsigned review of Austen-Leigh's acclaimed *Memoir* appeared in the *North British Review*. Simpson makes many of the points found in criticism of the post–World War II period. Austen's vision is ironic; her fiction reveals a pattern of coherent development; she is a moralist depicting personal self-discovery and the growth to maturity through interaction with others. In *Emma* she "perfects her processes for painting humorous portraits" (Southam, I, 259).

Others, too, regarded *Emma* as the summit of Jane Austen's achievement. The distinguished Shakespearean critic and professor of English at Liverpool, Glasgow, and Oxford Universities, A. C. Bradley (1851–1935), in a 1911 lecture given at Cambridge noted that *Emma* "is the most vivacious of the later novels, and with some readers the first favourite." Bradley thought that "as a comedy [*Emma* is] unsurpassed . . . among novels" (Southam, I, 237–238). Another essay anticipating much subsequent criticism is by Reginald Farrer (1880–1920), writing in the *Quarterly Review*, July 1917. Farrer regards *Emma* as "the Book of Books." He writes, "this is *the* novel of character, and of character alone, and of one dominating character in particular"—Emma (Southam, II, 265–266). In a lengthy discussion of the novel he draws attention to its author's "delicate balance of sympathetic identifications and critical detachment in our response to her heroine" (Lodge, *Jane Austen's Emma*: 19).

D. W. Harding's "Regulated Hatred" essay published in *Scrutiny* in 1940 uses the treatment of Miss Bates to indicate its author's depiction of the "eruption of fear and hatred into the relationships

of everyday social life." In a later exploration of the novel, Harding points to an element of "civil falsehood" permeating the novel: "When social peace and comfort are maintained through one person's making allowances and being forbearing the cost is sacrifice of full personal equality" (Harding, *Regulated Hatred*: 10, 174). Writing in *Scrutiny* in 1941–42, Mrs. Q. D. Leavis sees *Emma* as the illustration of Jane Austen "at the climax of her art and in completest possible control over her writing" (Leavis, *Scrutiny*, 75). Subsequent critics are concerned with explaining why *Emma* is so important in Jane Austen's artistic achievement. As Edmund Wilson noted in 1944, *Emma* "is with Jane Austen what *Hamlet* is with Shakespeare. It is the book of hers about which her readers are likely to disagree most" (Wilson).

Two areas dominate recent critical discourse on *Emma*. First, assessment of the character of Emma. Second, the relationship of the world of the novel to the actual world. C. S. Lewis in 1954 believes that Austen's work is concerned with her heroines' discovering "that they are making mistakes both about themselves and about the world in which they live." In the case of Emma, it is her "awakening" to her mistakes that makes the ending possible (Watt, 27). Marvin Mudrick, unsympathetic to Emma, observes in *Jane Austen: Irony as Defense and Discovery* (1952), that at the conclusion "there is no sign that Emma's motives have changed, that there is any difference in her except her relief and temporary awareness" (200). Writing almost four years later in 1956, Edgar F. Shannon argues that Emma in the course of the novel undergoes a genuine transformation. *Emma* "discloses a valid progression of the heroine from callousness to mental and emotional maturity—a development psychologically consistent and technically consonant" (Lodge, 130–131). Marilyn Butler in *Jane Austen and the War of Ideas* (1975) regards *Emma* as "the greatest novel of the period" and sees Emma's role as "to survey society, distinguishing the true values from the false; and, in the light of this new knowledge of 'reality,' to school what is selfish, immature, or fallible in herself" (250). More recently, for Claudia Johnson in her *Jane Austen: Women, Politics and the Novel* (1988), "female authority itself is the subject of *Emma*." For Johnson, "with the exception of Mr. Knightley . . . all the people in control are women" (122, 126).

Critics such as Arnold Kettle are troubled by what they perceive as a limited vision of society presented in *Emma*. Kettle writes in his section on the novel found in the first volume of his *An Introduction to the English Novel* (1951), "We do not get from *Emma* a condensed and refined sense of a larger entity. Neither is it a symbolic work suggesting references far beyond its surface meaning." Lionel Trilling, in 1956, suggests, however, that it is false to assume that "Jane Austen's world really did exist" (Lodge, 24–25). Other critics such as Malcolm Bradbury in 1962 have seen the novel as "concerned with two kinds of world—the social world and the moral world—and their interaction, an interaction that is intimate, but also complete" (Lodge, 217). Alastair Duckworth in his *The Improvement of the Estate* (1971) sees Emma as preoccupied with class consciousness. Emma's subjective truth is continually tested by the external reality of Highbury.

Critics today pay greater attention to the world in which Jane Austen lived and worked, and to the subtle manner in which that world is reflected in a novel like *Emma*. The novel's relevance is reflected in the number of recent films based on it. Recently, other manifold perspectives have been brought to bear on the novel—for instance, *Jane Austen and the Body*, with its subtitle taken from "Emma, the picture of health" (*Emma* 39, 1992), by John Wiltshire, focuses on the emphasis in *Emma* and other Jane Austen novels, on physical health and its close relationship to psychological well-being. The same author's "Health, Comfort and Creativity: A Reading of *Emma*," in M. C. Folsom's *Approaches to Teaching Austen's Emma* (2004), focuses on the importance of Perry in a novel that "addresses issues of physical, psychological, even moral health that are vital to life itself" (178).

CHARACTERS

Abbotts, Misses (Chapter 9) Two pupils at Mrs. Goddard's school in Highbury. According to Harriet, she and they "ran into the front room and peeped through the blind when [they] heard he [Elton] was going by" (75).

Abdy, Old John (Chapter 44) Ex-clerk to the former vicar of Highbury, the Reverend Bates. Miss Bates tells Emma, "Poor old John. I have a great regard for him; he was clerk to my poor father twenty-seven years; and now, poor old man, he is bed-ridden, and very poorly with rheumatic gout in his joints" (383).

Abdy, John (Chapter 44) Old John's son, head man, hostler at the Crown Inn. According to Miss Bates, conveys information about Frank Churchill's departure to Richmond (383).

Bates, Mrs. (Chapters 2–3, 12, 19–21, 23, 25–27, 28, 33, 37, 38, 41, 44, 48, 52) The "widow of a former vicar of Highbury, was a very old lady, almost past everything but tea and quadrille" (21). Her habit of falling asleep is taken advantage of by Frank Churchill. He uses Mrs. Bates's presence to flirt with Jane Fairfax while her grandmother sleeps. Friend of Mr. Woodhouse. She appears frequently in *Emma*.

Bates, Miss Hetty (Chapters 2, 3, 10, 12, 19–21, 23–30, 33, 38–39, 41, 43–45, 48, 42–53) The garrulous daughter of Mrs. Bates. She "enjoyed a most uncommon degree of popularity for a woman neither young, handsome, rich nor married . . . She had never boasted either beauty or cleverness. Her youth had passed without distinction, and her middle of life was devoted to the care of a failing mother, and the endeavour to make a small income go as far as possible. And yet she was a happy woman, and a woman whom no one named without good will" (21). A friend of Mr. Woodhouse, she is a conveyor of gossip and, as such, she is important to the plot. She is a litmus test for the patience and charitable nature of the other characters and especially Emma, as witnessed by the Box Hill incident. Miss Bates appears frequently throughout *Emma*.

Bates, Jane (1) *See* Fairfax, Jane (1) (née Bates)

Bickerton, Miss (Chapter 39) A "parlour boarder at Mrs. Goddard's" (333) school in Highbury. She panics when out walking with Harriet the night following the Crown Inn ball and leaves Harriet alone to face the Gypsies. Frank Churchill rescues Harriet and expresses anger at "the abominable folly of Miss Bickerton" (335).

Bird, Mrs. (Chapter 32) She and a Miss Milman, a sister of Mrs. James Cooper, an acquaintance of Mrs. Elton who uses her (with Mrs. Cooper and Mrs. Jeffreys) as examples of women "too apt to give up music" (277) after they have married.

Bragge, Mr. (Chapter 36) A very wealthy cousin-in-law of Mr. Suckling living near Maple Grove, near Bristol. Used by Mrs. Elton to illustrate her comment to Mr. Weston "what is distance . . . to people of large fortune? . . . twice in one week [Mr. Suckling] and Mr. Bragge went to London and back again with four horses" (306).

Bragge, Mrs. (Chapter 35) Mr. Suckling's cousin living near Maple Grove, near Bristol. Mentioned by Mrs. Elton as having "such an infinity of applications; every body was anxious to be in her family, for she moves in the first circle" (299–300).

Brown, Mrs. (Chapter 22) After a dinner given in Bath by a "Mr. Green," the relationship between Mr. Elton and Miss Augusta Hawkins is assisted by "the party at Mrs. Brown's" (182).

Campbell, Colonel and Mrs. Campbell (Chapters 12, 20, and mentioned elsewhere 19–21, 23–24, 26–28, 33, 35, 38, 41, 44, 46, 48, 52, 54, and 55) Colonel Campbell, army officer and friend of Lieutenant Fairfax, to whom he is indebted for saving his life during a camp fever outbreak. As a debt of obligation and thanks, he and his wife adopt Jane when she is nine as a companion for their own younger daughter and to educate her. His fortune is not enough to leave anything to Jane, who receives nothing but kindness from them and enough education to live respectably in the future as a governess. She becomes their second daughter, and "Living constantly with right-minded and well-informed people, [Jane's] heart and understanding had received every advantage of description and culture." On the marriage of their own daughter to

Mr. Dixon and settlement in Ireland, the Campbells are very reluctant to part with Jane, wishing her to be with them "for ever." However, their better judgment informs them that "what must be at last, had better be soon" (164–165). When they holiday with the Dixons in Ireland, Jane stays with her grandmother and aunt at Highbury. Frank Churchill, to hide their engagement, refers to them as the donors of Jane's piano. Jane goes to live with them in London until she marries. Neither actually appears in the novel.

Campbell, Miss. *See* Dixon, Mrs.

Churchill, Mr. (mentioned in chapters 2, 11, 14, 18, 25–26, 30–31, 36–37, 42, 45–47, 50, 54–55) Does not actually appear in the novel. Of Enscombe in Yorkshire, he is the very wealthy uncle and subsequently Frank Churchill's guardian. Apparently he disapproved of his late sister's marriage to Captain Weston, but their estrangement seems more his snobbish wife's doing than his. Childless, Churchill and his wife reach "a sort of reconciliation" (16) with his sister before her death. After she dies, he and his wife bring up Frank, her sister's son, as their own, implicitly making him their heir. Following Mrs. Churchill's death, he agrees to Frank's marriage to Jane Fairfax and is pleased to share Enscombe with them, which suggests a more accommodating temperament than his wife's. According to Weston, Churchill's "is a quiet, indolent gentleman-like sort of pride that would harm nobody, and only make himself a little helpless and tiresome" (310).

Churchill, Mrs. (Chapter 2; mentioned in chapters 11, 14, 25–26, 30–31. 36–37, 42, 45–57, 50, 52) Does not actually appear in the novel, yet her arrogance influences it. According to Weston's account, an "upstart," she married into the very wealthy Churchill family. She then "out-Churchill'd them all in high and mighty claims." For Weston, her "arrogance and insolence" (310) were the real reason for the estrangement between her husband and his sister, resulting in the estrangement between the Westons and the Churchills. Her domineering impact on Frank propels much of his deception and wish to keep secret his engagement to Jane Fairfax. Her death results in the final unraveling of the plot of the novel. Weston says that "she has no more heart than a stone to people in general; and the devil of a temper" (121).

Churchill, Miss. *See* Weston, Mrs. née Churchill.

Churchill, Frank (Chapter 2; mentioned in chapters 14, 18, 20, 23–31, 34–43, 46–51, 54–5) The son of Mr. Weston and his first wife (a Miss Churchill), adopted when he was three years of age on the death of his brother by the exceedingly wealthy Mr. and Mrs. Churchill of Enscombe, Yorkshire. Emma on their first meeting, which does not take place until chapter 23 (book 2) thinks "he was a *very* good looking man; height, air, address, all were unexceptionable, and his countenance had a great deal of the spirit and liveliness of his father's; he looked quick and sensible" (190). Indulged by the Churchills, and Mrs. Churchill likes to have Frank near her when unwell. The Churchills move to London and then to Richmond—her illnesses, whether physical, psychological, or both, are not a creation of Frank's. When he initially appears in the novel, he is 23 and by reputation admired in Highbury, where his presence is eagerly awaited.

While in Highbury, he is engaged in an elaborate game of deception to conceal his commitment to Jane Fairfax, whom the Churchills would not approve of. He and Emma flirt, although Knightley has reservations about his character, finding it surprising that he visits his father Weston so infrequently and is so dominated by his stepmother. His character is the subject of a disagreement between Emma and Knightley. The former uses Frank as the center for her imaginative schemes, by for instance planning that he will be attracted to Harriet Smith. Frank dallies with Emma, he enjoys riddles, and continually flatters. He traveled 16 miles to London for a haircut, although this is an excuse to purchase a piano for Jane Fairfax. Frank enjoys dancing, especially waltzing. Knightley views him as a "chattering coxcomb" (150) possessing "smooth plausible manners" who leads a "life of mere idle pleasure" (148–149). Knightley, once Frank's relationship

with Jane has been made known, condemns him as "a disgrace to the name of man" (426).

In spite of his duplicitous behavior, his comings and goings in and out of Highbury, and his manipulation of Jane's difficult position, Frank is on the whole excused by most of those he is acquainted with in Highbury. "Jane Fairfax's character," according to Knightley, "vouches for her disinterestedness; every thing in his favour . . . Frank Churchill is, indeed, the favourite of fortune. Every thing turns out for his good" (428). The writer of the longest letter in the novel, one in which he explains to the new Mrs. Weston his actions and requests forgiveness (436–443), three of the central voices in the novel remain somewhat mixed in their feelings toward him. Frank Churchill plays a crucial role at some of the key moments of the novel; for instance, he rescues Harriet from the Gypsies, quarrels with Jane on the day of the Donwell strawberry-picking party, and behaves curiously at Box Hill. His attitudes are implicitly contrasted with Knightley's. The latter represents England, Churchill wants to leave England as quickly as he can: "I am sick of England—and would leave it to-morrow, if I could" (365). At the conclusion of *Emma*, Frank and Jane, his bride, return to live at Enscombe, Yorkshire, where they are joined by Mr. Churchill.

Cole, Mr. and Mrs. (Chapters 9–10, 19, 21–22, 25–28, 33, 41–42, 44–45, 53) Residents of Highbury, "very good sort of people—friendly, liberal and unpretending; but, on the other hand, they were of low origin, in trade, and only moderately genteel." Settled in Highbury for a good many years, they are respected members of the local community. Mr. Cole worked with Knightley, Weston, and others on parish business. Mrs. Cole is a close friend and helper of Miss Bates, her mother, and Jane Fairfax, whom she protects from Emma. With the increase in their trade and consequent prosperity, "they added to their house, to their number of servants, to their expenses of every sort, and . . . were, in fortune and style of living, second only to the family at Hartfield" (207). Emma snobbishly considers them below her, owing to their origins in trade, and plans to refuse an invitation to their dinner party. Owing to the fineness of the expression of the invitation, the fact that Frank Churchill plans to attend, and their consideration to her father's needs, she accepts. "Mr. Cole never touches malt liquor" (210). The Coles possess "a new grand pianoforté in the drawing-room." Mrs. Cole is unable to play, and their "little girls . . . are but just beginning." For Mrs. Cole, Jane Fairfax "is mistress of music" and her husband "so particularly fond of music" (215–216).

Cooper, Mrs. James (née Milman) (Chapter 32) An acquaintance of Mrs. Elton, she gave up music after marriage (*see* also Mrs. Bird and Mrs. Jefferies)

Cox, Mr. (Chapter 26) "The lawyer of Highbury" (214).

Cox, William (Chapter 27) The eldest son of Mr. Cox, referred to by Emma when thinking of possibly eligible bachelors for Harriet Smith, "William Coxe—Oh! no, I would not endure William Coxe—a pert young lawyer" (137).

Cox, Miss (Chapter 29) Sister of William Cox, with her sister, she attends the Westons' ball at the Crown Inn, Highbury (248).

Cox, Anne (Chapter 27) Another Cox sister, she and her sister are described by Emma as "without exception, the most vulgar girls in Highbury." Anne is associated with Robert Martin, who consulted her father "upon some business, and he asked him to stay to dinner." Anne sat next to Robert Martin and found him "very agreeable." According to Miss Nash, "either of the Coxes would be very glad to marry" Robert Martin (232–233).

Dixon, Mr. (Chapters 19, 20) Described by Miss Bates as "a most amiable, charming young man" (160). The rich owner of Balycraig in Ireland, he marries Jane Fairfax's adopted sister, Colonel and Mrs. Campbell's daughter. Jane Fairfax's Highbury visit is partly the consequence of the Campbells' visiting their daughter in Ireland. During a visit to Weymouth, Dixon saves Jane from being thrown overboard from a boat. Emma constructs a secret relationship between Jane and Dixon. On learning that he is musical, she believes that he is responsible for sending Jane the Broadwood piano.

Dixon, Mrs. (née Campbell) (Chapters 12, 19, 20) Described by Miss Bates as "absolutely plain—but extremely elegant and amiable" (161). Has a very "warm attachment" to Jane, and encouraged her parents to adopt Jane, with whom she lives as a sister and with "unabated regard" (165).

Elton, Mrs. Augusta, née Hawkins (Chapter 21, 22, 32; also featured in chapters 33–36, 38, 42, 50–53, 55) The younger of two daughters of a Bristol merchant, she and her family spent some of their winters in fashionable Bath. Has an independent fortune "of so many thousands as would always be called ten" (181). According to Emma, "Her person was rather good; her face not unpretty; but neither feature, nor air, nor voice, nor manner, were elegant." After visiting her following her marriage, Emma is "quite convinced that Mrs. Elton was a vain woman, extremely well satisfied with herself, and thinking much of her own importance; . . . she meant to shine and be very superior, but with manners which had been formed in a bad school, pert and familiar" (270, 272). Following her marriage to Mr. Elton and Emma's hostility, she sets herself up as a social rival to Emma. She continuously refers to her wealthy elder sister, Selina, and her brother-in-law, Mr. Suckling of Maple Grove, near Bristol; her speech is laden with foreign phrases. She refers to her husband as "caro sposo" (Italian, "dear husband") (278–279, 302, 356), although her poor grammar ("Neither Mr. Suckling nor me": 321) reveals her lack of education. However she is capable of citing poetry and misquoting lines from Thomas Gray. She believes incorrectly that the ball planned by Weston was in her honor and considers that the talents of Jane Fairfax, to whom she "took a great fancy," are wasted "on 'the desert air'" (282). Her too conscientious efforts to find Jane Fairfax a governess position considerably annoy Frank Churchill. She and her husband seem suited to each other, and she has the final spoken words in the novel. Hearing from her husband the details of Emma and Knightley's wedding, she "thought it all extremely shabby, and very inferior to her own—'Very little white Satin, very few lace veils; a most pitiful business!—Selina would stare when she heard of it" (484). Poplawski observes, "Vain, showy, insensitive, and rude, she represents a classic early example of the vulgar nouveau riche character who would become such a mainstay of later" 19th-century fiction (129). She has some discernment, however, regarding Knightley as "quite the gentleman" (278).

Elton, Mr. (Rev. Philip) (Chapter 1, 13–14; appears also in chapters 3–4, 6, 8–10, 13–17, 19, 21–22, 26, 31–34, 36, 38, 40, 52–53, 55) Around 26 or 27. Emma thinks "he was reckoned very handsome; his person much admired in general, though not by her, there being a want of elegance of feature which she could not dispense with." He was "quite the gentleman himself, and without low connections" (35). After a year in Highbury as its clergyman, he made the vicarage livable. Emma tries to find him a suitable wife, perceives his liking for Harriet Smith, and makes every effort to encourage the relationship. Elton, "a young man living alone without liking it," willingly exchanges "any vacant evening of his own blank solitude for the elegancies and society of Mr. Woodhouse's drawing-room and the smiles of his lovely daughter" (20). He is anxious to please, and John Knightley comments, "I never in my life saw a man more intent on being agreeable . . . when he has ladies to please every feature works" (111). At the Westons' reception, Elton was "continually obtruding his happy countenance on [Emma's] notice" (118). On the way home, probably because "he had been drinking too much of Mr. Weston's good wine," he seizes Emma's hand and makes "violent love to her" (129).

Following his rejection by Emma, Elton goes to Bath and after a month returns to Highbury engaged. At the Crown Inn ball, he attempts to gain revenge on Emma by deliberately snubbing Harriet Smith. Emma "did not think he was quite so hardened as his wife, though growing very like her" (328). Elton's speech is replete with affected compliments. When he had turned his attentions to Emma, he tells her that in her inaccurate draw-

ing of Harriet "the attractions you have added are infinitely superior to what she received from nature" (42). In short, Elton is a social climber willing to flatter. His observations on the wedding of Emma and Knightley, at which he officiated, are deliberately aimed at pleasing his wife, who "thought it all extremely shabby, and very inferior to her own" (484).

Fairfax, Lieutenant (Chapter 26) An infantryman, he married Miss Jane Bates. He died shortly after "in action abroad . . . an excellent officer and most deserving young man," Lieutenant Fairfax's wife "sinking under consumption and grief soon afterwards." His commanding officer, Colonel Campbell "had been indebted to him for such attentions, during a severe camp-fever, as he believed had saved his life." Consequently, Campbell and his wife bring up Fairfax's daughter as their own (163).

Fairfax, Jane (1) (née Bates) (Chapter 20) Wife of Lieutenant Fairfax, a younger sister of Hetty Bates, she died of "consumption and grief soon" after the death of her husband, leaving a very young daughter, Jane (163).

Fairfax, Jane (2) (Chapters 10, 12, 20; also 14–21, 23–24, 26–28, 30–31, 33–35, 38, 41–45, 47–48, 51) Orphaned at the age of three, daughter of Lieutenant and Jane Fairfax, she is brought up by her aunt Hetty Bates and her grandmother, and the Campbells, and destined to become a governess. "She had . . . been given an excellent education. Living constantly with right-minded and well-informed people, her heart and understanding had received every advantage of discipline and culture" (164). A very talented pianist, she is disliked by Emma, who had known her since they were children. Ironically, in view of Frank Churchill's secret engagement to Jane, Emma confesses to him, "we should have taken to each other whenever she visited her friends. But we never did. I hardly know how it has happened; a little, perhaps, from that wickedness on my side which was prone to take disgust towards a girl so idolized and so cried up as she always was, by her aunt and grandmother, and all their set. And then, her reserve—I never could attach myself to any one so completely reserved" (203).

Emma perceives her as "very elegant, remarkably elegant . . . her face, her features—there was more beauty in them all together than [Emma] had remembered; it was not regular, but it was very pleasing beauty" (167). Following the Campbells' decision to extend their visit to their daughter in Ireland, Jane chooses to stay with her aunt and grandmother in Highbury. She is especially reserved because of her secret engagement to Frank Churchill, who is unable to make the engagement public because he is afraid that his rich aunt will disinherit him. Jane is irritated by Frank's overattentiveness to Emma and her refusal to walk with him after the Donwell Abbey visit leads him to behave erratically at Box Hill. Jane breaks their engagement and accepts Mrs. Elton's help in finding her a governess position. After knowing this, Frank reveals the engagement to his uncle, whose approval he gains following the death of Mrs. Churchill. Secrecy and deception cause Jane to become ill, and she refuses to see Emma. However, when the news of the engagement is made public, she quickly recovers, apologizes to Emma, and they form a friendship.

Primarily viewed through Emma's viewpoint, Jane is admired by Knightley. At one point, Emma thinks that he is likely to marry Jane, leading Emma to realize that she must marry him. Knightley tells Emma that "I am very ready to believe [Frank's] character will improve, and acquire from [Jane's] the steadiness and delicacy of principle that it wants" (448). Deirdre Le Faye notes that Jane Austen told her family that "the letters placed by Frank Churchill before Jane Fairfax, at the end of the irritating alphabetgame . . . which she swept away unread, contained the word 'pardon.'" Additionally, Jane Fairfax "only lived another nine or ten years after her marriage—succumbing, no doubt, to an inherited tendency to tuberculosis" (227).

Ford, Mrs. (Chapters 21, 27; also chapters 23 and 24) The proprietor of Ford's, "the principal woollen-draper, linen-draper, and haberdasher's shop united; the shop first in size and fashion in" Highbury (178). Mrs. Ford is "obliging" (235). Har-

riet Smith meets the Martins at Ford's, a shop frequented by Mr. Weston on his regular visits to Highbury.

Gilbert, Mrs. (Chapters 29, 38) As a member of the Highbury social group, she is at the Coles' dinner party and also the Crown Inn ball. At this event, Elton, pointedly, mentions her as the only partner he is able to dance with. In this way, he counters Mrs. Weston's efforts to get him to dance with Harriet Smith.

Gilbert, Miss (Chapter 29) "Expected at her brother's, and must be invited with the rest" (248) to Mr. Weston' ball.

Gilberts, the two (Chapter 29) Mrs. Gilbert's sons, eligible dancing partners. "There will be the two Gilberts" (248) who can make up the numbers at Mr. Weston's ball.

Goddard, Mrs. (Chapter 3; also mentioned in chapters 4, 7, 13, 15, 17, 21, 23, 25, 27, 39, 49, 54) The mistress of the local boarding school, "a plain, motherly kind of woman," she "gave the children plenty of wholesome food, let them run about a great deal in the summer, and in winter dressed their chilblains with her own hands. It was no wonder that a train of twenty young couple now walked after her to church" (22). Her "parlour boarder[s]" (333) include Harriet Smith and Miss Bickerton. She enjoys a game of cards, especially piquet, with Mr. Woodhouse and introduces Harriet Smith to Emma. She is "almost always at the service of an invitation from Hartfield" (20).

Graham, Mr. (Chapter 12) According to Emma, she "did not thoroughly understand what" Mr. John Knightley was "telling" his brother concerning his friend "Mr. Graham's intending to have a bailiff from Scotland, to look after his new estate. But will it answer? Will not the old prejudice be too strong?" (104), i.e., anti-Scottish bias on the part of the English.

Green, Mr. (Chapter 22) A Bath "dinner at Mr. Green's" is one of "the steps so quick" (182) in the rapid progress of the courtship of Mr. Elton and Augusta Hawkins.

Hannah (Chapter 1) The daughter of James, Mr. Woodhouse's coachman. Mr. Woodhouse recommends her for employment with Mr. and Mrs. Weston at the Randalls. Mr. Woodhouse tells Emma, "I am sure she will make a very good servant; she is a civil, pretty-spoken girl; I have a great opinion of her." He adds, "Whenever I see her, she always curtseys and asks me how I do, in a very pretty manner; and when you have had her here to do needlework, I observe she always turns the lock of the door the right way and never bangs it." Moreover, "it will be a great comfort to poor Miss Taylor to have somebody about her that she is used to see," and when James visits her at the Randalls, he can convey "how we all are" (9).

Harry (Chapter 32) A servant of Knightley at Donwell criticized by Mrs. Elton. She tells Emma "the Donwell servants . . . are all, I have often observed, extremely awkward and remiss.—I am sure I would not have such a creature as his Harry stand at our sideboard for any consideration" (458).

Hawkins, Miss Augusta. *See* Elton, Mrs.

Hodges, Mrs. (Chapters 27, 32, 52, 53) Miss Bates relates to Emma that Hodges, Knightley's Donwell housekeeper, is annoyed with Knightley for giving away the last of his apples: "She could not bear that her master should not be able to have another apple-tart this spring." Also, "Mrs. Hodges *would* be cross sometimes" (239). She is also among the Donwell servants castigated by Mrs. Elton. "And as for Mrs. Hodges, Wright [Mrs. Elton's housekeeper] holds her very cheap indeed.—She promised Wright a receipt, and never sent it" (458). When she learns of Knightley's impending marriage to Emma, Mrs. Elton is "not at all sorry that [she] had abused the housekeeper [Mrs. Hodges] the other day" (469).

Hughes, Dr. and Mrs. (Chapter 38) Guests at the Crown Inn ball.

James (Chapter 1; also chapters 3, 14–15, 23, 25–26, 29, 37, 54) The coachman at Hartfield whom Mr. Woodhouse seems most anxious to protect: "The carriage! But James will not like to put the horses to for such a little way" (8). James's daughter Hannah becomes the Westons' housemaid on Mr. Woodhouse's recommendation.

Jeffereys, Mrs. (Chapter 32) "Clara Partridge that was." According to Mrs. Elton, she and "the two Milmans, now Mrs. Bird and Mrs. James Cooper," Bath acquaintances, after marriage gave up music (277).

Knightley, Bella (Chapters 6, 12) The John Knightleys' second child.

Knightley, Emma (Chapter 12) The youngest of the four John Knightley children: "a nice little girl about eight months old . . . making her first visit to Hartfield, and very happy to be danced about in her aunt's arms" (98).

Knightley, George (1) (referred to throughout the novel) "A sensible man about seven or eight-and-thirty" (9), owner of Donwell Abbey and much of the Highbury parish. He "serves as the catalyst for Emma's growth" (Auerbach, 220). An old and very close friend of the Woodhouse family, he has known Emma since she was born and has always taken a very close interest in her. John, his younger brother, married Emma's older sister, Isabella. Plainspoken, he is not afraid to criticize Emma when he considers she has acted incorrectly. "Mr. Knightley, in fact, was one of the few people who could see faults in Emma Woodhouse" (11). For instance, he is far from pleased when she persuades Harriet to stop seeing Robert Martin and encourages her to court Mr. Elton. A gentleman farmer, Knightley is most conscientious about his civic duties, as for instance being a magistrate or looking after his tenant farmers and other employees. He participates fully in the life of Highbury, is kind, considerate, and highly respected. Kind to Miss Bates and her mother, he annually sends them his best cooking apples and brings his carriage to take them and Jane Fairfax to the party at the

Coles. Perceptive, he notices, for instance, Frank Churchill's overattentiveness to Emma. Emma's treatment of Miss Bates results in his chastising her. His jealousy of Frank Churchill, whom he regards as an "Abominable scoundrel" (426) owing to his flirtation with Emma, leads to his visiting the Knightleys in London. He finds them too happy and Isabella too much like Emma. His proposal to Emma is unpremeditated. The concern then is how they are able to marry "without attacking the happiness of her father," which he discusses "in plain, unaffected, gentleman-like English" (448). The solution is for him to live at Hartfield.

Auerbach writes that "Austen contrasts Mr. Knightley's character with that of all the other versions of 'gentleman' in the novel" (221). His speech is plain and frequently monosyllabic, contrasted, for instance, with Frank Churchill's French-influenced "manoeuvring and finessing" (146). He has known Emma for so long that it is hardly surprising their relationship will be "something so like perfect happiness" (432). The final words of the novel refer to "the perfect happiness of the union" (484). According to Le Faye, "Jane Austen told her family . . . that Mr. Woodhouse survived his daughter's marriage, and kept her [Emma] and Mr. Knightley from settling at Donwell about two years" (277).

Knightley, George (2) (Chapter 6) The third son of the John Knightleys. Emma draws him, commenting, "I am rather proud of little George" (45).

Knightley, Henry (Chapter 9) Mr. Woodhouse tells Harriet Smith, "Henry is the eldest, he was named after me, not after his [John Knightley] father. . . . Isabella would have him called Henry, which I thought very pretty of her. And he is a very clever boy, indeed" (80).

Knightley, Isabella (née Woodhouse) (Chapters 1, 11. Also see Chapters 7, 11–17, 23–26, 45, 49, 52–55) Emma's elder sister, has five children: "a pretty, elegant, little woman, of gentle, quiet manners, and a disposition remarkably amiable and affectionate; wrapt up in her family. . . . She was not a woman of strong understanding or

any quickness." She is rather like her father, she "was delicate in her own health, over-careful of that of her children, had many fears and many nerves" (92). On health matters, she defers to a Mr. Wingfield; her father defers to Mr. Perry.

Knightley, John (1) (Chapters 5, 11; also chapters 12–17, 34–36, 45, 49, 52–55) George Knightley's younger brother, and husband of Isabella, Emma's older sister, a London lawyer, "a tall, gentleman-like, and very clever man; rising in his profession, domestic, and respectable in his private character; but with reserved manners which prevented his being generally pleasing; and capable of being sometimes out of humour" (92). Lacks patience with some of his wife's whims and Mr. Woodhouse, and consequently does not always see eye to eye with Emma. Prefers his domestic comforts to a winter's evening spent at the Westons'.

Knightley, John (2) (Chapter 9) The Knightleys' second son, according to Mr. Woodhouse "very like his mamma" and "named after his father" (80).

Larkins, William (Chapter 27; also chapters 28, 30, 51–52, 54) Mr. Knightley's protective bailiff on the Donwell estate. Trusted by Knightley, he manages his accounts, "thinks more of his master's profit than any thing." Brings Miss Bates a sack of his master's best apples: Miss Bates describes him as "such an old acquaintance!" (239).

Martin, Mrs. (Chapter 4) Robert and Elizabeth Martin's mother, who treats Harriet Smith with kindness during her two-month visit to the Martins' Abbey Mill Farm. According to Harriet's account, Mrs. Martin has "*two* parlours, two very good parlours indeed . . . [and] a little Welch cow, a very pretty little Welch cow, indeed." The Martins have "a very handsome summer-house in their garden . . . a very handsome summer-house, large enough to hold a dozen people" (27).

Martin, Elizabeth (Chapter 4) One of the Martin sisters and a school friend of Harriet Smith.

Martin, Robert (Chapters 3, 4; see also chapters 7–8, 12, 26, 21–23, 27, 43, 47, 54–55)   Aged 24, Mr. Knightley's successful tenant farmer. According to Emma, "His appearance was very neat, and he looked like a sensible young man, but his person had no other advantage" (31–32). Mr. Knightley, on the other hand, finds him "open, straight forward, and very well judging" (59). Following consultation with Mr. Knightley, he proposes to Harriet Smith, who rejects him as being unworthy—her head has been turned by Emma. Knightley considers Robert Martin too good for Harriet. Martin's feelings for Harriet remain constant, and encouraged by Knightley, he calls on her during his stay with the John Knightleys in London. Harriet accepts him and at the end of the novel, they marry.

Harriet Smith tells Emma that Robert Martin "reads the Agricultural Reports" (29), suggesting that he "made a serious study of farming techniques and developments" (Pinion, 255). Robert Martin appears infrequently in the novel; we hear of him mainly in connection with Harriet. Norman Page notes that "the letter in which Robert Martin proposes to Harriet Smith is described though not quoted"; he satisfied "the prerequisite of grammatical correctness" and "he produced a satisfactory 'compositon'" (184). According to Emma, his proposal "would not have disgraced a gentleman" and he writes in "plain . . . strong, and unaffected" language (51).

Mitchell, Farmer (Chapter 1)   A Highbury farmer. Mr. Weston met Emma and Miss Taylor in Broadway lane "when, because it began to mizzle [Mr. Weston] darted away with so much gallantry, and borrowed two umbrellas for us from Farmer Mitchell's." This action of Weston's "made up [Emma's] mind on the subject. I planned the match from that hour" between Weston and Miss Taylor (12).

Nash, Miss (Chapters 4, 9)   Head teacher at Mrs. Goddard's school whose sister married a linen draper. A great collector of riddles, she gives Harriet the idea of making a collection of them and charades. A fervent admirer of Mr. Elton since he appeared in Highbury, she has written down all his texts and admires his yellow vicarage curtains.

Otway, Mr. and Mrs, Miss Caroline, George and Arthur (Chapter 38)   Guests at the Crown Inn ball.

Partridge, Mrs. (Chapter 32)   Claimed by Mrs. Elton as "my particular friend," she has "always resided with when in Bath" (275). She has a daughter, Clara (*see* Jeffereys, Mrs. Clara). Mrs. Elton offers to give Emma a letter of introduction to her.

Patty (Chapters 21, 27)   The Bateses' only servant.

Perry, Mr. (Chapter 2; and see also Chapters 7, 9, 12–13, 15, 19, 21, 25, 27, 29, 32, 41, 45, 49–50, 52–54)   The Highbury apothecary. His visits are "one of the comforts of Mr. Woodhouse's life," who regards him as an oracle of wisdom on all health matters. Mrs. Perry is a friend of the Bateses' who told Miss Bates that her wish is for her husband to have a carriage in bad weather. Jane Fairfax apparently repeats this in a letter to Frank Churchill, who carelessly mentions it in conversation. Mr. Perry agrees with Mr. Woodhouse that wedding cake might be unpleasant if eaten in excess; however, "there was a strange rumour in Highbury of all the little Perrys being seen with a slice of Mrs. Weston's wedding cake in their hands" (19). Perry "is . . . mentioned in *Emma* every twenty or so pages in one connection or another." Perry is "significant as a pointer to some of the novel's leading concerns. His very activity, which is also movement up the social scale, forms a telling contrast with the genteel inertia of his principal patient in the community, Mr. Woodhouse." He also points to the novel's fascination with "matters of health" (Wiltshire in Fulsom, 169–170).

Prince, Miss (Chapter 4)   One of the teachers at Mrs. Goddard's school.

Richardson, Miss (Chapter 4)   One of the teachers at Mrs. Goddard's school.

Saunder's John (Chapter 27)   Miss Bates intends to take her mother's spectacles to Saunders for repairs when a rivet falls out. She does not have the time to do so, and Frank Churchill offers to do it so he can spend more time with Jane Fairfax.

Serle (Chapters 3, 21) The cook at Hartfield. According to Mr. Woodhouse, she "understands boiling an egg better than any body" (24). She also is an expert at boiling a pork leg.

Smallridge, Mrs. (Chapter 42) A wealthy lady living near Bath, a neighbor of the Sucklings, with whom Mrs. Elton arranges a governess position for Jane Fairfax. She has three young daughters.

Smith, Harriet (Chapter 3, 4–10, 12–17, 19, 21–23, 25–27, 31–33, 38–40, 42–43, 45–59, 51–55) A "parlour-boarder" (23) at Mrs. Goddard's, where she was placed by an unknown father. She "certainly was not clever, but she had a sweet, docile, grateful disposition; was totally free from conceit; and only desiring to be guided by any one she looked up to" (26). "She was short, plump and fair, with a fine bloom, blue eyes, light hair, regular features, and a look of great sweetness" (23). Seventeen years old, "the natural daughter of somebody" (22), who by the end of the novel is revealed to be a respectable tradesman. "She proved to be the daughter of a tradesman, rich enough to afford her the comfortable maintenance which had ever been her's and decent enough always for concealment" (481–482). Emma mistakenly imagines that she may have a genteel heritage. Before being taken up by Emma, she spends two happy months with the Martins and was attracted by the young farmer Robert Martin. Taking Emma's advice, she turns Martin down and, encouraged by Emma, aspires to Elton. She is easily influenced by the socially superior Emma to become a participant in her mistaken schemes. Knightley treats her kindly, especially at the Crown Inn ball, where she is snubbed by Elton. Emma arranges for her to stay with the John Knightleys in London, where Robert Martin calls on Knightley's behalf, and proposes to her again. This time she accepts, having gained in the novel awareness of her social limitations, admitting that "she had been presumptuous and silly, and self-deceived" (481). For Knight-

ley, Harriet has "very seriously good principles," looking forward to "the affections and utility of domestic life" (474).

Stokes, Mrs. (Chapter 29) The landlady of the Crown Inn. Mr. Woodhouse asks Frank Churchill "If I could be sure of the rooms being thoroughly aired—but is Mrs. Stokes to be trusted? I doubt it. I do not know her, even by sight" (252).

Suckling, Mr. (1) (Chapter 36) Father of the owner of Maple Grove. Mrs. Elton is "almost sure that old Mr. Suckling had completed the purchase before his death" (310).

Suckling, Mr. (2) (Chapters 22; 32, 36) Elton's very wealthy brother-in-law, "who has been eleven years a resident at Maple Grove," near Bristol, "and whose father had it before him" (310). The younger Suckling married Selina Hawkins, the elder sister of the future Mrs. Elton. He maintained *two* carriages, one of which was the very fashionable barouche-landau boasted about by Mrs. Elton.

Suckling, Mrs. née Hawkins (Chapters 22, 32) The older sister of Mrs. Elton, she made a very advantageous marriage.

Taylor, Miss. *See* Weston, Mrs. Anne

Tom (Chapter 44) A servant probably at the Randalls. When Frank Churchill wishes to leave early following the Box Hill outing, "Tom had been sent off immediately for the Crown chaise" (383).

Tupmans, the (Chapter 36) According to Mrs. Elton, "there is a family in that neighborhood [Maple Grove] who are such an annoyance to my brother and sister from the airs they give themselves! . . . People of the name Tupman, very lately settled there, and encumbered with many low connections, but giving themselves immense airs, and expecting to be on footing with the old established families . . . They came from Birmingham, which is not a place to promise much" (310). They live at West Hall.

Wallis, Mrs. (Chapter 27) The wife of the Highbury baker, she bakes the Bateses' apples for them. Miss Bates tells Emma, "they are extremely civil and obliging to us, the Wallises, always—I have heard some people say that Mrs. Wallis can be uncivil and give a very rude answer, but we have never known any thing but the greatest attention from them." She adds, "it cannot be for the value of our custom now, for what is our consumption of bread you know?" (236–237).

Weston, Mr. (Chapters 1, 2; see also chapters 4, 5, 9, 11, 13–15, 18, 23–26, 29–32, 34–36, 38, 41–43, 45–46, 48, 51, 53, 54) "Mr. Weston was a native of Highbury, and born of a respectable family, which for the last two of three generations had been rising into gentility and prosperity." He succeeded "early in life to a small independence," joined the county militia, and rose to the rank of captain: he "was a general favourite" (15). Knightley describes Weston as "A straight-forward, open-hearted man" (13). He has a son, Frank, from his marriage to the wealthy Miss Churchill from Enscombe, Yorkshire, which "did not produce much happiness" (15). He agreed to Frank being adopted by the Churchills. Leaving the militia, followed his brothers into trade. After 20 years in London he purchased "a little estate adjoining Highbury" (16) and married for a second time, Miss Taylor who was Emma's governers. Every year he met his son, Frank Churchill, in London and was proud of him. He and his new wife hope that one day Frank will marry Emma and arrange the ball at the Crown Inn for them. John Knightley tells Emma, "Mr. Weston is rather an easy, cheerful tempered man, than a man of strong feelings; he takes things as he finds them, and makes enjoyment of them somehow or other" (96).

Weston, Anna (Chapter 53) The newborn girl of the Westons.

Weston, Mrs. Anne, née Taylor (Chapters 1, 2, 5–6, 9, 11, 13–14, 18, 23–24, 26–36, 38, 41–43, 56, 48, 50–55) The novel opens with "Poor Miss Taylor" (8), as she is still called by Mr. Woodhouse, and her marriage to Captain Weston. She has been the governess and friend of Emma, whom she brought up, for 16 years. Following Isa-bella, Emma's sister's, marriage, she has been a sister to Emma. She was one "such as few possessed, intelligent, well informed, useful, gentle, knowing all the ways of the family . . . one to whom [Emma] could speak every thought as it arose, and who had such an affection for her as could never find fault" (6). Knightley regards her as "a rational unaffected woman" (13). Mrs. Weston has let Emma have "rather too much her own way" (5). Mrs. Weston, Knightley believes, received "a very good education from *her* [Emma], on the very material matrimonial point of . . . doing as you were bid" (38). She defends Emma's character, saying "she has qualities which may be trusted; she will never lead any one really wrong; she will make no lasting blunder" (40). She can make incorrect judgments, such as when she believes that Knightley is attracted to Jane Fairfax and suspects that the piano was sent by him. She hopes that Emma and Frank Churchill will get together, but at the end of the novel, "with her baby [daughter] on her knee," foretells "a union of the highest promise of felicity" (468) between Emma and Knightley.

Weston, Mrs. née Churchill (Chapter 2) The deceased mother of Frank Churchill, who was rejected by her family when she married Captain Weston. She was "of age" and possessed "the full command of her fortune." The marriage "was an unsuitable connection, and did not produce much happiness." Mrs. Weston "had resolution enough to pursue her own will . . . but not enough to refrain from unreasonable regrets . . . nor from missing the luxuries of her former home." She and Weston "live beyond their income." She died after three years of marriage: "she wanted at once to be the wife of Captain Weston, and Miss Churchill of Enscombe" (15–16).

Weston, Frank. *See* Churchill, Frank.

Wingfield, Mr. (Chapter 11) Isabella Knightley "was fond of her own Mr. Wingfield in town as her father could be of Mr. Perry" (92). Her father questions the advice of Wingfield, her London apothecary, saying she should rather consult his Perry in Highbury.

Woodhouse, Emma (appears throughout the novel) The eponymous heroine, closely attached to her father, "handsome, clever and rich, with a comfortable home and happy disposition, seemed to unite some of the best blessings of existence; and had lived nearly twenty-one years in the world with very little to distress or vex her" (5). The narrative is mainly viewed from her perspective. There are two exceptions. In the fifth chapter of the first volume, Mr. Knightley and Mrs. Weston talk about Emma when she is not present (36–41). In the fifth chapter of the third volume, Knightley watches the behavior of Jane Fairfax and Frank Churchill over a game of cards (343–349). Otherwise, Emma is the lens through which the narrative is presented, and as the story unfolds the limitations of her character, she had "rather too much her own way" (5), become evident. Emma perceives, or misperceives, herself as vital to the community and able to arrange marriage for others. For instance, *she* notices Harriet Smith: "she would improve her; she would detach her from her bad acquaintance. . . . she would form her opinions and her manners" (23–24).

As the novel develops, assisted by Mr. Knightley's honesty with her, Emma slowly begins to be aware of her "insufferable vanity" and "unpardonable arrogance" (412–413), trying to arrange the lives of others such as Harriet Smith and Robert Martin, and rudeness to Miss Bates at Box Hill. She becomes aware that she has to be less of an "imaginist" (335), indulging in fantasies concerning others and their emotions, and "more rational, more acquainted with herself" (423). Emma's is also a love story as much as a voyage of self-discovery. During her planning of the romance of others, she gradually becomes aware of the depth of her feelings for Knightley; her awareness of her real feelings for him coexist with her recognition of her misplaced judgments. She wishes "to grow more worthy of him, whose intentions and judgment had been ever so superior to her own" (475). She dismissed, for example, the tenant farmer Robert Martin as unsuitable to marry Harriet Smith, whom she took, erroneously, to be a gentleman's daughter. Emma realizes Martin's "sense and worth" and approves of his marriage to Harriet. However, she

recognizes that their relationship "must sink," for Harriet will be a farmer's wife. Following the discovery that Harriet "proved to be the daughter of a tradesman," Emma reflects that if Harriet had married Knightley, Frank Churchill or Elton—one of the three Emma or Harriet had pretensions Harriet might marry—"the stain of illegitimacy, unbleached by nobility or wealth" would have entered into their family (481–482).

The novel concludes with Emma's wedding to Knightley. The final words of *Emma* predict "the prefect happiness of the union" (484) between Emma and Knightley. For Claudia Johnson, Emma "does not think of herself as an incomplete or contingent being whose destiny is to be determined by the generous or blackguardly actions a man will make towards her" (124). However, for Alastair Duckworth, "Emma is so egotistical that she seems unaware that other characters have as real an existence as she" (cited McDonald, 110).

Woodhouse, Mr. Henry (Chapter 1 and throughout the novel) The wealthy owner of Hartfield in Highbury, Surrey, a widower, the "most affectionate, indulgent" (5) father of the married Isabella and of Emma: "having been a valetudinarian all his life, without activity of mind or body, he was a much older man in ways than in years; and though everywhere beloved for the friendliness of his heart and his amiable temper, his talents could not have recommended him at any time." Further, "he was a nervous man, easily depressed, fond of every body that he was used to, and hating to part with them; hating change of every kind" (7). Throughout much of the novel he resists change, agreeing to Knightley's living at Hartfield at its conclusion only because he can offer protection from the poultry thieves. A hypochondriac, he continually relies on the advice of the local apothecary, Mr. Perry, who appears to respond to Mr. Woodhouse's every whim. Exceedingly careful of what he eats, "his horror of late hours and large dinner-parties made him unfit for any acquaintance, but such as would visit him on his own terms" (20). Food is prepared only in the way he is used to: Serle boils pork or egg better than anyone else. His son-in-law, John Knightley is too rough with Mr. Woodhouse's grandchildren. He is fearful of people catching cold. According to Le Faye, the author told her family "that Mr. Woodhouse survived his daughter's marriage, and kept her and Mr. Knightley from settling at Donwell, about two years" (277).

Wright (Chapter 38)   Mrs. Elton's housekeeper at the Highbury Vicarage.

BIBLIOGRAPHY

Primary Texts

Austen, Jane. *Emma*. Edited by R. W. Chapman. *The Novels of Jane Austen*. 3d ed. Vol. 4. Reprint. Oxford: Oxford University Press 1986. (All textual references are to this edition.)

———. *Emma*. Edited by R. Cronin and Dorothy McMillan. *The Cambridge Edition of the Works of Jane Austen*. Cambridge: Cambridge University Press, 2005.

———. *Emma*. Edited by James Kinsley, an introduction and notes by Adela Pinch and Vivien Jones. Oxford: Oxford University Press, 2003.

———. *Jane Austen's Letters*. Collected and edited by Deirdre Le Faye. Oxford: Oxford University Press 3d ed., 1995.

Secondary Works

Auerbach, Emily. *Searching for Jane Austen*. Madison: University of Wisconsin Press, 2004.

Bradbury, Malcolm. "Jane Austen's *Emma*," *Critical Quarterly* 4 (1962): 335–346.

Burrows, J. F., *Jane Austen's* Emma. Sydney: Sydney University Press, 1968.

Butler, Marilyn. *Jane Austen and the War of Ideas*. Oxford, U.K.: Clarendon Press, 1975.

Copeland, Edward, and Juliet McMaster, eds. *The Cambridge Companion to Jane Austen*. Cambridge: Cambridge University Press, 1997.

De Rose, Peter L., and S. W. McGuire. *A Concordance to the Works of Jane Austen*. 3 vols. New York and London: Garland, 1982.

Duckworth, Alistair M. *The Improvement of the Estate: A Study of Jane Austen's Novels*. Baltimore and London: Johns Hopkins University Press, 1971.

Folsom, Marcia McClintock. "The Eight Major Scenes," "The Chronology of *Emma*." In *Approaches to Teaching Jane Austen's* Emma, edited by Marcia McClintock Folsom, xxx–xxxii, 10–12. New York: MLA, 2004.

Gilson, David. *A Bibliography of Jane Austen*. New introduction and corrections by the author. Winchester: St. Paul's Bibliographies; New Castle, Del.: Oak Knoll Press, 1997.

Harding, D. W. *Regulated Hatred and Other Essays on Jane Austen*. Edited by Monica Lawlor. London and Atlantic Highlands, N.J.: Athlone Press, 1998.

Hardy, Barbara. *A Reading of Jane Austen*. London: Peter Owen, 1975.

Honan, Park. *Jane Austen: Her Life*. London: Weidenfeld and Nicolson, 1987.

Johnson, Claudia L. *Jane Austen: Women, Politics, and the Novel*. Chicago and London: University of Chicago Press, 1988.

Kettle, Arnold. *An Introduction to the English Novel*. Vol. 1. London: Hutchinson's University Library, 1951.

Lane, Maggie. *Jane Austen and Food*. London and Rio Grande, Ohio: Hambledon Press, 1995.

Lascelles, Mary. *Jane Austen and New Art* Oxford, U.K.: Clarendon Press, 1939.

Leavis, Q. D. "A Critical Theory of Jane Austen's Writings (1)," *Scrutiny* 10 (1941–1942): 61–87.

Le Faye, Deirdre. *Jane Austen: The World of Her Novels*. New York: Harry N. Abrams, 2002.

Lewis, C. S. "A Note on Jane Austen," *Essays in Criticism* 4 (1954): 359–371.

Lodge, David, ed. *Jane Austen's Emma: A Casebook*. Nashville, Tenn., and London: Aurora, 1970.

McDonald, Richard. "'And Very Good Lists They Were'. Select Critical Readings of Jane Austen's *Emma*." In *A Companion to Jane Austen Studies*, edited by Laura Cooner Lambden and Robert Thomas Lambden. Westport, Conn.: Greenwood Press, 2000: [97]–114.

Marsh, Nicholas. *Jane Austen: The Novels*. New York: St. Martin's Press, 1998.

Mudrick, Marvin. *Jane Austen: Irony as Defense and Discovery*. Princeton, N.J.: Princeton University Press, 1952.

Olsen, Kirstin. *All Things Austen: An Encyclopedia of Austen's World*, 2 vols. Westport, Conn.: Greenwood Press, 2005.

Page, Norman. *The Language of Jane Austen*. Oxford, U.K.: Basil Blackwell, 1972.

Phillipps, K. C., *Jane Austen's English*. London: Andre Deutsch, 1970.

Pinion, F. B. *A Jane Austen Companion: A Critical Survey and Reference Book*. London: Macmillan, St. Martin's Press, 1973.

Poplawski, Paul. *A Jane Austen Encyclopaedia*. Westport, Conn: Greenwood Press, 1998.

Shannon, Edgar F., Jr. "*Emma*: character and construction," *PMLA* 71 (1956): 637–650.

Southam, B. C., ed. *Jane Austen: The Critical Heritage*. 2 vols. London: Routledge and Kegan Paul, 1979, 1987.

Stokes, Myra. *The Language of Jane Austen*. Basingstoke, Hants, U.K.: Macmillan, 1991.

Trilling, Lionel. "*Emma* and the Legend of Jane Austen," Introduction. *Emma*. Boston: Houghton-Riverside, 1956, v–xxvi.

Vorachek, Laura. "The Instrument of the Century:' The Piano as an Icon of Female Sexuality in the Nineteenth Century," *George Eliot. George Henry Leaves Studies* 34–35 (2000): 26–43.

Watt, Ian, ed. *Jane Austen A Collection of Critical Essays*. Englewood Cliffs, N.J.: Prentice Hall, 1963.

Wiesenfarth, Joseph. *The Errand of Form: An Assay of Jane Austen's Art*. New York: Fordham University Press, 1967.

———. "A Likely Story: The Coles' Dinner Party." In Marcia McClintock Folsom, *Approaches to Teaching Austen's Emma*. New York: MLA, 2004, 151–158.

Wilson, Edmund. "A Long Talk about Jane Austen." *New Yorker*, October 13, 1945.

Wiltshire, John. "Health, Comfort and Creativity: A Reading of Emma." In Marcia McClintock Folsom, *Approaches to Teaching Austen's Emma*. New York: MLA, 2004, 169–178,

———. *Jane Austen and the Body: "The picture of health."* Cambridge: Cambridge University Press, 1992.

Evelyn (1951)

COMPOSITION AND PUBLICATION

Its author transcribed this unfinished fantasy into the notebook known as *Volume the Third*, probably between May 6 and August 1792. The notebook was given to her father on May 6, 1792, and the work following, *Catharine*, is dated August 1792. The manuscript shows evidence of a changed date, to August 19, 1809. *Volume the Third* is dedicated to "Miss Mary Lloyd," a close friend. Jane Austen abandoned *Evelyn* after 20 pages, but she left the next nine pages blank before beginning *Catharine*. Sutherland notes that at some later stage these blanks were filled, and "Evelyn" was completed in seven pages in a hand which closely resembles that of the mature James Edward Austen-Leigh, brother of Anna Elizabeth LeFroy. Anna provided a "four-page continuation to 'Evelyn,'" which is "loosely inserted" into the notebook. These additions, "initialed 'JAEL' . . . since Anna did not marry Benjamin LeFroy until 1814 . . . were made at least twenty-two years after Austen began the story in 1792" (*Textual Lives*, 225).

The manuscript of *Volume the Third* passed into the Austen-Leigh family until 1963, when it was deposited on loan to the British Library, where it was examined by B. C. Southam, who in addition to recording "the date given at the front of the notebook, 6 May 1792," notes that "an inscription inside the front cover refers to the contents of this manuscript as 'Effusions of Fancy by a very Young Lady Consisting of Tales in a Style entirely new,' a description that fits this work . . . for 'Evelyn' is fanciful and original in every respect" (Southam, *Literary Manuscripts*, 36). The manuscript was then sold at Sotheby's London on December 14, 1976, and returned to the British Library, where it was catalogued early in 1991.

The text of "Evelyn" was first published in R. W. Chapman's 1951 Oxford edition of *Volume the Third* by Jane Austen. Anna LeFroy's continuation is also included at the conclusion of the volume. Three years later, "Evelyn" appeared in the sixth volume of R. W. Chapman's Oxford edition of *The Works of Jane Austen*, revised by B. C. Southam in 1969. It is also published in Margaret Anne Doody and Douglas Murray's 1993 edition of *Catharine and Other Writings* ([174]–185), and in a Juvenilia Press edition published in 1999, edited by Peter Sabor and others.

SYNOPSIS

Frederic Gower describes a Sussex village "called Evelyn, perhaps one of the most beautiful spots in the south of England" (180). The village is free of sickness, misery, or vice. Consequently, Frederic wishes to rent a house but finds that none is available. He is staying at an inn, and its landlady, Mrs. Willis, sends him to visit a Mr. and Mrs. Webb. At the Webbs' he receives a warm reception, is well fed, and given money, and they agree to give Frederic Gower possession of their house and its grounds. Before leaving, the Webbs agree to Frederic's marrying Maria, their eldest daughter, to whom they provide a substantial dowry.

Following some idyllic months, Frederic sees a fallen rose. This rose reminds him of Rosa, his sister, and consequently the reason why he came to Evelyn from his home at Carlisle, in the north of England. He traveled to seek out the family of Rosa's deceased lover, Henry, and to get a picture of him for Rosa. Henry's family prevented the marriage and parted them by sending Henry to the Isle of Wight, hoping that the "Absence in a foreign Country" would cure him of his love for Rosa. Henry, however, died during a storm at sea. Frederic, in one of several letters in the text, writes to Rosa apologizing for his delay in writing to her. His sister Maria replies to Frederic, telling him that "poor Rose . . . has been dead these six weeks. Your long absence and continual Silence gave us all a great uneasiness and hastened her to the Grave."

The letter results in "a fit of the gout," and Frederic rides to the castle of Henry's parents "wishing to find whether his Lordship [Henry's father] softened by his Son's death, might have been brought to consent to the match, had both he and Rosa been alive. Frederic harangues both parents over the death of Rosa and Henry, and following a lengthy emotional speech, leaves the Castle, "leaving the whole Company unanimous in their opinion of his being Mad."

It is night; terrified of "seeing either Gipsies or Ghosts, he rode at full gallop all the way" back to Evelyn, where he finds that his wife, so upset by his departure, died of a broken heart just three hours after he left on his journey to the Castle. Following arrangements for her funeral, he departs for "Carlisle, to give vent to his sorrow in the bosom of his family." Arriving home, to "his surprise on entering the Breakfast parlour [he sees] Rosa his beloved

Rosa seated on a Sofa." Further, he learns that she is married to a Mr. Davenport, who arrived in Carlisle two days previously and, following the news of the death of Henry, proposed to her.

Frederic Gower goes into Carlisle for a drink at an inn. He is served by Mrs. Willis from Evelyn, who is in Carlisle visiting her cousin. Frederic proposes to her on the spot: "The next morning they were married & immediately proceeded to Evelyn." He forgot to inform the Webbs that their daughter "Maria is no more" and writes to them to tell them. Back at Evelyn "Mr. & Mrs. Gower resided many years at Evelyn enjoying perfect happiness the just reward of their virtues." In the last sentence of the incomplete manuscript, Frederic's sister Rosa and her husband come to Evelyn and "settled there in Mrs. Willis's former abode & were for many years the proprietors of the White Horse Inn—" (185–191).

CRITICAL COMMENTARY

Various areas of interest in "Evelyn" have attracted critical attention. These include the use of dialogue, metonymic examples, and the illustration "of the plot of narcissism" (Spacks, 129). A. Walton Litz includes "Evelyn" among "the most interesting of" its author's juvenilia because of the "glimpse" into "the writing to come. The dialogue exposes individual personalities, not stock characters," and the narration in its close relationship to the consciousness of Frederic comes close to free indirect speech (Litz, 5). The use of metonymy is found in, for instance, Mr. Gower's rose, "a metonymy for the name of a sister he had utterly forgotten. For someone so abstracted and unchallenged, a metaphor simply will not do: it takes a very heavy pun to anchor Mr. Gower's disconnected mind" (Martin, 93). For Patricia Meyer Spacks, in "Evelyn" "narcissism meets only the slightest obstacles [and] Mr. Gower stands alone in his customary solipsism." His "self-regard has eliminated his capacity for rationality," and this is exhibited in his visit to the Castle and the bereaved parents lamenting the death of their son.

Spacks writes that "Probability, that shibboleth of eighteenth-century novel critics, has nothing to do with such a work as 'Evelyn'" (129–130).

Others have also commented on the uniqueness of "Evelyn" among Jane Austen's work, especially noting its atmosphere. On the one hand, "it is a delicious fantasy aimed at satirizing such features in romantic novels" ranging from "love at first sight, instant declarations, and almost instant marriages," plus oppressive parents preventing marriages, "fainting fits; romantic Gothic settings; incredible surprises; and absurd acts of generosity." On the other, "Evelyn" takes its readers "into a new and enchanting world" (Pinion, 63–64). Textual references are thoroughly annotated in Doody and Murray's "Explanatory Notes" (342–346).

CHARACTERS

Davenport, Mr. (190–191) He marries Rosa Gower two days after telling her of the death of her "beloved Henry." They settle in Evelyn as "proprietors of the White Horse Inn" (190–191).

Gower, Frederic (180–191) The self-obsessed, forgetful central figure of "Evelyn."

Gower, Maria (née Webb) (183, 189) The wife of Frederic Gower, daughter of the Webbs of Evelyn, who befriends Gower when he first comes to Evelyn. They provide their daughter with a large dowry. She dies of a broken heart about three hours "after his departure" for Henry's parents' castle.

Gower, Rosa (later Davenport) (184, 186, 189–191) The "beloved" (185) sister of Frederic Gower. The "thirteenth daughter" and "the darling of her relations—From the clearness of her skin & the Brilliancy of her Eyes," she has "one of the finest heads of hair in the world" (184). Her brother Frederic visits Evelyn to seek out the parents of her deceased lover, Henry; their marriage had been prevented by Henry's parents. Mistakenly taken to be dead, her brother finds her alive when he returns to the family home at Carlisle. She marries Davenport and moves to Evelyn with her husband to run the White Horse Inn.

Henry (185, 187–188) Henry is "a young Man whose high rank and expectations" (185) lead to objections from his family to his marriage to Rosa. He is sent to the Isle of Wight but dies in a shipwreck. Frederic Gower visits the Castle of his parents an unnamed Lord and Lady in Sussex to inform them of his death.

Lord and Lady (Henry's unnamed Parents) (187–189) Visited by Frederic Gower in their Castle, "situated on a woody Eminence commanding a beautiful prospect of the Sea." Frederic wants to know from the Lord, if Henry and Mr. Gower's sister Rosa were still alive, would he have approved the marriage. The Lord finds such a question meaningless: A "well-bred Man," his Lady "felt a deeper sorrow at the Loss of her Son." He replies, "This is a very odd question" and "No one can more sincerely regret the death of my Son than I have always done." The perceived insensitivity of such a reply leads to Gower's "anger" and departure (187–188).

Webb, Mr. and Mrs. (181, 189, 191) Exceedingly wealthy and generous residents of Evelyn who have two daughters. The elder marries Mr. Gower and dies. Following a letter from Gower, Mrs. Webb (Anne Augusta) sends Gower "a draught on our banker for 30 pounds, which Mr. Webb joins with me entreating you & the amiable Sarah [Willis] to accept" (191).

Willis, Mrs. Sarah (later Mrs. Gower) (180–181, 191) The "remarkably amiable" ([180]) Landlady of the Evelyn Alehouse, where Frederic first stays on his visit to Evelyn. She recommends Frederic to the Willises. Following the death of Frederic's wife, he re-meets Sarah serving in Carlisle, where she is visiting a cousin. They marry the following morning and return to Evelyn to live happily.

BIBLIOGRAPHY

Primary Texts

Austen, Jane. "Evelyn." In *Volume the Third, by Jane Austen*, edited by R. W. Chapman. Oxford, U.K.: Clarendon Press, 1951, 4–27.

———. "Evelyn." In *The Works of Jane Austen*, Vol. 6. *Minor Works*, edited by R. W. Chapman. Oxford: Oxford University Press, 1986. [All textual references are to this edition.]

———. "Evelyn." In *Jane Austen's* Catharine *and other Writings*, edited by Margaret Anne Doody and Douglas Murray. Oxford: Oxford University Press, 1993, [174]–185.

———. *Evelyn, by Jane Austen at 16*, edited by Peter Sabor and others. Edmonton, Alberta, Canada: Juvenilia Press [Department of English, University of Alberta], 1999.

Secondary Works

Litz, A. Walton. "Jane Austen: The Juvenilia." In *Jane Austen's Beginnings: The Juvenilia and* Lady Susan, edited by J. David Grey. Ann Arbor, Mich., and London: UMI Research Press: [1]–6.

Martin, Ellen E. "The Madness of Jane Austen: Metonymic Style and Literature's Resistance to Interpretation." In *Jane Austen's Beginnings: The Juvenilia and* Lady Susan, edited by J. David Grey. Ann Arbor, Mich., and London: UMI Research Press: [83]–94.

Pinion, F. B. *A Jane Austen Companion.* London: Macmillan, 1973.

Spacks, Patricia Meyer. "Plots and Possibilities: Jane Austen's Juvenilia." In *Jane Austen's Beginnings: The Juvenilia and* Lady Susan, edited by J. David Grey. Ann Arbor, Mich., and London: UMI Research Press: [123]–134.

Frederic & Elfrida, a Novel (1954)

COMPOSITION AND PUBLICATION

The first of Jane Austen's youthful tales found in her *Volume the First*, probably written early in the 1787–90 period. A dedication to her close friend Martha Lloyd was added following spring 1789, after they first became friends. *Frederic & Elfrida, a Novel* (FE) consists of five brief chapters and is included in the sixth volume of R. W. Chapman's edition of Jane Austen's *The Works*. FE is also found in Margaret Ann Doody and Douglas Murray's 1993 edition of *Catharine and Other Writings* ([3]–10). There is a Juvenilia Press edition, *Frederic & Elfrida by Jane Austen at 11 or 12*, edited by Peter Sabor, Sylvia Hunt, and Victoria Kortes-Papp, published in 2002. The manuscript is in the Bodleian Library, Oxford.

SYNOPSIS

The five brief chapters of *FE* BURLESQUE contemporary novels of the time read by the young Jane Austen. For example, there is an exaggeration of the archetype in which young lovers encounter parental objections. In this instance, the lovers are not young: Rebecca Fitzroy is 36 and Captain Rogers, her suitor, is much older at 63! Her mother objects "on account of the tender years of the young couple" (7). She gives her consent at dagger point. The marriage of the eponymous hero and heroine, Frederic and Elfrida, cousins, is delayed for two decades owing to Elfrida's sensitivity—she is unable to face up to the shock of naming a wedding date. A specific date is precipitated by the return of Rebecca and Roger to the comically named Crankhumdunberry ("of which sweet village her [Charlotte Drummond's] father was rector" [5]) with their 18-year-old beautiful daughter, Eleanor. Frederic begins to fall for Eleanor; Elfrida then presses him to marry her the following day. He refuses, but following a series of family fits "that she had scarcely patience enough to recover from once before she fell into another" (11), Frederic changes his mind and they are married.

Three families interact in *FE*: the Fitzroys, the Drummonds, and the Falknors. They know one another so well that they feel free enough "to kick one another out of the window on the slightest provocation" (6). Charlotte Drummond is so concerned with keeping everyone happy that during a visit to her aunt's London house, she agrees to marry not one but two different suitors during the same evening. The following morning, aware of what she has agreed to, she drowns herself. The stream takes her body to Crankhumdunberry, where she is buried by her friends to the accompaniment of a doggerel they have composed that is her epitaph. The first two lines of her epitaph read: "Here lies our friend who having promis-ed| That unto two she would be marri-ed," and there are two similar lines (9).

CRITICAL COMMENTARY

Critics draw attention to the very young Jane Austen's comic absurdity, her use of parody, and remarkable knowledge of contemporary fictional devices in *FE*. Other areas of interest include the author's use of one letter in the story and the depiction of complex family relationships and interactions. Susan Pepper Robbins writes that "the wisdom of Elfrida's parents gives structure and stability to the tale." The single letter contains Elfrida's commission to Charlotte to purchase a bonnet, which she does. "The narrator's closure—'so ended this little adventure, much to the satisfaction of all parties' [5]—confirms the 'effectiveness' of the letter." The letter's "function is to document request-compliance in a stable community" (Robbins, 217). Austen's parody of the manner in which young girls are expected to behave has been commented on by Claudia L. Johnson. She indicates (51) Charlotte's "willingness to oblige every one" (4), she is "too good-temper'd & obliging" (7), and is unable to refuse both offers of marriage. The consequences are serious indeed—suicide!

CHARACTERS

Drummond, Rev. (5) He is the father of Charlotte Drummond and the rector of the comically named Crankhumdunberry.

Drummond, Charlotte (4, 7–9) Too willing to please everybody, too accommodating, she places herself in an impossible situation by agreeing in a single evening to accept two different marriage proposals. The next morning she commits suicide. She has "a willingness to oblige every one" (4).

Falknor, Elfrida (4–7, 9, 11–12) Elfrida, the heroine, and her cousin Frederic "were exceedingly handsome and so much alike, that it was not every one who knew them apart" (4).

Falknor, Frederic (4–5, 7, 9, 11) Frederic, the hero "in any threatening Danger to his Life or Liberty . . . was as bold as brass yet in other respects his heart was as soft as cotton" (11).

Fitzroy, Mrs. (6) Mrs. Fitzroy, a neighbor of Frederic and Elfrida, has two daughters.

Fitzroy, Jezalinda (6) Mrs. Fitzroy's eldest daughter with an "engaging Exterior & beautifull outside." She "ran off with the Coachman" (6).

Fitzroy, Rebecca (6) Mrs. Fitzroy's younger daughter, aged 36 and highly praised as "Lovely & too charming" in spite of a "forbidding Squint . . . greazy tresses & . . . swelling Back." She apparently has "engaging Qualities of . . . mind" (6).

Roger, Captain (6–7, 9–11) The Captain marries Rebecca Fitzroy. He is from Buckinghamshire and a "little more than 63" (7). They have a "beautiful Daughter of eighteen" (11).

Roger, Eleanor (11) The daughter of Captain Roger and Rebecca. Frederic becomes attracted to her.

Williamson, Mrs. (8) She is Charlotte Drummond's aunt and lives in the fashionable and expensive part of London called Portland Place.

BIBLIOGRAPHY

Austen, Jane. "Frederic and Elfrida." In *The Jane Austen Library. Volume the First*, edited by R. W. Chapman, with a foreword by Lord David Cecil, a preface by Brian Southam, and a preface by R. W. Chapman. London: Athlone Press, 1984, 5–19.

———. "Frederic and Elfrida." In *The Works of Jane Austen*, Vol. 6, *Minor Works*, edited by R. W. Chapman. Oxford: Oxford University Press, 1986. [All textual references are to this edition].

———. "Frederic and Elfrida." In *Jane Austen's Catharine and other Writings*, edited by Margaret Anne Doody and Douglas Murray. Oxford: Oxford University Press, 1993, [3]–10.

———. *Frederic and Elfrida by Jane Austen at 11 or 12*, edited by Peter Sabor, Sylvia Hunt, and Victoria Kortes-Papp. Edmonton, Alberta, Canada: Juvenilia Press [Department of English, University of Alberta], 2002.

Johnson, Claudia L. "'The Kingdom at Sixes and Sevens': Politeness and the Juvenilia." In *Jane Austen's Beginnings: The Juvenilia and* Lady Susan, edited by J. David Grey. Ann Arbor, Mich., and London: UMI Research Press, 1989, [45]–58.

Robbins, Susan Pepper. "Jane Austen's Epistolary Fiction." In *Jane Austen's Beginnings: The Juvenilia and Lady Susan*, edited by J. David Grey. Ann Arbor, Mich., and London: UMI Research Press, 1989, [215]–224.

Henry & Eliza (1933)

COMPOSITION AND PUBLICATION

This piece of juvenilia was included in the author's "Volume the First." First published in Chapman's 1933 edition, it is the fourth story and "humbly dedicated to Miss Cooper by her obedient Humble Servant The Author" (33). Jane Cooper was a childhood friend who visited the Austens around the beginning of 1789. Southam in his *Jane Austen's Literary Manuscripts* places the composition of *Henry & Eliza* (HE) at the 1787–90 period (16). In addition to inclusion in the sixth volume of R. W. Chapman's edition of Jane Austen's *The Works, HE* may be found in Margaret Anne Doody and Douglas Murray's 1993 edition of *Catharine and Other Writings* (31–36). Karen L. Hartnick with others prepared an illustrated Juvenilia Press edition published in 1996.

SYNOPSIS

The short narrative written in the third person contains a "song" in four lined rhymed couplets and two brief letters. The apparently childless Sir George and Lady Harcourt discover "a beautifull little Girl not much more than 3 months old" in their "Haycock." Adopting the baby, calling it Eliza, she is brought up as the Harcourts' and receives a good education. Taught to be virtuous, admired by all, doted on by her parents, Eliza lives until the age of 18 a life of "uninterrupted Happiness." She is "one day to be detected in stealing a banknote of 50£" and is "turned out of doors by her inhuman Benefactors."

Eliza then turns to her best friend, the local inn proprietor, Mrs. Wilson, who introduces her to the "Dutchess of F." (33–34). She takes Eliza in as a companion and with her daughter Harriet treats her as a part of the family. Harriet is just about to marry Henry Cecil. He and Eliza are immediately

attracted and secretly married by the chaplain to the Duchess—being obsessed with Eliza, the Chaplain will do anything she wants. The young couple elope to France, where they are pursued by 300 armed men hired by the Duchess to bring them back dead or alive. They live in France for three years, Eliza gives birth to two sons, and Henry dies.

Destitute, Eliza returns to England, where she is imprisoned in a prison built by the Duchess especially for Eliza, "a snug little Newgate" (36). Eliza escapes and with her two little boys returns to the town where the Harcourts had brought her up. She approaches a carriage stopped outside an inn and asks for charity. Inside are the Harcourts. Lady Harcourt suddenly realizes that Eliza is her natural daughter born while her husband had been in America and hidden because she was a girl rather than a boy. She had forgotten this and Eliza's pleading voice reminds her. Sir George, her husband, buys his wife's tale and forgives Eliza for stealing his money. She and the young boys return to Harcourt Hall. Eliza "then raised an Army, with which she entirely demolished the Duchess's Newgate, snug as it was, and by that act, gained the Blessings of thousands, & the Applause of her own Heart" (39).

CRITICAL COMMENTARY

Elements arousing critical interest in *HE* include its use of the epistolary form, its family theme, humor, parody, use of metonymy, presentation of the parental theme, and social commentary. The parallels between the fictional Eliza and the life of Jane Austen's cousin have also been the subject of interest. ELIZA DE FEUILLIDE, née HANCOCK, frequently visited the Austens at Steventon during the 1780s. An eccentric personality, a product of the "dissipated life she was brought up to," she was like the fictional Eliza, widowed when young, married to a Henry, and left with young sons to bring up. The real Eliza's first husband "was guillotined in 1794 during the Reign of Terror." Eliza then "married Jane's 'favorite brother' Henry in 1797" (Hartnick, xv–xvi).

HE provides early instances of its author's use of letters in her work. In this case there are two letters, one from Sara Wilson, a letter of introduction to her friend "the Dutchess of F" asking her to "Receive into your Family, at my request a young woman of unexceptional Character" and a brief note from "Henry & Eliza Cecil" telling the Dutchess "We are married & gone" (34–36). Relationships and reaction to parents or those acting as parents are conveyed in such a cryptic communication. Ellen E. Martin notes that "Lady Harcourt voices a parental amnesia that may be as true as it is whimsical" (93). Lady Harcourt comments to her husband: "Satisfied within myself of the wellfare of my Child, I soon forgot I had one, insomuch that when, we shortly after found her in the very Haycock, I had placed her. I had no more idea of her being my own, then you had" (39). Martin comments, "Reality's only sure home seems to be in the metonymic Haycock," and that "History consists less in what happens than in what is told"—Lord Harcourt believes his wife's explanation—"fiction is the accessible metonymy of an unknowable history" (Martin, 94).

Unsurprisingly, the humor, wit, parody, and social criticism of *HE* have not gone unnoticed. For a commentator such as Hartnick, Lord and Lady Harcourt anticipate Sir Thomas Bertram in *Mansfield Park* "whose self-contradictions bring havoc to his family" (xvii). There are parallels between *HE* and Fanny Burney's *Evelina*, a "History of a Young Lady's Entrance into the World," in which the tale "of the traditional novel heroine" is inverted. Among other literary parallels are Charlotte Lennox's (1720–1804) *The Female Quixote* (1752), in which "French romances, credulous readers, and girls who sought to be heroines" dominate. The absurdity underlining *HE* is reinforced at its conclusion when its heroine discovers her true mother, and probably father. She triumphs over her enemy—but the story concludes "not with the heroine's marriage, but with Eliza raising an army and demolishing a prison. . . . Only in the juvenilia would Jane Austen allow her heroine a hero's reward" (Hartnick, xiii, xvii, xiii).

CHARACTERS

Cecil, Henry (35–36) Lady Harriet's "lover" who deserts her to marry Eliza Harcourt. The reader is told nothing more except that he elopes with Eliza to France, is the father of her two sons,

and dies leaving her destitute and that they had "lived to the utmost extent of their Income" (36).

F., Dutchess of (35–36, 39) A friend of Mrs. Wilson, "was about 45 & a half; Her passions were strong, her freindships firm & her Enmities, unconquerable. She was a widow & had only one Daughter" (35). She immediately gives Eliza a home, but upon Eliza's elopement becomes an implacable enemy, sending "300 armed Men" to get Eliza and Henry "dead or alive," and if alive to have them "put to Death in some torturelike manner, after a few years Confinement." She captures Eliza when she returns destitute to England. Eliza escapes from "a snug little Newgate of their Lady's, which she had erected for the reception of her own private Prisoners" (36). Eliza finally gains her revenge by demolishing "the Dutchess's Newgate . . . and by that act, gained the Blessings of thousands" (39).

Harcourt, Eliza (33–39) An apparent foundling, ungrateful heroine of the story, who steals and is ejected from her protector's home. She steals another's "Lover" (35) in her second adopted home, elopes abroad, has two sons, returns home destitute, escapes from prison, and discovers her real mother. "A mutual Reconciliation . . . took place," and she returns to where she grew up at Harcourt Hall to raise an Army to demolish her enemy's "Newgate" (39).

Harcourt, Sir George (33–34, 37–39) The gullible owner of Harcourt Hall, who adopts Eliza. After she has been caught stealing, he ejects her. He believes his wife's story that they had forgotten that "when you [Sir George] sailed for America, you left me breeding" (38), and that Eliza is their daughter; they are reconciled.

Harcourt, Lady Polly (33–34, 37–39) The natural mother of Eliza, whom she had found in a "Haycock" while they are "superintending the Labours of their Haymakers, rewarding the industry of some by smiles of approbation, & punishing the idlenss of others, by a cudgel" (33). She seems to have forgotten that she "was delivered of this girl, but dreading your [her husband's] just resentment at her not proving the Boy you wished, I took her to a Haycock & laid her down" and soon forgot she had a child (38–39).

Wilson, Mrs. Sarah (34–35) The landlady of the Red Lion, near Harcourt Hall, and Eliza's "most intimate freind," to whom she goes for help, Mrs. Wilson writes to her friend "the Dutchess of F" to look after Eliza (34).

BIBLIOGRAPHY

Primary Texts

Austen, Jane. "Henry and Eliza." In *The Works of Jane Austen*. Vol. 6, *Minor Works*, edited by R. W. Chapman. Oxford: Oxford University Press, 1986. [All textual references are to this edition.]

———. "Henry & Eliza." In *Jane Austen's* Catharine *and other Writings*, edited by Margaret Anne Doody and Douglas Murray. Oxford: Oxford University Press, 1993, 31–37.

———. "Henry & Eliza." Edited by Karen L. Hartnick et al. Edmonton, Alberta, Canada: Juvenilia Press [Department of English, University of Alberta], 1996.

Secondary Texts

Martin, Ellen E. "The Madness of Jane Austen: Metonymic Style and Literature's Resistance to Interpretation." In *Jane Austen's Beginnings: the Juvenilia and Lady Susan*, edited by J. David Grey. Ann Arbor, Mich., and London: UMI: Research Press, 1989, [83]–94.

Southam, Brian C. *Jane Austen's Literary Manuscripts. A Study of the Novelist's Development through the Surviving Papers*. London: Athlone Press, 2001.

The History of England from the reign of Henry the 4th to the death of Charles the 1st
(1922)

COMPOSITION AND PUBLICATION

The *History of England (HE)* follows *Lesley Castle* in the second of the three notebooks in Jane Austen's handwriting into which she copied her childhood compositions. Dedicated to her elder sister, CASSANDRA, who at 18 drew the illustrations accompanying the text completed on Saturday November 26, 1791, when its author was 15. Following Jane Austen's death, the manuscript went to Cassandra and subsequently remained in family hands. On July 6, 1977, it was sold at Sotheby's auction house in London and then purchased by the British Library.

HE was first published in 1922 in an edition containing a preface by G. K. Chesterton (1874–1936). Subsequently, it appeared in the sixth volume of R. W. Chapman's Oxford edition of *The Works of Jane Austen*, first published in 1954 and revised by B. C. Southam in 1969. Southam also edited Jane Austen's *Volume the Second*, published in 1963, which contains *HE*. More recent appearances include Margaret Anne Doody and Douglas Murray's 1993 edition of *Catharine and Other Writings* ([134]–144), and in the same year Deirdre Le Faye edited the text with an introduction by A. S. Byatt, published by Algonquin Books in Chapel Hill, North Carolina. Jan Fergus with students produced an illustrated, well-annotated edition in the Juvenilia Press series published in 1995 and reissued in 2003.

SYNOPSIS

In her dedication to her sister, Jane Austen describes herself as "a partial, prejudiced, & ignorant Historian." Her parody of popular national histories begins with Henry IV, who "ascended the throne of England much to his own satisfaction in the year 1399," (139), and devotes a paragraph each to his successors, including Mary, who is succeeded by Elizabeth I. She, in a way Jane Austen's heroine, received two lengthy paragraphs. The Stuarts such as "James the 1st" have three paragraphs followed by a brief comic "SHARADE" devoted to his "principal favourites" (148). Jane Austen's comic history concludes with "Charles the 1st" and somewhat appropriately, given her sympathy toward the Stuart dynasty and anti-Elizabeth I stance, with the words "he was a STUART" (149).

CRITICAL COMMENTARY

According to Jan Fergus, *HE* offers its readers "a view of Jane Austen and her sister as collaborators." Furthermore "it is like all the other juvenilia in being full of literary jokes and private family references, intended for the pleasure of her audience of family and friends" (Fergus, iii). There has been speculation concerning the collaboration between Jane and her sister. Margaret Anne Doody writing on Austen's juvenilia implies that it was "written in cahoots with Cassandra" (101), that Jane Austen's elder sister did more than provide the informative illustrative portraits of monarchs. Other critics draw attention to ironic allusions in *HE* to SHAKESPEARE's history plays and to, for instance, RICHARD BRINSLEY SHERIDAN's *The Critic* (1779). In the late 20th and early 21st century, the focus has turned to "The sisters' major revision to conventional Tory British history . . . in their pointed inclusion of women." Jane Austen includes in *HE* "twenty two citations of women [and] thirty-four men" (Fergus, iv, xi). Not all the women are portrayed sympathetically. She blames, for instance, the events during the reign of Mary more on "the Kingdom" itself rather than on the person—Mary. The narrator, not without a touch of irony, adds that it might have been "foreseen that as she died without children, she would be succeeded by that disgrace to humanity, that pest of society, Elizabeth." Jane Austen, possibly with her tongue in her cheek, minimizes the number of those killed during Mary's reign for their religious beliefs: "Many were the people who fell martyrs to the protestant Religion during her reign; I suppose not fewer than a dozen" (144–145).

Christopher Kent, in his "Learning History with, and from, Jane Austen," explicates thoroughly *HE*'s relationship to Jane Austen's subsequent work, such as Catharine Morland's perceptions in *Northanger Abbey*, and the textbooks available to Jane Austen on her readings of English history. He also pinpoints "the main feature of" *HE*, "its exuberant wit" (64). Kent draws attention to the contemporary debate between the historians David Hume (1711–76) and William Robertson (1721–93) and John Whitaker, (1735–1808) who in his *Mary Queen of Scots Vindicated*, published in three volumes in 1782, came to Mary's defense and incriminated Elizabeth. Kent also explains Jane Austen's parody of OLIVER GOLDSMITH's The

History of England, from the Earliest Times to the Death of George II, published in 1771. The young Jane Austen extensively annotated her copy (see Sabor: 316–351). Jane Austen's title, *The History of England from the reign of Henry the 4th to the death of Charles the 1st*, echoes Goldsmith's. Her sympathy for the Stuarts has its origins in her "extensive family associations," with the Stuarts significantly on the female side through "her mother's ancestors" (Kent, 64). The textual references are extensively annotated in Doody and Murray's edition (328–332).

BIBLIOGRAPHY

Primary Texts

Austen, Jane. "History of England." In *Love & Freindship and other early works, now printed from the original Ms. by Jane Austen, with a preface by G. K. Chesterton.* New York: Frederick A. Stokes, 1922, 105–121.

———. "History of England." In *The Works of Jane Austen.* Vol. 6, *Minor Works,* edited by R. W. Chapman. Oxford: Oxford University Press, 1986. [All textual references are to this edition.]

———. "History of England." In *Volume the Second, by Jane Austen,* edited by B. C. Southam. Oxford, U.K.: Clarendon Press, 1963, 128–149.

———. "History of England." In *Jane Austen's, Catharine and other Writings,* edited by Margaret Anne Doody and Douglas Murray. Oxford: Oxford University Press, 1993, [134]–144.

———. *The History of England.* Edited by Deirdre Le Faye, with an introduction by A. S. Byatt. Chapel Hill, N.C.: Algonquin Books, 1993.

———. *The History of England.* Edited by Jan Fergus and others. Edmonton, Alberta, Canada: Juvenilia Press [Department of English, University of Alberta], 1995, reissued 2003.

———. "The History of England," in *Jane Austen Juvenilia.* Edited by Peter Sabur. Cambridge: Cambridge University Press, 2006: 176–186.

Secondary Texts

Doody, Margaret Anne. "Jane Austen, that disconcerting 'child.'" In *The Child Writer from Austen to Woolf,* edited by Christine Alexander and Juliet McMaster. Cambridge: Cambridge University Press, 2005, [101]–121.

Kent, Christopher. "Learning History with, and from, Jane Austen." In *Jane Austen's Beginnings: The Juvenilia and* Lady Susan, edited by J. David Grey. Ann Arbor, Mich., and London: UMI Research Press, [59]–72.

Jack and Alice (1933)

COMPOSITION AND PUBLICATION

Jane Austen's manuscript notebook "Volume the First," today at the Bodleian Library, Oxford University, contains 14 stories. *Jack & Alice* (JA) is the second of these. It "is respectfully inscribed to Francis William Austin Esqr Midshipman on board his Majesty's Ship the Perseverance by his obedient humble Servant The Author" (12). FRANCIS WILLIAM AUSTEN, the author's elder brother, at the age of 12 went to the Royal Naval Academy at Portsmouth, and in December 1788, the month his sister turned 13, he sailed for the East Indies as a volunteer on board HMS *Perseverance*. He remained in the East Indies for four years. B. C. Southam, in his *Jane Austen's Literary Manuscripts*, dates JA to the period between its author's 13th and 16th birthdays (15–16).

JA consists of nine brief chapters and parodies of contemporary novels. It was first published in 1933 in an edition edited by R. W. Chapman of the material found in Jane Austen's *Volume the First*, and was based on the manuscript then still in Austen family hands. Chapman included it in the sixth volume of *The Works*, which focused on the *Minor Works* (1954). It was reprinted with revisions by B. C. Southam from 1969 onward. Juliet McMaster introduced a Juvenilia Press edition published in 1992 and reprinted two years later. A more extensive Juvenilia Press edition, edited by Joseph Wiesenfarth and others, appeared in 2001. JA is also to be found in Margaret Ann Doody and Douglas Murray's 1993 edition of *Catharine and Other Writings* (11–27).

SYNOPSIS

Each of the short chapters contains characters who are representative of dominating features of a vice or a virtue. For instance, the Johnson family, central figures in JA, are "addicted to the Bottle & the Dice," and the three Simpson girls are respectively ambitious, spiteful and envious, vain and affected, and so on. The opening chapter presents a masquerade party held to celebrate the 55th birthday of Mr. Johnson—everybody is carried home "Dead Drunk" (13–14). Chapters then focus on various topics. For instance, Alice Johnson is infatuated with Charles Adams, who seems to have no interest in her. Alice takes counsel with Lady Williams, who, pretending to be sympathetic, goads Alice into a rage. However, addicted to Lady Williams's claret, Alice continues to visit her. Exploring the grounds of Charles Adams's estate, they find an attractive girl, Lucy, a tailor's daughter, caught in a mantrap. They hear Lucy's story; she has also become obsessed with Charles Adams, who is a North Wales neighbor. She has broken her leg in the trap. Lady Williams mends the leg, and Lucy miraculously walks back to the house with them. Lady Williams has her reasons for not wanting Lucy and Alice to be too friendly, and she tells Lucy that Alice is an ill-tempered drunk. Three Simpson girls call the following day inviting Lucy to join them on a visit to Bath. This is encouraged as Lady Williams can get rid of another potential competitor for Charles Adams's affection.

In chapter 7, the presumed hero of JA, Jack Johnson, Alice's brother, makes a brief nonappearance. The reader is told "that he never did anything worth mentioning" (25) and drank himself to death. Alice, now heiress to the family fortunes, persuades her father to propose to Charles Adams on her behalf, and he does so. Adams expects "Perfection" and responds by outlining Alice's vices. Alice, on hearing of the rejection, "flew to her Bottle & it was soon forgot."

Meanwhile in Bath, Lucy quickly forgets Charles Adams and becomes engaged to a Duke, "an elderly Man of noble fortune whose ill health was the chief inducement of his Journey to Bath" (26). This arouses the intense jealousy of one of the Simpson girls—Sukey, who poisons Lucy. The Duke mourns Lucy for two weeks and then marries Sukey's sister Caroline, who becomes a Duchess. Sukey is "speedily raised to the Gallows." "In the mean time the inhabitants of Pammydiddle" (a portmanteau word consisting of "Pam," a card game with the pam, the jack of clubs, as the trump card, and "diddle," meaning or implying cheating)—where the Johnsons live—"were in a state of the greatest astonishment & Wonder, a report being circulated of the intended marriage of Charles Adams"—"to Lady Williams" (29).

CRITICAL COMMENTARY

In addition to the youthful author's verbal fecundity, critics have commented on the "craziness in Austen's tale that rivals the madness of a Monty Python skit" (Wiesenfarth, ix): its characterization, humor, literary parody, play on sentimentalism, the literary influences upon it, and the way it anticipates its author's subsequent work. In her introduction to *Catharine and Other Writings* (1993), Margaret Anne Doody isolates what she believes to be specific allusions in *JA* to the writings of Jane Austen's contemporaries and 18th-century literary predecessors, such as FANNY BURNEY, HENRY FIELDING, and Charlotte Smith, among others. Jocelyn Harris, in Appendix 2 "*Sir Charles Grandison* in the juvenilia," to her *Jane Austen's Art of Memory* (1989), gives specific examples of parallels between Richardson's novel and Jane Austen's early writing, especially the juvenilia. Illustrations from *JA* are found on pages 228–30 of Harris's study. For instance, in Richardson's novel, Sir Charles Grandison "proves irresistible to women: 'Five Ladies . . . declared that they would stand out by consent, and let you pick and choose a wife from among them'" (II, 43: cited Harris, 230). The "hero" of *JA* is "the lovely, the lively, but insensible Charles Adams," whose "person had subdued the hearts of so many of the young Ladies, that of the six present at the Masquerade, but five had returned uncaptivated" (15–14).

In his introduction to the Juvenilia Press edition, Wiesenfarth writes that in *JA*, "In the world of worldly nonsense, Jane Austen . . . had an attentive ear to the meaninglessness of words in polite society." He provides various examples. For instance, "The duke mourns Lucy's death with 'unshaken constancy' but he marries Caroline Simpson two weeks later." Also, "Lady Williams continually calls Alice 'dear' while describing her as drunk." He also draws attention to Lady Williams, regarding "it as *bigamy* to have her servant say she's not at home when she is" (x). Harris makes a similar observation when she cites from *JA* chapter 2 the narrator's direct reference to Richardson's novel. Lady Williams, "like the great Sir Charles Grandison scorned to deny herself when at Home, as she looked on that fashionable method of shutting out disagreeable Visitors, as little less than downright Bigamy" (15, Harris, 228). Regarding the characterization in *JA* and Austen's other juvenilia, Patricia Meyer Spacks notes that they are obsessive and move in "sequences . . . of violent, haphazard action, as if to say that no pattern of resolution can issue from people unable to acknowledge the importance of anyone besides themselves" (131).

Jane Austen's parody of literature, novels in particular, and advertising is seen when a "lovely young Woman lying apparently in great pain beneath a Citron-tree" says, "I am a native of North Wales & my Father is one of the most capital Taylors in it!" (20). Brian Southam in his preface to the 1984 reprint of *Volume the First* regards the tales within it as "little literary personal jokes" and "trifles indeed" [xi–xii]. But others, while not making too many claims for *JA* and the other early stories, have found in them much of interest. *JA* is "not witty beyond words; it's witty because of words—words that Jane Austen uses wondrously well" (Wiesenfarth, xv).

CHARACTERS

Adams, Charles (13 and throughout) Described as "an amiable, accomplished & bewitching young Man, of so dazzling a Beauty that none but Eagles could look him in the Face" (13). Irresistible to women of all ages, pursued by them he escapes to his country estate. He plays hard to get and, of course, is tracked down on his estate. Lucy, for instance, when he does not reply to her letters, "choose[s] to take, Silence for Consent" and is caught in a mantrap: "Oh! Cruel Charles to wound the hearts & legs of all the fair" (22). At the end he is caught by an older woman, Lady Williams.

Dickins, Miss (17) She "was an excellent Governess" and "instructed [Lady Williams] in the Paths of Virtue. . . . She eloped with the Butler" (17).

Johnson, Mr. (25–26) The father of the "hero" and "heroine." The story begins with the celebration of his 55th birthday, which turns out to be a drunken revel. He proposes to Charles Adams on his daughter Alice's behalf and is "a man of few words" (25).

Johnson, Alice (13, 25–26) The drunken "heroine" from "a family of Love, & though a little addicted to the Bottle & the Dice, had many good Qualities" (13). She, in common with other ladies, becomes infatuated with Charles Adams. In rejecting her father's proposal to Adams on her behalf, Mr. Johnson is told, "Your Daughter Sir, is neither sufficiently beautifull, sufficiently amiable, sufficiently witty, nor sufficiently rich." As a consequence, Alice "flew to her Bottle & it was soon forgot" (26).

Johnson, Jack (25) Alice's brother, the "hero" or "anti-hero" who is not mentioned until chapter 7, "oweing to his unfortunate propensity to Liquor, which so compleatly deprived him of those faculties Nature had endowed him with, that he never did anything worth mentioning." He dies and Alice becomes the heir to the family fortune (25).

Jones, Mr. and Mrs. (12–13) Guests at Mr. Johnson's birthday party, they "were both rather tall & very passionate, but were in other respects, goodtempered, well behaved People" (12–13).

Lucy (25, 27–28) Lucy has a "perfect form . . . beautifull face, & eloquent manners" (23) and is obsessed with Charles Adams. A tailor's daughter, she pursues him, is caught in his mantrap, her broken leg is repaired by Lady Williams, who, to get rid of a rival, encourages Lucy to accept an invitation to Bath. There she becomes engaged to a very wealthy old Duke, and is poisoned by a jealous rival, and "Thus fell the amiable & lovely Lucy whose Life had been marked by no crime" (28).

Simpson, (Miss) Caroline, Sukey, and Cecilia (13, 27–29) Neighbors of the Johnsons, the eldest "Miss Simpson was pleasing in her person, in her Manners & in her Disposition; an unbounded ambition was her only fault. Her second sister Sukey was Envious, Spitefull & Malicious. Her person was fat & disagreeable. Cecilia (the youngest) was perfectly handsome but too affected to be pleasing" (13). Sukey, jealous of Lucy, frequently "endeavoured to cut [her] throat" and poisons her to death; she is "speedily raised to the Gallows." Caroline, "beautifull but affected," marries the Duke (27, 29).

Susan, Mrs. (21) Charles Adams's cook.

Watkins, Mrs. (17) A distant relation of Lady Williams's father, "a Lady of Fashion, Family & fortune; she was in general esteemed a pretty Woman." Lady Williams, however, "never thought her very handsome" as "she had too high a forehead, Her eyes were too small & she had too much colour" (17).

Williams, Lady Kitty (13 and throughout) "In Lady Williams every virtue met. She was a widow with a handsome Jointure & the remains of a very handsome face. Tho' Benevolent & Candid, she was Generous & sincere; Tho' Pious & Good, she was Religious & amiable, & Tho' Elegant & Agreable, she was Polished & Entertaining" (13). The adviser to the infatuated Alice Johnson, she manipulates her and Lucy for her own ends, which basically consist of ensnaring Charles Adams. At the conclusion of *JA*, "he was publicly united to Lady Williams" (29).

BIBLIOGRAPHY

Primary Texts

Austen, Jane. "Jack & Alice." In *Jane Austen's* Catharine *and other Writings*, edited by Margaret Anne Doody and Douglas Murray. Oxford: Oxford University Press, 1993, 11–27.

———. "Jack & Alice." Edited by Juliet McMaster and the students of English 659 at the University of Alberta, Edmonton, Canada: Juvenilia Press [Department of English, University of Alberta], 1992.

———. "Jack & Alice." Edited by Joseph Wiesenfarth et al. Edmonton, Alberta, Canada: Juvenilia Press [Department of English, University of Alberta], 2001.

————. *Volume the First.* Edited by R. W. Chapman. Oxford: Clarendon Press, 1933. Reissued with a foreword by Lord David Cecil and a preface by Brian Southam. London: Athlone Press, 1984.

————. "Jack & Alice." In *The Works of Jane Austen.* Vol. 6, *Minor Works,* edited by R. W. Chapman. Oxford: Oxford University Press. 1986. [All textual references are to this edition.]

Secondary Texts

Harris, Jocelyn. *Jane Austen's Art of Memory.* Cambridge: Cambridge University Press, 1989.

Southam, Brian C. *Jane Austen's Literary Manuscripts. A Study of the Novelist's Development through the Surviving Papers.* London: Athlone Press, 2001.

Spacks, Patricia Meyer. "Plots and Possibilities: Jane Austen's Juvenilia." In *Jane Austen's Beginnings: the Juvenilia and Lady Susan,* edited by J. David Grey. Ann Arbor, Mich., and London: UMI Research Press, 1989, [123]–133.

Lady Susan (1871, 1925)

COMPOSITION AND PUBLICATION

What is today known as *Lady Susan* was unpublished and untitled when Jane Austen died. Cassandra, the author's sister, gave the manuscript to Jane Austen's favorite niece, Fanny Knight (Lady Knatchbull). In 1871, she allowed James Edward Austen-Leigh to publish a transcription as an appendix to the second edition of his *A Memoir of Jane Austen,* in which it was titled *Lady Susan,* after its main character. It consists of a novel of 41 letters with a narrative conclusion transcribed from a fair copy in the author's hand, in other words, one she copied from another version. Two of the leaves of the manuscript, now at the Pierpont Morgan Library in New York, where it has been since 1947, have an 1805 watermark. R. W. Chapman transcribed the work and printed it in 1925 under the title *Lady Susan, by Jane Austen: written about 1805, first published in 1871* and reprinted in the sixth volume, *Minor Works,* of his *The Works of Jane Austen.* Kathryn Sutherland, writing in her *Jane Austen's Textual Lives,* repeats that the manuscript "is a fair-copy, almost free from correction or erasures, and laid out with scrupulous attention to paragraphing and speech demarcation, quite unlike Austen's habit in her working manuscripts." She quibbles with Chapman's collapsing of speeches together, consequently "curbing the visual expression of the work's energetic virtuosity in favour of the composure of the reporting voice" (207).

The dating of the manuscript has been controversial. Chapman assigns it to the 1805 period, as the tale is "very unlike [that of] a novice" (*Facts and Problems,* 52). Brian Southam, in his study of *Jane Austen's Literary Manuscripts,* assigns the story an earlier dating of around 1795. He writes, "the style, structure, and characterization indicate early composition close to 'Catharine'" and to Jane Austen's Juvenilia. He also assigns an earlier dating for its "Conclusion" (46). Christine Alexander and David Owen in their edition of *Lady Susan,* one of the superb "Juvenilia Press Editions," begun at the University of Alberta in Edmonton and continued at the University of New South Wales, Sydney, "believe that the 'Conclusion' is likely to have been written at the time the fair copy was made." Further, "this may well have been even later than" 1805. This was the year of the death of Jane Austen's father "and the necessary reassessment of the family's economic situation; the subject of her brilliant *Lady Susan* is less likely to have interested Austen at this time." She returned to revise her earlier writings in 1809 and may simply have drawn upon 1805 watermarked paper then (xi). Austen-Leigh in his *Memoir* notes that according to family tradition, *Lady Susan* constitutes an "early production," and Alexander and Owen accord "a composition date of about 1794" (xii).

SYNOPSIS

The majority of the 41 letters are written by the 35-year-old Lady Susan, or by her sister-in-law Mrs. Vernon. At the opening, Lady Susan has been a widow for four months and has depleted her late husband's finances. She writes an account of a relationship with one man and a flirtation with another. The main interest is the conflict between Lady Susan and Mrs. Vernon, who attempts to save her younger brother Reginald from Lady Susan's tentacles and rescue Frederica, Lady Susan's daughter, from her dominance. The narrative expressed in the letters relates how, following her husband's death, Lady Susan focuses her attention on the married Mr. Manwaring of Langford. In a very brief period, she can twist him around her little finger. She has also turned the wealthy Sir James Martin against Miss Manwaring with the intention of getting him for her daughter Frederica. To compensate for her neglect of Frederica's education, Lady Susan places her in an expensive London establishment so that she can learn deportment and manners to prepare her for suitable male suitors.

Lady Susan then goes to stay with Charles, her brother-in-law, and his family at their home, Churchill, in Sussex. Her brother-in-law's wife, Catharine née De Courcy, is deeply suspicious of Lady Susan, especially as it emerges that six years previously, Lady Susan attempted to prevent her brother-in-law from marrying as she did not wish to lose control of a portion of the Vernon family fortune. Reginald De Courcy, her nearly 23-year-old brother, came to Churchill to meet Lady Susan and is captivated by her. She is attempting to gain his inheritance but prefers the more experienced but married Mr. Manwaring.

In London, Lady Susan's close trusted friend Alicia Johnson, to whom she writes 17 of the 41 letters of the novel, is given the task of encouraging the foolish Sir James Martin to pay court to Frederica. Her daughter, however, takes an instant dislike to the weak Sir James and runs away from school. Lady Susan, who had assumed that her daughter had inherited her husband's "Milkiness" is surprised to discover elements of herself in the "little Devil" (268). After being refused readmittance to the London school, Frederica is taken to Churchill. Sir James sheepishly follows her. Frederica has confidence in Reginald De Courcy and reveals her fears to him. Lady Susan manages to assuage his fears for Frederica and gets rid of Sir James.

Lady Susan has other plans for the much younger Reginald. From London she writes to Reginald, who has returned to his Kent home, that it would be unwise for them to marry quickly. At the conclusion of her letter, she says that she needs

amusing, is in low spirits, and that the Manwarings are also in London. Reginald takes the bait and comes to London. He wishes to call on Lady Susan at the same time as she is expecting a visit from Mr. Manwaring. She sends him instead to Mrs. Johnson's, who is visited at the same time by Mrs. Manwaring, who has come to tell her guardian, Mr. Johnson, the tale of Lady Susan's manipulative activities. Reginald learns enough to ensure that Lady Susan's attempts to regain his affections are not returned. Lady Susan renews attempts to marry her daughter to Sir James Martin, and Miss Manwaring has designs on him—and Frederica hopes to marry Reginald. At the conclusion of the letters, Mrs. Vernon tells Lady De Courcy that Reginald has parted from Lady Susan for good. The plan to match Reginald and Frederica has been forestalled by Lady Susan, who has taken Frederica away, much to her distress, and as a consequence, "the poor girl's heart was almost broke at taking leave of us" (310).

The narrative of the third-person Conclusion relates that Mr. and Mrs. Vernon eventually rescue Frederica from her mother. She returns to Churchill and lives with them. Three weeks later Lady Susan marries the much younger Sir James—she is 35, "ten years older" (251) than Sir James—for his money. Regarding Lady Susan's future: "The World must judge from Probability. She had nothing against her, but her Husband & her Conscience." As for Frederica, she becomes part of the Vernon family until "such time as Reginald de Courcy could be talked, flattered & finessed into an affection for her"—this should take a year (313).

CRITICAL COMMENTARY

Richard Holt Hutton reviewing J. E. Austen-Leigh's *Memoir* in 1871 considers *Lady Susan* as "interesting only as the failures of men and women of genius are interesting." Hutton finds Jane Austen's use of the epistolary form curious, but the "feline, velvet-pawed, cruel, false, licentious" Lady Susan clearly has aroused his interest. Writing in the centenary year of Jane Austen's death, Reginald Farrer regards *Lady Susan* as "important to the study of its author's career and temperament." Farrer judges the book to be "not good; it is crude and hard, with the usual hardness of youth," but "the cold unpleasantness of 'Lady Susan' is but the youthful exaggeration of that irreconcilable judgment which is the very backbone of Jane Austen's power." Farrer adds, "and which, harshly evident in the first book, is the essential strength of all later ones" (Southam, *Critical Heritage*, II: 171, 258).

Q. D. Leavis in her "A Critical Theory of Jane Austen's Writings," published in *Scrutiny* in the early 1940s, reads *Lady Susan* as a trial run for *Mansfield Park*. Brian Southam in the appendix "Theories of Composition for *Mansfield Park* and *Emma*" to his *Jane Austen's Literary Manuscripts* (2001) takes issue with Leavis and the contention that "*Lady Susan* is drawn from life," on the grounds of lack of evidence for compositional transformation (149 and following). R. W. Chapman in his *Jane Austen: Facts and Problems* (1948) anticipates subsequent critical commentary: The novel is "as brilliant as its central figure," while other "characters are not very well individualized. But the hard polish of the style creates a vivid illusion" (52).

Marvin Mudrick in his *Jane Austen: Irony as Defense and Discovery* (1952) regards *Lady Susan* as its author's "first completed masterpiece" and as "a quintessence of Jane Austen's most characteristic qualities and interests" (138). For Mudrick, the "primary irony" is concentrated not on Lady Susan but on Mrs. Vernon, her sister-in-law. Mudrick observes that Mrs. Vernon fails to realize "the reasons for her impotence, never understands . . . that Lady Susan succeeds because their world is negative and anti-personal." Furthermore, "the veneer of gentility over the materialist base reflects manners but not motives, sentiments," as opposed to "feeling, propriety but not character, because, in such a society, inevitably, the individual exists to use and be used, not to know and be known" (136–137).

Similar observations are made by A. Walton Litz. His *Jane Austen: A Study of Her Artistic Development* (1965) contains one of the most extended studies of *Lady Susan* to date. Litz's emphasis is on Lady Susan rather than Mrs. Vernon, although he believes that the former is remote from reality and too self-assured. Her "hypocrisy," as opposed

to what he refers to in a subsequent Jane Austen heroine as "duplicity" or "insincerity," reveals that the author "borrowed . . . the proper manners to clothe her creation . . . from the literature of earlier decades" (41). Litz writes that "the manners and motives [of *Lady Susan*] belong more to the world of Richardson or the early Fanny Burney than to the world Jane Austen knew in the 1790s" (41). For Litz, *Lady Susan* is "a dead end, an interesting but unsuccessful experiment in a dying form based upon outmoded manners" (45).

J. David Grey's *Jane Austen's Beginnings: The Juvenilia and Lady Susan* (1989) includes several articles on *Lady Susan*, revealing that it attracts eclectic perceptions. The British novelist and critic Margaret Drabble observes in her foreword to the volume that "the astonishing anti-heroine, Lady Susan . . . has now, predictably, been adopted by some feminist critics as an example of a 'free woman,' unhindered by the usual concepts of female and more particularly material duty." Drabble perceptively adds that Lady Susan "remains an isolated, an alarming creation, from another fictional universe" (xiv).

Terry Castle in her introduction to a 1990 Oxford University Press edition of *Northanger Abbey, Lady Susan, The Watsons and Sanditon* believes that Jane "Austen is captivated" by Lady Susan "almost in spite of herself." For Castle, "Lady Susan is a villain, prone to near melodramatic cruelties. But she is also a survivor, a woman who refuses to be a passive victim." She adds, "Austen half-identifies with her heroine's incorrigible will to power, her gaiety, her erotic rebelliousness, her triumphant contempt for all the 'romantic nonsense' that keeps other women subservient" (xxvii–xxviii).

Three main areas of interest emerge from a review of reactions to *Lady Susan*: its date of composition; the consideration of Jane Austen's use of the epistolary form; and the fascination of Lady Susan herself. The most succinct review of these issues, including an assessment of the probable literary sources drawn on by the author, and a detailed discussion of the manuscript, may be found in Christine Alexander and David Owen's introduction to the 2005 Juvenilia Press edition of the novel. They write: "In Lady Susan the young Austen explores the psychology of evil: the allure of a witty, intelligent, but corrupt and malicious personality." Alexander and Owen's introduction concludes with the judgment that "in *Lady Susan,* the nineteen-year-old" author controls "her natural exuberance" and moves "towards a clearer moral structure, a new psychological richness and a sophisticated use of the epistolary mode that should be applauded" (xv, xxiv).

CHARACTERS

Clarke family (268) In letter 16 written by Lady Susan to Mrs. Johnson, the Clarkes, who live near Vernon Castle in Staffordshire (Lady Susan's former home), appear to be Frederica Vernon's only friends. Lady Susan assumes that Frederica will attempt to stay with them after running away from school.

De Courcy, Catherine. *See* Vernon, Mrs. Catherine, née De Courcy.

De Courcy, Lady C (246–248) From letters three and four, it emerges that Lady De Courcy is the wife of Sir Reginald De Courcy and the mother of Reginald and Mrs. Catherine Vernon.

De Courcy, Reginald (247–248, 254, and throughout) Catherine Vernon's brother, about 23 years of age, is according to Lady Susan in a letter (seven) to Mrs. Johnson "a handsome young Man, who promises me some amusement." She adds that "There is something about him that interests me, a sort of sauciness, of familiarity which I shall teach him to correct." In addition, "He is lively & seems clever." Initially enamored of Lady Susan, who wishes to subdue his "insolent spirit" (254) and make him subservient to her, he begins to see through her. Reginald has doubts concerning Lady Susan's treatment of her daughter Frederica, and his eyes are opened when he discovers that she is all the while conducting an affair with Manwaring. Consequently, he is "detesting" women (313) and disillusioned with love. The "Conclusion" leads readers to believe that eventually he will marry Frederica.

De Courcy, Sir Reginald (256, 260) The father of Reginald and Mrs. Catherine Vernon, Sir Reginald owns the Parkland estate and "is very infirm." Consequently, he is "not likely to stand in" Lady Susan's "way long" in her designs on his son and his inheritance (256).

Hamiltons, the (298) Friends of Alicia Johnson who visited the Lake District.

James (283) Reginald de Courcy's male servant.

Johnson, Alicia (244 and throughout) Married and living in London, she is the closest friend and confidante of Lady Susan. Seventeen of the 41 letters of the novel are addressed to her, and Lady Susan uses her as a cover for her correspondence with Manwaring. Lady Susan expresses at times her real feelings and motives to Alicia, whom she trusts. Alicia tries to retain Sir James Martin's interest in Lady Susan's daughter Frederica while she is at school in London.

Johnson, Mr. (245, 249, 298) Husband of Alicia, who is told by Lady Susan, "what a mistake were you guilty in marrying Man of his age!—just old enough to be formal, ungovernable & to have the Gout—too old to be agreable & too young to die" (298). Guardian of Mrs. Manwaring, and disliking Lady Susan, he refuses to invite her to his home and subsequently forbids his wife from corresponding with Lady Susan. He reveals that Lady Susan has been having an affair with Manwaring to Reginald de Courcy and provides him with the proof concerning her other outrageous activities.

Manwaring, Maria (245, 248) The sister of Mr. Manwaring. Her desire to marry Sir James Martin is thwarted by Lady Susan's intervention, initially on Frederica's behalf, and subsequently on her own behalf—Lady Susan marries him.

Manwaring, Mr. (243–245, 250, 256–258, 269, 295–296, 298–299, 302–303, 307–308) Married, he is obsessed with Lady Susan and starts their intimate relationship during her stay at his Langford family home. His wife's jealousy leads to

Lady Susan's departure to stay with the Vernons at Churchill. Manwaring, "so uncommonly pleasing," according to Lady Susan, moves to London to continue their affair. As a result, he and his wife eventually separate. Lady Susan tells Mrs. Johnson, "I have admitted no one's attentions but Manwaring's," (244) and seems to have a real affection for him.

Manwaring, Mrs. (245, 257, 296, 301, 307) Mrs. Johnson observes to Lady Susan: "Poor Manwaring gives me such histories of his wife's jealousy!—Silly Woman, to expect constancy from so charming a Man! But she was always silly; intolerably so, in marrying him at all." Alicia adds, "She, the Heiress of a large Fortune, he without a shilling! *One* title I know she might have had, besides Baronets. Her folly in forming the connection was so great" (296). She follows her husband to London in a failed attempt to curtail his relationship with Lady Susan. Following their separation, she goes to the house of Mr. Johnson, her former guardian. Her distress contrasts with Lady Susan's frivolity and refusal to see the consequences of her actions.

Martin, Sir James (245, 275–276) A young, exceedingly wealthy, but in Lady Susan's words "contemptibly weak" (245) man who is putty in the experienced, manipulative Lady Susan's hands. To divert his attentions from Maria Manwaring to her daughter Frederica, at Langford she flirts with him then gets Sir James to pay Frederica attention. After having refused to marry him, she yet again removes him from Maria and marries him for his money.

Smith, Charles (248, 264) A friend of Reginald De Courcy, whom he attempts to warn about Lady Susan's unacceptable behavior at Langford. Reginald, under Lady Susan's influence, tells his father, "I blame myself severely for having so easily beleived [*sic*] the scandalous tales invented by Charles Smith to the prejudice of Lady Susan" (264).

Summers, Miss (246) Lady Susan takes her daughter Frederica "to Town, where I shall deposit

her under the care of Miss Summers in Wigmore Street" (246).

Vernon, Charles (243, 246–247) The "amiable & mild" (247) younger brother of Lady Susan's deceased husband. Mild-mannered and kind, he is easy for Lady Susan to manipulate. He lives at Churchill in Sussex, although Lady Susan and her husband hoped to retain the family seat, Vernon Castle, by keeping Charles a bachelor, living with them and supporting them. His marriage means that they are forced, owing to Lady Susan's depletion of her husband's fortune, to sell the castle. Charles attempted to promote the marriage of his wife's brother Reginald to Frederica.

Vernon children (243, 250) There appear to be several of these, although only two, Catherine and Frederica, are specifically named. Lady Susan is friendly with them as a way of ingratiating herself into the family circle.

Vernon, Frederic (deceased (244, 249, 252) Charles Vernon's elder brother and Lady Susan's dead husband, "to whom her own behaviour was far from unexceptionable" (252). She depleted his fortune, forced him, owing to debts, to sell his ancestral home, Vernon Castle, in Staffordshire, and probably sent him to an early grave.

Vernon, Frederica Susanne (244, 250, 252–254, 269–270, 279, and throughout) The 16-year-old daughter of Lady Susan, described by her mother as "a stupid girl, & has nothing to recommend her" (252). Found "tiresome" (254) by her mother, who prefers affairs and other entertainments, she is sent to a finishing school in London to obtain "Grace & Manner" (253) and to become suitable for marriage and the social round. Frederica, however, has more of the "Milkiness" (268), and softness of her father's family rather than her mother's manipulativeness. She dislikes her mother's choice for her, Sir James Martin, and runs away from school. She is rescued by Charles Vernon, her uncle, and his wife takes a great liking to her, as does her brother Reginald De Courcy. Eventually Reginald sees through Lady Susan's subterfuge, and the Conclusion to the novel suggests that eventually he and Frederica will marry. Frederica is central to one of the important moral themes of *Lady Susan*: rescuing a daughter from a malevolent mother whose sole aim is to exploit her for her own nefarious purposes.

Vernon, Lady Susan (243 and throughout) The central voice of the novel, the heroine, or its anti-heroine. The wife of the late Frederic Vernon and mother of Frederica. She has at least three lovers during the narrative as related in the letters: the younger Reginald De Courcy; Sir James Martin, whom she eventually marries for his money; and more continuously, the mature, married Manwaring. A central problem in interpreting *Lady Susan* is how to perceive the presentation of Lady Susan. Is she an exploration of "the psychology of evil: the allure of a witty, intelligent, but corrupt and malicious personality" (Alexander and Owen, xv)? Or are there redeeming features? Her adversary, Mrs. Vernon, grants that "this dangerous creature . . . possesses an uncommon union of Symmetry, Brilliancy and Grace." In the same letter (six), Mrs. Vernon confides to Reginald De Courcy that the 35-year-old Lady Susan "is really excessively pretty. However you may chuse to question the allurements of a Lady no longer young, I must for my own part declare that I have seldom seen so lovely a Woman as Lady Susan." She describes her as "delicately fair, with fine grey eyes & dark eyelashes; & from her appearance one would not suppose her more than five & twenty, tho' she must in fact be ten years older." These endearments are the words of Lady Susan's fiercest enemy.

Her only confidante is Miss Alicia Johnson, and her letters to her reveal that Lady Susan can "make Black appear White." She has a "happy command of Language" (250–251). Aware of her abilities, Lady Susan confesses to Alicia (letter 16), "If I am vain of anything, it is my eloquence. Consideration & Esteem as surely follow command of Language, as Admiration waits on Beauty. And here [at Churchill, the home of Charles Vernon and his family] I have opportunity enough for the exercise of my Talent, as the cheif [*sic*] of my time is spent in Conversation" (268).

Manipulating her own daughter, relatives, late husband, and lovers, she is "tired of submitting my will to the Caprices of others—of resigning my own Judgement in deference to those, to whom I owe no Duty, & for whom I feel no respect" (308). In this same letter (39), her last, she tells Alicia that she has no regrets. "I never was more at ease, or better satisfied with myself & everything about me, than at the present hour" (307). In the Conclusion, the narrator somewhat equivocally observes that "She had nothing against her, but her husband, & her Conscience" (313).

Some critical voices regard Lady Susan's cruelty toward her daughter Frederica as taking "Lady Susan's crimes to a higher level." She bullies Frederica, and acts from the assumption that all males are akin to her in regarding "the relationship between the sexes as a sport, a contest to be won, and if her daughter will not play to win she must be forced to do so." In spite of Frederica's act of defiance, her refusal to marry Sir James, whom her own mother marries purely for mercenary reasons, "the focus remains on her cruel and calculating mother!" Mrs. Vernon, on the other hand, is a contrast morally and in maternal attitudes, and her 11 letters to her mother, Lady De Courcy, commenting on Lady Susan's conduct provide a counterpoint to Lady Susan's self-revelatory letters to Alice Johnson. Lady Susan's letters to young Reginald "reveal her hypocrisy in action so" that readers "gain the most complete psychological portrait Jane Austen had yet drawn" (Alexander and Owen, xvii–xviii).

Vernon, Mrs. Catherine, née De Courcy (243, 246, 274, and throughout) The wife of Charles Vernon, and the antithesis and antagonist of Lady Susan, who writes that she "dearly loves to be first, & to have all the sense & all the wit of the Conversation to herself" (274). Catherine Vernon's 11 letters to her mother, Lady De Courcy, show that she is one of the few who have no illusions about Lady Susan's character and motives. She describes Lady Susan as "Mistress of Deceit" (284). Highly sympathetic and protective toward Frederica, for whom she provides a home, she has children of her own. Her opposition to Lady Susan comes from experience, as six years prior to the main narrative related in letters, Lady Susan had tried unsuccessfully to prevent Catherine from marrying Charles Vernon. Lady Susan's motives are to retain control of some of the Vernon family assets. Mrs. Vernon attempts to prevent her brother Reginald from being seduced by Lady Susan and manipulated by her. Catherine "acts in some ways as the resisting and questioning voice of the reader—the resisting moral voice of the text—in the face of Lady Susan's sometimes bewitching appeal" (Poplawski, 303).

Wilson (284)   A servant at Churchill, the Vernon home, who according to Mrs. Vernon tells Lady Susan "that we are going to lose Mr. de Courcy" (284).

BIBLIOGRAPHY

Primary Texts

Austen, Jane. *Lady Susan.* Edited by R. W. Chapman. Oxford, U.K.: Clarendon Press, 1925.

———. *Lady Susan.* In *The Works of Jane Austen.* Vol. 6, *Minor Works,* edited by R. W. Chapman. Oxford: Oxford University Press, 1986. [All textual references are to this edition.]

———. *Lady Susan,* edited by Christine Alexander and David Owen, with illustrations by Juliet Macmaster. Sydney: Juvenilia Press (University of New South Wales), 2005.

———. *Northanger Abbey, Lady Susan, The Watson, and Sanditon.* Oxford World's Classics. Edited by James Kinsley and John Davie, with an introduction and notes by Claudia L. Johnson. Oxford: Oxford University Press, 2003.

Austen-Leigh, J. E. *A Memoir of Jane Austen and Other Family Recollections.* Edited and with an introduction and notes by Kathryn Sutherland. Oxford: Oxford University Press, 2002.

Secondary Works

Castle, Terry. Introduction to *Jane Austen. Northanger Abbey, Lady Susan, The Watsons, and Sanditon,* edited by John Davie, vii–xxxii. Oxford: Oxford University Press, 1990.

Chapman, Robert W. *Jane Austen: Facts and Problems.* Oxford, U.K.: Clarendon Press, 1948.

Drabble, Margaret. Foreword to *Jane Austen's Beginnings: The Juvenilia and Lady Susan,* edited by J.

David Grey, [xii]–xiv. Ann Arbor, Mich., and London: UMI Research Press, 1989.

Farrer, Reginald. "Jane Austen *ob.* July 18, 1817," *Quarterly Review* 228 (July 1917): 1–30.

Hutton, Richard Holt. "Miss Austen's Posthumous Pieces." *Spectator,* July 22, 1871, 891–892.

Leavis, Q. D., "A Critical Theory of Jane Austen's Writings," *Scrutiny* 10 and 12 (1941–1945). In her *Collected Essays,* I, *The Englishness of the English Novel,* edited by G. Singh. Cambridge: Cambridge University Press, 1983.

Litz, A. Walton. *Jane Austen: A Study of Her Artistic Development.* New York: Oxford University Press, 1965.

Gilson, David J., and J. David Grey. "Jane Austen's Juvenilia and *Lady Susan: An Annotated Bibliography.*" In *Jane Austen's Beginnings: The Juvenilia and* Lady Susan, edited by J. David Grey, 243–260. Ann Arbor, Mich., and London: UMI Research Press, 1989.

Mudrick, Marvin. *Jane Austen: Irony as Defense and Discovery.* Princeton, N.J.: Princeton University Press, 1952.

Poplawski, Paul. *A Jane Austen Encyclopedia.* Westport, Conn.: Greenwood Press, 1998.

Southam, Brian C. *Jane Austen; The Critical Heritage,* 2 vols. London: Routledge and Kegan Paul, 1979, 1987.

———. *Jane Austen's Literary Manuscripts,* revised edition. London: Athlone Press, 2001.

Sutherland, Kathryn. *Jane Austen's Textual Lives: From Aeschylus to Bollywood.* Oxford: Oxford University Press, 2005.

Lesley Castle an unfinished Novel in Letters (1922)

COMPOSITION AND PUBLICATION

Lesley Castle an Unfinished Novel in Letters (LC) follows *Love and Freindship* in the second of the three notebooks in Jane Austen's handwriting into which she copied her childhood compositions. The first of the 10 letters constituting *LC* is dated January 3, 1792, and the last, April 3, 1792, when Jane

Austen was 17. Following the author's death, the manuscript went to her sister, CASSANDRA, and remained in family hands. On July 6, 1977, it was sold at Sotheby's auction house in London, then purchased by the British Library.

LC is dedicated to Jane Austen's fourth brother, HENRY THOMAS AUSTEN. The 10 letters constituting *LC* were first published in 1922 in an edition containing a preface by G. K. Chesterton. Subsequently, *LC* appeared in the sixth volume of R. W. Chapman's Oxford edition of *The Works of Jane Austen*, first published in 1956 and revised by B. C. Southam in 1969. Southam also edited Jane Austen's *Volume the Second*, published in 1963, which contains *LC*. The work also appears in Margaret Anne Doody and Douglas Murray's 1993 edition of *Catharine and Other Works* (107–133). Jan Fergus with students produced a most informative illustrated edition in the Juvenilia Press series published in 1998. Fergus assigns the dating of *LC* to around 1790, when its author was just 15 years old.

SYNOPSIS

The 10 letters loosely focus on the second marriage of Sir George Lesley to Susan Fitzgerald (Lady Lesley) and its consequences on his two grown-up daughters, Margaret and Matilda. The chief correspondent is Charlotte Lutterell, who knows both Margaret Lesley and Susan Lady Lesley. In the letters, differing perspectives are presented. Sir George spends a good deal of time being entertained in London, while his two daughters live a happy but inactive life at Lesley Castle near Perth, Scotland. Sir George returns to Lesley Castle to introduce his new wife to his daughters. The new Lady Lesley finds the castle remote and socially isolated. Inevitably, there are conflicts between her and her stepdaughters, so all of them move to London, where the incomplete "novel" finishes.

The eighth letter is written by Eloisa Lutterell to Mrs. Marlowe and the ninth by Mrs. Marlowe to Eloisa. They relate the story of the broken-hearted Eloisa Lutterell, Charlotte's sister. In addition to a different letter and writer, the mood has transformed from the parodic mode and tone of the other letters to the very serious.

CRITICAL COMMENTARY

LC has created a reasonable amount of critical observation. The stylistic differences between letters eight and nine and the other letters have not gone unnoticed. For instance, B. C. Southam in his *Jane Austen's Literary Manuscripts* draws attention to parallels between SAMUEL RICHARDSON's *Familiar Letters* (1741), "designed to guide correspondents in meeting the difficulties of public and private life" (Southam, 33–34), and Eloisa's eighth letter. Eloisa writes that she hopes that Mrs. Marlowe will not consider her as too "girlishly romantic" in looking for a "kind and compassionate Freind who might listen to my sorrows without endeavouring to console me" (132). For Southam, "the diction and thought of the letter verge upon sentimentalism, but the sentence movement is dignified." Further, Eloisa's self-examination is genuine "and her emotion bears no hint of exaggeration, indulgence or literary falsification." Mrs. Marlowe's reply, the ninth letter, except for the closing paragraph and postscript, and the ending of the second paragraph, in which the writer exposes different kinds of "pretence and insincerity illustrated throughout the" other letters, is entirely appropriate in tone (Southam, 34).

Critics have noted "the contrast between the rhetorical manner of popular fiction and the artificiality of society slang and gush" (Southam, "Juvenilia": 252) in, for instance, the opening sentence of Charlotte Lutterell's reply to Margaret Lesley—the second letter in the sequence. *LC* is regarded as its author's first "ambitious attempt at the novel in epistolary form. It presents a number of interestingly contrasted characters, but [they] . . . suffer in varying degrees of eccentricity from the comical to the melancholy" and "present continually shifting impressions of the characters we wish to know . . . The technique of presenting characters through the eyes of others is one that Jane Austen was to use most effectively" (Pinion, 61). *LC* is a prefiguring text especially regarding subsequent characters, for instance, Sir George Lesley, vain and aging, as a trial run for Sir Walter Elliot in *Persuasion*.

The incomplete nature of *LC* may be viewed as a deliberate tactic on the part of the young Jane Austen. She writes in her dedication to her brother "That it is unfinished, I greive; yet fear that from me, it will always remain so" (109). In other words, she "does not want to turn her fictions into moral tales by visiting closure and poetic justice on her energetic transgressors" (McMaster, 182). In addition to its incomplete nature and use of the epistolary form, critics have drawn attention to its author's use of food as a reflection of character and excess that permeates *LC*. Charlotte Lutterell is an "insanely fixated cook" whose reaction to the fatal horse-riding accident of her sister's fiancé consists of "a series of energetic suggestions as to how they must now eat the food prepared for the wedding" (Doody, "Jane Austen, that disconcerting 'child'": 115). The food consists of an excessive feast. *LC* delights in self-indulgence and at times celebrates the immoral. In the final letter the reader is told of the resumed friendship between a deserted young husband, Lesley, and his former wife. She has deserted him for two other men, "the worthless Louisa . . . has turned Roman-catholic, and is soon to be married to a Neapolitan Nobleman of great and Distinguished merit." Lesley "says, that they are at present very good Freinds, have quite forgiven all past errors and intend in future to be very good Neighbours" (138).

CHARACTERS

Burton, Louisa (Lesley) (111, 119, 137–138) Described as "worthless" (112, 138), she marries Mr. Lesley, has a daughter, Lesley, grows tired of her husband, and elopes. She converts to Catholicism to marry a "Neapolitan Nobleman," and according to her former husband, he and she "are at present very good Freinds" (138).

Cleveland, Mr. (121–122) "A brother of Mrs. Marlowe . . . a good-looking young Man, and seems to have a good deal to say for himself" (121–122).

Danvers (111) Louisa Lesley leaves her husband, "her Child and reputation . . . in company with Danvers and dishonour" (111).

Dishonour, Rakehelly, Esqre. (111) Another name for Danvers, or for Danvers's companion.

Drummond, Colonel and Mrs. (117) They live in Cumberland and the Colonel is the cousin of the Lesleys.

Fitzgerald, William (123–125 and elsewhere) The brother of Lady Susan Lesley, described as "certainly one of the most pleasing young Men [Margaret Lesley] ever beheld" (123).

Flambeaus, Lady (137) The Lesleys dine with "Lady Flambeaus who is . . . intimate with the Marlowes" (137).

Gower, Sir James (137) Sir James Gower is just one of Margaret Lesley's "too numerous Admirers." He "is one of the most frequent of our Visitors, and is almost always of our Parties" (137).

Hervey, Diana (Mrs.) (129) The aunt of Henry Hervey; she settles near the Lutterells in Sussex about a year before the events recorded in *LC* take place.

Hervey, Henry (113–114, 129) He is Eloisa Lutterell's fiancé and dies of a fall from his horse, creating much inconvenience for Charlotte Lutterell, who has prepared a wedding feast.

Kickabout, the Honourable Mrs. (136) A lady who holds a "Rout," or wild party attended by Margaret and Matilda Lesley "escorted by Mr. Fitzgerald" and "accompanied [by] Lady Lesley" (136).

Lesley, Mr. (111, 119, 137–138) The 25-year-old brother of Margaret and Matilda, he has "given himself up to melancholy and Despair" following the desertion of his wife, "the Worthless Louisa" (111). Louisa and he "are at present very good Freinds" (138).

Lesley, Sir George (111 and following) Father of Margaret, Matilda, and the 25-year-old Mr. Lesley. He is described as "fluttering about the streets of London, gay [happy], dissipated and Thoughtless at the age of 57" (111). His second wife is much younger than he, and his bringing her to Lesley Castle to visit his ancestral home and daughters propels the plot.

Lesley, Margaret (110 and throughout) The not so young, youngest daughter of Sir George and one of the chief correspondents in *LC*. She and her sister Matilda are called by their new stepmother "two great, tall, out of the way, over-grown girls, just of a proper size to inhabit a Castle almost as Large in comparison as themselves" (124).

Lesley, Matilda (110 and throughout) The no longer young elder daughter of Sir George. When she and Margaret are invited by Lesley to visit him in Naples, they will be escorted on their journey by their admirer William Fitzgerald. "Matilda had some doubts of the Propriety of such a scheme— she owns it would be very agreeable." Margaret adds, "I am certain she likes the Fellow"—William Fitzgerald (138).

Lesley, Lady Susan (née Fitzgerald) (115 and following) She is the friend of Charlotte Lutterell and writer of six letters in addition to a postscript to the second letter, in which she announces that she married Sir George. The marriage, and Lady Susan's subsequent visit and reactions to Lesley Castle and its inhabitants, form the plot foundation. Much younger than her husband. Charlotte Lutterell claims to provide "an exact description of her [Lady Susan's] bodily and mental charms. She is short, and extremely well-made; is naturally pale, but rouges a good deal; has fine eyes, and fine teeth, as she will take care to let you know as soon as she sees you, and is altogether very pretty." Charlotte adds that Susan is "remarkably good-tempered when she has her own way;" she is "extravagant and not very affected" (120).

Lutterell, Charlotte (110 and throughout) One of the main correspondents, source of information, friend of Margaret Lesley and Lady Susan Lesley, she acts as a linking device throughout *LC*, tying the characters and actions into some kind of pattern. Obsessed with food and its preparation, which she prefers to her own "matrimonial Projects," she informs Margaret Lesley "I never wish to act a more principal part at a Wedding than superintending and directing the Dinner" (122).

Lutterell, Eloisa (113 and following) Charlotte's sister, her fiancé is killed just before their marriage by falling from his horse. The wedding meal cancellation provokes a frenzy of activity in her sister Charlotte. Eloisa's sorrows become the subject of a transformation of tone in the eighth and ninth letter of *LC* from the parodic and comic to the sad and melancholy.

M'Leods, M'Kenzies, M'Phersons, M'Cartneys, M'Donalds, M'Kinnons, M'Lellans, M'Kays, Macbeths, and Macduffs (111) Perthshire neighbors of the Lesleys, whom they visit.

Marlowe, Mr. and Mrs. (121) During Charlotte and Eloisa's stay in Bristol, they encounter "but one genteel family since we came. Mr. & Mrs. Marlowe are very agreable people; the ill health of their little boy occasioned their arrival here." Mrs. Marlowe has a brother, a Mr. Cleveland, who is "with them" (121).

William (114) One of the Lutterells' servants.

BIBLIOGRAPHY

Primary Texts

Austen, Jane. "Lesley Castle." In *Love & Freindship and other early works, now printed from the original Ms. by Jane Austen, with a preface by G. K. Chesterton*. New York: Frederic A. Stokes, 1922, 57–100.

———. "Lesley Castle." In *The Works of Jane Austen*. Vol. 6, *Minor Works*, edited by R. W. Chapman. Oxford: Oxford University Press, 1986. [All textual references are to this edition.]

———. "Lesley Castle." In *Volume the Second, by Jane Austen*, edited by B. C. Southam. Oxford, U.K.: Clarendon Press, 1963, 68–125.

———. "Lesley Castle." In *Jane Austen's Catharine and other Writings*, edited by Margaret Anne Doody and Douglas Murray, 107–133. Oxford: Oxford University Press, 1993.

———. *Lesley Castle, by Jane Austen at c. 15*. Edited by Juliet McMaster and others. Edmonton, Alberta, Canada: Juvenilia Press (Department of English, University of Alberta), 1998, reissued 2005.

Secondary Texts

Doody, Margaret Anne. "Jane Austen, that disconcerting 'child.'" In *The Child Writer from Austen to Woolf,* edited by Christine Alexander and Juliet McMaster, [101]–121. Cambridge: Cambridge University Press, 2005.

McMaster, Juliet. "The Juvenilia: Energy Versus Sympathy." In *A Companion to Jane Austen Studies,* edited by Laura Cooner Lambdin and Robert Thomas Lambdin, [173]–189. Westport, Conn.: Greenwood Press, 2000.

Pinion, F. B. *A Jane Austen Companion: A Critical Survey and Reference Book.* London: Macmillan, 1973, 61–62.

Southam, Brian C. "Juvenilia." In *The Jane Austen Companion,* edited by J. David Grey, A. Walton Litz, and Brian Southam, 244–255. New York: Macmillan, 1986.

———. *Jane Austen's Literary Manuscripts: A Study of the Novelist's Development through the Surviving Papers.* New edition. London: Athlone Press, 2001.

letters, Austen's

COMPOSITION AND PUBLICATION

Of Jane Austen's letters, 161 survive. The earliest surviving letter was written when she was 20 years old, dating from January 1796. The last surviving letter dates from the end of May 1817, six weeks or so before her death at the age of 41. So there are no known letters from the first 20 years of her life, no letters from 1797, and only six letters in each year from 1799 and 1800. There are no letters extant from June 1801 to September 1804, only one letter for 1804 as a whole, and one letter (in verse) from 1806. Three letters only survive from 1807, whereas there are no letters from July 1809 to April 1811, and only two from June 1811 till January 1813. There are 83 letters extant from the last three and a half years of her life, accounting for just over half of those that survive.

These represent a fraction of the letters she probably wrote. Deirdre Le Faye, the editor of Jane Austen's letters, comments: "at a conservative estimate, Jane Austen probably wrote about 3,000 letters during her lifetime" (Le Faye, "Letters," 33). Those that survive are found from all over the world, from Australia to North America. The majority are in the Pierpont Morgan Library in New York, the British Library has 13, and there are some in private hands. The publication history of the letters is complicated, and her sister, CASSANDRA, according to CAROLINE AUSTEN, "looked them over and burnt the greater part . . . 2 or 3 years before her own death," (*Memoir,* 174).

An early published source for Jane Austen's letters, Edward 1st Lord Brabourne's two-volume *Letters of Jane Austen* (1884), contains 14 letters that have subsequently disappeared. Other subsequent notable editions include R. W. Chapman's 1932 two-volume *Jane Austen's letters to her sister Cassandra and others.* This reclassified Brabourne's dating and ordering of the letters. In 1952, Chapman published a second edition of his 1932 edition. The later edition included an additional five letters that had come to light. In 1990, Jo Modert produced *Jane Austen's Manuscript Letters in Facsimile.* In 1995, Deirdre Le Faye produced a third new edition of *Jane Austen's Letters,* which remains the authoritative edition. The letters are placed in chronological order and numbered. In addition to a "Preface to the Third Edition" there are extensive notes, source listings, and detailed biographical and topographical indexes, plus a thorough "General Index."

CRITICAL COMMENTARY

Lord Brabourne in 1884 observed "that the letters . . . show what [Jane Austen's] own 'ordinary, everyday life' was, and . . . afford a picture of her such as no history written by another person could give so well." Further, "amid the most ordinary details and most commonplace topics, every now and then sparkle out the same wit and humour which illuminate" her fiction (I: xii–xv). So the letters are of biographical and historical interest. They can provide insight "as to the source of [Jane Austen's] plots or the origins of her characters, and social historians seek for precise information on the life of the middle-ranking professional classes of the period." For Le Faye the letters "fall into several clearly defined groups, the style and content of which are appropriate to the recipient" (Le Faye, "Letters," 38). To her brother FRANCIS, who is far away from home at sea, she sends family information that a close relative absent from home for a long time needs to know. Her youngest brother, CHARLES, was also at sea, and a number of letters from his sister are noted as being received in his diary. Unfortunately, only one has survived—written at the period of her last illness, on April 6, 1817. No letters to another brother, HENRY, are extant.

In spite of Cassandra's destruction of letters, 95 letters survive written to Jane Austen's beloved sister. These letters range from the earliest one dating from January 9–10, 1796, to one of the last known to be written by Jane Austen, dated April 27, 1817. Jane Austen died on July 18, 1817. The subject range of these letters is extensive: domestic gossip, fashion, shopping, health, mutual friends and their activities, household activity, household moves, accounts of public events, financial anxieties, among many other topics. In a letter of January 3, 1801, to Cassandra, Jane writes, "I have now attained the true art of letter-writing, which we are always told, is to express on paper exactly what one would say to the same person by word of mouth; I have been talking to you almost as fast as I could the whole of this letter" (*Letters,* 68). Her letters to Cassandra reflect their writers' changing moods and attitudes.

Jane Austen's letters to a younger generation, to her nieces and nephews as they grow up, are replete with advice. Those to her niece Anna Lefroy, who is attempting to become a novelist, contain specific information on writing and the composition of a naturalistic fictional work. She writes on September 9–18, 1814: "You are now collecting your People delightfully, getting them exactly into such a spot as is the delight of my life;—3 or 4 Families in a Country Village is the very thing to work on" (*Letters,* 275). The letters to her niece Fanny Knight contain advice on marriage and the vulnerability of single women—a major theme and concern of Jane Austen's novels. In one of her last letters, dated March 13, 1817, she writes to Fanny: "Single Women have a dreadful propensity for being poor—which is one very strong argument in favour of Matrimony, but I need not dwell on such arguments with *you* . . . Well, I shall say, as I have often said before, Do not be in a hurry; depend upon it, the right Man will come at last" (*Letters,* 332). In fact, Fanny did not marry until three years after Jane Austen's death. She became the second wife of Sir Edward Knatchbull, had nine children, and lived into her 89th year in 1882.

Outside her immediate family, Jane Austen writes gossipy letters to her old friends Martha Lloyd, and Alethea Bigg, and to her governess at Godmersham, Anne Sharp. There are business letters to her publishers, Crosby & Co., and to JOHN MURRAY. She responds to letters from the Reverend JAMES STANIER CLARKE. These letters to Clarke reveal at times her fictional preferences (see, for instance, to Clarke, April 1, 1816, *Letters,* 312). In short, the just over 160 surviving letters provide a window into Jane Austen's world, to her daily life, activities, and preoccupations.

BIBLIOGRAPHY

Primary Texts

Austen, Jane. *Letters of Jane Austen.* Edited with an introduction and critical remarks by Edward, Lord Brabourne, 2 vols. London: Richard Bentley & Son, 1884.

———. *Jane Austen's Letters to her Sister Cassandra and Others.* Collected and edited by R. W. Chapman, 2 vols. Oxford, U.K.: Clarendon Press, 1932; 2d edition. London: Oxford University Press, 1952.

———. *Jane Austen's Manuscript Letters in Facsimile . . .* [edited by] Jo Modert. Carbondale: Southern Illinois University Press, 1990.

———. *Jane Austen's Letters.* Collected and edited by Deirdre Le Faye. 3d edition. Oxford: Oxford University Press, 1995. [All textual references are to this edition.]

Secondary Works

Jones, Vivien. "Introduction" to *Jane Austen Selected Letters.* Oxford: Oxford University Press, 2004.

Le Faye, Deirdre, "Letters." In *Jane Austen in Context,* edited by Janet Todd, 33–40. Cambridge: Cambridge University Press, 2005.

Moss, Stephanie. "Jane Austen's Letters in the Nineteenth Century: The Politics of Nostalgia." In

Laura Cooner Lambdin and Robert Thomas Lambdin, *A Companion to Jane Austen Studies*, [259]–274. Westport, Conn.: Greenwood Press, 2000.

Love and Freindship (1922)

COMPOSITION AND PUBLICATION

Love and Freindship (*LF*) is in the second of the three notebooks in Jane Austen's handwriting into which she copied her childhood compositions. The dating 1790–92, that is, when she was between 15 and 17 years of age, appears in the notebook. Following the author's death, the manuscript went to her sister, CASSANDRA, and remained in family hands. On July 6, 1977, it was sold at Sotheby's auction house in London and then purchased by the British Library.

Entitled "Love and Freindship. A novel in a series of Letters," with the inscription "Deceived in Freindship & Betrayed in Love," and completed on June 13, 1790, the work was dedicated to ELIZA DE FEUILLIDE, Jane Austen's cousin. The spelling "Freindship" has been retained, as this was the author's own childhood spelling; however, she subsequently corrected this to "Friendship."

The 15 letters constituting *LF* were first published in 1922 in an edition containing a preface by the distinguished British man of letters G. K. Chesterton (1874–1936). Subsequently, *LF* appeared in the sixth volume of R. W. Chapman's Oxford edition of *The Works of Jane Austen*, first published in 1954 and revised by B. C. Southam in 1969. It was also published in Margaret Anne Doody and Douglas Murray's 1993 edition of *Catharine and Other Writings* ([75]–106). Juliet McMaster with students produced a highly informative illustrated edition in the Juvenilia Press series published in 1995.

SYNOPSIS

LF contains a letter from Isabel to Laura, her friend, Laura's reply, and 13 letters from Laura to Marianne. The letters are a comic imitation, or BURLESQUE, by the young Jane Austen of SENTIMENTAL FICTION read by the author and her contemporaries in the last decades of the 18th century. Laura, the chief writer, is the no longer youthful heroine of the sentimental novel, but aged 55. She is retelling her experiences to instruct Marianne, the daughter of her friend Isabel. In her letters, Laura ridicules literary conventions. These include "Perfections" in heroines (letter 3); curious names and origins (letters 3, 11, 15); attacks on parental judgments (letters 6, 9, 12); the romanticizing of illegitimate birth (letter 15); and excessive fainting. When the husbands of Laura and her friend Sophia reunite in letter eight, the two women "fainted Alternately on a Sofa." This is appropriate, for both the young Laura and Sophia are "all Sensibility and Feeling," witnessing events "too pathetic for the feelings," and they had "exchanged vows of mutual Freindship for the rest of our Lives, instantly unfolded to each other the most inward Secrets of our Hearts" (85–86).

Swooning, combined with temporary memory loss, occurs in letters nine and 10, in addition to letter eight. Here Jane Austen is no doubt referring to an episode in ANN RADCLIFFE's popular novel *The Mysteries of Udolpho* (1794), in which the heroine "paused again, and then, with a timid hand, lifted the veil." She, however, "instantly let it fall—perceiving that what it had concealed was no picture and, before she could leave the chamber, she dropped senseless on the floor." Radcliffe's narrative continues, "When she recovered her recollection, the remembrance of what she had seen had nearly deprived her of it a second time" (248–249).

There are other elements burlesqued in *LF*. Lovers in the novel are beyond the law; for instance, they can steal. In letter nine, the impoverished Augustus has, against the wishes of his father, married the young Sophia. During the first "few months" of their marriage, "they had been amply supported by a considerable sum of Money which Augustus had gracefully purloined from his unworthy father . . . a few days before his union with Sophia." However, such "Exalted Creatures! scorned to reflect a moment on their pecuniary Distresses and would have blushed at the idea of paying their Debts." Laura's letter continues, "Alas! what was their Reward for such disinterested Behaviour! The beautifull Augustus was arrested and we were all undone." Laura observes, "Such perfidious Treachery on the merciless perpetrators of the Deed will shock your gentle nature" (88). So morality is reversed: It is not the thief who is criticized, but those who arrest Augustus.

In the 13th letter, set in Scotland, the runaway "Sophia was majestically removing the 5th Banknote from the Drawer [in Macdonald's Library]" after having broken into it following the removal of the owner's keys. Sophia "was suddenly most impertinently interrupted in her employment by the entrance of Macdonald himself, in a most abrupt and precipitate Manner." The emphasis is upon Macdonald, who is "unblushing . . . without even endeavouring to exculpate himself from the crime he was charged with, meanly endeavoured to reproach Sophia with ignobly defrauding him of his Money" (96). Sophia is not the guilty party: It is Macdonald who is at fault!

In letters 11, 12, and 15, two young rakes, Gustavus and Philander, the third and fourth grandchildren of the elderly Lord St. Clair respectively, are described as "Gracefull Youth" (92). Lord St. Clair gives his four grandchildren, Sophia, Laura, Gustavus, and Philander, 50-pound banknotes each. This produces a fainting fit on the part of the girls. When they recover, they discover that the two youths have disappeared with their money! They are left to starve! Not literally, of course!

Other features of sentimental contemporary novels include, as indicated, temporary memory loss on the part of the heroines. In letters 10 and 13 the heroines, such as Laura and Marianne, forget the apparent severity of their situation. In letter 10, for instance, Laura writes: "in the Distress I then endured, destitute of any Support, and unprovided with any Habitation, I . . . never once . . . remembered my Father and Mother or my paternal Cottage in the Vale of Uske" (89). The contemporary novels burlesqued in *LF* also include the creation of romantic landscape environments for melancholic reflection. For instance, in letter 13 Laura and Sophia "left Macdonald Hall, and after having walked about a mile and a half we sate down by the side of a clear limpid stream to refresh our exhausted limbs. The place was suited to meditation.—; a grove of full-grown Elms sheltered us

from the East—A Bed of full-grown Nettels from the West," and so on (97).

There are also, as in contemporary novels, coincidental meetings. In letter 14 Laura, following her friend Sophia's death from consumption, travels by stagecoach for Edinburgh. It is too dark to see whom she is traveling with; however, at daybreak, she discovers that she is traveling with her "nearest Relations and Connections" whom she "inform[s] . . . of the whole melancholy Affair" (103–104)— what has happened to her. Also, to give one further illustration of the way the narrative reflects the fiction it is burlesquing, in the 13th letter Laura tells Marianne, "For two Hours did I rave." The context is "the lucky overturning of a Gentleman's Phaeton," from which two men are thrown out, both lying "weltering in their blood." Sophia and Laura recognize their own husbands, Edward and Augustus. "Sophia shrieked & fainted on the Ground—I screamed & instantly ran mad" (100, 98–99).

Laura, as the writer of the letters, is looking back, reflecting in late middle age, on events in which she was a crucial protagonist. Born in Spain, having an Irish father, an illegitimate mother, Scottish and Italian, Laura was convent-educated in France. She returned at age 18 to her parents' home in Wales, in the Vale of Uske, where she becomes friendly with the 21-year-old and more experienced Isabel. Laura married poor Edward, whose father comments that he has been "studying Novels" (81), as opposed to living in the real world. She and her friend Sophia persuade Janetta, the 15-year-old daughter of Sophia's cousin Macdonald, not to marry the sensible, agreeable Graham. The reason is that "he had no soul, that he never read the Sorrows of Werter [Goethe's 1774 novel written in letter form dealing with the loves of a young idealist] . . . that his Hair bore not the slightest resemblance to auburn" (or a romantic tinge, 93), Laura accepts the advice of Sophia as she lies dying and accepts £400 a year from her mercenary father-in-law, an "unsimpathetic" baronet, and goes to live in an isolated but romantic Highland village. In her final letter, she tells Marianne that she "took up my Residence" where she has "ever since" lived. She is "uninterrupted by unmeaning Visits," and can "indulge in a melancholy solitude, my unceasing Lamentations for the Death of my Father, my Mother, my Husband, my Freind." The final, 15th letter is dated "June 13th 1790"—when Jane Austen was 14 and a half (108–109).

CRITICAL COMMENTARY

In his preface to the initial printing of *LF*, G. K. Chesterton refers to it as a "rattling burlesque" and believes that its author's inspiration "was the gigantic inspiration of laughter" (x, xv). Subsequent critical commentary has also focused on its standing among its author's other JUVENILIA, the ways in which it anticipates Jane Austen's subsequent writings, its verbal and epistolary style, depiction of women, and of the relationships between parents and children. Other areas of interest range from examination of the nature of *LF*'s humor, parody, and treatment of family relationships, marriage, or even food.

Putting to one side the issue of whether Jane Austen wished to see her "Juvenilia" published, Marvin Mudrick has been one of the foremost exponents advocating *LF*'s significance. In his *Jane Austen: Irony as Defense and Discovery* (1968), he explores the targets of Jane Austen's irony in *LF*. These include Elizabeth Nugent Bromley's three-volume novel *Laura and Augustus: An Authentic Story: In a Series of Letters*, published in 1784. This is for Mudrick the chief victim of the parody in *LF*. However, Austen's tale became more widely accessible through its inclusion as a text in Sandra M. Gilbert and Susan Gubar's *The Norton Anthology of Literature by Women: The Tradition in English*, first published in 1985 and subsequently available as a college textbook throughout North America. Six years earlier the same editors devoted space in *The Madwoman in the Attic* to a feminist reading of *LF*. They pay particular attention to the fact that Jane Austen, as a young female writer, creates Laura and Sophia as a pair of independent-minded young female heroines who exercise independence of spirit.

A leading exponent of the vitality of *LF* is Juliet McMaster. In her "Teaching 'Love and Freindship,'" in J. David Grey's *Jane Austen's Beginnings: The Juvenilia and Lady Susan* (1989), she discusses the ways in which she teaches *LF*, its burlesque, its

"many interpolated narratives within Laura's narrative," the "different verbal styles," the nature of its comedy, and its relationship to Jane Austen's major work. This relationship extends from the exploration of "the rival claims of reason and emotion" to that of experience, the treatment of literature and its relationship to life, Jane Austen's use of letters, and other areas. For McMaster, "although it [*LF*] is the product of subtle perceptions and shows a subtle artist in the making, it is itself gloriously obvious" (142, 144, 148, 151).

McMaster's and her students' Juvenilia Press edition of *LF*, in addition to a critical and explanatory introduction, contains extensive notation of the sources probably drawn on by Jane Austen. McMaster writes in her preface that *LF* "is arguably the funniest short work of fiction in the English language. Here we find a young genius gloriously and uninhibitedly letting her hair down, piling joke upon joke, hyperbole on hyperbole." McMaster adds, "The memorable restraint of her mature novels for which Austen is famous is either not yet developed, or thrown to the winds" ([v]).

CHARACTERS

Agatha (92) Mother of Gustavus, and the youngest daughter of Lord St. Clair.

Augustus (86) Edward Lindsay's friend who extends Laura and Edward hospitality following their elopement.

Bertha (92) Lord St. Clair's third daughter, mother of Philander, she is "the amiable Bertha" (92).

Bridget (100) The daughter of a widow, she shelters Laura and Sophia. Described as "very plain & her name was Bridget . . . Nothing therefore could be expected from her" (100).

Claudia (81) Laura's mother, of Scottish-Italian ancestry.

Dorothea, Lady (81, 109) Laura in letter six recounts how Edward Lindsay told her that his father "insisted on my giving my hand to Lady Dorothea.

No never exclaimed I. Lady Dorothea is lovely and Engaging; I prefer no woman to her; but know Sir, that I scorn to marry her in compliance with your Wishes! No! Never shall it be said that I obliged my Father" (81). She marries Sir Edward and produces an "Heir to his Title and Estate" (109).

Graham, Mr. (93) The fiancé of Janetta Macdonald: "Sensible, well-informed, and Agreable; . . . but [Sophia and Laura] were convinced he had no soul" (93).

Gustavus (92) A grandson of Lord St. Clair, Agatha's son, "a Gracefull Youth." Teaming up with Philander, they steal 50-pound banknotes. He eventually becomes a successful actor and then a stagecoach driver.

Isabel (76–77) Writer of the first letter and recipient of the second, she is Laura's closest "freind" (76); most of the letters are written by Laura to Isabel's daughter Marianne.

Jones, Philip (106) "It is generally beleived that Philander, is the son of one Philip Jones a Bricklayer" (106).

Lindsay, Augusta (82) Sister of Edward Lindsay, her sister-in-law, Laura "found her exactly what her Brother had described her to be—of the middle size." She receives Laura with "a disagreeable Coldness and Forbidding Reserve" (82).

Lindsay, Edward (80 and throughout) Laura describes him as "the most beauteous and amiable Youth" she has ever seen. His real name "was Lindsay—for particular reasons" Laura "conceal[s] it under that of Talbot" (80). His mother having died, the son of a Bedfordshire baronet, Edward/Talbot has left home for his aunt's home following an argument with his father, who wished to force him to marry a Lady Dorothea. Edward proposes to Laura, they marry, and they go to his aunt's home, where he argues with Augusta, his sister. Edward, in response to her question of how he hopes to feed his wife and support her without his father's assistance, replies using his "nobly contemptuous Manner," asking her

"Can you not conceive the Luxury of living in every Distress that Poverty can inflict, with the object of your tenderest Affection?" His father arrives, Edward with "undaunted Bravery" (83–85) says that he has married without his father's consent and leaves with Laura for the home of his close friend Augustus. He too has rashly married, and here Laura meets a kindred spirit, Sophia. Edward goes to London to find assistance after Sophia and Augustus have gone into debt. Edward and Augustus reappear in *LF* lying "weltering in their blood" (99) from an overturned vehicle somewhere in Scotland. Laura and Sophia rush to assist them but Edward dies, and Laura lives on continually remembering him. In this sense, he perhaps is a figment of her fantasies, the product of reading too many sentimental novels!

Lindsay, Sir Edward (81, 105, 108–109) Edward's father, who "seduced by the false glare of Fortune and the Deluding Pomp of Title," (81), tries to force his son to marry Lady Dorothea. His son gives him little opportunity to respond to the announcement that he has married Laura. She re-meets Sir Edward on a stagecoach following her husband's death. Sir Edward, Augusta, and Lady Dorothea have come to tour Scotland, having been inspired by the description in "Gilpin's Tour of the Highlands." This is WILLIAM GILPIN's *Observations, Relative Chiefly to Picturesque Beauty . . . On Several Parts of Great Britain; Particularly in the High-Lands of Scotland*, published in 1789 (letter 14; 105). In Edinburgh he acknowledges Laura as "the Widow of his Son" and "desired I would accept from his Hands of four Hundred a year." Mindful of his obligations, his duties, "Sir Edward in hopes of gaining an Heir to his Title & Estate . . . married Lady Dorothea—. His wishes have been answered" (108–109).

Lindsay, Laura (76 and throughout) The chief letter writer in *LF*, who tells Marianne in a letter, "In my Mind, every Virtue that could adorn it was centered; it was the Rendez-vous of every good Quality and of every noble sentiment" (78). Isabel in the first letter, asks the aging, 55-year-old Laura, the friend from her youth, to retell for the purposes of instructing Isabel's young daughter Marianne, "the Misfortunes and Adventures of your life" (76).

Laura's assumption is that she is to appear as a positive example for Marianne: "May the fortitude with which I have suffered the many afflictions of my past Life, prove to be to her a useful lesson" (77). The daughter of an Irish father and an illegitimate opera singer of Scottish-Italian ancestry, she recounts her tale, her marriage, her trip with Sophia her great friend to London and Scotland, her husband's death, and amid other adventures, her final retreat to an isolated Highland village. Apart from a warning regarding unnecessary fainting fits (102), she seems to have learned little from her experiences: "I had always behaved in a manner which reflected Honour on my Feelings and Refinement" (104). She lives in a past world, a world of self-delusion and of the creative imagination, transforming assumed past happenings nurtured by an annual income of £400 allowed her by her late husband's father's generosity.

Macdonald, Mr. (92–93) "Sophia's cousin" (92), he shelters her and Laura after they are discarded by Lord St. Clair. MacDonald behaves oppressively toward his daughter and ejects Laura and Sophia when he catches Sophia removing banknotes from his drawer.

Macdonald, Janetta (93) She is the 15-year-old daughter, "naturally well-disposed, endowed with a susceptible Heart, and a simpathetic Disposition," but unappreciated by her father. "She *did like* Captain M'Kenzie *better* than any one she knew besides" (93–94).

M'Kenzie, Captain (94) Encouraged by Laura and Sophia, he elopes with Janetta to Gretna Green. His "modesty . . . had been the only reason of his having so long concealed the violence of his affection for Janetta" (95).

Marianne (76–77) The daughter of Laura's great friend Isabel, to whom Laura addresses her past adventures for her moral instruction. In Laura's letter to Isabel, she says, "I will gratify the curiosity of your Daughter; and may the fortitude with which I have suffered the many afflictions of my past Life, prove to her a useful lesson for the support of those which may befall her in her own" (77).

Matilda (91) The eldest daughter of Lord St. Clair and Sophia's mother.

Philander (91, 109) He is the illegitimate grandson of Lord St. Clair and "a most beautifull Young Man," (91), son of his third daughter, Bertha. With Gustavus, he purloins banknotes from Laura and Sophia and becomes a wandering actor, using the stage name Lewis.

Polydore (81) Laura's Irish father, who lives in the Vale of Uske in Wales.

St. Clair, Lord (91) The Scottish nobleman and grandfather of the four leading participants in *LF*: Sophia, Laura, Philander, and Gustavus.

St. Clair, Lady Laurina (91) Wife of Lord St. Clair, and a former Italian opera singer.

Sophia (85 and throughout) Laura's special friend, to whom she is attracted when they meet. She ran away with Edward [Lindsay]'s friend Augustus, and when Laura first sees her, she reminisces: "A soft languor spread over her lovely features, but increased their Beauty. . . . she was all Sensibility and Feeling. We [Laura and Sophia] flew into each others arms and after having exchanged vows of mutual Freindship for the rest of our Lives, instantly unfolded to each other the most inward Secrets of our Hearts" (85). Sophia and Laura take refuge with Sophia's Scottish relatives. A granddaughter of Lord St. Clair, she and Laura are removed from her relative's house. They discover their husbands thrown out of an overturned phaeton, and they faint. Sophia falls ill, suffers from consumption, and dies. Her final, anticlimatic words consist of advice to Laura to "Beware of swoons . . . Run mad as often as you chuse; but do not faint—" (102).

Staves, Gregory (106) Augustus's father, he is "a Staymaker of Edinburgh" (106), or maker of "stiff waistcoat[s] made of whale-bone worn by ladies" or of "Ropes in a ship to keep the mast from falling aft" (McMaster, ed., 43).

William (81) Edward Lindsay's manservant.

BIBLIOGRAPHY

Primary Texts

Austen, Jane. *Love & freindship and other early works, now first printed from the original MS. by Jane Austen, with a preface by G. K. Chesterton.* New York: Frederick A. Stokes, 1922, 1–51.

———. "Love and Freindship." In *Volume the Second,* edited by B. C. Southam, [3]–66. Oxford, U.K.: Clarendon Press, 1963.

———. "Love and Freindship." In *The Norton Anthology of Literature by Women. The Tradition in English,* edited by Sandra M. Gilbert and Susan Gubar, 206–232. New York and London: W.W. Norton, 1985.

———. "Love and Freindship." In *The Works of Jane Austen.* Vol. 6, *Minor Works,* edited by R. W. Chapman. Oxford: Oxford University Press, 1986. [All textual references are to this edition.]

———. "Love and Freindship." In *Jane Austen's Catharine and other Writings,* edited by Margaret Anne Doody and Douglas Murray, [75]–106. Oxford: Oxford University Press, 1993.

———. "Love & Freindship." Edited by Juliet McMaster and the students of English 659 at the University of Alberta. Edmonton, Alberta, Canada: Juvenilia Press (Department of English, University of Alberta), 1995, reissued 1997.

Secondary Works

Gilbert, Sandra M., and Susan Gubar. *The Madwoman in the Attic: The Woman Writer and the Nineteenth Century Literary Imagination.* New Haven, Conn., and London: Yale University Press, 1979, 107–145.

McMaster, Juliet. "Teaching 'Love and Freindship.'" In *Jane Austen's Beginnings: The Juvenilia and Lady Susan,* edited by J. David Grey, [135]–151. Ann Arbor, Mich., and London: UMI Research Press.

Mansfield Park (1814)

COMPOSITION AND PUBLICATION

Jane Austen's "Plan of a novel" agrees with Cassandra Austen's notes on the dating of the composition of her sister's novels. *Mansfield Park (MP)* was "begun sometime about Feby 1811—Finished soon after June 1813" (Lefaye, *Record,* 197). Letters written by Jane Austen in 1813 suggest prior knowledge on Cassandra's part of the plot. For instance, on January 29, 1813, when Cassandra was staying with their elder brother JAMES AUSTEN, a clergyman, Jane Austen refers in her letter to information she has requested to be confirmed: "I am glad to find your enquiries have ended so well," she tells Cassandra. "If you [could] discover whether Northamptonshire is a Country of Hedgerows. I [should] be glad again" (*Letters,* 202). Probably this refers to Fanny's observation in the second volume, chapter 4: "Three years ago, this was nothing but a rough hedgerow" (208). Such precision of detail has suggested to

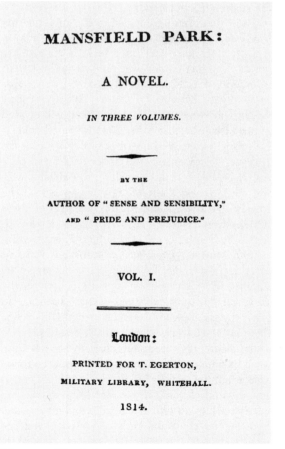

Title page of the first edition of *Mansfield Park*

some scholars that there was an earlier version of the novel (Litz, 179).

However, according to general consensus, *MP* is the first of Jane Austen's later novels to be written after what appears to be a six-year period lacking in productivity. The novel was probably finished and offered to the publisher THOMAS EGERTON late in 1813. Her brother HENRY AUSTEN read the novel, probably in proof in March 1814. On March 2, 1814, Jane Austen wrote to Cassandra that Henry "says it is very different from the other two, but does not appear to think it at all inferior" to her other work (*Letters*, 255). Egerton's terms were to charge his author Jane Austen a 10 percent commission on all sales. Jane Austen retained the copyright. *MP* was published in three volumes by Egerton on May 9, 1814, priced at 18 shillings for the three volumes. The manuscript of this edition has not survived.

The publisher John Murray subsequently "expressed astonishment that so small an edition of such a work should have been sent into the world." The first edition was probably published in an edition of 1,250 copies (Gilson, 49). Jane Austen wrote to her niece FRANCES AUSTEN (Fanny Knight) on November 18, 1814: "You will be glad to hear that the first Edit: of M.P." is all sold.— Your Uncle Henry [Austen] is rather wanting me to come to Town, to settle about a 2^d Edit" (*Letters*, 281). Egerton was unwilling to publish a second edition, and JOHN MURRAY stepped into the breach. A three-volume edition of 750 copies was published on February 19, 1816, again at 18 shillings. On December 11, 1815, Jane Austen wrote to John Murray, "I return . . . 'Mansfield Park,' as ready for a 2^d edit: I beleive, as I can make it" (*Letters*, 305). The author kept the copyright, the work was probably published at her expense, and John Murray took a 10 percent commission. The three volumes were offered to wholesale firms at a special prepublication subscription for 12s 6d a copy. In spite of such a price reduction, the second edition did not sell. In December 1817, 588 copies remained unsold, and in January 1820, there were still 498 copies unsold. These were sold off at 2s 6d. Allowing for the publisher's commission and the advertising costs, the author's profits were £118. 18. 4d (Gilson, 59–60).

No contemporary reviews of the novel have surfaced. Between June 15 and 20, 1814, Georgiana Dowager Lady Vernon wrote to Mrs. Phyllis Frampton: "I now recommend you 'Mansfield Park,' if you meet with it. It is not much of a novel, more the history of a family party in the country, very natural, and the characters well drawn." On November 7, 1814, Lady Anne Romilly wrote to the novelist MARIA EDGEWORTH, "Have you read Mansfield Park? It has been pretty generally admired here [i.e., London], and I think all novels must be that are true to life which this is, with a good strong vein of principle running tho' [through] the whole." She adds, however, "It has not . . . that elevation of virtue, something beyond nature, that gives the greatest charm to a novel, but still it is real natural every day life, and will amuse an idle hour in spite of its faults" (Gilson, 49–50).

It is hardly surprising that, given the lack of success of this second edition, no additional printings are known before the initial American publication. The Philadelphia publishers Carey and Lea published *MP* in three volumes in a run of 1,250 copies on December 1, 1832. Based on the second edition, it was reissued in one-volume form in Philadelphia in 1838 and again in 1845. In London, Richard Bentley published it in a single volume priced at six shillings. There were French translations published in Geneva, Switzerland, in 1815 and a year later in Paris. The novel continued to be published in London and New York throughout the 19th century. Hugh Thomson's illustrations, with Austin Dobson's introduction, were published by Macmillan in London and New York in 1897. The Everyman Library edition published by J. M. Dent in London and E. P. Dutton in New York appeared in [1906]. R. Brimley Johnson's editor's note is a partial reprint of his 1892 10-volume *Novels of Jane Austen* with additions. Other distinguished 20th-century editors include R. W. Chapman of 1923, with Mary Lascelles's "small changes and additions mostly based on Dr. Chapman's papers" included in the 1966 reprint ([xiv]).

There are significant differences in technical details, spelling, and publication between the first and second editions. Chapman's edition, (which has been used here for parenthetical page references), is a mixture of the two. Most reprints are based on the second edition. *The Cambridge Edition of the Works of Jane Austen* volume, edited by John Wiltshire, published in 2005, "is based on the second edition . . . [and] also includes variant readings drawn from the 1814 edition of the novel, published by Thomas Egerton" (Wiltshire, lxxxv).

SYNOPSIS

Volume 1

The novel opens with the family history of the extremely wealthy Sir Thomas Bertram and his wife's family. Lady Bertram, from an untitled family, had about 30 years previously "had the good luck to captivate Sir Thomas Bertram, of Mansfield Park, in the county of Northampton" (1) and married him. Her sister, however, had been less fortunate, making a foolish marriage to an irresponsible naval lieutenant, a Mr. Price. This marriage had been the reason for a lack of contact between Mrs. Price for a considerable number of years with her sisters, Lady Bertram and Mrs. Norris, the wife of the rector of Mansfield Park, the Reverend Norris. Expecting her ninth child and unable to deal with her growing family, Mrs. Price has written to her sister requesting assistance. Lady Bertram, considerably influenced by her dominating sister, Mrs. Norris, persuades Sir Thomas to offer a home to Fanny, the 10-year-old eldest Price daughter.

Very nervous, anxious, and withdrawn when she arrives, Fanny finds it difficult to adjust to her new grandiose environment and cousins—Tom, aged 17; Edmund, 16; Maria, 13; and Julia, aged 12. Edmund is kind to Fanny, befriends her, encourages her to read, and helps her to write to her beloved elder brother William, to whom she is close and who is about to embark on a naval career. Sir Thomas, hearing of Fanny's homesickness and attachment to William, invites him to spend a week at Mansfield Park. By the age of 15, Fanny regards Mansfield as her only real home and has earned the respect of Maria and Julia, who initially regarded her as stupid.

Mr. Norris dies, and there is a possibility that Fanny will have to live with Mrs. Norris, which depresses her as neither likes the other. However, Mrs. Norris, although responsible for Fanny's com-

ing to Mansfield Park initially, has not contributed to her upkeep, and has no intention of doing so now. Edmund intends to enter the church, and the living of Mansfield held by Mr. Norris was intended for him. Sir Thomas, however, is forced to sell it to help pay off the debts incurred by his eldest son and heir, Tom, through his extravagant lifestyle. The new incumbent is a Dr. Grant, who has purchased the living, although after him it can be repurchased. Sir Thomas's financial problems are compounded by difficulties with the properties he owns in Antigua in the West Indies. When Fanny is 16, Sir Thomas leaves for the Caribbean with Tom to try to resolve the issues.

Maria and Julia are old enough to attend the balls and lead an active social life chaperoned by Mrs. Norris, who represses Fanny, keeping her at home to look after Lady Bertram. She is couchbound, surrounded by her small dogs. The only member of the family who cares about Fanny is Edmund, and Fanny's feelings for him increase when he exchanges one of his own horses for one Fanny is able to ride after the death of her beloved pony. Tom returns to Mansfield Park after nearly a year. His father remains in distant Antigua. Maria, partly under pressure from Mrs. Norris, becomes engaged to the very wealthy Rushworth of Sotherton, the owner of one of the largest houses and estates in the area. Edmund feels that she has accepted him only for his money, as he has only his wealth to recommend him.

New characters in the form of the wealthy, socially adept, and attractive Henry and Mary Crawford appear. They come to stay with their relative Mrs. Grant at Mansfield parsonage. Maria and Julia both find Henry attractive. Mary at first finds Tom more interesting, but transfers her interest to Edmund, who is infatuated with her. Edmund goes as far as offering her the horse he has bought for Fanny to ride. Fanny is deprived of regular exercise and remains at Mansfield Park with Lady Bertram while the others go out riding.

Edmund, feeling guilty about the horse, is insistent that Fanny be included in the party to tour Rushworth's Sotherton estate. He even offers to remain at Mansfield with his mother, and eventually Mrs. Grant agrees to stay with Lady Bertram.

Mrs. Rushworth proudly displays Sotherton house, indicating its long history. In the private chapel, Mary Crawford, unaware that Edmund intends to become a clergyman, makes negative remarks about the clergy. The party then divides into groups for a tour of the Sotherton grounds. Edmund goes with Mary and Fanny, Maria with Rushworth and Henry, Mrs. Rushworth with Mrs. Norris and Julia. Mary, as they walk in the woods, is very surprised at Edmund's decision to enter the church and makes it clear that she has little respect for such a profession. Edmund, supported by Fanny, tries to persuade her of his deep commitment to his choice and its importance to the moral welfare of the nation. Mary is unable to comprehend and has little sympathy.

Fanny is tired and rests on a bench, leaving Edmund and Mary to walk on. She is joined by Maria, Rushworth, and Henry Crawford. Maria and Henry wish to go through a locked gate to the park beyond. Rushworth offers to return to the house to fetch the key. In his absence, Maria and Crawford—witnessed by Fanny—go off by themselves, having squeezed through the gate and into the park. Julia then arrives, and annoyed at being separated from Crawford, she is determined to catch up with Maria and Crawford, and also squeezes past the locked gate. Rushworth, too, sits by Fanny and complains to her about his fiancée's behavior. Fanny then goes in search of Henry and Maria, who promised to return within 10 minutes but have been gone an hour. They, too, have been in the park. Everyone returns to Sotherton for dinner. The day concludes with a rapprochement between Julia and Rushworth. For the homeward journey, Julia rides beside Henry, and Maria agrees to Rushworth's assisting her into the barouche.

There is a new visitor to Mansfield Park, a well-connected associate of Tom Bertram, the Honorable John Yates. He is obsessed with amateur theatricals. Edmund at first opposes the idea of organizing a play at Mansfield Park, as he knows his father would not approve. Fanny, too, disapproves. On hearing that Mary has agreed to participate, he agrees to do so, too. The choice of play, *Lovers' Vows*, is risqué and shocks Edmund and Fanny, but Edmund goes along with it, Fanny being the only one to hold out. Henry and Maria get closer during

"Mr. Yates rehearsing," illustration by William Cubitt Cook, *Mansfield Park,* London: Dent, 1892

the rehearsals, much to Julia's annoyance. Edmund and Mary also frequently rehearse together. This is observed with distress by Fanny, who has agreed to listen to their lines.

Volume 2

Sir Thomas returns from Antigua early and by surprise. He immediately stops the theatricals and removes the evidence of their presence at Mansfield Park. Sir Thomas is furious with Mrs. Norris for having approved such activities. Fanny is the only one who receives his approval, as she had the good sense not to become too involved. Yates is told to leave. Julia, in reaction to being snubbed by Henry, has been flirting with Yates. Sir Thomas initially approves of Maria's engagement to Rushworth, but after meeting him and becoming aware of Maria's indifference to him, urges her to break off the engagement. Maria, annoyed by Henry's treatment of her and having tasted freedom when her father was away, decides to go through with the marriage. This takes place; Maria, with Julia as accompaniment, goes on her honeymoon to Brighton and then London.

Fanny becomes the center of attention at Mansfield. She becomes friendlier with Mary. Invited to dine at the parsonage—much to Mrs. Norris's snobbish disapproval—with Edmund, she finds that Henry Crawford has returned. Fanny is startled by his impropriety in returning so early and his seeming lack of awareness of the problems he has caused. He speaks slightingly of Rushworth and without respect of Sir Thomas. For this Fanny admonishes him.

Much to Mary Crawford's annoyance, Edmund is to take holy orders shortly and become priest at the neighboring Thornton Lacey. Fanny meanwhile is blossoming in appearance. Henry and Mary devise a plan to get her to fall in love with him. He clearly enjoys such games but has not taken into account Fanny's strength of character and is unaware that she loves Edmund.

Following seven years at sea, William, Fanny's brother, returns home on leave and is invited by Sir Thomas to Mansfield Park. After hearing of Fanny's wish to see the now grown-up William dance, Sir Thomas arranges a ball to be held at Mansfield Park. This is Fanny's "coming-out" ball. William has given her the only piece of jewelry she possesses, an amber cross, but she lacks a chain to wear it on. So she consults Mary Crawford, who persuades Fanny to accept a fancy gold necklace, saying that it had been a gift from Henry to her. Learning this, Fanny attempts unsuccessfully to return it, as she has begun to suspect that Mary may well be acting on Henry's behalf.

Fanny returns to her Mansfield Park room to find Edmund writing a note to her to go with the gift he has for her. This is a gold chain for her amber cross and is just what Fanny wanted. She asks Edmund for advice regarding Mary's gift. He persuades her to retain it, as he does not wish there to be any ill feeling between "the two dearest objects I have on earth." Fanny has mixed emotions; she realizes that Edmund is seriously considering asking Mary to marry him; she loves him and still hopes to marry

him. She seizes his note "as a treasure beyond all her hopes" (264–265).

The next day witnesses another of Henry's schemes to gain favor with Fanny. Henry offers to take William, who is about to leave, to London in his carriage rather than having to endure the lengthy journey by mail coach. Further, Henry will introduce him to the influential Admiral Crawford, who may well be able to advance William's career. This pleases Fanny, who meets the dispirited Edmund on the stairs as she goes to dress for the ball. Edmund tells her that Mary has told him that as she does not approve of clergyman, this will be the final time they dance. He confides to Fanny that "it appears as if" Mary's "mind itself was tainted" (269). Fanny dresses in high spirits for the

Fanny receives a chain from Edmund. Illustration used as the frontispiece to *Mansfield Park* (London: Routledge, 1883)

"Joined at the chain and cross and put them round the neck." Illustration by Edmund H. Garrett, frontispiece to Volume 2, *Mansfield Park (Boston: Little, Brown, 1898)*

ball and wears Mary's necklace, William's cross, and Edmund's chain.

At the ball, Sir Thomas praises her for her appearance. Fanny is embarrassed to discover that she is expected to lead the opening dance and open the ball. Henry Crawford engages her for the first two dances and continually attracts her attention. Fanny is very happy to dance with the unhappy Edmund, who has parted badly with Mary in "mutual vexation" (279).

The following day after an early breakfast, Fanny says farewell in tears to William, who leaves for Portsmouth via London with Henry. Edmund also leaves for Peterborough to stay with his friend Mr. Owen. Both are to be ordained. Mary discovers that Owen has three grown sisters and feels jealous.

She goes to Fanny for reassurance. Fanny appears certain that Edmund has made no plans to marry. Henry returns to Mansfield to tell an amazed Mary that he has really fallen in love with Fanny and is no longer playing games with her. Mary sees advantages in this as she will be close to Edmund.

Early the next morning, Henry goes to visit Fanny to tell her that through the good offices of his uncle Admiral Crawford, William has been promoted to the rank of lieutenant. Fanny is overjoyed and profuse in her thanks, but after Henry proposes to her and makes a confession of love, she becomes distressed. She does not believe him or wish to believe him and runs in tears from the room to her own upstairs room. When Henry has left, she comes downstairs to share the news of William's promotion. Sir Thomas has invited Henry to dinner. He arrives bringing a note from Mary congratulating her and urging her to accept Henry's marriage proposal as a serious one. Fanny is again confused and writes a note for Mary, which she hands to Henry, saying that she has no intention of accepting Henry. The evening is very unpleasant for Fanny.

Volume 3

Henry makes another early-morning visit to Mansfield Park, this time to ask Sir Thomas for his consent to his marriage with Fanny. Sir Thomas goes to Fanny's room to find out her feelings and is very surprised to learn that she has rejected Henry. Fanny is unable to tell Sir Thomas that Henry has been playing games, too, with his daughter's emotions. Sir Thomas finds it difficult to believe that Fanny will reject such an advantageous proposal, given her marriage prospects. He loses patience with her and accuses Fanny of being ungrateful. Fanny is now most distressed and in tears. Sir Thomas sends Henry home, believing that after reflection Fanny will change her mind. He visits her the following day and she has not changed her decision. However, a consequence of his visit to her room is that Sir Thomas orders a fire to be lit daily—a sign of Fanny's improved status.

The next evening, Henry comes to renew his proposal, impressing Fanny with his sincerity and the change that has come over him, but his assumption that eventually Fanny will fall in love with him annoys her. Lady Bertram is pleased for Fanny when she hears of Henry's proposal. Mrs. Norris is annoyed that Fanny, rather than Julia, is preferred by Henry Crawford. Edmund returns as a clergyman from Peterborough and is surprised to see Mary still at Mansfield and the warmth of her reception of him. Sir Thomas enlists Edmund's help in attempting to persuade Fanny to accept Henry's proposal. Edmund is as unsuccessful as his father. Just as she is about to leave for London, Mary visits Fanny to urge her brother's case and reveals that she gave Fanny the necklace on Henry's behalf. Fanny is pleased to see both Crawfords depart for London but concerned that Edmund will eventually marry Mary.

William is at Mansfield having 10 day's shore leave. Sir Thomas feels it will be a good idea for Fanny to accompany him to Portsmouth and stay for a period with her family. It will reveal to her "the value of a good income" (369). Fanny views the visit from another perspective as providing a worthwhile opportunity to revitalize the family bonds that were severed when she came to Mansfield Park. She eagerly looks forward once again to seeing her parents, sisters, and brothers. Further, a separation from Edmund will lessen the pain of seeing him tempted into a marriage with Mary Crawford.

Sir Thomas's hopes are justified by Fanny's experiences at Portsmouth. She is surprised by the cramped conditions, dirt, and noise of her parent's house. Fanny finds that they have no time for her, and that her father lacks manners and is coarse, and that her mother is a "slattern" (390) without order or willpower. Her sole consolation comes in her bonding with Susan, her 14-year-old sister, whom she finds willing to be educated. After a month or so, Fanny is surprised to receive a visit from Henry Crawford. His manners and polish favorably contrast with the crudeness of the Price household. He tells her that he has been to his Everingham Norfolk estates and become more involved in its appropriate management to assist the tenants. Fanny is impressed but detects signs that Henry is yet again playing a role to impress, in this instance, her. Henry tells Fanny that Edmund is in London and in communication with Mary.

Fanny assumes that their forthcoming engagement is inevitable.

Fanny receives a letter from Mary Crawford full of irrelevant gossip but revealing that Edmund has not proposed to her. The letter, with its focus on external appearance, reveals Mary's essential inappropriateness for Edmund. Mary relates details of a party at which Henry, her brother, will re-meet Maria for the first time since her marriage. Fanny then receives a letter from Edmund written not from London but from Mansfield Park. He is disappointed by Mary's frivolous behavior in London and finds that her friends are vain and lacking in feeling. He is, however, still considering proposing to her. He reports seeing Maria and Henry at a party but apparently they exchanged hostile glances.

Lady Bertram has now been writing almost daily to Fanny with news and wishing that she would return home quickly, especially as neither of her daughters wishes to be at home. Sir Thomas, however, seems unwilling to arrange transportation for Fanny to come home. Lady Bertram is very distressed as Tom is very ill, falling from his horse and drinking excessively. Another letter is received from Mary shedding crocodile tears over Tom's expected death and looking forward to Edmund's eventually inheriting the estate, and implying that if this occurs she will overlook the fact that he is a clergyman and marry him. Mr. Rushworth is away from London and her brother Henry and Maria are seeing each other often. The letter disgusts Fanny.

Yet another letter from Mary arrives suggesting that a scandal involving Henry and Maria is about to occur and Fanny is not to believe it. Mr. Price the following day reads in his newspaper that Henry and Maria have eloped. Fanny anxiously waits for another letter bringing news. Three days later one arrives from Edmund postmarked from London. He confirms the story. Maria and Henry cannot be found; furthermore, Julia and Yates have eloped to Scotland. Sir Thomas has asked Edmund to collect Fanny the next day and to bring her home to look after Lady Bertram. He invites Susan to accompany them.

Back at Mansfield Park, a grateful Lady Bertram pours her heart out to Fanny. Edmund too confesses that he has broken with Mary once and for all. He found her lax attitude to Maria and Henry's behavior inappropriate. He also disapproved of her mocking Edmund's moral stance on the affair. Edmund reveals to Fanny how he misread Mary's and Henry's characters; he is dejected as he cannot envision loving anyone else. "Fanny's friendship was all that he had to cling to" (460). Fanny is happy in spite of the depressed atmosphere of Mansfield Park. She has been restored to her uncle's good graces, as he realizes that compared with the behavior of his two daughters, Maria and Julia, Fanny's has been outstanding.

After a time spent with Henry Crawford, Maria realizes that he has no intention of marrying her and the two split up badly. Rushworth meanwhile divorces her. Sir Thomas feels he is partially to blame as he should have paid more attention to his daughters and their activities. The bulk of his anger falls on Mrs. Norris, whom he considers to be directly responsible for his daughters' disgraceful conduct. After a while, he sends Maria and Mrs. Norris away from Mansfield Park to live in social isolation, with only each other to deal with.

Julia's marriage turns out to be better than expected. She and Yates ask Sir Thomas's forgiveness. Yates, it emerges, is wealthy and has more good sense than originally thought. Tom Bertram's health takes a turn for the better, and he determines to be less selfish and more responsible. Edmund at last realizes how much he needs and cares for Fanny, proposes, and is accepted, then Sir Thomas approves of the marriage. Sir Thomas supports William Price in his now promising naval career. Susan is asked to remain at Mansfield and replaces Fanny, who lives with Edmund at Thornton Lacey. In the future, the reader is informed, Dr. Grant dies and Edmund's birthright is restored. He becomes the Mansfield rector. As a married couple, Fanny and Edmund "must appear as secure as earthly happiness can be" (473).

CRITICAL SYNOPSIS AND COMMENTARY

Chapter 1

In common with *Northanger Abbey* but unlike *Emma, Persuasion,* and *Pride and Prejudice,* the novel opens with a paragraph of omniscient narration. There is an absence of short-clipped dialogue or focus on a single character. The emphasis is on place, making a suitable marriage, rising up the class ladder, money, status, and income. These are to be among the major themes of *Mansfield Park* (*MP*). The first four words refer to "about thirty years ago." Given that *MP* was published in 1814 and probably started three years earlier, chronologically the reference is to around the early 1780s, a period before the outbreak of the wars with France that so dominated English life during the final decade of the 18th century and the opening decade and a half of the new century. So historically the novel is to encompass the prewar and war years. The remainder of the first sentence focuses, first, on "Miss Maria Ward of Huntingdon," who is distinguished in rank, name, and fortune from "Sir Thomas Bertram, of Mansfield Park, in the country of Northampton." She is "Miss," not a Lady, with "only seven thousand pounds" [3]—not an insignificant amount of money—from a country town in the midland county of Northamptonshire. It is not without significance that Huntingdon's claim to fame is as the birthplace of Oliver Cromwell (1599–1658), the Puritan general who defeated the Royalists in the English Civil Wars of 1642–49 and who, after the execution of Charles I, became lord protector of England. The opposition between Puritanism, represented, for instance, in a distaste of the theater, leading to its closure, and hedonism, represented by the Royalists, is to surface in *MP*.

Sir Thomas Bertram, on the other hand, is not from a town but a county—Northamptonshire, and a property. He is a titled landowner. Sir Thomas is from Northampton, which "featured as the bedrock of [the] English community in Samuel Richardson's novel *Sir Charles Grandison* (1753–4), a favorite with the Austen family." In this epistolary novel, the mild-mannered hero is attracted to two women: one is Puritanical and virtuous, the other from a Catholic family. The hero, Grandison, performs many deeds of charity and kindness. He assists Sir Thomas Mansfield and his family (Stabler, 393). Miss Maria Ward "had the good luck to captivate" him. Luck, good fortune, and gambling also play their role in the novel in the way in which events unfold and their consequences on human destiny. This ability to captivate "thereby raised [her] to the rank of a baronet's lady, with all the comforts and consequences of an handsome house and large income." A baronet held an hereditary title, so his son or his heir became a baronet on his death. However, he sat in the lower house of Parliament, the House of Commons, not in the House of Lords.

A second sentence conveys reaction to the marriage and information concerning Maria Ward's family. Her uncle is a lawyer; in other words, her family are not from the landed gentry but from the professions largely based in the town. The lawyer "allowed her to be at least three thousand pounds short of any equitable claim," suggesting that he legally drew up the terms of marriage in which the sum of "seven thousand pounds" would pass to her husband once they were married. However, "at least three thousand pounds short" is ambiguous. It suggests that she was unable, owing to family circumstances, to give her husband the full sum. Or it might mean that she brought the full sum and, not being the eldest Ward sister, deprived her sisters of their full marriage portions. These sisters, "Miss Ward and Miss Frances," would "be benefited" by their sister's "elevation," her fortunate marriage.

The author tells her readers "there certainly are not so many men of large fortune in the world, as there are pretty women to deserve them." This is the first of many instances throughout *MP* of authorial observation on human activities and character. Clearly, "Miss Ward," unlike her sister Maria, had not similar "good luck" for six years after Maria's marriage, she is "obliged" (a common word in Jane Austen's work used 305 times), here almost meaning "forced," to marry a clergyman with connections to the family, "a friend of her brother-in-law." Moreover, he had "scarcely any private fortune." Sir Thomas gave "his friend an income in the living of Mansfield." In other words, Sir Thomas provided his sister-in-law and her husband a rent-free house for life with servants and income from tithes or rates collected from the local residents and the profits from farming the land belonging to the church.

The remainder of this sixth sentence is ambiguous and ironic: "Mr. and Mrs. Norris began their career of conjugal felicity with little less than a thousand a year." Miss Ward was "obliged" to marry Mr. Norris—hardly a foundation for a subsequent happy relationship. The word "career" (used only 6 times in Jane Austen's work) contains the sense of rushing into, as well as a profession. Miss Ward may well have rushed into the marriage as a career move; marriage was her livelihood, her life's work. An obvious instance of this may be seen in *Pride and Prejudice,* where Charlotte Lucas's acceptance of another clergyman, Mr. Collins, is perceived at least by Elizabeth Bennet as a mercenary move.

But "Miss Ward's match ... was not contemptible," contrasted, for instance, with her sister Miss Frances's action, which is a product of emotion rather than calculated self-interest. She "married, in the common phrase, to disoblige her family, and by fixing on a Lieutenant of Marines, without education, fortune, or connections, did it very thoroughly." The following sentence reinforces the negative tone: "She could hardly have made a more untoward choice." There are several areas of interest in these sentences. First, the use of the verb "to disoblige" (the sole instance in Jane Austen's work), rather than, for instance, the verbs "to spite" or "to annoy." Here the social consequences of Miss Frances's actions are suggested rather than the purely personal ones suggested, for instance, by "spite" or "annoy." Frances's actions are to have profound consequences on her and her children and their position in society, their prospects, and the unforeseen results of her actions form a major preoccupation of the novel. In the following sentence, Jane Austen uses the reinforced negative "untoward" rather than "worse choice," again emphasizing the social aspects. Frances has behaved in an inappropriate manner, not in the way expected from someone of her social status and rank. As "a Lieutenant of the Marines" (3), her husband's task was a policing one on ships and in the naval dockyards at Portsmouth, on the south coast of England—the important port during the Napoleonic Wars. The marines were regarded as a "subordinate and inferior branch of the Navy." Mr. Price is "an evident failure, since the average rate of promotion was from second to full lieutenant within the first year, and to captain seven or eight years later" (Southam, *Navy*: 202, 206).

Miss Frances's choice of husband lacks "connections." He lacks contacts with those who can suitably advise him or assist him in his career. The focus in the paragraph then moves back to the person of influence, power, position, status, and wealth—Sir Thomas Bertram. He "had interest," in other words, the ability to secure positions. This he was willing to exercise "for the advantage of Lady Bertram's sister." His motives are "from principle as well as pride, from a general wish of doing right" and also "a desire of seeing" that anybody connected with his family, his "respectability," was looked after. Otherwise, the situation of an impoverished, ill-connected relative might well reflect badly on him. The words "interest" and "principle" are interesting. Both are frequently found in Jane Austen's work: "interest," 247 times, and twice in the opening chapter, 53 times in the novel; "principle," less so, 37 instances. They have moral as well as financial implications. "Interest," as noted, can well imply self-interest. "Principle" occurs 13 times in *MP*, and four times in the first chapter. Its use is frequently as an abstract noun for the wish to do the right thing, implying moral conduct, an activating core behind religious belief, self-interest, and, in common with "interest," financial gain. If the correct moral action is taken, then wealth, "principal," and "interest" (3–4) will accumulate. It is a key word in the novel.

The Catch-22 is that Sir Thomas's sphere of interest, his "interest" does not in reality extend into the lowly marines "regarded as inferior, socially and professionally to the naval officers" (Wiltshire: 640). Furthermore, "before he had time to devise any other method of assisting" his sister-in-law and her husband, "an absolute break between the sisters had taken place." This argument is not only the consequence of personality conflict, but Jane Austen as narrator tells her readers, "It was the natural result of the conduct of each party, and such as a very imprudent marriage almost always produces." Frances, now Mrs. Price, did not inform her family of her intended marriage until "actually married." Character difference is now introduced. "Lady Bertram . . . a woman of very tranquil feel-

ings, and a temper remarkably easy and indolent, would have contented herself with merely giving up her sister." On the other hand, "Mrs. Norris had a spirit of activity," not in itself a negative quality, but one that controls her as it "could not be satisfied till she had written a long and angry letter to Fanny," as she is now known. Even her name has changed from "Ward" to "Price" and from "Frances" to the much more colloquial, common "Fanny," a name not without bawdy connotations. The whole novel may be seen as exploring the price she has to pay for her physical desires. Mrs. Norris's letter is "a long and angry" one pointing out "the folly" of Fanny's "conduct and threaten[ing] her with all its possible ill consequences." The reply from Fanny "was injured and angry" and "put an end to all intercourse between" Fanny and her sisters "for a considerable period." This distance no doubt increased by the account of the "very disrespectful reflections on the pride of Sir Thomas, as Mrs. Norris could not possibly keep to herself."

The opening paragraph provides the historical underpinning for the framework of the story. The second paragraph encompasses a separation of 11 years between the sisters and their families. They are separated by distance. There appears to be some communication with Mrs. Norris for, she tells Sir Thomas and Lady Bertram, "in an angry voice [no doubt a result of jealousy as Mrs. Norris is childless] that Fanny had got another child." The narrator then tells her readers that after 11 years, "Mrs. Price could no longer afford to cherish pride or resentment, or to lose one connection that might possibly assist her." The reasons are given: "A large and still increasing family, an husband disabled for active service," that is, unable to serve on a ship engaged in the naval conflict with France, "but not the less equal to company and good liquor, and a very small income to supply their wants." These factors "made her eager to regain the friends she had so carelessly sacrificed." It is clear that the author has little sympathy with Frances, Fanny Ward, now Price, the word "sacrificed" being especially strong, implying to give up, to renounce for something else—in this instance, personal preference rather than social responsibility, duty and common sense. "Friends" in this context relates to family and to those of financial and social status who are in the position to assist her.

Fanny writes to her sister Maria, now Lady Bertram, "in a letter" full of "contrition and despondence, such a superfluity of children, and such a want of almost every thing else, as could not but dispose them all [the Bertrams and Mrs. Norris] to a reconciliation." Fanny is just about to have her ninth child, and she asks for their assistance "as sponsors to the expected child" and "the future maintenance of" the other eight. She asks if Sir Thomas can find a position for her eldest child, "a boy of ten years old." She asks, "was there any chance of his being hereafter useful to Sir Thomas in the concerns of his West Indian property? No situation could be beneath him—or what did Sir Thomas think of Woolwich? or how could a boy be sent out to the East?" This paraphrasing of her questions emphasizes the information in the questions asked. The reader learns that Sir Thomas has property in the West Indies. Subsequently in the narrative (I, chapter 3, p. 30), it is revealed that he has an estate in Antigua. It is not suggested in the novel that Sir Thomas's wealth solely came from this source. Most of Britain's sugar supply came from the West Indies, and its estates provide the source for the income of some of the English gentry. The reference to Woolwich is to an important Royal Navy dockyard that also housed the Royal Arsenal (named by George III in 1805). It could have offered job opportunities, as might the East India Company controlling and administering India and other Southeast Asian territories.

In the shortest paragraph of the novel so far, the consequences of the letter are revealed: It "was not unproductive. It re-established peace and kindness. Sir Thomas sent friendly advice and professions." In other words, he sent assurance of future assistance. Also, "Lady Bertram dispatched money and baby-linen"—necessities—whilst "Mrs. Norris wrote the letters." Such a blunt comparative contrastive statement on the part of the author reveals that her sympathies are not with Mrs. Norris.

The consequences, in this novel of consequences, emerge in the next and fourth paragraph. Mrs. Norris, in a passage of free indirect speech, suggests that her sister "should be relieved from

the charge and expense of one child entirely out of her great number. 'What if they were among them to undertake the care of her eldest daughter, a girl now nine years old, of an age to require more attention than her poor mother could possibly give?'" Mrs. Norris adds that "the trouble and expense of" such an adoption "to them, would be nothing compared with the benevolence of the action." The key word here is "benevolence" (4–5), one used on 15 occasions and twice in *MP*. The words "partly as a result of the influence of" David Hume "and other" 18th-century "moral philosophers" had "a great deal of cultural credibility" at the time Jane Austen was writing. "Aligned with charity, benevolence betokened distinct moral value and sensibility in those who professed to feel or exercise it" (Wiltshire, 642). In the case of Mrs. Norris, self-interest also has to be taken into consideration. A daughter offered her the opportunity of acquiring the child she never had, without the expense. Her sister and her husband, Sir Thomas and Lady Bertram, would see to that.

Sir Thomas does not grant ready assent; he weighs up the consequences of such an action: the expenses, the emotional implications, the "cruelty instead of kindness in taking" the child "from her family." Then there are the implications for his own family, on "his own four children—of his two sons—of cousins involved, &c." In England, marriage between cousins had been legal since the time of Henry VIII in the 1530s and 1540s, and such marriages are sympathetically treated in literature. In Jane Austen's own family there were cousin marriages. So perhaps Sir Thomas's reservations have a material foundation: Such a marriage would not in this instance produce a dowry or social connections.

Sir Thomas's objections are immediately countered by Mrs. Norris in the first direct speech of the novel. Highly intelligent, and not afraid to flatter where necessary, she compliments Sir Thomas on his caution before focusing on each of his objections. To provide for the child is to act appropriately, it is a matter of "propriety"—a word occurring 61 times in Jane Austen's work. Thirteen of these in *MP*: Again, with its implications of appropriate, correct social behavior, it acts as a key epithet in the novel.

Mrs. Norris is not unaware of her own motivations, telling Sir Thomas that she "should be the last person in the world to withhold my mite upon such an occasion." The word "mite" (5–6) is used only twice by Jane Austen, both instances being in *MP*, the other in the second book, chapter 13 (305). The noun conveys both a minute insect and something small and insignificant. It also recalls a passage in the New Testament in the "Book of Mark," chapter 12, verses 42–44. Here "there came a certain poor widow, and she threw in two mites, which make a farthing." Jesus then says unto his disciples, "Verily I say unto you, That this poor widow hath caste more in, than all they which have cast into the treasury." There is usually with Mrs. Norris a self-righteous, religious implication underlying her actions or sentiments. She adds, however, that she has "no children of [her] own," and appeals to her own husband's sense of justice, implying that he does not hold her lack of a child against her, although Mrs. Norris may well be implying the opposite.

Mrs. Norris tells Sir Thomas, "Give a girl an education, and introduce her properly into the world, and ten to one," appropriately she uses a gambling or betting metaphor, "but she has the means of settling well, without farther expense to any body." The girl "would" not be "so handsome as her cousins," but the "human probability," the odds are, that as "a niece of our's," being brought up by them, "under such very favourable circumstances," these "would get her a creditable establishment." In other words, being introduced "properly into the world," meeting through Sir Thomas and Lady Bertram the appropriate social connections, she would find a suitable husband. Mrs. Norris then tries to throw cold water on the possibility of a closer relationship developing between the girl and Sir Thomas's sons, Tom or Edmund. Of course, in the light of what subsequently occurs in the novel, Mrs. Norris's assertion of such a relationship being "morally impossible" or virtually impossible proves to be incorrect. She is not without an element of vulgarity, either. She tells Sir Thomas to "breed her up," or bring the adopted girl up almost like a young pheasant or young horse, "and she will never be more to either than a sister." How wrong she is, as the unfolding of the plot will reveal.

Sir Thomas's reply is conveyed in the seventh paragraph of the first chapter. Basically, he is in agreement with Mrs. Norris, although not inconsiderate of the long-term consequences, especially if the girl does not find a suitable match. Sir Thomas is aware of the serious consequences of what is being proposed: "it ought not to be lightly engaged in." He is willing "as circumstances may arise," if a suitable marriage is not found, "to secure . . . the provision of a gentlewoman"—that is, to ensure that the girl has a secure future even if she remains unmarried.

Mrs. Norris in her response again flatters Sir Thomas. She says that she "could never feel for this little girl the hundredth part of the regard I bear your own dear children, [an exaggeration], nor consider her, in any respect, so much my own," she "should hate [herself] if [she] were capable of neglecting her." She then proposes that the 10-year-old Fanny Price journey from Portsmouth to London, which in the "coach" or basic public transport without any frills, took approximately 10 hours. She would undertake a journey of around 72 miles, or 115 kilometers, alone. Then she would stay in London with a total stranger, with "Nanny," unknown to her, and Nanny's "cousin," also unknown to the 10-year-old girl. After London, there is another 70 miles or so to travel to Mansfield. Even where she is to stay in London is reduced, a "less economical rendezvous being accordingly substituted." Frugal, childless, she has "no real affection for her sister, it was impossible for her to aim it more than the credit of projecting and arranging so expensive a charity" as bringing up the young girl. She is concerned with "the credit," a word used 108 times in Jane Austen and 27 times in this novel. It is yet another instance of its author using a noun with financial and emotive implications. Mrs. Norris would gain "credit," the approval from others for her actions.

Mrs. Norris's "views," her plans, are "more fully explained" in the following paragraph in response to Lady Bertram's first spoken words in the novel, the practical "calm inquiry of 'Where shall the child come to first, sister, to you or to us?'" Mrs. Norris, the source of the idea of taking a child from the harassed Mrs. Price, finds reasons for not taking in the child: "the little girl's staying with them, at least as things then were, was quite out of the question." The immediate reason is that her husband's "indifferent state of health made it an impossibility." Her excuses are followed by Lady Bertram's direct, "Then she had better come to us," a sentiment quickly reinforced by Sir Thomas with "dignity. . . . 'Yes, let her home be in this house. We will endeavour to do our duty by her.'" He adds, "she will at least have the advantage of companions of her own age, and of a regular instructress."

Mrs. Norris continues to arrange matters even to the point of which room the girl should have. The three, Sir Thomas, Lady Bertram, and Mrs. Norris, consider what to do if "she will prove" not to be "a well-disposed girl." Sir Thomas, if this is the case, will not "continue her in the family." Sir Thomas anticipates, given the circumstances of her first 10 years, "gross ignorance, some meanness of opinion, and very distressing vulgarity of manner." Lady Bertram reveals a superficial side to her personality by saying, "I hope she will not tease my poor pug." Her major concern seems with her miniature bull dog. They further consider "how to preserve" in an appropriate manner the distinction in terms of social status between the Bertram daughters, and the girl: "how, without depressing her spirits too far, to make her remember that she is not a *Miss Bertram*. . . . Their rank, fortune, rights, and expectations, will always be different."

The opening chapter of this novel so preoccupied, as other Jane Austen novels, with "rank, fortune, rights, and expectations," concludes with Mrs. Price's reaction to the request conveyed by letter from Mrs. Norris that Sir Thomas and Lady Bertram will take one of the children. "Mrs. Price seemed rather surprised that a girl should be fixed on." In her reply she assures "them of her daughter's being a very well-disposed, good-humoured girl. . . . as somewhat delicate and puny." In the final sentence of the first paragraph, the author yet again, as she is to do frequently in *MP*, directly intrudes into the narrative. "Poor Woman! She probably thought a change of air might agree with many of her children."

The first chapter of *MP* moves from the introduction of character placed in the perspective of place, Mansfield Park, to the decision to take in a child from an impoverished environment into a privileged one. The consequences of irresponsible, individual conduct upon others and children are introduced. Human motivation in the case of Mrs. Norris, for instance, is exposed. In short, the main factors influencing the narrative thread, themes, and preoccupations of the novel are found in its opening chapter: the concern with wealth, status, and rank; motivation; the consequences of ill-considered actions; the impact of the environment on the individual human being; and the nature versus nurture motif.

Chapter 2

In the first chapter, the reader encounters Sir Thomas and Lady Bertram, the owner of a wealthy estate and home; Mrs. Norris, the sister of Lady Bertram; and Mrs. Price. She has made a foolish marriage to a drunken, indigent marine lieutenant and has eight children. Her marriage is the cause of her separation from the rest of her family. After a period of 11 years, she has reconnected with her estranged sisters as she is unable to cope with her growing family and is expecting her ninth child. The Bertrams are persuaded by Mrs. Norris to take in Mrs. Price's eldest daughter.

This daughter and her introduction into her new home and surroundings are the subject of the second chapter. The first paragraph relates that "the little girl performed her long journey in safety" and then focuses on Mrs. Norris, who met her. Mrs. Norris, ironically, gains "the credit" for "being foremost to welcome her." Interesting words in this opening sentence, all referring to Mrs. Norris's actions, are "regaled," "credit," "importance," "leading," and "recommending." The ambiguity of "credit," with its financial implications in addition to that of gaining recognition, has been noted. A word used only once in Jane Austen, unlike the frequently used "credit," is "regaled," meaning enjoyed and took delight, with the implication of "regal," relating to royalty or authority. Combined with words such as "importance," "leading," and "recommending," this creates a false perception of Mrs. Norris's real authority.

The second paragraph describes "Fanny Price" (12), whose name, according to a critic, "may derive from George Crabbe's *Parish Register* (1807), part II, where 'Fanny Price' is a virtuous and long-suffering young woman pursued by a rakish gentleman" (Johnson, 11 n. 1). She is very shy and diffident but is "received . . . very kindly" by Sir Thomas and Lady Bertram: The former has to work harder than the latter at this. Lady Bertram, "by the mere aid of a good-humoured smile, became immediately [to Fanny] the less awful of the two," or less frightening.

The third and fourth paragraph introduce the Bertram family and their reception of Fanny. There are two sons aged "seventeen and sixteen, and tall of their age, had all the grandeur of men in the eyes of their little cousin." There are two younger daughters, whose "confidence increasing from their cousin's total want of it . . . were soon able to take a full survey of her face and her frock in easy indifference." The family is described as "remarkable fine," or good. The girls are "forward of their age," with the preposition "of" meaning here "for." Their manner of presenting themselves and way of speaking is in contrast to the exceedingly shy Fanny—"there was in fact but two years between the youngest and Fanny." The reader learns the daughters' names and ages: "Julia Bertram was only twelve, and Maria but a year older." However, Fanny "was as unhappy as possible. Afraid of every body, ashamed of herself, and longing for the home she had left." This state is the consequence of many factors, including the behavior of Mrs. Norris, who "had been talking to her the whole way from Northampton," stressing "her wonderful good fortune," her "gratitude," and consequent "good behaviour." Her unhappiness is increased by the sense "of it being a wicked thing for her not to be happy." Further, the journey has tired her.

The lengthy final sentence of the fourth paragraph contains repetitions of "in vain" followed by "vain." This reinforces Fanny's plight and state, especially as the three adults are trying, but "in vain," to assist her. The three descriptive epithets of the manner in which they try to help Fanny highlight character. Sir Thomas is full of "well-meant condescensions." Mrs. Norris's help is characterized by "officious prognostications"—the sole instance in Jane Austen of the word "prognos-

tications," meaning foretelling, predicting. Lady Bertram tries other methods, the soft touch. She smiles and makes Fanny "sit on the sofa with herself and pug." Even "gooseberry tart" inducements are "in vain."

When Fanny has gone to bed, Mrs. Norris comments on the situation, emphasizing her strictures to Fanny on the way to Mansfield Park. She also implies a negative in Fanny's personality by deliberately attempting to be impersonal, preferring an impersonal phrase, "I wish there may not be a little sulkiness of temper" rather than "Fanny has a sulky temper." She adds that Fanny's "poor mother had a good deal" of that quality. Mrs. Norris's comments conclude with "there is moderation in all things," probably designed to impress Sir Thomas. He would be familiar with the Latin saying "*est modus in rebus,*" of which the words are a literal translation.

Fanny "required a longer time . . . than Mrs. Norris was inclined to allow, to reconcile" herself to the new environment and surroundings. The two younger girls begin to see that she lacks certain things such as many sashes, "had never learnt French," and toys. Fanny is "forlorn" and fearful. Fanny's reactions are conveyed in a sentence containing three clauses. "She was disheartened by Lady Bertram's silence, awed by Sir Thomas's grave looks, and quite overcome by Mrs. Norris's admonitions." The triple clause sentence gains its particular effect in its final word—the sole instance of the use of "admonition/s" in singular or plural form in Jane Austen's work. The first two sentences of this eighth paragraph present Fanny's perspective. A lengthy final sentence contains Fanny's views of Edmund and Miss Lee, who is the Bertram governess. In class terms and status, Miss Lee is nearest to Fanny. It is not without significance that Fanny's room is next to that of the lowest on the totem pole, the governess, usually in such homes treated as a servant.

Not only the people but the house itself in its "grandeur" reinforces Fanny's sense of alienation. She retreats "towards her own chamber to cry." In the drawing-room she is described "as seeming so desirably sensible of her peculiar good fortune." In other words, she seems aware or conscious of her particular "good fortune." Here there is a direct correlation of moral value, "good," with "fortune," fate, position, and economic well-being. After a week in this unhappy state, she is comforted "by her cousin Edmund, the youngest of the sons," who found Fanny "sitting crying on the attic stairs." The choice of situation, "The attic stairs," rather than, for instance, the "bedroom" stairs, adds to the pathos of the situation; she wishes to escape, not to be seen.

Edmund's first words to her convey sympathy: "My dear little cousin," rather than a peremptory "Cousin" or a less formal but stilted "My dear cousin." The introduction of "little" is ironic but kind and accurate. Through persistent questioning, Edmund elicits information from Fanny. Her first direct words in the novel "William did not like she should come away" refer to her eldest brother, Fanny's "constant companion and friend; her advocate with her mother." It will emerge in the narrative that Edmund will replace William in the role of Fanny's protector. Her first words convey her vulnerability through a now curious use of English: the use of a noun clause object following the verb "like" today being rarely used if at all. Edmund discovers that she lacks paper and is even lacking a trust that any letter she writes will be posted. Edmund reassures her: "it shall go with the other letters; and as your uncle will frank it, it will cost William nothing." Here Edmund is referring to a privilege of his father. As a member of parliament, Sir Thomas was able to post letters without payment.

Edmund's thoughtfulness and kindness is reinforced. He assists Fanny "with his penknife or his orthography," using his penknife to sharpen the tip of the quill pen when it becomes blunt. In addition to sending "his love to his cousin William," Edmund "sent him half a guinea under the seal." A "half a guinea" (12–16), or half a pound sterling, would represent an enormous sum of money to the young William Price. It was a thin, small gold coin "which could be hidden under the wax seal that Sir Thomas would use to close the sheets of the letter" (Wiltshire, 644). It is through such actions that Fanny and Edmund are drawn together, and "From this day Fanny grew more comfortable. She felt that she had a friend, and the kindness of her cousin Edmund gave her better spirits with every body else." Adaptable, even at the age of 10, Fanny quickly learns whom to trust and not to trust.

Sir Thomas and Mrs. Norris perceive that Fanny "showed a tractable disposition, and seemed likely to give them little trouble." The general consensus is that "Fanny could read, work, and write, but she had been taught nothing more." In other words, she is a product of her impoverished upbringing, brought up to sew, to do needlework, to make and mend clothes, to read and write. She, however, "cannot put the map of Europe together" (17–18). This refers to a teaching tool in which "maps broken into pieces, resembling jig-saw puzzles, were often used to teach children geography" (Wiltshire, 644–645). The Bertram girls demonstrate Fanny's apparent stupidity by telling their "Aunt" Norris that Fanny is unable to tell them how to reach Ireland and refers to the Isle of Wight, an island off the south English coast directly opposite Portsmouth, as "*the Island,* as if there were no other in the world." From Fanny's point of view, growing up in Portsmouth, the Isle of Wight would indeed be "the Island": The ignorance here is that of the Bertram girls in their lack of perspective and imagination. At Mansfield Park, Fanny's education and her interaction with Edmund illustrate *MP*'s preoccupation with the imagination rather than mere book learning. This kind of learning by rote is exemplified in the comment to Aunt Norris from the Bertram girls that it is a long time "since [they] used to repeat . . . the Roman emperors as low as Severus; besides a great deal of the Heathen Mythology, and all the Metals, semi-Metals, Planets, and distinguished philosophers." The references here are to common classroom textbooks used at the time from which facts were learned by rote.

Fanny's further "great want of genius and emulation," (18–19), or lack of "inherent ability, aptitude, and inclination for study and for developing the mind" (Phillipps, 24) is additionally illustrated by her apparent lack of a memory of and seeming disinclination "to learn either music or drawing." Mrs. Norris's subtle, and less than subtle, downgrading of Fanny in the minds of her young cousins complements their lack, according to the narrator, "of self-knowledge, generosity and humility. In every thing but disposition, they were admirably taught." The word "disposition" meaning state of mind or feelings toward another is used on 132 occasions in Jane Austen's work. Thirty-four of these instances are found in *MP*, in which the word is used more frequently than in any other of her works. Sir Thomas "did not know what was wanting," and Lady Bertram ignores her daughters' education.

The period of Fanny's growing up until she is 15 is conveyed in transitional paragraphs at the conclusion of the second chapter. She has transferred "her attachment to her former home" to Mansfield Park and is not unhappy, although "often mortified" by the young Bertram girls, Maria and Julia's treatment of her. The adjective "mortified" has here the sense of deep humiliation and embarrassment. Fanny is in these paragraphs the sole focus of attention. Lady Bertram "in consequence of a little ill-health, and a great deal of indolence," or sheer laziness, "gave up the house in town." Families such as the Bertrams were expected to have a London residence in addition to their home in the country. With the exception of Sir Thomas, who is a member of the House of Commons and consequently has to spend some time in London, the other Bertrams remains in the country, where they "continue to exercise their memories." This word is used on six occasions in Jane Austen's work, three of them in *MP*. "Memory" is used 45 times, nine of which are in *MP*. In this immediate context, the narrator is being ironic at the expense of the Bertram girls. Subsequently memory, and especially Fanny's remembrance of what is due to Sir Thomas, her memory of Portsmouth, of life at Mansfield Park, become significant—they act as moral touchstone for Fanny's actions.

Sir Thomas's function is clearly presented in chapter 2. His perceptions of his children are shown to be accurate. For instance, "his eldest son was careless and extravagant." It is his duty for his daughters' sake to "extend . . . respectable alliances" so that they can marry well socially and financially. On the other hand, Edmund, his younger son, due to "his strong good sense and uprightness of mind," all essential positive characteristics meeting Jane Austen's total approval, "bid most fairly for utility, honour, and happiness to himself and all his con-

nections." In short, Edmund's destiny is clear. "He was to be a clergyman," that is, the regular professional route for younger sons, university-educated, who would not inherit their father's title or estates.

Before going to sea, Fanny's brother William spends a week with his sister at Mansfield Park. Edmund's consideration during this visit cements their friendship. Edmund "never failed her" even when he moved from Mansfield Park to the great public school of Eton, where he was a boarder, and then to Oxford University. The final paragraph of the chapter reinforces Edmund's fidelity to Fanny while the rest of the family "kept [her] back." It is Edmund who "knew her to be clever, to have a quick apprehension as well as good sense and a fondness for reading." Miss Lee, the governess, "taught" Fanny French "and heard her read the daily portion of History." It was the custom to read on a daily basis a historical account focusing on patriotic deeds: Miss Lee's text is more than likely Oliver Goldsmith's two-volume *History of England*, published in 1764. It is, however, Edmund who "encouraged" Fanny's "taste, and corrected her judgment." The chapter concludes on a slightly humorous note. "In return for such services" as encouragement and ego boosting, Fanny "loved" Edmund "better than any body in the world except William; her heart was divided between the two" (19–22).

Chapter 3

The third chapter is concerned with change. Initially it focuses on the potential consequences for Fanny of "the first event of any importance in the family . . . the death of Mr. Norris." This occurred "when Fanny was about fifteen." It heralds change. The consequences of Mr. Norris's death are initially felt by his widow. She leaves "the parsonage, removed first to the park, and afterwards to a small house of Sir Thomas's in the village." Mrs. Norris's pragmatism, with its element of cynicism, is conveyed in the information that she "consoled herself for the loss of her husband by considering that she could do very well without him." Further, she would deal with "her reduction of income by the evident necessity of stricter economy."

The second paragraph explains that his death has consequences for other reasons. The Bertrams possess two "family-livings," that is, clergy positions that also are able to support a family. Initially, one of the livings "was hereafter for Edmund." However, the "extravagance" of Tom, the older brother, means that the Mansfield living has to be sold to pay for his debts. Sir Thomas is obviously placed in a difficult situation. He tells Tom directly: "You have robbed Edmund for ten, twenty, thirty years, perhaps for life, or more than half the income which ought to be his." In the future, "it may . . . be in [their] power . . . to procure [Edmund's] better preferment," in other words, through using connections to advance Edmund's church position and consequently give him an increase in income. However, instead of the Mansfield living being given to Edmund, Sir Thomas is forced to sell it to Dr. Grant, and Edmund will have to wait until Dr. Grant dies to obtain it with its additional income. Tom's irresponsibility is reflected in his finding positives in the situation. Tom's refusal seriously to face up to what he has done is also conveyed through his colloquial observation regarding Dr. Grant: "no, he was a short-neck'd, apoplectic sort of fellow, and, plied well with good things, would soon pop off."

Conscious of his responsibilities, Sir Thomas is also aware of the passing of his time. The seventh paragraph conveys important information concerning the subsequent narrative and the fate of the characters as seen through his lens. First, there has been "the change in Mrs. Norris's situation," although Fanny hasn't been living with her, "and the improvement in [Fanny's] age." Second, Sir Thomas has experienced "some recent losses on his West India Estate" (23–24). The actual losses are unspecified. His estate "could be losing money for several reasons; decreased crop production stemming from exhausted soil; increased competition from other sugar-producing islands; and/or increased production costs resulting from the abolition of the slave trade in 1807" (Johnson, 19). Third, there is "his eldest son's extravagance." Given these factors, "it became not undesirable to himself to be relieved from the expense of [Fanny's] support and the obligation of her future provision." The reasons are utilitarian, a result of economic loss rather than due to anything Fanny has done. At the end of the paragraph, Lady Bertram tells Fanny through a factual statement and then a question, potentially shattering information: "So, Fanny, you are going to leave us, and live with my sister. How shall you like it?" Fanny, however, "must come up [to Mansfield Park] and take on [Lady Bertram's] patterns all the same." That is, she will with temporary stitching "tack" onto the clothes patterns used in embroidery or patchwork. The dichotomy between Fanny's physical and emotional move in Lady Bertram's mind and her concern with trivia, the insignificant, is here well evinced.

Fanny's reaction is conveyed in a succinct paragraph. "The news was as disagreeable to Fanny as it had been unexpected. She had never received kindness from her aunt Norris, and could not love her." Fanny immediately turns to Edmund for counsel in the situation. He only sees positives, believing that his aunt's "love of money does not interfere" with the proposal. Edmund mistakenly believes that his aunt has changed her conduct and that "when [Fanny is] her only companion, [she] *must* be important to her." This produces a self-pitying lack of confidence response by Fanny. "I can never be important to any one," and she explains why, revealing a good deal of self-awareness: "my situation—my foolishness and awkwardness." This confession leads Edmund to reassure her of positive strengths: "good sense and a sweet temper" combined with "a grateful heart." To this Fanny reveals her attachment to Edmund and how much she needs him: "Oh! cousin, if I am to go away, I shall remember your goodness, to the last moment of my life."

Edmund is aware that at Mansfield Park, Fanny has not been given the opportunity to shine: "*Here,* there are too many whom you can hide behind." Edmund's analysis is that his aunt "is much better fitted . . . for having the charge of [Fanny] now." Once "she really interests herself" in someone, she will really help her. Fanny responds, "I cannot see things as you do," but defers to Edmund's mistaken perception of his aunt, as the reader will discover. She is only too aware that at Mansfield Park "I know I am of none, and yet I love the place so well." She is reminded by Edmund that she will still have access to Mansfield Park, to its "park and gardens." Change in her is illustrated through her change from fear to affection of her pony and riding.

Mrs. Norris's adroit avoidance of "taking" Fanny reveals her own manipulative cleverness and also Fanny's age: She is now "a girl of fifteen!" Mrs. Norris, however, manages to retain her servants and "will have six hundred a year." Relatively, this is a considerable sum for a widow such as Mrs. Norris, allowing her to maintain three servants, so consequently her attitude and behavior toward Fanny are both mean and cruel. She is concerned, pointing out to Lady Bertram, her sister, that "Sir Thomas's means will be rather straightened, if the Antigua estate is to make such poor returns." Antigua was one of the earliest British West Indian colonies. The island's economy was almost entirely focused in sugarcane cultivation. Jane Austen had family ties with Antigua. Her father acted as a trustee of an estate on Antigua belonging to James Langford Nibbs. In the later 18th century, sugar production profits declined, and from 1807 onward planters operated at a loss. This is perhaps why the mean but shrewd Mrs. Norris questions whether Sir Thomas will be able to keep her in the style to which she has been accustomed.

Lady Bertram's response, "Oh! *that* will soon be settled. Sir Thomas has been writing about it, I know," prepares readers for his imminent departure for Antigua. Sir Thomas "grew reconciled" to Mrs. Norris's refusal to allow Fanny to live with her. Mrs. Norris cleverly let Sir Thomas and Lady Bertram know "that whatever she possessed was designed for their family." As a consequence, "Fanny soon learnt how unnecessary had been her fears of a removal." Mrs. Norris moves to the White house and "the Grants arrived at the parsonage, and these events over, every thing at Mansfield went on for some time as usual."

Change, however, is indicated in seemingly insignificant detail. Dr. Grant, for instance, "was very fond of eating, and would have a good dinner every day." Mrs. Grant "gave her cook as high wages as they did at Mansfield Park." Such lavishness seems inappropriate. "A fine lady in a country parsonage was quite out of place," and Mrs. Norris is unable to ascertain the source of Mrs. Grant's

income. Lady Bertram, however, is less interested in economy than in Mrs. Grant's not "being handsome." Again, seemingly insignificant matters are juxtaposed with more serious ones. In the same paragraph as these opinions being expressed, the reader is told that in a year, "Sir Thomas found it expedient to go to Antigua himself, for the better arrangement of his affairs, and he took his eldest son with him in the hope of detaching him from some bad connections at home." He and Tom "left England with the probability of being" away a year.

From Sir Thomas's point of view, his concern is with "leaving his daughters to the direction of others at their present most interesting time of life." On the positive side, the trip may do his eldest son good. Mrs. Norris's "watchful attention," combined with "Edmund's judgment," he believes, make up for Lady Bertram's insufficiencies. From Lady Bertram's perspective, being an optimist, she is not "disturbed" as she thinks only of herself. His daughters do not see their father as an "object of love," as "he had never seemed the friend of their pleasures, and his absence was unhappily most welcome," the reason being that "they were relieved from all restraint." Fanny's emotions are mixed and involved with inviting her beloved brother William the following winter to visit "as soon as [his] squadron," the group of ships sailing together, return to England.

The chapter concludes with Fanny's being misperceived. Sir Thomas grants his permission for William's visit but reminds her that she "may be able to convince" her brother that the years they have spent apart "have not been spent on [Fanny's] side entirely without improvement." He unnecessarily adds, "I fear he must find his sister at sixteen in some respects too much like his sister at ten." Fanny responds by crying "bitterly over this reflection when her uncle was gone." Consequently, "her cousins, on seeing her with red eyes, set her down as a hypocrite" (24–33).

The third chapter documents many changes. Fanny has moved into young womanhood. Her dependence on Edmund and lack of confidence are revealed. Mrs. Norris displays her nastiness and adroitness. Sir Thomas shows himself to be responsible and thoughtful but at times harsh. The economic background upon which the well-being of Mansfield and its environs depends emerges. Individual folly, Tom's gambling, the death of Mr. Norris, problems far away in Antigua, all these have their impact on the characters of the story. Crucial themes of the novel emerge: time and change, whether they be natural or economic, and their impact on characters.

Chapter 4

Edmund quickly replaces Tom and Sir Thomas in arranging business affairs at Mansfield Park. The second paragraph of the chapter consists of a lengthy single sentence with subordinate clauses. Mrs. Norris had been "indulging in very dreadful fears, and trying to make Edmund participate them whenever she could get him alone." Here "participate," meaning to share them, is used as a transitive verb. Perhaps more interesting is the information concerning "the travellers' safe arrival in Antigua after a favourable voyage." The passing of time is conveyed rapidly: "The winter came and passed without their being called for." This is followed by economic information that has a primacy: "the accounts continued perfectly good." Consequently, the family is able to focus upon everyday matters, especially Mrs. Norris's activities "in promoting gaieties for her nieces . . . and looking about for their future husbands." Maria and Julia "were now fully established among the belles of the neighbourhood" and are chaperoned by Mrs. Norris, who has, however, "Mrs. Grant's wasteful doings to overlook," or to retain a jealous eye on. Mrs. Norris replaces Lady Bertram, who is "too indolent" to stir herself beyond her couch and her pugs (small, effete pedigree dogs). Mrs. Norris "desired nothing better than a post of such honourable representation," as she is representing the Bertram family and its social position.

The sixth paragraph moves in focus to Fanny, who is excluded from the social activities enjoyed by Maria and Julia and is left at Mansfield Park with Lady Bertram. Miss Lee has evidently fallen victim to the economies forced upon the family by the economic downturn and "left Mansfield." Consequently, Fanny "became every thing to Lady Bertram during the night of a ball or a party. She

talked to her, listened to her, read to her." Fanny's presence "was unspeakably welcome" to somebody like Lady Bertram whose mind "had seldom known a pause in its alarms or embarrassments" (34–35), meaning "perplexities or hesitations due to shyness or timidity" (Wiltshire, 648). Taking all things into consideration then, although William, her brother, had not returned to England, "it was a comfortable winter to" Fanny. She listened to accounts of the balls "and whom Edmund had danced with," although she "thought too lowly of her own situation to imagine she should ever be admitted to the same."

The seventh paragraph focuses on Fanny, the loss of "her valued friend the old grey poney," the coming of spring, and the conflict for power and authority at Mansfield Park among Mrs. Norris, Lady Bertram, and Edmund. The battle is fought over the replacement of Fanny's pony. Mrs. Norris "could not but consider it as absolutely unnecessary." It would place Fanny on equal footing with her cousins and prove to be an additional expense. Edmund, on the other hand, asserts, "Fanny must have a horse," and this position is taken too by Lady Bertram. Part of Edmund's reasoning is that a horse provides for Fanny "the immediate means of exercise, which he could not bear she should be without."

The eighth paragraph concentrates upon Edmund's exchange of one of his three horses to secure a horse that Fanny "might ride . . . the new mare proved a treasure." It soon replaces "the old grey poney" in Fanny's affections. The final two sentences of the paragraph focus on Fanny's sense of indebtedness toward Edmund for his kindness. The "horse" serves as a narrative link from spring, to summer, and then to September, when Sir Thomas was expected to return. Mrs. Norris had tried to delay the horse decision until the time of Sir Thomas's return, but Edmund's action prevented this delaying tactic. "Unfavourable circumstances had suddenly arisen at a moment when [Sir Thomas] was beginning to turn all his thoughts towards England." Sir Thomas's situation is one of "very great uncertainty." Instead of Sir Thomas returning, he sends his son Tom home instead. Mrs. Norris consequently "could not help feeling dreadful presentiments" and spends "the long evenings of autumn . . . haunted by these ideas, in the sad solitariness, of her cottage, as to be obliged to take daily refuge in the dining room of the park." Winter heralds more social engagements. The result is for Mrs. Norris to believe, in a passage of direct quotation of her thoughts, that if Sir Thomas did not return "it would be peculiarly consoling to see their dear Maria well married."

A fresh character is introduced, a Mr. Rushworth, "who had recently succeeded to one of the largest estates and finest places in the country." Here "places" refers either to a mansion or to a large country house and its surrounding estates. The grander the property and its accompanying grounds, the more social and political clout its owner has. An insincerity in the character of Mr. Rushworth is conveyed by the word "fancied" in the opening sentence of the 10th paragraph of the chapter: he "soon fancied himself in love," the word "fancied" here implying imagined. This paragraph too conveys the motives underlying the pressure to marry. Maria is not 21 years old. She "was beginning to think matrimony a duty." The marriage to Rushworth would provide her with "a larger income than her father's," for the marriage will "ensure her the house in town, which was now a prime object." There is nothing here about compatibility, let alone love. Maria is assisted by Mrs. Norris's schemes. She and Mrs. Rushworth, the mother of the intended prey, join forces to promote the match. Maria was "perfectly faultless—an angel," according to Mrs. Norris, and "Mr. Rushworth appeared precisely the young man to deserve and attach her." The operative word here is "appeared."

Their engagement is conveyed in a single-sentence paragraph. It follows the appropriate "dancing with each other at a proper number of balls." The engagement was regarded by the neighborhood and the families as one of "expediency." Somewhat curiously, the word "expediency" is used only nine times in Jane Austen's work. Sir Thomas's consent is received after "some months"—in this manner his distance yet importance is conveyed. The sole dissenting voice is that of Edmund: "he was not pleased that her happiness should centre in a large income; nor could he refrain from saying to himself, in Mr. Rushworth's company, 'If this man had

not twelve thousand a year, he would be a very stupid fellow'" (35–40). Such a sum "is an above average income for a wealthy member of the gentry." It makes Rushworth wealthier than Mr. Darcy in *Pride and Prejudice* who has £2,000 a year. Both men can readily purchase a house in London and in the country.

Sir Thomas's assent in the 14th paragraph also conveys underlying social reasons for matrimonial alliances. "It was a connection exactly of the right sort; in the same county, and the same interest." The word "interest" in this context probably refers to similar political parties, or grouping, that is, the Tories representing the landed gentry rather than the Whig businessmen centered in London or the commercial concerns of the East India Company and the slave traders. Sir Thomas's only condition helps to convey the passage of time. "The marriage should not take place before his return." His response is written in April, and he hopes to leave "Antigua before the end of the summer."

Fanny has just turned 18 when new characters appear in the shape of "the brother and sister of Mrs. Grant, a Mr. and Miss Crawford, the children of her mother by a second marriage." Again in Jane Austen, as for instance with Frank Churchill or Jane Fairfax in *Emma,* the sons and daughters of another marriage, or one where one or both of the parents have died, set up warning signals to the reader, especially if they have inherited wealth. In this instance, "they were young people of fortune. The son had a good estate in Norfolk" and "the daughter twenty thousand pounds." Such a relatively large sum means that she can expect to marry a wealthy man, as she brings a lot in her dowry. Both were brought up by "a brother of their father," and his wife.

The paragraph conveying information concerning the young Crawfords states how their lives already had been blighted by death, first of their parents, then in the case of Miss Crawford, the death of her protector, Mrs. Crawford: "it was the lady's death which now obliged her *protégée,* after some months further trial at her uncle's house, to find another home." The narrator, Jane Austen, then uses an adjective that occurs only on one other occasion in her work. "Admiral Crawford was a man of *vicious* [my italics] conduct, who chose, instead of retaining his niece, to bring his mistress under his roof." The forceful adjective "vicious" means nasty with the implication of physical and mental violence. So Miss Crawford goes to Mrs. Grant, her sister, childless and "very much in want of some variety at home." No information is given in this paragraph, the 14th of the chapter, about the actual characters of either of the young Crawfords: A hint is given at the end concerning the "young woman who had been mostly used to London" and the ways of the large city, as opposed to those of the country.

More is revealed about character in the next paragraph. "To any thing like a permanence of abode, or limitation of society, Henry Crawford had, unluckily, a great dislike." Clearly the circumstances of his upbringing have made him restless. On the other hand, his escorting his sister "with the utmost kindness into" Northamptonshire illustrates more positive characteristics. The bond between sister and brother is revealed in her attempt "to persuade her brother to settle with her at his own country-house" and his commitment "to fetch her away again at half an hour's notice, whenever she were weary of the place."

The viewpoint conveying the meeting of Mrs. Grant with the young Crawfords switches from Miss Crawford's to focus on Mrs. Grant's perspective and then back to Miss Crawford's. She "found a sister [Mrs. Grant] without preciseness or rusticity—". Here Jane Austen uses a word associated with Dr. Johnson, "preciseness" (40–41), meaning "exactness, rigid nicety" (Wiltshire, 649), whose manners are polished and not those of the country, or "rustic." Mrs. Grant's focus is on "appearance," the external and superficial: "Mary Crawford was remarkably pretty: Henry, though not handsome, had air and countenance." In other words, he has all the appearance of a gentleman. Mrs. Grant "was delighted with each, but Mary was her dearest object." She is beautiful whereas Mrs. Grant is not, and Mrs. Grant already plans to match Mary Crawford with Tom Bertram. Such a plan accords with Mary Crawford's wishes: "Matrimony was her object, provided she could marry well"—her

motives are clearly mercenary in spite of her wealth. Also she had "seen Mr. Bertram in town"—in London. Mrs. Grant also has plans for Henry Crawford: "you shall marry the youngest Miss Bertram."

Mary Crawford then tries to warn her sister Mrs. Grant about her brother: "If you can persuade Henry to marry, you must have the address of a French woman. All that English abilities can do, has been tried already" (42). The reference to "a French woman" is perhaps to character description in MARIA EDGEWORTH's novel *Ormond* of 1817. The hero re-meets "his childhood sweetheart," who in addition to marriage has "improved in coquetry by Parisian practice and power" (Wiltshire, 649). Mary Crawford does tell her sister that "very clever women," among others, "have taken to reason, coax, or trick" her brother Henry "into marrying" without success. "He is the most horrible flirt that can ever be imagined."

The chapter closes with a dialogue among Mrs. Grant, Henry, and Mary Crawford on the subject of marriage. Henry's precociousness is quickly established. He praises marriage, claims to be "of a cautious temper, and unwilling to risk [his] happiness in a hurry." He even transforms Milton's lines in the fifth book of *Paradise Lost* (1667). "Heaven's *last* best gift," which is used by the biblical Adam in *Genesis* to describe Eve as *the* ultimate gift from God, to his own ends, as a comment defending delaying a marriage. In the last line of the chapter, Mary Crawford's tendency toward materialism emerges. She believes that "every body [should] marry if they can do it properly," and she adds that "every body should marry as soon as they can do it to advantage." Her emphasis is upon her final noun—the benefit or gain.

Chapter 5

The opening two paragraphs of the chapter present the Miss Bertrams' perspective on Miss Crawford and then her brother. The engagement of Maria to Rushworth makes Henry Crawford "the property of Julia, of which Julia was fully aware, and before he had been at Mansfield a week, she [Julia] was quite ready to be fallen in love with." In other words, she was available. The third paragraph presents an interesting example of Jane Austen's use of the technique of free indirect speech. Maria's reflections are conveyed within direct speech marks: "There could be no harm in her liking an agreeable man—every body knew her situation—Mr. Crawford must take care of himself" (44). Here brief speeches appear to be conflated, or the words within the dashes represent a truncated version of a much longer sequence. In both instances, there is the effect of the mixture of "the dramatic quality of direct speech with the succinctness of the indirect form" (Page, 126).

This gives way to a dialogue between Henry and Mary Crawford as to which Bertram sister they prefer. Henry appears to prefer Julia, while noting that "An engaged woman is always more agreeable than a disengaged." She is safe, having obtained her object—marriage: "All is safe with a lady engaged; no harm can be done." Mary believes that Maria has affection for Rushworth. Her brother, although unstated, believes, as Edmund, that she has accepted Rushworth only for his financial worth. Addressing his sister and Mrs. Grant, Henry Crawford's cynicism, or disappointment from perhaps a sad personal experience, emerges when he says that marriage "is, of all transactions, the one in which people expect the most from others, and are least honest themselves." This elicits the comment, "Ah! You have been in a bad school for matrimony, in Hill Street" (45–46). The allusion is to Hill Street, a fashionable wealthy part of London in Mayfair, where the majority of grand houses were finished in 1745: "the address probably signals fast living and scandal" (Wiltshire, 650).

The reply acknowledges that marriage is frequently an object obtained by trickery: "speaking from my own observation, it [marriage] is a manoeuvring business." The gerund is even used as a title by Maria Edgeworth for her 1812 novel, *Manoeuvring*, in which a mother, rather in the manner of Mrs. Bennet in *Pride and Prejudice*, schemes to secure wealthy marriage partners for her children. Mrs. Grant reminds Mary that there are positives and negatives in the human situation: "if one scheme of happiness fails, human nature turns to another; if the first calculation is wrong, we make a second better; we find comfort somewhere." The reply is to "Honour your *esprit de corps*," or her

group spirit. This is just one of many uses of French expressions by the Crawfords and indicates their worldly attitude, their cosmopolitanism, in contrast to the sedate provincialism of Mansfield Park and its environs.

Mrs. Grant sees Mansfield as a "cure" for both Henry and Mary: "without wanting to be cured [they] were very willing to stay." Mr. Grant does not object to their visit. His reason is conveyed in a passage in which the author uses a present participle: "A *talking* [my emphasis] pretty young woman like Miss Crawford, is always pleasant society to an indolent, stay-at-home man." The narrator adds, "and Mr. Crawford's being his guest was an excuse for drinking claret wine every day."

Julia and Maria Bertram's "admiration" or attraction for Henry Crawford's physical features are much greater than Mary Crawford's for either of "the Mr. Bertrams," although "she *should* like the eldest [Tom] best," given his time in London and having "more liveliness and gallantry than Edmund." The fact that Tom will inherit the Mansfield estate and already has rights to it, "the reversion of Mansfield Park, and a baronetcy, did no harm." Mary's perspective of Mansfield Park differs from that of the nervous, frightened Fanny. Mary's opinion of Tom is determined by whether he will fit into her own plans. She is concerned with Tom's social status and appearance and the place reflected by "any collection of engravings of gentlemen's seats in the kingdom" and whether Mansfield Park will fit into these represented by, for instance, [William Angus's] *The Seats of the Nobility and Gentry. In a collection of the most interesting and picturesque views, engraved by W.A. With descriptions of each view* (London, 1779–86). She even begins "to interest herself a little about the horse which he [Tom] had to run at the B—races." This is a reference to the horse Tom probably owns and runs at the race courses such as Banbury, Bedford, or Buckingham, not too far from Northampton. At the time the popularity of horse racing was increased by the prince regent's love for it. Horse racing was a worldly activity noted for gambling, corruption, and bribery.

Shortly after the Crawfords' visit to the Grants, Tom is called away "for many weeks" to the races.

Mary, in spite of attempts to get her to the races, does not join him, and the narrative attention is transferred to Fanny. The narrator asks a rhetorical question, switching her focus from Mary to Fanny: "And Fanny, what was *she* [Jane Austen's emphasis] doing and thinking all this while? and what was *her* [author's emphasis] opinion of the new-comers?" The author here intervenes on Fanny's behalf, inviting her readers to be interested in Fanny's "opinion." At 18, she is still very reticent, acknowledges Mary Crawford's "beauty," and "still continued to think Mr. Crawford very plain, in spite of her two cousins[']" contrary view. Fanny's enigmatic quality puzzles Mary Crawford. "She [Fanny] dined at the parsonage, with the rest of you, which seemed like being *out* [author's emphasis]; and yet she says so little, that I can hardly suppose she *is*" [author's emphasis]. On one level the observations refers to a young woman's formally being presented socially as mature and marriageable—she has entered the marriage market. On another level, it reminds the reader of Fanny's ambivalent status at the Bertrams.

Edmund, who hardly sees Fanny objectively, responds, "My cousin is grown up. She has the age and sense of a woman, but the outs and not outs are beyond me." This elicits a lengthy reply from Mary containing information about young ladies who have not yet been introduced to society. They would wear "a close bonnet . . . looks very demure, and never says a word." The "close bonnet" is a hat having a stiff brim that projects around the face and is often tied with a ribbon under the chin to suggest modesty. Her reply is so elaborate concerning what is expected of young ladies that Edmund believes Mary is "quizzing," or teasing, him. This leads into a conversation of a young lady, a Miss Anderson and her brother, who live in a very fashionable part of London, Baker Street. Before she was "out," she would hardly speak. After she was "out," she "stared" Mary Crawford "out of countenance," or embarrassed her by her own sudden extroverted behavior.

A conversation follows on the upbringing of young women. Edmund emphasizes "motives of vanity" and "real modesty." An instance is given from a recent visit to Ramsgate in Kent, a resort on

the south coast and its just built (in 1795) Albion Place, a fashionable wealthy square. Attention was incorrectly given to the youngest daughter "who was not *out*" [Jane Austen's emphasis], and" consequently Edmund "had most excessively offended the eldest." He has "never" been forgiven. At the end of the chapter, Mary Crawford asks Edmund whether Fanny Price goes "to balls? Does she dine out every where, as well as at" the Grants'? Edmund's reply of "No" produces Mary Crawford's assertive, "Miss Price is *not* [Jane Austen's emphasis] out" (47–51).

Chapter 6

An opening paragraph presents affairs largely through Mary Crawford's eyes. Tom Bertram has "set off for—", an unstated place, probably the races. She remains at the Grants', but "almost daily" sees the Bertrams. Rushworth now makes "his appearance at Mansfield for the first time since the Crawfords' arrival" (52), and he mentions his estate at Sotherton. Discussion of Sotherton and its need for repair brings out the conflict between Dr. Grant and Mrs. Norris, who "were seldom good friends; their acquaintance had begun in dilapidations, and their habits were totally dissimilar." Here there is a pun on "dilapidations" (55), which means decay and also the sums levied to repair damage to church property and possessions during an incumbency. Naturally the stingy Mrs. Norris would not have allowed her husband to make even little if any repairs during their time in church property.

The conversation between the characters during Rushworth's first visit to Mansfield Park centers on Sotherton and serves to reveal character. Fanny, for instance, who has been hitherto silent, "attentively listening," is forced to speak, although "in a low voice," when the subject of tree cutting on a large scale is introduced. "Fanny who was sitting on the other side of Edmund, exactly opposite Miss Crawford" whispers to Edmund, "Cut down an avenue! What a pity! Does not it make you think of Cowper? 'Ye fallen avenues, once more I mourn your fate unmerited'" (56). Fanny is citing from one of Jane Austen's favorite poems, WILLIAM COWPER's *The Task* (i. 338–339). In these lines the poet compares a walk of trees with the arched roof of a Gothic cathedral. In chapter 8 as they enter Rushworth's estate at Sotherton, they see that the avenue "is oak entirely" (83). So Fanny's regret reveals not only her lament for the destruction of the past but patriotism and feeling for those such as her brother who are serving in the war against Napoleon. Oak was a symbol of England as a nation and was used as an important element in shipbuilding.

Edmund's description of Sotherton and its history attracts Mary Crawford, who "said to herself, 'He is a well bred man; he makes the best of it,'" and Fanny expresses the wish to visit Sotherton. This leads Mary Crawford to describe a summer visit three years previously to "a cottage at Twickenham," an increasingly fashionable village approximately 10 miles to the southwest of London on the banks of the river Thames. The location of the poet ALEXANDER POPE's (1688–1744) residence, during the early years of the 19th century, more and more elegant riverside villas such as the house of the painter J. M. W. Turner (1775–1851), were being built there. However, her uncle, the admiral's cottage needed "to be improved" (56–57). In a similar fashion, Rushworth believes that Sotherton needs "improvement" (53), or in other words modernizing or bringing up to date at the hands of an "improver" (52). Mary Crawford notes that "for three months we were all dirt and confusion, without a gravel walk to step on, or a bench fit for use." Her strictures "did not suit [Edmund's] sense of propriety, and he was silenced," although "he was much disposed to admire" Miss Crawford.

Mary informs Edmund and Fanny that she has "tidings of my [her] harp at last" (57). Such an instrument as the harp had become very fashionable, especially after 1810, when Sebastien Erard patented a double-action harp. Mary tells Edmund at length about the difficulties of finding suitable transportation in the country. For one thing, she is avoiding "Dr. Grant's bailiff," or farm manager. Edmund explains that the farmers require their horses and carts for their hay making. Mary Crawford replies, "I shall understand all your ways in time; but coming down with the true London maxim, that every thing is to be got with money, I

was a little embarrassed at first by the sturdy independence of your country customs."

Mary's reply invites a contrast between London values and those of the country. Her "true London maxim, that every thing is to be got with money," (58) may well have reminded some of Jane Austen's readers of a passage in Samuel Johnson's *Adventurer*: "We who have lived long amidst the convenience of a town immensely populous, have scarce an idea of a place, where desire cannot be gratified by money" (67: June 26, 1753). Mary "was a little embarrassed at first," or puzzled "by the sturdy independence of your country customs." Her tone remains high-handed and patronizing. She seems unable to understand that "in harvest, it must be quite out of their [the farmers'] power to spare a horse." In other words, the rural economy depends on the horse and its absolute usefulness during the harvest. The horse needs the grass to feed and the farmers need grass for their carts. Mary does not realize that in the country money depends on hard labor on the land, rather than in the town, where money is to be spent. Although she proves to be a fine musician on the harp, the harp and music are luxuries.

Mary then turns her thoughts to letter writing. She complains that her brother, "who loves me, consults me, confides in me . . . has never yet turned the page in a letter." This leads Fanny to remark that when brothers "are at a distance from all their family . . . they can write long letters." She assumes that her audience is aware that a 1795 parliamentary act gave ordinary seamen permission to send single letters for the price of a single penny, which was paid in advance. These letters had to be countersigned by the commanding officer. Mary confesses to being acquainted with admirals but to "know very little of the inferior ranks." Her negative attitude to the naval profession forces Edmund to change the topic of their conversation "to the harp."

Jane Austen's narrative focus of attention then moves from Mary, Edmund, and Fanny to Mrs. Grant, Julia Bertram, and Henry Crawford. Mrs. Grant asks Henry about improvements on his Everingham estate. She observes, "Everingham as it *used* [Jane Austen's emphasis] to be was perfect in my estimation; such a happy fall of ground, and such timber! What would not I give to see it again!" Here "timber" is a reminder that existing standing trees represent real wealth. They can always at some future time be cut down and made into income when the timber, the wood, is sold for ship and house construction. Henry, however, points out that he "had not been of age three months before Everingham was all that it is now. My plan was laid at Westminster—a little altered perhaps at Cambridge, and at one and twenty executed." Westminster School in London was mostly fee-paying and attracted the sons of wealthy, middle-class families. Wickham in *Pride and Prejudice* and Henry both go to Cambridge University, whereas Edmund, in common with Jane Austen's father and James and Henry, her brothers, studied as undergraduates at Oxford.

Crawford is urged to give Rushworth the benefit of his experience. Mrs. Norris naturally plans the trip. She adds, "Edmund can go on horseback, you know, sister, and Fanny will stay at home with you," that is, Lady Bertram. The distinction between "can" and "will" reveals Mrs. Norris's sense that she can only suggest to Edmund, whereas she can order and intimidate Fanny. In the last paragraph of chapter 6, "every one concerned in the going, was forward in expressing their ready concurrence, excepting Edmund, who heard it all, and said nothing" (58–62).

In this chapter character is revealed against a backdrop of rural change. In the first paragraph of the chapter, seating at the Bertram dining table is a reflection of social status. As the chief guest, Rushworth sits at the top of the table with Lady Bertram, the hostess. Maria sits next to her fiancé, Rushworth, and Edmund sits next to Maria. Mary's "chosen place near the bottom of the table" is facing Edmund, whereas Fanny, who isn't mentioned having the least prestige and social position, sat at the foot of the table.

Before arriving at Mansfield Park, Rushworth visited "a friend . . . and that friend [had] recently had his grounds laid out by an improver." This is a reference to a landscape designer who was hired to make large-scale changes to the layout of a country house and its surroundings. One of Jane Austen's central preoccupations in *Mansfield Park* is with improvement, either on a superficial level or a much deeper, personal level. There were different schools and kinds of "improvement." In this chapter, "Mr. Repton" is mentioned (52–53). HUMPHRY REPTON was perhaps the most fashionable of landscape improvers. He worked on Stoneleigh Abbey, the home of Jane Austen's cousin Thomas Leigh. In chapter 6 Edmund voices a more conservative view to these changes, stating a preference for "an inferior degree of beauty, of my choice, and acquired progressively" (56). Jane Austen probably agreed with him. In HENRY AUSTEN's Biographical Notice, she was "enamoured of Gilpin on the Picturesque" from a young age (140–141). She was an admirer of the Reverend WILLIAM GILPIN, who advocated "irregularity and artificial intervention to shape the landscape" (Stabler, 398).

Repton's fees were high: "His terms are five guineas a day." A guinea was worth £1. 1s. A few paragraphs later there is a reference to "a moor park," or "a good apricot." Owing to the climatic conditions, these were very difficult to grow until successfully done so by Sir William Temple (1628–99). He spent his honeymoon at Moor Park in Hertfordshire in 1655. In 1760, the admiral of the fleet, Lord Anson, commissioned the landscape improver Capability Brown (1716–83) to improve Moor Park, and Anson introduced a new apricot strain, "a moor park" (54: Stabler, 399, n. 43).

Lady Bertram mentions another 18th-century development when she refers to "a shrubbery." The shrubbery developed in the middle of the century and provided seats for "the comfort of ladies in general" in the garden. Mr. Rushworth mentions "a good seven hundred . . . water meadows." In other words, he has 700 acres and meadows on which at times a stream washes over them. He tells Lady Bertram "that Repton, or any body of that sort, would certainly have the avenue at Sotherton down." For Capability Brown, Repton, and other improvers, the view from and toward the house had to be uninterrupted. Sotherton is an old edifice, "the house was built in Elizabeth's time," that is, during the reign of Elizabeth I (1558–1603). It has "a stream, which," Mary Crawford comments, "might be made a good deal of" (55–56). Improvers such as Repton and others frequently dammed and widened a stream in front of the house. For instance, at Pemberley, in *Pride and Prejudice* "a stream of some natural importance was swelled into greater" (245).

Following Fanny's revelation that her brother is at sea, Mary Crawford asserts, "In the King's service of course." Her assumption is that William serves in the Royal Navy, which may well be the avenue to fame or wealth (see PERSUASION), rather than the merchant service, which offered no such opportunities. Fanny refers to "the foreign stations", William "had been on." These are the overseas ports where his ship docked for repairs and was supplied with provisions. Such visits may well last a few weeks. Mary mentions "Post captain," or captains distinguished from the inferior commander of a small ship. Mary is aware of "their bickerings and jealousies," as they frequently went to law concerning prize money. She then observes, "Of *Rears*, and *Vices* [Jane Austen's emphasis], I saw enough. Now, do not be suspecting me of a pun, I entreat" (60). This remark and the pun has led to a good deal of critical discussion. Earlier, in chapter 4, there has been mention of her uncle's "vicious conduct" (41), and subsequently in the novel he is revealed to be an adulterer. Certainly her comment, whether she is aware of it or not, suggests that "she is referring to the Navy's reputation for sodomy, or less scandalously, to large bottoms and general bad behaviour" (Stabler, 400 n. 48). Edmund in response felt "grave" (60) rather than shocked. Wiltshire notes that "it is inconceivable, given the proprieties of the period, that, consciously [Jane Austen] would introduce such a subject into her text" (657).

Chapter 7

This is the first chapter in the novel to open with a sustained conversation, a discussion between Edmund and Fanny. Edmund agrees with Fanny concerning Mary Crawford's "impropriety in making . . . public" her negative observations relating to her uncle the admiral. In spite of her defects, Edmund regards Mary Crawford as "perfectly feminine." Authorial narrative then takes over. Although Edmund, "having formed [Fanny's] mind and gained her affections, he had a good chance

of her thinking like him." In other words, he has heavily influenced Fanny, but "there began now to be some danger of dissimilarity, for he was," the reader is told, "in a line of admiration of Miss Crawford, which might lead him where Fanny could not follow." The verb "might" here is interesting. Jane Austen, as narrator, does not use the more definite "will," preferring to leave the situation open. She adds, "Miss Crawford's attractions did not lessen. The harp arrived, and rather added to her beauty, wit, and good humour" (63–64). The perspective has shifted imperceptibly to Edmund's. The choice of the harp as musical instrument is suggestive, as the female performer is able to show her upper body and arms and, to quote from Sir Walter Scott's *Marmion* (1809), "Ever her bosom's rise and fall | Was plainer given to view" (canto 5).

The opening three sentences of the paragraph beginning "A young woman, pretty, lively, with a harp as elegant as herself," serve to place Mary Crawford among the background of the Grant parsonage. Nature in the form of "the rich foliage of summer" and the harp enrapture Edmund and reveal his vulnerability to Mary's superficial charms. "Elegant" associates the musical instrument with its performer and further alludes to the harp manufacturer Erard's decorations. In short, "the season, the scene, the air, were all favourable to tenderness and sentiment," also "Mrs. Grant and her tambour frame were not without their use." A "tambour frame" is a round-shaped frame consisting of a hoop fitting into another hoop. Across this cloth is stretched to make needlework easier. In other words, while Mrs. Grant is otherwise occupied, Edmund is able, seemingly unnoticed, after a week "to be a good deal in love." The perspective then transfers to Mary Crawford and her view of Edmund.

Mary's fickleness is conveyed in the last sentence of the paragraph: Its staccato effect is noticeable. "She did not think very much about it, however; he pleased her for the present; she liked to have him near her; it was enough." The next paragraph begins from Fanny's perspective. Inverted auxiliary verb order helps to convey her unease: "She would gladly have been there too [at the Grants'], *might she have gone* in uninvited" [my emphasis].

Fanny "scrupled to point out her own remarks" to Edmund. She is hurt, however, by his offering Mary the horse he bought for Fanny to ride and she is left with Lady Bertram while the others go riding. Mary Crawford "made her first essay," her initial riding attempt, "with great credit." Her "enjoyment of riding was such that she did not know how to leave off." To avoid Mrs. Norris, Fanny "look[s] down to the park, [to] command a view of the parsonage and all its demesnes, gently rising beyond the village road; and in Dr. Grant's meadow" to see the riders. The "demesnes" refers to the land adjacent to the parsonage and its property farmed by Dr. Grant. What she sees isolates her. She is excluded from "the sound of merriment." Her jealousy and disapproval, plus sense of alienation, is reinforced when she views Edmund assisting Mary onto the horse. Physical contact—he takes Mary's hand—adds to Fanny's unhappiness: "she saw it, or the imagination supplied what the eye could not reach" (65–67). The description echoes Cowper's melancholy line in *The Task*: "I gazed myself creating what I saw" (book 6, line 290). The final section of the last sentence of the paragraph reinforces a sense of pathos and self-pity: "if she were forgotten the poor mare should be remembered."

Once they have returned, Fanny then has the opportunity to ride, to exercise. Even then she has to watch "the others . . . walking down the hill together to the village." She hears "her attendant" praise Mary Crawford's riding skills: "I never *see* one sit a horse better . . . Lord bless me! how you *did tremble* when Sir Thomas first had you put on!" (67–69: my emphasis). Following further praise of Mary Crawford's horsemanship and the comment "that good horsemanship has a great deal to do with the mind," contrasting Fanny's inertia and withdrawn personality with Mary's extrovert performance, Edmund displays some interest in Fanny. He asks her "whether she meant to ride the next day." She replies that she does not know as Edmund may "want the mare." Edmund's reply shows that Fanny is not his first consideration: "Miss Crawford would be glad to have" the mare "for a longer time—for a whole morning in short. She has a great desire to get as far as Mansfield common." Fanny accedes to his wishes and is con-

sequently unable to ride for "four fine mornings" until Maria Bertram is excluded and Rushworth is absent, putting Maria into a "sullen" state and one that "throw[s] as great a gloom as possible over . . . dinner and desert." Edmund and Julia then return from their ride with Mary Crawford, and Edmund asks "But where is Fanny?" Her response receives a "scolding" from Mrs. Norris, who tells Fanny, "If you have no work of your own, I can supply you from the poor basket." In other words, Fanny, rather than Maria and Julia, can use the calico, the cheap, long-lasting Indian cotton, to make clothes for the poor of the parish.

Mrs. Norris's strictures arouse even Julia's sympathies, and Edmund asks Fanny rhetorically, "I am sure you have the headach?" While the others rode, neither Fanny, her tormentor Mrs. Norris, Lady Bertram, nor Maria has stayed at home. "Fanny cut the roses . . . It was shady enough in the alcove." The alcove was the summer-house, or flower garden. Mrs. Norris subsequently suggests that her sister Lady Bertram "let [Fanny] have [her] aromatic vinegar" for her headach. Edmund's feelings for Fanny reemerge in his agitated "What! . . . has she [Fanny] been walking as well as cutting roses; walking across the hot park to your house [Mrs. Norris's], and doing it twice, ma'am?—No wonder her head aches." Lady Bertram replies that "when the roses were gathered your [Edmund's] aunt wished to have them" in order that they could be dried and subsequently used as an air freshener.

It is revealed that Fanny has been distracted, for instance, she "forgot to lock the door of the room and bring away the key, so she was obliged to go again." Edmund regards this as "a very ill-managed business" and wonders why a servant could not "be employed on such an errand!" Mrs. Norris claims that she "had promised John Groom"—a generic name for a groom or servant—to write a letter for him. She argues that the distance, according to her, of Mansfield Park from her house, is "not much above a quarter of a mile," so consequently what has occurred "was not unreasonable to ask." This reveals that Mrs. Norris is not averse to manipulating the "truth" for her own purposes. As Mrs. Norris is in the village, it is farther than the parsonage from

Mansfield Park, and certainly more than "a quarter of a mile," more likely three-quarters of a mile.

Edmund wishes that "Fanny had half" Mrs. Norris's "strength." Mrs. Norris points out that if Fanny exercised more, she "would not be knocked up so soon," or exhausted. Fanny has "*being stooping* [my emphasis] among the roses"—her activity is described through the use of the expanded present participle. In so doing, Fanny "caught the headach"—another interesting usage, as today headaches are not "caught"! Lady Bertram admits to not being able to assist Fanny, as she was too preoccupied with the welfare of her pet dog, "Pug." Edmund's remedy is to bring Fanny "a glass of Madeira," a very sweet Portuguese white wine.

The final two paragraphs of the chapter focus on Edmund and then Fanny. Edmund is "vexed," and "angry with himself." He feels "ashamed"—an important word in Jane Austen's vocabulary, conveying the strong sense that a wrong has occurred. He "very seriously resolved . . . that it should never happen again." The three-sentence final paragraph moves from Fanny going "to bed with her heart as full as on the first evening of her arrival at" Mansfield Park, through her "feeling neglected," to her using the sofa as a retreat so that "the pain of her mind had been much beyond that in her head" to an awareness of "Edmund's kindness." This has made for "the sudden change" in her. At the start of the paragraph "her heart [is] as full," at its end, "the pain of her mind" seems external to her "head." The workings of the "mind," the "head" and the "heart" are areas explored through the novel in which Edmund's "love" for Mary Crawford is revealed as ephemeral in contrast to his real feelings for Fanny (70–74).

Chapter 8

The recommencement of "Fanny's rides" is briefly described in the opening paragraph, as is Mr. Rushworth's visit to Mansfield Park and the "properest" way for him to arrange a visit to his home at Sotherton. In the next paragraph, Mrs. Rushworth tries to persuade "Lady Bertram to be of the party" to visit Sotherton. Mrs. Norris considers that the journey of "ten miles there, and ten back" will "be too much for [her] sister." Although Mrs. Rush-

worth "should have been extremely happy to have seen" Miss Price too, Mrs. Norris asserts that "Lady Bertram could not possibly spare" Fanny. Lady Bertram assents to this: "I cannot do without Fanny." Edmund, on his return, learns of the plans and suggests that they use the family carriage for the planned visit. Julia objects: "go box'd up three in a post-chaise in this weather, when we may have seats in a barouche!" (75–77). Her comment is a marker of wealth. She compares her mother's carriage with the post chaise. To own a carriage "required an income of £800–£1,000 a year and the ownership of this mode of transport was a crucial indicator of wealth" (Stabler, 401 n. 61). Julia's objection concerning the discomfort of using the post chaise may also have something to do with her wish to sit next to Henry Crawford.

The discussion as to the mode of transportation to Sotherton continues for some time. Mrs. Norris's overfamiliarity with her servants is illustrated in her comment: "between ourselves, coachman is not very fond of the roads between this and Sotherton." Here the definite article "the" is dropped before "coachman." She follows this with the remark "and you know *one should* not *like* to have dear Sir Thomas when he comes home find all the varnish scratched off" [my emphasis]. This is an interesting example of the use of "should" where today "would" would be used. Here the indefinite pronoun "one" is the equivalent of "I." They settle on the "barouche box," and, as Edmund points out, "there can be no objection then" to Fanny's accompanying them as there will be "room for her." Edmund counters Mrs. Norris's and his mother's objections by saying that he will remain at home especially as "Fanny has a great desire to see Sotherton." Mrs. Norris still protests: She "had no affection for Fanny, and no wish of procuring her pleasure at any time." Further, she still opposes Edmund on this matter as she has already made the arrangements. Edmund however has already informed Mrs. Rushworth that Fanny "would probably be of the party."

A two-sentence paragraph describes Fanny's gratitude when she hears of the plan. On the one hand, "she felt Edmund's kindness with all, and more than all, the sensibility which he, unsuspicious of her fond attachment, could be aware of."

On the other hand, "her own satisfaction in seeing Sotherton would be nothing without him." Mrs. Grant offers herself as a companion to Lady Bertram, so Edmund is able to join the Sotherton party. Wednesday, the day for the planned visit, is a "fine" day. As is not unusual in Jane Austen, seemingly small matters of precedence occur. In this instance, who is to occupy "the envied seat" in the barouche. Mrs. Grant decides that Julia should drive with Henry, thus making a "Happy Julia!" and an "Unhappy Maria!" The author also enjoys comic detail. The carriage departs to "the barking of pug in his mistress's arms."

The 10-mile drive is initially viewed through Fanny's lens. It "was through a pleasant country." Here *country* means countryside. Fanny is experiencing "all that was new," and in keeping with her character and situation: "her own thoughts and reflections were habitually her best companions." Her appreciation for the landscape and setting only needed "Edmund to speak to of what she felt." The one thing she and Mary Crawford, "who sat by her," share is their mutual regard for Edmund. Fanny's empathy for nature is contrasted with Mary's lack of concern for "nature, inanimate nature." Fanny's "attention" on the other hand, "was all for men and women." Mary's focus is "for the light and lively." Here, as in other passages, the narrator clearly indicates her preference for one character, in this instance Fanny, over the other, Mary.

Maria has other concerns. The "conversation and merriment" between Julia and Henry Crawford is an offence to "her own sense of propriety." However, at the approach to Sotherton "it was better for" Maria, "who might be said to have two strings to her bow," or in other words, "she had Rushworth-feelings, and Crawford-feelings." The nearer to Sotherton they get, the more pronounced are her "Rushworth-feelings." On the other hand, "it was a pleasure to increase with their approach to the capital freehold mansion, and ancient manorial residence of the family, with all its rights of Court-Leet and Court-Baron." The references here need explaining. The "capital freehold mansion" means that Rushworth's family own the property and can do what they like with it. The "mansion"

and the "ancient manorial residence" do not really relate to size or luxuriousness but to the property's status. It has been in the family for generations. This "ancient" ancestral element is emphasized in the allusion to the "Court-Leet," the last word meaning law, which gave the owner priority as the chief landowner and judge of the surrounding area. In short, these descriptions stress just how much power Rushworth can exercise through the ownership of Sotherton.

As they approach Sotherton "no more rough road[s]" are encountered as Rushworth "has made it since he succeeded to the estate"—that is, the road has been tarred and sealed. "Alms-houses" are indicated: These are cottages or small houses provided by the local landowner, such as Rushworth for the poor and indigent of the neighborhood. They also "are coming to the lodge gates." These were common to 18th-century and earlier country houses and were placed in the front of the drive to the house. Alongside them would be a house lodging the gatekeeper in charge of them.

A running commentary (probably on the part of Rushworth's fiancée, Maria, although the speaker is not clearly identified) as the party approach Sotherton observes that in the village, the "cottages are really a disgrace." Mrs. Norris is "all delight and volubility." Fanny is so excited by the new surroundings that she asks questions: "Where is the avenue?" In the final single-sentence paragraph, Maria is able to "speak with decided information of what she had known nothing about." When Rushworth asks "her opinion . . . her spirits were in as happy a flutter as vanity and pride could furnish" (77–83). Such is the effect of money and property upon a human being such as Maria. The consequences of her "vanity and pride" will be revealed subsequently in the narrative.

Chapter 9

The party visit Sotherton House and are shown around it by Mrs. Rushworth. She is very proud of its history. They go into what was the private chapel, where Mary Crawford speaks disparagingly of clergymen without being aware that Edmund intends to enter holy orders. The party then divides into three groups: Edmund, Mary, and Fanny; Mr. Rushworth and Henry; Mrs. Rushworth, Mrs. Norris, and Julia. Mary, when they walk in "the wilderness," expresses to Edmund her "surprise" at his choosing to be a clergyman for a profession. For Mary "a clergyman is nothing." Edmund, on the other hand, tries to persuade her of the importance of a clergyman. He "has the charge of all that is of the first importance to mankind, individually or collectively considered, temporally and eternally . . . the guardianship of religion and morals." Edmund adds, "No one here can call the *office* nothing" [Jane Austen's emphasis]. Fanny has his approval and empathizes with Edmund's sense of the importance of his chosen profession. Mary Crawford is less convinced, saying to Edmund: "Come, do change your mind. It is not too late. Go into the law" (90–93). During the walk, Fanny becomes tired; realizing this, Edmund takes her arm. She is left in the shade seated on a bench while Edmund and Mary continue their walk.

In the opening paragraph the visitors enter "into the appointed dining-parlour, where a collation was prepared with abundance and elegance." The word "collation" is used three times in Jane Austen's work and refers to a meal usually of cold meats and some delicacies. Also in the same paragraph, in a passage bordering on indirect speech, Rushworth is reported as asking "How would Mr. Crawford like, in what manner would he choose, to take a survey of the grounds?—Mr. Rushworth mentioned his curricle," or his light two-wheeled carriage carrying only two people. Instead, Mrs. Rushworth in the second paragraph proposed taking also "the chaise," or the family carriage. This suggestion is not well received, as Crawford will be unable to ride in it. Mrs. Rushworth then proposes "shewing the house," which "was more acceptable." In other words, in the manner of Mrs. Reynolds showing Elizabeth Bennet and the Gardiners around Pemberley in *Pride and Prejudice*, they too would be given the grand tour of the house.

In the third paragraph, they see rooms "amply furnished in the taste of fifty years back, with shining floors, solid mahogany, rich damask, marble, gilding and carving." Mahogany, imported from the southern colonies of North America and Cuba, became fashionable between 1725 and 1750. Carv-

ings were popular for interiors during the late 17th century. This suggests that Sotherton House is a mixture of antiquated architectural styles. Further, the narrator says, "Of pictures there were abundance, and some few good." Here the use of the plural "were" is curious.

In this third paragraph, Mrs. Rushworth "addressed herself chiefly to" Mary Crawford and Fanny, "to whom every thing was almost as interesting as it was new." Mary Crawford, on the other hand, "had seen scores of great houses." Fanny "attended with unaffected earnestness to all that Mrs. Rushworth could relate" of the past history of Sotherton, of "regal visits and loyal efforts." This suggests that Sotherton is based on Stoneleigh Abbey in Warwickshire, which was owned by the Leigh family, to whom Jane Austen's mother was related. The family had remained loyal to Charles I during the English Civil War and in 1642 sheltered him. Certainly Fanny learns by listening intently to what Mrs. Rushworth relates of the past of Sotherton House.

The west front has "tall iron palisades," or a fence consisting of iron stakes. Its many rooms "could be supposed to be of any other use than to contribute to the window tax" (84–85). In a letter dated August 13, 1806, Jane Austen's mother noted that the new west wing built in the early 18th century of Stoneleigh, housing its chapel, had "45 windows in front" (Le Faye, *Family Record*: 157). Historically, the window tax was initially introduced in 1696, and during the Napoleonic Wars was considerably increased. It was based on the numbers of glass windows calculated on each property. Fanny imagines "a mere, spacious, oblong room, fitted up for the purpose of devotion"— exactly as the Stoneleigh chapel is in reality. She is disappointed, telling Edmund, "Here are no aisles, no arches, no inscriptions, no banners. No banners, cousin, to be 'blown by the night wind of Heaven?' No signs that 'a Scottish monarch sleeps below.'" She is citing lines from the description of Melrose Abbey in the second canto of Sir Walter Scott's *The Lay of the Last Minstrel* (1805). Edmund has to remind her that the Sotherton Chapel was not the medieval one imaged in Scott's poem but one built much later. Mrs. Rushworth is even more precise: "This chapel was fitted," she says "up as you see it, in James the Second's time." This is lacking in "banners and atchievements," or armorial designs commemorating chivalric achievements, when "the pews were only wainscot" or very expensive imported oak and the "cushions . . . only purple cloth" or not silk or velvet.

The chapel dating from "James the Second's time" (85–86) was built during the period 1685–88, when the last Stuart king briefly reintroduced Catholicism officially to England. Such a reference "underlines the royalist affiliations of the Rushworth family" (Wiltshire, 664) and the fact that they represent long-standing traditions. The family even kept a "domestic chaplain" who would have acted as a family confidant and tutor to the children in addition to officiating at family prayers. This practice ceased with Rushworth's father. Fanny regrets "that the custom should have been discontinued. It was a valuable part of former times." She adds, "There is something in a chapel and chaplain so much in character with a great house, with one's ideas of what such a household should be! A whole family assembling regularly for the purpose of prayer, is fine!" (86). Her words echo Dr. Johnson's definition of a family as "Those who live in the same house, household" (Wiltshire, 664). Mary Crawford, on the other hand, argues that "Every generation has its improvements," and ironically that "It must do the heads of the family a great deal of good to force all the poor housemaids and footmen to leave business and pleasure, and say their prayers here twice a day, while they are inventing excuses themselves for staying away." She adds that "it is safer to leave people to their own devices on such subjects." Mary's objections are to "formality," "restraint," and "obligation." The differences between her and Fanny, between order and respect for the past, and Mary's concern for the self, for the individual rather than community, reverberate throughout the novel. As will be seen shortly in the novel when the representatives of the old order and authority are absent, such as Sir Thomas, the family disintegrates into personal gratification, personal vendettas, and indulgence, as in the theatricals scene: continuity is replaced by anarchy.

Mary Crawford makes cynical remarks defending individual liberty, the discontinuance of tradi-tional values, and is flippant about the clergy, who "were not worth looking at—and in those days, I fancy parsons were very inferior even to what they are now." Edmund's reply is far from witty. He tells Mary, "Your lively mind can hardly be serious even on serious subjects." Here the adjective "serious" is used in the sense, first, of meaning direct or straightforward, and, second, in the sense of religious matters. While these two continue to argue over the appropriateness of place, the "closet" or the chapel, "the rest of the party" enters the chapel. Henry Crawford jokingly objects to seeing "Miss Bertram so near the altar." Maria's reaction by asking Crawford "if he would give her away?" anticipates subsequent developments in the novel. Her sister, Julia, carries "on the joke," which has serious underpinning, by remarking "it is really a pity that it should not take place directly, if we had but a proper license." Here "proper" refers to a license that is appropriate so that they could marry in their own house, in this case at Sotherton. Such a license was obtainable only from the archbishop of Canterbury and consequently extremely expensive.

Julia, not fully understanding the seriousness of what is involved, thinks that Edmund, if he "were but in orders!," that is, "ordained" as a minister in the Church of England, could perform the ceremony. She adds tactlessly, "Mr. Rushworth and Maria are quite ready." This makes Mary Crawford realize that Edmund is "to be a clergyman." He affirms this: "Yes, I shall take orders soon after my father's return—probably at Christmas." It is Edmund who reminds the other characters and the readers of the absence and subsequent return of the missing authority figure, Sir Thomas, and of the passing of time intruding upon the action of the novel.

As the party moves from the house to outside, Henry Crawford remarks, "I see walls of great promise," and Mrs. Rushworth says to her son, James, "I believe the wilderness will be new to all the party" (86–90). Her remark refers to an area in the garden, or park, that has been "planted with trees, and laid out in an ornamental or fantastic style, often in the form of a maze or labyrinth" (Stabler, 401 n. 71). Henry Crawford's comment too indicates change:

The "walls of great promise" imply a vision of transformation of Sotherton House and its surroundings. They walk in the grounds and divide into three groups, Julia, the younger Bertram daughter, was "the only one out of nine not tolerably satisfied with their lot"; she finds it hard to maintain the appropriate forms of social conduct by which "she had been brought up to practise as a duty." These qualities are "politeness," "just consideration of others, . . . knowledge of her own heart, that principle of right." It is these essential principles that are shortly to be shown in the novel to disintegrate.

In his defense of the role of the clergyman to Mary Crawford, Edmund tells her, "he must not . . . set the tone in dress," or fashion, and that "No one here can call the *office* nothing" [author's emphasis]. In other words, the public role of the clergyman as distant from his private personal character—Mary's response reveals that she has some knowledge at least of sermons. She mentions "Blair's," thereby displaying awareness of Hugh Blair's (1718–1800) five-volume *Sermons*, published between 1777 and 1801. Edmund responds by saying that Mary's perceptions are largely determined by "the metropolis," that is, London. He tells Mary, and the listening but largely silent Fanny, "We do not look in great cities for our best morality." In the country people know each other and their clergy, whereas this cannot be so in London, where "the clergy are lost there in the crowds of their parishioners." So in this sense, the country represents stability, and London represents change. Edmund tells his listeners that the clergy can influence "manners." He explains: "The *manners* I speak of, might rather be called *conduct*, perhaps, the result of good principles; the effect, in short, of those doctrines which it is their duty to teach and recommend" (author's emphasis). As noted, "manners" and "conduct" are key words and values reverberating through *Mansfield Park* and Jane Austen's writings as a whole.

Other references that need explicating in chapter 9 are "bon mot"; "At Oxford I have been a good deal used to have a man lean on me for the length of a street"; "a furlong in length"; "within compass"; "a ha-ha"; and "doing this morning." A "bon mot" is a witticism. The Oxford reference is to the custom of the students to walk arm in arm. "A furlong in length" is an eighth of an English mile, or approximately 200 meters. "I must speak within compass" means that Mary Crawford speaks within the range of possibilities. A wide trench or fence built to prevent livestock wandering is a "ha-ha," or hidden boundary. Boundaries are indeed important themes in a chapter in which Henry and Maria have been flirting, and even Julia has been attracted to Henry, and Mary has been more guarded toward Edmund after learning that his desire to be a clergyman who will earn very little is a serious one. Finally, Edmund's observation that he is not surprised that Fanny "should be tired now" in view of "what we have been doing this morning" reveals his concern for her, understanding of her needs and the passing of time (91–96).

Chapter 10

This chapter opens with the sense of time having passed. Time is presented in the chapter through varying perspectives. Fanny is left alone, while Maria and Henry Crawford go off alone in the park, Rushworth having gone to find the key to the locked gate. Julia joins Fanny briefly, annoyed at being separated from Henry. Determined to find Maria and Henry, she too manages to get around the locked gate. Rushworth returns and sits with Fanny to complain about Maria's behavior before he is persuaded to go in pursuit of the others. Fanny's "thoughts" are "engrossed by the two," Edmund and Mary, "who had left so long ago," and she goes in search of them. She had "been left a whole hour" while Edmund "talked of only a few minutes" absence. The appearance and disappearance, pairings and isolation of Fanny had taken "an hour and half" since they all left Sotherton House to tour its grounds. They return to the house for dinner, although it "seemed, to Fanny's observation,"—most of the events of the chapter are seen through her perspective—"too late for re-establishing harmony" (103–104). The chapter concludes on "a beautiful evening, mild and still" with "a silent drive." The participants' "spirits were in general exhausted—and to determine whether the day had afforded most pleasure or pain, might occupy the meditations of almost all" (106).

In the fourth paragraph of the chapter, Henry sees "a knoll" from which he and the others can see the house. Access to this small hill, part of the estate improvements, is the reason why Rushworth leaves to find the key. To get to it, Maria and Henry squeeze around the locked gate and go off alone. Maria tells Crawford that he is "too much of a man of the world," to which he replies, "I am afraid I am not quite so much the man of the world as might be good for me in some points." The phrase "man of the world" is ambiguous. It could well refer to sexual and worldly experience and Maria is perhaps being suggestive in referring to Crawford in that way. His response shows that he is at times aware of its meaning and his limitations. He tells her that his "feelings are not quite so *evanescent* [my emphasis], nor my memory of the past under such easy dominion as one finds to be the case with men of the world." This is the only use of the adjective "evanescent" in Jane Austen's work, which means lacking in permanence.

In fact, it is Henry's "evanescent" quality that Maria will discover to her personal cost and one that will have drastic consequences for her. Such foreshadowing is subsequently conveyed by her remark "unluckily that iron gate, that ha-ha, give me a feeling of restraint and hardship. I cannot get out as the starling said" (98–99). Her last sentence is found in Laurence Sterne's *A Sentimental Journey Through France and Italy* (1768). In a chapter entitled "The Passport, The Hotel at Paris," Sterne's narrator Yorick, who has arrived in Paris during a period of unrest without his passport, thinks of the Bastille, if he is caught without appropriate documents. The Bastille is a building he "cannot get out of," and as he thinks this, he hears a starling and attempts in vain to set the bird free. In a sense, the garden becomes a metaphor for Maria and her situation. She is entrapped in an engagement with Rushworth, will squeeze around the locked gates in an attempt to free herself, and by the end of the novel as a consequence of her attempt at liberation, find herself permanently entrapped, like the starling in Sterne's novel.

Henry seems to offer an alternative. He tells her, "I think you might with little difficulty pass round the edge of the gate, here, with my assistance" (99).

He is no doubt holding back some of the hedge brambles so that Maria can squeeze around them. Subsequently, his offer of freedom proves to be an illusion, or "evanescent" (98), short-lived. An additional literary allusion to freedom and imprisonment occurs when Julia, "hot and out of breath," returns and asks Fanny, "Hey-day! Where are the others?" The exclamation "Hey-day!" (100) is used only on two other occasions in Jane Austen and echoes the second scene of the second act of *The Tempest*, when Caliban has the illusion that he has found release from Prospero: "Freedom, high-day! high-day, freedom!" (line 176).

In the meantime, Rushworth, searching for the key, "was posting away," or searching as quickly as he can in his pursuit. Julia too "scrambled across the fence," whereas her sister, Maria, previously had squeezed, with Henry's assistance, around the gate. Rushworth joins the solitary Fanny and his jealousy of his rival, Henry Crawford, is made evident when he replies to Fanny's observation concerning Henry, "I do not think him at all handsome." He responds: "Handsome! Nobody can call such an under-sized man handsome. He is not five foot nine. I should not wonder if he was not more than five foot eight" (101–102). Implicitly Rushworth in his hostility has reduced Crawford's class status by reducing him in size: gentlemen in the early 19th century "were normally several inches taller than men of lower social standing" (Wiltshire, 671).

Mrs. Norris reappears toward the conclusion of the chapter. "She had found a morning of complete enjoyment" by dictating to the Sotherton domestic staff. For instance, "she had set" the gardener "right as to his grandson's illness, convinced him it was an ague and promised him a charm for it." The "charm" either refers to a cross to be worn around the neck or to herbal remedies. Mrs. Norris is here shown to be recommending antiquated remedies. In return for her advice, the gardener "presented her with a very curious specimen of heath," or species of plant with apparently herbal healing qualities.

While the party waits inside for "the arrival of dinner," they look at the "Quarterly Reviews," or the periodical/serial reviews such as the Whig *Edinburgh Review* or the Tory *Quarterly Review*, containing the latest literary reviews and political opinion.

Mrs. Norris, in addition to insisting that Fanny carry parcels for her, shocks the Sotherton housekeeper, Mrs. Whitaker, by asking her "whether wine was allowed at the second table." This suggests that wine may well have been served at the servants' table. Underlying this is Mrs. Norris's belief in pettiness toward those she considers beneath her in order to satisfy her own ego and preserve what she perceives to be the old-fashioned values represented by the ruling social hierarchy. Such a sense is reinforced by Mrs. Norris's comment that Mrs. Whitaker "turned away two housemaids for wearing white gowns." It was the custom for servants to be dressed in dark clothes, although transformations in textile technology made white cotton dresses much more affordable. For Mrs. Norris, social differences have to be upheld.

Maria has seen through Mrs. Norris and directly asks her at the end of the chapter, "What else have you been spunging!" In other words, what else apart from "beautiful pheasant's eggs," and "cream cheese" has she appropriated parasitically from Sotherton and its servants, whom she wishes to keep in their place. Appropriately in the final two-sentence paragraph of the chapter "when Mrs. Norris ceased speaking," the drive back to Mansfield Park is one of silence (104–106).

Chapter 11

Anticipation of impending events preoccupies the opening of the chapter. Maria especially, and Julia, are not looking forward to the return of Sir Thomas, expected in November. The third paragraph moves from direct authorial narration of their reactions to his return into indirect discourse conveying the "gloomy prospect" from Maria's point of view, in which she counts the months before her father's return. At the start of the fourth paragraph, one of Jane Austen's key words occurs. "Sir Thomas would have been deeply *mortified* [my emphasis] by a suspicion" that his daughters did not entirely welcome him home. He would indeed have been "shocked." This same fourth paragraph presents another point of view on his return. Mary Crawford, somewhat tactlessly, as the group gathers together for "the evening at Mansfield Park" following the Sotherton adventure, remarks, "How happy Mr. Rushworth looks! He is thinking of November," that is, when Sir Thomas returns, and his forthcoming marriage to Maria, the one thing Maria is not looking forward to.

The rest of the chapter follows a pattern with Fanny as a silent witness and then departs from this as she is given some of the lengthiest speeches she has so far expressed in the novel. Mary Crawford, Edmund, and Fanny discuss his decision to enter the church. Mary thinks that Edmund's decision has been influenced because he knows that "there is a very good living kept for [him] . . . hereabouts." Edmund, in spite of Fanny's brief denial, responds, "I see no reason why a man should make a worse clergyman for knowing that he will have a competence early in life," or enough income to live comfortably. But this is not the main reason for his choice. He does ask Mary whether she thinks that "the motives of a man who takes orders with the certainty of preferment," or the certainty of social, political, or financial gain, "may be fairly suspected"? Ever the realist, Mary replies, "What! take orders without a living! No, that is madness indeed, absolute madness!" Their debate touches on the hiring of curates to do all the clergyman's "work." Fanny thinks of the kindness her own brother, William, has experienced from "the chaplain of the Antwerp" although she does not express her thought. Despite the fact that Fanny names William's ship, this reference to "Antwerp" (108–110) serves as a reminder of several external realities forming the backdrop to the events of the novel. First, naval chaplains during a time of war were in short supply. Second, "the capture of Antwerp, an important naval base . . . was a consistent tenet of British foreign policy during the Napoleonic Wars. Between July and September 1809, the English Navy attacked" Antwerp unsuccessfully, losing 4,000 men while doing so (Wiltshire, 673).

Mary Crawford provides an example of a clergyman, Dr. Grant. While "most kind and obliging to" her, she sees him "to be an indolent selfish bon vivant," or hedonist. Indeed, "disappointment about a green goose, which [Dr. Grant] could not get the better of" forced her and her brother from the house to Mansfield Park that evening. The reference is to a goose killed when very young. In this instance, the goose was eaten in August rather than at Michaelmas some months later. This, for Mary, is another instance of Dr. Grant's preferment for the possibility of good food rather than waiting for a religious observance such as Michaelmas.

Fanny, in her longest speech so far in the novel, responds to Mary's using Dr. Grant's behavior as a marker for all clergy. She ceases to be a listener and observer and becomes instead a teller, and one who disagrees: "No . . . we need not give up his profession for all that," she tells Mary and Edmund. Her hesitation with them centers on self-knowledge, "that knowledge of himself." She tells them "whatever profession Dr. Grant had chosen, he would have taken a—not a good temper into it." She adds, "I think more would have been made unhappy by him as a sailor or soldier than as a clergyman." In other words, given the kind of human being he is, Dr. Grant would not have done well. However, Fanny believes that as a clergyman, his routine and duties "must make him think, and I have no doubt that he oftener endeavours to restrain himself than he would if he had been anything but a clergyman."

The maturity of Fanny's insight into another human being produces an anticipatory response from Mary Crawford. She wishes Fanny "a better fate . . . than to be the wife of a man whose amiableness depends upon his own sermons" (111–112). Her words echo Portia's to Nerissa in the second scene of the first act of *The Merchant of Venice*. Portia tells her companion, "It is a good divine that follows his own instructions" (line 14). The words in the instance of Fanny are ironic in that she will end up by marrying a clergyman, Edmund.

The final section of the chapter centers on Edmund and Fanny. Mary Crawford leaves them "to join in a glee," or drawing-room musical singing in parts, its subject frequently being love. Mary "tripped off to the instrument leaving Edmund looking after her in an ecstasy of admiration" extending to her "graceful tread" (112). Again there are literary allusions here. In this instance, to John Milton's "L'Allegro," where the poet notes that his nymph does "Come and trip it as you go| On the light fantastic toe" (lines 33–34). Left alone together, Fanny and Edmund both look at each other and

out the window. This leads Fanny to express "her feelings." She says, "When I look out on such a night as this, I feel as if there could be neither wickedness nor sorrow in the world" (113). Her words echo those between the lovers Lorenzo and Jessica at the start of the final act of *The Merchant of Venice*. Lorenzo tells Jessica: "The moon shines bright, In such a night as this,| When the sweet wind did gently kiss the trees" (V.i. 1–2). Lorenzo goes on to refer to Troilus's love for Cressida. All four, Lorenzo and Jessica, Troilus and Cressida, are involved directly or indirectly in betrayal—a motif that recurs in *Mansfield Park*.

Fanny also sees "on such a night as this . . . the sublimity of Nature." She stresses the world beyond the self. Her emphasis is on harmony rather than discord. Nature is good for the self also, it acts toward inner peace: "Here's what may tranquilize every care, and lift the heart." There is a contradiction here. On the one hand, "the sublimity of Nature" leads to forgetting the self. On the other, it "lift[s] the heart to rapture!" Her "enthusiasm" results in Edmund's praise and temporarily diverts his attention from Mary. He sees "Arcturus looking very bright," Arcturus being known then as the most radiant star in the heavens. To which Fanny, replies displaying her knowledge of the solar system, "Yes, and the bear. I wish I could see Cassiopeia," or another constellation in the northern sky. She is not adverse from going outside "star-gazing" with Edmund.

However, her romantic illusions are interrupted by the beginning of the "glee," and Edmund leaves her to hear Mary Crawford and the singers. She responds to this with a strong word in Jane Austen's vocabulary: "mortification," a variant of which has occurred earlier in the chapter. In the final 16-word single-sentence paragraph of the chapter, Fanny is once again by herself: "Fanny sighed alone at the window till scolded away by Mrs. Norris's threats of catching cold" (113).

Chapter 12

The time for Sir Thomas's return to Mansfield Park draws closer. The beginning of the game-shooting season, the first day of September, brings news of Henry Crawford. As a landowner, it was expected that he would be host for festivities among his tenants to celebrate the completion of the gathering in of the harvest. Tom Bertram, on the other hand, arrives back at Mansfield Park "to be gay," or happy, "to tell of races and Weymouth," the fashionable sea-bathing resort in the west of England for the gentry and aristocracy.

The second paragraph, and the lengthy second sentence of the two-sentence initial paragraph, are presented from Mary Crawford's point of view. She prefers Edmund to Tom Bertram, finding the latter egocentric and making "it perfectly clear that he did not care about her." Even if he were extremely wealthy and the immediate "owner of Mansfield Park . . . she did not believe she could accept him." Such sentiments indicate that while Mary Crawford is not totally a materialist, she is a realist. "The season and duties which brought" Tom Bertram "back to Mansfield took" Henry Crawford "into Norfolk." He has to attend to business affairs and to entertain his tenants. However, after two weeks he returns to Mansfield: "thoughtless and selfish from prosperity and bad example, he would not look beyond the present moment."

His return has its consequences on the emotions of the committed Maria and Julia. The former is bored by Rushworth, her fiancé; indeed, she is "doomed"—a word used only five times by Jane Austen in her work—"to the repeated details of his day's sport . . . his jealousy of his neighbours, his doubts of their qualification, and his zeal after poachers." His concern seems to be with the rights of "his neighbors" to take game such as hares and partridges. This right was limited to those whose properties were worth above a certain minimum. Poaching, on the other hand, was frequent as it was a way in which the poor survived in rural areas. In short, Maria has no "attachment" toward Rushworth, to whom she is committed. "Julia, unengaged and unemployed, felt all the right of missing" Henry Crawford "much more," and "Each sister believed herself the favourite." In this fourth paragraph, the narrator clearly indicates that "Maria by the hints of Mr. Crawford himself" is the one he prefers.

Fanny in her role of observer sees a relationship developing between Maria and Henry: "judging candidly," impartially, she tries to communicate her fears to Edmund. He does not, in spite of Mrs. Grant's opinion, believe that there is much attachment between Henry and Julia. He counters Fanny's fears that Henry admires Maria over Julia by asserting incorrectly, "Crawford has too much sense to stay" at Mansfield "if he found himself in any danger from Maria."

Fanny's "first ball" (114–117) provides her with another opportunity to observe Henry, and Maria's and Julia's behavior. She does so somewhat ironically through the lenses of the older escorts to the young: "the venomous Aunt Norris, the inveigling Mrs. Rushworth, and the comatose Lady Bertram guarding the morals of the young" (Stabler, 403 n. 93). The adherence to "the common forms" of changing dancing partners following dancing a set of two dances, and who are "the couple above," in other words, those at the top and bottom of the dancing rows, are commented on. When Mrs. Rushworth and Mrs. Norris see "Miss Julia and Mr. Crawford" in that situation, their conversation naturally turns to the extent of Crawford's "property."

Able to "listen no farther," Fanny, as the chapter concludes, is joined by Tom Bertram, who dances with her to avoid playing cards with Dr. Grant and Mrs. Norris. In his conversation with Fanny, he refers to "so many couple[s] of lovers—all but Yates and Mrs. Grant." This is the first introduction in the novel to Yates, who is not described in this chapter. Tom also says, "A strange business this in America, Dr. Grant." This could be a reference to one of the naval skirmishes between Britain and America that led up to the Anglo-American War of 1812–14. Or it could be a specific reference to the June 17, 1812, American declaration of war against Britain. It is another instance of an external reference to political and social events found throughout *Mansfield Park.*

While Mrs. Norris and Dr. Grant play "a rubber" of whist, a card game requiring four players and popular as a family entertainment since the 1740s, Fanny is forced to listen to Tom Bertram. He spends his time, at Fanny's initial ball, when she should be dancing and enjoying herself, speaking ill of Mrs. Norris and how fortunate he is to have found Fanny so that he can dance and speak to her. Once again, she is found to be useful, the silent observer of others' activities, whom others can use for their own purposes.

Chapter 13

This chapter and subsequent ones of the first volume of the novel are largely dependent on intertextual references to another literary work, a play. The consequences of its choice reverberate throughout the remainder of *Mansfield Park*. Tom Bertram's "new friend," to whom there was a brief mention in the previous chapter, comes to visit Mansfield Park. John Yates is "The Honourable," a title accorded to the younger sons of peers of the realm. He has "a tolerable independence," in other words, he is of independent means and does not have to wait until the death of a wealthy relative to inherit wealth. The appearance of John Yates reinforces the theme of theatricality. He came to Mansfield "on the wings of disappointment, and with his head full of acting." He had been staying with friends, and "was within two days of representation when the sudden death" of a near connection of the family he was staying with deprived him of the opportunity to perform. He was "so near happiness, so near fame, so near the long paragraph in praise of the private theatricals at Ecclesford, the seat of the Right Hon. Lord Ravenshaw, in Cornwall." So-called "private theatricals" (121), dramatic performances became local events involving neighbors and sometimes actors and actresses from the London stage. They were at times written up in the local newspapers.

Yates's persuasive enthusiasm, his "love of the theatre" (121) infected the others at Mansfield Park. After some debate as to choice, the play he was to have appeared in in Cornwall becomes the one to be performed at Mansfield Park. The choice of drama, *Lovers' Vows* by August von Kotzebue, a German writer, has considerable significance. First performed in 1791, it was adapted by Mrs. Inchbald for the London theater in 1798. During the period at which Britain was at war with France, many German plays were translated into English, and German influence on the English stage was fashionable. August von Kotzebue at the time was also better known in England than, for instance, Goethe or Schiller. *Lovers Vows* expressed political

radicalism using "the conventions of sentimental comedy. It was not shocking to an English audience to find the villains aristocrats, but it was dangerous to the aristocracy as a class denounced as villains." As Avrom Fleishman indicates, Mrs. Inchbald's adaptation, the one used at Mansfield Park, "for all its banality, is by virtue of its glancing blows at social values—the unpunished profligacy of the aristocrats and their hypocritical anathemas against those they seduce—an effective condemnation of the ruling classes" (27).

The plot of the play revolves around past behavior, the immorality of Baron Wildenhaim (to be performed at Mansfield by Yates). Before the action of the play takes place, he had seduced and then left a lower-class woman, Agatha (played by Maria Bertram). In the play, he is encouraging the marriage of his legitimate daughter (he has other illegitimate children) Amelia (played by Mary Crawford) to the wealthy but stupid Count Cassel (played by Tom Bertram). At the conclusion, class barriers are transcended as the Baron's conscience (assisted by Anhalt the clergyman, played by Edmund Bertram) makes Agatha honest, and legitimate, as it does its hero, Frederick (Henry Crawford), their son. As Penny Gay notes, "In the scene" in the play "in which Amelia/Mary and Anhalt/Edmund discuss the emotional bonds of marriage, 'Liberty!' is the one desire of the imagined couple in an unhappy marriage." Gay observes that Jane Austen "uses this idea with a conservative slant" (105). Maria Bertram, as noted, "has locked herself into the cage of a prudential marriage and 'cannot get out' as the starling said" (*MP*, 99). Subsequently, "when she frees herself, assisted by Henry Crawford, she transgresses moral codes and "her 'liberty' finally only leaves her in the purgatory of a remote private establishment with Mrs. Norris" (Gay, 105–107), with whom she is entrapped and imprisoned.

Yates is unable in Cornwall to play the role of Count Cassel, as "the poor old dowager could not have died at a worse time." They were left in Cornwall with "An after-piece instead of a comedy": a reference to a short piece added for the purposes of light relief following the central five-act drama. In this instance, the piece was a musical farce called *My Grandmother*, by Prince Hoare (1794), on the program at the Theatre Royal, Bath, in February 1795. Tom Bertram mentions a "jointure," or property jointly owned by a husband and wife, which on the death of the husband passes to the wife, and thence, as in this instance, to the dowager's son. It is Tom who initiates the theatrical proceedings at Mansfield by suggesting, "Yates, I think we must raise a little theatre at Mansfield, and ask you to be our manager," which is flattering as it assigns to Yates the chief organizational role.

Tom, who is "now master of the house," Mansfield Park, has the suggestion taken up and strongly endorsed by his sister "and Henry Crawford, to whom, in all the riot of his gratifications, it [theatrical performance] was yet an untasted pleasure." The use of "riot" (122–123) here suggests wildness and that Henry is an experienced man of the world. As Shakespeare's Prince Hal says in the third scene of the fourth act of *Henry IV Part 2,* "his headstrong riot hath no curb . . . When means and lavish manners meet together" (lines 62–64). Shakespearean allusions continue when Henry Crawford declares that he is foolishly to "undertake any character that ever was written from Shylock to Richard III": Both of these are tragic figures regarded as villains. Further, he could "cut capers in any tragedy or comedy in the English language," in other words, dash about the stage.

It is Tom Bertram who suggests "a few yards of green baize for a curtain." Their erection probably means tampering with the existing decor. Somewhat sarcastically, Edmund expresses his opposition to the whole plan by suggesting that they should "do nothing by halves" but have "a theatre completely fitted up with pit, box, and gallery." Furthermore, he suggests that they perform "a German-play" or one associated at the time with dubious morality. This includes "a figure-dance, and a horn-pipe, and a song between the acts." It was fashionable during the first decade of the 19th century to include music and dancing in the middle of a five-act drama. He also reminds the others that acting is a "trade" undertaken by professionals rather than those "who have not been bred to" it. He tries to prevent the theatricals through such means, although Tom envisions the "billiard-room" as ideal for a theater with his

"father's room" serving as "an excellent green-room" (123–125).

Edmund clearly states to his brother, Tom, why the theatricals at Mansfield Park are "very wrong." In "a general light private theatricals are open to some objections." These include placing the female performers in inappropriate situations. In the circumstances, however, there are other objections. These begin with his father's absence. He is "in some degree in constant danger." This alludes to the fact that, to return home, Sir Thomas has to undergo a dangerous and lengthy sea voyage made especially hazardous during wartime. Also, he reminds his brother of Maria's "very delicate . . . extremely delicate" situation. She is unofficially engaged to Rushworth, and the public announcement of the engagement will not be made until Sir Thomas officially returns.

Tom counters Edmund's objections, and their mother is no help. "Lady Bertram, sunk back in one corner of the sofa . . . just falling into a gentle doze." So Edmund is left to assert that he is "convinced that my father would totally disapprove of" the theatricals. Tom takes the opposite view, reminding Edmund that when they were boys Sir Thomas "encouraged" them in acting. Tom instances from childhood the mourning speech "over the dead body of Julius Caesar," in which Marc Anthony uses his rhetorical powers to display the treachery of Brutus, supposed to be acting for honorable motives. Another instance is from Hamlet's "*to be'd and not to be'd*" [Jane Austen's italics] soliloquy of self-doubt in another play full of betrayal, treachery, and deceit. Tom also mentions the line "My name is Norval," (126) from the second act of John Home's 1757 tragedy, *Douglas.* On one level, Norval's words celebrate heroism, and on another recognition and acknowledgment of origins. Norval, it emerges "is in fact the long-lost son of . . . the play's tragic heroine" (Wiltshire, 681–682). So again, the theme of deception emerges.

Edmund counters by reminding Tom of their father's "sense of decorum" or appropriateness. To this Tom reminds his brother that he is in charge: "Manage your own concerns, Edmund, and I'll take care of the rest of the family." Edmund realizing that he is unable to prevent the theatricals tries to limit them by hoping they "will be in a very small and quiet way." To this Tom responds that the "house shall not be hurt"—of course, ironically it is, and that he has "as great an interest in being careful of his house" as Edmund: Here "interest" is clearly financial, referring to material interest in the property. He is, however, suggesting changes, or "innovation[s]," such as changing the functions of rooms and moving furniture around. Reminded of the expense involved, Tom directly questions his brother's judgment, telling him, "Don't imagine that nobody in this house can see or judge but yourself." There are other perceptions and values than Edmund's.

Fanny as silent observer "heard it all" and attempts to comfort Edmund, even to the point of assuming that Mrs. Norris will be against theatricals. Edmund tells Fanny that Mrs. Norris "would" side with him, but he then reveals his awareness of the deep divisions within his family and that "aunt Norris . . . has no influence with either Tom or my sisters that could be of any use." Edmund adds, "Family squabbling is the greatest evil of all, and we had better do any thing than be altogether by the ears." He is here using a metaphor from dog fighting. As he anticipates, his sisters are "quite as unyielding to his representation," his serious pleading, against the play acting, "quite as determined in the cause of pleasure, as Tom." Further, Lady Bertram does not object, and they were not afraid of their father's disapprobation.

Julia appears aware "that Maria's situation might require particular caution and delicacy" but is motivated by selfish reasons. Julia wants to play the part opposite Henry Crawford. So popular is the idea of the theatrical performance that there are "no want of under strappers," or helpers. Mary Crawford is "happy to take the part of any old Duenna or tame Confidante." This is in the case of a "Duenna," a part in which an older, more experienced woman acts as a protector of a younger one: A "confidante" is a trusted friend who delivers information to friends or the audience. In this way, Edmund is "silenced" even to admitting that the "charm of acting might well carry fascination to the mind of a genius." In other words, a lively mind as opposed to one of taste.

The final paragraph of chapter 13 focuses on Mrs. Norris. Instead of opposing the proceedings, she uses them to her own advantage. She saves money by moving into Mansfield Park from "her own house" in order to help with the preparations for the play. In the activities "she foresaw . . . all the comforts of hurry, bustle and importance." She will be needed and save money: "she was, in fact exceedingly delighted with the project" (128–129).

Chapter 14

The final chapters of the first volume of *MP* are concerned with the preparations leading up to the performance of *Lovers' Vows*. Chapter 14 focuses on the selection of a play, and who is to perform which role. Henry Crawford tells Julia that she is unsuitable to take on the main heroine, Agatha, essentially a tragic part. He feels that Maria would be more appropriate for the role, as does Tom as director. He assigns a minor role, the Cottager's wife, to Julia, whose vanity is pricked, and jealous of Maria, she storms from the room exclaiming that she does not want to participate if she cannot be Agatha. In the final paragraph of chapter 14, "Fanny, who had been a quiet auditor of the whole," of the squabbles and arguments, is once more "alone." She reads the text of the chosen play, *Lovers' Vows*, is astonished by it, considering the text "so totally improper for home representation" in terms of "situation," and "language." She perceives both to be "so unfit to be expressed by any woman of modesty." Fanny believes that both the main female participants, Maria and Mary Crawford, will be "roused as soon as possible by the remonstrance which Edmund would certainly make" (136–137).

The second paragraph of chapter 14 makes it clear that the intended performers, Yates, Tom, and Henry, Maria, Julia, and Mary, "are not seriously interested in the play as an artistic production, but as an opportunity for a feast of misrule, for showing off and bringing themselves into various piquant and intimate relationships" (Lodge, 108). Yates's reaction to Tom's assigning of what Yates perceives as "the most trivial, paltry, insignificant part; the merest common-place—not a tolerable speech in the whole" (134), that of the Cottager's wife, to Julia reveals his partiality toward her. Similarly, Henry's favoring of Maria to play opposite him as his lover, Agatha, reveals his desires.

A catalogue of various plays are presented as possibilities for consideration in the third paragraph. The references to *Hamlet, Macbeth,* and *Othello* are clear. John Home's *Douglas* has been mentioned in the previous chapter. Other possibilities include "the Gamester . . . the Rivals, the School for Scandal, Wheel of Fortune, Heir at Law" (131). *The Gamester* (1753) is a tragedy by Edward Moore with which the great actress Sarah Siddons (1755–1831) was associated. Jane Austen's November 30, 1814, letter to her eldest niece, FANNY KNIGHT, shows that she was familiar with the career of Sarah Siddons and the roles she was noted for (*Letters,* 287). Two SHERIDAN comedies are mentioned: *The Rivals,* which was performed at Steventon in July 1794, and *The School for Scandal.* Jane Austen probably performed the role of Mrs. Candour in an 1808 performance (Wiltshire, 683). The other two references are to comedies: Richard Cumberland's *Wheel of Fortune (1795) and* George Colman the Younger's *Heir at Law* (1808). Shortly Tom Bertram makes a reference to two comic characters in Colman's drama: Lord Duberly, an imposter who is easily bribed, and his tutor, Dr. Pangloss, who tried to teach Duberley correct English (131).

Other references in need of explication include the use of the word "rant" in the eighth paragraph of the chapter. The noun is used only four times in Jane Austen's work, and three of these instances occur in *MP.* In this context it refers to a declamatory style of acting associated with the early 18th-century dramatist and actor Colley Cibber (1671–1757). Yates's preference for it shows that he has not kept up with London dramatic tastes, as the "rant" was by the early 19th century already something of the past in terms of fashions and tastes in acting. In the same paragraph, Maria was "feeling all the interest of an Agatha" (132). Agatha was a part performed by Sarah Siddons. She opens *Lovers' Vows* by pleading for food as a beggar. She had been a long time ago forced into a life of impoverishment and unhappiness when Baron Wildenhaim (played by Yates), with whom she has had a relationship, deserts her. However,

shortly after *Lovers' Vows* opens, she sees Frederick (Henry Crawford), a soldier, in fact her illegitimate son.

Chapter 15

This chapter is interested in the reactions *Lovers' Vows* evokes. In terms of basic narrative, Mary Crawford accepts the part of Amelia and Yates, Baron Wildenhaim. Edmund, when he hears of the choice of the drama, expresses strong disapproval. Lady Bertram arouses herself from her usual stupor by telling Maria: "Do not act any thing improper, my dear . . . Sir Thomas would not like it" (140). Maria, however, refuses to see anything inappropriate in the part she is performing. In an indirect reply to Edmund, when he asks her what part she has agreed to play, she says "I take the part which Lady Ravenshaw was to have done" at Ecclesford. She adds, and the four words within the parenthesis appear to be the narrator's intervention in the dialogue "and (with a bolder eye) Miss Crawford is to be Amelia" (139). Here she indicates that she is aware of Edmund's partiality toward Mary Crawford and by implication, of the nature, the content of the role of Agatha. As Lodge judiciously observes, "All through this episode, the behaviour of Maria and Julia illustrates how notions of social correctness which are not animated by moral principle can be twisted to suit the selfish purposes of the individual" (110–111).

In chapter 15, Mrs. Norris agrees to the continuation of the play; otherwise, the cost of what already has been spent on the preparation will be wasted. Furthermore, her role in the preparation allows her the power to exercise her role as the petty tyrant, which she relishes. For example, she catches the 10-year-old son, Dick, of the carpenter at Mansfield Park, Christopher Jackson, performing during lunchtime an errand for his father. Dick Jackson carries "bits of deal board," or cheap timber. He is "a great lubberly fellow" (142), or lazy and large. Mrs. Norris asserts, "I knew what all this meant" (142). She is determined to prevent the young boy from having a free meal with the other servants.

Edmund assumes that the others will agree with him on his objections to *Lovers' Vows;* he turns to them "as if hardly doubting a contradiction" (139). Mary Crawford, after accepting the role of Amelia, asks, "Who is to be Anhalt?"—a role played by Edmund. She continues, "What gentleman among you am I to have the pleasure of making love to?" (143). Her question relates to addressing Anhalt in a flirtatious manner, and is not to be taken literally. Mary refers to Edmund as "a disinterested adviser" (144), a role, although not a "disinterested" one, taken at times by Fanny. She is described as a "creepmouse" (145), an expression used only once in Jane Austen's work, and a word seemingly created for this occasion to express Fanny's excessive shyness and reticence. Interestingly, shortly after she is called this, Fanny becomes the only one speaking when she tries to "excuse" herself from her assigned role, that is, of the Cottager's wife. She has low expectations. It is Mrs. Norris who "is always wishing that Fanny should play the role of the poor relation, humble, grateful, helpful, obedient, even servile." Fanny is in a real dilemma. "Her diffidence makes it almost unimaginable for her to perform," and her integrity means that she cannot act what she is not. However, she cannot be ungrateful to those who have brought her up and sheltered her (Hardy, 29).

It is Mary Crawford who shows kindness to a tearful and humiliated Fanny, Edmund being "too angry to speak," and it is Mary's decency to Fanny in her difficult situation that restores Mary to "Edmund's favour." At the conclusion of the chapter, outsiders such as Charles Maddox are brought in to play roles. Edmund "said nothing." Julia is hostile toward the others. In the final paragraph, Mary Crawford tells Fanny "in an under voice" that she will curtail some of Maddox's speeches, lamenting, "It will be very disagreeable, and by no means what I expected" (149). Her objections are not Edmund's, but to the fact that she appears not to have got what she wanted, that is Edmund to play opposite her in the role of Anhalt.

Chapter 16

This is an important chapter centering upon Fanny alone in her room at Mansfield Park with her dilemma. Unlike the previous chapter, she is not in the company of others. One other char-

acter appears in the chapter, Edmund; he then departs and Fanny is once again alone. In the first paragraph, the narrator tells her readers that Fanny "had recourse . . . to another apartment, more spacious and more meet," or more suitable. This had been Miss Lee's, the governess, first to Maria, then to Julia, and to Fanny, quarters until "she had quitted them," a victim of Mrs. Norris's suggested economies. These rooms at the top of Mansfield Park were too small and humble for the Miss Bertrams. Fanny has use of them, according to Mrs. Norris, "having stipulated for there never being a fire in it on Fanny's account." Mrs. Norris, even on this occasion, exhibits a fundamental meanness.

The first two lengthy paragraphs of the chapter convey space and its occupant's personality. Fanny collects "plants, her books." The objects in the room are disparate but coalesce together by Fanny's nature. "The whole . . . now so blended together, so harmonized by distance, that every former affliction had its charm." In other words, Fanny's collecting, "her writing desk, and her works of charity and ingenuity," alleviate the effects of "the pains of tyranny, of ridicule, and neglect" to which she has been subject from the likes of Mrs. Norris. The fourth sentence of the second paragraph conveys Fanny's collection of painful remembrances. The fifth sentence moves through similar subordinate clause structures. It describes the hostility she had experienced, "her aunt Bertram," as a positive "Edmund had been her champion and her friend." The hostility and support are "now so blended together." The objects she has collected become an archive representing Mansfield Park. These objects include "a faded footstool of Julia's work . . . three transparencies made in a rage for transparencies" (150–152). These are pictures that have been "drawn on transparent material to be hung in windows and illuminated by daylight" (Stabler, 406 n. 120). The transparencies represent "Tintern Abbey," "a moon-light lake in Cumberland," and "a cave in Italy." "Tintern Abbey" was described in Gilpin's *Observations on the River Wye* (1782; 5th ed., 1800) as "a very enchanting piece of ruin" (p. 50, cited Wiltshire, 686). It is perhaps better known as a meditative ode on memory and its power by Wordsworth (1798). The Cumberland reference is also probably to a book by Gilpin published in 1786, his *Observations . . . on Several Parts of England; Particularly the Mountains, and Lakes of Cumberland and Westmoreland.* The "cave in Italy" (152) is a similar representative of the imagination.

Following these paragraphs in which the objects in the attic room convey their occupant's principles and tastes, a third paragraph interweaves omniscient narration and free indirect discourse. Fanny's inner turmoil, her conflicts, are depicted through a series of questions following authorial description: "she had begun to feel undecided as to what she *ought to do* . . . Was she *right* in refusing what so warmly asked, so strongly wished for?" (Jane Austen's emphasis). She has obligations to please those who have helped her: "to whom she owned the greatest complaisance." In her room, for instance, "the table between the windows was covered with work-boxes and netting-boxes, which had been given her at different times principally by Tom" (153). Netting here means crochet work. The questions, and their nature, illustrate "Jane Austen's insight into the difficulty of judging the correct line of action in complex situations" (Lodge, 112).

Fanny's thoughts are followed by Edmund's appearance. He has come to seek Fanny's "opinion." He wants her "advice." Basically Edmund wants justification from Fanny that he should participate in the theatrical performance. He believes that the situation will be made worse if somebody from outside such as Charles Maddox joins the cast. Edmund tells Fanny, "It does appear to me an evil of such magnitude as must, *if possible*, be prevented." Fanny, of course, objects to Edmund's decision: "I must take Anhalt myself. I am well aware that nothing else will quiet Tom." He tells her, "If I can be the means of restraining the publicity of the business, of limiting the exhibition, of concentrating our folly" or limiting it, "I shall be repaid."

Fanny, alone again with her thoughts when Edmund has gone, in the final paragraph in which inner thought processes combine with omniscient narration, asks in a series of questions: "Could it be possible? Edmund so inconsistent. Was he not deceiving himself? Was he not wrong? Alas, it was

all Miss Crawford's doing. She [Fanny] had seen her influence in every speech, and was miserable." In the closing sentences of the chapter, Fanny is in despair and fatalistic: "Things should take their course; she cared not how it ended"—self-delusion, "It was all misery *now*" (Jane Austen's emphasis) (156–157).

In his last speech, Edmund opens some of the books on Fanny's shelves. He asks her, "How does Lord Macartney go on?" (156). This is a reference to George Lord Macartney's (1737–1806) *Journal of the Embassy to China* and initially published in Sir John Barrow's *Some Account of the Public Life, and a Selection of the Unpublished Writings of the Earl of Macartney* (1807). Macartney was sent on a failed mission to open up trade between England and China. His "dignified refusal to capitulate to the Chinese authorities highlights Edmund's failure to hold to his principles and anticipates Fanny's own moment of resistance" (Stabler, 407 n. 123).

Chapter 17

Chapter 17 highlights Fanny's isolation. She and Julia are "two solitary sufferers" (163). The first two paragraphs describe Tom and Maria Bertram's celebration of their "victory over Edmund's discretion." Their perceptions of the motives underlying Edmund's change of mind accord with the narrator's: "he was to act, and he was driven to it by the force of selfish inclinations only." The atmosphere among most of the participants is "all good humour and encouragement." Thus "Mrs. Norris offered to contrive his dress," and Edmund is "assured" by Yates "that Anhalt's last scene with the Baron admitted a great deal of action and emphasis." In this scene Anhalt (performed by Edmund) manages to get Baron Wildenhaim (Yates) to marry Agatha (Maria Bertram). Anhalt forces the Baron to confess that he had seduced Agatha.

Tom makes a final attempt to get Fanny to participate, but Edmund tells him that "She certainly will not act," and with this "not another word was said," so that Fanny is left isolated from the proceedings. Mrs. Grant, "with her usual good humour agreed to undertake the part for which Fanny had been wanted." Mary Crawford is very kind to Fanny, according to Edmund, and this only increases Fanny's unhappiness. Her situation is summed up in the words "She alone was sad and insignificant." The other "sufferer" is Julia, who, although performing in *Lovers' Vows*, becomes increasingly aware that "Henry Crawford had trifled with her feelings" and knows that Henry prefers her sister, Maria. Mrs. Grant "entreat[s]" Henry "not to risk his tranquility by too much admiration there," that is, being sexually attracted to Maria. Mrs. Grant discusses the issue with Mary Crawford and advises her to tell Julia to direct her attentions to Rushworth, who will offer her wealth and security, and not be around too much. "When Sir Thomas comes, I dare say he [Rushworth] will be in for some borough, but there has been nobody to put him in the way of doing any thing yet." She overestimates Sir Thomas's influence by assuming that he can find a seat in the House of Commons for him. Rushworth, although wealthy and from an ancient family, apparently does not have the appropriate connections Mrs. Grant believes Sir Thomas has.

Mary Crawford's response reveals her preference for 18th-century political satire and the poetry of skepticism, as opposed, for instance, to Fanny's preference for early romantic literature expressing personal rather than political feelings. Mary imitates two lines from Isaac Hawkins Browne's *A Pipe of Tobacco: In Imitation of Six Several Authors* (1736): "Blest leaf! whose aromatic gales dispense | To Templars modesty, to Parsons sense." Mary Crawford's witty imitation: "Blest Knight!" referring to Sir Thomas, "whose dictatorial looks dispense | To Children affluence, to Rushworth sense," comments effectively on Mrs. Grant's expectations.

The concluding portion of this short chapter shifts attention to Julia's thoughts, aligning her with Fanny. This is not before Mary Crawford has thrown more cold water on Mrs. Grant's speculation. Mary realistically tells her, "I would not give much for Mr. Rushworth's chance, if Henry stept in before the articles were signed." She is pointing here to the important financial aspects of marriage. Before the actual marriage ceremony, the intended wife brings her "portion," and the prospective husband settles money on his future wife in case of his death. However, Julia's unhappiness is conveyed in the third paragraph before the conclusion of the

chapter, in a passage largely of authorial narration conveying Julia's state of mind. "Her heart was sore and angry, and she was capable only of angry consolations." Fanny has empathy for Julia, but "Julia made no communication, and Fanny took no liberties." They are "connected only by Fanny's consciousness."

The final paragraph relates the preoccupation of the others with theatrical concerns. The lengthy final sentence focuses on Mrs. Norris, who is "too busy in contriving and directing the little matter of the company," and saving money, to pay attention to her real responsibilities. The "absent Sir Thomas" is mentioned in the final clauses of the chapter. Mrs. Norris is too preoccupied "to have leisure," an ironic word given her inclination to meddle in others' affairs, "for watching the behaviour, or guarding the happiness of his daughters" (158–163). So the play that should have united people leads to their retreat into their own private worlds in which the consequences on others are ignored in the preoccupation of the moment. Mary Crawford's poetic imitations with their observations on human folly and vanity, and references to patronage fixing parliamentary seats through the exercise of influence, serve as reminders of another world, a public one, beyond the self-absorbed one of the Mansfield theatricals.

Chapter 18

The concluding chapter of the first volume culminates in the final preparations for the first complete rehearsal of three acts of *Lovers' Vows*. Perspectives on the proceedings fluctuate in the opening three paragraphs from Fanny's to Edmund's, then return to Fanny in her role as "a very courteous listener." These give way to Mrs. Norris's further attempts to bully Fanny into doing her bidding. In this instance she is rescued by "her kinder aunt Bertram." Through acting as a sympathetic ear, Fanny has moved to the center of attention and is needed by the other participants. Alone for a moment, "in her wish of retreat" she is joined by Mary Crawford, who manages to persuade Fanny to read rather than act the part that was to have been played by Edmund. They are joined by Edmund, who too "was seeking Fanny, to ask her to rehearse with him and help him prepare for the evening." Fanny then observes Edmund and Mary acting before being "again alone" with her thoughts.

Just before "the first regular rehearsal of the three first acts was" to take place, Mrs. Grant is unable to participate, Dr. Grant having suddenly taken ill apparently. All turn to Fanny at least to read the part of the cottager's wife, to have been performed by Mrs. Grant. Once again placed in a serious dilemma, she wavers but agrees to "do her best." In the final paragraph "They *did* begin" [Jane Austen's emphasis] but are "too much engaged in their own noise" to hear Julia appear "with a face all agast" and explain somewhat formally and factually, "My father is come! He is in the hall at this moment." The chapter and first volume conclude with a climactic moment, the reappearance of the unexpected Sir Thomas. The conclusion is appropriately dramatic in being unanticipated by most of those at Mansfield Park.

Intertextuality plays an important role in this chapter, which has various references to the text of *Lovers' Vows*. In the second paragraph, Fanny observes the "needlessly" repeated "rehearsal of the first scene between [Maria] and Mr. Crawford." In this scene, Frederick, played by Henry Crawford, offers money to the starving Agatha (Maria). They recognize each other as mother and son and embrace, making actual physical contact. In another instance, "it was a pleasure" for Fanny "to creep into the theatre, and attend the rehearsal of the first act—in spite of the feelings it excited in some speeches for Maria." This is probably a reference to Agatha's fervid memory of her actual seduction by the youthful Baron, which still excites her. Later on in the chapter, Fanny does not look forward to the rehearsal of the third act, in which Edmund and Mary Crawford participate in a scene: "the whole subject of it was love—a marriage of love was to be described by the gentleman [Edmund], and very little short of a declaration of love be made by the lady [Mary]."

Fanny becomes the vehicle for the others' expression of satisfaction, or unhappiness. She also is able to judge the play and the action, being an observer upon the individual rehearsals. Hers has once again been a learning process. She has learned through

viewing about the attraction between Maria and Henry Crawford. She has witnessed the jealousy felt by Julia over Henry's preference for her sister, suffered at the hands of an intimidating Mrs. Norris, and been the involved third party present at the rehearsal between Edmund and Mary Crawford. Once again, she has been placed in an impossible situation, torn between her own awareness that to participate in any way in the dramatic performance is wrong, and the wishes of others. She is unable to resist Edmund's "repeated . . . wish" that she participate to which "she must yield" and her own physical feelings, "a most palpitating [the only instance of the use of this form of the word in Jane Austen's fiction] heart." At the final moment she is saved by the return of Sir Thomas, who has power over her—her substitute father (164–172).

Volume 2, Chapter 1 (Chapter 19)

The first chapter of the second volume is preoccupied with the reactions to Sir Thomas's unexpected return home and to his reaction to what he finds at Mansfield Park. The narrator uses an exclamatory voice to indicate Sir Thomas's return: "How is the consternation [the sole use of the noun in this novel; it is used on four other occasions in Jane Austen's work] of the party to be described?" The question, directed both to the reader and to the characters, is answered in the next sentence: "To the greater number it was a moment of absolute horror." The first paragraph continues to speculate on the participants' reactions. Those of two of the visitors and nonmembers of the family become speculative: "Mr. Yates might" as "Mr. Rushworth might imagine it a blessing." Members of the Bertram family respond differently, especially in their expressions and their silence.

Julia's reaction is confused by "jealousy and bitterness," which seem to have "been suspended," even though her sister Maria's hand was still "pressing . . . to [Henry's] heart." The return of Sir Thomas somewhat ironically unites the hitherto arguing actors: "selfishness was lost in the common cause." Apart from "the Crawfords and Mr. Yates," with whom Fanny is left, as an outsider from the inner family circle, the other Bertrams, with Mrs. Norris and Rushworth, go to meet Sir

Thomas. When she plucks up the courage to enter the drawing room and joins "the collected family," Fanny is surprised by the warmth of her reception. Sir Thomas refers to her affectionately as "my little Fanny," and "his dear Fanny." As usual, she has conflicting emotions. "She was quite oppressed. He had never been so kind, so *very* kind to her in his life. His manner seemed changed" [Jane Austen's emphasis]. Unlike his previous, reticent, silent self, Sir Thomas is now the center of attention. He "was indeed the life of the party," concerned to relate his adventures even though Fanny "saw that he was grown thinner and the burnt, fagged [tired], worn look of fatigue and a hot climate."

Sir Thomas relates that "his business in Antigua had latterly been prosperously rapid, and he came directly from Liverpool," the large port city on the northwest English coast. Before the 1807 Abolition Act, it was the leading port for slaves trading to and from the West Indies and elsewhere. Even Lady Bertram is so pleased to see him that she "put away her work," she "move[s] Pug from her side, and give[s] all her attention and all the rest of her sofa to her husband." He relates "the most interesting moment of his passage to England, when the alarm of a French privateer was at the height." At this point in his story, Mrs. Norris, running true to form, "burst through his recital with the proposal of soup." Her selfish intrusion should not detract from the specific allusion to the naval conflict then being fought in the Atlantic. Britain's enemies, such as the French and the Americans, were harassing its commercial shipping often through the use of privateers. These were armed ships authorized by the French or American authorities to capture and plunder the enemy's merchant ships.

In spite of her self-absorption, Mrs. Norris is quick-witted enough to have hidden theatrical evidence such as "Rushworth's pink satin cloak" when Sir Thomas appeared. Although not as happy as her sister to see him, she at this moment was not "incommoded [a word occurring six times in Jane Austen and only once in *MP*] by many fears of Sir Thomas's disapprobation." As will emerge, she is mistaken. It is not she but her sister who initially brings up the subject of acting. Tom tries to change the subject by referring to the fact that

they are well into the game and pheasant shooting season, which started at the beginning of October. Although subsequently it has rained, on the first day he and Edmund "brought home six brace before us," or 12 pheasants. Following tea, Sir Thomas goes "into his own dear room," where he encounters Yates rehearsing the role of Baron Wildenhaim. Ironically, Sir Thomas's appearance, combined with Yates's acting, makes "a piece of true acting," which Tom Bertram, not aware sufficiently of the seriousness of what he has allowed to happen, "would not have lost upon any account." He is, however, aware that "in all probability the last scene on that stage" has been performed.

Sir Thomas, well schooled in public behavior as opposed to the expression of his private feelings, receives Yates "with all the appearance of cordiality which was due to his own character" as a guest in his house. Although he requires "all the forbearance it could supply, to save Sir Thomas from anger on finding himself thus bewildered in his own house," and "making part of a ridiculous exhibition in the midst of theatrical nonsense." Sir Thomas also notices "the ceiling and stucco of the room," which too may well have been altered for the theatricals. The erection of a proscenium arch most likely meant damaging the fine plaster of the ceiling. Yates, insensitive to Sir Thomas's "ideas of decorum," chatters on "without discernment to Sir Thomas'" sensibility, values or judgment. Tom tries to imply that Yates's values were an "infection from Ecclesford," a disease introduced to Mansfield from somewhere else.

Sir Thomas's immediate reproach is to Edmund: "On your judgment, Edmund, I depended; what have you been about?" To this Fanny "knelt in spirit to her uncle, and her bosom swelled to utter, 'Oh! not to *him*. Look so to all the others, but not to *him*!'" [Jane Austen's emphasis]. As Wiltshire observes, Fanny here has probably been influenced by her reading of *Lovers' Vows*. In the second scene of the fourth act, "for instance, Amelia begs her father to be allowed to marry Anhalt. 'Dear father! I shall never be able to love another—Never be happy with any one else' [throwing herself on her knees]" (692).

At the conclusion of the chapter, Sir Thomas makes one of several serious misjudgments of character. He judges Rushworth "as a well-judging steady young man" (186). Earlier he has laid all the blame for the theatricals on Edmund, who, as the narrator demonstrated, attempted to prevent them and entertained serious misgivings about their proceeding. Another misjudgment, as noted, is Mrs. Norris's. She is not "incommoded by many fears of Sir Thomas's disapprobation" (179). On the other hand, his appreciation of Fanny since he has been away has increased.

Volume 2, Chapter 2 (Chapter 20)

The morning following his father's return, Edmund attempts to explain to Sir Thomas why he went along with the theatrical schemes. Edmund tells Sir Thomas, "we have all been more or less to blame . . . every one of us, excepting Fanny. Fanny is the only one who has judged rightly throughout, who has been consistent." After shaking hands with Edmund, and not entering "into any remonstrance with his other children," believing "they felt their error," Sir Thomas methodically purges Mansfield Park of "every object" associated with the performances and restores it "to its proper state."

He confronts Mrs. Norris, the "one person . . . in the house whom he could not leave to learn his sentiments merely through his conduct." More than two lengthy paragraphs are devoted to the meeting between the two. The first is largely reported speech, the second a lengthy self-justification in the form of a speech from Mrs. Norris. Admonished by Sir Thomas for her activities and support for the theatricals, she changes the subject to emphasize her positive achievements, for instance, the marriage she claims to have arranged between Maria and Rushworth. This is ironic in light of Maria's real affection and Rushworth's stupidity. Mrs. Norris's language reveals her narcissism. She tries to flatter Sir Thomas and to placate him, even appealing to their mutual concern for horses, catching a cold in his service, concern with economies, and their mutual admiration for Rushworth. In short, "Sir Thomas gave up the point, foiled by her evasion, disarmed by her flattery."

The paragraph describing Sir Thomas's return to the business affairs of his estate and the following one opening with "Mr. Yates was beginning now to understand Sir Thomas's intentions" convey interesting illustrations of words rarely used in Jane Austen's work. Sir Thomas "had to reinstate himself in all the wonted concerns of his Mansfield life." He has "to see his steward and his bailiff—to examine and compute." This is the sole instance of "compute" in her work. The verb here is used in the sense of to reckon or to calculate. After dismissing "the scene painter," whose damage to Mansfield Park was limited to "the floor of one room," the destruction of "the coachman's sponges," and making "five of the under-servants idle," Sir Thomas turns his attentions "to wipe away every outward momento of what had been." His actions are compulsive and obsessive: "even to the destruction of every unbound copy of 'Lovers Vows' in the house, for he was burning all that met his eye."

A paragraph is preoccupied with Yates and his perspective. For instance, "he believed he should certainly attack the Baronet on the absurdity of his proceedings and argue him into a little more rationality." He has enough common sense, however, not to "pursue" the matter but perceives Sir Thomas as "so unintelligibly moral, so infamously tyrannical." The word "tyrannical" is used only on this occasion in Jane Austen, similarly the word "unintelligibly." Yates reveals his partiality for "his fair daughter Julia," a preference not reciprocated.

Yates's perspective is followed by a paragraph from Maria's perspective reflecting the difference between public appearance and private emotion: "The evening passed with external smoothness, though almost every mind was ruffled." Maria is hoping from Henry Crawford "immediate eclaircissement," meaning clarification. The use here of a French word is ironic during a period of national conflict with France, especially as éclaircissement implies clearing matters up from a situation of ambiguity. Maria's feelings for Henry Crawford are left in no doubt, he is "the man she loved." He makes it clear that he is leaving the Mansfield area immediately , and tells Tom, "I may perhaps get as far as Banbury to-day," that is, approximately 30 or 40 miles, traveling southwest to the town of Banbury between Northampton and Oxford, from Mansfield. He is prepared to return if *Lovers' Vows* is performed. Maria retains, after hearing this, her public facade in spite of her own emotions. "She had not long to endure what arose from listening to language, which his actions contradicted, or to bury the tumult of her feelings under the restraint of society." His leaving ends "all the hopes his selfish vanity had raised in Maria and Julia Bertram."

A brief paragraph conveys Julia's point of view. For selfish reasons, she "could rejoice that he was gone" and "could even pity her sister." The final three paragraphs are seen from the perspectives of Fanny, Sir Thomas, and Mrs. Norris. Fanny, too, is happy that the Crawfords have left. Mrs. Norris only regrets that her plan of "his falling in love with Julia had come to nothing"—again she is concerned with herself. Meanwhile, Rushworth outstays his welcome, almost pushing Sir Thomas's public facade of politeness beyond endurance. The only person who appears really to profit from the *Lovers' Vows* fiasco, and who has preserved some of it as a memento, is Mrs. Norris. At the end of the chapter, she "contrived to remove one article from [Sir Thomas's] sight that might have distressed him." Even her pilfering is done to please others! "The curtain . . . went off with her to her cottage, where she happened to be particularly in want of green baize." The emphasis on *particularly,* the finesse of detail in description of what ultimately survives from the theatrical is superb. Ironically, Mrs. Norris performs the role of the preserver, the conservator, of something—"green baize."

Volume 2, Chapter 3 (Chapter 21)

Sir Thomas withdraws from society, from the Grants and from Mary Crawford, too. Fanny only is fascinated by his information about the West Indies, and Edmund tells her that Sir Thomas admires her: "Your complexion is so improved!—and you have gained so much countenance!—and your figure." In other words, while relaying Sir Thomas's compliments, Edmund himself reveals his awareness that Fanny has become a "pretty woman" to whom he is attracted.

After initially liking Rushworth, Sir Thomas revises his opinion and concludes that he is "an inferior young man" toward whom Maria is "careless and cold. She could not, did not like him." This allows him to give her the opportunity to break her engagement. As Maria has not heard

from Henry Crawford, she decides out of "pride and self-revenge" upon marrying Rushworth. She will not allow Crawford to "destroy her credit, her appearance, her prosperity." In Maria's case, she believes that marriage will afford her the opportunity to escape from the confines of Mansfield Park and her father. She intends as a consolation to discover "fortune, and consequence, bustle and the world." The marriage takes place and she and Rushworth, accompanied by her sister, Julia, with whom she has once again grown close, leave for Brighton. The absence of the two sisters leaves "a chasm" at Mansfield.

Of interest in this chapter is the lengthy discussion at its beginning between Edmund and Fanny. There is a mention of "the slave trade," a subject that has produced much critical discussion. The slave trade was abolished in 1807 but in reality continued in Antigua and elsewhere in the British-dominated West Indies. Edmund tells Fanny, "It would have pleased [Sir Thomas] to be inquired of further." This is ambiguous, suggesting that Sir Thomas has an interest in the subject. This interest could be both a practical one, as he owns property in Antigua, and political. Slavery was opposed by the Evangelicals, and Sir Thomas's excessive reaction to the theatricals and lack of humor, "his reserve," however, strongly associates him with Puritanism. He values "quietness," and as Fanny tells Edmund, "I cannot recollect that our evenings formerly were ever merry, except when my uncle was in town."

There are several elements at work in the conversation between Edmund and Fanny. First, they discuss different lifestyles. Fanny and Sir Thomas prefer an ordered life based at Mansfield. Edmund appears to desire more excitement. Second, their conversation is dominated by the subject of Sir Thomas. It is his perception of Fanny's physical attractiveness, one confirmed by Mary Crawford's opinion, that allows Edmund to introduce the subject. Fanny admires Sir Thomas's regularity, he is "serious," there was "never much laughing." The values are those of "quietness" and "repose." Edmund finds that Fanny is "too silent," and Fanny refers to "a dead silence" when she asks Sir Thomas "about the slave trade." Edmund, on the other hand, refers to Mary Crawford as "lively" and having "liveliness." Later on in the chapter, Maria believes that by marrying Rushworth she can escape. "Independence was more needful than ever; the want of it at Mansfield more sensibly felt. She [Maria] was less and less able to endure the restraint which her father imposed." The question then remains, has Sir Thomas in his desire for order enslaved Mansfield Park and his family? He and his possessions provide security. What they are based on is not made clear. Are his attempts to preserve what he has realistic, or even commendable? The question is not answered; neither is, in this chapter, Edmund's exclamation to Fanny: "I wonder what she thinks of my father!" The "she" here is the lively Mary Crawford. Edmund partially answers that "she has talents to value his powers." She, Mary, will appreciate Sir Thomas's authority and wealth (196–204).

Volume 2, Chapter 4 (Chapter 22)

Fanny once again is the focal point of the chapter, "The only young woman" remaining at Mansfield Park, her "consequence increased." She is needed more than ever. "Not only at home did her value increase, but at the Parsonage too." Mary too has become isolated and also needs Fanny, and a "sort of intimacy" develops, "resulting principally from Mary Crawford's desire of something new, and which had little reality in Fanny's feelings." Again, Mary Crawford is associated with the "desire of something new," whereas in the previous chapters, readers have seen that Sir Thomas especially and Fanny are related to conservative values—as is Mrs. Norris, but ironically so. The closer association between Fanny and Mary is naturally greeted "with particular pleasure" by Edmund.

In this chapter, Fanny is given some of her longest speeches in the novel. These become near monologues centered on the endurance of nature represented by "shrubbery" and "the evergreens." Nature for Fanny is associated with praise of "the operation of time and the changes of the human mind!" She remembers the Parsonage garden before its shrubbery came into existence and before the Grants occupied the Parsonage. The memory between them is reinforced by the strength of sur-

vival of both trees and the human mind. In a lyrical passage, Fanny says, "Every time I come into this shrubbery I am more struck with its growth and beauty. Three years ago, this was nothing but a rough hedgerow." It has been transformed, "converted into a walk." She speculates on the future "and perhaps in another three years we may be forgetting—almost forgetting what it was before." Such words are more potent placed in the perspective of the previous chapters of the second volume, in which Sir Thomas has tried to obliterate all evidence and memories of the theatricals, and Mrs. Norris, for her own purposes, has preserved a small remnant of what took place at Mansfield Park.

Mary Crawford's response to Fanny's philosophical reflections on time, change, memory, and nature is insensitive. She is "untouched and inattentive, had nothing to say"—she is transformed into the silent one, whereas Fanny is now the talker, the communicator and verbal recorder. When she does say something, Mary reveals her snobbery. "Till I came to Mansfield," she tells Fanny, "I had not imagined a country parson ever aspired to a shrubbery or any thing of the kind." Fanny, however, continues to praise the Parsonage garden. "I am so glad to see the evergreen thrive!" is her reply to Mary's cold, unenthusiastic reaction. Thoughts of the "evergreens" lead to reflections on the diversity of nature: "When one thinks of it, how astonishing a variety of nature!" Fanny's thoughts transcend the narrow world of the Grants' garden, Mansfield Park, and its environs to encompass the wider one. "In some countries we know the tree that sheds its leaf is the variety, but that does not make it less amazing, that the same soil and the same sun should nurture plants differing on the first rule and law of their existence." No wonder Fanny says to Mary, "You will think me rhapsodizing" or exaggerating; she is indeed in a "wondering strain."

Mary Crawford's subsequent remark reflects a skeptical tradition of thought. If Fanny's reflections are more akin to late 18th-century/early 19th-century thinking, Mary's belong to another tradition. Mary tells Fanny, "To say the truth . . . I am something like the famous Doge at the court of Lewis XIV; and may declare that I see no wonder in this shrubbery equal to seeing myself in it." Mary here reveals, not for the first time in the novel, that she is well read. She is aware of the work of the French Enlightenment thinker Voltaire (1694–1778). In his *Le Siècle de Louis XIV* (1751), a Venetian judge ("the famous Doge") is asked his opinion about the gardens and palace at Versailles built by Lewis (Louis) XIV. The Doge replies that what most struck him was to see himself there. Such a response reflects Voltaire's skepticism and criticism of religious belief. The gardens and palace at Versailles are not necessarily a reflection of God's handiwork, but of the human self.

During their conversation, Mary Crawford reveals her materialistic attitude to marriage and to life in general. For instance, she defends the loveless marriage between Maria and Rushworth on the grounds of its social benefits: "Such a match as Miss Bertram has made is a public blessing, for the first pleasures of Mr. Rushworth's wife must be to fill her house, and give the best balls in the country." She prefers the formality of "Mr. Bertram" to Fanny's "Edmund." Fanny tells her: "How differently we feel! . . . To me, the sound of *Mr.* is so cold and nothing-meaning—so entirely without warmth and character!" (Jane Austen's emphasis). She continues by extolling the "nobleness in the name of Edmund," associating it with traditions of the past "of heroism and renown—of kings, princes, and knights; and seems to breathe the spirit of chivalry and warm affections."

According to Mary's scale of values, "A large income is the best recipé for happiness I ever heard of," which places Edmund beyond her reach. The chapter concludes with Edmund rushing after Fanny, who has left the Vicarage for home. Before departing they encounter the food-obsessed Dr. Grant, who invites Edmund "to eat his mutton with him the next day," or to dine with him. Mrs. Grant extends the invitation to Fanny (205–216).

Volume 2, Chapter 5 (Chapter 23)

The chapter opens with a display of further selfishness from Lady Bertram, who has become so dependant on Fanny that she questions why she should be invited to dine at the Grants'. Lady Bertram even goes to Sir Thomas to seek his opinion on the matter. There are several areas of interest in this chapter. Fanny refers openly to the Bertrams as "my mother" and "my father," while it is made clear that however sympathetic and kind Sir Thomas is toward Fanny, he still regards her as his "niece." Second, increasingly in the narrative, Fanny's inner thoughts are being conveyed rather than being related. This is done through a series of questions she asks herself, such as: "she was anxious, she knew—more anxious perhaps than she ought to be—for what was it after all whether she went or staid?" Third, the invitation to dine at the Grants' represents Fanny's initial dinner invitation, her invitation as it were to a wider social world beyond the confines of that she has known since coming to Mansfield Park: "and though now going only half a mile and only to three people, still it was dining out." In the world of a Jane Austen novel, seemingly small, insignificant events have consequences and larger implications for others. The invitation represents a stepping-stone in Fanny's life.

Naturally, Mrs. Norris creates the biggest fuss and difficulties. She makes Fanny feel "almost . . . a criminal" for accepting the invitation. Mrs. Norris reminds Fanny that the invitation is not really for her, but for her uncle and aunt and Mrs. Norris! She also tells Fanny that "people are never respected when they step out of their proper sphere." Her perception of conservative values is repeated when she tells Fanny of "The nonsense and folly of people's stepping out of their rank and trying to appear above themselves," and she reminds Fanny, "Remember, wherever you are, you must be the lowest and the last." Such viciousness and techniques of humiliation are shown up when, following Mrs. Norris's reminding Fanny that the carriage "will not be out," and that she will have to walk home whatever the weather, Sir Thomas appears and offers Fanny the carriage!

Fanny, accompanied by Edmund, rides in the family carriage to the Grants'. On the way, Edmund once again praises Fanny's appearance. Somewhat appropriately, Fanny "is all in white"—white being a symbol of virtue. Edmund's compliment is somewhat confused and rather lacking in diplomacy as he asks Fanny, "Has not Miss Crawford a gown something the same?" Surprisingly, there is another visitor at the Grants'—Henry Crawford, who has unexpectedly returned from Bath. Fanny is not pleased to see him but believes "there might be some advantage in his presence, since every addition to the party must rather forward her favourite indulgence of being suffered to sit silent and unattended to."

Fanny is surprised by Crawford's return so quickly after playing with the Bertram sisters' affections. She is angered by his observation about Julia and Maria and celebration of the theatricals. He observed, "I never was happier" than participating in them. His memory is taken with them: "I shall always look back on our theatrical with exquisite pleasure," so much so that he wishes that Sir Thomas's return home had been delayed: "if Mansfield Park had had the government of the winds just for a week or two about the equinox, there would have been a difference." This is a reference to, in this instance, September 22 or 23, the date on which the night and day are of the same duration. The "equinox" traditionally is associated with unpredictable weather. Henry Crawford immediately adds: "Not that we would have endangered" Sir Thomas's "safety by any tremendous weather— but only by a steady contrary wind, or a calm."

Such comments result in Fanny's answering Crawford back in words of anger and admonishment: "As far as *I* am concerned, sir, I would not have delayed his return for a day. My uncle disapproved it all so entirely when he did arrive, that in my opinion, every thing had gone quite enough" [Jane Austen's emphasis]. As the narrator relates, Fanny "had never spoken so much at once to him in her life before, and never so angrily to any one." Her anger is the result of the insult to her uncle and Henry Crawford's totally different hedonistic values.

The Crawfords' priorities emerge when the dinner conversation turns to Edmund's forthcoming ordination. For Henry, "the most interesting in the world" to discuss is "how to make money—how to turn a good income into a better." He is an unabashed venture capitalist, or entrepreneur. Cynically, he does not believe that Edmund will do much as a clergyman. "He will have a very pretty income to make ducks and drakes with," or to spend money. Henry is aware of the social reali-

ties; he is aware of Edmund's situation as a younger son. "Birthright and habit must settle the business." The chapter concludes with Mary Crawford's inner reaction to the reality of Edmund's taking orders. "She was very angry with him. She had thought her influence more." She regards his "situation" as a clergyman as beneath her, as one "she would never stoop to" and decides to distance herself from Edmund (217–228).

Volume 2, Chapter 6 (Chapter 24)

Henry tells his sister that during the time he is staying with her, he will "amuse" himself and exercise his mind. His plan "is to make Fanny Price in love with" him as he does "not like to eat the bread of idleness" (229). His citation is appropriately from Proverbs 31:26–27, where "a virtuous woman" is characterized. "She looketh well to the ways of her household, and entereth not the bread of idleness." He has noticed that Fanny "is quite a different creature from what she was in the autumn." She has matured, "her tout ensemble [whole appearance] is so indescribably improved!" His sister, Mary, tells him that he is attracted to Fanny because she does not care about him, and requests that he "will not be making her really unhappy." She "will not have [him] plunge her deep," (230–231), that is, make Fanny profoundly unhappy. The words are from a song attributed to Robert Burns ending in the line "And plunged me deep in woe" (Wiltshire, 699). Henry is puzzled by Fanny's indifference toward him. He asks his sister, "Is she queer?—Is she prudish?"—in other words, is Fanny odd?

Jane Austen as omniscient narrator cannot help but comment with irony on Fanny's situation. Fanny is not "one" of the "unconquerable young ladies of eighteen (or one should not read about them) as are never to be persuaded into love against their judgment" (230–231). Fanny is human, unlike, for instance, heroines such as Laura Montreville in Mary Brunton's novel *Self-Control* (1810). In that novel, Laura, a "pious Christian" heroine, consistently resists the attempts of "the handsome and charming Colonel Hargrave" to seduce her (Wiltshire, 699). Fanny would have found Henry difficult to resist "had not her affection been engaged elsewhere." Fanny regards him with "disesteem" (231), the only time the word is used in Jane Austen's writing. It means lack of respect for another's good character. As Stabler observes, "It was a serious failing to sink in someone's esteem and by applying the concept of disesteem to Henry," the author "makes clear that although Fanny can appreciate his taste and powers of expression, . . . she has a very low regard for his moral integrity" (410 n. 181).

Attention is diverted from Henry Crawford's elaborate game to make "a small hole in Fanny Price's heart" (229) by the reappearance of Fanny's brother William, who, at home on leave, is invited once again to Mansfield Park after an interval of seven years. His reintroduction into the novel is accompanied by naval references in need of explication. William's ship the *Antwerp* is "at anchor, in Spithead," or the anchorage between the Isle of Wight and Portsmouth. His ship returned "from the Mediterranean," where during the Napoleonic Wars much British naval activity was spent in blockading the ports so that the enemy was unable to attack British shipping and supplies. William has a lowly rank, "he was still only a midshipman."

The closeness of the attachment between brother, and sister, is demonstrated. In the earlier section, Henry openly tells his sister, Mary, of his intentions to pursue Fanny and to play games with her affections. Mary knows her brother well enough to advise him to temper or restrain his game so as not to hurt Fanny too much. The closeness between Fanny and William resurfaces in spite of their being separated by at least seven years and the different experiences they have had. Jane Austen overtly expresses understanding for such a relationship, saying that if they "are even entirely outlived" that is regrettable: "Too often alas!"

William likes Fanny's "queer fashion" (232, 233, 235), her habit of combing her hair back and "to be held in bands around the head" (Wiltshire, 700). William saw such styles "at the Commissioner's at Gibraltar." The Commissioner was responsible for the administration of affairs at a British supply port such as Gibraltar, on the southern tip of Spain. William as "young as was . . . had already seen a great deal. He had been in the Mediterranean—in the West Indies—in the Mediterranean again." This

suggests that his ship had taken part in Nelson's pursuit of French naval ships from the Mediterranean to the West Indies across the Atlantic and back again between May and June 1805.

Henry Crawford reacts to William's account of his adventures with envy. "He longed to have been at sea, and seen and done and suffered so much." There follows a superlative alliterative passage describing Henry's feelings: "His *h*eart *w*as *w*armed, his *f*ancy *f*ired." The repetition of *h*, *w*, and *f* is reinforced. "He *f*elt the *h*ighest respect for a lad *w*ho, before *h*e was twenty, *h*ad gone through such bodily *h*ardships" [my emphasis]. In the final paragraph of the chapter, Edmund, Crawford, and William bond—in spite of Fanny's fears—by going fox hunting. Sir Thomas has such faith and trust in William that he has loaned him "a high-fed hunter" (235–237)—a very expensive horse to feed and maintain.

Volume 2, Chapter 7 (Chapter 25)

Sir Thomas has no objections to socializing with the Grants and Henry and Mary Crawford. Following dinner at the Parsonage, they play cards, Henry instructing Lady Bertram and Fanny how to play. Sir Thomas adopts Fanny's role as observer and notices how much Fanny engages Henry's attention. As conversation proceeds, so does a card game in which Mary Crawford takes enormous risks and bids: "No cold prudence for me," she declares, "I am not born to sit still and do nothing. If I lose the game, it shall not be from not striving for it." She wins. "The game was hers, and only did not pay her for what she had given to secure it."

Discussion between Henry and Edmund focuses on Edmund's future dwelling. Henry reveals that during a recent hunting expedition his horse "flung a shoe," had become separated from the rest of the party, and made "the best of his way back" to Mansfield Park. By accident, he found himself in Edmund's prospective parish, Thornton Lacey. He has many suggestions for its improvement. His ideas are not dissimilar to the ones he made about Sotherton. First, he and Edmund agree that "the farm-yard must be moved" so that the Parsonage House can be displayed to its full advantage. This is all they agree on. Henry wants more full-scale transformations: "the house must be turned to front and east instead of north." Edmund's ideas are far less extravagant: "I think the house and premises may be made comfortable, and given the air of a gentleman's residence without any very heavy expense."

In a speech, Henry Crawford, omitting to say where the expenses are to come from, tells Edmund, Fanny, and the other listeners that the house "From being the mere gentleman's residence . . . becomes by judicious improvement, the residence of a man of education, taste, modern manners, good connections." The values that grandeur conveys, political and social superiority, underlie such ambitious plans for somebody else's home. Crawford is so taken with his own schemes that he wishes to "rent the house himself." But Edmund has other ideas, telling Henry, "I have no idea but of residence." In other words, he is not going to be absent from his parish and responsibilities, an attitude meeting Sir Thomas's full approval. The narrative focus then switches to the effect this has on Mary Crawford and Fanny. Mary realizes that Edmund will not live in the kind of splendor she requires. Fanny, on the other hand, ponders "with downcast eyes on what it would be, *not* to see Edmund every day" (Jane Austen's emphasis).

The metaphor of sight is prevalent in this chapter. Henry Crawford watches Fanny, Sir Thomas observes them both; the card game acting as a backdrop to the conversations requires that the participants watch their cards, their hands as well as what the other participants do. At the conclusion of the game, Fanny and William are "the most detached," removed from the others. William reflects that if he were that evening in Portsmouth, it "is the Assembly night." This is an allusion to the Thursday evening balls held on a fortnightly basis, providing the opportunity for tradespeople, professionals, and naval people to mix freely with the gentry. As William notes, "The Portsmouth girls turn up their noses at any body who has not a commission. One might as well be nothing as a midshipman. One *is* nothing indeed" (Jane Austen's emphasis). Slightly earlier in the chapter Mrs. Norris attempts unsuccessfully to take advantage of William. She suggests that he visit the Rushworths' home in Brighton.

William's geography is slightly inaccurate when he tells her "Brighton is almost by Beachey Head." This is about 17 miles from Brighton and very visible to ships in the English Channel. William adds that he "could not expect to be welcome in such a smart place as that—poor scrubby [insignificant, low] midshipman as I am."

In spite of Fanny's attempt to reassure William, he tells his sister, "I begin to think I shall never be made lieutenant. . . . Every body gets made but me." He reminisces about their past happiness together, their jumping "about together . . . when the hand-organ [a very popular kind of street entertainment throughout the 19th century in London and other towns such as Portsmouth] was in the street." At the end of the chapter, Mrs. Norris, running true to form, tries to place pressure on Fanny by hurrying her up. Although Sir Thomas would like to "dissent" from Mrs. Norris's perception of who initially ordered the coach and horses, Mrs. Norris's memory is conveniently selective and she appears to gain the upper hand. As does Henry, who in the last single-sentence paragraph is quicker than Edmund in putting Fanny's shawl around her shoulders (238–251).

Volume 2, Chapter 8 (Chapter 26)
Sir Thomas, in order to please William, and in spite of Mrs. Norris's objections, decides to hold a ball at Mansfield Park. In effect this will be Fanny's "coming out" (267) into society ball. Fanny has only "a very pretty amber cross which William had brought her from Sicily" (254) and worries what she should wear at the ball. Sicily at this time was a Royal Naval base used to make incursions into French-controlled Italy. Jane Austen's brother Charles Austen presented Jane and her sister, Cassandra, with "Gold chains & Topaz Crosses" he purchased from his share of the prize money from the capture of a French ship in the Mediterranean (see Jane Austen's letter to Cassandra, May 27, 1801: *Letters*, 91). William, as a midshipman, without prize money, could afford only "amber" rather than gold or topaz.

Fanny is unable to consult Edmund. He "was at this time particularly full of cares" concerned with "two important events now at hand, which were to fix his fate in life—ordination and matrimony." His ordination is to take place the following week and he is worried whether Mary Crawford will accept him or not. Edmund is to be ordained at "Peterborough . . . in the course of the Christmas week." Peterborough is a cathedral city approximately 35 miles northeast of Northampton. It was expected that the clergyman have a "wife who was to share, and animate, and reward those duties' (255) Edmund is going to be called to. The ordination service requires Edmund "'to frame and fashion' the life of his family as well as of himself" (Wiltshire, 706).

The coming ball is not high on Edmund's list of priorities. The day before the ball, a Wednesday, a chance encounter with Mary Crawford leads Fanny to consult her on what she should wear, and they find "a comfortable coze" to discuss the matter. This is the only instance of the word "coze" in Jane Austen, or indeed recorded in the *OED*. Mary offers Fanny a gold necklace, which she "more frequently placed before [Fanny's] eyes than the rest" she is offering her. The necklace Mary reveals had been a present to her from her brother, Henry. Fanny attempts to return it, but Mary urges her to keep it for herself. Fanny is shocked by the thought of taking "what had been the gift of another person—of a brother, too—impossible." Mary's words of apparent reassurance take on an insidious application. Henry, Mary tells Fanny, "would be too much flattered by seeing round your lovely throat an ornament which his money purchased three years ago, before he knew there was such a throat in the world?" to be offended. The repetition of "throat" here implies an underlying sense of entrapment.

The penultimate paragraph of the chapter, interweaves authorial description with inner thought processes, Fanny reflects that Henry "wanted, she supposed, to cheat her of her tranquility as he had cheated" her cousins. She thinks "whether he might not have some concern in this necklace!— She would not be convinced that he had not." Fanny's suspiciousness emerges "for Miss Crawford, complaisant as a sister, was careless as a woman and a friend."

In the last paragraph of the chapter, Fanny returns to Mansfield Park from her conversation with Mary Crawford at the Parsonage, "reflecting and doubting, and feeling that the possession of what she had so much wished for, did not bring much satisfaction." She returns "home again" (258–260), less happy and more troubled than she had been before setting out. Such a state foreshadows what is to occur to Fanny in the narrative before its conclusion.

Volume 2, Chapter 9 (Chapter 27)

This chapter divides into several sections, with Fanny largely the center of attention. In the first she encounters Edmund in her room writing a letter to her. Edmund seeks her advice regarding Mary Crawford. The next day, Henry uses a ploy to gain Fanny's favor by offering William a place in his coach. Fanny prepares for her ball, dispirited when she once again meets Edmund, who confides yet again his problems and fears regarding Mary. In the final section, Fanny, reassured by what Edmund has told her, dresses for the ball managing to wear William's amber cross, Edmund's chain, and Mary's (Henry's) necklace.

At the start of the chapter, Edmund has appeared to give Fanny "a plain gold chain perfectly simple and neat," reflecting its giver and Fanny and a contrast to the ornate necklace Mary has given her. Fanny honestly confesses to Edmund, "this is the only ornament I have ever had a desire to possess." Both are brought back to reality by the need for advice: Fanny from the "heavenly flight" of her mind following the gift from Edmund, he from his "reverie," his "fond reflection" of Mary. There follows a curious passage replete with negatives; nine instances of the word "not" are succeeded by an assertive "No" in the space of three short paragraphs. They relate to Fanny's desire to return the necklace to Mary and Edmund's response, in which he disagrees with Fanny, telling her to wear Mary's gift for the one night and reserve his gift "for commoner occasions."

Edmund's revelation yet again of the strength of his feelings for Mary leaves Fanny alone "to tranquillise herself as she could." This is the only instance of the verb "tranquillise" in Jane Austen's work—meaning to calm, to soothe. Fanny responds to what Edmund has told her, as "a stab," and demonstrates that she still is immature. Jane Austen once again uses irony at the appropriate time. In this chapter, Fanny is preparing for her "coming out ball," her coming of age at 18. On the other hand, "she had all the heroism of principle, and was determined to do her duty." She will act maturely. However, "she seized the scrap of paper on which Edmund had begun writing to her, as a treasure beyond all her hopes." This will serve as a memento, a preservation of memory. It provides evidence for "the researches of the fondest biographer."

Thursday, the day of the ball arrives. Again a written communication, this time in the form of a note from Henry Crawford to William, occupies a prominent place in the chapter. Henry's note is another attempt to gain Fanny's approval. The paragraph describing its content has several references needing explanation. Henry's uncle, an admiral, has a "late dinner-hour": dinner hour in London was usually later than the earlier dining time at Mansfield Park. William "enjoyed the idea of travelling post," or by the quickest and most expensive form of transport, having new fresh horses at each stage of the journey. Such a form of quick transportation was used by officers "going up [to London] with dispatches," or naval communications. Originally William was to "go up by the mail," or by the regular public stagecoach service, which also carried the mail. While Northampton is north of London, the expression "go up" is still used.

Fanny prepares herself for the ball, to being "regarded as the Queen of the evening." Noticeable at this point in the chapter is the use of Fanny's family name, "Price," which compliments "the trade of *coming out*" (Jane Austen's emphasis). An 18th birthday ball announced publicly to the world that a girl was now on the marriage market looking for an eligible, preferably rich, suitor. It not only heralds her own coming of age but what she can bring with her in addition to physical looks— what she can offer a suitor in terms of connections, political and social, as well as her dowry. In 1805, a contemporary of Jane Austen, Hannah More, published a pamphlet: "The White Slave Trade, hints towards forming a bill for the Abolition of the White Female Trade, in the Cities of London and Westminster."

Fanny yet again encounters Edmund, this time symbolically "standing at the head of a different staircase"—each staircase representing their respective destinies. Edmund, after showing concern for Fanny, and holding her hand, tells her that she is "a kind, kind listener." He confides that Mary Crawford "does not *think* evil, but she speaks it—speaks it in playfulness—and though I know it to be playfulness, it grieves my soul" (Jane Austen's emphasis) (262–269). Edmund's words, appropriately for someone about to be ordained, echo the New Testament passage in which "the unrighteous speak evil of the things that they understand not" (2 Peter 2: 12–15).

Edmund reinforces the *motif* of memory, which echoes throughout the novel whether in the form of Mrs. Norris taking home green baize, or Fanny secreting away Edmund's letter. He tells her, "there will be nothing to be remembered by either you or me, that we need be afraid of." He has confided in her that while Mary Crawford has agreed to dance the first two dances with him, "She never has danced with a clergyman she says, and she never *will*" (Jane Austen's emphasis). Edmund's unhappiness restores Fanny's "happier feelings." Previously, "there had been no comfort around, no hope within her. Now, every thing was smiling." She wears all her gifts. The final paragraph of the chapter demonstrates her self-sufficiency. She does not need the services of her aunt Bertram's personal maid to assist her (268, 270). To send a personal maid is an indication of the high esteem in which she is now held in the Bertram household.

Volume 2, Chapter 10 (Chapter 28)
The focus of the chapter is the ball and Fanny's role in it. Sir Thomas sees "with pleasure the general elegance of her appearance and her being in remarkably good looks" (272). Henry Crawford claims her for the first two dances, although she is bothered by his "attentions" (278) and disconcerted by "his eye glancing for a moment at her necklace—with a smile—she thought there was a smile—which made her blush and feel wretched." Continually observed by Sir Thomas, to her surprise she discovers "that *she* was to lead the way and open the ball" (Jane Austen's emphasis). Fanny

finds herself being "conducted by Mr. Crawford to the top of the room, and standing there to be joined by the rest of the dancers." According to the custom a ball would begin with the leading couple, in this instance Fanny and Henry Crawford, dancing and watched by the others: the idea of being watched runs through the chapter.

Fanny finds out from Mary Crawford that Henry is going to London the next day "purely for the pleasure of conveying [her] brother and talking of [Fanny] by the way." This leads to "confusion." Fanny "was happy whenever she looked at William," but not when she considered Henry Crawford and his "attentions." She looks forward to dancing with Edmund. When this takes place "his mind was fagged" and her happiness arises from his unhappiness. He tells her that he is "worn out with civility" and requests from Fanny "the luxury of silence." Subsequently they dance "together with such tranquility as might satisfy any looker-on that Sir Thomas had been bringing up no wife for his younger son"—words that, in the light of the ending of the novel, become highly ironic and inaccurate. The cause of Edmund's unhappiness is his encounter with Mary Crawford: "she had ridiculed—and they had parted at last with mutual vexation."

William and Sir Thomas notice how tired Fanny is at "three o'clock" in the morning. In spite of their protestations, Fanny insists in getting up early to say good-bye to her brother. Sir Thomas, much to Fanny's silent displeasure, invites Henry Crawford "to join the early breakfast party . . . instead of eating alone." The narrator writes explicitly that "Mr. Crawford was in love with Fanny" and Sir Thomas "had a pleasing anticipation of what would be." Sir Thomas uses his "absolute power." He advises Fanny "to go immediately to bed." As she leaves the dancers, Fanny is described as "stopping at the entrance door, like the Lady of Branxholm Hall, 'one moment and no more' to view the happy scene" (274–275; 277–280). The reference is to the first canto of Walter Scott's *The Lay of the Last Minstrel* (1805). In the poem "The Ladye forgot her purpose high," which is for her knight to recover the treasure buried in the tomb at Melrose Abbey, "One moment and no more;| One moment gaz'd

with a mother's eye,| As she paused at the arched door" (verse 20). Again the metaphor of seeing is used: Fanny looks at "the happy scene," is viewed by the others, and especially by Sir Thomas, who has watched Fanny and Henry closely during the ball. As she leaves she is "pursued by the ceaseless country-dance, feverish with hopes and fears, soup and negus." Balls included a supper with soup: "negus" is a hot spiced wine.

The final two sentences of the chapter make up its last paragraph. The focus is on Sir Thomas's motivation in sending Fanny to bed. He is not "thinking merely of her health." There is a possibility that he perceives that Henry Crawford "had been sitting by [Fanny] long enough, or he might mean to recommend her as a wife by shewing her persuadableness." There are three instances of the conditional past tense "might" at work in this final paragraph containing the meaning of a possibility (280–281).

Volume 2, Chapter 11 (Chapter 29)

The first of the two-sentence opening paragraph of the chapter conveys the passing of time and the speed of William's departure from Mansfield Park. There is a brief, factual sentence punctuated by a parenthesis and a semicolon suggesting the brevity of what has taken place: "The ball was over—and the breakfast was soon over too; the last kiss was given, and William was gone." Fanny is left "to grieve over the melancholy change" and "she sat and cried *con amore*" (Jane Austen's emphasis), or from the heart. Following "the second breakfast," or second meal, Edmund departs too and Fanny is left with Lady Bertram and Sir Thomas. They "played at cribbage," a card game for two to four players with a board with holes and pegs for scoring purposes. Mansfield Park is now quiet and underpopulated. The effects of time and change are conveyed through the lack of people and activity, and through Fanny. She "thought and thought again of the difference which twenty-four hours had made in that room, and all that part of the house." The "hope and smiles, bustle and motion" have gone to be replaced by "languor, and all but solitude." This sense is doubly reinforced by the season, "the tranquility of the present quiet week." It is in fact

Christmas time; Edmund leaves for Peterborough on December 23.

Lady Bertram especially misses Julia, who has obtained "permission to go to town with Maria." Fanny's usefulness to Lady Bertram and Sir Thomas has increased: "she is now a very valuable companion" for both of them. The rest of the chapter is taken up with contrasting the different reactions of Fanny and Mary to Edmund's absence and the change at Mansfield Park: "What was tranquillity and comfort to Fanny was tediousness and vexation to Mary." An impatient Mary goes to visit Fanny to see if she has any news of Edmund, who has deferred his return, "having promised to remain some days longer with his friend!" (282–286). Mary has heard that Edmund's friend Owen, with whom he is staying at Peterborough, has three grown-up sisters. Mary is jealous and her cynicism emerges when she tells Fanny, "It is every body's duty to do as well for themselves as they can." She adds that in the marriage cattle market, Edmund "is their lawful property, he fairly belongs to them." Fanny's silence puzzles Mary. "You don't speak Fanny—Miss Price you don't speak." Here Fanny's silence speaks volumes, revealing her deepest feelings for Edmund. Mary says to Fanny, "perhaps you do not think [Edmund] likely to marry at all—or not at present." Fanny's answer almost through her "blush" in responding, "No, I do not," breaks down the public face she has adopted in suppressing her internal feelings for Edmund. Mary's reply, "He is best off as he is" reveals her own sense of inadequacy and regret (289–290).

Volume 2, Chapter 12 (Chapter 30)

Henry returns from London to tell Mary that he is "quite determined to marry Fanny Price." His sister is surprised and also "not displeased with her brother's marrying a little beneath him." This chapter consists of their discussing Fanny's character, with Henry praising her and his sister becoming convinced of her brother's sincerity. Her initial materialistic response, "Lucky, lucky girl! . . . what a match for her!" and comment, "You will have a sweet little wife: all gratitude and devotion. Exactly what you deserve," is tempered by the insight that Fanny will not marry "*without love*; that is, if there

is a girl in the world capable of being uninfluenced by ambition, I can suppose it her" (Jane Austen's emphasis).

Henry reveals his plans to Mary. He has not yet told them to his surrogate father, the admiral. He will "let Everingham and rent a place in this neighbourhood." Mary will be able to spend six months of the year with him and Fanny. Both Henry and Mary reveal considerable insight in this chapter into Fanny's character. Henry tells Mary that at present Fanny "is dependent, helpless, friendless, neglected, forgotten"—only half true as Mary points out. She tells Henry: "Edmund never forgets her." When Henry marries her, she "will feel a difference indeed, a daily, hourly difference in the behaviour of every being who approaches her." Henry is more accurate in the last paragraph of the chapter when he tells Mary that Sir Thomas is "a rich, superior, longworded, arbitrary uncle," although he has returned from Antigua chastened.

There are several interesting references in this chapter. In the opening paragraph, Mary meets her brother "in the sweep," to the curved carriage drive leading up to the front of the Parsonage. Henry is unable to tell Mary, "How the pleasing plague had stolen on him," that is, when he first fell in love with Fanny as opposed to playing with her affections. The line is from a song by William Whitehead (1715–85) found in Robert Dodsley's very popular anthology *A Collection of Poems by Several Hands*. The context of Whitehead's line is very similar to the situation Henry finds himself in: a misogynist, in the manner of his uncle and surrogate father, the admiral, his distrust or hatred of women has been transformed, in this instance by Fanny, into love.

Henry tells Mary of Fanny's "good principles," and "he expressed what was inspired by the knowledge of her being well principled and religious" (294). The word "religion" is used on only three occasions in Jane Austen: two of these instances are in *MP* (92, 463). "Religious" is used on four instances, and this is the only occasion in *MP*. In other words, Fanny is sincere and pious: It is perhaps ironic that it is the misogynist Henry Crawford who should recognize these qualities in Fanny, he being so lacking in principles. Two other references should be noted. Henry tells Mary that he intends to settle in Northamptonshire, he shall "rent a place in this neighbourhood—perhaps Stanwix Lodge," that is, at Stanwick, to the northeast of the county town Northampton. Henry sees Mary "only as the supposed inmate of Mansfield Parsonage": "inmate" (295) in this context means a guest, or temporary resident, not a prisoner.

Volume 2, Chapter 13 (Chapter 31)

A lot occurs in this final chapter of the second volume. The morning following his arrival in Mansfield Park, Henry goes to visit Fanny. He tells her that through the good offices and connections of his uncle, the admiral, William has been promoted to the rank of "second lieutenant of H.M. Sloop Thrush" (299). According to Southam, a "sloop [is] a ship of between ten and eighteen guns, the humblest of vessels, which offered none of the opportunities of prize-money and distinction to be enjoyed in frigates" (*Jane Austen and the Navy*, 97). Price will earn around £100 a year, representing approximately a 40th of Henry Crawford's annual income, but William has become an officer, the initial step in the promotion ladder in the Royal Navy. Fanny is overjoyed to hear such news and very grateful to Henry for what he has done on behalf of her brother. Henry then presses his personal suit, "offering himself, hand, fortune, every thing to her acceptance." Fanny's response is a negative one: "'No, no, no.' she cried, hiding her face. 'This is all nonsense. Do not distress me. I can hear no more of this.'"

Henry persists with his proposal, so that Fanny is forced to "burst away from him" and leaves to be alone to deal with the tumult of her emotions. After she hears that Henry has left, she returns downstairs to share the intelligence of William's promotion with Sir Thomas and the others. She finds out that Sir Thomas has once again invited Henry to dine with the family "that very day." For Fanny, "this was a most unwelcome hearing." When Henry comes he has a note addressed to Fanny from Mary in which she congratulates Fanny, and urges her to accept Henry, she has Mary's "most joyful consent and approval." During dinner Fanny attempts to hide behind "her aunt Norris, who . . . screened her

a little from view." She is all too conscious of being watched and is "more silent than ever."

Fanny's thoughts range from her gratitude to Henry, and she half hears the dinner conversation, especially Mrs. Norris's remark that "William must not forget [her] shawl if he goes to the East Indies." Forever on the watch for an opportunity to gain something, Mrs. Norris is aware that fine shawls were found in the "East Indies." Fanny is preoccupied with "trying to understand what Mr. and Miss Crawford were at"—what their real motives were, or if they are "being serious." Crawford urges her to reply to her sister's note. Fanny does so and in a hurried reply she gives to Henry, she tells Mary "I have seen too much of Mr. Crawford not to understand his manners; if he understood me as well, he would . . . behave differently." She adds, "it would be a great favour of you never to mention the subject again." Fanny's attempt to hide, not to look directly at Henry, becomes an important element in the chapter. As he leaves, she "with averted eyes walked towards the fireplace." On the one hand, she feels confusion toward him; on the other, she does not wish to give Henry false signals by looking directly at him. Also, she has insight into his character and has made a negative assessment concerning him.

The final paragraph conveys her conflicting emotions. "Fanny thought she had never known a day of greater agitation, both of pain and pleasure," the latter relates to "William's advancement." In spite of what must be regarded as an "ill-written" note that "would disgrace a child . . . at least it would assure" the Crawfords "both of her being neither imposed on, nor gratified by Mr. Crawford's attentions" (299, 301–303, 305, 307–308). In this chapter, there are several interesting examples of Jane Austen's use of free indirect speech to convey such thoughts. For instance, when Henry is about to propose to Fanny, "He was after her immediately. 'She must not go, she must allow him five minutes longer,' and he took her hand and led her back to her seat." Henry Crawford's largely monosyllabic words convey his sense of the importance of what he is to do. The total sentence in which they appear conveys the unexpectedness from Fanny's point of view. When he initiates the proposal, a whole paragraph beginning "She was feeling, thinking, trembling, about everything" and concluding with a question: "if they meant but to trifle?" conveys her state of mind, her thoughts without her actually speaking (301–303).

Volume 3, Chapter 1 (Chapter 32)

The opening chapter of the third and final volume contains some of the longest instances of direct speech in the novel. These are given to Sir Thomas Bertram. The chapter also presents differing perceptions: those of Sir Thomas articulated as he discovers that Fanny is resolved to reject Henry Crawford; Fanny's perceptions of Henry not expressed to Sir Thomas, although the reader is aware of them, and of her depth of feeling for Edmund. In the opening paragraph of the chapter, Fanny's feelings are conveyed through the interweaving of interior monologue followed by authorial observation: "if Mr. Crawford would but go away!—That was what she most earnestly desired." Instead of writing, "Fanny was astonished" at Crawford's reappearance early the next morning, the adverse effect that Crawford's arrival has on Fanny is conveyed through the negative, "she could not but be astonished to see."

To avoid Crawford, Fanny retreats into her room. She "trembled at" the knock of her uncle on her door. He is surprised that following Mrs. Norris's instructions, there is no fire in Fanny's room in spite of the snow outside. He has come to tell Fanny that Crawford has come to ask him for her hand in marriage. In a mixture of authorial narration and direct speech, Sir Thomas tells Fanny what Crawford has said. She deliberately avoids eye contact with him. It gradually dawns on Sir Thomas that Fanny means to refuse Crawford. She tells Sir Thomas, "I—I cannot like him, Sir, well enough to marry him." Her refusal presents a challenge to Sir Thomas's authority and perceptions. In what is probably Fanny's longest direct articulation in the chapter, a very brief one compared to Sir Thomas's, she gives a contrary reading of what occurred the day before between herself and Henry Crawford. She tells Sir Thomas, "I gave him no encouragement yesterday." She then stresses, "On the contrary, I told him." She then becomes less sure of herself, "I cannot recollect my exact words."

Then after another parenthesis, she says, "I am sure I told him that I would not listen to him." In such a clause and the two following, she rapidly conveys what she did say, "it was very unpleasant to me in every respect, and that I begged him never to talk to me in that manner again."

Fanny's hesitancy reveals how difficult she finds it to oppose Sir Thomas, to whom she is so indebted. He replies that "There is something in this which my comprehension does not read." Fanny is presenting a set of values totally opposed to his vision of reality and how things are done. He reminds Fanny what Crawford has done for her brother, and she felt a "fresh shame." She cannot tell Sir Thomas that she thinks "ill of" Crawford's "principles" as "Her ill opinion was founded chiefly on observations," which in order to protect Maria and Julia, "she could scarcely dare mention to" Sir Thomas. He then crushes her in an accumulation of nouns conveying his perception of her selfishness. Sir Thomas "thought" Fanny "peculiarly free from willfulness of temper, self-conceit, and every tendency to that independence of spirit, which prevails so much in modern days, even in young women." Sir Thomas's is the ideology of the conservative male landowner.

To make matters worse, he accuses Fanny of disregarding her family, who "might be benefited." He would have been pleased to see his own daughters married to Crawford. In a giveaway remark, he describes Maria as "nobly married," rather than "happily married." Sir Thomas tells Fanny that he regards her refusal as "a gross violation of duty and respect." All she can do is to articulate her sorrow through tears: "She was miserable for ever." Sir Thomas returns to Fanny's room to tell her that Crawford has left the house, and following this advises her that she go into "the shrubbery" for a breath of fresh air. When she returns she finds that her uncle has ordered, contrary to Mrs. Norris's instructions, "a fire lighted and burning" in her room. During dinner she has to yet again suffer Mrs. Norris's bullying. At the end of the chapter, Mrs. Norris refuses to accept that Sir Thomas's butler Baddeley requests that Sir Thomas wants Fanny rather than her. Fanny, however, obeying the instructions, "found herself, as she anticipated, in another minute alone with Mr. Crawford" (311, 315, 317–319, 321–322, 325).

Volume 3, Chapter 2 (Chapter 33)

In another chapter focusing on differing perspectives, Henry Crawford continues his courtship of Fanny. Her refusal increases his determination to marry her. His misperception of Fanny's feelings emerges when the author conveys his thought: "He knew not that he had a pre-engaged heart to attack, of *that* he had no suspicion" (Jane Austen's emphasis). Fanny, "who had known too much opposition all her life," has a different view of Crawford, although she detects a change in him since his toying with Maria's and Julia's affections during the theatricals. Henry's refusal, however, to accept her *no* rouses anger in her: "some resentment did arise at a perseverance so selfish and ungenerous."

Sir Thomas decides that "upon her [Fanny's] disposition . . . kindness might be the best way of working." Since Henry Crawford has no qualms about making public his courtship of Fanny, Sir Thomas does so too. Not before he has ironically told her that her "happiness and advantage are" the object he has "in view" for her. Fanny, "when considered how much of the truth was unknown to" Sir Thomas, understood why he acted as he did. Especially as "romantic delicacy," or an appreciation for positive feelings—love—"was not to be expected from" Sir Thomas. The narrator seems to side with Sir Thomas rather than with Fanny, in pointing out that she is "only eighteen" and could also change "her own fancy."

Once Sir Thomas has made Henry's proposal public, Mrs. Norris, in deference to Sir Thomas's wish for her to remain silent, "only looked her increased ill-will" rather than in an open expression of hostility. She is furious that Fanny has been preferred by Crawford to Julia. Lady Bertram, on the other hand, "took it differently"—illustrating the motif of differing perceptions. From Lady Bertram's viewpoint, "she had been a beauty, and a prosperous beauty, all her life; and beauty and wealth were all that excited her respect." In urging Fanny to accept the proposal, she "feels a sort of credit" in it. The proposal reflects her own decision to let her personal maid, Chapman, help Fanny for the ball. At the end of the chapter there is a somewhat confusing reference to one of her dogs. Perhaps Lady Bertram is in her usual stupor, although she is very materialistic in urging Fanny to marry Henry Crawford. She tells Fanny, "more than I did for Maria—the next time pug has a litter you shall have a puppy" (326–333). Earlier in the novel in the first volume, chapter 7, Pug is a "him" (74), so he seems to have undergone a sex change, unless, of course, Lady Bertram has more than one "pug"! Or unless she is just confused or absentminded.

Volume 3, Chapter 3 (Chapter 34)

This chapter opens with yet another perspective. This time the focus is on Edmund, who returns from Peterborough as a newly ordained clergyman. To avoid Mary Crawford, "his absence" from the Mansfield environs "had been extended beyond a fortnight." Mary greets Edmund cordially, and Sir Thomas informs him of Henry's proposal to Fanny. Edmund is not surprised by Fanny's refusal, yet feels that given time she will accept him. For Edmund, "Fanny was worth it all; he held her to be worth every effort of patience, every exertion of mind."

Henry stays for the evening at the Bertrams'. His reading of a passage from Shakespeare's *Henry VIII* "was truly dramatic" and makes such an impression on Fanny that her "eyes which had appeared so studiously to avoid him throughout the day, were turned and fixed on Crawford, fixed on him for minutes, fixed on him in short till the attraction drew Crawford's upon her." At this point, Fanny "was shrinking again into herself." The reading from *Henry VIII* with the character of "the King, the Queen, Buckingham, Wolsey" and Cromwell, has intertextual significance. Wolsey's speech in the third act, scene 2, "Farewell, a long farewell to all my greatness," is an example of a proud man realizing that his situation is hopeless. The King is torn between his faithful wife of long standing in a loveless marriage and the promise held out by the younger and physically more attractive Anne Bullen. In a sense, Fanny represents the old values of reticence and sobriety, and Henry Crawford those of the emerging generation, of enjoyment and hedonism. He appears to be prepared to renounce these for the values Fanny represents of integrity.

Lady Bertram assumes that Henry will have a theater in his house at Everingham. Looking at Fanny, he is even prepared to renounce this pleasure. Edmund and Henry engage in a discussion on the art of reading, and Henry asks Edmund a series of questions about the church. These focus on the subject of preaching. Henry, in order to demonstrate "seriousness on serious subjects," confesses that he has "never listened to a distinguished preacher in my life, without a sort of envy." It is necessary for Henry to "have a London audience," as he can preach only "to the educated" and "not for constancy." Edmund retreats into reading the advertisements on the front page of a newspaper, while Henry tries to engage a reluctant Fanny on the subject of "constancy." He tells her that his "conduct shall speak for" him although she is "infinitely [his] superior in merit" but he shall win her: "It is he, who sees and worships your merit the strongest, who loves you most devotedly," who will be successful.

At the end of the chapter, Fanny is rescued by the appearance of the butler Baddely with tea, coffee, and cakes. The last paragraph consisting of two sentences is viewed not through either Fanny or Henry's eyes, but Edmund's. He was "inclined"—implying doubt of some nature—"to hope that so much could not have been said and listened to, without some profit of the speaker," Henry. Earlier in the chapter, the two-sentence paragraph beginning with a short, factual sentence, Henry and Edmund are concerned with "the subject of reading aloud." The following sentence beginning "The two young men were the only talkers," and concluding "and Fanny was listening again with great entertainment," embraces various subjects. These include "the ordinary school-system for boys," that means the public school system for which families paid: There was no universal education. There is also a reference to terms in logic such as "secondary causes" and "first cause." The sentence in this way reflects in its convoluted fashion its very subject: how to read aloud correctly.

Edmund tells Henry that "there is now a spirit of improvement abroad." He is referring to the impact of the Evangelical movement on the Anglican Church. Since his ordination, Edmund "had

already gone through the service once"—probably he helped with the Christmas services where his friends the Owens lived. Crawford mentions "our liturgy," or in other words, the Anglican order of service. He then proceeds before Fanny to outline what should be in a good sermon and the qualities needed in a fine preacher. These include "the preacher who can touch and affect such an heterogeneous mass of hearers, on subjects limited, and long worn thread-bare in all common hands."

In this chapter, Henry Crawford demonstrates his serious side and exhibits his knowledge of the Anglican Church and preaching. Once again, it is Fanny who, although on the whole remaining verbally silent, is the focus of attention of both Henry and Edmund. The key images are again perception, sight, and insight. Fanny deliberately tries to avoid looking at Henry and Edmund. Henry is not far wrong when he tells her, "You have some touches of the angel in you, beyond what—not merely beyond what one *sees*, because one never *sees* any thing like it—but beyond what one fancies might be" (my emphasis) (334, 336–337, 340–344, 339–341, 344).

Volume 3, Chapter 4 (Chapter 35)

Following Sir Thomas's request, Edmund tries to persuade Fanny to accept Henry Crawford's proposal and to discover what her objections are. Edmund tells Fanny that she cannot "imagine [him] an advocate for marriage without love?" He then describes the complimentary qualities of Fanny and Henry. They have, for instance, "moral and literary tastes in common. You have both warm hearts and benevolent feelings." Fanny, however, finds it difficult to excuse Henry's behavior toward Maria and Rushworth. "I must say, cousin, that I cannot approve his character." Edmund replies, "let us not, any of us, be judged by what we appeared at that period of general folly." He particularly blames himself. Fanny tells him that "As a by-stander . . . perhaps I saw more than you did." Responding to Fanny's observation concerning Henry, "I am persuaded that he does not think as he ought, on serious subjects"; Edmund distinguishes between "serious" thought and "feelings" (346–351). Such a debate reflects a long-standing one in the Anglican Church between those who "believed mankind to be endowed with natural affection and instinctive benevolence, and the main Anglican tradition, which contended . . . that 'good feelings' alone cannot be relied upon" (Wiltshire, 716).

Fanny, in one of her longest speeches in the novel, tells Edmund, "In my situation, it would have been the extreme of vanity, to be forming expectations on" Henry, and that she cannot form "an attachment" to him "at his service." She tells Edmund that he has a very limited and misleading idea "of the nature of women" if he assumes that they are "so very soon capable of returning an affection as this seems to imply." Edmund jumps to the conclusion that Fanny rejects Crawford, because with her "habit had most power, and novelty least." His assessment of her character is correct; what is incorrect is his analysis of why she rejects Crawford's proposal. Edmund adds to the "weariness and distress" he sees in Fanny's face by telling Fanny that Mary Crawford approves of the match with her brother. Fanny cunningly ascertains whether he found the Owen daughters, with whom he stayed, attractive. He responds that they "will not do for a man who has been used to sensible women." Constant reference to Mary Crawford leaves Fanny at the end of the chapter "oppressed and weary" (353–355).

Volume 3, Chapter 5 (Chapter 36)
Edmund tells his father to give Fanny "time" to return Henry Crawford's affection. Sir Thomas is "less willing than his son to trust to the future," but "there was nothing to be done . . . but to submit quietly, and hope the best." Fanny is "in continual terror of" the inevitable visit from Mary Crawford. When she does come, they go "up stairs" to Fanny's "now always fit for comfortable use" apartment. This is where Mary rehearsed with Edmund and Mary goes into "a reverie of sweet remembrances" of the scene between them concerning the idyllic depiction of a devoted couple and an unhappy marriage in which both partners (as Julia) long for liberty. Following her recollection, Mary tells Fanny that she does not realize what a "conquest" she has made, how many female admirers Henry has, and how jealous they are of Fanny. She also describes

the unhappy marriages she knows. Mary reveals the truth behind the gift of Henry's necklace she had given to Fanny. Mary "was delighted to act on his proposal, for both your sakes." Mary confesses to Fanny that she believes that Henry "loves you [Fanny] with all his heart, and will love you as nearly for ever as possible."

Mary reminds Fanny of what Henry has done for her brother William, and then takes her leave of her with "so much apparent affection." Fanny is relieved by Mary's departure, especially as "Her secret was still her own," that is her love for Edmund. At the conclusion of the chapter, the usually talkative Henry "scarcely said any thing," and "When it came to the moment of parting, he would take [Fanny's] hand" yet is silent. The next day both Crawfords leave for London (356–359, 362–365). A French expression meaning hard to please, "exigeant" is used. "Blues" is a reference to the Royal Regiment of Horse Guards, who have their headquarters in London and wear dark blue uniform jackets. A commission to such an elite regiment was very expensive. To "jilt" someone in the "Blues" is an act of either folly or daring (361).

Volume 3, Chapter 6 (Chapter 37)
Sir Thomas observes Fanny carefully: "she was always so gentle and retiring, that her emotions were beyond his discrimination." Edmund is surprised that Fanny does not miss Mary, "who was now the chief bane of Fanny's comfort." Fanny believes that it is now more likely than previously that Edmund will propose to Mary, although during their "last conversation" Mary had "still shewn a mind led astray and bewildered . . . darkened, yet fancying itself light" (366–367). It is appropriate, given Fanny's love and deep empathy for the newly ordained Edmund, that her thinking reflects biblical language.

William, her brother, arrives at Mansfield on 10 days' leave. "The happiest of lieutenants," he is able only to "describe his uniform," which he can only wear on duty. William is only a "2nd lieutenant" and compared with higher ranks and uniforms "it would be sunk into a badge of disgrace." This sense that things are relative underlies Sir Thomas's "scheme" that Fanny "should accompany her brother back to

Portsmouth, and spend a little time with her own family." In this way, she can place Mansfield and the proposal from Henry Crawford into perspective. Sir Thomas "wished her to be heartily sick of home before her visit ended" and "her Father's house would, in all probability, teach her the value of a good income." Fanny has a different perspective, seeing her visit as an opportunity to renew "her earliest pleasures" with her parents, brothers, and sisters. She also thinks that an absence from Edmund for some time "must do her good," especially as the pain of his probable marriage to Mary will be "hard to bear." William prepares Fanny for what is to occur, telling her in something of an understatement, "we seem to want some of your nice ways and orderliness at my father's . . . The house is always in confusion."

There are references needing explication in this chapter. Fanny misleadingly believes that "leisure and inclination for every comfort" (368–372, 371), provided by her visit to her mother, will alleviate the pain caused by Mary marrying Edmund. As Wiltshire observes, "Fanny imagines not merely ease, but assistance or support and spiritual sustenance" (718). She will discover that this is not the case. William is about to undertake "his first cruise," or voyage looking for prize money. He also longs to show his sister "several improvements in the dockyard." This refers to the construction under Sir Samuel Bentham's (1757–1831), direction of two deep docks during the years 1795 and 1801. As Fanny and William start their Portsmouth journey, "Sir Thomas actually give[s] William notes for the purpose." This refers to the 1797 Bank of England notes made legal tender for any amount. In the last sentence of the third from last paragraph, phrasing reminiscent of Dr. Samuel Johnson, "The vicissitude of the human mind had not yet been exhausted by her" (372, 374), in Wiltshire's words "underlines the slight absurdity of [Fanny's] . . . thinking she might have seen every thing" (719).

Volume 3, Chapter 7 (Chapter 38)
The Portsmouth scenes are some of the most interesting in the novel. In a well-known essay, David Lodge observes that "up to Fanny's visit to Portsmouth—character is revealed in trivial actions."

In contrast with her experience at Mansfield Park, the world of Portsmouth encountered by Fanny is one "in which the social values which govern behaviour are highly prized . . . but only when they are informed by some moral order of value which transcends the social" (98, 101–102). Arriving at her parents' home in Portsmouth after traveling for two days, Fanny is surprised by the difference in size between where they live and Mansfield, as exemplified by the "narrow street" and the "small house" where she and William are greeted by a "trollopy-looking maid-servant." She tells them that William's ship, the *Thrush*, has "gone out of harbour" and that William is needed immediately. Indeed, Mr. Campbell, who turns out to be the ship's surgeon, is going to collect him at six the same evening. Received by her mother and by two of her sisters, Susan, "a well-grown fine girl of fourteen," and Betsey, "the youngest of the family, about five," Fanny goes "into the parlour, so small that her first conviction was of its being only a passage-room to something better."

Fanny quickly learns that her parents have no time for her. Her mother is so involved with William, that she has not made a meal and even tea is difficult to organize. When she has time, Fanny's mother confesses, "what a sad fire we have got, and I dare say you are both starved with cold." Her father, Mr. Price, ignores Fanny and retreats into reading a neighbor's newspaper and greeting his son with the information concerning the progress of the *Thrush*. In short, "Fanny was almost shunned. The smallness of the house, and thinness of the walls, brought every thing so close to her . . . she hardly knew how to bear it." She begins to miss Mansfield and the values it represents contrasted with the noise, smallness, dust, and chaos of her Portsmouth house. "In her uncle's house there would have been a consideration of times and seasons, a regulation of subject, a propriety, an attention towards every body which there was not here."

The only comfort Fanny can draw upon is from Susan, who like William "had an open, sensible countenance." Problems with servant help remind Fanny of "a very pretty little girl . . . who had died a few years afterwards" at Mansfield, and who in fact was a relative of one of the servants at her parents' house. The shock of mortality is combined with shock at a conflict between the younger sisters over a knife. The quarreling shocks Fanny's "every feeling of duty, honour and tenderness" and sense of relationship between mother and daughter. At the conclusion of the chapter, "Fanny fatigued and fatigued again, was thankful to accept the first invitation of going to bed." She is to share with Susan a "confined and scantily-furnished chamber." This combined with "the smallness of the rooms" achieves her uncle, Sir Thomas's purpose, in allowing her to accompany her brother. "She soon learnt to think with respect of her own little attic at Mansfield Park, in *that* house reckoned too small for anybody's comfort" (Jane Austen's emphasis).

Portsmouth, and her parents' house is a great disappointment to Fanny. The language used by her mother and father is coarse. The father tells William in a speech replete with short sentences concerning the *Thrush*: "But by G—, you lost a fine sight by not being here . . . I would not have been out of the way for a thousand pounds." Blasphemy is followed by betting metaphors and idiomatic expression: "she had slipped her moorings and was coming out." The chapter is full of localized references, although at its beginning these are literary. In the third paragraph, William is described as being "of an age to be all for love." This is a clear allusion to the title of John Dryden's reworking of Shakespeare's drama, appropriately renamed *Anthony and Cleopatra, All For Love, or the World Well Lost* (1678). William is idealistic about love. From Sir Thomas's point of view, Fanny by rejecting Henry Crawford and his wealth has indeed "the World Well Lost"!

William and Fanny travel to Portsmouth "in the dirty month of February" via Oxford with "a hasty glimpse" of Edmund's former college. As they enter Portsmouth, "they passed the Drawbridge," which serves to illustrate that during the Napoleonic War period Portsmouth was a heavily guarded town and port. William's ship is moored near the *Canopus* and the *Elephant*, ships that participated in the Battle of Copenhagen in 1801. Jane Austen's own brother, FRANK AUSTEN, captained the *Elephant* and in 1805–06 served on the *Canopus*. Her younger brother CHARLES AUSTEN had been a mid-

shipman and then a lieutenant on the *Endymion* before assuming command of the *Cleopatra* in 1810. Fanny's father tells his son that his friend "was saying just now, that he thought you would be sent first to the Texel." This was an important area for the Royal Naval blockade of the Dutch mainland. The Dutch during this period were enemies of Britain. Her father "was upon the platform for two hours this afternoon," or a high point overlooking Portsmouth harbor from which naval activity could be seen. One of Fanny's brothers serves as a "midshipman on board an Indiaman," that is, a merchant ship probably belonging to the East India Company. Another, although much younger brother, Sam, has a "voice louder than all the rest!" His father observes, "That boy is fit for a boatswain." The "boatswain," who kept order and discipline on ship, and was responsible for the management of the rigging and sails, needed a loud voice, as much of his work was done by shouting or yelling.

Campbell, the ship's surgeon, and William leave for "the sally port," or the gap in the sea wall's protection allowing the officers and crew to join their ships moored offshore. Finally, not a naval reference, but one relating to domestic servants. Fanny believes that her mother means "to part with" a difficult servant "when her year was up." This assumes that there was some kind of written agreement, as there might well have been at Mansfield, that domestic servants were employed for a year. The rough-and-ready nature of existence at the Price home is reinforced by Mrs. Price's rejoinder to Fanny: "Her year! . . . I am sure I hope I shall be rid of her before she has staid a year" (375–387). This chapter then is unique in Jane Austen's work in its direct depiction of lower-class speech and attitudes.

Volume 3, Chapter 8 (Chapter 39)

The contrast between Mansfield Park and Fanny's new surroundings is pursued in a relatively brief chapter of 12 paragraphs, seen through Fanny's perspective without the dialogue of the previous chapter. The positives outlined in the lengthy initial sentence of the opening paragraph quickly give way to negatives: "it was all disappointment." Such a sense is conveyed in the third sentence of the chapter's second paragraph and its fourfold repetition of "no" followed by "nothing." William's parting words to his mother, "Take care of Fanny, mother. She is tender, and not used to rough it like the rest of us," fall upon deaf ears as the chapter demonstrates. The verb "lounges" is used to describe Mr. Price's activities, meaning strolling or sauntering around, almost without purpose. The time spent with William has been all too short. They have not even been able to "walk on the ramparts" or visit "the dock-yard." So Fanny is unable to view the protective ramparts built around Portsmouth. She also has not been able to visit the main Royal Naval shipyard.

Sir Thomas is correct. Her childhood home is "in almost every respect, the very reverse of what she could have wished." The Price home "was the abode of noise, disorder, and impropriety." She has no respect for her parents. Her father "was more negligent of his family, his habits were worse, and his manners coarser, than she had been prepared for." His reading is limited to "the newspaper and the navy-list," or the official published listings of promotions, officers, naval rules, and regulations. His talk is restricted to the navy and "the Motherbank," or the stretch of narrow water where ships sheltered in rough weather. Furthermore, "he swore and he drank, he was dirty and gross." Her mother had her hands full. The natural affection or bond between mother and daughter, "the instinct of nature was soon satisfied. . . . Her heart and her time were already quite full; she had neither leisure nor affection to bestow on Fanny." Mrs. Price's "days were spent in a kind of slow bustle, always busy without getting on, always behind and lamenting it, without altering her ways." Her mother is a mixture of the qualities of her two sisters but "very much more resembled Lady Bertram than Mrs. Norris." In a very telling sentence revealing the impact of wealth and character, Jane Austen writes that Mrs. Price "might have made just as good a woman of consequence as Lady Bertram, but Mrs. Norris would have been a more respectable mother of nine children on a small income."

Fanny does her best to be useful "and not to appear above her home." She feels alienated from the younger boys and the indulged Betsey "and

of Susan's temper, she had many doubts." Fanny misses "The elegance, propriety, regularity, harmony—and perhaps, above all, the peace and tranquillity of Mansfield." The noise, the lack of "good sense and good breeding" even place Mrs. Norris's "irritations" in a positive light. The chapter concludes with Fanny's temptation to apply to her Portsmouth and Mansfield homes "Dr. Johnson's celebrated judgment as to matrimony and celibacy, and say, that though Mansfield Park might have some pains, Portsmouth could have no pleasures." The negatives of one far outweigh the other. The Johnsonian reference is to chapter 26 of his fictional *Rasselas* (1759). In the eighth chapter of the third volume of *MP*, Jane Austen captures the balanced tone of her great predecessor. The sentences on the whole are straightforward. There is little if any dialogue, the use of semicolons and commas convey the measured but sure tone of judgment and condemnation. At Fanny's parents' home, "nobody sat still and nobody could command attention" (388–392).

Volume 3, Chapter 9 (Chapter 40)

Another relatively short chapter with almost no dialogue is yet again set in the Prices' home at Portsmouth, with Mary and then Fanny the central viewpoints. Fanny receives a gossipy letter from Mary Crawford that in Fanny's "present exile from good society" is very welcome. Mary's account, containing French expressions such as "passionnées," meaning ardent or affectionate, reveals that her brother, Henry, is in Norfolk at his Everingham estate. Maria and Julia are in London, and Yates continues to pay attention to Julia. Maria takes exception to Fanny's name. Edmund has not yet visited London. Julia has "the best looks of the two"—an indication that not all is well in Maria's marriage. But her husband is very wealthy; Maria, "will open one of the best houses in Wimpole Street," one of the most fashionable and expensive central London districts.

Mary writes Fanny, "Your cousin Edmund moves slowly," adding that "There may be some old women. . . . to be converted." In other words, "converted" to be Evangelicals. According to Mary, Yates is only "a poor honourable" who "is no catch," that is, being the younger son of a lord, he may have title but insufficient income. Mary's letter preoccupies the first two paragraphs of the chapter, which subsequently reverts to Fanny's reaction on reading it and her negative feelings toward her new surroundings, where "The men appeared to her all coarse, the women all pert, every body under-bred." She is perceived as having "airs," she did not for instance wear "fine pelisses" or a mantle of silk velvet reaching down to the ankles.

Consolation comes to Fanny from Susan, who tries to improve matters at home, has the quality of "reason," displays "delicacy," and "was inclined to seek [Fanny's] good opinion and refer to her judg-ment." She and Susan take refuge, sitting "together up stairs," as Fanny had done at Mansfield Park. Fanny needs books again: "wealth is luxurious and daring—and some of hers found its way to a circu-lating library. She became a subscriber," whereas previously at Mansfield Park she'd been surrounded by books. Circulating libraries developed in the mid-dle of the 18th century and the cost of borrowing a book was not cheap but something of a luxury.

Fanny wishes to share her own initial pleasures of reading with Susan, who "had read nothing." Fanny wishes to "inspire" in Susan "a taste for the biography and poetry which she delighted in her-self." Reading is an escape. In reading, Fanny hopes "to bury some of the recollections of Mansfield" that surface when her mind is not busy. She is also concerned now that she supposes Edmund has reached London. In the final sentence of the chap-ter, she is afraid of "the postman's knock within the neighbourhood." The postman knocks twice to receive payment. Fanny's unstated fear is that she will receive a letter from Mary saying that she and Edmund are engaged. The final word of the chap-ter, like its opening sentence, contains a positive sentiment rather than the negatives dominating the chapter: "if reading could banish the idea [of a "postman's knock"] for even half an hour, it was something gained" (393–398).

Volume 3, Chapter 10 (Chapter 41)

Largely using omniscient narration, this chapter focuses on Henry Crawford's surprise visit to Ports-mouth to see Fanny. Her mother's manners "were also at their best" in response to his "perfect" man-ners, and she expresses her "gratitude" to Craw-ford for helping William. Henry tells Fanny that "he set off" for Portsmouth following a brief stop in London, from Everingham, his Norfolk estate, where he had been on business. Edmund was in London. On hearing this, "the words 'then by this time it is all settled' passed internally" in Fanny, who assumes that Edmund has proposed to Mary. Henry, accompanied by Susan and Fanny, takes a walk and meets Mr. Price, who "was a very differ-ent man, a very different Mr. Price in his behaviour to the most highly-respected stranger." He behaves as "an attached father, and a sensible man." There is authorial intervention in the narrative when using the first person; Jane Austen writes, "and I believe, there is scarcely a young lady in the united kingdoms, who would not rather put up with the misfortune of being sought by a clever agreeable man, than have him driven away by the vulgarity of her nearest relations."

Mr. Price offers to show Henry Crawford the dockyard. As they walk around it, Henry tells Fanny and Susan about his estate business at Ever-ingham, his charitable efforts to help some of his tenants from being cheated by his agent, or lawyer, responsible for the estate finances. All this leads Fanny to think "him altogether improved since she had seen him; he was much more gentle, obliging, and attentive to other people's feelings than he had ever been at Mansfield." Henry also speaks of Mansfield Park and tells Fanny that he has come to speak to her. Much to Fanny's relief, Henry rejects an offer to dine at the Prices' but will see them the next day. The second sentence of the sixth paragraph from the end of the chapter indicates through its repetitive usage of the pronoun "he" three times that Henry Crawford is still preoccupied with himself. This sense is further reinforced in the final sentence of the paragraph, "*She* was nice only from natural delicacy, but *he* had been brought up in a school of luxury and epicurism" (Jane Austen's emphasis). The first word of the sentence could refer solely to Fanny, or to her whole family, or to Mrs. Price, the "*he*" is Henry, who represents a totally different set of values based on wealth and self-gratification.

Yet again in encounters between Henry and Fanny, there is emphasis on sight. When Henry appears unexpectedly, he "was wisely and kindly keeping his eyes away." Subsequently, as Fanny's attitudes become slightly more sympathetic toward Henry, "she was tolerably able to bear his eye." Henry's visit to Portsmouth is to see Fanny; it is not "a visit to the port-admiral, nor the commissioner." Henry stays at one of the largest inns, the "Crown" on the High Street. When they walk, they do so "at that season of the year," that is, early March and spring. "Portsmouth was a sad place." There would be few opportunities, especially for women, to leave the house in a naval port well known for prostitution, crime, and drunkenness. They encounter Fanny's father, "whose appearance was not the better from its being Saturday." In other words, he has probably been drinking with friends, not working. As they tour the dockyard, there is a reference to "the number of three deckers now in commission," or to the largest ships in the Royal Navy, having three gun decks. Other naval allusions include "a vessel in the stocks," or a ship being built or repaired.

Henry visits Everingham "at this unusual time of year," during the London season of parties and balls calculated to demonstrate to Fanny how thoughtful and socially conscious of his duties he has become. He also mentions the houses at "Mansfield, Sotherton, and Thornton Lacey," adding "perhaps, a fourth may be added, some small hunting-box in the vicinity of every thing," or somewhere where he and his friends can go hunting. Henry's social public awareness goes so far and no further: He must accommodate his own pleasures (399–407).

Volume 3, Chapter 11 (Chapter 42)

Henry Crawford goes with the Price family "to the Garrison chapel" near the sea, serving the officers and men of the Portsmouth Garrison. "Sunday," and the word is repeated three times in the second and third sentences of the second paragraph of the chapter, provides the opportunity for Mrs. Price and her family to be released from their domestic confines. So much so that the "no inconsiderable share of beauty" possessed by the Price family reveals itself. Fanny reflects on the consequences

of "circumstances" on her mother and Lady Bertram. Her mother, younger than Lady Bertram, has "an appearance so much more worn and faded, so comfortless, so slatternly, so shabby." On such a beautiful spring day, Fanny appreciates Henry Crawford's arm. Henry has perceived that being enclosed within the confines of the small Price home is not good for her health. In the sixth paragraph of the chapter, Fanny becomes "almost careless of the circumstances." She responds positively and spontaneously to nature, to "the ever-varying hues of the sea now at high water, dancing in its glee and dashing against the ramparts with so fine a sound." Indeed, "but for Mr. Crawford and the beauty of the weather [she] would soon have been knocked up [exhausted, unwell] now."

Fanny, forever trying to be accurate, responds to Henry's observation that "You have been here a month, I think?" with "It is only four weeks tomorrow." He, however, is convinced that at Portsmouth it "could not be salutary for her." This is the only instance in Jane Austen's work of the word "salutary," meaning healthy. Henry is afraid that the longer she stays at the Prices', the more she will be forgotten at Mansfield, and "that she ought never to be long banished from the free air, and liberty of the country." He is seeking her advice on matters concerning his Everingham estate responsibilities, although Henry is aware of his ultimate power and authority over Maddison, his agent. Fanny's response, "We all have a better guide in ourselves," reflects Evangelical thought relating to the conscience and inner light. Henry offers to take Fanny home to Mansfield whenever she requests it.

Henry returns to "the best dinner that a capital inn afforded," while Fanny returns to the "many privations" of the Price household. Henry's visit leaves her "very low," for "after being nursed up at Mansfield, it was too late in the day to be hardened at Portsmouth." She believes, "fancied," she has detected in Henry Crawford a "wonderful improvement," and "she was quite persuaded of his being astonishingly more gentle, and regardful of others, than formerly." Fanny poses a question to herself "that he would not much longer persevere in a suit so distressing to her?" (408–414).

Volume 3, Chapter 12 (Chapter 43)

Most of this chapter concerns Fanny's reaction to a letter she receives from Mary Crawford. Mary's letter includes incidental London gossip and, as an afterthought, Edmund is mentioned as being in London. Henry is preoccupied with estate business, but Mary is insisting that she stay until after a party, when "she will see the Rushworths." Mary's friends consider Edmund's physical appearance very favorably. She tells Fanny "my dear little creature, do not stay at Portsmouth to lose your pretty looks." Fanny concludes that Mary will accept Edmund when he proposes to her. "She would hesitate, she would teaze, she would condition, she would require a great deal, but she would finally accept." If Mary collects Fanny from Portsmouth, she will show her London and "the inside of St. George's Hanover-Square," a very fashionable church frequented by the wealthy but with a dull interior. Mary adds, "Only keep your cousin Edmund from me at such a time, I should not like to be tempted." So she is teasing Fanny and clearly treading on sensitive ground. However, Fanny concludes that "nothing yet decisive had yet taken place" between Mary and Edmund.

Fanny takes refuge at the Prices' in her relationship with her younger sister Susan, whom she considers "had an innate taste for the genteel and well-appointed." Fanny and Susan read together Oliver Goldsmith's "history" (see book 1, chapter 18), and Fanny is concerned about Susan's future once she, Fanny, leaves Portsmouth, or secures "her own release." The metaphor implies that her parents' home has become a prison for her. Fanny would ideally like to take Susan back to the civilizing influence of Mansfield Park. She begins to consider that Henry Crawford would not object to Susan's presence. In the last sentence of the chapter, Fanny thinks that Henry "was really good-tempered." Significantly, the final words of the sentence are "most pleasantly" and relate Fanny's mind to Henry Crawford and to Susan (415–419).

Volume 3, Chapter 13 (Chapter 44)

Chapter 44 contains a rambling self-confessional letter from Edmund, a letter from Lady Bertram followed by almost daily accounts from her, and Fanny's reactions to these letters. The contrasting styles between Mary Crawford's playful letters and Edmund's serious ones are evident. Fanny serves as the recipient of the letters in these chapters and reacts privately to them, Susan being her "only companion and listener." Fanny "might now be said to live upon letters," but she does not respond to them in kind.

Mary has written from London, Edmund from Mansfield Park, having returned from spending three weeks in London. He informs Fanny that his "hopes" of marrying Mary "are much weaker." To Edmund Mary is different in London, more "playful" and influenced by friends who are advocates of "every thing mercenary and ambitious, provided it be only mercenary and ambitious enough." Mary is influenced by the external, and although Edmund has not yet proposed to her, "She is the only woman in the world whom I could ever think of as a wife." Edmund fears "the habits of wealth." Edmund has seen Maria and Henry at a London party but they seemed to be distant. The Grants are leaving Mansfield and the vicarage to go to Bath, leaving Lady Bertram with limited companionship.

Following Fanny's reactions to Edmund's letter and news, Lady Bertram writes to tell her that Tom Bertram is very ill following a bout of drinking and a fall from a horse at Newmarket racecourse. Tom has been taken to Mansfield Park, and Lady Bertram is "so shocked to see him, that I do not know what to do." She writes to Fanny "in the same, diffuse style, and the same medley of trusts, hopes and fears, all following and producing each other at hap-hazard." In short, "Lady Bertram wrote her daily terrors to her niece."

In the final paragraph of the chapter conveying information to Fanny, that information is placed in its perspective: "So long divided, and so differently situated, the ties of blood were little more than nothing." What is important to Fanny cannot be so important and meaningful to the Prices and similarly if "three or four Prices might have been swept away, any or all, except Fanny and William, and Lady Bertram would have thought little about it." When she thinks that Tom Bertram might be so ill that he is dying, "the purity of [Fanny's] principles added yet a keener solicitude, when she considered how little useful . . . his life had (apparently) been." In other words, she is afraid that Tom will go to Hell (420–428).

Volume 3, Chapter 14 (Chapter 45)

This chapter focuses on two letters, one from Edmund, the other from Mary Crawford. Edmund's letter, apart from its postscript, is reported, Mary Crawford's quoted directly. Edmund's letter is revealing concerning his apparently unchanged feelings toward Mary Crawford; her letter provides insight into her real nature. In the opening paragraph, Lady Bertram seems more confident concerning Tom's condition, but Edmund's letter imports the true state of affairs. There are "some strong hectic symptoms, which seemed to seize" Tom's body "on the departure of the fever" and the family "were apprehensive for [Tom's] lungs." Fanny is aware, given her analysis of Mary's character, of "her selfishness and vanity," that for Mary "it would be good luck to have Edmund the only son." By marrying him she can consequently secure wealth and status.

Time passes slowly for Fanny stuck in Portsmouth: "Easter came—particularly late this year." However, in the years 1808–09, when the action of *MP* takes place, Easter was not late. In 1811 and 1812, the time Jane Austen was probably writing or rewriting *MP*, Easter was late, occurring at the close of April. Sir Thomas does not come to collect Fanny. "She supposed he could not leave his son, but it was a cruel, a terrible delay to" Fanny. At the end of April she will have been at Portsmouth "almost three months instead of two," and "her days had been passing in a state of penance." In other words, she had been at Portsmouth during the 40 days of Lent, a period in which renunciation is expected as a remembrance of Jesus' fasting in the wilderness before his crucifixion. Fanny has learned where she belongs, where her home is. She is so eager, longing so much to be at Mansfield that lines from William Cowper's poem "Tirocinium: Or, A Review of Schools" (1785) come to Fanny's mind. The last lines of the four-line "Th[e] indented stick, that loses day by day| Notch after notch, 'till all are smooth'd away,| Bears witness, long ere his dismission come,| With what intense

desire he wants his home," is "continually on [Fanny's] tongue." The context of Cowper's poem concerns a boy sent away to school who realizes how estranged he has become from his home for which he is, as is Fanny, "yearning."

The question of what is Fanny's true home has been resolved through her Portsmouth visit. "It must be applied to Mansfield. *That* was now her home. Portsmouth was Portsmouth; Mansfield was home" (Jane Austen's emphasis). Words in a letter from Lady Bertram, "I trust and hope, and sincerely wish you may never be absent from home so long again," become Fanny's "private regale," or treat. There then follows another lyrical passage conveying Fanny's response to her loss of "all the pleasures of spring. She had not known before what pleasures she *had* to lose in passing March and April in a town" (Jane Austen's emphasis). She misses "the earliest flowers," "the opening of leaves," "the glory of the woods," this is "because she was in the midst of closeness and noise, to have confinement, bad air, bad smells, substituted for liberty, freshness, fragrance and verdure, was infinitely worse."

While she is thinking how "useful" she could be at Mansfield, a letter comes from Mary Crawford in London. She speaks of Tom's death using language echoing 1 Samuel, 2:33. Mary writes, "To have such a fine young man cut off in the flower of his days, is most melancholy." The biblical tones reinforce the elegiac qualities of time, change, imminent loss, the movement of the seasons, clearly evident in the chapter and in *MP*. Mary speaks openly of the consequences of Tom's upcoming death of the "wealth and consequence" entailed for Edmund and her as his future wife, so that she can ignore the fact that Edmund is a clergyman. She also tells Fanny that Henry, her brother, has visited Maria Rushworth while Rushworth, her husband, was away at Twickenham and Richmond, fashionable towns on the Thames near London. The letter leaves Fanny with a sense of "disgust," and she finds the letter to reflect Henry's "conduct—*her* [Mary's] cold-hearted ambition—*his* [Henry's] thoughtless vanity" (Jane Austen's emphasis). In short, Fanny "was mortified." Fanny rejects Mary's offer to assist her return home. In the final paragraph of the chapter, Fanny reflects that as far as Mary is concerned, "Edmund would be forgiven for being a clergyman; it seemed, under certain conditions of wealth." Mary "had only learnt to think nothing of consequence but money" (429–436).

Volume 3, Chapter 15 (Chapter 46)

Two letters, an arrival and a departure, dominate this chapter. Fanny receives a letter from Mary urging her to "hear nothing, surmise nothing, whisper nothing, till" she writes "again." Mary says that "a most scandalous, ill-natured rumour has just reached" her. It involves her brother. According to Mary, "Henry is blameless, and in spite of a moment's *etourderie* [a thoughtless action or careless mistake: the choice of a French word "displays a worldly negligence of the gravity of the situation" (Stabler, 418 n. 343)] thinks of nobody but" Fanny. Until there is further news, Fanny remains in a "very uncomfortable" situation. She hears more, from a most unlikely source, that is, her father's newspaper reading. As it is early May and the light during the day draws out, there is no longer a need for a candle. However, "there was neither health nor gaiety in sun-shine in a town." Fanny sits "in a blaze of oppressive heat, in a cloud of moving dust." Her father reads in the newspaper of what has occurred. His response is to utter an expletive, and to give Maria "the rope's end." For Mr. Price, "a little flogging for man and woman too, would be the best way of preventing such things." Blows from "the rope's end" were a common form of punishment on board ship, whereas "flogging" was ceremonial, a punishment carried out usually by officers before an assembled crew. Newspapers usually published reports of elopements, and used a standard linguistic descriptive formula: for instance, including "the lists of hymen" to refer to a recent marriage.

On hearing the news of Maria's elopement, Fanny experiences "shame," and is in a "sort of stupefaction." Fanny "passed only from feelings of sickness to shudderings of horror" and she thinks of Henry's "unsettled affections, wavering with his vanity." She then thinks, in a passage of interior monologue, of the consequences of the elopement of Maria and Henry: "Whose peace could it not cut up for ever? Miss Crawford herself—Edmund." Another powerful word with resonance, "annihilation," comes to Fanny's mind when she thinks of Maria. Fanny does not receive a second letter from Mary but instead one from Edmund. He tells her that Julia has eloped "to Scotland with Yates," her father "is anxious" for Fanny to return home "for [his] mother's sake," and that he will collect Fanny from Portsmouth the next morning. Further, Sir Thomas "wishes [Fanny] to invite Susan to go with" her to Mansfield Park. In response to such news, "Never had Fanny more wanted a cordial," or a restorative. There is irony and antithesis in her situation: "She was, she felt she was, in the greatest danger of being exquisitely happy, while so many were miserable. The evil which brought such good to her!"

The remainder of the chapter is preoccupied with her hasty preparation to leave Portsmouth with Susan. Authorial comment is present in such a sentence as "There is nothing like employment, active, indispensable employment for relieving sorrow." Fanny "was ready to sink, as she entered the parlour" to see Edmund. The use of "sink" here implies collapse, and deference with an erotic undercurrent. Edmund "looked very ill," and Fanny's final "meal in her father's house" was similar to "her first; she was dismissed from it as hospitably as she had been welcome." As she and Susan "passed the barriers of Portsmouth," both experience "joy," in Fanny's case as if released from entrapment. Fanny is not afraid to catch Edmund's eye, whereas she averted herself from catching Henry's. Edmund "took her hand" on the way home to "the beloved place," Mansfield Park.

Susan is anxious, "meditating much upon silver forks, napkins, and finger glasses." The "finger glasses," the glass bowls of water used to rinse the fingers following the eating of fruit or dessert, for Susan represent gentility—a world she is not used to. Finally, in this chapter in the last paragraph, after they have arrived at Mansfield Park, Lady Bertram "came with no indolent step; and, falling on her neck, said 'Dear Fanny! now I shall be comfortable.'" There are here biblical overtones. When Joseph is reunited with his father, who had believed him dead, "Joseph . . . went up to meet his father . . . and he fell on his neck, and wept on his neck a good while," in Genesis, 46:29 (437–447).

Volume 3, Chapter 16 (Chapter 47)

Mrs. Norris particularly is "the greatest sufferer," as Maria was her favorite and is now "an altered creature." Fanny finds that everybody at Mansfield "had been all solitary, helpless, and forlorn alike." Mrs. Norris, and later on in the chapter, Mary Crawford, place the blame on Fanny: "had Fanny accepted Mr. Crawford, this could not have happened." Lady Bertram, on the other hand, receives Susan "with quiet kindness" and finds relief in pouring out her heart to Fanny. Lady Bertram was "to be listened to and borne with, and hear the voice of kindness and sympathy in return." Lady Bertram tells Fanny what has happened in her absence. Maria went to Twickenham to be with friends who happened also to be friends of Henry Crawford. Julia in the meantime has eloped with Yates. Moreover, Rushworth's mother is "unmanageable" and hostile. In the midst of this, "Tom's complaints had been greatly heightened by the shock of his sister's conduct, and his recovery so much thrown back by it."

Fanny believes that Sir Thomas must rely "on Edmund alone," especially in view of her rejection of Henry Crawford's proposal: "She was mistaken, however, in supposing that Edmund gave his father no present pain." Following a few days' silence, Edmund opens up to Fanny, telling her that Mary Crawford's attitude "had shocked him" during what turned out to be their final encounter. Mary's lack of seriousness concerning what happened, and the content of her words, "great anger at the *folly* of each" (Jane Austen's emphasis) alienates Edmund. He tells Fanny that Mary "reprobated her brother's folly in being drawn on by a woman whom he never cared for, to do what must lose him the woman he adored." Edmund says, "Oh! Fanny, it was the detection, not the offence which she reprobated."

Edmund's confession to Fanny is both in direct dialogue and reported speech. Fanny responds in much fewer words, and these are largely reported speech. Edmund is particularly incensed by what he perceives as Mary's mockery of his serious moral stance. She says to Edmund after hearing him out, "A pretty good lecture upon my word. Was it part of your last sermon?" When he left the room, she tries with "a saucy playful smile" to invite him to return "in order to subdue" him. Edmund resists the temp-tation and "such has been the end of our acquaintance." His words to Fanny are only stopped by "Lady Bertram's rousing thoroughly up"—she had been sleeping throughout. At the end of the chapter, the omniscient narrator observes that "Time would undoubtedly abate somewhat of his sufferings." This penultimate chapter of the novel closes with the comment, "Fanny's friendship was all that he had clung to."

Mrs. Norris wishes to charge Fanny "as the daemon of the piece," or as an agent of the devil, an evil spirit. Sir Thomas hopes to rescue his daughter Maria "from farther vice, though all was lost on the side of character"—in other words, her reputation was totally ruined. Edmund "received a note from Lady Stornaway to beg him to call" and to meet Mary Crawford. Social etiquette forbade an unengaged lady such as Mary from directly writing herself to Edmund. During his confiding to Fanny what took place, Edmund says, "This is what the world does," and he adds, "Spoilt, spoilt!" The "world" here refers to the "world" of fashionable London society and also to material as distinct from spiritual values. Edmund tells Fanny that Mary commented that her brother, Henry, "has thrown away . . . such a woman as he will never see again. She would have fixed him, she would have made him happy for ever." Mary also suggested "that what remained now to be done, was to bring about a marriage between them," i.e., Maria and Henry. Mary is alluding to the divorce act dissolving a marriage and allowing those involved to remarry. Finally, Mary when she appears to scorn Edmund's professional calling, tells him somewhat sarcastically, "When I hear of you next, it may be as a celebrated preacher in some great society of Methodists" (448–460). The Methodists followed the teachings of John and Charles Wesley and they broke away from the Anglican church in 1795 to appeal "to the illiterate and powerless." Wiltshire notes that "Mary is thus mocking both Edmund's religious fervour and his descent into a lower class" (735).

Volume 3, Chapter 17 (Chapter 48)

The final chapter of the novel ties up its loose ends and uses authorial direct commentary. The author dispenses in the very opening paragraph with any pretense of fictional realism, making it clear that Jane Austen is determining the destiny of her characters. "Let other pens dwell on guilt and misery. I [Jane Austen] quit such odious subjects as soon as I can." She is "impatient to restore every body, not greatly in fault themselves [as the reader learns, this excludes Mrs. Norris, Maria, and to some extent Henry Crawford], to tolerable comfort, and to have done with all the rest." The only character she literally kills off is Dr. Grant, the epicurean who somewhat appropriately dies through overeating. This conveniently allows Mary Crawford to live with her sister Mrs. Grant, and Edmund and Fanny to acquire the Mansfield Parsonage.

The second paragraph of the chapter focuses, as has so much of the novel, on Fanny, who now openly is "My Fanny," the author's Fanny. There are four sentences in this paragraph. The first three are short, the fourth lengthy, with clauses separated by semicolons. The paragraph contains eight instances of the use of the pronoun "she," and five of these are in the final lengthy sentence. The "she" is Fanny. The use of the auxiliary allocation "must" expressing compulsion and inevitability, determined by the author, occurs twice in the opening two short sentences of the paragraph. Jane Austen the author writes, "I have the satisfaction of knowing, must [Fanny] have been happy in spite of every thing." In other words, Fanny is Jane Austen's creation and as creator her Fanny, "My Fanny . . . must have been a happy creature." The possessive "My" refers to the author's creation and to something she is protecting.

Each character is accounted for in this final paragraph. Edmund "was very far from happy himself" and is in the third paragraph seen through Fanny's perspective. Sir Thomas "was the longest to suffer." Julia has redeeming qualities, as does Yates. Tom "gradually regained his health, without regaining the thoughtlessness and selfishness of his previous habits." Edmund, "after wandering about and sitting under trees with Fanny all the summer evenings," begins to be restored to cheerfulness. Sir Thomas realizes there "had been grievous mismanagement" of both Maria and Julia. He is not totally to blame. Mrs. Norris resolves to leave Mansfield

"and devote herself to her unfortunate Maria," and they move to "another country," not somewhere out of England but removed from London. "Mrs. Norris's removal from Mansfield was the great supplementary comfort of Sir Thomas's life." Maria's feelings toward Henry Crawford transform into something "like hatred." Her husband procures a divorce—an expensive lengthy process but in the case of a wife's adultery not impossible. Rushworth is then free to be "duped at least with good humour and good luck." Henry Crawford, although financially and socially secure, having lost Fanny, with whom "there would have been every probability of success and felicity," is punished as he "lost the woman whom he had rationally, as well as passionately, loved." Unlike Maria or Mrs. Norris, he is not isolated socially. The author comments, "*his* share of the offence, is, we know [again directly addressing her readers and assuming they agree with her] not one of the barriers, which society gives to virtue. In this world, the penalty is less equal than could be wished" (Jane Austen's emphasis). The implication is that in the next world there may be another "penalty."

The people who do benefit at the end of the novel are the eldest Price children, Fanny, William, and Susan; Sir Thomas; Lady Bertram; and Edmund. Finally realizing what Fanny means to him, Edmund "became as anxious to marry Fanny, as Fanny herself could desire." This is preceded by an ironic indirect authorial comment: "I purposely abstain from dates on this occasion, that every one may be at liberty to fix their own" when Edmund finally saw the light and proposed to Fanny. Her brother William experiences "rising fame" in his career, and Susan stays permanently at Mansfield. Sir Thomas, "sick of ambitious and mercenary connections, prizing more and more the sterling good of principle and temper," consents to the marriage of Edmund and Fanny. Even here financial worth is not far away, seen in the use of the word "sterling," which relates to silver and its value, as well as to moral qualities. In the final single-sentence paragraph, Fanny and Edmund married, move into the Mansfield Parsonage. Seen through "her [Fanny's] eyes" (461–473), the novel comes full circle.

In the first chapter Sir Thomas is "the real and consistent patron" of Fanny (8). At the very end of the novel, the Mansfield Parsonage, which Fanny previously "had never been able to approach but with some painful sensation of restraint or alarm," is transformed and becomes "as thoroughly perfect in her eyes, as every thing else, within the view and patronage of Mansfield Park, had long been." So the novel concludes not with the marital happiness of Edmund and Fanny, which "must appear as secure as earthly happiness can be"—the reservation reminding Jane Austen's readers of the fragility and impermanence of human life—the subject of the penultimate paragraph of *MP*. It concludes with "Mansfield Park" (473).

CRITICAL COMMENTARY

The publication of *MP* was passed over in silence by contemporary periodical reviewers. Jane Austen wrote down the opinions of her own immediate family. Their mixed opinions reflect the subsequent afterlife of the novel. Jane Austen's mother is reported as saying, "Not liked it so well as P. & P. [*Pride and Prejudice*]—Thought Fanny insipid—Enjoy Mrs. Norris." Cassandra, Jane's sister, "thought it quite clever, tho' not so brilliant as P. & P.—Fond of Fanny. Delighted much in Mrs. Rushworth's stupidity." Martha Lloyd "preferred [*MP*] altogether to" her other work. On the other hand, Fanny Cage, the niece of Edward [Jane Austen's brother] "did not much like it—not to be compared to P. & P.—nothing interesting in the characters—Language poor . . . Improved as it went on." Charles, Jane's brother, preferred *Pride and Prejudice*, too, and thought *MP* "wanted Incident."

There were some positive voices. Mrs. Cooke (Cassandra Leigh, 1743/4–1826), Jane's godmother and her husband the Reverend Samuel Cooke (1741–1820), were "very much pleased with" the novel, "particularly with the manner in which the Clergy are treated—Mr. Cooke called it 'the most sensible Novel he had ever read.'" THOMAS EGERTON, the publisher of the first edition, praised *MP* "for its morality & for being so equal a Composition—No weak Parts" (Southam, *Heritage*: I, 48–50). The Reverend JAMES STANIER CLARKE, the

prince regent's librarian, wrote that "in particular Mansfield Park" of Jane Austen's novels "reflect[s] the highest honour of your Genius & your Principles" (Rogers, 73). Jane Austen replied to Clarke in a letter dated December 11, 1815, "I am very strongly haunted by the idea that to those Readers who have preferred [*Pride and Prejudice*] it [*Emma*] will appear inferior in Wit, to those who have preferred [*Mansfield Park*], very inferior in good Sense" (*Letters*, 306).

Jane Austen's most influential advocate and literary voice proclaiming her qualities, SIR WALTER SCOTT, does not mention *MP*. On the whole during the 19th century, *MP* received less attention than *Emma*, *Pride and Prejudice*, *Sense and Sensibility*, *Northanger Abbey*, and *Persuasion*. A notable exception is RICHARD WHATELY, who in his *Quarterly Review* essay on Jane Austen published in 1821 devotes space to the novel. Whately, who became archbishop of Dublin, praises *MP*. He finds within it some of the author's "best moral lessons, as well as her most humorous descriptions." Whately reserves his most fulsome praise for Jane Austen's "insight . . . into the peculiarities of female character," and draws attention to Fanny's "restlessness and jealousy," in short, to her complexity (Southam, *Heritage*: I, 99–100).

Although writing more than three decades after Whately, GEORGE HENRY LEWES finds that "Aunt Norris and Lady Bertram are perfect . . . the scenes at Portsmouth . . . are wonderfully truthful and vivid." Lewes continues, "The private theatricals, too, are very amusing: and the days spent at the Rushworth's is a masterpiece of art" (Southam, *Heritage*: I, 166). Unfortunately, Lewes in his "The Novels of Jane Austen," published in *Blackwood's Edinburgh Magazine* (July 1859), does not elaborate. On the other hand, another Victorian admirer of Jane Austen, Margaret Oliphant, writing in March 1870 in the same venue, has probably even less to say: She finds *MP* "the least striking" of the novels "and though full of detached scenes, and still more of detached sentences, quite wonderful in their power of description, is dull and lengthy as a whole, and not agreeable" (ibid., 222). Richard Simpson too, in his influential 1870 essay on Jane Austen, devotes only a little space to *MP*. Simpson finds

MP and *NA* alike, for they both "attempt to show that true love is that which is founded on esteem, not on passion, and that passion should rather be the crown of the edifice than its foundation" (ibid., 255).

The great Shakespearean critic A. C. Bradley, in his 1911 lecture on Jane Austen given at Newnham College, Cambridge, anticipates an important strain in subsequent reactions to *MP*. He finds in Jane Austen's work "two distinct strains. . . . She is a moralist and a humourist." In being a "moralist," she is very much influenced by the style and tone of Dr. Samuel Johnson. She also has a "marked distrust of any indulgence in emotion or imagination where these are not plainly subservient to the resolve to do the right thing, however disagreeable or prosaic it may be." This results in Jane Austen's "approval of such heroines as Elinor Dashwood, Fanny Price, and Anne Elliot," and as readers "we share her approval." *MP*'s emphasis on morality and "unusual seriousness" is the least comic but most Johnsonian of her work—a judgment anticipating Mary Lascelles and Marilyn Butler—the most indebted to 18th-century prose. Bradley makes insightful character observations, too: "Why were the Bertram sisters what they were? Because their father was negligent and rather worldly, their mother a slug, and their aunt Mrs. Norris." For Bradley, *MP* it "is probably true that, of all the novels, it gains the most from repeated study" (Southam, *Heritage* II, 234–236, 238–239).

Reginald Farrer, in his 1917 *Quarterly Review* centenary tribute to Jane Austen, makes a negative observation about *MP*. He does note the effect of setting upon character: "the squalor of Portsmouth" has "a definite place in the evolution of Fanny." Still, Fanny's "two speeches . . . in the Vicarage shrubbery" are dismissed as "irrelevant flights of rhetoric . . . deliverances false in fact, trite in thought, turgid and sententious in expression." However, *MP* is its author's "*gran rifiuto.*" Farrer echoes Dante's *Inferno* in his depiction of those who at the very gates of Hell, made the great refusal or abdication. Farrer speculates that this is due to "the influence of the unhappiness through which" Jane Austen "had been passing." He writes, "None of her books is quite so brilliant in parts, none shows a greater technical mastery, a more audacious facing of realities, a more certain touch with character." But Farrer then adds, "Yet, alone of her books, [*MP*] is vitiated throughout by a radical dishonesty, that was certainly not in its author's own nature." Essentially "her own purpose of edification, being not her own, is always at cross-purposes with her unprompted joy in creation."

Fanny Price is "repulsive in her cast-iron self-righteousness and steely rigidity of prejudice." Mary "would be . . . most delightful as a wife." Fanny is a "penniless dull little nobody" (ibid., 252, 254, 262–264). This comment echoes that of D. W. Harding, who calls Fanny Price "a dreary, debilitated, priggish goody-goody" (Harding, 122). Harding, in his early essay "Regulated Hatred," published in 1940, isolates the Cinderella theme in *MP*, and in common with Farrer, finds the ending highly unsatisfactory. Harding stresses the fantasy elements and role playing in the novel. Lascelles, writing a year earlier, plays close critical attention to the text of the novel and emphasizes its author's deft handling of emotion and of the novel's catastrophe, Maria Bertram's elopement. Lascelles isolates its 18th-century elements and indicates the manner in which Jane Austen presents the "'calendar-time' of the world as we know it and 'personal time' of human beings as we know them" (Lascelles, 192).

In a lecture given at Cornell University in 1950, the novelist Vladimir Nabokov pinpoints what he perceives to be deficiencies in the structure of *MP*. These include the prolongation of Edmund's intended proposal to Mary Crawford, necessary for Henry's pursuit of Fanny and then the affair with Maria. The "slowness becomes something of a farce." For Nabokov "the whole play theme in" the novel "is an extraordinary achievement" (Nabokov, *Lectures*: 50, 30). Four years later, Lionel Trilling's essay on the novel appeared in the *Partisan Review* and gained greater currency being reprinted a year later in the fifth volume of *The Pelican Guide to English Literature*. In addition to placing emphasis on the wider moral context of the novel, comparisons being made with Wordsworth, George Eliot and others, Trilling asserts "Nobody, I believe, has ever found it possible to like" its heroine. "To outward seeming, Mary Crawford . . . is another version of

Elizabeth Bennet," but the author turns against her in favor of Fanny Price. "Yet" the novel "is a great novel, its greatness being commensurate with its power to offend." For Trilling, Fanny Price "is a Christian heroine" and that essentially is her problem. The theatricals are at the core of the dilemma of the novel as they represent fashionable London values as opposed to those of the country and the contemplative life exemplified by Fanny, Edmund, and Mansfield Park itself (Trilling, 127–129).

Tony Tanner, in his influential introduction to the Penguin edition of the novel, extends Trilling's argument that the novel does appear "to speak for repression and negation, fixity and enclosure." Tanner writes that in the character of Fanny, "we should perceive the pain and labour involved in maintaining true values [such as integrity and principles] in a corrosive world of dangerous energies and selfish power-play." For Tanner, by the time Jane Austen came to write *MP*, "much of the lightness and brightness has gone of the world and, although Jane Austen's incomparable comic sense is as alive as ever, she now seems more aware of the real evils and real sufferings inextricably involved in life in society" (Tanner, 460–462).

Avrom Fleishman's *A Reading of Mansfield Park: An Essay in Critical Synthesis* (1967) is devoted to a new critical explication of the novel, paying careful attention to its structure, the psychology and presentation of characters, and its central themes of "the values and dangers of feeling" (50). Fleishman's fifth chapter, "The Structure of the Myth," is noteworthy for presenting a detailed analysis of "the Cinderella myth," or pattern in the novel as represented by Fanny Price (59). David Lodge's reading in his *The Language of Fiction* (1966) brilliantly draws attention to the use of key vocabulary such as "duty" and "principle" (101) in the novel. Alistair Duckworth's *The Improvement of the Estate* (1971) places great emphasis on *MP*. For Duckworth, Mansfield and what it represents stand for "an inherited culture endangered by forces from within and from without" (Duckworth, 71). Duckworth sees the novel, especially in its depiction of landscape gardening and the management of a rural estate, as upholding conservative values. Such a reading is reinforced four year later in Marilyn

Butler's *Jane Austen and the War of Ideas.* She notes the way in which Fanny's values are contrasted with the materialism of Sir Thomas Bertram and the Crawfords' cynicism. Fanny's attitude represents conservative 18th-century values contrasted with those circulating after the French Revolution. Portsmouth and London stand for the materialistic world, Mansfield and Fanny stand for the altruistic world of duty and service.

Dominant readings in the last decades of the 20th century may be viewed as feminist and postcolonialist. Claudia Johnson's chapter "*Mansfield Park*: Confusions of Guilt and Revolutions of Mind" in her *Jane Austen, Women Politics and the Novel* (1988) probably represents the most sophisticated and extensive of the feminist readings. For Johnson, *MP* is a work pervaded with deception and self-interest and "demystification" containing "an enquiry into the moral wardrobe" (100) of authority figures. Playacting is one of its central metaphors. Edward Said, on the other hand, in an 1989 essay emphasizes the "comfort" of Mansfield Park, which, Said argues, is based on exploitation of slave labor on Sir Thomas Bertram's estate in Antigua. Fanny Price, too, is a "transported commodity," and Sir Thomas's burning of the unbound copies of *Lovers' Vows* fits the pattern of the slave master (106). Certainly, Said's work propelled investigations into the historical and political context of *MP*.

Said's is a contentious reading of the novel. Pat Rogers judiciously observes "the history of the reception of" the novel "shows that it has always been read according to the attitudes and preoccupations of the times." Consequently, the focus "on a dark and troubled novel goes with a parallel tendency in" the study of biography. The tradition of a happy family in "Austen studies has been replaced by an almost dysfunctional household riven by guilty secrets and hidden animosities" (83–84). What readings of the once neglected novel hold in store is open to conjecture. If 20th-century patterns are anything to go by, some hitherto largely neglected facet of the work will resurface. No critic yet, to the present writer's knowledge, has, for instance, made a case for either Mrs. Norris or Henry Crawford as the representatives of the central values of *MP*!

CHARACTERS

Anderson, Miss (Chapter 5) The sister of Charles Anderson. Tom Bertram met her when she "was not *out*" in society. Tom "could hardly get a word or a look from the young lady—nothing like a civil answer—she screwed up her mouth, and turned from me with such an air!" He reencountered her a year later when she was *"out"* (Jane Austen's emphasis), claiming Tom "as an acquaintance." She embarrassed him by her extrovert behavior and became an example of the wrong way mothers have of "managing their daughters," and of "an altered young lady."

Anderson, Charles (Chapter 5) The elder brother of Miss Anderson. A friend of Tom Bertram, Charles and his sister live in "Baker Street," a fashionable London area neighborhood.

The Aylmers (Chapters 45–47) Maria (Bertram) Rushworth spends Easter at Twickenham, southwest of London, with the Aylmers, "pleasant people." They are "a family whom" Maria "had just grown intimate with—a family of lively, agreeable manners, and probably of morals and discretion to suit—for to *their* house Mr. Crawford had constant access at all times" (Jane Austen's emphasis). Henry Crawford has a house nearby and uses his visits to the Aylmers to develop his affair with Maria.

Baddeley (Chapters 19, 32) Sir Thomas Bertram's butler at Mansfield Park.

Bertram, Edmund (Chapter 1 and throughout) The younger son of Sir Thomas Bertram of Mansfield Park, he is mostly the model for correct judgment and principles in the novel. Destined for the church, "he was not pleasant by any common rule, he talked no nonsense, he paid no compliments, his opinions were unbending, his attentions tranquil and simple" (65). Edmund's kindness and consideration are demonstrated when the 10-year-old Fanny Price first comes to Mansfield Park, where he befriends, protects, and advises her. So much so that he becomes the formative influence on the development of her personality. In spite of his subsequent romantic obsession with Mary Craw-

ford, his "friendship never failed" (21) Fanny. He leaves Fanny while he goes riding with Mary and allows her to use the mare he allowed Fanny to use. Edmund tells Fanny not to worry unduly about the enduring relationship between Maria, Julia, and Henry Crawford. To please Mary, he allows himself, against his better judgment and awareness of his father's disapproval, to participate in the theatricals. As Tony Tanner points out, "Edmund has chosen to be a clergyman by profession," and consequently "Edmund at this moment symbolically abandons his profession, his role in life, to play at being a stage clergyman indulging in a love affair (for such is his part!)." Tanner adds, "it involves an abdication of true self in order to indulge a passionate impulse" (458). Yet in spite of Mary's arguments and disdain for his decision to enter the church, Edmund does not waver in his calling and defends the clergy, emphasizing the spiritual and social role of the clergyman.

After visiting Mary in London and seeing her with her friends, Edmund begins to realize her superficiality and lack of principle. Following her less than serious reaction to her brother's behavior and his elopement, he breaks with Mary and begins to realize that Fanny is his real soul mate. Their relationship was that of protector and protected, "a regard founded on the most endearing claims of innocence and helplessness" (470). It is reversed at the conclusion of the novel. On his return to Mansfield from London, Edmund becomes dependent on Fanny, who is his comforter and adviser. He marries Fanny, and they initially live at Thornton Lacey, his first parish. On the death of Dr. Grant, they move to the Mansfield Parsonage.

The lengthiest praise of a name in Jane Austen's writings is Fanny's on the name of Edmund. In spite of "Edmund" being the name of the evil brother in Shakespeare's *King Lear,* Jane Austen was fond of the name "Edmund." While Edmund represents the values of restraint, consideration, and duty, his weakness in giving way to Mary and obsession with her has not gone unnoticed. Claudia L. Johnson described him as "dimsighted"; he "shares his father's [Sir Thomas's] tendency to invest personal desires with the dignity of moral imperatives." He is given to self-righteousness (111, 115) and to what Fleishman calls "righteousness indignation," which is "as a substitute for sexual fulfillment" (53). Few, however, would go as far as the English novelist and critic Kingsley Amis. Writing on the novel in *The Spectator* magazine in 1957, he finds Fanny and Edmund "both morally detestable." Amis adds, "to invite Mr. and Mrs. Edmund Bertram round for the evening would not be lightly undertaken" (Rogers, 78).

Bertram, Julia (Chapter 1 and throughout) The younger daughter of Sir Thomas and Lady Bertram, Julia is a year younger than her sister, Maria, and two years older than Fanny Price. Educated with Maria by her aunt Norris, whose values are "give a girl an education [a superficial one], and introduce her properly into the world, and ten to one but she has the means of settling well, without further expense to any body" (6). She is indulged by her aunt to grow up believing she and her sister are "the finest young women in the country" (44). Being the younger daughter, she is not spoiled as much as Maria by Mrs. Norris, and is more controllable. She is jealous of Maria when she becomes, in spite of being engaged, Henry Crawford's favorite, and as a result she refuses to participate in the Mansfield theatricals. She finds some compensation in flirting with Mr. Yates. Following Maria's wedding, she makes up with her and goes with Maria on her honeymoon to Brighton and subsequently to London. In London, she meets Yates again, whom she allows, although without too much enthusiasm, to court her. Following Maria's elopement with Henry Crawford, and fearful of the consequences for her father's severity, she agrees to elope with Yates. "She had not eloped with any worse feelings than those of selfish alarm. It had appeared to her the only thing to be done. Maria's guilt had induced Julia's folly" (467). Too bound up with her own pursuit of pleasure, in short a hedonist, she is unable to return to Mansfield to comfort her brother in his illness, or to be a friend to Fanny. Somewhat surprisingly, following her marriage to Yates, "she was humble and wishing to be forgiven" (462).

Julia has received scant critical attention except as a foil to her sister and as an example of a jealous sister, whose temper was "more controulable"

than Maria's (466). She is not seen in a conversation with her sister, with whom she competes unsuccessfully to play the role of a lover, in the performance of *Lovers' Vows*. She too is subject to Henry Crawford's flattering attention but emerges unscathed from him and is eventually contrite. Given her self-absorption and selfishness, unlike her sister Maria, Julia gets off relatively lightly at the end of the novel.

Bertram, Lady Maria, née Ward (Chapters 1–4, 8, 15, 19, 24, 27, 29, 33–34, 37, 44, 46–48) The subject of the opening sentence of *MP* and the most fortunate of her sisters, she "was a woman of very tranquil feelings, and a temper remarkably easy and indolent" (3–4). She is characterized with "all her incompetency and languor" (338). She displays more interest in her pug (whose gender she is confused about) and her sofa, than in her four children. Under Sir Thomas's direction, "she thought justly on all important points" (449) and leaves her sister Mrs. Norris to educate the children. Not shown to be malevolent, she is too stupid to play the card game Speculation. During her husband's absence in Antigua, she abandons her position as mistress of Mansfield Park, allows Mrs. Norris to accompany Maria and Julia to balls, and lets her choose a most inappropriate husband for Maria. Upon her husband's return after being away for over a year, she "*almost* fluttered for a few minutes, and still remained so sensibly animated as to put away her work, move Pug from her side, and give all her attention and all the rest of her sofa to her husband." Jane Austen, as narrator, adds "She had no anxieties for any body to cloud *her* pleasure" (Jane Austen's emphasis) (179).

Toward the conclusion of the novel, she is shocked into activity. In letters written "in the language of real feeling and alarm" (427), she keeps Fanny informed of Tom's condition during his illness. Dependent on Fanny, whom she somewhat takes for granted until she misses her while away in Portsmouth, Lady Bertram is genuinely pleased to see her return to Mansfield Park. She would not miss Fanny if she were married to Henry Crawford. His proposal "by convincing her that Fanny *was* (Jane Austen's emphasis) very pretty, which she had been doubting about before, and that she would be advantageously married . . . made her feel a sort of credit in calling her [Fanny] niece." Lady Bertram's ideal is to have "a handsome family," she has no sense of intrinsic values. At the end of the novel, she does not wish to lose Fanny, her "dear Fanny" but takes quickly to Susan (332–333, 427).

Lady Bertram fails to comprehend what is going on around her as evinced by her introducing the subject of *Lovers' Vows* to Sir Thomas on the evening of his return from his trip to Antigua. A foster parent, she bears a large responsibility for Maria's eventual disgrace, Julia's elopement, Tom's profligacy, and to some extend Edmund's fascination with Mary Crawford. Each of her children exhibits her values of prizing beauty and the superficial above morals, and immediate gratification above spirituality. Sally B. Palmer, in "Skipping the Leash: Lady Bertram's Lapdog," asks, is a deeper meaning than the comic and ridiculous behind "including Lady Bertram's pug in almost every Bertram family scene?" "Is the pug simply a stereotypical signifier of wealthy and indolent women, and an aspersion on Lady Bertram's neglectful motherhood?" Palmer sees the sexually ambiguous Pug as a symbol of "the colonized and enslaved even the marginalized because of sex," sexual ambiguity, and in a feminist reading, asserts that "the pug points the finger; or . . . the paw, of blame at the patriarchy for keeping women like Lady Bertram confined and bored into a lifetime stupor" (Palmer, 1, 4).

Bertram, Maria (Chapter 1 and throughout)

The eldest daughter of Sir Thomas and Lady Bertram, Maria is Mrs. Norris's favorite. She is three years older than Fanny Price, and her personality is influenced more by her mean and materialistic aunt than by her expensive education, governess, or parents. Persuaded by aunt Norris to become engaged to the wealthy and well-connected Mr. Rushworth in order to escape her parents and Mansfield Park, she has no affection for him. She takes the leading role in the theatrical performance of *Lovers' Vows* from her sister, and in revenge for Henry Crawford's accompanying Julia on the box to Sotherton, shamelessly flirts with him during

the theatricals. She is the first to break out of the restraints of her marriage and elopes with Henry Crawford. Rushworth divorces Maria, and she quarrels bitterly with Henry Crawford, who refuses to marry her. She is forced to return home. Her father punishes her by sending her to live away from Mansfield Park with her aunt Norris. Ironically, then her "hatred of home, restraint and tranquillity" is transformed at the end of the novel into imprisonment. She is forced to live with her aunt: "where, shut up together with little society, on one side no affection, on the other, no judgment, it may be reasonably supposed that their tempers became their mutual punishment" (202, 465).

Attention has already been drawn to the use of the metaphors of the locked gate and "the wounded spirit" longing to be liberated from confinement with reference to Maria. She "cannot get out, as the starling said" (202, 99). Kathryn Sutherland attributes what happened to Maria, and to some extent Julia, as due to the focus of their respective educations focusing on "accomplishments" rather than the "self-knowledge" possessed by Fanny: "Maria Bertram, in particular, is a study in imprudent unforgetting, and her tenacity turns her into a tragic figure" (xxi). For Sutherland, "Maria Bertram is ruthlessly sacrificed," she "is self taunted to her own destruction," not realizing the strength of her own feelings and passions. Maria is also sacrificed by Jane Austen "and confined within a definition of femininity that contemporary readers may have recognized as a critical glance at the turbulent heroines of the 1790s' radical romances." In other words, "Heroines like Mary Wollstonecraft's Maria, who 'wished to be only alive to love' but whom 'marriage had bastilled'" (xxxvi).

Claudia Johnson's feminist reading of *MP* sees Maria, and to a lesser extent Julia, attempting desperately to free themselves from "a code of female propriety" imposed by their father, who misreads his daughters. Johnson writes that her father's "confidence that Maria will cooperate in an alliance advantageous to himself without any ill effects is preposterous." She adds that Maria "never really attended to lessons in female modesty in the first place, nor is her disposition so placid as he wishfully fancies." She, Maria, is forced "to conceal rather than sublimate the rebelliousness of her temper." In this reading, Maria is a late 20th-century feminist straining against the restraints imposed on her by others and struggling to find her real self. The fact that she is doomed to live out her life in social ostracism, entrapped with her aunt, reveals the limitations of Jane Austen's own world. However Maria's adultery is an assertion of "the volatility of female desire outside established modes of social control" and "subvert[s] the law of the father in" *MP* (103, 112).

Bertram, Sir Thomas (Chapters 1–4, 11–13, 17–21, 23–29, 31–37, 44, 46–48) "Master at Mansfield Park," (370) a baronet and a member of Parliament, Sir Thomas is the wealthy owner of Mansfield Park. He appears to be the model of good sense and estate management. Father of Tom, Edmund, Maria, and Julia, he is also the guardian and benefactor of Fanny Price, his niece. Very serious in his deportment, he is distant from his children and pays little if any attention to their education and development, relying instead for his daughters' education on their aunt Mrs. Norris. He is kind to Fanny Price and attempts to help her mother financially when her sons need career assistance. Indulgent to his wife, he is away a lot from Mansfield with his London parliamentary duties. The owner of property in Antigua in the West Indies, he travels there and is absent from home for almost two years to deal with estate problems. While he is away, his strict regime at Mansfield Park disintegrates, problems occur, and private theatricals, of which he would not approve, are arranged.

He returns to Mansfield Park unexpectedly and reacts strongly to the theatricals, eradicating as many traces of them as he is able. On his return, his attitude to Fanny becomes kinder; however, his "good opinion" (314) is put to the test when she insists on refusing Henry Crawford. Fanny is grieved to hear Sir Thomas's "accusations, so heavy, so multiplied, so rising in dreadful gradation" (319). It is Sir Thomas who thinks that a visit to Portsmouth and her former family will give Fanny a sense of how fortunate she has been to live at Mansfield Park and lead her to accept Crawford.

His concern with appearance, morality, and reserve leads him to ignore the inner being, and he is sorely tested by Maria's and Julia's elopements and his eldest son's lack of character. At the conclusion of the novel, "sick of ambitious and mercenary connections" (471) threatening Mansfield Park and his family, he welcomes Fanny as his daughter-in-law. Sir Thomas's expulsion of Mrs. Norris "from Mansfield," who, he has come to realize, has been responsible for a good deal of what has gone wrong with his children, "was the great supplementary comfort of Sir Thomas's life" (465).

Sir Thomas has intrigued readers of *MP* from its initial reception. Jane Austen records John Pemberton Plumtree, (1791–1864) a family friend from Kent, as saying, "Sir Tho[ma]s is very clever, & his conduct proves admirably the defects of the modern system of Education" (Southam, *Heritage*: I: 50). To move forward, almost a century and a half, Vladimir Nabokov in his Cornell University lectures on *Mansfield Park* regards Sir Thomas as important to the formal structure of the novel. He does in passing anticipate a subsequent critical preoccupation, noting that "the source of the Bertram money" resides in the "cheap slave labor" operating Sir Thomas's Antiguan plantations. For Nabokov, the "West Indies Estate" is functionally necessary to the structure of the novel, which requires Sir Thomas to leave Mansfield Park. Similarly, he is absent from the chaperoned trip to Sotherton and the private theatricals. These events are part of the causation of the novel. Nabokov writes that it is Jane Austen's plan as the creator of *MP* "to remove Sir Thomas from Mansfield Park in order to have the young people of the book overindulge their freedom," and then subsequently to reintroduce Sir Thomas two years later "at the height of the mild orgy . . . the rehearsal" (18) of *Lovers' Vows*. Each detail has a function in the overall structure, propelling the narrative.

For Nabokov, details such as Sir Thomas's Antigua possessions are not in *MP* so that Jane Austen can make a pointed critique of Britain's colonial empire and practices, or the wealth of the Bertram family and how they use and misuse their wealth. Such details do engage Edward W. Said, who uses *MP* in the opening chapter of his *Culture and Impe-*

rialism (1993), a reprint of his 1989 essay. Said's aim, simply put, is to show that colonialism plays an important role in a novelist not regarded as political or ideological. For Said, the Bertram fortunes are sustained by exploitation of slave labor on Sir Thomas's Antigua estates and plantations. Further, Fanny Price herself is a "transported commodity" (106).

Claudia L. Johnson (1988) agrees with Marilyn Butler (1975) and Alistair Duckworth (1979), that Sir Thomas is the representative of conservative, 18th-century values embodied in his patriarchal views. However, Johnson argues that *MP* "erodes rather than upholds" (114) his values. She writes that the "paternal authority invoked . . . throughout the novel remarkably fails. Sir Thomas's gravity operates only as an external check, not as an internal inhibition upon the behavior of his children" (97). Sir Thomas is a performer sustaining his own self-interest and self-image.

Tony Tanner (1966) indicates when the others "complain of the gloom Sir Thomas brings into" Mansfield Park that Fanny responds, "I think he values the very quietness you speak of, and that the repose of his own family-circle is all he wants" (*MP*, 196). Tanner observes that "in standing for 'quietness' and 'repose,' Sir Thomas is upholding two of the major values in the world of the book" (Tanner, 448). Tanner and Avrom Fleishman (1967) both draw attention to the fact that "the theatricals provide the core of" *MP*. Tanner writes that they "represent the culmination of the irresponsible license indulged in during Sir Thomas's absence," and "in a deeper sense Mansfield Park is all but destroyed once 'the inclination was awakened'" (Tanner, 456; *MP*, 123). Fleishman draws parallels between Sir Thomas's situation with his daughters and Shakespeare's King Lear. Fanny represents to Sir Thomas "a new daughter to substitute for his lost ones: 'Fanny was indeed the daughter he wanted'" (*MP*, 472). Sir Thomas's "is the situation of Lear after his two elder daughters have proved to be harpies" (Fleishman, 62).

Bertram, Tom (Chapters 1–4, 12–19, 27, 32, 34, 45, 47–48) A hedonist and actor, Tom Bertram is the eldest son and heir. He "had easy man-

ners, excellent spirits, a large acquaintance, and a great deal to say." Fond of horse racing, betting, and perhaps other more dissolute activities, for Tom, his "younger brother" Edmund must help to pay for the pleasures of the elder. His debts and extravagance lead to the disposal of the living at Mansfield intended for Edmund. His father, Sir Thomas, takes him to Antigua hoping that the visit will encourage his elder son to become more seriously concerned with his responsibilities. The young Tom is sent home early and, in spite of being aware that his father would not approve, suggests performing a play at Mansfield Park. He prefers a comedy and chooses the provocative, suggestive *Lovers' Vows.*

Tom demonstrates force of character from the determination that he displays in promoting, organizing, and participating in the theatricals. This shows that his energies are misspent and that with discipline and direction could well be directed toward his social duties and responsibilities as head of the Mansfield estate during his father's prolonged absence. At the age of 26, be becomes a chastened character. A fall from a horse at Newmarket and a resulting illness, which becomes serious, leads him to return to Mansfield. He is thus removed form the temptation of London and perhaps the mercenary nature of Mary Crawford's desire to latch on to wealthy elder sons. His closeness to death leads to a transformation: "He had suffered, and he had learnt to think, two advantages he had never known before. . . . He became what he ought to be, useful to his father, steady and quiet, and not living merely for himself" (47, 23, 462).

At the end of the 20th century, Tom is viewed as more than simply the dissolute elder son and heir to the estates who undergoes a remarkable transformation at the conclusion of the novel. For a feminist critic such as Johnson, for instance, his mode of conduct revealed through his duplicitousness or double talk, is part of "the ugly facts about power" underpinning the novel. She cites the instance where Tom has been forced to play whist and "fumes against polite formulations that give with one hand what they take away with the other!" Tom says, "*That* is what I dislike most particularly . . . to have the pretense of being asked, of being given a choice, and at the same time addressed in such a way as to oblige one to do the very thing—whatever it be!" Johnson writes that "the 'pretense' of choice Tom resents is essential to the paternalistic discourse represented in [*MP*] because it enables people to compel others without having to regard themselves as bullies" (*MP*, 120; Johnson, 102).

Brown, Mrs. (Chapter 24) Presumably the wife of an officer stationed at the Gibraltar Garrison whose hairstyle William Price regarded as very strange; worn by "Mrs. Brown, and other women at the Commissioner's and Gibraltar." He adds, "Fanny can reconcile me to any thing" (235).

Campbell, Mr. (Chapter 38) Campbell is William Price's friend and the surgeon on the *Thrush*, the ship William is assigned to as a second lieutenant. Campbell is "a very well behaved young man" (384). He calls for William shortly following his arrival in Portsmouth with Fanny so that they both can join their ship.

Chapman, Mrs. (Chapter 27) Lady Bertram's personal maid whom, as a special favor, she sends up to assist Fanny to dress for her first ball. She is, however, "too late of course to be of any use" (271).

Charles (Chapter 20) One of the Mansfield Park grooms who acts as a postilion when members of the house travel: the postilion rides the leading horse, which draws or pulls the coach.

Charles, Sir (Chapter 31) A friend of Admiral Crawford who arranges William Price's promotion to lieutenant. This is done because Henry Crawford, the admiral's nephew, wishes to impress Fanny Price and to influence her.

Crawford, Admiral (Chapters 4–7, 21, 24, 27, 30, 31, 36, 43, 47) The uncle and guardian of Henry and Mary Crawford. He is described as "a man of vicious conduct, who chose, instead of retaining his niece [on the death of his wife], to bring his mistress under his own roof." Conse-

quently, Mary has to live with his half sister, Mrs. Grant, at Mansfield. Unhappily married, the only thing that unites the Crawfords is their affection for Henry and Mary. It is Mary who comments scathingly on the "circle" of admirals she met at her uncle's London home who spent their time on "the graduation of their pay, and their bickerings and jealousies" (41, 60). The admiral does assist young William, but there is irony here. He is appointed "to a sloop, a ship of between ten and eighteen guns, the humblest of vessels," offering almost no opportunity for "prize-money and distinction." Even in the dispersing of favors, Admiral Crawford is mean (Southam, *Navy*: 197). According to Henry Crawford, "the Admiral has his faults, but he is a very good man, and has been more than a father to me. Few fathers would have let me have my own way half so much" (296).

"Admiral and Mrs. Crawford, though agreeing in nothing else, were united in affection for" Henry and Mary, "or at least were no farther adverse in their feelings than that each had their favourite, to whom they showed the greatest fondness of the two." The narrative reveals that "The Admiral delighted in the boy" and that the mistreated, abused "Mrs. Crawford doated [*sic*] on the girl" (40).

Crawford, Henry (Chapters 4–15, 17–21, 23–26, 40–47) Regarded by many as the villain of *MP*, some of Jane Austen's family made interesting observations about him. Mrs. JAMES AUSTEN, (Mary Lloyd), the wife of the author's elder brother, remarked that she "thought Henry Crawford's going off with Mrs. Rushworth very natural." In a letter of March 2, 1814, written to her sister, Cassandra, Jane Austen noted that her brother HENRY AUSTEN "is going on with [*MP*]. He admires H. Crawford: I mean properly, as a clever, pleasant man" (Southam, *Heritage*: I: 48. 52).

Educated at Westminster and Cambridge, Henry brings his younger sister, Mary, to be with her half sister, Mrs. Grant, to the Mansfield Parsonage, when Fanny Price is 18 years old. Wealthy and restless, Henry has an estate at Everingham in Norfolk. "Though not handsome, had air and countenance," and is very flirtatious with sophisticated manners and taste. Following advice from

Admiral Crawford, only "the address of a French-woman," suggesting someone sexually experienced and charming, would be required to persuade Henry to marry. Experience in estate improvements results in his Sotherton visit and extensive but uncalled for advice on Thornton Lacey, the parish near Mansfield where Edmund receives his initial living, or position. Forever playing a part, acting, performing, he seems to wish his own self, his own personality and position, would disappear. Thus when he listens to William, he desires to be in his place and to be a sailor. When he listens to Edmund, he wishes to be a clergyman and to preach in the most fashionable London churches. Able to converse with almost everyone about his or her interests, he is a good listener and an outstanding actor in the Mansfield theatricals. Even though she does not approve of the theatricals, Fanny admires Henry's performance, and when she is most suspicious of him she is fascinated by his readings from Shakespeare.

Henry obviously enjoys tempting women into relationships and leading them up the garden path. He plays games with Julia's feelings and flirts remorselessly during the theatricals with Maria, giving her misleading signals, although he is aware of her engagement to Rushworth. He is stimulated by challenge: Maria nearly married, Fanny's seriousness. The only person he is honest with, too honest, is his sister, Mary. He means "to amuse himself," his "plan is to make Fanny Price in love with me," cynically to make "a small hole in Fanny Price's heart." As his sister tells him, "you must have a somebody." He wants Fanny to "feel when I go away that she shall be never happy again," and he destroys Maria's happiness without thinking through the consequences. Henry brings his restlessness to his behavior with women. Mary is convinced that he loves Fanny, and Sir Thomas is impressed by the constancy of his pursuit of her in spite of her refusal. His successful effort to secure her brother's promotion and his Portsmouth visit may be seen as an extension of his vanity: a refusal to accept a negative response. Even Fanny admires his wit: "Such a man could come from no place, no society, without importing something to amuse" when he visits her and her family in Portsmouth.

Henry helps twice to destroy the tranquility of Mansfield Park: through his participation in the theatricals and his elopement with the married Maria, whom he refuses to marry. He pursues Fanny and proposes to her, placing her in a difficult situation with her Mansfield family. Maria is punished for life, but Henry's only punishment seems to be that he does not marry Fanny, who seems to have been the only "probability of success and felicity for him." He has, however, been "ruined by early independence and bad domestic example," and "indulged in the freaks of a cold-blooded vanity a little too long." Henry is "entangled by his own vanity" and "in this world, the penalty is less equal than could be wished" (41–42, 229–231, 404, 467–468).

For a commentator such as Kathryn Sutherland, Henry and Mary Crawford's "is a world of metropolitan tastes, conspicuous consumption, self-gratifying acts of improvement, of wit and dandyism—the costume drama of the Regency" (xxxiii). As Tony Tanner observes, the "main focus" in the novel "is on the relations between the Crawfords and Fanny and Edmund. Henry decides to flirt with Fanny, but then he finds himself in love with her and eager for marriage." Henry and his sister "are far from villains," and the author endears "them with many of the most superficially attractive qualities in" *MP*. Both, however, "have been spoilt and subtly corrupted by their prolonged immersion in the immoral fashionable London world." These contrast with the values inherent in Mansfield Park and the conservative values of the country estate. Tanner argues that *MP* "reveals a battle between worlds as well as concentrating on the relationships of a few characters." The conflict is between the cynical, hedonistic world of London, represented by Henry and Mary Crawford, and the quiet, tranquil world of Mansfield Park. This world, or order, has to undergo upheaval, such as the theatricals and the exile of Maria, before it can restore itself to "quietness" and "repose" (Tanner, 442, 446–448).

Crawford, Mary (Chapters 4–19, 21–31, 34–38, 40, 42–47) After reading *MP*, one of Jane Austen's own nephews was "interested by nobody but Mary Crawford" (Southam, *Heritage:*

I: 48). Independently wealthy, having an income of £20,000, vivacious, pretty, and witty, she possesses a "true London maxim, that every thing is to be got for money." For Mary, happiness is bound up with a large income. Her skeptical materialism comes into conflict with Edmund's determination to be a clergyman. Unable to divert him into another choice of profession, "she would henceforth admit his attentions without any idea beyond immediate amusement." Her attitude softens later in the novel when she realizes that with Tom's illness, there is a stronger possibility that Edmund will inherit the Mansfield estates and possessions. Mary wishes to control when she refers to Henry Crawford's falling in love with Fanny as "the glory of fixing one who has been shot at by so many" (58, 46, 228, 363).

An important part of her role in the novel is as a temptress, to get others to indulge in "forbidden" pleasures. For example, she tempts Edmund to participate in the theatricals (with this she is successful), and to give up his vocation to become a clergyman. In this she is unsuccessful, and Mary fails to get Edmund to marry her. Mary's observation on Maria's elopement as a mere indiscretion, her attempt to place the blame for Henry's behavior on Fanny, lead Edmund to judge her as having a "corrupted, vitiated mind." However, Edmund does add that Mary's faults are not those that would "voluntarily give unnecessary pain to any one" but are faults of principle. Mary regrets leaving Mansfield for London, where she goes to live with her half sister Mrs. Grant. At the end of the novel, Mary was "long in finding among the dashing representatives, or idle heir apparents, who were at the command of her beauty, and her 20,000*l* any one who could satisfy the better taste she had acquired at Mansfield" (264, 456, 367, 469).

Critically, Mary has been paired with her brother, Henry, as the representatives of London metropolitan values. Mary is the attractive antithesis of the heroine, Fanny Price. For instance, Fanny is fearful of horses and riding. Mary, on the other hand, is "active and fearless, and, though rather small, strongly made, she seemed formed for a horsewoman." She is described as "gifted by nature with strength and courage"; she was "not born to sit still and do nothing." Rather than admit defeat

at a card game, she says, "I will stake my last" and wins. She too is widely read and enjoys witty puns (66, 69, 243). She frequently uses French phrases in conversation, unlike the plain-spoken Edmund, or the all too reticent Fanny. She associates herself with "the decadence and selfishness of French culture" by comparing "herself to the narcissistic Doge in the court of Louis XIV" (Emily Auerbach, 181). She is more than proficient on the harp and tells Fanny, "Selfishness must always be forgiven you know, because there is no hope for a cure" (68). Her cynicism knows no bounds, and she has insight into other characters such as Dr. Grant, whom she sees as more a glutton than a clergyman. She is "one of the most discerning and self-aware characters in Austen's fictional universe." Emily Auerbach adds, "an orphan raised by a debauched admiral and his embittered wife in a metropolis teaming with corrupted people, Mary has been robbed of faith. [She] *could* have been truly admirable had she been given a moral education to counter the inescapable corruption of the world around her" (182). In short, with her independent income and spirit Mary Crawford is as close as her creator comes to depicting some of the qualities of some modern educated, highly paid, early 21st-century feminists.

The Duke (Chapter 13) A participant in the private theatricals held at Lord Ravenshaw's home, Ecclesford, in Cornwall. According to the Honorable John Yates, "the duke was thought very great by many" (122).

Ellis (Chapter 1) The personal maid to Maria and Julia Bertram at Mansfield Park. When Fanny Price first arrives, Mrs. Norris observes to Lady Bertram and Sir Thomas, "I suppose you would not think it fair to expect Ellis to wait on her as well as the others" (10).

Fraser, Mr. (Chapter 36) A reasonably well-off widower who marries the much younger Janet Ross, a friend of Mary Crawford. According to Mary, "he turns out ill-tempered, and *exigeant* [demanding]; and wants a young woman, a beautiful young woman of five-and-twenty, to be as steady as himself" (361).

Fraser, Mrs. Janet, née Ross (Chapters 36, 43–44) A close friend of Mary Crawford for many years. Anxious to get her stepdaughter married, especially to Henry Crawford, jealous of the wealth and status of her sister Lady Stornaway, she had married an older man only for financial reasons. Mary regards "the Frasers to be about as unhappy as most other married people. And yet it was a most desirable match for Janet at the time. We were all delighted." Mary adds that her friend "does not manage" her husband well, "she does not seem to know how to make the best of it. There is a spirit of irritation, which, to say nothing worse, is certainly very ill-bred." Mary then adds that "poor Janet has been sadly taken in." She did not rush into the marriage, "she took three days to consider his proposals" (361). Edmund, however, tells Fanny in a letter that Mrs. Fraser "is a cold hearted, vain woman, who has married entirely from convenience" and blames her unhappy marriage on "her being . . . less affluent . . . than her sister" (421).

Dr. Grant (Chapters 3–6, 11–12, 17–18, 20–23, 25–26, 28, 35–36, 48) Dr. Grant succeeds Mr. Norris as rector of Mansfield. There is irony in a gourmand replacing the mean Norrises. Dr. Grant is 45, with a short neck and "apoplectic" (24). Mary Crawford describes her half sister's husband as "an indolent selfish bon vivant, who must have his palette consulted in every thing, who will not stir a finger for the convenience of any one" (111). More concerned with the epicurean side of life, with food and fine wine, he is something of a scholar and clearly has the right connections as he becomes a dean of Westminster. Somewhat appropriately, "Dr. Grant had brought on apoplexy and death, by three great institutionary dinners in one week" (469). Clearly, Dr. Grant is the total professional antithesis to the serious Edmund Bertram.

Mrs. Grant (Chapters 3–6, 11–12, 17–18, 20–23, 25–26, 28, 35–36, 48) Wife of the older Dr. Grant, the half sister, they have the same mother, of Mary and Henry Crawford. She is a good-humored and kindly person, aged about 30, but has "no chil-

dren" (24). Mrs. Grant accepts the part in *Lovers' Vows* that Fanny Price refuses to take. When moving to London, she regrets leaving Mansfield and the friends she has made. Perhaps overindulgent to her gluttonous, selfish husband, following his death she lives with Mary Crawford, who was "in need of the true kindness, of her sister's heart, and the rational tranquillity of her ways" (469).

Mr. Green (Chapter 7) Presumably a worker on the Mansfield estate or at Mansfield Park. Mentioned by Mrs. Norris as an excuse to Edmund in order to justify her decision to send Fanny on an errand on a very hot day: "Unless I had gone myself indeed; but I cannot be in two places at once" (73).

Gregorys, the (Chapter 25) They are a Portsmouth family known to Fanny and William when they were children. When he is still a midshipman, William tells Fanny that "Portsmouth girls turn up their noses at any body who has not a commission . . . You remember the Gregory's; they are grown up amazing fine girls, but they will hardly speak to *me* [Jane Austen's emphasis], because Lucy is courted by a lieutenant" (249).

Groom, John (Chapter 7) A generic name referring to a specific job. Mrs. Norris claims to Edmund that she "promised John Groom to write to Mrs. Jefferies about his son" (73).

Harding, Mr. (Chapter 47) He is an old London friend of Sir Thomas Bertram who alerts him twice about Maria's relationship with Henry Crawford and the consequent unfolding scandal.

Harrison, Colonel (Chapter 29) Attends the Mansfield Park ball for Fanny. Lady Bertram is "not sure whether Colonel Harrison had been talking of Mr. Crawford or of William, when he said he was the finest young man in the room" (283).

Henry, Sir (Chapter 13) Someone Yates met at Lord Ravenshaw's house party. "Sir Henry thought the duke not equal to Frederick, but that was because Sir Henry wanted the part himself" (122).

Holford (Mrs.) (Chapter 5)   A London acquaintance of Tom Bertram. At her house, he is embarrassed by Miss Anderson's behavior.

Jefferies, Mrs. (Chapter 7)   Apparently known to Mrs. Norris. She is to write a letter to her recommending John Groom's son.

Lascelles, Lady (Chapter 40)   Maria Bertram following her marriage sets up in a house on the fashionable Wimpole Street, London. Its previous tenant had been Lady Lascelles, with whom Mary Crawford had stayed.

Lee, Miss (Chapters 1–4, 15, 16)   Governess at Mansfield Park who teaches Maria and Julia Bertram and then Fanny Price. She "taught [Fanny] French, and heard her read the daily portion of History" (22). She is a victim of a cost-cutting exercise at Mansfield (28).

Maddison (Chapters 41, 42)   Maddison is Henry Crawford's estate manager, his agent at Everingham, Norfolk. Henry "suspected his agent of some underhand dealing" (404). Henry tells Fanny that he is "not satisfied about Maddison—I am sure he still means to impose upon me if possible, and get a cousin of his own into a certain mill" (411). Henry confesses that Maddison "is a clever fellow," and Henry does "not wish to try to displace him." Henry is trying to impress Fanny by showing her that he is a concerned, responsible landlord. "The mischief such a man does on an estate, both as to the credit of his employer, and the welfare of the poor, is inconceivable" (412).

Maddox, Charles (Chapters 15, 16)   According to Tom Bertram, "Charles Maddox" from Stoke "is as gentlemanlike a man as you will see anywhere" (148). Tom proposes that he play the part of Anhalt, the clergyman in *Lovers' Vows*.

Maddoxes, the Miss (Chapter 29)   Guests at the Mansfield Park ball, sisters of Charles Maddox and mentioned in passing by Lady Bertram after the ball.

Marshall, Captain (Chapter 6)   Captain Marshall is the captain of William Price's ship, the *Antwerp*, when William is a midshipman.

Maxwell, Mrs. (Chapter 38)   The silver knife that Susan and Betsey Price quarrel over was a gift to Mary Price from "her good god-mother, old Mrs. Admiral Maxwell, only six weeks before she was taken for death" (387).

Nanny (Chapters 1, 32)   Mrs. Norris's trusted housekeeper who escorts Fanny Price back to London following her visit there. Nanny has in London a cousin, "the sadler's" (8). Mrs. Norris gives her "orders" (323).

Norris, Mrs. née Ward (mentioned throughout)   Mrs. Norris fits the epithet used to describe her: "life seems but a quick succession of busy nothings." Jane Austen's mother "Enjoyed Mrs. Norris," and relatives were "delighted with Mrs. Norris" (Southam: *Heritage*, I: 49–50). A. C. Bradley blames Mrs. Norris, among others, for the Bertram sisters' being "what they were," adding that Jane Austen "must have detested Mrs. Norris. We all do. Who could say a good word for her?" He answers his own question. "Jane Austen could," explaining that her actions in living with the expelled Maria reveal that Mrs. Norris, "this intolerable woman had strong affections, and we admit that the story has implied this all along, though our hatred of her may have made us blind to it." To Reginald Farrer, who has little positive to say about *MP*, Jane Austen's depiction of Mrs. Norris is one of its redeeming features (Southam, *Heritage*: II: 236–237, 258).

Mrs. Norris does not figure predominantly in late 20th-century new critical, historical, and feminist accounts of *MP*. She interests Vladimir Nabokov as an enthusiastic letter writer serving as the household chronicler. Writing letters is an "activity" allowing her to play a significant part in family affairs. She writes down Sir Thomas's "advice and professions" (5). Her letter writing principally exists to relay information and/or make arrangements, as distinct from communicating through a letter with someone absent.

Johnson notes that Mrs. Norris undergoes a "bitter expulsion . . . as the villain of the piece." She observes, "Throughout the novel . . . Mrs. Norris has been treated with a peculiar superabundance of opprobrium: no occasion passes that she is not debased with sarcasm." Yet Mrs. Norris's "offenses are authorized, indeed sometimes are even requested, by Sir Thomas himself." Johnson points out that Sir Thomas "directs her to cooperate with him in maintaining the superior 'rank, fortune, rights, and expectations' [11] of his daughters at Fanny's expense." Sir Thomas "approves Maria's marriage with a great family. Mrs. Norris . . . is less a villain in her own right than an adjutant." Sir Thomas's worst qualities appear in her, including "officiousness . . . family pride," and his meanness (114). Johnson, however, refrains from commenting on Mrs. Norris's excessive meanness and nastiness, bordering on bullying, toward Fanny.

The husband of Lady Bertram's elder sister was a close friend of Sir Thomas. Generous in proposing welfare schemes for others to implement, she supports the idea that Fanny Price should come to live at Mansfield Park. Her husband apparently is too unwell for Fanny to live with them at the Parsonage. When widowed, she takes a small cottage in the village too small to put up visitors, although she has one room for friends and a servant. She has a reasonable annual income of £600 but is frugal, she claims, for the sake of the Bertram children. Mrs. Norris becomes the guardian and mentor of Julia and Maria, whom she spoils, favoring Maria, while treating Fanny Price very harshly. Sir Thomas later on in the novel blames Mrs. Norris for the disastrous way in which his daughters have turned out. She pushes the case for her beloved Maria to marry Rushworth, her material obsessions and concern for social status overriding other considerations.

Mrs. Norris does not object to the performing of *Lovers' Vows* at Mansfield Park, since she will be at the house and involved. At Fanny's ball she attempts to take some of the credit, and then she goes home "with all the supernumerary jellies to nurse a sick maid" (283). Angry at Henry Crawford's proposal to somebody she perceives as low down on the social pecking order, Fanny Price, she would have gone with Fanny to Portsmouth but remembers that she will have to pay for the return journey. Mrs. Norris finds it very difficult to come to terms with Maria's failed marriage and elopement, placing blame on Fanny for not accepting Henry Crawford. She joins Maria in another county where probably they both got on each other's nerves. Sir Thomas is very pleased to see her leave Mansfield Park. To Mrs. Norris's credit, she does contribute to the expense of William Price's commission. This does not excuse or condone her malicious treatment of Fanny. She is in Sir Thomas's words "an hourly evil" and nobody at Mansfield Park misses her: "She was regretted by no one at Mansfield," not even Fanny, who somewhat ironically at Portsmouth misses her! (465–466).

Norris, Rev. Mr. (Chapters 1, 3, 6, 22) The Reverend Mr. Norris was "a friend" of Sir Thomas Bertram with meager means. He and "Mrs. Norris began their career of conjugal felicity with very little less than a thousand a year" (3). Sir Thomas presents him with the Mansfield living. Mrs. Norris uses her husband's apparent delicate health as an excuse for not letting Fanny stay at the "Parsonage as a desirable companion to an aunt who had no children of her own." His wife claims that Mr. Norris "could no more bear the noise of a child than he could fly" (9). Mrs. Norris "consoled herself for the loss of her husband" when Fanny was about 15 "by considering that she could do very well without him, and for her reduction of income by the evident necessity of stricter economy" (23).

Oliver, Tom (Chapter 15) According to Tom Bertram, "a very clever fellow" (148). Tom Oliver lives at Stoke in the Mansfield neighborhood. He is considered very briefly for the role of Anhalt in the Mansfield Park performance of *Lovers' Vows*.

Owen, Mr. (Chapters 26, 29) A friend of Edmund Bertram from Lessingby near Peterborough in a similar situation, both being ordained during the Christmas week. Edmund spends Christmas and the post-Christmas period with Owen and his sisters.

Owens, the Miss (Chapters 29, 35) "His friend Mr. Owen had sisters—He might find them attractive" (286—287). Mary Crawford is jealous of them when Edmund extends his Christmas stay with the Owen family. According to Edmund, the Miss Owens are "Pleasant, good-humoured, unaffected girls" (355).Unlike Fanny and Mary Crawford, they lack common sense.

Prescott, Lady (Chapter 29) Lady Prescott is a guest at the Mansfield Park ball held for Fanny. Lady Bertram cannot remember "What it was that Lady Prescott had noticed in Fanny" (283).

Price, Betsey (Chapters 37–40, 46) Betsey Price is five years old when Fanny returns to visit her former Portsmouth home. The youngest of the Price children and her mother's favorite. Spoiled by her, she appears to have been "trained up to think the alphabet her greatest enemy" (391). Betsey argues with Susan over a "silver knife" (396). She was "left to be with the servants at her pleasure, and then encouraged to report any evil of them" (391). Fanny feels she is not able to improve or change her character. Somewhat ironically, the spoiled Betsey is associated with Mrs. Norris, who sends her a prayer book as a present: uninhibited, she is, even at a very early age, as selfish as Mrs. Norris.

Price, Charles (Chapters 38, 39) The Prices' sixth son, he is "about eight" years old, and like his brother Tom, "ragged and dirty" and noisy. He "had been born since Fanny left Portsmouth" (381). He goes to school, and in common with his brothers, for Fanny he is "quite untameable" (391).

Price, Fanny (throughout the novel) Probably the least liked of all Jane Austen's heroines, whose own mother "thought Fanny insipid," although some of her close family circle found Fanny "a delightful Character!" Fanny Knight "delighted with Fanny;—but not satisfied with the end—wanting more Love between her & Edmund." Throughout the 19th century there is little critical attention paid to Fanny. Hostility is exhibited in Reginald Farrer's July 1917 *Quarterly Review*

assessment in which he calls Fanny a "penniless dull little nobody." Henry Crawford "had a very lucky miss. . . . How he could ever seriously have wanted to marry her, in fact, becomes a puzzle, for she is the most terrible incarnation we have of the female prig-pharisee" (Southam, *Heritage*: I: 49–48; II: 263–264). Lionel Trilling (1957) declares, "Nobody, I believe, has ever found it possible to like the heroine of" the novel and proceeds to declare that Fanny is close to saintliness. Such a view is taken by Tony Tanner (1966), who sees Fanny as "never, ever wrong." Ignoring the irony of the novel, the novel celebrates quiet and peace. Fanny Price "suffers in her stillness. For righteousness' sake" (Wiltshire, lxvi–lxix).

Marilyn Butler (1975) writes that "Portsmouth is Fanny's exile in the wilderness, her grand temptation by the devil Mammon" on the part of Henry Crawford. Fanny chooses another world, "Mansfield, promises her a social life of affectionate service, together with an inner life of meditation" (Butler, 237, 245). Although feminist and political readings of the novel have focused attention away from Fanny, critical reactions have still to encompass the hostility she inspires. Perhaps the most judicious recent summary of Fanny is found at the conclusion of John Wiltshire's introduction to his edition of the novel in *The Cambridge Edition of the Works of Jane Austen* (2005). Wiltshire writes, "Fanny is not an ideal figure of moral righteousness" and that her "final happiness is contingent, a fallout from the motives, projects and passions of the rival figures whose lives have been so tellingly intertwined with hers" (lxxxiv).

What then of Fanny? She is only 10, small and physically fragile, when she is sent to Mansfield Park. Her absence from her Portsmouth family gives her a tremendous feeling of being alone and, except for Edmund's kindness, mistreated. Her "quiet, passive manner" covers fear and nightly tears. She especially misses her slightly older brother, William. Edmund tells her, "There is no reason in the world why you should not be important where you are known." Fanny becomes the chief companion of Lady Bertram, to whom she often reads. She is most sensitive to Edmund's kindness and his neglect when Mary Crawford arrives on the scene. She believes, unlike Mary, in his choice of the church as a career and does not agree with the theatricals in the absence of Sir Thomas, refusing to participate in them.

The central consciousness of the novel from whose perspective most, if not all, of its events are seen, she perceives that Henry Crawford is playing games with Maria's and Julia's affections. A Cinderella figure, she previously looked upon Sir Thomas Bertram with fear and trepidation, and continually suffers from the mean treatment bordering on bullying of Mrs. Norris. Upon his return from Antigua, Sir Thomas's attitude toward her is transformed into one of considerable kindness, especially after he learns that she alone has refused to be part of the theatrical activities. Fanny shows a considerable affinity for nature and gardens, their naturalness and development. She rejects Henry Crawford's proposal, as her heart is "pre-engaged," although she does not reveal this to Edmund. She perceives Henry again to be trifling with her affections in the manner he had trifled with Maria and Julia.

There are various stages in her progress in the novel. The first is Fanny's Cinderella-like move to Mansfield Park from Portsmouth. The second is the return home of Sir Thomas following his overseas trip. This stage includes his throwing a ball especially in her honor and culminates in Crawford's proposal. In the third stage of her development, Fanny returns with her beloved brother, William, to her Portsmouth home, where she spent her early years. This visit is an important part of her bildungsroman, her growing up and maturing. She imagines at Portsmouth she will "feel affection without fear or restraint" and dreams at last of being "at peace." A good deal of the novel depicts her dreaming and inner thoughts. Contrary to her expectations, she finds "closeness and noise . . . confinement, bad air, bad smells." She quickly "lost ground as to health," revealing her negative reaction to her new environment. It is only when she returns to Mansfield Park, to reconciliation with Sir Thomas, and to the awareness that "Edmund was no longer the dupe of Mary Crawford" that she recovers physically. In this fourth and final stage in her development, she is united with her

Prince Charming, although still "timid, anxious, doubting as she was." However, she has obtained "a delightful happiness" (15, 26, 326, 370, 432, 409, 461, 471). In the words of John Wiltshire in his *Jane Austen and the Body* (1992), the author's "representation of Fanny's psychology is so full and intricate" and "the physical and emotional aspects of her being are seen as inextricably interrelated" (108). Fanny is indeed a most complex heroine; it is no wonder that she has provoked diverse reactions since the days of her initial creation. She becomes "Mrs. Bertram" and hence (pun intended) "Price-less"!

Price, John (Chapter 38) Another brother of Fanny. He does not appear in *MP*. He lives in London and works in a public office as a clerk.

Price, Mary (deceased) (Chapter 38) Mary was around four when Fanny left home for Mansfield Park. She died without seeing Fanny again. "Only two hours before she died," she gave her mother the silver knife she received from her godmother Mrs. Maxwell to give to Susan. Little Betsey however keeps playing with the knife and it is "such a bone of contention" between the two (386).

Price, Mr. (Chapters 1, 37–42, 44–46) Fanny's father, "a Lieutenant of Marines, without education, fortune or connections" who had 10 children and "disabled for active service, but not the less equal to company and good liquor, and a very small income." Clearly, Price had qualities that initially attracted Miss Frances Ward to marry him in spite of all the obstacles to promotion in the marines. When he is introduced to Henry Crawford in Portsmouth, Price's "manners, now, though not polished, were more than passable; they were grateful, animated, manly; his expressions were those of an attached father, and a sensible man." At home, however, he presents a different face: "he swore and he drank, he was dirty and gross." His interests and conversation are confined to the Portsmouth dockyard, harbor, and the navy. During her visit, he does not treat Fanny with kindness; he "scarcely ever noticed her, but to make her the object of a coarse joke."

Price displays a brutal side. He prescribes the application of "the rope's end" and "a little flogging" for the eloping Henry Crawford and Maria Bertram (Rushworth). We are told very little of his actual service at sea. "He did not want abilities, but had no curiosity" (3–4, 402, 389, 440, 389) apart from his own masculine world. His language is violent, replete with swearing, although his "account of the *Thrush* leaving the harbour [is] packed with detail" and "offers a convincing pastiche of nautical expression and defines the narrow boundaries of Mr. Price's mental world." Southam adds that Jane Austen has focused on "the identity Mr. Price has created for himself as a fixated naval man, his horizons limited to naval matters and the world of Portsmouth" (Southam, *Navy*: 208, 206).

Price, Mrs. Frances, née Ward (Chapters 1, 37–44, 46) Fanny's mother and the younger sister of Lady Bertram and Mrs. Norris. "To disoblige her family," she married beneath her class. "She could hardly have made a more untoward choice," and she eventually severs all contact with her family. This distance continues for 11 years. Some reconciliation takes place following a letter she writes to Lady Bertram. She requests assistance, as she finds herself with more children and an unemployed "disabled" husband. The chief consequences of the letter are the adoption by the Bertrams of Fanny, the second-oldest child. At the time Fanny leaves Portsmouth for Mansfield Park, Mrs. Price has seven other children, and she is pregnant again. She subsequently gives birth to her 10th child, Betsey. Returning to Portsmouth eight years after leaving, Fanny is both shocked by the chaos she finds and by her mother. Initially warm toward Fanny, she has no time for her. She has become "a dawdle, a slattern, who neither taught nor restrained her children." Mrs. Price has "no talent, no conversation, no affection towards [Fanny]; no curiosity to know her better, no desire of her friendship, and no inclination for her company that could lessen her sense of such feelings."

The source for these deficiencies was her desire to marry Mr. Price, whose lack of status, position, and money plus crudeness have an adverse effect on his wife. Fanny is upset by the contrast between her real mother and Lady Bertram. The experience of meeting her natural mother again, amid the chaos and impoverishment of her own home in Portsmouth, reinforces for Fanny the values of order, quietness, and tradition embodied at Mansfield Park. Ironically, Fanny's mother does what Maria and Julia do later on in the novel—but in each instance they chose partners of wealth and social position. Maria pays the price, Julia luckily escapes. Frances Ward, who married for love, reaps the bitter fruits of her rebellion. At least three of her children, Fanny, William, and Susan, appear to some extent, not to pay the full price of the negative consequences (3, 4, 390).

It is revealing that Mrs. Price is ignored by Jane Austen's family and friends and largely ignored in the subsequent critical history of the novel. Although not mentioned specifically, Mrs. Price is part of George Henry Lewes's astute observation made in 1859 that "the scenes at Portsmouth, when Fanny Price visits her home after some years' residence at the Park, are wonderfully truthful and vivid" (Southam, *Heritage*: I, 166). Later, 20th-century critics, however, have problems with accommodating Mrs. Price: a failure who makes her choice, made her bed, and has to lie on it. She has not the luxury of income, family planning, childcare, or job opportunities.

Price, Sam (Chapters 38, 39) Sam, Fanny's 11-year-old brother, departs for his naval career on the same ship as his elder brother William, the *Thrush*, while Fanny stays in Portsmouth. He possesses a loud voice, and his father comments, "that boy is fit for a boatswain," or someone who controls the rigging on board a ship (383).

Price, Susan (Chapters 37–44, 46–48) Fourteen years old when Fanny goes back to Portsmouth, Fanny and Susan bond and Fanny realizes that Susan "had an innate taste for the genteel and well-appointed." Fanny grew "very fond of her" and became "her oracle." She introduces Susan to good reading. Fanny "began to feel that when her own release from Portsmouth came, her happiness would have a material drawback in leaving Susan behind." Fanny adds, "That a girl so capable of being made, every thing good, should be left in such hands, distressed her more and more" (418–419). Sir Thomas invites Susan to accompany Fanny on her return to Mansfield Park, and she becomes "perhaps, the most beloved" of Lady Bertram's companions (472) and remains at Mansfield Park.

Price, Tom (Chapters 38, 39) The Prices' fifth son, aged "about . . . nine." Fanny remembers helping to nurse Tom, whom "she wanted to keep by her, to try to trace the features of the baby she had loved, and to talk to him of his infant preference of herself. Tom, however, had no mind for such treatment . . . he came home . . . to run about and make a noise" (381).

Price, William (Chapters 1–4, 6–7, 11, 15–16, 19, 24–29, 31, 33, 36–39, 47) William, the eldest of the Price children and a year older than Fanny, serves as the bridge between the worlds of Portsmouth and Mansfield Park. There is a strong bond of affection between William and Fanny. In childhood, he was "her constant companion and friend, her advocate with her mother . . . in every distress." When Fanny initially goes as a girl to Mansfield Park, William is the member of her Portsmouth family whom she most misses. He is the sole member of her Portsmouth relatives to visit Fanny at Mansfield. William does so before going to sea at around 12 years of age. He sees her seven years later when aged 19; he "had known every variety of danger, which sea and war together could offer." As a midshipman serving on the *Antwerp,* and far from England, William remains a good correspondent, even sending his sister a pretty amber cross from Sicily.

William impresses those whom he meets, being well mannered, unpretentious, and generous. Sir Thomas Bertram is impressed with William's "good principles, professional knowledge, energy, courage, and cheerfulness." William makes a passing observation that he has not seen Fanny dance, and Sir Thomas reacts by arranging a ball in Fanny's honor. Not intimidated by Mansfield Park, its inhabitants, or atmosphere, he finds a ready audience in narrating his naval experience and thus serves as a vehicle through which Jane

Austen is able to remind her readers that there is a world beyond the confines of Mansfield and even Portsmouth, and that there is a war going on with France mainly enacted at sea in naval confrontations. Henry Crawford is so impressed by what William has experienced by the age of 20 that he envies him. Partly out of respect for William, but largely to impress Fanny, Henry Crawford influences his uncle, Admiral Crawford, to use his naval contacts to secure a promotion for William, who rises from being a humble midshipman, whom the young women will not look at, to becoming a lieutenant. Fanny returns to Portsmouth accompanied by William, who is immediately called away to serve on the sloop *Thrush.*

On the final page of the novel, the reader learns of "William's continued good conduct and rising fame" (15, 236, 473). His function in the novel is to demonstrate that, in common with Fanny, chaotic, impoverished backgrounds, such as those provided by the Price Portsmouth menagerie, are not a personal impediment, provided they are tempered by other environments: in William's case the navy, in Fanny's case Mansfield Park. His close relationship with Fanny reminds readers, in B. C. Southam's words, that in *MP,* he is "the figure of 'fraternal love' [235], a bond that Jane Austen places above all others, even above 'the conjugal tie' [234]" (Southam, *Navy:* 200). It is this relationship that Nina Auerbach calls "the vivid heart of the book" (*ELH,* [1972]: 119). Gilbert Ryle in his "Jane Austen and the Moralists" regards William "as the real hero of the story," seeing "their brother-sister love" as "the paradigm against which to assess all the others. Fanny's love for her cousin Edmund had begun as a child's love for a deputy-William'" (cited Southam, *Navy:* 200)

Ravenshaw, Lord (Chapter 13) Lord Ravenshaw of Ecclesford, in Cornwall, has a house party where Yates has been before he arrives at Mansfield Park. Lord Ravenshaw was organizing a private performance of *Lovers' Vows* that was canceled on the death of his grandmother. Lord Ravenshaw was going to take the role of Baron Wildenhaim. Yates comments, "he should have so mistaken his powers, for he was no more equal to the Baron! A little man, with a weak voice, always hoarse after the first ten minutes!" (122).

Rebecca (Chapters 38, 47) Mrs. Price's difficult, inefficient, incompetent servant. According to Fanny, she is "without a single recommendation" (385).

Robert (Chapter 23) Works as a nurseryman at Mansfield Parsonage. Mrs. Grant complains about his habit of leaving "some of [her] plants" outside without taking into account changes in the weather (212).

Rushworth, Mr. (Chapter 9) (deceased) James Rushworth's father, briefly referred to by his widow, Mrs. Rushworth, while showing visitors to Mansfield Park around the ancient family chapel at Sotherton Court. The deceased Mr. Rushworth ended the tradition conducted since the time of James II (1685–88) of holding regular family prayer there. Mary Crawford somewhat ironically refers to this as "improvements" (186). Rushworth's son too follows his father in destroying the past. Certainly, the family prayers suggest Recusant or Catholic sympathies, as James II briefly restored Catholicism to England.

Rushworth, Mr. James (Chapters 4–12, 14–15, 17–21, 23, 25, 35–36, 44–47) He is a fine example where pedigree, station, wealth, and ownership do not go with strength of character. James Rushworth has recently inherited Sotherton Court, 10 miles from Mansfield Park. He is described as "a heavy young man," and "heavy" refers both to his intelligence and his physical appearance. He has, according to the narrator, "not more than common sense," and Edmund says "if this man had not twelve thousand a year, he would be a very stupid fellow." Owing to the influence of Mrs. Norris, he and Maria quickly become engaged. Observing his friend Smith's improvements at Compton, he also changes the grounds at his estate, and destroys the work of nature over generations. Rushworth eagerly participates in *Lovers' Vows* but finds the learning of his part, with its "two-and-forty speeches" a problem and rehearsal rekindles his jealousy of Henry

Crawford. He abandons the play, which raises him temporarily in Sir Thomas's eyes, although even he realizes eventually that "the indignities of stupidity, and the disappointments of selfish passion, can excite little pity." During the theatricals, Rushworth reveals a delight in dressing up in splendid costumes. Despised by his wife, Maria, who elopes with Henry Crawford, his marriage lasts only six months. He "had no difficulty in procuring a divorce" and lives to "be duped at least with good humour and good luck" (38, 40, 224, 464).

Rushworth, Mrs. (Chapters 4, 8–10, 12, 16, 21, 40, 45, 47) James Rushworth's mother, "a well-meaning, civil, prosing, pompous woman, who thought nothing of consequence, but as it related to her own son's concerns" (75). She has tremendous pride in Sotherton Court, makes every effort to learn its history from her housekeeper, and acts as the guide to her guests from Mansfield. When her son James marries Maria Bertram, she goes to Bath but is in his company in Wimpole Street in London when there is strong suspicion that Maria has eloped with Henry Crawford. She disagreed with Maria, whom she disliked, and uses her maidservant to make sure that the relationship with Henry is not kept a secret.

Sally (Chapter 38) The slow, lower on the pecking order of the two Price household servants, "an attendant girl [of] inferior appearance" (383).

Scholey, Old (Chapter 38) One of Mr. Price's Portsmouth friends with some naval experience.

Smith (Chapter 1) A friend of Rushworth from Compton in a neighboring Northamptonshire county, who has just seen his estate through "improvement" directed by Humphry Repton (53).

Sneyds, the (Chapter 5) Tom Bertram tells Edmund and Fanny Price that his friend Sneyd and he went to visit Ramsgate. There Sneyd introduced Tom to "his father and mother and sisters," both of whom seemed to be "out" in society. Tom paid his attention to the younger sister, Augusta, who "ought not to have been noticed for the next six months." Consequently, the eldest Miss Sneyd "has never forgiven" him for such a social gaffe or impropriety (51).

Stephen (Chapter 19) One of the Bertram grooms, who is "steady" at driving their coach (189).

Stornaway, Lady, Flora Ross (Chapters 36, 43–44, 47) Formerly the "most particular friend" (359) of Mary Crawford in London, and sister to the now Mrs. Fraser. At Mansfield Park, Mary claims not to care for either as they had married for purely mercenary reasons, and both sisters are unhappily married. According to Mary, the then Flora Ross was "dying for Henry [Crawford] the first winter she came out" (362) in society. She jilted a "nice young man" (361) in a very fashionable Regiment, the Blues, for the sake of wealth and status represented by Lord Stornaway.

Stornaway, Lord (Chapters 36, 43) Mary Crawford tells Fanny Price that she distrusted Lord Stornaway before her friend Flora Ross married him. Following the marriage, her reservations have been confirmed. He is "horrid" and "has about as much sense . . . as Mr. Rushworth, but much worse looking, and with a blackguard character" (361). However, writing to Fanny from London, Mary seems to have had a change of heart: "I fancy Lord S. is very good-humoured and pleasant in his own family, and I do not think him so very ill-looking as I did, at least one sees many worse" (416).

Walsh, Captain (Chapter 38) One of Mr. Price's Portsmouth friends with naval experience.

Whitaker, Mrs. (Chapter 10) The Sotherton housekeeper, who shows Mrs. Norris around the dairy, provides her with a cream cheese recipe, cream cheese, and four pheasant eggs. Whether in fact Mrs. Norris has "been spounging" [took] these from "old Mrs. Whitaker," is left undecided (105–106).

Wilcox (Chapters 8, 20, 25) Contrary views are expressed concerning the old Mansfield Park coachman. Maria describes him as "a stupid old fellow, [who] does not know how to drive" (77). Surprisingly, Mrs. Norris seems to be concerned for him when she hurries Fanny after dining at the Parsonage: "Quick, quick. I cannot bear to keep old Wilcox waiting. You should always remember the coachman and horses" (251). According to Mrs. Norris, Wilcox suffers from "rheumatism which [she] had been doctoring him for" and he insisted on driving the Bertrams to Sotherton in "the middle of Winter" (189).

Yates, the Honourable John (Chapters 12–15, 17–20, 23, 40, 46–48) The Honorable John Yates forms a remarkably rapid friendship with Tom Bertram when they spend 10 days together in the same company at Weymouth. They are described rather ambiguously as "intimate friend[s]." Tom invites Yates to Mansfield Park, where he unexpectedly arrives following the early curtailment of Lord Ravenshaw's plans for a private theatrical performance of *Lovers' Vows*. Yates is the initial impulse behind the Mansfield Park theatricals, and he is cast in the role of Baron Wildenhaim. Previously, the death of his host's grandmother prevented this performance, and once again Yates's acting pretensions are curtailed, this time by the sudden appearance of Sir Thomas, who considers Yates "trifling and confident, idle and expensive" and "the worst object" associated with the theatricals. Yates in his turn regards Sir Thomas as "unintelligibly moral" and "infamously tyrannical." Considering himself a fine actor, Yates is generally perceived "to rant dreadfully," and somewhat ironically Mary Crawford observes, "[I]f his rents were but equal to his rants!" Subsequently, it is discovered that Yates is far wealthier than he appears.

Yates seems to have nothing to commend him "beyond habits of fashion and expense, being the younger son of a lord with a tolerable independence." He fails to realize that during the theatrical rehearsals, Julia Bertram is flirting with him to make Henry Crawford jealous. After leaving Mansfield Park, Yates surfaces again in the novel. In London, he once again pursues Julia, with whom he is besotted. Fearing increased restraints at Mansfield Park following the elopement of Maria and Henry, Julia elopes with Yates to Scotland, where they marry.

The marriage is "a less desperate business" than Sir Thomas thought, especially after it emerges that he has less debts than he believed and more money. While perceived as "not very solid," he may become "less trifling" and "at least tolerably domestic and quiet." In short, Yates is not fully a materialist in pursuit of wealth. He is an example of the maxim that appearances are frequently deceptive (117, 194, 191, 164, 394, 121, 462).

BIBLIOGRAPHY

Primary Texts

Jane Austen's Letters. Collected and edited by Deirdre Le Faye. 3d ed. Oxford: Oxford University Press, 1995.

Mansfield Park. Edited by R. W. Chapman. *The Novels of Jane Austen, III.* 3d ed. London: Oxford University Press. 1988 reprint of 1934, 3d ed. Referred to by page number in the text.

Mansfield Park. Edited by Claudia L. Johnson. New York: W.W. Norton, 1998.

Mansfield Park. Edited by James Kinsley, with an introduction and notes by Jane Stabler. Oxford World Classics. Oxford: Oxford University Press, 2003.

Mansfield Park. The Cambridge Edition of the Works of Jane Austen. Edited by John Wiltshire. Cambridge: Cambridge University Press, 2005.

Mansfield Park. Edited by Kathryn Sutherland. London: Penguin Books. 2003.

Secondary Works

Amis, Kingsley. "What Became of Jane Austen?" *Spectator* (October 4, 1957): 339–340. Reprinted in *Jane Austen: A Collection of Critical Essays,* edited by Ian Watt, 141–144. Englewood Cliffs, N.J.: Prentice Hall, 1963.

Auberach, Nina Joan. "'O Brave New World': Evolution and Resolution in *Persuasion,*" *ELH* 39 (1972): 112–128.

Auerbach, Emily. *Searching for Jane Austen.* Madison: University of Wisconsin Press, 2004.

Bradley, A. C. [On Jane Austen] 1911. In Southam, *Heritage,* II: 233–239.

Butler, Marilyn. *Jane Austen and the War of Ideas.* Oxford, U.K.: Clarendon Press, 1975.

Duckworth, Alistair M. *The Improvement of the Estate: A Study of Jane Austen's Novels.* Baltimore: Johns Hopkins University Press, 1971.

Farrer, Reginald. "Jane Austen, ob. July 18, 1817," *Quarterly Review* July 1917. In Southam, *Heritage:* II: 245–272.

Fleishman, Avrom. *A Reading of Mansfield Park: An Essay in Critical Synthesis.* Minneapolis: University of Minnesota Press, 1967.

Gay, Penny. *Jane Austen and the Theatre.* Cambridge: Cambridge University Press, 2002.

Gilson, David. *A Bibliography of Jane Austen. New Introduction and Corrections by the Author.* Winchester and New Castle, Del.: St. Paul's Bibliographies. Oak Knoll Press, 1997.

Harding, D. W. *Regulated Hatred and Other Essays on Jane Austen.* Edited by Monica Lawlor. London and Atlantic Highlands, N.J.: Athlone Press, 1998.

Harris, Jocelyn. *Jane Austen's Art of Memory.* Cambridge: Cambridge University Press, 1989.

Johnson, Claudia L. *Jane Austen: Women, Politics, and the Novel.* Chicago and London: University of Chicago Press, 1988.

Jones, Vivien. *How to Study a Jane Austen Novel.* Houndmills, Basingstoke, Hampshire, U.K.: Macmillan, 1987.

Lascelles, Mary. *Jane Austen and Her Art.* Oxford: Oxford University Press, 1949.

Le Faye, Deirdre. *Jane Austen: A Family Record.* 2d ed. Cambridge: Cambridge University Press, 2004.

Lewes, George Henry. "The Novels of Jane Austen," *Blackwood's Edinburgh Magazine* (July 1859): 99–113. In Southam, *Heritage:* I: 148–166.

Litz, A. Walton. *Jane Austen. A Study of Her Artistic Development.* New York: Oxford University Press, 1965.

Lodge, David. "The Vocabulary of *Mansfield Park.*" In his *Language of Fiction. Essays in Criticism and Verbal Analysis of the English Novel,* 94–113. London: Routledge, 1966.

Nabokov, Vladimir. "*Mansfield Park* (1814)." In *Lectures on Literature,* edited by Fredson Bowers, 9–60. New York and London: Harcourt Brace Jovanovich, Bruccoli Clark, 1980.

Page, Norman. *The Language of Jane Austen.* Oxford, U.K.: Basil Blackwell, 1972.

Palmer, Sally B. "Slipping the Leash: Lady Bertram's Lapdog," *Persuasion On-Line* 25, no. 1 (Winter 2004). Online journal. Available online. URL: www.

jasna.org/pesuasions/on-line/vol25no1/palmer.html. Accessed April 24, 2007.

Phillipps, K. C. *Jane Austen's English.* London: Andre Deutsch, 1970.

Rogers, J. Pat. "The Critical History of *Mansfield Park.*" In *A Companion to Jane Austen Studies.* Edited by Laura Cooner Lambdin and Robert Thomas Lambdin, [71]–86. Westport, Conn.: Greenwood Press, 2000.

Said, Edward W. "Jane Austen and Empire." In *Raymond Williams: Critical Perspectives,* edited by Terry Eagleton. Boston: Northwestern University Press, 1989, 150–164. Reprinted in his *Culture and Imperialism.* New York: Knopf, 1993, 80–97.

Southam, B. C., ed. *Jane Austen: The Critical Heritage.* 2 vols. London: Routledge and Kegan Paul. 1978–1979.

———. *Jane Austen and the Navy.* London: Hambledon and London, 2000.

Tanner, Tony. Introduction to *Mansfield Park.* Penguin Classics Edition, Harmondsworth, Middlesex, U.K.: Penguin Books, 1966. Reprinted as an appendix to K. Sutherland, 2003. [My Tanner references are to this reprint].

Trilling, Lionel. "*Mansfield Park.*" In *Jane Austen A Collection of Critical Essays* edited by Ian Watt, 124–140. Englewood Cliffs, N.J.: Prentice Hall, 1963.

Wiltshire, John. *Jane Austen and the Body.* Cambridge: Cambridge University Press, 1992.

Memoirs of Mr. Clifford An Unfinished Tale (1925)

COMPOSITION AND PUBLICATION

The seventh in order of appearance in Jane Austen's Juvenilia *Volume the First,* probably written in 1788 when its author was age 13. Described as "An Unfinished Tale," the short six-paragraph work is also dedicated to her younger brother CHARLES JOHN AUSTEN. *Memoirs of Mr. Clifford* (MC) is included in the sixth volume of R. W. Chapman's edition of Jane Austen's *The Works,* and in Margaret Anne Doody and Douglas Murray's 1993 edition of *Catharine and Other Writings* (40–41). To date, no Juvenilia Press edition exists. The manuscript is in the Bodleian Library, Oxford.

SYNOPSIS

The brief *Memoir* recalls a coach visit by Mr. Clifford in his youth from Bath to London. He has not visited London and the journey begins well; he covers "nineteen miles, the first Day," stopping the first night at Devizes. The next day, the traveler's pace is much slower, and "in the course of 3 days hard labour" he reaches Overton, where he becomes ill and is forced to spend "five months" being cared for by its "celebrated Physician." After being cured, he takes some time to reach Basingstoke, where apparently he stays with "Mr. Robins's." the memoir then ends (43–44).

CRITICAL COMMENTARY

MC has attracted some comment. Patricia Meyer Spacks notes that it "uses the familiar narrative metaphor of the journey as structural principle for a story about a man who does nothing whatever of interest. . . . The narrator reports" small details of the journey including "the boiled egg [he] shares with his servants at Devizes. This kind of detail is essential, since . . . essentially nothing happens to" the protagonist "from beginning to end." In fact, "Mr. Clifford appears to possess neither inner nor outer life" (125). Juliet McMaster remarks on "a gargantuan delight in plethora" found in MC and other juvenilia. So in this instance, the wealthy Mr. Clifford maintains "not just a coach and four" but "a great many Carriages of which I do not recollect half" and various other vehicles (McMaster, 124). The text is extensively annotated in Doody and Murray (301–303).

CHARACTERS

Clifford, Mr. (43–44) A very wealthy young man in delicate health, owner of various vehicles and probably the narrative "I" of MC.

Physician (43) A "celebrated" Overton physician who treats and cures Mr. Clifford.

Robins, Mr. (43) Lives near "the bottom of Basingstoke Hill," visited by Mr. Clifford (44).

BIBLIOGRAPHY

Primary Texts

Austen, Jane. "Memoirs of Mr. Clifford." In *The Jane Austen Library. Volume the First.* Edited by R. W. Chapman, with a foreword by Lord David Cecil, a preface by Brian Southam, and a preface by R. W. Chapman, 78–80. London: Athlone Press, 1984.

———. "Memoirs of Mr. Clifford." In *The Works of Jane Austen*, Vol. 6, *Minor Works*, edited by R. W. Chapman. Oxford: Oxford University Press. 1986. [All textual references are to this edition.]

———. "Memoirs of Mr. Clifford." In *Jane Austen's Catharine and other Writings*, edited by Margaret Anne Doody and Douglas Murray, 40–41. Oxford: Oxford University Press, 1993.

Secondary Works

McMaster, Juliet. "The Juvenilia: Energy Versus Sympathy." In *A Companion to Jane Austen Studies*, edited by Laura Cooner Lambdin and Robert Thomas Lambdin, [173]–189. Westport, Conn: Greenwood Press, 2000.

Spacks, Patricia Meyer. "Plots and Possibilities: Jane Austen's Juvenilia." In *Jane Austen's Beginnings: The Juvenilia and Lady Susan*, edited by J. David Grey, [123]–133. Ann Arbor, Mich., and London: UMI Research Press, 1989.

The Mystery, an Unfinished Comedy (1933)

COMPOSITION AND PUBLICATION

The 11th in order of appearance in Jane Austen's Juvenilia *Volume the First.* Dedicated to her father, the Reverend GEORGE AUSTEN, probably written around 1788, when she was 13, in three brief scenes; according to the author's dedication, it is "as *complete* a *Mystery* as any of its kind" (55). James Edward Austen-Leigh includes *The Mystery* ([M]) in the second edition of the *Memoir*, published in 1871 as an example "of her juvenile effusions . . . as a specimen of the kind of transitory amusement which Jane was continually supplying to the family party" (Austen-Leigh, 40). M is included in the sixth volume of R. W. Chapman's edition of Jane Austen's *The Works* and in Margaret Anne Doody and Douglas Murray's 1993 edition of *Catharine and Other Writings* (53–55). "It was also reprinted in two early works of biographical criticism" (Sutherland, *Textual Lives*: 206 n. 17). The manuscript is in the Bodleian Library, Oxford.

SYNOPSIS

There are three very short scenes in this one-act comedy. The first is set in a garden, the second and third in a parlor indoors. There are four male characters, three female characters, and a cameo part, "Corydon." In the first scene, Corydon is "interrupted" by "old Humbug his Son." In the second, the three ladies converse in very short sentences, and in the third, Colonel Elliott, searching for his daughter, finds Sir Edward Spangel "reclined in an elegant Attitude on a Sofa, fast asleep." The Colonel "whispers him, & Exit's" (55–57).

CRITICAL COMMENTARY

For Penny Gay, M "consists of an inspired riff on the trope of stage secrecy: the eight characters in the three scenes drop hints, nods and winks, and tantalizing unfinished sentences—but nothing material is actually revealed to anyone, on or off stage" (2). John McAleer points to affinities between "the two whispering scenes" (15) in M and SHERIDAN's drama *The Critic* (1779). Ellen E. Martin describes M as "the purest example of free-floating signs of meaning." She explains that the reader and audience "witness the passage of meaning from imminent revelation to its final resting place in the sleeping part of our brain, the aristocratic unconscious, draped gracefully, even as silently" (91–92), and she quotes from the stage direction to the final scene: "in an elegant Attitude on a Sofa" (*Minor Works*, 57).

CHARACTERS

Corydon (55) Appears in the first scene of M, speaks a single line, "But Hush! I am interrupted," and disappears. Described in the "Dramatis Personae" as a male (55), "Corydon" is a generic name in pastoral poetry for a rustic or simple country person.

Daphne (55–56)   Another classically based name, a character in the second scene of M. Classically, the name refers to a type of flowering shrub, a laurel, and is associated with virginity and shyness.

Elliott, Colonel (50–57)   Appears at the conclusion of M searching apparently for his daughter.

Elliott, Fanny (55–57)   Appears in the second scene of M; daughter of the Colonel.

Humbug Family (55–56)   Old, young, and Mrs. Humbug, or nonsense, appear in the first two scenes of M.

Spangle, Sir Edward (55, 57)   Appears in the third scene of M "reclined in an elegant Attitude on a Sofa, fast asleep" (57).

BIBLIOGRAPHY

Primary Texts

Austen, Jane. "The Mystery, An Unfinished Comedy." In *The Jane Austen Library. Volume the First,* edited by R. W. Chapman, with a foreword by Lord David Cecil, a preface by Brian Southam, and a preface by R. W. Chapman, 100–103. London: Athlone Press, 1984.

———. "The Mystery, An Unfinished Comedy." In *The Works of Jane Austen,* Vol. 6, *Minor Works,* edited by R. W. Chapman. Oxford: Oxford University Press. 1986. [All textual references are to this edition.]

———. "The Mystery, An Unfinished Comedy." In *Jane Austen's Catharine and other Writings,* edited by Margaret Anne Doody and Douglas Murray, 53–55. Oxford: Oxford University Press, 1993.

———. "The Mystery, An Unfinished Comedy." In J. E. Austen-Leigh, *A Memoir of Jane Austen and Other Family Recollections,* edited with an introduction and notes by Kathryn Sutherland. Oxford: Oxford University Press, 2002. 40–42.

Secondary Works

Gay, Penny. *Jane Austen and the Theatre.* Cambridge: Cambridge University Press, 2002.

Martin, Ellen E. "The Madness of Jane Austen: Metonymic Style and Literature's Resistance to Inter-
pretation." In *Jane Austen's Beginnings: the Juvenilia and Lady Susan,* edited by J. David Grey, [83]–94. Ann Arbor, Mich., and London: UMI Research Press, 1989.

McAleer, John. "What a Biographer Can Learn about Jane Austen from Her Juvenilia." In *Jane Austen's Beginnings: the Juvenilia and Lady Susan,* edited by J. David Grey, [7]–25. Ann Arbor, Mich., and London: UMI Research Press, 1989.

Southam, Brian C. "The Manuscript of Jane Austen's *Volume the First,*" *The Library,* 5th series 17 (1962): 231–237.

Sutherland, Kathryn. ["Explanatory Note"] *A Memoir of Jane Austen and Other Family Recollections,* edited with an introduction and notes by Kathryn Sutherland. Oxford: Oxford University Press, 2002. 217–218.

———. *Jane Austen's Textual Lives: From Aeschylus to Bollywood.* Oxford: Oxford University Press, 2005.

Northanger Abbey (1817)

COMPOSITION AND PUBLICATION

According to Cassandra, Jane Austen's sister, *Northanger Abbey* (NA), probably the third written of her early novels, was composed in 1798 and 1799. Cecil S. Emden suggests "that the main body of the novel was written in about 1794, and that the main sections burlesquing the horror-novels, and Mrs. Radcliffe's *The Mysteries of Udolpho* in particular, were added some four years later" (Emden, [279]). The novel was originally called *Susan,* was sold to the London bookseller Crosby & Co. for £10 in 1803 and advertised "In the Press" under the title "Susan." By 1809, it still had not been published. In a letter to Crosby & Co. dated Wednesday April 5, 1809, and written under the pseudonym of "Mrs. Ashton Dennis," Jane Austen wrote, "Six years have passed, & this work of which I avow myself the Authoress, has never to the best of my knowledge, appeared in print, tho' an early publication was stipulated for at the time of Sale." Jane Austen continues: "I can only account for such an extraordinary circumstance [i.e. the failure to publish] by supposing the MS. by some carelessness to have been lost." Jane Austen offers "to supply" the publishers "with another Copy if you are disposed to avail yourselves of it, & will engage for no further delay when it comes into your hands." She ends her letter, "Should no notice be taken of this . . . I shall feel myself at liberty to secure the publication of my work, by applying elsewhere."

In his reply of Saturday April 8, 1809, Richard Crosby, the publisher, offered to sell back the "MS . . . for the same as we paid for it." He points out "there was not any time stipulated for its publication, neither are we bound to publish it" (*Letter*, 174). Crosby had published ANN RADCLIFFE's *The Mysteries of Udolpho* in 1794. However, the matter dropped until after Jane Austen had successfully published four novels in print and in 1816, following the publication of *EMMA*, her brother HENRY AUS-

TEN bought back the original manuscript (its present whereabouts unknown) from Crosby. According to James Edward Austen-Leigh's *Memoir*, "when the bargain was concluded and the money paid, but not till then, the negotiator had the satisfaction of informing him [the publisher] that the work which had been so lightly esteemed was by the author of 'Pride and Prejudice'" (*Memoir*, 106).

In 1809, *Susan,* an anonymous novel, was published by the London publisher John Booth in two volumes. It then seems that Jane Austen reworked her manuscript and changed the name of the heroine from "Susan" to "Catherine." Following the recovery from Crosby of the original manuscript, Jane Austen thought of a quick publication. Her single paragraph "ADVERTISEMENT" preface to the novel on its posthumous publication was probably written in 1816. She describes its genesis: "This little work was finished in the year 1803, and intended for immediate publication." She recounts subsequent events. "It was disposed of to a bookseller, it was even advertised, and why the business preceded no farther, the author has never been able to learn." She comments "That any bookseller should think it worth while to purchase what he did not think it worth while to publish seems extraordinary."

The last two sentences of her "Advertisement" are very close to a statement of Jane Austen's authorial program. "But with this," she writes, "neither the author nor the public have any other concern than as some observation is necessary upon those parts of the work which thirteen years," that is since 1803, "have made comparatively obsolete. The public are entreated to bear in mind that thirteen years have passed since it was finished, many more since it was begun, and that during that period, places, manners, books, and opinions have undergone considerable changes" (*NA*, [12]). Traumatic changes had taken place on the political landscape between 1789, the year of the Revolutionary Terror in France, culminating in the execution of the French royal family and aristocracy and 1815–16. Napoleon had risen and been defeated; 22 years of war with France had finished in 1815 with the Battle of Waterloo. On a more mundane level, young ladies' fashions had changed, and so

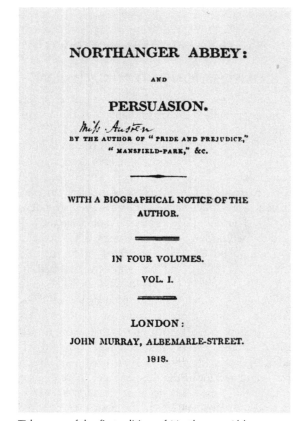

Title page of the first edition of *Northanger Abbey*

had the roads. John McAdam's road surfaces, for example, had speeded up road travel, so even John Thorpe's dreams of fast speeds in his gig might well become a reality by 1816.

In spite of this "Advertisement," the novel still did not appear. On March 13, 1817, Jane Austen writes to her niece Fanny Knight, "Miss Catherine is put upon the Shelve for the present, and I do not know that she will ever come out" (*Letters*, 333). Following Jane Austen's death in July 1817, Henry Austen took the manuscript, which with PERSUASION was published by John Murray in December 1817. Prefaced with Henry Austen's "Biographical notice" of his sister, under presumably his title *Northanger Abbey*, it was published as the first two volumes of the four-volume work, the final two volumes consisting of PERSUASION. The terms were the same as those of Jane Austen's other works published by John Murray: at the author's expense and 10 percent commission to the publisher. In December 1817, 1,750 copies were printed and published on December 20. The four volumes cost 24 shillings and were advertised as "Northanger Abbey, a Romance; and Persuasion, a Novel."

Its publication history follows that of *Persuasion's*, except that a separate edition of *Northanger Abbey* was published with the short biographical notice of the author by Carey, Lea, and Blanchard, the Philadelphia publishers, in January 1833 in two volumes. In 1824, it was translated into French by Hyacinthe de Ferrières, and there were two other French translations in the 19th century. Separate American editions were published in 1845 and 1881. The first separately published *Northanger Abbey* in Britain seems to have been in 1901, with an introduction by E. V., Lucas published by Methuen in London. Six years later, Dent in London, and Dutton in New York, published it with 24 colored illustrations by C. E. Brock. A year later (1906), *NA* was published with *Persuasion* as Everyman's Library No. 25, with an editor's note by R. Brimley Johnson. R. W. Chapman's edition of 1923 published the novel with *Persuasion*—this is the text in its third edition (with revisions) published in 1965. Page references used in this book are to this edition. A separate edition edited by Kathleen M. Metcalfe, an Oxford English lecturer

and wife of R. W. Chapman, was published by the Clarendon Press, Oxford, in 1923.

SYNOPSIS

Volume 1

Catherine Morland is the fourth of 10 children and the first daughter of a country clergyman. She is brought up in the protected environment of Fullerton, a village in Wiltshire in the southwest of England. There is nothing special about her. Catherine enjoys sport and outdoor activities; the only books she reads are romantic gothic fantasies. By the time she is 17 years of age, she still has led a dull existence apart from living in a happy family. Things begin to look up when she is invited by wealthy neighbors of the Morlands, Mr. and Mrs. Allen, to join them on a visit to Bath, the nearest large town and a center of fashion and social activity. Catherine eagerly awaits her introduction into fashionable society, especially with Mrs. Allen, who has "a trifling turn of mind" and an obsession with the latest fashions (20).

Catherine's first ball is a disappointment as Mrs. Allen does not know anybody. At the second ball, she meets Henry Tilney, who is around 25 years, a clergyman whom she is attracted to. He does not appear subsequently at social gatherings. However, Catherine is cheerful again at the Pump Room the morning after the ball as Mrs. Allen encounters an old school friend, Mrs. Thorpe. She has three daughters—Isabella, Anne, and Maria. James, Catherine's elder brother, is at the same Oxford College as their brother John, and the two are friends. Isabella, the 21-year-old eldest Thorpe daughter, strikes up a friendship with Catherine and they spend much time together, a shared interest being sensational gothic novels, which they read and discuss.

James arrives in Bath with John Thorpe. James has fallen in love with Isabella, and both attempt to unite Catherine with John Thorpe. She, however, is not attracted to him, finding him rude and foolish. At a ball the next day, Henry reappears. Catherine has to refuse his offer to dance as she has already agreed to dance with John Thorpe. She also meets Eleanor Tilney, Henry's sister, and hopes that Henry will ask her again, but John

Thorpe will not leave her company. The following day, John Thorpe takes Catherine for a ride in his gig. Isabella and James follow in a different carriage. Catherine's attitude to John Thorpe and his boorishness remains unchanged. He is anxious to ascertain how wealthy the Allens are. Back at the Allens' house, Catherine regrets that she has missed the Tilneys, whom Mrs. Allen met on a walk with Mrs. Thorpe.

The next day, Catherine renews her friendship with Eleanor Tilney at the Pump Room and is glad to hear that she and her brother will be at the next ball. At the ball, she attempts successfully to avoid the preying John Thorpe and enjoys dancing and talking with Henry Tilney, who points out his father, General Tilney, to her. Before leaving, she and Eleanor again talk and arrange to go for a country walk with Henry, meeting at midday the following day. Catherine is ecstatic.

The Tilneys, due to the unsettled weather, fail to arrive on time the next morning for the outing. Instead, John and Isabella Thorpe arrive and persuade Catherine to join her and James on a drive to Bristol, Clifton, and also Blaize Castle, which Catherine believes will be like the other castles she has read about in gothic novels, such as Mrs. Radcliffe's *The Mysteries of Udolpho*. John Thorpe misleads Catherine by informing her that he has just seen the Tilneys drive off in a phaeton. Believing him, she agrees to join the Thorpes and James. As they set out, they see Eleanor and Henry walking along the street. Eleanor sees Catherine, who is angry with John Thorpe. She urges him to stop so that she can apologize; Thorpe ignores her and drives

The Pump Room at Bath, from R. Warner, *The History of Bath,* 1801

on faster. Catherine is miserable and they do not even reach Blaize Castle before returning home.

The next morning, Catherine goes to apologize to the Tilneys but is told Eleanor is unavailable and then sees her leave the house with her father. At the theater that evening, Henry Tilney comes to talk to her and Catherine is able to apologize and explain what happened. Henry also explains that General Tilney is impatient and insisted on Eleanor going out with him. They agree that their walk should take place soon. Catherine sees John Thorpe talking to the General and learns that Thorpe plays billiards with him, and the General thinks Catherine to be the finest young lady in town.

On Sunday afternoon walking in the Bath Crescent, Catherine meets Eleanor and Henry and they agree to walk the next morning. Catherine is then approached by her brother James and the Thorpes, who insist that she accompany them on another attempt to go to Clifton and Blaize Castle. John Thorpe walks away to return to say that he has spoken to Eleanor Tilney and she has agreed to postpone their walking expedition. A furious Catherine rushes after the Tilneys to explain, sees them entering their house, and she goes directly to the drawing room, where they are all gathered. She explains in a rushed, confused manner. General Tilney is very polite to her and even invites her to stay for dinner. Catherine is unable to, owing to a prior commitment with the Allens, but is pleased to find that they approve of her action. Mr. Allen tells her that it is inappropriate for a young, unchaperoned woman to drive alone with young men in a carriage. Mrs. Allen agrees, leaving Catherine surprised that she had not told her this previously.

The walk with the Tilneys at last takes place and they have a spirited discussion on art, history, and novels. Isabella Thorpe asks to see Catherine and tells her that James, her brother, has proposed. He is on his way to his father to request his consent and find out how much income he has to live off so that he can marry. The next day he writes that his father approves. John Thorpe indicates to Catherine that he also wishes soon to marry and has a potential wife in mind. Catherine pretends not to understand him.

Volume 2

Catherine dines at the Tilneys, but finds them in a depressed mood, although General Tilney tries to do his best to make her feel welcome. Catherine wonders why, however, at another ball she finds Henry and Eleanor back to their usual friendly selves. They are with their elder brother, Captain Frederick Tilney, who has the handsome Tilney demeanor without Henry's refinement. Isabella, who gave the impression of reluctantly attending the ball, is attracted to Captain Tilney and they dance.

James Morland writes to tell Isabella details of the financial settlement his father has agreed to. Mr. Morland promises £40 per annum to be realized in two and a half years. James will also inherit an estate of the equivalent value or more. Isabella and her mother divert attention from their dissatisfaction with what they regard as the paucity of the sum by focusing on their unhappiness with the length of the engagement.

The Allens' Bath stay is extended and Catherine is invited to say with the Tilneys at Northanger Abbey. She can indulge "her passion for ancient edifices," which is "next in degree to her passion for Henry Tilney" (141). Isabella tells Catherine that John Thorpe, her brother, has written to her about his love for Catherine. She tells Isabella that she is unable to reciprocate Thorpe's affection. Captain Tilney then appears and sits next to Isabella at what is a prearranged meeting. Catherine suspects that Isabella, in spite of her engagement to her brother James, is encouraging Tilney. Catherine discusses the matter with Henry Tilney, who reassures her that his brother's Bath stay is temporary and that his feelings toward Isabella are not serious as she does not possess a fortune.

Catherine, Eleanor, and Henry leave for Northanger Abbey. For the first part of the journey, Catherine rides with Eleanor and her maid. On the second half, she joins Henry, who plays on her gothic and romantic preconceptions of the abbey. He tells her that he lives there for only a part of the year and spends the rest at Woodston Parson, his house, 20 miles from the Abbey. Catherine's initial perceptions of Northanger Abbey are disappointing, as it is not what she expected, being modern rather than antique. During her first night, there is a tremendous storm that gives vent to Catherine's gothic fantasies, especially after she finds an old cabinet in her room containing papers. She is unable to examine them as the wind blows out the candle, and she has to wait until the morning to read them. The howl from the wind and the storm make Catherine restless and her imagination wanders. In the morning, calm returns and the sun streams in, the content of the documents being but laundry bills!

General Tilney at breakfast drops hints about a possible marriage between Catherine and Henry, which Catherine does not pick up. She is shown the Abbey grounds, the General leaving Eleanor and Catherine to walk together after remarking that Catherine must be used to larger grounds. Eleanor takes Catherine to walk on her late mother's favorite route. She died nine years ago when Eleanor was 13. Her portrait is in Eleanor's bedroom, and the General does not use the route. The General, when Catherine is being shown around the Abbey, prevents her from seeing his late wife's rooms. Catherine's overactive imagination speculates that there is something to hide, especially after Eleanor tells her that her mother died suddenly and that Eleanor had not been home at the time. Catherine speculates that Mrs. Tilney must have been murdered or is still alive and kept a prisoner by her husband.

Catherine finds a way to inspect the restricted areas and finds a well-furnished contemporary apartment, with no prisoner. Ashamed, she is leaving as she encounters not the General but Henry, who has returned from Woodston earlier than expected. Henry realizes that she has been letting her imagination run riot, tells her that his mother died of natural causes, and that he and his brother were present. Furthermore, his father loved Mrs. Tilney and mourns her deeply. Catherine, full of remorse, feels she has lost Henry's affection; this is not the case and she is determined to act henceforth with greater common sense.

James sends Catherine a letter saying that his engagement to Isabella is broken and that he expects she will soon be engaged to Captain Tilney. An upset Catherine now realizes that Isabella is

mercenary. Henry and Eleanor tell her that their brother will not marry her and that their father will not approve of such a marriage, as Isabella has no fortune. Catherine becomes concerned with how the General will react if Henry proposes to her, as she too has no money. The General takes Catherine and Eleanor to visit Henry's Woodston home, which delights Catherine. Then the General strongly hints that she may well be the mistress of it one day. Catherine receives a letter from Isabella that makes clear that Captain Tilney has jilted her and she is trying to use Catherine to persuade her brother James to restore the engagement. Catherine, however, sees through Isabella.

General Tilney departs for London for a week and Catherine enjoys Eleanor and Henry's company. She is urged by Eleanor to remain with them. However, a carriage arrives before the end of the week and the General reappears. He sends Eleanor to tell Catherine that the whole family is leaving for Herefordshire immediately and that Catherine must return home to Fullerton the next morning. He does not even make proper arrangements for her to leave. Eleanor is very upset and unable to explain her father's behavior. An upset Catherine makes the 11-hour journey home alone and unattended by a public post chaise.

At Fullerton, after an 11-week absence, Catherine is welcomed back with open arms. Her parents are upset by General Tilney's treatment of her and especially because she had to travel home unaccompanied. For two days, Catherine is unable to forget Henry, and is very distressed. On the third morning her mother goes upstairs to find a journal article and returns to discover Henry Tilney with her. He apologizes to Mrs. Morland for his father's behavior and then suggests that Catherine should show him the way to the Allens' house. Henry tells Catherine that his father had been misled by John Thorpe into thinking that she was very wealthy. In London, he once again believed John Thorpe, who now told him the opposite, that she is not wealthy. Consequently, in a rage, he rushed back from London and ejected Catherine from the house. Henry returned from Woodston to find out what took place, argued with his father, refused to go to Herefordshire, and insists that he will marry Catherine.

In the meantime, he has proposed to Catherine, even though he does not have his father's consent.

The Morlands are surprised but happy to hear the news, but they too have to withhold their consent to the marriage until the General gives his. In the meantime, it emerges that Eleanor secretly has had an admirer for some time who apparently lacked wealth. He unexpectedly inherits a fortune and title and the now Viscountess Eleanor has no difficulty in getting her father to approve of the match between Henry and Catherine, especially as it emerges that Catherine is not as poor as first appeared. John Thorpe's information proves to be incorrect, and there is even a possibility that she may inherit the Allen estate at some future date. Following General Tilney's consent, the wedding of Henry and Catherine takes place "within a twelve-month from the first day of their meeting," and "to being perfect happiness at the respective ages of twenty-six and eighteen is to do pretty well" (252).

CRITICAL SYNOPSIS AND COMMENTARY

Chapter 1

The opening of *Northanger Abbey* (NA) offers its readers contradictory views of its subject, Catherine Morland. Moreover, the paragraph introduces a major theme of the novel: Appearances are deceptive. The opening sentence may be read in a variety of ways. "No one who had ever seen Catherine Morland in her infancy would have supposed her born to be an heroine," can be taken to mean that those who saw her after she was an infant can regard her as a "heroine." Or did she become a "heroine" despite initial appearances? Or, indeed, that there was never any doubt that she would be a "heroine"?

Such ambiguities of meaning run through the novel. The noun *heroine* occurs 20 times in Jane Austen's work. Seventeen of these are in *NA*, three in the first chapter, and by the end of the chapter, they call into question not only whether the word is appropriate for Catherine Morland but whether it should be applied to someone else. The authorial tone is authoritative. The author is informing her readers emphatically about Catherine Morland.

In spite of the emphasis, the ambiguity is reinforced. The second sentence accumulates negatives concerning Catherine. First, "her situation in life." Second, "the character of her father and mother." Third, "her own person and disposition." These "were all equally against her." The third sentence conveys information about her father. Professionally "a clergyman," he is named "Richard," ([13]) a private family allusion and joke. Jane Austen wrote to her sister, Cassandra, on September 15, 1796, "Mr. Richard Harvey's match is put off, till he has got a Better Christian name, of which he has great hopes" (*Letters*, 10). Physically, her father "had never been handsome." He is not wealthy; neither Catherine nor her father was "neglected," one assumes, socially or personally, neither is an orphan wanting for affection. The father is "a very respectable man": "Respectable" being an adjective of high commendation in Austen's novels.

More is learned about her father from the fourth sentence. "He had a considerable independence," meaning that he is not subservient to a local grandee as Collins is in *Pride and Prejudice*. The financial sense of "independent" is strengthened by the knowledge that he had "two good livings," in other words, he has a house and income from land granted to clergymen during their lifetime. The rest of this sentence strikes an ironic note: "he was not in the least addicted to locking up his daughters." The allusion could be to someone known to the author and her family, or also to occurrences in Samuel Richardson's *Clarissa* (1747–48) and Henry Fielding's *Tom Jones* (1749). These are just two of the novels mentioned in *NA*: a novel replete with literary allusions.

A key word in the opening sentence is "supposed," drawing an inference that may or may not be borne out. Catherine's mother appears as "Mrs. Morland." She possesses positive attributes in Jane Austen's world: "useful plain sense . . . a good temper . . . a good constitution." In other words, she is very healthy and has 10 children in an age when death during childbirth was not infrequent. Catherine is her first daughter after her mother has given birth to three sons. Her children are "plain," that is, lacking in beauty.

The opening paragraph is rather lengthy for the first paragraph of a Jane Austen novel and describes Catherine up to the age of 10. Unattractive, she prefers games usually attributed to boys rather than girls. She "greatly preferred cricket not merely to dolls, but to the more heroic enjoyments of infancy" such as "nursing a dormouse, feeding a canary-bird, or watering a rose-bush." The reference to "cricket" is interesting. The game was not developed during Jane Austen's lifetime as the national English summer obsession it subsequently became. It was, however, largely a game played by boys/males rather than females. Catherine has a short attention span. She "never could learn or understand any thing before she was taught; and sometimes not even then, for she was often inattentive, and occasionally stupid." For example, it took her three months of repetition by her mother to teach Catherine "to repeat the 'Beggar's Petition,'" ([13]–14), a poem by the Reverend Thomas Moss from his *Poems on Several Occasions* (1769), frequently "used as a recitation piece in children's education lessons" (Johnson, 357).

Catherine, however, is not stupid, only "occasionally." As usual with Jane Austen, there is balance and antithesis. Catherine has the ability to learn "the fable of 'The Hare and many Friends,' as quickly as any girl in England." In other words, she is able to learn a story in John Gay's *Fables* of 1712 concerning a hare who is deserted by his friends when a hound pursues him. The reference prefigures what happens to Catherine in the course of the novel: Her friends desert her at a time of trouble. Also, "she was very fond of tinkling the keys of the old forlorn spinet." But here again there is another side. Catherine learned for a year and "could not bear it." Her shrewd mother did not subsequently force her to play the instrument, and "the day which dismissed the music-master was one of the happiest of Catherine's life."

She also displayed no great talent for drawing. Her father taught her "writing and accounts," in other words, how to manage household accounts in preparation for the time when she would be married and control the finances in the household. She displayed no great ability in this or in the French taught by her mother. All three negatives relate to Catherine at 10 years old. On the positive side, Catherine "had neither a bad heart," "nor a bad temper." Further, she "was seldom stubborn, scarcely ever quarrelsome," and was "very kind" to her younger brothers and sisters. She objects to constraints of any kind, "was moreover noisy and wild, hated confinement and cleanliness." Her favorite occupation was in "rolling down the green slope at the back of the house." Dirt and the fear of it are frequent in the first volume of *NA*.

The lengthy opening paragraph depicts Catherine at the age of 10, her character, physical appearance, behavior, and family circumstances. The second paragraph encompasses five years, in which time she has gained a certain amount of "plumpness" and "her love of dirt gave way to an inclination for finery, and she grew clean as she grew smart." This paragraph now moves into her perspective, she hears "her father and mother remark on her personal improvement": "Catherine grows up quite a good-looking girl, she is almost pretty today." It is the qualifying "almost" with its implication of reservation, which ironically "is an acquisition of higher delight to" Catherine. For "the first fifteen years of her life" she "had been looking plain." These physical changes depict the movement into womanhood and sexual growth. Catherine "began to curl her hair and long for balls."

The third paragraph focuses on Catherine's enforced self-sufficiency. Her mother was frequently pregnant and giving birth. Catherine's mother's time was taken up with "teaching the little ones." Consequently, Catherine and the elder daughters were left to "shift for themselves." Catherine's tastes changed when she was 15, as did her manner of occupying herself. Previously she preferred "cricket, base ball, riding on horseback, and running about the country at the age of fourteen, to books." This description of her activities includes "base ball," a game then not unfashionable in England. As the 19th century developed, it was replaced in popularity by cricket and almost ceased to be played in the country. Interestingly, the *Oxford English Dictionary* attributes the first use of the name "base ball" to this instance in Jane Austen's *NA*.

Catherine does not object to books providing they are "all story and no reflection." From the age of 15 to 17, "she was in training for a heroine." Again, the word occurs ironically as in the opening paragraph. Catherine learns lines from literature, from ALEXANDER POPE, Thomas Gray, James Thomson, and SHAKESPEARE, not from experience. The lines she learns will provide a commentary on what she and the reader are to discover in the course of the novel.

Words learned from Pope's "Elegy to the Memory of an Unfortunate Lady," published in 1717, refer to "those who 'bear about the mockery of woe'" whom she is "to censure." Pope's words and poem dwell on personal and female unhappiness. His poem focuses on "an Unfortunate Lady" preferring to commit suicide than suffer unrequited love. She will die without friends. In death, to quote from the poem, "beauty, titles, wealth and fame" are irrelevant. No one will ever pretend to mourn for her, to indulge in "the mockery of woe." The poetic words prefigure an important lesson Catherine must learn. She has to distinguish between true and false values and friends. Isabella, for instance, may appear to be a friend, but as Catherine discovers, she really is not.

The second poetic lines are from Gray's "Elegy Written in a Country Churchyard," 1751. These are a powerful evocation of personal isolation and lack of opportunity: "Many a flower is born to blush unseen, / And waste its fragrance on the desert air." Gray's poem contains strictures warning against worldly vanity, ambition, and "the pomp of power." All end up in the grave. Later on in *NA*, characters obsessed with fashion, materialism, or the abuse of power such as Mrs. Allen, the Thorpes, and General Tilney appear.

The third of this set of poetic references in the first chapter, in a novel replete with literary allusions, consists of two lines from James Thomson's "The Seasons" and specifically from the section "Spring" 1728: "It is a delightful task / To teach the young idea how to shoot," (14–15). These lines, in spite of their being from a section of "Spring," are instead "preoccupied with death, loss, misery, deprivation, and . . . [are] designed to awaken one's feelings for the landscape and for one's fel-

low human beings" (Gaull, 11 n. 10). In addition, they echo themes that run throughout *NA*: that of innocence, experience, and education.

The lines from 18th-century poetry are followed by passages from Shakespeare. The first "great store of information" gained by Catherine are lines spoken by the villainous Iago from *Othello*. "Trifles light as air, / Are to the jealous, confirmation strong, / As proofs of Holy Writ" (3.2.322–3). Ironically, the "Trifles" of these lines, as "light as air," refer to the serious theme of jealousy that in the great tragedy results in murder. The "proofs of Holy Writ" are false ones as Othello misreads the false evidence, so cunningly presented by Iago, and as a consequence strangles his wife, Desdemona, who is innocent of what she is accused. Iago's lines signal the elements of deception and the dichotomy between appearances and reality reverberating through *NA*. Jane Austen is erecting signposts for her readers to look out for falsity, deception, dishonesty, and jealousy as her story proceeds.

The second Shakespearean lines are spoken by Isabella in *Measure for Measure*. She is pleading with her brother Claudius to accept that he will die rather than that Isabella, in order to save his life, should have sexual relations with Angelo, who has condemned him to death. Isabella tells her brother, "The poor beetle, which we tread upon, / In corporal sufferance feels a pang as great/ As when a giant dies" (3.1.78–80). Isabella, of course, is being hyperbolic. She is exaggerating, but she is an innocent who wishes to preserve her "virtue." Her fictional namesake Isabella also indulges in hyperbolic comments but is not an innocent. She is, on the contrary, a manipulator. Both she and Catherine seem to believe that everything is a crisis when it is not: They have almost no idea about the reality of human suffering.

The third Shakespearean quotation is lines also spoken by a "heroine." In this instance Viola in *Twelfth Night*. Disguised, out of self-protection, as a page, she speaks to the Duke Orsino. He complains that women are fickle and inconstant, "they lack retention" (2, 4, 95). On the contrary, to use Jane Austen's words, "a young woman in love always looks"—she then cites Viola's lines— "like Patience on a monument / Smiling at Grief"

(2.4.114–15: 16). The dramatic situation is replete with irony. Viola, a woman, dressed in masculine attire, puts a powerful man, a duke, in his place. In her novel, Jane Austen's heroine is outspoken; as the novel proceeds, she asserts to herself, and she is the first to fall in love.

Such citations guide the reader to important themes and preoccupations that will occur in the narrative. In the penultimate paragraph of chapter 1, the author's use of key words, antithesis, and pointers toward recurring elements throughout the novel, is evident. Catherine is judged and found wanting in relatively small matters and in far more important ones. Catherine "had a notion of drawing . . . At present she did not know her own poverty, for she had no lover to pourtray." The identification between "poverty" and not having a "love to pourtray" is comic. It indicates, however, that she is ready to be married and experience a relationship with a man. There is no suitable partner in her neighborhood, which has "not one lord . . . no not even a baronet"—a fine status distinction emphasizing that Catherine is ready to make a suitable and appropriate marriage. Not only is there a "poverty" of suitable male partners, there is even where she lives a lack of unsuitable ones: "not one young man whose origin was unknown. Her father had no ward, and the squire of the parish no children."

A key word recurs in this paragraph and in the short two-sentence paragraph following it: "heroine" and variations upon it. The reader is told that in drawing and in the search for a lover, Catherine "fell miserably short of the true heroic height." Yet "when a young lady is to be a heroine, the perverseness of forty surrounding families cannot prevent her." Jane Austen adds that "something must and will happen to throw a hero in her way."

To find a husband Catherine must leave the confines of her village and go out into the wider world, to the nearest large city, Bath, where there are eligible men and husbands in waiting. Hers is to be, in common with heroes and heroines of the 18th-century novels, a voyage from innocence to experience, from the country to the city. Ill health, as so often in Jane Austen's novels (as, it may be added, in life), becomes a marker for influencing individual destiny. The "chief" owner "of the prop-

erty about Fullerton, the village in Wiltshire where the Morlands lived, was ordered to Bath for the benefit of a gouty constitution." His wife invites Catherine to accompany them, "probably aware that if adventures will not befall a young lady in her own village, she must seek them abroad." The innocent Catherine is going to Bath deliberately to seek experience and "adventures."

In this final sentence of the chapter, the author returns to Mr. and Mrs. Morland. They "were all compliance" in this plan, and their daughter "all happiness" on going to encounter the unknown. She is the anticipated "heroine" but is not yet a "heroine." She is "all happiness" (14–17) for what she does not know. She is innocent but wishes to experience and, like Jane Austen's readers, encouraged to read on.

Chapter 2

The opening paragraph of the second chapter embellishes what has already been "said of Catherine Morland's personal and mental endowments" in the first chapter. She is "about to be launched into all the difficulties and dangers of a six weeks' residence in Bath." She is taken to Bath by Mrs. Allen as a salable new commodity on the marriage market. The focus in the paragraph is less on Catherine but on the author and what she intends to do in the rest of her narrative. "The reader's" are directly mentioned, and Jane Austen is concerned "lest the following pages should otherwise fail of giving any idea of what her character is meant to be." The author adds that Catherine's "heart was affectionate, her disposition cheerful and open, without conceit or affectation of any kind." Furthermore, Catherine's "mind" is "about as ignorant and uninformed as the female mind at seventeen usually is." In other words, Catherine is an innocent voyaging into experience in Bath.

The second paragraph presents in extravagant language the perspective of Catherine's mother: "A thousand alarming presentiments of evil to her beloved Catherine from this terrific separation must oppress her heart with sadness, and drown her in tears for the last day or two of their being together." Hyperbole is often used in this novel, which includes among its themes the search for the true emotions as distinct from artificial ones, and which parodies contemporary novels of exaggeration. The third sentence of the paragraph alludes to "the violence of such noblemen and baronets as delight in forcing young ladies away to some remote farm-house." Such actions occur more in fiction than in reality. The author directly addresses her readers, asking them "Who would not think so?" She suggests that Mrs. Morland is naive and "wholly unsuspicious of danger to her daughter from their machinations"—of "lords and baronets." On the contrary, there is an element of bathos in Mrs. Morland's concern for her daughter. She tells Catherine to "wrap yourself up very warm about the throat, when you come from the Rooms at night." In other words, she is more concerned with Catherine's catching a cold than being whisked away by "noblemen and baronets." Mrs. Morland's other concern is with her daughter's management of money. She must make sure she tries "to keep some account of the money" she will spend. Financial management was taught to girls as a key element in their education. Further, the reference is also probably an allusion to FANNY BURNEY's heroine in the novel *Camilla* (1796). She grossly exceeds her allowance, consequently involving herself and her family in considerable inconvenience. *Camilla* is alluded to on several occasions in *NA*.

Catherine's younger sister is mentioned in the opening sentence of the third paragraph of the chapter. "Sally, or rather Sarah," as, the author remarks, it is a habit of "young lad[ies] of common gentility" to alter "her name as far as she can." Jane Austen does not say what a "young lady" of uncommon "gentility" will do! The younger sister inevitably must be "at this time the intimate friend and confidante of her sister." In this instance, however, "she neither insisted on Catherine's writing by every post, nor exacted her promise of transmitting the character of every new acquaintance, nor a detail of every interesting conversation that Bath might produce." So in this way, *NA* is to be a different novel from a lengthy 18th-century novel such as, for instance, Samuel Richardson's epistolary *Clarissa,* in which the entire narrative is enacted through an exchange of letters.

Catherine's departure for Bath is focused on the mundane, "the common feelings of common life," rather "than with the refined susceptibilities" or overinflated emotions. Catherine's father did not give "her an unlimited order on his banker" but instead "gave her only ten guineas, and promised her more when she wanted it." "Only" is ironic: "ten guineas" is a very generous sum equivalent to around $10,000 in today's money. Even the journey to Bath was unadventurous. Instead of "robbers" or storms, the only event of note was Mrs. Allen's having to return to the inn, where she "left her clogs." Catherine's carriage is not subject to "one lucky overturn to introduce them to the hero." In Ann Radcliffe's *The Mysteries of Udolpho,* such an event introduces the heroine to the hero of the novel. Catherine is fascinated by Bath: "she was come to be happy, and she felt happy already."

At this point, the author intrudes again to discuss the creation of her characters and the ways in which her readers may assess their effect on each other. The sixth paragraph is devoted to this. The focus is on Mrs. Allen, with whom Catherine has gone to Bath. Information will be given so that "the reader may be able to judge, in what manner her actions will hereafter tend to promote the general distress, of the work." Mrs. Allen may "by her imprudence, vulgarity or jealousy—whether by intercepting her [Catherine's] letters, ruining her character, or turning her out of doors," ruin Catherine. In Radcliffe's *The Mysteries of Udolpho,* villainy is not confined to men. The heroine's aunt Madame Montini plays an important part in producing "distress" for the heroine. Similarly, in Radcliffe's *The Italian* (1797), it is the mother of the heroine's sweetheart, the Marchesa di Vivaldi, who causes the heroine "distress."

Mrs. Allen is described as "one of that numerous class of females, whose society can raise no other emotion than surprise at there being any men in the world who could like them well enough to marry them." Then the reader is informed, "She had neither beauty, genius, accomplishment nor manner." "Genius" here means not as it does today, very exceptional talent. Instead, the abstract noun refers to qualities of the mind. She possesses "a trifling turn of mind," a quality that might have attracted her husband. The description of Mrs. Allen becomes an attack on female ignorance, superficiality, and vanity: "Dress was her passion." Her husband may well have chosen her to give himself a sense of superiority.

The sixth sentence focuses on "our heroine's entrée into life." The French term rather than the English word "entrance" conveys the element of pretension and superficiality in what is taking place, although there is an underlying serious side as well. Catherine's entry into society marks her search for a suitable husband and a journey from innocence to experience. It is another literary allusion. In Frances Burney's first novel, *Evelina, or a Young Lady's Entrances into the World* (1778), the heroine moves from a sheltered village into the wider world. Mrs. Allen acts as Catherine's "chaperon," teaching her "what was mostly worn." Again, a French word is used to describe an older woman who will educate a younger woman, such as Catherine, as to what is socially accepted. In this manner, Catherine is prepared for her initial rite of passage, which will occur at "the Upper Rooms" at Bath. These were built in 1771 by John Wood the younger, and weekly dances as well as concerts were held there. Ironically, her speciality preparation in terms of dress and hair is not to make her stand out for others. She "hoped at least to pass uncensured through the crowd" and, she hoped, remain self-sufficient: "As for admiration, it was always very welcome when it came, but she did not depend on it."

The remainder of the chapter is devoted to the first ball for Catherine. Her initial impression is that of "a mob" and "a struggling assembly" with "friend's . . . torn asunder" from each other. The Bath assembly rooms were indeed crowded. Catherine moves through the mob to gain "a comprehensive view of all the company beneath her," discovering "a splendid sight." Mr. Allen has escaped to the card room, and Catherine's excitement turns to "disappointment." She becomes "tired of being continually pressed against by people." Individuality has been lost: "the generality of whose faces possessed nothing to interest, and with all of whom she was so wholly unacquainted, that she could not relieve the irksomeness of imprisonment by the exchange of a syllable with any of her fellow captives." The assembly for which she was so well prepared and dressed has become a prison and the other people attending it, the "mob," her fellow inmates captured by illusions of meetings and effecting a suitable marriage.

Mrs. Allen's concern is with congratulating herself "on having preserved her gown from injury." She is preoccupied with herself, telling Catherine in the first words of dialogue in the novel that she has "not seen any thing I like so well in the whole room" as her "delicate muslin" dress. Catherine's short response, her first words in the novel, convey an opinion. She tells Mrs. Allen, "How uncomfortable it is . . . not to have a single acquaintance here!" She asks Mrs. Allen for advice "What shall we do? . . . Had not we better go away as it is?" Mrs. Allen's advice is to stay. Her reasons are purely selfish: "I think we had better sit still, for one gets so tumbled in such a crowd! How is my head, my dear?" In other words, she asks Catherine, "How is my hairdo, my coiffure?" She is not concerned with Catherine but with her own appearance. Mrs. Allen, appearances to the contrary, knows nobody at the Assembly and is unable to "get [Catherine] a partner."

Mr. Allen reappears on the scene "when the dance was over." His first words are highly ironical and receive a dishonest response from Catherine. He asks her "I hope you have had an agreeable ball." Catherine responds, "'Very agreeable indeed,' she replied, vainly endeavouring to hide a great yawn." Somewhat ironically, once "the company began to disperse when the dancing was over," Catherine begins to be noticed. "Every five minutes, by removing some of the crowd, gave greater openings for her charms." However, "no whisper of eager inquiry ran round the room, nor was she once called a divinity by any body." In the fiction of Jane Austen's contemporaries, the heroines frequently are addressed in hyperbolic terms as divinities or angels. As the narrator reminds her readers, Catherine, however, is transformed from what she had previously been "three years before."

The final paragraph of the chapter draws attention to Catherine's vanity, to her wish for attention, to the literary allusions pervading *NA*, and to the realities of Bath existence. She is praised by "two gentlemen;" consequently, "her humble vanity was contented." She "felt more obliged to the two young men for this simple praise than a true quality heroine would have been for fifteen sonnets in celebration of her charms." Although she is not yet "a true quality heroine," she leaves the Assembly and "went to her [sedan] chair in good humour with every body." Reality has once again intruded on the heroine's dreams and fantasies. In Bath, owing to the narrow streets, sedan chairs were preferred to horse-drawn carriages.

Chapter 3

The opening paragraph of chapter 3 encompasses Catherine's and Mrs. Allen's explorations of the world of Bath and beyond the "Pump-room." Their social isolation is reinforced: "They paraded up and down for an hour, looking at every body and speaking to no one." The first sentence of the second paragraph sees a turn in "fortune" for "our heroine" Catherine. She and Mrs. Allen appear at "the Lower Rooms." These were to the south of the Upper Rooms nearer to the Abbey and the Pump Rooms. Weekly balls and concerts were held there. Catherine is "introduced" by "the master of ceremonies to . . . a very gentlemanlike young man as a partner;—his name was Tilney." Tilney is described as "about four or five and twenty . . . rather tall, had a pleasing countenance, a very intelligent and lively eye." There is a qualification: "if not quite handsome, was very near it." Clearly Tilney too is on the marriage market, having come to Bath to find a wife. His situation is not unlike Elton's, another clergyman, who in *Emma* also goes to Bath to find a wife.

The description of the initial meeting between Catherine and Tilney is reported through authorial narration: "she found him as agreeable as she had already given him credit for being. He talked with fluency and spirit." On the other hand, "there was an archness and pleasantry in his manner which interested, though it was hardly understood by her." So there is still a mystery about him. His opening words in the novel parody the manner of polite conversation between the sexes. Tilney's words "sendup" or poke fun at what is expected in polite society. The language is verbose: "I have

hitherto been very remiss, madam, in the proper attention of a partner here," Tilney tells Catherine. He continues, "I have not yet asked you how long you have been in Bath," and he awkwardly repeats twice the conjunction "whether."

Actual dialogue between Catherine and Tilney is short, punctuated by a lengthy speech from Tilney. His language and tone are exaggerated, and he plays with words. He replies to Catherine's information that she has been in Bath "About a week, sir" with "Really!" said "with affected astonishment." Tilney assumes that Catherine keeps a "journal" and that he will appear in it. He makes satirical comments on journals and letter writings: "I know exactly what you will say," he tells Catherine. "Friday, went to the Lower Rooms; wore my sprigged muslin robe with blue trimmings" (25–26). In the previous chapter, Mrs. Allen's concern was more for her "delicate muslin" gown and that it did not get torn, than for Catherine's welfare (22).

Catherine simply denies that she will write or say what Tilney assumes she will. She is factual and literal, while Tilney is verbally playful. She tells him that she "danced with a very agreeable young man, introduced by Mr. King." King was in fact Master of Ceremonies from 1785 until 1805. In 1805 he became Master of Ceremonies at the Upper Room. In a lengthy speech to Catherine, Tilney conveys his perception of "young ladies' ways." He tells her: "It is this delightful habit of journalizing which largely contributes to form the easy style of writing for which ladies are so generally celebrated." Tilney adds, "Every body allows that the talent of writing agreeable letters is peculiarly female." Catherine exhibits slowness in responding to his assertion "that the usual style of letter-writing among women is faultless, except in three particulars" with "And what are they?" To this opening he responds, "A general deficiency of subject, a total inattention to stops, and a very frequent ignorance of grammar." By "stops" is meant punctuation (27). As Marilyn Gaull observes, "This discussion is a self-parody: Austen wrote voluminous letters and framed her early works in the popular epistolary form, as a collection of letters" (21).

Before their conversation is interrupted by Mrs. Allen, Tilney concedes that "excellence is pretty fairly divided between the sexes." The reappearance of Mrs. Allen provides the opportunity for him to display his knowledge of muslin and women's clothing. This impresses Mrs. Allen, who has her own preconceived notions of men, as Tilney appeared to have of women. She is "quite struck by his genius," insight, or acumen. Asked what he thinks "of Miss Morland's gown," his reply is both flattering and practical: "It is very pretty madam . . . but I do not think it will wash well; I am afraid it will fray." Catherine finds his response "strange" and is surprised by his knowledge of female clothing; he admits to purchasing his "own cravats."

Mrs. Allen then complains about the lack of shops in the country, although "we have very good shops in Salisbury." The town is "eight miles" from where they live. This "is a long way," and to get there "is such a fag," in other words, hard work and an inconvenience in early 19th-century contemporary slang. Tilney "was polite enough to seem interested in what" Mrs. Allen was saying. He and Catherine dance again and her response that she "was not thinking of any thing" again provides an opportunity for her partner Tilney "to tease [her] on the subject whenever we meet, and nothing in the world advances intimacy so much." The subject of his teasing will be that she "was not thinking of any thing."

The final paragraph of this chapter is taken up with Catherine's reactions. Jane Austen directly addresses her readers in the first person. "Whether she thought of him so much, while she drank her warm wine and water, and prepared herself for bed, as to dream of him when there, cannot be ascertained; but I hope it was no more than a slight slumber or a morning doze at most." She closes her reflection on her heroine's possible thoughts by directing her readers' attention to a literary allusion: "a celebrated writer has maintained, that no young lady can be justified in falling in love before the gentleman's love is declared." Austen adds in her only noted allusion in the novel, that her reference is to Samuel Johnson's journal *The Rambler*, number 97, the second volume (1751). "That a young lady should be in love, and the love of a young gentleman undeclared, is an heterodoxy which prudence, and even policy, must not allow.

But thus applied to, she is all resignation to her parents. Charming resignation, which inclination opposes not."

Jane Austen is attacking the conventional notion that women should not form or even confess to an emotional attachment to a member of the opposite sex until the gentleman concerned has secured her father's permission and then may address her. In Richardson's novel *Sir Charles Grandison* (1754), the heroine is openly in love with Sir Charles before he formally requests her hand. In *NA*, Catherine displays her love for Henry Tilney and this encourages him.

Practicalities are never far from the surface of a Jane Austen novel and reemerge at the end of this third chapter. Mr. Allen, having seen Catherine and Tilney together, "had early in the evening taken pains to know who her partner was, and had been assured of Mr. Tilney's being a clergyman, and of a very respectable family in Gloucestershire" (28–30). So by the conclusion of the chapter, Catherine has moved from the country to the city, Bath. She has been to a ball, become acquainted with Bath, and found a male admirer.

Chapter 4

This chapter introduces other characters and another family into the narrative. So far, *NA* has been populated by Catherine, her family, Mr. and Mrs. Allen, and Henry Tilney. Now the Thorpes appear. The first paragraph highlights Catherine's isolation among the crowds of Bath. "With more than usual eagerness" she goes the day after meeting and dancing with Mr. Tilney to the "Pump-room" to see him again. Rebuilt between 1792 and 1796, the Bath Pump-room was a fashionable meeting place not dissimilar to a modern atrium-covered mall. From early in the morning, an orchestra played, and dancing, card games, and billiards were available. Her disappointment in Tilney's nonappearance is well conveyed by the omniscient narrator: "crowds of people were every moment passing in and out, up the steps and down; people whom nobody cared about, and nobody wanted to see; and he only was absent." The narrative voice and Catherine's thoughts coincide with "and he only was absent." The repetition of "nobody" and the inversion of "only he" reinforce Catherine's alienation and disappointment. Her mood is ironically highlighted by Mrs. Allen's comment to her in the last sentence of the paragraph: "What a delightful place Bath is." Mrs. Allen adds, "how pleasant it would be if we had any acquaintance here." A topographical feature of Bath inserted in the narrative by Jane Austen is found in this sentence: Catherine and Mrs. Allen "sat down near the great clock, after parading the room till they were tired." This is a reference to the Tompion Clock in the Pump-room, which was given to the city of Bath in 1709 by the distinguished clockmaker Thomas Tompion (1639–1713).

In the second paragraph, Mrs. Allen's wish to meet someone she knows is satisfied. Mrs. Allen remembers a rhyme, "despair of nothing, we would attain," as "unwearied diligence our point would gain." She is remembering an old lesson found in Thomas Dyche's *A Guide to the English Tongue* (1707) and frequently reprinted. Its purpose was to teach children correct pronunciation and spelling using instructional verses that they copied and memorized. She meets Mrs. Thorpe, "a former school-fellow and intimate, whom she had seen only once since their respective marriages, and that many years ago." They have not met for 15 years, and their self-absorption is exposed: "talking both together, far more ready to give than to receive information, and each hearing very little of what the other said." Mrs. Thorpe has children, Mrs. Allen not. Her three sons' careers, or intended careers, are not unrepresentative of those from their class and background: "John was at Oxford, Edward at Merchant-Taylor's,'" a prestigious London school founded in 1561 by members of the London merchants' guilds, "and William at sea." The navy, as shown in *Persuasion* and in Jane Austen's LETTERS, is an established choice for younger sons. She also has daughters: Mrs. Thorpe "expiated on the talents of her sons, and the beauty of her daughters." All this serves to silence Mrs. Allen, she "had no similar information to give." All she can do is to discern with "her keen eye . . . that the lace on Mrs. Thorpe's pelisse was not half so handsome as that on her own" (31–32). Mrs. Allen is reduced to noticing the difference between her own and Mrs. Thorpe's

ankle-length cloak. Jane Austen was interested in the pelisse, observing to her niece Anne in a letter of November 22, 1814, "Mrs. Clement [the wife of a local attorney] walks about in a new Black velvet Pelisse lined with Yellow & a white Bobbin-net-veil, & looks remarkably well in them" (*Letters*, 282).

The three Thorpe girls now appear: "the tallest is Isabella, my oldest; is she not a fine young woman?" Mrs. Thorpe observes, adding "I believe Isabella is the handsomest." These additions to the marital market stakes temporarily eclipse Catherine, until Isabella, who will play a not insignificant role in the story, notes the physical similarities between Catherine and her brother. This is repeated by Mrs. Thorpe and temporarily surprises Catherine, who then remembers that "her eldest brother," James, "had lately formed an intimacy with a young man of his own college." Furthermore, "he had spent the last week of the Christmas vacation with his family, near London." In this way through chance meetings, facial recognition, and memory, interconnections between characters are established within the texture of a Jane Austen novel.

In the sixth paragraph, relationships are established and Catherine pairs off with Isabella: the start of a friendship from which much is to be learned. An anticipatory hint of what subsequently is to happen in the narrative is humorously presented in the second sentence of the paragraph with the observation: "Friendship is certainly the finest balm for the pangs of disappointed love" (32–33). Claudia L. Johnson observes that here the writer "is mimicking the voice of gothic and sentimental novels, which are frequently peppered with sententious bromides on the consolations of friendship." She adds that in *NA*, "female friendship is clearly secondary, if not merely instrumental, to the romantic love plot," and draws attention to Austen's juvenile "satirical sketch" "LOVE AND FREINDSHIP," which "also sends up such clichés" (361–362).

There then follows a reported conversation between Catherine and Isabella. The emphasis is upon Isabella's greater experience of life: "being four years older than Miss Morland, and at least four years better informed." She is more knowledgeable concerning "balls, flirtations, and quizzes," or a witticism; a jest or something that is curious. Also Isabella "could compare the balls of Bath with those of Tunbridge; its fashions with the fashions of London." Tunbridge Wells, in Kent, is like Bath, a fashionable spa town. Catherine's innocence and Isabella's sophistication are displayed in the comment that Isabella "could discover a flirtation between any gentleman and lady who only smiled at each other." In this way, the author suggests to her readers that they should be prepared for some kind of duplicity from Isabella. She is capable of interpreting a smile. Isabella's "powers received due admiration from Catherine, to whom they were entirely new," and she adopts Isabella as a guide and role model through the maze of Bath. The conclusion of the paragraph reveals how gullible Catherine is. After they have seen each other, from the window Catherine "admired the graceful spirit of her walk, the fashionable air of her figure and dress, and felt grateful, as well she might, for the chance which had procured her such a friend."

The economic plight of the Thorpes is succinctly conveyed in the two-sentence penultimate paragraph of the chapter. The narrator tells us, "Mrs. Thorpe was a widow, and not a very rich one." As for her character, "she was a good-humoured, well-meaning woman, and a very indulgent mother." She spoiled her children. "Her eldest daughter had great personal beauty" and her younger sisters imitated her.

Mrs. Thorpe's history and Jane Austen as narrator, as writer, occupy the final paragraph of chapter 4. Jane Austen's contemporary readers "might" expect "long and minute detail from Mrs. Thorpe herself, of her past adventures and sufferings." These details include "the worthlessness of lords and attornies," which "might be set forth." The conditional "might" is repeated twice in this paragraph, "minute" once, and "minutely" once. Jane Austen, in a somewhat sarcastic tone, assures her readers that she is not going to repeat "minutely" what "had passed twenty years before" (33–34). Unlike the narratives of gothic fiction, she is not going to dwell on the negative activities of attornies and others who frequently cheat the innocent or the virtuous, especially widows, out of their fortunes.

Chapter 5

This short chapter contains Jane Austen's defense of the literary form she uses, literary and other allusions. One of these occurs in the first sentence with its reference to the "theatre." Catherine goes to the Theatre Royal, an important provincial English theater. On Orchard Street in Bath, it was built in 1749, was small, and Jane Austen herself went to its performances. In chapter 12 of *NA*, the Theatre Royal is more fully described. Some idea of its small size may be glimpsed in the first sentence. Catherine looked "in every box which her eye could reach . . . she looked in vain" for Henry Tilney. Some hint of his antisocial side is revealed in the authorial observation, "Mr. Tilney was no fonder of the play than the Pump-room." Her theater visit was on a Saturday. The next day was "a beautiful morning" when she hoped to see him, especially as Jane Austen, speaking from personal experience, writes "a fine Sunday in Bath empties every house of its inhabitants, and all the world appears on such an occasion to walk about and tell their acquaintance what a charming day it is."

Somewhat ironically, central Bath becomes too crowded. For the Thorpes and Allens, who have joined one another after church, "divine services," the Pump-room is "insupportable . . . there was not a genteel face to be seen." This overcrowding "every body discovers every Sunday throughout the season." Consequently, to escape the crowds and to join a better class of people, "they hastened away to the Crescent, to breathe in the fresh air of better company." They went to the Royal Crescent, built between 1767–74 in Palladian style with town houses at the summit of the hills, where there were views of the city and the surrounding countryside. Here dwelled the wealthy, and the center gardens were the setting for those who were to be seen to parade on a Sunday.

In this setting, "Catherine and Isabella, arm in arm, again tasted the sweets of friendship in an unreserved conversation." Catherine does not see Tilney in spite of a search for him in the other areas of Bath. The narrative uses verb inversion to convey Catherine's feeling. "They talked much, and with much enjoyment; but again *was* Catherine disappointed" [my emphasis]. She tries to explain his absence in terms of the fiction she knows. It is a "sort of mysteriousness, which is always so becoming a hero." She receives no information about him from the Thorpes, and her friend "Isabella was very sure that he must be a charming young man," although she has not met him. Catherine's friend "liked him better for being a clergyman." She confesses to being very "partial to the profession and something like a sigh escaped her as she said it." This "sigh" adds a note of mystery; it may, of course, be a sigh of relief that he is not wealthy and that she has not "fallen" for a clergyman. The final sentence of the second paragraph speculates on Isabella's reaction: "Perhaps Catherine was wrong in not demanding the cause of" her friend's reaction. The focus of the sentence then transfers to Catherine's inexperience "in the finesse of love, or the duties of friendship." Her innocence causes her not "to know when delicate raillery was properly called for," or in other words, when she is being laughed at. Catherine is not experienced enough in human relationships to know "when a confidence should be forced" in friendship.

The narrative focus in the third paragraph turns from Catherine and Isabella to Mrs. Allen. She is happy in Bath, having found "the family of a most worthy old friend" and also "friends by no means so expensively dressed as herself." Mrs. Allen was "Never satisfied with the day unless she spent the *chief* of it by the side of Mrs. Thorpe" (my emphasis). Here "chief" means "the main part" and is an interesting example of Jane Austen's changing an adjective into a noun. Further, "in what they called conversation . . . Mrs. Thorpe talked chiefly of her children, and Mrs. Allen of her gowns." Both are here succinctly summed up. The effect is achieved through the use of "called" and the contrast between "children" and "gowns."

The fourth and final paragraph moves from the friendship of Catherine and Isabella to their escape from the "wet and dirt" of Bath to the world of fiction and Jane Austen's most sustained defense of her form, the art of fiction, in her work. She acknowledges that the novel provides a form of escape. The two friends "shut themselves up, to read novels together." They are on "Christian name" terms. In the early 19th century strict rules governed forms of address. Using a Christian name or first name such as "Catherine" or "Isabella" without "Miss" and/or a surname or family name indicates a close relationship. Isabella soon returns to the more formal "Miss Morland," indicating the essentially superficial nature of her friendship with Catherine. Jane Austen then directly addresses her readers by using the first person "I" rather than the third person. She also uses "we" to express solidarity with her fellow novelists, saying "Let us not desert one another; we are an injured body."

There are many elements of interest in this paragraph. Jane Austen writes in the first person plural, and she uses theatrical metaphors, the word "performances" twice and "productions." She attacks "the press," "Reviewers," and a "thousand pens" who chose only male writers. She refers, in a direct address to the reader, to those who degrade the work of female writers: "It is only Cecilia, or Camilla, or Belinda." These are the heroines of Fanny Burney's novels *Cecilia* (1782) and *Camilla* and MARIA EDGEWORTH's *Belinda* (1801). On the one hand, Jane Austen as the author may be defending these novels and her art, that of the novelist. On the other hand, she may well be taking the side of her speaker with her direct address, "'Oh! it is only a novel!' replies the young lady; while she lays down her book with affected indifference, or momentary shame.—'It is only Cecilia, or Camilla, or Belinda.'" Part of Jane Austen's greatness is that she is constantly ironic, leaving matters open for different perspectives or viewpoints.

Earlier in the paragraph, she refers to "the abilities of the nine-hundredth abridger of the History of England" (35–38). Here the reference may be to Oliver Goldsmith's well-known *History of England* (1771), published three years later in abridged form. Or the reference may be to David Hume's frequently reprinted *History of England* (1754–61), mentioned again in chapter 14 of *NA*, not by Catherine but by Eleanor Tilney (109). Jane Austen herself produced a comic parody, the HISTORY OF ENGLAND in 1791. This early Jane Austen burlesque accords with Catherine's reading: "the men all so good for nothing, and hardly any women at all—it is very tiresome" (108).

In the same category in this fifth chapter as "the History of England," the narrator comments on "the man who collects and publishes in a volume some dozen lines of Milton, Pope, and Prior, with a paper from the Spectator, and a chapter from Sterne," and these "are eulogized by a thousand pens." These 17th- and 18th-century poets, novelists, and journal essayists (in the *Spectator*, an 18th-century journal) are all male. Even they are misrepresented by another male "who collects" only a small selection, "some dozen lines . . . a paper from the Spectator, and a chapter from Sterne."

Toward the beginning of this complex final paragraph of chapter 5, Jane Austen, directly addressing her readers, writes: "Yes, novels;—for I will not adopt that ungenerous and impolitic custom so common with novel writers, of degrading by their contemptuous censure the very performances, to the number of which they are themselves adding" (37). She will, in other words, apparently not follow, for instance, Maria Edgeworth, who in the advertisement to her novel *Belinda* (1801) attacks her fellow novelists, accusing them of "so much folly, error and vice" (Grogan, 59 n. 1).

Three novels and a literary journal are singled out in this paragraph for special attention. The three novels, *Cecilia, Camilla,* and *Belinda,* are all by women. They are praised with superlatives: "greatest . . . most thorough . . . happiest . . . liveliest . . . best chosen." All three exhibit "powers of the mind . . . knowledge of human nature . . . [which] are conveyed to the world." The three novels have in common attention to social conventions and center on young women deficient in social manners and behavior. Akin to Catherine or Emma Woodhouse, they lack right guidance in such matters.

The lengthy final elaborate sentence of the chapter appears to praise "the Spectator" in what is "the best chosen language," yet, on the other hand, parodies the language. Read closely, the sentence attacks the *Spectator* for being a "voluminous publication" in which "the substance of its pages so often consist[s] in the statement of improbable circumstances, unnatural characters, and topics of conversation, which no longer concern, any one living." Further, the "language too, [is] frequently so coarse as to give no very favourable idea of the age that could endure it."

In short, this chapter moves from narrative, Catherine and her escort Mrs. Allen settling in Bath, Catherine looking for her young man, the developing of "friendship" between Catherine and Isabella, to an authorial disquisition on the novel. This reasonably lengthy authorial address presents conflicting perspectives of the novel and reactions to it. By its end, the narrator has come down firmly on its side and has attacked previous prose models found, for instance, in a journal such as the *Spectator*. In the novel, for the narrator, "the liveliest effusions of wit and humour are conveyed to the world in the best chosen language" (37–38).

Chapter 6

In this chapter, Jane Austen returns to the narrative of the novel. She illustrates the nature of the relationship between Catherine and Isabella that has emerged "after an acquaintance of eight or nine days." Again, things are not what they seem. A close reading of the dialogue between the two shows that "their very warm attachment . . . delicacy, discretion, originality of thought, and literary taste," although containing "reasonableness," is more complex than it appears. The dialogue is that of questions and answers, statements and reactions to them. The main contrast highlighted in the dialogue is between Catherine's innocence and Isabella's experience. The narrative is detached, providing "a specimen" for the reader to examine of the relationship between the two. Isabella exaggerates, indulges in hyperbole, and is trivial and indelicate. She uses expressions such as "at least this age," "these ten ages," "an hundred things to say to you," "agonies." Her language is replete with inflated clichés. Isabella's prime concern seems to be with wealth and the latest fashions: "I was so afraid it would rain this morning . . . it looked very showery, and that would have thrown me into agonies!" In one of the shops along one of the most fashionable shopping areas of Bath, "in a shop window in Milsom-street," Isabella saw "the prettiest hat you can imagine . . . very like" Catherine's "only with coquelicot ribbons instead of green" (39). In other words, it is the color of red poppies. Jane Austen wrote to her sister, Cassandra, on December 18, 1798: "Coquelicot is to be all the fashion this winter" (*Letters*, 26).

As a contrast to Isabella's inflated language, there is Catherine's directness, her lack of sophistication. The conversation between the two moves from fashion and shopping to literature. Isabella asks Catherine, "Have you gone on with Udolpho?" To which the reply is, "Yes, I have been reading it ever since I woke; and I am got to the black veil." She is reading one of the most fashionable novels of the day, Ann Radcliffe's *The Mysteries of Udolpho*, which is parodied and used throughout *NA*. In chapter 6 of the second volume of *Udolpho*, the heroine faints when she lifts a black veil covering a large picture. She believes that it conceals the skeleton of Lady "Laurentina." Isabella claims to have read the novel and will not "for the world" reveal "what is behind the black veil." Catherine, Jane Austen, or her printer confuse "Laurentina's" name with that of Laurentini in the novel (39–40). As Catherine discovers when she finished *The Mysteries of Udolpho*, its heroine incorrectly assumes that what she sees behind the veil is Laurentini's body. She really sees the waxen figure covered in a shroud and eaten by worms, not the skeleton. To add to the irony, Lady Laurentini emerges as a perpetrator of horrific violence, not its victim. This episode, and Catherine's imagined re-creation of what she has not read, anticipate the passage later on in *NA* when her overactive imagination overresponds to a chest in a room at Northanger Abbey.

The knowledgeable Isabella has prepared a list of seven similar novels that Catherine should read. These begin with Eliza Parson's (1748–1811) *Castle of Wolfenbach* (1793). The third on the list is her *Mysterious Warnings*, published three years later. The plots are highly improbable, depend on the intervention of the supernatural, and depict depravity plus incest. Mrs. Parsons produced 60 such novels to feed her children after her husband died, leaving little money to support his family. The second novel Isabella recommends is Regina Marie Roche's (1746?–1845) *Clermont* (1798), in which a heroine attempts to discover her noble ancestry. The fifth choice, Francis Lathom's (1774–1832) *The Midnight Bell* (1798), contains in addition to

a depraved monk, a hero seeking his origins. The fourth and six recommendations, Peter Teuthold's *Necromancer of the Black Forest* (1794) and Eleanor Sleuth's *Orphan of the Rhine: A Romance* (1798), are of German origin. Her final recommendation, also a translation from German, Peter Will's *Horrid Mysteries* (1797), focuses on an aristocrat initiated against his will into a secret society named the Illuminati and his efforts to free himself from the society and its many crimes.

Interestingly, Jane Austen's father borrowed *The Midnight Bell* from a local library. All the other novels have the same publisher, "the Minerva Press, one of the principal publishers of the popular novels for women in the later 18th and early 19th centuries." As Claudia L. Johnson observes, "These gothic novels differ in style, from the violent and sensational to the picturesque and haunting, where (in the manner of Radcliffe) the lurid is implied and suspected rather than depicted" (363). Catherine reacts to the recommendations by asking Isabella, "are they all horrid, are you sure they are all horrid?" This was the intended effect of gothic fiction: to create a shuddering fear in the reader. The word is not used here in the negative sense of the novels not being any good.

Isabella has a short attention span. She is unable to say anything about her recommendations except that they are endorsed by her friend, a Miss Andrews, whom she briefly describes in inflated language. Miss Andrews "one of the sweetest creatures in the world, has" according to Isabella, "read every one of" the novels. Isabella then focuses briefly on her friend's "netting" activities rather than reading: "she is netting herself the sweetest cloak you can conceive." In other words, making tiny fancy-work items. Isabella is "so vexed with the men for not admiring her!" She adds, "I scold them all amazingly about it." Asked by Catherine to elaborate, she replies in a highly exaggerated manner that should have created warning signs for Catherine: "There is nothing I would not do for those who are really my friends . . . My attachments are always excessively strong."

Isabella then praises Catherine: "*you* are just the kind of girl to be a great favourite with the men" (Jane Austen's emphasis). At the same time, after she has sworn undying fidelity to Miss Andrews, she disparages her: "I must confess, there is something amazingly insipid about her." Isabella reveals her personal faults to the readers but not apparently to Catherine, who is naive and too trusting. Isabella tells Catherine that she is "indifferent to every body's admiration except that of one gentleman, who shall be nameless." She tells Catherine that her "feelings are easily understood," that she is open, unlike, implicitly, Isabella herself, who is playing games and attempting to disguise her real feelings and self. There are, however, positive features to Isabella. She encourages Catherine to be optimistic about seeing Tilney again. Catherine, on the other hand, admits to having her attention more focused on fiction than the real Tilney and yet again attempts, although indirectly, to discover the ending of *Udolpho* and what is "behind" the "black veil."

Isabella deflects the attempt, expressing instead surprise that her friend "should never have read Udolpho before," adding, "I suppose Mrs. Morland objects to novels." Catherine's reply is interesting. Her mother "very often reads Sir Charles Grandison herself; but new books do not fall in our way." Isabella finds Samuel Richardson's seven-volume epistolary novel published between 1753 and 1754 "an amazing horrid book," that is, one likely to make its readers afraid or to shudder with fear. She does add, however, that "Miss Andrews could not get through the first volume." The reference to Richardson's novel is interesting. Jane Austen dramatized it for her family to perform. It depicts a virtuous man resisting temptation who offers wise counsel and whose wisdom rescues two women from disastrous marriages and reunites them with their alienated parents.

Again, Isabella diverts the conversation from the literary to other matters such as dress and fashion. She is "determined at all events to be dressed exactly like" Catherine. "The men take notice of *that* sometimes you know" (Jane Austen's emphasis). Then in response to Catherine's "it does not signify if they do," Isabella denies that she takes "to mind" what men "say." Isabella regards men as "the most conceited creatures in the world" and then asks her friend whether she prefers "them best

dark or fair?" To this question Catherine replies, "Brown—not fair, and not very dark." The answer elicits Isabella's identification of Tilney and request for Catherine not to "betray" when she reveals her own masculine preferences. The curious response, revealing a suspicious nature, causes Catherine "some amazement" and reduces her temporarily to silence before she is about to revert "to what interested her at that time rather more than any thing else in the world, Laurentina's skeleton."

During the conversation, the setting, the Pump-room in the afternoon, has been forgotten. It emerges again when Isabella draws her attention to "two odious young men who have been staring at me [not Catherine] this half hour" and requests that they move. Following her instructions, "to the book" or to the letter, "they walked to the book," where "the arrivals" sign in their names to the Pump-room, and also give their addresses. Isabella, on the one hand, seems afraid they are being followed. On the other hand, she wonders where the young men have gone. Dishonestly she says, "Well, I am amazingly glad I have got rid of them!"

Isabella's duplicity is revealed further when she suddenly announces that she wishes "to [be] going to Edgar's Buildings" to look "at my new hat." Edgar's Buildings are a fashionable location at the top of Milsom Street and in the direction taken by the young men she was so anxious to avoid. Her actions at the conclusion of the chapter clearly reveal to the readers, but not apparently to Catherine, the disparity between Isabella's words and her deeds: "they set off immediately as fast as they could walk, in pursuit of the two young men" (40–43).

Chapter 7

The lengthiest chapter so far opens with the description of traffic congestion in Bath. The account is topographically precise and must have come from experience. Isabella and Catherine, pursuing the two young men, are impeded "by the approach of a gig," a light carriage on two wheels that carried up to two people and was drawn by a horse. They left "the Pump-yard to the archway opposite Union-passage; but here they were stopped." Before 1807, Union-passage was known as Cock Lane, but in that year Union Street, running parallel, opened. Such knowledge reveals that Jane Austen could not have written this passage until 1807. She makes a direct appeal to her readers' general knowledge when she writes, "Every body acquainted with Bath may remember the difficulties of crossing Cheap-street at this point." She also personifies the street: "it is indeed a street of so impertinent a nature . . . that a day never passes in which" holdups do not occur.

The two gentlemen Isabella and Catherine are following disappear into the crowd, out of which emerge, as Isabella exclaims, "Mr. Morland and my brother!" The meeting causes a horse "almost" to cause an accident—an example of Jane Austen's wry humor, her delight in the incongruous. The horse's erratic action is a result of "catching the young men's eyes." It is "the bright eyes of Miss Thorpe [which are] incessantly challenging [the] notice" of Catherine's brother James. A French expression, "devoirs" or obligatory, dutiful greetings, is used to convey James's response to his sister Catherine. Wrapped up in herself and "engrossed by her own" feelings, she seems oblivious to the obvious attraction her brother has for Isabella.

John Thorpe is described in greater detail than James. On Catherine "he bestowed a whole scrape and a half a short bow." His greeting of his sister is more perfunctory: "he slightly and carelessly touched the hand of Isabella." "He was a stout young man of middling height." He has "a plain face and ungraceful form." Further, he "seemed fearful of being too handsome unless he wore the dress of a groom, and too much like a gentleman unless he were easy where he ought to be civil, and impudent where he might be allowed to be easy."

His first words are addressed to Catherine. He asks her, "How long do you think we have been running it from Tetbury, Miss Morland?" In other words, he asks Catherine how long she thinks it took them to travel from Tetbury, a village 22 miles northeast of Bath. His response to James Morland's "twenty-three miles" distance is to exaggerate: "five and twenty if it is an inch." Akin to his sister Isabella, he too takes liberties with the truth. Morland points out to him that he even confuses the time they left Tetbury in order to attempt to demonstrate how quickly he rode the distance. Thorpe then appeals to Catherine to

"look at my horse; did you ever see an animal so made for speed in your life?"

In a lengthy speech addressed to Catherine, then to Morland, and then again to Catherine, Thorpe moves rapidly from subject to subject. He starts by praising the horse that "had not turned a hair till we came to Walcot Church." This is located in the north of Bath. The church is where Jane Austen's own parents married in 1764 and where her father was buried in 1805. Thorpe then asks Catherine's opinion of his gig. His question is followed by its history. The vehicle "was built for a Christchurch man"—Christchurch being one of the older Oxford colleges founded by Cardinal Wolsey in 1525. Thorpe then proceeds to tell Catherine how he acquired it. The account is punctuated by swearing: "'Oh! d—' said I, 'I am your man: what do you ask?' And how much do you think he did, Miss Morland?" (44–46). Claudia L. Johnson observes that "it is worth noting that John Thorpe is one of the few characters in Austen's fiction who swears." She adds, "More than characterization may be at stake here. Given the novel's pervasive concern with examining the proper uses of language, Thorpe's speech is a non-gothic instance of coarseness and exaggeration" (364).

Thorpe tells Catherine that his gig is "Curricle-hung" with a "seat, trunk, sword-case, splashing-board, lamps, silver-moulding, all you see complete." He is boasting about his purchase, as today somebody might about obtaining an expensive motorcycle complete with extra equipment. He paid "fifty guineas," to which information Catherine, as honest as ever, confesses, "I know so little of such things that I cannot judge whether it was cheap or dear." Thorpe confesses to "hate haggling and poor Freeman," from whom he bought the gig, "wanted cash." Catherine, always looking positively at things and people, replies, "That was very good-natured of you." The response reveals again the negative side of Thorpe's character. After swearing "Oh! D—it," he says "when one has the means of doing a kind thing by a friend, I hate to be pitiful." The word "pitiful" here means "mean" or "scrimping" with vulgar implications.

Thorpe's initial conversation or series of rantings has not shown him in a favorable light. Catherine's reactions again display her lack of sophistication and her good nature and honesty. Dialogue gives way to narrative reportage. Thorpe and James Morland accompany Isabella and Catherine back to Edgar's Buildings to "pay their respects to Mrs. Thorpe." Isabella walks with James. On their way, "they overtook and passed the two offending young men in Milsom-street." Isabella "was so far from seeking to attract their notice, that she looked back at them only three times." This is a wonderful illustration of Jane Austen's ironic humor at the expense of Isabella.

John Thorpe continues talking to Catherine about horses and carriages, the only subjects he seems to be interested in, and his negotiations to purchase the gig. He refuses an offer for his purchase from "Jackson of Oriel"—Oriel, founded in 1326 by Edward II, being one of the oldest of the Oxford Colleges. After swearing yet again, he further offends against propriety by inviting Catherine unaccompanied to drive with him the next day to Landsdown Hill, above Bath on its northwestern boundary. As inexperienced as she is, Catherine reveals that she is not as stupid as she may appear. "'Thank you,' said Catherine, in some distress, from a doubt of the propriety of accepting such an offer." Catherine asks him, "but will not your horse want rest?" To gain what he wants, Thorpe changes his previous insistence on the miles from Tetbury. What had been 25 miles now becomes two fewer. Truth is irrelevant to his securing his own way.

Thorpe's sister is complacent, encouraging her brother by pointing out that he "will not have room for a third" person in his gig. The focus of the narrative turns to Catherine and her inner thoughts conveyed by authorial observation. She is "fearful of hazarding an opinion of its own in opposition to that of a self-assured man." Cleverly she attempts "to vary the subject" and transfer it to the literary matters "which had been long uppermost in her thoughts." She asks Thorpe, "Have you ever read Udolpho"? His reply reveals him to be inane: "Udolpho! Oh, Lord! not I; I never read novels; I have something else to do" (at times talking about horses and gigs!). His sense of self-importance prevents Catherine for apologizing "for her question." Thorpe adds, "Novels are all so full of nonsense

and stuff." He claims to have read some: "There has not been a tolerably decent one come out since Tom Jones"—as this novel by Henry Fielding was published in 1749, it will be difficult to assume that Thorpe could speak about it and subsequent novels with any authority whatsoever. He compounds his stupidity by adding "except the Monk; I read that t'other day; but as for all the others [again, implicitly claiming to have read them] they are the stupidest things in creation" (44–48).

According to HENRY AUSTEN's *Biographical Notice of the Author,* Jane Austen expressed "reservations" concerning Fielding, "presumably on the [account] of his ribaldry" (Johnson, 365). Interestingly, there are affinities between Fielding's *Tom Jones* and *NA.* Fielding's novel depicts a voyage from innocence to experience by a not so innocent hero and an innocent heroine. In common with *NA,* the theme of social snobbery occurs. Both heroines are victims of misrepresentation and machinations, both travel from the country to the city—the journey is a learning experience. In the case of Sophia Weston, the heroine of Fielding's novel, she travels to London and retains her virtue in spite of great temptation. In both novels, the authors indulge in moral comments on various issues, including the value of the novel as a form. Of course, Thorpe is no doubt unaware of the deeper side of *Tom Jones,* and, as has been said, it is highly unlikely that he has actually read any of it!

M. G. Lewis's gothic thriller *The Monk* was published in 1796. It is noted for graveyard antics and a monk preying upon a woman and committing murder. Thorpe preys upon women but is not given the opportunity to commit murder. In his comments to Catherine, he again displays his ignorance, apparently being unaware that Mrs. Radcliffe wrote *Udolpho.* He is corrected by Catherine and then comments, "Aye, I remember, so it was." He adds, "I was thinking of that other stupid book, written by that woman they make such a fuss about, she who married the French emigrant." Jane Austen's humor lies in her highlighting Thorpe's self-exposure of ignorance and prejudiced innuendos. John Thorpe is not incorrect in his comment. Frances Burney married a refugee, General d'Arblay, who had fled from the French Revolution. England was now at war with France. His tone is contemptuous and bigoted. Catherine responds, "I suppose you mean Camilla?" His bigotry is reflected in his reply, "as soon as I heard she had married an emigrant, I was sure I should never be able to get through it" (48–49). Thorpe reveals also that he has read no further than the first three or four chapters of Burney's *Camilla, or a Picture of Youth,* published in 1796. He refers to episodes in those chapters in which "the endearing but disastrously incompetent Sir Hugh Tyrold plays with his brother's children and attempts to educate himself. Austen particularly admired Burney's skillful characterization of Sir Hugh" (Johnson, 365).

Jane Austen cannot resist poking fun at Thorpe's expense at the opening of the following paragraph. She points out, "This critique, the justness of which was unfortunately lost upon Catherine . . . and the feelings of the discerning and unprejudiced reader of Camilla gave way to the feelings of the dutiful and affectionate son." So there appear to be some positives to his character. These are quickly dispelled when his remarks to his mother are laced with sarcasm and uncomplimentary quips: "Ah mother! . . . where did you get that quiz of a hat, it makes you look like an old witch?" "Quiz" here means eccentric, odd. Thorpe's vulgarity is expressed in his ungrammatical "Here is Morland and I come to stay a few days." At the end of the paragraph, he bluntly "observes that they both looked very ugly"—referring to his sisters.

Catherine's innate common sense is contrasted with her inexperience in society and in dealing with people. "These manners did not please Catherine." However, "he was James's friend and Isabella's brother." In addition, "her judgment was further bought off by Isabella" appealing to her vanity, telling Catherine "that John thought her the most charming girl in the world." The narrator comments, "Had she been older or vainer, such attacks might have done little . . . it requires uncommon steadiness of reason to resist the attraction of being called the most charming girl in the world." So that when asked by her brother James how she likes Thorpe, "instead of answering, as she probably would have done, had there been no friendship and no flattery" at work, she answers in the affirmative.

The response from her brother is not entirely positive. For James, Thorpe is "good-natured" but "a little of a rattle." The word "rattle" is used only six times in Jane Austen's work and primarily to refer to noise. It is rarely used in the sense it is here of silly, vain, or someone who chatters too much. James unfortunately negates his insight by adding a negative antifeminist remark: "but that will recommend him to your sex I believe." He also displays a lack of insight when he refers to Isabella as having "so much good sense . . . thoroughly unaffected and amiable" and encouraging the friendship between his sister and her. His want of judgment is compounded by the remark, "She is a most amiable girl, such a superior under-standing!" The unfolding of the narrative will reveal just how wrong James is.

The chapter concludes with Catherine oblivious to her surrounding's, engrossed in her reading and in the world of her imagination. Following her brother's departure, she is "left to the luxury of a raised, restless and frightened imagination over the pages of Udolpho, lost from all worldly concerns of dressing and dinner." She is even "incapable of soothing Mrs. Allen's fears on the delay of an expected dressmaker" (49–51).

The pattern revealed in this chapter is representative of the narrative structure of *NA* as a whole. Something is said, meetings take place within the background of Bath, John Thorpe changes his story over the distance Tetbury is from Bath partly to impress Catherine, and thereby he reveals how little he can be trusted. John says he does not read novels, disparages them, and then claims knowledge of selected novels. Catherine is persuaded against her better instinct to speak favorably of someone. She will learn more during the course of the novel. At the end of the chapter, she is back in the world of the imagination. In the novel as a whole, she journeys to Bath and encounters people, and she learns to judge characters such as Isabella and John Thorpe. She will meet a character such as General Tilney, who is also motivated by his vanity and greed. Catherine is flattered by the General as she is by Isabella. She is insulted by the General, who is akin to John Thorpe in his high-handed treatment of others. In essence, hers is a learning process in which the imagination is tempered by experience. The controlling narrator's irony erects signposts to her readers as to what is to occur subsequently in the novel.

Chapter 8

The eighth chapter of the first volume of *NA* is similar to the previous chapter in length. The seven chapters so far have presented Catherine's relation to the other main characters. In this chapter, all the characters come together at a ball, which takes place at the Octagon Rooms where balls were held regularly on Mondays and Thursdays. By the conclusion, Catherine has begun to stand up for herself and to make decisions. She is forced to turn down Henry Tilney's invitation to dance as she has previously committed herself to dance with John Thorpe. He is late and rude. She in turn reject's Thorpe's invitation to dance more than two dances with her.

Previous character behavior is reinforced in this chapter. Catherine is left alone in spite of Isabella's declaration that she will not dance till her "dear love" Catherine has done so. John Thorpe also acts in a thoroughly selfish manner. Despite his previous commitment to dance with Catherine, he disappears to discuss "horses and dogs" plus "a proposed exchange of terriers" with a friend, keeping Catherine waiting. His rudeness is contrasted with Catherine's politeness, "no murmur passed her lips," and Henry Tilney's immaculate behavior. The disparity between what Isabella says and what she does is clearly demonstrated. She refers to Catherine as her "dear love" but deserts her as soon as the opportunity presents itself. Catherine, on the other hand, is sincere in her actions. She is loyal to Isabella and sincere in her regret at being unable to dance, because of a previous commitment, with Henry Tilney.

The chapter interweaves omniscient narration with closeness to Catherine's perspective on the proceedings at the ball. When Isabella, reassurances to the contrary, leaves her, "Catherine, though a little disappointed, had too much good-nature to make any opposition." Here Jane Austen is reminding her readers that Catherine has a nicer nature then Isabella. In the third paragraph, Henry

Tilney "looked as handsome and as lively as ever." This must be very close to what Catherine thinks and feels toward Tilney. In spite of deliberately inflated, exaggerated language, readers' sympathies are directed toward Catherine's situation. In the penultimate sentence of the second paragraph, to be left alone at a ball is not "to be disgraced in the eye of the world, to wear the appearance of infamy." On the other hand, what has happened to Catherine does reinforce the fact that "her heart is all purity, her actions all innocence, and the misconduct of another the true source of her debasement." Literally, the "heroine" has been the victim of Isabella's selfishness; she has not been debased, only left alone at a ball.

At the ball, Catherine has been the victim of others' selfishness and social conventions. The social conventions force her to turn down Henry Tilney's offer to dance, although she really wishes to dance with him. His offer "produced severe mortification to the lady"—Catherine has now become a "lady," aware of the rules of social convention. She is no longer a simple country girl. For instance, Darcy, following Elizabeth's rejection of his first proposal to her and accusation that he should have "behaved in a more gentleman-like manner," reacts with "mingled incredulity and mortification" (192–193). Catherine, like Elizabeth in *Pride and Prejudice*, and Tilney like Darcy, learn to distinguish truth from falsity.

The rituals of meeting, the social proprieties are stressed in the first meeting between Catherine and Tilney's sister. They went "through the first rudiments of an acquaintance, by informing themselves how well the other liked Bath, how much she admired its buildings and surrounding country, whether she drew, or played or sang, and whether she was fond of riding on horseback" (56).

Although a character, a "heroine" such as Catherine, has to distinguish between appearance and reality, there is an emphasis on style. As D. A. Miller notes, "A female character can hardly be introduced without her being instantly placed in an intricately graduated relation to style or one or more of its stand-ins (elegance, wit, beauty, fashion)" (41). For example, when Tilney's sister is introduced, the narrator tells us, "Miss Tilney had a good figure, a pretty face, and a very agreeable countenance; and her air, though it had not at all the decided pretension, the resolute stilishness of Miss Thorpe's, had more real elegance." The following sentence emphasizes key positive attributes in Jane Austen's fiction. "Her manners shewed good sense and good breeding." A distinction is made among "manners," "appearance," and Eleanor Tilney. As the novel develops, she becomes the true friend of Catherine, in contrast to the insincerity of Isabella.

An interesting word usage occurs at the end of the chapter. Catherine tells John Thorpe that she will not dance again. He replies by saying that "I will shew you the four greatest quizzers in the room; my two younger sisters and their partners." The uses of the agent-noun "quizzers" (56, 52, 59) has been the subject of comment. R. W. Chapman, in the notes to his early 20th-century edition of *NA*, writes, "*quizzers* should perhaps be *quizzes,* for the context shows that the speaker regards his sisters as *objects* of ridicule" (268).

The lengthy paragraph in the middle of the chapter beginning "Here they were interrupted by a request" is stylistically of considerable interest. Attention in the paragraph transfers from Mrs. Thorpe, Mrs. Allen, Mrs. Hughes, and Miss Tilney, to Catherine and her decision not to dance with Tilney. The third to seventh sentences convey her reactions to "her denial" to Tilney. The turmoil in her emotions is conveyed through the repetition and interaction of the pronouns "her" and "he" referring to Catherine and Thorpe. Not only has the object of her true feelings been removed through her decision, a result of the actions of others, but etiquette has forced Tilney to dance with another group. Catherine, toward the conclusion of the paragraph is roused from her thoughts. By being introduced by Mrs. Hughes to Miss Tilney, she regains her identity: "her" is replaced by her name, "Miss Morland." The "proper sense of . . . . goodness" in the person of Miss Tilney has a restorative influence upon her.

The final paragraph of the chapter finds Catherine alone. Tilney has been "drawn away," Miss Tilney "did not sit near her." Isabella, in spite of her earlier protestations to stay with Catherine, is too preoccupied "in conversing" with James Morland. She "had no leisure to bestow more on her friend than one smile, one squeeze, and one 'dearest Catherine.'" In short, her insincerity has been fully exposed (54–55, 59) in a chapter that focuses on private and public roles, behavior and emotions. These are some of the central themes of *NA*.

Chapter 9

The narrative events of this chapter are relatively straightforward. Catherine returns depressed from the ball, "earnestly longing to be in bed." Fortunately, she "fell into a sound sleep which lasted nine hours, and from which she awoke perfectly revived, in excellent spirits, with fresh hopes and fresh schemes." In spite of her better inclinations, she accompanies John Thorpe in his gig. James and Isabella follow in a different vehicle. Again, Catherine is bored by his chatter. He attempts to find out how wealthy Mr. Allen is, and she is very pleased when the trip is over. Catherine returns to the Allens to discover yet again that she has missed Henry Tilney, and this time he is accompanied by his family, who met Mrs. Allen during her walk with Mrs. Thorpe.

In the opening paragraph, there are references to time. Catherine wishes initially "to improve her acquaintance with Miss Tilney," and she resolves to "seek her . . . in the Pump-room at noon." A few sentences later the narrator reveals that Catherine's "plan for the morning" includes "quietly" reading *Udolpho* "till the clock struck one" (60). Chapman and others are puzzled by what for them appears to be an inconsistency. He writes: "It is possible that the text is corrupt, and that *at noon* represents some phrase containing the word *afternoon*. . . . The pump room was most frequented while the band played and this (at least in 1819 . . .) was between the hours of one and half past three" (268).

The rest of this lengthy sixth sentence of the first paragraph contains a superb account of Mrs. Allen. The description conveys the boredom of Catherine's morning combined with "the decided limitation of Mrs. Allen as a companion." This is achieved through a "see-saw structure" (Page, 94). Mrs. Allen "whose vacancy of mind and incapacity for thinking were such, that as she never talked a great deal, so she could never be entirely silent." The sentence continues: "and, therefore, while she sat at her work, if she lost her needle or broke her thread, if she heard a carriage in the street, or saw a speck upon her gown, she must observe it aloud, whether there were any one at leisure to answer her or not." The syntax is controlled by the pairing of the clauses, for example "as she never talked a great deal," and "so she could never be entirely silent."

Upon leaving the ball depressed and arriving home, Catherine is described as at "the extreme point of her distress." Unlike the heroines of gothic novels, who seem disinterested in food and unable to sleep, Catherine eats and sleeps. John Thorpe refers to "a famous ball last night." By "famous" he means well known locally rather than universally noted. Thorpe reminds Catherine that they "are going up Claverton Down," three miles southeast of Bath. Previously, he suggested that they went elsewhere—to Lansdown Hill. Thorpe tells Catherine: "What a dust you would have made, if I had not come." By "dust" he means "disturbance." The narrator tells her readers that Catherine "thought there could be no impropriety in her going with Mr. Thorpe as Isabella was going at the same time with James," her brother. In other words, she was not breaking social convention by going unaccompanied with a male into the country.

Thorpe, true to form, is preoccupied with his horse and himself. He tells Catherine that the horse "will, most likely, give a plunge or two, and perhaps take the rest for a minute." This does not mean that the horse will pause for a rest but react to being checked by Thorpe, the driver. Catherine's reaction reveals her inexperience: "It was too late to retreat, and she was too young to own herself frightened." This is followed by a lengthy sentence beginning, "Catherine, though she could not help wondering that" and concluding "with the consciousness of safety." In this sentence, Catherine's reactions to the journey, to the "relation of" the horse's "tricks" and the actual "enjoyment of air and exercise," during the ride are described.

This is followed by Thorpe's revealing his selfishness, his capacity for insult and bigotry. He asks

Catherine, "'Old Allen is as rich as a Jew—is not he?' Catherine did not understand him—and he repeated his question." Thorpe's bigotry and Catherine's innocence are clearly revealed. Thorpe is attempting to pry information from her concerning Allen's wealth and also how much financially Catherine—whom he incorrectly assumes to be Allen's goddaughter—is worth. Thorpe also assumes that Allen drinks, a "bottle a- day." This provokes a corrective reaction from Catherine: "Why should you think of such a thing? He is a very temperate man." There follows a series of denials on Thorpe's part concerning the amount of alcohol consumed in Oxford. Catherine's assumption that her brother " James does not drink so much" produces such an effusion of "frequent exclamations" from Thorpe that she concludes that there is "a great deal of wine drank in Oxford."

The narrative returns to the subject of the gig, as does the conversation. Thorpe refers to James's gig as "a little tittupy thing"—in other words, a flimsy, easily overturned, unsteady vehicle. He then gives Catherine a different account of it: "Oh, curse it! the carriage is safe enough, if a man knows how to drive it," adding "a thing of that sort in good hands will last about twenty years after it is fairly worn out." Clearly, Thorpe's assertions are not to be relied upon. Catherine "knew not how to reconcile two such different accounts of the same thing." She is unable "to know how many idle assertions and impudent falsehoods the excess of vanity will lead." Thorpe's use of language, his contradictions, his exaggerations, expose his indifference to truthfulness.

Thorpe's diction is contrasted in Catherine's mind with that of "her own family," who "were plain matter-of-fact people who seldom aimed at wit of any kind; her father, at the utmost, being contented with a pun, and her mother with a proverb." The use of language is a guide to veracity: "they were not in the habit, therefore, of telling lies to increase their importance, or of asserting at one moment what they would contradict at the next" (60–66). The emphasis on transportation in this chapter anticipates Catherine's subsequent return home to her family toward the conclusion of the novel "in a hack post-chaise" (232).

Thorpe's language reveals his self-absorption. As the narrator discloses in a comment identifying authorial narration with Catherine's thoughts, "all the rest of his conversation, or rather talk, began and ended with himself and his own concern." As inexperienced as she is, "little as Catherine was in the habit of judging for her self, and unfixed as were her general notions of what men ought to be, she could not entirely repress her doubt, while she bore with effusions of his endless conceit, of his being altogether completely agreeable." The assonance of "the effusions of his endless conceit" appropriately accords with the content and conveys the vacuity of Thorpe's speeches.

Dialogue between Catherine and Mrs. Allen predominates toward the end of the chapter. Catherine relates to Mrs. Allen an interesting observation by Mrs. Thorpe about the scarcity of veal: "There was hardly any veal to be got at market this morning, it is so uncommonly scarce." Mrs. Thorpe's lament is in itself a comment about the deficiencies of Bath, where veal is difficult to obtain, unlike implicitly in the country. The conversation inevitably turns to economic realities relating to the marriage market. Catherine assumes that the Tinleys "are very good kind of people, and very rich"—the indefinite article "a" being omitted.

The last paragraph of the chapter is not dialogue but reported speech: "Mrs. Allen had no real intelligence to give, and that she was most particularly unfortunate herself in having missed such a meeting with both brother and sister." The chapter ends with Catherine lamenting "her ill-luck." All she can do is to "think over what she had lost." The final word of the paragraph, "disagreeable," indicates that Catherine is beginning to form independent judgments with narrator and character perspectives in accord: "it was clear to her, that the drive had by no means been very pleasant and that John Thorpe himself was quite disagreeable" (66–69).

Chapter 10

"The Allens, Thorpes, and Morlands, all met in the evening at the theatre." Catherine and Isabella sit together. The artificial environment at the theater is matched by the artificial nature of Isabella's hyperbolic expressions of affection for Catherine.

She is "my beloved," and there are "many thousand things which had been collecting within her for communication" with Catherine. Isabella's language is replete with artifice. She asks Catherine, "How have you been this long age?" and refers to her as a "mischievous creature." She tells Catherine that her "brother is quite in love with [her] already," as is Tilney, who "is coming back to Bath" especially for her. Isabella's attention turns toward gowns and dress. Yet there is a serious side to her conversation when she adversely contrasts Bath existence with living in the country: "Do you know I get so immoderately sick of Bath," she tells Catherine, adding that she and Catherine's brother "soon found that our tastes were exactly alike in preferring the country to every other place." The contrast between the country and Bath is taken up again in this chapter in a conversation between Tilney and Catherine. She asserts, "Who can ever be tired of Bath?" This attitude will change by the end of the novel.

The next morning at the Pump-room, Catherine encounters Eleanor Tilney, who "met her with great civility." Eleanor and Catherine behave correctly: "and though in all probability not an observation was made, nor an expression used by either which had not been made and used some thousand of times before . . . yet the merit of their being spoken with simplicity and truth, and without personal conceit"—unlike, for instance, in the case of the language of John and Isabella Thorpe—"might be something uncommon." Catherine genuinely compliments Eleanor's brother Henry on the way he dances. She hears from Eleanor that when he "had the pleasure of seeing" Catherine, "he was in Bath but for a couple of days . . . to engage lodgings for us." This is something that "never occurred to" Catherine. She displays her interest in Henry and jealousy of others who may have danced with him. Catherine looks forward to meeting the Tilneys "at the cotillion ball to-morrow."

Jane Austen may be read as intervening moralistically in the narrative when Catherine returns "home very happy" from her encounter with Isabella and looks forward to "the evening of the following day" when the ball is to take place. "What gown and what head-dress she should wear on the occasion became her chief concern." The next two sentences read: "She cannot be justified in it. Dress is at all times a frivolous distinction, and excessive solicitude about it often destroys its own aim" (73). These sentences may be read literally or they may be read as parody: "Austen is mimicking the hortatory discourse of didactic literature here, contrasting the kinds of reading Catherine encountered at Fullerton," where she grew up "with the experience and reading she encounters in Bath" (Johnson, 365–366). Although Catherine had been "read . . . a lecture on the subject" last Christmas, "she lay awake ten minutes on Wednesday night debating between her spotted and her tamboured muslin" (73). An additional fashion point of detail is made in this paragraph beginning "she went home very happy." The moralizing tone, whether meant as parody or not, is found in narrator observations such as "man only can be aware of the insensibility of man towards a new gown," and the sentence such as "Woman is fine for her own satisfaction alone." The paragraph concludes with "But not one of these grave reflections troubled the tranquility of Catherine."

The rest of the chapter is concerned with the Thursday evening ball. Catherine tries to avoid John Thorpe and is worried in case Henry Tilney fails to ask her to dance once again. Just at the moment she senses that Thorpe is about to occupy her attentions, Tilney, to her pleasure and relief, asks her to dance. Thorpe hovers behind her while she is dancing and attempts to engage her in yet another of his monologues, in the guise of conversations, on his usual subject of horses, carriages, and hunting. Fortunately, the crowd forces him to move along. Catherine is then left alone to enjoy the company of the partner of her choice, Tilney. Her attention is drawn to "a very handsome man, of a commanding aspect, past the bloom"—a word that will be used forcibly to relate to Anne Elliot, the heroine of *Persuasion*—"but not past the vigour of life." This is Henry's father, General Tilney. Before leaving the ball, Catherine speaks again with Eleanor Tilney. They arrange the following day to go with Henry for a walk together in the country. Following the ball, the reader is told, Catherine is so happy that "she danced in her chair all the way home" (74, 80–81).

The description of the ball has several elements of interest. Jane Austen as narrator directly appeals to her female readers and asks them to identify with Catherine. She hopes that Tilney "should ask her a third time to dance, her wishes, hopes, and plans all centered in nothing less." Jane Austen adds, "Every young lady may feel for *my* [my emphasis] heroine in this critical moment, for every young lady has at some time or other known the same agitation." She places emphasis upon her readers identifying with Catherine by repeating "all" three times "*All* have been, or at least *all* have believed themselves to be, in danger from the pursuit of some one whom they wish to avoid, and *all* have been anxious for the attentions of some one whom they wish to please" [my emphasis].

The conversation between Catherine and Henry Tilney while they dance contains several areas of interest. Henry gives a "definition of matrimony and dancing" involving a perception of the power struggle between the sexes. "Man has the advantage of choice, woman only the power of refusal." He goes on to state the gender roles as he understands them as a product of his class, time, and place: "In marriage, the man is supposed to provide for the support of the woman; the woman to make the home agreeable to the man; he is to purvey, and she is to smile" (77). Claudia L. Johnson in *Jane Austen: Women, Politics and the Novel* notes that the gothic novels read by Catherine in Austen's *NA* depict "a strange world of broken promises and betrayed trusts." In his talk with Catherine, Tilney "explicitly raises the issue of promises, and his . . . conceit jocularly likening marriage to a country dance is striking for the anxiety it persistently evinces about infidelity" (43). Tilney refers to "mutual agreeableness," to "solely to each other," to "without injuring the rights of the other." He adds, "I consider a country-dance as an emblem of marriage. Fidelity and complaisance are the principal duties of both."

Other serious subjects are raised between them such as the quality of life in London, Bath, and the country. Their conversation clearly contrasts with John Thorpe's limited attempts at dialogue. These are confined, as noted, to gigs, horses, and hunting. Tilney warns Catherine that she "ought to be tired at the end of six weeks" in Bath. Catherine, on the other hand, still relatively fresh to Bath, finds there "a variety of amusements, a variety of things to be seen and done all day long, which I can know nothing of there," that is, in the country. Back home in the country, Catherine "can only go and call on Mrs. Allen." This comment amuses Tilney, who pokes fun at Catherine's expense: "What a picture of intellectual poverty! However, when you sink into this abyss again, you will have more to say. You will be able to talk of Bath, and of all that you did here."

There are several linguistic elements of interest, apart from a repetition of John Thorpe's hyperbolic, blasphemous language, at work in the latter section of this chapter. He asks Catherine, "Does he want a horse? Here is a friend of mine, Sam Fletcher, has got one to sell that would suit any body" (76, 79, 76). In addition, there are the use of "Latinate words which remind us of Augustan prose rather than our own when they occur so frequently." One of these is "felicity" (Phillipps, 87). Catherine "In chatting with Miss Tilney . . . a new source of felicity arose to her"—felicity meaning pleasure or happiness.

Other points worthy of attention toward the close of the chapter relate to Catherine's affection for her family. She tells Henry Tilney: "If I could but have papa and mamma, and the rest of them here, I suppose I should be too happy!" Her "more established friend, Isabella, of whose fidelity and worth she had enjoyed a fortnight's experience," has all but disappeared during the ball. Finally, time and the weather reassert themselves. She enjoins Eleanor Tilney to "remember—twelve o'clock," the time for their meeting the next day. Eleanor had agreed to the country walk, providing "it did not rain, which Catherine was sure it would not." The next chapter will reveal whether Eleanor remembers the time and whether Catherine's confidence that it will "not rain" (80–81) is justified.

Chapter 11

The next morning, the weather is not good and the clouds indicate rain. The Tilneys do not call for Catherine at noon. Half an hour later, the sun starts to emerge. Catherine does not know whether they will call on her. John and Isabella Thorpe

appear accompanied by James to persuade Catherine to join them on a drive to Bristol, a port town 11 miles northwest of Bath, and to Clifton, a fashionable village two miles west of Bristol. Following considerable pressure from the Thorpes, who tempt Catherine with the prospect of a visit to Blaize Castle, which John Thorpe incorrectly claims is the oldest castle in the country, she almost agrees to go with them. John Thorpe then dishonestly tells Catherine that he has just seen Henry and Eleanor Tilney driving away in a phaeton. Catherine then agrees to go with them. As they start out, they pass Henry and Eleanor walking in the street. Eleanor sees Catherine, who is upset when she considers how very rude she must appear for not having waited at home for Eleanor and her brother. Furious at John Thorpe for lying to her, she angrily insists that she be let down so that she can go and apologize. Her pleading is futile and only results in Thorpe's urging the horses to go faster. Upset for the rest of the drive, Catherine is unable even to visit Blaize Castle, which is in reality a folly or a pseudo-ruin. It was built in the shape of a triangular tower in 1766 by Thomas Farr as an imitation old castle. The party makes such slow progress that on John Morland's insistence they return home, as the day is getting late.

In addition to locations around Bath, there is a gothic literary reference to "the night that poor St. Aubin died!" Catherine is thinking of St. Aubert, the father of the heroine Emily in chapter 8 of *The Mysteries of Udolpho*. Another literary echo occurs when Catherine pleads with John Thorpe to let her down from the carriage so that she can apologize to the Tilneys: "Stop, stop, I will get out this moment and go to them." Her pleading falls on deaf ears: "But to what purpose did she speak? Thorpe only lashed his horse into a brisker trot . . . and Catherine, angry and vexed as she was, having no power of getting away, was obliged to give up the point and submit" (87). As Claudia Johnson notes, "abduction scenes are standard fare in late eighteenth-century fiction." In addition, "Catherine's experience" recalls that "of Evelina at the hands of Sir Clement Willoughby in" letter 21 of the opening volume of Fanny Burney's novel *Evelina*. Another association recalled here is "The instance of Ellena's abduction at the hands of ruf-fians in" the sixth chapter of the opening volume of Ann Radcliffe's *The Italian* (366).

"Dirt" occurs 19 times in Jane Austen's work, "dirty" 27 times. Five of these occurrences for each are found in this 11th chapter of *NA*. The words provide a comment on John Thorpe's dishonesty toward Catherine when he deliberately misinforms her about the Tilneys' behavior. From another per-spective, *NA* "is a novel recurringly preoccupied with dirt and the fear of dirt," especially in its first volume, which is "largely set in a rain-soaked Bath" (D. Jones, 56–57).

Following Catherine's, James's, and the Thorpes' return to the Allens', "Catherine was disturbed and out of spirits; but Isabella seemed to find a pool of commerce, in the fate of which she shared, by private partnership with Morland." She and Cathe-rine's brother play "commerce," a popular card game akin to poker, with the barter and its exchange of cards. At the end of the chapter, somewhat ironi-cally, it is Catherine who wins the game. She is told by Isabella, "Good Heavens! what a delightful hand you have got! Kings, I vow!" This is ironic in the sense that compared with Isabella, Catherine is an innocent who, as the chapter reveals, values honesty. Isabella, however, will treat her suitors as cards in a game, not hesitating to exchange a lower-numbered card for a higher-numbered one, or a poorer suitor (such as James Morland) for a richer one.

True to character, John Thorpe in the chapter refuses to listen to what he is being told and hears only what he wishes to hear. Catherine tells him that her brother "could not afford" to maintain "a horse and gig of his own." The direct statement that James, and by implication the Morlands, are not wealthy falls on deaf ears. Thorpe says "something in the loud, incoherent way to which he had often recourse, about its being a d—thing to be miserly; and that if people who rolled in money could not afford things, he did not know who could."

An interesting instance of variation on direct speech is found in this chapter. In the morning, it begins to rain: "The clock struck twelve, and it still rained." Catherine refuses to "despair yet. I shall not give it up till a quarter after twelve. This is just

the time of day for it to clear up, and I do think, it looks a little lighter. There, it is twenty minutes after twelve, and now I *shall* give it up entirely" (83, 89). Clearly then, Catherine cannot be speak-ing directly at once, in spite of the use of quota-tion marks, to Mrs. Allen. These are "intervening remarks which" have been omitted. This is "not a transcript of conversation but a selection from it, a number of speeches . . . conflated within a single set of quotation marks for the sake of vividness and economy. The author has performed . . . an edito-rial rather than a purely recording function" (Page, 120–121).

Chapter 12

The following morning, Catherine visits the Til-neys' house to apologize. It is believed that Eleanor is at home; Catherine presents her card and then is told that Eleanor has gone out. Catherine sees Eleanor leaving the house with her father, General Tilney. At the theater in the evening, she looks for Henry Tilney, who appears to ignore her. He does, however, come to speak to her, and she then has the opportunity to explain what happened. Henry's expression reveals how pleased he is with the expla-nation. He tells Catherine that Eleanor had not in fact deliberately ignored her when she called and wished to apologize for what must have seemed an impoliteness. However, Eleanor and her father, just as Catherine called, were going out, and impatient General Tilney insisted that the visitor should not be received. Happy again, Catherine and Henry rearrange the proposed walk so that it takes place sooner rather than later. As they talk, to Cath-erine's surprise, she sees John Thorpe in earnest conversation with General Tilney. She appears to be the subject. Subsequently, John Thorpe joins her and she asks him how he knows the General. Thorpe replies that they played billiards together. He informs Catherine that the General thinks her "the finest girl in Bath." Thorpe concurs with this opinion; however, Catherine is pleased only by the General's compliment and not by Thorpe's. Mrs. Allen suggests that Catherine put "on a white gown." She adds, "Miss Tilney always wears white." Eleanor, elegant and dignified, is associated with "white." The color contrasts effectively with the "dirt" of Bath highlighted in the previous chapter. In the third paragraph, there is an instance of the use by the narrator of free indirect speech. Calling at the Tilneys', Catherine is met by a servant: "The man believed Miss Tilney to be at home, but was not quite certain. Would she be pleased to send up her name?" The question keeps the form of direct speech, but is part of the narrative so that there is no need to introduce a very minor character who has a direct speech.

Penny Gay points out in her *Jane Austen and the Theatre* that it is probable that the theater described in this chapter 12 is the Orchard Street Theatre in Bath. Gay writes, "In a theatre only 40 feet wide, Catherine and Henry are opposite each other at a distance of perhaps 32 feet. No wonder she feels snubbed" (9). When she does have the opportunity to confess to Henry Tilney, Catherine's language is loose and hyperbolic, affected perhaps by her friendship with Isabella and her being forced to listen too much to John Thorpe. Catherine has "been quite wild to speak to" Henry. She "had ten thousand times rather have been with you [Henry]." Catherine's patent honesty, however, produces a "more natural smile into [Henry's] countenance." His reply is "in a tone which retained only a little affected reserve." Catherine's expression of feeling toward Henry, her openness, seems to extend the boundaries of what was expected from her gender. In the fiction of her time and social conventions, honesty of expression on the part of females, the initiation of declarations of affection, is rare. These are usually assigned to the male.

Somewhat ironically, the display of genuine emotion takes place in the theater, the setting for performance and feigned emotions in which the actors pretend to be what they are not. When Henry does speak to Catherine, she tells him, "I am sure by your look, when you came into the box, you were angry." The close physical proximity of people in the theater allows Catherine to read Henry's real rather than artificial feelings and emotions.

The chapter concludes with Thorpe's overinflated language. In answer to Catherine's question concerning where he met General Tilney, Thorpe responds, "I have met him for ever at the Bedford. . . . we had a little touch together." Thorpe met Henry's father at the Bedford Coffee House in the Covent Garden area of London. This was a noted coffee house during the 18th century as a place where writers and actors such as Henry Fielding, Alexander Pope, Richard Brinsley Sheridan, and David Garrick, among others, drank and socialized. Thorpe claims to have played "a little touch," or game of billiards, with the General. Somewhat predictably, Thorpe's bigotry and stereotyping emerge. He once again assumes that all wealthy people must be Jewish. Thorpe tells Catherine that the General is "A very fine fellow; as rich as a Jew."

In the concluding paragraph, Catherine is very pleased that apparently General Tilney "should admire her." Ironically, in view of what subsequently happens in the novel, "She joyfully thought, that there was not one in the family whom she need now fear to meet." At this juncture, however, her confidence has been boosted. There is also irony in the previous paragraph, where Thorpe "continued . . . delicate flattery" toward her. The word "delicate" is difficult to apply to the coarse, bigoted, and selfish Thorpe (93–96).

Chapter 13

In this chapter, Catherine asserts her independence. On Sunday afternoon, she walks in Bath Crescent and arranges with Eleanor and her brother Henry to go for their delayed walk the next morning. Shortly after she has done this, on a walk with her brother James and the Thorpes, they tell her they are going to drive to Clifton the next day and insist Catherine go with them. This time, Catherine refuses; she will not again say no to the Tilneys. John Thorpe breaks away from the walk, returns to say that he has spoken to Eleanor, and she has agreed to their walk being postponed. Catherine reacts angrily to his yet again interfering in her plans and making her seem rude to the Tilneys; she also no longer believes Thorpe. She disengages herself from the walking party and rushes after the Tilneys to explain what has happened. She sees them entering their house and brushes past the servant; then she goes into their drawing room. Ignoring formal niceties, Catherine almost without pausing to breathe explains what has happened and apologizes. The Tilneys find her explanation difficult to comprehend but appreciate Catherine's spirit. Catherine is formally introduced to General Tilney, who is especially polite toward her, and annoyed at his servant's actions, until Catherine explains that she rushed past him. Catherine has to decline an invitation to stay for dinner and spend the rest of the day. She is expected by the Allens but agrees in the very near future to spend another day with them. Catherine returns to the Allens, who approve of what she has done concerning the Thorpes and the Tilneys. Mr. Allen, however, informs Catherine about the inappropriateness of an unaccompanied young lady driving alone with a young man in an open carriage. Mrs. Allen agrees with her husband. Catherine is surprised that she had not told her this earlier, as she would not have gone with John Thorpe.

The chapter begins with a parody, an imitation of the protagonist's repetitive correspondence and journal entries found in the novels of, for instance, Frances Burney and Samuel Richardson. Stylistic elements of interest in the chapter include the use of free indirect speech. General Tilney "was quite angry with the servant whose neglect had reduced her to open the door of the apartment herself. 'What did William mean by it? He should make a point of inquiring into the matter.'" Style reflects character in the case of John Thorpe. A further illustration of his coarseness is found in his attempted description of Catherine. He is about to tell James Morland, "She is as obstinate as—." However, as the narrator relates, "Thorpe never finished the simile, for it could hardly have been a proper one."

The chapter shows that Catherine is no longer an innocent country girl. She clearly sees John Thorpe for what he is: dishonest and full of hot air. Catherine tells Isabella, "Mr. Thorpe had no business to invent any such message . . . and did I know that Mr. Thorpe has—," in other words, actually done what he says he has. "He led me into one act of rudeness by his mistake on Friday." In this instance there is a note of irony at work as it emerges that John Thorpe has actually done what he says he did and spoken to Eleanor Tilney. Catherine literally has to assert her independence of

mind by physically releasing herself from the hold of John and Isabella Thorpe: "she broke away and hurried off." Catherine has told the Thorpes, "It does not signify talking. If I could not be persuaded into doing what I thought wrong, I never will be tricked into it." In other words, talking will make no difference, she will not be diverted from what she intends to do. Catherine stayed "a quarter of an hour" at the Tilneys', the correct amount of time for a polite visit. She does not overstay her welcome. After she has left the Tilneys' and been introduced to General Tilney, her emotional relief is reflected in the way in which she walks: "Catherine delighted by all that had passed, proceeded gaily to Pulteney-street; walking, as she concluded, with great elasticity." She walks by herself in Bath with a lively, unaffected energy that conveys her happiness.

The last section of the chapter reflects some of the major themes of Jane Austen's novels: appropriate conduct and the conflict between different generations. Catherine has to learn how to behave in the world of Bath. She tells Mrs. Allen, "I always hoped you would tell me, if you thought I was doing wrong," that is, not behaving in the correct, socially accepted manner. Mrs. Allen's response is understandable: "young people do not like to be always thwarted." Mr. Allen tells Catherine that all he can do is to "only advise" her. He tells his wife, "You had better leave her alone, my dear, she is old enough to know what she is about; and if not, has a mother to advise her." In the final paragraph, Catherine, alone with her thoughts, is concerned with "what would the Tilneys have thought of her" and her own sense of right and wrong: "if she had been guilty of one breach of propriety, only to enable her to be guilty of another?" (97–105).

Chapter 14

The events of this chapter can be described briefly. Catherine and Eleanor, and Henry Tilney take their delayed walk to Beechen Cliff. This is quite a walk south of Bath and offers a fine view of the whole city. The three friends have a lively discussion on fiction, history, and art. The chapter is replete with allusions that need explanation. Catherine uses the adverb "amazingly" to describe her perception of reactions to fiction. She tells Henry,

"But I really thought before [that] . . . young men despised novels amazingly." He responds by repeating the adverb: "It is *amazingly*; it may well suggest *amazement* if they do—for they read nearly as many as women. . . . . Do not imagine that you can cope with me in knowledge of Julias and Louisas," in other words, the heroines of the novels Catherine has been identified with since the start of *NA*. Henry's objection to Catherine's inappropriate use of the adverb (it is also Isabella Thorpe's favorite word) is mixed with his confession that he, too, in common with other men, "read nearly as many" similar novels "as women."

In the same paragraph, Henry displays his knowledge of *The Mysteries of Udolpho*. He refers to Emily, the novel's heroine, who "herself left poor Valancourt [her true love] when she went with her aunt to Italy" upon the death of her father. Catherine responds by asking Henry: "do not you think Udolpho the nicest book in the world?" Tilney replies "The nicest;—by which I suppose you mean the neatest. That must depend upon the binding." He is criticizing Catherine's use of "nice" as agreeable instead of "discriminating." According, however, to the *OED*, Catherine's usage is appropriate. "Nice" (107) was in use from the middle of the 18th century as an adjective meaning something "that one derives pleasure or satisfaction from; agreeable, pleasant, satisfactory, attractive" (*OED*).

Eleanor tells Catherine, "The word 'nicest' as you used it, did not suit" her brother, "and you had better change it as soon as you can, or we shall be overpowered with Johnson and Blair all the rest of the way" (108). Samuel Johnson's *Dictionary of the English Language* was published in 1755, among the other objects of Johnson's aim was to secure the correct use of language. Hugh Blair (1718–1800), too, in his influential *Lectures on Rhetoric and Belles Lettres*, published in 1783, had a similar purpose. So Eleanor's reference to both of them in the context of assumed incorrect word usage is not without relevance. She is telling Catherine that she had better choose her words carefully, otherwise her brother will, so to speak, throw the books at her!

Eleanor Tilney displays different literary tastes than her brother or Catherine. She is "fond of history" and reads "a speech" if it "be well drawn up . . . with pleasure, by whomsoever it may be made—and probably with much greater pleasure if the production of Mr. Hume or Mr. Robertson, than if the genuine words of Caractacus, Agricola, or Alfred the Great." She is responding to Catherine's remark that "a great deal of [history] must be invention" (108, 109). Eleanor is telling Catherine that she approves of the habit found in David Hume's *History of England* (1754–61), and William Robertson's *History of Scotland* (1759), "of assigning eloquent thoughts and speeches to historical personages" (Johnson, 367).

The conversation moves from different authors, and the virtues of the writing of Mrs. Radcliffe, to the aesthetics of the landscape. The Tilneys "were viewing the country with the eyes of persons accustomed to drawing and real taste." The narrator adds, "Here Catherine was quite lost. She knew nothing of drawing—nothing of taste" (110). The allusions are to the picturesque or the judging of natural scenery as "if it might appear in a painting, especially by one of three eighteenth-century . . . artists, Claude Lorrain, Nicholas Poussin and Salvator Rosa." Paintings and landscape need to "include specific elements of the picturesque: mountains, small figures, a winding stream, a dot of red, a weathered tree, sometimes from a hill top . . . all carefully layered into a fore-ground, middle distance, side-screen, and so on" (Gaull, 259). Catherine is "heartily ashamed of her ignorance," however, for in the next sentence the author says, "A misplaced shame" and adds "Where people wish to attach, they should always be ignorant." Moreover, "A woman especially, if she have the misfortune of knowing anything, should conceal it as well as she can." This is a curious observation. Eleanor Tilney has been as much engaged as her brother in observing the picturesque.

Further, as the narrator ironically notes at the opening of the next paragraph, "The advantages of natural folly in a beautiful girl have been already set forth by the capital plan of a sister author." This is a reference to Frances Burney's Indiana Lynmere in *Camilla*, who is attractive but stupid. Jane Austen notes, not without irony, "imbecility in females is a great enhancement of their personal charms." Eleanor and Henry refer to "side-screens and perspectives—lights and shades" (110–111). This is a reference to the oeuvre of William Gilpin. In his *Three Essays: On Picturesque Beauty* (1792), the "picturesque features irregularity, rugged textures, and varieties of light and shade" (Johnson, 367).

References toward the end of chapter 14 move from the aesthetic to the political. Henry refers to the "inclosure" of land or, in other words, to the increasing fencing in during the Napoleonic Wars of land that had been used for pasturage and collecting of wood for fuel. The enclosures led to great hardship among the rural poor. Henry tells his sister that he has "heard that something very shocking indeed, will soon come out in London." He mentions "the riot," which is not "a new publication which is shortly to come out." Henry laughs at his sister for imagining "a mob of three thousand men assembling in St. George's Fields; the Bank attacked, the Tower threatened, the streets of London flowing with blood, a detachment of the 12th Light Dragoons . . . called up from Northampton"—where the cavalry barracks were built in 1796 not too far from London—"to quell the insurgents" (111–113). Eleanor is not imagining too much. St. George's Fields was a starting point for the Gordon Riots of 1780, and there were, during the last decade of the 18th century, frequent disturbances in London and elsewhere over the cost of basic food and heavy-handed political repression. Jane Austen's cousin Eliza de Feuillide, two months before visiting her at Steventon, had herself fled from a serious London riot in June 1792.

It is not surprising that this chapter has attracted critical attention. The focus is on Henry Tilney's praise of the novel, his occasional patronizing remarks against women, and to quote Penny Gay, "the Tilneys' employment of fashionable jargon" to describe the landscape. This alerts readers "to the theatricalising of the English landscape. . . . The danger of such a sophisticated fashionable educated perception as Henry Tilney's is that it encourages seeing the whole world as a stage set." Further, "what Henry so complacently offers as instruction to Catherine is at best unhelpful and at worst radically misleading" (Gay, 68–69).

Chapter 15

The final chapter of the first volume begins with an account of a brief note from Isabella asking Catherine to visit her as soon as she can. On the visit, Catherine is told that James, her brother, has asked Isabella to marry him and is about to ask his father's consent and find out how much of an income he will have to get married on. James writes the following day to say that his father has given his consent and blessing to the proposed marriage. John Thorpe then tells Catherine that he is considering marriage and considers her as his future wife. However, Catherine appears to ignore the implications of what he is saying.

In the opening paragraph of the chapter several expression need explicating. Maria Thorpe is reported as referring in her account to Catherine of the Thorpes' outing the previous day, to their laying "out some shillings in purses and spars; thence adjourned to eat ice at a pastry-cook's." The "purses and spars" (116) mean that money was spent on trinkets, small pieces "of lustrous stones, or geological specimens, to be purchased as ornaments and souvenirs" (Phillipps, 99). Isabella tells Catherine that on her first meeting James, a potential rival for James's affections, a "Miss Andrews drank tea with us that evening and wore her puce-coloured sarsenet" or a soft fine fabric.

The chapter is pervaded with irony. At this juncture, Isabella claims not to care too much for money, although she tells Catherine, "we must not expect such disinterestedness in many. As for myself, I am sure I only wish our situations were reversed." Her assumption is that the Morlands are very wealthy. Catherine, still immersed in the world of books as opposed to reality, places such a "charming sentiment" in the context "of all the [fictitious] heroines of her acquaintance." All Isabella requires is "a cottage in some retired village," adding, "There are some little villas about Richmond." The "cottage" in the late 18th century was a glamorized dwelling; Isabella's desire quickly transforms from a simple, lowly "cottage" to a "little villa" situated in Richmond, an extremely wealthy outer London suburb.

In the previous chapter, Henry Tilney objects to Catherine's use of language. Part of her education is to learn to use language appropriately. Faced with the news of her brother James's engagement, she is bereft of words. Her feelings and thoughts are conveyed in her expressions, in a face that "the eight parts of speech shone out most expressively" from "her eyes." Isabella, on the other hand, will demonstrate, as the narrative unfolds, that words for her bear little relationship to reality and are mere pretense. She has promised to marry James Morland and insisted that "the smallest income in nature would be enough for me." This will prove to be an illusion. Similarly, John Thorpe's comment to Catherine, "I hate the idea of one great fortune looking for another. And to marry for money I think the wickedest thing in existence" (118–120, 119, 124) is most disingenuous. He is without money and his interest in Catherine reflects his sister Isabella's in James. Both are under the misleading impression that the Morlands are very wealthy.

Volume 2, Chapter 1 (Chapter 16)

The second volume begins with an account of Catherine fulfilling her promise to dine with the Tilneys as soon as she has the opportunity. Catherine's high expectations from the visit are somewhat dimmed by the reserved reception she receives. Puzzled by Eleanor and Henry's coolness toward her, and General Tilney's excessive politeness, she attends a ball the same evening. Eleanor and Henry at the ball are back to their usual friendly selves toward her and are accompanied by Captain Frederick Tilney, their elder brother. Catherine, comparing him with Henry, notices similar family features and less refinement in behavior. She is also surprised by Isabella, who has come with her to the ball—James being way at Fullerton. Initially claiming that she does not wish to dance, Isabella quickly agrees to dance with Frederick as soon as he pays attention to her.

Following the dance, at their next meeting Catherine learns from Isabella that she has heard from James. The financial arrangements agreed to by Mr. Morland include the promise of an annual living (for a clergyman) of approximately £400 per year. James will have to wait another two and a half years for this. In the long term, he will also inherit an estate worth just as much from his father. Isabella and her mother disguise their disappointment at the smallness of the sums involved by focusing on the length of time Isabella and James have to wait until they can be married. She tells Catherine, "There's the sting. The long, long, endless two years and half that are to pass before your brother can hold the living" (136).

In the opening paragraph of the chapter, Catherine thinks "That he [General Tilney] was perfectly agreeable and good-natured, and altogether a very charming man, did not admit of doubt, for he was tall and handsome, and Henry's father." This is illogical and reflects Catherine's lack of maturity, clear thinking, and increasing obsession for Henry. He becomes the focal point of her judgment of others. Henry, too, is by no means unaware of Catherine's abilities. The immediate occasion is when she confesses to him: "Me?—yes; I cannot speak well enough to be unintelligible." Henry's reply, "Bravo!—an excellent satire on modern language," acknowledges the unintentional common sense and basic wisdom of Catherine's words (129–130, 134–135, 129, 133).

Volume 2, Chapter 2 (Chapter 17)

This relatively brief chapter is important in terms of narrative movement. It is now nearing the end of the six weeks the Allens plan to be in Bath. Catherine is not happy to return home. She is growing increasingly attached to the Tilneys. The Allens, however, extend their Bath stay for an additional fortnight. Catherine begins to hope that her relationship with Henry Tilney may well flourish; however, her dreams are once again crushed. General Tilney has to return home with Eleanor and Henry at the end of a further week. Catherine is invited to accompany the Tilneys to Northanger Abbey for an extended stay. This makes Catherine very happy. It will allow her to be closer to Henry and also indulge "Her passion for ancient edifices [which] was next in degree to her passion for Henry Tilney." The chapter concludes with a brief description of the history and physical condition of Northanger Abbey (141–142).

At the end of the first paragraph of the chapter, Jane Austen's "fondness for the abstract noun as complement to convey a general impression" (Phillipps, 162) displays itself. For Catherine, "The past suspense of the morning had been ease and quiet to the present disappointment." Austen occasionally uses an archaic word. General Tilney tells Catherine, "We leave Bath, as she has perhaps told you, on Saturday se'nnight."—a week, or seven nights. Such usage conveys an element of pomposity and excessive desire for correctness on the part of the speaker.

Catherine is excited as much by the prospect of Northanger Abbey as by the opportunity her visit affords to spend more time with Henry. The language used to convey her reactions to her invitation contains elements of sexuality and desire: "Northanger Abbey!—These were thrilling words, and wound up Catherine's feelings to the highest point of extasy." Catherine is full of eager expectation: "Her grateful and gratified heart could hardly restrain its expressions within the language of tolerable calmness." The narrative continues: "Every thing honourable and soothing, every present enjoyment, and every future hope was contained in it." The repetition of "every" is not only an illustration of her excited anticipatory state, but a narrative statement of fact. Catherine's future will, as the unfolding of the story reveals, be inexorably bound up with her visit. Her excitement is an expression of this awareness. Northanger Abbey does indeed contain the key to her fate (138–140).

Volume 2, Chapter 3 (Chapter 18)

"Two or three days" later at the Pump-room, Catherine is told by Isabella that she has received a letter from John Thorpe. Her brother declares his love for Catherine. She reacts with "astonishment" to this news and protests "her innocence of every thought of Mr. Thorpe's being in love with her, and the consequent impossibility of her having ever intended to encourage him." Following Catherine's protestations, Captain Tilney "approached immediately, and took the seat to which her [Isabella's] movements invited him." The meeting is apparently prearranged: "It seemed to [Catherine] that Captain Tilney was falling in love with Isabella, and Isabella unconsciously encouraging him." Catherine is jealous for the sake of her brother and increasingly becoming aware of the "thoughtlessness," the lack of consideration in Isabella,

who "had said many things which she [Catherine] hoped had been spoken in haste, and would never be said again."

This relatively short chapter contains several areas of interest. Grammatical usage reflects thematic concerns. The importance of money pervades Jane Austen's work. Isabella, ironically in view of her past behavior, displays a degree of honesty. Telling Catherine that her brother is in love with her, Isabella observes "I thought it a very foolish, imprudent business, and not likely to promote the good of either." Her reasons are economic and practical: "for what are you to live upon, supposing you came together?" Isabella adds: "You have both of you something to be sure, but it is not a trifle that will support a family now-a-days; and after all that romancers may say, *there is* [my emphasis] no doing without money" (143–144, 148, 146). Such hardheaded realism finds its grammatical expression in the gerund usage—one of Jane Austen's favorite constructions. In this context it has "its occurrence in negative contexts after *there is,* to express the idea of impossibility" (Phillipps, 135).

Jane Austen as narrator directly intervenes in her dialogue. Isabella and Captain Tilney are engaged in a coquettish tête-à-tête with Catherine as observer or playing the role of chaperone. Tilney tells Isabella, "if we have not hearts, we have eyes; and they give us torment enough." To which Isabella, replies, "Do they? I am sorry for it; I am sorry they find any thing so disagreeable in me. I will look another way. I hope this pleases you, (*turning her back on him,*) [my emphasis] I hope your eyes are not tormented now." The words in parentheses in her reply are not Isabella's but the narrator's. Jane Austen here follows the practice of her 18th-century predecessors such as Samuel Richardson and James Boswell by using the present participle "*turning*" [my emphasis] (147) "to indicate parenthetically the attendant circumstances of direct speech" (Phillipps, 143).

Volume 2, Chapter 4 (Chapter 19)

The focus is on Catherine's perceptions of Isabella's "unsteady conduct" regarding Captain Tilney. Catherine is startled by what she regards as Isabella's "wilful thoughtlessness" and disregard for the feelings of James, her fiancé. Catherine seeks Henry Tilney's counsel on the matter. Henry tells Catherine that he has told his brother "that Miss Thorpe is engaged." Henry adds that his brother "knows what he is about, and must be his own master." Henry suggests to Catherine that Isabella cannot be fully committed to James if she behaves as she does to Frederick, his brother. On another level, the conversation between Catherine and Henry is about their own developing depth of feeling for each other. Henry attempts to reassure Catherine by saying that Frederick will probably not stay long in Bath: "His leave of [army] absence will soon expire, and he must return to his regiment." Henry adds, "The mess-room will drink Isabella Thorpe for a fortnight, and she will laugh with your brother over poor Tilney's passion for a month." Catherine defers to Henry's perceptions. His observations "carried her captive. Henry Tilney must know best" (149–150, 152–153).

In this last citation quotation marks are absent. The comments, clearly Catherine's, are intertwined with the narration and illustrate Jane Austen's use of free indirect speech, which is a prominent feature of her later work. D. W. Harding writing on *NA* draws attention to the "natural but subtly organized dialogue . . . found in [this] very short chapter." The chapter demonstrates Henry's avoiding Catherine's direct questions concerning his brother's faults, yet also "leading her a step towards insight into Isabella and her behaviour with James and Frederick." For Harding, the chapter is replete with the "skilful management of tone and the practised command of dialogue."

Volume 2, Chapter 5 (Chapter 20)

Catherine and the Tilneys leave Bath for the 30-mile journey to Northanger Abbey. Catherine spends the first half of the journey traveling with Eleanor in her chaise. Following "the tediousness of a two hours' bait [food] at Petty-France, in which there was nothing to be done but to eat without being hungry," or stop at a small village where the horses rest and are fed, she travels with Henry in his curricle. He teases her about what she may well discover at their destination. Henry plays on Catherine's imagination, which has been stimulated by her readings in romantic and gothic

fiction. Henry also conveys factual information to Catherine about his life: "Northanger is not more than half my home; I have an establishment at my own house in Woodston, which is nearly twenty miles from my father's, and some of my time is necessarily spent there."

Catherine's high expectations of Northanger Abbey fueled by Henry's playing on her fantasies are disappointed. The Abbey is singularly lacking in high Gothic windows and antique chimneys: "So low did the building stand, that she found herself passing through the great gates of the lodge into the very grounds of Northanger, without having discerned even an antique chimney"—which her reading has led her to expect. Even the furniture has the "elegance of modern taste." Catherine's expectations of the fireplace based on her fictional readings do not conform with the reality she is confronted with: "the ample width and ponderous carving of former times, was contracted to a Rumford, with slabs of plain though handsome marble, and ornaments over it of the prettiest English china." In other words, it, too, is modern, based on the design of the American Benjamin Thompson, Count Rumford (1753–1814), the inventor of a fireplace with a back sloping in order to preserve the heat and stop smoke from getting into the room.

Several passages in this chapter are in need of explication. As noted, on the drive to the Abbey, Henry deliberately plays on Catherine's fictionally based delusions of what to expect. By doing so, he too displays knowledge of the popular novels of the time. Henry asks Catherine whether she is "prepared to encounter all the horrors that a building such as 'what one reads about' may produce?—Have you a stout heart?—Nerves fit for sliding pannels and tapestry?" Henry plays upon the fearful wind gusts, the blood-soaked daggers, foreboding furniture, the sleepless nights, found for instance in Radcliffe's *The Mysteries of Udolpho*. He tells Catherine, "How fearfully will you examine the furniture of your apartment!—And what will you discern? . . . over the fire-place the portrait of some handsome warrior, whose features will so incomprehensibly strike you, that you will not be able to withdraw your eyes from it." Henry plays upon Catherine's perceptions or rather misperceptions, her suppositions, she will "examine," she will "discern," something will "strike you [her]." The journey to the Abbey, the expectations aroused, will shortly be transformed into hard reality. This is part of Catherine's learning experience. On one level, she does not live in a novel, but in the real world.

There are direct parallels to passages in fiction. For instance, when she is almost entering her destination, "A sudden scud of rain driving full in her face, made it impossible to observe anything further, and fixed all her thoughts on the welfare of her new straw bonnet." In *The Mysteries of Udolpho*, the heroine, Emily, flees Udolpho Castle to escape the ubiquitous Montini. Her "appearance excited some surprise" from the local population, as "she was without a hat, having had time only to throw on her veil before she left the castle." Before continuing, she obtains a "necessary article of dress . . . a little straw hat, such as was worn by the peasant girls of Tuscany." Further, Jane Austen does not give an extensive, detailed description of the approach to the Abbey. In this way, she deliberately departs from the practice of contemporary novelists such as Ann Radcliffe or Charlotte Smith (*The Mysteries of Udolpho*, 444–445; cited Grogan, 164 n.1 and see also n.2).

The authority controlling the Abbey is revealed in the penultimate paragraph of this chapter. It is not Catherine's fiction-fueled fantasy or the modern architectural transformations that dominate the scene. General Tilney, in the middle of discussing the virtues of his home, "taking out his watch, he stopped short to pronounce it with surprize within twenty minutes of five!" (162). This is an example of the autocrat using the time to dictate prompt attention to his militarily precise commands. The General offers hospitality, not gothic fantasies, although Catherine initially allows herself to indulge in these. He also exercises dictatorial powers over his children and their guest. Jane Austen's setting, Northanger Abbey, may not have its lascivious preying Italian count from whom the heroine must flee. Instead, the landscape is dominated by a melancholy, brooding authoritarian.

Volume 2, Chapter 6 (Chapter 21)

Catherine's imagination is fueled by "an immense heavy chest" she finds in "her apartment." She manages to pry it open only to discover within it "a white cotton counterpane." She is then summoned to dinner by General Tilney. Her initial night at the abbey is accompanied by a violent storm. This "brought to her recollection a countless variety of dreadful situations and horrid scenes," or the gothic possibilities of her position. Her preparations for bed are accompanied by a certain amount of uncertainty and fear. She sees the curtains moving in the wind but receives reassurance from the fact "that Miss Tilney slept only two doors from her . . . and her spirits were immediately assisted by the cheerful blaze of a wood fire." However, in her room "she was struck by the appearance of a high, old-fashioned black cabinet," and Catherine begins to speculate upon its contents. After considerable difficulty, she manages to open the cabinet, only to find its drawers empty; there is in addition a locked inner compartment. "It was some time however before she could unfasten the door . . . but at length it did open," and "her quick eyes directly fell on a roll of paper." This apparently was "pushed back into the further part of the cavity, apparently for concealment." In a highly excited state anticipating revelations, she accidentally extinguishes her candle. She is unable to read what is on the roll of paper, and "Darkness impenetrable and immoveable filled the room." She is left with no choice but to wait anxiously until daylight to satisfy her curiosity concerning the contents of the piece of paper. The darkness, accompanied by "the storm too abroad," the sound of the wind, and other accompanying hoarse sounds, leads to a night in which Catherine "shuddered, tossed about in her bed, and envied every quiet sleeper." At the end of the chapter, "she unknowingly fell fast asleep."

Compared with the previous chapters of the second volume of *NA*, there is very little direct speech in this chapter. Quotation marks are used to convey Catherine's thoughts, and the remarks of Eleanor Tilney on the "curious old chest" Catherine finds in her room. General Tilney barks out commands as if he is still in the army. "General Tilney was pacing the drawing-room, his watch in his hand, and having on the very instant of their entering, pulled the bell with violence, ordered "Dinner to be on the table *directly*!"

The first object to capture her attention is "An immense heavy chest!" and in a passage enclosed by quotation marks, she describes it and speculates on its origin, asking, "by what strange events could it have fallen into the Tilney family?" The third paragraph dramatizes Catherine's efforts to open the chest: "Her progress was not quick, for her thoughts and her eyes were still bent on the object so well calculated to interest and alarm." After all her efforts the opening is an anticlimax. Fantasy again must give way to reality: "Her resolute effort threw back the lid, and gave to her astonished eyes the view of a white cotton counterpane, properly folded, reposing at one end of the chest in undisputed possession!" The chest with "a mysterious cypher" on the lid reveals the commonplace, the innocent, the clean and unspoilt.

The actual reality of the "immense heavy chest" is followed by an encounter with another piece of furniture. The "high, old-fashioned black cabinet" now becomes the object of Catherine's active imagination. The cabinet reminds her of the ebony cabinet in Henry Tilney's gothic tale told on the journey to Northanger Abbey: "It was not absolutely ebony and gold; but it was Japan, black and yellow Japan . . . and as she held her candle, the yellow had very much the effect of gold." Her description of the object is precise. The contents prove to be nonromantic and down to earth, practical. Such a revelation does not occur until the following chapter, for before she can discover what is inside the chest "her candle . . . was extinguished" (163–171). Gothic melodramatic writing, suspense, the play of Catherine's overexcited imagination, combine with realism. The furniture takes on an animistic quality of its own to reflect Catherine's nervous state. The weather too is turbulent, also mirroring the heroine's highly charged condition.

Volume 2, Chapter 7 (Chapter 22)

Catherine awakes to find that "a bright morning had succeeded the tempest of the night." Turning to her discovery of the previous night, she finds it to be "a washing-bill," and other mundane, everyday lists including "An inventory of linen." Her wild imaginings dashed, "She felt humbled to the dust." Indeed, "Nothing could now be clearer

than the absurdity of her recent fancies." The breakfast conversation with the Tilneys contains hints, overlooked by Catherine, from General Tilney relating to a possible engagement and marriage between Catherine and Henry. The General discusses the breakfast set: "He trusted however, that an opportunity might ere long occur of selecting one—though not for himself." He also refers to Henry's living and income at Woodston. The General with Eleanor shows Catherine around the grounds of the abbey. Catherine is impressed by its size. "She was struck . . . by the grandeur of the Abbey," and "had seen nothing to compare with it." The General, however, while admitting to loving gardens, implies that Catherine is used to larger ones. Eleanor expresses an interest in taking Catherine on her "favourite walk." The General makes an excuse not to join them on "a narrow winding path through a thick grove of old Scotch firs." Eleanor tells Catherine that "It was my mother's favourite walk." Her mother died when Eleanor "was only thirteen." In response to questions about Mrs. Tilney, Catherine finds out that her picture is not in "the drawing-room" or the General's room but rather hangs in Eleanor's "bed-chamber." Combining this information with the fact that the General took a different walk, Catherine's hyperactive imagination concludes that "His cruelty to such a charming woman made him odious to her." She is forced to walk with him again. Sensing a change in her attitude, General Tilney becomes concerned "for her health."

Instances of different word meaning than normally used today occur. Jane Austen, as omniscient narrator, relates of the General: "If he had a hobbyhorse, it was *that*. He loved a garden" (Jane Austen's emphasis) The expression "hobby-horse" means to indulge in a favorite past-time, or "hobby." The General excuses himself from following Eleanor and Catherine on taking what emerges as his late wife's "favourite walk." He tells them, "The rays of the sun were not too cheerful for him, and he would meet them by another course." The abstract noun "course" in this context refers to a specific definite path or route taken. An interesting example of Jane Austen's truncation of dialogue occurs toward the end of the chapter. Catherine asks Eleanor a series of questions concerning her mother: "Was she a very charming woman? Was she handsome? Was there any picture of her in the Abbey? . . . were questions now eagerly poured forth;—the first three received a ready affirmative, the two others were passed by." The questions more than likely were not asked all at once but separately. Jane Austen chooses to run them together probably to draw attention to Catherine's inquisitiveness and not to interrupt the narrative with unnecessary dialogue.

Various references in this chapter need explication. In the second paragraph, Catherine discovers an "inventory of linen." Among the items are "breeches-ball" and "a farrier's bill," in addition to "hair-powder." The latter, "hair-powder," by the turn of the 18th century and beginning of the 19th, had gone out of fashion. The "breeches-ball" was a special ingredient for cleaning breeches or trousers. The "farrier's bill" refers to the blacksmith's costs. Shortly after, Catherine exclaims to Henry, "What beautiful hyacinths!" and adds, "I have just learnt to love a hyacinth" (172–180). As Marilyn Gaull notes, "Forcing bulbs for ornamental flowers indoors was a recent fashion in country homes, and, because bulbs were expensive, a great luxury" (137). They are, however, unrelated to General Tilney, and one of the very few indications in the Abbey of the emergence of spring: It is "the leafless month of March." The General is responsible for the choice of the breakfast crockery: "and for his part, to his uncritical palate, the tea was as well flavoured from the clay of Staffordshire, as from that of Dresden or Sève." The reference to Staffordshire pottery is that produced by Josiah Wedgwood in his factory from the late 18th century onward and is preferred by General Tilney to the competing French or Austrian products.

In the grounds of the Abbey, "two sides of the quadrangle, rich in Gothic ornaments, stood forward for admiration. The remainder was shut off by knolls of old trees, or luxuriant plantations" (175, 177); the term "plantations" is "a pretentious word for gardens, in this case an ornamental kitchen-garden. Such detail," Gaull observes, "reveals General Tilney's self-indulgence and lack of social conscience, his growing tropical fruits when much of England . . . was starving or subsisting on horse

flesh, turnips, even nettles." Further, the General's "re-arranging functional land for the view, instead of crops, excluding other people, was recommended by Humphry Repton." His *Fragments on the Theory and Practice of Landscape Gardening* was published in 1816, when Jane Austen was possibly revising NA (Gaull, 140 n. 5). The General tells Catherine that his "pinery had yielded only one hundred in the last year." Assuming that Catherine is from a very wealthy family, he adds, "Mr. Allen . . . must feel these inconveniences" too. In fact, producing 100 pineapples in the pinery, the hothouse where they were grown, is not a bad crop and certainly more than enough for the General and his servants to consume. The General asks Catherine, "How were Mr. Allen's succession-houses worked?" (175, 177–178). This is a reference to "a series of hot-houses with different temperatures for forcing plants out of season, another sign of luxury and excess" (Gaull, 141 n. 7).

Volume 2, Chapter 8 (Chapter 23)

Catherine's imaginative suspicions of the General are increased when, during the tour of the Abbey, the General stops Eleanor from showing Catherine some rooms including the bedroom where Mrs. Tilney died. Eleanor tells Catherine that her mother's death was a sudden one and that she had not been at home when it occurred. This plays upon Catherine's vivid imagination. She begins to speculate that the General may well have murdered his wife or that Mrs. Tilney is kept a prisoner by her husband in a secret prison related to the room she was not allowed to visit. At the end of the chapter, Catherine is "sometimes startled at the boldness of her own surmises," but as "the clock struck twelve" she "had been half an hour asleep."

There are fewer references to explicate than in the previous chapter. In the fourth paragraph of the chapter, during her tour of the Abbey, "Wherever they went, some pattened girl stopped to curtsey, or some footman in dishabille sneaked off." The servant girls wear overshoes to protect their feet from the muddy garden. On the other hand, "dishabille" is probably a misprint for "déshabillé," meaning out of uniform or undressed, A few paragraphs later, after Eleanor's revelation that she was away from home when her mother died, Catherine's imagination once again runs riot. She compares General Tilney with Montoni. He has "the air and attitude of a Montoni," the villain in *The Mysteries of Udolpho* who tries to force the heroine, Emily, into an inappropriate marriage, for his financial gain.

In the fourth paragraph of the chapter, the one in which the General gives Catherine a tour of the Abbey, there is an interesting stylistic interplay between their perspectives and the introduction of *erlebte Rede.* Quotation marks are not used and different attitudes give way to one another. The General is less interested in the old than in the new. This is reflected in the conveniences. Catherine, on the other hand, is searching for the old: "The new building was not only new, but declared itself to be so; intended only for offices, and enclosed behind by stable-yards, no uniformity of architecture had been thought necessary." Consequently, "Catherine could have raved at the hand which had swept away what must have been beyond the value of all the rest, for the purposes of mere domestic economy." The viewpoint in this sentence then switches to the General's: *"but if he had a vanity, it was in the arrangement of his offices,"* (my emphasis, the italicized words indicate the General's thoughts) General Tilney's preoccupation is with order, appropriateness, and economy: Catherine's with the ancient and romantic (188–189; 184; 187; 184).

Volume 2, Chapter 9 (Chapter 24)

In this lengthy chapter, Catherine's fantasy is almost given a free rein. Catherine sees in the family church "the sight of a very elegant monument to the memory of Mrs. Tilney." In spite of this, she is convinced of General Tilney's guilt. She attempts once again to see Mrs. Tilney's former rooms, but at the last moment the General appears. She then in secret visits them: "She beheld what fixed her to the spot and agitated every feature." Instead of a shrouded unlit monument to murder, "she saw a large, well-proportioned apartment," and "the warm beams of a western sun gaily poured through two sash windows!" Reality is different from her horrible imaginings, "a shortly succeeding ray of common sense added some bitter emotions of shame." Catherine "was sick of exploring," and as

she leaves Mrs. Tilney's rooms, she hears someone "with swift steps" ascending the staircase. Terrified she encounters not the General but Henry, who has returned from Woodston earlier than expected.

The ensuing dialogue between them reveals that the staircase is the "nearest way from the stable-yard to" Henry's "own chamber." Catherine tells Henry that she has seen his mother's room. Isabella's name is briefly raised only to be swept aside by Henry, who then explains at length to Catherine the circumstances of his mother's "death [which] *was* sudden. The malady itself, one from which she had often suffered, a bilious fever—its causes therefore constitutional." He and his brother Frederick were with her during her final days, "Poor Eleanor *was* absent" [Jane Austen's emphasis]. His father, the General, "loved her. I [Henry] am persuaded, as well as it was possible for him to. . . . His value of her was sincere; and, if not permanently, he was truly affected by her death." At the end of the chapter, Henry confronts Catherine and asks her "to consider the dreadful nature of the suspicions [she has] entertained." He asks her, "What have you been judging from?" In the single-sentence final paragraph, "They had reached the gallery; and with tears of shame she ran off to her own room."

Catherine's idea that the General has entombed his wife is based on her readings in gothic fiction. At the end of the second paragraph of this chapter, her suspicions gather momentum: "Were she even to descend into the family vault where her ashes were supposed to slumber, were she to behold the coffin in which they were said to be enclosed—what could it avail in such a case? Catherine had read too much not to be perfectly aware of the ease with which a waxen figure might be introduced, and a supposititious funeral carried on." In chapter 14 of Ann Radcliffe's *Sicilian Romance* (1790), the Marquis Mazzini incarcerates for 15 years his first wife following a mock funeral in his castle's deserted south wing. Weekly and then monthly food supplies and other provisions are delivered by his servant Vincent or by the Marquis to the prison. They enter his wife's room through a series of secret tunnels and passageways.

In the spacious apartment of the deceased Mrs. Tilney, Catherine sees "an handsome dimity bed" and "a bright Bath Stove." A "dimity bed" is one covered with a firm cotton fabric with raised striped or fancy figure weaving. The "Bath Stove" is a fireplace with an iron plate above the fire affording a small opening producing a draught. There are also interesting stylistic features and ambiguities in this chapter. In the first paragraph, Catherine misreads "the highly-strained epitaph" on the "elegant monument to the memory of Mrs. Tilney" in the family chapel. The language arouses Catherine's suspicions. She forgets that many epitaphs at the time were deliberately restrained. When she at last enters Mrs. Tilney's quarters, Catherine "beheld what fixed her to the spot and agitated every feature." Her excessive emotion is caused not by the extraordinary, the horrific, but by the ordinariness of what she encounters.

Passages in this chapter have aroused considerable critical attention. In the penultimate paragraph, Henry reminds Catherine to "Remember the country and the age in which we live. Remember that we are English, that we are Christians." He adds, "Does our education prepare us for such atrocities? Do our laws connive at them?" and adds, "Where every man is surrounded by a neighbourhood of voluntary spies, and where roads and newspapers lay every thing open?" (190–198). On the one hand, Henry's remark may be considered as containing elements "of paranoia . . . badly out of tune" with his "astonishing generosity and nobleness of conduct." Also, given the violence of the times, riots and the navel recruiting activities, the comment concerning "Christians" may well be read ironically. Yet as B. C. Southam notes, "In the period following the end of the Napoleonic Wars in 1814 an extensive 'Spy-System' (as it was known) was maintained by the government." Also, "in the 1790s, . . . the spy-system was being used against the earliest radical groups, in an attempt to stifle the spread of democratic and revolutionary thinking" (Southam, *Casebook*: 123–124). In whichever ways this passage is read, it certainly provides an instance of Jane Austen's multiple levels of meaning.

Volume 2, Chapter 10 (Chapter 25)

The short opening sentence of the chapter encapsulates Catherine's situation. "The visions of romance were over. Catherine was completely awakened." She is most embarrassed by the stupid "extravagance of her late fancies" and is "humbled." She is also afraid that she has forfeited Henry's high opinion of her. Fortunately, this is not so, as he continues to treat her with great consideration and does not refer to the incident again. In keeping with *NA* as a record of Catherine's growing up, she gains self-knowledge from what has happened, acknowledging "that it had been all a voluntary, self-created delusion" largely due "to the influence of that sort of reading which she had there indulged"—that is in her past. Her readings in "all Mrs. Radcliffe's works" and others focused on "the Alps and Pyrenees." The situation in England, "at least in the midland counties of England," was entirely different. Consequently, "her resolution formed, of always judging and acting in future with the greatest good sense." She is assisted by "Henry's astonishing generosity and nobleness of conduct." Furthermore, "the anxieties of common life began soon to succeed to the alarm of romance."

She receives a letter from James her brother who has returned to Oxford. James tells her "that every thing is at an end between Miss Thorpe and me." He fully expects that her engagement to Captain Tilney will be announced and reveals that Isabella's "duplicity hurts [him] more than all" and concludes with a warning to his sister: "Dearest Catherine, beware how you give your heart." Eleanor and Henry at breakfast observe Catherine's "distress," although General Tilney seems impervious to it. She shares the news with them and they discuss Isabella's background: her father was a lawyer and she is not from "a wealthy family." Henry assures Catherine that her brother's "marrying Miss Thorpe was not probable." Eleanor and Henry agree with Catherine's analysis of Isabella Thorpe as fickle. They do not respond to Catherine's observation that General Tilney "only valued money as it allowed him to promote the happiness of his children." For Catherine, she "never was so deceived in any one's character in [her] life before." The chapter concludes with Henry and Eleanor comforting Catherine in her distress.

Catherine confesses that her perceptions have been unduly influenced by her reading of Mrs. Radcliffe's novels. She admits that her country, "the central part of England," and her friends demonstrate that Mrs. Radcliffe's writings are mere word construction bearing little relation to the realities around her. The fifth sentence of the third paragraph reads: "Murder *was not* tolerated, servants *were not* slaves, and *neither poison nor sleeping potions* to be procured like rhubarb from every druggist" [my emphasis]. This reference to "rhubarb," (199–202; 204–206; 200), is two-edged. It was "commonly grown in English gardens from the early eighteenth century." However, "the medicinal rootstock of the species of rheum [was] grown in China and Tibet and for a long period imported into Europe though Russia and the Levant, and used as a purgative." Consequently, Catherine, wakening "from her delusions, admits to herself that poisons and sleeping potions were not to be procured, 'like rhubarb,' from every druggist" (Lane, 75–76).

Another interesting facet of this chapter is its use of a letter: Catherine is not at home for a good deal of the novel and must make contact with her parents through letters. For instance, she writes to request permission to stay at Northanger Abbey as a guest of the Tilneys. Earlier in the novel, Henry Tilney passes satirical remarks on feminine letter writing and the habit of keeping journals (27–28). James Morland's letter to his sister, Catherine, is one of the few instances of the full citation of a letter in the novel. It contains important information: the breakup of his engagement and his jilting by Isabella. This will have consequences for the plot as it becomes evident that Isabella has left him for someone she considers to have more money. In turn, this will reveal Catherine's own lack of wealth.

Volume 2, Chapter 11 (Chapter 26)

Henry, Eleanor, and Catherine "frequently" discuss the prospect of Isabella marrying Captain Tilney. Henry and Eleanor "were perfectly agreed in considering Isabella's want of consequence and fortune as likely to throw great difficulties in the way of marrying their brother." Further, "the General would, upon this ground alone . . . oppose the connexion." This makes Catherine sense that "She was as insignificant, and perhaps as portionless as Isa-

bella." Henry delays telling his father what has happened and Frederick, his brother, does not come to visit them. The General accompanies Eleanor and Catherine on a visit to Henry at Woodston. Catherine is "delighted" by Henry's home and surroundings. The General hints that one day she may well be mistress at the house. For him, "the drawing room," which Catherine finds "the prettiest room in the world! . . . waits only for a lady's taste!" Catherine leaves for Northanger Abbey "at six o'clock" precisely with the General: "could she have felt equally confident of the wishes of his son," as she evidently does of the General, she "would have quitted Woodston with little anxiety as to the How or the When she might return to it."

Some references in the chapter need explication. Before the General agrees to visit Woodston, Catherine's thoughts are conveyed: "Now, there was nothing so charming to her imagination as the unpretending comfort of a well-connected Parsonage." Here, "well-connected" means conveniently designed. On the journey to Woodston from the Abbey, there are "all the little chandler's shops which they passed." These are general stores selling candles as well as dry goods. The General, when describing the Parsonage where his son Henry lives, professes an "aversion" to "patched-on bow." This is a reference to contemporary bow windows added to the house to catch the light in the winter and the breezes in the summer. Catherine admires at Woodston "a sweet little cottage . . . among the trees." This is probably a reference to the fashion of the time of country gentleman improving their estates by removing laborers' cottages from near the main house. These cottages had been placed nearer to the main house since feudal times for the sake of mutual protection.

This chapter reveals the General's peremptory nature. He decides to visit Henry at Woodston, and tells Henry, "Well, well, we will take our chance some one of those days. There is no need to fix." He then does just that, as if he is planning a military campaign: "Let me see; Monday will be a busy day with you, we will not come on Monday. . . . But on Wednesday, I think, Henry, you may expect us." Catherine is puzzled by his eating habits, and she asks herself, in an *erlebte*

Rede passage "why he should say one thing so positively, and mean another all the while, was most unaccountable! How were people at that rate, to be understood?" The only one, from Catherine's point of view, who seems to be "aware of what his father was at" (208–215), is Henry. She has still much to learn, as the narrative will unfold.

Volume 2, Chapter 12 (Chapter 27)

Most of this chapter consists of an unexpected letter from Isabella Thorpe addressed to "my dearest Catherine." Isabella's letter reveals her character and is replete with the "strain of shallow artifice," full of inconsistencies. Apparently for Isabella, her relationship with Catherine is unchanged. She plays down her "misunderstanding" with James Morland. Catherine is "dearer to me than any body can conceive," and James "is the only man I ever did or could love." It emerges that Isabella has been cast aside by Captain Tilney, whom she calls "the greatest coxcomb I ever saw, and amazingly disagreeable." She wishes Catherine to intercede with James on her behalf and to restore their broken engagement. Catherine is no longer fooled by Isabella. She has learned her lesson and sums her up as "a vain coquette" and will not do as Isabella wishes. She confides all this in Henry. Catherine says to Henry, "I do not understand what Captain Tilney has been about all this time." Henry does not attempt to defend his brother; he tells Catherine, "he has his vanities as well as Miss Thorpe." Henry's words succeed in Catherine being "complemented out of further bitterness."

At the end of the chapter, Henry compliments Catherine's honesty. He tells her "your mind is warped by an innate principal of general integrity, and therefore not accessible to the cool reasonings of family partiality or a desire of revenge." Interestingly, this is the sole usage in Jane Austen's work of "warped," which usually has the negative meaning of twisted out of shape. Here it is used by Henry in an ironical sense to mean influenced. Another word of interest is Isabella's use in her letter of "dearer": Catherine is "dearer to" her "than any body can conceive." Isabella has a motive for ingratiating herself with Catherine: jilted, the poorer James at least holds out the promise of some future

security. So "dearer" plays upon the double meanings of affection and economic wealth (216–219).

Volume 2, Chapter 13 (Chapter 28)

General Tilney "found himself obliged to go to London for a week" on unspecified business. It emerges that, among other things, he is checking up on Catherine's family. Catherine, during his absence, spends a very happy period in the company of Eleanor and occasionally Henry. Eleanor encourages Catherine to stay longer at the Abbey. Before the end of the week, just as Eleanor and Catherine are about to go to bed, at "eleven o'clock, rather a late hour at the Abbey," they hear a carriage arriving. Eleanor believes that the visitor is her brother Frederick, who has the habit of appearing unexpectedly. The late arrival is not Frederick but the General, who requests that Eleanor inform Catherine that her "father has recollected an engagement that takes our whole family away on Monday." Catherine is to leave for her home at Fullerton early the next morning. Eleanor relates to Catherine her father's commands: "not even the hour is left to your choice; the very carriage is ordered, and will be here at seven o'clock, and no servant will be offered you." Eleanor is very distressed at her father's rudeness: "to have you driven out of the house without the consideration even of decent civility! Dear, dear Catherine, in being the bearer of such a message, I seem guilty myself of all its insult." All Eleanor can say is that her father "is greatly, very greatly discomposed," or upset by something. She adds, "His temper is not happy, and something has now occurred to ruffle it in an uncommon degree."

Catherine spends a sleepless night wondering what she could have done to provoke such treatment: "And all this by such a man as General Tilney, so polite, so well-bred, and heretofore so particularly fond of her!" Eleanor helps her "soon after six" in the morning to prepare for the journey home. Catherine reflects on what has passed between her and Henry, who is at Woodston. She thinks it best that she and Eleanor do not write, although Catherine then changes her mind. Eleanor makes sure that Catherine is "provided with money enough for the expenses of her journey home." Catherine "upon examining her purse, was convinced that but for this kindness of her friend, she might have been turned from the house without even the means of getting home." The carriage arrives, and she leaves "her kind remembrance for her absent friend" Henry. Catherine departs "hiding her face as well as she could with her handkerchief," and "she darted across the hall, jumped into the chaise, and in a moment was driven from the door"—literally as well as figuratively.

Catherine's is a learning experience. Previously, her mind had been preoccupied with storms and haunted chambers conjured up by her readings in gothic fiction. Now "Her anxiety had foundation in fact, her fears in probability." She is the victim of General Tilney's peremptory decision, one based, Catherine and the reader will discover, on his discovery that she is not rich. At this stage in her development, "though the wind was high, and often produced strange and sudden noises throughout the house, she heard it all as she lay awake, hour after hour, without curiosity or terror" (220–229). The actual victim of human malevolence as opposed to imaginings created by literary reading, Catherine has learned some control over her emotions.

Volume 2, Chapter 14 (Chapter 29)
Following a journey of almost 11 hours, Catherine returns home unexpectedly to Fullerton after spending 11 weeks away. Her reception is "beyond any thing that she had believed possible. So surrounded, so caressed, she was even happy!" It is difficult and painful for her to retell "the particulars of her sudden return" from Northanger Abbey. She does not wish her parents to think negatively of Henry and Eleanor. They feel that "General Tilney had acted neither honourably nor feelingly—neither as a gentleman nor as a parent." Catherine's mother feels "sorry for the young people . . . but as for any thing else, it is no matter now; Catherine is safe at home, and our comfort does not depend upon General Tilney." Catherine, on the other hand, cannot dismiss what has happened so lightly. Her parents "never once thought of her heart." She writes with difficulty to Eleanor and cannot help thinking of Henry: "She could never forget Henry Tilney."

In an "expedient for restoring her spirits," Catherine's mother suggests that they visit their neighbors the Allens. At Mrs. Allen's, the discussion turns to James, Mrs. Morland saying, "it could not be a desirable thing to have him engaged to a girl whom we had not the smallest acquaintance with, and who was so entirely without fortune." Mrs. Allen too, like General Tilney and Isabella, regards money as a preeminent factor in a suitable marriage. Catherine reflects how "three months" have changed her. She set out with the Allens to Bath "looking forward to pleasures untasted and unalloyed, and free from the apprehension of evil as from the knowledge of it. Three months ago had seen her all this; and now, how altered a being did she return!" Mrs. Allen dwells to Catherine's discomfort on the General's behavior and draws attention to the "silk gloves" she has purchased in Bath and fine Flanders Mechlin lace. In the final paragraph of the chapter, Catherine's mother tries "to impress on" her "the happiness of having such steady well-wishers as" the Allens nearby. In spite of the "great deal of common sense" in her mother's attitudes, "Catherine's feelings contradicted almost every position her mother advanced." Catherine is unable to get Henry out of her thoughts.

There are several stylistic features of interest in this chapter. Catherine is obsessed with Henry: "How Henry would think, and feel, and look . . . was a question of force and interest to rise over every other, to be never ceasing, alternatively irritating and soothing." The tense expansions convey here the increased emotion and the sensual nature of her feelings for Henry. These are also conveyed through the use of the infinitive as an adjectival phrase describing a noun: "*to rise . . . to be* never *ceasing*" (my emphasis).

The last two sentences of the paragraph beginning "A heroine returning at the close of her career" continue the note of ironic parody evident in the opening words of the paragraph. Catherine after all is just 17 and at the start rather than "the close of her career." The sentences focus on Catherine: "A heroine in a hack post-chaise [a rented vehicle] is such a blow upon sentiment, as no attempt at grandeur or pathos can withstand. Swiftly therefore shall her post-boy drive through the village, and the gaze of Sunday groups, and speedy shall be her descent from it." Instead of a glorious homecoming in a fine carriage, Catherine, the heroine, returns home alone in a shabby rented carriage.

This chapter recapitulates the time frame of the story. Catherine has been away from home for "three months." Specific events have occurred: James's engagement to Isabella and its breaking off, Catherine's own involvement with the Tilneys, the Allens' behavior in Bath. At times, Jane Austen uses allusion or a subtext without expanding implied meaning. General Tilney's action is so reprehensible because it subjects Catherine to danger. The chapter opens, "Catherine was too wretched to be fearful. The journey in itself had no terrors for her; and she began it without either dreading its length, or feeling its solitariness" (230–239). Her situation places Henry Tilney's earlier words of reassurance, "Remember that we are English, that we are Christians" (197), in a somewhat ironic light. Her trip home would have lasted around 11 hours. She was undertaking it by herself in a public vehicle used to carry mail. "In both 1798 and in 1817, discharged soldiers, homeless beggars, and vagrants, robbers, criminals of all sorts, were common on the roads. [Those] who traveled in public coaches were in great danger, especially a defenseless young girl" such as Catherine "traveling alone. Alert to imaginary dangers, she fails to recognize the real ones" (Gaull, 181 n. 1).

Volume 2, Chapter 15 (Chapter 30)

There is very little dialogue and mostly reported speech in this penultimate chapter of the novel. Catherine for a remaining two days remains depressed: "in her silence and sadness she was the very reverse of all that she had been before." As she is unable to focus, and "dissatisfied," her mother tries to restore her daughter's spirits by fetching from upstairs a "clever Essay in one of the books ... about young girls that have been spoilt for home by a great acquaintance." The essay is in *The Mirror*, edited by the journalist and author of the popular novel *The Man of Feeling* (1771), Henry McKenzie (1745–1831). Mrs. Morland refers to Essay 12, "Consequences to little folks of intimacy with great ones in a letter from John Homespun,"

in the March 6, 1779, issue. In the essay, John Homespun believes that his daughters have been spoiled by a recent visit to a titled lady. He thinks that they have stayed up too late, copied her fashion, used French phrases, played cards, and even questioned the very basis of religious belief. On her return downstairs, Mrs. Morland finds Henry Tilney with Catherine. She is no longer depressed but is "the anxious, agitated, happy, feverish Catherine [with] glowing cheek and brightened eye." In other words, Henry's presence has transformed her spirits. Henry apologizes to Mrs. Morland for his "father's misconduct" and then suggests that Catherine show him where the Allens live: "if she would have the goodness to shew him the way."

On the walk to the Allens', Henry proposes, and after "a very short visit to Mrs. Allen, ... [Catherine] in the contemplation of her own unutterable happiness, scarcely opened her lips." On the return journey from the Allens', Henry explains the reasons for his father's behavior and subsequent events. John Thorpe misled the General into believing that Catherine was very rich, that she would inherit "ten to fifteen thousand pounds which her father could give her ... [in] addition to Mr. Allen's estate." In other words, the General believed that Catherine was "handsomely legacied" and "the almost acknowledged future heiress of Fullerton." This belief was the reason why General Tilney had invited Catherine to the Abbey, to develop a match between Henry and Catherine, whom he believed to be very wealthy. But while on his visit to London he meets John Thorpe again, "Irritated by Catherine's refusal" of his marriage offer, and "yet more by the failure of a very recent endeavor to accomplish a reconciliation between Morland and Isabella," Thorpe "hastened to contradict all that he had said before to the advantage of the Morlands." Condemning the family as "necessitous," or poor, Thorpe tells the General that the Morlands seek "to better themselves by wealthy connexions; a forward, bragging scheming race." In the context "race" means family.

Accepting Thorpe at his word, the General, "Enraged with almost every body in the world but himself, ... he set out the next day for the Abbey, where his performances have been seen." Henry returns to the Abbey from Woodston to learn what his father has done: summarily expelling Catherine from Northanger Abbey. "The conversation between [Henry and his father] at Northanger Abbey had been of the most unfriendly kind." Henry refuses to go with his father to Herefordshire, refuses to be intimidated by him, and insists on marrying Catherine. "The General was furious in his anger, and they parted in dreadful disagreement." The General refused his consent to the marriage "and on the afternoon the following day, [Henry] had begun his journey to Fullerton."

This chapter has various stylistic elements of interest, ranging from small matters of detail to larger ones. At the start of the chapter, a low-spirited Catherine "applied to her work." Here "applied" means to concentrate and is used as an intransitive verb, whereas today it is used intransitively in the sense of an application form. Another interesting usage of a verb is found when Henry calls unexpectedly at the Morlands'. He addresses Catherine. Henry, "on *developing* [my emphasis], from amidst all her perplexity of words in reply, the meaning, which one short syllable would have given," then requests that she show "him the way" to Mrs. Allen's. Here the verb "developing" means to discover rather than the usual meaning of a gradual unfolding. A further instance of a word being used in a way it would not be at the beginning of the 21st century is when Thorpe had been "in daily expectation of Morland's engaging Isabella." The gerund "engaging" means becoming engaged.

The third from last paragraph of the chapter has three sentences. The first two begin with a direct address from the narrator to the reader: "I leave it to my reader's sagacity" and an explanation of what happened by using reported speech for Henry's explanation to Catherine. "I have united for their ease what they must divide for mine." In other words, the writer has selected what it was possible for Henry to communicate at this time to Catherine.

Catherine's only crime is an economic one: "She was guilty of only being less rich than he [the General] had supposed her to be." If the General's behavior is understandable, Henry's is complicated. In another direct authorial narrative intrusion, we read, "I must confess that his [Henry's] affection originated in nothing better than gratitude, or, in other words, that a persuasion of her [Catherine's] partiality for him had been the only cause of giving her a serious thought." This authorial comment throws into doubt the depth of Henry's feelings for Catherine; perhaps the author is being ironic and playing with her readers. Ambiguity is compounded in the next sentence, which draws the reader's attention to the distinction between literary form and real life: "It is a new circumstance in romance, I acknowledge, and dreadfully derogatory of an heroine's dignity; but if it be as new in common life, the credit of a wild imagination will at least be all my own"—that is, Jane Austen, the narrator of *NA* (240–248).

Volume 2, Chapter 16 (Chapter 31)

The novel concludes not at Bath or Northanger Abbey but where it began, in the country at Fullerton and at Woodston. Catherine, the heroine after her adventures in the town and at the Abbey, moves from one rectory, her parents', to her husband's. The loose ends are tied up in seven paragraphs of omniscient narration. The Morlands are very surprised to be asked by Henry Tilney "for their consent to his marrying their daughter." They are willing "to sanction the engagement" but cannot do so until the General gives his consent, too. This approval is speeded up by the marriage of Eleanor "with a man of fortune and consequence." Eleanor kept her relationship a secret owing to her lover's lack of wealth, the "inferiority of [his] situation." But "his unexpected accession to title and fortune [he becomes a viscount, she a viscountess] had removed all his difficulties," and the barriers to the marriage disappear. "The influence of the Viscount and Viscountess in their brother's [Henry's] behalf" helps to change General Tilney's hostility to the marriage of Henry and Catherine. Further, the General learns "that Catherine would have three thousand pounds. This was so material an amendment of his late expectations, that it greatly contributed to smooth the descent of his pride." In addition, "the Fullerton estate, being entirely at the disposal of its present proprietor, was consequently open to every greedy speculation." So there is the strong suggestion that Catherine will inherit the Fullerton estate.

In the final paragraph of the novel, "Henry and Catherine were married, the bells rang and every body smiled; and . . . this took place within a twelve-month from the first day of their meeting." Henry is 26 and Catherine is 18. The narrator concludes that the General's "unjust interference" rather than being negative was a positive for it improved "their knowledge of each other, and [added] strength to their attachment." The novel ends on an ambiguous note: "I leave it to be settled by whomsoever it may concern, whether the tendency of this work [NA] be altogether to recommend parental tyranny, or reward filial disobedience."

There are several areas of interest to note in this final chapter. First, the General becomes the villain of the novel. He gives his permission for the marriage of Henry and Catherine only by deferring to rank and fortune: Eleanor has become a "Viscountess" and he, the General, can "be a fool if he liked it!" He also makes Henry "the bearer of his consent, very courteously worded in a page full of empty professions to Mr. Morland." The General is to the end insincere. The author, on the other hand, is also a manipulator of words. She has to tie up her loose ends and to unite Henry and Catherine. She can do so by introducing a secret relationship in the very last chapter, that between Eleanor and a "gentleman . . . long withheld only by inferiority of situation." Unlike her fictional General, Jane Austen as author confesses to her artifice. She tells her readers directly: "I too have only to add—(aware that the rules of composition forbid the introduction of a character not connected with my fable)" that Eleanor's gentleman's "negligent servant left behind him" the washing bills discovered by Catherine at Northanger Abbey. This suggests a clandestine relationship between Eleanor and her suitor at the Abbey!

Jane Austen, as has been noted, is not afraid to be honest with her readers and to address them directly. She says that although Henry and Catherine are in a state of "anxiety," this need not apply, "I fear, to the bosom of my readers, who will see in the tell-tale compression of the pages before them, that we are all hastening together to perfect felic-

ity." Jane Austen, the supreme artist, remains in total control of her narrative (249–252).

CRITICAL COMMENTARY

NA was first published with *Persuasion* in December 1817. A brief notice in the *Gentleman's Magazine* (July 1818) observes that *NA* "is decidedly preferable to" *Persuasion*, "not only in the incidents, but even in its moral tendency." There is a substantial review in the *British Critic* of March 1818. This finds fault with the depiction of General Tilney: "not a very probable character . . . not pourtrayed with our author's usual taste and judgement." This assessment is close to that of Jane Austen's fellow novelist Maria Edgeworth. In a letter of February 1818, she writes, "The behaviour of the General . . . packing off the young lady without a servant of the common civilities which any bear of a man, not to say a gentleman, would have shown, is quite outrageously out of drawing and doubt of nature." Archbishop Richard Whately, in an unsigned review of *NA* and *Persuasion* in the *Quarterly Review* (January 1821), pays more attention to *Persuasion* but does find space to praise "John Thorpe, with his horse that *cannot* go less then 10 miles an hour, his refusal to drive his sister 'because she has such thick ankles,' and his sober consumption of five pints of port a day," Whately adds, "altogether the best portrait of a species, which, though almost extinct cannot yet be classed among the Palaeotheria, the Bang-up Oxonian." In addition, "Miss Thorpe, the jilt of middling life, is, in her way, quite as good, though she has not the advantage of being the representative of a rare or a diminishing species" (Whately's emphasis). Henry Crabb Robinson (1775–1867), a literary man, diarist, and recorder of his times, notes in his diary entry for September 23, 1842, that he has just finished reading *Persuasion* and *NA*: "These two novels have sadly reduced my estimation of Miss Austen. They are little more than galleries of disagreeables and would-be heroes and heroines are scarcely out of the class of insignificants" (Southam, *Heritage* I: 16–17, 86, 101–102).

Somewhat similar views are found in the observations of two Victorian novelists and admirers of Jane Austen. Margaret Oliphant (1828–1897) is not surprised that Jane Austen is little read as her work is "so calm and cold and keen." She is, however, full of praise for *NA*: "Such a picture of delightful youth, simplicity, . . . and absurdity and natural sweetness, it is scarcely possible to parallel." Writing in her *The Literary History of the Nineteenth Century* (1882), Oliphant is full of enthusiasm for Catherine Morland, who "with all her enthusiasm and her mistakes, her modest tenderness and right feeling, and the fine instinct which runs through her simplicity is the most captivating picture of a very young girl which fiction, perhaps, has ever furnished." Oliphant draws attention to Jane Austen's use of *The Mysteries of Udolpho* in *NA* and its influence on Catherine: "Miss Austen makes her laughing assault upon Mrs. Radcliffe." When she can turn her attention away from Catherine for a moment, Oliphant notes that "the machinery of the story is wonderfully bad, and General Tylney [*sic*] an incredible monster, but all the scenes in Bath—the vulgar Thorpes, the goodhumoured Mrs. Allen—are clear and vivid as the daylight." She returns to Catherine, who "herself throughout always the most delightful little gentlewoman, never wrong in instinct and feeling, not withstanding all her amusing foolishness" (Southam, *Northanger Abbey*: 21, 53–54).

Oliphant's fellow novelist Julia Kavanagh (1824–77), writing in her *English Women of Letters* (1862), devotes more than six paragraphs to *NA*. Kavanagh writes that Jane Austen "laughed at her . . . heroine Catherine Morland . . . and described her by negatives." Kavanagh has reservations about Jane Austen, whose "powers so great should fail somewhere." Jane Austen's "Irony, though gentle, was a fault, and the parent of much coldness." She thought *NA* the least satisfactory of Jane Austen's novels. Kavanagh's discussion is limited to exhibiting Austen's satire in depicting Catherine and the Thorpes.

Writing in 1870 following the publication of James Edward Austen-Leigh's *A Memoir of Jane Austen*, Richard Simpson (1820–76) presents a more complex picture of the novel that anticipates subsequent critical reactions. Simpson, in an unsigned review of Austen-Leigh in the *North Brit-* ish *Review* (April 1870), sees *NA* as a reflection of its author's readings in Goldsmith, Hume, and Robertson, as well as Richardson and Dr. Johnson. *NA* "retains the traces and flavour of" its writer's early juvenilia and in particular "her parodies . . . designed not so much to flout at the style as at the unnaturalness, unreality, and fictious morality, of the romances she imitated." The novel's "heroine is a girl who thinks that Mrs. Radcliffe's novels give a real picture of life," and has a "polemical intention," of exposing the limitations of such novels. Simpson also has interesting observations on characterization in *NA*, drawing attention to other characters besides Catherine. "Miss Thorpe the flirt, and young Thorpe the fast Oxford Man . . . are fools rather on their moral than on their intellectual side" (Southam, *Critical Heritage*, I: 178, 196, 242, 255, 261).

The prolific man of letters George Saintsbury (1845–1933), in his preface to the 1894 illustrated edition of *Pride and Prejudice*, summed up the critical problems felt by so many regarding *NA*: "To some the delightful freshness and humour of [the novel], its completeness, finish and *entrain* [narrative flow], obscure the undoubted critical facts that its scale is small, and its scheme, after all, that of burlesque or parody, a kind in which the first rank is reached with difficulty."

Fresh perspective on the novel is provided by Reginald Farrer. In an essay published on the centenary of Jane Austen's death in the *Quarterly Review* (July 1917), Farrer devotes two paragraphs to *NA*, which he regards as superior to *Sense and Sensibility* and *Pride and Prejudice*. For Farrer, the novel is a work of transition between its author's early and late work. He writes, "in [the novel] Jane Austen takes a big stride forward. Developing her taste for technical problems, she here tackles a very difficult one . . . that of interweaving two motives, of parody and serious drama." Also she focuses "with her three great personal outbreaks—on Novels, on Folly in Females, and on the Vanity of Feminine Motives in Dress." Farrer regards Catherine as "our most delightful of all *ingénues* [unsophisticated young woman], but her story is kept so constantly comic that one has not time to concentrate on its chief figure."

In his introduction to the Oxford University Press 1930 World Classics edition of the novel, the scholar and novelist Michael Sadleir (1888–1957) gives a detailed account of the gothic novels mentioned in *NA*. Such literary historical emphasis in discussions of *NA* has lasted to the present time. Two years later, another novelist, Rebecca West (1892–1983, pseudonym of Cicely Isabel Fairfield) in her introduction to a Jonathan Cape edition of the novel published in 1932 and revised in 1940, draws attention to two other considerations subsequently also to preoccupy critics: the historical elements and its "feminism." Jane Austen through "indirectness" draws attention to the French Revolution and "the Napoleonic wars that were ravaging Europe during the whole of her adult life." Her "feminism" is seen in the depiction of Catherine Morland, and "shows us how the good creature was flattered by the romantic conception of love and womanhood.... To these illusions Jane Austen opposes the truth in her bitter invention of General Tilney's mercenary pursuit of Catherine and his unmannerly dismissal of her" (Southam, *Heritage,* II: 215, 261, 294, 295).

Mary Lascelles, in *Jane Austen and Her Art* (1939), argues that the parody, burlesque elements of the novel are not integrated with General Tilney's behavior toward Catherine. D. W. Harding, in his "Regulated Hatred: An Aspect of the Work of Jane Austen" (1940) and a subsequent essay on the novel, finds structural weaknesses between the literary elements in *NA* and the Catherine Henry–Eleanor Tilney plot. On the other hand, Marvin Mudrick, in his *Jane Austen: Irony as Defense and Discovery* (1952), argues that Jane Austen deliberately created a contrast between these two elements in order to demonstrate the superiority of the realistic elements to the literary ones (Southam, *Northanger Abbey:* 22).

Joseph Wiesenfarth, in his chapter on *NA* in his *The Errand of Form: An Assay of Jane Austen's Art* (1967), emphasizes the importance of words "throughout ... because their choice and their relation to reality distinguish true from false and good from bad." For Wiesenfarth, "in no novel is [Jane Austen's] concern for words as morally and [a]esthetically persuasive as it is in [*NA*], where mastery of language becomes the outward aspect of Catherine Morland's radical human effort to mature" (28–29).

NA as a novel of education is the focus of, for instance, Howard S. Babb's treatment of the novel in his *Jane Austen's Novels: The Fabric of Dialogue* (1962) and Alastair M. Duckworth in his *The Improvement of the Estate: A Study of Jane Austen's Novels* (1971). Duckworth argues that *NA* is a fiction of education in which its heroine Catherine learns to make "moral choices." He instances in the first volume three tests or trials: her invitation to Claverton Down, the Blaize Castle episode, and Clifton. From these experiences, she begins to resist temptation (94–95).

The 18th-century literary and historical contexts of the novel are thoroughly explored in the seventh chapter of Marilyn Butler's *Jane Austen and the War of Ideas* (1975). Further, *NA* "establishes the antiphonal role of dialogue and free indirect speech which is to be so important in [Austen's] career." For Butler, *NA* "subjects the conventional matter of the ... subjective novel to consistently critical handling." Jane Austen's achievement "is to rethink the material of the conservative novel in terms that are at once naturalistic and intellectually consistent" (177, 180–181). A similar literary historicist approach is taken in Jocelyn Harris's *Jane Austen's Art of Memory* (1989). *NA,* she writes, "far from being the slightest of her novels, dramatizes" the ideas found in John Locke's *Essay Concerning Human Understanding,* published posthumously in 1706. Harris shows how much the language and the ideas in *NA* reflect Locke's and "displays the powers of human understanding. It shows how they work, and describes to what ends they are given" (ix, 24).

Other influential diverse readings of *NA* include Claudia L. Johnson's. In her *Jane Austen: Women, Politics, and the Novel* (1988), she views *NA* as "an alarming novel to the extent that it, in its own unassuming and matter-of-fact way, domesticates the gothic and brings its apparent excesses into the drawing rooms of 'the midland counties of England'" (47: *NA,* 200). Its radical critique of English life depicted in the irony of gothic fantasy has not gone unnoticed. Edward Neill, in his *The*

Politics of Jane Austen (1999), writes that *NA* "is not only a novel about the novel, but also about fictions as well as fiction, about imaginary relations to real existences" epitomized by the attitudes of General Tilney—dictatorial and mercenary (28). Others, such as Griffin (1963), perceive the novel as "an extensive examination of the process of novel-reading" (34). Wallace (1988) believes that its real subject is parody (262); Gary Kelly, on the other hand, in his "Jane Austen, Romantic Feminism, and Civil Society" (1995), views *NA* in terms of Jane Austen's complex views of women in a society during a period of transition.

Feminism, gothic, and earlier literary traditions, education, satire, and issues of unity are ongoing reactions to *NA*. A survey of its reception should not ignore continuing discussion as to its composition and dating. As noted, this raises several issues as to its relationship to Jane Austen's juvenilia, specifically to CATHARINE, OR THE BOWER (1792), the manuscript called LADY SUSAN ([1794]), gothic fiction, and whether Jane Austen continually revised *NA* over a 20-year or so period. Another issue is why she doubted in her letter to Fanny Knight dated March 13, 1817, "that she [the novel] will ever come out" (*Letters*, 333). C. S. Emden's "The Composition of [*NA*]" (1968) remains the fullest discussion of such issues.

CHARACTERS

Alice (Chapter 28)   Just before leaving Northanger Abbey, Catherine is asked by Eleanor to write to her "at Lord Longtown's, and I must ask it, under cover to Alice" (228). Eleanor is fearful of being found out by her father, General Tilney. Alice is probably Eleanor's maidservant or the daughter or maidservant of Lord Longtown, an old friend of General Tilney.

Allen, Mr. (Chapters 1–4, 7–15, 18, 20, 22, 29)   The principal landowner in the Fullerton neighborhood, Mr. Allen is "a sensible, intelligent man" (20). He has to go to Bath "for the benefit of a gouty constitution" (17). He lives a quarter of a mile from the Morlands. The Bath visit is the reason for Catherine's visit, as she is invited by Mrs. Allen to accompany her and Mr. Allen. Although

not actively interfering in the arrangements his wife makes for Catherine, he gives her useful counsel when appropriate. At Bath, he tends to retreat from the assembly "mob" (20) into the peace and quiet of the card room.

Allen, Mrs. (Chapters 1–4, 7–15, 18, 20, 22, 29)   The childless wife of Mr. Allen, she "was one of that numerous class of females, whose society can raise no other emotion than surprise at there being any men in the world who could like them well enough to marry them. She had neither beauty, genius, accomplishment, nor manner." The author adds, "The air of a gentlewoman, a great deal of quiet, inactive good temper, and a trifling turn of mind, were all that could account for her being the choice of . . . Mr. Allen." She is attached to Catherine, and it is her idea to invite Catherine to join her and her husband during their visit to Bath. "Dress was her passion. She had a most harmless delight in being fine," and "In one respect she was admirably fitted to introduce a young lady into public, being fond of going every where and seeing every thing herself as any young lady could be" (20). Her conversation revolves around fashion or the trivial or commonplace. Most of her time is spent in "busy idleness" (67). In the role of Catherine's chaperon in Bath, she is rather heedless of the company kept by Catherine, and her advice is at times unwise, for instance, on the subject of Catherine's accompanying John Thorpe alone in an open phaeton. She is more preoccupied with her own clothes than "the comfort of her protégée" (21). She illustrates Jane Austen's sense that intelligent men such as Mr. Allen prefer women with a "trifling turn on mind" (20), as they pose no threat to their sense of superiority. She writes, "A woman, especially if she have the misfortune of knowing any thing, should conceal it as well as she can." But then she undermines this by referring to "the capital pen of a sister author" (111). Nowhere in the novel is it suggested that Mrs. Allen is malevolent.

Andrews, Miss (Chapters 6, 16)   Miss Andrews, probably from Putney (a suburb southwest of London), where the Thorpes live (205), is "a particular friend of" Isabella Thorpe. She reads all the "horrid" novels she can but "could not get through the first volume" (42) of Samuel Richardson's *Sir Charles Grandison; or, The Happy Man*, which contains an attempted seduction and opens with a discussion of clothing and fashion in hats. According to Isabella, Miss Andrews is "a sweet girl, one of the sweetest creatures in the world." She is spending her time "netting herself the sweetest cloak you can conceive." Further, Isabella "think[s] her as beautiful as an angel, and [is] so vexed with the men for not admiring her" (40–41). Isabella subsequently tells Catherine that she "remember[s] too Miss Andrews drank tea with us . . . and wore puce-coloured sarsenet [soft fine fabric]; and she looked so heavenly, that I thought your brother [James Morland] must certainly fall in love with her" (118). She is, in short, indicative of the superficial, insipid young women with whom Isabella Thorpe keeps company.

Corteney, General (Chapter 17) A former fellow military man and "very old" friend of General Tilney. His failure to show up in Bath means that "there is nothing to detain me [General Tilney] longer in Bath" (139).

Davis, Charlotte (Chapter 27) According to Isabella, at the conclusion of Captain Tilney's stay at Bath, "he was always by the side of Charlotte Davis: I pitied his taste, but took no notice of him" (217). Tilney clearly prefers her company to that of Isabella.

"Dorothy" (Chapter 20) A fictitious "ancient housekeeper" created by Henry Tilney as a character in his parody of the gothic romantic novels, he tells Catherine Morland as they travel from Bath to Northanger Abbey. "Dorothy," he tells Catherine, "no less struck by your appearance, gazes on you in great agitation, and drops a few unintelligible hints . . . that the part of the abbey you inhabit is undoubtedly haunted, and informs you that you will not have a single domestic within call." Catherine, however, is not as incredulous as it may seem. She tells Henry Tilney, "This is just like a book!" and "I am sure your housekeeper is not really Dorothy" (158–159).

Emily (1) (Chapter 14) As Catherine walks "round Beechen Cliff," she tells Eleanor and Henry Tilney, "It always puts [her] in mind of the country that Emily and her father travelled through" in Ann Radcliffe's *The Mysteries of Udolpho*. Henry too mentions that "Emily herself left poor Valancourt [her true love] when she went with her aunt into Italy" (106–107). Emily, the heroine of Radcliffe's novel, is sent away on the death of her father. Auerbach notes that Catherine's reference to Emily "carries double irony as Austen mocks Catherine for being reminded of French scenery when she only has read about it in a book by an English author who never went to France!" (90).

Emily (2) (Chapter 14) One of "two of the sweetest girls in the world." She "had been [one of Anne Thorpe's] dear friends all the morning." Catherine is "glad that Anne should have the friendship of Emily and a Sophia to console her" after her exclusion from the Clifton excursion trip (115).

Fletcher, Sam (Chapter 10) A friend of John Thorpe who has a horse to sell: "A famous clever animal for the road—only forty guineas." He and Fletcher "mean to get a house in Leicestershire" for the next hunting season (76).

The Lady Frasers (Chapter 26) Neighbors of General Tilney who, during Catherine's visit to the Abbey, "wished the Lady Frasers had been in the country," but they "were not in the country," otherwise probably they would have provided her with entertainment (209).

Freeman (Chapter 7) An acquaintance of John Thorpe from Christ Church College, Oxford. He sells his gig to Thorpe for "fifty guineas." According to Thorpe, "the iron-work was good as new, or better." Thorpe "hate[s] haggling, and poor Freeman wanted cash" (46).

Hart, Captain (Chapter 6) A dancing partner of Isabella Thorpe. She told him, she claims in a conversation with Catherine, that at a winter assembly at their Putney home "that if he was to tease me all night, I would not dance with him, unless he would allow Miss Andrews to be as beautiful as an angel" (40). Such observations reveal the superficial nature of the speaker, Isabella Thorpe.

Hodges, the (Chapters 6: 27) Friends in Bath of Isabella Thorpe. She tells Catherine, "Charles Hodges will plague me to death I dare say; but I shall cut him very short" (130–131). Subsequently, when Captain Tilney has left her, Isabella goes to a play "with the Hodges's, for a frolic, at half-price: they teased me into it," she writes Catherine, "and I was determined they should not say I shut myself up because Tilney was gone" (217)

Hughes, Mrs. (Chapters 8, 9) An acquaintance of both Mrs. Thorpe and an old school friend of the late Mrs. Tilney. She is part of the Tilney party during their Bath visit. Her information on the Tilney family is provided at secondhand by Mrs. Thorpe and Mrs. Allen. According to Mrs. Allen, the late Mrs. Tilney, when Miss Drummond, "had a very huge fortune," and "Mrs. Hughes saw all the clothes after they came from the warehouse." She is the source of information that "there was a very beautiful set of pearls that Mr. Drummond gave his daughter on her wedding-day." Mrs. Hughes too says that Henry Tilney "is a very fine young man" (68–69). At the second ball, she accompanies Eleanor to the dance floor and finds a place for her beside Catherine; this provides the opportunity for their first conversation.

Jackson (Chapter 7) An Oxford associate of John Thorpe, Jackson, from Oriel College, bid 60 guineas for Thorpe's new gig and horse (47).

King, Mr. (Chapter 3) James King was the actual master of ceremonies, the gentleman who met every visitor and made the appropriate introductions in the Lower Room at Bath from 1785 to 1805. He first introduces Henry Tilney to Catherine Morland (27).

Longtown, Marquis of (Chapters 17, 28) General Tilney is disappointed that "the Marquis of Longtown," one of his "very old friends," is not in

Bath (139). He subsequently uses as an excuse, "We are going to Lord Longtown's near Hereford for a fortnight" (224), to dismiss Catherine Morland from Northanger Abbey.

"Matilda" (Chapter 20) "The wretched Matilda" (160) is a character Henry Tilney has created in his parody of gothic novels during his journey with Catherine to Northanger Abbey from Bath.

Mitchells, the (Chapters 11, 27) A family acquainted with the Thorpes in Bath (90). Following her breakup with James Morland, Isabella writes to Catherine that they were spiteful toward her when she "happened to sit by" them at a play. Isabella says, "Anne Mitchell had tried to put on a turban like mine, as I wore it the week before at the Concert, but made wretched work of it" (217).

Morland, Catherine (1) (referred to throughout the novel) The eldest daughter of the Morlands of Fullerton. The author somewhat ironically comments in the opening chapter: "her heart was affectionate, her disposition cheerful and open, without conceit or affectation of any kind—her manners just removed from the awkwardness and shyness of a girl; her person pleasing, and, when in good looks, pretty—and her mind about as ignorant and uninformed as the female mind at seventeen usually is" (18). As a girl, she was plain and without accomplishments, loving boys' games including cricket. At 15, "appearances were mending; she began to curl her hair and long for balls; her complexion improved, her features were softened by plumpness and colour, her eyes gained more animation, and her figure more consequence" (14–15).

There is unfortunately no mysterious lover awaiting her at home. The reader is told in a sentence not without allusions to 18th-century novels such as Henry Fielding's *Tom Jones*: "There was not one family among their acquaintance who had reared and supported a boy accidentally found at their door—not one young man whose origin was unknown. Her father had no ward, and the squire of the parish no children" (16). Her neighbors the Allens invite Catherine to accompany them to Bath, where she meets people and goes to her first ball. These meetings with Isabella and John Thorpe, Eleanor and Henry Tilney, are to have a profound impact on Catherine. The novel "is really as much 'about' Catherine Morland's growth to maturity, her moral education, as it is about her going to Bath and finding a husband" (V. Jones, 23).

The narrative focuses on Catherine, her experiences in Bath, then Northanger Abbey, and her subsequent return home. Events are recounted from her point of view although modulated by the omniscient narrator. For instance, following her first ball, Catherine is becoming more critical of John Thorpe, especially following a drive with him. Jane Austen as narrator conveys her growing awareness of his limitations: "Little as Catherine was in the habit of judging for herself, and unfixed as were her general notions of what men ought to be, she could not entirely repress a doubt, while she bore with the effusion of his endless conceit, of his being altogether agreeable" (66). The novel begins with the ironic narrator telling her readers that the central character, Catherine, and the plot of her novel has little relationship if any to real life: "No one who had ever seen Catherine Morland in her infancy would have supposed her born to be an *heroine* [my emphasis]" ([13]). Catherine, however, is called a heroine 20 times in the novel. "In all, Austen uses *heroine, hero, heroism, heroic, heroines* more times in" this novel "than double that of [her] other novels combined" (Auberach, 72).

Catherine does not speak in the opening chapter. It is the author as narrator who tells her readers about her. Catherine's first words occur in the second chapter at the Bath Upper Rooms, and at her first ball she whispers to Mrs. Allen, "How uncomfortable it is . . . not to have a single acquaintance here! . . . What shall we do? . . . Had not we better go away as it is?" (22). Catherine is naive and honest. She also is trusting, for instance, failing to perceive for some considerable time that Isabella is a false friend. When friendly with Isabella Thorpe, she is reading Ann Radcliffe's *The Mysteries of Udolpho.* This reading, as opposed to her real-life experience with other people, subsequently is to influence her reactions at Northanger Abbey.

At Bath, John Thorpe attempts to gain Catherine's affection, but her integrity and lack of sophis-

tication draw her to Henry and Eleanor Tilney. She is invited to Northanger Abbey by their father, General Tilney. Catherine's reaction, "her passion for ancient edifices was next in degree to her passion for Henry Tilney" (141), reveals that she is still living in the world of imagination rather than reality. Her judgment is affected by "visions of romance" (199), by her reading of gothic literature. They fill her with suspicion and lead her, especially with regard to the death of Mrs. Tilney and the General's alleged role in her death, to unfounded conclusions. She is at a moment's notice sent home without escort or explanation by the General, who hitherto treated her with the utmost consideration and kindness.

The reason for her expulsion from Northanger Abbey is the discovery by General Tilney that Catherine is not, as he thought, a rich young heiress. In spite of what she experiences and learns, Catherine's "mind is warped by an innate principle of general integrity" (219). Henry Tilney defies his father, follows Catherine to Fullerton, and proposes. His father is reconciled finally to the marriage. His opposition, "so far from being really injurious to their felicity, was perhaps rather conducive to it, by improving their knowledge of each other, and adding strength to their attachment" (252). In short, Catherine is crucial to the structure and the plot of the novel, which resolves around her education to reality. Mrs. Morland comments, "we must live and learn" (236) "and this is just what Catherine does in" *NA* (Wiesenfarth, 22).

Morland children (Chapters 1, 13, 28) Catherine, the eldest daughter, has two sisters and three brothers who have names in the work. The sisters are Harriet (four) and Sarah (Sally) (16). The brothers are Richard (older but no age given; Mrs. Morland refers to "poor Richard's cravats [240]), James (another older brother), and George (six). In the opening paragraph of the novel, the narrator tells her readers they are "A family of ten children ([13]).

Morland, James (Chapter 4, 6, 7, 10, 11, 13, 15, 16, 19, 25, 29) James Morland, Catherine's elder brother, plays an important role in the structure of *NA*. Physically James and his sister Catherine are "exceedingly like" (32). At Oxford, he was a college friend of John Thorpe and stays with the Thorpe family at their Putney home for the final week of the Oxford vacation. At Putney, he meets John Thorpe's sister Isabella, with whom he has formed an attachment. He and John visit Bath in February. John becomes attracted to Catherine, and James is infatuated with Isabella, to whom he becomes engaged. James returns home to secure his financial position. Isabella, upon realizing that he is not from a wealthy family, jilts him for Captain Tilney. This is a bitter blow to James, who breaks off their engagement and returns to Oxford. His mother observes that James "will be a discreeter man all his life, for the foolishness of his first choice" (237). His mother believes "it could not be a desirable thing to have him engaged to a girl . . . who was so entirely without fortune" (236). James, during the Bath period, gives little if any counsel to his younger sister Catherine. His experience with Isabella highlights one of the central messages of the book: appearances are deceptive and money plays a crucial part in human affairs.

Morland, Mrs. (Chapters 1, 2, 15–17, 28–31) Catherine Morland's mother had 10 children. She "was a woman of useful plain sense, with a good temper, and, what is more remarkable, with a good constitution" ([13])—in other words, she is healthy. She "was a very good woman, and wished to see her children every thing they ought to be; but her time was so much occupied in lying-in and teaching the little ones, that her elder daughters were inevitably left to shift for themselves" (15). Wisely, following Catherine's abrupt return home from Northanger Abbey, Mrs. Morland observes, "I am sorry for the young people . . . they must have a sad time of it; but as for any thing else, it is no matter now; Catherine is safe at home, and our comfort dos not depend upon General Tilney" (234).

Morland, Rev. Richard (Chapters 1, 2, 17, 28–31) Catherine's "father was a clergyman, without being neglected, or poor, and a very respectable man . . . he had never been handsome. He had a considerable independence, besides two good liv-

ings—and he was not in the least addicted to locking up his daughters" ([13]). Sensible and cautious, when Catherine goes to Bath, "instead of giving her an unlimited order on his banker, or even putting an hundred pounds bank-bill into her hands, gave her only ten guineas, and promised her more when she wanted it" (19). Otherwise, he rarely makes an individual appearance in the novel, either as a speaker or as the subject of the narrator's observations. He is indissolubly tied to his wife as "Mr. and Mr. Morland" (see, for instance, 234). He is away from home when Henry Tilney calls at Fullerton, so is unable to "support" his wife "in giving encouragement, as in finding conversation for her guest" (242). He and Mrs. Morland are "surprise[d] on being applied to by Mr. Tilney, for their consent to his marrying" Catherine. They are agreed "that the General should come forward to solicit the alliance" between Catherine and Henry. Both Catherine's parents' "tempers were mild, but their principles were steady" (249). Apart from being the object of the narrator's humor at the start of the novel concerning his name being the all too common one of Richard ([13]), nothing negative is said about Richard Morland.

Parrys, The (Chapter 2) Friends of the Allens who did not "come, as they talked of once" (23), to the first Ball Catherine attends in Bath.

Parry, George (2) Catherine "might have danced with" (23) him at her first Bath Ball, if his family had attended it.

Robinson (Chapter 26) During Catherine's visit to Woodston Parsonage with General Tilney, she admires "a sweet little cottage . . . among the trees. . . . It is the prettiest cottage!" The General responds "You like it—you approve it as an object;—it is enough. Henry, remember that Robinson is spoken to about it. The cottage remains" (214). Robinson is probably the head gardener or responsible for the General's estate management.

Skinner, Dr., and family (Chapters 2, 8) The Skinners are neighbors of the Allens at Fullerton. They "were here [in Bath] last year" (22). Dr.

Skinner was in Bath "for his health last winter" for three months "and came away quite stout" (54), or in good health, rather than obese.

Smith, Miss (Chapter 8, 10) The "young lady" Henry Tilney "danced with on Monday" at the Bath assembly. She is "an acquaintance of Mrs. Hughes" (73). On the Monday Catherine had looked for Henry, she is free to dance with him after reluctantly having to refuse his offer to dance, because of a prior engagement with John Thorpe. However, "she saw [Henry] leading a young lady [Mrs. Smith] to the dance" (58). She is "disappointed and vexed" (59) that he does not renew the offer to dance. Catherine here is revealing her growing attachment to Henry Tilney.

Sophia (Chapter 14) With Emily, one of Anne Thorpe's new friends made very quickly "to console her" (115) following her exclusion from the excursion to Clifton.

Thorpe, Anne (Chapters 4, 14) Mrs. Thorpe's second daughter, she is left out of the excursion to Clifton. Catherine encounters her "loitering towards Edgar's Buildings [in Bath] between two of the sweetest girls in the world [Emily and Sophia], who had been her dear friends all morning." She overplays her lack of concern and exaggerates, telling Catherine "there is not a soul at Clifton at this time of the year." Catherine is glad that Anne "should have the friendship of an Emily and a Sophia to console her" (114–115).

Thorpe, Edward (Chapter 4) Mrs. Thorpe's second son, "at Merchant Taylors'" school (32).

Thorpe, Isabella (Chapters 4, 13, 27) Aged 21, she is the eldest of the three Thorpe sisters. She serves as a very useful learning experience for Catherine Morland. Isabella has "great personal beauty" (34) combined with "decided pretension . . . resolute stilishness" (55), and was "ungenerous and selfish, regardless of every thing but her own gratification" (98). Isabella "purposely misuse[s] words to deceive." Like her brother John, she has "no regard for the meaning of words or for pro-

priety in using them." Isabella "is a great offender with adjectives and adverbs and has affection for superlatives" (Wiesenfarth, 14, 17). For instance, "dearest, sweetest Catherine" is transformed into her "best and oldest friend" (98). Following her engagement to James, she says that she is "the happiest of mortals" (121). A favorite word of Isabella is "amazingly." She uses the adverb on 16 occasions: "I scold them all amazingly" (40); "something amazingly insipid about her" (41); and to instance two other examples, she tells Catherine somewhat disingenuously that she finds Captain Tilney "amazingly conceited" (135); and she tells Catherine that "young men especially . . . are so amazingly changeable, and inconstant" (146). This, ironically in light of her apparent change of affections from James Morland to Captain Tilney after she has discovered that James has not the fortune she thought he had, and then seemingly back to James after Tilney has jilted her, could well be applied to her.

Her misuse of language is paralleled by her actions. She dances with Frederick Tilney in spite of her reassurances to Catherine that in the absence of James Morland, she will not dance with anybody. She promised to marry James and decides that "the smallest income in nature would be enough for me" (119). She soon breaks the engagement, saying that "it is not a trifle that will support a family now-a-days; and after all that romancers may say, there is no doing without money." She tells Catherine, "What one means one day, you know, one may not mean the next. Circumstances change, opinions alter" (146).

Isabella has an important role in Catherine's voyage from innocence to experience of people and the world. She quickly affects to be Catherine's closest friend. Initially Catherine is taken in by her chatter concerning fashion and how to deal with men. She also finds Isabella's apparent interest in gothic fiction fascinating. Isabella is incapable of reading anything but pot-boiling romances, and she dismisses Richardson's *Sir Charles Grandison*. She attempts rather clumsily at times to match Catherine with her uncouth brother, John, and to disengage Catherine from Eleanor and Henry Tilney. Her flirtation with Frederick Tilney, and shabby treatment of James Morland, reveal to Catherine

Isabella's "strain of shallow artifice." After reading Isabella's lengthy letter defending her actions and her attempt to get Catherine to intercede with James on her behalf, Catherine tells Henry and Eleanor, "She must think me an idiot.... I see what she has been about. She is a vain coquette, and her tricks have not answered" (218).

Thorpe, John (Chapters 4, 7, 15, 18, 30) John Thorpe is the eldest of the Thorpe children and a fellow student with James Morland at Oxford. He is "a stout young man of middling height, who, with a plain face and ungraceful form, seemed fearful of being too handsome unless he wore the dress of a groom, and too much like a gentleman unless he were easy where he ought to be civil, and impudent where he might be allowed to be easy" (45). Boorish, inept in social manners, he seems obsessed with his horse, carriage, gig, buying, and selling—in short, horse and carriage trading. Continually exaggerating and bragging, he plays an important plot function as his claims mislead General Tilney into believing that Catherine Morland is from an exceedingly wealthy family. Following Catherine's rejection of his awkward proposal and the collapse of an attempt to reconcile Isabella and James Morland, he encounters General Tilney in London. He now describes the Morlands as a "necessitous family," they were "aiming at a style of life which their fortune could not warrant; seeking to better themselves by wealthy connexions; a forward, bragging, scheming race" (246). He is believed by General Tilney, who, returning to Northanger Abbey, instantly dismisses Catherine from his home.

John Thorpe claims to have read M. G. Lewis's gothic thriller *The Monk*, calling it a "tolerably decent" work, although he had just previously asserted, "I never read novels; I have something else to do. . . . Novels are all so full of nonsense and stuff" (48). In common with his sister, his exaggerated use of language has little relation to the truth. He constantly blasphemes: "O! d—said I,' 'I am your man'"; "O! d—it, when one has the means of doing a kind thing by a friend, I hate to be pitiful" (46–47); and to give one more example from several instances: "No, if you do not go; d—me, if I do" (99). Prejudiced, he asserts that all Jewish

people are wealthy (63). In short, Thorpe "is quick to damn and to insult, and slow to perceive and to understand" (Wiesenfarth, 18). Pleased by his own use of words, he is dishonest to Catherine concerning the Tilneys in order that he may take her to Clifton. He lies also to the Tilneys, telling them that Catherine has a prior engagement, his motive being to go with her again to Blaize Castle. He has an important function in the novel: Catherine learns not to trust what he says. He is important for her education and destiny. Without his lying about her wealth, General Tilney would not have cultivated her and encouraged Catherine's relationship with his younger son Henry and daughter Eleanor.

Thorpe, Maria (Chapters 4, 14) With Anne, one of Isabella's "underprivileged younger sisters" (121). The youngest, she too imitates her older sister in dress and manners. She goes with John Thorpe to the Clifton outing "quite wild to go. She thought it would be something very fine" (115).

Thorpe, Mrs. (Chapters 4–5, 8–9, 15, 25, 29) "Mrs. Thorpe was a widow, and not a very rich one; she was a good-humoured, well-meaning woman, and a very indulgent mother" (34). A school friend of Mrs. Allen, "they had been contented to know nothing of each other for the last fifteen years" (32) After meeting again by chance at the Bath Pump-room, they renew their friendship. Mrs. Allen has no children. Mrs. Thorpe six grown-up ones. She is talkative and she has three daughters with her in Bath. She lives at Putney, and her husband was a lawyer. Two of her children, Isabella and John, play an important role in Catherine's growth to awareness of others and the world beyond Fullerton.

Thorpe, William (Chapter 4) Mrs. Thorpe's third son—"at sea" (32).

Tilney, Eleanor (Chapter 8 and throughout) "Miss Tilney had a good figure, a pretty face, and a very agreeable countenance; and her air, though it had not all the decided pretension, the resolute stilishness of Miss Thorpe's [Isabella's], had more real elegance." The narrator adds, "Her manners shewed good sense and good breeding; they were neither shy, nor affectedly open." Unlike Isabella or John Thorpe, Eleanor is "without exaggerated feelings of extatic delight or inconceivable vexation" (55–56). Sister of Frederick and Henry Tilney, she is introduced to Catherine Morland at the Upper Rooms in Bath. She represents a sharp contrast in manners and behavior to Isabella Thorpe, proving to be a true friend to Catherine rather than a false, deceiving one. Eleanor makes Catherine very welcome at Northanger Abbey and is distressed by her father's conduct toward Catherine. She does everything she can to comfort and help her, and she gives her money so that Catherine can get home safely to Fullerton from the Abbey.

In addition to being a moral contrast to Isabella and a true friend to Catherine the heroine, Eleanor exemplifies Jane Austen's irony at work in *NA*. The author parodies in her novel gothic romance novels and their conventions of horror, sensation, and romantic intrigue. Ironically, Northanger Abbey itself during Catherine's visit becomes the setting for both, with Eleanor playing a central role. Catherine incorrectly believes that Eleanor's mother has either been imprisoned or worse by General Tilney, her father. General Tilney creates a sensation by summarily evicting Catherine. She is somewhat rescued by Eleanor, who helps her on the journey home. In the last chapter of the novel, the reader learns of Eleanor's secret meetings with her impoverished lover, who then becomes extremely wealthy and gains a title. Eleanor's marriage to "a man of fortune and consequence" (250) meets with her father's approval.

The narrator comments at the conclusion of *NA*: "I know no one more entitled, by unpretending merit, or better prepared by habitual suffering, to receive and enjoy felicity" (251). Eleanor Tilney proves indeed to be an appropriate role model for Catherine Morland.

Tilney, Captain Frederick (Chapters 14, 16, 18–20, 24–27)

According to Catherine's far from objective point of view, Captain Tilney's "air was more assuming, and his countenance less prepossessing. His taste and manners were beyond a doubt decidedly inferior" to those of his younger

brother Henry. General Tilney's eldest son is "a very fashionable-looking, handsome young man" (131). Isabella Thorpe pretends to dislike him, and she overtly flirts with him. Isabella, who deceives Catherine in her excessive display of affection for her and her brother James, is in her turn deceived, too. Captain Tilney's flirtation with her results in her breaking off her engagement with James in the misperception that Tilney will marry her. He soon, however, becomes interested in Charlotte Davis, whose company he clearly prefers at the end of his Bath visit. Assigned little dialogue in the novel, he leaves Bath to rejoin his regiment, the 12th Light Dragoons. Catherine Morland's reading of his character as being "decidedly inferior" (131) to Henry his brother, is revealed to be correct.

Tilney, General (Chapters 10, 12, 13, 16–17, 22–26, 28–31)

A widower whose marriage to a Miss Drummond, the school friend of Mrs. Hughes, brought him to enormous fortune. Father of Henry, Frederick, and Eleanor Tilney, he is "a handsome man, of a commanding aspect, past the bloom, but not past the vigour of life" (80). However, he is a dominating father "accustomed on every ordinary occasion to give the law in his family" (247), inflexible, and concerned with financial and class status. He comes to Bath apparently for health reasons but curtails his stay when he realizes that his friends the Marquis of Longtown and General Courteney are not in Bath. Misled by John Thorpe's exaggeration into believing that Catherine Morland is very wealthy, he is excessively polite toward her and anxious to encourage the friendship between her and his son Henry and daughter Eleanor. He appears in Bath to be "such an agreeable, worthy man" (238).

He invites Catherine to Northanger Abbey. On the journey from Bath to the Abbey, Catherine notices that he is "always a check upon his children's spirits" (156). At the Abbey, he continues to treat Catherine well. Her visit is characterized by "His anxiety for her comfort—his continued solicitations that she would eat" although he insists on regimental punctuality over meal times and Captain Tilney arouses the General's "impatience" (154). He chooses to visit Woodston, where Henry lives, and accompanied by Catherine and Eleanor, he informs Henry: "Well, well, we will take our chance some one of those days. There is no need to fix." He then proceeds to "fix," telling his son, "But on Wednesday, I think . . . you may expect us." Catherine is puzzled by this and other inconsistencies including contradicting attitudes to food. She asks herself: "but why he should say one thing so positively, and mean another all the while, was most unaccountable! How were people, at any rate, to be understood?" (210–211).

Such behavior adds to Catherine's vivid imagination, stimulated by her readings in gothic novels. She speculates concerning the death of Mrs. Tilney and believes that in common with the villainous actions in the novels she has read, the General has either imprisoned or murdered his wife. The irony of this is that the General does act in a villainous manner. He leaves for London for a week, "and he left Northanger earnestly regretting that any necessity should rob him for even an hour of Miss Morland's company" (220). Meeting John Thorpe in London and believing what he is now told, contrary to previously, that the Morlands are not wealthy, he returns home and summarily evicts Catherine from his home. He violates the rules of hospitality and chivalry, simply because he believes that she is not rich. Catherine then believes that "she had scarcely sinned against his character or magnified his cruelty" (247).

Eleanor's marriage to a wealthy, titled man meets with his full approval. There is little difficulty in obtaining his approval for the marriage of Henry and Catherine, especially when he learns that Catherine will bring a not inconsiderable sum to the marriage. In short, the General is primarily motivated by wealth. Dictatorial, at home he is moody, "slowly pacing the drawing-room for an hour together in silent thoughtfulness, with downcast eyes and contracted brow" (187). Contrary to Catherine's perceptions, she learns from Henry that the General "loved" his late wife "as well as it was possible for him to." Henry adds, "His value of her was sincere; and, if not permanently, he was truly affected by her death" (197). Notwithstanding Henry's observations, the General "has all the integrity of a John or Isabella Thorpe." Henry, his son, "knows exactly

how to deal with him" (Wiesenfarth, 24). The General's letter to Mr. Morland giving his consent to the marriage of Henry to Catherine, the reader is informed in the last paragraph of the novel, is "very courteously worded in a page full of empty professions" (252). In short, "to the very end" of this novel "the abuse of language distinguishes the insincerity of General Tilney as it had that of the Thorpes before him." The General, in company with the Thorpes, exemplifies a major concern of *NA*: the exposure of "the vices of vanity and avarice, expressed in the hypocrisy and lies of the general and John and Isabella." (Wiesenfarth, 28).

Tilney, Henry (Chapter 3 and throughout) The clergyman and apparent hero of the novel. When first introduced to Catherine Morland, "He seemed to be about four or five and twenty, was rather tall, had a pleasing countenance, a very intelligent and lively eye, and if not quite handsome, was very near it" (25). However, there are contrary perceptions. Eleanor, for instance, judges her brother to be "more nice than wise" (108).

The younger son of General Tilney, he holds the living of Woodston, 20 miles from Northanger Abbey. Well educated and well read, he and his sister genuinely like Catherine and take great pleasure in her company. He enjoys teasing Catherine with wordplay and is not afraid to make fun of her romantic illusions. It says much for his empathy for Catherine that he overlooks the seriousness of her accusations against his father's treatment of his mother. He is attracted by Catherine's lack of sophistication and by her honesty. When he learns of his father's behavior to her at the Abbey, he rushes to Fullerton for assurance of her safe return home and declares his affection for her. Henry refuses to go with his father to Lord Longtown's. He remains loyal to Catherine in spite of his father's initial refusal to give him consent to their marriage.

Henry Tilney acts as a normative character in the novel in the sense that he sets standards by which other characters are judged. For instance, his precise use of language stands in stark contrast to the use of language by Isabella and John Thorpe, and General Tilney. He instructs Catherine but is not adverse from playing elaborate word games with her and elaborately compares dancing to marriage (77–78). He deplores "the common cant" (38) and, unlike many of the other characters in the novel, dislikes Bath, telling Catherine "Bath, compared with London, has little variety, and so every body finds out every year" (78).

But Henry Tilney is a more complex hero than it may appear. He is a foil to the egocentricity of James Morland and the idle talk of John Thorpe, but he tells Catherine that his sister Eleanor is "stupid" (113). He is, according to Claudia Johnson in *Jane Austen: Women, Politics and the Novel*, "a self-proclaimed expert on matters feminine, from epistolary style to muslin" (37). From the very first encounter with Catherine, he assumes to know what is best for her and tends to doubt her word, for instance, when she tells him "perhaps, I keep no journal" (27). His self-confidence and self-assurance silence Catherine. She is "fearful of hazarding an opinion" in his presence "in opposition to that of a self-assured man" (48).

Henry in his verbal games with Catherine carried out, for instance in the carriage ride from Bath to Northanger Abbey, plants ideas in her mind. He has overheated her imagination, something that Catherine herself recognizes when obsessing over the cabinet and its contents, she reflects: "How could she have so imposed on herself? . . . And it was in a great measure his [Henry's] own doing, for had not the cabinet appeared so exactly to agree with his description of her adventures, she should never have felt the smallest curiosity about it" (173).

Henry's patriotism, his "short disposition on the state of the nation" conducted on the Beechen Cliff walk, is partly to bring Catherine "to silence" (111). Subsequently, when Catherine is found by Henry in his late mother's bedroom and he realizes that she suspects his father, General Tilney, of foul deeds, he launches into a defense of middle England: "Remember the country and the age in which we live. Remember that we are English, that we are Christians." He adds, "Does our education prepare us for such atrocities? Do our laws connive at them?" Henry then confesses in a highly ironic passage that such conduct could not be possible in a country "where every man is surrounded by a neighbourhood of voluntary spies" (197–198).

As noted, Henry's motives for marrying Catherine are even called into question: "he felt himself bound as much in honour as in affection to Miss Morland" (247). An ambiguous hero, he is loyal and faithful toward Catherine and refuses to be bullied by his father in giving her up. Antifeminist he may be at times and domineering, "within a twelve-month from the first day of their meeting," he marries Catherine, "to begin perfect happiness" at the age of "twenty-six" (252).

Tilney, Mrs. (née Drummond) (deceased) (Chapters 9, 25) The deceased wife of General Tilney and mother of Henry, Eleanor, and Frederick Tilney. She possessed "a very large fortune; and when she married," according to Mrs. Allen, whose source is Mrs. Hughes, a "school-fellow" of Miss Drummond, "her father gave her twenty thousand pounds [an enormous sum] and five hundred to buy wedding-clothes." She also received on her wedding-day "a very beautiful set of pearls" now in the possession of Eleanor Tilney (68–69). She died from a "malady . . . one from which she had often suffered, a bilious fever" (196), nine years before the start of the novel. According to Henry Tilney, She was "loved" by the General, her husband, and by her children (197). Catherine's fantasies concerning the fate of Mrs. Tilney constitute much of the gothic comedy and irony at Northanger Abbey.

Viscount, the (unnamed) (Chapter 28) The secret admirer of Eleanor Tilney. He is not able to marry her until "his unexpected accession to title and fortune had removed all his difficulties" and gained her father's assent. He "was really deserving of her [Eleanor]; independent of his peerage, his wealth, and his attachment, being to a precision the most charming young man in the world" (251). The reader also learns in the final chapter that the Viscount's forgetful servant had left behind the laundry bills Catherine finds in the bedroom cabinet at Northanger Abbey. The unnamed Viscount is a brilliant device to resolve plot entanglements. His sudden ascending to wealth and title allow Eleanor to marry as they do Catherine and Henry.

BIBLIOGRAPHY

Primary Texts

Jane Austen's Letters. Collected and edited by Deirdre Le Faye. 3d ed. Oxford: Oxford University Press, 1995.

Northanger Abbey. Edited by Barbara Benedict and Deirdre Le Faye. *The Cambridge Edition of the Works of Jane Austen.* Cambridge: Cambridge University Press, 2006.

Northanger Abbey and Persuasion. Edited by R. W. Chapman. *The Novels of Jane Austen, V.* 3d ed. London: Oxford University Press, 1965 reprint (with revisions) [Page numbers in Roman numerals refer to this edition.]

Northanger Abbey. Edited by Marilyn Gaul. "A Longman Cultural Edition." New York and London: Pearson, Longman, 2005.

Northanger Abbey. Edited by Claire Grogan. Broadview Literary Texts Reprint. Peterborough, Ontario, Canada: Broadview Press, 1998.

Northanger Abbey . . . Edited by James Kinsley and John Davie, with an introduction and notes by Claudia L. Johnson. Oxford World's Classics. Oxford: Oxford University Press, 2003.

Secondary Works

Auerbach, Emily. *Searching for Jane Austen.* Madison: University of Wisconsin Press, 2004.

Austen-Leigh, J. E. *A Memoir of Jane Austen and Other Family Recollections.* Edited by Kathryn Sutherland. Oxford World's Classics. Oxford: Oxford University Press, 2002.

Butler, Marilyn. *Jane Austen and the War of Ideas.* Oxford: Clarendon Press, 1975.

Duckworth, Alistair M. *The Improvement of the Estate.* Baltimore. Johns Hopkins University Press, 1971.

Emden, Cecil S. "The Composition of *Northanger Abbey,*" *Review of English Studies,* NS. 19, no. 75 (August 1968): 279–287.

Gay, Penny. *Jane Austen and the Theatre.* Cambridge: Cambridge University Press, 2002.

Griffin, Cynthia, "The Development of Realism in Jane Austen's Early Novels," *English Literary History* 30 (1963): 36–52.

Harding, D. W. *Regulated Hatred and Other Essays on Jane Austen.* Edited by Monica Lawlor. London and Atlantic Highlands, N.J.: Athlone Press, 1998.

Harris, Jocelyn. *Jane Austen's Art of Memory.* Cambridge: Cambridge University Press, 1989.

Johnson, Claudia L. *Jane Austen: Women, Politics, and the Novel.* Chicago and London: University of Chicago Press, 1988.

Jones, Darryl. *Jane Austen.* Houndmills, Basingstoke, Hampshire, U.K.: Palgrave Macmillan, 2004.

Jones, Vivien, *How to Study a Jane Austen Novel.* Houndmills, Basingstoke, Hampshire, U.K.: Macmillan, 1987.

Kelly, Gary. "Jane Austen, Romantic Feminism, and Civil Society." In *Jane Austen and the Discourse of Feminism,* edited by Devoney Looser, 19–33. New York: St. Martin's Press, 1995.

Lane, Maggie. *Jane Austen and Food.* London: Hambledon Press, 1995.

Miller, D. A. *Jane Austen, or The Secret of Style.* Princeton, N.J., and Oxford: Princeton University Press, 2003.

Neill, Edward. *The Politics of Jane Austen.* London and New York: Macmillan and St. Martin's Press, 1999.

Page, Norman. *The Language of Jane Austen:* Oxford, U.K.: Basil Blackwell, 1972.

Phillipps, K. C. *Jane Austen's English.* London: Andre Deutsch, 1970.

Southam, B. C., ed. *Jane Austen: Northanger Abbey and Persuasion: A Case Book.* London: Macmillan, 1976.

———. *Jane Austen: The Critical Heritage.* 2 vols. London: Routledge and Kegan Paul, 1978–1979.

Wallace, Tara Ghoshai. "*Northanger Abbey* and the Limits of Parody," *Studies in the Novel,* 20, no. 3 (Fall 1988): 262–73.

Wiesenfarth, Joseph. *The Errand of Form: An Assay of Jane Austen's Art.* New York: Fordham University Press, 1967.

"Ode to Pity" (1933)

COMPOSITION AND PUBLICATION

The final item in Jane Austen's *Volume the First* is dedicated to her sister, CASSANDRA. This parody of a conventional poetic form is followed by the "June 3d 1793" dating and represents an example of Jane Austen's late juvenilia, being written when she was 18. Included in the sixth volume of R. W. Chapman's edition of Jane Austen's *The Works* and in Margaret Anne Doody and Douglas Murray's 1993 edition of *Catharine and Other Writings* (70–71), it also is found with a commentary in David Selwyn's edition of *Jane Austen Collected Poems and Verse of the Austen Family* (1996). The manuscript copy is now in the Bodleian Library, Oxford.

CRITICAL COMMENTARY

The "Ode to Pity" consists of two rhymed verses. The first verse has seven lines rhyming irregularly; the second verse also rhymes irregularly and has nine lines. The "Ode" imitates the odes of the 18th-century poets William Collins (1721–59) and Joseph Warton (1722–1800). "The Myrtle Grove" in the second line of the first verse is probably a reference to "the Myrtle Shed," the opening line of Collins's well-known "Ode to Pity." In the second verse, the use of "brawling" in the opening line relates to the "flowing with the noise and commotion, as a brook." In line 14 of the poem "the Abby too a mouldering heap" echoes lines in Joseph Warton's "Ode to Fancy"—"to some abbey's mouldering towers." Selwyn observes that the 18-year-old Jane Austen inverts "the picturesque melancholy of [the] imagery" of Collins and Warton. In her poem, "silent" streams "brawl down the turnpike road," and abbeys "conceal'd by aged pines . . . rear" their heads to "take a peep." Selwyn writes, "The final joke is of course that, for all its language of generalized sympathy, the poem never alludes to pity at all" (78).

BIBLIOGRAPHY

Primary Texts

Austen, Jane. "Ode to Pity." In *The Works of Jane Austen*, Vol. 6, *Minor Works*, edited by R. W. Chapman. Oxford: Oxford University Press, 1986. [All textual references are to this edition.]

———. "Ode to Pity." In *Jane Austen's* Catharine *and other Writings*, edited by Margaret Anne Doody and Douglas Murray, 70–71. Oxford: Oxford University Press, 1993.

———. *Collected Poems and Verse of the Austen Family.* Edited with an introduction and notes by David Selwyn, 3, 78. Manchester, U.K.: Carcanet Press, 1996.

———. "Ode to Pity." In *The Jane Austen Library. Volume the First*, edited by R. W. Chapman, with a foreword by Lord David Cecil, a preface by Brian Southam, and a preface by R. W. Chapman, 137–138. London: Athlone Press, 1984.

———. "Ode to Pity." In *Juvenilia. The Cambridge Edition of the Works of Jane Austen.* Edited by Peter Sabor. Cambridge: Cambridge University Press, 2006, 96–97.

Secondary Works

Lambdin, Laura Cooner, and Robert Thomas Lambdin. "Humor and Wit in Jane Austen's Poems and Charades." In *A Companion to Jane Austen Studies*, edited by Laura Cooner Lambdin and Robert Thomas Lambdin, [275]–281. Westport, Conn: Greenwood Press, 2000.

"Opinions of Emma"

"Opinions of *Emma*," together with "Opinions of *Mansfield Park*," consists of collections of comments made by Jane Austen from letters to her and what she heard and from family remarks relating, on the one hand, to *Emma*, and on the other, to *Mansfield Park.* The undated manuscript is now in the British Library and probably belongs to the 1816 period. The opinions on *Emma* reflect those of the work's earliest readers.

The "Opinions of *Emma*" was first published in William and Arthur Austen-Leigh's *Jane Austen: Her Life and Letters* (1913), then in R. W. Chapman's *Plan of a Novel* (1926), then in his *Minor Works*, where they are annotated. They are also to be found in the first volume of B. C. Southam's "Critical Heritage" volume, published in 1979. Extracts are found also in J. Austen-Leigh's 1871 *Memoir*.

BIBLIOGRAPHY

Austen, Jane. "Opinions of *Emma*." In James Edward Austen-Leigh's *A Memoir of Jane Austen and Other Family Recollections* [1871], edited by Kathryn Sutherland, 114. Oxford: Oxford University Press, 2002.

———. "Opinions of *Emma*." In William and Arthur Austen-Leigh, *Jane Austen: Her Life and Letters*, 328–331. London: Smith Elder, 1913.

———. "Opinions of *Emma*." In *Plan of a novel according to hints from various quarters, by Jane Austen, with opinions on* Mansfield Park *and* Emma *collected and transcribed by her . . .* , edited by [R. W. Chapman], [14–19]. Oxford, U.K.: Clarendon Press, 1926.

———. "Opinions of *Emma*." In *The Works of Jane Austen*, vol. 6, *Minor Works*, edited by R. W. Chapman. Revised and edited by B. C. Southam, [436]–439. Oxford: Oxford University Press, 1986.

———. "Opinions of *Mansfield Park*." In *Jane Austen Volume I, 1811–1870. The Critical Heritage*, edited by B. C. Southam, 55–57. London and New York: Routledge, 2 vols., 1979, 1987.

"Opinions of *Mansfield Park*"

"Opinions of *Mansfield Park*" together with "Opinions of *Emma*" consists of collections of comments made by Jane Austen from letters to her and what she heard and from family remarks relating, on the one hand, to *Mansfield Park*, and, on the other, to *Emma*. The undated manuscript is now in the British Library. The *Mansfield Park* opinions reflect those of the work's very earliest readers and date from 1814 and 1815.

The "Opinions" were initially published in R. W. Chapman's *Plan of a Novel* (1926), then in his *Minor Works*, where they are annotated. They are also to be found in the first volume of B. C. Southam's "Critical Heritage" volume, published in 1979. Extracts are found also in J. Austen-Leigh's 1871 *Memoir*.

BIBLIOGRAPHY

Austen, Jane. "Opinions of *Mansfield Park*." In James Edward Austen-Leigh's *A Memoir of Jane Austen and Other Family Recollections* (1871), edited by Kathryn Sutherland, 106. Oxford: Oxford University Press, 2002.

———. "Opinions of *Mansfield Park*." In *Plan of a novel according to hints from various quarters, by Jane Austen, with opinions on* Mansfield Park *and* Emma *collected and transcribed by her . . .* , edited by [R. W. Chapman], [10–13]. Oxford, U.K.: Clarendon Press, 1926.

———. "Opinions of *Mansfield Park*." In *The Works of Jane Austen*, vol. 6, *Minor Works*, edited by R. W. Chapman. Revised and edited by B. C. Southam [431]–435. Oxford: Oxford University Press.

———. "Opinions of *Mansfield Park*." In *Jane Austen Volume I, 1811–1870. The Critical Heritage*, edited by B. C. Southam. London and New York: Routledge, 2 vols., I: 48–51. 1979, 1987.

Persuasion (1817)

COMPOSITION AND PUBLICATION

Jane Austen began the last novel she was to finish, which was called *Persuasion* after her death, on August 8, 1815. The first draft was completed on July 18, 1816. James Edward Austen-Leigh recalls that his aunt was dissatisfied with what she had written and especially how the lovers' reunion is effected.

> She thought it tame and flat, and was desirous of producing something better. This weighed upon her mind, the more so probably on account of the weak state of her health, so that one night she retired to rest in very low spirits. But such depression was little in accordance with her nature, and was soon shaken off. The next morning she awoke to more cheerful views and brighter inspirations; the sense of power revived; and imagination resumed its course. (Le Faye. *Jane Austen: The World of Her Novels*: [278]).

She revised the last two chapters, completing them on August 6, 1816. The holograph manuscript of these concluding original chapters, now in the British Library, is the only manuscript in existence of her six major novels. In a letter to her niece Fanny Knight dated March 13, 1817, Jane Austen, probably referring to this novel, writes, "I have a something ready for Publication, which may perhaps appear about a twelvemonth hence. It is short." She also wrote to Fanny Knight on March 23,

1817, "Do not be surprised at finding Uncle Henry acquainted with my having another ready for publication. I could not say No when he asked me, but he knows nothing more of it.—You will not like it, so you need not be impatient. You may *perhaps* like the Heroine, as she is almost too good for me" (*Letters*, 333, 335: Jane Austen's emphasis).

The delay in seeing the novel published may be due to a number of factors. Her brother Henry recalls that his sister was slow to begin the publication process. He writes, "For though in composition she was equally rapid and correct, yet an invincible distrust of her own judgment induced her to withhold her works from the public, till time and many perusals had satisfied her that the charm of recent composition was dissolved." There may also have been financial and health reasons leading to delay. Jane Austen died on July 18, 1817. Henry, who also probably gave it the title *Persuasion,* steered the novel through publication. There was a Jane Austen "family tradition that" she "referred" to the work "as *The Elliots*" (Le Faye, 278).

John Murray published *Persuasion* with *Northanger Abbey* in two volumes and Henry Austen's "Biographical notice" of his sister, on December 10, 1817, although 1818 is on the title page of the joint four-volume edition. *Persuasion* was volume 3 and 4. The work was published at its author's family's expense. The publisher John Murray received a 10 percent commission on sales. Some 1,750 copies were printed. Sales were good, as only 321 copies remained with publishers by the end of 1818. The total profit for the Austen family came to £515.17.7. Some of the remaining copies were exported to Australia. There is an advertisement in the *Sydney Gazette,* June 9, 1821, announcing a copy (Gilson, 85).

Carey and Lea, the Philadelphia publishers, produced the first American edition on November 8, 1832, in an edition of 1,250 copies. A French translation by Mme Isabelle de Montolieu was published in Paris in 1821 under the title *La Famille Elliot, ou L'Ancienne Inclination. Persuasion* was included in Bentley's cheap Standard Novels series, published in 1833 and reprinted frequently during the 19th century. R. Brimley Johnson's first Everyman library edition was published in 1892. Subsequently, *Persuasion* has been frequently reprinted.

Page references in the ensuing discussion will be to the third edition reprinted with revisions to volume 5 of R. W. Chapman's *The Works of Jane Austen: Northanger Abbey, Persuasion* (1965).

THE DATING OF *PERSUASION*

Persuasion differs from Jane Austen's other novels. Its action is specifically dated as taking place during the summer of 1814 and the middle of February 1815. The reader is told about the events that occurred during the summer of 1806, a year after the Battle of Trafalgar, when a young naval Commander, Frederick Wentworth, proposed to and was accepted by Anne Elliot. Under family pressure she breaks the engagement, and Wentworth returns to sea, "feeling himself ill-used" (28).

The action of the novel opens in Kellynch Hall, Anne's ancestral home in Somerset, in southwest England. There are various allusions in the novel to external events. In the early months of 1814, with the advance of anti-Napoleonic troops throughout France, it was clear that Napoleon would be defeated. In April 1814 he abdicated and was exiled to the island of Elba in the Mediterranean. On May 30, 1814, a peace treaty with France was signed in Paris. In June, various monarchs, politicians, and generals, including Alexander I of Russia and Frederick William III of Prussia, visited London to celebrate the victory over Napoleon.

Fortunes fluctuated in 1814 on a personal level. We learn from the opening chapter that the extravagant lifestyle of the vain Sir Walter Elliot left him deeply in debt and that he is forced to leave Kellynch Hall, the ancestral home, and to rent it out. On the other hand, 1814 is a very convenient moment for renting: "This peace will be turning all our rich Navy Officers ashore. They will be all wanting a home" (17). The heroine, Anne, however, is frequently transplanted to various locations, her travels reflecting social fragmentation and movement in a wider context. Such then is the international, national, and local context at which *Persuasion* begins.

SYNOPSIS

The action of *Persuasion* takes place between the summer of 1814 and the middle of February 1815;

therefore, approximately seven months are covered within its 24 chapters.

Volume 1

A family chronology is given of the Elliot family of Kellynch Hall in Somersetshire. As the novel begins, only one daughter, Mary, is married, the youngest. The elder Elizabeth, born June 1, 1785, and Anne, born August 9, 1787, are not. Their mother died in 1800 and Mary, born on November 20, 1791, married Charles Musgrove, the son and heir of a rich neighbor on December 16, 1810. They have two children, Charles and Walter, and live at Uppercross Cottage near Uppercross Hall, three miles from Kellynch, and home of the elder Musgroves. Sir Walter Elliot, born March 1, 1760, has no sons. The heir to Kellynch Hall is a nephew, William Walter Elliot. Around 1802–03, there was a possibility of a marriage between Elizabeth and Sir Walter's nephew, but she was snubbed and Elliot married someone much richer. Elizabeth is the first lady at Kellynch and at 29 in danger of remaining unmarried. She and her father are full of their own self-importance, the estate since Lady Elliot's death has been mismanaged, and they are in debt.

The second daughter, Anne, the main character in the novel, was close to her late mother, whom she resembles, and has "an elegance of mind and sweetness of character, which must have placed her high with any people of real understanding" (5). Her father and elder sister, Elizabeth, treat her with disdain, her younger sister Mary, a hypochondriac, uses her. Lady Russell, the close friend of her mother, truly values Anne, acts as a surrogate mother to her, and continues to advise the family. She and Anne are such close friends that when 19 in summer 1806, Lady Russell advised Anne to break off an attachment and she did so. Captain Frederick Wentworth, then 23, had few prospects and no connections to speak of. Anne knew that Lady Russell had her best interests at heart, but regrets breaking the engagement and pines for Wentworth. This is the reason given for the apparent loss of her good looks and vivacity, "her bloom" (6).

Mr. Shepherd, Sir Walter's agent, advises him to retrench, to let Kellynch Hall, and to move to more reasonable accommodation in Bath. Persuaded by Mr. Shepherd, Lady Russell, and Anne, Sir Walter agrees. In Bath, Lady Russell hopes Anne may find a suitable suitor and Sir Walter will break off the close friendship with Mr. Shepherd's widowed daughter, Mrs. Clay, who has undue influence over him. The Napoleonic Wars have just concluded, and returning naval officers who made fortunes during the wars return to England, looking for suitable property. Initially horrified by Shepherd's suggestion, Sir Walter agrees to Kellynch being rented to Admiral Croft, who has local connections. He is married to the sister of the previous curate of a neighboring parish, Edward Wentworth (brother of Captain Frederick Wentworth, Anne's former fiancé). Anne is concerned that Wentworth may soon visit Kellynch. He has risen in the ranks to become a captain, and Anne, who has followed his career in the newspapers and naval listings, is aware that he is now very wealthy and unmarried.

Sir Walter is to leave for Bath in September, the Crofts to move in shortly after. Mary Musgrove insists that Anne spend the autumn at nearby Uppercross helping her, as she is going to be unwell, and Anne is not really wanted in Bath. Anne welcomes this, preferring to stay in the countryside rather than Bath: at least with Mary she will be needed. Lady Russell is unsuccessful in removing Mrs. Clay's influence, as she is going with Sir Walter and Elizabeth to Bath. Anne tries to warn Elizabeth that Mrs. Clay has designs on their father, but she dismisses them, saying that Mrs. Clay has "freckles, and a projecting tooth, and a clumsy wrist" (34).

Sir Walter, Elizabeth, and Mrs. Clay go to Bath. After a few days with Lady Russell, Anne goes to stay with Mary. Although Mary is continually complaining, Anne enjoys the company of her lively children and the nearby Musgroves. They are friendly and have two very pleasant 19- and 20-year-old daughters, Louisa and Henrietta. The Crofts move into Kellynch Hall and come to pay their respects, while Anne discovers that Wentworth is shortly to visit and the Musgroves are anxious to pay respects to him. They had a son, Richard, who died at sea two years previously, and who served under Wentworth, who was kind to him. Wentworth visits Uppercross Hall and Anne avoids the meeting, but the next morning he visits the cottage. Anne finds that her feelings for him are the same as they were. The meeting clearly has unsettled her. The tactless Mary tells her that Wentworth remarked that Anne has changed so much that he hardly recognizes her. Anne is deeply hurt and realizes that she and Wentworth have no future with each other. From Wentworth's perspective, however, he is concerned about Anne and blames her for giving way to Lady Russell. He did not mean to meet her again and does not intend to court her. Having made his fortune, he fully intends to marry and settle down now that he has left the navy.

Wentworth regularly visits Uppercross. Henrietta and Louisa are infatuated with him. Charles Hayter, their cousin, part of a family of poor relations living at nearby Winthrop, is unhappy, as he and Henrietta are courting and he hopes to marry her eventually. Charles Musgrove, Mary's husband, likes Charles Hayter and prefers Wentworth to pay attention to Louisa. Anne is uncomfortable with the situation, especially as she is frequently in Wentworth's company, but he seems to ignore her and is very reserved toward her. One morning, Wentworth calls at Uppercross Cottage and helps Anne out of a difficult situation. She is unnerved by his close physical proximity and startled by his thoughtfulness for her situation. It seems increasingly as if an engagement will be announced between Wentworth and Louisa. Henrietta has taken herself out of contention by declaring her love for Charles Hayter.

The setting moves to Lyme Regis, where Captain Wentworth's wounded naval friend Captain Harville, with his family, has settled for the winter. Harville has been in indifferent health since being wounded in action two years previously. At the Harvilles is Captain Benwick, another of Captain Wentworth's fellow officers. Benwick was engaged to Harville's sister Fanny and is in mourning for her—she died the previous summer. Wentworth's account of a brief Lyme visit creates a will for the others to go also, so in mid-November he takes Charles, Mary, Anne, Henrietta, and Louisa to Lyme. Captain Benwick fails to

impress Anne, as he appears to revel in self-pity; Anne has been stoic following the breakup of her romance with Wentworth, which contrasts with Benwick's self-indulgence. The different attitudes are reflected in his quotations from romantic poetry and Anne's recommendation of the prose of "our best moralists" (101).

After a night at an inn, the Uppercross groups take a pre-breakfast stroll. They pass an elegant-looking gentleman who looks at Anne with admiration. At the inn, they see him again, Anne notes he is in mourning, and they discover that he is William Walter Elliot, her cousin. Mary Musgrove exults in this brief encounter with the future heir of Kellynch, while Anne is content to feel that her cousin appears to be sensible and respectable. Joined by Harville and Benwick, they go out walking again, this time to the Cobb, the ancient harbor wall. Louisa insists on jumping down some steps, but she falls on the hard stone pavement unconscious. Anne is the only one who does not panic, retains common sense, and organizes the distraught others to do something practical to help. Louisa is taken to the Harvilles' home and a surgeon calls to say that, apart from a severe concussion, she will be fine following a period of rest. Wentworth holds himself responsible, as he should have more firmly said no to Louisa's request to jump down the steps. Charles and Mary stay to look after Louisa, Wentworth goes back to Uppercross with Henrietta and Anne. He asks Anne about how they should tell the elder Musgroves and defers to her judgment. She is very flattered. Wentworth returns to Lyme; Anne stays at Uppercross Great House and then returns to stay with Lady Russell at Kellynch Lodge.

Volume 2

The second volume begins with the news that Louisa is not in danger any longer but needs time to recover. The Musgroves go to Lyme to be near her. At Kellynch, Anne is uncomfortable at having to give the news to Lady Russell and to tell her that she has been with Wentworth, whom she believes to be in love with Louisa. They visit Kellynch Hall and are warmly welcomed. Anne is amused to learn that Admiral Croft has removed most of the mirrors he discovered in Sir Walter's dressing room.

She privately reflects that Kellynch Hall has found more worthy occupants than its actual owners.

Mary and Charles return home to report that Louisa is steadily improving. Charles teases Anne about Benwick; he thinks that Benwick is in love with her. The elder Musgroves also return for Christmas with the hope that Louisa and Henrietta will be able to join them by the end of the holiday season. Wentworth has gone to stay with his brother Edward at his parish in Shropshire. Lady Russell and Anne move to Bath, the former to lodgings near Sir Walter and Elizabeth in Camden place, where Anne goes. Anne is surprised at the warmth of her reception; this, it emerges, is only because they wish to show off their new accommodation and reveal how Bath's high society seeks after them. Further, William Walter Elliot has renewed his relations with them, and Anne believes he is intending to court Elizabeth, although she is puzzled by his behavior. William Walter Elliot discovers that Anne is the lady he so admired at Lyme Regis. Anne is impressed by him and begins to compare him favorably with Wentworth, although she is still suspicious about his motives in becoming so friendly with them again. Lady Russell is more impressed by him and dismisses Anne's reservations. The difference between them emerges when he goes out of his way to be overly polite also to the Dowager Viscountess Dalrymple and her daughter the Honourable Miss Carteret, cousin of the Elliots, with whom they have not had contact for many years. Elliot reveals himself to be as snobbish and obsessed with status as Sir Walter and Elizabeth. The Dowager and her daughter lack elegance of mind and manners, yet apart from Anne, the rest including Lady Russell, seem obsessed by rank and apparent wealth.

In contrast to such society, Anne discovers in an impoverished area of Bath a former school friend, Mrs. Smith, whose husband died two years previously, leaving her all but destitute. She has developed rheumatic fever in her legs, leaving her crippled, yet she remains cheerful and resourceful in the face of adversity. Sir Walter disapproves of the visits to someone of Mrs. Smith's social standing, but Anne continues her visit. Mrs. Smith is looked after by the sister of her landlady, a nurse Rooke, who also helps a Mrs. Wallis, married to Colonel Wallis, a close friend of William Walter Elliot.

Lady Russell is convinced that once out of mourning for his first wife, Elliot intends to marry Anne. She, however, remains deeply suspicious of him. At the beginning of February, Admiral and Mrs. Croft appear in Bath. They bring a letter for Anne from Mary Musgrove with surprising information that Louisa is to marry Captain Benwick. Anne decides that poetry has brought them together and is relieved that Wentworth remains "unshackled and free" (167).

Wentworth arrives in Bath, encounters Anne sheltering in a shop from the rain, but finds the meeting emotional, and Wentworth recovers sufficiently to offer to accompany Anne home. However, Elliott reappears and Anne departs with him. The ladies accompanying Wentworth tell him the gossip that Anne and Elliot will at one time marry. Anne for her part looks forward to her next encounter with Wentworth; this occurs at a concert evening.

At the concert, Wentworth is more relaxed when they meet, speaking freely with her. Anne takes her seat knowing that his love has been rekindled but does not notice that Elliot has taken a seat beside her. A game of musical chairs occurs and Anne realizes that Wentworth is jealous of Elliot. This pleases Anne, yet she is uncertain how she can communicate to Wentworth that she loves him and dislikes Elliot.

The following morning, Anne again visits Mrs. Smith, who after hearing that she does not intend to marry Elliot, tells Anne that he is somewhat responsible for her poverty. Her husband had been influenced by him into a foolish, expensive lifestyle, and Elliot refused to act as a trustee on her husband's death and assist her in claiming benefit from a West Indian property. This confirms Anne's suspicions concerning William Walter Elliot; however, his character is even worse than she thought. Nurse Rooke has told Mrs. Smith that he found out from Mrs. Wallis that Elliot's interest in Anne and his sudden renewal of ties with his cousins are due to his fear that Sir Walter will marry Mrs. Clay, produce an heir, and disinherit him.

Later on in the day, Anne meets Elliot but is very reserved toward him. He is leaving Bath the following morning to visit friends. The next day, Anne sees him in conversation with Mrs. Clay, his apparent enemy. Anne has gone to the White Hart Inn to visit the Musgroves, who have unexpectedly come to Bath. They assume that Anne and Elliot are attached. She does her uttermost to let Captain Wentworth know that she prefers his company to Elliot's. Anne the following evening chooses to go with the Musgroves to the theater rather than attend a Camden Place party proposed by Elizabeth her sister.

At the Musgroves' lodgings the following day, Anne is with Wentworth and Captain Harville. Wentworth appears to be writing a letter while Harville and Anne discuss the apparent sudden transformation of affection on the grieving Benwick's part from Fanny Harville to Louisa. Anne tells Harville, with Wentworth listening, "All the privilege I claim for my own sex . . . is that of loving longest, when existence or when hope is gone" (235). Wentworth and Harville leave, Wentworth returns, using the excuse that he has forgotten his gloves, and gives Anne a letter. In this, he declares that he has not stopped loving Anne and asks for a reciprocal signal from her. She experiences "overpowering happiness" (238). Charles Musgrove offers to take her home as she appears to the others unwell. Wentworth catches up with them and offers to replace Charles, who has to see a gunsmith. Finally the two express openly their love for each other. Wentworth explains his foolishness in being involved with Louisa and is relieved when he hears of her engagement to Benwick. This frees him from obligations and he came to Bath to see Anne. He became jealous of Elliot and had almost given up hope.

At the Elliot party the same evening, they talk again. Anne reveals how much she regrets her decision of eight years previously, and if he had asked her again she would have accepted. Wentworth says that he nearly did when he began to amass a fortune but was too proud and resentful to do so. Wentworth is "no longer nobody" (248), has an outstanding reputation, and is wealthy, so Anne's family welcome the match. Lady Russell admits she was wrong in her advice to Anne and becomes affectionate toward Wentworth. She also is forced with the others to admit her error regarding William Walter Elliot, who has eloped with Mrs. Clay to London. As manipulative as he is, Elliot is in danger of being persuaded to marry Mrs. Clay. Mrs. Smith's income is improved as advised by Wentworth, and she is able to recover her husband's West Indian property. She becomes with Lady Russell a close friend of Wentworth and worthy to stand beside his own family. Anne and Captain Wentworth are very happy, her only fear being that Captain Wentworth might be called on to serve his country in the event of a war breaking out again.

CRITICAL SYNOPSIS AND COMMENTARY

Chapter 1

The opening of the novel depicts a man of apparent social standing, title, and property absorbed not with other people but with a book regarding past facts. The only volume Sir Walter Elliot looks at is that recording the past. The book is "the Baronetage," a probable reference to Debrett's *Baronetage of England*, which appeared in two volumes in 1808. From this Sir Walter finds "occupation" and "consolation" ([3]). The positive qualities are in the past, not in the present. From the past he can learn that in 1611 the rank of a baronet was initially created in England. The rank "occupies a marginal position between the gentry and the aristocracy which may help to explain [his] preoccupation with his precise" social position (Bree, 45)

Sir Walter's occupation, absorption, is with the past from which he derives "amusement," no doubt as a "consolation" from the "distressed" realities of the present. He focuses and "could read his own history" although he is "powerless" with all his status, name, title, and geographical location, "Kellynch-hall, in Somersetshire," to alter anything. So before turning to the specific, the author Jane Austen presents to her readers a man powerless and entrapped within a past, apparently distinguished in terms of social rank, which has gone forever. The "leaf" of the volume turns to his own family history and to specific dates. Sir Walter is the last of the line in a patriarchal society, as he has produced no living male heirs. His only son was "still-born," the year of the birth and death not being without significance: 1789, the year of the French Revolution, in which chaos reigned in France and the monarchy and nobility were executed by guillotine. The consequences leading to a power vacuum and the rise of Napoleon were well known to Jane Austen's readers. His navy and army by 1813–14, the period in which *Persuasion* is set, were defeated after years of war. The representative then of the old order, Sir Walter, cemented in the past, has lost his wife and produced three living children. These are all girls: Elizabeth, Anne, and Mary. The male "heir presumptive" is William Walter Elliot, the "great grandson of the second Sir Walter."

Specific names and dates are presented at the opening of the book. A symptom of Sir Walter's obsession with the past is seen in his adding to the printed page the details of his youngest daughter's marriage; "Dec. 16, 1810, Charles, son and heir of Charles Musgrove, Esq. of Uppercross in the county of Somerset" ([3]). His emphasis is on the male line and inheritance, although there is some reduction of status. His son-in-law is not a Baronet, but an "Esq," an owner of property "a landed gentleman who had no other title" (Phillipps, 213). Interestingly, the author precisely dates the marriage as "Dec. 16, 1810" on her own birthday. On December 16, 1810, she would have been 35 years old. Following this information, Sir Walter inserts "most accurately the day of the month on which he had lost his wife."

The third paragraph of the novel tells us "the history and rise of the ancient and respectable family," whose demise the reader is witnessing. Its claim to distinguished ancestry is reinforced by a reference in the first sentence. Sir William Dugdale's *The Ancient Usage in bearing of such Ensigns of Honour as are commonly call'd Arms, with a Catalogue of the present Nobility of England*, mentioned here, was published in 1682. Its function was to decide who was a genuine baronet. Sir Walter is frozen in time, his ancestors even prefigured "the first year of Charles II" ([3]–4), 1660, the year in which 159 Baronets had been newly created. The names of the 159 included Darcy, Morland, Willoughby,

Knightley, Bennet, and Crofts—all characters in Jane Austen's novels (Bree, 46).

Sir Walter's "heir presumptive" is another "Walter Elliot," with the added "William." Jane Austen describes Sir Walter's character in a paragraph of four sentences, beginning with "Vanity was the beginning and the end of Sir Walter Elliot's character, vanity of person and of situation." There are also double repetitive phrases—"The beginning and the end" and "of person and of situation"—as if to reinforce the fact that the historic inheritance concludes with Sir Walter. The second sentence draws attention to his personal appearance: "He had been remarkable handsome in his youth; and, at fifty-four, was still a very fine man." He is unchanging while change takes place all around him. Mutability and its consequences are a major preoccupation of *Persuasion*. The third sentence continues the balanced structural pattern: "Few women could think more of their personal appearance than he did; nor could the valet of any new made lord be more delighted with the place he held in society." The fourth and final sentence of the paragraph further exposes its subject's egoism and limited view of looking at the world, which is but a reflection of himself. "He considered the blessing of beauty as inferior only to the blessing of a baronetcy; and the Sir Walter Elliot, who united these gifts, was the constant object of his warmest respect and devotion." Sir Walter perceives that he "united these gifts" and was "the constant object of his [own] warmest respect and devotion." Transfixed in time, bankrupt, all Sir Walter can do is to contemplate his own navel, to examine himself in a mirror. The dual structure of the sentences mirrors its subject's self-reflexive absorption.

The succeeding paragraph opens with a description of past possibilities removed by death from Sir Walter, who "must have owed a wife of very superior character to anything deserved by his own." His obsession with possession is reinforced through the nearly repetitive "owed" and "own." The only fault the narrator attributes to Lady Elliot who "had been an excellent woman, sensible and amiable," is that a "youthful infatuation" had "made her Lady Elliot." For a period of 17 years until her death, "she had humoured, or softened, or concealed his failings." Clearly "not the very happiest being in the world herself . . . her duties, her friends, and her children . . . make it no matter of indifference to her when she was called on to quit them." Inheritance and legacy are reintroduced from different perspectives: "Three girls, the two eldest," Elizabeth and Anne, aged "sixteen and fourteen, was an awful legacy for a mother to bequeath" when she died in 1800. Not because of their gender but "an awful charge rather, to confide to the authority and guidance of a conceited, silly father," the onus being on Sir Walter rather than his deceased wife.

The reader is then introduced to a character, a close friend of Lady Eliot whose decisions, made in the past, profoundly affect the heroine of the novel. This "one very intimate friend, a sensible, deserving woman," Lady Russell, is described in positive language. She continues "the . . . maintenance of the good principles and instruction" given by Lady Elliot. Immediately Jane Austen assures us that "This friend and Sir Walter did *not* marry," (Jane Austen's emphasis) and tells us that "Thirteen years had passed away since Lady Elliot's death" in 1800. The close friend and Sir Walter "were still near neighbours and intimate friends; and one remained a widower, the other a widow."

The next paragraph begins with giving the reasons why Sir Walter did not remarry. Apparently he had tried to, "having met with one or two private disappointments in very unreasonable applications." A main reason given is his relationship with his single eldest daughter Elizabeth. At the age of 16 she "had succeeded . . . to all that possible, of her mother's rights and consequence." Further, "being very handsome, and very like himself, her influence had always been great, and they had gone on together most happily" (4–5). She shares her father's ageless quality: "she and her father are each other's mirrors, their relationship one of mutual narcissism, for each looks at the other and sees themselves . . . here we have the last and most coldly sterile of all Austen's incestuous relationships" (Jones, 178). The narrator states that Sir Walter "prided himself on remaining single for his dear daughter's sake."

A short sentence encapsulates Sir Walter's attitude to his other children and introduces the reader to the heroine. "His two other children were of very inferior value" (5). The last word has "the now obsolete sense of 'estimate and appreciation of, or liking for, a person or a thing'" (Phillipps, 46). Mary gains "a little artificial importance" as she has married Charles Musgrove. Lowest down in Sir Walter's hierarchy is Anne, who receives some of the author's most positive epithets. Unlike *Emma*, where the heroine is the focus of the opening sentence of the novel, the reader has to wait seven paragraphs until the central character of this novel is briefly described. In contrast with the opening of *Emma*, there is no ambiguity in the description: "But Anne, with an elegance of mind and sweetness of character, which must have placed her high with any people of real understanding, was nobody with either father or sister." Using the free indirect style common to *Persuasion*, the narrator adds, "her word had no weight; her convenience was always to give way." Through conveying what Sir Walter and Elizabeth think of her, it is significant that her name appears at the very end of the sentence and the paragraph: "she was only Anne." Isolation and the failure to recognize real worth is one of the central themes of *Persuasion*.

Somewhat ironically, the brief two-sentence paragraph that follows shows that Anne is not unappreciated. "To Lady Russell, indeed, she was a most dear and highly valued god-daughter, favourite and friend." Lady Russell takes on the role of a fairy godmother to Anne. "Lady Russell loved them all; but it was only in Anne that she could fancy the mother to revive again." Anne's is a Cinderella tale and, as will be revealed, she has taken the advice of her fairy godmother, advice that has profoundly influenced her life. The crucial experience of Anne's life has taken place in the past, before the novel opens. She is no longer youthful; she is neither Emma Woodhouse nor Elizabeth Bennet. "A few years before, Anne Elliot had been a very pretty girl, but her bloom had vanished early" (5–6). Emma, aged 21, had "a *bloom* of full health" (39: my emphasis); however, Anne Elliot's "bloom had vanished early" (6), the beauty and "fine complexion associated with young womanhood" had disappeared (Phillipps, 80). Even before it had withered, "her father had found little to admire in her," "so totally different were her delicate features and mild dark eyes from his own." Here the author interweaves a character's thoughts with her authorial description. Anne does not resemble him; consequently, "there could be nothing in them [her features] now that she was faded and thin, to excite his esteem." The narrative has moved from the author's praise of Anne's personal qualities and Lady Russell's appreciation of them, to the negative perceptions of a selfish father. His preoccupations are those of the opening of the chapter, "his favourite work." He has given up hope of Anne's name appearing in "any other page." His other daughter Mary "had merely connected herself with an old country family of respectability and large fortune." His obsession is with Elizabeth, who is most like him.

Narrative focus shifts from Anne to Sir Walter's preoccupation with himself and with Elizabeth. At "twenty-nine," Elizabeth is an example of "a woman [who] is handsomer . . . than she was ten years before." She has apparently not suffered from "ill health nor anxiety," and consequently "scarcely any charm" has disappeared. It is as if she, like her father, is frozen in time. She was "still the same handsome Miss Elliot that she had begun to be thirteen years ago." She is in pristine condition. Consequently, "Sir Walter might be excused . . . in forgetting her age, or at least, be deemed only half a fool, for thinking himself and Elizabeth as blooming as ever, amidst the wreck of the good looks of every body else." He and his daughter are forever young, while the remainder of his family grows older. The use of a metaphor related to the sea and a shipping "wreck" anticipate the naval element that becomes dominant in the novel. "Wreck" is used to suggest the folly of vanity inherent in people like Sir Walter.

Jane Austen adds that Sir Walter "could plainly see how old all the rest of his family and acquaintance were growing" apart from himself and Elizabeth. The final sentence of the paragraph enters into his perspective. Anne is "haggard." Her married sister Mary is "coarse," a not uncommon epithet in Jane Austen's work to describe a lack of delicacy. In Sir Walter's perspective, "every face in the neighborhood *worsting*" (6: my emphasis), an

example of Jane Austen's "conversions into verbs from common and abstract nouns, from adjectives and adverbs, even from proper names" (Phillipps, 200). At least he shows some personal concern for somebody else: "the rapid increase of the crow's foot about Lady Russell's temples had long been a distress to him."

Time and its consequences are a major preoccupation of the novel. These are movingly displayed in the paragraph focused on Elizabeth, in which her decay is conveyed by the author using repetitious phrases of biblical dimensions and elegiac associations echoing Wordsworth (1770–1850) and his obsession with memory. The passage of time for Elizabeth is conveyed in the repetition of "thirteen years" throughout the paragraph. The word "thirteen" occurs four times. Twice as "thirteen years," once as "thirteen winters' revolving frosts," and then "thirteen springs," which she remembers as "she had the consciousness of being nine-and-twenty." The mutability of her life, although "she was fully satisfied of being still quite as handsome as ever," is marked by a reference to "the book of books," with its biblical association and echo of her own father's similar self-absorption, with which the novel opens. "Always to be presented with the date of her own birth, and see no marriage follow but that of a youngest sister made the book an evil." Cruelly, in a passage blending narrative and dramatic style, "more than once, when her father had left it open on the table near her, had she closed it, with averted eyes, and pushed it away." The pronoun "it" repeated three times, standing for "the book of books," reinforces her father's stasis and Elizabeth's wish to "push it away." In the paragraph words such as "regrets," "apprehensions," "satisfied," "felt her approach to the years of danger," "rejoiced," "enjoyment," and "liked it not" (6–7) constitute "direct descriptions of feeling. There is also the more subtle account of feeling through action in the 'thirteen winters' revolving frosts' which had seen her opening local balls, and the 'averted eyes' with which she closes the Baronetage and pushes it away." As Barbara Hardy observes, "Feeling is stated and acted" (43).

A short paragraph of two sentences reinforces the sense of Elizabeth's failure expressed in the previous paragraph. Words and phrases are repeated that strengthen the "disappointment" and "disappointed" nature of Elizabeth's experience. "That book and especially the history of her own family, must ever present the remembrance of" the disappointment that has become permanent. "The heir presumptive, the very William Walter Elliot, Esq. whose rights had been so generously supported by her father, had disappointed her." The next two paragraphs tell the reader that Elizabeth had been rejected: "Instead of pushing his fortune in the line marked out for the heir of the house of Elliot, he had purchased independence by uniting himself to a rich woman of inferior birth." Money has motivated the heir rather than the dynastic ambition of Elizabeth's father.

Elizabeth's position as a breeder and participant in an auction where she has a definite role is reinforced by the description, first, not of her reaction to the rejection but the description of her father's reactions, which take precedence over hers. "Sir Walter had resented it." He is concerned with appearance, not with his daughter's feelings: "'For they must have been seen together' he observed, 'once at Tattersal's and twice in the lobby of the House of Commons'" (7–8). Tattersal's is a reference to a London auction house for trading horses that "became a popular meeting place for men interested in horses and betting." In addition, "Sir Walter, like some of his ancestors, is a Member of Parliament. Mr. Elliot is clearly not an MP—which would require a considerable private fortune—at this stage is his career" (Bree, 50).

Elizabeth's reactions are conveyed in the opening sentence of the paragraph that follows. She "had liked the man for himself," second, "still more for being her father's heir," and third, her feelings are a reflection her father. His "strong family pride could only see in *him*," Walter, "a proper match for Sir Walter Elliot's eldest daughter" (Jane Austen's emphasis). The heir, William Walter Elliot, like Sir Walter, had lost his wife. Although Elizabeth and her father have not seen him for many years, they are bound to display as relatives some mourning for his loss. Elizabeth "though she was at this present time (the summer of 1814) wearing black ribbons for his wife, she could not admit him to be worth thinking of again." What is taking place in her mind

is subordinated to social convention. Furthermore, Elliot, according to gossip, which is frequently relied upon, had "spoken most disrespectfully of them all, most slightingly and contemptuously of the very blood he belonged to." Such actions "could not be pardoned."

A sentence then conveys the futility of Elizabeth's existence in Kellynch-hall with its "sameness and the elegance, the prosperity and the nothingness." The unproductiveness of life is associated with the necessity to have money. Elizabeth is aware that her father does not retreat into the Baronetage, the "book of books" (7) for no reason. The escape into an existence now gone forever allows him "to drive the heavy bills of his tradespeople, and the unwelcome hints of Mr. Shepherd, his agent, from his thoughts." In short, "her father was growing distressed for money." The fault is Sir Walter's. "While Lady Elliot lived, there had been method, moderation, and economy." This "had just kept him within his income; but with her had died all such right-mindedness, and from that period he had been constantly exceeding it." He is forced to "retrench." Such a retrenchment will mean the disposal or renting of the ancestral home "the Kellynch property" (8–9).

Persuasion is a novel "about the miscarriages of life, about suffering and vulnerability." It is "a novel about 'the art of losing'" (Wiltshire, 196). In fact, "every character in" the novel "has suffered loss or adversity." How they adjust to loss that occurs "in at least one of five areas: property, status, connections, health and love" (Mooneyhan, 147, 146; Showalter, 183) is one of the preoccupations of *Persuasion*. Sir Walter reacts by asking Elizabeth, "Can we retrench? does it occur to you that there is any one article in which we can retrench?" However, he carries on as if nothing has occurred. Elizabeth's reaction is "to cut off some unnecessary charities," second, "to refrain from new-furnishing the drawing room," and third, she "added the happy thought of their taking no present down to Anne, as had been the usual yearly custom." These measures are "insufficient for the real extent of the evil." However, Sir Walter and Elizabeth refuse on "compromising their dignity or relinquishing their comforts."

The final two paragraphs of this opening chapter focus on economic necessity. The reader learns that Sir Walter "had condescended to mortgage as far as he had the power, but he would never condescend to sell. No; he would never disgrace his name so far." The advice of "two confidential friends," Mr. Shepherd and Lady Russell, has been sought on condition that it does not involve "the loss of any indulgence of taste or pride" (9–10). In this first chapter, the heroine Anne has only surfaced tangentially. The emphasis has been on her father, her sister Elizabeth, their vanity, obsession with the past, and the inevitability of change. These themes will recur.

Chapter 2

The second chapter opens with a description of Mr. Shepherd's reaction. He is "a civil, cautious lawyer" who deferred "to the excellent judgment of Lady Russell—from whose known good sense he fully expected to have just such resolute matters" related to the Elliots' financial difficulties "advised." There follows an assessment of the strengths and weaknesses of Lady Russell: "She was a woman rather of sound than of quick abilities." She has "strict integrity herself" and "a delicate sense of honour." On the other hand, "she was as desirous of saving Sir Walter's feelings, as solicitous for the credit of the family, as any body of sense and honesty could well be." Lady Russell "had a cultivated mind and was, generally speaking, rational and consistent." Yet her advice causes the heroine suffering and affects her life. "Not unlike Sir Walter," Lady Russell "had prejudices on the side of ancestry; she had a value for rank and consequence" in the sense of social place and what is due to it. Hence, this "blinded her a little to the faults of those who possessed them," such as Sir Walter and Elizabeth. Her "compassion and consideration" to Sir Walter are due to her being "the widow of only a knight," someone who ranked just below a baronet: "she gave the dignity of a baronet all its due." Sir Walter is also "an attentive neighbour, an obliging landlord, the husband of a very dear friend, the father of Anne and her sisters."

She "did not admit of a doubt" that "they must retrench." This must be "done with the least pos-

sible pain to" Sir Walter and Elizabeth. The "scheme of retrenchment" is undertaken in consultation with "Anne, who had never seemed considered by the others as having any interest in the question." Anne's priorities are "on the side of honesty against importance" or vanity. She prefers "a more complete reformation, a quicker release from debt, a much higher tone of indifference for every thing but justice and equity." Lady Russell refers to a plan undertaken by other "first families" in similar situations. Above all, "the person who has contracted debts must pay them." Honesty is a more important principle, according to Lady Russell, than "the feelings of the gentleman" (11–12). Anne agrees with Lady Russell, and her thoughts are reflections of her mother, who although aware of what was required of position and inheritance practiced "method, moderation, and economy" (9). For Anne, "duty" is part of "dignity," yet her insight "inclined her to think that the sacrifice of one pair of horses would be hardly less painful than of both" to her father and Elizabeth.

Anne's reaction to Lady Russell is conveyed in the use of free indirect speech. Her father's total rejection of the proposal is presented through the use of different kinds of presentation of speech. Authorial comment initially occurs. "How Anne's more rigid requisitions might have been taken, is of little consequence. Lady Russell's had no success at all—could not be put up with—were not to be borne" (13). The tone "is unmistakably imitative of Sir Walter's speech." Also, "the change of style is marked graphologically (by the dashes), lexically (by a more colloquial idiom) ["could not be put up with"], and syntactically." The free indirect speech moves into "telegraphic phrases condensing replies of perhaps much greater length." Through the use of quotation marks, Sir Walter's shocked reaction is conveyed. "There is no introductory verb of saying or attribution to a speaker" (Page, 135). His actual words appear to be used: "What! Every comfort of life knocked off! Journeys, London, servants, horses, table" (13). Yet the last "sentence of the paragraph [is] a clear example of free indirect speech, with verb and pronoun in the appropriate tense and person" (Page, 135). "No, he would sooner quit Kellynch-hall at once, than remain in it on such disgraceful terms."

An implied remark of Sir Walter's, "Quit Kellynch-hall," opens the next paragraph, which combines quotation marks indicating the reported speech of a previous conversation. Narrative and observation interweave with past-tense verbs and the use of the third person "he said." Mr. Shepherd seizes the opportunity suggested by Sir Walter's three words to make a decision. "Sir Walter would quit Kellynch-hall." There are three options: "London, Bath, or another house in the country." Anne prefers the latter option; "a small house in their own neighborhood" would give them "Lady Russell's society," they would "be near Mary," and close to "the lawns and groves of" their old home. She is overruled: "the usual fate of Anne attended her, in having something very opposite from her inclinations," her-wishes, "fixed on." Her home was to be a place "she disliked," Bath—a fashionable large town where the Elliots will have rank and entertainment.

Bath is preferable to London, where Sir Walter's lawyer, Shepherd, feels that his client "could not be trusted." Bath was nearer to Kellynch than London; Lady Russell also spent "some part of every winter there." Her "first views on the projected change had been for Bath." Here "for" is used to mean "in favour of." In this instance, as in other more important ones, Lady Russell opposes Anne's wishes. Her reasons relate to a sense of the descent into a small house "being too much for Sir Walter." Further, Anne herself "would have found the mortification of it more than she foresaw." Lady Russell's objections convey information concerning Anne's past. Her "dislike of Bath" is due to "the circumstance of her having been three years at school there, after her mother's death, and, secondly, from her happening to be not in perfectly good spirits the only winter which she had afterwards spent there with herself." Lady Russell personally prefers Bath, but the focus of narrative attention is gradually moving away from Sir Walter to Anne. Lady Russell's concern for her is conveyed through free indirect speech. "Anne had been too little from home, too little seen. Her spirits were not high. A larger society would improve them." A direct correlation between "health and spirits" is made: "a change . . . must do both . . . good." Then there

follows a sentence in which the author reports Lady Russell's thoughts: "She wanted her to be more known." The focus of narrative attention switches back to Sir Walter and then to Elizabeth. The fact that "Kellynch-hall was to be let" had to be kept "a profound secret," as "Sir Walter could not have borne the degradation of being known to deign letting his house." The act of "letting" rather than selling implies an unwillingness to let go, to hold on somehow to the past.

Another reason for wishing "Sir Walter and his family" removed from Kellynch-hall is that of an "intimacy" between Elizabeth and Shepherd's daughter. She has returned home "after an unprosperous marriage . . . with the additional burden of two children." In Jane Austen's world, the dissolution of the family structure through separation and marital breakdown is very rare. It is unclear whether Shepherd's daughter, a Mrs. Penelope Clay, is widowed or not. She has "the art of pleasing," an art that disturbs Lady Russell. The last two paragraphs of the second chapter focus on Lady Russell's lack of "any influence with Elizabeth," the "selfish arrangements which shut [Anne] out" from London visits and other occasions. They also focus on the "very dangerous companion" for Elizabeth that Lady Russell believes Mrs. Clay to be. Lady Russell's main reason, that she is convinced that Mrs. Clay has designs on Sir Walter, are not yet spelled out. Lady Russell "had never received from" Elizabeth "more than outward attention, nothing beyond the observances of complaisance" (14–16).

Chapter 3

Economic factors and social transformations dominate the opening paragraphs of the third chapter. The first paragraph, spoken by Shepherd, refers to "this peace" that "will be turning all our rich Navy Officers ashore." Shepherd also observes that "Many a noble fortune has been made during the war" and that there is the possibility of "a rich Admiral" coming their way. A "peace" did follow Napoleon's abdication in 1814. However, to speak of "peace" (17) was somewhat presumptuous. Jane Austen knew when she began to write her novel on August 8, 1815, something her characters are unaware of. Napoleon escaped from his exile on

Elba in March 1815 and was finally defeated at the Battle of Waterloo on June 18, 1815. The naval war, to all intents and purposes, was over by 1814. During the war at sea, large fortunes in the form of prize money could be made, especially by naval officers. The capture of an enemy vessel led to its inventory being taken and a "price" tag of contents. The victorious capturing ship's captain claimed as entitlement a considerable percentage of the value. The captain's commanding officer, frequently an admiral who was a considerable distance from where the boarding took place, and the ship's officers and men, also gained financially from a share in the booty. Brian Southam in his *Jane Austen and the Navy* observes that the opening section of this third chapter "is heavy with irony, the satire caustic. Having preserved the country throughout the war, the Navy, in the person of some 'rich Admiral,' as yet unknown, is now to save the bankrupt Baronet in time of peace. Opportunism, not gratitude, is in the air." He also notes that "there is no hint of patriotism, not even the slightest show of *amor patriae*" (267).

Sir Walter, Shepherd, and the attendant Mrs. Clay are sarcastic at the expense of the "gentlemen of the navy," who would regard Kellynch as a "prize" in the manner of an enemy vessel. They perceive naval attributes, which they can manipulate in a business transaction, not as "gallantry" or as brave qualities, but in terms of "responsible tenants." Naval officers are ironically perceived as having "very liberal notions" (17). Their enemy Napoleon represented post-revolutionary France and an ideology opposed to the old aristocratic, nondemocratic illiberal monarchist regimes. The Royal Navy was a hierarchical system ruled from above with the captain of a ship being God, Lord, and Master to all under his command. Lord Nelson, the victor at Trafalgar, was "'a dyed-in-the-wool reactionary,' 'a hanger-and-flogger and a proper-up of corrupt autocracies'" (D. Jones, 181, citing S. Schama, 113).

Sir Walter needs persuasion from Shepherd and his daughter Mrs. Clay to take senior naval officers as tenants. For Shepherd, their discretion can be relied on. Mrs. Clay's father had driven her over, "nothing being of so much use to Mrs. Clay's health

as a drive to Kellynch." She claims to "have known a good deal of the profession," to have considerable knowledge of senior naval officers. There is indeed much about Mrs. Clay and her past activities that the author deliberately leaves mysterious. She asserts that in the hands of naval officers, "Every thing in and about the house would be taken such excellent care of." In what appears to be the first formal address to Anne in the novel—although there is the possibility that she is speaking to her sister—Mrs. Clay says, "You need to be afraid, Miss Elliot, of your own sweet flower-garden's being neglected."

Sir Walter preempts a reply. He is reluctant to give a naval tenant use of his house and its grounds: "I am very little disposed to grant a tenant of Kellynch Hall any extraordinary favour, I assure you, be he sailor or soldier." He also addresses his daughter as "Miss Elliot," who should be on her guard with respect to her flower garden. Shepherd tries to reassure Sir Walter. Before he can reply, Anne makes her first speech in the novel. Her first words are "The navy," and she speaks in its defense. Anne draws attention to the plight of the newly demobbed (or released from service) sailor no longer fighting at sea "who have done so much for us." They "have at least an equal claim with any other set of men, for all the comforts and all the privileges which any home can give." She adds, "Sailors work hard enough for their comforts, we must all allow." Her words reveal her as the moral conscience of her family and Kellynch. They also indicate that her attitude to the navy and its men is far from neutral. As the narrative will indicate, her feelings for Wentworth, the naval officer she rejected through Lady Russell's persuasion, are still simmering below the surface.

The Shepherds agree with her. Sir Walter is not interested in people being rewarded for merit and achievement. His concern is usefulness to himself. He objects to the navy. First, it is "the means of bringing persons of obscure birth into undue distinction, and raising men to honours which their fathers and grandfathers never dreamt of" (18–19). His objection represents reactionary perceptions of blood and inheritance, ideas that in theory the French revolutionaries and the American Founding Fathers opposed. On another level, Sir Walter is afraid that his own baronetcy will be endangered. His baronetcy was a creation in 1660 of loyalty to Charles II. During 1814 and 1815, 30 new peerages were created, largely for "distinguished naval and military service" (Southam, 269). His second objection reflects his own self-love. The navy "cuts up a man's youth and vigour most horribly; a sailor grows older sooner than any other man; I have observed it all my life" (19). He is obsessed with perpetual beauty and looks. He objects, for instance, to Mrs. Clay's "freckles and a projecting tooth, and a clumsy wrist" (34). Admirals "are all knocked about," they appear to be "sixty" years of age but are in fact "forty."

Interestingly, in view of her subsequent subservient relationship to Sir Walter, Mrs. Clay begs to disagree with him, telling him that life inevitably involves decay. "The lawyer plods, quite care-worn; the physician is up at all hours, and traveling in all weather." The clergyman "is obliged to go into infected rooms, and expose his health and looks to all the injury of a poisonous atmosphere." On the other hand, only "those who are not obliged to follow any" profession, such as, by flattering implication, Sir Walter, "hold the blessings of health and a good appearance to the utmost." Mrs. Clay concludes by appealing to her experience of men. She knows "no other set of men but what lose something of their personableness when they cease to be quite young." Those who do not are the unproductive, "living on their own property, without the torment of trying for more." She adds, "it is only *their* lot . . . to hold the blessings of health and a good appearance to the utmost" (Jane Austen's emphasis). This is a compliment to the seemingly unchangeable Sir Walter, whom she is trying to entrap into marrying her. Mrs. Clay's speech highlights one of the major preoccupations of *Persuasion*: change and resistance to the inevitable. It is also an example that minor characters who appear intermittently, such as Mrs. Clay, should not be ignored. Their actions and speeches provide no less a commentary and insight into the richness of the novel than those given to more major players such as Sir Walter, Lady Russell, Admiral Croft, and others.

Immediately following his daughter's words, the reader is told that Shepherd has arranged for a ten-ant. The tenant, "Admiral Croft was a native of Somersetshire, who having acquired a very handsome fortune, was wishing to settle in his own country." Following the explanation, there follows a "cold suspicious inquiry" from Sir Walter: "who is Admiral Croft?" Shepherd's answer is briefly reported and indicates the Admiral's pedigree: "his being of a gentleman's family." Anne then makes her second intervention: "He is rear admiral of the white. [the second of the three ascending ranks for rear admirals: blue, white, and red] He was in the Trafalgar action, and has been in the East Indies since: he has been stationed there, I believe, several years." Her words reveal direct personal knowledge of the Admiral's activities and of naval hierarchies. The reader is not yet told the source of her knowledge. Her information is responded to by her father with remarks about Croft's physical appearance: "his face is about as orange as the cuffs and capes of my livery." Shepherd emphasizes the Admiral's ability to pay the rent and willingness to do so, his desire for "a comfortable home and to get into it as soon as possible." He had also inquired of "the deputation . . . but made no great point of it." This refers to permission to shoot game birds during the appropriate season.

Shepherd's point is that the tenant is a very responsible person. In addition, "He was a married man, and without children." In short, Shepherd's attempt to persuade Sir Walter conveys important information about characters who are to play a prominent role in the unfolding of the narrative. Shepherd tells the reluctant Sir Walter of the advantage of tenants without families. He extols the virtues of Mrs. Croft, who seemed "a very well-spoken, genteel, shrewd lady." The practical one, she "asked more questions about the house, and terms, and taxes, than the admiral himself, and seemed more conversant with business." Shepherd adds that he has local connections, a "sister to the gentleman who did live amongst us once." The name eludes him and he appeals to his daughter for help, addressing her by her first name, "Penelope." This is a highly ironic name. Penelope in Homer's *Odyssey* remains faithful over a 20-year period to her husband though she has received no news of him and is surrounded by suitors. Shepherd's daughter, as it emerges, is herself a flattering suitor after her prey whose history remains a mystery. Mrs. Croft's brother is in fact Wentworth, once engaged, as the reader discovers, to Anne. She and he, as it also emerges in the course of the narrative, have remained faithful to each other in spite of the years and barriers to their relationship.

Before the name is revealed, appropriately by Anne, Shepherd remembers that he "submitted to an amicable compromise" with a trespasser on his orchard. Wentworth was a curate, and is described by Shepherd as a "gentleman," to which Sir Walter, revealing his snobbery, responds, "You misled me by the term *gentleman* [Jane Austen's emphasis]." He then notes, "I thought you were speaking of some man of property; Mr. Wentworth was nobody, I remember"—if he does, he seems to have forgotten the past connection of the name with Anne, or is insensitive to that, thinking only of himself. Obsessed with ancestry, Sir Walter adds "quite unconnected—nothing to do with the Strafford family. One wonders how the many names of many of our nobility become so common" (20–23). This embodiment of snobbery refers to his family's baronetcy created by Charles II in 1660 from loyalty to the Stuart family during the 1642–49 civil war and their subsequent exile. The historical Thomas Wentworth (1593–1641), the first Earl of Strafford, initially a supporter of parliamentary rights and privileges, was executed by Parliament in 1641 for his actions on behalf of Charles I. Upon the restoration of his son to the throne in 1660, the Strafford honors were restored to Wentworth's son, who died without producing children. By 1791, the title had died out, although there were false claims to it during the 1820s, but these came to nothing (Bree, 63).

So within the space of a few paragraphs in the third chapter, there are two allusions: one to classical legend, to Penelope, the other to more recent English history, to Wentworth. Both reveal the variety of Jane Austen's narrative techniques in *Persuasion*. To return to its narrative, Shepherd perceiving that the Wentworth connection of "the Crofts did them no service with" the reactionary Sir Walter, all too aware of his dynastic history, he returns to appealing to his self-interest to persuade him to rent his property. "An admiral speaks his own consequence, and, at the same time can never make a baronet look small." He, Sir Walter Elliot, "must ever have the precedence."

He makes "a reference to Elizabeth," who agrees to the transaction. It is, however, not Sir Walter, Elizabeth, or Shepherd who closes the chapter, but Anne, the "most attentive listener to the whole." She had "left the room, to seek the comfort of cool air for her flushed cheeks." She walks "along a favourite grove" and to herself says, "a few months more, and *he*, perhaps may be walking here" (Jane Austen's emphasis). Again, Jane Austen uses a brilliant narrative device to gain the attention of her readers. Who the "*he*" (23–26), refers to is by no means clear, nor is Anne's past relationship. To gain further knowledge, the reader is induced to read on.

Chapter 4

The opening of the short fourth chapter provides an answer to the question. In a paragraph of omniscient narration, significant past events are all too briefly related. Unusually Jane Austen begins her chapter with an emphasized "*He*," providing readers with answers to the issues left hanging from the previous chapter. "*He* was not Mr. Wentworth, the former curate of Monkford, however suspicious appearances may be, but a captain Frederick Wentworth, his brother." The reader is then told that the brother was promoted to the rank of commander "in consequence of the action off St. Domingo." The "action off St. Domingo" (26) refers to events of February 1806, in which the British navy defeated the French navy off the coast of what is today the Dominican Republic. Wentworth took part in the action in which "two French ships were destroyed, and 760 of their men killed or wounded on three ships that were captured." British losses amounted to "64 killed and 294 wounded" (Bree, 65). Wentworth "not immediately employed," a command not yet being offered him, "had come into Somersetshire in the summer of 1806." An orphan, he lived for six months with his brother. He is described as "a remarkably fine young man, with a great deal of intelligence, spirit and brilliancy." Anne is described as "an extremely pretty girl with gentleness, modesty, taste, and feeling." Their attraction is partly explained: "for he had nothing to do, and she had hardly any body to love." But the relationship proved to be deeper. They fell "rapidly and deeply in love."

Jane Austen describes a romantic relationship based on feelings rather than social demands. Following an all too brief "period of exquisite felicity," problems occurred. "Troubles soon arose." Sir Walter's response was negative, one "of great astonishment, great coldness, great silence," and a refusal to assist Anne financially or emotionally. Lady Russell considered the relationship "a most unfortunate one." The third paragraph uses Lady Russell's point of view in "throw herself away at nineteen," "a young man, who had nothing but himself to recommend him." Lady Russell as Anne's surrogate mother is hostile: "It must not be, if by any fair interference of friendship, any representations from one who had almost a mother's love, and mother's rights, it would be prevented."

The fourth paragraph opens with the assertion, "Captain Wentworth had no fortune," but it presents his optimistic perspective—unlike Sir Walter Elliot, who is frozen in the past. The language is that of "lucky," "confident," "Full of life and ardour," and "wit." But the viewpoint switches into Lady Russell's point of view and her objections to him. She "saw it differently." Indeed, "his sanguine temper, and fearlessness of mind, operated very differently on her. She saw in it but an aggravation of the evil." To her way of thinking, "he was brilliant, he was headstrong," and "she deprecated the connexion in every light."

In these paragraphs, Lady Russell's objections largely center on material concerns. She refers to Anne's advantages, what she can offer a prospective suitor: "birth" and "beauty" and then her "mind." Wentworth is a "stranger without alliance or fortune," and has few if any hopes of "affluence." He is without "connexions." She is concerned for Anne's material welfare and position in society. Her attitude to marriage represents a prudent one, in which feelings play a subordinate role. They are closely allied to the attitude Charlotte Lucas adopts when she marries the Reverend William Collins in *Pride and Prejudice*. All Wentworth can offer is himself and his prospects, qualities that attract Anne and remain in her mind. It is ironic that he becomes successful and wealthy. In financial and social terms, Anne should have taken the gamble and gone with her feelings. She would not have been "sunk by him into a state of most wearing, anxious youth-killing dependence!" But neither Anne nor Lady Russell could have foreseen such an outcome, and what Lady Russell feared has occurred: Anne has lost her "bloom and spirits."

Paragraphs five and six focus on the internal conflict Anne experienced. The pressures on her are conveyed through the language of conflict and subjection. She is in a "combat" situation, which is difficult to "withstand." Anne "always loved and relied on" Lady Russell. She, Anne, is in a dependant situation. Anne is "self-denying," she and Wentworth experienced "the misery of a parting," and she had to "encounter all the additional pain of opinions" and suffering. Anne is at the center of a battleground: Wentworth and Lady Russell fighting over her with the latter emerging victorious. The isolated Anne "was persuaded to believe the engagement a wrong thing." The consequence is what Lady Russell wished to avoid. Anne's "attachment and regrets had, for a long time, clouded every enjoyment of youth, and an early loss of bloom and spirits had been their lasting effect." The word "bloom" (26–28) occurs 17 times in the course of *Persuasion,* more so than in any other Jane Austen novel. Six of these occurrences are in the first volume. A. Walton Litz, after indicating such a recurrence, believes that *Persuasion* is concerned with "the loss and return of 'bloom'" (Southam, *Casebook*, 231).

Persuasion's subject is not what has happened in the past, although this affects what happens subsequently. "In the novel the crucial passage of time is that which has elapsed since Anne was 'persuaded' to give up Wentworth and he disappeared into the navy" (Tanner, 211). The narrator tells her readers, "More than seven years were gone since this little history of sorrowful interest had reached its close; and time had softened down much." Unfortunately, Anne has been too isolated: "she had been too dependent on time alone" (28). Wentworth has not been replaced. *Persuasion* "is in effect a second novel." Tanner adds, "Part of its rare autumnal magic—not unlike that of Shakespeare's last plays—is that it satisfies the dream of a 'second chance' which must appeal to anyone who has experienced the sense of an irreparably ruined life owing to an irrevocable, mistaken decision" (Tanner, 211).

Anne has received another suitor. This was when she was 22 and "solicited" by Charles Musgrove. Lady Russell's perspective on this relationship is presented rather than that of Anne, who apparently refused the suitable match. Musgrove was from the right family, from "landed property," and "the eldest son of a man" holding "general importance" locally, just beneath her own father's social stature. Again, Lady Russell's values are those of status and property. Yet Lady Russell, without wishing "the past undone," is too realistic for that; she "began . . . to have the anxiety which borders on hopelessness for Anne's being tempted by some man of talents and independence." Charles Musgrove, in the meantime, had married Anne's younger sister, Mary.

The subsequent paragraph transfers viewpoint to Anne's and is presented through the use of free indirect narration to convey her thoughts "at seven and twenty," when she "thought very differently from what she had been made to think at nineteen." Anne does not "blame Lady Russell, she did not blame herself for having been guided by her," but she would counsel differently if approached. In spite of "every anxiety attending [Wentworth's] profession, all their probable fears, delays and disappointments, she should yet have been a happier woman in maintaining the engagement than she had been in the sacrifice of it." Wentworth has had a good war: "All his sanguine expectations, all his confidences had been justified. His genius and ardour had seemed to foresee and to command his prosperous path" (28–29). She has "taken damagingly outmoded advice from aristocrats. Wentworth, meritocrat that he is, has made his fortune off the back of the new world order" (D. Jones, 183). The detail of his promotion from the rank of Commander to that of Captain, and how he "made a handsome fortune," will emerge. Anne "could not doubt that his being rich; and, in favours of

his constancy, she had no reason to believe him married."

Anne clearly perceives the choices that she made. At 27, from experience, she now favors "early warm attachment, and a cheerful confidence in futurity, against that over-anxious caution which seems to insult exertion and distrust Providence!" In other words, Lady Russell's position. Anne "had been forced into prudence in her youth," yet "she learned romance as she grew older—the natural sequel of an unnatural beginning." The remainder of the chapter concerns Anne's coming to terms with the new reality, "that Captain Wentworth's sister was likely to live at Kellynch." Anne's isolation is reinforced by her sense that events of the past are "known to those three only among her connexions, by whom no syllable she believed, would ever be whispered." Lady Russell's silence was assured, her father's and sister Elizabeth's a consequence of ignoring Anne. Further, her other sister, "Mary, had been at school while it all occurred" and Mrs. Croft had been out of the country (28–31). So this short but important chapter has related, largely from Anne's perspective in "telescopic brevity" (Tanner, 211), events of seven years previously, blocked out by her vain father and sister, prevented by her well-meaning surrogate mother. The heroine of *Persuasion* must face the future alone.

Chapter 5

Chapter 5 begins with the visit of the Crofts to Kellynch-hall to arrange for their move to the property. Notably Anne deliberately misses their visit by going for a walk. Both Sir Walter and Admiral Croft treat each other with "hearty good humour." The depiction of their mutual reservations about each other is not lacking in sarcasm and humor. Sir Walter "declared the Admiral to be the best-looking sailor he had ever met with, and went so far as to say, that, if his own man might have had the arranging of his hair, he should not be ashamed of being seen with him any where." The Admiral tells his wife, "The baronet will never set the Thames on fire, but there seems no harm in him."

Anne at least is needed by her younger married sister, Mary, who declares that "Anne had better stay for nobody will want her in Bath." So she remains in the country with Mary during the early autumn while others, including Mrs. Clay, go to Bath. Dating at the start of chapter 5, detailing the arrangements for the Elliots' leaving Kellynch-hall and moving to Bath is very precise. There are "the possible heats of September in all the white glare of Bath." Reference to "The Crofts were to have possession at Michaelmas" (32–34) specifically relates to September 29, one of the four days traditionally assigned to the quarters of the year on which house tenancies were "usually begun and ended" (Bree, 71). Anne is associated here with autumn: "so sweet and so sad of the autumnal months in the country."

Reaction to Mrs. Clay accompanying Sir Walter and Elizabeth to Bath moves from Anne's perspective to Lady Russell's, who considers it an "affront" to Anne, and then back in a passage of free indirect style, to Anne's. She, "Anne herself was become hardened to such affronts." In an earlier passage in the 12th paragraph of the chapter, "Mrs. Clay had freckles, and a projecting tooth, and a clumsy wrist," yet "she was young, and certainly altogether well-looking."

The physical condition of Mrs. Clay with her "freckles," her "projecting tooth," and "clumsy wrist" (34) has led to speculation concerning her state of health. In the fourth chapter of the second volume of *Persuasion*, Sir Walter tells Anne, "I should recommend Gowland, the constant use of Gowland, during the spring months. Mrs. Clay has been using it at my recommendation, and you see what it has done for her. You see how it carried away her freckles." "Gowland" (146) was a skin lotion. Mrs. Clay's physical problems, "her personal misfortunes," her lack of beauty, "and that she reprobates all inequality of condition and rank more strongly than most people," are what attracts Elizabeth to her. Indeed, Elizabeth draws Anne's attention to her father's reaction. "You must have heard him notice Mrs. Clay's freckles." The verb "notice" (35) in this context means "to observe with the eye" and "to pass remarks about a thing in conversation" (Phillipps, 84). A response from Anne that "there is hardly any personal defect . . . which an agreeable manner might

not gradually reconcile one to" provokes an oversensitive response from her sister concerning her perception that she and Anne both lack beauty, are "plain," and she thinks "it rather unnecessary in you [Anne] to be advising me."

Sir Walter's leave of Kellynch-hall is feudal, while Anne's has "a sort of desolate tranquility." She moves in with Lady Russell, whose response to the departure is conveyed from her notion of the "break-up of the family," whose "respectability was as dear to her as her own." She also would miss her daily contact with the Elliots. Lady Russell finds it "painful to look upon their deserted grounds." She needs to "escape the solitariness and melancholy of so altered a village." Anne, on the other hand, is associated almost naturally with solitude; she is a creature of the new century and sensibilities. Lady Russell belongs to the world of the previous century, to a social world with ordered rules of conduct and behavior.

The contrast between these different sensibilities finds reflection in the description of architecture and place. Anne replaces Kellynch for Uppercross, the home of Mary, her sister. The Elliots and her sister's family frequently meet. Uppercross contains "only two houses superior in appearance to those of the yeomen and labourers." The first was that of the "squire," the second that of the parsonage. The former when he married was improved, and had "its viranda, French windows" and other elements as eye-catching as the "aspect and premises" of the home of Mary's in-laws, "about a quarter of a mile further on."

Scenic descriptions serve as a backdrop for the introduction of Mary Musgrove, Anne's younger sister. She is a continual complainer. Anne has come to stay with her to cheer her up. She is the mother of two children, and her first words to Anne are, "So, you are come at last!" She does not say, "So, you have come at last," or "Thank you for coming, Anne, it is good to see you. How are you?" Mary's words form a cumulative catalog of complaint. She continues, "I began to think I should never see you. I am so ill I can hardly speak. I have not seen a creature the whole morning" (35–37).

Jan Fergus indicates that "Mary uses 'never' five times and 'always' three times, each time reproachfully" in this initial scene with Anne (McMaster and Stovel, 70). She is, in common with her father, narcissistic; she had, as the narrator tells her readers, inherited "a considerable share of the Elliot self-importance." Suffering from mental anguish, Mary is unable to cope with her surroundings, her situation, or her children. Ironically confronted with a visit from Anne, Mary repeats four times in the space of a few paragraphs her central complaint about being lonely: "I have not seen a creature the whole morning"; "I have not seen a soul this whole morning"; "I have not seen one of them [the family] to-day"; "not one of them have been near me."

Mary's complaints reflect her inherited narcissism and attitude to her sister found in her father and Elizabeth. Mary responds to Anne's apology for not coming earlier, she "had so much to do," with "Dear me! What can *you* possibly have to do?" (Jane Austen's emphasis) Anne's explanation that she has been cataloguing "their father's books and pictures," making order in the garden, packing, fulfilling family responsibilities which her father should have undertaken, such as "going to almost every house in the parish, as a sort of take-leave," is received with the curt, "Oh! Well." This is followed by yet another complaint that Anne failed to ask "one word about our dinner at the Pooles yesterday."

Mary attributes her illness to being "crowded into the backseat with Henrietta and Louisa" (37–39), the two sisters of her husband, Charles, on their return in the carriage, which she was forced to share, from the Pooles' party. A hypochondriac, "she feels entitled to sit in the best seat." She truly feels "ill-used"; this occurs "with or without the hyphen . . . eight times in *Persuasion* . . . more than half the times it appears in all Austen's works." Fifty percent of its usages in the novel "refer to Mary's sense of it." Jan Fergus observes that the character of Mary Musgrove was especially "created for *Persuasion* . . . because the novel is to some extent about ways that people cope with the sense of ill-usage as well as with loss and grief" (McMaster and Stovel, 73, 74).

As soon as Anne has revived her sister's spirits, they pay a call on the Musgroves, her in-laws, at the "Great House" nearby. Its description com-

pares favourable with Kellynch-hall, where Sir Walter has his Baronetage and his hall of mirrors. At Uppercross, there is "a grand piano forte and a harp, flower-stands and little tables placed in every direction," suggesting disorder rather than order. Even the portraits "seemed to be staring in astonishment." The setting represents generational changes. "The father and mother were in the old English style, and the young people in the new." The older Musgroves are described as "a very good sort of people; friendly and hospitable, not much educated, and not at all elegant." They are not condemned, "Their children had more modern minds and manners." The sisters Henrietta and Louisa are seen through Anne's lenses: "living to be fashionable, happy and merry." She, Anne, is the meditative one: "she would not have given up her own more elegant and cultivated mind for all their enjoyments" (40–41).

Chapter 6

Chapter 6 moves from Anne's response to her transplantation to Uppercross, to her perception of Charles Musgrove, to Mary and their children, until the focus moves to Michaelmas and the Crofts' move to Kellynch-hall. The chapter concludes with the Crofts' visit to the Musgroves', talk of Wentworth, and a "pathetic piece of family history," (50) concerning the Musgroves' son Richard. The focus in the chapter is on the word "transplanted," with transitions in time, place, character, situation, and destiny. The word "transplanted" (43), is used on one other occasion in Jane Austen's novels—in *Emma*. Ironically, the speaker is Mrs. Elton, Anne's antithesis, complaining to Emma (273).

The opening paragraph of chapter 6 reveals Anne's awareness that "a distance of only three miles, will often include a total change of conversation, opinion, and idea." The move from Kellynch-hall to Uppercross, in terms of distance, is not a great one but reveals the limitations of being entrapped socially or within the self. Anne "must now submit to feel that another lesson, in the art of knowing our own nothingness, beyond our own circle, was become necessary for her." Anne was isolated at Kellynch-hall, with the exception "of having one such truly sympathising friend as Lady

Russell." Adapting to the transition brought about, "with the prospect of spending at least two months at Uppercross," she is willing to learn, to adapt to her new surroundings, to change and adapt to the people she is now with. Her sister "was not so repulsive and unsisterly as Elizabeth, nor so inaccessible to all influence of hers." "Repulsive" (42–43), used on only six other occasions in Jane Austen's novels, had for her readers milder connotations than it has today: "it generally means 'tending to repel by coldness of manner' rather than 'offensive' or 'loathsome'" (Phillipps, 23).

The implications of personal and situational transition are illuminated in the opening paragraph by a specific topographical reference. The Musgrove "young ladies" from their perspective remind their father that if they "shall be in Bath in the winter . . . we must be in a good situation—none of your Queen-squares for us" (44). A place, which from one perspective may appear to be positive, may not be so from other perspectives. Jane Austen herself had lodged in the Square with her parents during 1799. She wrote to her sister, Cassandra, on May 17, 1799: "I like our situation very much—it is far more cheerful than Paragon, & the prospect from the Drawingroom window at which I now write, is rather picturesque" (*Letters*, 41). The Miss Musgroves' negative attitude to it suggests that by 1814 the address was no longer fashionable (see Bree, 79). In any case, their attitude exemplifies the message of the opening section: transplantation opens up fresh perspectives and reveals "self-delusion" (42).

Anne's relationships in her new situation are very different: "She was always on friendly terms with her brother-in-law; and in the children, who loved her nearly as well, and respected her a great deal more than their mother, she had an object of interest, amusement, and wholesome exertion." She, Anne, previously had rejected Charles Musgrove, who, married to Mary, "did nothing with much zeal, but sport; and his time was otherwise trifled away, without benefit from books, or any thing else." This is an echo of the opening of the novel, in which Anne's father studies a book reflecting his own egoism and family destiny.

The fifth paragraph of chapter 6 makes it evident that Charles and Mary are incompatible. He has retreated out of doors and Mary complains of "lowness." To Anne's perspective, "they might pass for a happy couple." They "agreed in the want of more money, and a strong inclination for a handsome present from his father." From the isolation of her previous existence, Anne's situation has moved almost to the opposite extreme. She is "treated with too much confidence by all parties." Mrs. Musgrove even goes as far as addressing her, her daughter-in-law's sister, as "Miss Anne," halfway between familiarity and formality. In other words, she is regarded as part of the inner family circle.

Rank is never far from the surface of a Jane Austen novel. The young Musgroves speak to Anne "of rank, people of rank and jealousy of rank." They note "how easy and indifferent" Anne is "about it," although their mother is "so very tenacious." Anne's response to her difficult social situation as confidante reveals her acumen. The narrator asks, "How was Anne to set all the matters right?" a reflection of Anne's asking herself the same question. The answer is found in her role as a patient listener, her ability to "soften every grievance and excuse each to the other." The visit improves Anne's "own spirits," due to the "change of place and subject, by being removed three miles from Kellynch." Jane Austen displays great insight into the way companionship can transform a person's personality: "Mary's ailments lessened by having a constant companion." Essentially, however, Anne is alone. Her isolation is reflected in her playing the harp unappreciated by "either of the Miss Musgroves," who have "no voice, no knowledge of the harp." Anne "knew that when she played she was giving pleasure only to herself." Music is associated with her deepest emotional life and traumatic events: "never, since the age of fourteen, never since the loss of her dear mother [had she] known the happiness of being listened to, or encouraged by any just appreciation or real taste." At Uppercross, as at Kellynch-hall, Anne is forced to rely on her own inner resources: "In music she had been always used to feel alone in the world."

Her time at Uppercross is precisely marked out. She passes "the first three weeks" until Michaelmas in company, accompanying "country dances." At Michaelmas, Kellynch-hall intrudes once again into her life. Somewhat ironically, given her treatment by her father and elder sister Elizabeth, Anne regards Kellynch as "a beloved home made over to others." Associated with Kellynch are "all the precious rooms and furniture, groves, and prospects" that were "beginning to own other eyes and other limbs!" So it is objects such as furniture, rooms, scenery that she misses rather than human beings. She is reminded of the date September 29 by her hypochondriac sister, who, in spite of her self-obsession and unhappiness, is not presented unsympathetically. Anne "had this sympathetic touch . . . from Mary . . . 'Dear Me! is not this the day the Crofts were to come to Kellynch? I am glad I did not think of it before. How low it makes me!'"

The focus in chapter 6 transfers to the new inhabitants of Kellynch-hall, the Crofts. "The Crofts took possession with true naval alertness." Self-obsessed, "Mary deplored the necessity for herself. 'Nobody knew how much she should suffer.'" In other words, she shall suffer and "She should [meaning I shall] put it off as long as she could." However, it is the Crofts who visit first and "Mrs. Croft fell to the share of Anne." Mrs. Croft is viewed through Anne's eyes. The initial description of her is physical. She has a "reddened and weather-beaten complexion, the consequence of her having been almost as much at sea as her husband." This "made her seem to have lived some years longer in the world than her real eight and thirty." Unlike Anne's father, Sir Walter, Mrs Croft is subject to time and aging. She has "open, easy and decided manner," and displays "feelings of great consideration towards" Anne "in all that related to Kellynch."

Anne's perception that Mrs. Croft seems unaware of her previous connection with her brothers and especially Frederick rather than Edward leads to an ambiguity in Mrs. Croft's opening words. She tells Anne, "It was you . . . I find, that my brother had the pleasure of being acquainted with." The turmoil of Anne's emotions is revealed: "Anne hoped she had outlived the age of blushing; but the age of emotion she certainly had not." She receives another misperceived signal when Mrs. Croft adds, "Perhaps you may not have heard that he is married." The effect of these words is conveyed through Anne's reaction to them and relief that it was her brother Edward rather than Frederick that Mrs. Croft probably spoke of.

The note of narrative ambiguity is continued when Admiral Croft tells Mary that "a brother of Mrs. Croft" is expected on a visit. Anne again assumes this to be Edward. There is a distraction when Louisa Musgrove "came on foot, to leave more room for the harp, which was bringing in the carriage" (43–44, 46–50). The "use of the active form of the expanded tenses in a passive sense" (Phillipps, 115), in the relative clause "which was bringing," reinforce the depth of her emotional turmoil. It is only incidentally that she now learns that the visitor is to be Frederick Wentworth and not his brother.

The narrator interrupts the narrative to convey the story of Richard Musgrove. Initially, this is told by Louisa Musgrove, who uses the delivery of a harp to her mother, rather than a pianoforte, as a springboard for the tale sparked by the news that Captain Wentworth is shortly to visit. Wentworth "was the name of poor Richard's captain." Louisa as narrator gives way to Jane Austen as narrator. She does not mince words: "The real circumstances of this pathetic piece of family history were, that the Musgroves had had the ill-fortune of a very troublesome, hopeless son." There is no attempt to pass over Richard's feelings: "He had been sent to sea, because he was stupid and unmanageable on shore." In other words, a naval career is seen as an option for "a thick-headed, unfeeling, unprofitable" son. For six months of his "several years at sea," he had served under Captain Frederick Wentworth on his frigate, the *Laconia*. Wentworth influenced Richard to send "the only two letters" home received by his mother and father, or rather the "only two disinterested letters; all the rest had been mere applications for money."

This digression focusing on Richard Musgrove has several functions. It displays a secret within the Musgrove family; underneath the surface glitter there is a sadness that the parents attempt to cover. In addition, the digression reveals the positive nature of Wentworth's character. He has, for instance, been "only two perticular [*sic*] about the school-master" (50–52), which all naval ships were obligated to carry. Wentworth has been "more conscientious than many captains about the education of the boys under his care" (Bree, 88).

In this chapter the word "bursts" occurs once more: "the name of Wentworth as connected with her son" provokes Mrs. Musgrove to "one of those extraordinary bursts of mind which do sometimes occur." The Musgroves' emotional turmoil is paralleled by Anne's emotions toward Wentworth.

The frequent mention of the Wentworth the Musgroves met in Clifton, then as now, a fashionable part of Bristol, provides "a new sort of trial to Anne's nerves." Her reactions to his name and the fact that a meeting is unavoidable given the Musgroves' gratitude "for the kindness he had shewn poor Dick" (52), conclude chapter 6. The chapter has moved from Anne's transplantation to Uppercross, her adaptability to her new surroundings, through character description and family secrets. She, Anne, now awaits another meeting with the man she has rejected yet still feels for.

Chapter 7

The seventh chapter culminates in the first meeting after eight years between Anne and Wentworth. He is the focus of attention in the chapter. The first paragraph's viewpoint moves from Wentworth to Mr. Musgrove and his report to Anne of calling on Wentworth. According to her calculations, she and Wentworth "must meet" after a week. The encounter between them is influenced by the "bad fall" of one of her nephews, and she takes control of the situation. "Anne had everything to do at once." She sends for the apothecary, finds Musgrove, comforts her sister, who is almost in "hysterics—the servants to control—the youngest child to banish, and the poor suffering one to attend and soothe" (53).

In the fourth and fifth paragraphs, Anne learns more of Wentworth's visit from the younger Musgroves and Charles Musgrove. The wounded Musgrove is treated by the apothecary Robinson, who has in *Persuasion* a far less prominent role than Perry, his counterpart in *Emma*. The sixth and seventh paragraphs reveal movement "from objective narrative to the unspoken thoughts of a character, and back again" (Page, 132). Charles Musgrove's vulnerability, his sense of fatherly responsibility and

duty, quickly transform into a desire to meet Wentworth. The sentence "The child was to be kept in bed, and amused as quietly as possible; but what was there for a father to do?" reflects this. The first part of the sentence is formal narrative, a reflection of Robinson the apothecary's professional instructions. The second part of the sentence moves into free indirect speech indicated by Musgrove's question. This continues in the next sentence: "This was quite a female case, and it would be highly absurd in him, who could be of no use at home, to shut himself up." "It must be a work of time to ascertain that no injury had been done to the spine, but Mr. Robinson found nothing to increase alarm." Charles Musgrove's lack of seriousness contrasts with Robinson's serious language: "ascertain . . . to increase alarm." A transference in tone is also seen in the sentence, "His father very much wished him to meet Captain Wentworth, and there being no sufficient reason against it, he ought to go." Charles has moved his position. He has difficulties with being confined to the area of the house and watching over his son. He uses his father's presumed wishes to justify his own selfishness. The rest of the sentence following a semicolon after "go"; moves from Charles's thoughts to indirect speech: "and it ended in his making a bold public declaration, when he came in from shooting, of his meaning to dress directly, and dine at the other house."

Austen's stylistic versatility is additionally seen in her use of dialogue for the whole of paragraph eight of this seventh chapter. Charles's actions are justified through his lack of usefulness and reliance on Anne: "you see I can be of no use. Anne will send for me if any thing is the matter." This leads to a reaction from his wife, Mary, who reflects on the general selfishness of the male gender and their lack of feeling. Anne responds by reinforcing the role of women, as she perceives it: "Nursing does not belong to a man, it is not his province. A sick child is always the mother's property," she informs her sister. But Mary is still intent on meeting Wentworth and accompanying her husband. Anne offers to stay with the sick boy, Charles. This elicits a double-edged response from her sister: "You, who have not a mother's feelings, are a great deal the properest person. You can make little Charles do anything; he always minds you at a word." She also believes that Anne does "not mind being left alone."

Left alone, Anne reflects on her position: "She knew herself to be of the first utility to the child." Furthermore, "what was it to her if Frederick Wentworth were only half a mile distant, making himself agreeable to others?" Her sense of duty is a form of escape from the consequences of her past decision to reject Wentworth. She feels that if he had wished to see her, to renew their acquaintance, he would have visited her. This sense of his wishing to avoid her is reinforced by the report of the evening visits from Charles Musgrove and his wife. They have arranged to meet Wentworth the following morning at the Great House rather than at the Cottage. However, Wentworth insists on seeing how the ill patient is.

The emotional intensity of the meeting between Anne and Wentworth is indicated through the punctuation and sentence structure. There is a five-word sentence, "And it was soon over." Wentworth's appearance is conveyed through a sequence of semicolons, parentheses, a colon, and reiterated parentheses conveying the agitated thought sequence in Anne's mind. "Her eye half-met [not completely, as if they are both embarrassed] Captain Wentworth's; a bow, a curtsey passed; she heard his voice—he talked to Mary, said all that was right, said something to the Miss Musgroves, enough to mark an easy footing: the room seemed full—full of persons and voices—but a few minutes ended it." The emphasis is on time, the inherent vagueness of impression rather than citation of what is actually being said, reflecting the intense emotion on Anne's part.

This intensity of feeling and Anne's attempt to deal with it rationally is reflected in a passage of free indirect speech conveying her thoughts: "What might not eight years do?" she asks herself. Anne is trying persuasion: "Events of every description, changes, alienations, removals—all, all must be comprised in it; and oblivion of the past—how natural, how certain too!" A recurring theme of this novel is how people respond to the profound transformations that have taken place in their lives. Emotionally, how do they respond to

the resurrection, the reappearance in their lives of deep feelings from the past? How do they persuade themselves that past feelings have been suppressed? The tumult of emotions in Anne conveyed through the short sentences and staccato agitated punctuation reflect the turmoil in her emotional world.

Mary unfeelingly tells her sister Anne, "Captain Wentworth is not very gallant by you, Anne, though he was so attentive to me." Asked his opinion of Anne, he is reported as responding, "You were so altered he should not have known you again." Her reaction is of "silent deep mortification." To Anne, Wentworth has "not altered, or not for the worse." Her own sense of a lack of self-confidence is conveyed: "No; the years which had destroyed her youth and bloom had only given him a more glowing, manly, open look, in no respect lessening his personal advantages."

The emphasis here is on Anne's feelings. Without warning, the perspective switches for the first time to Wentworth. He "had used such words, or something like them, but without an idea that they would be carried round to her. He had thought her wretchedly altered, and, in the first moment of appeal, had spoken as he felt. He had not forgiven Anne Elliot. She had used him ill; deserted and disappointed him." Such reflections go on for the five paragraphs remaining in the chapter. It concludes with his inner thoughts. In the penultimate paragraph and its second sentence, it is revealed that "Anne Elliot was not out of his thoughts," especially when Wentworth "described the woman he should wish to meet with." She would possess "A strong mind, with sweetness of manner." This important chapter ends with his reflection, "I have thought on the subject more than most men" (55–62).

Chapter 8

Chapter 8 continues this pattern of shifting internal narrative. Anne is now the listener, the receiver of memories from eight years previously when she and Wentworth were close. In *Persuasion*, in common with other Austen novels, "there is always someone telling and someone listening." The reader moves "from the private to the public life through the constant narrative motion, utterances are joined with silences, and events become reflections." Furthermore, "there are . . . two levels of narration" taking place within the public dialogue and discussion. This is "accompanied, enlarged, qualified and contradicted by the words that are thought" (Hardy, 67).

Such a pattern may be seen in the opening four paragraphs of the chapter and in Louisa's reply to Wentworth and his response to her in recollections of his initial encounter with his sloop, the *Asp*. Wentworth entertains the Musgroves and appears to ignore Anne, who reflects, "Once so much to each other! Now nothing!" As he talks she remembers the past, as does Mrs. Musgrove, who thinks of her lost son. His words mean different things to the Musgrove girls, to Mrs. Musgrove, and to Anne, especially when Wentworth jests about the vulnerability of life at sea and its danger. As the narrator observes, "Anne's shudderings were to herself alone."

Records are again used in the novel, to evoke memory. In this instance, "the navy-list" induces memories of the *Asp* and the *Laconia,* on which the young Charles Musgrove served under Wentworth's command. The ship has positive memories for Wentworth, who recalls, "How fast I made money on her—A friend of mine, and I, had such a lovely cruise together off the Western Islands" (the Azores). The friend is Captain Harville, a former fellow officer on the *Laconia.* He and his family subsequently play a role in the narrative of *Persuasion.* For Mrs. Musgrove, the *Laconia* reminds her of her lost son. As silent observer, Anne detects from Wentworth's "momentary expression" that his perceptions of young Musgrove are not Mrs. Musgrove's. Wentworth reverts to his surface social charm, not revealing submerged feelings that are observed only by Anne. The inner self is left to her perceptions.

Austen is often direct, not covering up realities, however uncomfortable they may seem. She contrasts Mrs. Musgrove's physical condition with Anne's. The former is "of a comfortable substantial size." Anne has a "slender form, and pensive face." Mrs. Musgrove indulges in "large fat sighings over the destiny of a son, whom alive nobody had cared for." The two, the fat and the slim, are united in sorrow: "Personal size and mental sorrow have certainly no necessary proportions." She adds that "A large, bulky figure has as good a right to be in deep affliction, as the most graceful set of limbs in the world," although the Rubenesque are vulnerable to "ridicule."

Other listeners in the chapter are the Admiral and his wife. The Admiral was "thinking only of his own thoughts." The Admiral's "thoughts" are with the subject of women on board ship. Wentworth says, "I hate to hear of women on board, or to see them on board; and no ship, under my command, shall ever convey a family of ladies any where, if I can help it." This brings a response from Wentworth's sister, the Admiral's wife. Their conversation reintroduces Harville and his family and displays Wentworth's kindness: He "would assist any brother officer's wife that [he] could." The conversation turns on Wentworth's eligible state and the inevitability of his being married. However, Mrs Croft, the wife of the Admiral, has wisely observed in words that must have had an effect on the listening Anne and convey exactly her situation: "We none of us expect to be in smooth water all our days."

Wentworth removes himself, knowing that he disagrees with his sister and her husband concerning his reactions when he is married. The public discourse turns to Mrs. Croft's account of how many times she crossed the Atlantic and the places she visited and did not visit. For Mrs. Croft, "the happiest part of my life has been spent on board a ship. While we were together, you know, there was nothing to be feared." She recounts the only occasion in which she "ever really suffered in body or mind," and that was when she passed the winter alone at Deal on the Kent coast while her husband "was in the North Seas." The fears were imaginary. It is the imagination that preys on the isolated listener, Anne, as she accompanies the dancing that ends the evening: "her eyes would sometimes fill with tears as she sat at the instrument, she was extremely glad to be employed, and desired nothing in return but to be unobserved." In company, among dancing and music, she is alone with her thoughts.

The chapter concludes from Anne's perspective on a melancholy note. She perceives that there are contenders for Wentworth's affections: the Miss Hayters, "the females of the cousins" of the Musgroves, Henrietta and Louisa. The third paragraph from the end of chapter 8 conveys her dual performance. On the one hand, she performs musically; on the other hand, she is thinking of Wentworth. He spoke to her but is "negative." The final paragraph conveys Anne's perceptions. She "did not wish for more of such looks and speeches. His cold politeness, his ceremonious grace, were worse than anything." Public appearance and perception of private reality coalesce (63, 66–72).

Chapter 9

The opening two paragraphs of the ninth chapter interweave omniscient and indirect narration. Descriptions of Wentworth's activity—he "was to come to Kellynch as to a home, to stay as long as he liked"—are interspersed with his perspective. "There was so much of friendliness, and of flattery . . . the old were so hospitable, the young so agreeable." Consequently Wentworth, delays a proposed visit to his brother in Shropshire, a county on the border of England and Wales. His visits to Uppercross usually take place in the mornings, when "the Admiral and Mrs. Croft were generally out of doors together, interesting themselves in their new possessions, their grass, and their sheep."

The favorable consensus of Wentworth, "unvarying, warm admiration everywhere," is interrupted by the appearance at Uppercross of Charles Hayter, a clergyman, "the eldest of the cousins." He is described as "a very amiable, pleasing young man, between whom and Henrietta there had been a considerable appearance of attachment previous to Captain Wentworth's" appearance on the scene. "A short absence from home had left [Charles Hayter's] fair one [Henrietta] unguarded by his attentions at this critical period," and he returns home to find "very altered manners" on her part.

The differences in the lives of the two sisters and their children's are conveyed in a paragraph opening with a seven-word sentence. This sentence states facts: "Mrs. Musgrove and Mrs. Hayter were sisters." The following sentence is slightly more elaborate: "They had each had money, but their marriages had made a material difference in their

degree of consequence." In this the reader learns that owing to the economic circumstances of their parents, the Hayter children will be less fortunate than the Musgrove children. They "would, from their parents' inferior, retired, and unpolished way of living, and their own defective education, have been hardly in any class at all, but for their connexion with Uppercross." An exception is the "eldest son," Charles, "who had chosen to be a scholar and a gentleman." In addition, he "was very superior in cultivation and manners to all the rest." What is implicit, but not stated, is that he lacks money and property. His connections must come through the Musgroves.

Further, "the two families had always been on excellent terms." There seem to be "no pride on one side, no envy on the other." And "Charles's attention to Henrietta had been observed by her father and mother without any disappropriation." This variant of the Cinderella theme present in the story of the relationship between Anne and Wentworth is punctuated by the appearance of Wentworth on the scene and Henrietta's transference of her affections.

The narrative transfers to the silent observer, Anne, and her perception of "which of the two sisters were preferred by" Wentworth. Comparative adjectives are used to describe them: "Henrietta was perhaps the prettiest; Louisa had the higher spirits." Anne no longer knows, eight years later, which "were more likely to attract" Wentworth. Although the elder Musgroves at the "Mansion-house" seem to ignore the situation, the younger ones at the Cottage speculate on the possibilities. Anne is forced to listen while Charles Musgrove states Wentworth's preference for Louisa and "Mary for Henrietta." Both believe that a marriage for "either would be extremely delightful" from their point of view, but clearly not from that of the silent Anne.

Charles's favoring of Wentworth is based primarily on his fortune and future earning prospects. Charles is "sure that [Wentworth] had not made less than twenty thousand pounds by the war." Also, "in any future war," Wentworth will financially prosper and "distinguish himself" (73–75). Mary, Charles's wife, speculates on Wentworth's being made a baronet and his wife gaining social precedence over the daughter of a baronet. Her husband is influenced by money, Mary by social position and rank. Here "the possessive adjective second person *your*" is used "in a slightly contemptuous . . . usage" (Phillipps, 167) by Mary to downplay her husband Charles's future prospects. She tells him, "I never think much of your new creations." In reality Mary "looked down very decidedly upon the Hayters" and so favors Henrietta. The snobbishness of the Elliots reasserts itself in her reaction. She thinks in terms of its being "quite a misfortune to have the existing connection between the families renewed—very sad for herself and her children."

Mary's views reflect those of her father, Sir Walter, yet are attitudes that influenced Anne's decision to reject eight years previously the impecunious Wentworth. They are values found throughout Jane Austen's fiction, seen, for instance, in Darcy's initial resistance to Bingley's affection for Jane Bennet and his own attitude toward his attraction to Elizabeth Bennet in *Pride and Prejudice*. Mary tells her husband, with Anne in attendance as the listener: "I do not think any young woman has a right to make a choice that may be disagreeable and inconvenient to the *principal* part of her family" (Jane Austen's emphasis). She adds, "and be giving bad connections to those who have not been used to them." She regards Charles Hayter with the disdain with which Wentworth was treated. "And, pray, who is Charles Hayter? Nothing but a country curate. A most improper match for Miss Musgrove, of Uppercross."

Snobbery reverberates throughout Jane Austen's novels. Anne must be aware, as Mary gives her opinion, that she herself rejected Wentworth as a consequence of her giving way to similar opinions expressed, for instance, by Lady Russell.

Mary's husband, in a lengthy speech to her and Anne, outlines the material benefits Charles Hayter as an elder son would bring to such a marriage: an approximately 250-acre estate plus a farm near Taunton, where his father lives. Charles Musgrove concludes that he will be "very well satisfied," if "Louisa can get Captain Wentworth." After her husband has left them, Mary speculates on Wentworth's assumed preferences for Henrietta over Louisa to a silent Anne. To avoid Wentworth, to "escape from being appealed to as umpire," Anne remains at the Cottage rather than going with the others to dinner at the Musgroves'.

In a free indirect passage, Anne meditates on Wentworth's preferences. The narrative then modulates to a passage of omniscient narration in which the reader is informed that Charles Hayter had the opportunity he has wished for: a curacy in Uppercross. Neither Henrietta nor Louisa seems at all interested in such information. Their attention is focused on whether Wentworth will make an appearance. He does but at the Cottage, where only Anne "and the little invalid Charles" are present. The awkwardness between them is not made easier by the appearance of Charles Hayter and the two-year-old Charles. He refuses to remove himself from Anne, who is rescued by Wentworth's resolutely bearing him away.

The final paragraph of chapter 9 conveys the tumult of Anne's reaction in lengthy staccato sentences. Anne's turmoil gives way to her sense of hostility between Charles Hayter and Wentworth. But her feelings are not on this but on her own: "She was ashamed of herself, quite ashamed of being so nervous, so overcome by such a trifle; but so it was." The chapter ends with a variant use of the verb "recover": "and it required a long application of solitude and reflection to recover her" (74–80). The verb has no personal object. The focus is on Anne, who has not spoken a word in the chapter.

Chapter 10

The 10th chapter demonstrates the experience of deeply felt personal isolation in the midst of company. The first paragraph makes fine distinctions between "admiration" and "love." The differences are based on Anne's "memory and experience[s]" of Wentworth. Her longing "for the power" to warn Louisa and Henrietta of "what they were about" is another reflection of Anne's social and personal isolation. Toward the end of the paragraph, she exonerates Wentworth from awareness "of the pain he was occasioning. There was no triumph, no pitiful triumph in his manner," especially as Wentworth "had, probably, never heard, and never thought of any claims of Charles Hayter" upon Henrietta.

Anne's sole criticism of Wentworth is confined to his "accepting the attentions . . . of two young women at once."

Charles Hayter disappears from the scene only to reappear subsequently. The use of the gerund preceded by "a" in "Charles Musgrove and Captain Wentworth being gone a shooting together" reflects 18th-century usage and Austen's attempt to convey the speech inflections of country gentlemen. In the fourth and subsequent paragraph of the chapter, she superbly combines the description of a November walk, the scenery and atmosphere of late autumn, and the coming of winter, to accord with Anne's emotional state. Anne is forced to join the company, to become part of "family-habits" with "every thing being to be done together, however undesired and inconvenient," although she is on her own (82–83).

In this chapter, the "symbolic use of the natural setting" and Anne Elliot's "melancholy . . . are continuously presented through the imagery of autumn" (Litz, *Jane Austin*, 151). Joined by Charles Musgrove and Wentworth, whose "time and strength, and spirits, were, therefore, exactly ready for this walk, and they entered into it with pleasure," Anne is forced to join the party. Charles and Wentworth join as a consequence of the unexpected behavior of "a young dog, who had spoilt their sport." This is one of a series of unexpected happenings that occur throughout the chapter and elsewhere in the novel and affect Anne, whose wish is to be alone at home. On the walk her "object was, not to be in the way of any body." The "last smiles of the year upon the tawny leaves and withered hedges" (83–84) reflect the mood found especially in the poetry of Jane Austen's romantic contemporaries such as Byron, Wordsworth, and Scott. "Nature has ceased to be a mere backdrop; landscape is a structure of feeling which can express, and also modify, the minds of those who view it" (Litz, *Jane Austen*, 153).

Anne herself associates "the sweet scenes of autumn" with poetry, "some tender sonnet, fraught with the apt analogy of the declining year, with declining happiness, and the image of youth and hope, and spring, all gone together, blessed her memory" (85). The association is with Shakespeare's Sonnet 73 with its opening lines "That

time of year thou mayst in me behold/When yellow leaves, or none, or few do hang / Upon those boughs which shake against the cold." The final couplet of the sonnet, as will be seen in *Persuasion*, confirms the strength of love even in isolation. "This thou perceiv'st, which make thy love more strong, / To love that well, which thou must leave ere long." At the end of the chapter, in yet another accident unanticipated by Anne, Wentworth rescues her from tiredness and forced conviviality by finding her room in his sister and brother-in-law's carriage.

The landscape is described to reflect Anne's emotional state. There are "ploughs at work, and the fresh-made path spoke the farmer, counteracting the sweets of poetical despondence, and meaning to have spring again." Spring follows the bleakness of winter. So Anne's hope will be renewed at the end of this chapter and at the conclusion of *Persuasion*.

Places reflect perceptions. The Hayters are seen as lower on the social scale than the Musgroves. Their home, Winthrop, in the winter is "without beauty and without dignity . . . an indifferent house." The marriage of the Admiral and Mrs. Croft is seen as an ideal one. Louisa tells Wentworth, "If I loved a man, as she loves the Admiral, I would be always with him, nothing should ever separate us, and I would rather be overturned by him, than driven safely by anybody else."

These words are echoed in the chapter. Anne is once again the silent listener. By accident she hears Wentworth use the metaphor of a "nut" to Louisa when he gives her the benefit of his experience. He tells her that "*yours* is the character of decision and firmness itself" (Jane Austen's emphasis). Wentworth continues, "It is the worst evil of too yielding and indecisive a character, that no influence over it can be depended on.—You are never sure of a good impression being durable. Every body may sway it; let those who would be happy be firm." Wentworth then exemplifies by taking "a nut . . . from an upper bough." The nut, which "has outlived all the storms of autumn," provides an illustration of the firmness of human beings and the constancy of emotions. Anne, protected by "a bush of low rambling holly" hears Louisa telling Wentworth that Charles Musgrove "wanted to marry Anne" and "that she refused him." Further, that "Lady Russell . . . persuaded Anne to refuse him." Anne's consciousness is the focus of the scene and the chapter. "The listener's proverbial fate was not absolutely hers; she had heard no evil of herself,—but she had heard a great deal of very painful import." She subsequently joins Mary. Anne's "spirits wanted the solitude and silence which only numbers could give."

Charles Hayter rejoins the party, and he and Henrietta are reconciled in a brief passage serving to leave the focus on Louisa and Wentworth. Anne is left with Charles and Mary. The former, however, "was out of temper with his wife." Anne is again on her own. A silent Wentworth rescues her. The walkers encounter the Crofts riding home. Anne "was in the carriage, and felt that he had placed her there, that his will and his hands had done it, that she owed it to his perception of her fatigue, and his resolution to give her rest." Anne believes "She understood him. He could not forgive her,—but he could not be unfeeling."

Even in the carriage, she is reminded of the past and of her present isolated situation. The Admiral reflects to his wife that Wentworth "certainly means to have one or other of those two girls." He then turns to Anne and tells her what she already knows: "We sailors . . . cannot afford to make long courtships in time of war." However, the chapter, one full of irony and the use of nature to convey human emotion and isolation, ends comically. The carriage, through Anne's guidance, avoids "a rut" and did not "run foul of a dung-cart." She gains "some amusement at their style of driving, which she imagined no bad representation of the general guidance of their affairs" (85–92).

Chapter 11

The opening of chapter 11 continues with Anne's perspective and her autumnal melancholic mood. Lady Russell's name reappears, and Anne is expecting to return to Kellynch. The second and third paragraphs of the chapter show Anne to be an isolated figure haunted by the past and living in a time of change. A return to Kellynch has its positives and negatives. "She wished it might be possible for her to avoid ever seeing Captain Wentworth at the hall;—those rooms had witnessed former meetings which would be brought too painfully before her." She is also only too aware that "Lady Russell and Captain Wentworth . . . did not like each other."

Yet again, Anne's plans are diverted from their original course. "Captain Wentworth after being unseen and unheard of at Uppercross for two whole days" reappears on the scene to tell them that he has visited his naval friend Captain Harville, who has "settled with his family at Lyme for the winter." Harville "had never been in good health since a severe wound which he received two years before" (93–94). Lyme had become fashionable in the opening years of the 19th century. A small town on the southwest coast of England, in Dorset, it quickly had emerged from sleepy obscurity as a spa and social center fed by the fashion for medicinal bathing and drinking of the seawater. On September 14, 1804, Jane Austen wrote to her sister, Cassandra, that she went to a ball at the Lyme Assembly Rooms, walked on the Cobb, the semicircular walk stretching out into the sea, and enjoyed "delightful" bathing (*Letters*, 94–95).

In spite of objections, "the young people were all wild to see Lyme." Consequently, "Charles, Mary, Anne, Henrietta, Louisa, and Captain Wentworth" depart for the seaside spa planning to spend one night there. In November, being out of season, there are "scarcely any family but of the residents left." The town itself and its surroundings are described in detail in the eighth paragraph of the chapter. The emphasis is on the coastal district "Charmouth, with its high grounds and extensive sweeps of country, and still more, its sweet retired bay, backed by dark cliffs, where fragments of low rock among the sands make it the happiest spot for watching the flow of the tide, for sitting in unwearied contemplation." The Pinny area is notable for "its green chasms between romantic rocks" (94–95).

The voice of the two lengthy sentences in this eighth paragraph is not Anne's but Jane Austen's. The language evokes that of the early Wordsworth, Scott, or Byron: "the sense of the passing of time, the taste for seclusion and 'for sitting in unwearied contemplation', the stress on firsthand experience and on the value of revisiting scenes, are essentially Wordsworthian." Echoes of Coleridge's *Kubla*

Khan are found in the "sweet," "wonderful," and "lovely" passage (Page, 11–12). The description echoes Anne's contemplative mood of the previous chapter, reflected by the November scenery. Human and natural aspects coalesce. Anne's life, as that of Wentworth's, is one of journeys, of shifting landscapes, from the past, the sea, the voyage of eight years to the present and the future: "many a generation must have passed away since the first partial falling of the cliff."

The narrative voice moves "down by the now deserted and melancholy looking rooms" to the "small house" where "the Harvilles settled." As often in the narrative of *Persuasion*, accidental meetings occur, this time the reappearance of Wentworth with the Harvilles and Captain Benwick. He is also from Wentworth's past, a young officer "whom he had always valued highly." After "a year or two waiting for fortune and promotion" he had gained "at *last*" (Jane Austen's emphasis) both. But his fiancée, "Captain Harville's sister . . . had died the preceding summer while he was at sea." Wentworth perceives Benwick's "disposition as of the sort which must suffer heavily" the loss. He united "very strong feelings with quiet, serious, and retiring manners and a decided taste for reading and sedentary pursuits."

In a switch from Wentworth's to her viewpoint, Anne sees affinities with Benwick. She "cannot believe his prospects so blighted for ever." An analogy from crops and vegetation "blighted" is once again used in the novel to convey human feelings. The author uses quotation marks to convey Anne's inner dialogue with herself on Benwick's state: "He is younger than I am; younger in feeling, if not in fact." She concludes, "He will rally again, and be happy with another." Descriptions follow of Benwick and Captain and Mrs. Harville. Authorial voice and Anne's coincide, for instance, "Captain Harville, though not equalling Captain Wentworth in manners, was a perfect gentleman, unaffected, warm, and obliging." Anne's perspective intrudes when she reflects that "these should have been all my friends" if she had eight years previously married Wentworth. Now in Lyme on the Cobb, by the sea, meeting them again, "she had to struggle against a great tendency to lowness."

Captain Harville's "ingenious contrivances and nice arrangements" in their small house are seen through Anne's eyes. A distinction is made between genuine invitations, "those who invite from the heart," and those whose invitations are insincere, socially motivated by duty. Physically disadvantaged by "lameness," Harville has found compensations. "He drew, he varnished, he carpentered, he glued; he made toys for the children, he fashioned new netting-needles and pins with improvements."

Anne's response to the visit is that "she left great happiness behind her." Louisa romanticizes the naval life: She "burst forth into raptures of admiration and delight." Anne, however, "found herself by this time growing so much more hardened to being in Captain Wentworth's company than she had at first imagined could ever be." She and he "never got beyond" the level of "common civilities," and his presence at the table "was become a mere nothing." A surprise night visit from Wentworth, Harville, and Benwick leads "to Anne's lot to be placed rather apart with Captain Benwick." They talk of literature, of moral work, "collections of the finest letters," biographical memoirs and contemporary poetical work, but novels are not mentioned. Scott's *Marmion* or *The Lady of the Lake*, Byron's *The Bride of Abydos* and *Giaour* (also referred to by Catherine Moreland, the heroine of *Northanger Abbey*) are discussed. Berwick's preference is for these two Byron works. All four poetic examples provide examples of the laments for a love, which has been lost, in the manner of *Persuasion* itself, although none of them offers remedies for recovering from loss.

In the final three paragraphs of the chapter, Anne, at last communicating with someone, "ventures to recommend a larger allowance of prose in his daily study." She recommends readings "calculated to rouse and fortify the mind by the highest precepts, and the strongest example of moral and religious endurances." Benwick "declared his little faith in the efficacy of any books on grief like his." In the final paragraph, Anne alone again reflects on her situation in which she has preached "patience and resignation" to someone younger than she is whom she has not met before. She is also aware that she is being hypocritical for "her own conduct would ill bear examination." She too has given way to sadness and self-pity (95–101).

Chapter 12

The final chapter of the first of the two volumes of *Persuasion* occurs at Lyme. Walking on the sands before breakfast, Anne listens to Henrietta Musgrove's praise of "the sea-air," and Henrietta is reminded of the life of Dr. and Mrs. Shirley, the now aging Rector of Uppercross. They "have been doing good all their lives, wearing out their last days in a place like Uppercross, where, excepting our family, they seem shut out from all the world." Perhaps her thoughts are evoked by reflections on her future with the clergyman Charles Hayter. She wished "Lady Russell lived at Uppercross and were intimate with Dr. Shirley." Henrietta has "always look[ed] upon her as able to persuade a person to any thing!" These words, echoing the title of the novel, also echo in Anne's memory: it was Lady Russell's persuasion that led her to break her engagement with Wentworth.

Their conversation, of which the reader only hears Henrietta's side, is interrupted by their "seeing Louisa and Captain Wentworth coming towards them." Louisa, remembering something she wishes to buy at a shop, asks them to return to town with her. On their way back, a chance encounter with "a gentleman" on the Cobb steps shows that Anne's spirits too have been somewhat restored. "Anne's face caught his eye . . . She was looking remarkably well; her very regular, very pretty features having the bloom" (102–104)—now no longer "faded" (16) as earlier in the novel—"and freshness of youth restored by the fine wind which had been blowing on her complexion, and by the animation of eye which it had also produced." Changed psychological states are reflected in changed physiological states.

It emerges that the stranger whose "earnest admiration" she attracted is a cousin: "a Mr. Elliot; a gentleman of large fortune." Their "father's next heir," he, like Benwick, is in mourning. A waiter is turned to for information, although he is unable to supply any. In a brief speech notable for its use of the negatives: "No, ma'am—he did not mention

no particular family"—indicating lack of education through grammatical incorrectness. Mary addresses Anne in a series of exclamations on Elliot, his resemblance to their family and "livery." Wentworth's response to all this is addressed as much to Anne as to Mary, and perhaps reflects just a note of jealousy. He tells them, "We must consider it to be the arrangement of Providence, that you should not be introduced to your cousin."

Perspectives switch back and forth from Anne to Mary. The former has "a secret gratification to herself . . . to know that the future owner of Kellynch was undoubtedly a gentleman, and had an air of good sense." Mary wishes the encounter to be mentioned to her father and sister now in Bath. Anne is opposed to this, and she is the correspondent with Elizabeth, not Mary.

After breakfast joined by Captain and Mrs. Harville, and Captain Benwick, they "take their last walk about Lyme." At first Anne is accompanied by Captain Benwick: "they walked together some time, talking as before of Mr. Scott and Lord Byron, and still as unable, as before, and as unable as any other two readers, to think exactly alike of the merits of either." She is joined by Captain Harville, who tells her that she has performed "a good deed in making" his friend "talk so much." Anne's response that time is a healer, and her allusion to the necessity to "remember" reflects her own situation. Harville then recounts the experience of how Benwick learned of his wife's death following his return from the Cape of Good Hope and appointment as captain of the *Grappler*. It was Wentworth whose ship had docked the week previously in Plymouth who "travelled night and day till he got to Portsmouth, rowed off to the Grappler . . . and never left the poor fellow for a week." He adds, "nobody else could have saved poor James" Benwick.

Anne's response is subordinated to Harville's strength of feeling on the subject. She is distracted by Mrs. Harville's wish that her husband return home. Anne and the others continue their walk. She is again joined by Benwick and the opening line of Byron's *The Corsair* (1814)—"O'er the glad waters of the dark blue sea"—or Canto II verse XVII of his *Childe Harold's Pilgrimage* (1812)—"He that has sail'd upon the dark blue sea" are echoed in "Lord Byron's 'dark blue seas' could not fail of being brought forward by their present view." Attention then turns to Louisa who, jumping, "was too precipitate by half a second, she fell on the pavement of the Lower Cobb and was taken lifeless!": "There was no wound, no blood, no visible bruise," is the first half of the sentence. In the second portion "her eyes were closed, she breathed not, her face was like death." In the second sentence, "The horror of that moment to all who stood around!" is strikingly conveyed.

Wentworth has Louisa in his arms. Mary screams and renders her husband "immoveable." Henrietta "lost her senses too" but is supported by Benwick and Anne. Wentworth's cry for help is answered by Anne, who implores Benwick to "go to him. Rub her hands, rub her temples" and supplies salts. Wentworth seems to have lost control of the situation yet is again rescued by Anne's call for "A surgeon" and suggestion that Benwick "knows where a surgeon is to be found." At this moment of crisis, Anne assumes command, "attending with all the strength and zeal, and thought, which instinct supplied" to the needs and requirements of others. Charles Musgrove directly appeals to her: "what is to be done next? What in heaven's name, is to be done next?" and "Captain Wentworth's eyes were also turned towards her" (104–111). Anne is no longer "identified with the blank dash '—' a notation of absence, of aposiopesis [silence] of being prematurely cut off at twenty-seven" (Tandon, 233). She now takes command in an emergency.

In the next paragraph the focus switches from Anne, Wentworth, and Musgrove to "the workmen and boatmen about the Cobb." Jane Austen's dry, ironic humor asserts itself: "many were collected near them, to be useful if wanted, at any rate, to enjoy the sight of a dead young lady." She adds, "nay, two dead young ladies, for it proved twice as fine as the first report."

Subsequently, Captain Harville "brought senses and nerves that could be instantly useful" after he has been alerted by seeing Captain Benwick "flying by" his house. Louisa is taken to the Harvilles' house and "under Mrs. Harville's direction, was conveyed upstairs, and given possession of her own bed." Her sister Henrietta, who previously had fainted and been revived, is "kept by the agitation of hope and fear, from return of her own insensibility." Another interesting word usage is found in the next paragraph. "They were sick with horror while" the surgeon "examined," "but he was not hopeless." The fact "that he did not regard it as a desperate case," and the subsequent relief, "the ecstasy of such a reprieve" with "fervent ejaculations of gratitude to Heaven" is conveyed through the general expression "may be conceived" by the reader.

Jane Austen presents differing perspectives as part of her all-embracing irony. An instance of this is found in the single-sentence paragraph which follows:

> The tone, the look, with which "Thank God!" was uttered by Captain Wentworth, Anne was sure could never be forgotten by her; nor the sight of him afterwards, as he sat near a table, leaning over it with folded arms, and face concealed, as if overpowered by the various feelings of his soul, and trying by prayer and reflection to calm them.

In addition to the religious references to "God," the "soul," and "prayer and reflection" (111–112), there is the issue of comprehension of the situation by Wentworth and Anne. She perceives Wentworth's response as an indication of his strong feelings for Louisa. Her perception on an initial reading of the chapter appears sensible, although Wentworth has been more attentive to her since Elliot, the heir to Kellynch, noticed her on the Cobb steps. In the penultimate chapter of the novel (II: 11), Wentworth tells Anne that her perception was incorrect and that his reaction revealed his love for her and not Louisa. He became aware that it was Anne only that he loved (242). So there are at least two ways of examining this paragraph. First, Anne's perceptions at the time he said, "Thank God!" Second, subsequently to be revealed in the novel. Appearances are deceptive: perhaps Anne's interpretation of Wentworth's reactions reveals her own lack of certainty of regaining Wentworth's love.

The following three paragraphs, beginning with "It now became necessary for the party to consider what was best to be done" and concluding with Wentworth's "Musgrove, either you or I must go

(112–113), focus on the consequences of Louisa staying with the Harvilles. Stylistically, they reveal their author's "unusual flexibility, combining the immediacy of speech with the unslackened narrative pace made possible by the free mingling of diverse elements" (Page, 128). The first two sentences of the paragraph beginning "It now became necessary" are *authorial narrative. Authorial observation* is found in the last sentence of the paragraph: "And all this was said with all truth and sincerity of feeling irresistible." Interspersed is *free indirect speech*, for instance, in the sentences "That Louisa must remain where she was … did not admit a doubt. Her removal was impossible." Other examples are "Captain Benwick must give up his room to them, and get a bed elsewhere … could accommodate no more"; and a lengthy passage of almost three sentences; "they could hardly bear to think of not finding room for two or three besides," and concluding "Between those two, she could want no possible attendance by day or night."

There is, in addition to narrative, authorial observation and free indirect speech, *direct speech* indicated by quotation marks. This occupies little space in the paragraph, and the individual speaker, probably one of the Harvilles, is not indicated before "putting the children away in the maids' room, or swinging a cot somewhere." The paragraph is followed by another in which the identity of the indirect speaker is again unclear. In the previous instance the words are probably the Harvilles'. In the next, the direct speech could belong to all three speakers. It is introduced by narrative: "Charles, Henrietta, and Captain Wentworth were the three in consultation, and for a little while it was only an interchange of perplexity and terror." Then follows a sequence of black dashes "Uppercross—the necessity of some one's going to Uppercross—the news to be conveyed—how, it could be broken to Mr. and Mrs. Musgrove—the lateness of the morning,—an hour already gone since they ought to have been off—the impossibility of being in tolerable time" (112–113). As Norman Page observes, "the exclamatory nature of the conversation is being conveyed by the use of nominal groups and subordinate clauses rather than complete sentences." Further, "the use of main verbs is suspended as action is temporarily paralysed by the shock of the accident, and only static, apparently unproductive expressions of dismay are possible" (Page, 130).

Direct speech is followed by the authorial observation, "At first, they were capable of nothing more to the purpose than such exclamations." This is followed by "but after a while, Captain Wentworth exerting himself, said." What he said is decisive and reveals character—he is able to assume a position of authority in a difficult situation. "We must be decided, and without the loss of another minute … Musgrove, either you or I must go." At this juncture, Anne reappears once again as listener. This time she hears words from Wentworth that are difficult to misconstrue following Wentworth's formal reference to "Mrs. Charles Musgrove [who] will, of course, wish to get back to her children." He refers to her by her Christian name, "but, if Anne will stay, no one so proper, so capable as Anne!" Sentiments of affection "warmly agreed to" by Charles and Henrietta.

Wentworth, on Anne's appearance, then addresses her using the affectionate "you" second-person singular, "You will stay, I am sure; you will stay and nurse her." The reaction to this becomes Anne's. Wentworth spoke "with a glow, and yet a gentleness, which seemed almost restoring the past." Following a parenthesis, the author intervenes with the descriptive, "She coloured deeply; and he recollected himself, and moved away."

Mary, however, rejects the plans. For Mary, "Anne … was nothing to Louisa, while she was her sister, and had the best right to stay in Henrietta's stead! Why was not she to be as useful as Anne?" Consequently, "the change of Mary for Anne was inevitable." Anne's viewpoint again becomes predominant. She and Benwick are again thrown together and "she felt an increasing degree of good-will towards him." Wentworth becomes the observer rather than Anne: "Captain Wentworth was on the watch for them." His reaction to "the substitution of one sister for the other" is reflected in his "evident surprise and vexation" and "the change of his countenance."

Attention transfers to Anne's reaction. "She endeavoured to be composed, and to be just. Without emulating the feelings of an Emma towards her Henry, she would have attended on Louisa" (113–116). The allusion is to Henry Prior's poem *Henry and Emma* (1709). This has as its foundation the ballad "The Nut-Brown Maid," celebrating the fidelity of the Maid who is tested by an assumed rival who does not exist, a reflection of Anne's own state of mind.

The focus on the journey back from Lyme is on Anne's reaction to Wentworth, whose appeal to God and expression, "Dear, sweet Louisa!" again are capable of misinterpretation by her. Anne believes that Wentworth must be comparing Louisa's "very resolute character" with her own "persuadable temper." She hopes that her actions at the Cobb and the Harvilles' might possibly lead to a change in Wentworth's perception of her. On the return journey, "there had been total silence among them for sometime." Henrietta appears to have "cried herself to sleep." Wentworth addresses Anne, seeking her assent to a plan of his that he break the news to the Musgroves while she remain with Henrietta. For Anne, "the appeal remained a pleasure to her—as a proof of friendship, and of deference for her judgment, a great pleasure."

At the end of the chapter and the first part of *Persuasion*, Anne is left at Uppercross Great House with the Musgrove family. Wentworth "announced his intent of returning in the same carriage to Lyme; and when the horses were baited, he was off" (116–117).

Volume 2, Chapter 1 (Chapter 13)

Anne is no longer alone. At Uppercross for two days, "she had the satisfaction of knowing herself extremely useful there." In terms of locations and characters, the chapter moves from Uppercross to Lady Russell's at Kellynch, and then to Admiral and Mrs. Croft at Kellynch-hall. The viewpoint through which these are centered is Anne's. The accident at Lyme and news of Louisa's health form a backdrop. Characters such as the Crofts and Lady Russell reappear, and mention is made of Mrs. Clay and Sir Walter Elliot.

Anne is the last to leave Uppercross; the Musgroves, at her persuasion, decide to go to Lyme to be with Louisa, and the former children's nurse,

Sarah, is brought from the neighboring town of Crewkherne "to go and help nurse dear Miss Louisa." The indirect speech echoes the Musgroves' and Anne's sentiments. Anne is separated from the family, who are referred to three times in the third person, "they," to emphasize the sense of her being left alone. Anne reflects on the situation: "A few months hence, and the room now so deserted, occupied but by her silent, pensive self, might be filled again with all that was happy and gay, all that was glowing and bright in prosperous love, all that was most unlike Anne Elliot!"

Place, the weather, and the season, "a dark November day, a small thick rain almost blotting out the very few objects ever to be discerned," reflect Anne's autumnal and melancholy mood. She is leaving Uppercross with its memories for Lady Russell, yet cannot leave "without a saddened heart— Scenes had passed in Uppercross, which made it precious." The dash once again in the narrative signals Anne's present isolation and memories. For her, Uppercross was the location "of many sensations of pain, once severe, but now softened; and of some instances of relenting feeling, some breathings of friendship and reconciliation, which could never be looked for again." These memories "could never cease to be dear. She left it all behind her; all but the recollection that such things had been."

The meeting again with Lady Russell and the visit with her at Kellynch lodge is less difficult than Anne had believed. Lady Russell's perception of Anne is complimentary: "either Anne was improved in plumpness or looks, or Lady Russell fancied her so." Not for the first time in an Austen novel, physical well-being reflects an inner state of improvement. Anne connects these "compliments . . . with the silent admiration of her cousin, and of hoping that she was to be blessed with a second spring of youth and beauty."

Attention turns to Lady Russell's concerns that "Mrs. Clay should still be with" her father and sister in Bath. Anne's mind is not with them but on the Harvilles and Captain Benwick. She is not too interested in the activities at "Camden-place," a new housing development built in the early 19th century north of the center of Bath. Jane Austen uses an interesting verb form to convey the introduction of an awkward subject between Anne and Lady Russell: "they must speak of the accident at Lyme" and Captain Wentworth. Anne misperceives Lady Russell's reaction to her assumption of an attachment between Wentworth and Louisa. Outwardly, Lady Russell wished "them happy; but internally her heart revelled in angry pleasure, in pleased contempt." She reflects "that the man who at twenty-three had seemed to understand somewhat the value of an Anne Elliot, should, eight years afterwards, be charmed by a Louisa Musgrove."

Lady Russell and Anne, following news from Lyme, as an act of social duty call on the Crofts at Kellynch-hall. Lady Russell had already formed "so high an opinion of the Crofts," who carry out their social and other responsibilities toward "the parish . . . and the poor" much better than its owners. Anne is unable to think, "These rooms ought to belong only to us . . . An ancient family to *be* so *driven* away!" The exclamatory infinitives (emphasized in the citation) do not apply to the Crofts. However, her entering Kellynch-hall does evoke memories for Anne of her dead mother, "and [she] remembered where she had been used to sit and reside."

"The prevailing topic" of conversation between the visitors and the Crofts is "the sad accident at Lyme." The description provides the only instance in Jane Austen's works of the use of the expression "yester morn." This evokes nostalgia and regret especially from Anne's perspective, as if to emphasize permanent loss: "each lady dated her intelligence from the same hour of yester morn, that Captain Wentworth had been in Kellynch yesterday." On the other hand, it had brought a note containing Wentworth's inquiry concerning Anne's welfare. The viewpoint is again hers, and characteristically dashes appear as punctuation forms "— This was handsome,—and gave her more pleasure than almost any thing else could have done."

The narrator's positive criteria referring to "a couple of steady, sensible women" is used for Mrs. Croft, Anne, or Lady Russell. Admiral Croft's "goodness of heart and simplicity of character" are appreciated by Anne, if not by the snobbish Lady Russell. Conversation between the Admiral and

Anne turns upon one of the few alterations that he has made to the house. The Admiral has "done very little besides sending away some of the large looking-glasses from [his] dressing-room, which was [Anne's] father['s]." Admiral Croft objects to "such a number of looking-glasses! Oh, Lord! there was no getting away from oneself." The Admiral's requirements are rather "with my little shaving glass." His lack of vanity contrasts sharply with the consummate egoism of Anne's father, Sir Walter Elliott, who the Admiral believes "must be rather a dressy man for his time of life."

The chapter concludes with "Lady Russell and Mrs. Croft . . . very well pleased with each other." The Crofts are "going away for a few weeks to visit their connexions in the north of the county." Anne consequently is in no "danger" of encountering Wentworth at Kellynch-hall. In the final sentence, she is alone with her thoughts that "Every thing was safe enough, and she smiled over the many anxious feelings she had wasted on the subject" of meeting Wentworth again ([121]–128).

Volume 2, Chapter 2 (Chapter 14)

This chapter begins at Uppercross, although attention is on what happened at Lyme. By its conclusion, the setting has moved to Bath, which remains the locale for the remainder of *Persuasion*. The chapter also focuses on characters in the novel other than Anne or Wentworth but indirectly illuminates them as well. The first three paragraphs relate to Charles and Mary's activities, Louisa's condition, and relationships between the Musgroves and the Harvilles, as well as a mention of Charles Hayter. Fashionable activities, too, are conveyed. Mary, for instance, "has bathed" although it is unclear whether she did so in the sea or in the indoor baths built in Lyme in 1804. Benwick and his activities become the focus of a discussion between Charles and Mary, with Anne as listener, as she initially "enquired after Captain Benwick." Charles and Mary perceive that Benwick is attached to Anne although they both interpret differently his motives for staying in Lyme. Their argument highlights how they can both misjudge Benwick's motives. It also reveals Lady Russell's judiciousness. In spite of Mary's prompting, she refuses to judge Benwick, saying, "I must see" him "before I decide." Further, her comment to Charles's sense that Benwick will call on them soon, "Any acquaintance of Anne's will always be welcome to me," is an ironic reminder of her previous treatment of Wentworth.

Differing perceptions of Benwick's character and Lady Russell's response to him elicit her sense of her own character as "steady and matter of fact" and determination "not to judge him [Benwick] before-hand." Mention by Mary of their meeting at Lyme with Mr. Elliot brings out a negative reaction from Lady Russell, who has "no wish to see" him. Two paragraphs then follow, revealing Jane Austen's subtle modulation of variety of tone and shift in narrative focus. Close attention to the six-sentence paragraph beginning "With regard to Captain Wentworth," concluding, "much more disposed to ride over to Kellynch," and the three-sentence paragraph beginning "There can be no doubt," concluding "been beginning to excite," exhibit Jane Austen's ability to reveal a complex subtext.

The first sentence of the first paragraph focuses on Wentworth, who is the subject of the rest of the paragraph. Anne is mentioned only once and that is in the first sentence. She "hazarded no enquiries" about Wentworth (130–133). This is the only use of the word "hazarded" in *Persuasion,* and its usage is limited to only seven other instances in Austen's novels. Here it implies an anxiousness to hear about Wentworth, combined with a sense of taking a chance, a gamble suggesting uncertainty over his feelings and situation. Earlier in the chapter, she had almost neutrally "enquired after Captain Benwick" (130). In the first four sentences of the paragraph, the speaker, probably Mary, reports that Wentworth's health has recovered as has Louisa's: "he was now quite a different creature from what he had been the first week." But the fourth sentence reveals that "Wentworth had not seen Louisa," and in this sentence of lengthy subclauses indicated by semicolons, Wentworth and Louisa become as dissociated, unlinked, and modified as the sentence structure. Mary expected him to see her, interprets Wentworth's actions, believing that he "was so extremely fearful of any ill consequence to her from an interview." However, "on the contrary,"

Wentworth "seemed to have a plan of going away for a week or ten days." The final fifth sentence reintroduces Benwick, whom Wentworth "wanted to persuade . . . to go with him" unsuccessfully to Plymouth. It concludes with Charles's speculation on Benwick's refusal to accompany Wentworth: a supposition that he "seemed much more disposed to ride over to Kellynch." The novel will reveal that it is not Anne who is the focus of Benwick's attentions but Louisa.

The following three-sentence paragraph focuses on Lady Russell's and Anne's thoughts on Benwick. Lady Russell, "after giving him a week's indulgence" and still not visiting them, "determined him to be unworthy of . . . interest." The accusative infinitive construction of "to be unworthy of" conveys her sense that he, Benwick, is not worth even thinking about. Anne's focus on him highlights her solitariness and social work. She could not "return from any stroll of solitary indulgence in her father's grounds, or any visit of charity in the village, without wondering whether she might see him or hear him." The short subsequent third sentence, "Captain Benwick came not, however," reveals that he, for Anne, is a preoccupation probably created to distract herself from thoughts of Wentworth.

Although "neither Henrietta, nor Louisa, nor Charles Hayter nor Captain Wentworth" were at Uppercross, the presence of the Musgroves and "the little Harvilles" make it, for Anne, "already quite alive again." A paragraph devoted to the Musgrove family is followed by a paragraph focusing on Anne's response and the author directly relating that "Louisa was now recovering apace." Readers are also told that "Captain Wentworth was gone, for the present, to see his brother in Shropshire."

The transfer of location from Uppercross to Bath is achieved through an authorial observation on sounds, the use of the word "innoxious" and the fine distinction between the "sort" and the "quantity" of noises. Lady Russell and Anne enter Bath crossing the Avon on the south side of the city, and to get to Camden-place, where the Elliots are, they have to travel through the city center. Lady Russell and Anne react differently to the city. The former finds its noises, "The bawling of newsmen, muffin men [sellers of muffins] and milkmen . . . the ceaseless clink of patterns ['overshoes with wooden soles supported on an iron ring to raise the wearer a few inches, this enabled women to walk on muddy roads without getting too much dirt on their clothes' (Bree, 157)]" relief from being in the country. For her and Mrs. Musgrove, "nothing could be so good for her as a little quiet cheerfulness."

Anne, on the other hand, "did not share these feelings." She views the building and the rain as "too rapid." Her isolation would increase—"who would be glad to see her when she arrived?" She looks back—looking back is a characteristic of Anne—"with fond regret, to the bustles of Uppercross and the seclusion of Kellynch." The sounds and activity of Bath, her return to her father and sister Elizabeth, will increase her isolation.

Jane Austen uses a letter from Elizabeth to convey information concerning Mr. Elliot, the heir to Kellynch-hall. He had called at Camden-place three times and wished to "proclaim the value of the connection" with his relatives "as he had formerly taken pains to shew neglect." Elliot makes a conscious effort in calling so frequently. Camden-place, where Anne, Elizabeth, and their father live, is not in the center of Bath and is up a steep hill. Lady Russell "was in a state of very agreeable curiosity and perplexity about" him. The narrator suggests skepticism concerning his motives by inserting a sentence concerning his calling activities. "This was very wonderful, if it were true": in other words, had "he really sought to reconcile himself like a dutiful branch" to the family he had previously scorned?

Anne's reaction is fairly neutral: "she felt that she would rather see [him] again than not." At the end of the chapter Anne "was put down in Camden-place; and Lady Russell then drove to her lodgings in Rivers street." The activities at Lyme and their consequences seem far away (133–136).

Volume 2, Chapter 3 (Chapter 15)

This chapter provides a different setting and fresh characters. It also highlights the vanity of Sir Walter and Elizabeth brought out by Bath. Kellynch-hall, its space, "duties and dignity of the resident land-holder" are discarded by Sir Walter and Elizabeth. Both, ironically from Anne's point of view, "finding extent to be proud of between two walls, perhaps thirty feet asunder." Somewhat surprisingly, Anne is welcomed by both her father and her sister, although neither had any "inclination to listen to her . . . Uppercross excited no interest, Kellynch very little, it was all Bath."

In addition to the resident "very pleasant and very smiling," but silent Mrs. Clay, they have too "many introductions" in a Bath where Anne "must sigh, and smile, and wonder too." In this world appearance seems to be all. The focus of attention is Mr. Elliot, the figure from the families' past, who had 10 years previously broken an engagement to Elizabeth. Elliot had repeatedly visited them. The pronoun "he" is used frequently, five times in the paragraph beginning, "But this was not all what they had to make them happy." It occurs on eight occasions in the following paragraph beginning, "They had not a fault to find in him." Such repetition emphasizes Elliot's role-playing. This sense of falsity is reinforced by the threefold reoccurrence of "such" in the description of Elliot's behavior: "such great openness of conduct, such readiness to apologize for the past, such solicitude to be received as a relation again."

Anne learns from the report of his visits, not from Elliot himself but from the reports of his "very intimate friend . . . a Colonel Wallis, a highly respectable man," an ambiguous account of Elliot's first marriage. The explanation concerns "A very fine woman, with a large fortune, in love with him!" It seems to allay Elizabeth's hostility: "though Elizabeth could not see the circumstance in quite so favourable a light, she allowed it be a great extenuation." Anne serves in the role of listener. A lengthy paragraph opening, "Anne listened, but without quite understanding it," through indirect speech, enters into her thoughts and reactions to Elliot. "Still, however, she had the sensation of there being something more than immediately appeared, in Mr. Elliot's wishing, after an interval of so many years, to be well received by them." She recalls Elliot's rejection of Elizabeth when younger, as if remembering her own breaking off with Wentworth, although for different reasons. "Most earnestly did she wish that he might not be too nice, or too observant, if Elizabeth were his object."

Anne's impressions of meeting Elliot at Lyme are little "attended to" by her father and sister. "They could not listen to her description of him. They were describing him themselves; Sir Walter especially." His description reveals his vanity. According to Sir Walter, Elliot "appeared to think that he (Sir Walter) was looking exactly as he had done when they last parted"—a decade earlier. Sir Walter described Mrs. Wallis, the wife of Elliot's close friend Colonel Wallis, "in daily expectation of her confinement" but "charming" and "said to be an excessively pretty woman, beautiful," hence, "worthy of being known in Camden-place," where appearance is the chief criterion of value. Sir Walter goes into a lengthy lament on the lack of "pretty women" he has encountered in Bath. The passage in which his observance is related is notable for its narcissism. The emphasis is on Sir Walter, what "He had," "He did," "He hoped." Indeed, "he" is repeated seven times to stress his vanity, and his obsession with personal appearances.

Sir Walter's delusions are interrupted by Anne's recollection of the late visit of Elliot. On their meeting on the steps in Lyme, "he had not been at all aware of who she was." In addition, "He looked completely astonished, but not more astonished than pleased; his eyes brightened, . . . he welcomed the relationship." Further, "He was quite as good-looking as he had appeared at Lyme . . . his manners were so exactly what they ought to be." Elliot has ceased to be himself and is role-playing. This role-playing is reinforced in the final paragraphs of the chapter, which repeat "he" and "his" with occasional allusions to his past behavior and his attempts to explain away his past actions.

Interestingly, "his reflections" are addressed to Anne, to whom he knew he "must not be addressing . . . alone." Anne contrasts Sir Walter and Elizabeth's interest in "an accident" at Lyme to Elliot's and Lady Russell's "in the wish of really comprehending what had passed, and in the degree of concern for what she must have suffered in witnessing it." The final two paragraphs focus on the passing of time and the "elegant little clock on the mantle-piece," appearing a fine object striking "eleven with its silver sounds." In the last paragraph of the chapter, a single sentence, "Anne could not

have supposed it possible that the first evening in Camden-place could have passed so well!" There is irony here: she has been surprisingly welcomed by her father and sister. She is the focus of attention—Elliot's (138–144).

There are interesting linguistic features in this chapter. The verb "to place" is found in the abstract sense of "to attribute" or "ascribe" followed by "in" (Phillipps, 64) when Elliot is described as "Placing his whole happiness *in* [my emphasis] being on intimate terms in Camden-place" (140). Sir Walter is told when he has observed that Mary "had a red nose"—"Oh! no that *must have been* [my emphasis] quite accidental." Here "uncommonly . . . the modern meaning of present supposition or certainty about the past" occurs (Phillipps, 124). A third illustration of interesting word usage may be seen. "*In* frequently occurs where *on* appears today; for instance *in his way*, for *on his way*" (Phillipps's emphasis, 192). Anne reacting to the late knock at the door thinks, "It was possible that he might stop in his way home" (142).

Volume 2, Chapter 4 (Chapter 16)

Rank and snobbery are predominant in this chapter. It starts and finishes with Anne's negative reaction to Mrs. Clay and hopes that the relationship between her and Sir Walter is not too strong. In the final paragraphs of the chapter she seems to have found a somewhat surprising ally in their dislike of Mrs. Clay—Elliot, who the narrative will reveal has his own motives for getting the better of Mrs. Clay. Appearance, looks, come to the fore when Anne is alone with her father, who recommends that his daughter use the same personal skin lotion, "Gowland," used by Mrs. Clay. Sir Walter, somewhat blinded by Mrs. Clay, believes that its usage "has carried away her freckles." To Anne, on the other hand, "it did not appear . . . that the freckles were at all lessened." However, regarding their relationship, from Anne's point of view, "every thing must take its chance" and if they married and Elizabeth did so too, Anne "might always command a home with Lady Russell."

From Lady Russell's perspective, "the sight of Mrs. Clay in such favour, and of Anne so overlooked, was a perpetual provocation." Even here,

Lady Russell's vexation is mitigated as she has much to do in Bath. People on a daily basis visit the Pump-room in order to drink a glass of the spring water. Her approval of William Elliot is couched in terms to remind Anne of his "steady, observant, moderate, candid" free from malice, qualities. These are different from those she discerned in Wentworth. Elliot, from Lady Russell's lenses, has "good understanding, correct opinions, knowledge of the world." He has no "pride or weakness" and is "never run away with by spirits or by selfishness, to what was amicable and lovely" (145–147). The qualities she discerns in Elliot "establish the priority of that most basic unit of the social structure, the patriarchal family . . . Of course Lady Russell is drastically wrong about Sir Walter's heir." In common with other "villanous gentleman and peers of . . . fiction," they "manipulate other people's domestic lives in order to secure their own power." Elliot "is out for himself" (Johnson, 149).

Anne has learned to "sometimes think differently" from Lady Russell, who, as Anne learns, and the narrative reveals, was so wrong about Wentworth. Lady Russell's views are contrasted with Anne's, who is more skeptical in her attitude to Elliot. In the Elliot household, "Elizabeth must be first," and precedence, "rank and connexion" so valued by William Elliot predominate. "The arrival of the Dowager Viscountess Dalrymple and her daughter, the Honourable Miss Carteret . . . cousins of the Elliots," exemplifies the excessive deference shown especially by Anne's father and elder sister to class and rank and reveals his snobbery. Anne sees her father and older sister lacking "pride" in their dealing with "nobility." The family connection had broken, owing to the absence of "letters of ceremony." The social rituals determine relationships. The Elliots at the time of the death of the "late Viscount" had omitted to send a formal condolence letter to the Dalrymples, who live in Ireland (147–148).

As Bree observes, "this indication that the Dalrymples are Irish is a further satire on Sir Walter's eagerness to renew the acquaintance, since the Irish nobility were often thought of as socially inferior to the English and Scottish nobility" (170 n. 2). Sir Walter receives but "three lines of scrawl from the Dowager Viscountess." His and Elizabeth's obsession with their cousins bring only shame to Anne, who sees in them "no superiority of manner, accomplishment, or understanding." To others, "because she had a smile and a civil answer for every body," Lady Dalrymple "acquired the name of a 'charming woman.'" In other words, superficial manners are the criteria of character. The daughter, "Miss Carteret . . . was so plain and so awkward, that she would never have been tolerated in Camden-place but for her birth."

Lady Russell "expected something better." Elliot defends the relationship in terms of "a family connection, as good company," and "their value." Anne tells Elliot that her "idea of good company . . . is the company of clever, well-informed people." Elliot responds by saying that "Bath and good manners are essential" and alludes to Pope's "A little Learning is a dang'rous Thing" (line 215) in *Essays on Criticism* (1711). Elliot tells Anne that "a little learning is by no means a dangerous thing in good company, on the contrary, it will do very well." His tone becomes more intimate toward Anne, but in spite of increasing familiarity, Elliot adheres to conservative values. He tells Anne, "rank is rank." To which Anne, objecting to her father's subservience to rank, responds, "I suppose (smiling) I have more pride than any of you."

In the final three paragraphs, Anne displays her opposition to the values important in Bath. She informs Elliot that she is "too proud to enjoy a welcome which depends so entirely upon place." The response from Elliot brings out both his seeming affection for Anne and an insight into his motives. He tells Anne, "I love your indignation" and refers to her as "my dear cousin." He informs Anne, "here you are in Bath, and the object is to be established here with all the credit and dignity which ought to belong to Sir Walter Elliot." He refers to his own pride and then, lowering his voice, feels "that every addition to your father's society, among his equals or superiors, may be of use in diverting his thoughts from those who are beneath him." This clear reference to Mrs. Clay brings approval, agreement with Anne. Both for their own reasons have the same object, "The view of defeating her"—Mrs. Clay (149–151).

Volume 2, Chapter 5 (Chapter 17)

The chapter moves from Anne's visit to a former school friend, "Miss Hamilton now Mrs. Smith," who "was said to have married a man of fortune" but "was a widow and poor . . . and in addition to these distresses, had been afflicted with a severe rheumatic fever, which finally settling in her legs, had made her for the present a cripple" (152). Anne's renewal of her friendship leads to discussion and adverse observation from her father, although Lady Russell "Sees nothing to blame in" (157) the acquaintance. The chapter concludes with Lady Russell's and Anne's differing perceptions of Mr. Elliot.

The introduction of Mrs. Smith so late in the novel has perplexed many: "Why . . . does Austen give the resilient survivor Mrs. Smith so much time near the end of the novel?" (Auerbach, 247). Mrs. Smith lives in a poor area of Bath and in lodgings. She is in "severe and constant pain" (154). She makes "two strong claims on [Anne's] attention, of past kindness and present suffering," reflecting Anne's own predicament. At school she "had shewn [Anne] kindness in one of those periods of her life when it had been most valuable" following the loss of her mother. As a 14-year-old girl, she had been comforted by "Miss Hamilton, three years older" who "had considerably lessened [Anne's] misery." So Anne is repaying a debt from her past. She is also exhibiting kindness and recognition that genuine worth transcends social status.

At her friend's lodgings, Anne discovers that Mrs. Smith is being treated by her landlady with kindness. Further, "neither sickness, nor sorrow seemed to have closed her heart or ruined her spirits" (152–153). With the help of her landlady nurse Rooke, "a shrewd, intelligent, sensible woman," she learns to accommodate. The nurse "taught me to knit . . . she put me in the way of making these little thread-cases, pin cushions and card racks," so that Mrs. Smith is helping those even less fortunate than herself. Mrs. Smith has considerable insight into her own condition. She tells Anne it is "weakness . . . that appears in a sick chamber; it is selfishness and impatience rather than generosity and fortitude, that one hears of." She reinforces what readers have witnessed Anne experiencing in the course of the novel: "There is so little real friendship in the world!" (155–156). She also leads Anne to reflect on what might have been and change—a theme pervading *Persuasion*.

Since she last saw Miss Hamilton, Mrs. Smith, "twelve years were gone since they parted, and each presented a somewhat different person from what the other had imagined." Essentially, "Twelve years had changed Anne from the blooming, silent, unformed girl of fifteen, to the elegant little woman of seven and twenty, with every beauty excepting bloom" (153). Her friend seems to have adjusted more to her plight than Anne, whose situation is so much better. Mrs. Smith has even created, with the help of her nurse and landlady, a cottage industry by selling "all the high-priced things [she has] in hand now" to a Mrs Wallis, "a mere pretty, silly, expressive, fashionable woman" who "has plenty of money."

Adaptability to change and kindness are illustrated by the introduction of Mrs. Smith, who is to play an important role in the plot of *Persuasion* by revealing the true side of William Elliot, Anne's seeming admirer. Positive moral values are demonstrated in Mrs. Smith, her nurse, and Anne's visits to them. Negative values are represented at Camden-place and in the activities of Sir Walter and Elizabeth Elliot and their associates. When he hears that his daughter Anne has been visiting such an unfashionable address as "Westgate-buildings," Sir Walter formally addresses her: "Upon my word, Miss Anne Elliot, you have the most extraordinary taste!" He objects to "low company, paltry rooms, foul air, disgusting associations." He objects to Mrs. Smith's age and condition, assuming, "she is old and sickly." Sir Walter, however, has never seen Mrs. Smith.

Sir Walter asks her age, "Forty?" Anne replies that "she is not one and thirty." He is in his fifties and proud of his appearance. Austen herself lived into her 42nd year, her sister, Cassandra, lived until she was 72 and a naval brother made it into his nineties. Sir Walter's comments are a further reflection of his total self-absorption. Even his friend Mrs. Clay "thought it advisable to leave the room" when he made such disparaging, snobbish observations. As the narrator somewhat ironically observes, "Mrs. Smith was not the only widow in Bath between thirty and forty, with little to live on, and no sirname of dignity" (157–158).

While Anne, against the wishes of her father and sister, revisits her friend, Sir Walter and Elizabeth invite both "Lady Russell and Mr. Elliot" to Camden-place. Both speak of Anne. "Her kind, compassionate visits to this old schoolfellow, sick and reduced, seemed to have quite delighted Mr. Elliot." Such sentiments persuade Lady Russell that he meant "to gain Anne in time, as of his deserving of her." So much so that in conversation with Anne, Lady Russell becomes Elliot's advocate. She tells Anne, "I think there would be every possibility of your being happy together." On the other hand, Anne remains unconvinced; she is not persuaded. She tells Lady Russell, "We should not suit."

Lady Russell uses subtle tactics to persuade Anne. She sees her "as the future mistress of Kellynch, the future Lady Elliot" and looks "forward [to seeing Anne] occupying [her] dear mother's place." This has an effect on Anne, and authorial narration combines with her point of view. "For a few moments her imagination and her heart were bewitched" (156–160). This last word is used on only one other occasion in Jane Austen's fiction, in *Pride and Prejudice,* when "Darcy had never been so bewitched by any woman as he was by" Elizabeth (52). Darcy and Anne are most reluctant to allow their reason to be overruled by their "imagination" or "heart." Admittedly, "the idea of becoming what her mother had been . . . was a charm which she could not immediately resist." However, Lady Russell "believed in short, what Anne did not believe." Anne "never could accept" Elliot, and her rationality takes over: "her judgment on a serious consideration of the possibilities of such a case, was against Mr. Elliot."

The three paragraphs, at the conclusion of the chapter beginning with "Though they had now been acquainted a month," and concluding "and yet Mrs. Clay found him as agreeable as anybody," are viewed through the narrator's and Anne's eyes. Terms such as "a sensible man, an agreeable man," "rational, discreet, polished," with the caveat "but he was not open," convey different aspects of individual behavior that conform to certain social norms. The assumption is that a person's character can be readily divided up into such categories. Anne's and the narrator's catalogue of personality traits consist of positive ones and negative ones. Anne "prized the frank, the open-hearted, the eager character beyond all others." But "Mr. Elliot was too generally agreeable . . . He endeared too well,—stood too well with everybody."

The chapter ends not with Anne's viewpoint, however, but with Lady Russell's. She is still hoping to persuade Anne of Elliot's positive qualities, still hoping, "seeing him receive the hand of her beloved Anne in Kellynch church, in the course of the following autumn." Lady Russell "saw nothing to excite distrust" (160–161). By the conclusion of the novel, these sentiments will be read ironically.

The chapter contains interesting word usage. Mrs. Smith is described as having "that elasticity of mind . . . which was from Nature alone" (154). Anne saw that Elliot "had been, at least, careless on all serious matters." Here "serious" implies "religious" (161). A few paragraphs earlier the adverb is used in a similar sense. Mrs. Smith tells Anne that "there are so many who forget to think seriously till it is almost too late" (156).

Volume 2, Chapter 6 (Chapter 18)

The seasonal reference to the "autumn," the last word of the previous chapter, gives way in the first sentence of chapter 6 to "It was the beginning of February." Anne, after a month in Bath, wished to hear the "news from Uppercross and Lyme." She knew that Henrietta Musgrove had returned home, and that her sister Louisa, although "recovering fast, was still at Lyme." A letter from Anne's younger sister, Mary, delivered from the Crofts, who were visiting Bath, to Anne conveys much information. The letter addressed to Anne and dated "February 1st," is an authorial device to convey what has taken place off stage.

Mary's letter reveals that the Harville children remained with the Musgroves at Uppercross. The weather has been "dreadful." Charles Hayter "has been calling much oftener than was welcome." She does not mention in her letter that he is Henrietta's suitor. Mary is pleased that Anne apparently finds "Mr. Elliot so agreeable," and notes the "immense time Mrs. Clay has been staying with Elizabeth!" In a postscript to the first part of her letter, Mary adds "that the butcher says there is a bad sore-throat about. I dare say I shall catch it." She tells Anne that Mrs. Croft offered to take her letter to her: "I shall therefore be able to make my letter as long as I like." The rest of Mary's letter is devoted to "something . . . that will astonish you [Anne] not a little." In essence, Captain Benwick's "being in love with Louisa" and asking Mr. Musgrove for her hand in marriage. Mary observes, "We are all very well pleased . . . for though it is not equal to her marrying Captain Wentworth, it is infinitely better than Charles Hayter." Mary's husband, Charles, wonders what Captain Wentworth will say: "but if you remember, I never thought him attached to Louisa." The narrator describes Anne's reaction to the news: "She had never in her life been more astonished . . . It was almost too wonderful for belief." Attempting to "preserve an air of calmness," Anne responds to questions from her father and sister. Epistolary form, the letter, gives way to indirect narration—"Sir Walter wanted to know whether the Crofts travelled with four horses"—and then to direct dialogue and questions: "'How is Mary?' said Elizabeth; and without waiting for an answer, 'And pray what brings the Crofts to Bath?'" Anne's reply concerning a possibility of gout on the part of the Admiral elicits a condescending response from Sir Walter. "Gout and decrepitude! . . . Poor old gentleman." For Sir Walter, all the Crofts will be known for in Bath is as "the renter of Kellynch-hall" and according to Elizabeth, the Crofts are not socially the right class to invite to Laura-place to meet Lady Dalrymple.

Snobbery and self-interest are depicted through dialogue; information concerning engagements and love interests are depicted through a letter. Following Mrs. Clay's "more decent attention, in an enquiring after Mrs. Charles Musgrove, and her fine little boys, Anne was at liberty." Alone "in her own room she tried to comprehend" the news in Mary's letter. Her first thoughts are with Wentworth's reactions and speculation on whether "he had quitted the field, had given Louisa up, had ceased to love, had found he did not love her." She wonders about the relationship between Captain

Benwick and Wentworth: "she could not endure the idea of treachery, or levity, or anything akin to ill-usage between him and his friend!"

Anne's thoughts are conveyed in passages akin to the stream of consciousness found, for instance, in the work of James Joyce when the author enters into the mind of the character. Such an instance occurs in the first seven sentences of the paragraph beginning, "Captain Benwick and Louisa Musgrove!" Staccato sentences concluding with exclamation marks, questions such as "Where could have been the attraction?" are followed by "The answer soon presented itself," which returns to indirect narration and then returns directly to Anne's thoughts, "It had been in situation." A lengthy sentence with subordinate clauses beginning "They had been thrown together several weeks" then follows. This reflects Anne's thought patterns. Indirect narration once again intrudes—"That was a point which Anne had not been able to avoid suspecting before"—giving way once again to Anne's consciousness. At the end of the paragraph, Anne concludes in words emphasizing the past tense. "He [Benwick] had an affectionate heart. He *must love* [my emphasis] somebody."

Anne perceptively sees the differences in character between the extrovert "high-spirited, joyous, talking Louisa Musgrove, and the dejected, thinking, feeling, reading Captain Benwick." She sees what has happened, however, through the perspective of consideration of Wentworth and how it affects him. Her feelings for him are clearly conveyed by direct authorial narration: "No, it was not regret which made Anne's heart beat in spite of herself, and brought the colour into her cheeks when she thought of Captain Wentworth unshackled and free."

Private wishes give way to social concerns. The initial meeting in Bath between Anne and the Crofts is related in a brief two-sentence paragraph. Another two-sentence paragraph conveys information as to which part of Bath they lodged in, that this was "perfectly to Sir Walter's satisfaction," and that Sir Walter "did, in fact, think and talk a great deal more about the Admiral, than the Admiral ever thought or talked about him." A paragraph is devoted to the Crofts' activities, their walking in

Bath, Lady Russell's taking Anne "out in her carriage almost every morning," and Anne's perception of the Crofts' mutual happiness together.

The remainder of the chapter focuses on a meeting Anne has with Admiral Croft. She encounters him staring "at a printshop window . . . in earnest contemplation of some print." An Admiral, a pragmatic, experienced leader of men, is fascinated by a print "of a boat" (162–169). He also has many acquaintances in Bath whom he refers to. Jane Austen constructs a special kind of speech for him "unlike that of any other character" in *Persuasion.* She manages to convey his "bluff heartiness" through "the use of unusually short and direct statements, a preference for concrete over abstract vocabulary, and the absence of description and analysis." He also on occasion uses naval language (Page, 140). Seeing a Captain Brigden approaching, he tells Anne, "Brigden stares to see anybody with me but my wife. She, poor soul, is tied by the leg. She has a blister on one of her heels, as large as a three shilling piece." Of Admiral Brand and his brother who are approaching, he comments, "Shabby fellows, both of them!" So, even if the Admiral is given to hyperbole, his wife's blister must be a large one! Of "old Sir Archibald Drew and his grandson," he comments to Anne: "he takes you for my wife. Ah! the peace has come too soon for that younker" (youngster).

The Admiral tells Anne information concerning Louisa Musgrove and his wife's surprise that "Miss Musgrove, instead of being to marry Frederick [Wentworth], is to marry James Benwick." Wentworth did not stay at Lyme but went to Plymouth and then to his brother Edward, the curate. Admiral Croft succinctly sums up Benwick's character and career as if he is giving judgment at the bridge of his ship. He is "a very active, zealous officer" and his "soft sort of manner does not do him justice." However, "James Benwick is rather too piano for me . . . Sophy and I cannot help thinking Frederick's manners better than his." The source of the information is a letter Wentworth wrote to his sister, the Admiral's wife, and Wentworth's source was his friend Captain Harville. This leads Anne to find out from the Admiral whether Wentworth feels "an ill-used man" from what has happened. Anne

seems to be concerned that any friendship between Wentworth and Benwick "should be destroyed, or even wounded, by a circumstance of this sort." The Admiral replies, "No, you would not guess, from his way of writing, that he had ever thought of this Miss (what's her name?) for himself." Anne is not totally reassured by such an answer but is unable to "press the enquiring further."

Chapter 6 concludes with the Admiral's concern for Wentworth. "Now he must begin all over again with somebody else. I think we must get him to Bath. . . . Here are pretty girls enough. I am sure." He asks Anne, "Do not you think, Miss Elliot, we had better try to get him to Bath?" (169–173). With all his insight, practical knowledge, and experience of dealing with men, Admiral Croft seems unaware that the ideal partner for Wentworth is Anne. It is hardly surprising that she remains silent and the chapter ends with his question.

Volume 2, Chapter 7 (Chapter 19)

The previous chapter concluded with Admiral Croft "expressing" to Anne "his wish of getting Captain Wentworth to Bath." Chapter 7 begins with Anne seeing Wentworth in Bath. Before they meet, four paragraphs following the introductory one are spent in direct authorial description of a game of musical chairs concerning who is and who is not out in a carriage during a short spell of rain. Out shopping, Anne encounters Mr. Elliot, Miss Elliot, Mrs. Clay, and others, plus Lady Dalrymple and her carriage. These chapters of *Persuasion* are replete with topographical detail of Bath. The third paragraph of the chapter conveys clues that Elliot's relationship with Mrs. Clay is complex: "her boots were so thick! much thicker than Miss Anne's, and, in short, her civility rendered her quite as anxious to be left to walk with Mr Elliot, as Anne could be." Such minutiae, as to who wishes to walk with whom, in spite of the rain, is suggestive.

Motive and the desire for relationship or renewal of relationships are strengthened when Anne reacts emotionally to the sight of Wentworth. "For a few minutes she saw nothing before her. It was all confusion. She was lost." Anne regards herself as "the greatest simpleton in the world, the most unaccountable and absurd!" Her sense of loss of identity and control is conveyed in the sixth paragraph of the chapter in which her name is not mentioned once. "Captain Wentworth" is mentioned twice and then as "he": "He was more obviously struck and confused by the sight of her, than she had ever observed before; he looked quite red." Additionally, from Anne's perspective, "she felt that she was betraying the least sensibility of the two. She had the advantage of him."

The encounter is reported through her perspective. No conversation is recorded. "Time had changed him, or Louisa had changed him. . . . He looked very well." Anne feels "grieved" when "there was complete internal recognition on each side" between Wentworth and her sister Elizabeth, yet they do not acknowledge each other. "She [Anne] had the pain of seeing her sister turn away with unalterable coldness."

Subsequently, Wentworth offers Anne his "new umbrella" and to accompany her in spite of the rain. Anne informs him that she is "only waiting for Mr. Elliot." Briefly, the narrative perspective transfers to Wentworth's viewpoint and his recollection of Elliot from "the steps at Lyme" before transferring to the direct authorial. "They walked off together, her arm under his, a gentle and embarrassed glance and 'a good morning to you,' being all that she had time for, as she passed away."

Rather than focusing on Wentworth's reactions to this, the reader is left to guess how he felt. Instead, direct remarks from "the ladies of Captain Wentworth's party" are given. These range from "Mr. Elliot does not dislike his cousin, I fancy?" to "the men are all wild after Miss Elliot. Anne is too delicate for them." Wentworth's silence is revealing and speaks volumes.

The focus shifts to Anne and her walk with Elliot. His conversation and observations are conveyed in summary form: "praise, warm, just, and discriminating of Lady Russell, and insinuations highly rational against Mrs. Clay." But Anne's thoughts are "only of Captain Wentworth. She could not understand his present feelings," and "She hoped to be wise and reasonable in time; but alas! alas! she must confess to herself that she was not wise yet."

No more is made of her walk with Elliot and attention is directed to Anne's thoughts on what would happen if and when Lady Russell saw Wentworth. A paragraph beginning "The following morning Anne was out with her friend" is devoted to Anne's wondering what Lady Russell's reaction to seeing Wentworth will be, but there seems to be a singular lack of reaction. Instead, Lady Russell claims that she "was looking after some window-curtains." What concerns Anne rather is "that in all this waste of foresight and caution, she should have lost the right moment for seeing whether he [Wentworth] saw them."

The chapter ends on an ambiguous note. The Elliots spend their evenings "in the elegant stupidity of private parties," and Anne, "wearied of such a state of stagnation, sick of knowing nothing, and fancying herself stronger because her strength was not tried," eagerly awaits a concert at which she persuades herself that Wentworth, "very fond of music," will attend. She notes that her sister "Elizabeth had turned from him, Lady Russell had overlooked him . . . she felt that she owed him attention." Before going to the concert, she has to tell Mrs. Smith, who has disappeared once again from the narrative, that she will be unable to spend the evening with her. Mrs. Smith asks Anne, "Who is your party?" or whom Anne will be going to the concert with. On hearing, Mrs. Smith replies: "I begin to have a foreboding that I may not have many more visits from you." The final one-paragraph sentence reaffirms the uncertainty experienced by Anne throughout this chapter. "Anne was startled and confused" and she hurries away (174–180).

Volume 2, Chapter 8 (Chapter 20)

Mrs. Smith's ambiguity is not explained in this chapter, which is set at the concert. It is attended by "Sir Walter, his two daughters and Mrs. Clay," Lady Dalrymple, Elliot, and Wentworth—some of the major players at this point in the narrative. The music they have come to hear is incidental to the drama unfolding among Anne, Wentworth, and the others. The interplay is among public appearance, social necessities, and private emotions. At the beginning of the chapter, the reader is told that Anne's sister at least recognizes Wentworth's existence. This reveals that Anne still seems to care about what her family perceives.

There are three central conversations in the chapter. The first is that between Anne and Wentworth before the concert begins, followed by Anne's reactions to what took place between them. The second is her explanation to Elliot, whom she is sitting next to, of the words of an Italian song and his subsequent comments. The third is after the first act finished, when there is an account, with very brief dialogue, of an encounter between Anne and Wentworth. This concludes the chapter.

In the first conversation, Wentworth recalls the events at Lyme and comments on what he perceives to be the inappropriateness of the alliance between Benwick and Louisa Musgrove. Part of his disapproval over Benwick's actions is a reflection of his own feelings. Wentworth tells Anne, "A man like him, in his situation! With a heart pierced, wounded, almost broken!" He recalls Fanny, Benwick's dead fiancée, and adds "A man does not recover from such a devotion of the heart to such a woman!—He ought not to—he does not." Implicitly, Wentworth is referring to his own love for Anne.

Anne's reaction to this confession is highlighted in spite of her surroundings. The private tumult of feelings is contrasted with the public world of noise and bustle: "the various noises of the room, the almost ceaseless slam of the door, and ceaseless buzz of persons walking through." In spite of these distractions, Anne "distinguished every word." The subsequent dialogue focuses on recollection, place, meaning, and the emotions they evoke. Anne tells Wentworth, "One does not love a place the less for having suffered in it, unless it has been all suffering, nothing but suffering—which was by no means the case at Lyme."

This private dialogue dealing with deeply felt personal emotion is conducted in a public place and interrupted by social conventions such as entrances and seating arrangements. In this, Anne "was divided from Captain Wentworth" and temporarily alone with her thoughts. The encounter and conversation with Wentworth has put her "in good humour with all," her "delightful emotions were a little subdued" when she sees that "he had disappeared." Her mood is contrasted with that of her sister Elizabeth. She depends on appearances,

"arm in arm with Miss Carteret, and looking on the broad back of the dowager Viscountess Dalrymple before her, had nothing to wish for which did not seem within her reach." Elizabeth's happiness depends on whom she is with socially. Hers is not a private but a public existence. Anne's happiness is the consequence of personal feeling: "the origin of one all selfish vanity, of the other [Anne] all generous attachment." A distinction is made here among selfishness, egocentricity, and "generous attachment," such as Anne's with another.

A lengthy paragraph of free indirect speech conveying Anne's thoughts follows. Its second brief sentence, "Her happiness was from within," encapsulates the previous distinction between "selfish vanity" and "generous attachment." This is reinforced by the switch from the personal name "Anne" at the start of the paragraph to the pronoun "her," then "she," to focus not on her but on the object of these thoughts. Wentworth is not named but becomes the more personal "His" as if to offset and belong to "her." Anne's thoughts are "all, all declared that he had a heart returning to her at least; that anger, resentment, avoidance, were no more." Her assessment of their encounter persuades Anne "He must love her."

The second important conversation occurs during "the interval succeeding an Italian song." Anne explains the words "the sense of an Italian love-song" to Elliot, who has sat next to her. "They had a concert bill between them." Such physical closeness, as will be seen in Wentworth's subsequent reactions in the third conversation at the end of this chapter, conveys erroneous signals. Elliot flatters Anne, he appeals to her vanity, referring to his knowing about her character a long time before actually meeting her: "No one can withstand the charm of such a mystery . . . Anne was all curiosity," wishing to know the source. She assumes it to be Wentworth's brother.

A new proposal from Elliot—"I would breathe any wishes that the name [Anne's] might never change"—is interrupted by Sir Walter and Lady Dalrymple referring to appearance: "A well-looking man." They are referring to Wentworth. Several paragraphs are preoccupied with Anne's reactions to Elliot's comments, and to hoping that

Wentworth would come to her. She receives some comfort: "She was persuaded by Lady Russell's countenance that she had seen him"—Wentworth. His absence adds to her sense of isolation even in public. She attempts to make herself less inaccessible by placing "herself much nearer the end of the bench than she had been before, much more within reach of a passer-by."

Jane Austen uses an interesting literary allusion. She writes that Anne "could not do so [rearrange her seating], without comparing herself with Miss Larolles, the inimitable Miss Larolles." This is a reference not to an actual Miss Larolles, but to a character in Fanny Burney's novel *Cecilia or, Memoirs of an Heiress*.

In the context of this chapter of *Persuasion*, Wentworth believes, because of his observance of the proximity of Anne and Elliot, that there is an attachment between them. There are other similarities between the novels. In each, a sensible but lonely heroine is placed in a household where the owners live beyond their means. Both suffer from a parent whose preoccupation is with social rank

The last encounter at the conclusion of the chapter with Wentworth contains minimum dialogue. But there is effective stylistic variation. There is direct speech. Anne, for instance, asks Wentworth, "Is not this song worth staying for?" There is Wentworth's reply: "No! . . . there is nothing worth my staying for." Free indirect speech is used, "she found herself accosted by Captain Wentworth, in a reserved yet hurried sort of farewell." The final paragraph of the chapter is also free indirect speech combined with authorial observation on Anne's thoughts concerning her perception of Wentworth's "Jealousy of Mr. Elliot!" Her thinking is interspersed with "For a moment the gratification was exquisite. But alas! There were very different thoughts to succeed." Anne's consciousness is then directly entered into: "How was jealousy to be quieted? How was the truth to reach him?" These questions are shortly to be answered (183–191).

There are several other interesting features in this chapter. The only usage in Jane Austen's writings of the word "scientific" is found in the description of Anne's thoughts after her first meeting at the concert with Wentworth: "she had feelings for the tender, spirits for the gay, attentions for the scientific, and patience for the wearisome" (186). The word is used here as an adjective in the sense of being characterized by "science" or trained skill (*OED*).

Volume 2, Chapter 9 (Chapter 21)

This is a lengthy chapter of revelations. In the first paragraph, Anne visits Mrs. Smith "to avoid Mr. Elliot." This becomes somewhat ironic, as he will be the subject of disclosure during her visit. The free indirect style conveys that Elliot's attention has flattered her. "How she might have felt, had there been no Captain Wentworth in the case, was not worth enquiry" (192). In the third two-sentence paragraph, "amusement sweetened by affection enters the commentary on the heroine's feelings" (Hardy, 179). Also present is Jane Austen's wry irony: "Prettier musings of high-wrought love and eternal constancy, could never have passed along the streets of Bath, than Anne was sporting with from Camden-place to Westgate-buildings. It was almost enough to spread purification and perfume all the way."

Mrs. Smith has already received an account of the concert from "a laundress and a waiter"—such is the speed and method of communication of local Bath gossip relating to special social events. As the narrator observes, "Everybody of any consequence or notoriety in Bath was well known by name to Mrs. Smith." The meeting between Mrs. Smith and Anne is conveyed largely through dialogue rather than indirect narration. Mrs. Smith knows the layout of the concert hall. She also tells Anne that her "countenance perfectly informs me—[Mrs. Smith] that you [Anne] were in company . . . with the person whom you think the most agreeable in the world, the person who interests you at this present time, more than all the rest of the world put together." This insight produces "a blush" on "Anne's cheeks."

While Anne is wondering "how any report of Captain Wentworth could have reached" Mrs. Smith, her companion asks Anne if Mr. Elliot knows that she is in Bath. Mrs. Smith has mistaken the object of Anne's affection: Elliot rather than Wentworth. Mrs. Smith cleverly gains further information concerning the context of Anne's relationship with Elliot. She assures Mrs. Smith that she "must consider me only as Mr. Elliot's relation," firmly telling her, "I am not going to marry Mr. Elliot." Anne's sentiments are not believed by Mrs. Smith, who using a shipping metaphor tells her, "Your peace will not be shipwrecked as mine has been. You are safe in all worldly matters, and safe in his character. He will not be lead astray, he will not be misled by others to his ruin."

Anne ascertains from Mrs. Smith that it is assumed that she will marry Elliot. Her source is Mrs. Rooke—Nurse Rooke, who "had had it from Mrs. Wallis herself." After repeated denials, it seems that Mrs. Smith's incredulity is conquered and she opens up regarding her past relationship with Elliot and her account of his character. These are conveyed in a passage of direct speech beginning "I beg your pardon, my dear Miss Elliot" (192–198), and concluding several paragraphs later with "He described one Miss Elliot, and I thought very affectionately of the other" (201).

Before describing what happened, Mrs. Smith condemns Elliot as "a man without heart or conscience; a designing, wary, cold-blooded being who thinks only of himself; who, for his own interest or ease, would be guilty of any cruelty, or any treachery, that could be perpetrated without risk of his general character. He has no feeling for others." She adds that he is totally amoral, being "beyond the reach of any sentiment of justice or compassion" (199). It has been observed correctly that this "description of the true Mr. Elliot is never challenged or controverted. It is the most unqualified summary of unmitigated evil in all Jane Austen's work" (Tanner, 227).

Mrs. Smith reveals to Anne that Elliot cheated her husband. Mrs. Smith still speaks affectionately of her late husband. Following his death, she has been left disabled and without means of support. Elliot, from an impoverished background, broke the rules. He destroyed families, friendships, and trust to gain wealth by whatever means possible. People were to be used and then cast off. He "had one object in view—to make his fortune, and by a rather quicker process than the law. He was determined to make it by marriage." After he learned that Anne's father and sister were planning a wealthy match, he drew away from the Elliot family as they were of no further use to him. Anne learns that Mrs. Smith, when she was friendly with Elliot, had been the source of information about her. Previously, Anne had thought that Wentworth's brother was the source of Elliot's knowledge of her. Mrs. Smith represents differing values that change with age and experience. She tells Anne, "When one lives in the world, a man or woman's marrying for money is too common to strike one as it ought." She "was very young [nineteen], and associated only with the young, and we were a thoughtless, gay set, without any strict rules of conduct. We lived for enjoyment." Older, she tells Anne, "I think differently now; time and sickness, and sorrow, have given me other notions."

Elliot's motivation was money. This "was all that he wanted." He wanted the "chance of the Kellynch estate . . . all the honour of the family he held as cheap as dirt." Elliot is an unadulterated materialist. Mrs. Smith then produces a letter dated "July 1803" to her husband from Elliot, written before her marriage, as evidence of his perfidy and lack of morality. In it he asks for money from Smith and disparages the Elliot family, especially Sir Walter. He is also ashamed of the name Elliot: "I wish I had any name but Elliot."

Anne is shocked by the sentiments concerning her father and a sense that she has committed "a violation of the laws of honour, that no one ought to be judged or to be known by such testimonies," in other words, "that no private correspondence could bear the eye of others." Anne's scruples highlight Elliot's lack of them. However, as Anne observes to her informant, what she has shown belongs to the past, so "why be acquainted with us now?" To this Mrs. Smith replies, "I will shew you him [Mr. Elliot] as he is now." She is unable to "produce written proof again, but I can give as authentic oral testimony as you can desire, of what he is now wanting, and what he is now doing." She continues, "He is no hypocrite now. He truly wants to marry you. His present attentions to your family are very sincere, quite from the heart."

Her source is Elliot's friend Colonel Wallis, to whom he speaks freely. Wallis then repeats everything to his wife, who then spills the information to Nurse Rooke, who in turn tells Mrs. Smith. Nurse Rook is her "historian." Anne regards such an authority, a gossip chain passing information at secondhand, as "deficient." Mrs. Smith then goes to considerable length to demonstrate that her authority from Nurse Rooke is not at all "deficient." She describes in detail Anne's acquaintance with Elliot and of Mrs. Clay's activities. Mrs. Clay is "a clever, insinuating, handsome woman, poor and plausible" who creates "a general idea among Sir Walter's acquaintance, of her meaning to be Lady Elliot."

Elliot himself is no longer motivated by material considerations: "having long had as much money as he could spend . . . he has been gradually learning to pin his happiness upon the consequence he is heir to." Self-obsessed, as narcissistic as Anne's father, "He cannot bear the idea of not being Sir William." His object in returning to Bath was "to watch Sir Walter and Mrs. Clay." Anne's response accords with Jane Austen's. Character and author speak as one although direct speech is used. Anne tells Mrs. Smith "there is always something offensive in the details of cunning. The manoeuvers of selfishness and duplicity must ever be revolting." Anne concludes that "Mr. Elliot is certainly a disingenuous, artificial, worldly man, who has never had any better principle to guide him than selfishness." She cannot add that he is just like her own father.

The ninth chapter of the second volume of *Persuasion* concludes with an account by Mrs. Smith of what had occurred after her marriage. This is told not as previously, through direct speech, but in common with passages elsewhere in the novel, by the extensive use of free indirect narration. Smith's ruin is conveyed through his widow's perspective, with admission of her own errors and supported by replies to letters she wrote to Elliot of "urgent applications" for support.

The perspective then transfers to Anne's: "It was a dreadful picture of ingratitude and inhumanity; and Anne felt at some moments, that no flagrant open crime could have been worse." Anne learns from Mrs. Smith "that some property of her husband in the West Indies . . . might be recoverable by proper measures." Alone, without money

and connections, Mrs. Smith is unable to take any action, and on this matter she "had hoped to engage Anne's good office with Mr. Elliot," especially after she understood, mistakenly, that Anne may well marry him. Inwardly, Mrs. Smith's "heart bled" for Anne, but she regarded Elliot as "sensible, he is agreeable, and with such a woman as you [Anne], it was not absolutely hopeless." After what she has heard, Anne is made to "shudder at the idea of the misery which must have followed" her marriage to Elliot.

Ironically, she reflects in the penultimate paragraph of the chapter, "It was just possible that she might have been persuaded by Lady Russell!" as she had been many years previously. In the last paragraph, "It was very desirable that Lady Russell should be no longer deceived." Anne leaves Mrs. Smith's with "full liberty to communicate to" Lady Russell what she has been told (200–211).

This important chapter explains the inclusion of Mrs. Smith at a late stage in the narrative as a conveyer of information and playing a crucial role in the denouement of the plot. Mrs. Smith exposes human perfidy and folly. Elliot is revealed as amoral. His ruthless pursuit of self-interest at the expense of other human beings is among its author's finest depictions of evil. Society is shown as depending on checks and balances. Set against the backdrop of Bath, Anne's father's egoism, and the games play of Mrs. Clay, the amorality of William Walter Elliot is exposed. Anne is thereby forced to assert her real self and wishes, her love for Wentworth.

Volume 2, Chapter 10 (Chapter 22)
The final three chapters of the novel were written to replace the original two final chapters completed on July 18, 1816. The revised chapters were completed on August 6, 1816. In the revised published 10th chapter, the perspective is primarily Anne's, blended with dialogue and some of the narrator's reportage. The chapter opens with Anne's reflections on what she had learned at Mrs. Smith's. Anne succeeded in her intention of avoiding Elliot. Her sister Elizabeth reveals that she is only too aware of the elaborate games played by people when courting. She tells Anne, "I have been rather too much used to the games to be soon overcome by a

gentleman's hints." Anne's response to a remark by Mrs. Clay exhibits a sarcastic side. Anne tells Mrs. Clay, "I lay no embargo on any body's words. If you will have such ideas!" She firmly denies that she is any more "sensible" of Elliot's "attentions being beyond those of other men." In response, Mrs. Clay retreats into "a convenient silence." Mrs. Clay is rescued from embarrassment by Anne's father, who addresses Mrs. Clay ironically as "dear Penelope"—the name of the faithful wife of Ulysses, who for more than 20 years resisted her suitors.

When Elliot does "enter the room," Anne's attitude has changed: "now she saw insincerity in every thing." Toward him, "she was accordingly more guarded, and more cool, than" previously. The perspective changes to Elliot's and then back to Anne's. She now sees the situation in stark hues: "It was bad enough that a Mrs. Clay should be always before her; but that a deeper hypocrite [Elliot] should be added to their party, seemed the destruction of every thing like peace and comfort." Compared to Elliot, "Mrs. Clay's selfishness was not so complicate [complicated] nor so revolting as his."

Elliot leaves Bath for a few days. On the Friday morning, Mrs. Clay leaves early and Elizabeth's attitude toward Lady Russell becomes more contemptuous: "Lady Russell quite bores one with her new publications." She also "thought her dress hideous the other night." The Elliots receive a surprise visit from Charles and Mary Musgrove. Anne learns that they are accompanied by Mrs. Musgrove, Henrietta, and Captain Harville, all of whom are staying in Bath at the White Hart. Henrietta took the opportunity "to come and buy wedding-clothes for herself and her sister." Her fiancé, Charles Hayter, had obtained "a very good living . . . only five-and-twenty miles from Uppercross." Consequently, their marriage need not be delayed. Anne tells Charles that both the Musgroves "should be happy in their children's marriages." She adds that his "father and mother seem so totally free from all those ambitious feelings which have led to such misconduct and misery, in both young and old!" Anne refers to "money" and its impact on marriage.

Charles tells Anne that Louisa since her illness "is altered: there is no running or jumping about, no laughing or dancing." On the contrary, Benwick

"sits at her elbow reading verses, or whispering to her, all day long." Elizabeth has a problem concerning propriety, whether or not "Mrs. Musgrove and all her party ought to be asked to dine with them." However, Elizabeth is only too aware of "the difference of style, the reduction of servants, which a dinner must betray." Again, she places appearances above other values. "It was a struggle between propriety and vanity; but vanity got the better."

Anne visits the party at the White Hart, where she finds "a heartiness, and a warmth, and a sincerity." Such genuineness of feeling is contrasted with "the sad want of such blessings at home." She, too, is wanted by Mrs. Musgrove and others. They are joined by "Captains Harville and Wentworth." Anne "feared from [Wentworth's] looks, that the same unfortunate persuasion [attitude, cast off mind], which had hastened him away from the concert room, still governed." Her maturity, the result of experience, is shown in her reaction. "She tried to be calm, and leave things to take their course." She and Wentworth "are not boy and girl, to be captiously irritable, misled by every moment's inadvertence and wantonly playing with our own happiness."

Mary sees Elliot and Mrs. Clay from the window. Anne doubts the information. Her reaction receives "smiles and intelligent glances" from some of the company, evidence that the rumors concerning an impending engagement between her and Elliot circulate. She sees for herself the meeting, though Elliot was supposed to be away from Bath for a few days. A dispute takes place in which Charles refuses to meet "Lady Dalrymple and her daughter and Mr. Elliot," preferring to go to the theater. Charles's response, "What is Mr. Elliot to me?" is a "careless expression" and "life to Anne." It also catches Captain Wentworth's "attention," who is "looking and listening with his whole soul."

Wentworth takes the opportunity to talk to Anne. He remembers that she was not a card player but observes, "time makes many changes." Anne replies, "I am not yet so much changed." Wentworth responds in a commentary upon the length of their separation, "It is a period, indeed! Eight years and a half is a period!" They are interrupted by other visitors, Sir Walter and Elizabeth. Their very entrance produces "a general chill" and on Anne "an instant oppression." The atmosphere, "the comfort, the freedom, the gaiety of the room" is replaced on their appearance by "cold composure, determined silence . . . insipid talk" in response to their "heartless elegance."

Elizabeth at last acknowledges Wentworth's presence and invites him and the others to Camden-place. She "had been long enough in Bath, to understand the importance of a man of such an air and appearance." In the world of Bath, appearance is all. "The past was nothing. The present was that Captain Wentworth would move about well in her drawing-room." Jane Austen's satire is directed at Elizabeth personally and at the place whose values she conforms to—Bath. As soon as Elizabeth and her father leave, the warmer atmosphere returns, "but not to Anne," who "saw disdain in [Wentworth's] eye" and "surprise" that he should, in spite of past treatment, accept the invitation. Anne sees Wentworth's "cheeks glow and his mouth form itself into a momentary expression of contempt" when Mary comments erroneously that Wentworth "cannot put the card out of his hand."

The chapter ends where it began, at Camden-place. Anne is again alone. She is debating with herself whether Wentworth will actually appear. The final two paragraphs concern her confrontation with Mrs. Clay, when Anne reveals that she has seen Elliot with her. They conclude with Mrs. Clay's utterances of duplicity, known to Anne, but not necessarily to Jane Austen's readers on an initial reading of *Persuasion* (213–228).

Volume 2, Chapter 11 (Chapter 23)

This penultimate chapter contains much information and much is resolved. The opening paragraph refers to "the Sultaness Scheherazade's head," which is likened to "Mr. Elliot's character," from *The Arabian Nights Entertainment*, circulated in various popular English translations during the 1790s. The sultan discovers his sultana's infidelity and decides to have a fresh wife every night and then have each new wife strangled at dawn. Scheherazade amuses him so much with her tales for a thousand and one nights that she lives another day to tell another story. Eventually, the Sultan revokes the decree and she survives.

When Anne reaches the White Hart Inn, in spite of the company, she is alone with her own thoughts, and is "outwardly composed" until Wentworth speaks to her. Anne's state is conveyed in a sentence showing through antithesis a conflict of expectancy: "She was deep in the happiness of such misery, or the misery of such happiness, instantly." At the White Hart, Wentworth is involved with Captain Harville in writing a letter. Mrs. Musgrove is conveying to Mrs. Croft "minutiae" of detail concerning Charles Hayter and her daughter's engagement. Both Mrs. Croft and Mrs. Musgrove "abominate . . . long engagement[s]." Words from Mrs. Croft appertaining to "an uncertain engagement" and "to begin without knowing that at such a time there will be the means of marrying," attract the attention of both Anne and Wentworth. Anne experiences "a nervous thrill," and Wentworth also reacts to the words, after Anne's eyes had "instinctively glanced towards" him. Wentworth's "pen ceased to move, his head was raised, pausing, listening, and he turned round the next instant to give a look—one quick, conscious look at her."

Mrs. Musgrove and Mrs. Croft's talk now becomes "only a buzz of words in [Anne's] ear, her mind was in confusion." She and Captain Harville, at Harville's suggestion, then begin conversing. This begins on the subject of "a small miniature painting" of Captain Benwick, and then broadens into a far-reaching discussion of men and women, which is absent from the earlier, discarded version of this chapter, and contains a good deal of irony. The irony resides in the fact that Anne argues that men are more likely than women to be inconstant. She has Benwick in mind but is also addressing Wentworth, who is not too far away in the same room and listening, a role performed by Anne in much of the novel. Anne tells Harville, "Man is more robust than woman, but he is not longer-lived; which exactly explains my view of their nature of attachments."

Their debate is interrupted. The third person in the debate, although so far a silent participant's, "pen had fallen down, but Anne was startled at finding him nearer than she had supposed" (229–233). Wentworth's dropping the pen has produced a flurry of critical opinion. He pauses to hear Anne's response and his proposal letter "is certainly the product of slippage, what happens when the pen of patriarchal authority falls from his hands." His letter of proposal resulting in "the resolution" of the novel "is so powerful . . . because it is *unauthorized*, not the product of authority." It is created by "a slip of the pen" (Darryl Jones, 187).

Harville tells Anne that he does "not think [he] ever opened a book in [his] life which had not something to say upon a woman's inconstancy . . . perhaps you will say, these were all written by men!" This is ironic, as Harville's words appear in a book written by a woman, Jane Austen, and Benwick has been an inconstant man! In an outburst of emotion overheard by Wentworth, Anne tells Harville: "All the privilege I claim for my own sex . . . is that of loving longest, when existence or when hope is gone." This is an assertion from the depths of her being, and she cannot speak afterward: "her heart was too full."

The irony is compounded in Mrs. Croft's leave taking, which interrupts the debate between Captain Harville and Anne. Mrs. Croft refers to her and Wentworth parting company, to his having "had a card too" and to his being "disengaged." Literally, Mrs. Croft and the others are to separate; Wentworth's hand is to be revealed to Anne. The result will be their engagement. Wentworth is involved with "folding up a letter in great haste," with "having sealed his letter with great rapidity," and leaving with "a hurried, agitated air." He is silent and leaves. His letter takes on greater import. He returns to the room with the excuse that "he had forgotten his gloves." Wentworth crosses the room and "drew out . . . a letter from under the scattered paper, placed it before Anne with eyes of glowing entreaty fixed on her for a moment." He then leaves the room; all is "the work of an instant!" The pen, its interruption, Wentworth's drawing out of a letter, Wentworth's "eyes of glowing entreaty" do have a sexual suggestiveness conveying the tumult of emotions felt by him and Anne.

From Anne's perspective, the importance of the content of the letter is emphasized: "On the contents of that letter depended all which this world could do for her!" Alone again, Anne "sinking into the chair which [Wentworth] had occupied, succeeding to the very spot where he had leaned and written, her eyes devoured the following words." Erotic implications are suggested by her action of "sinking," his leaving, withdrawing, and her eyes devouring his letter. The word "succeeding" (234–237) here means "following in, or occupying, a position vacated by another" (Phillipps, 66).

Wentworth's letter conveys written rather than spoken words. The letter expresses Wentworth's desire for Anne. It is written as Anne spoke, the writer Wentworth creatively responding to the spoken sentiments. There is an absence of irony in Wentworth's sentiments, a directness, and honesty of feeling. Wentworth tells Anne that he "can listen no longer in silence" and "must speak to [her] by such means as are within [his] reach"—not through speech but the pen. He is in a state of "half agony, half hope." Writing in the first person, Wentworth intermingles "I" and "you" in his letter. Wentworth's sentences are short, rarely extending beyond statements such as, "I have loved none but you" and "You alone have brought me to Bath. For you alone I think and plan." Clearly, "such a letter was not to be soon recovered from." Anne's wish to be alone with her thoughts, her "overpowering of happiness" is thwarted by the entrances of Charles, Mary, and Henrietta. Anne is forced unsuccessfully to adopt a social role. "They could see that she looked very ill—were shocked and concerned—and would not stir without her for the world." The next sentence enters Anne's thoughts: "This was dreadful!" All she wishes is to be by herself.

The remainder of the chapter may be divided into four sections. First, Anne's unsuccessful attempt to leave White Hart, alone, and to find Wentworth. Second, she is accompanied home by Charles Musgrove and meets Wentworth on the way. Thirdly, Musgrove, as he wishes to inspect "a capital gun," leaves Wentworth to accompany Anne home. Alone with each other after years of waiting, Anne and Wentworth find a "comparatively quiet and retired gravel-walk" to be together. The sentences describing their conversion and rewarding their happiness interweave the present and the past. They begin with the words, "There they exchanged," "There they returned again into the past," "And there, as they slowly paced" (234–238, 240).

Page indicates that there is a "remarkable degree" of construction upon the "Johnsonian principle of balance" (100) in the sentence "And there, as they slowly paced the gradual ascent, heedless of every group around them, seeing neither sauntering politicians, bustling house-keepers, flirting girls, nor nursery-maids and children, they could indulge in those retrospections and acknowledgements, and especially in those explanations of what had directly preceded the present moment, which were so poignant and so ceaseless in interest." The sentence contrasts the worlds of politics and domestic existence with Wentworth's and Anne's private world. The sentence prior to this beginning "There they returned again," in its urgency of tone, "seems to suggest the first intensity of" their feelings toward each other. The sentence that follows beginning "All the little variations" is an "expression of the calmer state which succeeded" (Page, 101; 240–241).

The rest of this third section of the penultimate chapter of *Persuasion* focuses on Wentworth's account of his fluctuating emotions toward Anne, including his "jealousy of Mr. Elliot." He confesses that "he had meant to forget" Anne but was unable to do so. He describes Anne as possessing "a collected mind," which is the only instance in Jane Austen of such a description of a character and its qualities. Anne's reactions to Wentworth's outpourings are brief and usually not conveyed, as his are in direct speech but in indirect form. For instance "It is something for a woman to be assured, in her eight-and-twentieth year, that she has not lost one charm of her earlier youth." Both characters use the keyword "persuasion." Wentworth tells her that, seeing the influence upon Anne of Lady Russell, he was reminded of "the indelible immoveable impression of what persuasion had once done." Anne tells him that "if [she] was wrong in yielding to persuasion once, remember, that it was to persuasion exerted on the side of safety, not risk."

The fourth and final section of the chapter finds Anne "at home again, and happier than any one in that house could have conceived." The chap-

ter concludes with the main characters gathered for "a card-party." The interaction of the public and the private is viewed through Anne's perspective. She is "glowing and lovely in sensibility and happiness" and no longer alone. She had "always, the knowledge of his being there!"—Wentworth. In the last paragraphs of the chapter, Anne and Wentworth again return to the past and reflect on it from their differing points of view. She defends her decision to submit to Lady Russell's wishes concerning their engagement on the grounds of duty and conscience. Wentworth speaks of his pride, of his being "too proud to ask again" for Anne's hand. He confesses to not understanding her. For Wentworth, "six years of separation and suffering might have been spared." This chapter of final reconciliation concludes with Wentworth's words: "I must learn to brook being happier than I deserve" (241–247).

Volume 2, Chapter 12 (Chapter 24)

The final chapter of *Persuasion* sees Wentworth and Anne finally united. The opening paragraph is Jane Austen's perspective on her narrative. In its first sentence, she addresses her readers, asking them, "Who can be in doubt of what followed?" Using the first person, she informs readers that financial considerations or foolishness will not stop "two young people" when they "take it into their heads to marry." She adds that "This may be bad morality, to conclude with, but I believe it to be truth." She emphasizes Wentworth's and Anne's "maturity of mind, consciousness of right and one independent fortune between them" before dealing with individual reactions to their marriage. Wentworth "with five-and-twenty thousand pounds, and as high in his profession as merit and activity could place him, was no longer nobody." Consequently, Sir Walter cannot object to Wentworth, especially as Sir Walter is a "foolish, spendthrift baronet." In a return to the opening of the novel, Sir Walter was able "at last to prepare his pen with a very good grace for the insertion of the marriage in the volume of honour."

Two paragraphs are devoted to Lady Russell's reaction. The first is from Anne's perspective, the second from an authorial viewpoint. From Anne's perspective, Lady Russell "must learn to feel that she had been mistaken with regard to both" her understanding of Elliot, and of Wentworth. It is necessary for her to admit in both instances "that she had been pretty completely wrong, and to take up a new set of opinions and of hopes." In the third paragraph of the final chapter, this is precisely what she does. Her previous rationality is trumped by her attachment to Anne. Lady Russell "was a very good woman, and if her second objective was to be sensible and well-judging, her first was to see Anne happy." Consequently, at the conclusion of *Persuasion*, "love" triumphs over rationality. Lady Russell "loved Anne better than she loved her own abilities." She becomes Wentworth's and Anne's surrogate mother.

Of the others, "Mary was probably the one most immediately gratified" by the marriage. In addition to having another sister married, Wentworth was "richer . . . than either Captain Benwick or Charles Hayter." A disadvantage for Mary was that while Anne was still single, Mary, although younger, gained precedence over her socially because she was married. She is envious of Anne's "landaulette"—four-wheeled carriage. There is also a possibility that Wentworth would become a baronet as baronetcies were being frequently bestowed at the conclusion of the Napoleonic War in 1815 as a reward for naval and military merit.

Elizabeth in addition "had soon the mortification of seeing Mr. Elliot withdraw." The marriage "deranged his best plan of domestic happiness." The "double . . . game [Elliot] had been playing" is now fully exposed when he leaves Bath, and Mrs. Clay also leaves the town. She is "next heard of as established under his protection in London." Their relationship will be ambiguous. Mrs. Clay "had sacrificed, for the young man's sake, the possibility of scheming longer for Sir Walter." Between her and Elliot "it is now a doubtful point whether his cunning, or hers, may finally carry the day."

The loss of Mrs. Clay "and the discovery of their deception in her" shocks Sir Walter and Elizabeth much more than Anne's marriage to Wentworth. Anne, however, is preoccupied by the lack of what she has to offer Wentworth apart from herself. She has "no relations to bestow on him which a man

of sense could value." His family welcomed her, she is unable to reciprocate: "the disproportion in their fortune was nothing" compared to that. Anne's sense of isolation remains with her. "She had but two friends in the world to add to his [Wentworth's] list, Lady Russell and Mrs. Smith." The former, Wentworth "could now value from his heart."

Interestingly, the last paragraphs of the novel are preoccupied with Mrs. Smith. Wentworth assists "her in the way of recovering her husband's property in the West Indies." So finally Mrs. Smith "might have been absolutely rich and perfectly healthy, and yet be happy" (248–252). There is always a qualification in Jane Austen's world. It is in this instance possible to be rich, very healthy, and also happy. As Emily Auerbach observes, "Running throughout *Persuasion* is the clear argument that happiness comes to those with patience and perseverance, a warm, unselfish generosity toward others, a desire to be useful, an awareness of other worlds, an openness to change" (263). The final two sentences in the novel do not foresee in the marriage of Anne and Wentworth children or permanent stability: There will be "the dread of a future war." Anne has to "pay the tax of quick alarm" for her marriage to a naval captain. *Persuasion* concludes, unlike *Pride and Prejudice* or *Mansfield Park*, with domestic happiness but with "national importance"—future uncertainty beyond the control of the individual (252).

The Cancelled Chapters of Persuasion
The only surviving manuscripts from Jane Austen's novels are the two original final chapters of *Persuasion*, now in the British Library. Chapter 10, volume 2, is dated at its beginning "July 8," and chapter 11, volume 2, at its conclusion "July 18–1816." This chapter was first published by her nephew J. E. Austen-Leigh in the 1871 second edition of his *Memoir of Jane Austen*, first published in 1870. Both chapters were published for the first time in R. W. Chapman's edition of the novel, published in 1923.

A quarter of chapter 10 was included almost word for word in the revised chapter 11. The canceled chapter 11 with also some changes to the wording became the revised final chapter 12. Jane

Austen, in transforming chapter 10 into the revised 11th chapter, altered the reunion between Anne and Wentworth. Its setting and actions are changed to accord with the qualities of tone prevailing in the rest of the novel.

The canceled 10th chapter presents a comic scenario. Admiral and Mrs. Croft, previously lacking guile, now act as a pair of matchmakers. Anne and Wentworth become the victims of coincidences, manipulations, and surprises that are out of character. Their independence of mind has disappeared. Anne encounters Admiral Croft. He invites her back to his lodgings, where she meets his brother-in-law, Wentworth. According to the Crofts, Anne will marry William Elliot and they will reside at Kellynch-hall. Anne tells Wentworth that this is untrue; he then proposes to her. No explanation is given why Wentworth assumes that Anne still has feelings for him. Such an ending, J. E. Austen-Leigh records in the 1870 *Memoir*, Jane Austen "thought . . . tame and flat, and was desirous of producing something better" (p. 218: cited Southam, *Literary Manuscripts,* 92). As Brian Southam observes in his detailed account of the revised endings, "Some of the major alterations are in the adjustment of tone, as if in anticipation of the graver mood which was to control the design of the new chapter 11." The new ending is free of irony, and "other major changes" found in the canceled chapters "strengthen the relationship of this chapter [11] to the earlier parts of the book" (Southam, *Literary Manuscripts,* 95–97).

Marilyn Butler points out that there is relatively less dialogue in *Persuasion* than in Jane Austen's other novels. The revised version involves less direct speech and more indirect reporting of thoughts. Consequently, the replacement of Wentworth's direct proposal in Gay-street Bath results in less direct confrontation between him and Anne and more internal thought processes. Wentworth uses the pen to propose instead, and "Anne speaks her thoughts as it were in soliloquy." The effect is in keeping with other techniques original to the novel, "for it puts a premium on expression of the self, and avoids direct communication between the self and another" (Butler, 283).

CRITICAL HISTORY AND COMMENTARY

Persuasion was initially published with *Northanger Abbey.* Early reviews spend more time on *Northanger Abbey* than *Persuasion.* Three appeared early in 1818. The *British Critic* for March 1818 was brief and negative, finding the novel "in every respect a much less fortunate performance than" *Northanger Abbey.* The *Gentleman's Magazine* published in July of the same year, noted that "*Northanger Abbey* . . . is decidedly preferable . . . not only in the incidents, but even in its moral tendency." The *Edinburgh Magazine* in May observed that the first novel "is the more lively, and the second the more pathetic. . . . There is the same good sense, happiness, and purity in both."

The most detailed contemporary review appeared in the *Quarterly Review* for January 1821. Written by Richard Whately, archbishop of Dublin, it is an overall assessment of the seriousness of Jane Austen's writings. For Whately, *Mansfield Park* is his favorite but *Persuasion* is "superior to all." He finds that it lacks somewhat "the humorous delineation of character" found in other novels; however, "it is one of the most elegant fictions of common life we ever remember to have met with." Whately pays tribute to Austen's "*economy* in the handling of plot and action, and her capacity to effect minute yet significant discriminations amongst a range of similar characters" (Southam, I, 84, 16, 267, 102, 19). Two years later an anonymous review in the *Retrospective Review* finds in the heroine. "A mind beautifully framed, graceful, imaginative, and feminine, but penetrating, sagacious and profound . . . one of the most beautiful female characters ever drawn . . . the heroine of *Persuasion*" (Southam, I, 110–111).

Writing some 30 years later, another anonymous reviewer in the *New Monthly Magazine,* May 1852, wished to introduce a neglected writer to the reading public. Jane Austen, the writer argues, has not "reaped her rightful share of public homage." This attempt to make her novels more popular notes her "felicitous irony . . . most caustic passages" and "the hardest hits and keenest thrusts of her satire." Singled out for especial praise is *Persuasion,* which "teems with individuality," instanced by Sir Walter Elliot, "Mrs. Clay, clever, manoeuvring, and unprincipled; Captain Wentworth, so intelligent, spirited, and generously high-minded." The heroine Anne is "the self-sacrificing and noble-hearted victim of undue *persuasion*," and Mary, her sister, compounds her problems by "fancying herself neglected and ill-used." The Crofts are "frank, hearty, and constitutionally good-natured" (I: 135–138).

George Henry Lewes's "The Novels of Jane Austen," published in *Blackwood's Edinburgh Magazine* in July 1859, is a detailed argument in defense of its author's judgment that Jane Austen "is an artist of high rank, in the most rigorous sense of the word" (149). Austen is compared to Shakespeare: "we never tire of her characters. They become equal to actual experiences" (153). *Pride and Prejudice* has "the best story, and the greatest variety of character." Lewes adds, "Even *Persuasion*, which we cannot help regarding as the weakest" of her novels, "contains exquisite touches, and some characters no one else could have surpassed" (165–166). The barrister William Frederick Pollock (1815–1888), writing around the same time as Lewes, in *Fraser's Magazine,* January 1860, praises *Persuasion*, finding it "memorable for containing Anne Elliot, the most perfect character and disposition of all [her] women" (173). For the prolific novelist and biographer, Julia Kavanagh (1826–1877) in her *English Women of Letters* published in 1862, "beyond any other of Miss Austen's tales, *Persuasion* shows us the phase of her literary character which she chose to keep most in the shade: the tender and the sad." Julia Kavanagh writes that "the shadow of a long disappointment, of secret grief, and ill-repressed jealousy will ever hang over Anne Elliot." Kavanagh anticipates subsequent perceptions of the novel by adding, "This melancholy cast, the result, perhaps of some secret personal disappointment, distinguishes *Persuasion* from Miss Austen's other tales. They were never cheerful, for even the gentlest of satire precludes cheerfulness; but this is sad" (194–195).

The anonymous critic writing in the *English-Woman's Domestic Magazine* for July–August 1866 has reservations about *Persuasion*. For the writer, "*Persuasion* has been called the latest and best of" Jane Austen's works, largely "because in the

character of Anne there is the nearest approach to a sentimental attachment." Yet "we cannot think that any one would give [the novel] a place above either *Mansfield Park* or *Pride and Prejudice*, and we ourselves would place it even lower." The characters in *Persuasion* are not so "finished or amusing as in most of her books" and are less "so well connected with each other, being more of separate studies than organised groups." However, in the "loves of Captain Wentworth and Anne . . . there is more natural romance of a sentimental character than in any other of her love sketches" (210).

The distinguished novelist Margaret Oliphant responded to J. E. Austen-Leigh's *Memoir of Jane Austen*, initially published in 1870, in a lengthy assessment of "Miss Austen and Miss Mitford in *Blackwood's Edinburgh Magazine* in March of the same year. She regards *Persuasion* as "very charming and full of delicate touches, though marked with the old imperfection which renders every character a fool except the heroic pair who hold their place in the foreground" (225). Writing the same year, Richard Simpson, reviewing the *Memoir* in the *North British Review*, while drawing attention to Jane Austen's genius and her power of ironic exposure of her society, compares her to Shakespeare. For Simpson, "Anne Elliot is Shakespeare's Viola," who "never tells her love or rather never talks of it." Jane Austen "must surely," Simpson believes, "have had Shakespeare's *Twelfth Night* in her mind while she was writing" *Persuasion* (256). The American critic and exponent of realism William Dean Howells, writing in 1901, on the other hand, in common with Mrs. Oliphant, associates the special quality of *Persuasion* with that of its heroine. "People will prefer Anne Elliot to Elizabeth Bennet according as they prefer a gentle sufferance . . . more than a lively rebellion." *Persuasion* he regarded as "imagined with as great a novelty and daring as *Pride and Prejudice*" (Southam, *Casebook:* 25).

A new edition of *Northanger Abbey* and *Persuasion* was published by Chapman and Hall in 1870 with a Tauchnitz English Language popular edition emanating from the Leipzig, Germany, publishers a year later. Hugh Thomson's illustrations, with an introduction by Austin Dobson (1840–1921) to both novels published together, appeared in 1897. In the same year, Adolphus Jack (1868–1945), in his *Essays on the Novel,* dismissed *Emma* and *Persuasion* as "these prim little moralizings of Miss Austen's later years" (Southam, *Heritage,* 11, 48). Somewhat surprisingly, the first separate publication of *Persuasion,* as distinct from its inclusion with another Jane Austen novel, does not occur until the Nelson's Classic's edition of [1926].

Twentieth-century critical responses to *Persuasion* increasingly find depth in the novel. It receives praise from fellow creative writers. Virginia Woolf, for instance, in *The Common Reader* (1925), discerns in *Persuasion* "a peculiar beauty and a peculiar dullness." The former is associated with Jane Austen's discovery toward the end of her life "that the world is larger, more mysterious, and more romantic than she had supposed." The "dullness" has its origins in her familiarity "with the ways of the world" (Southam, *Casebook,* 25). A fellow novelist, Elizabeth Bowen (1899–1973), in 1957 writes of *Persuasion* as "a masterpiece of delicate strength." She too finds in it an element "unheard hitherto" and relates the novel to "restraint" and "maturity." She also associated the novel with the "one mystery" of its author's "otherwise open life . . . her love affair" (26–27).

Setting biographical speculation aside, the sophisticated narrative techniques focusing on analysis are seen in a line of critical reactions to the novel extending from A. C. Bradley's 1911 lecture on Austen, with its "two distinct trains . . . a moralist and a humourist" (Southam, 234), to Mary Lascelles 1939 monograph and to R. S. Crane in 1957 and beyond. Lascelles writes of "new possibilities . . . opening out" in the novel, to "Jane Austen's maintenance of the consistent point of view in this novel" (Lascelles, 76, 204). The Chicago-based formalist critic R. S. Crane (1886–1967), analyzes *Persuasion* "as a serious comedy: a comedy in the general sense that its plot moves from unhappiness to happiness" centering on Anne and Wentworth. Crane traces in detail narrative patterns throughout the work (Southam, *Casebook,* II, 177).

Formalist approaches have continued through the latter years of the 20th century and into the new one. D. W. Harding in 1964 isolates the Cinderella motif pattern found in Austen's work. For Harding, Anne Elliot "is the most mature and profound of Cinderellas." *Persuasion* "is a . . . mature interpretation of . . . entirely unmerited wrongs. Anne has brought her chief misfortune on herself through a mistaken decision" (Harding, 148–149).

There has always been a diversity of approaches to *Persuasion.* Gilbert and Gubar, in *The Madwoman in the Attic* (1979), find a subtext of feminine discontent in the novel exemplified in the alienation from a male-centered social structure experienced by Anne Elliot. Marilyn Butler, on the other hand, reacts in her *Jane Austen and the War of Ideas* (1975), to what she perceives as readings of the novel celebrating Austen's social and moral universality while ignoring their historical and intellectual context. The novel has an "exclusively subjective viewpoint," but "for Jane Austen to treat the inner life for the first time with unreserved sympathy required her to rethink her form. For whatever reason . . . the result in *Persuasion* is muddle." Butler isolates "recurring imbalances in *Persuasion* between the inner and outer plains of reality" (Butler, 277, 290). Ultimately for Butler, *Persuasion,* as do Jane Austen's other works, affirms traditional values.

Claudia Johnson in 1988, on the other hand, perceives in *Persuasion* the sense that "stately houses and their proprietors are no longer formidable, and their intransigence is matched only by their vapidity" (Johnson, 165). John Wiltshire's section on *Persuasion* in his *Jane Austen and the Body* (1992) draws on various disciplines, including psychoanalysis, economic history, and gender studies. For Wiltshire, the novel deals with "the miscarriages of life," and is "about suffering and vulnerability. . . . The novel is shot through with recognitions of the body's fragility and mutability, and of the tenuousness of the emotions" (Wiltshire, 196). The novel's "treatment of desire" and "political inflexions" (Neill, 135) engage Edward Neill in his lively chapter "'Jane's Fighting Ships': *Persuasion* as Cultural Critique" in his *The Politics of Jane Austen* (1999). Finally, there are many references to *Persuasion* in Brian Southam's extensive, fully documented, historically based, detailed *Jane Austen and the Navy* (2000), and especially in the chapter "*Persuasion*: The Righting and Re-Writing of History" (257–298).

CHARACTERS

Alicia, Lady (Chapter 19: II: 7: 179)   A Bath acquaintance of Lady Russell. She especially admires "some window curtains" in Pulteney Street (179).

Atkinson, Miss (Chapter 19: II: 7: 177)   She once dined with Mr. Elliot "at the Wallises" and "says he is the most agreeable man she ever was in company with" (177).

Baldwin, Admiral (Chapter 3: I: 3: 20)   Sir Walter Elliot describes him as "the most deplorable looking personage you can imagine, his face the colour of mahogany, rough and rugged to the last degree, all lines and wrinkles, nine grey hairs of a side, and nothing but a dab of powder at top" (20). Baldwin is an example of Sir Walter's objection to the navy as a profession.

Benwick, Captain James (Chapters 2, 11, 13, 18, 20)   Engaged to Captain Harville's sister Fanny, who dies in June 1814, and lives with the Harvilles in Lyme. "Had been first lieutenant of the *Laconia*," where he served under Wentworth. Had waited "for fortune and promotion." The former came and "promotion, too . . . at *last*" (Jane Austen's emphasis), when he became commander of the *Grappler*, "but Fanny Harville did not live to know it." He is "an excellent young man and an officer . . . uniting very strong feelings with . . . a decided taste for reading [especially the poetry of Scott and Byron], and sedentary pursuits" (96–97). Initially attracted to Anne, he surprises everybody when he falls in love and marries Louisa Musgrove.

Brand, Admiral (Chapter 18)   Admiral Croft, walking with Anne Elliot in Milsom Street in Bath, sees Admiral Brand and his brother on the other side of the street. He describes them as "Shabby fellows" who played "a pitiful trick once" on Admiral Croft: they "got away some of my best men" (170).

Brigden, Captain (Chapter 18)   A friend of Admiral Croft whom he sees in Milsom Street in Bath.

Carteret, the Hon. Miss (Chapter 16)   The Elliots' Irish cousin. Daughter of the Viscountess Dalrymple, she "was so plain and so awkward, that she would never have been tolerated in Camden-place but for her birth" (150).

Clay, Mrs. Penelope (Chapters 2–3.5, 13, 15–17, 19–22)   Daughter of Sir Walter Elliot's lawyer and estate manager, Shepherd, "returned, after an unprosperous marriage, to her father's house, with the additional burthen of two children. She was a clever young woman, who understood the art of pleasing" (15). She "had freckles, and a projecting tooth, and a clumsy wrist . . . but she was young, and certainly altogether well-looking, and possessed, in an acute mind and assiduous pleasing manners, infinitely more dangerous attractions that any merely personal might have been" (34). She forms a strong friendship with Elizabeth Elliot and plans to become her father's second wife. William Elliot makes her his mistress—he is aware of the danger of being disinherited if she marries Sir Walter. She and William Elliot elope together to London.

Croft, Admiral (Chapters 3–8, 10, 13, 18, 23)   Retired senior naval officer, "A rear admiral" (21) who fought at the Battle of Trafalgar and then served for a time in the East Indies. He and his wife, to whom he is devoted, became tenants of Kellynch-hall, recommended to the Admiral by Mr. Shepherd after meeting him at the Taunton quarter sessions in 1814. "A native of Somersetshire," he "acquired a very handsome fortune." Honest and lacking in social airs and graces, the opposite of the vain and pretentious Sir Walter Elliot. Mr. Shepherd described him as "a very hale, hearty, well-looking man, a little weather-beaten, to be sure, but not much" (21–22).

"Admiral Croft" by Hugh Thompson, illustration to *Persuasion*, Macmillan edition, 1897

Croft, Sophia (née Wentworth) (Chapters 3–8, 10, 13, 18, 23)   Devoted wife of Admiral Croft, elder sister of Frederick Wentworth, with many West Country connections. Highly intelligent, described as "neither tall nor fat, had a squareness, uprightness, and vigour of form, which gave importance to her person." She had "been almost as much at sea as her husband." She was 38 years old, and "Her manners were open, easy, and decided, like one who had no distrust of herself, and no doubts of what to do." She was "without any approach to coarseness . . . or any want of good humour" (48).

Dalrymple, the Dowager Vicountess (Chapter 16)   Mother of the Honorable Miss Carteret. Widow of the Elliots' wealthy Irish cousin. "Spoken of as a charming woman" but lacking in "superiority of manner, accomplishment, or understanding . . . She had a smile and a civil answer for everybody" (149–150). The Elliots

wish to reestablish contact with her for social reasons following an estrangement.

Dalrymple, Viscount (Chapters 16)   Deceased Irish cousin of the Elliots, whose failure to send his widow a letter of condolence on his death resulted in an estrangement of the families.

Drew, Sir Archibald (Chapter 18)   An old friend of Admiral Croft spotted with his grandson walking on Milsom Street in Bath. Sir Archibald mistakes Anne Elliot for Admiral Croft's wife and "kisses his hand" (170) to her.

Durands, the little (Chapter 21)   Described by Mrs. Smith as regular Bath concertgoers "with their mouths open to catch the music; like unfledged sparrows ready to be fed. They never miss a concert" (193).

Elliot, Anne (appears throughout the novel)   The second daughter of Sir Walter and the deceased Lady Elizabeth Elliot, to whom she was very close and who died when she was 14 years old. Heroine of the novel and its main viewpoint, through which most of the actions and characters are perceived and judged. Twenty-seven years of age at its beginning in 1814, she was once very pretty. The breaking of an engagement with Frederick Wentworth at the age of 19 in 1806 under persuasion from Lady Russell, a surrogate mother, results in "an early loss of bloom and spirits" (28). When she was 22, Charles Musgrove proposed to her, but she rejected him, realizing that she would have been happier rejecting Lady Russell's advice. "She had been forced into prudence in her youth, she learned romance as she grew older—the natural sequel of an unnatural beginning" (30). She is "nobody" with her own father and elder sister, Elizabeth, "with an elegance of mind and sweetness of character" (5). The evolving reawakening of her relationship with Wentworth propels the plot and is the main interest of the novel. She gains in self-confidence and moves gradually to the center of the stage, being desired by William Walter Elliot, the heir of Kellynch. She is musical and prefers the country. When her father and Elizabeth move to Bath, she stays at Uppercross to help her younger sister, Mary, with her young children. Anne in "twelve years had changed . . . from the blooming silent, uniform girl of fifteen, to the elegant little woman of seven and twenty, with every beauty excepting bloom" (153). Reunited with Wentworth, whom she marries, she regrets that she "had but two friends in the world" to bring to him: "Lady Russell and Mrs. Smith" (251). During the novel, she has moved from Kellynch-hall, Uppercross, Kellynch-lodge, lodgings at Lyme and Bath, and then to marriage. However, the novel "declines to situate Anne's renewed happiness with Captain Wentworth in a home at all" (Sodeman, 790).

Elliot, Elizabeth (Chapters 1–2, 5, 12, 14–20, 22, 24) Eldest daughter of the Elliots, she is 29 at the start of the novel and for 13 years since her mother's death, has acted as the first lady of Kellynch-hall. A replica of her narcissistic father, she too is vain, proud, and snobbish, ignoring her younger sister Anne. Living in a time warp, she was "still the same handsome Miss Elliot that she had begun to be thirteen years ago" (6). Her life is one of "prosperity and . . . nothingness" (9). "She felt her approach to the years of danger" (7) and regrets her failure to find a husband. Ten years previously, she had been snubbed by her cousin Sir William Walter Elliot, whom "she could not admit him to be worth thinking of again" (8). However, when he appears in Bath, she assumes he is courting her and receives another humiliation at his hands when he elopes with Mrs. Clay. This is doubly ironic as Elizabeth has preferred Mrs. Clay to her sister Anne as her companion and confidant, exemplifying her lack of discernment.

Elliot, Lady Elizabeth, née Stevenson (Chapter 1) Deceased wife of Sir Walter Elliot. She died in 1800 after 17 years of marriage, when Anne, her second daughter, was 14 years old. She "had been an excellent woman, sensible and amiable; whose judgment and conduct, if they might be pardoned youthful infatuation which made her Lady Elliot, had never required indulgence afterwards" (4). Her

character was far superior to that of her vain husband, whose failings she conceded as a conscientious and dutiful but unhappy wife. Her careful frugal management of Kellynch-hall and the estate quickly disintegrated following her death. Anne inherited many of her positive qualities and greatly missed her. The novel begins 13 years after her death, and Lady Russell, her "very intimate friend" (5), tried to replace her as the source of sensible family advice and counsel.

Elliot, Mary   *See* Musgrove, Mary.

Elliot, Mrs. (Chapters 1, 15, 21)   Deceased wife of William Walter Elliot. The wealthy daughter of a grazier and a butcher's granddaughter, her husband married her for her money. "A rich woman of inferior birth" (8), she was "well educated, accomplished, rich, and excessively in love with" Elliot (139). However, according to Mrs. Smith, "she was too ignorant and giddy for respect, and he had never loved her" (211).

Elliot, Sir Walter, Bart (1) (Chapter 1)   The grandfather of Sir Walter.

Elliot, Sir Walter, Bart (2) (Chapters 1–5, 8, 15–18, 20, 22–24)   "Vanity" was the beginning and the end of Sir Walter's character, vanity of person and of situation. He had been remarkably handsome in his youth, and, at fifty-four, "was still a very fine man" (4). A baronet, perhaps Jane Austen's most sustained attack on inherited rank, he is a spendthrift and squanders away the well-managed estate his wife left when she died. A snob, obsessed by superficiality, he for instance objects to his daughter Anne's—whom he consistently ignores—visits to Mrs. Smith as she is a poor widow living in an impoverished area of Bath. Narcissistic, obsessed by his own looks and image in the mirror, he is prejudiced against the navy as he perceives that those who serve in it fail to retain their good appearance. He is not changed by the end of the novel, being "a foolish, spendthrift baronet, who had not had principle or sense enough to maintain himself in the situation in which Providence had placed him" (248). The father of three daughters,

Elizabeth, Anne, and Mary, he accepts Wentworth, whom he had previously snubbed, once he finds out he is wealthy.

Elliot, Sir William Walter (Chapters 1, 12–17, 19–24) The nephew of Sir Walter and heir presumptive to the baronetcy. Thirty-four years of age in 1814, 11 years earlier he became estranged from the Elliots, having snubbed Elizabeth and married as a poor law student "a rich woman of inferior birth" (8). His marriage provided him with wealth and independence. A chance meeting with Anne Elliot, to whom he is attracted, at Lyme propels the plot. A widower, he reestablishes contacts with the Elliot family, having heard that Mrs. Clay has designs on Sir Walter. If they married and produced an heir, this would prevent him from inheriting the baronetcy. He has a "very gentlemanlike appearance . . . air of elegance and fashion, his good-shaped face, his sensible eye, but, at the same time . . . very much under-hung" (141). Anne is flattered by his attentions. He is "rational, discreet, polished—but he was not open" and "too generally agreeable" (161). Mrs. Smith reveals to Anne that he "is a man without heart or conscience; a designing, wary, cold-blooded being, who thinks only of himself." The villain of the novel, "he is black at heart, hollow and black!" (199). Anne realizes that his attentions to her are motivated by a desire to be with Mrs. Clay. He seduces her away from Sir Walter and sets her up in London.

Frankland, Mrs. (Chapter 19) A Bath acquaintance of Lady Russell. She, with Lady Alicia, specially admires "some window-curtains" in Pulteney Street (179), *See also* Alicia, Lady.

Grierson, Lady Mary (Chapter 8) Wentworth once, if he had arrived "later at Lisbon . . . would have been asked to give a passage to Lady Mary Grierson and her daughters." However, he "hate[s] to hear of women on board, or to see them on board" (68–69).

Harville, Captain (Chapters 8, 11, 12–14, 22–23) A friend of Captain Wentworth, a fellow officer on the *Laconia*. Two years before the nov-

el's setting, he was wounded. He is "a tall, dark man, with a sensible, benevolent, countenance; a little lame" (97). Unlike Captain Benwick, he does not dwell on his problems. In spite of struggling to maintain a wife and three children, he remains cheerful and active, keeping busy by making toys for the children and furniture. Considerate and generous, he provides for his deceased sister's fiancé, Benwick, and arranges for Louisa Musgrove to be nursed following her accident on the Cobb. Anne is full of praise for him.

Harville, Fanny (Chapter 11) The deceased sister of Captain Harville and fiancée to Captain Benwick, to whom she had been engaged for some time while waiting for him to gain promotion and make his fortune at sea.

Harville, Mrs., and her three children (Chapters 8, 11) "Mrs. Harville, a degree less polished than her husband, seemed however to have the same good feelings" (97). An experienced nurse, despite looking after three children she also takes good care of Louisa Musgrove during her stay at Lyme.

Hayter, Mr. (Chapter 9: I) Married to the sister of Mrs. Musgrove (senior). He "had some property of his own, but it was insignificant compared with Mr. Musgrove's." He and his wife and family live at Winthrop, two miles from the Musgroves at Uppercross but live an "inferior, retired, and unpolished" life in comparison (74). Looked upon as poor relations, they remain on excellent terms with the Musgroves.

Hayter, Mrs. (Chapter 9: I) Sister of Mrs. Musgrove, by marrying Hayter she reduced her social rank and status.

Hayter, Rev. Charles (Chapters 9, 10, 13, 18, 22–23) The Hayters' elder son, "who had chosen to be a scholar and a gentleman, and who was very superior in cultivation and manners to all the rest" (74). He and his cousin Henrietta had an understanding until Wentworth appeared. However, her attachment to him returned. Charles goes to Lyme to see how Louisa Musgrove is recuperating. His hopes of becoming curate to the aging Dr. Shirley of Uppercross are stifled. He is offered a living for some years in Dorset, however, and consequently he and Henrietta can marry.

Hayters, the Miss (Chapters 8, 9) "The Miss Hayters, the females of the family of cousins" (71). They received a "defective education, have been hardly in any class at all, but for their connexion with Uppercross" (74). However, the young cousins get on well together.

Ibbotsons, the (Chapter 21) According to Mrs. Smith, a family attending a Bath concert.

Jemima (Chapter 6, 7, 18) Mrs. Mary Musgrove's nursery maid at Uppercross Cottage. Mary thinks her "the trustiest, steadiest creature in the world." Mrs Musgrove, her mother-in-law, thinks differently. She goes "gadding about the village" and is "a fine-dressing lady" (45).

Mackenzie (Chapters 5) The gardener at Kellynch.

Maclean, Lady Mary (Chapter 21) According to Mrs. Smith, "She never misses" a Bath concert (193).

Mary (Chapter 21) Maid to Mrs. Smith in her humble Bath lodgings.

Morley, Sir Basil (Chapter 3) According to Sir Walter Elliot, "a friend of mine" (20).

Musgrove, Charles (Chapter 1: 6; also chapter 7, 10, 12, 14, 18, 22, 23) Eldest son of Mr. and Mrs. Charles Musgrove of the Great House, or Mansion House, at Uppercross. Five years before the start of the novel, he proposed to Anne Elliot, who refused him. Subsequently he married Mary, her younger sister. They have two children, Charles and Walter, and live at Uppercross Cottage, near his parents: "civil and agreeable, in sense and temper he was undoubtedly superior to his wife." Also, "he did nothing with much zeal, but sport; and his time was otherwise trifled away, without benefit from books or any thing else"; he enjoys shooting (43).

Musgrove, Charles (the younger) (Chapters 5, 7) The older of Charles and Mary Musgrove's two sons. Dislocates his collarbone in a fall, allowing Anne Elliot to take charge and consequently delay her meeting after a separation of many years with Wentworth at Uppercross. Nursing Charles provides the excuse she needs.

Musgrove, Henry (Chapter 13) The younger, more spoiled, "the lingering and long-petted master Harry, sent to school after his brothers" (122) of the elder Mr. and Mrs. Musgrove of Uppercross Hall.

Musgrove, Henrietta and Louisa (Chapters 5, 7, 8, 9–13, 18, 20, 22, 23) The elder daughters of the Musgrove family. Louisa is 20 and Henrietta a year younger, but they are indistinguishable. Wentworth is unable to decide initially which he prefers, and Admiral Croft cannot distinguish between them. From school in Exeter, they gained "the usual stock of accomplishments" and are living as "fashionable, happy, and merry" (40). Both enjoy dancing and are attractive and attracted to Wentworth. This provides some respite for Henrietta, who is attached to her cousin Charles Hayter. Wentworth is perceived as paying attention to Louisa. Her fall at the Cobb places her in the company of Captain Benwick, with whom she falls in love. Her wedding to Benwick and Henrietta's to Hayter are expected to occur shortly after the close of the novel. Their switching of affections is meant to highlight Anne's maturity and constancy. Wentworth's flirtation with Louisa reveals his "angry pride" (242).

Musgrove, Mr. Charles (Chapters 1, 4–9, 11–14, 18, 20, 22–23) The wealthy landowner of Uppercross Hall in Somerset. Father of Charles, Louisa, and Henrietta. He and his wife are "a very good sort of people; friendly and hospitable, not much educated, and not at all elegant." Not overly ambitious for their children. Anne contrasts their sincerity and genuineness with the artificiality and lack of warmth of her own family. They "were in the old English style" (40).

Musgrove, Mrs. (Chapters 5, 8) Wife of the wealthy landowner of Uppercross Hall. Sister of

Mrs. Hayter. Physically "of a comfortable substantial size, infinitely more fitted by nature to express good cheer and good humour, than tenderness and sentiment" (68). Becomes maudlin over the death of her son Richard, and finds that her daughter-in-law Mary overindulges her children, whom she finds too troublesome to invite to the Great House. Is very welcoming to the Harville children during their stay.

Musgrove, Mrs. Mary née Elliot (Chapters 1, 4–7, 9–14, 18, 22–24) An "attention seeking hypochondria[c]" (Poplawski, 206), the younger sister of Elizabeth and Anne Elliot. Wife of Charles Musgrove, she has two little boys, Charles and Walter, whom she regards as out of control. Lacks the "understanding or temper" of Anne. "While well, and happy, and properly attended to, she had great good humour and excellent spirits; but any indisposition sank her completely; she had no resources for solitude; and inheriting a considerable share of the Elliot self-importance, was very prone to add to every other distress, that of fancying herself neglected and ill-used" (37).

Musgrove, Richard (Chapters 6, 7, 8) The "very troublesome, hopeless son" of Charles and Mrs. Musgrove, brother to Charles, Louisa, and Henrietta. He "had been sent to sea, because he was stupid and unmanageable on shore" (50). He served for six months under Captain Wentworth on the *Laconia* as a midshipman whom "every captain wishes to get rid of." During his time at sea, Wentworth persuaded him to write "two disinterested letters" (51) home not requesting money. "Poor Richard" (50) died abroad in 1812 before he reached the age of 20. Ironically, with time his mother, Mrs. Musgrove, made him the object of her grief with "her large fat sighings over the destiny of a son, whom alive nobody had cared for" (68).

Musgrove, Walter (Chapters 5, 9) The younger son of Charles and Mary Musgrove: "a remarkable stout, forward child of two years old" (79). His mother has little control over him. His climbing on Anne Elliot's back leads to her rescue by Captain Wentworth. His firm, gentle removal of him is the initial display of feeling displayed by Wentworth to Anne since their meeting again.

Musgroves, the younger (Chapters 5, 14) The Musgroves of Uppercross Hall have "a numerous family" (40) who go back to school after "the Christmas holidays" (129). The older children are Charles, Henrietta, and Louisa.

Pooles, the (Chapter 5) A family living near the Musgroves at Uppercross: The Musgroves attend a dinner party at the Pooles'. The crowded carriage conditions on the way lead to one of Mary Musgrove's regular "illness" episodes (39).

Robinson, Mr. (Chapter 7) The local apothecary called in to treat young Charles Musgrove's "collar-bone" (54).

Rooke, Nurse (Mrs.) (Chapters 17, 21) Mrs. Smith's friend and confidante: "a shrewd, intelligent sensible woman" (155). Also a source of gossip and news. She taught Mrs. Smith self-sufficiency, to knit, and how to make some money by selling knitted items to Mrs. Rooke's wealthier patients. She attends the wife of Colonel Wallis and brings information that Anne Elliot is to marry Mr. Elliot.

Russell, Lady (Chapters 1, 2, 4–6, 10, 12, 14, 16–24) Anne's close friend, substitute for her deceased mother, Lady Russell is "a woman rather of sound than of quick abilities . . . she was a benevolent, charitable, good woman, and capable of strong attachments; most correct in her conduct, strict in her notion of decorum, and with manners that were held a standard of good-breeding." Her advice to Anne to reject Wentworth propels the plot of the novel. Prejudiced on the side of "ancestry . . . rank and consequence" (11), she misjudges Mr. Elliot, not seeing through his status and superficial charm. Although Anne considers her an "excellent friend," she learns in the course of the novel that "she and her excellent friend could sometimes think differently" (147). On the other hand, Lady Russell consulted Anne on the future of Kellynch-hall and recommended tough economic measures. She did not approve of Mrs. Clay or Elizabeth's friendship with her. Anne travels to Bath with Lady Russell, whose custom it is to spend her winters in the city. At the end of the novel, Lady Russell exhibits integrity by accepting Anne's union with Wentworth. Lady Russell "was a very good woman, and if her second object was to be sensible and well-judging, her first was to see Anne happy. She loved Anne better than she loved her own abilities" (249).

Russell, Sir Henry (Chapters 2, 7) The deceased husband of Lady Russell. He is a knight rather than a baronet, hence his widow gives Sir Walter Elliot "the dignity of a baronet" (11)

Sarah (Chapter 13) Although the youngest Musgrove child, Henry, has left for school, Sarah, the family's nursemaid, still lives with the Musgroves at Uppercross Hall. She makes herself useful by mending clothes and treating minor injuries. Sarah goes to Lyme to look after Louisa after her fall.

Shepherd, John (Chapters 1–3, 5, 13) Sir Walter Elliot's very cautious legal agent, who advises him to let out Kellynch-hall to live in Bath rather than London, owing to the cost and to avoid temptation. Shepherd met Admiral Croft at the Taunton quarter-sessions, recommends him to Sir Walter, and draws up the terms of his tenancy at Kellynch-hall. His daughter is Mrs. Clay.

Shirley, Dr. (Chapter 9) The rector of Uppercross, "who for more than forty years had been zealously discharging all the duties of his office, but was now growing too infirm for many of them" (78). Charles Hayter is expected to assist him. Dr. Shirley's wife's cousins live at Lyme, the best place, according to Henrietta Musgrove, for him to retire.

Shirley, Mrs. (Chapter 12) The wife of Dr. Shirley with cousins at Lyme. According to Henrietta Musgrove, Mrs. Shirley and her husband "have been doing good all their lives." Henrietta does not want them "wearing out their last days in a place like Uppercross, where, excepting our family, they seem shut out from all the world" (102).

If they move, Charles then can become curate of Uppercross.

Smith, Charles (Chapters 17, 21) Deceased husband of Mrs. Smith: "A man of fortune" (152), weakness of character and too close a friendship with William Walter Elliot resulted in his financial ruin. Elliot, according to his widow, "was the intimate friend of my dear husband, who trusted and loved him, and thought him as good as himself" (199). Foolishly he made Elliot the executor of his will, and Elliot refused to assist his widow.

Smith, Mrs., née Hamilton (Chapters 18, 19, 21–22, 24) The former Miss Hamilton at the age of 17 befriended Anne Elliot during Anne's first school year. Three years older, Miss Hamilton realized how much Anne suffered from the loss of her mother and from being sent away from home for the first time. The following year when 18, Miss Hamilton left school and shortly after married Charles Smith. Anne has not seen her for 12 years and learns that Mrs. Smith "was a widow, and poor. Her husband had been extravagant; and at his death, about two years before, had left his affairs dreadfully involved." Further, "she had difficulties of every sort to contend with, and in addition to these distresses, had been afflicted with a severe rheumatic fever, which finally settling in her legs, had made her for the present a cripple" (152). Far from bitter, she possesses "the choicest gift of Heaven," (154) the ability to transform her afflictions into positives: "neither sickness nor sorrow seemed to have closed her heart or ruined her spirits" (153). It is Mrs. Smith who reveals William Walter Elliot's true character and motives. Wentworth helps her to recover "her husband's property in the West Indies," she experiences "some improvement of health . . . [and] her cheerfulness and mental alacrity did not fail her" (251–252). She remains very close to Anne and her husband, Wentworth.

Speed, Mrs (Chapter 21) The landlady at the Westgate Buildings in Bath, where Mrs. Smith lodges. Her sister is Mrs. Rooke, who helps Mrs. Smith.

Spicers, the (Chapter 9) A family who may be able to assist Charles Hayter in "getting something from the Bishop in the course of a year or two" (76).

St. Ives, Lord (Chapter 3) His father, according to Sir Walter Elliot, "we all know to have been a country curate without bread to eat." Sir Walter resents having "to give place" to him as he has gained a higher social rank, being "Lord St. Ives" (19–20).

Trent, Governor (Chapter 3) A former resident at Monkford near Kellynch and a man of property, a "gentleman" (23).

Wallis, Colonel (Chapters 15–17, 20–21, 23) "A very intimate friend" of William Walter Elliot, "a highly respectable man, perfectly the gentleman (and not an ill-looking man . . .) who was living in very good style" in Bath (139). A friend of Elliot's first wife, they had been friends for many years. He is also admired for "a fine military figure, though sandy-haired" (142), whom women find attractive. His wife, who is expecting a child, repeats what Elliot tells him without his knowledge, to Nurse Rooke, who passes the information to Mrs. Smith.

Wallis, Mrs. (Chapter 15) Wife of Colonel Wallis. According to William Walter Elliot "she was said to be an excessively pretty woman, beautiful" (141). However, Nurse Rooke tells Mrs. Smith that her only concerns are money and fashion. Expecting a child, she gossips to Nurse Rooke and repeats what her husband tells her, revealing Elliot's reasons for his warmth toward his uncle Sir Walter, Elizabeth, and Anne.

Wentworth, Edward (Chapters 3, 6, 9, 14, 18, 20, 23) Brother of Captain Frederick Wentworth, had been a curate at Monkford, Somerset, than married and settled in Shropshire, where his brother visits him. Anne Elliot first met his brother at Monkford, and he is the only person known to his brother to have knowledge of their short engagement. She is positive that he is very discreet.

Wentworth, Frederick (Chapters 4, 6–14, 18–20, 22–24) The central male character in *Persuasion*, he became a naval commander in February 1806, following the battle of St. Domingo (in which Jane Austen's brother Francis took part as a captain). Wentworth then stayed with his brother Edward at Monkford during the summer of 1806, when he met Anne. He was "a remarkably fine young man, with a great deal of intelligence, spirit and brilliancy" but with "a most uncertain profession, and no connexions to secure even his farther rise" in the navy and "no fortune" (26–27). He and Anne fell in love. She was persuaded by Lady Russell to reject Wentworth. Anne's caution angers Wentworth, who returns to sea, and gains promotion and fortune through capturing enemy vessels. He first commands the *Asp* and then the *Laconia*. In 1814, during a lull in the Napoleonic Wars, he visits his sister Mrs. Croft shortly after she has taken up residency at Kellynch-hall. Invited to Uppercross by the Musgroves, who remember his kindness to their son Richard, he reencounters Anne. He has not forgiven her and believes "her power with him was gone forever" (61). He learns that she rejected Charles Musgrove, and his kindness toward her deeply affects her, especially as he seemed to favor Louisa Musgrove.

The novel traces Wentworth's gradual restoration of his love for Anne (seen largely from her perspective). Wentworth is relieved when he hears that Louisa is engaged to Captain Benwick, and he is jealous of Anne's friendship in Bath with Elliot. For Wentworth, Anne exemplifies "the loveliest medium of fortitude and gentleness." He admits his "angry pride" (241–242) in not proposing to her again after he had been given command of the *Laconia*, two years after their separation. Blunt, yet with a strict code of honor, he writes to Anne: "You pierce my soul. I am half agony, half hope. Tell me not that I am too late, that such precious feelings are gone for ever. I offer myself to you again with a heart even more of your own, than when you almost broke it eight years and a half ago" (237). One of his first acts after his marriage to Anne and "in their settled life" (251) is to help her friend Mrs. Smith to regain some of her lost fortune.

BIBLIOGRAPHY

Primary Texts

Jane Austen's Letters. Collected and edited by Deirdre Le Faye. 3d ed. Oxford: Oxford University Press, 1995.

Northanger Abbey and Persuasion. Edited by R. W. Chapman. *The Novels of Jane Austen, V.* 3d ed. London: Oxford University Press, 1965 reprint (with revisions) [Volume, chapter, references and page numbers are to this edition.]

Persuasion. Edited by Linda Bree. Broadview Literary Texts. Peterborough, Ontario, Canada: Broadview Press, 1998.

————. Introduction by David Daiches. Norton Library. New York: W.W. Norton, 1958.

————. Edited by John Davie, with an introduction and notes by Claude Rawson. Oxford World's Classics. Oxford: Oxford University Press, 1998.

————. Edited by Patricia Meyer Spacks. A Norton Critical Edition. New York: W.W. Norton, 1995.

Secondary Works

Auerbach, Emily. *Searching for Jane Austen.* Madison: University of Wisconsin Press, 2004.

Butler, Marilyn. *Jane Austen and the War of Ideas.* Oxford: Clarendon Press, 1975.

Fergus, Jan. "'My sore-throats, you know, are always worse than anybody's': Mary Musgrove and Jane Austen's Art of Whining." In *Jane Austen's Business: Her World and Her Profession,* edited by Juliet McMaster and Bruce Stovel, 69–80. London and New York: Macmillan and St. Martin's Press, 1996.

Gilson, David. *A Bibliography of Jane Austen New Introduction and Corrections by the Author.* Winchester: St. Paul's Bibliographies; New Castle, Del.: Oak Knoll Press, 1997.

Harding, D. W. *Regulated Hatred and Other Essays on Jane Austen.* Edited by Monica Lawlor. London and Atlantic Highlands, N.J.: Athlone Press, 1998.

Hardy, Barbara. *A Reading of Jane Austen.* London: Peter Owen, 1975.

Honan, Park. *Jane Austen: Her Life.* London: Weiderfeld and Nicolson, 1987.

Johnson, Claudia L. *Jane Austen: Women, Politics, and the Novel.* Chicago and London: University of Chicago Press, 1988.

Jones, Darryl. *Jane Austen.* Houndmills, Basingstoke, Hampshire, U.K.: Palgrave Macmillan, 2004.

Le Faye, Deirdre. *Jane Austen: The World of Her Novels.* New York: Harry N. Abrams, 2002.

Litz, A. Walton. *Jane Austen: A Study of Her Artistic Development.* New York: Oxford University Press, 1965.

————. "*Persuasion*: Forms of Estrangement," in *Jane Austen: Bicentenary Essays,* edited by John Halperin. Cambridge: Cambridge University Press, 1975: 235–246.

Mooneyham, Laura G. *Romance, Language, and Education in Jane Austen's Novels.* London and New York: Macmillan and St. Martin's Press, 1988.

Neill, Edward. *The Politics of Jane Austen.* London and New York: Macmillan and St. Martin's Press, 1999.

Page, Norman. *The Language of Jane Austen*: Oxford, U.K.: Basil Blackwell, 1972.

Phillipps, K. C. *Jane Austen's English.* London: Andre Deutsch, 1970.

Poplawski, Paul. *A Jane Austen Encyclopaedia.* Westport, Conn: Greenwood Press, 1998.

Schama, Simon. *A History of Britain, Volume Three: The Fate of Empire, 1776–2000.* London: BBC, 2002.

Showalter, Elaine. "Retrenchments." In *Jane Austen's Business,* edited by J. McMaster and Bruce Stovel, 181–191.

Sodeman, Melissa. "Domestic Mobility in *Persuasion* and *Sanditon,*" *Studies in English Literature* 45, no. 4 (Autumn 2005): 787–812.

Southam, B. C. *Jane Austen and the Navy.* London: Hambledon and London, 2000.

————. *Jane Austen's Literary Manuscripts: A Study of the Novelist's Development Through the Surviving Papers.* New Edition. London: Athlone Press, 2001.

————, ed. *Jane Austen: Northanger Abbey and Persuasion: A Casebook.* London: Macmillan, 1976.

————, ed. *Jane Austen: The Critical Heritage.* 2 vols. London: Routledge and Kegan Paul, 1978–1979.

Tandon, Bharat. *Jane Austen and the Morality of Conversation.* London: Anthem Press, 2003.

Tanner, Tony. *Jane Austen.* Cambridge: Harvard University Press, 1986.

Wiltshire, John. *Jane Austen and the Body: The Picture of Health.* Cambridge: Cambridge University Press, 1992.

Plan of a Novel, according to hints from various quarters (1926)

COMPOSITION AND PUBLICATION

Jane Austen's *Plan of a Novel, according to hints from various quarters* (*Plan*) appears in R. W. Chapman's *The Works of Jane Austen VI Minor Works,* The manuscript is now in the Pierpont Morgan Library, New York An undated fair copy it was probably written in 1816. Extracts appeared in Austen-Leigh's 1871 *Memoir*. The first complete text of *Plan* is found in *Plan of a Novel and other documents,* edited by R. W. Chapman in a limited edition of 350 copies published by the Clarendon Press, Oxford, in 1926. Sutherland in her notes to "A Memoir," observes that "to appreciate the full flavour and sharpness of [the] comedy, the 'Plan' needs to be read with the complete text of" the Reverend James Stanier Clarke's letters to Jane Austen, as her "Plan" was probably a response to them (243).

SYNOPSIS

A single paragraph consists of a response replete with private jokes to James-Stanier Clarke's suggestions that Jane Austen write a novel focusing on a clergyman or a historical romance based on the Saxe-Cobourg family (Princess Charlotte had just become engaged to a Saxe-Cobourg). Jane Austen's *Plan* has a faultless, accomplished heroine (as Jane Austen indicates in her notes to *Plan*, like her niece Fanny Knight, later Lady Knatchbull, 1793–1882), "the Daughter of a Clergyman" (William Gifford, 1756–1826, editor of the *Quarterly Review* and JOHN MURRAY's reader for *Emma*). The father and daughter will converse in "long speeches, elegant Language." Much of the first volume is to be taken up with a life story, and this volume will close with the clergyman's "opinion of the Benefits to result

from Tythes being done away"—a suggestion of Clarke in a letter to Jane Austen.

The story will contain "a striking variety of adventures. . . . a wide variety of Characters." Father and daughter will travel continuously and the interest will come from those trying to influence them, such as "some totally unprincipled & heart-less young Man, desperately in love with the Heroine, & pursuing her with unrelenting passion." Jane Austen's "scene will be for ever shifting from one Set of People to another." The hero is referred to as "the anti-hero." She encounters another female, an equivalent to a Lucy Steele or Mary Crawford figure, "of Talents & Shrewdness" from whom the "Heroine shall shrink from the acquaintance." Totally isolated and impoverished, the heroine and her father "retreat into Kamschatka" in remote Siberia. Following the death of her father, the heroine "crawls back towards her former Country—having at least 20 narrow escapes of falling into the hands of the Anti-hero," and by chance meets the hero. Somewhat in contradiction to the Siberian experience, the penultimate sentence reads, "Throughout the whole work, [the] Heroine to be in the most elegant Society & living in high style" ([428]–430).

CRITICAL COMMENTARY

Commentary has focused on the relationship of the *Plan* to its author's annoyance with James-Stanier Clarke for his frequent requests found in his letters to her, the private allusions to members of Austen's family and circle, and her own work, plus its parodic references to other literary work. Further, the *Plan* has been viewed as an authorial manifesto. Kathryn Sutherland in her *Jane Austen's Textual Lives* observes that Jane Austen is "writing at a stage in her own publishing career when she can express with some confidence what she believes the novel should do, she here sets in ludicrous light many of the devices of contemporary fiction" (248). B. C. Southam in his chapter "The Plan of a Novel" in his *Jane Austen's Literary Manuscripts* writes that in the *Plan* Jane Austen presents, as she does "so consistently in [her] six novels . . . the subject-matter of observed and familiar life with naturalness and probability, an essential fidelity to common experience, without which her higher aims would never have been achieved" (Southam, 85). References in the *Plan of a Novel* are well explicated in Doody and Murray's "Explanatory Notes" (360–362).

BIBLIOGRAPHY

Primary Texts

Austen, Jane. ["Plan of a Novel"]. In James Edward Austen-Leigh, *A Memoir of Jane Austen and Other Family Recollections* [1871]. Edited by Kathryn Sutherland, 97–99, 243–244. Oxford: Oxford University Press, 2002.

———. *Plan of a novel according to hints from various quarters, by Jane Austen, with opinions on* Mansfield Park *and* Emma *collected and transcribed by her . . .* Edited by [R. W. Chapman]. Oxford, U.K.: Clarendon Press, 1926.

———. "Plan of a Novel." In *The Works of Jane Austen*, Vol. 6, *Minor Works*, edited by R. W. Chapman, revised edition by B. C. Southam, [428]–430. Oxford: Oxford University Press. 1986. [All textual references are to this edition.]

———. "Plan of a Novel." In *Jane Austen's* Catharine *and other Writings*, edited by Margaret Anne Doody and Douglas Murray, 230–232. Oxford: Oxford University Press, 1993.

SECONDARY WORKS

Southam, Brian. C. *Jane Austen's Literary Manuscripts: A Study of the Novelist's Development through the Surviving Papers*. New Edition. London: Athlone Press, 2001.

Sutherland, Kathryn. *Jane Austen's Textual Lives: From Aeschylus to Bollywood*. Oxford: Oxford University Press, 2005.

Prayers (Three Evening Prayers) (1940)

There are three undated "Prayers" attributed to Jane Austen based on two manuscripts at Mills College, Oakland, California. The first contains the inscription "Prayers composed by my ever dear sister Jane," probably in her sister Cassandra's hand, on paper watermarked 1818. The first prayer has a title: "Evening Prayer." The second manuscript is written in two different hands and contains the second and third prayers. The three were first published in 1940 by a private press in San Francisco run by a William Matson Roth. They are also in *Minor Works* ([453]–457) and in Doody and Murray ([247]–250). Le Faye suggests that the "Prayers" probably were a product of Jane Austen's last years (*Family Record*, 267).

The prayers are communal rather than personal. The first "Prayer" warns of "deceiving ourselves by pride or vanity" and requests permission to address God "with our hearts, as with our lips." There is an emphasis on introspection and self-examination: "May we now, and on each return of night, consider how the past day has been spent by us, what have been our prevailing thoughts, words and actions during it, and how far we can acquit ourselves of evil."

The second Prayer continues the inward-looking mode and takes up the concern with "neglected duties" and the deist belief that the individual is able to control his or her own life. Sins are the result of frailty, which we must fight. However, the prayer moves from pride and self-sufficiency to natural depravity: "to creatures so formed and situated . . . We are helpless and dependent."

The third Prayer begins with a consideration of our daily activity and that "for which we were before accountable"—this is important, and part of our duty. This third Prayer, in addition to repeating many of the sentiments of the first two Prayers, contains a plea for "fervent prayer" and the recognition of a greater power beyond ourselves: "We feel that we have been blessed far beyond anything that we have deserved." However, the conclusion of the Prayer is deistic, with its emphasis on the self: "may we . . . so conduct ourselves on earth as to secure an eternity of happiness with each other in thy heavenly kingdom" ([453]–457).

CRITICAL COMMENTARY

Marilyn Butler in her *Jane Austen and the War of Ideas* uses passages in *Prayers* twice in the context of discussing *Sense and Sensibility* and *Pride and Prejudice*. In the first instance, the second paragraph of the first Prayer is used as evidence to demonstrate that Jane Austen "as a Christian deplored" the fictional Marianne Dashwood's "doctrine of complacency and self-sufficiency" exhibited in the first part of *Sense and Sensibility* (189). Apropos of the actions of Darcy and Elizabeth Bennet in *Pride and Prejudice*, Marilyn Butler observes that Darcy "in theory . . . admits he is fallible, but the real impression left is one of pride. For Elizabeth, too, the quality that goes with severity about others is complacency towards the self." Butler uses the second sentence of the second paragraph of the third Prayer to illustrate Darcy and Elizabeth's sentiments: "this disposition to think well of the self and ill of others is the opposite of what she [Jane Austen] conceives to be the Christian's duty" (205–206).

Elton E. Smith's "Jane Austen's Prayers: Deism Becoming Theism" places the three Prayers within their theological and historical context. On the one hand, the "Prayers" have deist elements with their emphasis on the importance of human reason as distinct from revelation, the emphasis on individual morality and behavior. Deism was influential in late 18th-century England and elsewhere; it stressed the physical laws of the universe rather than the importance of a supreme creator. Theism, on the other hand, became much more influential during the first decades of the 19th century, as did the Evangelical influence, stressing self-scrutiny. The Creator, as opposed to the individual, is Supreme. The individual is sinful and should be full of remorse for sins committed each day and request forgiveness. For Smith, "when we discuss the three great written prayers of Jane Austen, we note deistic remnant and evangelical intrusion." The Prayers reflect the Anglican Book of Common Prayer, "their deist foundation; and . . . their evangelical innovation" (285). Essentially then, these three "Prayers" provide nonfictional evidence for the religious beliefs and observances of Jane Austen. In her *Jane Austen's Philosophy of the Virtues*, Sarah Emsley goes so far as to say that Jane Austen's "novels can be read in the light of the three prayers she composed" (8).

BIBLIOGRAPHY

Primary Texts

Austen, Jane. *Three Evening Prayers*. San Francisco: Colt Press, 1940.

———. "Prayers." In *The Works of Jane Austen*, Vol. 6, *Minor Works*, edited by R. W. Chapman. Oxford: Oxford University Press. 1986. [All textual references are to this edition.]

———. "Prayers." In *Jane Austen's* Catharine *and other Writings*, edited by Margaret Anne Doody and Douglas Murray. Oxford: Oxford University Press, 1993: [247]–250.

Secondary Works

Butler, Marilyn. *Jane Austen and the War of Ideas*. Oxford: Clarendon Press, 1975.

———. "History, Politics and Religion." In *The Jane Austen Companion*, edited by J. David Grey, A. Walton Litz, and Brian Southam, 190–208. New York: Macmillan, 1986.

Emsley, Sarah. *Jane Austen's Philosophy of the Virtues*. New York: Palgrave Macmillan, 2005.

Le Faye, Deirdre. *Jane Austen: A Family Record*. 2d ed. Cambridge: Cambridge University Press, 2004.

Smith, Elton E. "Jane Austen's Prayers; Deism Becoming Theism." In *A Companion to Jane Austen Studies*, edited by Laura Cooner Lambdin and Robert Thomas Lambdin, [283]–289. Westport, Conn.: Greenwood Press, 2000.

Pride and Prejudice (1813)

"It is a truth universally acknowledged that a single man in possession of a good fortune must be in want of a wife" [3]. So begins Jane Austen's arguably most enduringly successful novel—one that has been translated into at least 35 languages. At the heart of the novel lies irony—what appears to be so may indeed not be so. These words at the start of the novel are those of the author, who is a subtle commentator throughout the story. But they express precisely the sentiments of the anxious and fussy Mrs. Bennet, hardly noted in the rest of the novel for her wisdom or diplomacy. Her self-appointed task in life is to make sure that each of her five daughters secures a suitable that is, a financially sound, preferably very rich husband. Her observations reflect the key concern of *Pride and Prejudice:* the crucial importance of money and property in influencing human activity and relationships. The 20th-century British poet, playwright, and critic, Wystan Hugh Auden (1907–1973) summed up the qualities, pithily and brilliantly encapsulated in Mrs. Bennet's opening words at the start of *Pride and*

PRIDE

AND

PREJUDICE:

A NOVEL.

IN THREE VOLUMES.

BY THE

AUTHOR OF " SENSE AND SENSIBILITY."

VOL. I.

London:

PRINTED FOR T. EGERTON,
MILITARY LIBRARY, WHITEHALL.

1813.

Title page of the first edition of *Pride and Prejudice*

Prejudice. In his "Letter to Lord Byron" (1936), he wrote of Jane Austen:

> You could not shock her more than she shocks me;
> Beside her Joyce seems innocent as grass.
> It makes me uncomfortable to see
> An English spinster of the middle class
> Describe the amorous effects of 'brass',
> Reveal so frankly and with such sobriety
> The economic basis of society

COMPOSITION AND PUBLICATION

Pride and Prejudice, first published in 1813, is a novel obsessed with "the amorous effects of 'brass,'" or money, and revealing "so frankly and with such sobriety," in other words without pretense, honestly, "The economic basis of society" (Southam, II: 219). The second of Jane Austen's adult or mature fictions to be completed, it originally was entitled "First Impressions." The novel was composed between October 1796 and August of the following year, when its author was living at Steventon in Hampshire. At the start of writing the novel, Jane Austen was the same age as her heroine, Elizabeth Bennet. The author's father, the Reverend GEORGE AUSTEN, and the rest of her family were so impressed with what she had written that he approached a fashionable London publisher, Thomas Cadell, on November 1, 1797, asking if the publisher would consider publishing a "Novel comprised in three vols. about the length of Mrs. Burney's Evelina." The reference to Fanny Burney and *Evelina; or, a Young Lady's Entrance into the World,* a novel published in letters in 1778, creates speculation that "First Impressions" was also originally epistolary, in other words, written as a sequence of letters. Letters do play a prominent part in the text. George Austen's offering letter of "First Impressions" to Cadell the publishers was short and did not contain narrative detail or say that the novel was a comic one focusing on manners and the way people behave. Cadell's clerk declined the offer by "Return of Post" (Gilson, 24).

Jane Austen was not put off by this rejection. She did not burn or destroy her manuscript. Her correspondence reveals that the novel was very popular in her family circle and subject to family readings. For instance, in a letter to her elder sister, Cassandra, dated January 9, 1799, she writes somewhat sarcastically, "I do not wonder at your wanting to read *first impressions* again, so seldom as you have gone through it, & that so long ago"—not more than two years. Five months later, on June 11, she writes to Cassandra, not without a hint of irony, that she "would not let Martha" Lloyd—her close friend—"read First Impressions again upon any account, & am very glad that I did not leave it in your power.—She is very cunning, but I see through her design;—she means to publish it from Memory, & one more perusal must enable her to do it."

Resisting family pressure to publish it, Jane Austen kept the manuscript, "First Impressions," for more than 10 years. During this period, the London publisher Thomas Egerton published *Sense and Sensibility* on October 30, 1811. During the years 1810 to 1811 Jane Austen reworked "First Impressions," changing dates, and as she writes to Cassandra on January 29, 1813, she "lopt & cropt" her manuscript. She also had to change the title, as in 1800 a novel called *First Impressions* by one Margaret Holford was published in London by the Minerva Press. Jane Austen wrote to her niece Anna Austen on September 28, 1814, objecting to the phrase "vortex of Dissipation," an example of which is found in Holford's novel. Jane Austen found this "such thorough novel slang." Probably she found her antithetically phrased new title *Pride and Prejudice* while reading FANNY BURNEY's novel *Cecilia; or, Memoirs of an Heiress* (1782). In a letter to Martha Lloyd of November 29, 1812, she writes that she has sold the copyright (the ownership) of *Pride and Prejudice* to the Whitehall London publisher of the Military Library, THOMAS EGERTON. She received less than she wanted, being paid £110 rather than the sum she had requested of £150. Egerton published the novel in three-volume format on January 28, 1813. The price was 18 shillings for the volumes: "I want to tell you that I have got my own darling Child from London," Jane wrote to Cassandra a day later. She also told Cassandra that Egerton sent her five copies, the other four going to her brothers, Charles, Edward, James, and Frank (*Letters*, 35, 44, 202, 277, 197, 201).

In common with other Jane Austen novels published during her lifetime, the author's name is not on the title page. Published anonymously "By the Author of Sense and Sensibility," the book was a considerable success. Probably around 1,500 copies were printed. These were soon sold out and a second edition, the number of copies printed is unknown, was published in October 1813. JOHN MURRAY, the London publisher, issued in two volumes rather than three, a third edition four years later, in 1817. Again, the number of copies printed is not known. Jane Austen, who had sold the copyright, seems to have had no say in these subsequent printings. An American edition under the title "Elizabeth Bennet; or, Pride and Prejudice: A Novel in Two Volumes" by the "Author of 'Sense and Sensibility,'" published "from the Third London Edition," that is Murray's 1817 edition, was published in Philadelphia by Carey Lea in 1832. Twelve hundred and fifty copies were printed. The first complete translation in another language, into French, had occurred 10 years previously when, in 1822, "Orgueil et Prévention" was published in Paris in four volumes by Chez Maradan, Libraire, at 16 rue des Murais (Gilson, 113, 140).

Page references are to the 1988 Oxford reprint of R. W. Chapman's edition.

SYNOPSIS

Volume 1

Mrs. Bennet hears that Netherfield, a nearby country estate, has been rented by the young, wealthy, and single Mr. Bingley. She directs her husband to visit Bingley immediately to prepare for future relationships. The Bennets have five daughters, and Mrs. Bennet is anxious to find husbands for them. After some teasing, Mr. Bennet makes the visit and Bingley reciprocates, although the Bennet girls are out when he calls. He meets them at the next Meryton Ball—Meryton being the nearest large town—and is immediately attracted to Jane, the oldest and most attractive daughter.

Bingley is accompanied by his sisters Caroline and Mrs. Hurst, and her husband, Mr. Hurst. With them is the noble-looking, handsome, and exceedingly wealthy Darcy. He does not have Bingley's charm and is quickly judged "the proudest, most disagreeable man in the world" (11). He refuses to dance with anybody but Bingley's sisters and makes an enemy of Mrs. Bennet by making a disparaging remark about Elizabeth, the second daughter. Elizabeth also hears the remark, but she is high-spirited and confident, and the comment does not endear Darcy to her. Bingley continues to court Jane, and Darcy and Elizabeth are frequently in each other's company. Darcy revises his opinion of her and admires her wit, intelligence, and "fine eyes" (36). Sir William Lucas, a neighbor of the Bennets, throws a party that Darcy attends. Charlotte, Sir William's daughter, is a very close friend of Elizabeth who seems unaware of Darcy's interest in her. Caroline Bingley, who has designs on Darcy, becomes aware that Elizabeth is a rival and plays on Darcy's snobbery, reminding him of Mrs. Bennet's vulgarity.

The Bingley sisters invite Jane to spend an evening with them at Netherfield. Mrs. Bennet withholds the use of the family carriage, insisting that Jane go on horseback; she hopes that the possibility of rain will get an invitation for Jane to stay overnight. It rains sooner than anticipated, Jane catches a severe cold, and she is forced to spend some time at the Bingleys'. Elizabeth tramps three miles through muddy fields to visit her. The Bingley sisters consider such behavior inappropriate for a lady; Darcy silently admires the complexion the walk brings to Elizabeth's appearance. Elizabeth is invited to stay at Netherfield to nurse Jane. This brings Darcy and Elizabeth closer together, but the surprise visit of Mrs. Bennet and her irresponsible daughters, Lydia and Kitty, serves as a reminder to Darcy of the social barriers between him and the Bennets, and he begins to distance himself from Elizabeth.

As the Bennets have daughters, the estate will be inherited by Mr. Bennet's nephew, the Reverend William Collins. He visits their home at Longbourn apparently to heal the family rift but really to find a suitable wife from among the Bennet daughters. Collins is obsequious to his patron, the wealthy Lady Catherine de Bourgh of Rosings in Kent, who has advised him to marry. Foolish, full of self-importance, and tactless, he is the object of ridicule among the Bennets. Mrs. Bennet, how-

ever, sees him as a suitable prospect for one of her daughters. Thinking that Jane is spoken for, she directs his attention to Elizabeth.

Kitty and Lydia, the younger Bennet daughters, frequently visit Meryton, where the militia are stationed, and they use their Meryton aunt, Mrs. Phillips, as an excuse for their visits. Accompanied by Jane, Elizabeth, and Collins, they walk from Longbourn to Meryton to hear the latest gossip and meet an officer they know, a Mr. Denny, who is accompanied by the charming and handsome Mr. Wickham, newly arrived from London to take up a commission in Denny's regiment. Bingley and Darcy appear on horseback and come over to greet Jane and Elizabeth. As soon as Darcy and Wickham see each other, there is an evident awkwardness and Elizabeth realizes that they know each other. At a dinner party the following evening, Wickham and Elizabeth are mutually attracted and she asks him about Darcy. According to Wickham, Darcy destroyed his career by denying him a living in the church, reserved by Darcy's father. Apparently Darcy's motivation was pride and jealousy. Further, Lady Catherine de Bourgh's aunt and she have planned for a long time to unite their estates by arranging a marriage between Darcy and her daughter. Wickham's descripton of Darcy's character accords with Elizabeth's own first impressions; she believes Wickham's version of events and grows even more hostile to Darcy.

Bingley hosts a ball at Netherfield and Elizabeth looks forward to dancing with Wickham. Collins, to her surprise, tells her he will be at the ball, engages her for the first two dances, and clearly has designs on her. Wickham, to Elizabeth's disappointment, does not appear, and she believes that Darcy is the reason for his not coming. The behavior of Mrs. Bennet and Mary, who sings too much, confirms Darcy in his perceptions that a marriage with one of the Bennet daughters would be inappropriate. He resolves to take Bingley away from the area in spite of his love for Jane. Following the ball, Jane is distressed to receive a letter from Caroline Bingley saying that the Netherfield party has left for London and does not intend to return again until winter. Caroline mentions that there are hopes that Bingley will marry Georgiana, Darcy's sister.

Elizabeth believes that to be wishful thinking on Miss Bingley's part.

On the day following the ball, Collins proposes to Elizabeth and cannot accept her refusal, so that she has to leave the room. Mrs. Bennet insists that Mr. Bennet pressure Elizabeth to accept Collins, but Mr. Bennet takes Elizabeth's side. Mr. Collins's pride is restored by the appearance of Charlotte Lucas, who pays attention to him and is encouraging him. Charlotte openly admits to Elizabeth "I ask only a comfortable home" (125), and that her motives are mercenary. Mrs. Bennet is mortified. Her neighbors will have married off a daughter before she does. Their daughter one day will be mistress of Longbourn.

Volume 2

Jane receives another letter form Caroline Bingley telling her that her brother will remain in London for the winter and is seeing Georgina Darcy a good deal. Jane concludes that she is mistaken in supposing that Bingley loved her. Elizabeth tells her that Caroline wishes her to react that way. Jane is stoical and refuses to think ill of the Bingleys. Mrs. Bennet begins to think that her daughters will never marry. Wickham's presence and his relationship with Elizabeth is the sole ray of light in a depressed atmosphere. His apparent bad treatment by Mr. Darcy is widely known. Only Jane Bennet reserves judgment.

Christmas arrives and Mrs. Bennet's brother, the successful London tradesman Mr. Gardiner, and his wife stay at Longbourn for the holiday period. Mrs. Gardiner is close to Jane and Elizabeth, and she cautions Elizabeth to be careful regarding Wickham. They invite Jane to London in the hope that she may see something of the Bingleys, who will be in a more fashionable area of London than they are. Charlotte marries Collins and leaves for Kent after getting a promise from Elizabeth that she will visit her in March at Hunsford Parsonage. In London, Jane does not see Bingley and is twice snubbed by Caroline Bingley. Jane also gathers that Bingley will probably give up Netherfield for good.

It is now Elizabeth's turn to be disillusioned. Wickham has transferred his attentions to Miss King, a very wealthy young woman. Elizabeth remains in no doubt about Darcy but cannot blame Wickham too much, as he has acted in a similar fashion as her friend Charlotte. Elizabeth realizes that her feelings for Wickham were not too strong. Wickham's pursuit of the rich Miss King is unsuccessful.

Elizabeth spends a night with Jane and the Gardiners in London on her way to visit Charlotte. The Gardiners invite her on their summer tour during which they hope to travel as far north as the Lake District. At Hunsford, Elizabeth is warmly welcomed by Charlotte and surprised to see how well she has adjusted to her new surroundings. Hunsford is on the edge of Rosings Park, and about one and a half miles from Rosings House, home of Collins's haughty patroness, Lady Catherine de Bourgh. On the third day of her visit, Elizabeth, accompanied by the Lucases, visits Rosings House. Elizabeth is the only one not to be in awe of rank, money, and snobbery. Lady Catherine dominates the conversation and her sickly daughter, Miss de Bourgh, remains pale, oppressed, and silent.

Darcy and his cousin Fitzwilliam arrive to stay with Lady Catherine. In each other's company, Darcy and Elizabeth renew their verbal fencing, Elizabeth sees that he is not the least interested in Miss de Bourgh and is increasingly attracted by herself. She develops a friendship with Colonel Fitzwilliam, who inadvertently reveals that Darcy is responsible for separating Jane and Bingley, having just rescued a close friend from an inappropriate marriage. Later that day, Elizabeth is alone at the parsonage, brooding over Jane, and is surprised by Darcy. Agitated, he blurts out his love for her and wish to marry her in spite of her family status and "sense of her inferiority" (189). Elizabeth becomes angry, rejects Darcy, and gives as her reasons his treatment of Jane, interference in Bingley's affairs, ill-treatment of Wickham, and his high opinion of himself.

The following day Elizabeth receives a letter from Darcy. He explains that he did not perceive Jane to be as deeply in love with Bingley as he was with her, and that her family's lack of propriety, apart from Jane and Elizabeth, created problems. Darcy admits that he may well be in error regarding the depth of Jane's feelings for Bingley. He then explains at length that George Wickham is the son of a former trusted steward of the Darcy estate Pemberley in Derbyshire. In gratitude for his father's help, Darcy's father educated Wickham, settled a church living on the estate for him as Wickham intended to enter the church, and left him a legacy. Wickham turned out, however, to be unscrupulous and wasted the money. He had no intention of going into the church and asked Darcy for assistance which he refused. Further, Wickham had attempted to elope with Darcy's 15-year-old sister, Georgina, but had been forestalled.

Initially, Elizabeth has doubts about Darcy's explanation, but after reflection she becomes convinced of its truthfulness. She also begins to revise her own perceptions of him and feels that she may have been unnecessarily prejudiced. Her feelings toward Darcy are confused. The month of May has come, and Jane and Elizabeth return to Longbourn. Elizabeth tells Jane about Darcy's proposal and Wickham, whose regiment is shortly leaving Meryton for Brighton. They decide, in retrospect unwisely, not to expose further Wickham's character.

Lydia is invited to Brighton by Mrs. Forster, who has recently married the commander of Wickham's militia regiment, Colonel Forster. Elizabeth tries to persuade her father that Lydia is too young and irresponsible to go to Brighton. Her father overrules her: "We shall have no peace at Longbourn if Lydia does not go" (232). Elizabeth's summer tour with the Gardiners has to be curtailed, owing to Mr. Gardiner's business affairs. They will be able to travel as far north as Derbyshire and find themselves near Pemberley. It is mid-July and Elizabeth agrees to a visit to the house and grounds after finding out that Darcy is not in residence.

Volume 3

Elizabeth and the Gardiners tour Pemberley and are shown around the house by Mrs. Reynolds, the housekeeper, who has known Darcy since birth and reveals his generosity, responsibility, and warmheartedness. Seeing Darcy's portrait in the picture gallery, Elizabeth feels even more drawn to him. Darcy arrives home unexpectedly, is very courteous to Elizabeth and the Gardiners, invites Mr. Gardiner to go fishing in the lake, then brings his sister

and Bingley to visit them at their lodgings in the local inn. Elizabeth finds Georgina to be unassuming and pleasant, with no especial attachment to Bingley, who asks after Jane and her family.

They are invited to dinner at Pemberley, but before going Elizabeth receives two distressing letters from Jane. In the first, Jane reveals that Lydia and Wickham have eloped. The second letter reveals that they have not gone as expected, to Scotland, that Wickham has no intention of marrying Lydia, and that their present whereabouts are unknown. Darcy arrives and Elizabeth confides in him. Darcy listens in silence and offers some words of comfort and leaves. Elizabeth believes that she will not see him again and that "she could have loved him" (278).

The Gardiners and Elizabeth go to Longbourn to assist Mrs. Bennet and the family. Gardiner goes with Mr. Bennet to London to try to find Lydia and Wickham. Reports of Wickham's debts and profligacy flow in. Mr. Collins sends a pompous letter of condolence, advising Mr. Bennet to renounce Lydia and pointing out that his other daughters will find it very difficult now to find husbands. Mr. Bennet returns from London without success. A letter is received from Mr. Gardiner to say that Lydia and Wickham have been found and a marriage arranged. It is assumed that Mr. Gardiner has bribed Wickham. Mrs. Bennet is now unconcerned, delighted at having one daughter married. Elizabeth reflects on her own ruined marital opportunities.

After the wedding, an unrepentant Lydia and Wickham visit Longbourn. Lydia reveals that Darcy was present at the wedding. Elizabeth finds out from her aunt Gardiner that Darcy tracked the couple down, paid off Wickham's debts, and gave him a cash sum providing he marry Lydia. Mrs. Gardiner believes Darcy did it all for Elizabeth's sake. Mr. Bingley and Darcy soon after return to Netherfield and visit the Bennets. Elizabeth is ashamed by her mother's behavior to Darcy, but pleased by the renewal of the courtship of Bingley with Jane. Their engagement is announced and Mrs. Bennet is overjoyed at the prospect of having two daughters married.

Rumors circulate of an engagement between Darcy and Elizabeth. Lady Catherine de Bourgh arrives and confronts Elizabeth, insisting that she promise not to marry Darcy. Elizabeth refuses to give such an undertaking. Lady Catherine tells Darcy. This gives him fresh hope and he passionately, but without his previous pride, declares his love to Elizabeth. Elizabeth is no longer prejudiced against him, and accepts him. The news comes as a surprise to all the Bennets, and Mrs. Bennet rapidly changes her opinion of Darcy. Elizabeth and Darcy live at Pemberley and are especially close to the Gardiners, "the persons who, by bringing [Elizabeth] into Derbyshire, had been the means of uniting them" (388).

CRITICAL SYNOPSIS AND COMMENTARY

Chapter 1

The book opens at the home of the Bennet family, the fictional Longbourn House in the village of Longbourn Hertfordshire, now largely urban sprawl and a commuting corridor for north London and other parts of the capital city. In the late 18th century, it was rural, with country houses, estates, villages, and market towns. Mrs. Bennet, who has five daughters, hears that a nearby country estate has been "taken by a young man of large fortune from the north of England." The first chapter encapsulates Jane Austen's style, themes, and modes of characterization. The opening sentence of 23 words contains ambiguities of its own. Beginning with a generalization, an assumption pertaining to a "truth" apparently "universally acknowledged" by whom specifically we are not told: probably to Jane Austen's readers past, present, and future, from eclectic cultures and societies. The emphasis is on singularity, gender, male gender, marital state, and need. This need can be personal, imposed socially by others, by unstated social laws and mores, or a combination of both. Further, "possession" means ownership of property, land, and other commodities signifying wealth and station. These ingredients—an unmarried man who is financially and socially well connected—necessitate a wife. This need must be satisfied. The second paragraph indicates elements of a specific social situation by referring to "rightful property of some one or other of their daughters." This is an ironic reference to the

situation in which women found themselves after the passing into law of the Married Woman's Property Act of 1753. Under this law, all their property became that of their husband, upon whom they were financially dependent. On marriage they owned nothing. A wealthy, landowning, property-owning husband may well have been acquired for them. In effect, they subsequently owned nothing. They or their families did the catching in the contest for possession or acquisition of wealth; in reality following marriage, they owned nothing.

The second word of the first dialogue of the novel includes this application. The word "dear" may imply affection between Mr. Bennet and his wife. It also suggests something purchased at cost. We learn as the novel develops that Mr. Bennet has indeed paid dearly for his marriage: "his lady" conveys the sense of possession after marriage. Mr. Bennet owns Mrs. Bennet, financially. A lack of rapport between the two is indicated by Mr. Bennet's refusal to reply to his wife's information. When he does reply, the response is far from sympathetic and even on the caustic side. The "want," the need is on his wife's side not his; all he will do is listen. Acquiescence in hearing the information leads his wife into the longest sentence and speech of the novel so far. In it she imparts considerable useful information. As readers, we learn that according to a neighbor, Mrs. Long, the local large estate, Netherfield Park, the second specific mention of this property, has been rented: "taken by a young man of large fortune from the north of England."

So we are given his age, told the man is young, that he has wealth and geographically is not from the south or London, the capital city, but from the north, or, rather, north of Hertfordshire, where the Bennets live. Further, he inspected his new home on the first day of the week, a Monday. His mode of transport was "a chaise and four," that is, an enclosed four-wheeled carriage drawn by four horses. Ownership of such a vehicle indicated considerable wealth. We are also told that he agreed to tenancy terms immediately. Interestingly, the author does not tell us why Netherfield is vacant, and who the real owner is. The unnamed young man "is to take possession before Michaelmas," in other words, September 29, a quarter day, marking the beginning of a tenancy if payment is due in quarterly installments.

The paragraph is informative. A wealthy young man with servants has taken the tenancy of a local estate. Basic important information is conveyed briefly through clipped dialogue. First, a name must be assigned to the newcomer, and second, his marital status needs to be ascertained. Somewhat ironically and against expectation, it is Mr. Bennet who directly asks his wife the question, "Is he married or single?" To that we learn that the latter is the case. The reply reveals much: "Oh! single, my dear to be sure!" Again there are reverberations of the word "dear": expensive, costly, affectionate closeness of relationship, and "to be sure." This implies surety, guarantee, and positiveness like an insurance policy to be realized and collected. Three words that Mrs. Bennet frequently uses are "to be sure." They also occur in Richard Brimsley Sheridan's famous comedy *The School for Scandal* (1777) in the mouths of not one but several of the characters, especially when discussing others. So it is likely that Jane Austen is, in her use of the repetitive phraseology, drawing on a comic dramatic tradition known to some of her readers.

In the dialogue in this initial chapter and frequently throughout the novel, attributions such as "he said" or "she said" are omitted ([3]). In a letter to her sister, Cassandra, dated January 29, 1813, Jane Austen admits that "a 'said he' or a 'said she' would sometimes make the Dialogue more immediately clear—but I do not write for such dull Elves As have not a great deal of Ingenuity themselves" (*Letters*, 202). She expects her readers to display high intelligence and assumes that she is not writing for a stupid or dim-witted audience.

Not only does Mrs. Bennet tell her husband and readers that Mr. Bingley is young and single with a "large fortune" (4), she also has ascertained approximately how much that fortune may be. It is large indeed, among the largest of the admittedly not unwealthy diverse characters who parade through Jane Austen's novels. Edward Copeland, in his excellent "Money" assessment in *The Cambridge Companion to Jane Austen*, observes that "At two thousand pounds a year (the landed gentry income

of Mr. Bennet . . . domestic economy must still hold a tight rein, especially in *Pride and Prejudice* where there are five daughters in need of dowries." Further, "Incomes of four thousand pounds a year and above (Darcy's, Bingley's . . .) leave behind the cheese-paring cares of middle class income . . . to enter a realm of unlimited genteel comforts" (136–137). Given such facts, it is natural that Mr. Bingley should be ensnared, captured by one of the Bennet daughters! "What a fine thing for our girls!" Again we have the relationship between aesthetic value and commercial value. A dress or a painting may well be "a fine thing" in aesthetic terms. Its value is also material, financial, and economic.

Of course, Mr. Bennet is toying, verbally dueling, deliberately annoying his wife by feigning ignorance of her intentions. These are clear. She is "thinking of his marrying one of" their daughters. Mr. Bennet's response plays on an interesting, often-used 18th-century word associated with value and architectural planning—"design." Today the word is rarely used in the sense of "intention." The primary meaning in Mr. Bennet's response "Is that his design in settling here?" is associated with planning, especially of gardens, landscape, and buildings. It may well have religious associations in terms of "grand design" or "cosmic design." In this sense the metaphor has its genesis in the relationship between God as the designer, or architect of the universe, or its orderer in an ordered world that has a hierarchy based on class status. Mr. Bennet's question is not as curious as it may appear. Clearly, if Mr. Bingley is ensnared by one of the Bennet daughters, then the status of the family increases in terms of how they are perceived by their neighbors and the society around them, Also, of course, the life of the daughter is transformed immeasurably in terms of living conditions, economic wealth, and status. The children of any marriage are more or less guaranteed a much more secure and prosperous future than otherwise.

Interestingly, it is Mrs. Bennet who first introduces into the novel the modern concept of "love." The social acceptance of marriage for love is a product of 20th-century Western society. In other societies, "love," in terms of the strong bond of affection between woman and man, does not play a prominent or even a significant role. Marital alliances were often dynastic, formed by parents and families, with the children merely pawns or objects in economic and social alliances with no say in the future relationship in which they are the chief players or protagonists. Mrs. Bennet concedes that alliances cannot be forced. The onus, the decision lies with the male rather than with the female. She tells her husband, "it is very likely," more than possible, not probable—yet another example of which this book is full of Jane Austen's exceedingly careful choice of language and words—"that he *may* fall in love with one of them" (Jane Austen's emphasis).

For this to happen, contact and meetings must be formed. It is the function in this plan of Mr. Bennet to initiate this, as his wife tells him. He "must visit him as soon as he comes." Mr. Bennet's response teases his wife and also, somewhat sarcastically, flatters her. "You are as handsome as any of them, Mr. Bingley might like you the best of the party." The response exhibits a pandering to her vanity and conveys information. The reader learns why it is so important to find suitable husbands for the Bennet daughters.— There are five of them, and they are apparently "grown up" and of a marital age. In these circumstances, as Mrs. Bennet tells her husband, "When a woman has five grown up daughters she ought to give over thinking of her own beauty."

Mr. Bennet continues the verbal sparring, responding in a short, clipped sentence representative of many of his sentences, which often are one-liners, clipped in contrast with his wife's much more verbose observations. In his response to his wife, he tells her, "In such cases, a woman has not often much beauty to think of." It is no coincidence, hardly a surprise, that Mr. Bennet should professionally be an attorney, although in the novel we do not see him actually practice his profession. He seemingly has to be persuaded by an overanxious Mrs. Bennet to promise to visit, to introduce himself and subsequently his family, his eligible daughters, to the new neighbors. Mrs. Bennet plays to what she perceives to be his weakness: "Only think what an establishment it would be for one of them," in other words, what a splendid large home they would possess if one of the daughters managed

to marry Bingley. She also appeals to his sense of propriety. Others will visit Bingley, a neighborly knight of the realm, Sir William and Lady Lucas, will do so. Mr. Bennet is a commoner; Sir William Lucas his neighbor has a title. We subsequently learn that he also has an unmarried daughter. So there is competition for the newcomer, who has a choice of unmarried daughters in the area into which he has moved.

In spite of social differences and rivalries, Mr. Bennet continues to play with his wife's intentions to tease her, and lead her along. Rather than visiting, he will send his wife along with a letter of introduction in which he first gives his "hearty consent to his marrying which ever he chuses of the girls." Notice that it is Bingley who makes the decision concerning marriage. The girls seem to have no role in the process whatsoever. They are chosen rather than choosing. Second he shows a preference for one of his daughters: "I must throw in a good word for my little Lizzy." This is the first time the name, in this instance a nickname, of one of the daughters has been mentioned, and a parental preference expressed. Mrs. Bennet's response demonstrates different preferences. Lizzie she perceives as "not half so handsome as Jane, nor half so good humoured as Lydia." Mrs. Bennet uses a word "handsome," which subsequently is used of the male gender, or animals such as a horse rather than of a woman. The female is "beautiful" or "pretty," as opposed to handsome.

These parental preferences presented early in the narrative change little during the novel. Mr. Bennet's preference is for Lizzy, his wife's somewhat for Jane and decidedly for Lydia, who, we are to learn, is exceedingly foolish and threatens the reputation of the family. Mr Bennet finds that "Lizzie has something more of quickness than her sisters," in other words, she displays a quicker intelligence, although he has few illusions, unlike his wife, finding them "all silly and ignorant like other girls." Mr. Bennet's playful gender bias—his sexist remarks—are countered by his wife's; "how can you abuse your own children in such a way?" In this context, "abuse" means verbal disparagement in the verbal sparring between husband and wife, rather than anything more sinister and physical in a modern sense. Mrs. Bennet is aware that her husband is teasing her. "You delight in vexing me," she replies. "Vexing" has the implication of annoying. She adds, "You have no compassion on my poor nerves," providing Mr. Bennet the opening for which he verbally has been waiting. He tells his wife: "I have a high respect for your nerves. They are my old friends. I have heard you mention them with consideration these twenty years at least." This brilliant riposte conveys the information that they have been married for more than 20 years, and that the relationship between husband and wife is by no means a satisfactory one. Mrs. Bennet's repy is her shortest in the opening chapter: "Ah! You do not know what I suffer." The dialogue between them continues with Mr. Bennet teasing his wife twice that when there are other wealthy men in the area, he will visit them.

The chapter concludes not with short conversational dialogue but omniscient narration, with the author informing her readers of the characteristics of these two characters. Factually, we learn the Bennets have been married for 23 years and that they have little in common. His wife does not understand his character: "*Her* mind was less difficult to develope" (Jane Austen's emphasis). The word "develope" (2–5) is used in a sense rarely if ever used today, in the sense of "'to unfold or unfurl,' in this case suggesting that Mrs. Bennet's thought processes are not difficult to discern" (Stafford, 312) or understand. Significantly, the author appears to agree with her male character: "She was a woman of mean understanding, little information, and uncertain temper." These negatives represent inherited characteristics and not those imposed on her by gender and society. In addition, Jane Austen tells the reader, "When she was disconcerted she fancied herself nervous," the third reference to "nerves" pertaining to Mrs. Bennet in the first chapter. Yet nothing in the world of a Jane Austen novel is what it appears to be. Mrs. Bennet has a single preoccupation: "The business of her life was to get her daughters married; its solace was visiting and news" (5).

Chapter 2

The opening chapter of *Pride and Prejudice* tells the reader much about character, plot, and moti-

vation. The reader is told by the narrator at the opening of chapter 2 that "Mr. Bennet was among the earliest of those who waited on Mr. Bingley." The ironic nature of his treatment of Mrs. Bennet, evident from the close of the first chapter, is reinforced in the first paragraph of this second chapter. Mr. Bennet's intention to pay Mr. Bingley a visit is made evident, although he gave his wife opposite signals "to the last." Mr. Bennet even withholds disclosure of the visit until the following evening, and even then, the information is accidentally disclosed in information to Lizzie, his favorite daughter. The disclosure is then indirect and activated by a passing remark on headgear, as Mr. Bennet observes her "employed in trimming a hat" (6). Such behavior was fashionable during the period. In June 1799, Jane Austen wrote to her sister, Cassandra, "Eliza has a bunch of Strawberries, and I have seen Grapes, Cherries, Plumbs, Apricots." She also tells Cassandra somewhat amusingly, "I cannot help thinking that it is more natural to have flowers grow out of the head than fruit" (*Letters*, 42, 44).

Action by Elizabeth provides the main spring of the central dialogue of the second chapter, among father, wife, and daughter concerning behavior. In addition, the conversation conveys much information about what has taken place. Mr. Bennet's actions and attitudes, as well as those of his wife and daughters, reinforce what we know of the relationship between husband and wife. The father hopes that Mr. Bingley will approve of Elizabeth's fashion statement. His wife rises to her husband's bait, responding "resentfully" by challenging what she perceives to be her husband's assumption that they will be aware of Mr. Bingley's likes and dislikes. Her daughter Elizabeth tries to reassure her that they will meet Bingley "at the assemblies" and that a neighbor, Mrs. Long, will introduce them. Her reminder of the assemblies is a reference to the presence in English provincial towns and cities of rooms especially built or adapted for public balls or dances so that people could meet, the ostensible reason for introductions being dances. Mrs. Bennet is forever aware that there is competition among mothers of unmarried daughters to introduce them first to eligible, preferably wealthy, bachelors. Mrs. Bennet tells her husband that she does not "believe

Mrs. Long will do any such thing"—the reason being that "She has two nieces of her own." Further "she is a selfish, hypocritical woman." Mrs. Bennet then immediately contradicts herself, exhibiting just how prejudiced she is by adding, "I have no opinion of her." Mr. Bennet assents to this observation, turning it into something of the nature of a compliment to his wife. He is "glad to find that you do not depend on her serving you." Mrs. Bennet, unable to find a suitable reply, turns her frustration on her daughter Kitty by telling her to stop coughing and to "Have a little compassion on [her] nerves" as she "tears[s] them to pieces." Her nervous system has become a piece of discarded clothing ready to be recycled. Mrs. Bennet's remarks may well be perceived as a reflection of her own lack of self-esteem. She is perpetually a butt, an object of her husband's sarcasm and remarks aimed at lowering her value. So in a real sense, she has become a piece of discarded clothing.

Mr. Bennet is not able to resist a rejoinder to his wife, responding, "Kitty has no discretion in her coughs . . . she times them ill." To this the hapless Kitty replies that she does "not cough for her own amusement." Her coughing may well be a psychosomatic reaction to the incessant conflict she is forced to sit through between husband and wife fought out verbally. In this conflict, the father is the superior contestant and his wife the inferior, who takes out her frustration on the weaker object, her daughter Kitty. In the first edition of the novel, Kitty is named in the reply, "When is your next ball to be, Kitty?" The reply (whomever it is attributed to—Kitty or Lizzy) in subsequent editions becomes "To-morrow fortnight" and provokes a response from Mrs. Bennet, revealing that she has been gathering information relating to her neighbor Mrs. Long's activities and timetable. She "does not come back till the day before," consequently "it will be impossible for her to introduce" Mr. Bingley, "for she will not know him herself."

This provides Mr. Bennet with the opportunity further to annoy and frustrate his wife, an activity he appears to enjoy and use as an excuse for his own dissatisfaction with his marital situation. He replies with what must appear to his listeners to be the enigmatic "Then, my dear, you may have the advantage of your friend, and introduce Mr. Bingley to *her*"—the last word receiving emphasis typographically to indicate speech emphasis. As so often in a Jane Austen novel, one character has knowledge the others have not. In this instance, Mr. Bennet knows of his own visit to Bingley; the other members of his family do not. So this knowledge can be regarded as a situational irony. Mr. Bennet is aware of a situation, the others are not. There is in Mr. Bennet's specific reply to his wife, in the manner in which he addressed her, a further irony. He addresses his wife, not for the first time or for the last time, as "my dear." This, as has been indicated, draws attention to the nature of his perception of his relationship with his wife. On the one hand, they are close; on the other, the relationship is costly in economic and in psychological terms on a daily basis of interaction. Mrs. Bennet's reply indicates that she is well aware that her husband is playing games with her—"how can you be so teasing?" she asks him. In his reply, her husband provides his wife with an implicit compliment as he praises or honours "her circumspection." In other words, Mrs. Bennet's scepticism for, as she has correctly said to him, what he has requested is "Impossible" since she is "not acquainted with" Mr. Bingley.

Mr. Bennet then embarks on one of his longer dialogues in the chapter. Instead of one or two sentences, he is given four. The last sentence contains subordinate clauses and follows three sentences, which are each sequentially longer than the last. The four-word "I honour your circumspection" is followed by the seven-word "A fortnight's acquaintance is certainly very little"—emphasis placed on the final "little." There is then a 14-word epigrammatic "One cannot know what a man really is by the end of a fortnight." Underlying such a truism is the implicit critique of the system of values held by Mrs. Bennet that any eligible man is suitable for one of her daughters, provided he has money. For Mr. Bennet, there must also be knowledge of the man's character, or "what a man really is," and only time can reveal this. On the other hand, Mr. Bennet is a realist, aware of competition for wealthy, unmarried men among those who have daughters. He informs his wife and daughters, "But if *we* [this pronoun receiving typographical emphasis to indicate speech emphasis] do not venture [again, an example of Jane Austen's marvelous choice of vocabulary with its implication of an expedition and capital advantage. The action may well lead to marriage, which can result in financial advantage: a daughter will be well provided for, and there will be one fewer to feed, clothe, and maintain at home] someone else will; and after all Mrs. Long and her nieces must stand their chance. [Mr. Bennet is aware of competition, luck, and opportunity in the marital stakes]; and therefore, as she will think it an act of kindness if you decline the offer, I will take it on myself."

The response from the daughters is verbally one of silence. In terms of body language, they respond by staring "at their father." Mrs. Bennet, incredulous as ever, replies with the repeated, "Nonsense, nonsense!." This provokes her husband to convey information he has hitherto suppressed and to remind his family of the ground rules relating to etiquette. He has, as the father and head of the household, to pay a formal, official visit to Mr. Bingley and to introduce himself formally, before the rest of his family can do so. Before he imparts the information that he has visited Mr. Bingley, he addresses another daughter. In the way the reader's reaction to the daughter, in this instance, Mary, is manipulated. Her father regards her as "a young lady of deep reflection [who] read[s] great books and make[s] extracts." That is, she copies out passages from the books she reads. Mary's thoughtful, bookish nature is conveyed through her inability to reply to her father, immediately providing him with the opportunity to return to the subject of Mr. Bingley. His wife's frustrated explication that she is "sick of Mr. Bingley" provides the opening Mr. Bennet has been waiting for. Even when he at last reveals that he has actually visited Mr. Bingley, he tries to score points at the expense of his wife. He tells her that as he has "actually paid the visit, we cannot escape the acquaintance now." The response from the family and his wife is one of silence. Instead of dialogue between Mr. Bennet and Mrs. Bennet, the narrator takes over, telling the reader that "the astonishment of the ladies was just what he [Mr. Bennet] wished," that of Mrs.

Bennet "perhaps surpassing the rest" of the family. When the first tumult of joy was over, Mrs. Bennet "began to declare that it," the visit, "was what she had expected all the while." She begins by praising Mr. Bennet, the first compliment she has given him in the novel, yet turns the compliment to herself, saying that she was the negotiator and should gain the credit for his visit. She "knew [she] would persuade [him] at last." She was "sure" that her husband "loved [his] girls too well to neglect such an acquaintance." The word "love" here is used in the sense of caring for their future. She consequently praises her husband: "such a good joke, too, that you should have gone this morning, and never said a word about it till now."

The final four paragraphs of chapter 2, the first, third, and fourth, consist of one sentence each. In the first, Mr. Bennet leaves the room "fatigued with the raptures of his wife" and daughters. We are left to speculate on the consequences of what he has done. The two daughters who are not to occupy the subsequent central stage now come into prominence early in the novel. As he leaves, Mr. Bennet tells Kitty that she "may cough as much as [she] chuse[s]." The second and lengthier of these paragraphs of the concluding four of the second chapter is the longest. It consists of Mrs. Bennet's praise for her husband's actions and appreciation of the personal difficulty involved in taking the action that he took: for Mrs. Bennet "At [her and Mr. Bennet's] time of life, it is not so pleasant . . . to be making new acquaintance every day." However "for [their] sakes," their father and mother "would do anything." She then exhibits preference for one daughter over the other, by reassuring Lydia, who is her "love," that while she is "the youngest, [she] dare say[s] that Mr. Bingley will dance with [her] at the next ball." To which Lydia "stoutly" replies, "I am not afraid; for though I *am* the youngest, I'm the tallest," (Jane Austen's emphasis), which suggests early physical maturity and this physical sense is implied by the narrator's use of the adverb "stoutly" in Lydia's reply. Physicality is, however, not the subject of the concluding sentence and paragraph, for "the rest of the evening was spent in conjecturing how soon he would return Mr. Bennet's visit, and determining when they should ask him to dinner" (6–8). Interestingly, it is not Mr. Bennet who will invite Bingley to dinner but the invitation will be a collective one, with perhaps the implication that Mrs. Bennet will do the actual inviting.

So the opening two chapters set the scene, introduce the situation, and provide motivational explanation. To repeat, a family with daughters of a marriageable age has a necessity to consider the welfare of the daughters. Their future should be secured through finding them a suitable marriage. This can be greatly assisted if a wealthy, eligible, that is unmarried, man moves into the neighborhood.

Chapter 3

The opening of the third chapter contains the lengthiest paragraphs so far encountered in the novel. From it further information is conveyed concerning perceptions of the new neighbor, Mr. Bingley. In spite of various stratagems from Mrs. Bennet and her five daughters, they are unable to obtain "any satisfactory description of Mr. Bingley." This opening sentence of the third chapter is the first time the reader actually learns the number of daughters—five—in the Bennet family. The father's isolation from them and from his wife is reinforced: "he eluded the skill of them all." They are then "obliged to accept the second-hand intelligence of their neighbour Lady Lucas," who, the reader learns, has a husband, "Sir William." He tells his wife, the narrator reports, that Bingley is "quite young, wonderfully handsome, extremely agreeable." Also, "he meant to be at the next assembly with a large party." So the note of gregariousness is extended to the supposition that he is "fond of dancing," which "was a certain step towards falling in love." Consequently, expectations are aroused: "very lively hopes of Mr. Bingley's heart were entertained."

The paragraph concerned with the situation and speculation relating to the possibilities concerning the new neighbor, Mr. Bingley, has seven sentences. It is followed by a simple sentence-paragraph consisting largely of speech by Mrs. Bennet to her husband in which she reinforces—if reinforcement were necessary—her aspirations, not for herself but for her daughters. Again, there is irony in the fact that Mrs. Bennet's aspirations appear to be not for herself but for her daughters. Her wish is for them to be married to wealthy husbands. However, her desire can be perceived as selfish. With her daughters married to wealthy, well-connected husbands, there will be less competition for attention at home and fewer mouths to feed. Marriage will lead to greater social connections and relationships for Mrs. Bennet as mother-in-law and increase her social stature among the neighbors and in the surrounding society in which she lives. Viewed from this perspective, then Mrs. Bennet's wish to "see one of [her] daughters happily settled at Netherfield"—Bingley's family home—is far from altruistic. She adds, "and all the others equally well married. [She] shall have nothing to wish for." No doubt other wishes and desires will occur to her.

Jane Austen, as narrator, reports Bingley's approximately 10-minute visit to the Bennets to return Mr. Bennet's visit to him. There is no dialogue. Mr. Bingley "had entertained hopes of being admitted to a sight of the young ladies, of whose beauty he had heard much; but he saw only the father." On the other hand, "The ladies were somewhat more fortunate, for they had the advantage of ascertaining from an upper window, that he wore a blue coat and rode a black horse" (9). In other words, he wore the latest fashion in colors—blue. In William Combe's popular and socially indicative *The Town of Dr. Syntax or Search of the Picturesque*, published in 1812, there is a triplet: "One who was in full fashion drest / In coat of blue and corded vest / And seem'd superior to the rest" (canto xx). There is always in the world of Jane Austen's novels, indicative as they are, of the world generally, somebody "superior" to someone else. The emphasis here is on "seem'd": Appearance and reality are two different elements. This difference between the two, between appearance and reality, is an important undercurrent in the remainder of this third chapter and throughout the novel.

The chapter now focuses on the ball in the Assembly Rooms, where Mrs. Bennet and the other local mothers will meet their potential prey, the eligible Mr. Bingley, whom they hope to capture for one of their daughters. Even before the ball, rumors circulate "that Mr. Bingley was to bring twelve ladies and seven gentlemen with him to the assembly." In other words, there would be too many ladies and too much competition for the attention of too few eligible men. This rumor is unfounded, for "when the party entered the assembly room, it consisted of only five altogether; Mr. Bingley, his two sisters, the husband of the eldest, and another young man." The Bingley party's appearance is conveyed not through dialogue or the perceptions of one of the characters such as Mr. or Mrs. Bennet, for instance, but through the narrative. The narrator reports to readers a brief (fewer than one-sentence) description of the physical appearance and manners of Mr. Bingley and his sisters. The former "was good looking and gentlemanlike." In addition, "he had a pleasant countenance, and easy, unaffected manners." The reader is then told that "the sisters were fine women, with an air of decided fashion." The most extensive description in this paragraph is reserved for a character who has not yet entered the canvas of the novel but will play a central role within it—Bingley's friend Darcy. This description follows a very brief one of Bingley's brother-in-law Mr. Hurst, who "merely looked the gentleman;"—later in the novel, Mrs. Hurst, Bingley's older sister, will play a significant role in the plot development. Darcy attracts "the attention of the room by his fine, tall person, handsome features, noble mien." Darcy's physical appearance is not all that makes him the focal point of the attention. His appeal gains weight by the report "in general circulation within five minutes after his entrance" that he has "ten thousand a year"—he is an exceedingly wealthy man, possessing "a large estate in Derbyshire." This wealth is not founded, unlike Bingley's, on trade or merchandise, but on land in one of the most beautiful parts of the country. However, in this novel of contrasts, Darcy's vast wealth built on land cannot save him from disfavor for "his manners gave a disgust . . . for he was discovered to be proud, to be above his company, and above being pleased." "Disgust" in Jane Austen's time had a less negative connotation than today, implying distaste.

Darcy's behavior, his attitude, is contrasted with Mr. Bingley, who in today's language has the quali-ties of a sales representative. He is "amiable," in other words, "lively and unreserved, danced every dance, was angry that the ball closed so early, and talked of giving one himself at Netherfield" (10–11). Such qualities described as "amiable" are not always positive in the world of Jane Austen's novels. Frank Churchill in *Emma* "may be very 'amiable,' have very good manners, and be very agreeable; but he can have no English delicacy towards the feelings of other people" (149). The note of ambiguity implied by the use of "amiable" is not dwelled upon at this point in *Pride and Prejudice*. The emphasis here is on the negative perceptions of Darcy provoked by his behavior. Mrs. Bennet in particular takes an intense dislike of Darcy. This reaction is described as "the most violent against him," especially "by his having slighted one of her daughters." Repeatedly in a Jane Austen novel, an overheard conversation serves as a plot device. Elizabeth overhears a conversation between Bingley and his friend Darcy, whose first words in the novel are negatives: "I certainly shall not. You know how I detest it," that is, dancing. Darcy's reasons for this are given "unless I am particularly acquainted with my partner." These objections are about the social surroundings he is in and also to the specific company. Darcy, overheard by Elizabeth, says, "there is not another woman in the room, whom it would not be a punishment to me to stand up with." The assumption is that Darcy is referring to Jane Bennet. Bingley then draws Darcy's attention to Elizabeth, "sitting behind him." Although the reader has been given no precise physical description of Elizabeth, or for that matter of any of the sisters, according to Darcy, Elizabeth is "not handsome enough to tempt [him]." Darcy is "in no humour at present to give consequence to young ladies who are slighted by other men." As a consequence, Elizabeth, the reader is told, "remained with no very cordial feelings towards" Darcy. We as readers also learn that Elizabeth "had a lively, playful disposition, which delighted in any thing ridiculous."

The following paragraph contains a good deal of information conveyed in the past tense by the narrator. Much of it is seen through the eyes of Mrs. Bennet, whose impressions of the assembly room evening become the main focus of the narrative. Her eldest daughter, Jane, danced twice with Bingley and had been much admired by the party. "Elizabeth felt Jane's pleasure"—having a special affinity with her sister. Mary had been praised as "accomplished," the other sisters, "Catherine and Lydia," found partners to dance with. Their immaturity is emphasized: for finding "partners . . . was all that they had yet learnt to care for at a ball." Readers are also told that the Bennets are "the principal inhabitants" of the village of Longbourn, where they live. The narrative then moves in this paragraph from the general to the particular, from the macrocosm to the microcosm. Mr. Bennet awaits their return home. He is reading, for a book obliterates time for him. His expectations are that the ball and Bingley will disappoint his wife. His wife is gushing with enthusiasm, eager to relay the events of "a most excellent ball." She goes into detail about whom Bingley danced with and which dances in particular were danced. Such detail irritates Mr. Bennet, especially when his wife focuses on the lace on the dresses, and he continues to interrupt her, so much so that she "related with much bitterness of spirit and some exaggeration, the shocking rudeness of Mr. Darcy." The chapter ends with a short paragraph spoken by Mrs. Bennet in which she describes the "disagreeable, horrid man" Darcy. Her only regret is that her husband was absent and thus unable "to have given [Darcy] one of [his] set downs." In short, Mrs. Bennet "quite detest[s] the man" (12–13).

Before moving onto the fourth chapter, it is worth pausing to look more closely at the way Jane Austen uses prose in the third chapter. Norman Page indicates in his *The Language of Jane Austen* (1972) that chapter 3 contains "Jane Austen's mature narrative prose." Page adds,

> If we ignore one sentence of dialogue, the first four paragraphs of that chapter contain eighteen sentences, which range from five to ninety-one words in length, with an average of thirty words. A norm of moderate length, that is to say, is combined with a wide degree of variation. Since half the sentences contain between twenty and forty words, the norm is firmly enough established to give a stability to the prose which heightens by contrast the effect of the occasional wide depar-

tures from that norm. There are examples of both the simple sentence ('Mrs. Bennet was quite disconcerted.') and the double sentence ('In a few days Mr. Bingley returned Mr. Bennet's visit, and sat about ten minutes with him in his library.'). Most of the sentences are complex, however, and in the longer sentences a preference is shown for subordination over co-ordination. Even the longest sentence in the passage involves no loss of clarity, however, since the larger unit of ninety-one words is broken down into smaller units whose relation to each other is immediately apparent. This can be shown most clearly by taking some mild typographical liberties with the sentence in question:

> A.1. The gentleman pronounced him to be a fine figure of a man,

> A.2. the ladies declared he was much handsomer than Mr. Bingley, and

> A.3. he was looked at with great admiration for about half the evening,

> B. till his manners gave a disgust which turned the tide of his popularity;

> C.1. for he was discovered to be proud,

> > C.2. to be above his company,

> > C.3. and above being pleased;

> D.1. and not all his large estate in Derbyshire could then save him from having a most forbidding, disagreeable countenance,

> D.2. and being unworthy to be compared with his friend.

One sees very clearly here Jane Austen's fondness for three-part structures. A1.-3. record the initial reactions of the company assembled at Netherfield to Darcy, A.3. acting as a summary of the previous two clauses; all three are of approximately the same length. B. is only slightly longer but gains greater force from the two 'strong' nouns *disgust* and *popularity*, and acts as the pivot on which the sentence turns. C.1.-C.3. are parallel to A.1.-A.3., indicating the unanimous change of heart in response to Darcy's 'manners', and suggesting by their greater brevity an offended and dismissive attitude. The greater length of D.1.-D.2. gives an air of finality to this social judgment; it also has internal patterning in the ironic antithesis of 'large estate' and 'disagreeable countenance' (the implication being that the two are not, as a general rule, closely correlated), and D.2. looks forward to the next sentence, the subject of which is 'his friend.' (103–104: *Pride and Prejudice*, 9–10)

These opening three chapters are indicative of Jane Austen's style and technical devices in *Pride and Prejudice*. Dialogue is used to convey attitude and perceptions about other characters. The narrator sets up the dialogue, at times reports it, using the third-person narrative. Dialogue, in addition to commenting on the perceptions of one character concerning another, is also revealing about a character. For instance, Mrs. Bennet is garrulous; most concerned about the welfare of her daughters and herself; and has a complicated, not entirely satisfactory relationship with her husband. Dialogue also conveys information about others. Sometimes this is rumor, otherwise not. For instance, in the fourth chapter, Jane tells her sister Elizabeth that "Miss Bingley is to live with her brother and keep his house." Inner thoughts and reflections are presented through authorial reportage rather than dialogue. In the fourth chapter, Elizabeth's private reflections on the behavior of the Bingleys' suitors give way to narrative relation of information that is subsequently important in assessing motive and action. The Bingleys "were in the habit [of] spending more than they ought." In other words, they lived above their means. The exact amount of their income is provided in the narrative. In addition, they "had a fortune of twenty thousand pounds" (11–15). In other words, they probably had an annual income of approximately £1,000, or around U.S. $1,900. The Bingleys are relatively prosperous. "At this period, an agricultural labourer might earn around £45 per year, and a lawyer £450. After the death of her father in 1805, Austen lived with her mother and sister on an income of about £460" (Stafford, 314) or well under U.S. $1,000.

Austen conveys subtle class differences and distinctions in a variety of ways. Sometimes she uses dialogue. Sometimes she uses reportage. In chapter 4, Austen tells the readers that the Bingley fortune "had been acquired by trade." The foundation of their wealth is impressed on their memories. Families whose wealth was acquired from "trade" (15) were frequently perceived as lower in the social hierarchy than the older landed families. Unlike Darcy's inheritance, "Bingley's wealth is relatively new; and the family does not yet possess the estate that would secure its position within the ranks of the landed classes" (Stafford, 314).

Chapter 4

The fourth chapter conveys through the device of omniscient narration information about relationships outside the Bennet family. The reader is told about the Bingleys' family and fortunes. We also learn that Mr. Bingley is somewhat impetuous and prone to making quick decisions. For instance, "he was tempted by an accidental recommendation to look at Netherfield house. He did look at it and into it for half an hour, was pleased with the situation and the principal rooms, satisfied with what the owner said in its praise, and took it immediately." Jane Austen's repetitions of "it" are effective in conveying the sense of impetuosity: the house being transformed into a possession, an "it."

The next paragraph contrasts Bingley with Darcy and goes some way to explaining the nature of their friendship, "in spite of a great opposition of character." Antithesis is one of the important building blocks in Jane Austen's depiction of character and situation. "Bingley was endeared to Darcy by the easy, openness, ductility [an interesting choice of word, with its roots in chemistry, implying pliancy and flexibility]." The author adds that, "No disposition could offer a greater contrast to his own," Darcy's. This is in fact free indirect speech, the style *indirect libre* or *erleble Rede*. In other words, these could be Darcy's thoughts as well as Jane Austen's, the author. Bingley depends on Darcy for judgment and understanding. Jane Austen as omniscient narrator tells her readers that Bingley "was sure of being liked wherever he appeared, Darcy was continually giving offence." Darcy is, "haughty, reserved, and fastidious, and his manners, though well bred, were not inviting." Jane Austen in the two final paragraphs of chapter 4 conveys the reactions of Bingley and Darcy, Mrs. Hurst and her sister to the Meryton assembly. The attitudes of Bingley and Darcy are in antitheses: the former is positive; the latter, negative. Even Jane Bennet, whom Darcy "acknowledged to be pretty . . . smiled too much." Mrs. Hurst and her sister also "pronounced her to be a sweet girl." Consequently, the accommodating Bingley "felt authorised by such commendation to think of her as he chose," (16–17) the implication being that with someone so influenced by others' opinions, he could always have his mind changed.

Chapter 5

Chapter 5 is short and consists of an opening paragraph of four sentences of omniscient narration, a second and third paragraph of three short sentences and one sentence, and the dialogue with a concluding short sentence. The first paragraph conveys information about the Bennets' neighbor Sir William Lucas. He has formerly been in trade in Meryton, the local town, and has become the knighted owner of Lucas Lodge, "where he could think with pleasure of his own importance, and unshackled by business, occupy himself solely in being civil to all the world." Impressed by rank, unlike William Collins later in the novel, he is not "supercilious" and is "by nature inoffensive, friendly and obliging." His wife, the reader is told in the second paragraph, is "a very good kind of woman, not too clever to be a valuable neighbor to Mrs. Bennet." Her eldest daughter, Charlotte, "is a sensible, intelligent young woman, about twenty-seven" and "Elizabeth's intimate friend." The use of the adjective "sensible" (18) to describe her is interesting. Mr. Collins, whom she marries, "was not a sensible man" (70). In other words, he was not reasonable, judicious, and wise.

The remainder of the chapter consists of short dialogue. Austen's dialogue conveys much narrative information. Jane Austen's text uses single quotation marks to indicate direct speech between Charlotte Lucas, Mrs. Bennet, Jane Bennet, Elizabeth, Mary, and a "young Lucas," who speaks at the end of the chapter. Some of the dialogue turns on hearsay, who heard what and from whom about what someone may or may not have said—in this instance concerning whom Bingley considered the

most attractive woman in the room. Information is also conveyed through direct speech about others. For instance, Darcy's perceived nonresponse to the Bennets' neighbor Mrs. Long is attributed to the fact that she "does not keep a carriage, and had come to the ball in a hack chaise," indicating that she is of a lower social status than those who "keep a carriage." The last section of the dialogue consists of reflections on the meaning of "pride": Elizabeth Bennet can "forgive" Darcy's if he had not "mortified" hers. Again, there is a balance and antithesis at work in the fabric of Jane Austen's texture. In this instance, "pride" can be forgiven if it does not offend somebody else's personal "pride." However, there is, as the bookish Mary points out in a lengthy speech, a distinction between "vanity and pride." She says, "A person may be proud without being vain. Pride relates more to our opinion of ourselves, vanity to what we would have others think of us." The conversation takes on a different tone when Mary's pedantic distinction is swept aside with the assertion of one of the young Lucas boys, that if he had Darcy's wealth, "I should not care how proud I was. I would keep a pack of foxhounds, and drink a bottle of wine everyday." The chapter ends with the boy protesting that he would not drink too much, and Mrs. Bennet asserting that he would. His reference to foxhunting relates information about changes in country fashions, for in the later 18th century, foxhunting gradually replaced hare and stag hunting as the favourite pursuit of the well-off.

Jane Austen uses speech here, as in her work generally, to convey character difference. Mary is serious and pedantic, hence her sentiments on "pride." Mrs. Bennet is easily sidetracked into irrelevancy; consequently, she is more preoccupied with the young Lucas's potential overdrinking than with either Darcy or Bingley. Elizabeth is direct, yet capable of making fine distinctions. Charlotte Lucas shows her fondness for Elizabeth in expressing the wish that Darcy had danced with her. Jane exhibits a trusting nature in accepting at face value what Bingley's sister tells her (18–20).

Chapter 6

The sixth chapter contains a mixture of narration with dialogue and hurries the action. The focus is on Darcy's reaction to Elizabeth, placed within a specific social context—a party at Sir William Lucas's. Before the party, the Longbourn ladies pay a courtesy return visit to Netherfield. Elizabeth and her friend Charlotte discuss Jane and Bingley, and Darcy's thoughts are expressed through free indirect speech. The opening paragraph conveys different perceptions of Mrs. Hurst and Miss Bingley. Jane sees their attention as a positive. Elizabeth, on the other hand, "saw superciliousness in their treatment of every body." The fourth compound sentence of this paragraph interweaves free indirect speech with authorial direct narration, the separation between the two being the second semicolon dividing the two parts of the sentence. In the first part the reader enters into Elizabeth's thoughts concerning Jane: "It was generally evident that whenever they met, that he *did* admire her; and to *her* it was equally evident that Jane was yielding to the preference which she had begun to entertain for him from the first, and was in a way to be very much in love" (Jane Austen's emphasis). Then the author speaks more directly in her own voice, telling the reader "but she [Elizabeth] considered with pleasure that it was not likely to be discovered by the world in general," the reason being "since Jane united with great strength of feeling, a composure of temper and a uniform of cheerfulness of manner, which would guard her [Jane] from the suspicions of the impertinent."

A similar narrative technique is at work elsewhere in the chapter when the narrator tells us about Darcy's reactions to Elizabeth and then enters into his framework of thinking. On the one hand, Darcy "made it clear to himself and his friends that she [Elizabeth] had hardly a good feature in her face." Simultaneously, "he began to find it [her face] rendered uncommonly intelligent by the beautiful expression of her dark eyes." The word "clear" here in terms of clarifying and illuminating has a reverberating positive meaning in the sentiments that follow, as Darcy against his better judgment discovers other qualities. "To this discovery succeeded some others equally mortifying." They are presented as antitheses. On the one hand, there is "more than one failure of perfect symmetry in her form"; on the other, "he was forced to

acknowledge her figure to be light and pleasing." Again, although Elizabeth's "manners were not those of the fashionable world," on the other hand Darcy "was caught by their easy playfulness." Jane Austen, stylistically in this paragraph, at her very best, moves the focus, the perspective, from Darcy to Elizabeth. Her prejudiced viewpoint concludes this paragraph of shifting stylistic devices: "to her [Elizabeth] he was only the man who made himself agreeable no where, and who had not thought her handsome enough to dance with." The remainder of the chapter continues the focus on Darcy's reactions to Elizabeth. The setting is Sir William Lucas's. The techniques used are dialogue between Sir William and Darcy, reactions to Elizabeth's piano playing, and the performance of her sister Mary, Elizabeth's refusal to dance with Darcy, and dialogue between Elizabeth and Sir William and Mrs. Bingley. The chapter ends with a prophetic dialogue between Miss Bingley and Darcy, Miss Bingley telling Darcy that he "will have a charming mother-in-law indeed, and of course she will be always at Pemberley with" him (21–27).

Austen uses this chapter to make contemporary allusions. The Bingley ladies, for instance, prefer to play "Vingt-un" to "Commerce." They prefer one fashionable card game involving bartering and betting rather than another. Vingt-un is often called blackjack in America. Commerce, a somewhat more complicated game, is a form of poker. In it, the players buy individual cards from the dealer and barter for them with the other players. Shorter "Scotch and Irish airs," songs and dances played on the keyboard, are preferred by the younger generation to what appears to be "a long concerto." Darcy's reply to Sir William's comment that he considers dancing "as one of the first refinements of polished societies" is that dancing "has the advantage of also being in vogue amongst the less polished societies of the world—Every savage can dance" (23–25). This allusion echoes a passage from the *Lectures in Rhetoric and Belles Lettres*, 2 volumes (London 1783), written by Hugh Blair (1718–1800), the 18th-century Scottish political philosopher and literary critic. In his Lecture 38, "On the Origin and Progress of Poetry," Blair observes that in the "savage state . . . from the very beginning of society, there were occasions on which they met together for feasts, sacrifices and Public Assemblies, and on all such occasions, it is well known, that music, song, and dance, made their principal entertainment" (ii, 314).

Chapter 7

Underlying the world of polite manners and superficial appearances at Sir William Lucas's, games played for the highest stakes are being enacted. The winner will gain the highest hand in the marital stakes. This serious search for a suitable partner to continue the ancestral line, the economic basis of society, is reinforced at the opening of chapter 7. The narrator reveals the real state of affairs at the Bennet household and why Mrs. Bennet's quest to find suitable husbands for her daughters is not just a reflection of a scatterbrained, garrulous, unhappily married mother. The Bennet inheritance is restricted. The entailment stipulates that if Mr. Bennet has no son to continue the line, his property will pass to a male in another branch of the family: Longbourn will go to Mr. Bennet's cousin, the unmarried clergyman William Collins. Hence the utmost necessity for his five daughters to marry well. Mr. Bennet's income, "an estate of two thousand a year," would generate in modern currency about U.S. $66,000 in 1988. So with five potential dowries to fund, he was on a very tight rein. Mrs. Bennet's father, a lawyer, had left her "four thousand pounds," which is not enough to make a substantial difference materially in their way of life, or in their daughters' dowries. It would, of course, determine the quality of Mrs. Bennet's life once she became a widow. Mr. Bennet, although apparently by profession a lawyer, has inherited land and a far from wealthy income. Mrs. Bennet, on the other hand, is from the professional middle class of lawyers and businessmen. Her sister is married "to a Mr. Phillips, who had been a clerk to their father, . . . succeeded him in the business, and a brother settled in London in a respectable line of trade." Jane Austen precisely conveys the economic means and needs of her characters. Mrs. Phillips, for instance, is as anxious as her sister to marry the daughters off, and is only too ready to indulge the youngest Bennet girls, Catharine and Lydia, in their wish to meet members of the militia residing in the neighborhood.

The third paragraph of the seventh chapter moves skillfully from geographical location of residence, to shops in the local town, to hints of the wider world and potential conflicts. This is achieved through three references: to the precise distance of the village of Longbourn from the neighboring town; to a shop; and to the militia. Longbourn is "only one mile from Meryton," walking distance in fine weather; poor weather conditions affecting travel will shortly have an impact on the plot. The two youngest daughters were "tempted thither three times a week, to pay their duty to their aunt," whom the reader is told is as garrulous as their mother, and also to visit "a milliner's shop just over the way." These shops selling an assortment of fabrics, fancy materials, clothing, and various accessories and especially fashionable hats, were centers of gossip. Catharine and Lydia learned from their aunt Phillips of the "recent arrival of a militia regiment in the neighborhood; it was to remain the whole winter, and Meryton was the headquarters."

In common with many young women of their generation depicted in opera, drama, and literature of the early 19th century, their heads were turned by the militia. "They could talk of nothing but officers; and Mr. Bingley's large fortune, the mention of which gave animation to their mother, was worthless in their eyes when opposed to the regimentals of an ensign." The militia, a military force, consisted of volunteers. Its main object during the Napoleonic Wars was to be ready in the first line of defense in case of a French invasion. This fear was a real concern during the last decade of the 18th century and the first two of the new century. The reference is a timely reminder that for most of Jane Austen's life, England was at war with France. The south of the country was especially vulnerable to invasion, being the closest part of the country to France. Jane Austen's brother Henry was a member of the Oxford militia in 1793, and when war erupted with France, he served for seven years as an officer. The reference to "an ensign" is a typical piece of Jane Austen irony as the "ensign" is contrasted with "Bingley's large fortune." An ensign was the officer of the lowest rank in the army with insufficient fortune or connections to buy his way into a higher rank. Someone with Bingley's amount of money would have been able to purchase a far superior army ranking.

An important narrative device in a Jane Austen novel is the use of a letter as a means of communication. The first two letters of many in *Pride and Prejudice* occur in the seventh chapter. As has been noted, the novel originally was probably an epistolary novel in an earlier version. There are 44 letters in the novel, far more than in *Northanger Abbey* (nine instances), or *Sense and Sensibility* (21 instances). In *Pride and Prejudice*, they supply narrative information and detail, are a method of characterization, and provide an insight into the motives of the letter writer. They also give their writers and recipients the chance to reveal themselves and their motives. The first letter is from Caroline Bingley to Jane Bennet, asking Jane to dine with her and her older sister Louisa (Mrs. Hurst). The French "tête-à-tête" in the invitation reveals the writer's social pretensions; it also has the meaning of an intimate conversation. The invitation becomes an important springboard for plot development. Mrs. Bennet ingeniously ensures that the only coach the family possesses is not available, as Mr. Bennet requires it to work on the farm. Jane is thereby forced "to go on horseback," and because it rains, she has to stay overnight at Netherfield, the Bingley residence. The news that she has to spend more time away from home is conveyed in the second letter in the novel, again, a short, single-paragraph letter. This is from Jane to Elizabeth. The letter contains essential information. She got "wet through" and her "kind friends will not hear of [her] returning home till [she is] better," and the apothecary, Mr. Jones, is being called to see her. Apothecaries in rural areas were regarded by many as the equivalent of doctors; they both prescribed and dispersed "draughts," or medicines.

As a consequence, Elizabeth insists on visiting her sister and is forced to walk alone across the muddy fields three miles from Longbourn to Netherfield. "She was shewn into the breakfast-parlour." Through such a detail Jane Austen is able to convey the size of the Netherfield establishment as breakfast is held in a special room only used for that purpose. Elizabeth's act of walking three miles in difficult circumstances causes interesting reactions. "Elizabeth was convinced that" Mrs. Hurst and Miss Bingley "held her in contempt [as] her appearance created a great deal of surprise" as inappropriate behavior for a lady and exhibiting the Bennets' lower social status. Darcy's reactions are more complex, "divided between admiration of the brilliancy which exercise had given to her complexion, and doubt as to the occasion's justifying her coming so far alone." Elizabeth is also invited to stay at Netherfield to be with her sister. So the narrative focus in seven chapters has moved from Longbourn, to Assembly Rooms, to the home of the intended prey—Bingley (28–34).

Chapter 8

Chapter 8 is one of the longest so far, consisting of paragraphs of omniscient narration and then dialogue. The initial paragraph reveals details of social status and habits. The Bingleys dine "at half past six," a relatively late time but one kept in fashionable parts of London. Mr. Hurst, the narrator tells her readers, "was an indolent man, who lived only to eat, drink and play cards, who when he found her prefer a plain dish to a ragout, had nothing to say to" Elizabeth (35). Ragout was "a spicy meat and vegetable dish, imported from France in the late "17th century," since when it had become something of a byword for foreign influence and affectation. . . . Mr. Hurst's preference for a ragout is indicative of his interest in money and general ostentation" (Stafford, 317).

Another allusion in this chapter indicating character as well as social habits is that of a card game. In the evening, "on entering the drawing-room [Elizabeth] found the whole party [the Bingleys and Darcy] at loo, and was immediately invited to join them; but suspecting them to be playing high she declined it." Loo, a card game in which various players could participate, offered an opportunity to place bets. It was fashionable for women to play such a game, and cards might well serve as a replacement for conversation or reading. Elizabeth's negative attitude to the game, her resistance too, displays her candor, her intelligence, and her integrity.

Elizabeth's reluctance to play leads Caroline Bingley into conversation with Darcy concerning the depth, range, and extent of the library at his country estate at Pemberly. The ensuing conversation between Caroline Bingley, the younger sister of Bingley, who has designs on Darcy, Darcy, and Elizabeth, works on several levels, as do most of the dialogues in Jane Austen's novels. On one level, there is the surface meaning of what is said. In this instance, the "accomplishments" of young ladies are outlined. These extend from Bingley's "they all paint tables, cover skreens, and net purses." These accomplishments reflect considerable free time, and wealth—the servants performing many of the household duties. Darcy objects to the generalization that this applies to all women, as he "cannot boast of knowing more than half a dozen, in the whole range of [his] acquaintance." Miss Bingley and Darcy produce another list of accomplishments: "A woman must have a thorough knowledge of music, singing, drawing, dancing, and the modern languages, to deserve the word." Further, "she must possess a certain something in her air and manner of walking, the tone of her voice, her address and expressions, or the word will be but half deserved." The listing is as unrealistic as Bingley's was generalized. The words "greatly," "thorough," "certain something," and "half" reinforce the idealistic nature of such demands. Further physical accomplishments such as the ability to walk in a certain manner are juxtaposed with intellectual ones, such as a knowledge of music and modern languages. Darcy wants "something more substantial, in the improvement of her [a woman's] mind by extensive reading," revealing very high standards, and that he is exceedingly difficult to please.

Other layers of meaning underlie the apparently witty surface of the dialogue. Darcy's desire for "something more substantial" could be viewed as a reflection of his views concerning the perception of the superficiality of women's education. He rebukes Caroline Bingley for using "all the arts which ladies sometimes condescend to employ for captivation." This "cunning" he finds "despicable"—a strong word of condemnation in the vocabulary of Jane Austen's novels. On the other hand, he is searching "for something more substantial." So character

Caroline Bingley and Mrs. Hurst, in reaction to news that Jane Bennet has worsened, solace "their wretchedness by duets after supper." Illustration by C. E. Brock, from *Pride and Prejudice,* London: Dent Edition, 1907

competition, rivalry between characters, and as yet unrealized wishes are revealed through dialogue. Elizabeth by implication has provoked Darcy's interest. She has implicitly challenged him in her riposte to him, "you must comprehend a great deal in your idea of an accomplished woman." This has resulted in his expansion of the qualities he is looking for. Of course, underlying such a dialogue is a narrowly subscribed rigid structure of courtship and the marriage, capturing the right husband, the right prey, is the only way in which Jane Austen's heroines can land a secure existence. It is rare that disparities of class, income, and social status are bridged, in for instance a meeting of intellects.

Chapter 8 concludes on a note of fine social distinction. Initially, when Jane was taken ill, an apothecary was summoned. By the end of the chapter, the Bingleys are "convinced that no country advice could be of any service, recommended an express to town for one of the most eminent physicians" (37, 39–40). They do not regard a country apothecary as sufficiently competent to deal well with serious medical problems. This mirrors contemporary doubts concerning the status of apothecaries. In 1821, apothecaries formed an association to improve their station and education. Intense disputes in the medical world over status, competency, rights, and privileges in the provincial England of the 1829–31 prereform years are to find brilliant fictional depiction. George Eliot in *Middlemarch: A Study of Provincial Life* (1871–72), especially in the character of Lydgate, exposes a world of chicanery and deceit, his idealism crushed by the harsh realities of social existence.

Chapter 9

Jane Austen's narrative is hurried along in chapter 9. Mrs. Bennet, Lydia, and Kitty expose themselves as silly during a visit to Netherfield. Lydia reminds Bingley of his promise to give a ball. They demonstrate to Darcy the inferior social status to which Elizabeth Bennet belongs. The chapter contains some interesting observations. Darcy remarks that "In a country neighborhood you move in a very confined and unvarying society," to which there is the riposte, "But people themselves alter so much, that there is something new to be observed in them for ever" (42–43). These sentiments resemble Jane Austen's inevitable choice of the country for the canvas of her fiction. She writes on September 9, 1814, to her niece Anna, who is planning a novel, "You are now collecting your People delightfully, getting them exactly into such a spot as is the delight of my life;—3 or 4 families in a Country Village is the very thing to work on" (*Letters*, 275).

Chapter 10

Letter writing forms the subject of chapter 10. At the start of the chapter, Darcy's attempts to write a letter to his sister are continually thwarted by Caroline Bingley's overattentiveness. She constantly flatters Darcy to gain favor with him, complimenting him "on his hand-writing, on the evenness of his lines, or on the length of his letter." This results

in a four-way conversation among Darcy, Caroline, her brother Charles, and Elizabeth. In the dialogue, Elizabeth's sarcasm at Bingley's expense produces a response from Darcy on the theme of pride and humility that pervades the book. Elizabeth tells Bingley that his "humility . . . must disarm reproof." Darcy replies, "Nothing is more deceitful . . . than the appearance of humility. It is often only carelessness of opinion, and sometimes an indirect boast." The result is a lengthy dialogue consisting largely of a verbal sparring match between Darcy and Elizabeth with occasional interruptions from Bingley on intentions, "friendship and affection." At the conclusion, Elizabeth appears to have got the better of Darcy. She tells him that he "had much better fin-

"'No; stay where you are. You are charmingly grouped,'" from C. E. Brock, illustration to *Pride and Prejudice* (London: Macmillan edition, 1895)

ish his letter," and "Mr. Darcy took her advice and did finish his letter." Elizabeth becomes the object of Darcy's gaze, while Mrs. Hurst and her sister sang. Darcy then asks her to dance and Elizabeth gives an elaborate negative, her response relating to assumptions she has made concerning his intentions: "You wanted me, I know, to say 'Yes,' that you might have the pleasure of despising my taste." Elizabeth takes delight in "cheating a person of" [what she assumes to be] "their premeditated contempt."

Elizabeth's expectations are again proved to be formed incorrectly. She was "amazed at [Darcy's] gallantry." The narrator tells her readers "there was a mixture of sweetness and archness, in her manner which made it difficult for her to affront anybody." The use of "archness" is ambiguous, implying adroit cleverness. Consequently, "Darcy had never been so bewitched by a woman as he was by her. He really believed, that were it not for the inferiority of her connections, he should be in some danger." The awareness of Darcy's attraction to Elizabeth results in Caroline Bingley's jealousy. She will try to get "rid of Elizabeth" as quickly as possible. Caroline reminds Darcy of Elizabeth's mother and silly sisters "to provoke" [him] into disliking her. At the end of the chapter, Elizabeth exhibits her knowledge of appropriate taste. She deflects Darcy's attempt to apologize for the rudeness of Mrs. Hurst and Caroline Bingley with the observation, "You are charmingly group'd and appear to uncommon advantage. The picturesque would be spoilt by admitting a fourth" (67–53). The youthful Jane Austen was very fond of writers on the picturesque such as William Gilpin (1724–1804). For Gilpin, groups of three (a group of three cows is one of the examples given by Gilpin) are attractive because of their irregularity.

Chapter 11

In chapter 11, the verbal dueling between Darcy and Elizabeth continues assisted by Caroline Bingley. Her brother is preoccupied with talking to Jane, who has recovered sufficiently to leave her room and spend some time downstairs. In describing the scene, Jane Austen draws upon her favorite poet, William Cowper. "Mr. Hurst had . . . nothing to

do, but to stretch himself on one of the sofas and go to sleep" (54). Cowper at the opening of his poem *The Task* (1785) described the sofa "as a symbol of luxury and indolence" in his lines "Thus first necessity invented stools. / Convenience next suggested elbow chairs, / And luxury th'accomplished Sofa last" (i, 86–88). Against this background, Darcy and Elizabeth enact a contest of wills on "vanity and pride." Their conversation elicits some of their most memorable lines in the book. Elizabeth tells Darcy, "I hope I never ridicule what is wise or good. Follies and nonsense, whims and inconsistencies *do* divert me, I own, and I laugh at them whenever I can." (Jane Austen's emphasis) This results in a defense from Darcy of pride, which "where there is a real superiority of mind . . . will be always under good regulation." It also evokes a listing of his faults ranging from his "temper," which "is I believe too little yielding." He finds that he "cannot forget the follies and vices of others so soon as I ought, nor their offences against myself." These are sentiments that will soon be tested when Wickham appears on the scene. At this point, as Darcy tells Elizabeth, she "is willfully to misunderstand" everybody and especially him. By the end of the chapter, there has been a subtle change in Darcy's attitude to Elizabeth: "He began to feel the danger of paying Elizabeth too much attention" (54–58).

Chapter 12

A shorter chapter consisting of seven brief paragraphs of omniscient narration follows chapter 11, where dialogue dominates. The focus is on Jane and Elizabeth's departure from Netherfield and return to Longbourn. Mrs. Bennet does her best to forestall this without success. There is also attention to the impact of the stay, particularly on Darcy. In a passage of *erleble Rede* (free indirect speech), the reader learns that Elizabeth "attracted him more than he liked—and Miss Bingley was uncivil to *her,* and more teasing than usual to himself." Consequently, Darcy adopts a policy of disguise and deception: "he wisely resolved to be particularly careful that no sign of admiration should *now* escape him" (Jane Austen's emphasis). The chapter concludes with Elizabeth and Jane's return home. In the final paragraph, there is a pun. The sisters found their sister "Mary, as usual, deep in the study of thorough bass": the study of musical harmonies and also the study of human sin, or baseness. In the last sentence, (59–60), folly and frivolity gain the upper hand, with rumor circulating concerning goings on in the militia. Within two chapters, serious dialogue underlying a contest of wills between Darcy and Elizabeth has been replaced by trivia.

Chapter 13

A new character enters into the narrative in the next chapter through the device of an elaborate and character-revealing letter. He is introduced by a conversation between members of the Bennet family on the subject of Mr. Collins "who, when I [Mr. Bennet] am dead, may turn you all out of his house as soon as he pleases" (61). The reader is also told that there has been a long-standing family quarrel on the matter of inheriting Longbourn. Mr. Bennet reads his distant relative's letter, which is wordy, elaborate, pompous, pedantic, and replete with cliché. The letter consists of one paragraph of five lengthy sentences with elaborate subclauses: "the average sentence-length in this letter is 71.4 words" (Page, 186). It contains formulaic expressions such as "trespass on your hospitality," well-worn metaphors ("heal the breach," "the offered olive branch") superficial hollow phrases ("bounty and beneficence," "promote and establish"). The letter also reveals Collins's superciliousness and deference to his patron, "the Right Honourable Lady Catherine de Bourgh." Mr. Bennet seems to take Collins's sentiments in the letter at their face value, as the reflection of "a most conscientious and polite young man." Elizabeth, on the other hand, is more penetrating, aware of "his extraordinary deference for Lady Catherine." She thinks that "he must be an oddity," and finds his style to be "very pompous." She has doubts about his being "a sensible man" (62–64).

Chapter 14

The remainder of chapter 13 and all of chapter 14 are preoccupied with the Reverend Collins's visit to Longbourn. The ostensible reason for the visit is an attempt at a rapprochement between him and the Bennet family regarding the entail issue. The real reason has to do with the advice of his patroness, Lady Catherine de Bourgh of Rosings in Kent. "She had even condescended to advise him to marry as soon as he could, provided he chose with discretion." So his visit to Longbourn has another motive. He had received complimentary reports concerning the Bennet girls and wishes to marry one of them to please his patroness. Mr. Bennet concludes that "his cousin was as absurd as he had hoped" (66, 68), stupid, lacking tact, and full of his own self-importance.

Chapter 15

Jane Austen concurs with her character's judgment. She opens chapter 15 with the sentence, "Mr. Collins was not a sensible man, and the deficiency of nature had been little assisted by education or society" (70): he lacked common sense, reasonableness, and wisdom. Mrs. Bennet, true to form, can only think of the prospects Collins offers as an eligible match for one of her daughters. Believing Jane to be spoken for, to Bingley, she thinks that Elizabeth will make an appropriate match for Collins.

There are several interesting allusions in these chapters. Collins in his letter in chapter 13 tells Mr. Bennet that Lady Catherine de Bourgh "has preferred me to the valuable rectory" (63). Subsequently, the narrator reveals that "A fortunate chance had recommended [Collins] to Lady Catherine de Bourgh when the living of Hunsford was vacant" (70). Lady Catherine has allowed Collins to live in a parish and the house that went with it, which she controls. Collins, as a clergyman, would benefit from the house, allied income, and property gained from the parishioners of, for instance, other land belonging to the church. He and any family he may have can live comfortably and in style provided he is appropriately deferential to the controlling authority—in this instance, Lady Catherine de Bourgh. Collins is, of course, too deferential. In chapter 14 at Longbourn, Collins reads extracts from "Fordyce's Sermons" (68) to Lydia. This is singularly ironic. James Fordyce's *Sermons to Young Women* (1766) had attacked modern fiction for the harmful effects it had on the imagination of the young. As will be revealed, Lydia in particular is especially foolish and headstrong. In Mr. Bennet's library, Collins is attracted to "one of the largest folios in the collection." In other words, Collins is attracted to appearances, a folio being the largest of book sizes, rather than to content and quality. Lady Catherine attracts him as she has great wealth, status, and influence.

During Collins's Longbourn visit, other new characters are introduced into the story. Mr. Bennet retreats into his library; it is a place of escape, peace, and quiet. "In his library [Mr. Bennet] had been always sure of leisure and tranquillity; and though prepared, as he told Elizabeth, to meet with folly and conceit in every other room in the house, he was used to be free from them there." Narratively, the retreat to the library is used as a device to get Collins away from the house at Longbourn and allow him to join the Bennet girls on a walk to Meryton. In Meryton, they encounter Mr. Denny, the militia officer about whom rumors had been circulating. Denny is accompanied by a "young man [who] wanted only regimentals to make him completely charming. His appearance was greatly in his favour." The narrator adds, "he had all the best part of beauty, a fine countenance, a good figure and very pleasing address." These tributes are all to external qualities. Nothing is said about his internal behavior, his character. Denny introduces Wickham to the Bennet party, and as he is doing so, a coincidence occurs (Jane Austen sometimes uses coincidence as a plot device). The significance of such a device is often not immediately apparent and is frequently revealed on revisiting the novel or subsequently (as in this instance) as the plot unfolds. As Wickham is being introduced, Bingley and Darcy are seen on horseback. Immediately they come to greet Jane and Elizabeth. The latter, "happening to see the countenance of both" Darcy and Wickham "as they looked at each other, was all astonishment at the effect of the meeting. Both changed colour, one looked white, the other red." The effect of the chance encounter on each other and the discomfort it induced in both is appropriately viewed through Elizabeth's eyes. Her misperception of Darcy's actions and prejudice in Wickham's favor is to have serious plot consequences. Jane Austen uses free indirect speech to convey the impact on Elizabeth: "Mr. Wickham,

after a few moments, touched his hat—a salutation which Mr. Darcy just deigned to return. What could be the meaning of it?—It was impossible to imagine; it was impossible not to long to know" (71–73).

The answer to this question will be satisfactorily resolved only after much misunderstanding at the resolution of the novel. Through the use of a chance meeting, and the observance of it by one of the characters, who will be most affected by the history underlying the meeting, Jane Austen uses small fine detail that has the utmost significance. However, the narrative focuses directly not on this brief encounter; in fact, Darcy and Bingley ride on quietly. It moves to Mrs. Philips's reaction to her nieces and reception of Mr. Collins. By the end of the chapter, Mrs. Philips has invited the Bennets to dinner the next evening. Pressured by Lydia and Kitty, she also agrees to invite the new officer, Wickham, too.

Chapter 16

Their encounter with Wickham at the Philips's Meryton home is the subject of chapter 16. While the others play whist, Wickham and Elizabeth are able to talk and she asks him about Darcy. Wickham tells her that Darcy's father "was one of the best men that ever breathed, and the truest friend that [Wickham] ever had." Elizabeth finds it "quite shocking" when informed by Wickham that his career has been destroyed by Darcy, who ignored the wishes of his late father and denied Wickham "the best living in his gift." Elizabeth asks, "What can have induced [Darcy] to behave so cruelly?" According to Wickham, Darcy was jealous of him owing to "his father's uncommon attachment to" him, and his "pride." Wickham explains that he grew up with Darcy, they "were born in the same parish, within the same park, the greatest part of [their] youth was passed together." His father was the "most intimate, confidential friend" of Darcy's father. Wickham tells Elizabeth that "almost all [Darcy's] actions may be traced to pride;—and pride has often been his best friend." In the previous speech, somewhat ironically in the perspective of subsequent plot unraveling, Elizabeth refers to Darcy's actions as "abominable" and "dishonest":

She has accepted what Wickham has told her at face value and without verification.

Wickham refers to Darcy's brotherly concern and kindness. Darcy "has also *brotherly* pride, which with *some* brotherly affection, makes him a very kind and careful guardian of his sister" (Jane Austen's emphasis). Again Jane Austen places a hint in the narrative, a cue that subsequently is to grow in her story. Wickham tells Elizabeth that Darcy's "sister is nothing to [him] now," the implication being that there was a relationship. In response to Elizabeth's inquiry concerning the relationship between Bingley and Darcy, Wickham claims not to know Bingley, adding, "He is a sweet tempered, amiable, charming man. He cannot know what Mr. Darcy is." This can be read at several levels: as an untruth in that Bingley has recognized Darcy's strengths, Bingley has more to learn about Darcy's strength of character, or a true account of the state of affairs between them. Wickham, when hearing the name of Lady Catherine de Bourgh from Collins, informs Elizabeth that she is Darcy's aunt and wishes to combine her property with him. "Her daughter, Miss de Bourgh, will have a very large fortune, and it is believed that she and her cousin will unite the two estates" (78, 80–83). Elizabeth is impressed by Wickham; what he has told her reinforces her prejudices, her own sense of Darcy's character.

Chapter 17

In chapter 17, the omniscient narrator tells her readers that "Elizabeth felt herself completely taken in" by Wickham (87). The chapter opens with a discussion between Elizabeth and Jane on truth and deception. Jane makes excuses for Bingley, and he is included among those whom Darcy has mistreated. Jane is less certain than her sister, and is less inclined to rush to judgment. "One does not know what to think," she tells Elizabeth, who immediately replies, "One knows exactly what to think." Elizabeth finds it, ironically, difficult to believe "that Mr. Wickham should invent such a history as he gave me last night; names, facts, every thing mentioned without ceremony." She adds, "If it be not so, let Mr. Darcy contradict it. Besides, there was truth in his looks." At this

stage in the novel, Elizabeth is taken in by appearances, by surface charm and glitter. The sisters' discussion is interrupted by an invitation from "Mr. Bingley and his sisters" to "the long expected ball at Netherfield." Preparations for the event, with whom Elizabeth in particular is to dance, preoccupy the remainder of the chapter, most of which is omniscient narration. There is a self-serving, slightly ridiculous speech from Collins in which he solicits the first two dances in advance from Elizabeth. She had been dreaming that Wickham would be her partner. Instead, she finds herself the subject of Collins's increasing attention and chooses to ignore a "hint" from her mother that "the probability of their marriage was exceedingly agreeable to *her*," (Jane Austen's emphasis), that is, Elizabeth's mother, not Elizabeth. The upcoming Netherfield ball makes even the usually unbearable weather, "such . . . succession of rain as prevented their walking to Meryton once . . . endurable to Kitty and Lydia," the two youngest (85–86, 88).

Chapter 18

The Netherfield ball, which takes place in chapter 18, is the important social happening so far in the novel. There have been many social events already: visits, meals, walks, and assemblies. The upcoming ball is important, for most of the key characters are present except one, who is most conspicuous by his absence—Wickham. The ball has been carefully prepared and demonstrates Bingley's benevolence. He comes personally to Longbourn to deliver an invitation, and goes ahead with the plan for the ball in spite of his sister's and Darcy's objections to it. The ball also arouses expectations. At the event, Collins, Elizabeth, Jane, and Bingley hope to develop their relationships. Mrs. Bennet too expects that these courtships will be cemented in actual marital proposals. Elizabeth looks forward to seeing Wickham and gaining information that he is correct concerning Darcy. The actual ball does not prove to be a disappointment but ironically is not what the Bennets expected. Wickham is absent, the courtship of Bingley and Jane is not developed, Mr. Collins makes little if any headway with Elizabeth, and Elizabeth is unable to confront Darcy. She suspects that he is the reason why Wickham is absent but is unable to substantiate what remains a suspicion based on her prejudice against him. Darcy's view that the Bennet sisters are unsuitable marital partners is confirmed by the behavior of Mrs. Bennet and Mary, who sings far too much when asked to perform.

Chapter 18, the description of Netherfield, is lengthy. It operates on many levels and has consequences that reemerge in the novel. For instance, in Darcy's lengthy letter to Elizabeth after she has rejected his proposal of marriage, he refers to "the evening of the dance at Netherfield" (197). Through the advantage of hindsight, Elizabeth is in accord with Darcy's view of what occurred. The immediate consequences are that Jane receives a letter from Caroline Bingley telling her that their "whole party have left Netherfield . . . and are on their way to town; and without any intention of" returning (116). Jane is also told that Caroline and Louisa, her sister, are optimistic that there will be a marriage between Bingley and Georgina, Darcy's sister. Elizabeth attempts to reassure Jane that this is probably a mistake on Caroline Bingley's part and that Bingley is "in love with" her (119). However, before this letter has been received, the day following the ball, Elizabeth herself has been the subject of a proposal from Mr. Collins.

Before examining this, we briefly analyze the structure of the Netherfield Ball chapter. It opens with Elizabeth's disappointment at finding Wickham absent. There is then a dialogue between her and Darcy accompanying their dancing together. The subject of Wickham is raised by Elizabeth but they are interrupted by Sir William Lucas, who mentions the closeness of the relationship between Jane and Bingley and speculates that "a certain desirable event . . . shall take place." This "seemed to strike [Darcy] forcibly." There follows a conversation between Darcy and Elizabeth on the subject of reading, books, and prejudice during which there is a warning from Darcy to Elizabeth "not to sketch [his—Darcy's] character at the present moment, as there is reason to fear that the performance would reflect no credit on either." The actions of this chapter illustrate one of Jane Austen's continuing preoccupations in her work, to demonstrate that appearances are deceptive. Caroline Bingley then

tells Elizabeth, after she and Darcy have separated, that she should not believe what Wickham tells her: "George Wickham has treated Mr. Darcy in a most infamous manner." Elizabeth is so prejudiced in Wickham's favor and against Darcy that she refuses to believe Caroline. She is not even reassured by Jane's report of Bingley informing her of his defense of Darcy. The rest of the chapter is taken up with Collins's plan to introduce himself to Darcy, a relative of his patroness Lady Catherine de Bourgh, and elaborate prolix speeches by Collins to Elizabeth and others. Elizabeth is preoccupied with visions of the consequences of a marriage between Jane and Bingley. The reader is to learn later on that similar thoughts are engaging Darcy, hence his desire to separate the two, a reason being, the unsuitability of a marriage to someone with a mother such as Mrs. Bennet, who insists in making ridiculous observations overheard by Darcy. The family is further shown to disadvantage by Mary's singing. She becomes the subject of "derision" among the Bingley sisters.

The chapter ends with an unhappy Elizabeth, lengthy speeches from Collins, "a manoeuver" from Mrs. Bennet to delay the Bennet family departure, and Mrs. Bennet's certainty that "she should undoubtedly see her daughter settled at Netherfield, in the course of three or four months." Mrs. Bennet's irresponsible actions have partly contributed, as emerges, to the opposite taking place. The last paragraph also tells readers that "Elizabeth was the least dear to her [Mrs. Bennet] of all her children." "Dear" here is a term of endearment, of affection. It also has financial implications. Mrs. Bennet does not mind Elizabeth marrying the less wealthy Mr. Collins, who is "quite good enough for *her*" (Jane Austen's emphasis)—Elizabeth. Her "worth . . . was eclipsed by Mr. Bingley and Netherfield" (92, 94, 100, 102–103).

Chapter 19

The next five chapters focus not on Jane and Bingley, on Darcy or Wickham, but on Collins and his attention toward Elizabeth. Mr. Collins's proposal to Elizabeth is comic. The source of its being comedy is its incongruity. Collins proposes in a pedantic manner, as if he is delivering a Sunday sermon. He tells Elizabeth at some length his "reason for marrying," his home is "a humble abode," "music an innocent diversion," death a "melancholy event." He even informs Elizabeth that he "should hope to lead [her] to the alter ere long." His proposal is full of condescension and acute awareness of social rank. He is proposing because his patroness, Lady Catherine de Bourgh, has instructed him to do so. Collins is also actively aware of money and Elizabeth Bennet's financial state. He tells her on that matter he "shall be uniformly silent" after she has been made aware how perilous her financial situation is, "that one thousand pounds in the 4 per cents . . . will not be [hers] till after [her] mother's decease, is all that [she] may ever be entitled to." This will only generate an annual income of £40, which, compared to Mr. Bennet's present income of £2,000 annually and Collins's of a few hundred pounds, is not enough to live on. In any case, on Elizabeth's marriage the meager income will pass as capital to her husband. Elizabeth's money will become one of the sources of the income by which Collins's status is judged. In Collins's case, his status depends on his patroness Lady Catherine de Bourgh's good graces.

Chapter 20

Chapters 20 and 21 deal with the consequences of Elizabeth's rejection of Collins's offer. Mrs. Bennet naturally is mortified to hear that what she considers to be such a suitable marital proposal has been rejected. She turns to Mr. Bennet to support her and persuade Elizabeth to reconsider. Elizabeth is "summoned" to her father's sanctum, his retreat from his wife and other domestic inconveniences, the library. His response is ironic and in some respects egocentric. Mr. Bennet tells Elizabeth, "Your mother will never see you again if you do *not* marry Mr. Collins, and I will never see you again if you *do*" (Jane Austen's emphasis). He tells his wife to "allow [him] the free use of [his] understanding on the present occasion," in other words, that his wishes should be preeminent. Further, that he "shall be glad to have the library to [himself] as soon as may be." In other words, for selfish reasons he takes his daughter's part and wishes to be left

alone. His short, antithetically based sentences, his wit is used as a defensive mechanism.

Mrs. Bennet too retreats, not to the library, but to berating her daughters and Charlotte Lucas, who is visiting about her "nervous complaints" (105–106, 112–113).

Chapter 21

In the meantime, Jane relates in chapter 21 the contents of a letter she has received from Caroline Bingley. The rest of the chapter is taken up with Elizabeth and Jane's reactions to the letter as Jane reads passages from it to her sister. Elizabeth is concerned to reinforce Bingley's strength of genuine attachment to Jane in spite of what Caroline Bingley tells her. Jane is much less disposed to think negative thoughts or motives of anyone. She tells Elizabeth, "Caroline is incapable of wilfully deceiving any one; and all that I can hope in this case, is that she is deceived herself" (114). The reader, however, is largely presented with Elizabeth's perception of what has occurred.

Chapter 22

The final two chapters of the first volume of *Pride and Prejudice* concern a marriage not anticipated earlier in its narrative. The opening paragraphs of chapter 22 are sufficient to report Collins's proposal to Charlotte Lucas and her acceptance, "solely from the pure and disinterested desire of an establishment, [she] cared not how soon that establishment were gained." As Charlotte explains to Elizabeth, who has expressed incredulity at the engagement, she is "not romantic you know. I never was. I ask only a comfortable home." She is a realist, as she tells Elizabeth, "considering Mr. Collins' character, connections, and situation in life, I am convinced that my chance of happiness with him is as fair as most people can boast on entering the marriage state." Charlotte has no illusions, her "opinion of matrimony was not exactly" Elizabeth's, who would not "have sacrificed every better feeling to worldly advantage." Elizabeth perceives that her friend has disgraced herself. She, Charlotte, has lowered herself in "her esteem" and Elizabeth is convinced "that it was impossible for that friend to be tolerably happy in the lot she had chosen." Once again, subsequent events in the narrative are to demonstrate that Elizabeth's prejudgment of the situation is incorrect. Charlotte, who has realistically married for pragmatic reasons, is able to be "tolerably happy in the lot she had chosen." Charlotte's choice is a realistic reflection of the marriage market. It is a logical and a reasonable choice based not on desire and love but upon practicality.

Chapter 23

The last chapter of the first volume focuses on anxiety in the Bennet family. Mrs. Bennet, practical as ever, is "in a most pitiable state." She fears that the marriage between Charlotte and Collins, heir to the Longbourn estate, will have practical adverse consequences upon the Bennets: that Collins was "resolving to turn herself and her daughters out of the house, as soon as Mr. Bennet were dead." Mrs. Bennet's temper is not improved by a visit from her friend and neighbor Lady Lucas, who has "the comfort of having a daughter well married" before Mrs. Bennet has achieved such a desired goal. Further, neither Jane nor Elizabeth has heard any news of Bingley's whereabouts or of his return to Netherfield. In short, the first volume concludes on a downbeat note for the Bennet family with none of their expectations fulfilled (122, 125, 130, 127).

Volume 2, Chapter 1 (Chapter 24)

The second book opens with the summary of a letter Caroline Bingley has written to Jane. The contents of the letter are not relayed as on a previous occasion by Jane but by the author. They are then conveyed through each characters' reactions to the contents: in this instance, Jane's and primarily Elizabeth's. The latter's reactions are conveyed in *erlebte Rede,* or the indirect speech mode. Jane Austen subsequently uses dialogue between the sisters and then between Mr. Bennet and Elizabeth to convey reaction to the letter. The chapter concludes with a "dispelling [of] gloom, which the late perverse occurrences had thrown on many of the Longbourn family" by the regular presence of Wickham at Longbourn. Jane is left as the only person refusing to think ill of the Bingleys. She is the only one who has refused to condemn Darcy "as the worst of men." Caroline's letter confirmed that Bingley will spend the winter in London, and she suggests an attachment

between Bingley and Georgiana Darcy. Elizabeth distrusts Caroline's motives, attributing them to an attempt to make Jane believe falsely that she was misled in her impression of Bingley's strength of feeling toward her. Subsequently in the narrative, Elizabeth's insight into Caroline's motivation will be verified, and Jane shown to be too trusting but correct about Darcy.

Volume 2, Chapter 2 (Chapter 25)

New characters, the Gardiners, are introduced into the narrative. Gardiner, Mrs. Bennet's brother, is "a sensible, gentleman-like man, greatly superior to his sister as well by nature and education." He is successful in trade and his warehouse. He and his wife live in Gracechurch Street, London, in a part of the city associated with trade and money but socially acceptable. Mrs. Bennet's welcome for Mrs. Gardiner allows Jane Austen, through the use of a casual remark made in dialogue by Mrs. Bennet, to comment on the very latest fashion controversies. Mrs. Bennet is "very glad to hear what you [Mrs. Gardiner] tell us, of long sleeves" (138–140). In a letter to her sister, Cassandra, of March 9, 1814, Jane Austen writes, "I wear my gauze gown today, long sleeves & all; I shall see how they succeed, but as yet I have no reason to suppose long sleeves are allowable . . . Mrs. Tilson had long sleeves, too & she assured me that they are worn in the evening by many" (*Letters,* 261–262). This is just one small example of the way in which a Jane Austen narrative is littered with allusions to contemporary fashion and behavior.

On hearing of Jane's disappointment from Elizabeth, Mrs. Gardiner invites Jane to stay with her in London. The reader is informed that Mrs. Gardiner, too, before her marriage "spent a considerable time" where both Wickham and Darcy grew up, and her memory seems to confirm the prejudice against Darcy.

Volume 2, Chapter 3 (Chapter 26)

Mrs. Gardiner warns Elizabeth to be cautious about Wickham. Her caution is a practical one. In this respect, she is not dissimilar to Charlotte Lucas. Mrs. Gardiner tells Elizabeth, "if he had the fortune he ought to have, I should think you could not do better." But Elizabeth's "sense," her common sense, sensibleness should take priority over her "fancy," her selfish, impractical desires. Elizabeth promises not to rush into anything or to disappoint either her aunt or her father, but she believes that the days for making marriages based solely on financial or practical considerations are over: "young people are seldom withheld by immediate want of fortune, from entering into engagements with each other." Ironically, this indeed is the case in *Pride and Prejudice* and contrary to Elizabeth's expectations.

Charlotte is married and extracts a promise from Elizabeth to visit her and her new home at Hunsford in Kent. Charlotte's letters to Elizabeth are full of praise for "the house, furniture, neighbourhood and roads." Jane meanwhile has gone to London to stay with her aunt Gardiner; she sees Caroline Bingley briefly and then writes a lengthy letter to Elizabeth, which is quoted in full. Jane admits to having been duped by Caroline, and she and Elizabeth believe that "all expectation from" Bingley "was now absolutely over." Elizabeth has a disappointment of her own to contend with. Wickham has turned his attentions toward a Miss King, who has acquired an inheritance of 10,000 pounds, a sum much more than the amount Elizabeth can hope to inherit or bring to a marriage. She is still sympathetically disposed or prejudiced in Wickham's favor, telling her aunt that her sisters "Kitty and Lydia take his defection much more to heart" than she does. In this way, Jane Austen once again is placing hints in the narrative of what is to come. Elizabeth adds to her aunt that her sisters "are young in the ways of the world." Elizabeth, after her experience with Charlotte's actions, realizes that "handsome young men must have something to live on, as well as the plain."

Volume 2, Chapter 4 (Chapter 27)
In March, Elizabeth accompanies Sir William Lucas and his second daughter, Maria, on a visit to Charlotte Lucas at Hunsford in Kent. They interrupt the journey with a visit to the Gardiners at Gracechurch Street and to Jane. They also spend their time in London during "the morning in bustle and shopping, and the evening at one of the theatres." Before leaving her Aunt Gardiner's, Elizabeth agrees to accompany them on a tour of Derbyshire

and the Lake District—a popular venue for scenic travel. Further, Elizabeth in a dialogue with her aunt over Wickham's transfer of affection to Miss King, an heiress, is ready to accept his "mercenary" behavior as appropriate to "a man in distressed circumstances." Elizabeth is "sick of them all"—that is, men. The chapter ends on an optimistic note: "Adieu to disappointment and spleen" (142, 144–146, 149, 150, 152–153).

Volume 2, Chapter 5 (Chapter 28)
Collins greets his visitors to Hunsford Parsonage with a "formal civility." Elizabeth is impressed by how comfortable her friend Charlotte is and by her "evident enjoyment" of her new surroundings. She also notices how adroitly Charlotte manages her husband, encouraging, for instance, his gardening, which he enjoys and which also gets him out of the Parsonage. The Parsonage is situated near the boundary of Rosings Park, and Rosings House is within walking distance. The day following their arrival they have visitors. Humorously, Elizabeth mistakes Mrs. Jenkinson, Lady Catherine de Bourgh's companion, for the patroness herself. She "expected at least that the pigs were got into the garden, and here is nothing but Lady Catherine and her daughter!" Elizabeth is pleased that the daughter "looks sickly and cross" and hence will be a suitable match for Darcy (155, 157–158).

Volume 2, Chapter 6 (Chapter 29)
The next day, they visit Rosings and Lady Catherine de Bourgh. Collins shows his visitors Rosings Park. In spite of his superciliousness and exceeding deference to his patroness, Collins is practical and impressed by possessions. For instance, he enumerates the cost of the glazing at Rosings Park. Windows and glazing were very expensive as windows had been subject to tax since 1696, with additional taxes relating to the weight of glass being subsequently introduced. The amount and size of windows in a new property indicated the owner's wealth, and windows in general were a status symbol. Sir William Lucas and his daughter Maria are overwhelmed by the "grandeur surrounding" them. Lady Catherine, through her manner of receiving her visitors, does not hesitate to make them feel that they are of "inferior rank" to her.

Elizabeth remains aloof from being overawed by either Lady Catherine, her rank, her money, or her surroundings or from being reminded that her "father's estate is entailed to Mr. Collins." She is not phased by Lady Catherine's shock at learning that she, Elizabeth, did not have a governess. The reader learns through Lady Catherine's interrogation of Elizabeth that the latter is not yet "one and twenty." Elizabeth shocks Lady Catherine by speaking forthrightly to her and refusing to be overawed (162, 164, 166).

Volume 2, Chapter 7 (Chapter 30)

Sir William's Hunsford visit is only for a week. Elizabeth is left with Charlotte, who she discovers has found a way to accommodate her husband without too much interference from him. Charlotte even has arranged the Parsonage so that she and her husband have their own separate space. Lady Catherine manages even "the minutest concerns" of the parishioners who live nearby, being regularly informed of local developments by Mr. Collins. Lady Catherine is visited at Easter by her two nephews, Darcy and Colonel Fitzwilliam. The latter is Darcy's cousin and with Darcy guardian of Georgiana Darcy. The two soon call at the Parsonage. The meeting between Darcy and Elizabeth is a very brief one in the seventh chapter of the second volume. Most of the chapter is omniscient narration, with occasional interweaving into Elizabeth's perspective. Two instances of dialogue occur. Collins perceives that Darcy would not have visited the Parsonage so soon if Elizabeth had not been present. Elizabeth asks Darcy whether he happened to see Jane in town: the answer is not given.

Volume 2, Chapter 8 (Chapter 31)

The Lucases and Elizabeth are invited to Rosings after church on Easter evening. The focal point of chapter 8 is Elizabeth's performance at the piano during the visit, the responses this produces especially in Darcy, his attentiveness to her, and his embarrassment at "his aunt's ill breeding." Two key moments are evident in the encounter. Elizabeth tells Colonel Fitzwilliam when responding to his request to tell him "what [she has] to accuse [Darcy] of" (169, 173–174), that at his first ball, he danced only four times, in spite of the scarcity

of gentleman. This may be perceived as the reason for Elizabeth's initial prejudice against Darcy. The second key moment occurs when Elizabeth uses her piano performance to provide a counterpoint to Darcy's evident shyness and lack of social skills. In this chapter Darcy shows yet again that he is incapable of small talk. Jane Austen uses Elizabeth's apparently superficial conversation during her piano playing to reveal deep emotion and feelings. She has much to teach Darcy, who ironically appears not to hear the real import or context of what she is saying to him. If he had listened to her, he would not have immediately proposed and would have saved himself anguish. Elizabeth also learns in the chapter that Darcy apparently has no interest in developing a relationship with the sickly-looking Anne de Bourgh, the only daughter of Lady Catherine and heiress to the Rosings estate and properties.

Volume 2, Chapter 9 (Chapter 32)

Darcy's difficulty in expressing himself is further illustrated in chapter 9 when he visits the Parsonage and finds Elizabeth alone. Tongue-tied, he responds in brief sentences to Elizabeth's questions concerning Bingley and the possibility of his returning to Netherfield. He presents a more benevolent side of Lady Catherine than has surfaced previously by telling Elizabeth that she enlarged the Parsonage when Mr. Collins first appeared at Hunsford. Darcy seems genuinely concerned with the happiness of Charlotte, Elizabeth's friend. In the course of their conversation, Darcy "drew a chair a little towards her," revealing emotion and affection but his tone changes and they are interrupted. The chapter concludes with Elizabeth and Charlotte speculating as to "why Mr. Darcy came so often to the Parsonage" and why Colonel Fitzwilliam also appears so much. Elizabeth is aware of Darcy's "earnest, steadfast gaze" but dismisses Charlotte's suggestion of "the possibility of his being partial to her." In the last paragraph of the chapter, the indirect speech pattern focuses on Charlotte's thoughts rather than Elizabeth's. The attention is on Colonel Fitzwilliam's many positive attributes. But, as ever in a Jane Austen novel, there is a "counter balance" to his "advantages." These are, as is so often the case, practical and material: "Darcy had considerable patronage, in the church and his cousin could have none at all" (174, 180–181). In other words, Darcy had the real wealth, connections, and status, Fitzwilliam had none.

Volume 2, Chapter 10 (Chapter 33)

Chapter 10 of the second volume is well placed structurally to occur before Darcy's proposal to Elizabeth. It explains why she is so hostile toward him and plants signposts indicating that his proposal should not be a total surprise to the reader or even to Elizabeth, if she had read the signs correctly. Darcy finds every possible reason to meet her in the grounds of Rosings, on walks, to ask her questions about the happiness of the Collinses and her opinion of Rosings: "he seemed to expect that whenever she came into Kent again she would be staying *there* too." In terms of the perspective of the unfolding of the narrative, this turns out to be true. Elizabeth talks with Colonel Fitzwilliam, indicating to him the sense that Darcy enjoys "the power of doing what he likes." She also discovers that Darcy is exceedingly wealthy and that younger sons such as Colonel Fitzwilliam "cannot marry where they like." Estates were handed down from father to eldest son, and younger sons often went into the church or armed forces unless they married an heiress.

Fitzwilliam also explains to Elizabeth that he and Darcy have joint guardianship for Georgiana Darcy, Darcy's 16-year-old sister. There is a hint in Fitzwilliam's asking Elizabeth "why she supposed Miss Darcy likely to give them any uneasiness," that "she had somehow or other got pretty near the truth." This is not developed at this point in the novel. Fitzwilliam inadvertently reveals that recently Darcy has "saved a friend from the inconveniences of a most imprudent marriage, but without mentioning names or any other particulars." Elizabeth believes that this is a reference to Jane, and that Darcy has been "the cause of all that Jane has suffered, and shall continue to suffer." Moreover, Darcy "had ruined for a while every hope of happiness for the most affectionate, generous heart in the world." Elizabeth brooding upon this suffers a headache. Unwilling to see Darcy, she remains at the Parsonage as the Collinses go to Rosings. The chapter ends on a slight note of wry humor. Mr. Collins is not concerned with Elizabeth's health but with incurring Lady Catherine de Bourgh's displeasure "by her staying at home" (182–187).

Volume 2, Chapter 11 (Chapter 34)

Chapter 11 of the second volume has been regarded as the focal structural point of the novel. "Irony in *Pride and Prejudice* is more totally verbal in the first half of the novel than in the second . . . the verbal irony is necessary to the ambiguity that enables Darcy and Elizabeth so completely to misunderstand each other." Joseph Wiesenfarth, in *The Errand of Form: An Assay of Jane Austen's Art* (1967), argues that the plot of the novel "builds to a statement of problems that arise through verbal ambiguity. Darcy comes to think that Elizabeth loves him whereas" (63) she is very hostile to him, owing to the way she perceives he has treated Jane and Wickham. She is brooding on this treatment when Darcy appears at Hunsford and is most agitated. He confesses his love for her and requests her hand in marriage. Taken by surprise and shaken, she is unable to respond sufficiently. Constructing this as a positive, Darcy explains his own struggle against his pride, "his sense of her inferiority . . . of the family obstacles which judgment had always opposed to inclination" (189). Elizabeth rejects him and asks him to resolve, in Wiesenfarth's words, the "four problems that keep them apart: the problems of Bingley's separation from Jane, of Darcy's relation to Wickham, of the Bennet family's impropriety, and of Darcy's ungentlemanly manners." These problems are resolved in the second half of the novel (Weinsheimer, 51). Darcy's response to what is from his perspective a surprising rejection is that of total honesty, telling Elizabeth that "these offences might have been overlooked, had not your [Elizabeth's] pride been hurt by my honest confession of the scruples that had long prevented my forming any serious design." The chapter concludes with Elizabeth reflecting on Darcy's "abominable pride" and his refusal to explain his actions satisfactorily. Unable to face company, even Charlotte, somewhat in the manner of her father, who retreats to his library, she "hurried . . . away to her room" (192–194).

Volume 2, Chapter 12 (Chapter 35)

The following chapter focuses on the consequences of what has taken place. The next morning, Elizabeth goes on a different route to avoid meeting Darcy during the walk. However, he has anticipated her, meets her, and asks her to read a letter, the text of which takes up the rest of the chapter. Darcy dated it "from Rosings at eight o'clock in the morning" (192). He has adhered to social convention by delivering it "privately to avoid comprising Elizabeth's reputation," for the "letter breaks contemporary social convention since correspondence between" a man and a woman "was only acceptable if the couple were engaged" (Stafford, 325). The letter outlines in some detail the part Darcy has played in Bingley's separation from Jane, and it also explains Darcy's relationship with Wickham. Darcy tells Elizabeth that he perceived that at Netherfield, Jane's "look and manner were open, cheerful and engaging, as ever, but without any symptom of pecular regard" for his friend Bingley. Darcy "was desirous of believing her indifferent." Further, Darcy was in danger of connecting himself with a family who behaved with a "total want of propriety" not, as Elizabeth perceived, that they lacked suitable connections. He specifically refers to the conduct of Mrs. Bennett and to the "three younger sisters," not to either Jane or Elizabeth.

Most of the lengthy two-paragraph letter is taken up with Wickham's family history, conduct toward Darcy, and his sister Georgiana. Colonel Fitzwilliam is offered as collaborating witness to what Darcy relates about Wickham. Elizabeth is told that Wickham is the son of a most respected steward who served long and honorably in the family on the Darcy Pemberley estate in Derbyshire. Wickham was educated as a gentleman and promised a church living on the Pemberley estate if he stuck to his promise to become a clergyman. On the death five years previously of Darcy's father, Wickham was left a not inconsiderable legacy of £1000. However, Wickham had serious character defects. He gave up a career in the church for that of the law, but "his studying the law was a mere pretence," and in London, "being now free from all restraint, his life was a life of idleness and dissipation." When he had spent his legacy he asked

for the Pemberley living, but Darcy refused. Wickham turned his attentions to Darcy's young sister Georgiana, who "was then but fifteen." Wickham's attempt to elope with her, his "chief object was unquestionably my sister's fortunes, which is thirty thousand pounds . . . [and] . . . the hope of revenging himself on me," was foiled at the very last minute. At the end of the letter, Darcy asks "God [to] bless" Elizabeth and reveals his aristocratic Christian name "Fitzwilliam"—his mother being Lady Anne Fitzwilliam, the aunt of Colonel Fitzwilliam (197–198, 201–203).

Volume 2, Chapter 13 (Chapter 36)

The following chapter is preoccupied with Elizabeth's conflicting reactions to Darcy's letter, with the "contrariety of emotion" it "excited." She finds his explanation of the Jane-Bingley separation unsympathetic: "his style was not penitent, but haughty. It was all pride and insolence." However, assessing the evidence presented regarding Wickham, using her memory, she believes that she has been erroneous in her attitude toward Darcy. "She grew absolutely ashamed of herself—Of neither Darcy nor Wickham could she think, without feeling that she had been blind, partial, prejudiced, absurd." So much so that she revises her reaction to Darcy's explanation of the Jane-Bingley relationship: "She felt that Jane's feelings, though fervent, were little displayed, and that there was a constant compliancy in her air and manner." Elizabeth admits that "vanity, not love, has been my [her] folly" and is in accord with Darcy's judgment of her family's behavior. Two issues then remain to be resolved: the conduct of the Bennet family and Darcy's manner, his pride, his behavior (204, 208).

Volume 2, Chapter 14 (Chapter 37)

Elizabeth misses the farewell call from Fitzwilliam and Darcy to the Parsonage. Both leave Rosings. The Collinses and Elizabeth then visit Rosings. Lady Catherine, observing "that Miss Bennet seemed out of spirits," urges her to stay on at Hunsford Parsonage, telling Elizabeth, "you will have been here only six weeks. I expected you to stay for two months." Lady Catherine is most solicitous as to how women travel, for "Young women should always be properly guarded and attended, according to their station in life." She points out that the summer before last, when her "niece Georgiana went to Ramsgate . . . [she] made a point of her having two men servants go with her," a small detail the irony of which is not lost on Elizabeth in view of what Darcy has just revealed in his letter about Wickham's attempted seduction. This chapter following Darcy's letter then turns to Elizabeth's solitary reflections on it. She is unable to find a solution: Her sisters and mother and her "own past behaviour . . . were hopeless of remedy"; furthermore "Jane had been deprived by the folly and indecorum of her own family!" In short, Elizabeth leaves Rosings in a depressed state (211–213).

Volume 2, Chapter 15 (Chapter 38)
Chapter 15 of the second volume opens with Mr. Collins "paying [Elizabeth] the parting civilities which he deemed indispensably necessary." These are lengthy: "words were insufficient for the elevation of his feelings . . . Elizabeth tried to unite civility and truth in a few short sentences." She regrets leaving Charlotte in such a situation but recognizes her independence of spirit and spirit of self-reliance. She travels with Maria Lucas, who, no longer intimidated into silence by Lady Catherine and Rosings, exclaims "it seems but a day or two since we first came!—and yet how many things have happened!" She sums them up: "We have dined nine times at Rosings, besides drinking tea there twice!" adding "that much I shall have to tell!" Elizabeth to herself adds that she will have a good deal "to conceal." Elizabeth is in a "state of indecision" as to what she should reveal to Jane. There is the fear of grieving Jane, of "exceedingly astonish[ing] Jane," and there is little of Elizabeth's own vanity left (215–218).

Volume 2, Chapter 16 (Chapter 39)
Elizabeth, Jane, and Maria Lucas return to Hertfordshire in the second week of May. Immediately, the two older sisters are confronted by the adolescent behavior of their younger sisters Kitty and Lydia. Lydia has purchased a bonnet, a very fashionable adornment especially when taken home, as Lydia intends, to "pull it to pieces." Lydia relays the latest gossip to her sisters. This concerns the militia, who "are going to be encamped near Brighton," a fashionable seaside resort on the south English coast, 50 miles or so south of London. Brighton had a disreputable reputation, the prince regent having transformed his house at the resort into something much grander for his mistress Mrs. Fitzherbert. Lydia reveals that "there is no danger of Wickham's marrying Mary King," the heiress, as she has gone out of harm's way to Liverpool, a commercial center on the northwest coast. Lydia's questions to her sisters concerning what happened to them during their stay in London and Kent reveal that Jane "is almost three and twenty," with the implication that she "will be quite an old maid soon." Lydia confesses that she would be "ashamed" if she were not married before such an age, and that Aunt Philips "says Lizzy had better have taken Mr. Collins." She adds, however, that she does "not think there would have been any fun in it." Lydia's ambitions are to be married first. The chapter is preoccupied with Elizabeth and Jane's reception at Longbourn, Lydia's self-obsession and continued reference to Wickham, and attempts to go to Brighton to be with the officers (219–221).

Volume 2, Chapter 17 (Chapter 40)
Alone with Jane, Elizabeth is able to tell her of Darcy's proposal, her reaction, and George Wickham's perfidy. This has a serious effect on Jane, who is always trying to see the positive side of other people. She "would willingly have gone through the world without believing that so much wickedness existed in the whole race of mankind, as were here collected in one individual." She finds it difficult to make a choice between Darcy and Wickham. The two sisters both consider the implications of appearance and character. Elizabeth confesses her mistaken prejudice against Darcy to Jane, and they resolve to keep quiet about Wickham's character, especially as "the general prejudice against Mr. Darcy is so violent, that it would be the death of half the good people in Meryton, to attempt to place him in an amiable light." Although Elizabeth has told Jane about Darcy's proposal, her reaction to it, and Wickham, she has not told Jane about Darcy's attitude to her family or role in the separation of Bingley and Jane. The latter "was not happy" and "still cherished a very tender affection for Bingley." The chapter concludes with Mrs.

Bennet constantly reminding Elizabeth that Charlotte and Mr. Collins "will never be distressed for money" and that on the death of Mr. Bennet, they will occupy Longbourn.

Volume 2, Chapter 18 (Chapter 41)

The 18th chapter of the second volume consists of lengthy conversations between Elizabeth and Mrs. Bennet, Elizabeth and Wickham prefaced by quips from mainly Lydia and Mrs. Bennet, and concludes with accounts of Lydia's excitement at leaving for Brighton. Lydia believes that "A little sea-bathing would set [her] up for ever." Jane Austen probably agrees with her (229). She enjoyed her sea bathing at Lyme, writing to her sister Cassandra on September 14, 1804, "The Bathing was so delightful this morning . . . that I believe I staid in rather too long" (*Letters,* 95). Lydia receives "an invitation from Mrs. Forster, the wife of the Colonel of the regiment, to accompany her to Brighton." Kitty, of course, is jealous. Elizabeth tries to prevent the visit, making her father aware of "all the improprieties of Lydia's general behaviour." Further, "she will, at sixteen, be the most determined flirt that ever made herself and her family ridiculous." Mr. Bennet agrees with Elizabeth but will not stop the visit, telling Elizabeth, "We shall have no peace at Longbourn if Lydia does not go to Brighton." He believes that Colonel and Mrs. Forster "will keep her out of any real mischief."

The author tells us, "In Lydia's imagination, a visit to Brighton comprised every possibility of earthly happiness." As the narration unfolds, the very opposite of this occurs. Before Lydia leaves for Brighton, Wickham does too. Elizabeth and Wickham meet and she tries to confront him with revealing the truth of his relationship with Darcy. Wickham, however, bluffs his way through the conversation, insisting, ironically, that Darcy "is wise enough to assume ever the *appearance* of what is right" (Jane Austen's emphasis), and pointing out that Darcy's "pride" might well in future "deter him [Darcy] from such foul misconduct" as Wickham asserts he has experienced at Darcy's hands. There has been already a reversal in the plot. Elizabeth, earlier all too prepared to accept what Wickham said, is now no longer prepared to do so. At the end of the evening, "they parted at last with mutual civility, and possibly in mutual desire of never meeting again"—the word "possibly" having ironic implications. The penultimate chapter of volume 2 concludes with Lydia and her departure once again the focus of proceedings (230–235).

Volume 2, Chapter 19 (Chapter 42)

The final chapter (19) of the second volume serves something of a reviewing function from Elizabeth's perspective of what has taken place previously and also presages what is to happen. It opens with her assessment of the strengths and weaknesses of her father's character. She "had never been blind to the impropriety of her father's behaviour as a husband" and especially to his habit of "exposing his wife to the contempt of her own children." In view of the family situation, she looks forward to her upcoming "tour to the Lakes," and she wishes, too, that Jane could accompany her. Lydia promised before she left for Brighton to write home regularly, but her letters are late in coming and short. The arrival of summer meant that "Everything wore a happier aspect" in Longbourn and Meryton. However, a change in the Gardiner business plans means that they will be unable to travel as far north as planned, will have less time, and will "go no farther northward than Derbyshire." Elizabeth is very disappointed. The Gardiners arrive at Longbourn and leave their children, "two girls of six and eight years old and two younger boys . . . under the particular care of their cousin Jane" (236–239). Their destination is Lambton, a fictitious Derbyshire town where Mrs. Gardiner had once lived and "not more than a mile or two" away from Pemberley. The second volume concludes with Elizabeth about to visit Pemberly with the Gardiners. She agrees to do so after she has established that Darcy and his family will be away for the summer.

Volume 3, Chapter 1 (Chapter 43)

In the lengthy first chapter of the third volume, topography is used as a clear reflection of character. Pemberley and its grounds are largely perceived through Elizabeth's eyes. All is harmony, order, and propriety on the estate, with none of the ostentation of Rosings Park and Lady Catherine de Bourgh. Elizabeth's first impression of Pemberley's environs is so positive that "she felt, that to be mistress of Pemberley might be something!" (245). She has "come to recognize not merely the money and status of Pemberley, but its value in the setting of a traditional social and ethical orientation, its possibilities" (Gray, 311–312). Inside Pemberley, "Elizabeth saw, with admiration of his [Darcy's] taste, that it was neither gaudy nor uselessly fine; with less of splendor, and more real elegance, than the furniture at Rosings." She reflects that she "might have been mistress" of the place. In this setting, her objection to Darcy's manners disappears. She and the Gardiners are shown around the house by Mrs. Reynolds, the housekeeper, who has known Darcy "since he was four years old." They learn that Wickham "has turned out very wild" and Mrs. Reynolds observation on Darcy's generosity of spirit, charitableness, even-tempered nature, and kindness run counter to Elizabeth's perceptions of Darcy. Mr. Gardiner is "highly amused by the kind of family prejudice, to which he attributed [Mrs. Reynolds's] excessive commendation of her master," who is also "the best landlord and the best master . . . that ever lived." Elizabeth's reactions to Mrs. Reynolds's praise of Darcy are conveyed in *erlebte Rede,* indirect speech. She asks herself the question, "What praise is more valuable than the praise of an intelligent servant?" The servant's whole being, whole existence, depends on the person served.

As the Gardiners and Elizabeth are departing from Pemberley House and its immediate surroundings, Darcy appears unexpectedly. "Their eyes instantly met, and the cheeks of each were overspread with the deepest blush," and this reveals the depth of feeling between the two. Elizabeth is overcome by the "impropriety" (a sense of behavior she has become aware of from Darcy) of her being at Pemberley. Darcy also finds the meeting difficult and "at length, every idea seemed to fail him." He becomes speechless. Elizabeth is "overpowered by shame and vexation, . . . Never in her life had she seen his manners so little dignified, never had he spoken with such gentleness as on this unexpected meeting." Elizabeth's thoughts are now totally focused on what Darcy is thinking rather than on the beauties of the Pemberley grounds or even her

companions, her aunt and uncle. In the grounds they encounter once again Darcy, who waits to be introduced to the Gardiners, with whom he strikes up an immediate rapport. Darcy invites Mr. Gardiner to fish in the grounds "as often he chose" and offers him fishing tackle and indicates the best "parts of the stream" where to fish. They learn that Darcy has come ahead of "Mr. Bingley and his sisters" to see that all was prepared for their visit. He wishes them to meet his own sister. Darcy and Elizabeth walk together. In the carriage going to their lodgings, she and the Gardiners discuss her meeting with Darcy. Mrs. Gardiner is skeptical that Darcy "could have behaved in so cruel a way by any body, as he has done by poor Wickham." On the contrary, Darcy has "dignity in his countenance." The chapter ends with Mrs. Gardiner's renewing a former friendship in the Pemberley area and Elizabeth doing "nothing but think, and think with wonder, of Mr. Darcy's civility, and above all, of his wishing her to be acquainted with his sister" (246–259).

Volume 3, Chapter 2 (Chapter 44)

Darcy brings his shy sister "little more than sixteen, her figure was formed, and her appearance womanly and graceful" to visit Elizabeth and the Gardiners. They are followed shortly after by Bingley. It is evident to the Gardiners "that [Darcy] was very much in love with" Elizabeth; however, "of the lady's [Elizabeth's] sensations they remained a little in doubt." Elizabeth has noted the remarkable "improvement of manners" on Darcy's part, and she had not previously "seen [Darcy] so desirous to please, so free from self- consequence, or unbending reserve." There is even verification from mutual acquaintances of what Darcy said of Wickham, and they learn that Darcy had discharged Wickham's debts. Elizabeth reflects, "Such a change in a man of so much pride excited not only astonishment but gratitude—for to love, ardent love, it must be attributed" (261–266).

Volume 3, Chapter 3 (Chapter 45)

The Gardiners and Elizabeth revisit Pemberley, where Georgiana Darcy, Mrs. Hurst, Caroline Bingley, and Mrs. Annesley, with whom the latter lives in London, receive them. Darcy has been with

Gardiner and some others fishing on the estate. He joins them, and Caroline Bingley's attempts to speak ill of Elizabeth before Darcy, and to introduce by implication the name of Wickham, only produce Darcy's compliments concerning Elizabeth: "I have considered her as one of the handsomest women of my acquaintance" (271).

Volume 3, Chapter 4 (Chapter 46)
Volume 3, chapter 4 is concerned with the two letters Elizabeth receives from Jane and Elizabeth's confession of their content to Darcy. In the first of the letters, Jane tells Elizabeth that Wickham and Lydia have eloped, apparently to Scotland. In the second, Jane reveals that they have gone to London and that it is doubtful whether Wickham will marry Lydia. In short, their uncle Gardiner's advice is urgently needed. Just as Elizabeth is on her way to find her uncle, she encounters Darcy. In her obvious distress Elizabeth tells Darcy what has happened, observing, "*You* know him too well to doubt the rest. She has no money, no connections, nothing that can tempt him to—she is lost forever." She confesses to Darcy that she should have acted differently when her "eyes were opened to [Wickham's] real character." Darcy says little in response and Elizabeth feels a deep sense of shame: "her power was sinking; every thing *must* sink under such a proof of family weakness, such an assurance of the deepest disgrace" (Jane Austen's emphasis). She believes that she will not see Darcy again, and the rest of the chapter is taken up with her rumination on her feelings toward Darcy, Wickham and Lydia's actions, and concern for Jane to deal with "a family so deranged; a father absent, a mother incapable of exertions and requiring constant attendance" (277–278, 280). Accounts are quickly settled at the inn, and the Gardiners with Elizabeth return to London.

Volume 3, Chapter 5 (Chapter 47)
Discussion of Lydia's elopement between Elizabeth and the Gardiners forms the basis for the first part of the next chapter. Elizabeth reflects on the folly of her father's behavior, his lack of example, "indolence," and lack of attention to his family. She confesses to the Gardiners as they journey toward Longbourn, that she, too, "was ignorant of the truth" herself until she saw Darcy and Colonel Fitzwilliam at Rosings. Even then, "that *she*," her sister Lydia, "could be in any danger from deception never entered [Elizabeth's] head" (Jane Austen's emphasis). They return to a distraught Longbourn. Mrs. Bennet overreacts and believes that her husband will be killed in a duel with Wickham and "the Collinses will turn [them] out" of their house "before he is cold in the grave." Mary remarks to Elizabeth "that loss of virtue in a female is irretrievable—that one false step involves her in endless ruin—that her reputation is no less brittle than it is beautiful—and that she cannot be too much guarded in her behaviour towards the undeserving of the other sex" (283–285, 287, 289). Meanwhile, Mr. Gardiner has gone to London to help Mr. Bennet in his search for Lydia and Wickham. Colonel Foster has reported that his wife, Harriet, received an irresponsible note form Lydia saying that they are going to Gretna Green, a town on the English-Scottish border well known for marriages of couples who have eloped. The chapter concludes with Jane's account of her father's attempts to locate the runaway couple.

Volume 3, Chapter 6 (Chapter 48)
The attitude to Wickham in Meryton has been rapidly transformed: "all seemed striving to blacken the man, who, but three months before, had been almost an angel of light." Notes of debt, intrigues, and attempted seduction emerge. Mrs. Gardiner receives a letter from her husband recounting what has occurred and wondering whether Elizabeth knows if Wickham has any relatives: "Elizabeth was at no loss to understand from whence this deference for authority proceeded." Perhaps this is a hint that Mr. Gardiner is aware that she has contact with Darcy, who, it emerges subsequently, is involved in the case. Anxiously awaiting news by letter, they receive a letter not from Mr. Gardiner but from Mr. Collins addressed to Mr. Bennet. Seemingly a letter of condolence, he advises Mr. Bennet "to throw off [his] unworthy child from [his] affection for ever," and tells Bennet that Lydia's action have damaged the marital prospects of his other daughters. Intelligence from Colonel Forster in Brighton is reported in a letter from Mr. Gardiner. Wickham has run up

enormous debts in Brighton and has been involved in gambling. On hearing of Mr. Bennet's impending return home, Mrs. Bennet, contrary to her earlier sentiments on her husband's welfare and worry about his death in a duel, now asks, "Who is to fight Wickham, and make him marry her, if he comes away?" Elizabeth reflects that if "she had known nothing of Darcy, she could have borne the dread of Lydia's infamy somewhat better." Mr. Bennet returns home, regretting his decision to allow Lydia to go to Brighton, but again displays a lack of direction and adroitness in dealing with his daughters, joking with Kitty that if she behaves "for the next ten years," he shall review a prohibition he has imposed on balls and army officers (294–300).

Volume 3, Chapter 7 (Chapter 49)
Jane and Elizabeth are walking together "in the shrubbery behind the house" when the housekeeper, Mrs. Hill, tells them that Mr. Bennet has received an express letter from Mr. Gardiner. He writes to say that Lydia and Wickham have been found and that a marriage between them has been arranged. The terms of the marriage he outlines at some length. The rest of the chapter presents differing viewpoints to news of the proposed marriage. Mr. Bennet reluctantly agrees to the terms, observing that "Wickham's a fool, if he takes [Lydia] with a farthing less than ten thousand pounds." Elizabeth assumes that the settlement, a bribe, has come from Mr. Gardiner. Jane is concerned to put a positive light on the affair, arguing that Wickham's "consenting to marry [Lydia] is a proof . . . that he is come to a right way of thinking." Elizabeth believes their conduct to be reprehensible. Mrs. Bennet, on hearing the news, is ecstatic: "She will be married at sixteen!" She is "in such a flutter," she tells Jane that she is unable to write, and goes to Meryton to "tell the good, good news." Elizabeth, on the other hand, "sick of this folly, took refuge in her own room." She reflects that Lydia's marriage will bring "neither rational happiness nor worldly prosperity" although she sees "all the advantages of what they had gained" (301, 304–307).

Volume 3, Chapter 8 (Chapter 50)
In the next chapter, the eighth of the third volume, Mr. Bennet wishes that he had been more sensible

in portioning his income and "laid by an annual sum, for the better provision of his children and his wife." He agrees to the Wickham-Lydia marriage settlement and then returns, the omniscient narrator relates, "to all his former indolence" after asking the Gardiners for the particulars of the settlement. Mrs. Bennet is preoccupied with wedding trivia. Mr. Bennet forbids Lydia from entering Longbourn and refuses to "advance a guinea to buy clothes for his daughter." Elizabeth's thoughts are on Darcy, and she regrets telling him what has happened; "She was convinced that she could have been happy with him; when it was no longer likely they should meet." Mr. Gardiner writes again to Mr. Bennet, pointing out that Wickham has the possibility of a commission in the regular army as opposed to the militia. He will be stationed at Newcastle in the north of the country. Jane and Elizabeth prevail on Mr. Bennet to receive Lydia and Wickham after the marriage and before they depart for Newcastle (308–311).

Volume 3, Chapter 9 (Chapter 51)
Following the wedding, the couple is received coolly by Mr. Bennet at Longbourn. "Elizabeth was disgusted . . . Lydia was Lydia still; untamed, unabashed, wild, noisy, and fearless." Wickham, too, behaves as if nothing amiss has taken place. Elizabeth is also so distressed by Lydia's behavior that "she got up, and ran out of the room" (315, 317). Lydia describes the wedding and reveals a secret that Darcy attended. Elizabeth immediately writes to her aunt Gardiner for more information.

Volume 3, Chapter 10 (Chapter 52)
Most of the following chapter is taken up with Mrs. Gardiner's detailed explanation of events leading to the wedding and Darcy's role in it. He had found Wickham, whom he persuaded to marry Lydia. Wickham's considerable "debts are to be paid . . . another thousand in addition to her own settled upon *her* [Lydia], and his commission purchased." All of this is Darcy's work, for Darcy considered it "his duty to step forward, and endeavor to remedy an evil, which had been brought on by himself" owing, Darcy says, "to his mistaken pride." Darcy and Mr. Gardiner had jointly arranged the wedding. Mrs. Gardiner concludes her letter by saying how

much she likes Mr. Darcy, who "wants nothing but a little more liveliness, and *that*, if he marry *prudently*, his wife may teach him" (324, 322, 324–325).

The rest of chapter 10 is taken up with Elizabeth's reaction to the letter and an encounter with Wickham. A lengthy passage of indirect speech conveys Elizabeth's reactions. "Her heart did whisper, that he had done it for her," but Darcy as "Brother-in-law of Wickham! Every kind of pride must revolt from the connection." Elizabeth personally was "humbled, but she was proud of" Darcy. She then encounters Wickham, who speaks to her openly about Darcy and his family. Elizabeth lets Wickham know clearly that she no longer believes his account of past affairs and relationships, yet as she and he "are brother and sister," she parts with him on not unfriendly terms (326, 329).

Volume 3, Chapter 11 (Chapter 53)

At the start of the next chapter, Elizabeth "was pleased to find that she had said enough to keep [Wickham] quiet." Mr. Bennet is no longer unfavorably disposed toward Wickham. "He simpers, and smirks, and makes love to us all." Mr. Bennet adds that he defies "even Sir William Lucas himself, to produce a more valuable son-in-law," words that will prove to be ironically incorrect by the end of the novel, when the extremely wealthy Mr. Darcy becomes a son-in-law. News reaches Longbourn that Bingley is to return to Netherfield. This time, unlike at the start of the novel, Mr. Bennet refuses to call on him. Three days after his arrival at Netherfield, Bingley and Darcy call on the Bennets at Longbourn. Elizabeth had concealed from Jane Darcy's role in Lydia's marriage "or to relate her own change of sentiment towards him." Darcy is largely silent during the visit, and Elizabeth "in such misery of shame" has to listen to her mother reveling in the news of the marriage of Lydia and Wickham. Elizabeth's "misery, for which years of happiness were to offer no compensation, received soon afterwards material relief, from observing how much the beauty of her sister re-kindled the admiration of her former lover" (330, 334, 337).

Volume 3, Chapter 12 (Chapter 54)

Volume 3, chapter 12, focuses on the fortunes of Elizabeth and Jane Bennet at "a large party assem-bled at Longbourn" (340). Jane spends the evening singled out by Bingley for his special attention. Elizabeth and Darcy are able to spend but brief moments together.

Volume 3, Chapter 13 (Chapter 55)

In the following chapter, Darcy leaves for 10 days in London, and Bingley continually calls on Jane at Longbourn. Elizabeth "smiled at the rapidity and ease with which an affair was finally settled, that had given them so many precious months of suspense and vexation." The engagement is announced and Elizabeth is careful not to mention to Jane the role of Darcy in parting her and Bingley previously, "for, though Jane had the most generous and forgiving heart in the world, [Elizabeth] knew it was a circumstance which must prejudice [Jane] against him [Darcy]." The chapter ends with a paragraph remarking upon the remarkable reversal of "misfortune" that had occurred to the Bennet family within a few weeks of Lydia's elopement (347, 350).

Volume 3, Chapter 14 (Chapter 56)

In the next chapter, Lady Catherine de Bourgh, responding to "a report of a most alarming nature," visits Longbourn to insist that Elizabeth make a promise *not* to marry Darcy. The two walk outside the house, and Lady Catherine de Bourgh confronts Elizabeth, who refuses at first to respond to the questions concerning a marriage between herself and Darcy. Lady Catherine asserts that Darcy "is engaged to my *daughter*" (Jane Austen's emphasis). She follows this dogmatic assertion with a lengthy catalogue of reasons why Elizabeth should not marry Darcy and why her daughter should. These range from the gratitude due to her for entertaining Elizabeth, her own "determined resolution," Lady Catherine's sense that her daughter and Darcy "are formed for each other." She then tells Elizabeth that her life as Darcy's wife will be miserable: "honour, decorum, prudence, nay, interest [in the financial as well as the emotional sense] forbid it," in short, the "alliance will be a disgrace," and will "ruin [Darcy] in the opinion of all his friends, and make him the contempt of the world." Elizabeth responds in a spirited manner to these insults and arguments. She counters them. Lady Catherine has no right to concern herself with Elizabeth's affairs; Elizabeth is socially equal to Darcy, the world will have "too much sense" to be outraged by the marriage. Elizabeth is "only resolved to act in that manner, which will in my [her] opinion, constitute my [her] happiness." Lady Catherine leaves Longbourn without sending "compliments" (353–356, 358) to Mrs. Bennet. To the very end, she is insulting.

Volume 3, Chapter 15 (Chapter 57)
Chapter 15 opens with Elizabeth's private reaction to the visit. She feels that Darcy's "notions of dignity" would probably outweigh other considerations and that she will not see him again. The family are surprised at Lady Catherine's visit. Mr. Bennet tells Elizabeth that he has received a letter from Mr. Collins congratulating him on Elizabeth's marriage, too. Mr. Bennet offends Elizabeth with his comments concerning a "Mr. Darcy, who never looks at any woman but to see a blemish, and who probably never looked at *you* in his life!" (Jane Austen's emphasis). Collins proceeds to tell Mr. Bennet how he would have dealt with Lydia, commends his Christian sense of "forgiveness," and adds that Charlotte, his wife, is pregnant: a male heir would eventually inherit Longbourn on Mr. Bennet's death. At the end of the chapter, however, in spite of what he considers to be his wit, Mr. Bennet "had most cruelly mortified [Elizabeth] by what he had said of Mr. Darcy's indifference, and she could do nothing but wonder at such a want of penetration" (361, 363–364).

Volume 3, Chapter 16 (Chapter 58)
Darcy appears with Bingley at Longbourn. The family go for a walk and Darcy and Elizabeth are together, and Elizabeth thanks him for his "unexampled kindness to [her] poor sister" Lydia. Darcy explains that his actions were taken out of consideration for her, Elizabeth, alone. Elizabeth tells Darcy that "her sentiments" have utterly transformed toward him. Darcy tells her that Lady Catherine told him of her visit to Elizabeth. This has the opposite effect of what Lady Catherine intended, as it provides Darcy with hope, for, if Elizabeth had "irrevocably decided against [Darcy, she] would have acknowledged it to Lady Catherine, frankly and openly." Darcy recollects their past misun-

derstandings and tells Elizabeth of his objects and motives for his actions. Both of them review the relationship of Bingley and Jane. She, Elizabeth, has told Darcy that "all her former prejudices [against him] had been removed" (365–366, 368).

Volume 3, Chapter 17 (Chapter 59)
Elizabeth tells an incredulous Jane that she and Darcy are engaged and she tells Jane of Darcy's "share in Lydia's marriage." Darcy and Elizabeth agree that he shall ask for Mr. Bennet's consent, although they are unsure how Mrs. Bennet will take the news. After Darcy has spoken to Mr. Bennet, her father asks Elizabeth, "what are you doing? Are you out of your senses, to be accepting this man? Have not you always hated him?" Her father's real concern is with Elizabeth's happiness. She confesses, "I love him." On hearing this, Mr. Bennet gives his consent. He says that he knows she "could be neither happy nor respectable, unless you truly esteemed your husband." Elizabeth reassures him and tells him "what Mr. Darcy had voluntarily done for Lydia." Her mother, on hearing the news from Elizabeth, reacts unlike her usual self. She "sat quite still, and [was] unable to utter a syllable." Mrs. Bennet quickly changes her opinion of Darcy and "stood in such awe of her intended son-in-law, that she ventured not to speak to him." Mr. Bennet regards Wickham as "perhaps" his "favourite" son-in-law but tells Elizabeth that he "shall like *your* husband quite as well as Jane's" (Jane Austen's emphasis) (374, 376–379).

Volume 3, Chapter 18 (Chapter 60)
The final two chapters tie up the loose ends. Elizabeth gets "Darcy to account for his having ever fallen in love with her." Darcy explains that "Lady Catherine's unjustifiable endeavours to separate [them] were the means of removing all [his] doubts." Elizabeth sends her aunt Gardiner a letter inviting her and her family to spend Christmas at Pemberley. Darcy informs Lady Catherine of the upcoming marriage, and Mr. Bennet does likewise to Mr. Collins. Charlotte arrives back at Lucas lodge "to get away till the storm was blown over." Elizabeth "looks forward with delight to the time when" she and Darcy can be at Pemberley (380–381, 383).

Volume 3, Chapter 19 (Chapter 61)
In the final chapter, the author tells her readers that Bingley purchased an estate "within thirty miles of" Pemberley. Kitty spent most of her time with Jane or Elizabeth and "Mary was the only daughter who remained at home." Lydia and Wickham live "unsettled," unhappy lives. Georgiana Darcy and Elizabeth drew closer to each other. Lady Catherine "condescended to wait on them at Pemberley" and with the Gardiners who "had been the means of uniting" Darcy and Elizabeth, they were always "on the most intimate terms" (385–388).

CRITICAL COMMENTARY

Immediate reactions of readers to *Pride and Prejudice* echo subsequent ones pointing to the novel's enduring qualities and critical heritage. Carey and Lea's 1832 American edition was noticed by the *National Gazette and Literary Register,* published in Philadelphia. The journal concludes its observations by noting, "If the American world will read novels, let us have those of which the moral is good, the text pure, and the instructiveness practical and domestic; entertaining and ingenious, but free from all poison." In 1815, the editor of John Murray's journal, the *Quarterly Review,* William Gifford, notes similar qualities on the other side of the Atlantic. He too thought that the novel would not corrupt morals and lacked the melodramatic qualities evident in gothic novels by Mrs. Radcliffe and others parodied by Jane Austen in her posthumously published *Northanger Abbey* (1817). Gifford wrote to John Murray, "I have for the first time looked into 'Pride and Prejudice'; and it is really a very pretty thing. No dark passages; no secret passages; no wind-howlings in long galleries; no drops of blood upon a rusty dagger-things that now should be left to ladies' maids and sentimental washer women," in other words, the ingredients of the gothic novel written by Mrs. Radcliffe and others. The dramatist Richard Brinsley Sheridan advised a Mrs. Sherriff, whom he met at a dinner party around the time of the first publication of *Pride and Prejudice,* "to buy it immediately, for it was one of the cleverest things he ever read."

In the preface to the *Memoir* of his sister Jane, Henry Austen writes that when the novel was first published, "a gentleman, celebrated for his literary attainments, advised a friend of the authoress to read it, adding, with more point than gallantry, 'I should like to know who is the author, for it is much too clever to have been written by a woman.'" Other contemporary readers were drawn to the characterization. John William Ward, the first Earl of Dudley (1781–1833), drew the attention of the wife of the Scottish philosopher Dugald Stewart (1753–1828) to Mr. Collins: "There is a parson," he wrote "quite admirable." Anne Isabella Milbanke, who was to marry Lord Byron, in 1813 described *Pride and Prejudice* as "at present the fashionable novel. It . . . contains more strength of character than other productions of this kind." But not all were pleased. Sir Humphry Davy (1778–1829), the distinguished chemist, wrote, "'Pride and Prejudice' I do not very much like. Want of interest is the fault I can least excuse in works of mere amusement, and however natural the picture of vulgar minds and manners is there given, it is unrelieved by the agreeable contrast of more dignified and refined characters occasionally captivating attention. Some power of new character is, however, ably displayed, and Mr. Bennett's [sic] indifference is in truth not exaggerated." Davy had literary interests and was acquainted with Wordsworth and Coleridge. However, he is not remembered today for his literary criticism but as a distinguished chemist and inventor primarily of laughing gas and a safety lamp for use in coal mines (Gilson, 104, 27, 26, 25, 26).

Jane Austen was critical of *Pride and Prejudice,* writing in a letter to her sister, Cassandra, on February 4, 1813, that it "is rather too light & sparkling;—it wants shade" (*Letters,* 203). However, critics and general readers have looked most favorably on the novel since its initial publication. After outlining the plot of a "very agreeable novel" in an unsigned review in the journal *Critical Review* shortly following its publication, the reviewer observes

The above is merely the brief outline of this very agreeable novel. An excellent lesson may be learned from the elopement of Lydia:—the work also shows the folly of letting young girls have their own way, and the danger which they incur in associating with the officers, who may be quartered in or near their residence. The character of Wickham is very well pourtrayed;—we fancy, that our authoress had Joseph Surface [a character in Sheridan's play *The School for Scandal* who seems to be charming and upright but in fact is a thorough going villain] before her eyes when she sketched it; as well as the lively Beatrice, when she drew the portrait of Elizabeth. Many such silly women as Mrs. Bennet may be found; and numerous parsons like Mr. Collins, who are every thing to every body; and servile in the extreme to their superiors. Mr. Collins is indeed a notable object.

The sentiments, which are dispersed over the work, do great credit to the *sense* and *sensibility* of the authoress. The line she draws between the prudent and the mercenary in matrimonial concerns, may be useful to our fair readers. . . . We cannot conclude, without repeating our approbation of this performance, which rises very superior to any novel we have lately met with in the delineation of domestic scenes. Nor is there one character which appears flat, or obtrudes itself upon the notice of the reader with troublesome impertinence. There is not one person in the drama with whom we could readily dispense;—they have all their proper places; and fill their several stations, with great credit to themselves, and much satisfaction to the reader (Southam, I: 46–47).

Sir Walter Scott, a most astute critic, wrote in his journal on March 14, 1826, that he reread

> for the third time at least, Miss Austen's very finely written novel of *Pride and Prejudice*. That young lady had a talent for describing the involvements, and feelings, and characters of ordinary life, which is to me the most wonderful I ever met with. The Big Bow-wow strain I can do myself like any now going; but the exquisite touch, which renders ordinary commonplace things and characters interesting, from the truth of the description and the sentiment, is denied to me. Scott adds, "What a pity such a gifted creature died so early!" (Gilson, 475).

Charlotte Brontë also recognizes Jane Austen's ability to convey the realities of everyday life. However, in a letter to the critic George Henry Lewes (1817–79), she asks him why he "like[s]" Jane Austen "so very much" and expresses reservations about Lewes's suggestion that *Pride and Prejudice* should be regarded as a model for her own writing. For Charlotte Brontë, the novel gives "an accurate, daguerreotyped portrait of a commonplace face! a carefully-fenced, highly-cultivated garden, with neat borders and delicate flowers." Regrettably, there is "no glance of a bright, vivid physiognomy, no open country, no fresh air, no blue hill, no bonny beck. I should hardly like," she writes to Lewes on January 12, 1848, "to live with her ladies and gentlemen, in their elegant but confined houses" (Southam, I: 126–128).

Lewes, in an essay, "The Novels of Jane Austen," in *Blackwood's Edinburgh Magazine* in 1859, compares Jane Austen to Shakespeare. For Lewes, Jane Austen "makes her very noodles [comic characters such as Mr. Collins, Lady Catherine de Bourgh, Mrs. Bennet, and others] inexhaustible amusing, yet accurately real. We never tire of her characters." He praises, as does Scott, her realism and ability to depict everyday life (Kaminsky, 91–92). In a review of *Jane Eyre* written 12 years earlier, Lewes refers to "the greatness of Miss Austen," to "her marvellous dramatic power" (Ashton, 82). Another Victorian admirer of Jane Austen, herself a fine novelist, Margaret Oliphant, observes in "Miss Austen and Miss Mitford," *Blackwood's Edinburgh Magazine* (March 1870), that "Lady Catherine de Bourgh and the housekeeper at Pemberley—conventional types of the heaven above and the abyss below—are the only breaks which Miss Austen ever permits herself upon the level of her squirearchy." For Mrs. Oliphant, "Nothing could be more lifelike, more utterly real" than the Bennet family. She particularly admires the portrait of Mr. Collins who "stands before us tall and grave and pompous, wrapt in a cloud of solemn vanity, servility, stupidity and spitefulness, but without the faintest gleam of self-consciousness or suspicion of the ridiculous figure he cuts." Yet Mrs. Oliphant wonders "whether our author is in reality the gentle cynic she has concluded her to be, or if she has produced all these marvels of selfish folly unawares, without knowing what she was doing, or meaning anything by it" (Southam, I: 215, 219, 221).

In a lecture "The Lesson of Balzac" given in 1905, Henry James notes Jane Austen's "little touches of human truth, little glimpses of steady vision, little master-strokes of imagination." These elements of artistry have been ignored in the "beguiled infatuation, a sentimentalized vision" embodied in the popular view of "our dear, everybody's dear Jane" (Southam, I: 32). Virginia Woolf, writing in the *Common Reader*, also draws attention, like Henry James, to Jane Austen as "mistress of a much deeper emotion than appears on the surface" (142). The serious nature of Jane Austen's art and in particular its exemplification in *Pride and Prejudice* is fully explored in Mary Lascelles's *Jane Austen and Her Art* (1939). With Lascelles's work, "the day of the 'amateur' essayist addressing 'the common reader' was now past. Henceforth, criticism was seen to be a serious activity" (Grey, 108). Lascelles stresses Jane Austen's narrative art and form based on "the symmetry of correspondence and antithesis. . . . This pattern is formed by diverging and converging lines, by the movement of two people who are impelled apart until they reach a climax of mutual hostility, and thereafter blend their courses towards mutual understanding and amity" (Lascelles, 160).

D. W. Harding's "Regulated Hatred: An Aspect of the Work of Jane Austen" was originally presented as a lecture to the Literary Society of Manchester University on March 1939. Published in *Scrutiny* 8 (1940), it emphasizes the satirical element in her work. Jane Austen uses "caricature" in, for instance, her depiction of characters such as Mr. Collins and Lady Catherine de Bourgh. "The implications of her caricatures as criticism of real people in real society," he writes, "is brought out in the way they dovetail into their social setting." Charlotte, who is "decent, stodgy . . . puts up cheerfully with Mr. Collins as a husband; and Elizabeth can never quite become reconciled to the idea that her friend is the wife of her comic monster" (Harding, 13–14). Harding's focus on the satirical and ironic elements of Austen's art becomes

a framework for much subsequent criticism, especially in the period of close reading, of attention to the words on the page, which lasted from the 1930s to the middle 1970s. For instance, Dorothy Van Ghent in her *The English Novel: Form and Function* (1953) isolates in the opening chapter of *Pride and Prejudice* the use of the words "property," and "fortune," "possession," "establishment," and "business." These words have, she writes, "consistently been setting up the impulsion of economic interest against those nonutilitarian interests implied by the words 'feelings' and 'love'" (Grey, 302).

Irony and its implications is the focus of Marvin Mudrick's *Jane Austen: Irony as Defense and Discovery* (1952). In his chapter on *Pride and Prejudice*, as in her other work, Jane Austen "deals with the distinction between false moral values and true," but she is dealing with something more complex, the relationship between the self and society (107). In his introduction to *A Collection of Critical Essays* (1963), Ian Watt recognizes that "in general, the criticism of Jane Austen in the last two decades is incomparably the richest and most illuminating that has appeared." Watt also noted that "recent criticism has perhaps failed to give the nature of Jane Austen's social and moral assumptions an equally exacting analysis" (13). Subsequent studies attempted to remedy this want of emphasis. For instance, linguistic perspectives were used in Norman Page's *The Language of Jane Austen* (1972), which has chapters on "Style in Jane Austen's Novels," her use of syntax, and the way in which she uses letters in her novels. Jane Austen's vocabulary, sentence structure, and "Modes of Address are the subject of K. C. Phillipps's *Jane Austen's English* (1970), with its most useful index to the words actually used in her novels (225–229). Both these studies place Jane Austen's use of language within a specific historical framework and make clear the historical antecedents at work in her application of words and phrases. To take one example from many, Barbara Hardy's *Reading of Jane Austen* (1975) is a subtle exploration by a superb close critical reader of Jane Austen's "flexible medium, a capacity to glide easily from sympathy to detachment, from one mind to many minds, from solitary scenes to social gatherings" (14).

There are studies that placed Jane Austen within a historical and literary context. Frank W. Bradbrook's *Jane Austen and Her Predecessors* (1966) demonstrates how thoroughly her novels are permeated by contemporary literary allusions. Alistair M. Duckworth's *The Improvement of the Estate: A Study of Jane Austen's Novels* (1971) places her subject within an 18th-century "providential" novel and a more contemporary tradition. Duckworth uses the word "estate" as a central metaphor in Jane Austen's novels, in which there is an inherent conservatism. The union of Darcy and Elizabeth, for instance, represents "the vitalized reconstitution of a social totality, the dynamic compromise between past and present, the simultaneous reception of what is valuable in an inheritance and the liberation of the originality, energy and spontaneity in the living moment" (Grey, 314). A similar perspective is conveyed in Marilyn Butler's influential *Jane Austen and the War of Ideas* (1975), which treats its subject's political, educational, and literary frameworks, concluding that *Pride and Prejudice* is essentially a "conservative novel" (214). However, such studies give way in the 1970s and after to works increasingly influenced by theoretical considerations. Thus, for instance, Steven Cohan and Linda M. Shires's *Telling Stories: A Theoretical Analysis of Narrative Fiction* (1988) focuses on structuralist and poststructuralist methodology. It instances *Pride and Prejudice* as an example of a narratological perspective to fiction. In recent years, feminist perspectives have focused prominently on Jane Austen. Patricia Meyer Spacks's *The Female Imagination* (1975) argues that Elizabeth Bennet's development in the novel is a "paradigm of adolescent potential fulfilled." Spacks writes that Elizabeth in the course of the novel learns to appreciate "the positive advantages of maturity over childishness, even in a society whose rigidities offer protection to the continued immaturity . . . characteristic of most of its members" (155). Nina Auerbach, in her *Communities of Women: An Idea in Fiction* (1978), writes that Jane Austen's perspective of women is a negative one. In the world of *Pride and Prejudice* "the malevolent power of the mother is ennobled by being transferred to the hero, and the female community of Longbourn, an oppressive blank in a dense society, is dispersed with relief in the solidity of marriage" (55).

Feminist ideas circulating in the 18th century, the writings of Mary Wollstonecraft, Fanny Burney, and Maria Edgeworth, form the context of discourse in a study such as Alison Sulloway's *Jane Austen and the Province of Womanhood* (1989). For Sulloway, the marriages at the end of *Pride and Prejudice*, the union of Darcy and Elizabeth, Jane and Bingley, exemplify that "Christian hope" and "infectious joy" . . . "triumph over [Jane Austen's] rational social cynicism," which recognizes, as D. W. Harding and others have acknowledged, "the bizarre compensatory equations built into every marriage" (217). Claudia L. Johnson, on the other hand, in *Jane Austen: Women, Politics, and the Novel* (1988), views *Pride and Prejudice* as exhibiting a "conservative yearning for a strong, attentive, loving, and paradoxically perhaps, at times even submissive authority" (73).

Pride and Prejudice has been the recipient of eclectic perspectives, from those emphasizing power structures, Marxist analyses, class issues, and cultural concerns, among other approaches. To instance five other readings from many, Joseph Wiesenfarth's chapter "*Pride and Prejudice*: Manners as Self-Definition" in his *Gothic Manners and the Classic English Novel* (1988) refines earlier observations on the novel found in his *The Errand of Form: An Assay of Jane Austen's Art* (1967) and "Austen and Apollo" in *Jane Austen Today* (1975). Drawing on ideas in the writings of Mikhail Bahktin, Wiesenfarth judiciously observes that "Jane Austen make a case in *Pride and Prejudice* for a prudent marriage and against a mercenary marriage" (25). He concluded his analysis, "Jane Austen classically articulates *Pride and Prejudice* as a novel of manners by casting it in the form of a case that dramatizes the development of the cardinal virtues in two individuals of complementary character whose freedom to love each other satisfies society's concern for . . . coherence and continuity" (40). Oliver MacDonagh, in his *Jane Austen: Real and Imagined Worlds* (1991), views Charlotte's marriage as a "career" move based on mercenary, pragmatic calculation. Juliet McMaster's "Talking about Talk in *Pride and Prejudice*," in *Jane Austen's Business: Her World and Her Profession*

(1996), focuses on speech and the use of language in the novel. She agrees with Tony Tanner's summary of *Pride and Prejudice* as "a novel in which the most important events are the fact that a man changes his manners and a young woman changes her mind" (Introduction, *Pride and Prejudice* [1995]. 7). She adds that "these changes were not accidental: each [Darcy and Elizabeth] effects the change in the other, and through their powers in language" (93).

Two other readings of the novel, both published in the year 2004, suffice to demonstrate the protean quality of recent approaches that this deeply admired novel generates. The distinguished German critic of 19th- and 20th-century fiction in English, Paul Goetsch, finds earlier antecedents for the various kinds of "laughter" found in *Pride and Prejudice*. Goetsch follows an analysis of laughter in the novel with the comment "that women and men like [it] for different reasons." The former may prefer "Jane Austen's sensitivity to the position of women in society and the moments of autonomy and freedom from social restraints the Elizabeths and Lydias of her world enjoy." On the other hand, men may prefer Jane Austen "because the fascinating, defiant female protagonist can be tamed after all." Goetsch concludes, "It is of course equally possible that both women and men like to read the novel for the same or some of the same reasons" ("Laughter in *Pride and Prejudice*," in *Redefining the Modern*, 40, 41). Emily Auerbach's chapter "The Liveliness of Your Mind: *Pride and Prejudice*," in her *Searching for Jane Austen*, presents a many-faceted perspective on the novel and its author. She concludes that "the humor between Elizabeth and Darcy will enrich, not polarize, their union. . . . Like Elizabeth and Darcy blending liveliness and judgment, Austen's own fiction offers sparkling amusement and serious instruction, barbed wit and gentle wisdom" (165).

CHARACTERS

Annesley, Mrs. (Chapter 45) Elizabeth and the Gardiners meet Mrs. Annesley on their visit to Pemberley. Mrs. Annesley is "a genteel, agreeable-looking woman" with whom Georgiana Darcy lives in London. Her "endeavor to introduce some kind of discourse proved her to be more truly well bred than either" Mrs. Hurst or Caroline Bingley (267).

Bennet, Mr. (Chapters 1–3, 7, 13–15, 18, 20, 22–24, 39, 41–42, 47–53, 55, 59–61) Mr. Bennet is a complex character. An attorney, he has an annual income of £2,000 and five unmarried daughters, all of whom live at home, Longbourn. He "was so odd a mixture of quick parts, sarcastic humour, reserve and caprice, that the experience of three and twenty years had been insufficient to make his wife understand his character." He frequently retreats into his library to escape his family, and especially his wife, to whom he is particularly sardonic and satirical, telling her, for instance, that he has "a high respect for [her] nerves. They are my old friends. I have heard you mention them with consideration these twenty years at least" (5). Elizabeth is his favorite daughter: When Darcy asks formally for her hand, Mr. Bennet is anxious to discover the extent of Elizabeth's true feelings for him (376). As he has no male heir, his Longbourn estate is "entailed . . . on a distant relation" (28), a fact that causes Mrs. Bennet much distress. Lydia's irresponsibility makes him realize that he should have taken much more interest in the development of his daughters. He participates in making sure that she marries Wickham (with Darcy's assistance) but is still somewhat deficient in dealing with Kitty, who remains at home. Mr. Bennet returns "to all his former indolence" (309).

Bennet, Mrs. (Chapters 1–3, 5, 7, 9–10, 12–15, 17–26, 37, 39–42, 47–56, 58–59, 61) Mrs. Bennet (née Gardiner) is a comic character, the mother of five daughters, and the daughter of a Meryton attorney. "She was a woman of mean understanding, little information, and uncertain temper. When she was discontented she fancied herself nervous. The business of her life was to get her daughters married; its solace was visiting and news" (5). Her relationship with her husband is clearly not an easy one; she is continually being teased by him and he retreats into his library, leaving her to deal with their daughters. Lydia is her favorite daughter. Garrulous throughout most of the novel, she is silent when learning of the engagement of Elizabeth and Darcy, quickly changing her previously hostile attitude toward him. She "stood in such awe of her intended son-in-law, that she

"Mrs. Bennet and her two youngest girls," from Hugh Thompson, illustration to *Pride and Prejudice (London: George Allen edition of 1894)*

ventured not to speak to him" (379). Earlier her indiscretion had been a reason for Darcy's trying to distance himself and Bingley from the Bennet family. Her "values are mindlessly bourgeois" (Wiesenfarth, *Gothic Manners:* 36).

Bennet, Catherine (Kitty) (Chapters 2, 14–15, 17, 19–20, 23, 26, 39, 41–42, 46–49, 53, 55–56, 58–59, 61) The fourth Bennet daughter, who, according to her father, "has no discretion

in her coughs . . . she times them ill" (6). When he leaves the room Mr. Bennet gives her permission to "cough as much as you chuse" (8). As a weak-willed, easily influenced girl, she is led astray by Lydia, her younger sister. She is "weak-spirited, irritable, and completely under Lydia's guidance." In common with Lydia, she is "ignorant, idle, and vain" (12, 13). However, she can be influenced for the good, and once Lydia has left home, there are possibilities for improvement. At the conclusion of the novel, she, "to her very material advantage, spent the chief of her time with her two elder sisters," Jane and Elizabeth. "In society so superior to what she had generally known, her improvement was great." Catherine's, or Kitty's, temper was not "so ungovernable" as Lydia's "and, removed from" Lydia's influence, "she became, by proper attention and management, less irritable, less ignorant, and less insipid" (385). She was not allowed to visit Lydia (Mrs. Wickham). For Emily Auerbach, "the fretful Kitty . . . seems to have inherited her mother's frenzied nerves" (*Searching*, 144).

Bennet, Elizabeth (mentioned throughout the novel) Elizabeth's perspective is at the core of the narrative, which revolves around her, and "the structure of the novel" may be conceived "in terms of Darcy's two proposals to Elizabeth" (*Gothic Manners*, 31). The second daughter of the Bennets, 20 years old, she is the heroine of *Pride and Prejudice*. "She had a lively, playful disposition, which delighted in any thing ridiculous" (12). Most of the plot centers around her developing and changing relationship with Fitzwilliam Darcy, who finds that her face "was rendered uncommonly intelligent by the beautiful expression of her dark eyes" (23). At the close of the novel, they marry. She speaks to Darcy, who is lacking in "liveliness" in a "lively, sportive" (387) way and he is attracted to her because of her "liveliness of mind" (380). The author Jane Austen identified with many of Elizabeth Bennet's characteristics, writing to her sister, Cassandra Austen, on January 29, 1813, "I must confess I think [Elizabeth] as delightful a creature as ever appeared in print, & how I shall be able to tolerate those who do not like *her* at least, I do not know" (*Letters*, 201 Jane Austen's emphasis). Resilient, she "was not formed for ill humour," and when Wickham, against her expectations, fails to appear at the Netherfield ball, Elizabeth "could not dwell long on her spirits . . . she was soon able to make a voluntary transition to the oddities of her cousin" Mr. Collins (90). She was adaptable, and "it was her business to be satisfied—and certainly her temper to be happy" (239). Courageous and at times opinionated, she is not easily intimidated. She observes, "There is a stubbornness about me

that never can bear to be frightened at the will of others. My courage always rises with every attempt to intimidate me" (174), and she will not be bullied or cowed by Lady Catherine de Bourgh. Her father's favorite, she has prejudices; for instance, she is taken in, as are so many others, by Wickham's superficial charms.

An optimist, united with Darcy, she tells him, "You must learn some of my philosophy. Think only of the past as its remembrance gives you pleasure" (368–369). When Elizabeth is confronted with real distress such as Lydia's disgrace, Jane's sorrow, her own mortification and self-reproach, she no longer laughs her problems away, and refuses to dwell on the past. At times, her judgments of people and situations—Wickham is the most obvious example—are shown to be incorrect. She is, however, not afraid to admit that she has been wrong, and she cares deeply for her elder sister, Jane. For instance, when the family learns of Lydia's shameful behavior, Elizabeth, who is staying at Lambton near Pemberley, "was wild to be at home—to hear, to see, to be upon the spot, to share with Jane in the cares that must now fall wholly upon her, in a family so deranged" (280). Quick to rush to judgment, she believes that her close friend Charlotte Lucas, when she agrees to Collins's proposal of marriage, has sacrificed "every better feeling to worldly advantage" (125) and finds it hard to accept that Charlotte is able to find contentment in her marital situation.

Bennet, Jane (Chapters 1, 3–13, 15, 17–18, 20–21, 23–27, 30, 32–34, 36–42, 44, 46–61) The eldest and most beautiful Bennet daughter, Jane is 22 years old. Elizabeth tells her, "You are too good. Your sweetness and disinterestedness are really angelic. . . . *You* wish to think all the world respectable, and are hurt if I speak ill of any body. *I* only want to think *you* perfect" (Jane Austen's emphasis: 134–135). Mr. Bennet tells her and her fiancé, Bingley, "You are each of you so complying, that nothing will ever be resolved on; so easy, that every servant will cheat you; and so generous, that you will always exceed your income" (348). Her love for Bingley, separation from him, and eventual union with him form an important component of the plot and of Elizabeth's evolving response to Darcy. An optimist, she is willing to see positives even in Caroline Bingley, who she believes "is incapable of wilfully deceiving any one" (119). Elizabeth has quickly seen through Caroline: Elizabeth has "more quickness of observation and less pliancy of temper than her sister" (15). Jane is more pragmatic than Elizabeth. She is not so opposed to Charlotte Lucas's engagement to Collins as her sister, telling Elizabeth, "Remember that she [Charlotte] is one of a large family: that as to fortune, it is a most eligible match; . . . she may feel something like regard and esteem for our cousin" (135). During Bingley's absence, "whatever she felt she was desirous of concealing" and she has a "steady mildness" (129).

Bennet, Lydia (Chapters 1–3, 7, 9, 12–18, 20, 26, 37, 39, 41–42, 46–67, 51–53, 61) Irresponsible, "self-willed" (213), and spoiled, a younger version of her mother, Lydia is the youngest of the Bennet daughters. She is "a stout, well-grown girl of fifteen, with a fine complexion and good-humoured countenance; a favourite with her mother, whose affection had brought her into public at an early age" (45). She has a "disdain of all restraint" (231), coupled with an "ungovernable . . . temper" (385), and a "sort of natural self-consequence" (45). Elizabeth warns her father of the dangers if "he will not take . . . trouble of checking her exuberant spirits" (231), and she proves to be correct, for Lydia is "absolutely resolved" (322), to be with Wickham in spite of her "disgraceful situation . . . She cared for none of her friends, she wanted no help of [Darcy's], she would not hear of leaving Wickham. She was sure they should be married some time or other, and it did not much signify when" (322–323). She is unrepentant and unashamed and boasts of being the first to be married. At the conclusion of the novel, "Lydia was Lydia still," untamed, unabashed, wild, noisy, and fearless (315).

Elizabeth is aware of the underlying reasons for Lydia's behavior: "She has never been taught to think on serious subjects . . . she has been given up to nothing but amusement and vanity. She has been allowed to dispose of her time in the most idle and frivolous manner" (283). Spoiled by her mother and ignored by her father, she is the "silliest" (29) girl in the area. The "ignorance and emptiness of her mind" (231) causes Elizabeth to despair. "Oh! thoughtless, thoughtless Lydia!" when she reads the letter sent to Harriet Forster on her elopement with Wickham (7, 17, 5). Somewhat ironically, Lydia and Elizabeth have much in common. Both are attracted to the same charming rogue, Wickham. Elizabeth, as well as Lydia, is capable of acting with a "total want of propriety" (198). Both form opinions quickly and are unafraid of authority. Elizabeth confesses, "I dearly love a laugh" (57). However, Jane Austen "distinguishes between" Elizabeth and Lydia "by using the word 'fun' only in association with Lydia, not Elizabeth. Lydia titters, 'we had such fun,' 'it was such fun,' 'such a good piece of fun' . . . even when describing her own disgraceful behaviour" (220). She "seems impervious to any emotion other than impatience and fun" (*Searching,* 138–139). Of course, the role Darcy plays in her marriage to Wickham is an important element in the development of the relationship between Darcy and Elizabeth. It puts their new relationship to a test and "deepens it through empathy" (*Errand of Form,* 70). And it demonstrates to what lengths Darcy is prepared to go for love of Elizabeth.

Bennet, Mary (Chapters 2–3, 5–6, 12–13, 17–18, 22, 29, 47, 55, 61) Mary is the third Bennet daughter. She "piqued herself upon the solidity of her reflections" (20). The omniscient narrator informs her readers that "Mary, who having, in consequence of being the only plain one in the family, worked hard for knowledge and accomplishments, was always impatient for display." Willing to sing or play the piano, she "had neither genius nor taste." Her time is spent reading what appear to be moralistic works. Further, "though vanity had given her application, it had given her likewise a pedantic air and conceited manner, which would have injured a higher degree of excellence than she had reached." She likes to show off in public with her "accomplishments" (25), as opposed to her looks or liveliness. Lydia and Kitty perceive her as a bore. At the end of the novel, "Mary was the only daughter who remained at home," where "she was necessarily drawn from the pursuit of accomplishments by Mrs. Bennet's being quite unable to sit alone." She "was obliged to mix more with the world." Although "she could still moralize over every morning visit . . . she was no longer mortified by comparisons between her sisters' beauty and her own" (386). She shows a liking for Mr. Collins. She "might have been prevailed on to accept him" if circumstances had been different. "She rated his abilities much higher than any of the others" did (124).

Bingley, Caroline (Chapters 3–4, 6–12, 17–18, 21, 24, 26, 33, 43, 45, 55, 60–61) Younger sister of Bingley, she and her sister, Louisa (Mrs. Hurst), "were in fact very fine ladies; not deficient in good humour when they were pleased . . . but proud and conceited. They were rather handsome, had been educated in one of the best private seminaries in town, had a fortune of twenty thousand pounds, were in the habit of . . . associating with people of rank." From "a respectable family in the north of England [this] circumstance [was] more deeply impressed on their memories than that their brother's fortune and their own had been acquired by trade" (15). Caroline has designs on Darcy and is jealous of Elizabeth Bennet when she perceives Darcy's preference for her. She "was very deeply mortified by Darcy's marriage: but as she thought it advisable to retain the right of visiting at Pemberley, she dropt all her resentment" (387).

Bingley, Charles (Chapters 1–4, 8–12, 15, 17–18, 21, 23–25, 33–37, 40, 43–44, 53–55, 58–59, 61) He is described by the author as possessing "the easiness, openness, ductility" of temper. Bingley, who "inherited property to the amount of nearly a hundred thousand pounds from his father . . . had the firmest reliance, and of his [Darcy's] judgment the highest opinion." Unlike his friend Darcy, "Bingley was sure of being liked wherever he appeared" (15–16). Elizabeth notes Bingley's "want of proper resolution which now made him the slave of his designing friends" (133), and Darcy writes to Elizabeth, "Bingley has great natural modesty, with a stronger dependence on my judgment than on his own" (199). He falls in

love with Jane almost the first time he sees her, but allows his sisters and Darcy to convince him that their relationship would be inappropriate. Bingley's feelings for Jane continue, and they are reunited and marry. Mr. Bennet tells her, "Your tempers [Jane's and Bingley's] are by no means unlike. You are each of you so complying, that nothing will ever be resolved on; so easy, that every servant will cheat you; and so generous, that you will always exceed your income" (348). After their marriage, Bingley "bought an estate . . . and Jane and Elizabeth, in addition to every other source of happiness, were within thirty miles of each other" (385).

Carter, Captain (Chapters 7, 9) Before Wickham joins the militia in Meryton, Lydia Bennet expresses her "admiration of Captain Carter, and her hope of seeing him . . . as he was going the next morning to London" (29). He is a device to demonstrate the foolishness of Lydia.

Chamberlayne, Mr. (Chapter 39) Another militia officer stationed in Meryton used to illustrate the irresponsibility of Lydia and her sister Kitty Bennet. A junior officer in Colonel Forster's regiment, at one of the Colonel's and Mrs. Forster's house parties, Lydia tells Elizabeth and Jane that she and Kitty "dressed up Chamberlayne in woman's clothes, on purpose to pass for a lady,—only think what fun! . . . and you cannot imagine how well he looked! . . . Lord! how I laughed!" (221).

Collins, William (Chapters 13–30, 32–33, 37–38, 48, 56–57, 60) The clergyman nephew of Mr. Bennet and heir to Meryton. "He was a tall, heavy looking young man of five and twenty. His air was grave and stately, and his manners were very formal" (64). Further, he "was not a sensible man and the deficiency of nature had been but little assisted by education or society." An exceedingly prolix letter writer, "the greatest part of his life having been spent under the guidance of an illiterate and miserly father," a "fortunate chance" recommendation secured for him the reasonably wealthy rectorship of Hunsford in Kent. Dependent on the good graces of Lady Catherine de Bourgh, "the respect which he felt for her high rank . . . his veneration for her as his patroness, mingling with a very good opinion of himself, of his authority as a clergyman, and his rights as a rector, made him altogether a mixture of pride and obsequiousness, self-importance and humility" (70). Servile to those he perceives as his superiors, Collins is a snob, pompous, and arrogant to those he feels are inferiors. An object of Jane Austen's humor and satire, he is cut down to size by Elizabeth's rejection of his marriage proposal. Collins quickly rebounds to propose to Charlotte Lucas, who succeeds in taming him.

Darcy, Lady Anne, née Fitzwilliam (deceased) (Chapters 16, 56)   The late mother of Fitzwilliam Darcy, sister of Lady Catherine de Bourgh, and the daughter of an earl. Apparently Lady Anne and Lady Catherine planned a marriage between their children, Fitzwilliam and Anne, shortly after their births. This is the "tacit engagement" insisted on by Lady Catherine when she tries to prevent Elizabeth from marrying Darcy (355).

Darcy, Fitzwilliam (Chapters 3, 5–12, 15–21, 24–26, 29–37, 40–47, 50–61)   The exceedingly wealthy "hero" of the novel, with an annual income of £10,000 a year. When he initially appears at the Meryton ball, he "soon drew the attention of the room by his fine, tall person, handsome features, noble mien; and the report which was in general circulation within five minutes after his entrance, of his having ten thousand a year." However, "he was discovered to be proud, to be above his company, and above being pleased" (10). The perception that he is arrogant, snobbish, and aloof alienates Elizabeth Bennet and others. Her initial dislike of him gains reinforcement through Wickham's account of Darcy's apparent mistreatment of him. Elizabeth, however, undergoes a transformation in her perception of Darcy, who is shown to have integrity, nobility, and sensitivity. Others reveal his real role regarding Wickham's activities, his outstanding qualities as the guardian of Pemberley. His discreet handling of the Wickham-Lydia affair, his bringing Bingley and Jane back together, and other revelations change Elizabeth's attitude toward him. He confesses to Elizabeth, "I cannot fix on the hour,

or the spot, or the look, or the words, which laid the foundation" of his love for her. "It is too long ago. I was in the middle before I knew it *had* begun" (380: Jane Austen's emphasis). He and Elizabeth are equals enjoying debate.

Darcy, Georgiana (Chapters 8, 10, 16, 23–24, 29, 33, 35, 37, 43–46, 52, 54, 58, 60–61)   Darcy's younger sister. "Miss Darcy was tall, and on a larger scale than Elizabeth; and though little more than sixteen, her figure was formed, and her appearance womanly and graceful. She was less handsome than her brother, but there was a sense of good humour in her face, and her manners were perfectly unassuming and gentle" (261). The initial information in the novel about her is from Wickham, who tells Elizabeth Bennet that "she is too much like her brother,—very, very proud. . . . Since her father's death, her home has been London where a lady lives with her, and superintends her education" (I: 16). Later the reader discovers that she is shy rather than proud, unassuming, and good-natured. When first in London, she was looked after by a Mrs. Younge, who on a trip to the seaside resort of Ramsgate with Georgiana, then 15, assisted Wickham in gaining her affection. Loyal to her brother, Darcy, Georgiana told him of the situation and Darcy saved her from the entanglement, Wickham's intention being to gain her £30,000 fortune. At the end of the novel, she makes her home at Pemberley: she "had the highest opinion in the world of Elizabeth; though at first often listened with an astonishment bordering on alarm, at her lively, sportive, manner of talking to her brother" (387–388).

Darcy, Mr. (deceased) (Chapters 16, 35)   Darcy's father, who owned Pemberley and has been dead for five years before the narrative unfolds. Wickham describes him "as one of the best men that ever lived" (78). Wickham's father was the steward of his Pemberley estates and was most efficient, so much so that Mr. Darcy senior became the godfather of George, his son. He "liberally bestowed" kindness on young George, paid for his schooling and time at Cambridge University, and also informally provided for him in his will. Wickham kept his "vicious propensities" (199–200) from Darcy's father.

Dawson (Chapter 37) Lady Catherine de Bourgh's long-suffering maid. She "does not object to the Barouche box," the driver's box in which she is happy to travel, according to Lady Catherine, to make room inside the Barouche carriage for others (II: 14).

De Bourgh, Lady Catherine (Chapters 13–14, 16, 19, 26, 28–32, 37, 48, 56–58, 60–61) Fitzwilliam Darcy's aunt, "a tall, large woman with strongly-marked features, which might once have been handsome. Her air was not conciliating, nor was her manner of receiving them [Sir William Lucas and Elizabeth Bennet], such as to make her visitors forget their inferior rank." In addition, "She was not rendered formidable by silence; but whatever she said, was spoken in so authoritative a tone, as marked her self-importance" (162). Owner of Rosings and its surroundings, she is a snob and a bully. She tries to intimidate Elizabeth Bennet into not marrying Darcy. Elizabeth's integrity, refusal to be cowed, and high intelligence are contrasted with Lady Catherine's snobbish, arrogant, and dictatorial assumptions. For Lady Catherine, her daughter, Miss Anne, and Darcy "are destined for each other by the voice of every member of their respective houses." As she tells Elizabeth, "and what is to divide them? The upstart pretensions of a young woman without family, connections, or fortune. Is this to be endured!" (356). She makes things worse for herself by telling Darcy of Elizabeth's defiant response. This encourages him to renew his courtship of her. Lady Catherine is a micromanager poking her nose into other people's affairs. At Rosings "whenever any of the cottagers were disposed to be quarrelsome, discontented or too poor, she sallied forth into the village to settle their differences, silence their complaints, and scold them into harmony and plenty" (169). At the end of the novel, although "extremely indignant on the marriage of her nephew . . . she condescended to wait" on Darcy and Elizabeth "at Pemberley, in spite of that pollution which its woods had received, not merely from the presence of such a mistress, but

the visits of [Elizabeth's] uncle and aunt from the city" (388).

De Bourgh, Miss Anne (Chapters 14, 16, 19, 28–31, 37, 41, 48, 52, 56) According to Maria Lucas, "She is quite a little creature. Who would have thought she could be so thin and small!" Elizabeth sees her as "sickly and cross' (158). The only child of Lady Catherine, her companion is Mrs. Jenkinson, who spoils and overprotects her. Dominated by her mother, who with her late sister, Darcy's mother, has agreed to a "tacit engagement" of their children" (355) that comes to nothing.

De Bourgh, Sir Lewis (deceased) (Chapter 13) The deceased husband of Lady Catherine de Bourgh, mentioned briefly in a letter from William Collins to Mr. Bennet (62).

Denny, Mr. (Chapters 14–16, 18, 39, 41, 47) An officer in the militia based in Meryton under the command of Colonel Forster. Denny introduces his old friend Wickham into the militia regiment. It emerges that Denny, mentioned frequently by Lydia, had foreknowledge of Wickham's intentions toward her.

Fitzwilliam, Colonel (Chapters 30–36, 41, 47) The younger son of an earl "about thirty, not handsome, but in person and address most truly the gentleman" (171). Darcy's cousin and with Darcy joint guardian of Georgiana Darcy. Not as wealthy as Darcy, he must make a favorable marriage, paying "some attention to money." At Rosings, he forms a friendship with Elizabeth. As a younger son he is "inured to self-denial and dependence" (183). He is much less reserved than Darcy, "entering into conversation directly with the readiness and ease of a well-bred man, and talked very pleasantly" (171). He serves as a "counterbalance" to Darcy, who "had considerable patronage in the church, and his cousin could have none at all" (181).

Forster, Colonel (Chapters 6–7, 9, 12, 14, 39, 41–42, 46–48, 50) Commander of the militia regiment quartered in Meryton for the winter, and marries his much younger wife, Harriet, while in

Meryton. The regiment moves to Brighton, and Harriet invites Lydia to stay. Lydia then elopes with Wickham, a member of Forster's regiment. Forster has no involvement in Wickham's activities and demonstrates his integrity and honor by trying to track Wickham and Lydia down once they have eloped. He then "with kindest concern . . . came to Longbourn, and broke his apprehensions to us in a manner most creditable to his heart." Jane adds, "I am sincerely grieved for him and Mrs. F., but no one can throw any blame on them" (275).

Forster, Mrs. Harriet (Chapters 39, 41–42, 47, 50) Recently married to the older Colonel Forster, "a resemblance in good humour and good spirits had recommended her and Lydia to each other, and out of their *three* months' acquaintance they had been intimate *two*." She invites Lydia to join her in Brighton. Elizabeth's reservations about the friendship and the visit go unheeded by Mr. Bennet. "Little advantage," Elizabeth argues, "could derive from the friendship of such a woman as Mrs. Forster, and the probability [favored] her being yet more imprudent with such a companion at Brighton, where the temptations must be greater than at home" (230). Elizabeth proves to be correct: Harriet turns out to be an irresponsible companion for Lydia in Brighton.

Gardiner, Mr. Edward (Chapters 25–27, 38, 42–52, 60–61) F. B. Pinion writes "there are no characters in *Pride and Prejudice* more admirable, less open to criticism, than the Gardiners, even though in the eyes of the haughty they are degraded by being connected with trade" (*Companion*, 142). Mr. Gardiner, Mrs. Bennet's brother, is "a sensible gentlemanlike man, greatly superior to his sister as well by nature as education . . . a man who lived by trade, and within view of his own warehouses" (139). He is prosperous, living in Gracechurch Street, London. He and his wife invite Elizabeth Bennet to visit the Lake District, but this is curtailed to a tour of Derbyshire, where they visit Pemberley. The visit is crucial for Elizabeth's transformation of her perceptions of Darcy, who immediately takes to the Gardiners. Arrangements for Lydia's marriage settlement are made for Darcy by Mr. Gardiner's

lawyer, Haggerston. "Always on the most intimate terms, Darcy as well as Elizabeth, really loved them [the Gardiners]; and they were both over sensible of the warmest gratitude towards the persons who, by bringing her [Elizabeth] into Derbyshire, had been the means of uniting them" (388). Paul Poplawski writes, "Mr. Gardiner is also important as a relatively new fictional type in that he represents a positive picture of the self-made tradesman, able to hold his own with the gentry" (151).

Gardiner, Mrs. M. (Chapters 25–27, 38, 42–52, 60–61) "An amiable, intelligent, elegant woman, and a great favourite with all her Longbourn nieces" (139), Mrs. Bennet's younger sister-in-law, has two daughters and two sons. She plays a crucial role in the plot. She grew up in Derbyshire near Pemberley, and it is her revisiting her old haunts that reconciles Elizabeth and Darcy. She also, in lengthy letters to Elizabeth, keeps her informed of the efforts being made to find Lydia and Wickham and in so doing, lets Elizabeth know of Darcy's role in bringing the two together. Shrewdly, she writes Elizabeth that Darcy "wants nothing but a little more liveliness, and *that*, if he marry *prudently*, his wife may teach him (325).

Goulding Family (Chapters 50–51, 53) Neighbors of the Bennets living at Haye Park. Mrs. Bennet, when she learns of the Lydia-Wickham marriage, thinks they might live locally and that Haye Park would be most suitable "if the Gouldings would quit it" (310). Lydia, after her marriage, "overtook William Goulding in his curricle . . . took off my [her] glove, and let my [her] hand just rest upon the window frame, so that he might see the ring" (316).

Grantley, Miss (Chapters 10, 11) Darcy tells his sister, Georgiana, on Caroline Bingley's request, that she is "quite in raptures with her beautiful little design for a table, and I [Caroline] think it infinitely superior to Miss Grantley's" (48)—her acquaintance.

Haggerston (Chapter 49) The attorney who, on Gardiner's instructions, prepares "a proper settlement" (303) for Lydia and Wickham.

Harrington, Miss Harriet and Miss Pen (Chapter 39)   Young ladies living in the Meryton neighborhood, friends of Mrs. Forster, and known to Lydia Bennet, invited to Mrs. Forster's home for an informal dinner, "but Harriet was ill, and so Pen was forced to come by herself" (221).

Hill, Mrs. (Chapter 13)   The Bennets' housekeeper at Longbourn (13).

Hurst, Mr. (Chapters 3–4, 6–8, 10–11, 18, 21, 26, 33, 45)   Husband of Bingley's sister Louisa, has a house in Grosvenor Street, London, but prefers to sponge off his wife's relatives and friends. Seems to have married her for her money: "he was an indolent man, who lived only to eat, drink, and play at cards, who when he found [Elizabeth to] prefer a plain dish to a ragout, had nothing to say to her" (35).

Hurst, Mrs Louisa, née Bingley (Chapters 3–4, 6–8, 10–11, 18, 21, 26, 33, 45)   She and her sister, Caroline, "were fine women with an air of decided fashion" (10). Has a considerable fortune of her own but lives off her brother Bingley. Is conceited and proud.

Jenkinson, Mrs. (Chapters 19, 29)   "In whose appearance there was nothing remarkable," (162) formerly Miss de Bourgh's governess and now her companion. Has four nieces "most delightfully situated through [Lady Catherine de Bourgh's] means" (165).

John (Chapter 37)   Mr. Collins's manservant at Hunsford Parsonage.

John (Chapters 37, 46)   Servant of the Gardiners, accompanies them on their Derbyshire visit.

Jones, Mr. (Chapters 7, 15)   The Meryton apothecary called on to see Jane Bennet when she is unwell at Netherfield Park. His "shop boy" tells Mrs. Philips that Jane has returned to Longbourn from Netherfield Park (73).

King, Miss Mary (Chapters 3, 26–27, 36, 39)   A young Meryton lady who inherits £10,000 and then attracts Wickham's attention. Lydia describes her as "such a nasty little freckled thing." Her family remove her from Meryton: "She is gone down to her uncle at Liverpool; gone to stay" (220).

Long, Mrs. (Chapters 1–2, 5, 49, 53–54)   A neighbor of Mrs. Bennet. She has two nieces and is the first to tell Mrs. Bennet that the eligible Mr. Bingley has arrived at Netherfield. When Mrs. Bennet perceives her as competing for Bingley, she calls Mrs. Long "a selfish, hypocritical woman" (16). Subsequently, she can be more generous, referring to Mrs. Long as "as good a creature as ever lived—and her nieces are very pretty behaved girls, and not at all handsome" (342).

Lucas, Charlotte (Chapters 3, 5–6, 9, 13, 18, 20–22, 24, 26–33, 36–38, 40, 56–57, 60)   "Intimate friend" of Elizabeth Bennet, the eldest of the Lucas daughters. "A sensible, intelligent young woman, about twenty-seven" (18), she has a totally different perspective on marriage than Elizabeth, and views Mr. Collins as her "pleasantest preservative from want" (122). She "instantly set out to meet him accidentally in the lane" (121). The "prudent, steady" (135) Charlotte develops her own ways to handle her husband. At the end of the novel, she and Collins are expecting "a young olive-branch" (364).

Lucas, Maria (Chapters 3, 26–29, 32, 37–39, 58)   The younger daughter of Sir William and Lady Lucas. She is "a good humoured girl, but as empty-headed as himself [her father], [she] had nothing to say that could be worth hearing" (152). She accompanies Elizabeth to Rosings, where she is "frightened almost out of her senses" and "thought speaking out of question" (162–163). She has a younger brother as well as younger sisters.

Lucas, Sir William and Lady Lucas (Chapters 1, 3, 5–6, 9, 18, 22–23, 27–30, 35, 39–40, 47, 49, 51, 56–57, 60)   Lady Lucas is "not too clever to be a valuable neighbour to Mrs. Bennet." She has a number of children and doesn't hesitate to make the Bennets aware that she has a daughter who has married before any of them.

Her husband, Sir William, the neighbor of the Bennets "had been formerly in trade in Meryton, where he had made a tolerable fortune and risen to the honour of knighthood by an address to the King during his mayoralty." Overawed by wealth and rank, he is "inoffensive, friendly and obliging" (18).

Metcalfe, Lady (Chapters 29) Known to Lady Catherine de Bourgh. Lady Catherine recommended Miss Pope as a governess to Lady Metcalfe. Lady Metcalfe calls at Rosings to thank Lady Catherine for such a "treasure" (165).

Millar, Colonel (Chapter 41) Mrs. Bennet remembers that 25 years previously, she "cried for two days together when Colonel Millar's regiment went away. I thought I should have broke my heart" (229). Mrs. Bennet is empathizing with her daughters Kitty and Lydia over the departure of Colonel Forster's regiment.

Morris, Mr. (Chapter 1) The man from whom Bingley leases Netherfield Park; whether he is the agent or the owner is not clear.

Nicholls, Mrs. (Chapters 11, 53) Mr. Bingley's cook and possibly housekeeper.

Phillips, [Philips] Mr. (Chapters 7, 10, 14–16, 21, 39–41, 47–48, 51, 53, 55, 60) Mrs. Bennet's sister is "married to a Mr. Phillips, who had been a clerk to their father, and succeeded him in the business." An attorney in Meryton, he regularly visits the militia officers stationed in Meryton and thus opening "to his nieces a source of felicity unknown before" (28–29). Elizabeth finds the officers "superior to the broad-faced stuffy uncle Phillips, breathing port wine" (76).

Phillips [Philips], Mrs. née Gardiner (Chapters 7, 10, 14–16, 21, 39–41, 47–48, 51, 53, 55, 60) A source of intelligence concerning the officers in the militia stationed at Meryton. Vulgar and a gossip, she has married her father's clerk. She encourages Lydia's and Kitty's flirtatious activities, organizing supper parties for them and the officers.

Pope, Miss (Chapter 29) Recommended as a governess by Lady Catherine de Bourgh to Lady Metcalfe, she is, according to the latter, "a treasure" (II: 6).

Pratt, Mr. (Chapter 39) An officer in Colonel Forster's regiment, a friend of Denny and Wickham with whom Lydia became friendly.

Reynolds, Mrs. (Chapter 43) At Pemberley, "the housekeeper came; a respectable-looking, elderly woman, much less fine, and more civil, than [Elizabeth] had any notion of finding her" (246). She shows the Gardiners and Elizabeth around Pemberley House and is full of praise for Darcy. This marks a turning point in Elizabeth's attitude to him.

Richard (Chapter 14) The Phillipses' servant; Lydia tells her mother, "Do you know, mama, that my uncle Philips talks of turning away Richard, and if he does, Colonel Forster will hire him" (68).

Robinson, Mr. (Chapter 5) A gentleman living in the Meryton neighborhood who asks Mr. Bingley "how he liked our Meryton assemblies, and whether he did not think they were a great many pretty women in the room, and *which* he thought the prettiest?" (Jane Austen's emphasis). Bingley immediately answers "Oh! the eldest Miss Bennet beyond a doubt, there cannot be two opinions on that point" (19).

Sally (Chapter 47) A maidservant at Mrs. Forster's at Brighton. After Lydia has eloped with Wickham, she writes to Mrs. Forster. Lydia asks her to "tell Sally to mend a great slit in [her] worked muslin gown" (292).

Sarah (Chapter 45) One of the Bennets' maidservants at Longbourn.

Stone, Mr. (Chapter 51) Described by Lydia as "that horrid man," a business associate of Mr. Gardiner who calls him "away upon business" on Lydia's wedding day. Lydia adds "when once they get together, there is no end of it" (319).

Watson, Miss (Chapter 7) A Meryton resident. Lydia tells her mother that Mrs. Phillips reports "that Colonel Forster and Captain Carter do not go so often to Miss Watson's as they did when they first came" (80).

Webbs, the Misses (Chapter 29) There are three of them known to Lady Catherine de Bourgh, all playing musical instruments, and their father has not so good an income as Elizabeth Bennet's.

Wickham, Mr. (deceased) (Chapters 16, 34, 43) "The late Mr. Darcy's steward" (247), who died five years before the main action of the novel. Began as an attorney "but he gave up every thing to be of use to the late Mr. Darcy, and devoted all his time to the care of the Pemberley property." His son, Wickham adds, in one of the few accurate observations he makes, that his father "was most highly esteemed by Mr. Darcy, a most intimate, confidential friend" (81). Before his death, Mr. Darcy promised old Wickham that he would provide for his son.

Wickham, George (Chapters 15–18, 21, 24–27, 34–36, 39, 41, 43, 46–53, 61) "His appearance was greatly in his favour; he had all the best part of beauty, a fine countenance, a good figure, and a very pleasing address" (72). When she has learned better, Elizabeth tells her Aunt Gardiner, "we all know that Wickham has every charm of person and address that can captivate a woman" (284). Wickham "smiled, looked handsome, and said many pretty things" (330). He came to Meryton with his friend Denny after taking a commission in the militia. Elizabeth is taken in by his charm and good looks and believes Wickham's story that Darcy has treated him badly. He turns his attention to Miss King as soon as he learns that she has a fortune. Educated by Darcy's father at school and Cambridge, he turns down a church living and accepts £3,000 instead from Darcy. Pretending to study law in London, Wickham quickly spends the money. He attempts to elope with the 15-year-old Georgiana Darcy, his motive being her £30,000 inheritance. He leaves gambling debts of up to £1,000 when he elopes with Lydia Bennet.

Darcy settles the debts, buys him a commission in the north of England, and makes sure he marries Lydia, upon whom he settles £1,000. "His affection for [Lydia] soon sank into indifference; her's lasted a little longer" (387). In short, Wickham is a man of "vicious propensities," and "the want of principle"; he leads "a life of idleness and dissipation" (200–201). Elizabeth's change in perceptions of him reflects her growth in awareness of Darcy's virtues; she moves from prejudice, partly induced by believing Wickham, into real appreciation and love for Darcy.

Younge, Mrs. (Chapters 35, 52) Appointed Georgiana Darcy's companion when she was sent to London at the age of 15. She "proved to have been a prior acquaintance" (202) of Wickham and assists him in his plans to elope with her charge, Georgiana (II: 12). She is dismissed from her position but reappears in the story. Darcy goes to her, as "he knew [she was] intimately acquainted with Wickham" for knowledge of his and Lydia's whereabouts. She had taken "a large house in Edward-street, and has since maintained herself by letting lodgings" in London. She has to be bribed before she "procured the wished for direction" (322) as to Wickham and Lydia's location.

BIBLIOGRAPHY

Primary Texts:

Jane Austen's Letters. Collected and edited by Deirdre Le Faye. 3d ed. Oxford: Oxford University Press, 1995.

Pride and Prejudice. Edited by R. W. Chapman. *The Novels of Jane Austen, II.* 3d ed. Oxford: Oxford University Press, 1998 reprint [Page references are to this edition.]

———. Edited by Donald Gray. A Norton Critical Edition. 3d ed. New York: W.W. Norton, 2000.

———. Edited by James Kinsley, with an introduction and Notes by Fiona Stafford. Oxford: Oxford University Press, 2004.

———. Edited by Pat Rogers. *The Cambridge Edition of the Works of Jane Austen.* Cambridge: Cambridge University Press, 2006.

———. Introduction by Tony Tanner. Harmondsworth, U.K.: Penguin Books, 1975.

Secondary Works

Ashton, Rosemary, ed. *Versatile Victorian Selected Writings of George Henry Lewes.* Bristol, U.K.: Bristol Classical Press, 1942

Auerbach, Emily. *Searching for Jane Austen.* Madison: University of Wisconsin Press, 2004.

Auerbach, Nina. *Communities of Women: An Idea in Fiction.* Cambridge: Harvard University Press, 1978.

Babb, Howard. *Jane Austen's Novels: The Fabric of Dialogue.* Columbus: Ohio State University Press, 1962.

Butler, Marilyn. *Jane Austen and the War of Ideas.* Oxford, U.K.: Clarendon Press, 1975.

Copeland, Edward, and Juliet McMaster, eds. *The Cambridge Companion to Jane Austen.* Cambridge: Cambridge University Press, 1997.

Gilson, David. *A Bibliography of Jane Austen: New Introduction and Corrections by the Author.* Winchester Hamshire, U.K.: St. Paul's Bibliographies; New Castle, Del.: Oak Knoll Press, 1997.

Goetsch, Paul. "Laughter in *Pride and Prejudice.*" In *Redefining the Modern: Essays on Literature and Society in Honour of Joseph Wiesenfarth,* edited by William Baker and Ira B. Nadel, 29–43. Cranbury, N.J.: Associated University Presses, 2004.

Grey, David J., A. Walton Litz, and Brian Southam, eds. *The Jane Austen Companion.* New York: Macmillan, 1986.

Harding, D. W. *Regulated Hatred and Other Essays on Jane Austen,* edited by Monica Lawlor. London and Atlantic Highlands, N.J.: Athlone Press, 1998.

Hardy, Barbara. *A Reading of Jane Austen.* London: Peter Owen, 1975.

Johnson, Claudia L. *Jane Austen: Women, Politics, and the Novel.* Chicago and London: University of Chicago Press, 1988.

Kaminsky, Alice R. *Literary Criticism of George Henry Lewes.* Lincoln: University of Nebraska Press, 1964.

Langland, Elizabeth. "*Pride and Prejudice*: Jane Austen and Her Readers." In Lambdin, Laura Cooner, and Robert Thomas Lambdin, 41–56. *A Companion to Jane Austen Studies.* Westport, Conn.: Greenwood Press, 2000.

Lascelles, Mary. *Jane Austen and Her Art.* London: Oxford University Press, 1939.

McMaster, Juliet. "Talking About Talking in *Pride and Prejudice.*" In *Jane Austen's Business; Her World and Her Profession,* 81–94. London: Macmillan; New York: St. Martin's Press, 1996.

Mudrick, Marvin. *Jane Austen: Irony as Defense and Discovery.* Princeton, N.J.: Princeton University Press, 1952.

Page, Norman. *The Language of Jane Austen*: Oxford, U.K.: Basil Blackwell, 1972.

Phillipps, K. C. *Jane Austen's English.* London: Andre Deutsch, 1970.

Pinion, F. B. *A Jane Austen Companion.* London: Macmillan, 1973.

Poplawski, Paul. *A Jane Austen Encyclopaedia.* Westport, Conn: Greenwood Press, 1998.

Selwyn, David. *Jane Austen and Leisure.* London: Humbledon Press, 1999.

Southam, B. C., ed. *Jane Austen: Sense and Sensibility, "Pride and Prejudice" and "Mansfield Park": A Case Book.* London: Macmillan, 1976.

———. *Jane Austen: The Critical Heritage.* 2 vols. London: Routledge and Kegan Paul, 1978–1979.

Spacks, Patricia Meyer. *The Female Imagination: A Literary and Psychological Investigation of Women's Writing.* New York: Knopf, 1975.

Sulloway, Alison G. *Jane Austen and the Province of Womanhood.* Philadelphia: University of Pennsylvania Press, 1989.

Watt, Ian P., ed. *Jane Austen: A Collection of Critical Essays.* Englewood Cliffs, N.J.: Prentice Hall, 1963.

Wiesenfarth, Joseph. "Austen and Apollo." In *Jane Austen Today,* edited by Joel Weinsheimer, 46–63. Athens: University of Georgia Press, 1975.

———. *The Errand of Form: An Assay of Jane Austen's Art.* New York: Fordham University Press, 1967.

———. *Gothic Manners and the Classic English Novel.* Madison: University of Wisconsin Press, 1988.

Woolf, Virginia. *The Common Reader.* New York: Harcourt, Brace and World, 1925.

Sanditon (1925)

COMPOSITION AND PUBLICATION

Roughly 24,000 words divided into 12 chapters survive in manuscript form now at King's College, Cambridge, of a novel posthumously called *Sandi-*

ton. According to tradition, Jane Austen intended to call the novel *The Brothers*. The manuscript is dated by Jane Austen, "27 January 1817," on the first leaf and then "18 March 1817" when it was put aside. She died on July 18, 1817. Toward the end of 1816, her illness was in remission and she probably felt well enough to begin a new novel. The manuscript remained in the Austen family. J. E. Austen-Leigh's 1871 *Memoir* contains extracts approximating roughly one-sixth of the total manuscript; there it is called *The Last Work*. In 1930, the manuscript was presented by a descendant of Jane Austen's family to King's College, Cambridge, where it resides today.

First published in 1925 by Oxford University Press and edited anonymously by R. W. Chapman, *Sanditon* was included in the sixth volume of Chapman's edition of *The Works of Jane Austen,* published in 1954 and subsequently with revisions. A facsimile reproduction introduced by B. C. Southam appeared in 1975. The manuscript is characterized by unparagraphed folios, or manuscript pages, which contain many insertions, erasures, and abbreviations. As Southam observes in his introduction to the facsimile, there appear to be three kinds of changes in the manuscript. First, there "are concurrent changes made at the time of writing," for instance, "at the bottom of page [29] where 'being' is cancelled in preference of 'having.'" Second, there are changes "which seem to have been made at the end of the days work, when" the author reviewed what "she had just written, making corrections with the same pen." Third, there are changes "made at a later re-reading." These are "identifiable by a difference in pen strokes and the inking" (ix–x). There are also shorthand forms used for names, for instance, "E. Bourne" (363) for Eastbourne, and initials for names such as "H" for Heywood (368), and so on.

SYNOPSIS

In the opening scene, "A gentleman & Lady [are] travelling from Tunbridge towards that part of the Sussex Coast which lies between Hasting & E[ast] Bourne." They "being induced by Business to quit the high road, & attempt a very rough lane, were overturned" (363). Mr. Parker, a land speculator from Sanditon in Sussex, is on his way home with his wife from London. In response to an advertisement for a new medical practice they read in yesterday's newspaper, they leave the main road to influence a Willingden (a village) surgeon to come to Sanditon. In this way, they can increase its appeal as a family resort. As a consequence of the coach overturning, Mr. Parker has a serious ankle sprain. A local farmer, Mr. Heywood, convinces Parker that he was aiming for the incorrect Willingden; the advertisement referred to one seven miles away. As a result of his injury, the Parkers are forced to stay at the Heywoods' for a fortnight. In return for the Heywoods' hospitality, the Parkers take the 22-year-old Charlotte, the eldest of the Heywoods' 14 children, to Sanditon to stay with them.

On the journey back to Sanditon, Mr. Parker tells Charlotte about Sanditon and the various people she will encounter. Of these, the most important is Lady Denham of Sanditon House. She is a co-developer of Sanditon, and there are two families related by marriage to this elderly widow hoping to inherit her fortune. Mr. Parker hoped that Lady Denham's nephew, Sir Edward Denham, and his sister would be the main beneficiaries of the will. But there is also a relative called Miss Brereton who has a claim on the Denham wealth. Two miles from their destination, they pass the Parkers' former very attractive home, which Charlotte perceives, "Seems to have as many comforts about it as" (379) her own home in Willingden. Mrs. Parker seems to regret leaving their old house for the new one, Trafalgar House, which sits "on the most elevated spot . . . about a hundred yards from the brow of a steep, but not very lofty Cliff" (384).

During the journey, Mr. Parker has also spoken a good deal about Sidney, his witty brother, and a younger brother, Arthur, who appears to be a hypochondriac. He also has two sisters, Susan and Diana. Diana has contacted her brother to say that she cannot come to Sanditon; however, she is hoping to persuade two families to stay at Sanditon. Following dinner, the Parkers take Charlotte to the town and the circulating library. As they are leaving the library, they encounter Lady Denham and Clara Brereton, whom they invite to Trafalgar House for tea.

The following morning, Lady Denham's second husband's nephew, Sir Edward Denham, and his sister Esther pay the Parkers a fleeting visit. The Parkers leave with Charlotte to continue their tour and find the Denhams seated on the terrace with the "two superior Ladies" (395) seated at one end of the bench and Sir Edward with Clara Brereton at the other. They decide to walk together, and Sir Edward tells Charlotte of his fascination with the sea. In a rapid transition of his attitude toward women, he declares that for him love is above all "prosaic Decencies" (398). It is also revealed that "Sir Edward *must* marry for money" (Jane Austen's emphasis) and that his sister "Miss Esther must marry somebody of fortune, too—She must get a rich Husband" (400–401). In the eighth chapter, the narrator tells her readers that "Sir Edw[ard's] great objective in life was to be seductive. . . . it was Clara alone on whom he had serious designs; it was Clara whom he meant to seduce" (405).

Diana Parker appears at Sanditon without warning. She has left her brother Arthur and sister Susan to find lodgings and sort out the luggage. The main object of her visit was to find accommodation for one of the families she has persuaded to reside in Sanditon. This family is shortly to arrive. Charlotte meets Susan and Arthur in their accommodation in a terrace house. In spite of its being "a very fair English Summer-day," (413) there was not one window open. The "invalides" (409) are seated by a fire, victims of their imaginary ailments. Arthur seeks remedies in laziness, wine, and fine food.

It emerges that the two families who are expected are one and the same: West Indian and from a ladies' boarding school from Camberwell in Surrey. They arrive in two carriages, and Diana discovers that she is responsible for an expensive house for a week. The families, a Mrs. Griffiths with her three girl charges, two Miss Beauforts and Miss Lambe, a wealthy but delicate West Indian heiress, prefer cheaper lodgings. They are all quickly introduced to the Parkers and the Denhams.

On a misty morning, Charlotte and Miss Parker walk to Sanditon House. They meet a carriage on its way to Sanditon; in it is Sidney Parker, Mrs. Parker's brother-in-law. He has driven over from Eastbourne on the Sussex coast to spend a few days with friends at a Sanditon hotel. Charlotte is impressed by his pleasant manner, and she and Mrs. Parker walk along discussing Mr. Sidney Parker until they enter the Sanditon House grounds. Charlotte, taller than Mrs. Parker, sees Clara Brereton in what appears to be an intimate conversation with Sir Edward Denham. Charlotte assumes that this is a secret lovers' encounter and does not say anything to Mrs. Parker.

The unfinished novel breaks off with Charlotte and Mrs. Parker at Sanditon House. They wait for Lady Denham in the elegant sitting room in which Mrs. Parker indicates the paintings of Lady Denham's former husbands. There is a full-length one of Sir Harry Denham over the mantelpiece and a miniature of Mr. Hollis among other miniatures. The manuscript concludes with Charlotte feeling sympathy for "Poor Mr. Hollis! . . . to be obliged to stand back in his own House & see the best place by the fire constantly occupied by Sir H[arry] D[enham]" (427).

CRITICAL COMMENTARY

Two of the fullest accounts of *Sanditon* to date are found in Southam in his study of *Jane Austen's Literary Manuscripts* (2001), his introduction to the facsimile edition of *Sanditon* (1975), and Kathryn Sutherland's *Jane Austen's Textual Lives* (2005). Southam and others notice the differences between *Sanditon* and its author's other work. In the introduction to the facsimile edition, Southam writes, "from the very opening of *Sanditon* we can see that Jane Austen has abandoned her usual framework—the regular and established way of life of country gentry conducted at a quietly domestic tempo." On the other hand, in *Sanditon* "she gives us a story of change and movement, with a succession of accidents, mistakes and surprises, with eccentrics hard driven by their manias and obsessions." Other differences include an emphasis on the elements—nature, the wind, the sun, and the sea. There is a fresh focus on "the economic and social facts of life," shopkeepers and their activities, the payment of suppliers, the development and exploitation of the countryside, and land speculation. "For the first time in Jane Austen, the sense of *place* is strong and deeply rooted, not only topographically but socially, historically, and morally" (xi–xii).

John Burrows in his *Computation into Criticism* (1987) calculates that in *Sanditon* there are "only 1211 words of character narrative, of which a thousand are divided almost equally between Charlotte and Mr. Parker" (169). Southam, on the other hand, in his *Jane Austen's Literary Manuscripts* argues that "Each stage of the work is dominated by one of the strongly drawn figures—Mr. Parker, Diana, Arthur, Sir Edward, and Lady Denham— the passages being linked by Charlotte's experience as the point of view through which much of the action is observed" (112). J. E. Austen-Leigh in his *Memoir* published in 1871 included only a fraction of the work in the form of indirect discourse. He was following the lead set by Anna Lefroy, a close friend and relative by marriage of the author, who wrote to Austen-Leigh, August 8, 1862, that "I think those parts ought to be a good deal trimmed, & softened down" (quoted Sutherland, 175). R. W. Chapman in his detailed *Jane Austen: Facts and Problems* (1948) believes that had Jane Austen lived, "she would have smoothed these course strokes, so strikingly different from the mellow pencillings of *Persuasion*" (208). In other words, she would have rewritten some of her caricatures found in the manuscript in the writing of Mr. Parker, Diana his sister, Lady Denham, and Sir Edward.

Francis Warre Cornish in his *Jane Austen* in the "English Men of Letters Series" writes that *Sanditon* "contains some promising sketches; but it would be useless, if not impertinent, to pass an opinion on a work so obviously incomplete" (231). Writing not in 1913 as in the case of Cornish, but in 1986, Tony Tanner concludes a nearly 36-page extensive analysis of *Sanditon*, by persuasively arguing that Jane Austen is in "a world where she can no longer control or occupy the centre, because it has no centre, no organising values." The work "is not mere burlesque. She is writing herself out of the world she is writing about." Tanner adds, "If, as author, she is necessarily and unavoidably omniscient, she counterbalances that fact by demonstrating that as curator and admonisher of values, she is now effectively impotent" (284). Other facets of *Sanditon* are found in Deirdre Le Faye's *Jane Austen:*

The World of Her Novels (2002). Le Faye points out that with the end of the Napoleonic Wars, "French warships no longer posed a threat to transatlantic sea travel, the *nouveaux riches* plantation owners from the West Indies were able to come unhindered to England, with a view to buying their way into society." They appear in *Sanditon* toward its conclusion in the guise of Miss Lambe, the 17-year-old, extraordinarily wealthy, half mulatto. Le Fay also points to Lady Denham's possession of some of the very latest technological inventions, including "a chamber horse—which was the Regency equivalent of an exercise bicycle or similar fitness machine" (305–307).

Another recent critic who makes interesting observations on *Sanditon* is John Wiltshire. The final chapter, "*Sanditon*: The Enjoyments of Invalidism," of his *Jane Austen and the Body* (1992), is taken up with a detailed commentary on the unfinished work and its depiction of hypochondria. For Wiltshire, it is not merely the characters and narrative, but the physical appearance of the manuscript that are revealing: "the text seems actively to dwell on, to call attention to, the amazing behaviour of the hypochondriacal body." Wiltshire adds, "this writing is bringing out the fact that where relations between the body and imagination are concerned, ordinary criteria go by the board" (214).

An extensive analysis of the manuscript at King's College, Cambridge, its history, interpretation, and attempts at continuation, may be found in Kathryn Sutherland's *Jane Austen's Textual Lives*. She observes that the manuscript exhibits revision of the overusage of the adverb "much," revision of an "initial reliance for constructing the scene on verbal participles," and an elimination of duplication and "verbal participles" such as "quitting," "toiling," and "looking" (187). Sutherland notes "what seems different and disturbing in *Sanditon* is less the fact that objects have their solid existence apart from our possessive purposes as the frequency with which they resist all active inquiry. Where objects go, people follow." Further, characters are "adrift in their own language-loop, [they] deny by their robust self-absorption an underlying principle of consensus. There is none" (193–194). For Sutherland, *Sanditon* "seems from the outset to abandon plot in favour of local embellishment and thematic obsessions" (195).

Attempts to continue *Sanditon* include Anna Lefroy's, which probably began "after 1845 when the manuscript came into her possession" (251). Lefroy's addition is roughly the same length as Jane Austen's manuscript, making a total of 40,000 words. She enlarges the topography of Sussex and the potential of the seaside resort for tourist purposes. A Mr. Tracy is introduced, Sidney Parker's holiday companion who turns out to be mysterious and sinister. There are other changes, too: Charlotte and Sidney Parker are toned down. However, Lefroy's continuation too is incomplete. It remained unpublished until 1983, when it was transcribed and edited by Mary Gaither Marshall (see Sutherland, 250–257).

Section J of David Gilson's *A Bibliography of Jane Austen* describes two *Sanditon* continuations. The first by Alice Cobbett, published in 1932, uses Jane Austen's manuscript as the foundation "for a melodramatic plot featuring Sir Edward Denham's association with smugglers, his kidnapping of Clara Brereton and her rescue by Charlotte Heywood." A few new characters are introduced; a good deal of the action is transferred to Hastings on the Sussex coast. Miss Lambe "is developed into a flamboyant creature named Lorelia, who plays a large part in the story." Gilson also describes a 30-chapter version published anonymously in 1975, probably by Marie Dobbs (427).

CHARACTERS

Andrew (Chapters 381–382) Lady Denham's old gardener at Sanditon House. According to Mr. and Mrs. Parker, "as to Gardenstuff . . . any accidental omission is supplied in a moment" by Andrew; however, "we ought to go elsewhere upon such occasions," for instance, when gales occur. As Mr. Parker has encouraged the Stringers to come to Sanditon, they could also go to Stringer. The cook "is always complaining of old Andrew now, & says he never brings her what she wants." This represents then a dilemma: Mr. Parker is a paternalistic estate owner who wants to follow tradition by using Andrew. On the other hand, he is a venture capitalist wishing to stimulate local business by using, for instance, the Stringers (381–382).

Beard, Mr. (Chapter 389) A visitor to Sanditon and on the circulating library subscription list. He is a solicitor from Gray's Inn, London.

Beaufort, Miss, and Letitia (Chapter 421–423) Among the students at Mrs. Griffith's seminary visiting Sanditon. They are "very accomplished & very Ignorant, their time being divided between such pursuits as might attract admiration, & those Labours & Expedients of dexterous Ingenuity, by which they could dress in a stile much beyond what they *ought* to have afforded" (421 Jane Austen's emphasis).

Brereton, Clara (Chapters 375, 377–379, 391, 405, 426–427) Described as "Elegantly tall, regularly handsome, with great delicacy of complexion & soft Blue eyes, a sweetly modest & yet naturally graceful Address. Charlotte could see in her only the most perfect representation of whatever Heroine might be most beautiful & bewitching, in all the numerous vol[ume]s" in the Sanditon circulating library (391). Initially invited to Sanditon House to stay for six months, Clara is found so acceptable that her visit is extended. Others fear that she might well inherit a goodly portion of the Denham estate. Consequently, Sir Edward Denham has "serious designs" on her. Toward the end of the novel she and he are glimpsed in what appears to be a compromising situation. Clara, however, "saw through him, & had not the least intention of being seduced" (405).

Brown, Dr. and Mrs. (Chapter 389) Visitors to Sanditon and included on the subscription library listing.

Capper, Miss (Chapter 408) "Miss Capper, the particular friend of [Diana Parker's] very particular friend Fanny Noyce;—now, Miss Capper is extremely intimate with a Mrs. Darling" (408).

Darling, Mrs. (Chapter 408) According to Diana Parker, "the West Indians" include a connection with "Miss Capper," who "is extremely intimate with a Mrs. Darling, who is on terms of constant correspondence with Mrs. Griffiths herself" (408). Mrs. Griffiths runs a girls' school that has a very wealthy West Indian student, Miss Lambe.

Davis, Mrs. (Chapter 389) A Sanditon visitor included among the names of the circulating library list of subscribers.

Denham, Lady, née Brereton (Chapters 375–377, 391–393, 399–402) Both of the wealthy Lady Denham's husbands have died. She is "of middle height, stout, upright & alert in her motions, with a shrewd eye, & self-satisfied air—but not an unagreeable Countenance" (391). She owns a good deal of Sanditon and is involved financially in fostering its development as a leading seaside resort. A Miss Brereton, born into wealth but inadequately educated, the elderly Mr. Hollis was her first husband. He owned a good deal of property, including much of Sanditon and its surroundings. Sir Harry Denham of Denham Park near Sanditon was her second husband, and from him she gained the title Lady Denham. Sir Harry, against his expectations, gained little from the marriage. Lady Denham is now 70 years old. The Brereton, Denham, and Hollis families are seeking her favors to benefit from her will. She describes herself as not a "Woman of Parade" and maintains Sanditon House to preserve "poor Mr. Hollis's memory." The development of Sanditon and its environs interests her for the financial profit it will bring. She objects to its having a doctor, as that will encourage "our Servants the Poor to fancy themselves ill" (393). Charlotte Heywood considers her to be "thoroughly mean" (402).

Denham, Miss Esther (Chapters 394, 396, 406–407, 412–413, 420–423) "A fine young woman, but cold & reserved, giving the idea of one who felt her consequence with Pride & her Poverty with Discontent" (394). Sir Edward Denham's sister and perceived by Lady Denham to be anxious to be invited to Sanditon House with her brother. In Lady Denham's presence, her personality changes, and instead of being "cold & reserved," she is "listening & talking with smiling attention or solicitous eagerness." She attempts to ingratiate herself with her wealthy older relative. Her personality change

may be perceived as "very striking—and very amusing—or very melancholy, just as Satire or Morality might prevail" (394, 396).

Denham, Sir Edward, Bart. (Chapters 398–405) The nephew of Sir Harry, Lady Denham's second husband, his "great object in life was to be seductive.—With such personal advantages as he knew himself to possess, & such Talents as he did also give himself credit for, he regarded it as his Duty—He felt that he was formed to be a dangerous Man—quite in the line of the Lovelaces" (405), the seducer from SAMUEL RICHARDSON's *Clarissa, or, the History of a Young Lady* (1747–48). Well read, he affects the pose of a literary character of low morals but high birth. His language also imitates his literary models; he speaks of ROBERT BURNS, for instance, as "all ardour & Truth!—His Genius & his Susceptibilities might lead him into some Aberrations . . . It were Hyper-criticism, it were Pseudo-philosophy to expect from the soul of high toned Genius, the grovellings of a common mind." Lady Denham wishes that a suitable young heiress would appear in Sanditon who would be appropriate for Sir Edward. Charlotte believes she sees him in a compromising situation with Clara Brereton: Charlotte does not trust him, thinking of him as "downright silly" (398). There is a possibility that he might have transferred his attentions to the young wealthy Miss Lambe.

Denham, Sir Harry, Bart. (deceased) (Chapters 375, 427) Lady Denham's second husband, deceased, whom apparently she had married for his title. He was uncle of Sir Edward and Esther Denham, and his portrait still occupies pride of place in the Sanditon House sitting room, implying that Lady Denham was not ill-disposed to his memory.

Dupuis, Mrs. Charles (Chapter 411) Diana Parker's friend, acquainted with Mrs. Griffiths of a Camberwell girls' school, to whom she recommended Sanditon.

Fisher, Miss and Mrs. Jane (Chapter 389) Sanditon visitors whose name appears on the circulating library subscribers listing.

Griffiths, Mrs. (Chapters 408, 420–421) The proprietor of a Camberwell girls' school, she brings three of her pupils to stay at Sanditon, which has been recommended by friends of Diana Parker. The pupils include the Beaufort girls and the West Indian heiress, Miss Lambe. Mrs. Griffiths has a cousin with a financial interest in tonic pills, which she gives Miss Lambe.

Hanking, Rev. (Chapter 389) A Sanditon visitor whose name appears on the circulating library subscribers listing.

Heeley, William (Chapter 383) Thomas Parker observes to his wife, Mary, as they walk through Sanditon: "Look at William Heeley's windows.— Blue shoes, & nankin Boots!—who w[ould] have expected such a sight at a Shoemaker's in old Sanditon!—This is new within the Month" (383).

Heywood, Mr. (Chapters 365, 370) Described as "a well-looking Hale, Gentlemanlike Man, of middle age" (365), in fact 57, who has lived his entire life at Willingden in Sussex, where he farms. He has a comfortable home although not rich, and is kind, giving hospitality to the Parkers when their carriage overturns. He and his wife have not traveled far from home and do not accept Mr. Parker's invitation to visit Sanditon. The Heywoods do not object, however, to sending their daughter Charlotte with the Parkers to Sanditon.

Heywood, Mrs. (Chapters 365, 370, 373) Married to Mr. Heywood, "older in Habits than in Age" (373), she has 14 children. She and her husband are content with their unostentatious way of living. Both are most generous hosts to the Parkers when they stay with them for a fortnight.

Heywood, Charlotte (Chapters 374 and throughout) The protagonist of *Sanditon* has one of the main but not the only narrative perspective. She is "a very pleasing young woman of two and twenty" (374). The Heywoods' eldest daughter, she accompanies the Parkers back to Sanditon. Perceptive and "Sober-minded," she initially finds

Sir Edward Denham "agreable & did not quarrel with the suspicion of his finding her equally so," although "I [the author] make[s] no apologies for my Heroine's vanity.—If there are young Ladies in the World at her time of Life, more dull of Fancy & more careless of pleasing, I know them not, & never wish to know them" (395). Yet Charlotte becomes aware of Sir Edward's manipulativeness and she reacts against what she considers to be Lady Denham's meanness. Tony Tanner notes in his *Jane Austen* that "the plentiful use of free, indirect speech when it comes to transcribing what is going on in Charlotte's head—what she is saying to herself—indicates that she and Jane Austen share the same discourse, speak with one voice, as it were" (284). But Charlotte's is by no means the only perspective in *Sanditon*; her perspective is in itself limited. A good example of this is when she thinks she sees, or partially sees, Clara and Sir Edward in what possibly could be a compromising situation on the grounds of Sanditon House at the end of the fragment. Charlotte "instantly felt she had nothing to do but to step back again, & say not a word" (426). Not a gossip, she has the insight to recognize that her perceptions may not be accurate.

Hillier, Mr. and Mrs. (Chapters 380–381) A tenant farming family occupying Thomas Parker's former house outside Sanditon and two miles from the sea.

Jebb (Chapter 381) Possibly a milliner. Mrs. Parker talks about buying her daughter "a large Bonnet at Jebb's" (381) in Sanditon.

Lambe, Miss (Chapters 408, 421) A student at Mrs. Griffith's school: "about 17, half Mulatto, chilly & tender, had a maid of her own, was to have the best room in the Lodgings, & was always of the first consequence in every plan of Mrs. G[riffith]" (421). She is very wealthy and the source of the misunderstanding that a West Indian family are coming to Sanditon. Lady Denham, when hearing of Miss Lambe's presence, instantly tries to arrange a match with Sir Edward Denham, her nephew, and the heiress.

Little, Captain (Chapter 389) Yet another name read by Mr. Parker on the Sanditon circulating library subscribers listing. Captain Little is a visitor from Limehouse in the London dock area.

Mathews family (Chapter 389) The names of "Mrs. Mathews—Miss Mathews, Miss. E. Mathews, Miss H. Mathews" (389) are on the Sanditon circulating library subscribers listing.

Merryweather, Miss (Chapter 389) Another Sanditon visitor found on the circulating library subscribers listing. She also appears to be from Limehouse.

Morgan (Chapter 389) The Parkers' butler at their Trafalgar House Sanditon home.

Mullins family (Chapter 423) Mr. Parker suggests that Lady Denham be informed of "the poor Mullins's situation," and she be sounded out "as to a Subscription for them." Parker adds, "their distress is very great" (423)

Noyce, Fanny (Chapter 408) Diana Parker's "very particular friend," belonging to the "short chain" of correspondence that links Diana and Mrs. Griffith's presumed West Indian family.

Parker, Arthur (Chapters 371, 385, 413–416) Twenty-one, "quite as tall as his Brother [Thomas] & a great deal Stouter—Broad made & Lusty—and with no other looks of an Invalide, than a sodden complexion" (413–414). Now poor, he has decided that he is too sickly to work in a profession. He complains of his livery, being rheumatic and "subject to Perspiration" (416). His nerves are such that green tea is liable to give him paralysis in his right side. He is very loquacious until the food arrives; then he stops talking and devours toast and cocoa. During the summer months at Sanditon, he sits as close as he can to a brisk fire with all the windows closed.

Parker, children, including Mary (Chapters 371, 381) Thomas and Mary Parker have four young children. The first three were born in the old family house and within the last two years, the fourth, in the new Sanditon house. Mary Parker can buy for baby "Mary a little Parasol, which will make her as proud as can be" (381).

Parker, Diana (Chapters 371, 385–387, 406–407) Described as "about 4 & 30, of middling height & slender; delicate looking rather than sickly; with an agreable face, & a very animated eye; her manners resembling her Brother's [Thomas] in their ease & frankness, thought with more decision & less mildness in her Tone" (407). An interfering busybody, she is very loquacious, and four pages (407–410) are taken up on her arrival at Sanditon with her account of herself and her activities. She has a "chain" (408) of correspondents, "Wheel within wheel" (387), frequently producing inaccurate information. Her language "is a kind of hypochondriac's hyperbole" (Wiltshire, 210). For instance, she declares with reference to employing a Sanditon doctor, "Had you the most experienced Man in his Line [medicine] settled at Sanditon, it w[ould] be no recommendation to us. We have entirely done with the whole Medical Tribe" (386). Wiltshire observes that "what makes Diana so risible is the combination of specificity and the wildly improbable, a specificity that suggests both her energy of mind and at the same time the eccentricity of its application" (210).

Parker, Mr. Thomas (Chapters 363, 366–367, 372, and throughout) Approximately 35 years old, married for seven years with four young children, he is one of the main property owners and landowners in Sanditon and its environs. Thomas Parker is the leading entrepreneur determined to transform Sanditon and its surrounds into a fashionable bathing resort. The eldest son, he has inherited land and property, including the family estate and a reasonable though not excessive fortune. Described as "generally kind-hearted, Liberal, gentleman-like, easy to please; of a sanguine turn of mind, with more Imagination than Judgement" (372), his energies are preoccupied with speculation and attempting to advertise the merits of Sanditon. As Tanner notes, "his speech is conspicuously marked by asyndeton (i.e., omitting particles which usually begin sentences)." This is appropriate, "for in his hurry he does 'omit' (forget) 'beginnings' and connectives" (260). Constantly in a rush, his language is replete with repetition, of continually attempting to sell something. He even admits to reading the newspapers incorrectly. For instance, at the beginning of the story, he is on the wrong road as there are "two Willingdens" (366). This is Thomas Parker's error: "the advertisements did not catch my eye till the last half hour of our being in Town;—when everything was in the hurry confusion which always attend a short stay there." He adds, "One is never able to complete anything in the way of Business you know till the Carriage is at the door" (367). The Sanditon circulation library list serves as a potential listing of visitors' names he can use to sell Sanditon and what he feels it has to offer.

Sanditon opens with Thomas Parker hurrying to the wrong Willingden, traveling on a rough lane and his carriage overturning. As a consequence, he sprains his ankle and is forced to spend with his wife Mary two weeks, not doing very much, at the Heywoods', whose settled life represents the antithesis of his own. In return, the Parkers take Charlotte Heywood to stay with them at Sanditon. The overturning of his carriage and sprained ankle might serve as a warning of Mr. Parker's fate if his speculation fails. However, he also has qualities, such as kind-heartedness and liberality, more appropriate to an old-fashioned, good-natured country squire than to an aggressive exploiter of the environment.

Parker, Mrs. Mary (Chapters 363, 372) Wife of Thomas Parker, with four young children. She "was as evidently a gentle, amiable, sweet tempered Woman, the properest wife in the World for a Man of strong understanding, but not of capacity to supply the cooler reflection which her own Husband sometimes needed, & so entirely waiting to be guided on every occasion, that whether he were risking his Fortune or spraining his Ancle, she remained equally useless" (372). Such a description, especially at its conclusion, is not lacking in irony.

Parker, Sidney (Chapters 371, 382, 425) Thomas Parker's younger brother, 27 or 28 years old, who "lives too much in the World to be set-

tled." He is "a very clever Young Man,—and with great powers of pleasing" (382), with a sense of humor and reasonable wealth. Just before the end of the manuscript, Charlotte and Mrs. Parker meet him briefly. He drives on, and they are "to meet again within a few hours" (425). The meeting does not take place as the manuscript stops.

Parker, Susan (371, 385, 413) The younger sister, "more thin & worn by Illness & Medicine, more relaxed in air, & more subdued in voice" (413) than her sister Diana or the hyporchondriacal Arthur. She suffers from bad teeth and has three of them extracted following an attempt to find solace from a headache by applying six leeches a day for 10 days. She is very nervous and surrounds herself with bogus medicines, but when Charlotte meets her, she thinks that her apparent illnesses can be cured by using commonsense methods.

Pratt, Richard (389) Another Limehouse visitor to Sanditon, noted by Mr. Thomas Parker as on the circulating library subscription list.

Sam (407) An "old" porter at the Sanditon hotel who helps the Parker hypochondriacs with their luggage. In fact, Diana Parker helps Sam "uncord the Trunks" (407).

Scroggs, Miss (389) Yet another name of a Sanditon visitor found by Mr. Thomas Parker on the circulating library subscribers listing.

Sheldon, Mrs. (386) Apparently a friend of Diana Parker living in Hampshire. Her coachman sprained his ankle and Diana claims to have "rubbed his Ancle with my own hand for six Hours without Intermission" (386).

Smith, Lieutenant (389) A Sanditon visitor from the Royal Navy whose name appears on the circulating library subscribers listing.

Stringer, Mr. and Son (381–382) Mr. Stringer is the owner of a Sanditon fruit and vegetable business that he operates with his son. Mr. Thomas Parker encouraged him to set up in Sanditon and has doubts about not giving the Stringers enough of his own business.

Whitby, Miss (390) The daughter of the proprietress of the lending library and Sanditon bookstore. In order to serve Charlotte Heywood, she is "hurried down from her Toilette, with all her glossy Curls & smart Trinkets" (390).

Whitby, Mrs. (381, 389) Proprietress of the Sanditon library and bookstore. She is "sitting in her inner room, reading one of her own Novels, for want of Employment," (389) when the Parkers call, with Charlotte Heywood, at the library on their initial evening back at Sanditon.

Woodcock, Mr. (407) The proprietor of the hotel in Sanditon.

BIBLIOGRAPHY

Primary Texts

Austen, Jane. [*Sanditon*] *Fragment of a Novel Written by Jane Austen January–March 1817*. Edited by R. W. Chapman. Oxford, U.K.: Clarendon Press, 1925.

———. *Sanditon* in *The Works of Jane Austen*. Vol. 6, *Minor Works*, edited by R. W. Chapman. Oxford: Oxford University Press, 1986. [All textual references are to this edition.]

———. *Sanditon. An Unfinished Novel*. Reproduced in Facsimile from the Manuscript in the Possession of *King's College, Cambridge*. Introduction by B. C. Southam. Oxford, U.K.: Clarendon Press; London: Scholar Press, 1975.

———. *Sanditon*, [*by*] *Jane Austen and another lady* [*Marie Dobbs*]. Boston: Houghton Mifflin, 1975.

———. *Northanger Abbey, Lady Susan. The Watsons and Sanditon*, edited by James Kingsley and John Davie, with an introduction and notes by Claudia L. Johnson. Oxford: Oxford University Press, 2003 [Oxford World's Classics].

———. *Somehow lengthened, by Alice Cobbett: a development of "Sanditon"* (*Jane Austen's fragmentary last novel*). London: Ernest Benn, 1932.

Austen-Leigh, J. E. *A Memoir of Jane Austen and Other Family Recollections*. Edited with an introduction and notes by Kathryn Sutherland. Oxford: Oxford University Press, 2002.

Gilson, David. A *Bibliography of Jane Austen: New Introduction and Corrections by the Author*. Winchester Hampshire, U.K.: St. Paul's Bibliographies; New Castle, Del.: Oak Knoll Press, 1997.

Secondary Texts

Burrows, John F. *Computation into Criticism: A Study of Jane Austen's Novels and Experiment in Method*. Oxford, U.K.: Clarendon Press, 1987.

Chapman, Robert W. *Jane Austen: Facts and Problems*. Oxford, U.K.: Clarendon Press, 1948.

Cornish, Francis Warre. *Jane Austen*, "English Men of Letters" Series. London: Macmillan, 1913.

Le Faye, Deirdre. *Jane Austen: The World of Her Novels*. New York: Harry N. Abrams, 2002.

Southam, Brian C. *Jane Austen's Literary Manuscripts*. Rev. ed. London: Athlone Press, 2001.

Sutherland, Kathryn. *Jane Austen's Textual Lives: From Aeschylus to Bollywood*. Oxford: Oxford University Press, 2005.

Tanner, Tony. *Jane Austen*. Houndmills, Basingstoke, Hants., U.K.: Macmillan, 1986.

Wiltshire, John. *Jane Austen and the Body: "The picture of health."* Cambridge: Cambridge University Press, 1992.

"Scraps" (1992)

COMPOSITION AND PUBLICATION

"Scraps" consists of five brief pieces that complete the second of the three notebooks in Jane Austen's handwriting into which she copied her childhood compositions. The dedication to her newly born niece FRANCES (FANNY) CATHERINE AUSTEN is written "in a fine, beautifully formed copper-plate script" (Southam, *Literary Manuscripts:* 17). The dating of the five pieces has been attributed to January 1793. Following the author's death, the manuscript went to her sister, CASSANDRA, and remained in family hands until it was sold at Sotheby's on July 6, 1977. It is now in the British Library.

"Scraps" were first published in G. K. Chesterton's edition. Subsequently, they appeared in the sixth volume of R. W. Chapman's Oxford edition of *The Works of Jane Austen*, revised by B. C. Southam in 1969. Southam also published them in his edition of Jane Austen's *Volume the Second,* and they appear in Margaret Anne Doody and Douglas Murray's 1993 edition of *Catharine and Other Writings* (194–208).

SYNOPSIS

The first "Scrap" consists of a single-paragraph letter from "The Female Philosopher—" Arabella Smythe to Louisa Clarke and describes the family, the Millars, mutual acquaintances. "The Female Philosopher" is the 18-year-old Julia Millar, an "amiable Moralist" who makes "most sensible reflections" and "Sentiments of Morality" (171–172).

The second "Scrap" is "The First Act of a Comedy," made up of four brief scenes with five male characters, including a "Chorus of ploughboys" and the classical figure "Strephon," and five females, including a "Cook" and the classically based "Chloe." Four characters are traveling to London with servants and inn staff. There is a mix-up; Popgun, the father of Pistoletta, is taking his daughter to marry Strephon. Strephon is traveling to marry Chloe, who is also on her journey to London expecting to marry Strephon!

The third "Scrap" consists of a single paragraph elaborately titled "A Letter from a Young Lady, whose feelings being too strong for her Judgement led her into the commission of Errors which her Heart disapproved." In her letter, Anna Parker confesses to her "beloved Elinor" her many crimes. These include the murder of her parents, repeated perjury, and forgery. She concludes her letter with the words, "I am now going to murder my Sister" (173–175).

The fourth "Scrap" is a short paragraph of eight sentences written by Elizabeth Johnson to her friend Clara entitled "A Tour through Wales—in a letter from a Young Lady." Much is packed into the paragraph, including, for instance, the detail, "My Mother rode upon our little poney & Fanny & I walked by her side or rather ran, for my Mother is so fond of riding fast that she galloped all the way."

The fifth "Scrap" is "A Tale." The first paragraph describes how "a Gentleman whose family name I shall conceal, bought a small" Pembrokeshire cottage. The second and third paragraphs focus on the selling of this dwelling to the buyer's brother, who visits it with his wife, two sisters, and their servants. "A Tale" essentially is a parody of the trend among Jane Austen's contemporaries to purchase picturesque country cottages. In this instance, when the brother, Robertus, arrives with his family and servants, there is no room for them. So Wilhelminus, the seller, puts some of his brother's family up in two tents: "A couple of old blankets, each supported by four sticks" (176–178).

CRITICAL COMMENTARY

Critical interest in each of the "Scraps" has varied, with the main attention being paid to the first and second "Scraps." Elizabeth Bennet's younger sister Mary Bennet reads profusely and reflects deeply: a "preliminary sketch of the philosophical Mary is found in Julia Millar of" the first of the "Scraps" (Pinion, 203). John Halperin notes that in the first of the five items, "there appear two sisters [Charlotte and Julia] two years apart in age—roughly the distance in age . . . between Jane Austen and her sister Cassandra." Halperin considers the younger Charlotte "as a laughingly complacent self-portrait" of the author Jane Austen (37). Charlotte "has a pleasing plumpness . . . She is fair and her face is expressive sometimes of softness the most bewitching, and at others of Vivacity the most striking," and so on (171).

The second "Scrap," entitled "The first Act of a Comedy," Penny Gay describes as consisting "of an inspired riff on the trope of stage secrecy: the eight characters in the three scenes drop hints, nods and winks, and tantalizing unfinished sentences—but nothing material is actually revealed to anyone, on or off stage." Further, "The first Act" is a parody of "the burletta or comic opera of the day" (2).

There is surprisingly little critical comment on the other "Scraps." Anna Parker's self-confession of heinous criminal atrocity seems ripe for further observation. Elizabeth Johnson's account of "A Tour through Wales" is clearly a burlesque of the fashionable travelogues of Jane Austen's contemporaries, and the fifth "Scrap" is a satire aimed, as is *Sanditon,* at commercial exploitation and false advertising. Textual explication is to be found in Doody and Murray's "Explanatory Notes" (339–342).

BIBLIOGRAPHY

Primary Texts

Austen, Jane. "Scraps" in *Love & Freindship and other early works, now printed from the original Ms. by Jane Austen, with a preface by G. K. Chesterton.* New York: Frederick A. Stokes, 1922, [161]–174.

———. "Scraps" in *The Works of Jane Austen.* Vol. 6, *Minor Works,* edited by R. W. Chapman. Oxford, U.K.: Oxford University Press, 1986. [All textual references are to this edition.]

———. "Scraps" in *Volume the Second, by Jane Austen.* Edited by B. C. Southam. Oxford, U.K.: Clarendon Press, 1963, 194–208.

———. "Scraps" in *Jane Austen's Catharine and other Writings,* edited by Margaret Anne Doody and Douglas Murray. Oxford: Oxford University Press, 1993, [165]–172.

Secondary Works

Gay, Penny. *Jane Austen and the Theatre.* Cambridge: Cambridge University Press, 2002.

Halperin, John. "Unengaged Laughter: Jane Austen's Juvenilia." In *Jane Austen's Beginnings: The Juvenilia and Lady Susan,* edited by J. David Grey. Ann Arbor, Mich., and London: UMI Research Press, [29]–44.

Pinion, F. B. *A Jane Austen Companion: A critical survey and reference book.* London: Macmillan, 1973.

Sense and Sensibility (1811)

COMPOSITION AND PUBLICATION

Probably around 1795, Jane Austen experimented with a novel entitled *Elinor and Marianne* written in the form of letters. In this, according to family tradition, the sisters were parted, whereas in *Sense and Sensibility,* "Elinor and Marianne are never parted, even for a single day." According to CASSANDRA AUSTEN's noting of composition dates for Jane Austen's novels, "Sense & Sensibility begun Nov. 1797." This was revised for publication in 1809–10 but HENRY AUSTEN, Jane's brother, comments that "it was with extreme difficulty that her friends . . . could prevail on her to publish her first work." This reluctance may have been due to the fact that *First*

Impressions (the earlier version of PRIDE AND PREJUDICE) was rejected for publication. *Susan* (the earlier version of NORTHANGER ABBEY), although sold to a publisher, remained unpublished.

JAMES and Henry AUSTEN's connections with the London publisher THOMAS EGERTON led to his publishing the work. It was "published on commission 'for the author'," with Jane Austen "paying expenses and taking the receipts—subject to payment of a commission to the publisher for handling the book—while retaining the copyright." The author believed, Henry Austen writes, that the sale of the novel "would not repay the expense of pub-

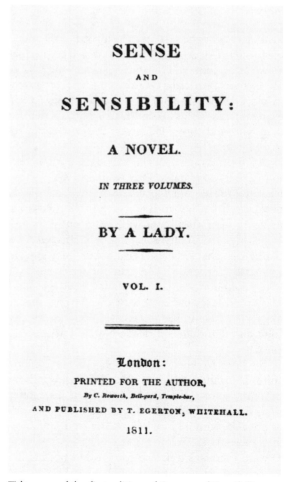

Title page of the first edition of *Sense and Sensibility*

lication, that she actually made a reserve from her very moderate income to meet the expected loss." In April 1811, Jane Austen corrected proofs. *Sense and Sensibility* was published at the end of October 1811 in three volumes priced at 15 shillings. The title page attributed authorship to "By A Lady." The first edition, either of 1,000 or 750 copies, sold out before July 1813. Egerton produced a second edition in November 1813 at 18 shillings. Jane Austen still received royalties from the volume in March 1817 (Gilson, 7–8).

Page references are to the 1943 Oxford reprint of R. W. Chapman's edition of the novel.

SYNOPSIS

Volume 1

Old Mr. Dashwood of Norland Park in Sussex and his heir, his nephew Henry Dashwood, have died. Henry married twice. By his first marriage, he has a son, John. John and his four-year-old son, Henry, are in their own right wealthy and by a provision in old Dashwood's will, they are the heirs to his estate. Henry by his second marriage has a dependant wife and three daughters: Elinor, Marianne, and Margaret.

As soon as Henry Dashwood is buried, the John Dashwoods move into Norland Park. John's wife, the selfish and egocentric Fanny Dashwood, persuades John not to honor a verbal promise he made to his father to provide sufficiently for his stepmother and daughters. Elinor is attracted to Fanny's brother Edward Ferrars, but knows he is financially dependent on his snobbish mother, who would not countenance such a marriage. Mrs. Dashwood loses patience with the distant, supercilious treatment she receives from Fanny and John and determines to leave Norland as soon as she can.

Sir John Middleton of Barton Park in Devonshire, a distant relation, invites the Dashwoods to become tenants of Barton Cottage on his estate. Mrs. Dashwood and her daughters move as soon as possible, without tangible assistance from Fanny and John. Mrs. Dashwood makes it evident that Edward Ferrars is welcome to visit, but not his sister or her husband, although she goes through the motions of inviting them.

The Dashwoods move to Barton Cottage, meet an almost overwelcoming Sir John Middleton and his more reserved wife. At Barton Park, they meet Lady Middleton's mother, Mrs. Jennings, and Colonel Brandon of Delaford in Dorsetshire. The Colonel is very attentive to Marianne and her piano playing, but she makes it clear after he has gone that at 35 he is too old and boring to be a suitor.

The Dashwoods quickly settle into the rhythms and routines of country life. One morning Marianne and Margaret set off for a walk, the weather turns suddenly, and to avoid the heavy rain they are forced to turn back. They run down the hill to the garden gate, but in doing so Marianne falls and twists her ankle. A gentleman out hunting comes to her rescue, takes her in his arms, and carries her to the cottage. Her rescuer is John Willoughby, living at nearby Allenham. He calls the next day to enquire about her. Marianne idealizes him as the type of hero she meets only in fiction. Sir John tells her that he is high-spirited and lacks "moderation" but evidently is "well worth catching" (45–44). He has property in Somersetshire and is the heir of Mrs. Smith, the elderly aunt of the nearby Allenham Court.

Willoughby frequently visits Barton Cottage. Marianne, infatuated with him, gives Willoughby a lock of her hair. Elinor gently attempts to warn her not to commit herself too much until she knows more about him. Willoughby's adverse comments on Colonel Brandon, whom Elinor has grown to respect and admire, trouble her, especially as she is aware that Brandon has fallen in love with Marianne.

Willoughby and Marianne continue to defy convention by openly displaying their mutual attraction, and an engagement is expected. Willoughby, however, suddenly announces his imminent departure for London. He leaves quickly, giving no return date, and a distraught Marianne waits in vain for a letter from him. Edward Ferrars spends a week at Barton Cottage but is reserved and uneasy toward Elinor. In contrast to her sister, she exercises self-control and does not exhibit her true feelings.

Two newly discovered relations of Mrs. Jennings, Anne and Lucy Steele, stay as guests of the

Middletons at Barton Park. Both are fashionable ladies. Anne is nearly 30 and plain, while Lucy is younger and superficially smart. Elinor discovers that Lucy and Edward have secretly been engaged for four years. Edward was a pupil of her uncle in Plymouth, and they have kept the engagement a secret as Lucy is without a fortune and Edward's mother would not approve. Elinor is initially unable to accept that Edward would attach himself to someone as superficial as Lucy, but from what she knows of his family, she comes to accept the situation and is silently "wretched" (135).

Volume 2

Elinor does not display her feelings and guesses that on Edward's part, the engagement was part of a youthful infatuation. She learns from Lucy that they both have grown tired of each other, but Edward is too honorable to break off the promise to her, and Lucy refuses to give up a potentially wealthy match. Mrs. Jennings invites Elinor and Marianne to spend the winter season in London. Owing to a promise to Lucy, Elinor has withheld information about the secret engagement and not informed Marianne. But she has to listen to her sister's distress regarding Willoughby. Against her better judgment, she allows herself to be persuaded by her mother and sister to accept the London invitation, and they leave for London with Mrs. Jennings during the first week of January.

Marianne writes to Willoughby and receives no answer. The Middletons arrive in London and organize a ball, to which Willoughby has been invited but fails to appear. They then attend a large gathering with Lady Middleton, where they encounter Willoughby accompanied by a very fashionable lady. Willoughby is very cool and barely polite toward Marianne, who almost faints and is prevented by Elinor from rushing after him to demand an explanation. Elinor tells Lady Middleton that her sister is unwell. They return home at once with Marianne in "silent agony" (178).

The following day, a distraught Marianne writes to Willoughby and receives an immediate reply. In the same reserved tone as the previous day, Willoughby denies slighting her or having

Elinor and Marianne, on the frontispiece to *Sense and Sensibility (London: Routledge, c. 1875)*

given her a reason to think that there was an attachment between them. He returns her letters as she requested, along with her lock of hair. Furthermore, he is engaged to be married. Mrs. Jennings, who is back from her usual morning gossip with acquaintances, confirms that Willoughby is shortly to marry and adds that, having spent his fortune rashly, he is marrying Miss Grey, an heiress.

Colonel Brandon reveals to Elinor that Willoughby seduced and deserted Brandon's 16-year-old ward, Eliza Williams. She is the illegitimate daughter of Brandon's deceased sister-in-law, Elizabeth Brandon, with whom Brandon was in love. Willoughby is exposed as "expensive, dissipated and worse than both" (210). Marianne, rather than finding consolation in this, is even more depressed as she has lost Willoughby and also her romantic ideals. But she begins to view Brandon more sympathetically.

Mrs. Dashwood persuades Elinor and Marianne to stay in London, as at Barton Cottage Marianne will be reminded too much of Willoughby. Further, the John Dashwoods will soon be in London, and the girls should spend time with them. Two weeks after Willoughby's letter, early in February, Willoughby marries and leaves London. The Steele girls arrive, as do the John Dashwoods. In a jeweler's shop one morning, without knowing who it is, Elinor and Marianne observe the vain Robert Ferrars fastidiously selecting a toothpick case. They also meet John Dashwood, who makes lame excuses for not having called on them but wishes to meet the well-connected wealthy Middletons. He arrives without his wife the next day at Mrs. Jennings', where Brandon is visiting. John Dashwood then walks with Elinor to the Middletons' residence. During the walk his mercenary nature emerges. He encourages Elinor to pursue Brandon for his wealth, speaks of Marianne's reduced opportunities to marry well, and reveals his plans to make enclosures in Norland Commons on his estate. Mrs. Ferrars plans to marry Edward Ferrars to a wealthy heiress, the Honorable Miss Morton.

John Dashwood gives his wife such a favorable report of Mrs. Jennings and Lady Middleton that she agrees to visit them and bonds with the egocentric Lady Middleton. Mrs. Jennings, Elinor, Marianne, and Brandon are invited to dinner at the Middletons'. In addition to Anne and Lucy Steele, they meet Mrs. Ferrars. She is especially disdainful of Elinor, whom she suspects of still having designs on Edward. Elinor finds this ironic, since if Mrs. Ferrars knew Edward was already secretly engaged, she would be outraged. Mrs. Ferrars slights Elinor's drawing and receives a rebuke from Marianne. Colonel Brandon particularly admires Marianne for this display of an "affectionate heart" (236).

In the last chapters of volume 2, Anne and Lucy Steele are invited to stay at John and Fanny Dashwood's Harley Street residence. Elinor perceives this as a signal that Lucy has succeeded in flattering Fanny and she will support her in making public the news of her engagement to Edward.

Volume 3

This opens with the news that the Steele girls have been thrown out of the Harley Street house. Anne Steele reveals the secret engagement, and Fanny Dashwood reacts with horror and a fit of "violent hysterics" (259). Elinor reveals her own situation to Marianne, who begins to be aware of just how difficult it has been for Elinor. Mrs. Ferrars has given Edward an ultimatum. If he marries Lucy, he will be disowned and disinherited; if he breaks the engagement and agrees to marry Miss Morton, she will increase his fortune. Edward has made it clear that he will keep his word to Lucy. He has been dismissed from his mother's house and she has arranged through lawyers to transfer the estate due to him to Robert, the younger brother. Three days later, Anne Steele tells Elinor that Edward offered Lucy a release from the engagement but she refused. The following morning, Elinor receives a letter from Lucy stating that she had offered Edward the opportunity to break off the engagement but he had refused.

Colonel Brandon, hearing of Edward's financial difficulties, offers him an unfilled position in the church as a clergyman on his Delaford estate. It is early April, and Elinor and Marianne leave London for Barton. On their way, they visit the Palmers at Cleveland in Somersetshire, where they travel with Mrs. Jennings. Cleveland is only 30 miles from Willoughby's Combe Magna, and Marianne is overcome with nostalgia. She goes out in spite of the rain on long walks, catches cold, which becomes pneumonia, and falls dangerously ill. She is inadequately treated by Mr. Harris, the Palmers' apothecary. Colonel Brandon leaves to fetch Mrs. Dashwood from Barton, and Elinor remains with the very ill Marianne.

Elinor's devoted nursing sees her sister through the worst of the crisis. Later in the evening on the fifth day of the illness, Elinor hears a carriage. Instead of the expected Mrs. Dashwood and Colonel Brandon, Willoughby appears. He has dashed from London, having heard that Marianne is dying, to try to explain his actions and asks for forgiveness.

He acknowledges to Elinor his behavior to Eliza Williams and mercenary marriage to Miss Grey. His last letter to Marianne was dictated by his wife, whom he neither loves nor respects. Elinor grants Willoughby a degree of forgiveness and pities the long, loveless unhappy years ahead of him. She also agrees to convey his story to Marianne once she has recovered sufficiently.

Her mother arrives with Colonel Brandon, who on the journey confessed his love for Marianne. Mrs. Dashwood will do all she can to promote it, and she tries to make up for her former encouragement of Willoughby by trumpeting Brandon's praises. Marianne and Elinor return to Barton with their mother. Marianne undergoes a period of intense self-reflection. Elinor tells her of Willoughby's visit, and she concludes that she could not have been happy with him. Marianne determines to be less emotional and to exercise greater self-control.

Mrs. Dashwood's manservant Thomas returns from a visit to Exeter with the news that Edward Ferrars and Lucy Steele are married. Marianne on hearing the news looses self-control. Elinor retains control but is clearly distressed. Mrs. Dashwood realizes how much she has neglected Elinor and paid too much attention to Marianne. Elinor clearly still loves Edward and has hoped they may marry in spite of the obstacles. Edward arrives unexpectedly at the cottage. Elinor thinks he has come to announce his marriage to Lucy. He explains that it was not him at Exeter but his brother Robert. Lucy had quickly transferred her attentions to Robert once she learns that he will inherit the estate and has married Robert before even breaking the engagement with Edward. They maliciously tricked Edward in Exeter.

Edward comes to Barton to ask for Elinor's hand. She accepts and they are partially reconciled with Mrs. Ferrars, who gives consent for them to marry but keeps the settlement of the estate on Robert in spite of his marriage to Lucy. Elinor and Edward marry at Barton in the autumn and settle at Delaford, where the generous Brandon has improved the parsonage. All scheme to persuade Marianne to see Brandon as a suitor and she at last accepts his proposal. They are married within a year of Edward

and Elinor's marriage. The couples live happily at Delaford in regular contact with Mrs. Dashwood and Margaret at Barton. The lives of Lucy and Robert, Mrs. Ferrars, Willoughby, and his wife, and John and Fanny Dashwood are full of "disagreement between themselves" (380).

CRITICAL SYNOPSIS

Chapter 1

The opening paragraph of the first chapter introduces some of Jane Austen's favorite themes: money, inheritance, and family conflict. One generation passes and gives way to another. A distinction is made between selfish interest and "goodness of [the] heart." The reader is not introduced to a specific time but to a family—the Dashwoods. The second paragraph introduces the gender distinction. One generation of male Dashwoods are sufficiently taken care of, whereas their sisters are not. Practically the estate is "tied up for the benefit [of] a small child." Jane Austen creates warning signs concerning this child, who had "an earnest desire of having his own way." The three girls are "left" with "a thousand pounds a piece," relatively paltry sums. The young John Dashwood "was not an ill-disposed young man," although even this is qualified by Jane Austen with the comment "unless to be rather cold hearted, and rather selfish, is to be ill-disposed." There are a number of other reservations concerning the character of John Dashwood in spite of his conducting "himself with propriety in the discharge of his ordinary duties." In other words, he conducted himself appropriately, but his Achilles' heel is his wife, whom he married when he was young. He was "very fond of his wife. But Mrs. John Dashwood was a strong caricature of himself;—more narrow-minded and selfish."

The eighth paragraph of the chapter contains a sequence of inner thought processes conveying Dashwood's intentions toward his half-sisters in the form of quotation marks used to separate thoughts he is saying to himself. The remainder of the chapter moves from the funeral of Henry Dashwood to the young Mr. John Dashwood's unannounced appearance at Norland Park, the Dashwood residence. There clearly is no love lost between John Drummond's stepmother and her stepson's wife.

The mother remains at Norland only after listening to her eldest daughter, Elinor, regarding "the propriety" or appropriateness "of going and her own tender love for all her three children." She wishes to "avoid a breach with" the family.

The last four paragraphs of the chapter describe the differing personalities of the daughters. The eldest, Elinor, clearly is able to influence her mother. She is 19 yet "possessed strength of understanding, and coolness of judgment." She has an "eagerness of mind," which may be perceived as "imprudence," for instance, by the young Mrs. Dashwood. Unlike her mother, Elinor knows how "to govern" her feelings, a quality "which one of her sisters had resolved never to be taught."

If Elinor represents common sense, then Marianne, her sister, is the embodiment of "sensibility." Marianne too is "sensible and clever," but in addition "eager in every thing; her sorrows, her joys could have no moderation." In other words, "she was every thing but prudent." The penultimate paragraph describes the sisters' and mother's different reactions to their situation. Marianne and her mother "gave themselves wholly up to their sorrow." Although also "deeply afflicted," Elinor is able to control her feelings, "she could exert herself," and is able to undertake appropriate social duties such as treating her stepbrother's wife upon arrival at Norland Park in the correct manner and encouraging her mother to exercise "similar forbearance."

The chapter ends with a brief single paragraph describing Margaret, the younger sister, who is only 13. Like Marianne, "she had already imbibed a good deal of [her] romance, without having much of her sense" and does not appear "at a more advanced period of life" to "bid fair to equal her sisters" ([3]–7). So essentially, Elinor is associated with qualities aligned to "sense," or 18th-century neoclassicism, such as a middle way, rationality, moderation, the control of feelings, social responsibility and values, duty, and charity. Marianne, on the other hand, her mother, and younger sister Margaret represent characteristics associated with romanticism, such as the open expression of feelings, giving the imagination free rein, excess, and individual, as opposed to social, concerns. The novel may be viewed as an interaction or dialogue between these values. By its completion they intermingle.

Chapter 2

The second chapter largely consists of a debate between John Dashwood and his wife, Fanny, as to how much his stepmother and sisters should practically receive. Their discussion moves from the subject of annuities and their limitations, to whether they should abide by his late father's request to grant each of the daughters 1,000 pounds each. The reader learns that once Mrs. John Dashwood had "installed herself mistress of Norland . . . her mother and sisters-in-law were degraded to the condition of visitors." They are treated more kindly by John Dashwood than by his wife. Mrs. Dashwood is unhappy because Norland reminds her of what was rather than what is—she lives in the past rather than the present. She has an optimistic outlook on life, a "sanguine expectation of pleasure which is happiness itself."

Mrs. Fanny Dashwood's point of view is conveyed at some length, especially in the third paragraph of the chapter, and continued in discussion between her and her husband. Her meanness is disguised by her consideration for "the fortune of their dear little boy": Any payment to her husband's relatives implies taking money from their young son. Her husband feels a debt of obligation to his father's wishes. This is soon whittled away by Mrs. Fanny Dashwood. She objects to the annuity, as her husband's stepmother "is very stout and healthy, and hardly forty." So by the conclusion of the chapter, John Dashwood decides, being influenced by his wife, "that it would be absolutely unnecessary, if not highly indecorous, to do more for the widow and children of his father, than such kind of neighbourly acts as his own wife pointed out." Even "The china, plate and linen" of Stanhill, Mrs. Dashwood's former home, remains. As the young Mr. Dashwood observes, "That is a material consideration undoubtedly. A valuable legacy indeed!" and adds, "And yet some of the plate could have been a very pleasant addition to our own stock here."

The second chapter contains a mixture of omniscient narration and dialogue, presenting counter-arguments between John Dashwood and his wife, Fanny, of which Fanny, Mrs. John Dashwood, gets the better of the argument. So an intended legacy of 3,000 pounds for each daughter is pared down to acts of charity. "Material consideration[s]" (8–13) reverberate through the novel.

Chapter 3

A brief chapter moves through several perspectives. The first four paragraphs focus on the older Mrs. Dashwood. Her "eldest daughter," Elinor's "steadier judgment rejected several houses too large for their income, which her mother would have approved." The second paragraph concentrates on Mrs. Dashwood's mistaken reliance on the "liberality of his intentions" of the young John Dashwood. The third paragraph conveys the "contempt" she "felt for her daughter-in-law," which is exacerbated by "a growing attachment between" Elinor "and the brother of Mrs. John Dashwood," Edward Ferrars. Elinor's mother's motives for encouraging "the intimacy" between them are shown by the narrator not to be those of self-interest. "Edward Ferrars was the eldest son of a man who had died very rich"; however, somewhat unusually, "the whole of the fortune depended on the will of his mother." The deceased Mr. Ferrars left his fortune to his wife rather than to a male descendant, unlike, for instance, in the case of the dead Mr. Dashwood, who leaves his second wife and three daughters in a dependent situation.

Mrs. Dashwood, in contrast to most of the other characters in the novel, ignores disparities created by wealth: "It was enough for her that he appeared to be amiable, that he loved her daughter, and that Elinor returned the partiality." The narrator adds, "It was contrary to every doctrine of her's [Jane Austen here uses a variant form of "hers"] that difference of fortune should keep any couple asunder who were attracted by resemblance of disposition."

The sixth paragraph shifts the point of view to that of the author and then to that of "his mother and sister." Edward Ferrars is described through negatives: He is "not recommended to their good opinion . . . He was not handsome," he is "diffident" or shy. Edward fails to conform to his mother and sister's expectations: "they wanted him to make a

fine figure in the world in some manner or other." His mother wishes to see him in Parliament and his sister wishes to see him driving a "barouche," or a four-wheeled open carriage, a modern equivalent being an extremely expensive car. But Edward's "wishes centered in domestic comfort and the quiet of private life." The final sentence of the paragraph is a fine example of authorial irony. It seems to be a comment by the author but encapsulates Mrs. Ferrars's materialistic outlook and values: "Fortunately he had a younger brother who was more promising," one who would make more of a splash, a show in the world.

To Elinor's mother, "she saw only that [Edward] was quiet and unobtrusive." A discussion between Elinor and her mother reveals that the mother has much in common with the attitudes of her younger daughter Marianne, being unable "to separate esteem and love." Dialogue between Marianne and her mother closes the chapter. It reveals the impulsive, selfish driven younger daughter for whom external appearances are important. She "could not be happy with a man whose taste did not in every point coincide with [her] own." As her mother reminds her in the last paragraph of the chapter, she is "not [yet] seventeen." Marianne's relationship with her mother is very open. She assesses Edward's character impulsively according to her perception of his apparently lukewarm reading aloud of lines from the poet WILLIAM COWPER, one of Jane Austen's favorite authors. She complains to her mother, "To hear those beautiful lines which have frequently almost driven me wild, pronounced with such impenetrable coldness, such dreadful indifference!" Edward's reading aloud of literature becomes a basis for character assessment (14–18).

Chapter 4

The chapter contains a lengthy speech by Elinor to her sister and the description of the contents of a letter from a distant relation of Elinor's offering her mother and sister a home. This is the first instance of a letter in the novel playing a significant role. This chapter, important for plot development, opens with Elinor and Marianne discussing Edward Ferrars's character in terms of his reactions to drawing, revealing that the sisters disagree aesthetically but also over the nature of love. Elinor's sense that Edward has reservations about their relationship, "the longer they were together the more doubtful seemed the nature of his regard," prefigures subsequent events in the narrative. Mrs. Ferrars's "contempt" toward Mrs. Dashwood, when she broaches the subject of a possible marriage between Elinor and Edward, results in the desire to leave Norland, as "her beloved Elinor should not be exposed another week to such insinuations"—of ensnaring him for mercenary reasons.

The "cold and unfeeling behaviour" Mrs. Dashwood receives at the hands of her relatives by marriage encourages her to accept an invitation made in a letter from a distant relative, Sir John Middleton of Barton Park. Although living in Devonshire, in the west of England, far away from Norland, Sussex, and Edward, "to quit the neighbourhood of Norland was no longer an evil; it was an object of desire; it was a blessing." Elinor, in spite of her as yet apparently unreciprocated attachment to Edward, "thought it would be more prudent for them to settle at some distance from Norland." Here she exercises common sense rather than personal feeling and "made no attempt to dissuade her mother from sending her letter of acquiescence"— or somewhat reluctant acceptance of Sir John's offer (19–24).

Chapter 5

In this short transitional chapter of eight paragraphs, Mrs. Henry Dashwood announces her move from Norland. John Dashwood, in spite of his promise to his late father, makes no real effort to assist, and his wife even wishes to deprive her husband's relatives of "any handsome article of furniture." The young Dashwoods are invited to visit Barton. Edward regrets that they will be "so far from" Norland. Elinor helps her mother prepare for the quick move: "the furniture was all sent round by water," a common means of transportation during the early 19th century. Elinor's "wisdom" limits "the number of their servants to three."

In the first paragraph the word "incommode," or inconvenient, occurs for the only time in Jane

Austen's work. It conveys the sense of the rapid transition from one home to another. This sense of transition is also movingly conveyed through the perspective of Marianne Dashwood in the last paragraph of the novel. Just before leaving Norland, Marianne pays homage to the house where she has spent most of her childhood: "Dear, dear Norland! . . . when shall I cease to regret you!—when learn to feel a home elsewhere!" Such addresses to houses or parts of nature holding especial sentimental meaning and memory were common in gothic literature and found in the work of Jane Austen's contemporaries such as Scott and Wordsworth. However, Marianne's feelings are genuine: "No leaf will decay because we are removed, nor any branch become motionless, although we can observe you no longer!" Although *Sense and Sensibility* (SS) is about the interaction of two qualities as reflected through the personalities of Elinor and Marianne, it is also a novel about growing up. The novel depicts the process of change in human beings as they experience the world against the background of nature and its cyclical pattern of change and renewal (25–27).

Chapter 6

This is another short chapter, mostly of authorial narration conveying the journey from Sussex to Devon, the initial impressions of the new home, and meeting with Sir John and Lady Middleton. The first paragraph is concerned with the journey. Initially "melancholy" as they move closer to their new home, the environment—"It was a pleasant fertile spot, well wooded, and rich in pasture"— creates a change in mood, to "cheerfulness." This is in spite of the smallness of Barton: "a small green court was the whole of its demise in front," or extent of the property.

The second and third paragraphs interweave the macrocosm and the microcosm, the larger picture of Barton Cottage and its place in the world with specific details such as the "window shutters" and the walls, contrasted with those of Norland. The sense of the importance of individual response to the environment is continued. Barton Cottage's "situation" regarding its immediate location, the "high hills [which] rose immediately behind," gives way descriptively to "the village of Barton," and the external perspective in the third paragraph, the internal and differing reactions to it. Mrs. Dashwood admits that the house "is too small for our family," then makes impractical suggestions for improvements. The change in personal situation and mood is reflected in the seasons: "It was very early in September; the season was fine"—even the weather is sympathetic, kindly. Improvements are planned for the spring.

The last five paragraphs of the chapter introduce the Middletons, who have rented at a very cheap rate Barton Cottage to their distant relatives. Sir John Middleton's kindness and consideration is backed up by actual deed, "within an hour after he left them, a large basket full of garden stuff and fruit arrived from the park." This "was followed before the end of the day by a present of game." However, "his entreaties were carried to a point of perseverance beyond civility." On the other hand, the Dashwoods find the much younger Lady Middleton more "reserved, [and] cold" than her husband. Their eldest child is very shy, and the chapter concludes with Sir John being unable to leave the Cottage "without securing the promise of dining at the park the next day" (28–31).

Chapter 7

This is yet another brief chapter consisting of nine descriptive paragraphs of direct authorial narration without dialogue. The Dashwoods visit the Middletons at Barton Park, "about half a mile from the cottage." The smallness of the cottage is highlighted by Barton Park, which "was large and handsome; and the Middletons lived in a style of equal hospitality and elegance." Both "strongly resembled each other in that total want of talent and taste which confined their employments . . . within a very narrow compass." They are described: "Lady Middleton piqued [prided] herself upon the elegance of her table, and of all her domestic arrangements." Her husband enjoys society and especially "young people" and young ladies. His criteria of approval is that a "pretty girl" should be "unaffected," without pretension, and natural, although his nieces, as he and the reader will discover, are far from "simple." He has "a good heart," and apparently prefers girls

to "sportsmen," as they will be interested also in shooting, which is his territory. Sir John has been able to invite "only one gentleman" to Barton Park to welcome the Dashwoods, as "it was moonlight and every body was full of engagements." This refers to transportation problems during the period. In the country, moonlight evenings made visits to venues some distance away from home practical, as the moonlight provided natural lighting.

They are introduced to Lady Dashwood's mother, Mrs. Jennings, who, in addition to being "merry, fat" and elderly, "talked a great deal, seemed very happy, and rather vulgar." She subjects Elinor and Marianne to "common-place raillery," or good-natured ridicule, especially on the "subject of lovers and husbands," and "hoped they had not left their hearts behind them in Sussex." The other guest is "Colonel Brandon," who "was silent and grave" and perceived by Marianne and her younger sister, Margaret, as "an absolute old bachelor, for he was on the wrong side of five and thirty." The "cold insipidity of Lady Middleton" is disturbed only "by the entrance of her four noisy children after dinner."

The final two paragraphs of the chapter center around Marianne's performance at the piano and her singing songs requested, revealing considerable ability on her part to remember words and tunes. The others overpraise Marianne's performance. "Colonel Brandon alone, of all the party, heard her without being in raptures." Her response to him is mixed. On the one hand, it "was estimable when contrasted against the horrible insensibility of the others," whom she perceives as lacking musical taste. On the other hand, "a man" past 35 years of age "might well have outlived all acuteness of feeling and every exquisite power of enjoyment." Marianne's, is a total misjudgment as the novel reveals. For one so full of feeling and sensibility, she seriously misreads her fellow human beings.

Chapter 8

The opening paragraph focuses on Mrs. Jennings, "a widow, with an ample jointure," that is, money or property settled on her following her husband's death. She is convinced "that Colonel Brandon was very much in love with Marianne Dashwood." This conviction "supplied her with endless jokes against them both." Marianne, who is 17, points out that Colonel Brandon "is old enough to be *my* father." Elinor tells her sister that "if there should be any chance happen to be a woman who is single at seven and twenty, I should not think Colonel Brandon's being thirty-five any objection to his marrying *her*" [Jane Austen's emphasis]. The observation reinforces the sense that in Jane Austen's work, 27 is the age at which single women despair of finding a husband. Notably Charlotte Lucas in *Pride and Prejudice* is 27 when she captures the Reverend Collins, and Anne Elliot, the heroine of *Persuasion,* is the same age when she at last marries Wentworth.

The chapter is taken up with a dialogue among Elinor, Marianne, and their mother on marriage and whether marrying a man of 35 is "dooming Colonel Brandon and his wife to the constant confinement of a sick chamber." The wife of an older man will "submit to the offices of a nurse, for the sake of the provision and security of a wife." A similar observation is made in the third volume of SAMUEL RICHARDSON's *Sir Charles Grandison.* Marianne notes that Colonel Brandon "talked of flannel waistcoats" (36–38). Flannel, a woolen fabric of loose texture, was associated by Jane Austen with illness. She writes on June 19, 1799, to her sister, Cassandra, from Bath, "my Uncle is still in his flannels, but is getting better again" (*Letters,* 47).

Elinor unsuccessfully attempts to get Marianne to admit that she is not uninterested in Brandon. When Elinor leaves the room, Marianne and her mother discuss what appears to be Edward Ferrars's failure to visit them in their new home. Marianne believes that he may be ill. This results in an intimate and speculative discussion between mother and daughter on motives, character, and feelings. Marianne tells her mother that Elinor's "self-command is invariable." She asks, "When is she dejected or melancholy? When does she try to avoid society, or appear restless and dissatisfied in it?" Such unanswered questions posit questions in the mind of readers, who speculate as do the fictional characters. In this way, readers are encouraged to read on in the narrative to try to find the answers to the questions (38–39).

Chapter 9

This important chapter is placed in the perspective of plot development and the introduction of new characters. The Dashwoods settle down to their new existence and enjoy "ordinary pursuits" such as their garden and walking in the surrounding countryside, which "abounded in beautiful walks." The impulsive Marianne, accompanied by her younger sister, Margaret, ignores "one memorable morning" the warning signs of "driving rain" and goes out on a walk. Forced to turn back, they run "with all possible speed down the steep side of the hill which led immediately to their garden gate." Margaret makes it, but Marianne falls down and is carried home by "a gentleman" who is out shooting game birds and accompanied by two pointers, or dogs, bred to indicate or "point" to the location of the game. "He put down his gun and ran to her assistance [and] took her up in his arms without further delay, and carried her down the hill."

Such a chance encounter has important consequences. Elinor and her mother agree that Marianne's rescuer is "uncommonly handsome" and with good manners. Elinor discovers that his name is "Willoughby," currently living in a nearby house admired by the Dashwoods, Allenham Court, and he asks to be allowed to call the next day "to inquire after" Marianne. The 11th paragraph of the chapter, seen through Marianne's perspective, beginning with "His manly beauty" (40–43), conveys the attractiveness of appearance or "the cosmetic element in sexual attraction" (Hardy, 151). Willoughby's "person and air were equal to what" Marianne's "fancy had ever drawn for the hero of a favourite story." He appeals to her preconceptions. Further, "His name was good, his residence was in their favourite village, and [Marianne] soon found out that of all manly dresses a shooting-jacket was the most becoming" (43). The name is associated with pedigree, aristocracy, and class. In this paragraph, Jane Austen ironically reveals how the superficial and external joined with social image provide an "irresistible blend": It will take most of the novel for Marianne "to lose the romantic image of appearance in the reality of experience" (Hardy, 151).

Sir John visits the family and apparently speaks highly of Willoughby: "A very decent shot, and there is not a bolder rider in England," meet his criteria of "as good a kind of fellow as ever lived." Furthermore, he will inherit Allenham Court when his relative, "the old lady" residing there, dies. In other words, "he is very well worth catching." Mrs. Dashwood objects to this, observing, "Men are very safe with us, let them be ever so rich." Sir John stresses Willoughby's energy as seen in his dancing and hunting activities. Such qualities appeal to Marianne as "his eagerness . . . should know no moderation," and she objects to what she regards as Sir John's clichés concerning her "settling one's cap at a man" or "making a conquest." But in the last paragraph of the chapter, Sir John reminds her that Brandon "is very well worth setting your cap at, I can tell you, in spite of all this tumbling about and spraining of ancles" [sic]. Marianne, of course, ignores such wisdom (43–45).

Chapter 10

Marianne and Willoughby's relationship develops and becomes closer during his frequent visits to the Dashwoods' cottage. Elinor is more reserved toward him, perceiving that "he strongly resembled" Marianne in "saying too much what he thought on every occasion, without attention to persons or circumstances." Elinor attempts to defend Colonel Brandon, "for what could a silent man of five and thirty hope, when opposed by a very lively one of five and twenty?" Elinor "liked him—in spite of his gravity and reserve." For Willoughby, on the other hand, "Brandon is just the kind of man . . . whom everybody speaks well of, and nobody cares about; whom all are delighted to see, and nobody remembers to talk to." The chapter concludes with Willoughby offering Elinor "three unanswerable reasons for disliking Colonel Brandon." These are trivial: "he has threatened me with rain when I wanted it to be fine"; Brandon finds "fault with the hanging of my curricle," or the interior of his fashionable two-wheeled carriage; "and I cannot persuade him to buy my brown mare."

The chapter is replete with literary allusions. Margaret characterizes Willoughby as "Marianne's preserver" (46–52). In doing so, she is probably echoing Jane West's *A Gossip's Story*, published in 1796. In this novel, "a heroine called Marianne

is rescued by a handsome young man when the horse she is riding takes fright at a carriage. The young man, Clermont, is referred to as her 'preserver'" (Lamont, 307). In the fourth paragraph of the chapter, Elinor tells her sister that she knows what Willoughby "thinks of Cowper and Scott." She adds, "you have received every assurance of his admiring Pope no more than is proper" (47). Cowper and SCOTT are in accord with romantic taste and focus on human feeling stimulated by "suffering and by the passage of time" (Lamont, 307). The poetry of ALEXANDER POPE, on the other hand, focuses less on individuals than on individuals as social beings.

Elinor, in this fourth paragraph, tells Marianne that she and Willoughby will soon exhaust the subject of literature. She adds, "another meeting will suffice to explain his sentiments on picturesque beauty." This is an allusion to the fashion for assessing nature through the principles found in WILLIAM GILPIN's work. Gilpin stresses the primitive and nonstructured elements of nature and the powerful effect of light. Marianne's defense, "I have erred against every common-place notion of decorum; I have been open and sincere where I ought to have been reserved, spiritless, dull and deceitful," reveals her strong individualist, nonconformist spirit.

Willoughby tells Elinor that Colonel Brandon "is patronized by" her, or favored by her. Furthermore, Willoughby and Marianne believe that Elinor will accept whatever Brandon tells her, whether he refers to the "East Indies"—an expression used to refer to the Indian subcontinent in addition to the actual East Indies—or his observations on "the existence of nabobs, gold mohrs and palanquins." These expressions convey perceptions of India. According to the *OED*, the origins of "nabob" are from Urdu and mean the governor of a province but took on the meaning of someone returning from India with a fortune. The leading gold coin of northern India was a "mohr," and "palanquin" referred to a covered vehicle carried by bearers. Elinor tells Willoughby "that *his*," referring to Colonel Brandon's "observations had stretched much farther than *your* candour" (Jane Austen's emphasis). Here "candour" is used somewhat ironically in the now no longer used sense of freedom from malice or kindness. It emerges subsequently in the novel that Willoughby is less than kindly disposed toward Brandon (47, 50–51).

Chapter 11

This chapter describes the developing relations between Marianne and Willoughby, now publicly displayed, and Elinor's private reservations about it. Marianne flaunts conventional behavior. Elinor "only wished that" her sister's "affection" for Willoughby "were less openly shown; and once or twice did venture to suggest the propriety of some self-command to Marianne." The whirl of social activity and her devotion to Willoughby have even reduced Marianne's "fond attachment to Norland," her previous home. October has come, the time for "private balls," and "this was the season of happiness to Marianne."

On the other hand, "Elinor's happiness was not so great." She is uneasy about her younger sister, and "neither Lady Middleton nor [her mother] Mrs. Jennings could supply to her the conversation she missed." Lady Middleton's "reserve was mere calmness of manner with which sense," that is, the ability to make intelligent decisions, "had nothing to do." The only "new acquaintance" Elinor is able to form a friendship and discuss matters with is Colonel Brandon. She "had reason to suspect that the misery of disappointed love had already been known by him." His words to her, "Your sister, I understand, does not approve of second attachments," echoes a debate in RICHARDSON's *Sir Charles Grandison* relating to the idealistic opinion that a person can be in love twice. Elinor's contention with Marianne is a conservative one: "Her systems have all the unfortunate tendency of setting propriety at nought; and a better acquaintance with the world is what I look forward to as her greatest possible advantage."

At the conclusion of the chapter, Brandon almost opens up to Elinor and makes a personal revelation. He stops short of doing so, and Elinor does not attempt to pry out of him what he is concealing. Her reticence is contrasted by Jane Austen as narrator with how Marianne would react to the situation. "The whole story would have been speedily formed under her active imagination; and every thing established in the most melancholy order of disastrous love" (52–57).

Chapter 12

Marianne tells Elinor that Willoughby has given her a horse as a gift. She does not think, as Elinor indicates to her, of the implications of such a gift and her acceptance of it. Apart from the impropriety of receiving the gift from someone she has not known for long, Marianne impractically ignored the expense involved in the horse's upkeep, the necessity to "keep a servant to ride it, and [to] build a stable."

Elinor overhears Marianne telling Willoughby that she is forced to reject his gift. He responds by addressing her "by her christian name," and referring to the time when she "leave[s] Barton to form [her] own establishment in a more lasting home." From this Elinor perceives "an intimacy so decided, a meaning so direct" that she assumes a private engagement. However, the author's use of literary allusions are warning signals that not all is as it seems. Marianne is an impractical dreamer. She lives in a world of illusions. This is reinforced by Willoughby's remark, "Queen Mab shall receive you" (58–59). This is a reference to Mercutio's speech in *Romeo and Juliet* celebrating dreaming. "The fairies' midwife" leads people to believe in the fulfillment of their "dreams/ Which are the children of an idle brain/ Begot of nothing but vain fantasy,/ Which is as thin of substance as the air,/ And more inconstant than the wind" (I. iv. 53–54, 96–100).

In this chapter, literary allusions continue to serve as a warning. Margaret, who shows herself to be sensible and more discreet than she initially appeared, tells Elinor that she witnessed Willoughby cutting "off a long lock of" Marianne's "hair . . . he kissed it, and folded it up in a piece of white paper, and put it into his pocket-book." This is a reference to a passage in Alexander Pope's *The Rape of the Lock* (1714), where a highly erotic and suggestive passage at the conclusion of the third canto, a lock of the heroine, Belinda's, hair is cut during a card game following tea. Similarly, Willoughby has cut Marianne's hair "after tea"—tea being a social and public event. The detail of the "pocket-book" reinforces the sense of possession: Willoughby has possessed Marianne, appropriated her for his own selfish purposes in a very public manner.

The relationship between the sexes receives some comic treatment in an episode where Elinor's affections and the object of them are discussed by Mrs. Jennings, who attempts to pry out of Marianne and Margaret "who was Elinor's particular favourite," although Mrs. Jennings is really trying to get Marianne to confess. In response to Mrs. Jennings's comment "He is the curate of the parish I daresay," Marianne observes, "He is of no profession at all." If this is applied to Willoughby, as developments in the novel will reveal, unlike Willoughby, characters such as Edward Ferrars and Colonel Brandon take their responsibilities very seriously indeed.

After Margaret has tactlessly revealed that Elinor has a favorite "and his name begins with an F," Lady Middleton rapidly turns the subject to that of the weather. She is assisted by Colonel Brandon. At the end of the chapter they agree to visit the next day "to see a very fine place about twelve miles from Barton, belonging to a brother-in-law of Colonel Brandon," who is responsible for its upkeep "as the proprietor . . . was abroad" (58–62).

Chapter 13

Events take a somewhat surprising turn in this chapter. Letters will play an important role in the novel. During breakfast, Colonel Brandon receives a letter that, when he "looked at the direction" or address, caused him to change "colour." The letter "came from town," from London, and despite the pleadings of the others, Brandon leaves immediately and cannot say when he will return. He is forced to cancel the planned trip to Whitewell, his brother-in-law's house. Mrs. Jennings asks him, "What can you have to do in town at this time of year?" a reference to the fact that sportsmen, hunters, would be in the country in October. Elinor overhears Willoughby commenting to Marianne that the visit is Brandon's invention and wagering "fifty guineas the letter was of his own writing." Such a remark reveals his own nefarious caste of mind. In 1717, the value of a guinea, issued as gold coins for the use of traders in Africa, was fixed at a pound sterling and one shilling. The last minting of the guinea was in 1813. The word "guinea"

remained for professional fees, the cost of horses, and other items such as artworks.

New characters make their appearance—"the two Miss Careys [came] over from Newton." Brandon goes on horseback to Honiton, a town on the Exeter-to-London road, from where he will "go post," or in a fast but expensive means of transportation that stopped at posting inns to change the horses. Mrs. Jennings seems sure that she knows the reason for his abrupt departure, that "it is about Miss Williams," who, she tells Elinor, "is his natural daughter," or illegitimate. According to Mrs. Jennings, Miss Williams is "as like him as she can stare." This expression concerns the likeness of one to another—"as she can stare." She adds, "I dare say the Colonel will leave her all his fortune." Legally, a child born out of wedlock had no rights to the father's estate unless expressly stated in his will. In the first edition of SS, the passage continued, "Lady Middleton's delicacy was shocked; and in order to banish so improper a subject as the mention of a natural daughter, she actually took the trouble of saying something herself about the weather" (Lamont, 309–310).

Marianne and Willoughby disappear in his carriage for the morning. Marianne confirms to Elinor the information she received from "her own woman," her lady's maid, that she had spent the time at Allenham Court, currently occupied by Willoughby's sick and elderly aunt, Mrs. Smith. Marianne tells Elinor that she "never spent a pleasanter morning in [her] life." For Elinor, Marianne's going uninvited and unchaperoned is a serious breach of "decorum." To this Marianne responds, "we always know when we are acting wrong, and with such a conviction I could have had no pleasure." So she accords with the "sentimental" thinkers such as the Earl of Shaftesbury and others, Rousseau and Hume, for instance, and other 18th-century thinkers, who argued that personal feelings are the correct guide to right conduct. Elinor replies that Marianne's actions have "already exposed [her] to some very impertinent remarks."

The chapter concludes with Marianne conceding to her sister that "it *was* rather ill-judged in me to go to Allenham" (Jane Austen's emphasis). She then describes in some detail the beauty of the house and its surroundings, including "a beautiful hanging wood," or a wood on a steep slope of a hill (63–69).

Chapter 14

The opening paragraph consisting of two lengthy sentences, each subdivided by a semicolon, presents the perspective of Mrs. Jennings, who speculates on why Colonel Brandon left so suddenly for London. She believes that Brandon is not as wealthy as he appears, and that "his brother left every thing sadly involved," or in a financial mess. The narrative focus transfers in the third paragraph from Mrs. Jennings's "conjecture[s]" to Elinor's perspective. She is "engrossed by the extraordinary silence of her sister and Willoughby on the subject" of Brandon's sudden departure. Elinor thinks that Willoughby lives above his means and that "his poverty" must be the reason for the delay in announcing the engagement to Marianne.

A major portion of the chapter is taken up with Willoughby's praise of the virtues of Barton Cottage, for which, had he the money, he "would instantly pull Combe down, and build it up again in the exact plan of this cottage." This remark elicits Elinor's disbelief: "With dark narrow stairs, and a kitchen that smokes, I suppose," she tells him. He hopes that whatever occurs—a signal that he is aware that change is about to take place—Barton Cottage will not change. Willoughby sincerely believes for the moment in his own fantasies—in this way he is as much a dreamer as Marianne. He asks the Dashwoods to "always consider [him] with kindness which has made every thing belonging to you so dear to me." They assent to this, and the chapter ends with time and change looming—the planning of commitments for the next day (70–74).

Chapter 15

The chapter opens with Mrs. Dashwood, Elinor, and Margaret returning home to find Marianne in tears. They find Willoughby alone, and in an embarrassed, awkward manner, he announces that he must immediately leave for London. He leaves quickly, refusing to make a commitment to return to visit them. Mrs. Dashwood and Elinor are left to speculate on the reasons. Mrs. Dashwood refuses to think ill of him and tries to place a positive spin on what has happened and Willoughby's reasons. Elinor is more skeptical and suspicious.

To settle her nerves following Willoughby's abrupt departure, Mrs. Dashwood "sat down to work," that is, to sew. Elinor's "wish [is] to be candid in [her] judgment of every body." She uses the word "candid" in the sense used by Dr. Johnson, of being "free from malice; not desirous to find faults" (*OED*), but finds Willoughby's behavior very strange. Her fears, she tells her mother, will be lessened "if we find they correspond," that is, if Willoughby and Marianne write to each other. It was inappropriate, however, for a young unmarried woman to write to a man unless they were engaged. Her mother responds that Elinor is making "a mighty concession indeed!" Some of Jane Austen's readers no doubt would be reminded of the tragic consequences that followed Clarissa, the heroine of Samuel Richardson's novel, capitulating to family pressures, corresponding against her will, with the villain Lovelace.

At the conclusion of the chapter, Marianne reappears with "red and swollen" eyes. She "could neither eat nor speak . . . burst into tears and left the room." True to her beliefs, Marianne is unable to do anything in half measures: "She was without any power, because she was without any desire of command over herself" (77, 79, 80, 82).

Chapter 16

Marianne is upset by Willoughby's absence, especially when no letter is received from him. Her mother refrains from asking her whether she and Willoughby are formally engaged, telling Elinor, "I would not attempt to force the confidence of any one; of a child much less." Following "about a week" of solitary walks, Marianne is persuaded to join her sisters: "Elinor . . . greatly disapproved such continual seclusion." Elinor's reserve and sense of the necessity of company again emerge and contrast with Marianne's romantic sense of melancholy, brooding, remembrance of the past, and isolation. On their walk they encounter Edward Ferrars, who "walked back with them to Barton." They learn that "he had been in Devonshire a fortnight," and "his coldness and reserve mortified

[Elinor] severely," although "she avoided every appearance of resentment or displeasure." Unlike her sister Marianne, Elinor does not display her feelings for others to see.

In the second paragraph of the chapter the word "chief," meaning "the main part," is used. Indulging in memories of her home with Willoughby, Marianne sits at the piano "gazing on every line of music that [Willoughby] had written out for her." Willoughby here displays considerable musical ability, as copying music is a far from easy skill. Marianne's feelings receive little sympathy from "Sir John and Mrs. Jennings" who, unlike Elinor, Margaret, and her mother, "were not so nice" to her. They were not as reticent as her mother and sister. Her mother, however, is somewhat tactless when she tells Marianne, "We have never finished Hamlet" (83–85, 87–88). Tony Tanner comments: "One guesses that [they] had perhaps arrived at the part where Hamlet inexplicably rejects Ophelia" (93).

Marianne mistakenly thinks that "a man on horseback riding towards them" during their walk is Willoughby. Her sister Elinor "screen[s] Marianne from particularity." Here "particularity" is used in the obsolete sense of "peculiarity such as to excite surprise" (*OED*). Marianne transfers her thoughts to Willoughby, whom she contrasts with Edward, "his brother elect," that is, someone who is going to enter the office of being a clergyman. Edward comments to Elinor and Marianne that the area where they live "is a beautiful country . . . but these bottoms must be dirty in winter." By "bottoms" are meant low-lying areas that are probably going to be muddy.

In this chapter Elinor reacts differently to nature than her sister Marianne. Reflecting on Norland, Elinor responds stoically and factually to Marianne: "Dear, dear Norland . . . probably looks much as it always does at this time of year. The woods and walks, thickly covered with dead leaves." Marianne responds to nature vaguely in a romanticized way: "Oh! . . . with what transporting sensations have I formerly seen them fall! How I delighted, as I walked, to see them driven in showers about me by the wind!" The emphasis is on her and her feelings, rather than on Elinor's more literal description (86–88).

Chapter 17

Edward visits the Dashwoods at their cottage and during conversation relaxes somewhat after receiving "the kindest welcome from" Mrs. Dashwood. The discussion turns to wealth, how wealth would be spent, the character of Marianne, and Edward's "gravity and thoughtfulness." Edward acknowledges that he lacks "assurance," or self-confidence. He, Marianne, and Elinor discuss "competence," or the appropriate amount for a comfortable existence. Edward has "about eighteen hundred or two thousand a-year." To which Elinor responds, "*One* [thousand] is my wealth!" Interestingly, two thousand is the amount Colonel Brandon and Mr. Bennet in *Pride and Prejudice* receive annually. For Marianne, two thousand is insufficient to maintain "a proper establishment of servants, a carriage, perhaps two, and hunters, cannot be supported on less," in other words, "future expenses at Combe Magna"—Willoughby's home.

According to Edward, Marianne's financial gain would be "a happy day for booksellers, music-sellers, and print-shops!" Print shops sold engravings. She too would purchase books, "and she would have every book that tells her how to admire an old twisted tree." Such a description Marianne would read in the work, for instance, of WILLIAM GILPIN and his observations on romantic and picturesque landscapes with "old twisted tree[s]." Perceptively, Marianne tells Edward, "You are not very gay," or happy, "yourself" and at the conclusion of the chapter "he sat for some time silent and dull" (90–95).

Chapter 18

In this chapter, Edward Ferrars and Marianne are again the focus of attention. It opens with Elinor's perception of "the low spirits of her friend" Edward. Elinor, Edward, and Marianne walk in "the surrounding country" and give their opinion on the landscape. Edward tells Marianne that he disagrees with Gilpin's perceptions and that he has "no knowledge in the picturesque." For Edward tells her, "I shall call hills steep, which ought to be bold; surfaces strange and uncouth, which ought to be irregular and rugged," according to Gilpin, who frequently used the term "rugged" to apply to scenery. Furthermore, Edward continues that he will refer to "distant objects out of sight, which ought [according to Gilpin] only to be indistinct through the soft medium of a hazy atmosphere."

Edward's observations reveal, his protestations to the contrary, considerable knowledge of contemporary aesthetic ideas. Marianne tells him, "Every body pretends to feel and tries to describe with the taste and elegance of him who first defined what picturesque beauty was." In this chapter and elsewhere, Jane Austen is criticizing characters such as Marianne, who takes the values expressed by Gilpin too seriously. However, Jane Austen's brother HENRY AUSTEN noted that from "a very early age she was enamoured of Gilpin on the Picturesque; and she seldom changed her opinions on either books or men" (*Memoir*, 140–141).

Within the context of chapter 18, a function of the discussion between Edward and Marianne is to reveal his sense of balance and her exaggeration. Edward tends toward antiromanticism: "I have more pleasure in a snug farm-house than a watch-tower—and a troop of tidy, happy villagers please me better than the finest banditti [outlaws or bandits] in the world." Lacking ambition, he seeks peace and quiet domesticity. Marianne responds with a look of "amazement."

Another central feature of this chapter is speculation as to the source of a lock of hair that Edward is noted to have in a ring he is wearing. He says, "it is [his] sister's hair." Elinor and Marianne assume "that the hair was" Elinor's. Mrs. Jennings, who subsequently with Sir John visits the Dashwoods at their cottage, "was not long in discovering that the name of Ferrars began with an F. and this prepared a future mine of raillery against the devoted [doomed] Elinor." The expression "a future mine of raillery" is interesting. On the one hand, it provides a guide to future narrative developments: Elinor's feelings for Edward. Second, the industrial and military metaphor of mining and a mine contains the meaning of something waiting to explode when trodden on—such as Elinor's sensitivity as far as Edward is concerned.

The chapter transforms in mood and tone from serious aesthetic discussion on the countryside, revealing character differences, to jesting. It concludes with prefiguring irony and with Edward's

viewpoint, rather than as it opened, with Elinor's. Edward tells Marianne, "I guess that Mr. Willoughby hunts": words indeed that will ring true subsequently in the narrative, where it will emerge that Willoughby "hunts" more than rabbits, foxes, or game birds. Marianne's reply, "the time will come I hope," reinforces the irony. Edward's regret at the implications of his remark and Marianne's reactions to it form the subject of the last paragraph of chapter 18 (96–100).

Chapter 19

The opening of this chapter focuses on Edward, his departure after "a week at the cottage," and Elinor's putting a positive spin on his behavior. Her feelings, confined to herself, are contrasted with Marianne's more overt expression of feeling. The remainder of the chapter focuses on the Middletons and their visit to the cottage with their daughter and her husband.

In the opening paragraph, the narrator conveys Edward Ferrars's personal unhappiness: "He had no pleasure at Norland; he detested being in town; but either to Norland or London he must go." The emphasis here is on the imperative "must go." The narrative focus in the second paragraph moves to Elinor, who tries to justify Edward's "want of spirits, of openness, and of consistency." She attributes these "to his want of independence, and his better knowledge of Mrs. Ferrars's disposition and designs." For Elinor, Edward is "temporizing with his mother," that is, negotiating with her to gain time. Dialogue between Mrs. Dashwood and Edward takes place from the third paragraph of the chapter until his departure. Mrs. Dashwood tells him that he "would be a happier man if [he] had any profession to engage [his] time and give an interest to [his] plans and action." His career options include the law—"chambers in the Temple," or residence at one of the Inns of Court to become a barrister, or advocate, the army or the navy. However, as Edward admits, "I always preferred the church, as I still do. But that was not smart enough for my family." As he "had no inclination for the law" or the other alternatives open to him, he "entered at Oxford and have been properly idle ever since."

Mrs. Dashwood responds by saying that Edward's "sons will be brought up to as many pursuits, employments, professions, and trades as Columella's" (101–103). This is a reference to *Columella, or the Distressed Anchoret* (1779), a two-volume novel by Richard Graves (1715–1804). This is based on the story of Lucius Columella, a first-century A.D. Roman. Planning the future of his sons, he "flattered himself that [they] would be secured from that tedium and disgust of life which *he* experienced, and which he had brought upon himself by a life of indolence and inactivity" (II: 210). Edward responds to Mrs. Dashwood that his sons "will be brought up . . . to be unlike myself as is possible." Edward once again exhibits his own self-disgust, his masochism.

Once Edward has left, Elinor "busily employed herself the whole day" to divert her mind from "her own grief." Marianne, on the other hand, finds Elinor's "behaviour . . . so exactly the reverse of her own." Elinor, unlike Marianne, exercises "the business of self-command." She is interrupted from her inner thoughts, her "reverie . . . by the arrival of company." Sir John and Lady Middleton bring to the cottage, with Mrs. Jennings, "a gentleman and lady," their daughter and their husband, the Palmers. The remainder of the chapter diverts from the serious tone and mood of its first half to focus on Sir John's admiration of Marianne, Palmer's largely silent snobbery—he objects to the "very low pitched" ceiling—and trivial social matters. Elinor refers in the final paragraph of the chapter to the "frequent invitations" to the Middletons: "The alteration is not in them, if their parties are grown tedious and dull. We must look for the change elsewhere" (103–109).

Chapter 20

The tone of light relief in the guise of the Palmers is continued in this chapter. The setting moves from the cottage to Barton Park, the home of the Middletons. In spite of Elinor and Marianne's unhappiness, life goes on, and others are preoccupied too with their own issues, however trivial these may appear to be. Mrs. Palmer, for instance, is amazed at the Dashwoods' inability to visit London during the social season. She also complains about the lack of "a billiard room" at Barton Park. Conversation moves from Allenham (Willoughby's home), regarded by Mr. Palmer "As vile a spot as I ever saw in my life" to manners, who should be invited to Barton Park, and naturally the weather. This "makes every thing and every body disgusting." Here "disgusting" means displeasing or offensive.

Elinor uses Mrs. Palmer to gain more information about Willoughby. Before doing so, Mrs. Palmer has told her that her husband intends to enter Parliament and that "he will never frank for" her. In other words, he will not allow her to send letters post-free by addressing them in his own handwriting and after 1784 writing also the date. This privilege was abolished in 1840, when the penny post came into operation. Mrs. Palmer assumes, in response to Elinor's inquiry concerning Willoughby, that Marianne "is to marry him," adding "it is what every body talks of." She also says that her husband would not visit Willoughby "for he is in the opposition" (111, 114–115). This refers to Mrs. Palmer's belief that Willoughby is a "Whig," or supporter of the opposition in Parliament. During Jane Austen's lifetime, the majority of governments were "Tory." Also, when SS was begun "in its present form . . . the Prime Minister was William Pitt the Younger (1759–1806), in 1809–11, when [it] was finished it was Spencer Perceval (1762–1812)." Both were heads of Tory governments (Lamont, 314).

Mrs. Palmer's source of information concerning Marianne's supposed engagement is Colonel Brandon, whom she met in the fashionable London area of Bond Street. The source surprises Elinor, and Mrs. Palmer admits that she perceived from Brandon's looks that he confirmed the engagement. Mrs. Palmer adds, "Mama says *he* was in love with your sister too" (Jane Austen's emphasis)—she uses the past tense. The narrative reveals that Brandon continues to love Marianne. Her next remark that "it was a great compliment if he was, for he hardly ever falls in love with any body" followed by a question from Elinor concerning Willoughby, on rereading, reveals Willoughby's fickleness and Brandon's constancy, and the possibility of a previous "love" affair.

A chapter of gossip concludes with Charlotte Palmer saying that if the Middletons had "wished it very much," she could have married Brandon however she is under the illusion that she is "much happier as I am." Ironically, she adds that the sardonic, indifferent "Mr. Palmer is just the kind of man I like" (114–117).

Chapter 21

Two new characters, Anne and Lucy Steele, who Mrs. Jennings has just discovered are relatives, appear at Barton Park. They have been invited by Sir John, who met them while on a visit to Exeter. Fashionable ladies keen to please Lady Middleton, they flatter her and indulge her young children. Anne is nearing 30 and "very plain"; Lucy is in her early twenties and attractive. Elinor, however, "was not blinded by" Lucy's appearance and senses a "want of real elegance and artlessness." It emerges that they are acquainted with the Dashwoods and know the same people. Anne observes, "Norland is a prodigious beautiful place, is not it?" To which Lucy responds, "We have heard Sir John admire it excessively" (120, 124, 123). Chapman notes that Anne has "no business to know anything of beauty in Norland, and her sister is ready with an explanation; in which, however, she . . . overreaches herself," as Sir John has "never visited" Norland (384). Toward the end of the chapter, the Steele sisters reveal that they know one of the Ferrars brothers.

In the sixth paragraph of the chapter, Lady Middleton is "taking patterns of some elegant new dress," that is, she is making paper patterns to copy the dress. Her children's "work-bags" are searched; these are bags containing sewing equipment. One of the Steeles gives the children "sugar plums," or boiled sweets, and one bathes a child's wound "with lavender-water," or oil of lavender dipped in spirits, used to soothe head and nervous disorders. Marianne responds to Lucy Steele's overfriendliness "without any éclat" or exaggeration. Lucy tells Elinor and Marianne, "perhaps you young ladies may not care abut the beaux [young gentlemen] and had as lief be without them as with them," or as gladly be "without them." Anne Steele remarks to Elinor, "perhaps you may have a friend in the corner already," a secret admirer. Such remarks of the Steeles' are suggestive and imply that they know more than they reveal (120–123).

Chapter 22

The first volume of SS concludes with an important chapter in terms of revelation and the display of strength of character. Most of the chapter centers on a conversation between Lucy and Elinor. Lucy not only is acquainted with Edward Ferrars, she secretly has been engaged to him for a period of four years. He was student of Lucy's uncle in Plymouth where their relationship began, and because Lucy is poor and Edward's mother would not agree to the engagement, they have been forced to keep it a secret. Elinor initially is incredulous, but when Lucy shows her Edward's miniature, reveals that he stayed with the Steeles at "Longstaple" before visiting Elinor and Marianne, shows her a letter from Edward, and reveals that she "gave him a

Frontispiece by William Greatbatch, probably after George Pickering, to *Sense and Sensibility (London: Richard Bentley, 1833)*

lock of my hair set in a ring," Elinor "was mortified, shocked, confounded."

Elinor's reactions to Lucy's revelation reveal her strength, her ability to control her emotions. Initially disbelieving, Elinor then questions Lucy. In spite of "an exertion of spirits, which increased with her increase of emotion," she still appears calm and "did not feel very compassionate" when her tormentor, Lucy, "took out her handkerchief." She even manages to score a point with Lucy, telling her, "You must at least have felt that my being acquainted with it could not add to its safety." Such exchanges are accompanied by Elinor's looking "earnestly at Lucy, hoping to discover something in her countenance." Elinor and Lucy act as poker players: "Lucy's countenance suffered a change" and Elinor "is almost overcome—her heart sunk within her, and she could hardly stand," yet she manages to control herself (134–135, 130, 133, 132, 134). In this way, writes Barbara Hardy, "the totally unexpected revelation . . . Jane Austen's surprises" unite both her readers and her characters "in an overlapping response."

Lucy implies that she and Edward are in love. They are engaged; her story selectively told, as the narrative will reveal, comes as a surprise to both Elinor and the reader. Lucy's good manners, her asking her rival Elinor for advice, is part of her revenge, and she miscalculates Elinor's self-control. The confrontation between the two is a superb illustration of Jane Austen's pitting "one intelligence against the other. Each woman knows what is happening, speaks or hears the subtext" (Hardy, 72). Occasionally, Lucy's lack of education reveals itself in grammatical errors. She refers to "my sister and me" and uses a vulgar expression. Her determination "to set for it," or to give Edward a portrait, reveals also her poverty, for only the wealthy could afford to have their portraits painted.

The first volume of SS concludes, then, with revelation, and conflict between two characters, revealing the bitterness between them. In the concluding paragraph the Steeles leave and Elinor is left alone "at liberty to think and be wretched" (134–135).

Volume 2, Chapter 1 (Chapter 23)

The opening chapter of the second volume focuses on Elinor's reactions to the revelations of the previous chapter and her subtle planning for a further skirmish with her rival Lucy Steele to demonstrate that the news of the engagement has not upset her. The chapter conveys Jane Austen's narrative skill in manipulating a social setting, in this instance, the seemingly innocent occupation of basket making, to convey a verbal and nonverbal exchange of conflict.

The initial paragraphs of the first chapter consist of Elinor's interior monologue and thoughts. Personal pronouns such as "her" and "he" are frequent, the former being Elinor, the latter Edward, as are questions asked by Elinor to herself. Elinor "wept for him [Edward], more than for herself" and decides that his engagement was the consequence of youth: "could he ever be tolerably happy with Lucy Steele . . . be satisfied with a wife like her [Lucy Steele]—illiterate, artful, and selfish?" Elinor reveals insight into others and herself: "She was stronger alone, and her own good sense so well supported her, that her firmness was so unshaken." She is aware that "Lucy was disposed to be jealous of her" and understands Lucy's motives for revealing to her the engagement.

The chapter then moves from the solitary Elinor to her in society, with the Middletons, meeting "for the sake of eating, drinking, and laughing together, playing at cards, or consequences." The game of "consequences" becomes ironic. It is "a round game, in which a narrative of the meeting of a lady and a gentleman, their conversation, and the ensuing 'consequences,' is concocted by the contribution of a name or a fact by each of the players," who are ignorant of what the other players have contributed (*OED*). Elinor's plan is to engage Lucy in conversation while they undertake social functions and gather further information, with the consequences, from her. At the conclusion of the chapter, Elinor's opportunity comes following at Barton Park "a round game" (a game played together usually at a round table), the working of "fillagree" (rolled-paper work, in this instance constructing a basket for a spoiled child), the call "for some working candles" (candles giving additional lighting), the proposal of "a rubber of Casino" (a card game played with partners), and other forms of general civility. These Marianne pointedly ignores, going to play the piano, which forms a background to the verbal conflict directly to follow. Elinor, too, but more politely "cut[s] out" or does not play cards in order to maneuver Lucy into a situation where they can speak (139–145).

Volume 2, Chapter 2 (Chapter 24)

Most of the chapter is occupied with Elinor and Lucy's verbal and silent clash played out while they are basket making and with the sounds of Marianne playing the piano in the background. Elinor's plan to show that she is not jealous of her rival, and to gain further information, is only partially successful. She gains additional knowledge but her "politeness, sympathy, reserve and intelligence doom her to be a confidante in painful circumstances." Elinor herself, however, has no one to confide in (Hardy, 74–75). "The confidential discourse" between them closes when Elinor is "called to the card table." The chapter concludes with her reflection that Edward has no "affection for the person who was to be his wife" and "that he had not even the chance of being tolerably happy in marriage," as it is evident that "he was weary" of his engagement. Although "the visit of the Miss Steeles at Barton Park" is extended for "nearly two months" until the Christmas "festival," Elinor and Lucy do not revive the subject of the engagement.

It becomes clear during the dramatic dialogue between Elinor and Lucy, in which Lucy does more of the talking, that her motives for not breaking off her engagement to Edward are mercenary. She tells Elinor that they "must wait, it may be for many years" to marry as Edward "has only two thousand pounds of his own," which is enough to live off frugally but not lavishly. Lucy claims that she does not wish to deprive Edward "perhaps, of all that his mother might give him if he married to please her." Elinor is part of her plan to increase their prospects: "he should take orders as soon as he can, and then" she hopes that Elinor will persuade her "brother to give him Norland living"—a very prosperous one that included land. In short, Lucy is cunning and scheming, determined to secure a wealthy man and escape from poverty (151–152, 147, 149).

Volume 2, Chapter 3 (Chapter 25)

Money and property, in this instance through trading, form the foundation of Mrs. Jennings's prosperity. With the advent of January, she invites Elinor and Marianne to spend the winter season with her at her London home in the fashionable Portman Square area. Mrs. Jennings's intention is to "get one of" the sisters "well married." She claims that she needs the company instead of "poking by myself" or living by herself in a half-hearted way.

Much of the chapter is preoccupied with Elinor's change of mind. Initially, she is adamant about not going to London, whereas Marianne and their mother are enthusiastic. Marianne's enthusiasm, with the support of her mother, triumphs over Elinor's prudence. Marianne and Mrs. Dashwood cannot know a secret that is shared with the readers: that Edward is engaged to Lucy Steele. Elinor almost reveals this but her reticence gets the better of her when she responds to Mrs. Dashwood's observation in the middle of the chapter concerning Elinor's future "sister-in-law's family." Elinor's reply is received with "astonishment" by Marianne after Elinor has said that "it is a matter of perfect indifference to [her] whether I am ever known" to his family "or not." In such a way, Jane Austen is able to convey the way in which confidences are kept in families. In this instance, to repeat, readers, in addition to Elinor, are aware of Edward's engagement. At the end of the chapter, Mrs. Jennings's invitation is accepted with some of the other parties involved in the novel also to appear in London in January. The Middletons are "to follow" shortly, the Miss Steeles will come too "only with the rest of the family" (153–154, 157–158).

Volume 2, Chapter 4 (Chapter 26)

This chapter moves from the journey to London, to the arrival in London, the writing of letters (Elinor to her mother, Marianne to Willoughby), to visitors. The first is Brandon, followed by Mrs. Jennings's pregnant daughter, Mrs. Palmer. There is the inevitable expedition to a fashionable shopping area, in this instance to "Bond-street especially," followed by further visitors, "two elderly ladies of Mrs. Jennings's intimate acquaintance." Such rituals form the backdrop for Marianne's anxious wait for the arrival of Willoughby's reply to a letter she has written him—it fails to come.

The metaphor of "eyes" continues from the previous chapter, is applied again in the opening paragraph of the chapter to Marianne, and subsequently to Mrs. Palmer, "whose eye was caught by every thing pretty, expensive, or new" at the shops, making her "wild to buy all." Elinor's role as an intelligence gatherer, through observation or conversation with others, is highlighted during the three-day coach journey to London. Secrets come to the fore as Elinor does not know her sister writes to Willoughby, or whether they are engaged or not. Colonel Brandon's visit once again reveals his concern for Marianne and affinity with Elinor; they converse in a "calm kind of way." Mrs. Jennings's remarks to him reintroduce the subject of his rivalry with Willoughby over Marianne and the revelation that Mrs. Jennings "got a very good husband"—prosperous and kind—who "had been dead" for more than "eight years" (165, 162, 163).

Volume 2, Chapter 5 (Chapter 27)

The themes of secrecy and appearances dominate the chapter. It opens with the weather, Marianne's writing yet again to Willoughby, this time to his country residence at Combe Magna, the Middletons' arrival in London, social encounters, to Brandon's confession of his feelings for Marianne to Elinor. Several other matters emerge, including Mrs. Jennings's loyalty to "a few old city friends," or her husband's friends from the business areas, in spite of her daughter's snobbish objections. Sir John Middleton arranges "an unpremeditated dance" at which Marianne learns that Willoughby is in London and was invited to the event. Marianne continues to write to Willoughby, and Elinor's writing to her mother is interrupted by a visit from Colonel Brandon, who confides in her, as Lucy Steele has done. At the conclusion of the chapter, Elinor is alone "with a melancholy impression of Colonel Brandon's unhappiness" following his conviction that Willoughby and Marianne are engaged (168, 170, 174).

Volume 2, Chapter 6 (Chapter 28)

A few days later, Elinor and Marianne encounter Willoughby at a large gathering. He is "standing a few yards of them, in earnest conversation with a very fashionable looking young woman." Clearly embarrassed at even having to acknowledge Marianne, "her touch seemed painful to him, and he

held her hand only for a moment." He leaves the party—Marianne is preoccupied with herself, is stopped from speaking to him by Elinor, and is taken home, "where hartshorn," or the equivalent of smelling salts, "restored her a little to herself." The last two paragraphs of the chapter focus on Elinor's sense of her misperception of Willoughby's feelings and relationship with Marianne. She is at this point willing, owing to witnessing "embarrassment which seemed to speak of a consciousness of his own misconduct," not to believe that he has "been sporting with the affection of his sister from the first, without any design that would bear investigation." The last paragraph of the chapter interweaves the two sisters' reactions to what has taken place. Marianne is in "misery" and Elinor's "own situation" with Edward "gained in the comparison." She, Elinor, has not experienced with Edward "an immediate and irreconcilable rapture."

Up to this point in the novel, Marianne has disregarded social convention and modes of conduct in her passion for Willoughby. He, however, selfishly refuses to follow Marianne's behavior. His coldness to her, yet adherence to social rules in taking "her hand only for a moment," contrasts with Marianne's lack of restraint. She pleads with Elinor, "Tell him I must see him again—must speak to him instantly—I cannot rest—I shall not have a moment's peace." The threefold repetition of the personal pronoun "I," the use of the verb "must," reveals in Marianne's speech that she has lost control of her emotions. Marianne's experience in this chapter marks the start of a learning process concerning her relationships with others and society. This will be resolved by the conclusion of the narrative (176–179).

Volume 2, Chapter 7 (Chapter 29)

In this chapter, Jane Austen draws on the narrative device of using letters to reveal the correct version of what has occurred, as opposed to individual character perceptions and interpretation of others' actions. The opening sentence "Before . . . the sun gained any power over a cold, gloomy morning," with "little light," uses the weather to create the atmosphere and tone of the rest of the chapter, Elinor discovers her sister Marianne in a situation of deep distress. At breakfast, Mrs. Jennings's presence does not help the situation, as she believes that Marianne and Willoughby are about to marry. This leads to more anxiety on Marianne's part.

Elinor reads a letter Marianne receives from Willoughby. The text is given so that the reader is not responding to Elinor's perception of a letter selectively presented. In his letter, Willoughby pleads innocence to any offense he may have given: "I can assure you to have been perfectly unintentional." The narrator and character agree in their responses to the letter: "With what indignation such as a letter as this must be read by Miss Dashwood, may be imagined . . . a letter so impudently cruel . . . and which proclaimed its writer to be deep in hardened villainy." Willoughby's letter produces an extreme reaction in the normally calm Elinor: "so bitter were her feelings against him, that she dared not trust herself to speak" to her sister. In his letter, Willoughby returns "the lock of hair" Marianne gave him and tells her that his "affections have been long engaged elsewhere."

Following a revisit from Mrs. Jennings curtailed by Elinor, who tells the visitor that Marianne is unwell, both sisters comfort each other. Marianne admits that she assumed that she and Willoughby were engaged and that "he loved" her. She has been a victim of misperception. The reader and Elinor share the three notes Marianne had previously written to him when arriving in London. The letters reveal to Elinor the "impropriety," (180, 183–184, 187, 186, 188), the inappropriateness of their being written in the first place. Marianne has rejected social forms and conventions for her personal passion for Willoughby. She "felt [herself] . . . to be as solemnly engaged to him, as if the strictest legal covenant had bound us to each other."

At the conclusion of the chapter, Elinor resists Marianne's pleas to return home immediately, telling her sister that they have social obligations that must take precedence over personal ones: "civility of the commonest kind must prevent such a hasty removal." In the final paragraph, Marianne is finally "persuaded" to take a sedative, "some lavender drops," and "continued on the bed quiet and motionless." So a chapter that opened early in

the morning with a sleepless and restless Marianne closes with the "restless pain of [her] mind and body" stilled (188–191).

Volume 2, Chapter 8 (Chapter 30)

Mrs. Jennings learns from gossip that Willoughby "is to be married very soon—a good for-nothing fellow," he has squandered his inheritance. Without finances he is shortly to marry an extremely wealthy heiress, a Miss Grey. At the conclusion of the chapter, Brandon appears to corroborate further what Mrs. Jennings has learned; his source too is gossip.

Mrs. Jennings, in a down-to-earth fashion, sums up Willoughby's behavior. She tells Elinor, "when a young man, be he who he will, comes and makes love to a pretty girl, and promises marriage, he has no business to fly off from his word only because he grows poor, and a richer girl is ready to have him." She succinctly expresses Willoughby's motivation: "Fifty thousand pounds! and by all accounts it wo'nt come before it's wanted; for they say [gossip plays a leading role in this chapter] he is all to pieces." Rumor again is the foundation for an unfounded observation of Mrs. Jennings. Following her comment that Colonel Brandon "will have her [Marianne] at last," she adds, forever mindful of the materialist side of existence, "Two thousand a year without debt or drawback—except the little love child," a reference to an illegitimate child that she assumes to be Brandon's. The practical Mrs. Jennings comes up too with a solution: "she may be 'prenticed out at small cost," or apprenticed to a trade.

Mrs. Jennings's speech is littered with rich proverbial expressions such as "One shoulder of mutton, you know, drives another down." In other words, that one experience, such as falling in love, conjures up a similar experience. Her recommendation is "the finest old Constantia wine" to soothe the nerves and cheer up all. It was a remedy tried by her husband when he suffered from "a touch of his old cholicky gout," a painful illness of the joints. "Constantia wine," or a superior dessert wine from Constantia in the Cape Town region of South Africa, became very popular in the 19th century (192, 194, 196–198).

Volume 2, Chapter 9 (Chapter 31)

A chapter of revelation begins with Marianne's irritation toward Mrs. Jennings's kindness, which she perceives as a request for "gossip, and she only likes me now because I supply it." The opening paragraphs reveal Marianne's changeability and lack of reason. A letter comes from her mother conveying out-of-date news: She has not heard of Willoughby's engagement and disdainful treatment of Marianne. Only Elinor's counsel "of patience" prevents Marianne returning immediately to their mother in the country. Marianne observes Elinor writing a letter to her mother telling her what has happened.

She is interrupted by the arrival of Colonel Brandon, whom Marianne, ironically in view of what is to happen, commenting to Elinor, says, "We are never safe from *him*" (Jane Austen's emphasis). Brandon becomes her lifelong protector. The remainder of the chapter is largely a lengthy narrative on Brandon's part, with a few brief interjections from Elinor. Brandon relates the tragic tale of his dead sister-in-law, Eliza, whom he loved but she married at the age of 17 "against her inclination to my brother, . . . [who] did not even love her." She and Brandon were just prevented from eloping to Scotland where they could have married, being under 21, without parental consent. Brandon "procured my exchange," an army posting away from England and learnt of his brother and Eliza's divorce. Before 1857, these were extremely expensive as they had to be by parliamentary act.

Brandon returns to England three years later and finds Eliza "in a spunging-house," one for debtors, as her "legal allowance" following her divorce was inadequate. Further, his sister-in-law is totally altered, suffering from "consumption," or lung infection. All Brandon can do is prepare her "for death"—in other words, settle her affairs and give her counseling. He becomes the guardian of her child, Eliza, and following the death of his brother, "some five years ago," the young Eliza visited him regularly at Delaford—a visit misperceived by some. At 14 she was seduced and made pregnant by Willoughby, with whom Brandon fought a drawn duel as a matter of honor. Brandon hopes that by knowing this, Elinor might assist Marianne

to recover more easily from her disappointment. She has escaped the fate of Eliza and her mother (201–211).

Volume 2, Chapter 10 (Chapter 32)

The opening section of this chapter focuses on Marianne and her reaction to Willoughby's behavior. She does speak "with a kind of compassionate respect" toward Brandon; however "her mind did become settled, but it was settled in a gloomy dejection." Mrs. Dashwood recommends that her daughters remain in London as it provides "a variety of occupations, of objects, and of company" unavailable in the country at Barton. Elinor restrains Mrs. Jennings, Sir John, and Lady Middleton, and Mrs. Palmer from mentioning Willoughby in front of Marianne, although they denounce him when she is not present. "Early in February, within a fortnight from the receipt of Willoughby's letter, Elinor had the painful office of informing her sister that he was married." Elinor hopes now to persuade Marianne to leave the house and to become more sociable.

At the end of the chapter, Anne (Nancy) and Lucy Steele arrive in London. They visit Elinor, and tell her that they took a hired carriage for three passengers, "a post-chaise," to London accompanied by "a very smart beau," a Dr. Davies, who, it subsequently emerges, is a clergyman, not a medical doctor. In the last paragraphs, Elinor dissuades them from intruding on the apparently sick Marianne. She is aided, somewhat ironically, "by Lucy's sharp reprimand," which controls the wishes of her sister (212–219).

Volume 2, Chapter 11 (Chapter 33)

Marianne ventures out with Elinor, who is "carrying on a negociation for the exchange of a few old-fashioned jewels of her mother." They are kept waiting at the jeweler's by an exceedingly vain customer; his manner is described as "puppyism," or affectation. He insists on personally inspecting each of the "toothpick case[s]." This individual subsequently turns out to be Robert Ferrars, Edward's younger brother. Elinor and Marianne then meet their brother, John Dashwood. Most of the chapter is concerned with the exposure of his materialistic values: All is judged by price and value. He is convinced that Colonel Brandon is attached to Elinor; his main concern is whether Brandon is "a man of fortune?" and is disappointed by Brandon's apparently low income. John Dashwood conveys information. He tells Elinor that a "match" has been arranged for Edward Ferrars to an heiress, what he describes as "a very desirable connection."

Dashwood tells Elinor about his own apparent lack of wealth, although it emerges that he has been enlarging his country property. He has enclosed the commons, depriving the local small farmers of their grazing rights and purchased the land and farm "adjoining my own property." Further, Dashwood has "destroyed the old walnut trees," no doubt selling them at a high price, given their demand in wartime as a material for guns and rifles. He is not insensitive enough to ignore that Marianne "looks very unwell, has lost her colour, and is grown quite thin." In view of this, he believes that Elinor will make in financial terms a better match than Marianne. He calls on the Middletons: "Abundance of civilities passed on all sides." On the way back to his residence, John tells his sister "that Mrs. Jennings was the widow of a man who had got all his money in a low way." Snobbery and materialism intermingle, but material values triumph in this chapter, which exposes the values of vanity, conceit, and materialism (223–228).

Volume 2, Chapter 12 (Chapter 34)

The Middletons are invited to dinner by the Dashwoods. The setting for the chapter takes place in the Dashwoods' "very good house" in fashionable Harley Street. A social drama is enacted in three scenes: the dinner table, the drawing room when the ladies are alone after dinner; and when they are joined by the gentlemen. The participants include the Miss Steeles, Mrs. Jennings, Elinor and Marianne, Colonel Brandon, and Edward's mother, Mrs. Ferrars. Even before the formal social rituals, Lady Middleton and Mrs. Dashwood bond in their mutual "cold hearted selfishness" and "an insipid propriety of demeanor, and a general want of understanding." At dinner, misplaced flattery and exaggerated manners abound. Fanny Dashwood and Mrs. Ferrars ignore Elinor and are most respectful to Lucy, whom they perceive as wealthy and are unaware of her engagement to Edward.

Mrs. Ferrars, "not a woman of many words," possesses a "strong character of pride and ill nature." The "grand dinner" is matched by the "poverty" of the conversation.

This becomes "particularly evident" when the ladies are alone. In mixed company at least, as the author sarcastically indicates, "the gentleman *had* supplied the discourse with some variety—the variety of politics, inclosing land, and braking horses" (Jane Austen's emphasis). Left alone, the ladies descend into trivia: "the comparative heights" of the two little boys, "Harry Dashwood and Lady Middleton's second son William."

When they are joined by the gentleman, Marianne breaks down the social conventions by openly challenging Mrs. Ferrars's insulting behavior toward Elinor, who is suspected of having designs on Edward. Mrs. Ferrars, after learning that a drawing is by Elinor, slights it by unfavorably comparing it with the work of Miss Morton, the wealthy heiress whom she hopes Edward will marry. This provokes Marianne into an outburst of emotional feelings most inappropriate to social decorum. She tells Mrs. Ferrars: "what is Miss Morton to us?—who knows, or who cares, for her!—it is Elinor of whom *we* think and speak" (Jane Austen's emphasis). She is attacking the very foundation of Mrs. Ferrars's and the others' beliefs: money. No wonder "Mrs. Ferrars looked exceedingly angry, and drawing herself up more stiffly than ever, pronounced in retort this bitter philippic," or comment meant to crush the opponent, from the "Philippics" of the Athenian orator and Demosthenes (384–322 B.C.). She replies "Miss Morton is Lord Morton's daughter," as if money and status are all. Marianne collapses in tears and is comforted especially by Colonel Brandon and Elinor.

Marianne's defiance of Mrs. Ferrars and her tears have broken the social conventions governing the social niceties of the dinner party. John Dashwood, who started the trouble by using the painted screens to flatter Elinor's work and thus drawing Brandon's attention to her, concludes the chapter with inappropriate behavior. He comments to Brandon that Marianne "has not such good health as her sister—she is very nervous." He adds that Marianne "*has been* a beauty. . . . You would not think it perhaps. . . . Now you see it is all gone" (Jane Austen's emphasis). The irony of course is that Brandon sees things differently (229–237).

Volume 2, Chapter 13 (Chapter 35)

The social gathering of the previous chapter is transformed to one between Elinor, then Marianne (now much more talkative), Lucy Steele, and then Edward Ferrars, who comes to call on Elinor and Marianne. Lucy's reading of Mrs. Ferrars is amusing and highly ironic. She found her "so exceedingly affable," a word used by Jane Austen to describe that of superiors to their inferiors, and implying condescension. Lucy, however, finds in Mrs. Ferrars "no pride, no hauteur," or haughtiness of manners. For Lucy, she "is a charming woman." Elinor tries not to respond, "to make a civil answer." They are interrupted by Edward's visit, "a very awkward moment, and the countenance of each," Edward, Lucy, and Elinor, all of whom "looked exceedingly foolish."

Elinor manages briefly to extricate herself from the situation by fetching Marianne, who overenthusiastically greets Edward and speaks socially more than she has done for a considerable time. She even ignores a provocative observation by Lucy about the constancy of "young men." After Edward and Lucy have left, Elinor and Marianne discuss the situation. Elinor is unable, owing to "her promise of secrecy to Lucy," to tell her sister of the engagement between Edward and Lucy. All she can do is to "hope" that she will not be placed subsequently in such a difficult situation (238–245).

Volume 2, Chapter 14 (Chapter 36)

The final chapter of the second volume is again one of social encounters, counterpointed by Jane Austen's satire. Robert Ferrars, Edward's brother, demonstrates "that he was exactly the coxcomb [Elinor] had heard him described to be by Lucy" and is in fact "the very he, who had given them a lecture on toothpick-cases." He even gives Elinor his approval of a "cottage, there is always so much comfort, so much elegance about them," somewhat ironic words revealing that his actual experience of them is very limited. He attributes his bother Edward's "extreme *gaucherie*" (Jane Austen's emphasis), or awkwardness of manner, to his being

educated privately rather than, as in Robert's case, being sent "to Westminster," a school noted for its intellectual and social activities. He rejects plans drawn up by the most distinguished architect of the day, Joseph Bonomi (1739–1808), and chooses to build a cottage instead.

The beginning of the chapter highlights Lady Middleton's dislike of Elinor and Marianne: "their presence was a restraint, both on her and on Lucy." The announcement in the opening paragraph that Mrs. Palmer, Mrs. Jennings's daughter, has given birth to a boy, takes care of her, and leaves Elinor and Marianne in the company of Lady Middleton, the Steeles, and Mr. and Mrs. John Dashwood. Marianne has become more sociable: "it was become a matter of indifference to her whether she went or not." She has, however, "to her dress and appearance . . . grown so perfectly indifferent," and "douceur," or sweetness, is "considered by Marianne as the greatest impertinence of all."

Toward the end of the chapter, to avoid having Elinor and Marianne stay with her, Fanny Dashwood persuades her husband, John, to invite the Steele girls to remain in London with them. Lucy's "flattery had already subdued the pride of Lady Middleton and made an entry into the close heart of Mrs. John Dashwood." Elinor perceives the invitation to be natural, heralding the subsequent announcement of the engagement between Edward and Lucy. In the last paragraph, Fanny calls "Lucy by her christian name" and gives both Steele girls "a needle book, made by some emigrant." This snobbish allusion, the snobbery with a note of contempt implied in "some," probably refers to the many refugees in London fleeing from revolutionary France. After January 1792, their property had been confiscated by the revolutionary French government. In this manner, the second volume ends on a wider note than the mere social manners of a small portion of London society would imply. This final chapter of the second volume begins with a birth, and has for its theme human folly and vanity (246–254).

Volume 3, Chapter 1 (Chapter 37)

The opening chapter of the third and final book may be divided into three sections, each of which contains the imparting, or reporting of news, and reactions to the revelations. The news is communicated in the first section by Mrs. Jennings telling Elinor that Anne Steele has revealed to Fanny Dashwood that Lucy and Edward are engaged. An outraged Fanny throws the Steele girls out of her house. Mrs. Jennings conveys the news in an idiomatic fashion, interposing details of her little granddaughter's "red-gum," a rash or skin problem. She says that Anne is "no conjurer," or far from clever. She comments "what a taking poor Mr. Edward will be in when he hears of it," or he will be in a very agitated state.

In the second section, Elinor has the difficult task of telling Marianne that the secret she herself has been protecting is now public information. Elinor takes the opportunity to explain to Marianne her own reactions to what has occurred and why she behaved as she did. The focus is on the listener, Marianne, rather than on the speaker or messenger, Elinor. Marianne's "feelings" prevent Elinor from finishing, although she does manage to tell her sister that she too has "feelings" and has "suffered." Marianne has at this point in the novel developed sufficient self-restraint and agrees on not being overtly hostile to Edward when they meet.

The third section of the chapter consists of a visit from John Dashwood in which he tells Marianne, Elinor, and Mrs. Jennings what has subsequently taken place since Anne Steele revealed news of the engagement. Mrs. Ferrars tried to bargain with her son to break the engagement. If he married Miss Morton, "she would settle on him the Norfolk estate, which, clear of land-tax [a tax based on the rental values of landed property] brings in a good thousand a-year," or a reasonable annual income. Marianne does not react; "she remembered her promises [to Elinor] and forbore," so that she has begun to learn self-control. Dashwood's priorities are material: "he never wished to offend anybody, especially anybody of good fortune," in other words, wealthy. In short, Mrs. Ferrars has disinherited Edward when he refuses to break off the engagement, and he "is dismissed for ever from his mother's notice." Mrs. Ferrars has settled the estates on Robert, his younger brother. At the end of this chapter of information and reaction

to it, when Dashwood leaves them, "Marianne's indignation burst forth." She is "joined in a very spirited critique upon" Mrs. Ferrars's "conduct" ([258]–269).

Volume 3, Chapter 2 (Chapter 38)

Elinor is the focus of two encounters with each of the Steele girls. The first is a personal one, with Anne Steele, whom she meets three days after the events of the last chapter while in Kensington Gardens, and the second is in the form of a letter from Lucy to her. Both concern Edward. Anne relays information she has apparently acquired by listening at the door to a conversation she claims to have heard. In this, apparently Edward offered Lucy the opportunity to break the engagement, owing to his poverty. She, according to Anne, refused and they plan to marry when he has taken holy orders and found a living. Lucy's letter to Elinor received the next morning contradicts Anne's account: Lucy claims that Edward refused her offer to break the engagement.

This chapter begins and ends with Mrs. Jennings's reactions to the news. Her stupidity is complemented by Anne Steele's. While telling Elinor her account of what she claims to have overheard between Edward and Lucy, her language reveals her vulgarity: "'La!' I shall say directly." Here "La" is an exaggerated term for "Lord." In her letter to Elinor, Lucy also uses inappropriate language. Trying to imitate what she thinks will be Edward's vocabulary, she writes, "We have had great trials, and great persecutions." These refer to the sufferings of the early Christian martyrs. Elinor's skepticism, and a warning note to the reader not to take Lucy's words at their face value, are reinforced by the observation following her reading referring to "its writer's real design," or motivation. In the last paragraph, the idea of fantasy and ridiculousness is reinforced in Mrs. Jennings's excessive and, as it will emerge, undeserved praise of Lucy.

At the start of the chapter, Elinor meets Anne in the fashionable Kensington Gardens on a "beautiful" Sunday during "the second week of March" (270–278). Jane Austen herself, in a letter to her sister, Cassandra, dated April 25, 1811, refers to a walk in Kensington Gardens in the spring when "everything was fresh & beautiful" (*Letters*, 184).

Volume 3, Chapter 3 (Chapter 39)

Misperception and irony is the keynote of this chapter. Elinor accepts Palmer's invitation for the Dashwoods to join them at their Cleveland home in Somerset—Cleveland being a few miles from Bath and on the way to Barton. Marianne "sighed for the air, the liberty, the quiet of the country." Mrs. Jennings pretends not to try to overhear a conversation between Elinor and Colonel Brandon, although she reconstructs, or imagines, what she believes is being said. Jane Austen, as narrator, intervenes in the narrative to relate, "What had really passed between" Elinor and Colonel Brandon. Learning of Edward Ferrars's financial and other difficulties, Brandon offers him, through Elinor's good offices, a small rectory bringing in no "more than 200 . . . [£] per annum," but enough for him "to marry" and live very modestly. The irony is that Brandon entrusts the communication of his offer to Elinor. Brandon probably is unaware that Elinor is in love with Edward. He also incorrectly assumes that Lucy is "a very deserving young woman." His trust in Elinor once again places her in a very difficult situation—similar to that Lucy placed her in when she revealed her engagement to Edward.

Misperception is compounded in the last paragraph of the chapter. Mrs. Jennings, through eavesdropping and imagining what is taking place, perceives that Colonel Brandon has made Elinor "an offer of marriage" (279–284).

Volume 3, Chapter 4 (Chapter 40)

Misunderstandings abound in this chapter. It begins and ends with Elinor in the company of Mrs. Jennings. At the beginning, Mrs. Jennings believes that Colonel Brandon and Elinor are delaying their wedding and the announcement until Edward has been ordained so that he can marry them. After she has left, Elinor "sat deliberately over her paper, with the pen in her hand" considering what she is to write to Edward Ferrars when he appears. She tells him of Brandon's offer: "I am charged with a most agreeable office"; the difficulty of Elinor's situation is indicated by an authorial parenthesis "(breathing rather faster than usual as she spoke)." Edward responds, "I cannot be ignorant that to you, to your goodness, I owe it all," a misunderstanding

reinforced by his subsequent comment, "as you well know, I am no orator." This observation does not bode well for his subsequent career as a clergyman who will have to give sermons. The underlying unstated assumption is that Edward thinks that Elinor is to marry Colonel Brandon and has persuaded him to offer "the living of Delaford."

The chapter closes with Mrs. Jennings's return home to Elinor, who when Edward leaves reflects to herself, "When I see him again . . . I shall see him the husband of Lucy." A thought described with considerable narratorial irony as "this pleasing anticipation." Mrs. Jennings's "deception" that "the Colonel only marries [Elinor] for the sake of giving ten guineas to Mr. Ferrars!" is corrected by the end of the chapter. Mrs. Jennings makes plans to decorate the Delaford parsonage, where she will visit Lucy and Edward (285–292).

Volume 3, Chapter 5 (Chapter 41)

The opening two paragraphs of the chapter focus on Lucy's reactions to the news of the granting of the Delaford Rectory and her gratitude to Colonel Brandon and willingness to exploit him. Elinor once again becomes the center of narrative attention. She calls on Fanny Dashwood, is not allowed into the house, but accidentally meets her husband, John Dashwood, outside. On hearing the news of Brandon's gift, Dashwood asks, "What could be the Colonel's motive?" He calculates that Brandon could have made a considerable profit from selling the Delaford living. Elinor's explanation he finds simplistic—"to be of use to Mr. Ferrars"—and tells her that her "reasoning is very good, but it is founded on ignorance of human nature." Hesitantly, cautiously, he tells Elinor that Mrs. Ferrars had apparently said that a marriage between Elinor and Edward Ferrars would be "the least evil of the two," in other words preferable to one between Edward and Lucy Steele.

The conversation is interrupted "by the entrance of Mr. Robert Ferrars," with whom Elinor is left alone, "in silence and immovable gravity," expressing contempt for him with "her eyes" as he proceeds to poke fun at his brother Edward's "idea of . . . being a clergyman." He tells Elinor, "We may treat it as a joke." Robert regards Lucy as "the merest awkward country girl, without style or elegance, and almost without beauty," seriously underestimating her intelligence and cunning. In the last paragraph of the chapter, Mrs. John Dashwood appears and, influenced by her husband, attempts to welcome Elinor (293–300).

Volume 3, Chapter 6 (Chapter 42)

Chapter 6 opens with a single-sentence paragraph expressing good intentions on the part of John Dashwood to Elinor before she and Marianne travel to Cleveland. It is "very early in April" when they leave London with Mrs. Jennings, Mrs. Palmer, and her new baby. Marianne reflects on London and Willoughby; Elinor, on the other hand, is "more positive" about the departure. She is "pleased to be free herself from the persecution of Lucy's friendship."

Cleveland and its surroundings are described through Marianne's vision. There are "open shrubbery and closer wood walk" and a "Grecian temple," where she thought "of wandering from place to place in free and luxurious solitude." Elinor is given the opportunity to review her opinions of Mr. Palmer, whom she finds more sympathetic and contrasts "his Epicurism," or self-indulgence, with Edward's totally different character. Brandon visits and tells Elinor of Edward's activities. His visits suggest to Elinor through watching "his eyes" that he favors Marianne: Mrs. Jennings remains convinced of Brandon's attachment to Elinor.

Marianne's walking in the rain on the Cleveland grounds "where the trees were the oldest, and the grass was longest and wettest" leads to "a cold so violent" that "she went to bed" and becomes ill (301–306).

Volume 3, Chapter 7 (Chapter 43)

The gravity of Marianne's illness results in the departure of Mrs. Palmer and her baby and then Palmer. Elinor attends her sister through the vicissitudes of her illness. She is assisted by Mrs. Jennings and Brandon, who acts as a messenger to fetch Mrs. Dashwood from Barton. Marianne is treated incompetently by the local apothecary, Harris. The depiction of Harris contrasts unfavorably with the trust Mr. Woodhouse places in Perry in *Emma*. Jane Austen uses consonants most effec-

tively to convey Marianne's illness: "a day spent in sitting shivering"; "Poor Marianne, languid and low." The development of the crisis in her illness is conveyed through a precise chronological time line. Following the failure of Harris's medicines, and "the morning of the third day," from "about noon" precise bulletins occur. Harris arrives again "at four o'clock," two hours later "at six o'clock," when what appears to be a relapse occurs. An hour later "at six o'clock" Elinor leaves "Marianne still sweetly asleep" to drink something after such lengthy sick-room duties. The weather too reflects the ups and downs of Marianne's state: "The night was cold and stormy" and "The wind roared round the house, and the rain beat against the windows." Marianne's illness is presented largely through Elinor's perspective, and contrary to Elinor's expectations, "the clock struck eight" and unpredictably she hears a coach draw up late in the evening.

Elinor is expecting her mother but not so soon. Throughout the chapter, Elinor's strength of character, Mrs. Jennings's sensible advice, and Brandon's character are revealed. As the coach arrives, "Never in her life had Elinor found it so difficult to be calm as at that moment." Her characteristic external restraint is put to its test. She anticipates "perhaps" the "despair" of her mother. Instead, in a moment of superb narrative reversal and focus, the unexpected occurs. Elinor does not find her mother and Colonel Brandon in "the drawing-room." The four horses, indicating urgency, instead of the two, as were the custom, drawing the carriage, have brought, of all people, Willoughby! (307–316).

Volume 3, Chapter 8 (Chapter 44)

The chapter consists of Willoughby, in spite of Elinor's initial objections, telling his side of his story. He has heard from Sir John Middleton that Marianne is dying and he rides to Cleveland hoping to be able to explain himself and his version of events. According to Willoughby, he was going to ask Marianne to marry him at Barton. However, Mrs. Smith, when hearing of his seduction of Eliza Williams, told him to leave Allenham. Aware of his own lack of prospects and wealth and fearful of poverty, he is forced to marry for money. His letter to Marianne, he informs Elinor, was dictated by his wealthy wife. His deep feelings for Marianne, regret at his behavior, and unhappy marriage, past misdeeds, "the world had made him extravagant and vain," lead Elinor to assure Willoughby "that she forgave, pitied, wished him well."

Willoughby's lengthy tale is punctuated by Elinor's interruptions. The narrator does not allow Willoughby one long confession. Initially, Elinor is very reluctant to listen to him and thinks momentarily that he is "drunk." Willoughby's "steadiness of . . . manner and the intelligence of his eye as he spoke" force her to listen to him. She interrupts Willoughby following his claim that he has "lost every thing that could make [life] a blessing." Elinor is "a little softened" by Willoughby's words and evident sincerity. The narrator draws attention to the shifts in the listener's responses to what she is being told, as well as to the teller's—Willoughby's—telling. At points in the tale Willoughby comments on the ways in which language is used. For instance, he says that "every line, every word" of Marianne's unanswered letters to him "was—in the hackneyed metaphor which their dear writer, were she here, would forbid—a dagger to my heart." Jane Austen, as narrator, is careful to distinguish between ways of expression and depth of feeling. Similarly, Elinor as a character distinguishes between the depth of her inner feelings and her outward expressions of them. Willoughby in this chapter is pouring out his heart, and his feelings and his apparent motivation: vanity, fear of poverty, the need for a wealthy marriage, his unhappiness (317–332).

Volume 3, Chapter 9 (Chapter 45)
The chapter begins with Elinor's inner responses to Willoughby's confession after he has left her. It then moves to Mrs. Dashwood's appearance. Instead of finding a very sick Marianne, she finds a daughter well on the way to recovery. Mrs. Dashwood tells Elinor that on their journey to Cleveland, Colonel Brandon has revealed his love for Marianne. She will do all she can to encourage the match and tells a slightly amused Elinor that Brandon is a much more suitable husband for Marianne than Willoughby.

The opening paragraphs of the chapter convey Elinor's sense of "sadness" for Willoughby and for the waste it has produced in him and in others. There is fatalism in her reactions: "Elinor's heart was full. The past, the present, the future," a sense of irreversibility in what has taken place. Elinor has momentary feelings for Willoughby: "for a moment [she] wished Willoughby a widower." Her thoughts are complex. "Then, remembering Colonel Brandon, reproved herself, felt that to *his* sufferings and *his* constancy far more than to his rival, the reward of her sister was due" (Jane Austen's emphasis). In the remainder of the chapter, she is again a listener, reacting briefly to her mother's exposition of Brandon's virtues as Marianne's suitor and Willoughby's deficiencies (333–394).

Volume 3, Chapter 10 (Chapter 46)
Mrs. Dashwood, Marianne and Elinor return to Barton. Before doing so, Marianne gathers her strength after her serious illness. Before departing, Mrs. Jennings and Colonel Brandon go their separate ways. After a two-day journey, they reach Barton. Marianne is lost in her own recollections. Her near death experience, and the loss of Willoughby, make her aware that she has been selfish, especially when she thinks of Elinor's stoic, selfless behavior. Her illness was "entirely brought on by" herself, and "Had I died,—it would have been self-destruction." Marianne is determined "to shew that my spirit is humbled, my heart amended, and that I can practise the civilities, the lesser duties of life, with gentleness, and forbearance." Elinor's account of Willoughby's confession is briefly summarized. Marianne listens silently and with restraint (345, 347, 348).

There are several areas of interest in this chapter. Noteworthy is the use of imagery of "eyes," continuing from the end of the previous chapter, where Mrs. Dashwood observes, "there was always a something . . . in Willoughby's eyes at times, which I did not like" (338). In the second paragraph of chapter 10 of the final volume, Marianne's appearance following her serious illness is described as "strengthened by the hollow eye, the sickly sin, the posture of reclining weakness" (340). Recovering, Marianne turns to her piano and books, "the music on which her eyes first rested was an opera, procured for her by Willoughby." She adds, "That would not do" (342). As Elinor recounts Willough-by's confession, "Marianne said not a word—She trembled, her eyes were fixed on the ground" (347). Of course, "eyes" and sight reveal inner feelings and reactions. Elinor in this chapter is once again subjected to a personal confessional. In the previous chapter, it was Willoughby's, in this, it is her sister's, which is replete with religious and spiritual language and associations. These include specific reference to Henry VIII's dissolution of monasteries during the mid–16th century, as Marianne plans to "often go to the old ruins of the Priory" (343).

Volume 3, Chapter 11 (Chapter 47)

The chapter begins and concludes from Mrs. Dash-wood's perspective. At its opening she passes judgment on Willoughby, listens to Elinor's truncated account of what Willoughby told her, and at the end of the chapter regrets, after hearing the news from their servant, that Edward and Lucy are married, not having paid more attention to Elinor. For Elinor, like Marianne, too had been "suffering" (355). During the chapter Margaret, the youngest sister, returns "and the family were again all restored to each other" (352).

Elinor's retelling of Willoughby's tale, this time to her mother, involves condensation that reflects Elinor's sense of her listener, of what her mother can hear or tolerate, and Elinor's own developing reactions to what Willoughby has told her. For Elinor, Willoughby's actions have "been grounded on selfishness." She tells Marianne, "It was selfishness which first made him sport with your affection" and determined his subsequent actions. Elinor says, "His own enjoyment, or his own ease, was, in every particular, his ruling principle" (351). Marianne realizes that she would not have led a happy life with Willoughby even though they had married. After Elinor has spoken to her mother and Marianne of Willoughby, and Margaret's return to the family, she "grew impatient for some tidings of Edward" (351–352). Letters from her brother reveal very little.

The news from the servant of his marriage produces an extreme reaction from Marianne. She "gave a violent start, fixed her eyes upon Elinor, saw her turning pale, and fall back in her chair in

hysterics." Elinor, on the other hand, "recovered the use of her reason and voice" (353) to question the servant, Thomas, to gain more information. We as readers, as listeners to the evidence that sounds so confirmatory, know, if we have read the whole novel, indeed the next chapter, that it is once again mistaken information. The characters involved lack our knowledge, and suffer as a consequence personal distress, so much so that in the last paragraph, Mrs. Dashwood regrets that her attentions have been focused on "Marianne's affliction." She has forgotten "that in Elinor she might have a daughter suffering almost as much, certainly with less self-provocation, and greater fortitude" (356).

Volume 3, Chapter 12 (Chapter 48)

In this chapter the misinformation from the previous chapter, with its consequences, is corrected. Elinor is the focus of attention. Her imagination dominates the first seven paragraphs. She speculates on Edward and his marriage and on Lucy's actions: She would be "courting the favour of Colonel Brandon, of Mrs. Jennings, and of every wealthy friend" (357). Surprisingly, Edward arrives unexpectedly and alone. Elinor is speechless. Eventually the conversation between him and Mrs. Dashwood turns to the subject of his supposed marriage. He tells them that his younger brother, Robert, has married Lucy. Elinor, during this revelation, had retreated to work. Edward ironically "took up a pair of scissars . . . spoiling both them and their sheath by cutting the latter to pieces as he spoke." Unable to control her emotions any longer, Elinor "almost ran out of the room, and as soon as the door was closed, burst into tears of joy, which at first she thought would never cease." After she leaves, Edward falls "into a reverie," or silent trance, and he too leaves (360).

Volume 3, Chapter 13 (Chapter 49)

The book is now winding toward its close. Edward has come to Barton to propose to Elinor, who accepts him. Again, she is subject to a confessional, but one she has waited for and enjoys. Edward tells her of his early friendship with, and subsequent engagement to, Lucy, and how she "appeared everything that was amiable and obliging" (362).

The intimacy between Elinor and Edward is followed by Lucy's letter to Edward breaking off their engagement. John Dashwood writes to Elinor to tell her that Fanny, his wife, and Mrs. Ferrars have "suffered agonies of sensibility" (371) as a result of Robert's marriage to Lucy. Consequently, there is hope of reconciliation between Edward and his estranged mother. His letter has followed one from Mrs. Jennings venting "her honest indignation against the jilting girl" (370). At the end of the chapter, persuaded by Elinor, Edward goes to London to ask Fanny and John Dashwood to assist with reconciliation with his mother.

In addition to letters, the chapter is replete with intimate confidences between Edward and Elinor displaying the depth of their relationship. Her feelings when she learns that "Lucy was married to another" and he is at last "free" are anything but restrained: "She was everything by turns but tranquil." Jane Austen as narrator makes a fine distinction between "two rational creatures" and "lovers": "between *them* ["lovers"] no subject is finished, no communication is ever made, till it has been made at least twenty times over" (Jane Austen's emphasis: 363–364). The narrator, however, is on occasion ambiguous. When Edward proposes to Elinor, "he did not, upon the whole, expect a very cruel reception. It was his business . . . to say that he *did* and he said it very prettily" (Jane Austen's emphasis). The narrator adds somewhat cynically, "What he might say on the subject ["of his fate with" Elinor] a twelvemonth after [they are married] must be referred to the imagination of husbands and wives" (366). The implication is that all might not be bliss a year after the realities of marriage have set in.

Volume 3, Chapter 14 (Chapter 50)

In the last chapter of the novel, the loose ends are tied up and futures anticipated. Edward and Elinor marry and settle, with Colonel Brandon's assistance, at Delaford. Mrs. Ferrars is reconciled to Edward and to the marriage to allow a similar financial settlement she had given Fanny on her marriage to John Dashwood. Edward and Elinor consequently have "an income quite sufficient to their wants" (374). Lucy, on the other hand, cunningly ingratiates herself with Mrs. Ferrars to

become "a favourite child." Close to Mrs. Ferrars, to John, and Fanny, ironically the "frequent domestic disagreements between Robert and Lucy themselves . . . could exceed the harmony in which they all lived together."

Marianne, "with such a confederacy against her," of Mrs. Dashwood, Edward, and Elinor, at last marries Brandon. At the age of 19, she is "placed in a new home, a wife, the mistress of a family and the patroness of a village." Willoughby, on the other hand, "made her his secret standard of perfection in woman" but is comforted by his wife, who "was not always out of humour, nor his home always uncomfortable." In the last paragraph the realities of everyday existence intrude. Barton, the Ferrarses, and Delaford, the Brandons, constantly are in communication with one another; "they could live without disagreement between themselves." Further, "the happiness of Elinor and Marianne" did not produce "coolness between their husbands" (377–380).

CRITICAL COMMENTARY

Contemporary comments and reviews of *Sense and Sensibility* were largely laudatory. For instance, in a letter postmarked November 24, 1811, Henrietta, Countess of Bessborough, comments to Lord Granville Leveson Gower, "Have you read 'Sense and Sensibility'? It is a clever novel. They were full of it at Althorp [landed estate], and tho' it ends stupidly I was much amus'd by it" (Gilson, 9). Four years later, a French translation of *Sense and Sensibility* was published. Two very early reviews of the novel from 1812 are sympathetic. The review in the *British Critic* commends *Sense and Sensibility* to "female friends . . . [who] may peruse these volumes not only with satisfaction but with real benefits, for they may learn from them, if they please, many sober and salutary maxims for the conduct of life, exemplified in a very pleasing and entertaining narrative" (Southam, I: 40). The *Critical Review*, February 1812, noted, "both amusement and instruction" in the novel, and found Sir John Middleton amusing and admired Marianne, while observing that her excess at times "annoys everyone around her." The reviewer's observations concerning Marianne echo subsequent criticism. He fears that "there are too many" Mariannes, adding "but without her elegance and good sense, who play their feelings and happiness till they lose the latter . . . render the former perfectly ridiculous and contemptible" (Southam, I: 35, 37).

George Henry Lewes, writing in the *Westminster Review* in July 1852, praises Jane Austen's use of language in the novel. He uses Lucy Steele as an example, writing "Only cultivated minds fairly appreciate the exquisite art of Miss Austen," Lucy's "bad English [is] delicately and truthfully indicated" (Southam, I: 141). Julia Kavanaugh, on the other hand, in 1862 believes that Elinor and Marianne are "somewhat deficient in reality. Elinor Dashwood is Judgment—her sister Marianne is Imagination. We feel it too plainly. And the triumph of Sense over Sensibility, shown by the different conduct they hold under very similar trials, is all the weaker that it is the result of the author's will." Kavanaugh praises Jane Austen's "Delicate irony," especially in the depiction of the foolish Sir John Middleton and Mrs. Jennings, who brings elements of comic relief to the novel (Southam, I: 179, 181).

Margaret Oliphant, in 1870, objects to Marianne's "selfish and high-flown wretchedness" and the "foolishness" of Sir John Middleton, and says "the Miss Steeles are simply vulgar and disagreeable" (Southam, I: 222). Increasingly, among late 19th-century reactions to Jane Austen, the differences between her historical and literary period and the present, engage critical comments. For instance, Leslie Stephen, writing in 1875, comments that "there is not a single flash of biting satire. She [Jane Austen] is absolutely at peace with her most comfortable world. She never hints at a suspicion that squires and parsons of the English type are not an essential part of the order of things" (Southam, II: 174–175). These are observations found wanting in the critical perceptions of subsequent writers such as D. W. Harding and Claudia L. Johnson. On the other hand, Marilyn Butler and Jocelyn Harris find Jane Austen ideological and stylistically heavily indebted to her 18th-century predecessors.

Early 20th-century critics are largely fascinated by her characterization, although Richard Simpson's 1870 *North British Review* essay pointed the way to subsequent readings of the world of Jane

Austen's fiction as a "microcosm of some larger moral universe." Writing in the immediate post–World War II period, Ian Watt points to the values of Jane Austen's time that are lost to readers of later generations: for instance, Marianne and Willoughby's use of first names is much more suggestive than appears to Watt's contemporary readers. For Watt, the importance of the novel is not in the focus on Elinor and Marianne but in "their relation to a fixed code of values." Watt finds the concepts of "sense" and "sensibility" to be very complex, an insight that will be developed by subsequent critics such as Butler and Johnson. Watt writes that "Jane Austen developed for the first time a narrative form which fully articulated the conflict between the contrary tendencies of her age: between reason and rapture, between the observing mind and the feeling heart, between being sensible and being sensitive" (Watt, 47, 51).

C. S. Lewis, writing in 1954, slightly earlier than Watt, also points to serious elements underneath the seeming glittering surface of *Sense and Sensibility*. For Lewis, the scenes where Marianne comes to realize that her selfishness has given her sister Elinor pain are part of a pattern of "undeception" of heroines in Austen's novels. Selfishness, however, does not result in tragedy, but in "cheerful moderation" (Lewis, 185). The depiction of the realities of emotional experience in *Sense and Sensibility* are noted in an earlier 1919 essay by the Irish novelist George Moore (1852–1933). In a fine assessment of the strengths and weaknesses of the novel, Moore writes, "Remember that the theme of the book is a disappointment in love, and never was one better written, more poignant, more dramatic." Moore adds, "We all know how terrible these disappointments are, and how they crush and break up life, for the moment reducing it to dust" (Southam, II, 275).

Marilyn Butler's *Jane Austen and the War of Ideas* is a sophisticated placement of Jane Austen's work within the ideological and literary contexts in which it was written. She finds the structure of *Sense and Sensibility* to be very complex: the "novel advances on the assumption that what happens to one of the central characters must also happen to the other; at every turn the reader cannot avoid the appropriate conclusion" (183). For Butler, "Elinor is the first character in an Austen novel consistently to reveal an inner life" (189). Elinor represents "an active, struggling Christian in a difficult world" (192).

Reading the novel from a feminist perspective, Claudia Johnson insightfully sees *Sense and Sensibility* as a "radical critique of conservative ideology [as] an examination of the morally vitiating tendencies of patriarchy" (69). The story of the two Elizas, both of whom are used and abused, and unsuccessfully protected by Brandon, is central to her reading of the novel. For Johnson, "if this insert tale is never permitted to become central, it nevertheless is linked to the larger story" (55) in the novel of the dangers lurking beneath a protected world to which at the conclusion of *Sense and Sensibility,* Marianne and Elinor "withdraw" (72).

Money and property as determinates of personal worth in the novel have not been ignored. Oliver MacDonagh, for instance, points to the reality that not one of the characters in the novel actually earns any money. On the whole, *Sense and Sensibility* has not received the intense critical attention reserved for such novels as *Emma, Pride and Prejudice,* and *Mansfield Park.* Moreland Perkins's *Reshaping the Sexes in Sense and Sensibility* is an extensive, book-length study devoted to the novel and reactions to it. Perkins's work, a product of the late 20th-century critical industry, reveals that the novel, its characters, and ideas continue to engage almost two centuries after its publication.

CHARACTERS

Betty (Chapter 25) Mrs. Jennings's maid. Mrs. Jennings invites Elinor and Marianne to accompany her to London. However her "inconvenience . . . will only be sending Betty by the coach, and I hope I can afford *that*" (Jane Austen's emphasis, 153). Mrs. Jennings asks Elinor to recommend Betty's sister to Edward Ferrars and Lucy Steele, who seem to be getting married, as a housemaid.

Brandon, Colonel (Chapters 7–8, 10, 11–14, 20, 26–27, 30–34, 39–43, 46–47, 50) Brandon has too easily been dismissed as a "wooden and undeveloped character . . . unexciting and remote." He has been described as "a vacuum" and a "stolid sad sack" (cited Auerbach, 113). Akin to Elinor, he has difficulties with expression and is very reticent, telling Elinor "it would be impossible to describe what I felt" (199). The narrator describes him as "on every occasion mindful of the feelings of others" (62). He is a friend of Sir John Middleton, against whom his "silent and grave manner" curiously contrasts. Marianne subsequently refers to Brandon as an old, unwell man. Around 35 years of age, he is from the start of the novel described as "sensible" and "gentlemanlike" (34). Elinor quickly appreciates his "good-breeding and good nature," (51) combined with considerable strength of character, especially contrasted with the superficial nature of the rest of Barton society.

Brandon, when the Dashwood girls stay in London, visits them on a daily basis, and he makes little attempt to disguise his concern for Marianne and her welfare. Under Willoughby's influence, Marianne finds Brandon wanting in "genius, taste . . . spirit . . . brilliancy . . . ardour." Elinor, on the other hand, appreciates Brandon's experience of life, his genuineness, his knowledgeable "thinking mind" (51). She perceives that Brandon's reticence is the consequence of "some oppression of spirits" rather than a "natural gloominess of temper" (50).

Eventually Brandon reveals that he loved the 17-year-old Eliza Williams, not unlike Marianne in character. She married instead, against her wishes, his elder brother, and Brandon subsequently left for the East. Mistreated by the brother, she was unfaithful, and divorced, she ends up in poverty and sickness, before dying early. Brandon took care of her daughter, Eliza, who recently had eloped with, and been seduced by, Willoughby. Brandon challenged Willoughby to a duel from which both escaped unhurt. The seduction is the reason for his sudden unexplained departure from Barton.

Brandon's obvious pain is increased as he has fallen in love with the 17-year-old Marianne, who reminds him of Eliza. He is forced to remain silent while she becomes increasingly besotted by Willoughby, whom he knows to be disingenuous. Yet Brandon remains constant and selfless in his devotion to her. When he learns that Edward Ferrars has been disinherited by his mother, Brandon offers him a living on the Delaford estate he has inherited after the death of his brother. He drives at night to fetch Mrs. Dashwood from Barton when Marianne is seriously ill at Cleveland. On the return journey, he reveals his love for Marianne and gains Mrs. Dashwood's support for his suit. It becomes a "darling object" (378) for Mrs. Dashwood to bring Marianne and the Colonel together. She is successful in this object and they marry: "in Marianne" Colonel Brandon "was consoled for every past affliction."

In short, the romantic Marianne marries someone she regarded as boring, too old, and ridiculous as he wore a flannel waistcoat. He is the clear opposite to Willoughby, and she has learned to appreciate Brandon's fidelity and integrity. At the end of the novel, "Colonel Brandon was now as happy, as all those who best loved him, believed he deserved to be" (379).

Brandon, Fanny (Chapters 13, 14)   References to Colonel Brandon's sister are sparse. She is married to the owner of the Whitwell estate and apparently is unwell. She is believed to be with her husband "at Avignon" (70) when Sir John Middleton suggests a visit to the Whitwell grounds.

Brandon, Mr. (deceased) (Chapter 31)   The elder brother of Colonel Brandon, who married Eliza Williams, his cousin, for her wealth: "Her fortune was large, and our family estate much encumbered." He treated her with "great unkindness" (205–206). Dissipated, Brandon neglects his wife and, following her infidelity, divorces her. Brandon dies five years before the central events of the novel take place; his younger brother Colonel Brandon inherits Delaford, the family estate in Dorset.

Brandon, Mrs. Eliza, née Williams (deceased) (Chapter 31)   Seen through Colonel Brandon's narrative and recollections, "This lady was one of [his] nearest relations, an orphan from her infancy, and under the guardianship of [Brandon's] father . . . from our earliest years we were playfellows, and friends." According to Brandon, at 17 "she was married—married against her inclination to [his] brother" to save the Brandon family fortunes. Initially she resisted the marriage, attempting unsuccessfully to elope with her relative

Colonel Brandon. Treated badly by her husband, "without a friend to advise or restrain her"—Colonel Brandon had departed for the East Indies, and his "father lived only a few months after [their] marriage"—she was unfaithful. From her affair she had a little girl, Eliza, and her husband divorced her. Three years after these events, by accident Colonel Brandon found her living in a debtor's prison "so altered—so faded—worn down by acute suffering of every kind!" and dying of consumption. Brandon places her "in comfortable lodgings" and visits "her every day during the rest of her short life."

Related by Brandon, her tale has various functions. It serves as a warning for those like Marianne, and Brandon admits that she reminds him of Eliza, who have too much sensibility rather than sense. Concerning Eliza's behavior, Brandon tells Elinor, "can we wonder that with such a husband to provoke inconstancy, and without a friend to advise or restrain her?" she becomes a victim of the male sex. She is not given a "legal allowance . . . adequate to her fortune, nor sufficient for her comfortable maintenance." Following her divorce, she is left "to sink deeper in a life of sin" (205–207). For a feminist critic such as Claudia L. Johnson, "Eliza's story, like so much of the central matter in" the novel, "indicts the license to coercion, corruption and avarice available to grasping patriarchs and their eldest sons" (56).

Brandon, Old, Mr. (deceased) (Chapter 3)   Colonel Brandon's father, Eliza Williams's uncle and guardian. He forces her "against her inclination" to marry his eldest son to save the Brandon estate from financial ruin. He "lived only a few months after their marriage" (205–206). Old Mr. Brandon is today perceived by critics as a "grasping patriarch," manipulating his sons and relatives (Johnson, 56).

Burgess, Mrs. (Chapter 49)   Following her sister Lucy's elopement with Robert Ferrars, a stranded Anne Steele "goes to Exeter." There "she thinks of staying there three or four weeks with Mrs. Burgess," a friend, "in hopes . . . to fall in with the Doctor [Davies] again" (370–371), whom she believes is attracted to her.

Careys, the (Chapter 13) One of the Middletons' numerous acquaintances and neighbors living in Newton. "The two Miss Careys" come to Barton for the planned Whitwell party, and when this fails to materialize, they and other members of their family "came to dinner" at the Middletons' (65, 67).

Cartwright (Chapter 26) Associated with Mrs. Jennings in London, who has "had Cartwright to settle with" (163). He could be her lawyer, business adviser, housekeeper, or head servant.

Clarke, Mrs. (Chapter 38) "An intimate acquaintance of Mrs. Jennings" who meets her and Elinor in Kensington Garden. She is unable to convey any information concerning "the Willoughbys" or Edward Ferrars.

Courtland, Lord (Chapter 36) A friend of Robert Ferrars who "came to [him] . . . on purpose" seeking advice on building plans drawn up by the architect Joseph Bonomi. Robert Ferrars apparently throws the plans "into the fire" and tells Courtland to "build a cottage" instead (251–252).

Dashwood, Mr. (deceased) (Chapter 1) Described as a "single man, who lived to a very advanced age," owner of the "large" and long-established Dashwood estate in Sussex at Norland Park, "where, for many generations" the Dashwoods "lived in so respectable a manner, as to engage the general good opinion of their surrounding acquaintance." Following the death of his sister, "who for many years of his life had, [been his] constant companion and housekeeper" [3], he invited his nephew, and legal inheritor, Henry Dashwood, and his family to live at Norland.

Old Dashwood's death and will is the source for the complications of the plot of *Sense and Sensibility*. In his will, he disinherited his nephew Henry Dashwood's second wife and her three daughters, instead leaving the estate to the son of Henry's first marriage, John Dashwood, and his son, Harry Dashwood. Consequently, when Henry dies only a year following the death of old Mr. Dashwood, his second wife and daughters find they are without

rights at Norland and are soon forced to find somewhere else to live.

Dashwood, Miss (deceased) (Chapter 1) The unmarried sister of old Mr. Dashwood, his companion and housekeeper. Her death, a decade before the narrative begins, "produced a great alteration" at Norland, "for to supply her loss, he invited and received into his house the family of his nephew Mr. Henry Dashwood" [3].

Dashwood, Henry (deceased) (Chapter 1) Twice married. By his first wife he had a son, John, and by his second wife, three daughters, Elinor, Marianne, and Margaret. On the death of his uncle, he became owner of the Norland estate, but finds it secured to his son John and John's son, Harry, who is four years old. Henry Dashwood dies a year after his uncle, leaving a comparatively small sum, "ten thousand pounds, including the late legacies [of £3,000], was all that remained for his widow and daughters." Henry Dashwood possessed a "temper . . . cheerful and sanguine" (4).

Dashwood, Mrs. Henry (Chapters 1, 3, 10, 15–19, 25, 31–32, 45–47, 49–50) The second wife of Henry Dashwood, she is left with little money, and dependant on the goodwill of the son and his wife of her husband's first wife. She has three daughters, Elinor, Marianne, and Margaret. Due to the generosity of her cousin Sir John Middleton, she and her daughters leave Norland and live at Barton Cottage. According to the narrator, the ability to control her feelings was "a knowledge which [she] had yet to learn" (6). She admits that she "can feel no sentiment of approbation inferior to love" (16). Mrs. Dashwood "had an excellent heart; her disposition was affectionate, and her feelings were strong" (6). Restrained by her eldest daughter, Elinor, she encourages Marianne's enthusiasm for Willoughby, and, after she has met him for a week, anticipates their engagement. She persuades Elinor and Marianne to accept Mrs. Jennings's invitation to go to London. She hopes that their visit will reunite Willoughby to Marianne. At the conclusion of the novel, she regrets that she previously had not been more responsible for Marianne. To achieve her "darling object" (378), the marriage of Marianne and Colonel Brandon, she frequently takes her to Delaford. After her two eldest daughters marry, she is "prudent enough" (381) to stay at Barton cottage.

Mrs. Dashwood is vague and overromantic, intuitive rather than rational. She is uncertain about practical financial affairs, and is convinced that she sensed something unpleasant in Willoughby's eyes. As the novel proceeds, she begins gradually to appreciate Edward Ferrars's strengths, "an evolving appreciation that works against the grain of her spontaneous taste" (Perkins, 40). In short, as a widow in straitened circumstances with two daughters of marriageable age, and a younger daughter, existence in a male-dominated society is complicated and difficult. Lacking financial acumen, she is viewed by her own daughters and others as an indulgent parent. However, Barton Cottage becomes a place of retreat for Willoughby, Edward Ferrars, and Colonel Brandon—a place where they can feel happy and somewhat secure. For instance, Edward, after spending a week at Barton and the Dashwoods', "valued their kindness beyond any thing, and his greatest happiness was in being with them" (101). Mrs. Dashwood is fortunate that she has a distant relative such as Sir John Middleton to provide a comfortable roof for her and her daughters and congenial company with the appropriate social contacts at nearby Barton Park. She rarely speaks ill of anyone—apart from Willoughby when his trickery of Marianne emerges.

Dashwood, Elinor (throughout the novel)   The heroine and central consciousness of the novel. The eldest of the three Dashwood daughters, she "possessed a strength of understanding, and coolness of judgment, which qualified her, though only nineteen, to be the counsellor of her mother." Of the Dashwood women, she has the greatest "strength of understanding, and coolness of judgment" (6), combined with self-control. Unlike her younger sister Marianne, and her mother, she does not reveal her feelings to others. At Norland, before she has moved to Barton Cottage, she has fallen in love with Edward Ferrars but outwardly does not display her feelings for him. She perceives that he is not

wealthy enough to be an appropriate match for her, yet she retains her love for Edward and does not relinquish the hope that eventually they will marry. Even when discovering that he is engaged to Lucy Steele, in spite of her mortification and disappointment, she still maintains external appearances of calmness and keeps her emotions to herself. She analyzes Edward's situation and believes that he does not really love Lucy but is committed to her out of duty rather than love. Her reticence provides a remarkable contrast to Marianne's unbridled emotions at the loss of Willoughby. Elinor's fidelity to Edward and self-restraint at the end of the novel are rewarded. Lucy Steele married Robert Ferrars, allowing Edward at last to declare his love for Elinor, and they marry.

Elinor's closest friend, both in terms of character and fate in the novel, is Colonel Brandon. He, among others, has used Elinor as a confessor for his private fears and emotions. She proves in the novel to be a good listener and counselor. Elinor's self-restraint represents an alternative set of values to those embodied in the romantic, self-absorbed, sentimental Marianne or her mother, and the selfish hedonism of Willoughby or the manipulating duplicity of a Lucy Steele. Elinor represents the "sense" of the title of the novel, and her sister Marianne the "sensibility": The two, Elinor and Marianne, are complementary. Both have a good deal in common. They both are dreamers. Edward, following Lucy's elopement with his brother, knows that Elinor will accept him. Elinor admits to herself that "in spite of herself, she had always admitted a hope, while Edward remained single, that something would occur to prevent his marrying Lucy" (357). Her self-restraint and lack of public display of feelings may belong to the 18th-century Augustan virtues of moderation. Her dreams, and fidelity to her wish to marry Edward, represent romantic values.

Dashwood, Fanny, née Ferrars (Chapters 1–3, 5, 24, 32–34, 36, 37, 41–42, 49–50)   "A strong caricature of her [husband, John Dashwood]; more narrow-minded and selfish" (5). Sister of Edward and Robert Ferrars, Fanny is a snob, mean, materialistic, and calculating. Her ability to twist her husband around her little finger is demonstrated in the second chapter of the novel, in which she adroitly brings her husband to deprive his father's second wife and three daughters of any sufficient income. She persuades John Dashwood to do exactly the opposite of his late father's clear intentions. In this second chapter, almost every sentence starts with "Certainly" or "To be sure," "Undoubtedly," "I believe you are right," or "That is very true." Each phrase represents her paring away of the £3,000 due to Mrs. Henry Dashwood and her daughters. She encourages her mother's hostility toward her brother Edward to keep Elinor, her mother, and sisters in poverty and to humiliate them. Mrs. Jennings, not noted for sparing her opinion, regards Fanny's treatment of Lucy and Anne Steele as both cruel and lacking in reason. Fanny Dashwood regrets Edward's lack of ambition and finds Lady Middleton congenial: "There was a kind of cold hearted selfishness on both sides, which mutually attracted them; and they sympathized with each other in an insipid propriety of demeanour, and a general want of understanding" (229). In short, Fanny Dashwood has much in common with the vain, utterly selfish, and mean Sir Walter Elliot in PERSUASION, but she is much more manipulative and intelligent.

Dashwood, Harry (Chapter 1) The only son of John and Fanny Dashwood, to whom the old Mr. Dashwood took a shine, so much so "as to leave his estate" to Harry "a child of four years" when he died (4).

Dashwood, John (Chapters 1–3, 5, 24, 32–34, 36–37, 41–42, 49–50) The only son of Henry Dashwood by his first wife and consequently the half brother of Elinor, Marianne, and Margaret. Described as "not an ill-disposed young man, unless to be rather cold hearted, and rather selfish, is to be ill disposed; but he was in general, well-respected; for he conducted himself with propriety in the discharge of his ordinary duties" (5). Inheriting the Norland estate, he promised his father as he lay dying that he would look after his widow and half-sisters. Left comfortable by inheriting some of his mother's wealth, plus his estate's income, he could

reasonably have carried out his late father's wishes by giving his half sisters a thousand pounds each. However, John Dashwood, putty in the hands of his mean, selfish wife, is persuaded to deprive them of any money. Her hostility, in spite of John Dashwood's seemingly good intentions, causes his father's widow and daughters to leave Norland and go Barton Cottage.

Materialistic John Dashwood's behavior in London reveals that he is interested in others only if they have money. Owing to the high cost of keeping up appearances in London, he finds his Norland estate commitments too expensive, although he acquires another farm. John encourages Elinor to marry Colonel Brandon to gain wealth and status, and he manages to gain a legacy from Mrs. Jennings. He is unable to comprehend Brandon's altruistic motives in granting Edward Ferrars an appropriate living. His philistine obsession with money and status becomes more "a source of satiric humor than of serious moral censure" (Poplawski, 116).

Dashwood, Margaret (Chapters 1, 7, 10, 12, 15, 17, 21, 23, 45–46, 48, 50) The youngest Dashwood daughter is "a good-humoured well-disposed girl." However, the narrator warns her readers in the final paragraph of the first chapter, "as she had already imbibed a good deal of Marianne's [her sister's] romance, without having much of her sense, she did not, at thirteen, bid fair to equal her sisters at a more advanced period of life" (7). At the end of the novel, she remains with her mother at Barton Cottage, having "reached an age highly suitable for dancing, and not ineligible for being supposed to have a lover" (380).

Dashwood, Marianne (throughout the novel) The second Dashwood daughter, she is just 17 at the beginning of the novel. Her father had died, she is the middle sister with Elinor as her elder sister and Margaret as her younger one. The narrator tells her readers toward the conclusion of the opening chapter, "She was sensible and clever; but eager in every thing; her sorrows, her joys, could have no moderation. She was generous, amiable, interesting: she was every thing but prudent. The resemblance between her and her mother was strikingly great" (6). Her words to her mother concerning Edward Ferrars's reading of poetry and her direct appeal to Willoughby when she encounters him in London exemplify her unrestrained spontaneity. These qualities are also reflected in her indiscreet Allenham visit, an attempt to see Willoughby, presented in chapter 9, and her willingness to begin a relationship with him and her assumption that they are engaged, combined with her disregard for her own welfare at Cleveland when she catches fever after walking in a severe rainstorm. She is also rude to those around her: "her usual inattention to the forms of general civility" (144). On the whole, her ideas are incorrect. She objects to "second attachments," although, ironically, she marries Colonel Brandon, a "second attachment" (55) on her part and on his. She opposes what she regards as her sister Elinor's "doctrine" of "treat[ing] our acquaintance in general with greater attention," or paying more attention to the needs of others (94). Marianne is dogmatic and consistent in her romantic ideals.

Marianne is close to her mother, to whom she is most alike. She considers Edward Ferrars's aesthetic judgment wanting, and throughout most of the novel, until her serious illness, she looks on Colonel Brandon as close to the grave. In the three years encompassed in the time frame of the novel, the reader sees her maturing through disappointment and experience so that at the conclusion, she is ready to be Brandon's wife. Jane Austen uses her excesses of emotional response to satirize romantic extremes. To take two examples, Marianne appeals directly to the trees at Norland: "And you, ye well-known trees" (27). After Willoughby deserts her, her emotions know no restraint: the "nourishment of grief was every day applied" (83). In spite of these extremes, Marianne possesses fine artistic judgment and an astute awareness of language and style. She has no time for the trivial and second rate and unreservedly criticizes materialism and the ridiculous concern with status and social forms. She is resurrected from a life-threatening illness by the efforts and concern of her sister Elinor and Colonel Brandon, who loves her. In the final chapter, the narrator relates that Marianne "was born to

an extraordinary fate. She was born to discover the falsehood of her own opinions, and to counteract, by her conduct, her most favourite maxims." Essentially, "she was born to overcome" and to be happy. At the age of 19, "she found herself . . . submitting to new attachments, entering on new duties, placed in a new home, a wife, the mistress of a family, and the patroness of a village" (378–379).

Dashwood, Mrs. (deceased) (Chapter 1) The first wife of Henry Dashwood and mother of John Dashwood. Her "fortune" made ample provision for her son; it was a large fortune, "half of which devolved on [Henry Dashwood] on his coming of age" [3].

Davies, Doctor (Chapters 32, 38) A theological divine who traveled with Anne Steele and her sister to London. Anne Steele tells Mrs. Jennings that "every body laughs at me so about the Doctor." Her "cousins say that they are sure I have made a conquest" (218). She has something of an obsession with him, even to the point of wearing pink ribbons, apparently "the Doctor's favourite colour" (272).

Dennison, Mrs. (Chapter 36) One of Fanny Dashwood's London acquaintances whose visit to the Dashwoods' Harley Street residence coincides with the visit of Elinor and Marianne. She invites them to her musical evening by "mistake" (252), assuming that they are guests of Fanny Dashwood's. This necessitates Fanny sending her carriage for Elinor and Marianne and, "what was still worse" (248), creating the impression that she is treating them with consideration. At the musical evening, Elinor meets Edward's younger brother, Robert.

Donovan, Mr. (Chapter 37) A comic character. An apothecary or physician, he is called in by Mrs. Palmer regarding her child's apparent illness: "it was nothing in the world but the red-gum." He is asked by Mrs. Jennings whether he has any gossip. In reply, he hints that "For fear any unpleasant report should reach the young ladies under your care as to their sister's indisposition, I think it advisable to say, that I believe there is no great reason for alarm; I hope Mrs. Dashwood will do very well." This refers to the fact that Donovan has just visited Fanny Dashwood after she has fallen into hysteria over the news that her brother Edward Ferrars is secretly engaged to Lucy Steele. This news Donovan conveys to Mrs. Jennings (257–258).

Elliott, Sir, and Lady Elliott (Chapter 36)   Apparently friends of Robert Ferrars. They live near Dartford in a large house somewhat sarcastically referred to as "a cottage." Robert, when staying with them, shows them how to arrange their space so that they can hold a dance for "exactly eighteen couple[s]." He consequently disabuses them of the notion "that there can be no accommodation, no space in a cottage" (252).

Ellison, Mr. and Mrs. (Chapter 30)   The guardians of the wealthy Miss Grey. According to Mrs. Jennings, they "would not be sorry to have Miss Grey married, for she and Mrs. Ellison could never agree" (194).

Ferrars, Edward (Chapters 3–5, 8, 12, 16–19, 21–24, 32–41, 47–50)   Edward, the brother of Mrs. Fanny Dashwood and Robert Ferrars, is the oldest son of a father "who had died very rich." However, his inheritance depends on keeping in the good books of his selfish mother. Edward first met Elinor Dashwood soon after she and her family moved to Norland Park. His sister Fanny objected to their developing relationship, and this was one of the main reasons why Elinor, her sisters, and her mother left for Devon. Reserved in public and shy, well read, with "an open affectionate heart" (15), Edward wants a quiet life, but his mother is ambitious for him, wishing him to go into Parliament. Edward's preference is for the church. His family does not approve, and remaining unemployed, he enters Oxford University when 19 and has been idle subsequently.

Not sent to public school, he was privately tutored by a Mr. Pratt near Plymouth, on the southwest coast of England, for four years. At Mr. Pratt's he met his niece Lucy Steele, to whom he became secretly engaged, and subsequently came to regret the engagement, a "consequence of ignorance of the world—and want of employment" (362). Duty bound to uphold the engagement, Edward refuses his mother's offer of an estate in Norfolk worth £1000 a year if he agrees to marry Miss Morton, a wealthy heiress. Edward's secret commitment to Lucy Steele explains his curious behavior toward Elinor both at Norland and at Barton Cottage. After the engagement becomes public, his mother disowns and disinherits Edward. Meanwhile, Edward has taken holy orders, and it appears that he and Lucy have agreed to marry when he obtains a living. Colonel Brandon, after learning of the situation, offers Edward, through Elinor's good offices, the living of Delaford, which he accepts.

While Edward is at Oxford being ordained, Lucy Steele marries his brother Robert, consequently releasing Edward from "an entanglement which had long formed his misery" (361). At last able to declare his love for Elinor, Edward goes to Barton to explain everything and to propose. She accepts, and a near reconciliation with his mother following "an ungracious delay" (373) takes place. She grudgingly consents to the marriage and gives him a small allowance though by no means as much as Edward would have received if he had followed her wishes and married the heiress Miss Morton. At the end of the novel, the narrator reveals that Edward does not regret his comparative lack of wealth and is not jealous of the wealthy but argumentative existence of his brother Robert with Lucy, his sister, or mother. He finds professional satisfaction as a clergyman and "an increasing attachment to his wife and his home" (377).

Although often presented in negative terms, perceived as dull, Edward possesses wit and is not without irony. He claims to "have no knowledge of the picturesque" and does not "like crooked, twisted, blasted trees . . . ruined, tattered cottages . . . nettles, or thistles, or heath blossoms." Edward, with his tongue in cheek, tells Marianne that he prefers "a troop of tidy, happy villagers," "the finest banditti in the world." This amazes Marianne and makes Elinor laugh (96, 98). In addition to a sense of wit and irony, Edward has insight into character, telling Marianne, for instance, that if she was rich she "would buy [books] all over and over again; she would buy up every copy" (92). He also refuses to submit to his mother in spite of Elinor's urging on him "a little humility." He agrees to visit her but "still resisted the idea of a letter of proper submission" (372).

Ferrars, Mrs. (Chapters 17, 19, 22–24, 33–35, 37, 41, 49, 50) Mrs. Ferrars is described as "a little, thin woman, upright, even to formality, in her figure, and serious, even to sourness, in her aspect." In addition, "her complexion was sallow; and her features small, without beauty, and naturally without expression." Her chief characteristic is "pride and ill nature." She says little (232), but bullies others through the use of her enormous wealth, social connections, and excessive pride. Fanny Dashwood inherits her selfishness from her, and they conspire together to attempt to destroy Edward Ferrars's hope for a secluded, independent existence. Both patronize those who flatter them, such as the two Steele girls, and they humiliate Mrs. Henry Dashwood and her daughters at every opportunity.

Mrs. Ferrars promises to "do all in her power to prevent" her eldest son Edward's "advancing in . . . any profession" of his own choice (267). He is fortunate to find Elinor to support his interests and Colonel Brandon to assist him practically. There is some kind of reconciliation between Mrs. Ferrars and her eldest son and Elinor at the end of the novel. Yet the author's concluding ironic barb at Mrs. Ferrars's, and the materialistic values she represents, is contained in the observation that Edward and Elinor "were never insulted with her real favour and preference." That is reserved for the manipulative, scheming Lucy Steele and her husband, Robert (375).

Ferrars, Robert (Chapters 3, 22, 24, 33, 36–37, 41, 47–48, 50) The spoiled younger brother of Edward Ferrars. Before she has met him, Lucy Steele appositely sums him up: "I fancy he is very unlike his brother—silly and a great coxcomb" (148). Appropriately, he makes his initial appearance in the novel at Sackville Street jeweler's, fastidiously spending 15 minutes deciding on which toothpick case to select. Elinor observes that he is "adorned in the first style of fashion" and beneath

his pampered surface, she detects "the puppyism of his manner" with a face of "strong, natural, sterling insignificance" (221–220). Her impression is confirmed when she is formally introduced to him at Mrs. Dennison's musical evening. He is "exactly the coxcomb" and not deserving "the compliment of rational opposition."

A snob, he considers himself superior to his elder brother Edward, as he had the "advantage" (250–252) of being sent to a public school (probably Westminster), while Edward was privately schooled. He boasts of an apparent friendship with a Lord Courtland and of planning "magnificent cottages." His mother's favorite, he is suitable for the position of marrying the extremely wealthy Miss Morton when Edward refuses to do so. Believing he can persuade Lucy Steele to give up Edward, he is captivated by her. He is "proud of his conquest, proud of tricking Edward, and very proud of marrying privately without his mother's consent." Even this act of defiance fails to alienate his mother, and due to his wife's scheming he is "re-established . . . completely in her favour." He pays a high price, however, for his marriage as there were "frequent domestic disagreements" between him and Lucy (376–377).

Ferrars, Sir Robert (Chapter 36) Robert tells Elinor that he asks his mother, "Why would you be persuaded by my uncle, Sir Robert, against your own judgment, to place Edward under private tuition, at the most critical time of his life?" (251). Given the consequence of his education on the conceited, snobbish Robert, his uncle appears with such advice to be a sensible relative. Mrs. Ferrars listens, or defers, to Sir Robert, and he serves as another illustration of her connections and network of contacts in high social places.

Gibson, Old (Chapter 33) Shrewdly John Dashwood purchases "East Kingham Farm . . . where old Gibson used to live. The land was so very desirable . . . so immediately adjoining my own property" (225).

Gilberts, the (Chapter 20) The Gilberts are among the Middletons' neighbors at Barton Park. Following Sir John Middleton's complaint to his wife that she has not invited them to dinner, she points out that it is rather the turn of the Gilberts to invite the Middletons to dinner.

Godby, Miss (Chapter 38)   An apparent source for London gossip among the Steele girls' acquaintances. Anne Steele hears from Miss Godby that Edward Ferrars will give Lucy Steele up now that his mother has discovered that they are secretly engaged. "Miss Godby told Miss Sparks, that nobody in their senses could expect Mr. Ferrars to give up a woman like Miss Morton, with thirty thousand pounds to her fortune, for Lucy Steele that had nothing at all" (272).

Grey, Miss Sophia (Chapters 30, 44)   According to Mrs. Jennings, Sophia Grey is "a smart, stylish girl they say, but not handsome." Her one great asset is her wealth; she has "Fifty thousand pounds!" (194). Relations with her guardians, Mr. and Mrs. Ellison, seem to have been strained. Willoughby, who marries her for her money, describes her as "jealous as the devil" (327). It is Sophia who dictates his letter breaking off all contact with Marianne, who still remains his "secret standard of perfection in woman" (379).

Harris, Mr. (Chapter 43)   Harris is "the Palmers' apothecary" (307) who attends Marianne when she falls ill at Cleveland. An optimist, he unsuccessfully tries out various remedies.

Henshawe, Biddy (Chapter 29)   According to Mrs. Jennings, Biddy Henshawe is the aunt of Sophia Grey: "she married a very wealthy man" (194).

Jennings, Charlotte   *See* Palmer, Mrs.

Jennings, Marry   *See* Middleton, Lady.

Jennings, Mr. (deceased) (Chapters 11, 25, 30)   Husband of Mrs. Jennings, wealthy, he "had traded with success in a less elegant part of" London (153). His widow now lives in a much more fashionable part of town. Her husband was fond of old Constantia wine (197).

Jennings, Mrs. (Chapters 7–8, 9–14, 18–19, 21, 25–27, 29–34, 36–43, 46, 49–50)   A source for much of the gossip in the novel, she "was a good-humoured, merry, fat, elderly woman, who talked a great deal, seemed very happy, and rather vulgar" (34). She lives near Portman Square, a very fashionable part of London, and counts the Steele sisters among her relatives. Both her daughters are well married, so she turns to promoting the marriages of others, including Elinor and Marianne. In London, she is confident that she can find a husband for one of them, if not both. She expresses doubts about Colonel Brandon's past, implying that he has a secret love child; her gossip is often lacking in foundation. She interferes in others' affairs and is wanting in tact.

In spite of these defects, Mrs. Jennings is kind. She is prepared to assist Edward Ferrars and Lucy Steele if they marry. She pays the costs for Anne Steele's return journey to Exeter. Loyal to her friends, she is very kind to Marianne and sympathetic to Edward when she learns that his mother has disinherited him. Marianne regrets that she has treated her with disdain.

Middleton children (Chapters 7, 21)

Sir John and Lady Middleton have four spoiled and uncontrolled children. They range from John, who is six; William; Annamaria, who is three; to a younger, unnamed child. Lucy and Anne Steele manage to become friendly with the Middletons through paying attention to their children. Lady Middleton is obsessed with them, with a particular fondness for her "troublesome boys" (55).

Middleton, Lady Mary, née Jennings (Chapters 4, 6–7, 11–13, 16, 18–21, 23, 25, 27–28, 32–34, 36, 44, 46, 50)   The eldest daughter of the garrulous Mrs. Jennings, "not more than six or seven and twenty . . . though perfectly well-bred, she was reserved, cold, and had nothing to say for herself beyond the most common-place inquiry or remark" (31). She is elegant and graceful, and her interests are confined to "humouring" (120), or spoiling, her four children, whom she dotes on. The Dashwood girls find her "cold insipidity" (34) repulsive. In London, she becomes friendly with

Mrs. John Dashwood: their "cold hearted selfishness" (229) unites them.

Middleton, Sir John (Chapters 4, 6–7, 11–13, 16, 18–21, 23, 25, 27–28, 32–34, 36, 44, 46, 50) Mrs. Henry Dashwood's cousin who invites the Dashwoods to Barton and provides them with a cottage. "A good looking man about forty," an extrovert and very hospitable. He is "thoroughly good-humoured" (30), and "he delighted in collecting about him more young people than his house could hold, and the noisier they were the better was he pleased" (32). He is the opposite of his wife, and his chief pursuits, in addition to entertaining, are hunting and shooting, and he judges men by how competent they are as sportsman. He and his wife play an important narrative role in the novel. Their socializing provides the opportunities for people such as Willoughby and Marianne to meet each other. In London, their social activities and acquaintances provide the backdrop for the plot development.

Morton, Lord (deceased) (Chapter 33) His "only daughter," the Honorable Miss Morton, received "thirty thousand pounds" when he died (224).

Morton, Miss, the Honorable (chapters 33–34, 38, 41, 50) The heiress with £30,000, whom Mrs. Ferrars vainly hopes that, first, her son Edward and then Robert would marry.

Palmer, Mr. Thomas (Chapters 19–21, 26, 32, 36–37, 39, 42–43) Described as "a grave looking young man of five or six and twenty, with an air of more fashion and sense than his wife, but of less willingness to please or be pleased" (106). The husband of Charlotte, the younger daughter of Mrs. Jennings, they lived in the fashionable area of London in Hanover Square and at Cleveland near Bristol. He is socially perceived as affecting an attitude of "indifference, insolence, and discontent," and Elinor believes that he attempts to seem above others. "It was rather a wish of distinction she believed, which produces his contemptuous treatment of every body, and his general abuse of every

thing before him" (112). His wife, on the other hand, is cheerful and sociable. But at Cleveland, and following his son's birth, he seems more polite and attempts to be sociable. Their house in London provides a place where Elinor and Marianne can meet people. The Cleveland house, located midway between London and Barton, is where Marianne falls dangerously ill and Willoughby confesses to Elinor.

Palmer, Mrs. Charlotte, née Jennings (Chapters 19–21, 26, 32, 36–37, 39, 42–43) Mrs. Jennings's younger daughter, Lady Middleton's sister, recently married to Mr. Palmer, she is expecting their first child when she meets the Dashwood girls at Barton. Subsequently, she gives birth to a son at their London home. Younger than her sister, she is "totally unlike her in every respect. She was short and plump" (106) and very talkative. Her husband criticizes her vulgarities of speech, and she displays a curious logic, for example, "Oh! dear, yes; I know him extremely well . . . Not that I ever spoke to him indeed" (114). At Cleveland, she is very kind and considerate to Elinor and Marianne, displaying her "constant and friendly good-humour" (304). For Auerbach, her marriage is a "dreadful . . . one of insults and abuse on the one hand and escapist oblivion on the other" (121).

Parrys, the (Chapter 30) Numbered among Mrs. Jennings's numerous London acquaintances.

Pratt, Mr. (Chapters 21–23, 34, 36–38, 47–49) The uncle of Lucy Steele who lives at Longstaple near Plymouth in Devon. Edward Ferrars had been his pupil for four years and subsequently, while staying with Mr. Pratt, became secretly engaged to Lucy.

Richard, Cousin (Chapter 38) Miss Steele's cousin. Anne Steele tells Elinor "that when it came to the point, he [Cousin Richard] was afraid Mr. Ferrars would be off," that is, Edward would break his engagement to Lucy (272).

Richardsons, the (Chapter 38) Known to the Miss Steeles, they take Anne Steele to Kensington Gardens. According to Anne Steele "they are very genteel people He makes a monstrous deal of money, and they keep their own coach" (275).

Robert—, Sir (Chapter 36) The uncle of Edward and Robert Ferrars who persuaded Mrs. Ferrars "to place Edward under private tuition" (251) rather than sending him, as in the case of Robert, to a public school.

Rose, Mr. (Chapter 21) According to Lucy Steele, "there's Mr. Rose at Exeter, a prodigious, smart young man, quite a beau, clerk to Mr. Simpson" (123).

Sally (Chapter 47) A Barton Park maidservant. Thomas, a manservant, delivers a message from Sally to her brother at the Exeter New London Inn, where he sees "the youngest Miss Steele," a newly wed with "Mr. Ferrars" (354).

Sandersons, the (Chapter 30) Part of Mrs. Jennings's network of London friends and associates.

Sharp, Martha (Chapter 38) Anne Steele reveals to Elinor, "a year or two back, when Martha Sharpe and I had so many secrets together, she never made any bones of hiding in a closet, or behind a chimney-board, on purpose to hear what we said" (274). Anne uses this to justify her own activities secretly overhearing Lucy and Edward.

Simpson, Mr. (Chapter 21) Mr. Rose's employer at Exeter.

Smith, Mrs. (Chapters 9, 13–15, 44, 50) The infirm elderly cousin of John Willoughby on whom he is financially dependent. After she dies, Willoughby hopes to inherit Allenham Court in Devon, which she owns. Willoughby is staying at Allenham when he initially meets Elinor and Marianne.

Sparks, Miss (Chapter 38) A gossip, one of Anne Steele's London acquaintances.

Steele, Miss Anne (Chapters 21–25, 32, 34–38, 49) Anne, or "Nancy," Steele described by Mark Twain as "coarse, foolish, and disagreeable" (cited Auerbach, 300). The elder of the two Steele sisters, she is nearly 30, "with a very plain and not a sensible face, nothing to admire" (120). She is obsequious to those with money and socially above her. On the way from Exeter to London, she and her sister Lucy meet a theologian, Dr. Davies. Anne obsesses over him and believes without foundation that he is attracted to her. In London, she indiscreetly tells Mrs. John Dashwood about the engagement between Lucy and Edward Ferrars. As a result Edward is disinherited by his mother. Her speech is uncouth and vulgar. Not inappropriately, Mrs. Jennings observes: "poor Nancy had not seven shillings in the world." Mrs. Jennings gives her five guineas to go to Exeter. The last we as readers hear of her, she is thinking of staying temporarily in Exeter with a friend "in hopes, as [Mrs. Jennings tells] her, to fall in with the Doctor again" (370–371). With few friends, unmarried, and poor, her fate in the world inhabited by Jane Austen's characters is to be pitied.

Steele, Miss Lucy (Chapters 21–25, 32, 34–38, 47–50) Lucy, Anne's younger sister, is 23, with "considerable beauty; her features were pretty, and she had a sharp quick eye, and a smartness of air, which though it did not give actual elegance or grace, gave distinction to her person" (120). She has connections but lacks money. When young, after meeting Edward Ferrars at her uncle's home near Plymouth, she secretly becomes engaged to him. Staying at Barton Park, Lucy and her sister ingratiate themselves with the Middleton family by sycophancy and indulging the young children. Consequently, in spite of claiming many other social engagements, especially in Exeter, they stay two months and are invited to London. Lucy learns enough of Edward's affection for Elinor to be jealous but is unaware that his mother plans a match for Edward with the very wealthy Miss Morton. Owing to the indiscretion of her sister, Anne, in revealing the engagement, both sisters fall out of favor socially. Robert, Edward's brother, attempts to persuade Lucy to give his brother up, but the clever, manipulating Lucy attracts Robert. They marry secretly, with Robert "proud of his conquest"

(376)—he has been given a Norfolk estate worth £1000 a year by his mother when annoyed that Edward refuses to break with Lucy. Her "selfish sagacity," and "humility, assiduous attentions, and endless flattery" (375) make her a favorite of Mrs. Ferrars, although she and Robert are continually feuding.

Jane Austen as narrator reserves some of her fiercest satire in the novel for Lucy. In the concluding chapter, she observes: "The whole of Lucy's behaviour in the affair, and the prosperity which crowned it, therefore, may be held forth as a most encouraging instance of what an earnest, an unceasing attention to self-interest, however its progress may be apparently obstructed, will do in securing every advantage of fortune." She also adds, "with no other sacrifices than that of time and conscience" (376). Lucy is born with beauty and high intelligence and connections, but no money. She has to survive as best she can in a ruthless, materialistic world based on class, snobbery, connections, and money. Otherwise, her fate would have been that of her sister: vain hope and poverty dependent on others' favors.

Taylor, Mrs. (Chapter 30) A garrulous London acquaintance of Mrs. Jennings, who informs her that Willoughby is shortly to marry Sophia Grey.

Thomas (Chapter 38) Thomas, manservant to the Dashwoods, moves with them from Norland to Barton Cottage. On an errand to Exeter, Thomas sees Lucy Steele and Mr. Ferrars together in a carriage and assumes that they are married. He has not identified which Mr. Ferrars, and his information given to the Dashwoods causes grief to them all and especially to Elinor. She believes that her hopes of marrying Edward Ferrars have now finally been dashed. Fortunately, Thomas saw Robert Ferrars, not Edward.

Walker, Miss (Chapter 30) Yet another gossipy London acquaintance of Mrs. Jennings.

Westons, the (Chapter 20) Friends of the Palmers who are shortly expected to visit them at Cleveland.

Whitaker family (Chapter 18) A family living near Barton Park, and acquaintances of the Middletons.

Williams, Eliza, Miss (Chapters 11, 13–14, 21–22, 44, 47) The illegitimate daughter of Eliza, the wealthy orphan with whom Colonel Brandon when young had fallen in love. Against her will, to save the family estate, she was married to his elder brother. Following her infidelity, they were divorced and Brandon finds her and her daughter, Miss Eliza, living in desperate conditions. She dies leaving her daughter in Brandon's care. The girl, known as Eliza Williams, Mrs. Jennings believes to be Colonel Brandon's natural daughter. At the age of 16, following a Bath visit and nine months before Brandon's initial acquaintance with the Dashwoods, she disappears. It emerges subsequently that she eloped to London with Willoughby, who seduced her, then abandoned her. The letter telling Brandon this results in his abrupt departure from the Middletons' on the morning of the proposed Whitwell visit. Arriving in London, he finds her about to give birth to Willoughby's child. After fighting a drawn duel with Willoughby, Brandon then takes Eliza and her baby into the country, where he provides for them. Miss Eliza is extremely vulnerable, totally dependent on the protection of Brandon.

Williams, Eliza (Brandon) *See* Brandon, Mrs. Eliza.

Willoughby, John (Chapters 9–20; 26–32, 44–47, 50) A charming predator of women, he is the first of Jane Austen's tricksters to prey on others. These include George Wickham, Henry Crawford, Frank Churchill, and William Walter Elliot. Willoughby appears to possess "every advantage of persons and talents . . . a disposition naturally open and honest, and a feeling, affectionate temper" (331) who is most attractive to women. Elinor, however, also detects in him a "want of caution" (49). This perception proves to be correct when it emerges that he has seduced and deserted Colonel Brandon's ward, Eliza Williams, whom he has made pregnant.

Willoughby's behavior, Elinor explains, is the consequence of "too early an independence and its consequent habits of idleness, dissipation, and luxury" (331). So having frittered away his inheritance, he has little alternative but to flatter his aging relative Mrs. Smith, hoping to inherit Allenham Court after she dies. His other possibility is to marry an heiress. He is known as a good horse rider and a "decent shot" (43), with considerable musical talent that attracts him to Marianne—they have similar tastes.

All the characters including Elinor, although she has reservations, make excuses for him as they are taken in by his personal charm. Even Elinor at the conclusion of the novel has regrets on his behalf, and his fate is not a disaster. Having given up Marianne without telling her, in London his attentions transfer to the wealthy Sophia Grey, whom he loses no time in marrying. In his confession to Elinor upon hearing of Marianne's grave illness, Willoughby admits that he has to "rub through the world" (332), to accommodate as best he can, and that happiness at home is not for him. His is above all the "dread of poverty" (323). Ironically, his relative Mrs. Smith "gave him reason for believing that had he behaved with honour towards Marianne, he might at once have been happy and rich." Further, although he "could not hear" of Marianne's "marriage without a pang," Willoughby "lived to exert, and frequently to enjoy himself," taking refuge "in his breed of horses and dogs" (379).

BIBLIOGRAPHY

Primary Texts

Jane Austen's Letters. Collected and edited by Deirdre Le Faye. 3d ed. Oxford: Oxford University Press, 1995.

Sense and Sensibility. Edited by R. W. Chapman. *The Novels of Jane Austen:* I, 3d ed. Oxford: Oxford University Press, 1943 reprint. [All page references are to this edition.]

———, edited by James Kinsley, with an introduction and notes by Margaret Anne Doody and Claire Lamont. Oxford: Oxford University Press, 2004.

Secondary Works

Auerbach, Emily. *Searching for Jane Austen.* Madison: University of Wisconsin Press, 2004.

Austen-Leigh, J. E. *A Memoir of Jane Austen and Other Family Recollections.* Edited by Kathryn Sutherland. Oxford: Oxford University Press, 2002.

Butler, Marilyn. *Jane Austen and the War of Ideas.* Oxford, U.K.: Clarendon Press, 1975.

Gilson, David. *A Bibliography of Jane Austen New Introduction and Corrections by the Author.* Winchester, Hampshire, U.K.: St. Paul's Bibliographies; New Castle, Del.: Oak Knoll Press, 1997.

Hardy, Barbara. *A Reading of Jane Austen.* London: Peter Owen, 1975.

Johnson, Claudia L. *Jane Austen: Women, Politics, and the Novel.* Chicago and London: University of Chicago Press, 1988.

Lewis, C. S. "A Note on Jane Austen." In Walter Hooper, ed., *Selected Literary Essays by C. S. Lewis.* Cambridge: Cambridge University Press, 1969.

MacDonagh, Oliver. *Jane Austen: Real and Imagined Worlds.* New Haven, Conn.: Yale University Press, 1991.

Perkins, Moreland. *Reshaping the Sexes in* Sense and Sensibility. Charlottesville and London: University Press of Virginia, 1998.

Poplawski, Paul. *A Jane Austen Encyclopaedia.* Westport, Conn.: Greenwood Press, 1998.

Southam, Brian, ed. *Jane Austen: The Critical Heritage.* 2 vols. London: Routledge and Kegan Paul, 1978–79.

Tanner, Tony. *Jane Austen.* Houndmills, Basingstoke, Hants, U.K.: Macmillan, 1986.

Watt, Ian. "On Sense and Sensibility." In I. Watt, ed. *Jane Austen: A Collection of Critical Essays.* Englewood Cliffs, N.J.: Prentice Hall, 1963.

Sir Charles Grandison or The Happy Man, A Comedy in Five Acts (1980)

COMPOSITION AND PUBLICATION

Sir Charles Grandison (CG) is a relatively new arrival in the Jane Austen canon. Her family tradition ascribed the 53-page draft adaptation of SAMUEL RICHARDSON's novel, in five acts with stage directions, to ANNA AUSTEN, Jane Austen's niece. The manuscript came up at Sotheby's London auction house on December 13, 1977, and was purchased by Jubilee Books of Burford, Oxford,

England. Brian Southam inspected the manuscript and reattributed most of the writing to Jane Austen on the grounds of style, length, and compositional chronology. Southam dates the drama around the late 1790s and believes that the very young Anna Austen contributed no more than "inserting a word or two here and there, changing a phrase, bringing a character on stage" (11). Southam first published the text, and a transcription of the original, with a detailed introduction and a foreword by Lord David Cecil, in 1980.

CRITICAL COMMENTARY

For Southam, CG is an example of its author's Juvenilia. Essentially, the text is a reduction of Richardson's vast novel published in letter form in 1753–54 into five brief dramatic acts. The emphasis of CG is on women's lives, and the majority of the scenes take place in a drawing room. In Richardson there are 20 men and 16 women, in Jane Austen's version, 14 men and 15 women. "The essence of the joke in Jane Austen's" CG, Southam writes, "is the reduction of a mammoth novel to a miniature play . . . a comedy of abridgement" meant for family performance (21). CG is essentially an "allusive joke," a joke replete with literary allusions. Southam writes in the last chapter which is devoted to "Sir Charles Grandison" in the new edition of his *Jane Austen's Literary Manuscripts* (2001) that "the subtitle 'The Happy Man,' is in itself an important allusive joke." It is a "key phrase" in the novel, "referring to the hero in his happy state with the marriage ceremony and married life in prospect." In truth, however, this reiterated phrase "the Happy Man" becomes hollow placed in the perspective of the seven volumes of Richardson's novel, especially with their emphasis on conduct, and Jane Austen "mimics its less than subtle delivery" (139).

There are many private and family jokes in Jane Austen's version. Characters walk on and off the stage briefly and are unrelated to CG or to Richardson. There are snatches of dialogue present simply to give someone something to say. For instance, in the opening scene, a Mrs. Reeves chats with a milliner about dresses. There is no fictional source for this and the conversation is not developed in

the play. At least 29 characters appear in the play; to list them is pointless.

Essentially, the play revolves around the beautiful and virtuous Harriet Byron, whose arrival in London attracts the attention of the womanizer Sir Hargrave Pollexfen. Following her resistance, he kidnaps her at a masked ball and tries to get her to marry him in secret. Her continual defiance leads him to send Harriet in a carriage to his country estate. But on the journey, Sir Charles Grandison appears as an honorable gentleman who comes to Harriet's rescue. They fall in love but are unable to marry, unfortunately, because Grandison is attached to an Italian noblewoman, Clementina della Porretta. They have not married owing to religious differences, and Clementina has experienced a breakdown in her health. Grandison makes a trip to Italy to see her. His presence restores her health, but she believes that they should not sacrifice their religious convictions for the sake of their personal desires and passions. Grandison, released from his obligations, returns to England to marry Harriet.

Logan Speirs writes that "the main three characters . . . are always clearly defined—the bland, despotic Grandison, the depressed Harriet, the restive Charlotte"—the younger sister of Sir Charles. "Above all, Grandison is the hero of the play in much the same way as he is the hero of the novel" (35). Southam, in the new edition of his *Jane Austen's Literary Manuscripts*, comments that Jane Austen's "appreciation of [Richardson's] achievement was a fine mixture of admiration and irreverence; and her eye for absurdity was focused sharply on him as on any other of her literary idols" (140).

BIBLIOGRAPHY

Primary Texts

Austen, Jane. *Jane Austen's "Sir Charles Grandison."* Transcribed and edited by Brian Southam, with a foreword by Lord David Cecil. Oxford: Clarendon Press, 1980.

Secondary Texts

Southam, Brian C. *Jane Austen's Literary Manuscripts.* New edition. London: Athlone Press, 2001.

Speirs, Logan. "Sir Charles Grandison or the Happy Man. A Comedy," *English Studies* 66 (February 1985): 25–35.

Sir William Mountague (1933)

COMPOSITION AND PUBLICATION

The sixth in order of appearance in Jane Austen's juvenilia *Volume the First*, probably written during the year 1788 when its author was 13 and "humbly dedicated to Charles John Austen" (40)—her younger brother, CHARLES JOHN AUSTEN. *Sir William Mountague* [WM] is included in the sixth volume of R. W. Chapman's edition of Jane Austen's *The Works*. WM is also published in Margaret Anne Doody and Douglas Murray's 1993 edition of *Catharine and Other Writings* (38–39). To date, no Juvenilia Press edition exists. The manuscript is in the Bodleian Library, Oxford.

SYNOPSIS

The paragraphs related in the third person focus on the amorous activities of the wealthy young Sir William Mountague, who falls in love all too easily. Retreating to "a small Village near Dover," he falls in love there, too, and leaves for "a freind's House in Surry," where he "soon fell in love" with his friend's "beautifull Neice." After shooting the man she is about to marry, they plan to marry. Shortly before the wedding, he is visited by the sister of the deceased man, whom he "privately married." He is married but "a fortnight" when Sir William "became again most violently in love." (41–42).

CRITICAL COMMENTARY

Apart from the fact that there are three Miss Cliftons in the story, reinforcing Jane Austen's pattern of three marriageable young women in her work, WM has aroused little if any critical observation. There are detailed explanatory notes in Doody and Murray's 1993 edition (300–301).

CHARACTERS

Arundel, Miss (42) Sir William Montague shoots her "preferred" suitor, a Mr. Stanhope. She then has "no reason to refuse" Sir William, but Mr. Stanhope's sister intervenes. Miss Arundel is "beautifull" but "cruel" and the niece of Mr. Brudenell (42).

Brudenell, Mr. (41–42) A friend of Sir William's, he has a "House in Surry." He is described as "a sensible Man" with "a beautifull Neice"—Miss Arundel (42).

Miss Cliftons (41) "Sir William had not been long in the possession of his Estate before he fell in Love with the 3 Miss Cliftons of Kilhoobery Park." They were "young" and "equally handsome, equally rich & equally amiable" (41).

Mountague, Sir William (40–42) A wealthy and well-connected young man from an ancient family aged, "about 17" (41), who finds the opposite sex irresistible: He is also violent and enjoys hunting.

Percival, Lady (41) Described as "a young Widow of Quality, . . . accomplished & lovely." Sir William adores her and urges her to name a wedding day. She chooses the first day of the hunting season, "the first of September." She refuses to "delay the Wedding a short time [and] . . . enraged . . . returned to London the next Morning" (41).

Stanhope, Emma (42) The sister of the Mr. Stanhope who was shot, she demands money in recompense for her brother's death but the next day marries his killer.

Stanhope, Mr. (42) A gentleman preferred by Miss Arundel, and consequently shot by the hero/anti-hero, Sir William Mountague.

BIBLIOGRAPHY

Primary Texts

Austen, Jane. "Sir William Mountague." In *The Jane Austen Library. Volume the First*, edited by R. W. Chapman with a foreword by Lord David Cecil, a preface by Brian Southam, and a preface by R. W. Chapman, 74–77. London: Athlone Press, 1984.

———. "Sir William Mountague." In *The Works of Jane Austen*, Volume 6, *Minor Works*, edited by R. W. Chapman. Oxford: Oxford University Press. 1986. [All textual references are to this edition.]

———. "Sir William Mountague." In *Jane Austen's Catharine and Other Writings*, edited by Margaret

Anne Doody and Douglas Murray, 38–39. Oxford: Oxford University Press, 1993.

———. "Sir William Mountague." In *Jane Austen Juvenilia* (The Cambridge Edition of the Works of Jane Austen). Edited by Peter Subor. Cambridge: Cambridge University Press, 2006, 47–49.

Secondary Work

McAleer, John. "What a Biographer Can Learn About Jane Austen from Her Juvenilia." In *Jane Austen's Beginnings: The Juvenilia and Lady Susan*, edited by J. David Grey, [7]–27. Ann Arbor, Mich., and London: UMI Research Press, 1989.

The Three Sisters, A Novel (1933)

COMPOSITION AND PUBLICATION

The 12th of Jane Austen's youthful tales found in her *Volume the First*. It is dedicated "To Edward Austen," her third brother, who was adopted and brought up by a distant cousin. In December 1791, he married Elizabeth Bridges and moved to a small house named Rowling in Kent. Probably around this period, Jane Austen visited her brother and his new bride. Southam dates *The Three Sisters* (TS) to 1792, when its author was 16 (*Literary Manuscripts*, 26). Consisting of four letters, it is included in the sixth volume of R. W. Chapman's edition of Jane Austen's *The Works*. TS is also found in Doody and Murray's 1993 edition of *Catharine and Other Writings* (55–67). Juliet McMaster, with her students, prepared an illustrated Juvenilia Press edition in 1993 and reissued it in 1995. The manuscript copy is in the Bodleian Library, Oxford.

SYNOPSIS

The work contains four letters. The first is from Mary Stanhope to her friend Fanny. The second is also from Mary to Fanny. The third and fourth are from Mary's sister Georgina to her friend Jane. The letters focus on a serious subject that will reverberate throughout Jane Austen's work, although in TS it is treated comically: marrying for security rather than love. As Mary tells Jane, she has been proposed to by the rich and thoroughly unpleasant, aging neighbor Mr. Watts; "If I accept him I know I shall be miserable all the rest of my Life" (58), but she will be secure even if unhappy. Mary is the eldest of three Stanhope girls. Her mother tells Mary that she will not miss the opportunity of one of her daughters being married to a wealthy man, and she does not care which daughter it is. Mary, being the eldest, feels more pressure to marry rather than to be left on the shelf, and is tending to accept Mr. Watts's proposal.

Georgina's letters present the story from a different angle. The youngest and most intelligent of the sisters, she pokes fun at what she perceives to be Mary's foolishness. The three sisters, Mary, Sophy, and Georgiana, in common with most other people, agree on Mr. Watts's limitations: "Hideous in his person and without one good Quality to make amends for it." They all apparently are determined not to marry him: "were Beggary the only alternative" (62).

Georgina and Sophy play a trick on their elder sister. They pretend they will accept him if she refuses him; by doing so, they believe they are protecting themselves. As a result, Mary accepts Mr. Watts, as she does not wish to be upstaged by either the younger Georgiana or Sophy. Mr. Watts calls late in the day to hear Mary's decision and both of them haggle well into the early hours of the morning, concerning the precise nature of the marriage settlement. Mary insists on a new carriage, fresh horses, clothes, furniture, plus servants and "an infinite number of the most valuable Jewels" (65). She also wishes to spend time in Bath and London, in addition to going to other towns. Mr. Watts replies negatively and says that he will withdraw his proposal and instead ask Sophy, if Mary insists on her requests. Mary has to be content with a new carriage and even then they argue over its color. The following day, she goes to visit the Duttons, where she boasts about the benefits of her forthcoming marriage. Neither the Duttons nor her sisters are at all impressed or envious. Mary's sisters' attention has been diverted to the handsome and polite young Mr. Brudenell. Mary returns home, meets Mr. Watts, and quarrels with him. Mrs. Stanhope patches things up between them and Watts plans to make sure they get married quickly.

CRITICAL COMMENTARY

Among Jane Austen's juvenilia, *TS* has been praised for being a mature work. For Southam, "with its firm design and neatly-turned plot it reads like a short episode from a full-scale novel." Unlike most of her other early writing, *TS* "avoids lengthy passages of narrative or reported speech" in favor of "direct conversation." Passages in *TS* indicate "the direction [of] their author's art . . . Her aim is to show how character is formed and defined in the events of ordinary life, and how speech and behaviour are determined by a complex of personal and social considerations" (*Literary Manuscripts*, 34–35).

Frances Beer, in her introduction to the *Juvenilia of Jane Austen and Charlotte Brontë* (1986), similarly views *TS* as an important marker in its author's development. It is one representing "the movement away from a strict neoclassical reaction to a series of isolated foibles—and towards a romantic response to the individual as potential victim of a materialistic, claustrophobic society." This "is crucial to Austen's artistic development, and will be carried over and refined in her novels" (16).

TS anticipates elements in Jane Austen's later work. For instance, the Stanhope family is similar to the Dashwood family in *Sense and Sensibility*. In each, a mother lives with three unmarried daughters in straitened circumstances. In *Pride and Prejudice*, a mother is anxious that the three elder Bennet sisters marry well. Sibling rivalry occurs in *TS* and other Jane Austen works, and in *Persuasion*, Anne Elliot, ignored by her own family, has been persuaded largely from materialistic considerations to reject the proposal of the man she loves—Wentworth. Watts, in *TS*, has similarities to Collins in *Pride and Prejudice*. He is rude, Charlotte accepts him for the security he offers, and both are prepared to marry someone else if refused.

CHARACTERS

Brudenell, Mr. (67–70) According to Georgina Stanhope, after meeting him at the Duttons', he is "the handsomest Man I ever saw in my Life" (68).

"He is the son of Sir Henry Brudenell of Leicestershire," and "His Sister is married to John Dutton's Wife's Brother" (67).

Dutton, Kitty and Jemima (57–59, 69) Friends of the Stanhope girls, Mary Stanhope believes she has triumphed over them by accepting the wealthy Mr. Watts; a brother, John Dutton, is mentioned too.

Stanhope, Mrs. (58–60, 70) Mother of three daughters whom she is anxious to see comfortably married. She seems to have influence over Mr. Watts, who complains to her of Mary's "behaviour, & she had persuaded him to think no more of it" (70).

Stanhope, Georgina (58, 60–63, 67, 71) The youngest and most intelligent of the Stanhope sisters, she writes two of the four letters constituting *TS*. She devises the scheme that leads her elder sister Mary to accept Mr. Watts for fear of being the unmarried sister left on the shelf.

Stanhope, Mary (57–71) The eldest and perceived by her other sisters to be the most foolish. Anxious to marry to "triumph over the Duttons" her neighbors (57), she is persuaded to marry a man she "hates" as "she could not bear to have either of" her sisters "married before" she is (58). Argumentative, she haggles unsuccessfully over the terms of her marriage settlement and is forced to settle for a fraction of what she requested.

Stanhope, Sophy (58–63, 70) More likely to marry Mr. Watts than Georgiana, if her elder sister, Mary, refuses him; she is the youngest of the Stanhope girls.

Watts, Mr. (57–71) According to Mary Stanhope, "quite an old Man, about two & thirty," with "a large fortune." He "is very healthy . . . very ill tempered & peevish extremely jealous, & so stingy that there is no living in the house with him" (58). Her sister Georgiana describes his "figure [as] unfortunately extremely vulgar & his Countenance is very heavy," although she sees also "an open

Frankness in his Disposition" and "prudent" rather than "stingy" (62). More than equal to Mary in haggling, he is close to, and influenced by, Mrs. Stanhope and very anxious to marry Mary.

BIBLIOGRAPHY

Primary Texts

Austen, Jane. "The Three Sisters." In *The Works of Jane Austen*, Vol. 6, *Minor Works*, edited by R. W. Chapman. Oxford: Oxford University Press, 1986. [All textual references are to this edition.]

———. "The Three Sisters." In *Jane Austen's Catharine and Other Writings*, edited by Margaret Anne Doody and Douglas Murray, 55–67. Oxford: Oxford University Press, 1993.

———. Amelia Webster and The Three Sisters *Epistolary "Novels" by Jane Austen*, edited by Juliet McMaster and others. Edmonton, Alberta, Canada: Juvenilia Press [Department of English, University of Alberta], 1993, reissued 1995.

———. "The Three Sisters." In *Jane Austen Juvenilia* (The Cambridge Edition of the Works of Jane Austen). Edited by Peter Sabor. Cambridge: Cambridge University Press, 74–89.

Secondary Works

Beer, Frances. "Introduction." In *The Juvenilia of Jane Austen and Charlotte Brontë*, 7–19. Hammondsworth, Middlesex, U.K.: Penguin Books, 1986.

Southam, Brian C. *Jane Austen's Literary Manuscripts.* Revised edition. London: Athlone Press, 2001.

Verses (Collected Poems and Verse of the Austen Family) (1996)

David Selwyn's *Collected Poems and Verse of the Austen Family* (1996) contains at least 19 verses attributed to Jane Austen. The first three poems in his volume are "Songs and Verses from the Juvenilia." These include the four-line "Song" rhyming a, b, a, b, found in the first chapter of *Frederic & Elfrida*. The second referred to as "Epitaph" is a four-line rhymed couplet from the fourth chapter

of the same piece of "Juvenilia." The third is a four-line "Song" rhyming a, b, a, b. The fourth is another "Song" from "Juvenilia," in this case a four-line rhyming couplet from "Henry and Eliza," in which the heroine, Eliza Harcourt, amuses herself "happy in the conscious knowledge of her own Excellence . . . with making & singing the following lines," beginning "Though misfortunes my footsteps may ever attend" (*Minor Works*, 34). These are followed by two "songs," the first rhyming a, b, c, c, c, the second rhyming a, a, b, b, b. Both are from "The first Act of a Comedy."

The seventh poem is the "ODE TO PITY" found at the conclusion of *Volume the First* and discussed elsewhere. The eighth is entitled by Doody and Murray in their edition of *Catharine and Other Writings* (236) and by Selwyn "The little bag" (3–4). Chapman in *Minor Works* titles them as "Verses given with a Needlework Bag to Mrs. James Austen" (444–445). The autograph manuscript dated "Jan[uary] 1792" is in private hands. It is reproduced in *Country Life*, 172 (October 28, 1982), p. 1,323. The text was first published in chapter 5 of J. E. Austen-Leigh's *Memoir* (1870). The poem relates to the January 1792 move by Mary Lloyd, a childhood friend of the author who left the area where the Austens lived to move 15 miles away. As a going-away present, Jane Austen sent her a needlework bag or "This little bag," and the two verse quatrains.

The next poem has the lengthy title given it by Jane Austen's niece ANNA AUSTEN (Lefroy), "Lines written by Jane Austen for the amusement of a Neice (Afterwards Lady Knatchbull) on the arrival of Captain & M[rs.] Austen at Godmersham Park after their marriage July 1806." This refers to the marriage of Jane Austen's fifth brother, FRANCIS WILLIAM AUSTEN to Mary Gibson at Ramsgate on July 24, 1806. Jane Austen, who was at Clifton near Bristol in July 1806, sent the five verses of four-line rhyming couplets to her niece FANNY AUSTEN, who was at Godmersham, where the newlyweds spent their honeymoon. The manuscript in the writing of Anna Lefroy is in private hands, and was published in the *Times Literary Supplement* by Deirdre Le Faye on February 20, 1987, p. 185, and also published with "Explanatory Notes" in Doody and Murray (364).

The 10th poem in Selwyn is "Oh! Mr. Best, you're very bad" (5–6) and dated by Jane Austen "Clifton 1806." The 11 verses of four irregularly rhymed verse lines are found in a shortened version in *Minor Works* under the title "Lines to Martha Lloyd" (445). This text is from *Jane Austen: Her Life and Letters*, by William and Arthur Austen-Leigh. The manuscript of the poem was still in Jane Austen's descendants' hands when seen by Donald Greene, who discusses it in his "New Verses by Jane Austen" in *Nineteenth Century Fiction* 30 (1975), 257–260. The poem contains in the first line of its second stanza a reference to "Harrowgate," the north of England watering place and rival of Bath where the fashionable went for cures for assumed ailments. The last line of the ninth stanza—"From Newb'ry to Speen Hall"—refers to Newbury, almost 20 miles from Steventon, where Jane Austen lived, and Speen Hall is a mile outside of Newbury.

"On Sir Home Popham's sentence—April 1807" is an eight-line rhyming satirical couplet on a contemporary political subject, and in this sense is unusual in Jane Austen's work. The manuscript in the author's hand is now at the Bodmer Foundation in Cologny-Genève, Switzerland, and the text first appeared in the second volume of Edward, 1st Lord Bradbourne's *Letters of Jane Austen* published in 1884, p. 344. It is in *Minor Works*, p. 446, and also in Doody and Murray (p. 237). Popham (1762–1820) was accused of withdrawing his naval squadron without orders from the Cape of Good Hope. He argued his own case, gained sympathy, and his career was not handicapped; in fact, Popham was appointed Knight Commander of the Bath in 1815 and two years later to Commander in Chief of the Jamaica Station. He had connections with Francis Austen and lived near Jane Austen's relatives. Chapter 7, "Politics and the Navy: The Popham Poem," of Brian Southam's *Jane Austen and the Navy* (2000) contains a detailed account of the Popham trial.

"To Miss Bigg previous to her marriage, with some pocket hand[kerchiefs] I had hemmed for her" is a quatrain in rhyming couplets. The manuscript is now at the Jane Austen Memorial Trust at Chawton. It was published, with its companion, written "On the same occasion—but not sent" in Bradbourne (II, 344), in *Minor Works* (446–447) and also in Doody and Murray (238). Both verses are dated by the author "Aug[ust] 26, 1808." Miss Bigg is Catherine Bigg, and the sister of Harris Bigg-Wither. Jane Austen had accepted his marriage proposal on the evening of December 2, 1802. She changed her mind the following morning. His sister Catherine in October 1808 married the uncle of the poet ROBERT SOUTHEY, the Reverend Herbert Hill. The companion poem, "On the same occasion—but not sent," survives in a manuscript now at the Bodmer Foundation in Cologny-Genève. Its subsequent publication is similar to that of "To Miss Bigg." "On the same occasion . . ." consists of eight lines of alternative rhyming couplets concluding with "Slight be her Colds & few her Tears" (*Minor Works*, 447).

One of the longest poems we have of Jane Austen is her "To the Memory of Mrs. Lefroy, who died Dec[ember] 16—my Birthday—written 1808." A manuscript copy of the poem remained in the hands of Jane Austen's family until 1936, when a copy was given to the dean and the Chapel of Winchester Cathedral. Eleven quatrains were published in J. E. Austen-Leigh's *Memoir,* with the note that Jane Austen's close friend Anne Lefroy, to whom Jane Austen was devoted, was "killed by a fall from her horse on" the author's birthday, December 16, 1804. He adds that "The following lines to her memory were written by Jane four years afterwards, when she was thirty-three years old." Austen-Leigh observes, "They are given, not for their merits as poetry, but to show how deep and lasting was the impression made by the elder friend on the mind of the younger" (48). The 11 verses are also found in *Minor Works* (440–442), which also prints two additional stanzas (442), and the 13 verses are in Doody and Murray (238–240).

This lament for a dear lost friend is followed in Selwyn's edition of the *Collected Poems* by "Alas poor Brag, thou boastful Game!" The five lines are found in a letter Jane Austen sent to her sister, Cassandra Austen. The letter is dated January 17, 1809, and Jane Austen introduces the lines by writing to Cassandra, "I have just received some verses in an unknown hand, & am desired to forward them to my nephew Edw[ard] at Godersham." The "unknown hand" is a joke—the lines are accepted as Jane Austen's and are in her hand in the manuscript of her letter now in the Pierpont Morgan Library, New York. In a letter to Cassandra written on January 10, 1809, Jane Austen comments on the decline of the card game Brag in favor of the more fashionable game Speculation. This decline in Brag's popularity was experienced by Jane Austen during the card games played at Godmersham over Christmas 1809 (*Letters*, 165–168, 162–165). The lines were initially published in 1884 in Edward, 1st Lord Bradbourne's *Letters of Jane Austen*, and may also be found in Doody and Murray (240).

They are followed by "My dearest Frank, I wish you joy," dating from "Chawton, July 26—1809"—a verse letter of 52 rhyming lines that Jane Austen sent to her brother FRANCIS AUSTEN and his wife Mary. She congratulated them on the birth of their second of eight children and elder son, Francis William, on July 12, 1809, at Rose Cottage, near Alton. The copy of the poem is at the Jane Austen Memorial Trust at Chawton, and the actual verse letter is at the British Library. It was first published in R. W. Chapman's 1932 edition of *Jane Austen's Letters to Her Sister Cassandra and Others*, and may also be found with explanatory notes in Doody and Murray (240–242, 366, 367). Selwyn writes: "After a brief congratulatory opening, the main theme of the poem is not so much the baby as a loving reminiscence of Francis William's own characteristics as a child and a wish to see them extended into the new generation" (82).

J. E. Austen-Leigh's *Memoir* (75) is the only source for a "Mock Panegyric on a Young Friend," found also in *Minor Works* (442–443) under the title "In measured verse I'll now rehearse," in Doody and Murray (244–245), and simply called "In measured verse" in Selwyn (12–13). The seven-verse quatrains, according to the *Memoir*, are for Jane Austen's niece ANNA AUSTEN: the author "took it into her head to write the following mock panegyric on a young friend [Anna], who really was clever and handsome" (*Memoir*, 74). The context is probably the 17-year-old Anna's breaking off of an engagement during the summer of 1810. Anna was known to be temperamental, and her parents opposed the engagement. Jane Austen wrote to

Francis Austen on September 25, 1813, concerning Anna' subsequent engagement to Benjamin Lefroy, whom she married, "There is an unfortunate dissimilarity of taste between them in one respect which gives us some apprehensions, he hates company & she is very fond of it—This, with some queerness of Temper on his side & much unsteadiness, of hers, is untoward" (*Letters*, 231–232).

Early in February 1811, Jane Austen traveled to the town of Alton in Hampshire with Maria Beckford, who was the sister-in-law of Edward Austen Knight's tenant at the house he was renting out. On the journey, Miss Beckford had to consult an apothecary named Newnham "about some 'old complaint'" and "I've a pain in my head," or as Chapman titles it in *Minor Works*, "Lines on Maria Beckford" (448–449), "is supposedly their conversation 'as it actually took place'" (Selwyn, 13). The four-verse quatrains are found in various manuscripts in Jane Austen's hand and were first published in *Minor Works*. They also appear in Doody and Murray (242).

"On the Marriage of Mr. Gell of East Bourn to Miss Gill" in two four-line rhyming couplets was occasioned by a newspaper announcement of a forthcoming marriage on February 25, 1811, which appeared in the *Hampshire Telegraph and Sussex Chronicle*. The manuscript is in private hands; another of the poems is owned by the Bath City Council. The text was first published in the *Memoir* ([78]). It is published in *Minor Works* with "eyes" and "ease" at the end of the second and last lines of the second verse (444). Doody and Murray print the two verses as one verse, with the end of the third and last lines reading, "I'm the slave of your *iis*/ Oh, restore if you please, By accepting my *ees*" (243), which is the form in the *Memoir* and "restores pun and playfulness" (Doody, 280). This is also the form preferred by Selwyn (14).

"Between Session & Session" consists of six lines rhyming a, a, a, b, b, b, included by Jane Austen in a letter to her sister, Cassandra, dated "Tuesday 30 April 1811" (*Letters*, 185–187). First published in Bradbourne's *Letters* (Vol. 2: 97) and in Chapman's edition of her letters, the lines are also in Doody and Murray (243) and in *Minor Works* under the title "On the Weald of Kent Canal Bill" (449) and in Selwyn (15). The manuscript is at the Pierpont Morgan Library, New York. The context of the poem is political. In 1809, a plan was proposed to construct a canal between the Medway and Rother Rivers in Kent, with extensions into the Kentish heartland. An actual Parliamentary bill was proposed in 1811 and passed, receiving royal approval, but the plan was eventually abandoned.

In her letter, Jane Austen, before writing the six lines, tells her sister, "I congratulate Edward on the Weald of Kent Canal-Bill being put off until another Session." Why her brother EDWARD AUSTEN (KNIGHT) should be so opposed to the construction of the canal in unclear. Doody and Murray speculate that her brother perhaps felt that his own property or lands were threatened "or thought the region would deteriorate under the pressure of such industrial improvements." The author "assumes that the developers are looking only for gain at the expense of the country" (368). Certainly the lines and their context associate with SANDITON and its concern with commercial exploitation of the land.

"When stretched on one's bed" are five verses of six lines each with an aa, b, cc, b rhyme scheme, dated by the author "Oct[ober] 27, 1811." The dating is three days before the publication of SENSE AND SENSIBILITY—her first published novel published at her own expense. The second line mentions "a fierce-throbbing head," possibly due to "frustration over the delay" in publication "or anxiety as to any financial loss" (Selwyn, 15). The manuscript of the lines belongs to the Bath City Council, and the lines appear in *Minor Works* (447–448), in Doody and Murray (242), and in Selwyn (15–16).

"On the marriage of Miss Camilla Wallop & the Reverend [Henry] Wake" are four lines rhyming a, b, a, b. The lines first appear in *Memoir* (74) and subsequently in *Minor Works* under the title "A Middle-aged Flirt," with the additional title "On the Marriage of a Middle-Aged Flirt with a Mr. Wake, Whom, it was Supposed, She would Scarcely Have Accepted in her Youth" (444). The lines also appear in Doody and Murray (244) and in Selwyn (17). No manuscript is known to have survived. Jane Austen, in a letter to her friend Martha Lloyd dated November 29, 1812, writes, "The 4 lines on Miss W. which I sent you were all my own, but

James afterwards suggested what I thought a great improvement" (*Letters*, 196–197). Her brother JAMES AUSTEN changed the name Camilla in the poem to Maria and "handsome, and tall" for "merry & small." The lines then passed down in the Austen family circle, through Mrs. Benjamin Lefroy. On March 26, 1813, Miss Urania Wallop married an elderly curate, the Reverend Henry Wake. The poem's theme of not being left on the shelf to end up, as it were, as a Miss Bates (*Emma*), is one that occurs throughout Jane Austen's work.

"Written at Winchester on Tuesday the 15th July 1817" is one of Jane Austen's longer poems. The six verses rhyming a, b, a, b were written three days before her death. Two manuscripts of what is referred to as Jane Austen's "last poem exist" (Honan, 435), a copy at the New York Public Library (the Berg Collection) and one at Chawton. The poem first appeared in J. H. and E. C. Hubback's *Jane Austen's Sailor Brothers* (1906, p. 272), *Minor Works* (451–452)—here the poem is called "Venta" after the Roman name for Winchester— and in Doody and Murray (246). Park Honan, in his *Jane Austen, Her Life*, attributes the poem to a period of its author's recovery during what was her last illness (401–402). In the poem, Jane Austen has a vision of Lord and Ladies who have organized the races without asking for St. Swithun's (July 15 is St. Swithun's Day) permission for them to take place. St. Swithun was the bishop of Winchester, who died in 862; a legend grew up relating to the reburial of his bones on July 15, 971, when a storm erupted. This was taken as a sign that he was angry, and a tradition developed that the weather for the next 40 days was determined by the weather on his saint's day. The races indicated that "the good people forgot their old Saint" (451).

The first of the final two poems in Selwyn attributed to Jane Austen is "Riddles" (18). These are three quatrains each followed by the name "Jane." No manuscript is known to exist. Chapman in *Minor Works* prints the verses under the title "Charade" (450), an activity frequently performed by Jane Austen's family. The verses are found in *Charades written a hundred years ago by Jane Austen and her family*, published in 1895. The solution to the first charade is "Hemlock," to the second

"Agent," and to the third charade, "Bank Note" (*Minor Works*, 457). The final poem is also a "Charade" to "Miss" (Selwyn, 19), found in the ninth chapter of the first volume of *Emma* and consisting of three verses, the first two of four lines each and the third verse being a rhyming couplet. The solution is "Courtship" (Selwyn, 86). These verses are excluded from *Minor Works* and Doody and Murray, although the first verse of "Riddles" is in the latter under the title "Charades" (245).

Selwyn's *Jane Austen Collected Poems and Verse of the Austen Family* also contains verses under the heading "Family Verse" and poems attributed to the Austen family members: her mother, Mrs. AUSTEN (1739–1827); her brother JAMES AUSTEN (1765–1819); a relative JAMES LEIGH PERROT (1753–1817); her brothers and sister, CASSANDRA ELIZABETH AUSTEN (1773–1845); FRANCIS WILLIAM AUSTEN (1774–1865); CHARLES JOHN AUSTEN (1779–1852); HENRY THOMAS AUSTEN (1771–1850), her nephew GEORGE KNIGHT (1795–1867); her niece Anna Austen (1793–1872); her niece FANNY KNIGHT (1793–1882), JAMES EDWARD AUSTEN-LEIGH (1798–1874), and her niece CAROLINE MARY CRAVEN AUSTEN (1805–1880). In short, in the words of David Selwyn, "The handful of poems written by Jane Austen—impromptu, occasional, often arising from games—were the result not so much of the art which produced her novels as of a tradition of family verse-writing inherited from her mother" ("Poetry," 59).

BIBLIOGRAPHY

Primary Texts

Austen, Jane. *Charades &c Written a Hundred Years Ago by Jane Austen and Her family.* London: Spottiswoode & Co., [1895].

———. *Collected Poems and Verse of the Austen Family.* Edited with an introduction and notes by David Selwyn. Manchester, U.K.: Carcanet Press, 1996.

———. *Jane Austen's Letters.* Collected and edited by Deirdre Le Faye. 3d ed. Oxford: Oxford University Press, 1995.

———. *Jane Austen's Letters to her Sister Cassandra and Others.* 2 vols. Collected and edited by R. W. Chapman. Oxford, U.K.: Clarendon Press, 1932.

———. "Verses." In *Jane Austen's Catharine and other Writings,* edited by Margaret Anne Doody and Douglas Murray, 234–246. Oxford: Oxford University Press, 1993.

———. "Verses." In *The Works of Jane Austen,* Vol. 6, *Minor Works,* edited by R. W. Chapman. Oxford: Oxford University Press, 1986.

Austen-Leigh, J. E. *A Memoir of Jane Austen and Other Family Recollections.* Edited with an introduction and notes by Kathryn Sutherland. Oxford: Oxford University Press, 2002.

Austen-Leigh, William, and Richard Arthur. *Jane Austen: Her Life and Letters. A Family Record.* London: Smith, Elder & Co., 1913.

Brabourne, Edward, Lord. *Letters of Jane Austen.* 2 vols. Edited with an introduction and critical remarks by Edward, Lord Brabourne. London: Richard Bentley & Son, 1884.

Secondary Works

Gilson, David. "Jane Austen's Verses," *Book Collector* 33, no. 1 (Spring 1984): 25–37; 34, no. 3 (Autumn 1985): 384–385.

Greene, Donald. "New Verses by Jane Austen," *Nineteenth Century Fiction* 30 (1975): 257–260.

Honan, Park. *Jane Austen Her Life.* London: Weidenfeld and Nicolson, 1987.

Hubback, John Henry, and Edith Charlotte Hubback. *Jane Austen's sailor brothers, being the adventures of Sir Francis Austen, G.C.B., Admiral of the Fleet, and Rear-Admiral Charles Austen.* London: John Lane. The Bodley Head, 1906.

Selwyn, David. "Poetry." In *Jane Austen in Context,* edited by Janet Todd, 59–67. Cambridge: Cambridge University Press.

Southam, Brian. *Jane Austen and the Navy.* London and New York: Hambledon and London, 2000.

The Visit, a Comedy in 2 Acts (1934)

COMPOSITION AND PUBLICATION

The 10th in order of appearance in Jane Austen's juvenilia, *Volume the First.* Dedicated to her eldest brother JAMES AUSTEN, ordained in December 1787 and made a priest in June 1789. He organized theatricals performed during Jane Austen's childhood at the Steventon rectory between 1782 and 1789. *The Visit* (V) contains a reference to "my Grandmother's time" at the opening of its first act (50). B. C. Southam assigns a 1787 to June 1790 date for V, or before 1793, the year prior to the publication of Prince Hoare's popular musical play *My Grandfather*, which premiered in December 1793 (Southam, 16). V is included in the sixth volume of R. W. Chapman's edition of Jane Austen's *The Works* and in Margaret Anne Doody and Douglas Murray's 1993 edition of Catharine *and Other Writings* (47–52). The manuscript is in the Bodleian Library, Oxford.

SYNOPSIS

The play contains two acts. The first has two scenes set in "a Parlour" (50–51). The second act also has two scenes, the first set in "the Drawing Room," and the second set in "The Dining Parlour" (51, 53). Lord Fitzgerald has house guests but not enough chairs for them so they have to sit on each other's laps, thus becoming familiar with one another. Following a quick dinner, the characters confess love: Lord Fitzgerald proposes to Sophy Hampton, Stanly to Cloe Willoughby, Miss Fitzgerald to Mr. Willoughby, Sir Arthur Hampton's nephew. V concludes with Lady Hampton's, "And may you all be Happy!" (54).

CRITICAL COMMENTARY

Very little appears to have been written on V. Commentary is perfunctory, although Ellen F. Martin does indicate "a nice send-up of the common metonymy" of "giving one's *hand* in marriage" (91) at the conclusion of V: Miss Fitzgerald declares, "Since you Willoughby are the only one left, I cannot refuse your earnest solicitations—There is my Hand" (54). In her *Jane Austen and the Theatre*, Penny Gay draws attention to V's reference to Hoare's *my Grandfather*, "which is [also] the subject of Tom Bertram's theatrical pun in *Mansfield Park*" (168, n. 2). She notes that V "is set out in perfect compliance with the convention of the printed drama, with stage directions including asides and instructions for actors' movements." Further, V's text "is a hilariously deadpan

parody of society drama, in which polite clichés are exchanged and nothing of moment is said except by the Fitzgeralds" who place "all the shortcomings of the visit on the eccentricities of 'my Grandmother'" ([1]).

CHARACTERS

Fitzgerald, Lord (50–54)   The host of the V: He has not enough seating for his guests.

Fitzgerald, Miss (50–54)   Daughter of the host, who reverses social convention by proposing at the end of V to Willoughby.

Hampton, Sir Arthur (50–54)   A silent participant in V. Lord Fitzgerald tells him to "taste that Tripe." Sir Arthur "never touches wine" (53).

Hampton, Lady (50–54)   Tells her host what her husband and daughter prefer to eat.

Hampton, Sophy (50–54)   The Hamptons' daughter to whom Lord Fitzgerald proposes.

Stanly (50–54)   A participant who proposes to Cloe Willoughby but apparently does not drink.

Willoughby (50–54)   Proposed to by Miss Fitzgerald at the end of V, and Sir Arthur's nephew, she tells him, "I am afraid . . . you take no care of yourself" (53).

Willoughby, Cloe (50–52, 54)   Probably Willoughby's daughter, Stanly proposes to her.

BIBLIOGRAPHY

Primary Texts

Austen, Jane. "The Visit: A Comedy in 2 Acts." In *The Jane Austen Library. Volume the First*, edited by R. W. Chapman with a foreword by Lord David Cecil, a preface by Brian Southam, and a preface by R. W. Chapman, 90–99. London: Athlone Press, 1984.

———. "The Visit: A Comedy in 2 Acts." In *The Works of Jane Austen*, Vol. 6, *Minor Works*, edited by R. W. Chapman. Oxford: Oxford University Press. 1986. [All textual references are to this edition.]

————. "The Visit: A Comedy in 2 Acts." In *Jane Austen's Catharine and Other Writings*, edited by Margaret Anne Doody and Douglas Murray, 47–52. Oxford: Oxford University Press, 1993.

————. "The Visit." In *Jane Austen Juvenilia* (The Cambridge Edition of the Works of Jane Austen), edited by Peter Sabor, 61–68. Cambridge: Cambridge University Press, 2006.

Secondary Works

Gay, Penny. *Jane Austen and the Theatre*. Cambridge: Cambridge University Press, 2002.

Martin, Ellen E. "The Madness of Jane Austen: Metonymic Style and Literature's Resistance to Interpretation." In *Jane Austen's Beginnings: The Juvenilia and Lady Susan*, edited by J. David Grey, [83]–94. Ann Arbor, Mich., and London: UMI Research Press, 1989.

The Watsons (1871)

COMPOSITION AND PUBLICATION

The Watsons is an unfinished novel of approximately 17,500 words. J. E. Austen-Leigh in his 1871 *Memoir of Jane Austen* first published the work, which he titled *The Watsons*. R. W. Chapman examined the surviving manuscripts of the work in 1924 and recorded the manuscript alterations in his text of the novel published in 1927. The manuscript of the novel seems to be the sole instance of its author's manuscripts being split up. Basically, it passed in the Austen family until 1915, when William Austen-Leigh presented the first six leaves to a charity auction held at Sotheby's in London to aid the Red Cross in April of that year. These leaves passed into the hands of the London book dealer C. J. Sawyer, who sold them to the Pierpont Morgan Library of New York in 1926, where they are today. The remainder of the manuscript, 38 leaves in all, remained with the Austen family, although mostly on deposit in the British Museum, now the British Library, until 1978. Since 1988, it has been owned by Sir Peter Michael and on deposit at Queen Mary and Westfield College, University of London. Analysis of these drafts at the Pierpont Morgan Library

and in London shows that the manuscripts are heavily revised drafts and that some of the leaves are watermarked 1803. Furthermore, the manuscript lacks pagination and coherent paragraphing, and has "no separation of speaking parts from one another." More than "a third of the *Watsons* fragment is cast in direct speech." There are no chapter divisions (K. Sutherland, 145), and abbreviations, for instance "Eliz" for "Elizabeth," and "&" for "and" (*Minor Works*, 322), are used.

Questions about why the work is unfinished have led to speculation. It has been suggested that the death of the author's father on January 27, 1805, left her too depressed to continue with the work. Her personal distress at the time was compounded by the accidental death around December 16, 1804, of her close friend Madam Lefroy. Other reasons include the author's general unsettled state following the move from Steventon in 1801 and the move to Chawton eight years later. Most of the period was spent moving from place to place and mainly in the town—Jane Austen wrote best in the country. Also, she suffered from economic uncertainty—a major preoccupation of the unfinished *The Watsons*. B. C. Southam observes that her "failure to continue the work later was in recognition of its serious flaws." The author also "felt out of sympathy with the almost unrelieved bleakness of the social picture and the asperity of the satire." In *The Watsons*, the tale revolves around "a distressed heroine" (Southam, *Literary Manuscripts*, 63, 65).

SYNOPSIS

Emma Watson lived with a wealthy aunt and uncle Turner in Shropshire for 12 years. Two years after the death of her uncle, her aunt married an Irishman, Captain O'Brien, and made her home in Ireland. Emma, at the age of 19 is forced to return to her invalid widower father's home at Stanton, a village three miles from D[orking] in Surrey. Regarded by her aunt and uncle as a daughter and provided with every comfort, no direct provision was made for her in the event of her uncle's demise. There is a suggestion, unsupported by Emma, that O'Brien married her aunt for her money.

Emma's father is looked after by her elder sister Elizabeth. The family are genteel but not wealthy and unable to maintain an appropriate coach. One of her father's oldest friends is Mr. Edwards and his family. Richer, they maintain a coach, live in Dorking, and also invite the Watsons to spend the night in their home whenever there is a ball. One is to take place on Tuesday, October 13, and anybody who is anybody in the area will attend, including Lord Osborne of Osborne Castle.

The narrative opens with Emma, accompanied by Elizabeth, driving to the Edwardses' to prepare for the ball. On the way, she is "instructed & cautioned" by Elizabeth. She is 28 and tells Emma what to expect, how to behave, who is in love with whom, the schemes and disappointments of family members, and especially the activities of her other sisters, Penelope and Margaret, in their attempts to obtain a wealthy husband. She is warned that the flirtatious Tom Musgrave is "an universal favourite" (315). It quickly becomes apparent to Emma that her sister's primary object in life is to find a wealthy husband. Emma expresses a predominant concern running throughout Jane Austen's fiction: "To be so bent on Marriage—to pursue a man merely for the sake of situation—is a sort of thing that shocks me." Emma, inexperienced in the ways of the world, adds, "I cannot understand it, Poverty is a great Evil, but to a woman of Education & feeling it ought not, it cannot be the greatest." Emma "would rather be a Teacher at a school (and I can think of nothing worse) than to marry a Man I did not like."

Elizabeth's reaction to this is to observe, "I think I could like any good humoured Man with a comfortable Income" (318), and to conclude that her sister Emma is naive and hitherto has been brought up in too sheltered an environment. She tells Emma of Sam their brother's vain hope of marrying Mary Edwards, an only child with a wealthy inheritance. Sam, a surgeon, then a far from prestigious position, working in Guildford, has with his poor prospects, no chance of marrying Mary. Elizabeth, who is unable to attend the ball as she has to look after their invalid father, asks Emma to keep an eye on Mary and notice especially when she dances with Captain Hunter. Possibly, Elizabeth hopes that Sam may be as fortunate as their elder brother Robert, who is a prosperous lawyer in Croydon, and married to a relatively wealthy woman.

Emma's "conversation with Eliz[abeth]" gives "her some very unpleasant feelings, with respect to her own family" and how she will be perceived by the wealthy Edwards family, whom she has seen briefly only once before. She is received politely, but "The Mother [Mrs. Edward] tho' a very friendly woman, had a reserved air & a great deal of formal Civility." Her "daughter, a genteel looking girl of 22," treated Emma in the same manner as her mother. The father, Mr. Edwards, "had an easier & more communicative air than the Ladies of the Family." He tells them that "the Osbornes will certainly be at the Ball" as the horses and carriages have been ordered for them. As they dress, Mary and Emma grow to be more at ease with each other, and when they return to the parlor, Mary "asked Emma if she were not often reckoned very like her youngest brother" (322–324), Samuel. This brings a negative reaction from Mr. and Mrs. Edwards, including the former's "There is not the least likeness in the world." During dinner, Mr. Edwards asks Emma details of her aunt's new marriage to O'Brien, adding "Elderly Ladies should be careful how they make a second choice" (326), insinuating that O'Brien has mercenary motives in marrying the aunt.

Emma, who with the Edwardses has arrived early at the ball, spots Tom Musgrave and learns from Mary that his family regard him with suspicion, as he has "rather an unsettled turn," or temperament. He is, however, reasonably wealthy. Mary is engaged for the first two dances with Captain Hunter, and Emma, as a new person, is thoroughly scrutinized: "A new face & a very pretty one, could not be slighted." Lady Osborne; her son Lord Osborne, and daughter Miss Osborne; her friend a Miss Carr; Lord Osborne's former tutor, Mr. Howard, currently a local clergyman; Mrs. Blake, his widowed sister; and Charles, her 10-year-old son appear at the ball. Tom Musgrave displays himself publicly, apparently hanging around in the background to make his entrance with the Osbornes. Lady Osborne "tho' nearly 50 . . . was very handsome, & had all the Dignity of Rank," (328–329) observes that their early appearance is because young Charles enjoys dancing. Charles eagerly awaits his initial dance promised to him by

Miss Osborne, but she takes up instead with one of the officers, a Colonel Beresford. Emma rescues the 10-year-old boy from disappointment by dancing with him. Mrs. Blake is very grateful to Emma, and as they dance, the "Partnership . . . c[oul]d not be noticed without surprise." Charles tells Emma much about himself, and Lord "Osborne himself came & under pretence of talking to Charles, stood to look at his partner"—Emma (331).

Following tea, Mrs. Blake introduces her brother, Mr. Howard, to Emma, and he requests two dances with her. Before this, Emma overhears Lord Osborne instructing Tom Musgrave to dance with the "beautiful Emma Watson." Osborne's motive is that he may be introduced formally to Emma. Emma coolly rejects Tom's request for a dance by saying that she has a "prior Engagement" (333–334). Her two dances with Mr. Howard are most agreeable, and she regrets that she cannot dance with him more, as the Osbornes leave. Emma retires to bed after returning home "in charming Spirits, her head full of Osbornes, Blakes & Howards."

"The next morn[ing] brought a great many visitors" to Mrs. Edward's house, "as Every body wanted to look again at the girl who had been admired the night before by L[ord] Osborne." Tom Musgrave then appears carrying a note from Elizabeth, Emma's sister, to the effect that Emma's father has taken the family carriage to go to a religious ceremony and that she will have to find an alternative method of getting home. In "a verbal postscript" (337–338), Tom adds that Elizabeth agreed to his bringing Emma back home in his curricle. Emma considers this to be inappropriate, and Mrs. Edwards offers her the family coach. Back home, Emma tells her sister what has taken place. Elizabeth is most impressed to learn of Emma's friendship with such social superiors as the Osbornes and is mortified to learn of Emma's disapproval of Tom Musgrave. Their father returns home full of admiration for the preacher he had heard at the "Visitation." The preacher, it emerges, is Mr. Howard, who assisted Mr. Watson up some stairs to dinner and asked about one of his daughters, "but I do not know which."

"On the 3d day after the Ball" (343–344), Lord Osborne and Tom Musgrave take the household by surprise as Emma and Elizabeth prepare a nonformal parlor dinner. Emma, while flattered by the visit, is dismayed by her situation and the poverty of her surroundings. Tom engages Elizabeth in animated conversation, while Lord Osborne attempts to impress Emma. An awkward visit is concluded when Nanny, the Watsons' housekeeper, interrupts to say that the bedridden Mr. Watson is still waiting for dinner. Reflecting on the visit, "among other unsatisfactory feelings it once occurred to [Emma] to wonder why M[r.] Howard had not taken the same privilege of coming, & accompanied by his Lordship."

"A week or ten days rolled quietly away after this visit" (347–348). More of Emma's family appear, including her sister Margaret Watson, brother Robert, and his wife, Jane. They stay at Stanton for a few days to get to know their sister Emma. She finds them all obsessed with money. Her brother tells her, "A woman should never be trusted with money" (351), and Emma is upset when Robert speaks negatively of her beloved aunt and deceased uncle.

Later on in the evening, a visitor appears to relieve the gloom: "The door opened & displayed Tom Musgrave in the wraps of a Travellor" (355). He is returning from London and "loved to take people by surprise, with sudden visits at extraordinary seasons." His visit is appreciated by Emma as his charm is not unwelcome to her. Margaret persuades Elizabeth to invite him for the following evening to dinner. Tom is unable to commit himself, "And so, he departed, delighted with the uncertainty in which he had left it"—that is, the Watsons' company.

The following day Margaret, in an excited state, prepares for the dinner. However, Tom fails to appear, and "The Peace of the party for the remainder of that day, & the whole of the next, which comprised the length of Robert & Jane's visit, was continually invaded by her fretful displeasure, & querulous attacks." Consequently, Emma finds an "alternative of sitting . . . with her father," whom she finds "if ill . . . a Man of Sense and Education . . . if able to converse, a welcome companion." With her father, "Emma was at peace from the dreadful mortifications of unequal Society, & family Discord—from the immediate endurance of Hard-hearted prosperity, low-minded Conceit,

& wrong-headed folly, engrafted on an untoward Disposition." Emma is invited by Robert and Jane to accompany them to Croydon and to stay with them. She does not accept this invitation, and "the Visitors departed without her."

At this point, the manuscript concludes. There is a note in the second edition of J. E. Austen-Leigh's *A Memoir of Jane Austen* (1871) reading:

> When the author's sister, Cassandra, showed the manuscript of this work to some of her nieces, she also told them something of the intended story. . . . Mr. Watson was soon to die; and Emma to become dependent for a home on her narrow-minded sister-in-law and brother. She was to decline an offer of marriage from Lord Osborne, and much of the interest of the tale was to arise from Lady Osborne's love for Mr. Howard, and his counter-affection for Emma, whom he was finally to marry (360–363).

CRITICAL COMMENTARY

The text of *The Watsons* was unavailable until 1871. Many subsequent commentators have been concerned with why it remained unfinished. Richard Holt Hutton, reviewing J. E. Austen-Leigh's *Memoir* in the *Spectator*, July 22, 1871, finds *The Watsons* "full of promise" (Southam, *Heritage*, II: 17). William Makepeace Thackeray's daughter Anne, in an extensive 9,000-word review of the *Memoir* published in the *Cornhill Magazine* in 1871, in addition to praising the vivaciousness of *The Watsons*, anticipates Q. D. Leavis's "Critical Theory of Jane Austen's Writings," published in *Scrutiny* between 1941 and 1944. Anne Thackeray writes, "*The Watsons* is a delightful fragment, which might belong to any of her other histories. It is bright with talk, and character, and animation" (Southam, *Heritage*, II: 165–166). Both distinguished critical voices find parallels between *The Watsons* and the later *Emma* in terms of plot structure and characterization. Q. D. Leavis argues that Jane Austen used the materials of *The Watsons* afresh for *Emma*. This view is reiterated in her "Introduction" to the Illustrated Classics edition of *Sense and Sensibility, Lady Susan and the Watsons*, published in 1958.

B. C. Southam has challenged Leavis's belief that *The Watsons* was transformed into *Emma*. He admits that there are "resemblances." First, "The name Emma is common to both heroines"; second, Surrey is the setting in both; third, in both there "is a ball in which someone is rescued from acute embarrassment by an invitation to dance." Last, both "fathers are self-centred invalids." For Southam, however, "the fundamental difference is one of vision and personality." Differences between the two Emmas outweigh the similarities: "The earlier heroine is a study in sober perfection," while "the later heroine is a lively girl, at times willful and foolish, who has to learn slowly by her mistakes" (Southam, *Literary Manuscripts*, 151).

Virginia Woolf in *The Common Reader* (1925) finds *The Watsons* "second-rate" but fascinating, revealing difficulties confronting a writer. She claims "in this unfinished and in the main inferior story are . . . all the elements of Jane Austen's greatness." There is a caveat: "Those first angular chapters of *The Watsons* prove that hers was not a prolific genius." Woolf observes that in *The Watsons* Jane Austen "makes us wonder why an ordinary act of kindness [Emma's dancing with the young Charles Blake] . . . becomes so full of meaning" (Watt, 18, 21).

Inevitably, there have been sequels to *The Watsons*. The first, entitled *The Younger Sister*, was a three-volume novel published in 1850 by Catherine Hubback, a niece of Cassandra Austen. There were sequels published in 1923 and in 1928. The latter is *The Watsons by Jane Austen: Completed in Accordance with Her Intentions* by a great-grandniece Edith Hubback Brown with the assistance of Francis Brown. Jane Austen's fragment also accompanies the first of a 26-chapter 1977 reconstruction (Gilson, 424–425).

In spite of these speculative continuations, critical discussion, down to the modern period, has focused on three areas: the date of composition, why *The Watsons* was left incomplete, and its relationship to *Emma*. Approaches to these issues have been biographical, aesthetic, and a mixture of the two. B. C. Southam believes that Jane Austen left *The Watsons* unfinished because of its heroine's strength, not weakness. On the other hand, Joseph Wiesenfarth in his "*The Watsons* as Pretext" (1986), argues that Jane Austen was repeating herself, something she did not like doing. Wiesenfarth's is one of the most succinct and illuminating accounts of the unfinished work. He writes, "the central event . . . is the dance at which Emma takes young Charles Blake as her partner and becomes, in turn, the partner of Mr. Howard, whom we know Jane Austen intended her to marry." This scene recalls other balls in Jane Austen's work, for instance, the Meryton ball in *Pride and Prejudice* and also the Crown Inn ball in *Emma* (102). For Wiesenfarth, "Jane Austen never finished *The Watsons* because after writing the final drafts of *Sense and Sensibility* and of *Pride and Prejudice* she did not have to." Emma is "transformed into Jane Fairfax and . . . then the only remaining unused item of significance which was left from the fragment was . . . the case of the sister who is too nice in her ways to succeed in the common, everyday world that Jane Austen's fiction depicts." Wiesenfarth adds that the case of Emma Watson "was itself worked out in *Persuasion*" (105–106). Alistair Duckworth, in his *The Improvement of the Estate: A Study of Jane Austen's Novels* (1971), considers Emma Watson's marriage to Mr. Howard a "successful resolution," affirming an underlying propriety (223–226). Money and pragmatism concern Oliver MacDonagh's reading in his *Jane Austen: Real and Imagined Worlds* (1991) of the fragment.

Alison G. Sulloway, in her *Jane Austen and the Province of Womanhood* (1984), reads the ballroom scene in *The Watsons* as an illustration of its author's "ironic interest in dancing as a symbol of male domination" (150). Feminist readings have not ignored the incomplete work. To take two instances of this approach, Deborah Kaplan's *Jane Austen among Women* (1992) perceives Emma as resenting masculine power. For Kaplan, *The Watsons* is a detailed analysis of "the detrimental effects that women's social and economic dependence can have on feminine identities" (171). Camille Paglia, in her *Sexual Personae: Art and Decadence from Nefertiti to Emily Dickinson* (1990), goes so far as to assert that Emma has a "latent masculinity" (441). A. Walton Litz, in his *Jane Austen: A Study of Her Artistic Development* (1965), believes that *The Watsons* was unique in Jane Austen's output, Emma Watson being "subject to none of the misapprehensions and self-deception of the other heroines" (89). The debate continues today as to the status, stature, and significance of the fragment first published in 1871.

CHARACTERS

Beresford, Colonel (330) Miss Osborne breaks her promise to dance with little Charles Blake at the ball and instead dances "these two dances with Col[onel] Beresford" (330).

Betty (346) The Watsons' kitchen maid.

Blake, Mrs. (329–331) Mother of Charles and three other children. The widowed sister of Mr. Howard, she is "a lively and pleasant-looking little woman of 5 or 6 & 30" (330).

Blake, Charles (329–330) "A fine boy of 10 years old," son of Mrs. Blake. Emma Watson "was immediately struck with the fine Countenance & animated gestures of the little boy" (329–330), who loves dancing.

Carr, Fanny (329, 340) Friend of Miss Osborne, Tom Musgrave says she is "a most interesting little creature. You can imagine nothing more *naïve* or *piquante*" (Jane Austen's emphasis, 340).

Curtis, Mr. (321) The Guildford surgeon to whom Sam Watson is apprenticed.

Edward(e)s, Mr. (314, 323, 325) He is a well-off gentleman living in the town of Dorking in Surrey, with "a much easier & more communicative air than the Ladies of [his] Family" (323). He puts Emma at ease when she visits his home. Sociable, he "had lived long enough in the Idleness of a Town to become a little of a Gossip" (325). He appears to want to signal to Emma that her brother Sam is an inappropriate match for his daughter Mary. A member of the local whist club, which met three times a week at the White Hart, if winning, he always stayed late.

Edward(e)s, Mrs. (319, 322–323, 338–339) Initially "tho' a very friendly woman, had a reserved air & a great deal of formal Civility" (322) when Emma first comes to visit. She loosens up as the ball comes closer and takes place. On the day after, she comes to Emma's rescue, when the latter refuses to be driven home by Tom Musgrave, by saying, "Our Carriage is quite at your Service" (339).

Edward(e)s, Mary (320–323) The Edward(e)s' daughter who displays "the shew of good sense, a modest unpretending mind, & a great wish of obliging" (323). Twenty-one years of age and considered to be worth at least £10,000, she, like her mother, is initially reserved toward Emma but becomes friendlier. Emma's brother Sam is in love with her, but his sister Elizabeth feels that he has little chance with her, owing to the lowly status of the Watson family. At the ball, her chief partner is Captain Hunter. Her mother is disappointed that she prefers him to the banker's sons the Tomlinsons.

Harding, Dr. (317) Elizabeth tells Emma that their sister Penelope Watson "has been trying to make some match at Chichester" in Sussex, but "she won't tell us with whom, but I beleive [*sic*] it is a rich old Dr. Harding, Uncle to the friend she goes to see" (317).

Hemmings, Mr. (353) A Croydon acquaintance of Robert and Jane Watson who appears to "change" his "dress every day of" his life (353).

Howard, Rev. Mr. (330, 333, 343–344, 347, 363) Lord Osborne's former tutor, Mrs. Blake's brother, vicar of Wickstead, and intended hero of *The Watsons*. More than 30 years old, he dances with Emma: "there was a quietly-chearful gentlemanlike air in Mr. H which suited" her (333). Mr. Watson returns from a religious visitation and tells his daughter that the preacher was a Mr. Howard, who had "given them an excellent Sermon" (343). He had assisted Mr. Watson on "a pretty steep flight of steps" and "enquired after one of [his] Daughters" (344). According to a note at the conclusion of the 1871 edition, "much of the interest of" *The Watsons* "was to arise from Lady Osborne's love for Mr. Howard, and his counter affection for Emma, whom he was finally to marry" (363).

Hunter, Captain (320) He dances with Mary Edwards at the ball.

James (319) The Watsons' coachman.

Marshall, Mr. (353) A Croydon acquaintance of Robert and Jane Watson. Like Mr. Hemmings, he appears to change his "dress" (353) on a daily basis.

Musgrave, Tom (318–319, 331, 333, 335–336, 342–344, 347, 355, 357–358) Emma Watson observes, "I allow his person & air to be good—& that his manners to a certain point—his address rather—is pleasing.—But I see nothing else to admire in him" (342). When young, he came into a good deal of money, about £800–£900 a year. A friend of Lord Osborne, with whom he frequently went hunting, he has lived in the Guildford district for six years and is known for his charm, manners, and various flirtations. These include the three Watson girls—Elizabeth, Penelope, and Margaret. He is attracted to 19-year-old Emma, but she quickly sees through him and refuses his invitation to ride home in his carriage. At the White Hart assembly, he hangs around in the wings so that he can make a grand entrance with the Osbornes. When they leave early, he makes himself very comfortable at the White Hart with "a Barrel of Oysters" (335). Emma objects to his calling on her without warning with Lord Osborne. Elizabeth observes that unless he can marry "somebody very great" (319) like Miss Osborne, he will remain a bachelor.

Nanny (341, 344) A servant at the Watsons' house, she "brought in the dinner" (341) and the third day "after the Ball . . . Nanny at five minutes before three, was beginning to bustle into the parlour with the Tray & the Knife-case" (344) when Lord Osborne and Tom Musgrave appear.

Norton, Mr. (337) He is "a Cousin of Capt. Hunter's" (337) and one of Mary Edwards's dancing partners.

O'Brien, Captain (326) The second husband of Emma Watson's aunt who, following the marriage, sent Emma home to Stanton. He did not want Emma to go with them to Ireland. It is suggested that he might have married Miss Turner for her money, and it is probable that Emma will no longer inherit any of the money due to her.

Osborne, Lady (329, 357, 363)   At the ball, "of the females, L[ady] Osborne had by much the finest person;—tho'nearly 50, she was very handsome, & had all the Dignity of Rank" (329). The mother of Lord and Miss Osborne, she lives at Osborne Castle in the parish of Wickstead near Dorking in Surrey. "Much of the interest of" *The Watsons* "was to arise form Lady Osborne's love for Mr. Howard" (363).

Osborne, Lord (314, 329, 344–348, 363)   He is "a very fine young man; but there was an air of Coldness, of Carelessness, even of Awkwardness about him, which seemed to speak him out of his Element in a Ball room" (329). Uneasy socially, in spite of his high social status, he says very little. He is attracted to Emma Watson, but she finds his brusqueness and behavior off-putting, and "She was to decline an offer of marriage from" him (362).

Osborne, Miss (329, 340)   Tom Musgrave describes her as "perhaps . . . not critically handsome, but her Manners are delightful" (340). Lord Osborne's sister, at the ball she breaks her promise to the young Charles Blake, as soon as Colonel Beresford asks her to dance with him.

Purvis, Mr. (316)   Elizabeth tells her sister Emma that she "was very much attached to a young Man of the name of Purvis, a particular friend" of her brother Robert. She adds, "Every body thought it would have been a Match," but her younger sister Penelope split them apart by attempting to gain Purvis for herself. Elizabeth "will never love any Man as I loved Purvis." He subsequently married somebody else (316).

Richards, Rev. Dr. (344)   A clergyman at the religious visitation attended by Mr. Watson and especially kind to him.

Shaw, Mrs. (317)   Niece of Dr. Harding, Penelope Watson visits her frequently in Chichester.

Stokes, Jack (341)   He and his uncle are acquaintances of the Watson family. The uncle will deliver a letter from Elizabeth Watson to Sam in Guildford.

Styles, Mr. (337)   A "particular" friend of Captain Hunter and one of Mary Edwards's dancing partners.

Tomlinson, Mr. (322, 336)   He is the banker who "might be indulged in calling his newly erected House at the end of the Town with a Shrubbery & sweep in the Country" (322). His wife and two sons are mentioned subsequently in relation to the ball.

Tomlinson, Mrs. (327)   An early arrival at the Dorking assemblies.

Tomlinson, James (336–337)   One of the banker's sons who was supposed to have danced with Mary Edwards. She dances with Captain Hunter and his friends instead.

Turner, Mr. (deceased) (361)   Emma Watson's "Uncle who had formed her mind with the care of a Parent" (361).

Turner, Mrs. (315, 321, 326, 361)   Emma's aunt whom she remembers with "Tenderness," who brought Emma up "like a Child of her own" (326). Her "amiable temper had delighted to give [Emma] every indulgence" (361). Two years after her husband's death, she marries a Captain O'Brien and goes to live in Ireland. Mr. Edwards suggests that O'Brien married her for her money and comments, "When an Old Lady plays the fool, it is not in the course of nature that she should suffer from it many years" (326).

Watson, Mr. (315, 343–344, 354, 361–363)   Mr. Watson "was sickly & had lost his wife . . . only could profit by the kindness of his friends" (315). The father of Emma Watson, he has three other daughters, Elizabeth, Penelope, Margaret, and two sons, Robert and Samuel. Relatively poor, he has an old friend in the prosperous Mr. Edwards of Dorking. Emma finds in him solace and wisdom: "if ill, [he] required little more than gentleness & silence; &

being a Man of Sense and Education, was if able to converse, a welcome companion" (361). He "was soon to die" (362).

Watson, Augusta (350) Robert and Jane Watson's young daughter left in Croydon when they come to stay in Stanton.

Watson, Elizabeth (315, 317, 319–320, 328, 345, 353–354, 359, 361–362) The 28-year-old "eldest sister" of Emma "whose delight in a Ball was not lessened by a ten years Enjoyment, had some merit in chearfully undertaking to drive [Emma] & all her finery in the old chair to D[orking]" (315). Elizabeth remains at home, allowing Emma to go to the ball. She formed an attachment to a young man named Purvis, a friend of her brother Robert. But her sister Penelope wanted Purvis for herself, and he married someone else. A realist, she is aware that it was "very bad to grow old & be poor & laughed at" (317). She feels that she could accommodate to a man with humor and a reasonable income.

Watson, Emma (throughout) The central focus of *The Watsons*, she lived in Shropshire with her wealthy aunt for 14 years. On the marriage of her widowed aunt, who goes to live in Ireland, she is forced to return home to Stanton near Dorking and live in relatively impoverished circumstances with her invalid father and unmarried sisters. "It was well for her that she was naturally chearful; for the Change [in her circumstances] had been such as might have plunged weak spirits in Despondence" (362).

Attractive and refined, she is shocked to learn that one of her sisters, Penelope, attempts to marry a much older man for his wealth. Emma prefers to teach than marry a man she is not attracted to. At the first Dorking winter assembly and ball, her beauty, newness to the area, and kindness to the 10-year-old Charles Blake, with whom she dances after he has been let down, attract much attention. This leads Charles Blake's mother to introduce her to her brother, a tutor and clergyman, Mr. Howard. She dances with him and clearly finds him attractive. Mrs. Blake belongs to the party of the highly influential Osbornes, and in this way Emma also is introduced to

Lord Osborne and Tom Musgrave. Both unexpectedly call at Stanton to see her. Tom offers her a lift home in his carriage, which she displays common sense and strength of character in refusing. She also declines an invitation to stay in Croydon with her financially obsessed and snobbish brother, Robert, and his wife, Jane. Following her father's death, she is "to become dependent for a home on her narrow-minded sister-in-law and brother. She was to decline an offer of marriage from Lord Osborne" and "finally to marry" Mr. Howard (362–363).

Watson, Jane (319, 349) Emma's sister-in-law, married to her brother Robert, "the only daughter of the Attorney to whom he had been Clerk, with a fortune of six thousand pounds." She "was not less pleased with herself for having had that six thousand pounds, & for being now in possession of a very smart house in Croydon, where she gave genteel parties, & wore fine clothes." Furthermore, "in her person there was nothing remarkable; her manners were pert and conceited" (349).

Watson, Margaret (317, 319, 349) The youngest of the Watson daughters. Elizabeth tells Emma, "she is all gentleness & mildness when anybody is by.—But she is a little fretful & perverse among ourselves" (319). She imagines that Tom Musgrave is courting her when he calls to see Emma. She "was not without beauty; she had a slight, pretty figure, & rather wanted Countenance than good features;—but the sharp & anxious expression of her face made her beauty in general little felt" (349). She stayed for a second time in Croydon with her brother Robert in the belief that her absence would be noted by Tom Musgrave.

Watson, Penelope (316–317) The second Watson daughter. Elizabeth tells Emma "she has her good qualities, but she has no Faith, no Honour, no Scruples, if she can promote her own advantage" (317). Elizabeth does not trust her, as she had intervened in her relationship with Purvis, and he married somebody else. According to Elizabeth, she would stop at nothing to be married. Apparently, Tom Musgrave, after dallying with her affections for a time, transferred them to Margaret. Subsequently,

Penelope has been scheming to make a match with the old and wealthy Dr. Harding from Chichester.

Watson, Robert (316, 348–349, 352, 363) Emma's eldest brother, "an Attorney at Croydon, in a good way of Business; very well satisfied with himself for the same, & for having married the only daughter of the Attorney to whom he had been Clerk, with a fortune of six thousand pounds" (348–349). Always mercenary, he fails to understand why his uncle left his wealth to his wife, and consequently Emma had to go home "without a sixpence" (352). Following her father's death, Emma "became dependent for a home" with her "narrow-minded sister-in-law and" mean, financially obsessed brother.

Watson, Samuel (320, 324)   The younger Watson son. According to Mr. Edwards, he "is a very good sort of young Man, & I dare say a very clever Surgeon, but his complexion had been rather too much exposed to all weathers" (324). A surgeon with the Guildford-based Mr. Curtis, Mary Edwards appears to be more attracted to Captain Hunter than to Sam, who has loved her for two years. She seems to be too wealthy to wish to marry a young surgeon.

BIBLIOGRAPHY

Primary Texts

Austen, Jane. *Sense and Sensibility with Lady Susan and the Watsons.* Introduction by Q. D. Leavis and illustrations by Philip Gough. London: Macdonald, 1958.

———. *The Watsons.* In *The Works of Jane Austen,* Vol. 6, *Minor Works,* edited by R. W. Chapman. Oxford: Oxford University Press. 1986. [All textual references are to this edition.]

———. *Nothanger Abbey, Lady Susan, The Watsons, and Sanditon,* edited by James Kinsley and John Davie, with an introduction and notes by Claudia L. Johnson. Oxford: Oxford University Press, 2003 [Oxford World's Classics.]

———. *The Watsons* [completed by David Hopkinson]. London: Peter Davies, 1977.

———. *The Watsons,* completed in accordance with her intentions by Edith (Jane Austen's great grand-niece) and Francis Brown. London: Elkin Mathews, 1928.

Austen-Leigh, J. E. *A Memoir of Jane Austen and Other Family Recollections,* edited and with an introduction and notes by Kathryn Sutherland. Oxford: Oxford University Press, 2002.

Hubback, Catherine Anne. *The Younger Sister.* 3 vols. London: Thomas Cautley Newby, 1850.

Secondary Works

Duckworth, Alistair M. *The Improvement of the Estate: A Study of Jane Austen's Novels.* Baltimore: Johns Hopkins University Press, 1971.

Kaplan, Deborah. *Jane Austen Among Women.* Baltimore: Johns Hopkins University Press, 1992.

Leavis, Q. D., "A Critical Theory of Jane Austen's Writings," *Scrutiny* 10 and 12 (1941–1945), reprinted in her *Collected Essays,* Vol. 1, *The Englishness of the English Novel,* edited by G. Singh. Cambridge: Cambridge University Press, 1983.

Litz, A. Walton. *Jane Austen: A Study of Her Artistic Development.* New York: Oxford University Press, 1965.

McDonagh, Oliver. *Jane Austen: Real and Imagined Worlds.* New Haven, Conn.: Yale University Press, 1991.

Paglia, Camille. *Sexual Personae: Art and Decadence from Nefertiti to Emily Dickinson.* New Haven, Conn.: Yale University Press, 1990.

Southam, Brian C. *Jane Austen: The Critical Heritage.* 2 vols. London: Routledge and Kegan Paul, 1978–79.

———. *Jane Austen's Literary Manuscripts.* Revised edition. London: Athlone Press, 2001.

Sulloway, Alison G. *Jane Austen and the Province of Womanhood.* Philadelphia: University of Pennsylvania Press, 1989.

Sutherland, Kathryn. *Jane Austen's Textual Lives: From Aeschylus to Bollywood.* Oxford: Oxford University Press, 2005.

Watt, Ian, ed. *Jane Austen: A Collection of Critical Essays.* Englewood Cliffs, N.J.: Prentice Hall, 1963.

Wiesenfarth, Joseph. "The Watsons as Pretext," *Persuasions* 8 (1986): 101–111.

Woolf, Virginia. "Jane Austen." In her *The Common Reader.* New York: Harcourt, 1925.

PART III

Related Entries

See the list on page xi for commonly used abbreviations referring to important texts. Austen works cited are discussed in Part II.

Austen, Anna (June Anna Elizabeth Lefroy) (1793–1872)   Jane's niece, recipient of 15 extant letters from her aunt, daughter of Jane's brother James. Born at Deane on April 15, 1793, and died at Reading, September 1, 1872. She married at Steventon Church on November 8, 1814, Benjamin Lefroy (1791–1829), and had a son and six daughters. Following her husband's death, she and her children lived in rented accommodations. She wrote verse and attempted to write a novel. Anna was close to her aunt Jane, especially from the summer of 1812 until her aunt's death in 1817. She published a novella, *Mary Hamilton,* in 1833 and two children's books, *The Winter's Tale* (1841) and *Springtide* (1842). Anna attempted to complete the unfinished *Sanditon.* From around 1855, she wrote down her family history, which passed to her daughter Fanny Caroline (1820–85), who lived with her mother and was the only one of her children never to marry. The history was used in her half brother James Edward Austen-Leigh's *Memoir.*

Austen, Caroline Mary Craven (1805–1880) Jane Austen's niece, born at Steventon on June 18, 1805, the second child of James and Mary Austen. She lived with her mother, Mary, until she died in 1843 and then near her brother James Edward Austen-Leigh, whose large family of 10 children she helped bring up. She spent the last 20 years of her life at Frog Firle near Alfriston in Sussex, acting as hostess for James's two bachelor sons, Charles-Edward (1832–1924) and Spencer (1834–1913). She never married. The recipient of nine extant letters from her aunt Jane, whom she knew well, she composed her memories of her in 1867, *My Aunt Jane Austen: A Memoir* (published in 1952), drawn upon by her brother for his 1869 *Memoir* and her *Reminiscences* (published in 1986, written in 1872).

Austen, Cassandra Elizabeth (1773–1845)   Jane Austen's almost three-year-older sister, with whom she was very close, as the extant letters to her testify. Cassandra was Jane's main correspondent, heiress, and executrix. They grew up together and briefly attended school away from home at the Abbey School, Reading, from 1785 to 1786. In 1792, she became engaged to TOM FOWLE (1765–97) and increasingly spent her time away from Steventon with her fiancé and his family at Kingsbury in Berkshire. In autumn 1795, he accepted an offer from his patron, Lord Craven, to accompany him to the West Indies as his personal chaplain, sailing in mid-January 1796.

Jane formed an attachment with Tom Lefroy (1776–1869). Her sister, now 23, objected to her overfamiliarity with Tom, and in this rare instance Jane seems not to have deferred to her older sister's judgment. But Tom Lefroy left for London to resume his legal studies and in 1797 married the sister of a college friend, spending the rest of his very successful career in Ireland. In spring 1797, the news reached home that Tom Fowle had died from yellow fever caught at sea near St. Domingo in the West Indies. He was buried at sea in February 1797. Tom left his fiancée his savings, of £1,000, providing her subsequently with an income not to make her totally dependent on her family. Cassandra continued to attend balls and other social activities with Jane, with whom she became even closer. Cassandra remained a spinster.

As Mrs. Austen aged, Cassandra took on herself more and more family duties. In addition, she frequently visited her elder brother Edward to assist him with his ever-increasing family based at Godmersham in Kent. When Cassandra and Jane were apart, Cassandra received very conversational letters from her—a major source of our subsequent knowledge of Jane's life. As the years rolled on, the two sisters drew closer together. As Fanny Caroline Lefroy's Austen family history records: "They seemed to lead a life to themselves within the general family life, which was shared only by each other . . . their *full*, feelings and opinions were known only to themselves. They alone equally understood what each had suffered and felt and thought" (Fanny's emphasis; cited in *Family Record*, 104).

Following her father's decision to retire from his ecclesiastical duties, Cassandra returned home from an extended stay at Godmersham in February 1801 to assist with the move from Steventon to Bath. Following their father's death in January 1805, his widow and her daughters experienced financial difficulties. Tom Fowle's will in some ways protected Cassandra, who, early in March 1805, went to nurse a close family friend, Mrs. Lloyd, and to assist her daughter Martha. Following Mrs. Lloyd's death early in April 1805, Martha came to live with Mrs. Austen, Jane, and Cassandra. The relationship was broken only in 1817 by Jane's death, and 10 years later by Mrs. Austen's. Cassandra's Christmas and New Year's usually were spent at Godmersham. An uncertain period followed the Reverend George Austen's death. Jane, her mother, and Martha moved around, living, for instance, in Clifton near Bristol and then among other places to Southampton, sometimes

with Cassandra, who was assisting Edward's wife, Elizabeth, at Godmersham. In September 1808, Elizabeth gave birth to her 11th child and died shortly afterward. Cassandra remained at Godmersham until February 1809, assisting Fanny (the eldest daughter) and her father, Edward, with the running of a large house and caring for the 10 younger brothers and sisters.

In spring 1809, Jane and her mother moved to Chawton Cottage, their final home. They were joined by Martha and Cassandra. This "was a cheerful house" (*Memoir*, 170) and a very creative period for Jane. Cassandra also spent extended periods at Godmersham. In 1816, Jane's health declined; in May, she and Cassandra went to Cheltenham to the spa waters for a cure. Cassandra also accompanied Mary Lloyd to Cheltenham during August and early September: Mary Lloyd too was unwell. Cassandra returned from Cheltenham on September 21, 1816. In her will, made on April 27, 1817, Jane gave everything to "my dearest sister," Cassandra, who accompanied her on her final 16-mile journey to Winchester to consult a highly respected surgeon. Cassandra recorded a detailed account of hers sister's last few hours and words.

Cassandra and Martha stayed on at Chawton Cottage. Mrs. Austen died aged 87 on January 18, 1827. She left Cassandra a legacy of £600 per annum. Martha died in 1843. Cassandra lived on for another two years, preserving her sister's beloved memory. She "frequently stayed with her brothers and their families and in turn entertained nephews and nieces at the Cottage," and "it is thanks to Cassandra's contact with her brothers' children that traditions concerning Jane's life were preserved." In 1843, around the time she drew up her will, she burned some of her sister's letters and retained others. Cassandra "divided her monies equally between each branch of the family" and also distributed Jane's surviving manuscripts and effects.

A great-niece seeing Cassandra at a family christening in 1843 remembered her as "a pale dark-eyed old lady, with a high arched nose and a kind smile" (*FR*, 267–268, 271, 270). James Edward Austen-Leigh records in the *Memoir* that Jane and Cassandra "were not exactly alike. Cassandra's was the colder and calmer disposition; she was always prudent and well judging, but with less outward demonstration of feeling and less sunniness of temper than Jane possessed" (19).

Austen, Cassandra, née Leigh (1739–1827) Jane Austen's mother, who married in 1764 in Bath, the Reverend George Austen. Her family was a large, well-connected one based in Adlestrop in Gloucestershire. Another branch of the family owned Stonleigh Abbey in Warwickshire, and there was a family connection with the founder of St. John's College, Oxford—Jane's brothers went to the college on "Founder's Kin" scholarships. Another connection was with the Perrot family of Northleigh, Oxfordshire. James, Jane Austen's uncle, changed his name from Leigh to Perrot when he inherited the Perrot estate.

The father of Cassandra was from an early age a fellow of All Souls College, Oxford. Rector of Harpsden near Henley-on-Thames from 1731 until his death, he married Jane Walker in 1732 and had six children, two of whom died young, leaving James (1735–1817), Jane (1736–83), Cassandra, and Thomas (1747–1821), who was mentally disadvantaged and with Jane Austen's brother George looked after outside the family circle. Cassandra's father died in 1764 and her mother in 1768.

She was the mother of eight children born between 1765 and 1779, the first three born at Deane Parsonage, and the others at Steventon rectory, where she and her husband lived from 1768 until 1801. The Austens were not wealthy; she was very sociable, enjoying visits to Bath and London, family visits and balls, plus amateur theatricals. Following her husband's death in 1805, she left Bath with her daughters, living initially in Southampton with her son Frank and his wife from 1806 to 1809, then at Chawton, where she was looked after by Jane, and then Cassandra and Martha Lloyd. She died aged 87 on January 17, 1827.

Austen, Charles John (1779–1852) Jane Austen's youngest brother, whom she refers to in a letter to her sister, Cassandra, as "our own particular little brother" (January 21, 1799; her words being a misquotation from Fanny Burney's *Camilla; Letters,* 38, 367). A favorite, Charles had a very distin-

Rear-Admiral Charles Austen

guished naval career. Educated at the Royal Naval Academy, Portsmouth, 1791–94, he was promoted to midshipman in 1794, three years later to lieutenant, and then commander in 1804, taking part in several engagements with the French navy. A post-captain in 1810, on coastguard duties in Cornwall from 1820 to 1826, he became a rear admiral in 1846 and commander in chief of the East India and China Station in 1850. He died of cholera on October 7, 1852, while on active service in Burmese waters.

Charles married, first, in Bermuda on May 19, 1807, Frances Fitzwilliam Palmer, the daughter of a retired former attorney general of Bermuda. They had four daughters, and Frances died shortly after giving birth to her fourth daughter, who also died, in September 1814. Charles then went back to sea, commanding HMS *Phoenix,* and was involved in the naval conflict following Napoleon's escape from Elba in March 1815. In 1816, his ship was wrecked during a hurricane off the coast of Asia Minor near Smyrna. His crew was saved and Charles was cleared of all blame following a court-martial, but he had to wait another 10 years before going to sea again (*FR*, 234).

He remarried, much to his family's disapproval, his sister-in-law, Harriet Palmer (died 1867) in August 1820. They had three sons and a daughter. Charles was the dedicatee of two of Jane's juvenilia: "Sir William Mountague" and the "Memoirs of Mr. Clifford." Jane sent him a copy of *Emma*, and Charles wrote home from the Mediterranean, "Emma arrived in time to a moment. I am delighted with her, more so I think than even with my favourite Pride & Prejudice, & have read it three times in the Passage" (*FR*, 230). Only one letter from Jane Austen to Charles is extant—dated April 6, 1817 (*Letters*, 338–339), although he is mentioned frequently in Jane Austen's other surviving letters. Charles was unable to attend his sister's funeral. His diary contains mentions of his sister (*FR*, 251–252).

Austen, Edward (Knight) (1767–1852) Jane Austen's third brother, born on October 7, 1767, at Deane in Hampshire, shortly before his parents moved to Steventon Rectory. Thomas Knight II (1735–94), a distant relative of his father, visited Steventon with his new wife, Catherine, née Knatchbull (1753–1812). They took a fancy to Edward, took him with them for the rest of their wedding tour, thoroughly liked his company, and when it became clear that they would not have children, they decided to adopt Edward and make him their heir around 1783. He was educated by his father, then sent to a German university, and on a grand tour of Europe, which was seen as a necessary part of a young man's education. From 1786 to 1790, he visited Switzerland, Italy, and Dresden. On December 27, 1791, he married Elizabeth Bridges (d. 1808). Initially, they lived at Rowling near Goodnestone, Kent, and in 1797 moved to Godmersham Park. In 1812, he officially took the name Knight. Edward inherited three estates, those of Steventon and Chawton in Hampshire and Godmersham near Canterbury in Kent.

Edward and Elizabeth had six sons and five daughters. The eldest, FRANCES-CATHERINE (Fanny) (1793–1882), became the second wife of Sir Edward Knatchbull, of Kent, and they had nine children. Edward (1829–93), the first Lord Brabourne, edited the *Letters of Jane Austen* (1884). Elizabeth died a few weeks after giving birth to Brook John (1808–78), the youngest child. Edward and Elizabeth were especially close to Cassandra, Jane and Edward's sister, and Cassandra increasingly spent lengthy periods of time at Godmersham Park helping Edward with estate and family affairs and assisting Elizabeth with her frequent pregnancies. Jane Austen visited Godmersham frequently.

Following his wife's death, Edward increasingly spent more time at his Chawton estate to be close to his mother and sister and provided a house for them in Chawton village. He attended Jane's funeral. Jane's juvenile work "The Three Sisters," a burlesque of wedding plans, was dedicated to him. Appropriately as a country squire, he noted an error of his sister's description of the Abbey Mill Farm in *Emma*, with its "orchard in bloom" on the day of the Donwell Abbey strawberry party: "Jane, I wish you would tell me where you get those apple-trees of yours that come into bloom in July" (*FR*, 230). Edward did not remarry, and lived peacefully at Godmersham until his death in 1852. His daughter Marianne (1801–96) replaced her late mother as her father's hostess, remained unmarried, and on her father's death lived with her unmarried brothers Charles Bridges (1803–67) at Chawton, and then with Brook-John before living finally with her niece Cassandra Hill.

Austen, Elizabeth, née Bridges (1773–1808) One of the 13 children of Sir Brook Bridges, a neighbor of the Knights of Godmersham. She and her sisters were educated at a boarding school in Queen Square in Bloomsbury in London, run solely for the education of daughters of the nobility and gentry. Elizabeth married Edward (Knight) Austen on December 27, 1791, at a double wedding at which her sister Sophia married a William Deedes. Her other sister, Fanny, married too in the same month. The three sisters also became engaged in the same year, hence Jane Austen's early burlesque "The Three Sisters," dedicated to Edward her brother, Elizabeth's new husband. Elizabeth gave birth to 11 children and died shortly after the birth of her final child.

Austen, Frances (Fanny) Catherine (1793–1882) The eldest daughter of Edward and Elizabeth Austen (Knight), Fanny was Jane Austen's first-born niece, close to her aunt, and one of her favorites. Jane Austen wrote to her sister, Cassandra, on October 7, 1808, that she is "almost another Sister & could not have supposed that a neice would ever have been so much to me. She is quite after one's own heart" (*Letters*, 144). Two days afterward, on October 9, Fanny's mother died, and aged 16, she was left "to be companion to her father, mistress of a large household and surrogate mother to her [10] younger brothers and sisters" (*FR*, 170).

Jane Austen dedicated her juvenile pieces "Scraps" to Fanny. They regularly corresponded, and eight of their letters survive. Letters written during 1814–17, in which Jane Austen gives advice on matters of heart and marriage, provide an important insight into her personal perspectives on these subjects. Fanny herself married, in October 1820, the almost 12-years-older Sir Edward Knatchbull (1781–49), becoming his second wife. Sir Edward's first wife, Annabella-Christiana Honywood, died in 1814, leaving Sir Edward a widower with six children. Fanny and Sir Edward had nine children, their eldest son, Edward (1829–93), becoming in

Fanny Austen

1880 first Lord Brabourne. Fanny inherited most of the surviving letters of Jane Austen from Cassandra, her aunt. These were not available to James Edward Austen-Leigh for his 1869 *Memoir*. Following Fanny's death, they were used by Edward her son for his edition of the *Letters of Jane Austen* (1884).

Fanny provided four of the hints contained in Jane Austen's *Plan of a Novel, according to Hints from Various Quarters,* and her reaction to two of her aunt's novels are found in "Opinions of *Mansfield Park*" and "Opinions of *Emma*." Jane gave her as a Christmas present in 1804 a small diary, *The Ladies Complete Pocket Book.* Fanny wrote copious entries from 1804 to 1872, and the years 1804 to 1817 frequently refer to Jane and to other family activities. The diaries are at the Centre for Kentish Studies at Maidstone in Kent.

Austen, Sir Francis William (Frank) (1774–1865)

Frank, as he was known, was Jane Austen's fifth brother, who had the most adventurous and risky life of all the Austen children, whom he outlived by many years. He also lived longer than six of his 11 children. Educated at the Royal Naval Academy, Portsmouth, from just before his 12th birthday in April 1786, he left in December 1788 to go immediately to sea on the HMS *Perseverance,* returning home five years later. He rose rapidly in the ranks, a midshipman in 1791, the following year a lieutenant, a commander in 1798 and a post-captain in 1800. He returned to active service from 1804 to 1815, and in 1830 became a rear admiral. Knighted in 1837 and honored for his war service in 1815, in 1838 he was vice admiral, and 10 years later an admiral serving as commander in chief of the North American and West Indian station. In 1863 he became admiral of the fleet.

He returned to shore duties in 1814 and lived at Chawton Great House, where he was close to his mother and his sisters. In July 1806, he married Mary Gibson of Ramsgate (1785–1823). The first years of their marriage he was largely at sea, and Mary lived with Jane Austen, her mother, and Cassandra in Southampton. From Mary he had six sons and five daughters, number eight being Catherine-Anne (1818–71), who married John Hubback. She followed two of her sons, who emigrated to America in the 1870s. Between 1850 and 1863, she wrote 10

Admiral Sir Francis Austen, anonymous portrait, courtesy the Jane Austen House, Chawton

Frank attended Jane's funeral. He wrote of his sister that "it has been a matter of surprise to those who know her best, how she could at a very early age and with apparently limited means of observation, have been capable of nicely discriminating and pourtraying such varieties of the human character as are introduced in her works." He added, "In her temper, she was chearful and not easily irritated, and tho' rather reserved to strangers . . . yet in the company of those she loved the native benevolence of her heart and kindness of her disposition were forcibly displayed" (*FR*, 230, 273–274).

Following his wife's death in 1823, Frank married in 1828 the 63-year-old Martha Lloyd, the close friend of Jane and Cassandra. She died in 1843. Known as a devout officer, Frank according to the *Memoir* had "great firmness of character," with a "strong sense of duty, whether due from himself to others, or from others to himself. He was consequently a strict disciplinarian." His death in 1865, the last survivor of Jane Austen's generation that personally knew her, prompted James Edward Austen-Leigh's *Memoir* (17, 166).

Austen, George (1766–1838)   Jane Austen's second brother, born at Deane, August 26, 1766, about whom little is known. An epileptic from a young age, possibly deaf as well as dumb, he was unable to be part of the family activities. Boarded out locally, supervised by his parents, and later his brothers, he died on January 17, 1838. He remains unmentioned by name in Jane Austen's letters.

Austen, Rev. George (1731–1805)   Jane Austen's father, according to Henry Austen in his 1817 introduction to *Northanger Abbey* and *Persuasion*, was "a profound scholar" with "a most exquisite taste in every species of literature" ([3]). Indeed, by 1801, he had a library of approximately 500 volumes, which his children had access to. The family described George as "blessed with a bright & hopeful disposition which characterised him during the whole course of his life," with a "mildness and gentleness of temper, and . . . steadiness of principle" (*FR*, 4). Born May 1, 1831, at Tonbridge in Kent, his father, William Austen (1701–37), was a surgeon, and his mother was Rebecca (Walter)

novels, including a completion of *The Watsons*, and her eldest son, John Henry Hubback (1844–1939), collaborated with his daughter Edith Charlotte to write *Jane Austen's Sailor Brothers* (1906).

Frank was the recipient of various letters from his sister and preserved some of them; others he gave away. Six are extant. He was dedicatee of two of the juvenilia: "The Adventures of Mr. Harley" and "Jack and Alice." Jane wrote to him concerning the naming of ships in *Mansfield Park*. He liked the novel "extremely" but thought "that though there might be more Wit in P&P—& an higher Morality in MP—yet altogether, on account of it's peculiar air of Nature throughout, he preferred it [*Emma*] to either." Of *Persuasion*, he wrote, "I do not know whether in the character of Capt. Wentworth [Jane Austen] meant in any degree to delineate that of her Brother [Charles]: perhaps she might—but I rather think parts of Capt. Harville's were drawn from myself. At least some of his domestic habits, tastes and occupations bear a strong resemblance to mine."

Austen, née Hampson (c. 1695–1733). It was her second marriage; she had a son by her first and four from her second. George was the third child; the second, Philadelphia (1730–92), maintained contact with her younger brother and subsequently became part of Jane Austen's family circle.

George's mother died in 1732, and his father remarried in 1736, dying a year later. The children were sent to live with his brother Stephen (1704–51), a bookseller and publisher based in St. Paul's Churchyard, London. Apparently, Stephen treated the children harshly. At around 10 years of age, George returned to Tonbridge to live with an aunt; he became a pupil at Tonbridge School, the fees being paid by his wealthy bachelor uncle, Francis (1698–1791), a solicitor in Sevenoaks in Kent. In 1747, he gained a scholarship to St. John's College, Oxford, where he gained a B.A. degree in 1751. Two years later he gained another award, giving him another seven years in Oxford. In 1754, he obtained an M.A. and was ordained. Following a period as a curate and schoolmaster at his old school Tonbridge, he returned in 1758 to St. John's College. He was described as "Handsome," and "His eyes [were] not large, but of a peculiarly bright hazel . . . The complexion was clear, the countenance animated, & the whole appearance striking" (*FR*, 4).

George could have remained at St. John's for the rest of his life, provided he did not marry. In 1761, through family connections, he obtained the living at Steventon in Hampshire but remained in Oxford until 1764. He probably met his future wife, Cassandra Leigh, in the early 1760s at Oxford—her uncle being at the time the master of Balliol College. They married on April 26, 1764, and went to Steventon. The rectory needed repair, and their married life began in a rented parsonage at Deane, two miles from Steventon, where they lived until 1768, when they moved into a renovated and extended Steventon rectory. George was already supplementing his income by farming. Children began to appear; James, the first of eight who survived, was born in 1765, George in 1766, and Edward in 1767.

Early in 1773, the first daughter, Cassandra, was born, to be followed in December 1775 by Jane Austen. This was a period of financial difficulty,

and George began to take on boarding pupils until 1796, largely coaching them in the classics for university entrance. The financial situation was helped by a monetary gift from James Leigh Perrot, his wife's wealthy brother, and the purchase by Francis his uncle of the Deane living, bringing in additional income.

Although not wealthy, he was able to educate his children, to provide them with an extensive library, and to provide theatrical entertainment at home and musical instruments. His wife had good connections, and his pupils were often from wealthy, well-connected, titled families. In 1800, much to the shock of Jane and Cassandra, he decided to retire to the urban environment of Bath. In retirement, he appears not to have been unhappy and made family trips to the west country and Wales, and also visited Godmersham and Steventon, where his firstborn son, James, was now the curate. He died in Bath on January 21, 1805, leaving his wife but not his daughters provided for.

Clearly he encouraged Jane in her writing, even going so far as offering the early version of *Pride and Prejudice*, called "First Impressions," to the London publisher Cadell and Davies. Jane Austen wrote to her brother Frank the day after her father's death: "he was mercifully spared from knowing that he was about to quit the Objects so beloved, so fondly cherished as his wife & Children ever were—His tenderness as a Father, who can do justice to? . . . The Serenity of the Corpse is most delightful!—It preserves the sweet, benevolent smile which always distinguished him" (*Letters*, 97–98).

Austen, Henry Thomas (1771–1850) Jane Austen was close to her fourth brother, Henry, who acted as her literary representative and arranged for the publication of her novels. He had a varied career, experiencing both wealth and poverty, and displayed considerable flexibility when faced with variegated fortunes. Known for his wit, sociability, and considerable intelligence, he had a sanguine temperament. A relative wrote when meeting the young Jane that "she is very like her brother Henry, not at all pretty & very prim, unlike a girl of twelve."

Born on June 8, 1771, Henry entered St. John's College, Oxford, as a scholar in 1788. A relative wrote to Philadelphia Walter, Jane's father's sister, following a visit to Oxford: "I did not think you would know Henry with his hair powdered & dressed in a very *tonish* [fashionable] style, besides he is at present taller than his Father" (*FR*, 64). He took an active part in the Steventon theatricals, performing the leading roles. Jane dedicated her early "Lesley Castle" to him, dating from probably early 1792. At Oxford, he assisted his brother James with a literary journal, *The Loiterer*.

Graduating in 1792, he received an M.A. four years later and retained his connections with St. John's until 1798. Expected to follow his older brother James into the church, following the outbreak of war with France in 1793, he joined the Oxford militia as a lieutenant. The life clearly suited him, as in 1797 Henry became captain and adjutant. He made enough contacts in this position to resign his commission in 1808 and become a banker and army agent in London. Probably in 1796, he became engaged to Mary Pearson of Greenwich in London, the daughter of a naval captain. According to Henry's relative, she "is a most intolerable Flirt, and reckoned to give herself great Airs" (*FR*, 98). She broke off the engagement in autumn 1796. Ten years previously, Henry had been attracted to his cousin Eliza de Feuillide (1761–1813), who was married at the time. Her husband subsequently died, guillotined in 1794. Her young, sickly son, Hastings (b. 1786), lived with her. On her return from France, they renewed their friendship and married in London on December 31, 1797. She and Henry did not have children.

Clearly, Henry's banking and agency business prospered, as he formed banking partnerships in Alton Hampshire and Hyde in Kent, and in 1813 was appointed to the prestigious position of the receiver general for taxes for the county of Oxfordshire. During this period Jane Austen frequently stayed with him in London. Following the immediate period of his first wife Eliza's death in April 1813, Jane appears to have taken on the role of his housekeeper and confidante. Her letters to her sister, Cassandra, written from Henry's London addresses, reveal something of the nature of her close relationship with Henry.

As a consequence of the period of financial uncertainty following the conclusion of the Napoleonic Wars, Henry's banking activities collapsed, and in March 1816, he went bankrupt. Various members of the family who acted as surety or had money tied up in his ventures lost money. Jane, however, lost only about £13, having invested the profits from her first three novels elsewhere. Henry, forever adaptable, returned to his earlier vocation, the church. By December 1816, he was ordained as a deacon and became the curate at Chawton. He wrote and delivered, Jane wrote her elder brother James Edward on December 16, 1816, "very superior Sermons" (*Letters*, 323). Chaplain to the British embassy in Berlin, he delivered a series of *Lectures upon . . . the Book of Genesis* published in 1820. On the title page, Henry described himself as the domestic chaplain to some distinguished members of the aristocracy.

From the end of December 1819 until 1822, Henry was the Steventon rector. He remarried, in April 1820, Eleanor Jackson. There were no children from the marriage, and she survived him, living until 1864. From 1822 until 1827, Henry served as a curate at Farnham in Surrey and was also master of the grammar school. He and Eleanor lived near Alton in Hampshire, where he was a curate from 1824 until 1839. His last years were spent at Colchester, Essex, and in Tunbridge Wells in Kent, where he died on March 12, 1850.

Through his London contacts and belief in her abilities, Henry was the major force in getting his sister Jane's novels published. He was the first to provide biographical information about her and wrote the introduction to the posthumous publication of *Northanger Abbey* and *Persuasion* (1817/1818). He revealed her identity to the public, and wrote and negotiated on her behalf, repurchasing, for instance, "Susan" from Crosby, the publishers who held onto the copyright, in 1816. In her will, Jane Austen left him a legacy of £50 and according to family tradition "asked Henry to be her literary executor" (*FR*, 259). He attended his sister's funeral and preserved her memory most notably in his "Biographical Notice" of 1817.

Austen, James (1765–1819) Born at Deane on February 13, 1765, Jane Austen's eldest brother and regarded as the poet of the family. The producer of amateur theatricals at the Steventon Parsonage, he played a large part in Jane Austen's early reading and in the formation of her literary taste. Her juvenile playlet "The Visit, a Comedy in 2 Acts" was dedicated to James, who encouraged her following the publication of *Sense and Sensibility* by sending her encouraging verses. He did not attend Jane's funeral, "feeling that in the sad state of his own health and nerves, the trial would be too much for him" (*FR*, 189, 256), although he did compose an elegy "Venta! Within thy sacred fame," containing the couplet "And not a line she ever wrote/ 'Which dying she would wish to blot.'" The complement echoes Ben Jonson of Shakespeare: "in his writing (whatsoever he penned) he never blotted out a line." James Austen also in the poem wrote: "But to her family alone/ Her real & genuine worth was known" (Selwyn, 48–50, 100).

He was known as quiet and studious, and his mother compared him with Edward, his younger brother. Edward "has a most active mind, a clear head, & a sound Judgement, he is quite a man of Business—That my dear James was not—Classical Knowledge, Literary Taste, and the power of Elegant Composition he possessed in the highest degree; to these [Edward] makes no pretensions. *Both* equally good amiable and sweet-temper'd" (Cassandra Austen's emphasis: *FR*, 53).

James went at the early age of 14 in 1779 to St. John's College, Oxford, graduating in 1783 and obtaining an M.A. in 1788. After over a year traveling on the Continent, he entered the church, becoming in 1780 the curate of Stoke Charity in Hampshire. Other curacies followed, although he remained living in Oxford, where, in June 1789, he was ordained as a priest, moving back to the Steventon area in spring 1790 to become curate of Over-ton. In March 1792, he married the well-connected Anne Mathew (1759–95). The daughter of a distinguished general, she was more than 30 when she married James, giving her an allowance of £100 per annum. Other livings were presented to James on his marriage, and in 1792, he and Anne moved into the Deane Parsonage, where their daughter June-Anna Elizabeth (Anna) was born in 1793. She married, in November 1814, Benjamin, the youngest son of the Reverend Isaac Peter George Lefroy (1745–1806), had one son, and six daughters. She preserved the letters she received form her aunt and perpetuated her memory.

On May 3, 1795, James's wife, Anne Mathew then 36, died suddenly following a harsh winter. In January 1797, James remarried Mary Lloyd (1771–1843), whom Jane describes in a May 22, 1817, letter as "in the main *not* a liberal-minded Woman" (Jane Austen's emphasis: *Letters*, 340–341). James and Mary had two children, James Edward and Caroline Mary Craven. James Edward (1798–1874) wrote the *Memoir* of his aunt. His sister (1805–80) did not marry, was very close to her brother, and lived with her mother, then helped her brother with his large family.

Following his father's retirement in 1801, James took over at Steventon, succeeding him on his death in January 1805. James's health deteriorated in his later years, and he distanced himself from the rest of his family. There was a strain in family relations following his remarriage, and Mary Lloyd appears not to have treated her stepdaughter Anna well. Anna increasingly spent more time with Jane and Cassandra. Between January 1789 and March 1790, while at Oxford, James published a weekly periodical, *The Loiterer*. There are affinities in the attitudes toward money, education, and class found in *The Loiterer* and Jane Austen's early writings. Certainly, James encouraged his sister's literary taste and helped with her literary development.

Bath During the late 18th century and early years of the 19th century, Bath was a fashionable spa center offering medicinal baths that were supposed to have curative properties. It is situated 116 miles to the west of London on the road passing Maidenhead, Reading, Hungerford, and Devizes. Jane Austen visited Bath in 1797 and 1799, before her family moved there in 1801. They lived from 1801 to 1804 at 4 Sydney Place, then from 1804 to 1805 at 3 Green Park Buildings East. Following her father's death in January 1805, she and her mother found temporary lodgings at 25 Gay Street, and then probably from January to June 1806 in Trim Street. Jane Austen's wealthy relatives, the Leigh-Perrots, from 1797 rented 1 Paragon and then in 1810 purchased 49 Great Pultney Street.

There are extensive references to areas of Bath, to streets, places, and specific buildings and to its surroundings throughout Jane Austen's letters and other writings. These testify to the importance of Bath and its environs for her. It was a medicinal and social center, a place claiming to restore health, and one in which adults came to find appropriate wealthy marriage partners and social connections. The evidence from Jane Austen's fiction suggests that the author did not care for Bath. Probably in common with Anne Elliot, "She disliked Bath, and did not think it agreed with her—and Bath was to be her home" (*Persuasion*, 14). She found it oppressive and rainy and once the Assembly Room Balls had finished, boring, and she was relieved to leave the town. She writes to her sister, Cassandra, on

July 1, 1808, from Godmersham in Kent, where she is staying temporarily: "It will be two years tomorrow since we left Bath for Clifton [Bristol], with what happy feelings of Escape!" (*Letters*, 138).

During the second half of the 18th century, Bath experienced several housing booms. However, by the conclusion of the Napoleonic Wars in 1815, it was on the decline. Other attractions such as the sea drew visitors away from it, and the assemblies held at the Upper and Lower Rooms attracted fewer people. The wealthy upper middle class and aristocrats went elsewhere. Bath had thrived well as a spa center where people went for the curative properties (see, for instance, *Sense and Sensibility* [208–209] and *Emma* [275, 307]). In *Northanger Abbey*, Catherine and others visited "the Pump-Room, where the ordinary course of events and conversation took place; Mr. Allen, after drinking his glass of water," for which he paid, "joined some gentleman to talk over the politics of the day and compare the accounts of their newspapers." On the other hand, "the ladies walked about together, noticing every new face, and almost every new bonnet in the room" (71).

Not all the visitors were ill or claimed to be ill. Bath offered amenities (*Northanger Abbey*, 78–79) such as subscription libraries, weekly concerts, the theater, and excellent walks around it. Beechen Cliff figures in *Northanger Abbey* (106, 111). The Assembly Room elsewhere offered balls (see, for instance, *Northanger Abbey*, 130, 195, 201; *Emma*, 156; and *The Watsons*, 325). There were numerous

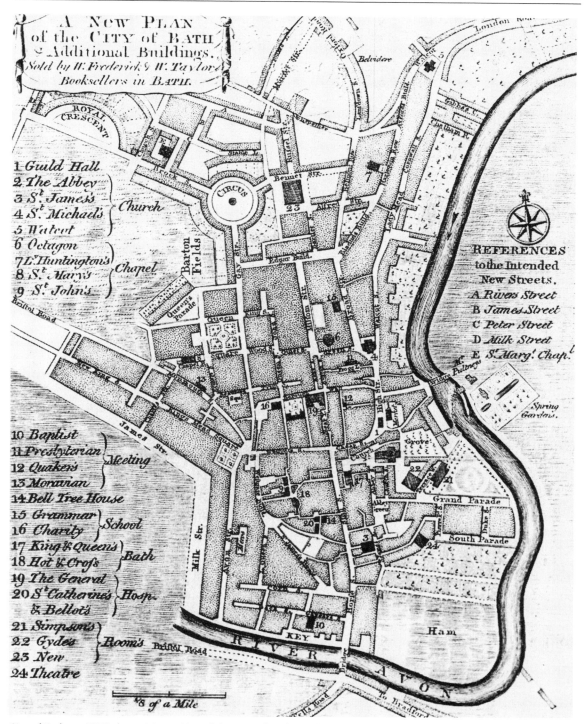

City of Bath, c. 1776, from *A New Plan of the City of Bath & Additional Buildings, 1776,* sold by W. Frederick and W. Taylor

churches of various denominations for worship and social meetings. Jane Austen's father married Jane's mother at Walcot Church in 1764, and in 1805 he was buried there. Leading attractions were the fashionable shops (see *Northanger Abbey*, 25, 29, 217, and *Persuasion*, 141). The town had a good number of stables (*Mansfield Park*, 193) and many clothing shops.

Northanger Abbey and *Persuasion* are especially noteworthy for specific descriptions of streets and the Pump Room, where visitors displayed themselves and the latest fashions. Near the old city and to its west was the Westgate Buildings, described in *Persuasion* (152–153, 157–158, 192). The Austens contemplated living there when they initially moved to Bath. Jane Austen wrote to Cassandra on January 3, 1801: "Westgate Buildings, tho' quite in the lower part of the Town are not badly situated themselves; the street is broad, & has rather a good appearance" (*Letters*, 67). The Leigh-Perrots rented a house at 1 the Paragon. Jane Austen found the place too dark. Near was Queen Square (*Persuasion*, 42). She stayed there in May–June 1799 and wrote to her sister, Cassandra, on May 17, 1799, the day after arriving: "I like our situation very much—it is far more chearful than Pargon, & the prospect form the Drawingroom window at which I now write is rather picturesque" (*Letters*, 41).

In short, Jane Austen's letters and other works are replete with references to Bath, which she knew intimately. It is the largest town where she spent a good deal of her life, the commercial, social, and recuperative center. Bath was the center of the marriage market, too, where eligible spouses were to be found and caught. In *Persuasion*, it becomes associated with decay, corruption, and narcissism, a place where Sir Walter Elliot can preen himself and indulge in a fantasy world of snobbery. On the other hand, it is also the home of Admiral and Mrs. Croft, who went there for medicinal purposes in an attempt to relieve the gout. So Bath is not totally identified with chicanery, vanity, and social climbing.

BIBLIOGRAPHY

Austen, Jane. *Jane Austen's Letters*, collected and edited by Deirdre Le Faye. Oxford: Oxford University Press, 1995.

———. *Emma*. Edited by R. W. Chapman. *The Novels of Jane Austen*. Vol. 4. 3d ed. Oxford: Oxford University Press.

———. *Northanger Abbey and Persuasion*. Edited by R. W. Chapman. 3d ed. *The Novels of Jane Austen*, II. Oxford: Oxford University Press, 1965.

———. *Sense and Sensibility*. Edited by R. W. Chapman. *The Novels of Jane Austen*, Vol. 1. 3d ed. Oxford, U.K.: Clarendon Press, 1943.

———. "The Watsons." In *Minor Works*, edited by R. W. Chapman. *The Works of Jane Austen*, VI. Reprint: 314–363. London: Oxford University Press, 1963.

Olsen, Kirstin. *All Things Austen. An Encyclopedia of Austen's World*. 2 vols. Westport, Conn: Greenwood Press, 2005: I: 54–71.

Pinion, F. B. *A Jane Austen Companion*. London: Macmillan, 1973, 195–200.

Bentley, Richard (1796–1871) Bentley was the founder of the publishing house Richard Bentley and Son (1829–98) and part of the complicated publishing history of *Pride and Prejudice*. The heirs of THOMAS EGERTON owned the copyright of *Pride and Prejudice*; HENRY AUSTEN owned the copyright of Jane Austen's five other published works. Bentley purchased the *Pride and Prejudice* copyright for £40 from Francis Pinkney, Egerton's executor, about whom we know very little. Bentley offered Henry Austen £250 for the other copyrights. Austen accepted the offer, but Bentley, a shrewd businessman, deducted the £40 he paid to Pinkney, and paid Austen on September 20, 1832, only £210.

The publishing house of Bentley published Jane Austen's works from 1832 until the six-volume Steventon Edition of 1882. Smith Elder bought the firm in 1898, and the rights later passed to Macmillan. "When Henry Austen sold his Jane Austen copyrights to Richard Bentley for a modest sum, he could not foretell that these quiet novels . . . would not only yield a substantial yearly profit throughout the century but would occupy a central position in English fiction" (Gettmann, 14).

BIBLIOGRAPHY

Gettmann, Royal A. *A Victorian Publisher: A Study of the Bentley Papers*. Cambridge: Cambridge University Press, 1960.

The Bible and the Book of Common Prayer The Authorized Version of the Bible, or the King James Version (1611), and the 1662 Book of Common Prayer were familiar to Jane Austen from a young age. She knew them from repetition in extract form on a daily basis. She read the Bible, and had the Bible read to her at home or as a part of the church service. She heard on a regular cyclical basis the passages for Sundays and for the religious festivals. Passages from the book of Psalms were used throughout the church services. She herself wrote prayers (see entry on *Prayers* in Part II).

Characters' names in her work, such as Mary, clearly have a biblical source. Interestingly, there are few biblical citations in her novels. An exception is found in *Emma*. Miss Bates misquotes, "We may well say that 'our lot is cast in a goodly heritage'" (174). She is referring to Psalm 16, verses 5–6, "The Lord is the portion of mine inheritance and of my cup: thou maintainest my lot. The lines are fallen onto me in pleasant places; yea, I have a goodly heritage." Often the most selfish and unsympathetic of her characters claim to be men of religion—for instance, Elton in *Emma* and Collins in *Pride and Prejudice*. However, Edmund in *Mansfield Park*, chooses the church as a vocation and takes his duties seriously. In the same novel, Henry Crawford objects to the "redundancies and repetitions" of church services (340).

Clearly biblical morality pervades Jane Austen's writing. For instance, biblical injunctions concerning vanity may be seen in Elizabeth Bennet's attitude toward Wickham, Emma's toward Harriet, and Sir Walter Elliot's self-absorption in *Persuasion*. Her relatively simple diction and clarity owe much to the King James version of the Bible. "In narrative passages," Jane Austen's "taste for brief declarative sentences is something she shares with the gospels. 'Henry and Catherine were married, the bells rang, and every body smiled' [*Northanger Abbey*, 252]. That is in its way a very New Testament sentence" (Grundy, 196).

BIBLIOGRAPHY

Austen, Jane. *Emma*. Edited by R. W. Chapman. *The Novels of Jane Austen*, Vol. 4. 3d ed. Oxford: Oxford University Press, 1986.

———. *Mansfield Park*. Edited by R. W. Chapman. *The Novels of Jane Austen*, Vol. 3. 3d ed. Oxford: Oxford University Press, 1988 reprint.

———. *Northanger Abbey and Persuasion*. Edited by R. W. Chapman. *The Novels of Jane Austen*, II. 3d ed. Oxford: Oxford University Press, 1965.

Grundy, Isabel. "Jane Austen and Literary Traditions." In *The Cambridge Companion to Jane Austen*, edited by Edward Copeland and Juliet McMaster, 189–210. Cambridge: Cambridge University Press, 1997.

Brabourne, Edward, first baron Brabourne (1829–1893) Edward Knatchbull-Hugessen, first baron Brabourne, was the first editor of Jane Austen's letters. Ninety-six of these came into his possession following the death of his mother, Fanny Knight, Lady Knatchbull (1793–1862), Jane Austen's favorite niece. The letters were largely from Jane Austen to her sister, Cassandra, who left them to Fanny on her death in 1845. There were also five letters from Jane Austen to Fanny Knight, nine to Anna Lefroy, one to Jane's niece Cassandra, the daughter of her brother Charles, and two from Jane's sister, Cassandra, to Fanny Knight. The letters were unavailable to James Edward Austen-Leigh at the time he wrote the *Memoirs* in the late 1860s. Following Lord Brabourne's death in 1893, most of the letters were sold to the Pierpont Morgan Library, New York. The *Letters of Jane Austen edited with an introduction and critical remarks by Edward, Lord Brabourne* were published in two volumes by Richard Bentley and Son in 1884.

Brontë, Charlotte (1816–1855) The early Victorian novelist and poet, author of *Jane Eyre* (1847), *Shirley* (1849), and *Villette* (1853). Her views on Jane Austen are considered a barometer of mid–19th-century critical opinions on her predecessor's achievement. Charlotte Brontë's attitudes to Jane Austen are found in her correspondence with the critic GEORGE HENRY LEWES (1817–78) and William Smith Williams (1800–75), the publisher's reader for Smith and Elder largely responsible for the acceptance of *Jane Eyre*.

Brontë's comments to Lewes in a letter dated January 12, 1848, are a reaction to his article on

"Recent Novels: French and English" in *Fraser's Magazine* (December 1847), in which he highly praised Jane Austen's achievement. Lewes called Jane Austen a "*prose* Shakespeare" (Lewes's emphasis), and proclaimed "that Fielding and Miss Austen are the greatest novelists in our language." For Lewes, Sir Walter Scott lacked "two Shakespearian qualities—tenderness and passion."

Brontë responds by asking Lewes, "Why do you like Miss Austen so very much? I am puzzled on that point. What induced you to say that you would rather written *Pride and Prejudice* or *Tom Jones* than any of the Waverley Novels?" She finds Austen's world too constricting, describing *Pride and Prejudice* as "An accurate, daguerreotyped portrait of a commonplace face [referring to engraved portraits of Elizabeth Bennet found, for instance, in the 1833 Bentley edition of the novel]; a carefully fenced, high-cultivated garden, with neat borders and delicate flowers." For Charlotte Brontë, the French novelist George Sand (1804–76) "is sagacious and profound. Miss Austen is only shrewd and observant." In a letter of January 18, 1848, she asks Lewes, "Can there be a great artist without poetry?" It is poetry that Jane Austen lacks. Charlotte Brontë adds that Jane Austen "being . . . without 'sentiment,' without *poetry*, may be *is* sensible (more *real* than *true*), but she cannot be great" (Brontë's emphasis).

In her April 12, 1850, letter to W. S. Williams, she comments on her reading of *Emma*, finding it wanting. Jane Austen "does her business of delineating the surface of the lives of genteel English people curiously well," but "the Passions are perfectly unknown to her." Charlotte Brontë adds that Jane Austen's "business is not half so much with the human heart as with the human eyes, both, hands and feet . . . what throbs fast and full, through hidden, what the blood rushes through, what is the unseen seat of Life and the sentient target of death—*this* Miss Austen ignores." Essentially, Jane Austen was "a very incomplete, and rather insensible (not *senseless*) woman" (Brontë's emphasis). To sum up, Charlotte Brontë's correspondence with Lewes and Williams "provides the key statement of the Romantic case against Jane Austen, a case determined . . . by a personal, temperamental incompatibility" (Southam, 1: 124–128, 24).

See also Henry Fielding, and Sir Walter Scott.

BIBLIOGRAPHY

Jane Austen. Volume I, 1811–1870: The Critical Heritage. Edited by B. C. Southam. London and New York: Routledge, 1979.

Brontë, Charlotte. *The Letters of Charlotte Brontë with a Selection of Letters by Family and Friends.* 3 vols. Edited by Margaret Smith. Oxford, U.K.: Clarendon Press, 1995–2003.

Brydges, Sir Samuel Egerton (1762–1837) Brydges, the writer and genealogist (no relation to Thomas Egerton), moved with his wife to Hampshire in 1786 to be near his sister, Jane Austen's friend and mentor, Anne Lefroy, née Brydges (1749–1804). He found Jane Austen at around the age of 14 to be "fair and handsome, slight and elegant, but with cheeks a little too full" (*Memoirs*, 44). Brydges wrote two novels, *Mary de Clifford* (1792) and *Arthur Fitz Albini* (1798). About the latter, Jane Austen comments to her sister, Cassandra, "it does not quite satisfy my feelings that we should purchase the only one of Egerton's works of which his family are ashamed. . . . There are many characters introduced, apparently merely to be delineated" (November 25, 1798: *Letters*, 22). In 1808, Brydges revised Collins's *Peerage of England*. The work's original compiler, Arthur Collins, using panegyrics, had dedicated volumes of this work to members of the nobility. Collins and Egerton may well have been the inspiration for the names and portions of the characters of Mr. Collins and Lady Catherine de Bourgh in *Pride and Prejudice*. Sir Egerton proudly traced his own family relationship to the "House of De Burgh."

In 1810, Brydges moved to Lee Priory near Canterbury in Kent and set up his own private Lee Priory Press in the servants' quarters. Four years later, he became a baronet, but owing to his extravagance, in 1818, he had to flee to the Continent.

BIBLIOGRAPHY

Austen-Leigh, J. E. *A Memoir of Jane Austen and Other Family Recollections.* Edited by K. Sutherland. Oxford: Oxford University Press [World's Classics], 2002.

Le Faye, Deirdre. *Jane Austen's Letters.* Edited by Deirdre Le Faye. 3d ed. Oxford: Oxford University Press, 1995.

Pinion, F. B. *A Jane Austen Companion: A Critical Survey and Reference Book.* London: Macmillan, 1973.

burlesque   A literary term applied to Jane Austen's early writing, her juvenilia, and to *Northanger Abbey.* M. H. Abrams in his *A Glossary of Literary Terms* defines a "Burlesque" as an imitation in "the manner (the form and style) or else the subject matter of a serious literary work or a literary *genre* . . . but makes the imitation amusing by a ridiculous disparity between the manner and the matter." There are various forms of burlesque. It can be a parody imitating the manner or the "characteristic features of a particular literary work, or the distinctive style of a particular author." For instance, Jane Austen's *Northanger Abbey* pokes fun at the genre of the gothic novel (27). The early juvenilia "Love and Freindship," "The History of England," and "Jack and Alice" are each instances of burlesque. "Love and Freindship" imitates the 18th-century epistolary novel. "The History of England" ridicules popular historical works such as Goldsmith's *History of England* (1764), and in "Jack and Alice," Jane Austen "mimics the inflated rhetoric, the rhythms and cliché diction of sentimental fiction" (Southam, 246). In her later work, the burlesque elements are "subtler, more allusive, and . . . more closely interwoven with the fabric of the story" (Lascelles, 64).

BIBLIOGRAPHY

Abrams, M. H. *A Glossary of Literary Terms.* 8th ed. Boston: Thomson, 2005, 27–29.

Lascelles, Mary. *Jane Austen and Her Art.* Oxford, U.K.: Clarendon Press, 1939, 55–66 [a detailed explanation of "burlesque."]

Southam, Brian. "Juvenilia." In *The Jane Austen Companion,* edited by J. David Grey, A. Walton Litz, and Brian Southam, 244–255. New York: Macmillan, 1986.

Burney, Mrs. Fanny (Mme d'Arblay: 1752–1840) Jane Austen's father in July 1796 subscribed to Fanny Burney's three-volume *Camilla* (1796), and she refers to it with admiration in her letters. On September 15, 1796, Jane Austen writes to Cassandra, "There are two Traits in" the "character" of a mutual friend "which are pleasing; namely, she admires Camilla, & drinks no cream in her Tea" (9). Somewhat ironically in *Northanger Abbey,* John Thorpe finds *Camilla* boring and stops reading it after the first few chapters: "such unnatural stuff! . . . there is nothing in the world in it but an old man's playing at see-saw and learning Latin" (49). *Camilla,* and the earlier *Cecilia* (1782), are used in *Northanger Abbey* to illustrate the achievement of fiction. In spite of this testament to her admiration for another female novelist of manners who was until the flop of *The Wanderer* (1814) a highly successful novelist, there are not many references to Fanny Burney in Jane Austen's letters or fiction. There are mentions of characters such as Captain Mirvan and Madame Duval in *Evelina,* published in 1778 (see, for instance, letters to Cassandra, November 26, 1815, February 8, 1807, *Letters,* 302, 120).

In a letter written ?mid-July 1814, to her niece Anna, who has started to write fiction, Jane Austen does not recommend to copy Lord Orville's style of "speaking [in the] 3d person [as a] Lover" in *Evelina* (*Letters,* 267). There are distinct plot resemblances between Burney's *Evelina* and Jane Austen's youthful, unfinished fragment "Catharine or the Bower." Both may "fittingly be subtitled 'The History of a Young Lady's Entrance into the World'" (Southam, 38). Both have as a heroine a girl who is brought up in rural isolation by a guardian, and both are subject to temptation while visiting London.

In a passage in *Northanger Abbey,* Jane Austen probably alludes to Fanny Burney's *Camilla* in the comment: "the advantages of natural folly in a beautiful girl have been already set forth by the capital pen of a sister author" (111). In *Sanditon* she recalls Camilla's being unable to stop herself buying trinkets she cannot afford. Austen's Charlotte "repressed farther solicitation. . . . She had not *Camilla's* youth, and had no intention of having her Distress" (Jane Austen's emphasis, 390). Probably Jane Austen took the title of *Pride and Prejudice* from the fifth volume and last chapter of *Cecilia*, "where the phrase 'Pride and Prejudice' is repeated three times in quick succession and given further prominence by being printed in capitals" (*Family Record*, 190). Thematic parallels between Jane Austen's work and Fanny Burney's are not difficult to find. They include the theme of education and self-control found in *Camilla* and in the later *The Wanderer*—an important element in *Sense and Sensibility*. Catherine Morland's relationship with her mother also owes something to *Camilla*, whose parents believe that Camilla "has been spoilt by high life" and Elizabeth Bennet "as a poor heroine destined to marry a wealthy aristocrat, resembles Evelina and Camilla." Also "Darcy as a 'patrician hero' has . . . affinity with Fanny Burney's Lord Orville and Edgar Mandlebert" (Butler, 179, 199). Essentially then, Jane Austen admired and learned from the art of Fanny Burney, who in 1793 married a French general exiled in England and from 1802 to 1812 was interned by Napoleon in France. However, "it is only by reading Fanny Burney that one can realize how far" (Pinion, 168–169) superior Jane Austen's own artistic achievement is.

BIBLIOGRAPHY

Austen, Jane. *Jane Austen's Letters.* Collected and Edited by Deirdre Le Faye. 3d ed. Oxford: Oxford University Press, 1995.

———. *Northanger Abbey and Persuasion.* Edited by R. W. Chapman. *The Novels of Jane Austen*, V. 3d ed. London: Oxford University Press, 1965.

———. *Pride and Prejudice.* Edited by R. W. Chapman. *The Novels of Jane Austen*, Vol. 2. 3d ed. London: Oxford University Press, 1965.

———. *Sanditon* in *Minor Works.* Edited by R. W. Chapman. *The Works of Jane Austen*, Vol. 6. London: Oxford University Press, 1963.

Butler, Marilyn. *Jane Austen and the War of Ideas.* Oxford, U.K.: Clarendon Press, 1963.

Pinion, F. B. *A Jane Austen Companion: A Critical Survey and Reference Book.* London: Macmillan, 1973.

Southam, Brian C. *Jane Austen's Literary Manuscripts: A Study of the Novelist's Development through the Surviving Papers.* New edition. London and New York: Athlone Press, 2001.

Burns, Robert (1759–1796)   Jane Austen probably read the work of the Scottish rural romantic love poet Robert Burns. His work is referred to, however, only in *Sanditon*. Sir Edward Denham says of Burns's "Lines to his Mary" that "there is Pathos to madden one!—If ever there was a Man who *felt*, it was Burns." He continues mentioning other poets such as JAMES MONTGOMERY (1771–1854), WILLIAM WORDSWORTH (1770–1850), and THOMAS CAMPBELL (1777–1844). "But Burns—I confess my sence [sic] of his Pre-eminence." When she is able to reply, the heroine Charlotte responds, "I have read several of Burns's Poems with great delight . . . but I am not poetic enough to separate a Man's Poetry entirely from his Character;—& Poor Burns's known Irregularities [a reference to his womanizing and predilection for the bottle] greatly interrupt my enjoyment of his Lines." She adds, "I have difficulty in depending on the *Truth* of his Feelings as a Lover. I have not faith in the *sincerity* of the affections of a Man of his Description. He felt & he wrote & he forgot." Sir Edward, in response, leaps to Burns's defense: "He was all ardour & Truth!—His Genius & his Susceptibilities might lead him into some Aberrations—But who is perfect?" (Jane Austen's emphasis, 397–398).

BIBLIOGRAPHY

Austen, Jane. *Sanditon.* In *Minor Works*, edited by R. W. Chapman. *The Works of Jane Austen*, Vol. 6. London: Oxford University Press, 1963.

Byron, George Gordon, sixth baron (Lord Byron) (1788–1824)   There are few references to the rebellious romantic poet Byron in Jane Austen's letters. On March 5, 1814, she begins a letter to her sister, Cassandra: "I have read the Corsair, mended my petticoat, & have nothing else to do" (*Letters*, 257). While she was writing *Persuasion*, Jane Austen copied out "Napoleon's Farewell," Byron's dramatic monologue written just before the ship carrying Napoleon to exile in St. Helena set sail. Captain Benwick self-indulgently in *Persuasion* displays a love for Byron, whom he compares with Scott, and lines from *The Corsair* (1816) are also quoted in the novel, as are references to other poems by Byron: *The Giaour* (1813) and *The Bride of Abydos* (1813) (107, 167, 109, 100).

Jane Austen's *Mansfield Park* and *Emma* were published by John Murray—Byron's publisher. Peter Knox-Shaw writes, "the scene on the Cobb" in *Persuasion* "unfolds a medley of Byronic motifs— leaps, strong arms, and 'lifeless' forms; and . . . the language too, is given a Byronic twist, even down to the negative and asyndeton [omission of conjunctions]" characteristic of Byron's early verse (233–234).

BIBLIOGRAPHY

Austen, Jane. *Jane Austen's Letters.* Collected and edited by Deirdre Le Faye. 3d ed. Oxford: Oxford University Press, 1995.

————. *Jane Austen: Collected Poems and Verses of the Austen Family.* Edited by David Selwyn. Manchester, U.K.: Carcanet Press, 1996.

————. *Northanger Abbey and Persuasion.* Edited by R. W. Chapman. *The Novels of Jane Austen*, Vol. 5. 3d ed. London: Oxford University Press, 1965.

Knox-Shaw, Peter. *Jane Austen and the Enlightenment.* Cambridge: Cambridge University Press, 2004.

C

Cadell and Davies This London publishing house was started by the bookseller Thomas Cadell the elder (1742–1802) and continued by his son Thomas Cadell the younger (1773–1836). From 1793, the firm operated as Cadell and Davies. Cadell earlier published, with the publisher William Strahan (1715–85), Gibbon's *Decline and Fall of the Roman Empire* (1776–1778), Mackenzie's *The Man of Feeling* (1771), and, among others, the poetry of ROBERT BURNS from 1787 onward.

In autumn 1797, Jane Austen's father offered Cadell her "First Impressions," a novel in letters. Her father failed to inform Cadell that this novel was a comedy dealing with manners. Cadell did not even bother to look at the manuscript and instructed his clerk to reject it immediately. "First Impressions" became *PRIDE AND PREJUDICE*.

BIBLIOGRAPHY

Le Faye, Deirdre. *Jane Austen: The World of Her Novels*. New York: Harry N. Abrams, 2002.

Campbell, Thomas (1777–1844) A line from the poet Thomas Campbell's "Pleasures of Hope" (1799) is quoted in *SANDITON*. Sir Edward Denham comments: "Campbell in his pleasures of Hope has touched the extreme of our Sensations—'Like Angel's visits, few & far between.'" Sir Edward adds, "Can you conceive any thing more subduing, more melting, more fraught with deep Sublime than that Line?" (397). There is here in the mention of "Sublime" a reference to a key concept relating to 18th-century thought. Edmund Burke, in the middle of the 18th century, attributed the origins of the sublime to things "in any sort terrible" and "fitted in any sort to excite the ideas of pain, and danger." Nature, such as the Alps and the Lake Country in England, were described as wild, stormy, and ominous—shades of the gothic depicted in *Northanger Abbey*. With the romantics, and a later generation, the sublime began to be related to internal perceptions of nature—see, for instance, Marianne Dashwood's responses in *SENSE AND SENSIBILITY* (Abrams, 317–318).

Today a neglected writer, Thomas Campbell, the son of a Glasgow merchant, was a prolific poet and continued producing into the early Victorian era, his last collection, *The Pilgrim of Glencoe*, appearing in 1842. He also composed nationalistic, and for a Scot, somewhat ironically titled songs celebrating military exploits, such as "Ye Mariners of England." Campbell's collection *The Pleasures of Hope* was published in 1799.

See also ROBERT BURNS, JAMES MONTGOMERY, and WILLIAM WORDSWORTH.

BIBLIOGRAPHY

Austen, Jane. *Sanditon*. In *Minor Works*, edited by R. W. Chapman. *The Works of Jane Austen*, Vol. 6. 363–427. London: Oxford University Press.

Abrams, M. H. *A Glossary of Literary Terms*. 8th ed. Boston: Thomson, 2005, 317–318.

Carnell, Geoffrey. "Campbell, Thomas (1777–1844)." In *Oxford Dictionary of National Biography*, 60 vols., edited by H. C. G. Matthew and Brian Harrison, 9, 863–866. Oxford: Oxford University Press, 2004.

chronology of Austen's composition There has been a lively critical debate concerning the actual dates at which Jane Austen is thought to have written her works. Apart from remarks made by her nephew James Edward Austen-Leigh in his *Memoir,* there is very little specific evidence to support precise dating. No manuscript of Jane Austen's six novels is known to be extant apart from two chapters of *Persuasion.* The other surviving manuscripts are of the juvenilia, such as *Lady Susan,* but these may have been revisions made at a later date. A rough draft of *The Watsons* survives, written on paper from 1803. Fanny Caroline Lefroy (1820–85), daughter of Anna (1793–1872), commented in 1883: "Somewhere in 1804 [Jane Austen] began 'The Watsons,' but her father died early in 1805, and it was never finished" (cited Sutherland, 15).

Following Jane Austen's death, her sister, Cassandra, drew up dates of composition (see *Minor Works:* facing p. 242). These dates are examined in considerable detail by Kathryn Sutherland (12–22). Essentially, she assigns the composition of the *Juvenilia* to c. 1787–93, the drafting of *Sir Charles Grandison* to 1790–1800, also to that period various "juvenilia" and the earliest drafts of *Sense and Sensibility, Pride and Prejudice,* and *Northanger Abbey.* The years 1803–09 are on the whole creatively fallow, and the following period, 1809–17, prolific (20–22).

In an appendix to his revised edition of *Jane Austen's Literary Manuscripts: A Study of the Novelist's Development through the Surviving Papers* (2001), Brian Southam takes issue with Q. D. Leavis's "A Critical Theory of Jane Austen's Writings," found in articles published in *Scrutiny* between 1941 and 1944. Leavis insists that an investigation into Jane Austen's compositional procedure is crucial, otherwise "no criticism of her novels can be just or even safe" (86). Her arguments are complex. She is concerned to demonstrate that Jane Austen was a dedicated professional writer working slowly and over a considerable time period. *Mansfield Park,* for instance, went through at least three stages, evolv-

ing from *Lady Susan* and *Emma* from *The Watsons* (see Kinch, 140–144, Southam, [141]).

Southam disagrees specifically concerning *Lady Susan* and *The Watsons,* believing that the "confusion . . . dates from the publication of *Sense and Sensibility*" (141–142). Essentially "stronger evidence of the change . . . from *The Watsons* to *Emma* is necessary" (153). Southam does not, however, dissent from Leavis in believing that Jane Austen was a serious dedicated professional writer. On the other hand, Sutherland places importance on the actual publication dates of the novels and "brings into focus and creative association the full range of the non-published writings" (13). Taking these into consideration, with Cassandra's notes and references in Jane Austen's letters, "*Sense and Sensibility* and *Pride and Prejudice,* must each have taken shape, wholly or partly, in more than one draft, between 1795–8 and 1810–12." For a period during 1811, Jane Austen had three novels in the works: *Pride and Prejudice, Mansfield Park,* and, in April 1811, she corrected proofs for *Sense and Sensibility.* "*Persuasion* was begun on 8 August 1815 and the first draft completed on 18 July 1816 (with a revised ending written by 6 August 1816)." Sutherland concludes that Jane Austen's compositional procedures include "alongside new ventures the mining over time of manuscript fragments and the revision of earlier completed writings, a pattern which leaves us with *Sanditon,* her final work, as the sequel to *Northanger Abbey,* one of her earliest" (17–20). In view of the lack of specific factual data, controversy and speculation will continue.

BIBLIOGRAPHY

Austen, Jane. *Minor Works,* edited by R. W. Chapman. *The Works of Jane Austen,* Vol. 6. London: Oxford University Press, 1963.

Kinch, M. B., William Baker, and John Kimber. *F. R. Leavis and Q. D. Leavis: An Annotated Bibliography.* New York and London: Garland, 1989, 140–145.

Leavis, Q. D. "A Critical Theory of Jane Austen's Writings (1)," *Scrutiny* 10 (June 1, 1941): 61–87.

Litz, A. Walton. "Chronology of Composition." In *The Jane Austen Companion,* edited by J. David Grey, A. Walton Litz, and Brian Southam, 388–391. New York: Macmillan, 1986.

Southam, Brian C. "Theories of Composition for *Mansfield Park* and *Emma*." In Brian C. Southam. *Jane Austen's Literary Manuscripts: A Study of the Novelist's Development through the Surviving Papers*. Revised edition, [141]–153. New York and London: Athlone Press, 2001.

Sutherland, Kathryn. "Chronology of Composition and Publication." In *Jane Austen in Context*, edited by Janet Todd, 12–22. Cambrdige: Cambridge University Press, 2005.

chronology within Austen's novels R. W. Chapman in his Appendix "Chronology of *Mansfield Park*" to his edition of the novel observes that "the only full date given is that of the ball at Mansfield Park, which was Thursday, 22 December . . . 22 Dec. was a Thursday in 1808." Chapman then writes: "We do not suppose that Miss Austen used an almanac for any purpose except that of convenience, or that she conceived the events of the story as necessarily belonging to an actual year" ([554]). Chapman proceeds to demonstrate a complex narrative chronology beginning with the Mansfield ball (253, 256) and concluding with Sunday May 7, 1809, with Edmund opening his heart to Fanny (556).

The novel in fact opens with Sir Thomas Ward marrying Miss Maria Ward "About thirty years ago" ([3]), then moving to about 26 years later and July when Fanny Price is 18 (40), and concluding in May of the following year—1809. The novel thus comes a full circle in terms of generations. The 20th-century novelist Vladimir Nabokov (1899–1977), in his Cornell University lectures given in the early 1950s on *Mansfield Park* and other works of fiction, creates his own chronology of the novel. It begins with the note "'About thirty years ago': 1811 (the year 'Mansfield Park' was begun)—30 = 1781" and concludes as Chapman's Chronology with "1809. Summer Edmund opens his heart to Fanny" (8, 61). Nabokov shows that the chronology of Austen's novel is intricate and essential to the fabric of her work.

Chapman's "Chronology of *Emma*," an appendix to his edition of the novel, also demonstrates a cyclical pattern beginning in late September and concluding the following autumn (September; October and November), in which three weddings occur (497–498). Marcia McClintock Folsom, in her "Teaching about *Emma*'s Chronology," shows that the chronology "is carefully constructed" and "that Austen conceives of the novel as taking place over fourteen months, during which Emma must have had a birthday, so that she would be twenty-one when she marries." The action of *Emma* moves from September 1813 through each of the subsequent months and concludes in November 1814 (11–12).

Sense and Sensibility starts "early in September," Elinor and Marianne are in London after Christmas, and over the Easter holidays at the Palmers' estate. The novel concludes with Elinor's wedding and her move to Delaford by Michaelmas (September 29): again, a cyclical pattern over a year's duration (28, 374). No specific date is given. Similarly, *Pride and Prejudice* begins in September, during the hunting season, Jane is in London after Christmas, Elizabeth spends Easter with the Collinses, she goes to the north Midlands during the summer, and then to Longbourn. The novel finishes in autumn—again a cyclical process. There is a scholarly consensus that the novel "is set in the 1811–1812 period" (Modert, 55).

Northanger Abbey has a more compressed time frame. The events occur largely during an 11-week period starting with Catherine's Bath visit. Seven weeks later, she visits the Tilneys to return home a month later (220). The novel concludes with her marriage to Henry Tilney "within a twelvemonth from the first day of their meeting" (252). Complete dates are absent from the novel, although the months of February, March, and April are named (63, 177, 216). The detailed "Chronology of *Northanger Abbey*" in Chapman's edition begins with "Three or four days . . . spent in learning what was mostly worn," moves to "Mon. '2' Feb. The Upper Rooms," and finished with "Wed. '22' April. Mrs. Morland looks for the *Mirror*, and makes the acquaintance of Mr. Henry Tilney" ([275]–277). No complete dates are given in the novel, and there is a scholarly dispute over the years in which the novel takes place (1798 seems to be the year having the majority opinion [Modert, 55]).

The only novel to begin with a specific year is *Persuasion*, and the time is summer 1814 (8).

The Elliots depart from Kellynch in September, and the Crofts move in at Michaelmas (33, 48, 206). Anne spends Christmas of 1814 with Lady Russell. She then goes to Bath, where the novel concludes either in later February or early March 1815. *The Watsons* is even more precise, beginning on "Tuesday Octr ye 13th" ([314]), with October 13 beginning on either 1801 or 1807. The important point is that Jane Austen's chronology is integral to her artistry and to the very structure of her novels, to the "development of events, one event causing another, a transition from one theme to another, the cunning way characters are brought in, or a new complex of action is started, or the various themes are linked up, or used to move the novel forward" (Fredson Bowers, in Nabokov, 16).

BIBLIOGRAPHY

Austen, Jane. *Emma*. Edited by R. W. Chapman. *The Novels of Jane Austen*, Vol. 4. 3d ed. Oxford: Oxford University Press, 1986.

———. *Mansfield Park*. Edited by R. W. Chapman. *The Novels of Jane Austen*, Vol. 3. 3d ed. Oxford: Oxford University Press, 1988 reprint.

———. *Northanger Abbey and Persuasion*. Edited by R. W. Chapman. *The Novels of Jane Austen*, Vol. 2. 3d ed. Oxford: Oxford University Press, 1965.

———. *Pride and Prejudice*. Edited by R. W. Chapman. *The Novels of Jane Austen*, Vol. 2. 3d ed. Oxford: Oxford University Press, 1932.

———. *Sense and Sensibility*. Edited by R. W. Chapman. *The Novels of Jane Austen*, Vol. 1. 3d ed. Oxford, U.K.: Clarendon Press, 1943.

———. "The Watsons." In *Minor Works*, edited by R. W. Chapman. *The Works of Jane Austen*, Vol. 6. London: Oxford University Press, 1963.

Folsom, Maria McClintock. "Teaching about *Emma's* chronology" in *Approaches to Teaching Austen's Emma*, edited by Marcia McClintock Folsom, 9–12. New York: MLA, 2004.

Modert, Jo. "Chronology within the Novels." In *The Jane Austen Companion*, edited by J. David Grey, A. Walton Litz, and Brian Southam, 53–60. New York: Macmillan, 1986.

Nabokov, Vladimir. *Lectures on Literature*. Edited by Fredson Bowers, with an introduction by John Updike. New York and London: Harcourt Brace Jovanovich, Bruccoli Clark, 1980.

Clarke, the Reverend James (James Stanier Clarke) (1767–1834)

The Reverend James Stanier Clarke was an author and biographer. From 1795 to 1799, he served as a naval chaplain and in 1799 began the *Naval Chronicle*, which lasted for 20 years. In the same year, he became the domestic chaplain and in 1805 the librarian to the Prince of Wales, subsequently the prince regent. In addition, from 1790 to 1834 he was a rector in Sussex and from 1808 until his death a Canon of Windsor. Clearly, someone with the highest social connections, he is of interest to students of Jane Austen. Three extant letters from her to him survive; he was responsible for Jane Austen dedicating *Emma* to the prince regent, and his letters to Jane Austen and "creative" suggestions to her provided the stimulus for her burlesque "Plan of a Novel."

The *Emma* dedication to the prince was the result of a chance encounter with one of the prince regent's physician, who was treating her brother Henry in the late autumn of 1815. Jane Austen had completed the novel and, with Henry, was negotiating publication terms with John Murray. Henry, however, fell dangerously ill. The chance meeting with one of the royal physicians led to an invitation to visit the royal residence at Carlton House. The librarian James Stanier Clarke told Jane that she could dedicate her next work to the prince. Jane wrote to him on November 15, 1815, requesting a clarification. The following day, Clarke wrote her a flowery reply confirming that she had permission to dedicate a work to the prince regent, who "has read and admired all your publications." In addition to thanking her "for the pleasure your volumes have given me," Clarke suggested that she write a novel based on "the habits of life, and character, and enthusiasm of a clergyman, who should pass his time between the metropolis and the country."

Jane Austen's December 11, 1815, reply informing Clarke of *Emma's* dedication to the prince suggests that she did so somewhat under pressure from her publisher, John Murray. She thanks Clarke for "thinking [her] capable of drawing such a clergyman as you gave the sketch" in his letter, "But I assure you I am *not*." She adds, "The comic part of the character I might be equal to, but not the good, the enthusiastic, the literary." Clarke wrote Jane Austen on December 21, 1815, praising *Emma* and again suggesting that she introduce "an English clergyman" and "Carry your Clergyman to Sea as the Friend of some distinguished Naval Character about a Court." Clarke's suggestions form the foundation for Jane Austen's PLAN OF A NOVEL (see Part II), probably meant as family entertainment and written around May 1816.

Clarke as the prince regent's librarian formally thanked Jane Austen for the presentation copy of *Emma* in a letter dated March 27, 1816. Another suggestion for a novel was made. The prince regent's daughter Princess Charlotte had become engaged to Prince Leopold of Saxe-Cobourg. Clarke wrote: "Perhaps when you again appear in print you may chuse to dedicate your Volumes to Prince Leopold: any Historical Romance, illustrative of the History of the august house of Coburg, would just now be very interesting." The reply, dated April 1, 1816, was polite but firm. Jane Austen admits that such a suggestion "might be much more to the purpose of Profit or Popularity; than such pictures of domestic Life in Country Villages as I deal in." However, she "could no more write a Romance than an Epic Poem.—I could not sit seriously down to write a serious Romance under any other motive than to save my Life, & if it were indispensable for me to keep it up & never relax into laughing at myself or other people, I am sure I should be hung before I had finished the first Chapter." She adds, "No—I must keep to my own style & go on in my own Way" (*Letters*, 296–297; 305–306, 311–312). Clarke does not seem to have replied. He did, however, possess a copy of the posthumously published *Northanger Abbey and Persuasion* (Gilson, A9, x, 89).

BIBLIOGRAPHY

Austen, Jane. *Jane Austen's Letters.* Collected and edited by Deirdre Le Faye. 3d ed. Oxford: Oxford University Press, 1995.

Austen-Leigh, J. E. *A Memoir of Jane Austen and Other Family Recollections*, edited by Kathryn Sutherland.
Oxford World's Classics. Oxford: Oxford University Press, 2002.

Gilson, David J. *A Bibliography of Jane Austen.* Winchester, Hampshire, U.K.; New Castle, Del.: St. Paul's Bibliographies: Oak Knoll Press, 1997.

clergy/church/religion In the 18th century, entering the church was a profession rather than a vocation. The clerical life was considered appropriate for a gentleman with education, as it offered generally reasonable living accommodation and power. The problem was to have sufficient contacts to find a parish where the parson was able to live in the manner of a country landowner. The clergy did not have fixed salaries, and their income had to be drawn from various sources. These included tithe payments—the parson received by right a 10th of the annual gross product from all the land cultivated in his parish. Fees were also charged for baptisms, marriages, and burials. A parish could offer more than one living. For instance, during the 1770s, the living at Steventon was assessed at £100 a year and the neighboring Deane one at £110. So Jane Austen's father, combining the two together, had a reasonable annual income to provide for his family. In addition, he tutored pupils in Greek and Latin at home for payment, preparing them for university entrance.

The clergyman's duties were by no means full-time. Though he had to attend his church on Sundays to conduct the morning and evening service, a sermon was not mandatory. On at least three occasions during the year he held the Holy Communion services. Sundays could also be the day for weddings and funerals. Baptisms, especially of unwell babies, had of necessity to take place on other days. There were yearly and irregular parish meetings to attend, and sick visiting was expected. Nonetheless, some livings or church properties were advertised as conducive to the best fishing, shooting, or hunting, and there were abuses.

Jane Austen's father seems to have taken his position seriously. In aristocratic families, the elder son managed the estate, the middle ones tended to enter the law or the church, and the younger sons entered the military. The Reverend George Austen was the third of four children, the son of a surgeon and the only son to survive. Because he was well educated and without an estate to manage, it is no surprise that after Oxford he should enter the church. Of Jane Austen's brothers, James, the eldest, after Oxford went into the church; her third brother, Edward, was adopted when young by a wealthy family and became a country gentleman. Her second brother, George, was disadvantaged and probably deaf. Henry, her fourth brother, joined the militia, became a banker, lost his money, and eventually became a curate. Her other younger brothers, Francis William, the fifth brother, and youngest brother Charles John, both had very successful naval careers.

The clergymen who figure in her works exemplify Jane Austen's perceptions of the Church of England. In *Sense and Sensibility,* the indecisive Edward Ferrars takes holy orders more or less as a last resort and is extremely fortunate that Colonel Brandon presents him with the Delaford living. In *Pride and Prejudice,* William Collins, "by fortunate chance" (70), receives from the wealthy, well-connected Lady Catherine de Bourgh the sumptuous Hunsford rectorship in Kent. Collins sees his main responsibility as not the service of his parishioners, but to serve only one of them. He flatters and is exceedingly servile to his patroness, Lady Catherine, considers others as inferiors, and will do whatever she demands. In *Northanger Abbey,* Henry Tilney serves the family living at Woodston by riding over to it for two or three days per week. In *Mansfield Park,* Mary Crawford is annoyed that Edmund Bertram intends to take his clerical duties seriously and take up full-time residence in Thornton Lacey, where his parish is. In *Emma,* Elton, although vain and mean, on the lookout for a wealthy, well-connected wife, does take the Highbury parish duties seriously. In *Persuasion,* Charles Hayter, "a very amiable, pleasing young man," intends to be a conscientious curate. He is succeeding the elderly Uppercross rector Dr. Shirley, who has "zealously" discharged his duties for over 40 years." Shirley and his wife are "excellent people . . . who have been doing good all their lives" (73, 102).

Edmund Bertram encapsulates the perception that the clergy should serve as local role models.

He says, "We do not look in great cities for our best morality . . . A fine preacher is followed and admired; but it is not in fine preaching only that a good clergyman will be useful in his parish and his neighbourhood." In London, "the clergy are lost . . . in the crowds of their parishioners," whereas in the country, they are known by their conduct and example (93). In *Mansfield Park,* the worldly and cynical Sir Thomas Bertram presents an alternative perception of what a "parish priest" (the sole use in the novels of the word "priest") should be doing. According to Sir Thomas, Edmund "might read prayers and preach," also "he might ride over, every Sunday, to a house nominally inhabited, and go through divine service." At Thornton Lacey, he "might be the clergyman . . . every seventh day, for three or four hours." Sir Thomas is aware that Edmund "knows that human nature needs more lessons than a weekly sermon can convey." He adds, "if he does not live among his parishioners and prove himself by constant attention their well-wisher and friend, he does very little either for their good or his own" (247–248).

Religion in Austen's work is that of the established Anglican Church, the Church of England. Her clergymen are Anglicans of one variety or another. Her letters also reveal that she was in some way influenced by Evangelicalism. This was a movement emphasizing conversion, acts of love, or charity, and a worldly existence apart from immorality and vice, in other words, renunciation. Jane Austen wrote to Cassandra on January 24, 1809: "I do not like the Evangelicals.—Of course I shall be delighted when I read it [Hannah More's novel *Coelebs in Search of a Wife* (1809)], like other people, but till I do, I dislike it." In More's evangelical novel, she found "pedantry & affectation" (*Letters,* 170, 172). In 1814, the year after she completed *Mansfield Park,* the work containing the fullest religious discussion she wrote, Jane Austen observes in a letter to her niece Fanny Knight that she was "by no means convinced that we ought not all to be Evangelicals, & am at least persuaded that they who are so from Reason & Feeling, must be happiest & safest" (November 18, 1814: *Letters,* 280).

There are differing religious reactions in *Mansfield Park.* Mary Crawford, personally affronted by

Edmund Bertram's faith and earnestness, accuses him of wishing to convert or reform the vulnerable (394, 458). On the other hand, the self-indulgent, unthoughtful Lady Bertram cries herself to sleep "after hearing an affecting sermon" (453). Fanny Price's positive affirmation of a moonlit night follows a theological tradition of revelation found, for instance, in the work of William Paley and his *Evidences of Christianity* (1794) and *Natural Theology* (1802). In the 1802 book, he opens his work by using the analogy of discovering a watch in a field. This reveals that the watch had a maker who created it with a purpose. Fanny observes: "When I look out on such a night as this, I feel as if there could be neither wickedness nor sorrow in the world." She adds, "there certainly would be less of both if the sublimity of Nature were more attended to, and people were carried more out of themselves by contemplating such a scene" (113).

See also BIBLE AND THE BOOK OF COMMON PRAYER, THE.

BIBLIOGRAPHY

Austen, Jane. *Jane Austen's Letters.* Collected and edited by Deirdre Le Faye. Oxford: Oxford University Press, 1995.

———. *Emma.* Edited by R. W. Chapman. *The Novels of Jane Austen,* Vol. 4. 3d ed. Oxford: Oxford University Press, 1986.

———: *Mansfield Park.* Edited by R. W. Chapman. *The Novels of Jane Austen,* Vol. 3. 3d ed. Oxford: Oxford University Press, 1988 reprint.

———. *Northanger Abbey and Persuasion.* Edited by R. W. Chapman. *The Novels of Jane Austen,* Vol. 2. 3d ed. Oxford: Oxford University Press, 1965.

———. *Pride and Prejudice.* Edited by R. W. Chapman. *The Novels of Jane Austen,* Vol. 2. 3d ed. Oxford: Oxford University Press, 1932.

———. *Sense and Sensibility.* Edited by R. W. Chapman. *The Novels of Jane Austen,* Vol. 1. 3d ed. Oxford: Clarendon Press, 1943.

Butler, Marilyn. "Austen's Religion: Anglicans and Evangelicals." In *The Jane Austen Companion,* edited by J. David Grey, A. Walton Litz, and Brian Southam, 202–207. New York: Macmillan, 1986.

Le Faye, Deirdre. *Jane Austen: The World of Her Novels.* New York: Harry N. Abrams, 2002, 79–81.

Olsen, Kirstin. "Clergy," "Religion." In *All Things Austen: An Encyclopedia of Austen's World.* 2 vols. Westport, Conn., and London: Greenwood Press: I: 145–158; II: 596–605.

Wheeler, Michael. "Religion." In *Jane Austen in Context,* edited by Janet Todd, 406–414. Cambridge: Cambridge University Press, 2005.

comedy   The critical emphasis on Jane Austen's essential seriousness tends to minimize her superb comic artistry. As a great novelist, she selects and manipulates her characters and materials to interest and amuse her readers. Jane Austen's works are not tragic in the sense of their concluding with death, and the motif of revenge is low down on her list of priorities. The worst that can happen in her works is a failure to marry the appropriate person, or elopement resulting in social isolation. Basic elements of classical comedy are found in Jane Austen's writing. There is *romantic comedy,* which has the basic ingredients of a heroine whose love has not a smooth passage, yet overcomes all difficulties to conclude in what the reader takes is a happy union. A good example is Anne Elliot and Frederick Wentworth in *Persuasion.* The relationship between Elizabeth Bennet and Darcy in *Pride and Prejudice* is somewhat of a variant of this pattern, as Elizabeth gradually realizes that she "loves" Darcy later in the novel and similarly with Darcy. Their emotions toward each other fluctuate.

The works are replete with *satiric* comedy. In *Pride and Prejudice,* for instance, Lady Catherine de Bourgh and Mr. Collins are the objects of ridicule on the part of the narrator and her characters. An element of satiric comedy is caricature, that is, "a verbal description" that "exaggerates or distorts, for comic effect, a person's distinctive physical features or personality traits" (Abrams, 28). Mrs. Norris, for instance, in *Mansfield Park,* is a caricature. Her excessive repetitive claims of disinterested benevolence and spurious reasons she gives for a refusal to do things—for instance, concern for her husband's health, and then the fact that she is mourning—mask her selfishness and nastiness. Her refusals under false claims are enveloped in lengthy sentences and speeches. Similar traits are revealed in the first few letters written by Lady

Susan in *Lady Susan.* Other instances range from Mrs. Elton to Mr. Woodhouse in *Emma.* His obsession with health also thinly disguises an essential selfishness.

There are also elements of the classic *comedy of manners* in Jane Austen's work. These focus on verbal *"repartee,* witty conversational give-and-take" or "verbal fencing match[es]" largely between the sexes and each representing differing social classes. They are combined with the violation of "social standards and decorum." Elizabeth and Darcy, and the Crawfords in *Mansfield Park* are evident illustrations of Jane Austen's exploitation of the comedy of manners. On the other hand, there is little *farce* evident in Jane Austen's world. The novels lack "sexual mix-ups, broad verbal humor, and physical bustle and horseplay" (Abrams, 39–40). There are exceptions, including John Thorpe's use of language in *Northanger Abbey;* Lady Catherine de Bourgh's antics in *Pride and Prejudice* border on the farcical, as do elements in the "juvenilia" including, for instance, events in *Lady Susan.*

Jane Austen's letters and novels are replete with ridiculously juxtaposed incidents. In her letters, she can move rapidly within a paragraph from theater visits, to "seeing the Indian Jugglers," to being "very glad to be quiet now till dressing time" and then to breakfast, dinner, the merits of someone's singing, to having a cold, to her "gauze gown," the fact that she has "lowered the bosom especially at the corners, & plaited black sattin ribbon round the top," and so on (to Cassandra Austen, March 9, 1814, *Letters,* 261). In other words, she is indulging in garrulous gossip. In the opening paragraph of chapter 17 of the final book of *Mansfield Park,* she comments, "Let other pens dwell on guilt and misery. I quit such odious subjects as soon as I can, impatient to restore everybody, not greatly in fault themselves, to tolerable comfort, and I have done with all the rest" (461). Jane Austen's is the world of Shakespearean comedy, not tragedy.

See also BURLESQUE.

BIBLIOGRAPHY

Austen, Jane. *Jane Austen's Letters.* Collected and edited by Deirdre Le Faye. Oxford: Oxford University Press, 1995.

———. *Mansfield Park.* Edited by R. W. Chapman. *The Novels of Jane Austen,* Vol. 3. 3d ed. Oxford: Oxford University Press, 1988 reprint.

Abrams, M. H. *A Glossary of Literary Terms.* 8th ed. Boston: Thomson, 2005, 28, 38–41.

Bayley, John, "Characterization in Jane Austen." In *The Jane Austen Companion,* edited by J. David Grey, A. Walton Litz, and Brian Southam, 24–34. New York: Macmillan, 1986.

Harding, D. W. "Character and Caricature in Jane Austen." In D. W. Harding, *Regulated Hatred and Other Essays on Jane Austen,* edited by M. Lawlor, [80]–105. London and Atlantic Highlands, N.J.: Athlone Press, 1998.

Wiltshire, John. "The Comedy of *Emma.*" In *Approaches to Teaching Austen's Emma,* edited by Marcia McClintock, 55–60. New York: MLA, 2004.

Cowper, William (1731–1800)   William Cowper, the 18th-century contemplative poet of rural life, was a poet of philosophical repose, traditional, conservative, yet noted for his opposition to the slave trade. Jane Austen's brother Henry remembered that his sister's "favourite moral writers were Johnson in prose, and Cowper in verse" (Le Faye, 57). In a letter to her sister, Cassandra, dated November 25, 1798, she mentions that "some money . . . is to be laid out in the purchase of Cowper's works." In another letter to Cassandra written less than a month later, on December 18–19, 1798, she tells her sister that "My father reads Cowper to us in the evening, to which I listen when I can." On February 8, 1807, she tells her sister that garden improvements are underway, but "I could not do without a Syringa, for the sake of Cowper's line" (*Letters,* 22, 27, 119)—a reference to "The Winter Walk at Noon," stanza 6, lines 149–150 in Cowper's *The Task* (1784). Fanny Price in *Mansfield Park* quotes lines from *The Task* when she objects to improvements at Sotherton (56). In another letter to Cassandra dated November 3, 1813, Jane Austen refers to the departure of a servant who "has more of Cowper than of Johnson in him, fonder of Tame Hares & Blank verse"—a reference to Cowper's main poetic technique and to his "Epitaph on a Hare"—"than of the full tide of human Existence at Charing Cross" (*Letters,* 250).

Another piece of biographical evidence should suffice to demonstrate Jane Austen's preference for the blank verse poet of rural contemplation, William Cowper. On June 29, 1808, she gave to her niece Fanny Catherine Austen as a present a copy of the two-volume 1808 edition of Cowper's *Poems* (Gilson, 434). Cowper is frequently quoted in her novels, especially by Marianne Dashwood in *Sense and Sensibility*, who tells her mother that Cowper's lines "have frequently almost driven me wild." Marianne judges Edward Ferrars's character negatively as he "pronounced [Cowper's lines] with such impenetrable calmness, such dreadful indifference!" (18). Fanny Price too is a great admirer of Cowper. In addition to remembering his lines from *The Task* in opposition to estate improvements, when she believes mistakenly that Portsmouth is where she really belongs, "her longings to be with [the Price family] were such as to bring a line or two of Cowper's *Tirocinium* for ever before her. 'With what intense desire she wants her home,' was continually on her tongue, as the truest description of a yearning" to find a place she can call home (431). The lines and feeling are ironic, as it is at Portsmouth that she realizes that her true place is at Mansfield. Self-resignation and deception underline Knightley's "remembering" of "Cowper and his fire at twilight," and the line "Myself creating what I saw" from the fourth book of *The Task* in *Emma*. Knightley judges correctly a "private understanding . . . between Frank Churchill and Jane [Fairfax]" (344).

At the end of the first chapter of *Sanditon*, Parker misquotes a line from Cowper's "Truth": "I fancy we may apply to Brinshore [a sea-side resort], that line of the Poet Cowper in his description of the religious cottager, as opposed to Voltaire—*She, never heard of half a mile from home*" (Jane Austen's emphasis). Cowper's praise of an old woman's strengths, her virtues, is applied to a seaside resort (370). The misappropriation, however, does draw attention to the rural English conservative and religious qualities of Cowper, as opposed to the worldly French cynicism of Voltaire. It is no wonder that Cowper's lines are quoted by fictional characters for whom Jane Austen clearly finds sympathy: Marianne Dashwood, Fanny Price, and Mr. Knightley.

BIBLIOGRAPHY

Austen, Jane. *Jane Austen's Letters*. Collected and edited by Deirdre Le Faye. 3d ed. Oxford: Oxford University Press, 1995.

———. *Emma*. Edited by R. W. Chapman. *The Novels of Jane Austen*, Vol. 4. 3d ed. London: Oxford University Press, 1986 reprint.

———. *Mansfield Park*. Edited by R. W. Chapman. *The Novels of Jane Austen*, Vol. 3. 3d ed. Oxford: Clarendon Press, 1988 reprint.

———. *Sanditon*. In *Minor Works*, edited by R. W. Chapman. *The Novels of Jane Austen*, Vol. 6. 3d ed. London: Oxford University Press, 1963.

———. *Sense and Sensibility*. Edited by R. W. Chapman. *The Novels of Jane Austen*, Vol. 1. 3d ed. London: Oxford University Press, 1943 impression.

Gilson, David. *A Bibliography of Jane Austen*. Winchester, Hampshire, U.K.; New Castle, Del.: St. Paul's Bibliographies, Oak Knoll Press, 1997.

Le Faye, Deirdre. *Jane Austen: A Family Record*. 2d ed. Cambridge: Cambridge University Press, 2004.

Crabbe, George (1754–1832) J. E. Austen-Leigh comments in the fifth chapter of *A Memoir of Jane Austen* that "among [Jane Austen's] favourite writers . . . Crabbe in verse . . . stood high." He adds, "She thoroughly enjoyed Crabbe; perhaps on account of a certain resemblance to herself in minute and highly finished detail; and would sometimes say, in jest, that if she ever married at all, she could fancy being Mrs. Crabbe" (71). Kathryn Sutherland, in her annotation to the passages in *A Memoir*, notes that "George Crabbe's metrical *Tales* (1812) are among Fanny Price's reading [*Mansfield Park*, 156], and her name may be taken from Crabbe's earlier poem *The Parish Register* (1807), a moralistic study of various levels of village life, in which Fanny Price is a 'lovely' and 'chaste' young girl" (231).

In Jane Austen's letters to her sister, Cassandra, there are several references to George Crabbe and to his wife, Sarah, who died on September 21, 1813. Crabbe, who practiced medicine at Aldeburgh on the Suffolk coast, visited London with his wife during the late summer of 1813. In a letter dated September 15–16, 1813, Jane Austen joked to Cassandra that she had not yet met Crabbe. In a letter to Cassandra of October 21, 1813 she wrote, "No;

I have never seen the death of Mrs. Crabbe. I have only just been making out from one of his prefaces that he probably was married. It is almost ridiculous. Poor Woman! I will comfort *him* as well as I can, but I do not undertake to be good to her children" (Jane Austen's emphasis, *Letters*, 218, 243).

Mansfield Park is the novel in which Jane Austen depicts scenes more often associated with Crabbe. The Portsmouth chapters, in their depiction of squalor among those associated with the sea, reflect the stark depiction of rural coast life and the degradation of poverty found in Crabbe's "The Village" (1783) and *The Borough* (1810). Crabbe's poem "Procrastination," with its lines "More luckless still their fate, who are the prey/ Of long-protracted hope and dull delay;/ Mid plans of bliss the heavy hours pass on,/ Till love is wither'd, and till joy is gone," might well "have contributed something to the genesis of *Persuasion*" (Pinion, 177).

BIBLIOGRAPHY

Austen, Jane. *Jane Austen's Letters.* Collected and edited by Deirdre Le Faye. 3d ed. Oxford: Oxford University Press, 1995.

———. *Mansfield Park.* Edited by R. W. Chapman. *The Novels of Jane Austen,* Vol. 3. 3d ed. Oxford, U.K.: Clarendon Press, 1988 reprint.

Austen-Leigh, James Edward. *A Memoir of Jane Austen and Other Family Recollections,* edited by Kathryn Sutherland. Oxford World's Classics. Oxford: Oxford University Press, 2002.

Pinion, F. B. *A Jane Austen Companion: A Critical Survey and Reference Book.* London: Macmillan, 1973.

Crosby, Richard Richard Crosby of Crosby & Co., publishers of Stationers' Court, Ludgate Street, London, purchased the manuscript of *Northanger Abbey* under the title *Susan* from William Seymour, acting on behalf of Henry Austen, Jane's brother, in the spring of 1803. They paid £10 for the manuscript, which they did not publish. Jane Austen wrote to them on April 5, 1809, asking for information relating to a possible publication date and saying that if the manuscript had been lost, she was willing to supply another one. Richard Crosby replied on April 8, 1809, saying that they had purchased the "MS novel entitled *Susan* . . . but there was not any time stipulated for its publication, neither are we bound to publish it, Should you or anyone else [*sic*] we shall take proceedings to stop the sale" (*Letters,* 174–175). Henry purchased the manuscript in the spring of 1816, and it was published posthumously under the title *Northanger Abbey*.

BIBLIOGRAPHY

Austen, Jane. *Jane Austen's Letters.* Collected and edited by Deirdre Le Faye. 3d ed. Oxford: Oxford University Press, 1995.

Sutherland, Kathryn. *Jane Austen's Textual Lives from Aeschylus to Bollywood.* Oxford: Oxford University Press, 2005, 221, 230, 235.

D

dancing, assemblies, and balls Jane Austen's letters are replete with references to dancing, assemblies, and balls. It is clear from her life and work that they constituted important social activities where eligible and appropriate partners could be met. The first of her known letters, written on January 9, 1796, to her sister, Cassandra, contains a detailed description of "an exceedingly good ball" Jane Austen attended the previous evening. The letters mention only one dance by name, the Boulanger. In yet another account of a ball she attended, Jane tells her sister, Cassandra, in a letter dated September 5, 1796: "in the Evening danced two Country Dances & the Boulangeries" (*Letters*, 1, 1, 8). This lively dance with its French origin is also mentioned at the opening of *Pride and Prejudice* (13). When she lived in Bath, Jane Austen attended large formal balls held in the fashionable Upper and Lower Rooms. Living in Southampton from 1806 to 1809, she decided to "go to as many Balls as possible" (*Letters*, December 9, 1808: 156). At Chawton Cottage in 1809 and subsequently, she was probably too old actually to participate in dancing. Her niece Anna became the center of her interest in balls. She writes to Cassandra on January 10, 1809: "The Manydown Ball was a smaller thing than I expected, but it seems to have made Anna very happy. At *her age* it would not have done for *me*" (Jane Austen's emphasis, 165).

Narrative description of dances—assemblies where public as opposed to private balls took place—and balls forms a tripartite structure approximating a basic musical or dance pattern. First of all, as part of the "A" musical pattern, there are sometimes elaborate preparations, discussions, and expectations before the actual ball. The central, or "B," section consists of the actual ball itself, and the final "C" section consists of the consequences, the "heightenings of imagination and all the laughs of playfulness which are so essential to the shade of a departed ball (*Mansfield Park*, 284). This "A-B-C" pattern is also seen in *Emma*. Here there are preparations for the Crown Inn ball, the postponements, changes in venue, and then the ball and its consequences (see book 3, chapter 2 and following).

Other important balls that have significant consequences for their participants occur in *Pride and Prejudice* and *Mansfield Park*. At the Netherfield ball in *Pride and Prejudice*, everything appears to go awry for Elizabeth and Jane Bennet, due to the inappropriate behavior of their sister and mother. "To Elizabeth it appeared, that had her family made an agreement to expose themselves as much as they could during that evening, it would have been impossible for them to play their parts with more spirit, or finer success" (101). The consequences propel much of the subsequent action of the novel. Largely due to his perceptions formed at this ball, Darcy, for instance, removes himself and Bingley from the Netherfield area. In *Mansfield Park*, on the other hand, in accord with the Cinderella motif of the tale, Fanny is given the opportunity to go to the ball. Indeed, Sir Thomas throws one for her and

A ball dress, 1820, *Courtesy of Ackermann's Costume Plates, 1818–1828*

Great House in the latter. There are assemblies, the large public balls in *Northanger Abbey* (74, 76–77) and *Emma* (229–245). Waltzes, on the other hand, are found in *Emma* to accompany the country dancing (229, 242). Most of these dances are social, in groups or pairs, without, unlike the waltz, too much physical contact.

The importance of dancing was as a social event, an activity, whether large as at the public assembly or privately arranged balls where people could meet. The men sought the partners and the women had the right to accept or refuse. If they refused, the custom was for the woman not to look at the gentleman she refused and largely not to dance for the remainder of the evening. Jane Austen wrote to her sister, Cassandra, on January 8, 1799, that "There was one Gentleman, an officer of the Cheshire, a very good looking young Man, who I was told wanted very much to be introduced to me;—but as he did not want it quite enough to take much trouble in effecting it, We never could bring it about." She adds, "One of my gayest actions was sitting down two Dances in preference to having Lord Bolton's eldest son for my Partner, who danced too ill to be endured" (*Letters*, 35). Jane Austen preferred on this occasion to place dancing skills above a potential well-connected marriage partner.

BIBLIOGRAPHY

Austen, Jane. *Jane Austen's Letters.* Collected and edited by Deirdre Le Faye. Oxford: Oxford University Press, 1995.

———. *Emma.* Edited by R. W. Chapman. *The Novels of Jane Austen,* Vol. 3. 3d ed. Oxford: Oxford University Press, 1986.

———. *Mansfield Park.* Edited by R. W. Chapman. *The Novels of Jane Austen,* Vol. 3. 3d ed. Oxford: Oxford University Press, 1988 reprint.

———. *Northanger Abbey and Persuasion.* Edited by R. W. Chapman. *The Novels of Jane Austen,* Vol. 2. 3d ed. Oxford: Oxford University Press, 1965.

———. *Pride and Prejudice.* Edited by R. W. Chapman. *The Novels of Jane Austen,* Vol. 2. 3d ed. Oxford: Oxford University Press, 1932.

———. *Sense and Sensibility.* Edited by R. W. Chapman. *The Novels of Jane Austen,* Vol. 1. 3d ed. Oxford, U.K.: Clarendon Press, 1943.

her brother William at which she becomes the belle of the ball (see book 2, chapter 10 and following). Subsequently, Fanny gains her prince charming.

Large public events in the shape of formal dances are absent from *Sense and Sensibility* and *Persuasion*, although in both informal dances take place, at Barton Park in the former and in the Uppercross

Grigsby, Joan. "Dancing, Balls and Assemblies." In *The Jane Austen Companion*, edited by J. David Grey, A. Walton Litz, and Brian Southam, 118–119. New York: Macmillan, 1986.

Olsen, Kirstin. "Dance." In *All Things Austen: An Encyclopedia of Austen's World*. 2 vols. Westport, Conn., and London: Greenwood Press: I: 195–206.

dress In *Northanger Abbey*, Jane Austen as narrator firmly asserts: "Dress is at all times a frivolous distinction, and excessive solicitude about it often destroys its own aim" (73). Somewhat curiously, however, there is a paucity of detail in her novels concerning the specific dresses and clothes worn by her characters. Her letters contain a plethora of observations on clothes, shopping for them, and

Evening Dress, 1820, *Courtesy of Ackermann's Costume Plates, 1818–1828*

specific details, for instance, of the cut of clothing. There were distinct transformations of fashion throughout Jane Austen's lifetime; partly a consequence of developments in cotton-spinning technology, and the price of wool grew rapidly. Muslins became fashionable in the last decades of the 18th century, and early in the new one. Henry Tilney buys "a true Indian" for his sister for only "five shillings a yard" (28).

In *Pride and Prejudice*, one of the first things Mrs. Gardiner did when she visits the Bennets "was to distribute her presents and describe the newest fashions" (139). There was considerable discussion over what to wear between family members and friends. In a letter to her sister, Cassandra, written on Christmas eve 1798, clothing is mentioned by Jane Austen several times: "My black Cap was openly admired." She tells Cassandra "that you should meditate the purchase of a new muslin Gown [is] delightful," and adds, "I am determined to buy a handsome one whenever I can, & I am so ashamed of half my present stock that I even blush at the sight of the wardrobe which contains them." Jane though "cannot determine what to do about my new Gown; I wish such things were to be bought ready made. I have some hopes of meeting Martha [Lloyd, Jane's closest friend], at the Christening [of James Edward Austen-Leigh] . . . next Tuesday, & see what she can do for me" (*Letters*, 30), in other words, whether she can copy clothing. Harriet Smith speaks in *Emma* of her "pattern gown," or copied one (235).

Elizabeth and Lydia Bennet alter their clothing; they trim their own bonnets (6, 219). Jane Austen was highly skilled with the needle and did her own alterations. On March 5, 1814, she informs Cassandra, "I have determined to trim my lilac sarsenet with black sattin [*sic*] ribbon just as my China Crape is, 6^d width at bottom, 3^d or 4^d at top—Ribbon trimmings are all the fashion at Bath, & I dare say the fashions of the two places [she is writing from London] are likely enough to content *me*" (Jane Austen's emphasis, *Letters*, 258). Dress increasingly became less formal and rigid in the first and second decade of the 19th century. Simple fine muslin dresses with high waists and emphasizing the bosom with the ancient Greek

Walking Dress, 1818, *Courtesy of Ackermann's Costume Plates, 1818–1828*

Walking Dress, 1818, *Courtesy of Ackermann's Costumes Plates, 1818–1828*

and Roman statues as an example became fashionable. The narrator warns in *Northanger Abbey* that a man's heart is not influenced "by the texture of their muslin." Catherine Morland is not untypical: she "lay awake ten minutes on Wednesday night debating between her spotted and her tamboured muslin" (74, 73).

For outside clothing, fashionable were the pelisse, a full-length long-sleeved jacket with a short waist. The spencer was the half-length version. These were made of velvet, woolen cloth, or silk. Indoors, cloaks and shawls were worn. Lady Bertram is anxious that her nephew bring her two when he returns from the East Indies (305). Veils were worn sometimes on formal occasions, although Mrs. Elton scorns the "very few lace veils" (484) worn at Emma's wedding. As a protection

from the sun, parasols were at times used (see *Sanditon*, 381).

As for footwear, this, too, could be put to practical use. In order to fall behind Harriet and Mr. Elton, Emma deliberately breaks off the lace of her boot (89). In nasty weather, when it was wet or muddy, woolen overshoes raised by an iron frame were worn. Anne Elliot finds their noise discomforting and objects to the "ceaseless clink of patterns" she hears in Bath (135).

In her letters, Jane Austen mentions women's underwear. She purchases a linen shift, or basic undergarment, and frequently silk stockings. Corsets also were worn. She writes to Cassandra on September 15, 1813: "the stays now are not made to force the Bosom up at all; *that* was a very unbecoming, unnatural fashion. I was really glad to hear that they are not to be much off the shoulders as they were" (Jane Austen's emphasis, *Letters*, 220).

There are far fewer references to male attire in her letters or novels. Shirts and cravats were made at home, and Jane, in company with her creations Fanny Price and Catherine Morland, spends considerable time sewing for their brothers

(*Letters*, 7: *Mansfield Park*, 390; *Northanger Abbey*, 240). Military uniform is attractive. William Price, for instance, dressed in a lieutenant's uniform evidently was "looking and moving all the taller, firmer, and more graceful for it" (*Mansfield Park*, 384). Those whose dress, whether male or female, displays ostentation, do not escape Jane Austen's satirical wit—for instance, Sir Walter Elliot, Robert Ferrars, or Mrs. Elton. On the other hand, Emma and Mr. Knightley, neither of whom had a "taste for finery or parade" (484), receive their author's approbation.

BIBLIOGRAPHY

Austen, Jane. *Jane Austen's Letters.* Collected and edited by Deirdre Le Faye. Oxford: Oxford University Press, 1995.

———. *Emma.* Edited by R. W. Chapman. *The Novels of Jane Austen,* Vol. 4. 3d ed. Oxford: Oxford University Press, 1986.

———. *Mansfield Park.* Edited by R. W. Chapman. *The Novels of Jane Austen,* Vol. 3. 3d ed. Oxford: Oxford University Press, 1988 reprint.

———. *Northanger Abbey and Persuasion.* Edited by R. W. Chapman. *The Novels of Jane Austen,* Vol. 2. 3d ed. Oxford: Oxford University Press, 1965.

———. *Pride and Prejudice.* Edited by R. W. Chapman. *The Novels of Jane Austen,* Vol. 2. 3d ed. Oxford: Oxford University Press, 1932.

———. *Sense and Sensibility.* Edited by R. W. Chapman. *The Novels of Jane Austen,* Vol. 1. 3d ed. Oxford: Clarendon Press, 1943.

———. "Sanditon." In *Minor Works,* edited by R. W. Chapman. *The Works of Jane Austen.* Vol. 6. London: Oxford University Press, 1963, 363–427.

Blank, Antje. "Dress." In *Jane Austen in Context,* edited by Janet Todd, 234–251. Cambridge: Cambridge University Press, 2005.

Byrde, Penelope. "Dress and Fashion." In *The Jane Austen Companion,* edited by J. David Grey, A. Walton Litz, and Brian Southam, 131–134. New York: Macmillan, 1986.

Olsen, Kirstin. "Clothing." In *All Things Austen: An Encyclopedia of Austen's World.* 2 vols. Westport, Conn., and London: Greenwood Press: I: 160–176.

Edgeworth, Maria (1767–1849) Jane Austen clearly admired the work of the Irish novelist and educational writer Maria Edgeworth. On September 28, 1814, she wrote to her niece Anna, who planned to write novels, "I have made up my mind to like no Novels really, but Miss Edgeworth's, Yours [Anna's] & my own" (*Letters,* 278). In the narrator's defense of fiction as a literary form in the fifth chapter of *Northanger Abbey,* Edgeworth's *Belinda* (1801) is included as an illustration of "some work in which the greatest powers of the mind are displayed, in which the most thorough knowledge of human nature, the happiest delineation of its varieties, the liveliest effusions of wit and humour are conveyed to the world in the best chosen language" (38). In a letter to her sister, Cassandra, dated August 23–24, 1814, Jane Austen refers to "one of my vanities, like your not reading *Patronage*" (*Letters,* 271)—a reference to Maria Edgeworth's novel published in 1814.

Maria Edgeworth was from a wealthy Irish family, and her novels earned far more than Jane Austen's, for whom she was something of a fellow female fiction role model. Edgeworth's story "Vivian," found in the second series of *Tales of Fashionable Life* (1812), has similar concerns that reverberate thematically through Jane Austen's own writing, and especially *Mansfield Park*: "moral motivation, and . . . insistence on the critical importance of education" (Pinion, 103). In the advertisement to *Belinda* (1801), Maria Edgeworth "repudiated the 'folly, error and vice . . . disseminated in books classed under this denomination'" (cited Stabler, 43). Jane Austen, as narrator, in *Northanger Abbey* refuses to "adopt that dangerous and impolitic custom so common with novel-writers of degrading by their contemptuous censure the very performances, to the number which they are themselves adding" (37).

Maria Edgeworth, from E. A. Duyckinck, *Portrait Gallery of Eminent Women, 1873*

Stylistically, Jane Austen, in common with Maria Edgeworth and FANNY BURNEY, "blended omniscient narration with Richardson's device of intimate letters to track the evolution of a courtship" (Stabler, 43). Further, Jane Austen's titles, *Sense and Sensibility, Pride and Prejudice,* and *Persuasion,* in addition to the title Jane Austen "preferred for her niece Anna's novel, 'Enthusiasm' . . . serve surely to advertise them as novels of the Edgeworth kind, novels that function also as moral fables" (Cronin, 293). In spite of such similarities, a critic such as GEORGE HENRY LEWES, writing on "The Novels of Jane Austen" in *Blackwood's Magazine,* in 1859, noted that Jane Austen's craftsmanship, her aesthetic skills, were superior to a contemporary such as Maria Edgeworth, and that her work would outlive Edgeworth's. Richard Whately, an Anglican minister, writing in 1821, preferred Jane Austen's novels to Edgeworth's as the former was a Christian and essentially more conservative than the radical Irish writer (Grey, 99, 195).

BIBLIOGRAPHY

Austen, Jane. *Jane Austen's Letters.* Collected and edited by Deirdre Le Faye. 3d ed. Oxford: Oxford University Press, 1995.

———. *Northanger Abbey and Persuasion.* Edited by R. W. Chapman. *The Novels of Jane Austen,* Vol. 5. 3d ed. London: Oxford University Press, 1965.

Cronin, Richard. "Literary Scene." In *Jane Austen in Context,* edited by Janet Todd, 289–296. Cambridge: Cambridge University Press, 2005.

Grey, J. David, A. Walton Litz, and Brian Southam, eds. *The Jane Austen Companion.* New York: Macmillan, 1986.

Pinion, F. B. *A Jane Austen Companion: A Critical Survey and Reference Book.* London: Macmillan, St. Martin's Press, 1973.

Stabler, Jane. "Literary Influences." In *Jane Austen in Context,* edited by Janet Todd, 41–50. Cambridge: Cambridge University Press, 2005.

education   Education in terms of the development of the self and the awareness of relationships with others, and the needs of others, is a central theme in Jane Austen's work. Much of the educational emphasis in her writing is on female growth and opportunities. These were severely limited in Jane Austen's world. Her brothers were educated outside of the home, at school, and at university, or trained for the navy. Two of her brothers became clergymen, two entered the navy, and one became through adoption a member of the gentry, or landed upper class. Jane and her sister were schooled or educated to become wives; in Jane's case and that of Cassandra, they took care of the household and relatives. In addition, Jane became a professional writer based at home. Women had very limited property rights within or outside marriage—there are exceptions: Lady Catherine de Bourgh in *Pride and Prejudice* and Lady Russell in *Persuasion* are individually very wealthy and wield considerable power and authority. To maintain the continuity of estates and property transfer, it was necessary for women to produce a male heir. Although the gender of the offspring was impossible to determine, the emphasis on child production & its importance was a part of education, and illegitimate heirs were discouraged as they produced highly expensive legal implications.

With the exception of Emma, most of Jane Austen's heroines are Cinderella figures. They brought to a marriage accomplishments inherited, such as high morality and ethical standards found in the case of Fanny Price, or other factors such as liveliness and high intelligence as in the instance of Elizabeth Bennet, rather than land, property, cash, or all three. Jane Austen's characters read, and the act of reading becomes a process of learning. Education, however, may be misguided. In *Mansfield Park,* the educated Bertrams, Rushworths, and Crawfords are involved in foolish estate improvements, foolish theatricals, and an improper "love" affair. On the other hand, the educated Edmund Bertram and Fanny Price culturally and morally reinvigorate the Mansfield estate.

Female education essentially emphasized household management, needlework, food preparation, tending the sick, and religious instruction. Schooling was largely at home, or, in more well-off families, through a governess or private tutor. Cassandra and Jane Austen are in some ways exceptions, as they attended briefly a boarding school. Governesses were inferior and dependent on the whim of their employers and charges—Jane Fairfax is preparing for such a fate. Education included learning to dance, to sing, and to play a musical instrument, usually the piano. Such skills exhibit a young woman's physical attributes on social occasions so that a suitor could be attracted. Cultural awareness and intellectual interests were displayed in drawing and painting skills, speaking languages such as French and Italian, and decorative needlework. Such accomplishments were valuable social assets. In *Pride and Prejudice,* thanks to their father, who has an extensive library, and the Gardiners, Jane and Elizabeth Bennet realize suitable, wealthy marriages. Catherine Morland, Emma Woodhouse, and Marianne Dashwood, on the other hand, are characters whose education has in one way or another gone awry, and the novels in which they figure depict their education or growth to appropriate realization of what they can or cannot do. Lydia, Mary Bennet, or Harriet Smith are less major figures whose education has left some important elements lacking and, in the instance of Lydia Bennet, has disastrous consequences.

Jane Austen somewhat ironically wrote to her niece Fanny Knight on March 23, 1817, that "pictures of perfection . . . make me sick & wicked" (*Letters,* 335). Education intrinsically cannot result in happiness or a suitable marriage. Maria Bertram is well educated but ends up unhappily. Fanny Price's education is a tougher one than Maria's, and her fate seems with Edmund to be a better one than Maria's. Similarly, Elizabeth Bennet's prospects are undoubtedly brighter than her younger sister Lydia's: both had similar educational opportunities. Jane Austen's novels are rarely inhabited by the "fallen" woman or the "improperly" educated Becky Sharpe or Moll Flanders personality. Also, Jane Austen, in common with many of her predecessors and contemporaries, wishes to educate her readers. She does this through direct narration, interior monologue, dialogue, and identification with her heroes and heroines. D. D. Devlin appropriately commented that all her "novels, and many of her minor works, unfinished works and juvenilia, are about education" (1).

BIBLIOGRAPHY

Austen, Jane. *Jane Austen's Letters.* Collected and edited by Deirdre Le Faye. Oxford: Oxford University Press, 1995.

Devlin, D. D. *Jane Austen and Education.* London: Macmillan, 1975.

Kelly, Gary. "Education and Accomplishments." In *Jane Austen in Context,* edited by Janet Todd, 252–261. Cambridge: Cambridge University Press, 2005.

Olsen, Kirstin. "Education." In *All Things Austen: An Encyclopedia of Austen's World.* 2 vols. Westport, Conn., and London: Greenwood Press: I: 227–236.

Egerton, Thomas A London publisher and printer who distributed James Austen's *The Loiterer,* which ran for 60 issues till March 20, 1790. For what he referred to as "the Military Library, Whitehall," Egerton published on Jane Austen's behalf *Sense and Sensibility* in three volumes in 1811, and a second edition two years later. Jane Austen wrote to her brother Francis on July 3, 1813, "every Copy of S. & S. is sold & that it has brought me £140—besides the Copyright" (*Letters,* 217).

Egerton offered her £110 for *Pride and Prejudice,* which he bought outright in November 1812. He gave Jane Austen five gratis sets of the three-volume novel anonymously published in January 1813. He issued in 1813, without Jane Austen's permission, a second edition and in 1817 a third edition. Richard Bentley in 1832 purchased the copyright from Francis Pinkney, Egerton's executor.

Egerton also published *Mansfield Park* on May 9, 1814, in an edition of 1,250 copies at 18 shillings each. He paid Jane Austen, who retained the copyright, £13.7 shillings for the first edition in three volumes, which was sold out by November 1814. Jane Austen was unhappy with Egerton, and commented in a letter to her sister, Cassandra, on January 29, 1813, on typographical errors in the first edition (*Letters*, 202). John Murray printed the second edition.

BIBLIOGRAPHY

Austen, Jane. *Jane Austen's Letters*. Edited by Deirdre Le Faye. 3d ed. Oxford: Oxford University Press, 1995.

————. *Mansfield Park*. Edited by John Wiltshire. *The Cambridge Edition of the Works of Jane Austen*. Cambridge: Cambridge University Press, 2005.

Gilson, David. *A Bibliography of Jane Austen*. Winchester, Hampshire, U.K, and New Castle, Del.: St. Paul's Bibliographies and Oak Knoll Press, 1997.

F

Feuillide, Elizabeth de, née Hancock (1761–1813) Born in Calcutta, the goddaughter of Warren Hastings, who in 1775 settled a large sum of money on her. She went with her mother, Philadelphia Hancock, to Germany and Belgium from 1777 to 1779. In 1781, she married Jean Capot de Feuillide (1750–94), a soldier and self-styled count. In 1786, she gave birth in London to her only child, Hastings, who was handicapped and died in 1801. Elizabeth, Jane's cousin, participated in the Steventon theatricals and formed a close friendship with Jane and especially Henry, her favorite brother.

Following the death of her husband, who was guillotined on February 22, 1794, she renewed her close friendship with Henry, whom she married on December 31, 1797. Jane dedicated "Love and Freindship" to her. Eliza remarked on Jane and Cassandra when she visited Steventon in 1792: "Cassandra & Jane are both very much grown. . . . They are I think equally sensible, and both so to a degree seldom met with, but still my Heart gives preference to Jane, whose kind partiality to me, indeed requires a return of the same nature." Jane attended her on her deathbed and was with her during the final days of her life. She was buried with her mother and her son; Henry's epitaph was "a woman of brilliant generous and cultivated mind" (*FR*, 76, 200).

See also HENRY THOMAS AUSTEN; JANE AUSTEN and her family; PHILADELPHIA HANCOCK.

Fielding, Henry (1707–1754) In his "Biographical Notice of the Author," Jane Austen's brother observes that "she did not rank any work of Fielding quite so high" as SAMUEL RICHARDSON's *Sir Charles Grandison.* He adds, "Without the slightest affectation she recoiled from every thing gross. Neither nature, wit, nor humour, could make her amends for so very low a scale of morals" (7). But in her first extant letter dated January 9, 1796, she exhibits detailed knowledge of the minutiae of Fielding's best-known novel, *Tom Jones* (1749). She knows the color of the clothes in which Jones was wounded, telling her sister, Cassandra, that a friend "is a very great admirer of Tom Jones, and therefore wears the same coloured clothes, I imagine, which *he* did when he was wounded" (Jane Austen's emphasis). This is a reference to *Tom Jones*, book 7, chapter 14 (*Letters*, 2, 354).

The text of *Northanger Abbey* contains in chapter 7 a discussion of fiction in which the boorish John Thorpe asserts, "Novels are so full of nonsense and stuff; there has not been a tolerably decent one to come out since Tom Jones, except the Monk" (a gothic horror novel by Matthew Gregory Lewis (1775–1818), published in 1796) (48). John Thorpe is crude and lacking in sophistication, so it is hardly a surprise that the grosser elements of Fielding's novels would appeal to him.

There appear to be no references to Fielding's other novels, such as *Jonathan Wild the Great* (1743) or *Amelia* (1751), but elements of the ebullience, parody, and sense of fantasy found in some of Jane Austen's *Juvenilia*, such as *Jack and Alice*, might have their origin in Fielding's dramatic burlesque *The Tragedy of Tragedies, or, The Life and Death of Tom Thumb the Great*, written in 1731. It was performed as one of the Steventon theatricals on March 22, 1788 (*Family Record*, 63). A critic such as Avrom Fleishman draws parallels between *Tom Jones* and *Pride and Prejudice*. The former contains the story of the young woman from the provinces who finally finds contentment. Elizabeth Bennet "is Sophia Western," Fielding's heroine, "grown up" (71, 73).

BIBLIOGRAPHY

Austen, Jane. *Jane Austen's Letters*. Collected and edited by Deirdre Le Faye. 3d ed. Oxford: Oxford University Press, 1995.

———. *Northanger Abbey and Persuasion*. Edited by R. W. Chapman. *The Novels of Jane Austen*, Vol. 5. 3d ed. London: Oxford University Press, 1965. [Includes "Biographical Notice of the Author".]

Fleishman, Avrom. *A Reading of Mansfield Park: An Essay in Critical Synthesis*. Baltimore and London. The Johns Hopkins Press, 1970.

Le Faye, Deirdre. *Jane Austen: A Family Record*. 2d ed. Cambridge: Cambridge University Press, 2004.

Films, Television, Radio, and Video Adaptations

According to the enumerative filmography available on the "Internet Movie Database" (IMDB) consulted on October 14, 2006, since 1940 there have been 34 adaptations of Jane Austen on screen. This list includes four for the year 2007: *Sense and Sensibility*, a mini-TV series in the preproduction stage; *Persuasion*, for TV, in preproduction; *Mansfield Park*, for TV and filming; *Northanger Abbey*, for TV and filming. From 2000 to 2005, there have been four films, including three of *Pride and Prejudice*, such as *Bride and Prejudice*, the Bollywood musical. The fourth, made in India in 2000, is of *Sense and Sensibility*.

The brief glimpse into Jane Austen's filmography reveals that there is an insatiable interest in her work and demand for it. Other evidence of this from the United Kingdom alone is reflected in the fact that *Pride and Prejudice* was one of the British Broadcasting Corporation's (BBC) all-time hit serials when it ran in 1995, and the book was second in a 2003 BBC Big Read Survey among the general British reading public. This 1995 version was adapted by Andrew Davis. Darcy was played by Colin Firth and Elizabeth Bennet by Jennifer Ehle.

Within a five-year period, 2000–2004, at least eight books focused on, or contained chapters on, Jane Austen on film, television, radio and video. Many drew upon the IMDB, and an account of those studies is informative. Erica Sheen's "'Where the garment gapes': faithfulness and promiscuity in the 1995 BBC *Pride and Prejudice*," is the opening essay following the introduction in *The Classic Novel from Page to Screen* (2000). This series of essays considers cinematic and television adaptations of 11 works from *Pride and Prejudice* to Dickens's *Pickwick Papers*, and *The Old Curiosity Shop*, to the 1996–97 adaptation of Michael Ondaatje's *The English Patient* (first published in 1992). Sheen's *Pride and Prejudice* essay ranges from a consideration of reviews of the film, which appropriate authority of their own: "the literary text is implicitly assessed, in relation to its adaptation, as what it actually only becomes when it leaves the academy and goes somewhere else, and that is a *property*" (3). Sheen argues that Jane Austen's "omissions and inventions," such as her omission of "active wedded promiscuity" (18), is partly responsible for her appeal and reflected for instance in Darcy's diving naked into a pond in Davies's production. She also discusses Carl Davis's music for the production.

Sheen focuses on a single text and production. The second edition of Linda Troost and Sayre Greenfield's *Jane Austen in Hollywood* (2001) contains, in addition to the editors' introduction "Watching Ourselves Watching," 14 essays by different contributors. Subjects range from Rachel M. Brownstein's consideration of the MGM 1940 film *Pride and Prejudice*, starring Laurence Olivier as Darcy and Greer Garson as Elizabeth Bennet; Carol M. Dole's reflections on "Austen, Class and the American Market"; to Suzanne Ferris's "Emma Becomes Clueless." The final contribution is the editor's consideration of "The Mouse That Roared: Patricia Rozema's *Mansfield Park*," released in 1999, made jointly by Miramax and

BBC films. Troost and Greenfield's volume is accompanied by 27 black-and-white still photographs from productions ranging from Ehle and Firth in *Pride and Prejudice* to Frances O'Connor as "the mousy Fanny Price" and Jonny Lee Miller as Edmund Bertram embracing (129 facing). There are two appendixes: "Austen Adaptations Available on Video" (205–207) and an enumerative, alphabetically arranged listing of "Selected Reviews, Articles, and Books on the Recent Films, 1995–2000" (208–212). The first appendix reveals the availability of four *Emma* videos ranging from a 1972 BBC One production, two in 1996 (Miramax and the BBC/A&E), plus *Clueless*, made by Paramount and distributed in 1995.

In *Jane Austen on Film and Television: A Critical Study of the Adaptations* (2002), Sue Parrill examines the history of the nearly 30 film and television adaptations of the six major Jane Austen novels available to her: *Sense and Sensibility*, *Pride and Prejudice*, *Emma*, *Mansfield Park*, *Persuasion*, and *Northanger Abbey*. There are chapters on each and a very useful "Appendix: Filmography of Austen Adaptations" (189–203) containing details of timings, who directed, who wrote the screenplay and produced, plus a cast listing of the adaptation Parrill considers. The oldest, not surprisingly, is Robert Z. Leonard's 1940 direction, produced by Hunt Stromberg with screenplay by Aldous Huxley and Jane Murfin of *Pride and Prejudice*. Parill's text is accompanied by black-and-white still photographs.

Suzanne R. Pucci and James Thompson edit a series of essays divided into four parts, *Jane Austen and Co. Remaking the Past in Contemporary Culture* (2003). The editors in their introduction, "The Jane Austen Phenomenon: Remaking the Past at the Millennium," note that they and their contributors are "concerned less with the notion of adaptation, less with the eventual similarity or difference between an Austen or other classical novel and the subsequent film, object or event. Instead, they are more involved in an inquiry into those cultural, social and pedagogical conditions that have motivated and shaped these remakes" (2). The first of the four parts focuses on classroom activities. The second, "In the Nation," has an essay on *Clue-*

less and one on comparing our perceptions of Jane Austen's England with "the present geographies of tourists who visit Austen-themed locations in" England at the end of the 20th century (111). The third part, "At Home," has an interesting account by Suzanne R. Pucci (133–155) of "The Internet site dubbed the 'Republic of Pemberley'" (133) [http://www.pemberley.com] entirely devoted to many aspects of Jane Austen. Virginia L. Blum's "The Return to Repression: Filming the Nineteenth Century" (157–178) is concerned with 1990s film perceptions and adaptations "of the nineteenth-century story of sexual repression" (159). Blum's focal Jane Austen adaptation is the 1995 BBC production of *Pride and Prejudice* and the remarks of Colin Firth, who performed Darcy: "This is where he wants to kiss her. This is where he wants to have sex with her right now" (163). Blum comments, that observing Colin Firth "struggling with his pent-up emotion is the centrepiece of the" film, and notes that the two principal actors, Colin Firth and Jennifer Ehle, "had an affair during the filming . . . an essential part of the story of our reception of this particular Austen adaptation that led to a phenomenon known as 'Darcymania' among British and North American women" (165).

The fourth part of the book encompasses similar terrain. Ruth Perry's "Sleeping with Mr. Collins" (213–218) uses the match between Charlotte Lucas and Mr. Collins as an *exemplum* of "our own reliance on the visual, or physical, 'chemistry' [which] . . falsifies the representation of the body, sexuality, and even marriage in Austen's own day" (213). Martine Voiret's "Books to Movies: Gender and Desire in Jane Austen's Adaptations" (229–245) generally considers cinematic and television Austen adaptations of the 1980s and 1990s in terms of the 1960s sexual revolution and the "male body as sexual object" rather than the female one (231). Costume dramas focusing on the rendition of *Persuasion* (BBC/WGBH, 1995) and *Mansfield Park* (BBC/Miramax, 1999), and others including "the continuing marginalization of women in contemporary films" (257), concern Madeleine Dobie in her "Gender and the Heritage Genre: Popular Feminine Turns to History" (247–259). An appendix to Pucci and Thompson, "Television, Film, and

Radio Productions of Austen" (261–263), lists the television and radio productions of Austen cited in the volume: This is followed by a listing of "Jane Austen's Radio Versions" taken from [http://www.geocities.com/Hollywood/Set/2484] (264–266), covering BBC productions. The earliest listed is *Love and Friendship,* broadcast on BBC Regional service on August 17, 1936. A BBC Third Program broadcast of *Love and Friendship,* on November 4, 1953, is also noted (266). Disappointingly, these are not discussed in the text of *Jane Austen and Co,* and neither are a 1948 and 1972 radio broadcast dramatization of *Lady Susan,* or a 1948 reading of *Sanditon.*

Jane Austen on Screen (2003), edited by Gina and Andrew Macdonald, is accompanied by 19 black-and-white illustrations from film adaptations of Jane Austen and an enumerative "Filmography" (260–265) arranged by the earliest date: the 1940 (MGM) *Pride and Prejudice* being the first item, Andrew Davies script of *Northanger Abbey* (2004), produced on London Weekend Television, being the last. In their "Introduction," the editors write: "the symbiosis between Jane Austen's prose fiction and its silver screen versions is a phenomenon worth exploring, for it is unique and rich in messages about current thinking, and not just about gender; the adaptations touch nerves concerning authenticity, social class, and literary sensibility" (1). The first chapter consists of three "short 'takes' on Austen: summarizing the controversy between literary purists and film enthusiasts" (9–21). Roger Gard comments generally, "A few skeptical thoughts on Jane Austen and film," observing "that what is often held to be the best film adaptation is of Austen's least complex work," *Sense and Sensibility,* starring Emma Thompson as Elinor Dashwood and Hugh Grant as Edward Ferrars (Columbia/TriStar, 1995). Gayline Preston focuses on "Ang Lee's sensitive screen interpretation of Jane Austen" in an account of this film adaptation of *Sense and Sensibility* (12–14). Kate Bowles, on the other hand, is concerned with "The Janeite culture of the Internet and commercialization through product and television series spinoffs." These include Jane Austen sites on the Internet, extending from "The Republic of Pemberley" [http://www.pemberley.com] to the "defunct Internet discussion list Austen-L" (15–17).

The impact of Jane Austen is the subject of Harriet Margolis's "Janeite culture: what does the name 'Jane Austen' authorize?" (22–43), which considers such areas as "Jane Austen in Hollywood," the nature of the author's appeal, the role of the BBC and the Public Broadcasting System in America in producing adaptations of Jane Austen's work. Margolis also writes on the author and director Amy Heckerling's 1995 film, *Clueless,* which uses Jane Austen. The differences between "Translation" and "imitation," between the former's insistence on "fidelity" (45) to the text, and "difference from the original" (51), are discussed by Jocelyn Harris in "'Such a transformation!': translation, imitation, and intertextuality in Jane Austen on screen" (44–68). Harris concludes that "the most satisfying Jane Austen movies are not just 'translations' but 'imitations' rejoicing in their difference" (66), such as Lee's *Sense and Sensibility,* Patricia Rozema's 1999 Miramax *Mansfield Park,* in which Frances O'Connor plays Fanny Price and Harold Pinter, Sir Thomas Bertram, "a violent oppressor to his slaves" (60), and *Clueless.*

The 1999 Miramax *Mansfield Park* and the 1983 BBC version of *Mansfield Park* are the subject of Jan Fergus's "Two *Mansfield Parks*: purist and postmodern" (69–89). Penny Gay pays special attention to Ang Lee's 1995 *Sense and Sensibility,* scripted by Emma Thompson in "*Sense and Sensibility* in a post feminist world: sisterhood is still powerful" (90–110). Sony Pictures Classics's release of *Persuasion,* Roger Michell's 1995 film adaptation, is the subject of Paulette Richards' "Regency romance shadowing the visual motifs of Roger Michell's *Persuasion,*" in which Ciaran Hinds is Captain Wentworth and Amanda Root is Anne Elliot (111–126). The same film is also the central focus of another essay, Tara Ghoshal Wallace's "Filming Romance: *Persuasion*" (127–143).

Douglas McGrath's 1995 film adaptation of *Emma* preoccupies Hilary Schor's "Emma, interrupted: speaking Jane Austen in fiction and film" (144–174). Ellen Belton writes on "Reimagining Jane Austen: the 1940 and 1995 film versions of *Pride and Prejudice*" (175–196), and David Monaghan considers "*Emma* and the art of adaptation" (197–227). Monaghan's essay encompasses

Andrew Davies's ITV (Independent Television) A & E 1996 adaptation of *Emma*, Amy Heckerling's Paramount Pictures 1995 *Clueless*, and the 1996 *Emma* "written and directed by Douglas McGrath for Miramax ... a curious hybrid in that it displays characteristics of both the BBC classic drama and the Hollywood film, more particularly *Clueless*" (199). In the final essay, *Clueless* antecedents are considered in John Mosier's "Clues for the clueless" (228–253), which concludes on a pessimistic note: "No film has yet been made worthy of Austen" (251).

Individual perspectives, rather than a collection of differing ones, are found in the last three discussions of Jane Austen's visual and sound representations to be considered as informative. Louise Flavin's 2004 book, *Jane Austen in the Classroom: Viewing the Novel/Reading the Film,* contains her perceptions of film adaptations and their classroom usage of "fourteen Jane Austen adaptations available on video that might be used in the classroom" (12). There are four versions of *Emma*: the 1972 BBC written by Denis Constanduros with Doran Godwin as Emma and John Carson as Knightley; the 1996 Miramax, Douglas McGrath film with Gwyneth Paltrow as Emma and Jeremy Northam as Knightley; and the 1996 Meridian [ITV] and A & E Andrew Davies, version with Kate Beckinsale as Emma and Mark Strong as Knightley; inevitably, the fourth is the 1995 *Clueless*. There are two versions of *Mansfield Park*: the 1983 BBC written by Ken Taylor with Sylvestra Le Touzel as Fanny, Nicholas Farrell as Edmund, the Miramax/BBC, 1999, Patricia Rozema version with Frances O'Connor as Fanny, Jonny Lee Miller as Edmund, and Harold Pinter as Sir Thomas Bertram. One version of *Northanger Abbey* is considered, the 1987 BBC and A & E produced by Louis Marks, with Katherine Schlesinger as Catherine Morland, Peter Firth as Henry Tilney, Robert Hardy as General Tilney, and Googie Withers as Mrs. Allen. Two *Persuasion*s are discussed: 1971 Granada ITV's written by Julien Mitchell with Ann Firbank as Anne, Bryan Marshall as Wentworth, and Basil Dignam as Sir Walter Elliot, and the 1995 BBC, WGBH Nick Dear (writer), Roger Michell (director) production.

Flavin considers three available videos of *Pride and Prejudice*: the 1940 MGM; the 1979 BBC written by Fay Weldon with Elizabeth Garvie as Elizabeth Bennet and David Rintoul as Darcy; the 1995 BBC/A & E Andrew Davies production with Jennifer Ehle as Elizabeth and Colin Firth as Darcy. She also writes about two *Sense and Sensibility* productions, the 1985 (BBC) written by the novelist and adapter Alexander Baron and directed by Rodney Bennet, with Irene Richard as Elinor Dashwood and Bosco Hogan as Edward Ferrars; and the 1995 Ang Lee version, written by Emma Thompson. At the conclusion of each discussion, times are given with the cast lists and other details.

Ang Lee's film version of *Sense and Sensibility* and Rozema's *Mansfield Park* are the subject of all too brief discussion in Lisa Hopkins *Screening the Gothic* (2004: 36–52). Hopkins's focus is on the gothic as opposed to "Austen's Enlightenment rationalism" (52). "The *Emma* films," with a focus on "the three *Emma* movies released in 1995 and 1996" (9) are mentioned in Marcia McClintock Folsom's *Approaches to Teaching Austen's* Emma. The volume also contains a contribution by Carol Dole entitled "Classless, Clueless: *Emma* Onscreen" (88–99). Dole suggests that classroom "teachers show excerpts of the two costume-drama versions of *Emma* in class and ask students to compare them with passages in the novel"—Miramax's version with Gwyneth Paltrow and Kate Beckinsale as Emma, in the telefilm written by Andrew Davies. She also "explains why Heckerling's *Clueless* is truer to the spirit of Austen's [novel] than the other two movies" (9).

BIBLIOGRAPHY

Internet Sites

http://www.imdb.com [Internet Movie Database]
This is user friendly. Just input "Jane Austen," or the name of the novel, the actor, or the director, and much information on films, television shows, and videos will be displayed.

http://www.pemberley.com
This supplements the IMDB site, although it does not supply any information about films and videos, which is not available on the IMDB site. However, pemberley.com is by no means confined to screen

representations of Jane Austen, and contains a plethora of information about the writer.

Books and Articles
The following books discussed in the main text contain extensive bibliographies and further documentation. For the latest Jane Austen adaptation, whether on film, TV, or video, *imdb.com* and *pemberley.com* should be consulted.

Dole, Carol M. "Classless, Clueless: *Emma* Onscreen." In *Approaches to Teaching Austen's* Emma, edited by Marcia McClintock Folsom, 88–99. N.Y.: MLA, 2004.

Flavin, Louise. *Jane Austen in the Classroom: Viewing the Novel/Reading the Film.* New York: Peter Lang, 2004.

Hopkins, Lisa. *Screening the Gothic.* Austin: University of Texas Press, 2005.

Macdonald, Gina, and Andrew Macdonald, eds. *Jane Austen on Screen.* Cambridge: Cambridge University Press, 2003. [Contains 11 chapters by various hands.]

McCrum, Robert. "Austen Powers." *Observer,* September 11, 2005.

Parrill, Sue. *Jane Austen on Film and Television: A Critical Study of the Adaptations.* Jefferson, N.C.: McFarland, 2002.

Pucci, Suzanne R., and James Thompson, eds. *Jane Austen and Co.: Remaking the Past in Contemporary Culture.* Albany: State University of New York Press, 2003. [Contains 12 chapters by various hands and a useful appendix: "Television, Film, and Radio Productions of Austen," 261–266.]

Sheen, Erica. "'Where the garment gapes': faithfulness and promiscuity in the 1995 BBC *Pride and Prejudice.*" In *The Classic Novel: From Page to Screen,* edited by Robert Giddings and Erica Sheen, 14–30. Manchester: Manchester University Press, 2000.

Troost, Linda, and Sayre Greenfield, eds. *Jane Austen in Hollywood.* 2d ed. Lexington: University Press of Kentucky, 2001. [Contains 14 chapters by various hands and two useful appendixes: "Austen Adaptations Available on Video" (205–207); the enumerative, "Selected Reviews, Articles and Books on Recent Films, 1995–2000" (208–212).]

food and meals Jane Austen wrote to her sister, Cassandra, on October 27, 1798, from Steventon Rectory where she had just arrived after a visit to her brother at Godmersham Park in Kent: "I carry about the keys of the Wine & Closet." She mentions the bad weather, the difficulties of "going to Town" shopping, and her mother's ill health. Even "the Dandelion Tea" had to be purchased "at Basingstoke." With the exception of tea, coffees, chocolate, wine, sugar, and dried fruit, the Austen family was dependent on locally produced food. These were obtained largely from her father's rented farm and lands attached to the rectory. On December 1, 1798, Jane Austen comments on her "father's mutton" and in other letters refers to chicken, ducks, guinea fowl, and turkeys (see, for instance, June 11, 1799: *Letters,* 16–17, 24, 25). The Austens grew in their garden such staples as potatoes and vegetables. Family and friends provided fish and game.

Meal contents depended on the weather and the seasons. The evidence in Austen's letters reveals that on occasions her mother fed 10 to 12 people three times a day, including her father's boarding pupils and the servants. The family kept a cook but not a housekeeper. Food and supplies were easier to obtain after the Austens moved to Bath, although the cost of food with their reduced income, and the necessity of purchasing more rather than producing it themselves, became an issue. Matters became somewhat easier when they moved once again to the country to Chawton. At Chawton, Jane Austen was responsible for the breakfast, usually consisting of toast, rolls, tea, coffee, or chocolate. This necessitated making toast and boiling the kettle on the fire.

The major meal of the day was dinner. Times for this differed. Evidence from the letters provides differing times. At Steventon, dinner was usually at half past three. In 1808 in Southampton, they dined at five. In *The Watsons,* Tom Musgrave knows that the Watsons dine at three and arranges to visit them just at three to embarrass them. He admits to dining at eight in the evening. At Northanger Abbey, the General dines at five precisely, and at the Mansfield Parsonage and at Longbourn, they dine half an hour earlier. At Netherfield, dinner is at half-past six. Late dinners required some midday refreshments. Willoughby, in a great hurry, takes a "nuncheon" at an inn (318). Sandwiches are given at the Mansfield Parsonage. The actual eating and serving of dinner was something of a ritual. For instance, during the Coles' party in *Emma*, the discussion between Emma and Frank Churchill is interrupted: "They were called on to share in the awkwardness of a rather long interval between the courses . . . but when the table was again safely covered, when every corner dish placed exactly right," they can resume their conversation (218).

Tea drinking is frequently mentioned in Jane Austen's letters and work. This is not afternoon tea time but tea drinking an hour or two following a meal, usually dinner, and often confined to the women while the men drank port in another room. Supper, the final meal of the day, was not necessarily a big meal, especially if there had been a large dinner. In *Emma*, Mr. Woodhouse naturally prefers supper "because it had been the fashion of [his] youth; but his conviction of suppers being very unwholesome made him rather sorry to see any thing put on it," that is, the supper table (24). Balls made supper important. In *Emma*, "A private dance, without sitting down to supper, was pronounced an infamous fraud upon the rights of men and women" (254). On November 20, 1800, Jane Austen wrote to Cassandra concerning a ball she went to: "We began at 10, supped at 1 . . . There were but 50 people in the room" (*Letters*, 60).

Food reveals character. Bingley, in *Pride and Prejudice*, insists when arranging a ball at Netherfield that his housekeeper should have enough time to prepare "white soup enough" for his guests (55). Such a soup contains very expensive ingredients and was fashionable in France. So Bingley's insistence on white soup is an elaborate compliment to his brother-in-law Mr. Hurst, who has expensive tastes, and to his friend Darcy, who has a French cook. The choice also demonstrates that Bingley is not too careful about how he spends his money. There are other examples in Jane Austen's work of character revelation through food, for instance, the self-indulgent Willoughby exhibits his chastened side when on his dash to see Marianne before what he assumes to be her death, he takes a quick lunch

at a Marlborough coaching inn. His lunch consists not of an elaborate, expensive meal, which would take time to consume, but cold beef and drink: a quick lunch before departing on his journey.

Emma is replete with references to food. Hartfield is a community where those with more food, such as Mr. Woodhouse and Emma, and Knightley, provide for the less fortunate. It becomes a gesture of love: Robert Martin collects walnuts to give to Harriet Smith. Miss Bates and her mother receive apples from Knightley at Donwell and port from the Woodhouses. A key scene in the novel is the Coles' dinner party, at which the two key components of the novel, sex and property, are demonstrated against a backdrop of the rituals of food, its serving, and eating (see Wiesenfarth). On the whole, however, "with the single exception perhaps of the pyramids of fruits at Pemberley (symbolic of the social pyramid which Elizabeth must conquer), any mention of a specific food stuff in Austen is made by a character who is thereby condemned for being greedy, vulgar, selfish or trivial" (Lane, "Food": 268).

BIBLIOGRAPHY

Austen, Jane. *Jane Austen's Letters*. Collected and edited by Deirdre Le Faye. Oxford: Oxford University Press, 1995.

———. *Emma*. Edited by R. W. Chapman. *The Novels of Jane Austen*, Vol. 4. 3d ed. Oxford: Oxford University Press, 1986.

———. *Pride and Prejudice*. Edited by R. W. Chapman. *The Novels of Jane Austen*, Vol. 2. 3d ed. Oxford: Oxford University Press, 1932.

———. *Sense and Sensibility*. Edited by R. W. Chapman. *The Novels of Jane Austen*, Vol. 1. 3d ed. Oxford, U.K.: Clarendon Press, 1943.

Lane, Maggie. *Jane Austen and Food*. London and Rio Grande, Ohio: Hambledon Press, 1995.

———. "Food." In *Jane Austen in Context*, 262–268. Cambridge: Cambridge University Press, 2005.

Olsen, Kirstin. "Food," "Travel." In *All Things Austen: An Encyclopedia of Austen's World*. 2 vols. Westport, Conn., and London: Greenwood Press, I: 255–290.

Wiesenfarth, Joseph. "A Likely Story: The Coles' Dinner Party." In *Approaches to Teaching Austen's*

Emma, edited by Marcia McClintock Folsom, [151]–158. New York: MLA, 2004.

Fowle, Tom (1765–1797) Tom Fowle was the second son of the Reverend Thomas Fowle (1726–1806), who was a university friend of Jane Austen's father. Tom was a pupil of Rev. George Austen at Steventon from 1779 to 1783. He went to St. John's College, Oxford, in 1783, and received an M.A. in 1794. From 1788 to 1789, he was a curate in Hampshire and Berkshire. From a relative, Lord Craven (1770–1825), he received another rectory, this time in Wiltshire.

Tom and Jane Austen's sister, Cassandra, grew attached when he studied with her father, and they probably became engaged late in 1792, but could not afford to marry. Tom was appointed a chaplain to Lord Craven, who as a lieutenant colonel in the army was sent to active military duties in the West Indies in 1795–96. Tom accompanied him but died of yellow fever off St. Domingo on February 13, 1797.

He had sensibly drawn up a will before departing for the West Indies and left Cassandra his savings of £1,000 a year, which if invested wisely made her less reliant on family charity if she remained unmarried. Cassandra never married, remained close to Tom's family, and cherished his memory.

French Revolution The cataclysmic events haunting the imaginations of many 19th-century creative minds that began in 1789 do not directly enter into Jane Austen's work. There is no mention of the removal of the French monarchy (1789) and the bloody events surrounding it, the executions of Louis XVI and Marie Antoinette, the butchery of the French aristocracy and consequent Reign of Terror. Jane Austen and her family were personally affected by these events. Her cousin Eliza de Feuillide married a French count, and she was in Paris in 1792 when the Tuileries (the royal palace) was stormed and the September massacres took place. It is hardly surprising that during a period of such upheaval, her royalist-sympathizing husband, the Comte de Feuillide, should be accused of antirevolutionary activity and guillotined on February 22, 1794.

"The cruel death of" her cousin's "husband brought the horrors of the French Revolution straight into the peaceful Steventon rectory and left Jane with a loathing of republican France for the rest of her life" (*FR*, 78). In a letter to Cassandra written on September 8, 1816, that is, after the Napoleonic Wars and the final defeat of Napoleon Bonaparte, Jane observes that their cousin Christopher Edward Lefroy (1785–1856), "is coming back from France, thinking of the French as one c^d wish, disappointed in every thing. He did not go beyond Paris." Jane also received a letter from the family servant: "she speaks of France as a scene of general Poverty & Misery,—no Money, no Trade—nothing to be got but by the Innkeepers" (*Letters*, 321). It may well be the fear of bloodshed and chaos that underlies the very prominent conservative element running through Jane Austen's work. For instance, in *Mansfield Park*, it is not only the nature of the subject matter of the play chosen for performance that is so disturbing to Sir Thomas Bertram, Edmund, and Fanny. The problem lies rather in the drama's disruption of the normal routines of existence and the daily rounds as if it is a harbinger of chaos—a chaos expressed in the events of the French Revolution.

BIBLIOGRAPHY

Austen, Jane. *Collected Poems and Verse of the Austen Family*. Edited by David Selwyn. Manchester, U.K.: Carcanet, 1996.

Le Faye, Deirdre. *Jane Austen: A Family Record*. 2d ed. Cambridge: Cambridge University Press, 2004.

Neill, Edward. *The Politics of Jane Austen*. London and New York: Macmillan and St. Martin's Press, 1999.

Olsen, Kirstin. "French Revolution." In *All Things Austen: An Encyclopedia of Austen's World*. 2 vols. Westport, Conn., and London: Greenwood Press, I: 294–301.

games Jane Austen's work is replete with many kinds of games that often are a charade for more serious basic human activities such as power play, manipulation of others, and the key activity of finding the appropriate partner to ensnare. *Emma* contains word games as a key ingredient in its plot development, especially relating to Jane Fairfax. The characters play "charades," a game in which the syllables of a word such as "courtship" are each signified by rhyming lines, for example "My first / second," and so on, concluding with "My whole" (76–78, 82). Such games played in the Austen family survive and are found in David Selwyn's edition of the *Collected Poems and Verse of the Austen Family* (see 18, 19, 21, 36, 51, 52, 54).

Card playing was also an important social activity in Jane Austen's family circle and in her work. Playing cards also transcended social and class barriers. In *Pride and Prejudice*, for instance, the Bingleys, and Phillips, Mrs. Bennet's brother-in-law and an attorney, after dinner, sit down to play cards (54, 84). In *Emma*, at the Crown, there is room "for a whist club established among the gentlemen and half-gentlemen of the place" (197). Various kinds of card games were played. Whist, involving four players, was common, as were round games played by any number. These were noisy and included casino, loo, vingt-un, and the most detailed in Jane Austen's writing, speculation. In 1813, it was a comparatively new game and, in the second book of *Mansfield Park*, chapter 7, becomes "a metaphor of the game Mary Crawford is playing with Edmund as

a stake" with its demands corresponding to Henry Crawford's cynical manipulative values (Selwyn, *Leisure*, 271–275). More traditional card games are cribbage, played by two, three, or four, and piquet, for two players (as, for instance, Mr. Woodhouse and Mrs. Goddard). Lady Catherine de Bourgh prefers quadrille, a well-established game played by four.

All these games involved gambling of one kind or another. Tokens, often used as a substitute for money, were known as "fish" (*Watsons*, 357; *Pride and Prejudice*, 84, 166). The sole noncard game occurring in the novels is backgammon, while surprising absences are chess, draughts, and dominoes. Card games and other indoor games were not restricted to one sex. For children, "Cricket, base ball, riding on horseback, and running about the country" (*Northanger Abbey*, 15) were, for instance, not confined to boys. These are physical games, whereas those played indoors are predominately mental. A change in Jane Austen's attitude toward them may be seen in *Persuasion*, generally regarded as her final novel. Sir Walter Elliot and Lady Dalrymple, examples of an older social structure, prefer the older card games, which have definite rules and structures. The emerging generation, such as Captain Wentworth and Anne Elliot, represent a differing set of values. Wentworth perceives Anne's dislike of playing cards as a representation of her fidelity, her constancy. Again, cards and games are used by Jane Austen for symbolic purposes and to reveal character.

BIBLIOGRAPHY

Austen, Jane. *Collected Poems and Verse of the Austen Family.* Edited by David Selwyn. Manchester, U.K.: Carcanet, 1996.

———. *Emma.* Edited by R. W. Chapman. *The Novels of Jane Austen,* Vol. 4. 3d ed. Oxford: Oxford University Press, 1986.

———. *Northanger Abbey and Persuasion.* Edited by R. W. Chapman. *The Novels of Jane Austen,* Vol. 2. 3d ed. Oxford: Oxford University Press, 1965.

———. *Pride and Prejudice.* Edited by R. W. Chapman. *The Novels of Jane Austen,* Vol. 2. 3d ed. Oxford: Oxford University Press, 1932.

———. "The Watsons." In *Minor Works,* edited by R. W. Chapman. *The Works of Jane Austen,* Vol. 6. London: Oxford University Press, 1963.

Burlin, Katrin Ristkok. "Games." In *The Jane Austen Companion,* edited by J. David Grey, A. Walton Litz, and Brian Southam, 179–183. New York: Macmillan, 1986.

Gay, Penny. "Pastimes." In *Jane Austen in Context,* edited by Janet Todd, 337–345. Cambridge: Cambridge University Press, 2005.

Olsen, Kirstin. "Cards," "Games." In *All Things Austen: An Encyclopedia of Austen's World.* 2 vols. Westport, Conn., and London: Greenwood Press, I: 87–99, 310–316.

Selwyn, David. *Jane Austen and Leisure.* London: Hambledon, 1999.

gardens and landscape   Jane Austen's brother Henry wrote in his "Biographical Notice" (1818), found in *Memoirs,* that his sister was "a warm and judicious admirer of landscape, both in nature and on canvas." From "a very early age she was enamoured of Gilpin and the picturesque" (140–141). GILPIN, REPTON, and other landscape improvers appear as names to be considered in her novels (see, for instance, *Mansfield Park,*: 55–56). James Edward Austen-Leigh in the *Memoirs* describes at some length the landscape of Chawton, where Jane Austen lived from 1808 onward (see *Memoirs,* 67–68). She also spent periods of time with her brother and his family at the large Godmersham Park estate in Kent. The house, not unlike its grander, fictional Pemberley, was in a park, and on either side were wooded downs and also a Doric temple. At Addlestrop in Gloucestershire, the home of her great-grandfather and his family, improvements had been made by Repton in 1799: The rectory gardens were landscaped and a stream was created, flowing through a summer garden and over rocks into a lake. Jane Austen was also familiar with Stoneleigh Abbey in Warwickshire, visited by her in 1806. Originally a Cistercian monastery founded in 1155, over the centuries it had witnessed internal and external transformations, including external remodeling early in the 18th century. This left it half-Elizabethan in appearance, with the river Avon running "near the house amidst Green Meadows, bounding [*sic*] by large and beautiful Woods, full of delightful Walks" (*FR,* 156).

Jane Austen displays an acute eye and appreciation of scenic landscape. After a visit to Esher Place, the manor house of Esher in Surrey, and rebuilt in 1805, she writes on May 20, 1813, to her sister, Cassandra: "there could not be a Wood or a Meadow or a Palace or a remarkable spot in England that was not spread out before us, on one side or the other" (*Letters,* 210).

Pemberley, Darcy's home, is described at some length and is a tribute to Darcy. It stands in a vast park on elevated ground among a rim of "woody hills." There are Spanish chestnuts over the lawn, and the stream has been enlarged. There are no buildings, such as a Doric temple, around the house. A bridge is undecorated and "in character with the general air of the scene" (245–246, 253–254). On the other hand, in *Mansfield Park* and *Northanger Abbey,* improvements based on Repton are attacked. The changes result in the destruction of magnificent avenues of ancient trees (see, for instance, *Mansfield Park,* 55–56, 82, 103, and *Northanger Abbey,* 177). She does, however, assent to the building of houses in protected valleys rather than on the crests of downs (*Sanditon,* 379–380). Jane Austen does not approve of improvers such as Henry Crawford, who neglects his social responsibilities while changing the landscape. General Tilney's transformation of Northanger Abbey not only does not appeal to Catherine Morland but is described as egocentric. John Dashwood in *Sense and Sensibility* exhibits his thoughtlessness and, in the manner of Henry

Crawford, an insensibility to human beings when he encloses the Norland common, removes ancient walnut trees, and replaces them with a flower garden and greenhouse for his wife. On the other hand, Delaford has not been improved or interfered with by Colonel Brandon and receives Jane Austen's approval. It is "a nice, old fashioned place, full of comforts and conveniences; quite shut in with great garden walls, that are covered with the best fruit trees in the country" (196–197). Donwell Abbey, too, in *Emma,* with its "old neglect of prospect" and "abundance of timber in rows and avenues, which neither fashion nor extravagance had rooted up," represents "English verdure, English culture, English comfort" at its zenith (358, 360).

In *Mansfield Park* and *Persuasion,* nature rather than landscape tends to be emphasized and frequently related to a character's moods or state of mind. In the earlier *Sense and Sensibility,* Marianne has a "passion for dead leaves" (88), and Emma, following her negative behavior to Miss Bates on Box Hill, enjoys "the exquisite sight, smell, sensation of nature, tranquil, warm and brilliant after a storm" (424). Anne Elliot in *Persuasion,* on the other hand, responds to "the sweet scenes of autumn" and to its melancholic qualities (85). Fanny Price reacts to the spring as "that season which cannot, in spite of its capriciousness, be unlovely" (432). With Fanny and Anne Elliot, the natural rhythms of the seasons accord with their very being. Anne experiences "the ploughs at work . . . the farmer, counteracting the sweets of poetical despondence and meaning to have spring again" (85)—the farmer does not improve the landscape, unlike Repton and his associates, but assists the natural cyclical season rhythms and patterns.

BIBLIOGRAPHY

Austen, Jane. *Jane Austen's Letters.* Collected and edited by Deirdre Le Faye. Oxford: Oxford University Press, 1995.

———. *Emma.* Edited by R. W. Chapman. *The Novels of Jane Austen,* Vol. 4. 3d ed. Oxford: Oxford University Press, 1986.

———. *Mansfield Park.* Edited by R. W. Chapman. *The Novels of Jane Austen,* Vol. 3. 3d ed. Oxford: Oxford University Press, 1988 reprint.

———. *Northanger Abbey and Persuasion.* Edited by R. W. Chapman. *The Novels of Jane Austen,* Vol. 2. 3d ed. Oxford: Oxford University Press, 1965.

———. *Pride and Prejudice.* Edited by R. W. Chapman. *The Novels of Jane Austen,* Vol. 2. 3d ed. Oxford: Oxford University Press, 1932.

———. "Sanditon." In *Minor Works,* edited by R. W. Chapman. *The Works of Jane Austen,* Vol. 6. London: Oxford University Press, 1963, 363–427.

———. *Sense and Sensibility.* Edited by R. W. Chapman. *The Novels of Jane Austen,* Vol. 1. 3d ed. Oxford, U.K.: Clarendon Press, 1943.

Austen-Leigh, James E. *A Memoir of Jane Austen and Other Family Recollections.* Edited and with an introduction and notes by Kathryn Sutherland. Oxford: Oxford University Press [World's Classics], 2002.

Duckworth, Alistair M. "Landscape." In *Jane Austen in Context,* edited by Janet Todd, 278–288. Cambridge: Cambridge University Press, 2005.

———. *The Improvement of the Estate: A Study of Jane Austen's Novels.* Baltimore and London: Johns Hopkins University Press [New Edition], 1994.

Grey, J. David. "Topography." In *The Jane Austen Companion,* edited by J. David Grey, A. Walton Litz, and Brian Southam, 380–387. New York: Macmillan, 1986.

Le Faye, Deirdre. *Jane Austen: A Family Record.* 2d ed. Cambridge: Cambridge University Press, 2004.

Olsen, Kirstin. "Gardens and Landscape." In *All Things Austen: An Encyclopedia of Austen's World.* 2 vols. Westport, Conn., and London: Greenwood Press, I: 316–324.

Gilpin, William (1724–1804) Henry Austen, in his "Biographical Notice of" his sister, observes that Jane Austen "was a warm and judicious admirer of landscape, both in nature and on canvass. At a very early age she was enamoured of Gilpin on the Picturesque; and she seldom changed her opinions either on books or men" (7). William Gilpin's *Three Essays: on Picturesque Beauty; Picturesque Travel and on Sketching Landscape* was published in 1792. His *Observations, relative chiefly to Picturesque Beauty, made in the Year 1776, on Several Parts of Great Britain; particularly the High-Lands of Scotland* was published three years earlier. Both find their way into Jane Austen's "Juvenilia." In letter 14 of "Love and Freindship," Augusta tells Laura "that having a considerable taste for the Beauties of Nature, her curiosity to behold the delightful scenes it exhibited in that part of the World had been so much raised by Gilpin's Tour to the Highlands, that she had prevailed on her Father to undertake a Tour to Scotland" (105). In "The History of England," which is replete with mock humor, "Edward the 6th" is "by no means . . . equal to those first of Men Robert Earl of Essex, Delamere, or Gilpin." The first, Robert Earl of Essex, was executed for rebellion; Delamere is the fictional antihero of Charlotte Smith's novel *Emmeline*, published in 1788, and "Gilpin" is the writer on landscape and art, William Gilpin (144).

Ironic allusions to Gilpin's work are by no means restricted to Jane Austen's "Juvenilia." In the 10th chapter of the first book of *Pride and Prejudice*, Elizabeth says that she will not accompany Darcy and the two Bingley sisters for a walk: "the picturesque would be spoilt by admitting a fourth" (53). The allusion here is to a passage and illustrations in Gilpin's *Observations* focusing on the Lake District, where he says that three cows, rather than four, constitute a group (II, 258–259). Again, in the 18th chapter of the opening volume of *Sense and Sensibility*, Gilpin's work forms the backdrop for the debate between Edward and Marianne on aesthetics. Edward somewhat disingenuously denies knowledge of the picturesque. Marianne, on the other hand, is aware that "admiration of landscape scenery is becoming a mere jargon" and that "Every body pretends to feel and tries to describe with the taste and elegance of him who first defined what picturesque beauty was"—that is, Gilpin (97). To return to *Pride and Prejudice*, the way taken by the Gardiners and Elizabeth Bennet in their excursion to Derbyshire (240) is precisely that taken by Gilpin on his visit to the Lake District in his *Observations*.

In *Northanger Abbey*, Henry and Elinor "talked of fore-grounds, distances, and second distances—side-screens and perspectives—lights and shades." Henry's "instructions were so clear that she soon began to see beauty in every thing admired by him" (111). Henry's views are those of Gilpin, who in his *Three Essays* comments on "that kind of beauty which would look well in a picture." Landscapes

may well stimulate a picture. This is different "from the 'beautiful' (whose harmonies and symmetries can look dull or flat when painted), the picturesque features, irregularity, rugged textures, and varieties of light and shade" (Johnson, 367).

BIBLIOGRAPHY

Austen, Jane. *Minor Works*. Edited by R. W. Chapman. *The Novels of Jane Austen*, Vol. 6. 3d ed. London: Oxford University Press, 1963 [Includes "Biographical Notice"; "The History of England"; "Love and Freindship."]
———. *Northanger Abbey and Persuasion*. Edited by R. W. Chapman. *The Novels of Jane Austen*, Vol. 5. 3d ed. London: Oxford University Press, 1965.
———. *Northanger Abbey, Lady Susan, The Watsons, and Sanditon*. Edited by James Kinsley and John Davie, with an introduction and notes by Claudia L. Johnson. Oxford: Oxford University Press, 2003 [Oxford World's Classics].
———. *Pride and Prejudice*. Edited by R. W. Chapman. *The Novels of Jane Austen*, Vol. 2. London: Oxford University Press, 1965. [Revised by Mary Lascelles.]
———. *Sense and Sensibility*. Edited by R. W. Chapman. *The Novels of Jane Austen*, Vol. 1. 3d ed. Oxford, U.K.: Clarendon Press, 1943 impression.
Duckworth, Alistair M. "Landscape." In *Jane Austen in Context*, edited by Janet Todd. Cambridge: Cambridge University Press, 2005, 278–288.

Goldsmith, Oliver (1730–1774)   Two works by the Anglo-Irish writer Oliver Goldsmith known to be owned by Jane Austen are recorded in Gilson's section K "Books Owned by Jane Austen" of his *A Bibliography of Jane Austen*. Gilson K10 is Goldsmith's eight-volume *An history of the earth and animated nature* (1774). The next item K11 is Goldsmith's four-volume *The History of England, from the earliest times to the death of George II* (1771). According to a Jane Austen family tradition, "the engraved portraits of monarchs in roundels at the chapter heads are coloured through in a childish fashion . . . by" (441) Jane Austen. On the other hand, "they may be the work of her sister, Cassandra, who illustrated Jane Austen's own juvenilia parody of schoolroom histories in her *The History of England from the Reign of Henry 4th to the Death of Charles 1st,*" by, as Jane Austen observes, "a partial, prejudiced, & ignorant Historian" (139). This is "a mock reabridgement of Goldsmith's *Abridgement* of his own full-scale *History of England*" (Southam, 188). In addition to countering Goldsmith's anti-Stuart bias, Jane Austen satirizes her model's popularization of history, seen, for instance, in her description of Henry IV. She writes that unlike Goldsmith, "it is not in my power to inform the Reader who was his Wife. Be this as it may" (139).

There are allusions to Goldsmith's history in Jane Austen's novels. Catherine Morland in *Northanger Abbey* read history "as a duty" (108)—the history she would have had access to included Goldsmith's popular *History*. In the third and final volume of *Mansfield Park,* Fanny Price and her sister Susan read Goldsmith, although "What Fanny told [Susan] of former times," that is, the past, "dwelt more on her mind than the pages of Goldsmith" (419). Somewhat curiously, there seems to be only two references to Goldsmith's popular novel *The Vicar of Wakefield*. In the final volume of *Emma,* the ninth chapter, the narrator asserts, "Goldsmith tells us, that when a lovely woman stoops to folly, she has nothing to do but die; and when she stoops to be disagreeable, it is equally to be recommended as a clearer of ill-fame" (387). Earlier in the novel, Harriet Smith tells Emma that Mr. Martin "has read the Vicar of Wakefield" (29).

Goldsmith, in his poem *The Deserted Village* (1770), depicts the decimation of traditional English rural village life, and he places the blame on the corrupting forces of commercialization. Goldsmith's poem may have been in Jane Austen's mind when she depicts estates such as Pemberly in *Pride and Prejudice,* Donwell Abbey in *Emma,* or Sotherton in *Mansfield Park,* as ideal places representing conservative values at their best and resisting changes brought about by commerce. Again in *Sanditon,* she seems to oppose the commercial exploitation of the landscape and what it represents.

See also MARGINALIA.

BIBLIOGRAPHY

Austen, Jane. *Emma.* Edited by R. W. Chapman. *The Novels of Jane Austen,* Vol. 4. 3d ed. Oxford: Oxford University Press, 1986 reprint.

———. *The History of England.* In *Minor Works,* edited by R. W. Chapman. *The Works of Jane Austen,* Vol. 6. London: Oxford University Press, 1963 reprint, 139–150.

———. *Mansfield Park.* Edited by R. W. Chapman. *The Novels of Jane Austen,* Vol. 3. 3d ed. Oxford: Oxford University Press, 1988 reprint.

———. *Northanger Abbey and Persuasion.* Edited by R. W. Chapman. *The Novels of Jane Austen,* Vol. 3. 3d ed. Oxford: Oxford University Press, 1965.

Gilson, David. *A Bibliography of Jane Austen.* Winchester, Hampshire, U.K., and New Castle, Del.: St. Paul's Bibliographies and Oak Knoll Press, 1997.

Southam, Brian. "Grandison." In *The Jane Austen Companion,* edited by J. David Grey, A. Walton Litz, and Brian Southam, 187–189. New York: Macmillan, 1986.

H

Hancock, Philadelphia, née Austen (1730–1792)   Philadelphia was the one-year-older sister of Jane Austen's father and the only member of her father's family with whom he retained regular contact. Both, on the death of their mother in 1732 and the subsequent remarriage of their father in 1736, were sent to Stephen, his brother in London, who treated them harshly. Philadelphia was apprenticed in 1745 on her 15th birthday to a London milliner. She completed her apprenticeship in 1750, and in January 1752 left England for Madras, India, probably in search of a husband. On February 22, 1753, she married Tysoe Saul Hancock (1723–75), the surgeon at an East India Company post. Philadelphia's daughter, her only child, Elizabeth, was born in Calcutta in 1761, where Tysoe had served since 1759. In Calcutta, the Hancocks became friendly with Warren Hastings (1732–1818), who subsequently became governor-general of Bengal (1773–85) before being impeached on political grounds.

Hastings was godfather to Elizabeth, and she was named after his own daughter, who had died. There were persistent rumors that Elizabeth was indeed his daughter and he provided for her and her mother. Tysoe returned to India in autumn 1768, having been back in London for three years. While he was away, Philadelphia and her daughter regularly visited the Austen family in Hampshire. In 1792, Warren Hastings set up a trust in Philadelphia's name. Three years later, in November 1795, Tysoe died while still in India. Warren Hastings was one of the executors and trustees of his will. In 1777, Philadelphia set off for the Continent, first going to Germany and Belgium, then to Brussels and, in autumn 1779, settling in Paris. Philadelphia spent some time in Paris with her daughter and her daughter's husband. She then returned to England, to London, developed symptoms of breast cancer, and died on February 26. She was buried in Hampstead churchyard on March 6, 1792. A relative wrote of her character, "I do not know a fault she has—so strictly just & honorable in all her dealings, so kind and obliging to all her friends and acquaintance, so religious in all her actions" (*FR*, 61).

BIBLIOGRAPHY

Le Faye, Deirdre, *Jane Austen: A Family Record*. 2d ed. Cambridge: Cambridge University Press, 2004.

houses and architecture   Catherine Morland in *Northanger Abbey* speculates on the nature of the house she has been invited to visit, "With all the chances against her of house, hall, place, park, court, and cottage, Northanger turned up an abbey" (141). There are many different kinds of houses in Jane Austen's work, a reflection of functions, size, and, on occasions, origin. Furthermore in the novels the diverse houses provide a satirical opportunity, especially for pretension. In *Pride and*

Prejudice, following his knighthood, Sir William Lucas moves to a house reflecting his new status: "denominated from that period Lucas Lodge" (18). Mary Crawford is pleased in *Mansfield Park* that Mansfield Park is genuine with "a real park five miles round" (48).

Jane Austen spent her youth and last years in the country. She grew up in Steventon Rectory, and most of her final years were spent in Chawton Cottage. During the years 1801 and 1809, she lived in towns, Bath and Southampton, and she also visited places such as the palatial house and estate at Godmersham Park in Kent, built in 1732. Northanger Abbey and Knightley's home in *Emma,* Donwell Abbey, are the oldest dwellings in her fiction. The former Northanger Abbey had "fallen into the hands of an ancestor of the Tilneys on its dissolution" (142) and becomes a place of entrapment. On the other hand, Donwell Abbey is presented positively and described as "covering a good deal of ground, rambling and irregular, with many comfortable and one or two handsome rooms" (358). Donwell has apples and strawberries and fertile grounds: General Tilney at Northanger Abbey has hot houses and cultivates pineapples. Also old is Sotherton Court in *Mansfield Park,* of Elizabethan origin: "a large, regular, brick building—heavy, but respectable looking, and has many good rooms." It is furnished "in the taste of fifty years back" (56, 84): Maria Rushworth prefers the London house in Wimpole Street.

The dating, the age of Pemberley in *Pride and Prejudice,* is not stated. There is a long gallery upstairs where family and other pictures are displayed. It is "standing well on rising ground," (245) and Elizabeth Bennet and the Gardiners find the grounds magnificent. The older properties in *Northanger Abbey, Mansfield Park,* and *Emma* are on low grounds. In *Sanditon,* Parker comments, "Our Ancestors, you know always built in a hole" (380). Jane Austen's heroines do not dwell in these but in more recently built ones. For instance, *Mansfield Park* is "a spacious modern-built house," also "modern, airy, and well

situated" (48, 447). Hartfield, too, where Emma lives, is "modern and well-built" (272), and in *Sense and Sensibility,* the Palmers live in "a spacious, modern-built house" (302). Even Rosings, Lady Catherine de Bourgh's house, is "a handsome modern building" (156).

The interiors of houses are rarely described, and then only when a move takes place. In *Sense and Sensibility,* the cottage the Dashwoods move to in Devonshire, Barton Cottage, is described in some detail (see 28). In other novels, dining, drawing, and, where appropriate, breakfast rooms appear (see, for instance, *Emma,* book 1, chapter 9). Mr. Bennet in *Pride and Prejudice* has a library and his wife a dressing room, as does Sir Thomas Bertram in *Mansfield Park.* Fanny by accident has one that she calls the "East Room," populated by mementoes, books, plants, and small pictures (Book 1, chapter 16).

As is evident in *Mansfield Park,* Jane Austen does not shy away from describing smaller dwellings and the discomfort and problems they bring, such as in squalor, bad odors, and people on top of one another. Fanny Price, however, unlike Anne Elliot in *Persuasion,* is not homeless. Anne's father lets out the ancestral house, Kellynch Hall, and moves into rented accommodation in Bath. With the exception of Emma, the loss of a house and all that it represents haunts her heroines. Mr. Parker in *Sanditon,* however, throws off his associations with the past. He is not financially strapped and constructs a new house, "Trafalgar House—which by the bye, I almost wish," he observes, "I had not named Trafalgar—for Waterloo is more the thing now" (380).

See also GARDENS AND LANDSCAPE, WILLIAM GILPIN, and HUMPHRY REPTON.

BIBLIOGRAPHY

Austen, Jane. *Emma.* Edited by R. W. Chapman. *The Novels of Jane Austen,* Vol. 4. 3d ed. Oxford: Oxford University Press, 1986.

———. *Mansfield Park.* Edited by R. W. Chapman. *The Novels of Jane Austen,* Vol. 3. 3d ed. Oxford: Oxford University Press, 1988 reprint.

———. *Northanger Abbey and Persuasion.* Edited by R. W. Chapman. *The Novels of Jane Austen,* Vol. 2. 3d ed. Oxford: Oxford University Press, 1965.

———. *Pride and Prejudice.* Edited by R. W. Chapman. *The Novels of Jane Austen,* Vol. 2. 3d ed. Oxford, U.K.: Oxford University Press, 1932.

———. *Sense and Sensibility.* Edited by R. W. Chapman. *The Novels of Jane Austen,* Vol. 1. 3d ed. Oxford, U.K.: Clarendon Press, 1943.

———. "Sanditon." In *Minor Works,* edited by R. W. Chapman. *The Works of Jane Austen,* Vol. 6. London: Oxford University Press, 1963.

Lamont, Claire. "Domestic Architecture." In *Jane Austen in Context,* edited by Janet Todd, 225–233. Cambridge: Cambridge University Press, 2005.

Olsen, Kirstin. "Architecture," "Furniture." In *All Things Austen: An Encyclopedia of Austen's World.* 2 vols. Westport, Conn., and London: Greenwood Press, I: 16–26; 301–306.

J

Janeites   The term "Janeites," or "Janites," appears to have been invented by the literary critic and professor George Saintsbury (1845–1933). In his *History of Nineteenth-Century Literature* (1896) and preface to *Pride and Prejudice*, illustrated by Hugh Thomson, published in 1894, Saintsbury distinguishes between "personal love" for Jane Austen and conventional admirers of the author—"loving by allowance." Confessing that he belongs to "the sect—fairly large and yet unusually choice—of Austenians or Janeites," he is ready "to live with and to marry" Elizabeth Bennet (1894: ix, xxiii).

Lovers of Jane Austen are by no means confined to her afterlife, to the late 19th century and beyond. For instance, the novelist and essayist, Jane Austen's near contemporary Mary Russell Mitford (1787–1855), is credited with having visited Bath and lived "far more in the company of Jane Austen's characters than in that of the actual celebrities of the place and found them 'much the more real of the two'" (Constance Hill, 106). A mid–19th century illustration of the cult of Jane Austen is provided by Charlotte Brontë. Writing to W .S. Williams, her reader at Smith, Elder, on March 23, 1853, following the publication of *Villette* (1853), she told him: "I had a letter the other day announcing that a lady of some note who had always determined that whenever she married, her elect should be the counterpart of Mr. Knightley in Miss Austen's 'Emma'—had now changed her mind." Brontë's correspondent "vowed that she would either find the duplicate of Professor Emanuel," Brontë's hero in *Villette*, "or remain forever single!!!" (*Brontë Letters*, 3: 138).

The "Janeites" received a considerable injection of enthusiasm from the publication in 1870 of James Austen-Leigh's *Memoir*, which coincided with the passing in the same year by the British Parliament of the Education Act. This made mandatory the statewide foundation of elementary schools, insisted on universal literacy and the use of literary teaching as a national heritage, and the fostering of the awareness of national pride. A consequence was the opening of a wider reading public for Jane Austen. A late Victorian Jane Austen publishing boom is represented by the 1870 *Memoir*. A deluxe *Steventon Edition of Jane Austen's Work*, the first collected edition of the novels, appeared in 1892 with a portrait of the author as a frontispiece, and woodcuts of Chawton Church and Steventon Parsonage. These suitably packaged its author as a marketable commodity. The London publisher Routledge in 1883 produced cheap editions, and three years later a sixpenny novel, so that Jane Austen was available to all. A gauge of Jane Austen's popularity, her marketability, is reflected in the fact that the London publisher Dent's 10-volume set introduced by R. Brimley Johnson (1867–1932) was reissued five times in five years (Gilson, 263–265).

Inevitably, there was a reaction. The elitist critic and author Henry James (1843–1916), in his "The Lessons of Balzac" published in the *Atlantic Monthly*, 96 (1905) dissected the genesis of Janeitism and its late 19th-century revival. James perceived it as an illustration of "a beguiled infatuation, a sentimentalized vision," a response to "the stiff breeze of the commercial." The "critical spirit" did not produce Janeitism. "Responsible, rather, is the body of publishers, editors, illustrators, producers of the pleasant twaddle of magazines; who have found their 'dear,' our dear, everybody's dear, Jane so infinitely to their material purpose, so amenable to pretty reproduction in every variety of what is called tasteful, and in what seemingly proves to be saleable form" (Southam, II: 230). Today, "saleable" commodities range from T-shirts (sweatshirts) with characters and/or the author emblazoned on them, card games, videogames, mugs, reading clubs, paperweights, kitsch, and groups dedicated to the cult of personality. A fine example is Karen Joy Fowler's *The Jane Austen Book Club*, published in 2004 and devoted to an account of various perceptions of Jane Austen put to "evil" and "useful" purpose (1) somewhere in the United States in the first decade of the 21st century.

Henry James admires Jane Austen's style; his attack focuses on her marketplace commodification, not her work. Nearly 30 years later, another great novelist, D. H. Lawrence (1885–1930), in his late work *À propos of Lady Chatterley's Lover*, published in the year of his death, describes Jane Austen unsympathetically. She is "this old maid" who "typifies 'personality' instead of character, the sharp knowing in apartness instead of knowing in togetherness, and she is," he writes, "to my feeling, thoroughly unpleasant, English in the bad, mean, snobbish sense of the word, just as Fielding is English in the good generous sense" (92–93).

Between James's 1905 remarks and Lawrence's comments around 1930, much had changed. English literature became increasingly institutionalized as a subject. On the political front, Europe witnessed profound transformation, and the destruction of much of its youth in bloody World War I. Further disasters were to follow in the shape of profound economic uncertainty and World War II. In terms of the justification of English literature as a valid university subject, it was necessary to establish a canon of great writers. Critics and university teachers such as A. C. Bradley (1851–1935), one of the founding figures of the

English Association in 1906, which advocated the importance of the subject, were intent on making Jane Austen an important part of the canon. In his 1911 English Association lecture on Jane Austen, Bradley opens with a confession. He trusts that the listeners "belong" with him "to the faithful," and he comments of Elizabeth Bennet, "I was meant to fall in love with her, and I do" (Bradley, 28). Virginia Woolf (1882–1941), writing in the *Nation* on December 15, 1923, saw the dangers inherent in attitudes represented by Bradley and others: "Anybody who has had the temerity to write about Jane Austen is aware . . that there are twenty-five elderly gentlemen living in the neighbourhood of London who resent any slight on her genius as if it were an insult offered to the chastity of their Aunts" (433).

Somewhat ironically, Jane Austen and the Janeites received a boost from the savagery of World War I. Reginald Farrer (1880–1920), in a centenary tribute to Jane Austen published in the *Quarterly Review* in July 1917, nearly a year before the 1918 armistice, opens his essay with the words, "The concluding storms of a great conflict had hardly died down." He continues, "when her world, almost unaware, bade farewell to Jane Austen." He is referring to the Napoleonic Wars: "now, amid the closing cataclysms of a conflict yet more gigantic, we celebrate the hundredth year of her immortality." He speaks of reading Jane Austen in a "water-logged trench" (Southam, II, 245–246).

Perhaps the most revealing exposition of Jane Austen's impact during the 1914–18 war and its aftermath is found in Rudyard Kipling's short story "The Janeites," published in 1924 and written in 1922–23. The story appears in a different form in his *Debts and Credits* (1926), with a concluding poem, "Jane's Marriage." In this Jane Austen, the author either goes to heaven or marries her fictional character Captain Wentworth. The story has as its setting a London Masonic Lodge in 1920. The speaker is the shell-shocked former soldier Humberstall, the survivor of a German attack on his artillery unit. In this unit, he was inducted by a Sergeant Macklin into a secret society of Jane Austen readers. Humberstall relates in his cockney dialect that one day the officers discussed whether or not "Jane" Austen died without leaving "direct an' lawful prog'ny." An exceedingly intoxicated Macklin, a lower rank, contradicts the officers' conversation: "She *did* leave lawful issue in the shape o' one son; an' 'is name was 'Enery James" (124). Macklin is not disciplined by the officers but carried to bed and looked after. The password of the club is from *Northanger Abbey:* "*Tilniz an' trap-doors,*" and Macklin reveals to Humberstall the delights of Jane Austen, which make the horrors of the trenches and the war endurable: "It *was* a 'appy little Group" (Kipling's emphasis, 132). Wounded, he tries to board a hospital train, is ejected, but is helped after telling the senior nurse "to make Miss Bates, there stop talkin' or I'll die" (136). The head nurse, a Janeite, assists Humberstall and manages to secure a blanket for him.

The male military Janeites are aware that Jane Austen's novels are "all about young girls o' seventeen . . . not certain 'oom they'd like to marry." However, there are other elements of interest: "dances, an' card parties an' picnics, and their young blokes goin' off to London on 'orseback for 'aircuts an' shaves." On the other hand, "there was nothin' *to*" the plots of the novels, "nor *in* 'em. Nothin' at all" (Kipling's emphasis, 128). Jane Austen's world, for Humberstall and his fellow Janeites, is not a world of fantasy and escape as it was for so many late Victorian and Edwardian readers and during World War II. Humberstall reads Jane Austen as her novels evoke the trenches and the war: "it brings it all back—down to the smell of the glue-paint on the screens. You take it from me, Brethren, there's no one to touch Jane when you're in a tight place" (137).

Claudia L. Johnson's reading of Kipling's story in her "Austen Cults and Cultures" draws attention to its references to "two exclusive societies—the Masons and the Janeites—but several details suggest that Austen's fiction promoted a secret brotherhood of specifically homoerotic fellowship, too" (216). Humberstall uses cockney spelling, chalking "De Bugg" rather than De Bourgh on a gun casement. His Sergeant Major accuses him of "writin' obese words on His Majesty's property" (131) and reports Humberstall to his superior officers.

They are fellow Janeites, secret ones, and dismiss the charges. Humberstall even names the artillery weapons of destruction after characters in Jane Austen's novel. His superior officer Macklin "reached up an' patted me on the shoulder." "You done nobly . . . You're bringin' forth abundant fruit, like a good Janeite" (130).

Austen's novels have a classless appeal, and in Kipling's tale become associated with the weapons of destruction. They were also used for healing purposes, being recommended to "severely shell-shocked" soldiers as part of the healing process. Kipling's story coincides with the real-life achievements of the Oxford academic Robert William Chapman (1881–1960), who during his artillery battalion wartime service in Macedonia, found relief in collating editions of Samuel Johnson and planning what would become definitive texts of the great English writers. He wrote in his "Reading Aloud" that "to restore, and maintain in its integrity, the text of our great writers is a pious duty," and he remembered "a series of summer evenings in Perthshire," Scotland, "when a lady read *Persuasion* to admiration" (46). His idea for an edition of Jane Austen's work "predated the war, but they were resituated by war." The attention and scholarly apparatus that had previously been brought to bear on classical texts were redirected to the texts of English authors such as Jane Austen. Chapman's "concern to establish an accurate text, after the careless reprint history of the later 19th century, not only inaugurated the modern critical engagement with Austen but also the serious scholarly investigation of the English novel (of any English novel) as a literary form." His "1923 critical edition of the Austen text is the first such treatment of an English novelist" (Sutherland, 26). Chapman's labors represent an escape from the horrors of war, a nostalgia for the past, an attempt to place English culture on a higher level, to give its literary texts classical status.

The years between the two world wars witnessed a reaction to the cult of Jane Austen in its various incarnations, represented most significantly by work published around the time of and during World War II. D. W. Harding (1906–93) in 1938 became senior lecturer in psychology at

Manchester University. From 1941 to 1944, he was engaged on war service and in 1945 became professor of psychology at London University. He is perhaps best known for his "Regulated Hatred: An Aspect of the Work of Jane Austen," a paper given at a March 1939 meeting of the Literary Society of Manchester University, and published subsequently in the Cambridge-based *Scrutiny* VIII (1940). Harding had been an undergraduate at Emmanuel College from 1925 to 1928, where he met F. R. Leavis (1895–1978) and his wife, Q. D. Leavis (1906–81), and from 1933 until 1947 served on the editorial board of the Leavises's *Scrutiny*, devoted to a serious critical review of the humanities, with special attention to literature. Harding's intention in his lecture was "to suggest a slightly different emphasis in the reading of Jane Austen," and to "claim the sort of readers who sometimes miss her." Harding aims at "those who would turn to her not for relief and escape [the Janeites] but as a formidable ally against things and people which were to her, and still are, hateful" (25). His focus is on her as a satirist, using "caricatures as criticism of real people in real society" (13). Harding also stresses "the fascination she found in the Cinderella theme, the Cinderella theme with the fairy godmother omitted" (16).

A year after Harding's lecture appeared, the first of four essays by Q. D. Leavis, "A Critical Theory of Jane Austen's Writings," appeared in *Scrutiny* (1941)—the last in spring 1944. These essays argued that Jane Austen was not the "inspired amateur" of conventional Janeite wisdom but "a dedicated professional writer who worked slowly and laboriously," drawing on her own family and other novelists for her raw materials. She reworked earlier versions of her own novels and prolifically wrote letters, read aloud in her family circle and then rewritten for fictional purposes. The publication of Jane Austen's letters revealed that she lacked a sense of innate correct behavior or propriety: "she made jokes about drunkenness, sweating, fleas in the bed and illicit sexual relations" (Kinch, 140, 144–145). She was not a model of good taste. It is Jane Austen's "intense moral preoccupation," and "her indebtedness to others" that, in the words of F. R. Leavis, writing in the opening chapter of

his influential *The Great Tradition: George Eliot, Henry James, Joseph Conrad* (1948), makes her "one of the truly great writers" (5).

Writing in 1954 in "A Note on Jane Austen," C. S. Lewis (1898–1963) follows in the D. W. Harding, Q. D. Leavis, and F. R. Leavis tradition. He attacks the Janeites; the novelist "is described by someone in Kipling's worst story as the mother of Henry James . . . I feel much more sure that she is the daughter of Dr. Johnson." For Lewis, Austen's work is underpinned by a "hard core morality" and seriousness, providing the foundations for real study as distinct form dilettante pursuits (cited Watt, 34).

World War II attitudes are reflected in the 1940 foundation of the Jane Austen Society of England, which made the restoration of Chawton Cottage, the author's home for the last eight years of her life, a priority, and by Sheila Kaye-Smith and G. B. Stern's *Speaking of Jane Austen*, published in 1943. *Speaking of Austen* treats characters as if they are real people. The author's imaginative creators are transformed into real creations populating the imaginations of a war-torn, bombarded population. The Jane Austen Society created during the Blitz, the German blanket bombing of London and other British cities, was preoccupied with conservation, preservation, and restoration, as if Jane Austen were a saint and her relics had at all costs to be safely maintained. Its activities reflect the sense of Jane Austen representing a nation whose privacy is being invaded and targeted. Chawton House from 1947 became part of the Jane Austen Memorial Trust, and it honors both the author and Philip John Carpenter, son of the founder of the trust and a victim of the war (Lynch, 115). Chawton House when purchased lacked Jane Austen's relics. These, such as the lock of her hair, had subsequently to be obtained. It had to be populated to make it real.

The purchase of Chawton House presaged a late 20th-century boom in "Austenism tourism" generated by "a nostalgic, anglophilic notion of 'heritage': the premise that Chawton, Steventon, Winchester and Bath . . . permit a kind of time-travel to the past." The reason is that "they preserve an all but vanished Englishness or set of 'traditional values'" (Lynch, 116). Such iconic perceptions have been reinforced by Jane Austen's radio, television, and cinematic and video status. The popular media has proved most adaptable to her work and widely decimated it, creating a fascination with houses, costumes, transportation, and other seeming re-creations of Jane Austen's world. Such developments have often paralleled the growth in education and mass literacy in the post-1945 world and the extension of the Jane Austen academic industry. Founded in 1979, the Jane Austen Society of North America (JASNA), on the one hand, organizes meetings that feature discussions of typical Janeite preoccupations, such as food, picnics, and dogs in Austen's work, and on the other hand, presents papers on essentially serious concerns published in its annual journal, *Persuasions*.

A popular element of Jane Austen meetings on both sides of the Atlantic are Jane Austen quizzes. The Janeite and academic elements, the popular, the trivial, and the serious are combined in *So You Think You Know Jane Austen? A Literary Quizbook,* containing four levels of quizzes: "Brass Tacks," "Factual but Tricky," "Very Tricky and Occasionally Deductive," and "The Interpretative Zone," inviting "deduction and speculation" ([ix]). The book too provides the answers. Published in paperback in 2005, aimed at a mass market as part of the Oxford World's Classics series, it is the work of an academic scholar and critic, the retired former Lord Northcliffe Professor of Modern English Literature at University College, London, John Sutherland, and the editor of *Jane Austen's Letters* (1995) and *Jane Austen: A Family Record* (1989; new edition 2004), the eminent Jane Austen scholar Deirdre Le Faye. In the same year, 2005, the first three volumes of *The Cambridge Edition of the Works of Jane Austen,* designed to bring the fruits of 75 years of textual scholarship and editing practice to bear on the texts since R. W. Chapman's editions of the 1920s, were published. Consequently, in *So You think You Know Jane Austen? A Literary Quizbook* and the Cambridge edition, the hopes of the Janeites, the lovers of Jane, have been realized. Her stature has been fully realized—she is immortalized for all time by *the* professionals who have also become her worshippers!

See also CHARLOTTE BRONTË.

BIBLIOGRAPHY

Bradley, A. C. "Jane Austen: A Lecture." In *Essays and Studies by Members of the English Association* 2 (1911): 7–36. Reprinted in Southam, II: 233–239.

Brontë, Charlotte. *The Letters of Charlotte Brontë with a Selection of Letters By Family and Friends.* Edited by Margaret Smith. 3 vols. Oxford, U.K.: Clarendon Press, 1995–2003.

Chapman, R. W. "Reading Aloud." In *The Portrait of a Scholar and Other Essays Written in Macedonia, 1916–1918.* London: Oxford University Press, 1920.

Farrer, Reginald. "Jane Austen, ob. July 18, 1817," *Quarterly Review* 228 (July 1917): 1–30. Reprinted in Southam, II: 245–272.

Fowler, Karen Joy. *The Jane Austen Book Club.* New York: G. P. Putnam's, 2004.

Gilson, David. *A Bibliography of Jane Austen.* Winchester, Hampshire, U.K. and New Castle, Del.: St. Paul's Bibliographies and Oak Knoll Press, 1997.

Harding, D. W. "Regulated Hatred: An Aspect of the Work of Jane Austen." In *Regulated Hatred and Other Essays on Jane Austen, by D. W. Harding,* edited by Monica Lawlor. London and Atlantic Highlands, N.J.: Athlone Press, 1998, 5–26.

Hill, Constance. *Jane Austen: Her Homes & Her Friends.* London and New York: John Lane, 1902.

James, Henry. "The Lessons of Balzac." In *Atlantic Monthly* 96 (105): 166–180. Reprinted in Southam, 2: 229–231.

Johnson, Claudia L. "Austen Cults and Cultures." In *The Cambridge Companion to Jane Austen,* edited by Edward Copeland and Juliet McMaster. Cambridge: Cambridge University Press, 1997, 211–226.

Kaye-Smith, Shelia, and Gladys Bronwen Stern. *Talking of Jane Austen.* London: Cassell, 1943.

Kinch, Maurice, William Baker, and John Kimber. *F. R. Leavis and Q. D. Leavis: An Annotated Bibliography.* New York and London: Garland, 1989.

Kipling, Rudyard. "The Janeites" (1926). In *Debts and Credits,* edited by Sandra Kemp. Harmondsworth, U.K., and New York: Penguin, 1987, 119–140. Quoted in Claudia L. Johnson, 214–217.

Lawrence, David Herbert. À *propos of Lady Chatterley's Lover.* London: Mandrake Press, 1930.

Leavis, Frank Raymond. *The Great Tradition: George Eliot, Henry James, Joseph Conrad.* London: Chatto & Windus, 1948.

Lewis, C. S. "A Note on Jane Austen," *Essays in Criticism* 4 (October 1954): 359–371. Reprinted in *Jane Austen: A Collection of Critical Essays,* edited by Ian Watt. Englewood Cliffs, N.J.: Prentice Hall, 1963, 25–34.

Lynch, Deirdre Shauna. "Cult of Jane Austen." In *Jane Austen in Context,* edited by Jane Todd, 111–120. Cambridge: Cambridge University Press, 2005. ["The Cambridge Edition of the Works of Jane Austen."]

Persuasions [annual journal, Jane Austen Society of North America], 1979—.

Saintsbury, George. "Preface" to Jane Austen, *Pride and Prejudice,* illustrations by Hugh Thomson. London: George Allen, 1894, ix–xxiii.

Southam, B. C., ed. *Jane Austen Volume 2, 1870–1940 The Critical Heritage.* London and New York: Routledge, 1987.

———. "Janeites and Anti-Janeites." In *The Jane Austen Companion,* edited by J. David Grey, A. Walton Litz, and Brian Southam, 237–243. New York: Macmillan, 1986.

Sutherland, Kathryn. *Jane Austen's Textual Lives: From Aeschylus to Bollywood.* Oxford: Oxford University Press, 2005.

Sutherland, John, and Deirdre Le Faye. *So You Think You Know Jane Austen? A Literary Quizbook.* Oxford: Oxford University Press [Oxford World's Classics], 2005.

Watt, Ian, ed. *Jane Austen: A Collection of Critical Essays.* Englewood Cliffs, N.J.: Prentice Hall, 1963.

Woolf, Virginia. "Jane Austen at Sixty." *The Nation,* December 15, 1923, 433. Reprinted in Watt, 15–24.

Johnson, Samuel (1709–1784) Henry Austen observes in his "Biographical Notice of the Author" that his sister's "reading was very extensive in history and belles lettres; and her memory extremely tenacious. Her favourite moral writers were Johnson in prose, and Cowper in verse" (7). Jane Austen's copy of the first edition, second volume of Johnson's didactic romance *Rasselas, Prince of Abissinia: A Tale* (1759) survives "with her name written on the title-page in a juvenile hand, showing that she made early acquaintance with Johnson's work" (*FR,* 57; Gilson, 443, K15). *Mansfield Park* contains a paraphrase of a citation from chapter 26 of *Rasselas.* The eighth chapter of the final volume of *Mansfield Park* concludes with a single-sentence paragraph exhibiting the quality of Johnson's balanced prose style: "In a review of the two houses"—Portsmouth and Mansfield Park—"as they appeared to her before the end of a week, Fanny was tempted to apply to them Dr. Johnson's celebrated judgment as to matrimony and celibacy, and say, that though Mansfield Park might have some pains, Portsmouth could have no pleasures" (392).

Earlier in the novel, Johnson's light-hearted semisatirical sketches, *The Idler,* contributed to the *Universal Chronicle, or Weekly Gazette* between April 15, 1758, and April 5, 1760, are mentioned as being among Fanny Price's reading (156). In *Northanger Abbey,* Henry Tilney's sister warns Catherine that they are in danger of being "overpowered with Johnson . . . all the rest of the way" on their walk as Henry Tilney challenges the use of "the word 'nicest'" (108): The allusion here is to Dr. Johnson's great *Dictionary,* first published in 1755, containing copious illustrations of English usage.

Jane Austen's letters refer to Johnson in the context of his companion and biographer James Boswell (1740–95). On November 25, 1798, she tells Cassandra, her sister, that she and her father "have got Boswell's 'Tour to the Hebrides,'" published in 1785, "and are to have his 'Life of Johnson,'" probably the 1793 second edition. Jane Austen concludes another letter to Cassandra, dated February 8, 1807, with a reference to Johnson's July 4, 1774, letter to Boswell: "but like my dear Dr. Johnson I believe I have dealt more in Notions than Facts." In a letter of November 3, 1813, Jane Austen makes a sophisticated allusion to Boswell's *Life of Johnson* (April 2, 1775) when she says that a friend "has more of" the poet "Cowper than of Johnson in him, fonder of Tame Hares & Blank Verse than of the full tide of Human Existence at Charing Cross" (*Letters,* 22, 362, 121, 250, 386, 427).

Jane Austen pays Samuel Johnson a very high compliment by praising him in a poem written "To the Memory of Mrs. Lefroy," a favorite friend of hers who died from falling from her horse in 1804. She includes two verses adapted from Boswell's *Life:*

At Johnson's Death, by Hamilton 'twas said,
"Seek we a substitute—Ah! vain the plan,
No second best remain to Johnson dead—
None can remind us even of the Man."

So we of thee—unequalled in thy race,
Unequall'd thou, as he the first of Men.
Vainly we search around thy vacant place,
We ne'er may look on thy like again.

Boswell is quoting Johnson's close friend the Rt. Hon. William Gerrard Hamilton (1727?–1796), who is supposed to have said, "Johnson is dead.—Let us go to the next best.—There is nobody—No man can be said to put you in mind of Johnson." This is found in the 1792 edition of Boswell's *Life* (Selwyn, 8, 81).

R. W. Chapman, in his listing "Of Literary Allusions" in Jane Austen's work, draws attention to a passage in the early "Love and Friendship: A novel in a Series of Letters" with the inscription "Deceived in Freindship and Betrayed in Love" (76). The passage "we left Macdonald Hall, and . . . sate down by the side of a clear limpid stream" (97), according to Chapman, "is a parody of a Johnson's description of his sitting in" Glen Sheil in *A Journey to the Western Islands* (1775). Furthermore, Jane Austen's "knowledge of the two Universities of Aberdeen" in the juvenilia *Lesley Castle* came from Johnson's description of that city in his *A Journey* (MW, [458]).

Critics have noted Johnsonian parallels in Austen's early and subsequent work. Peter De Rose writes that Johnson is "one of the few writers to whom Jane Austen explicitly and favorably alludes in her Juvenilia and in her major novels" (6). John Wiltshire notes that "the crusty medical men in the novels of her contemporaries may be versions of 'Dr. Johnson,' but Austen's incorporation of Johnson's intellectual disposition is far deeper." Wiltshire continues that it is "realized in her pervasive alertness to affectation, and that scorn and ridicule of medical narcissism which is powered by feeling for real distress" (315–316). Isobel Grundy notes, "Besides his minute particulars, Austen relished Johnson's habits of playful intertextuality and hidden meanings" (199). Perhaps above all, Johnson is a stylistic model. In the "Index" to Norman Page's

The Language of Jane Austen (1972) there are far more references to Johnson, his language, his style, than to any other of Jane Austen's predecessors or contemporary writers (207).

BIBLIOGRAPHY

Austen, Jane. *Jane Austen's Letters.* Collected and edited by Deirdre Le Faye. 3d ed. Oxford: Oxford University Press, 1995.

———. *Jane Austen Collected Poems and Verse of the Austen Family.* Edited with an introduction and notes by David Selwyn. Manchester, U.K.: Carcanet Press, 1996.

———. *Mansfield Park.* Edited by R. W. Chapman. *The Novels of Jane Austen,* Vol. 3. 3d ed. Oxford: Clarendon Press, 1988 reprint.

———. *Minor Works.* Edited by R. W. Chapman. *The Novels of Jane Austen,* Vol. 6. 3d ed. London: Oxford University Press, 1963.

———. *Northanger Abbey and Persuasion.* Edited by R. W. Chapman. *The Novels of Jane Austen,* Vol. 5. 3d ed. London: Oxford University Press, 1965. [Includes "Biographical Notice of the Author" ([3]–9) and Chapman's "General Index: I: Of Literary Allusions (295–307).]

De Rose, Peter. *Jane Austen and Samuel Johnson.* Washington, D.C.: University Press of America, 1980.

Gilson, David J. *A Bibliography of Jane Austen.* Winchester, Hampshire, U.K., and New Castle, Del.: St. Paul's Bibliographies: Oak Knoll Press, 1997.

Grundy, Isabel. "Jane Austen and Literary Traditions." In *The Cambridge Companion to Jane Austen,* edited by Edward Copeland and Juliet McMaster, 189–210. Cambridge: Cambridge University Press, 1997.

Johnson, Claudia L. *Jane Austen: Women Politics and the Novel.* Chicago and London: University of Chicago Press, 1988. [Extensive references to Jane Austen's indebtedness to Johnson.]

Le Faye, Deirdre. *Jane Austen: A Family Record.* 2d ed. Cambridge: Cambridge University Press, 2004.

Page, Norman. *The Language of Jane Austen:* Oxford: Basil Blackwell, 1972.

Wiltshire, John, "Medicine, Illness and Disease." In *Jane Austen in Context,* edited by Janet Todd, 306–316. Cambridge: Cambridge University Press, 2005.

juvenilia "Juvenilia" refers to Jane Austen's earliest writings produced approximately between around 1787 (she was 12 years old in December of that year) and 1793–94, when she was 17. Jane Austen "collected some twenty-nine of these early pieces, amounting to over 90,000 words, to transcribe them into books" referred to as "Volume the First," "Volume the Second," and "Volume the Third" (Southam, [1]). These were gathered together in R. W. Chapman's edition of her *Minor Works*, first published in 1954 and reprinted with revisions in 1963. To these should be added the draft adaptation in dramatized form of SAMUEL RICHARDSON's *Sir Charles Grandison or the Happy Man, a Comedy*, probably belonging to 1791–92, attributed to Jane Austen in 1977 and published in 1980. Many of Jane Austen's early writings have appeared individually in editions published by the Juvenilia Press, which "promote[s] the study of literary juvenilia . . . Its editions are slim volumes of early writing, by children and adolescents (up to the approximate age of 20)" (Alexander). Margaret Anne Doody and Douglas Murray's "World's Classics" edition of Jane Austen's *Catharine and Other Writings* (1993) usefully collects and introduces her "juvenilia" in a single volume. Peter Sabor's edition of the "Juvenilia" in *The Cambridge Edition of the Works of Jane Austen* appeared in 2006.

Interpretations of the "Juvenilia" has largely focused on the way in which they reflect her later work. Some attention has been paid, however, to their intrinsic merit and to the light they appear to throw on the young Jane Austen's opinions and state of mind. According to Margaret Anne Doody in her introduction to *Catharine and Other Writings*, "Jane Austen was not a child as a writer when she wrote these early pieces. She possessed a sophistication rarely matched in viewing and using her own medium" (xxxv).

The contents of the three volumes containing Jane Austen's transcription into three notebooks, corresponding to three volumes, are outlined below (separate entries for each individual title should be consulted as well as individual poems and SIR CHARLES GRANDISON).

Volume the First
Frederic & Elfrida, Jack and Alice, Edgar & Emma, Henry & Eliza, The Adventures of Mr. Harley, Sir William Mountague, Memoirs of Mr. Clifford, The Beautifull Cassandra, Amelia Webster, The Visit, The Mystery, The Three Sisters, A Beautiful Description, The Generous Curate, Ode to Pity

Volume the Second
Love and Freindship, Lesley Castle, The History of England, A Collection of Letters, The Female Philosopher, The First Act of a Comedy, A Letter From a Young Lady, A Tour Through Wales, A Tale

Volume the Third
Evelyn, Catharine, or the Bower

BIBLIOGRAPHY

Alexander, Christine. "The Juvenilia Press Editions" [facing title page]. *Lady Susan by Jane Austen*, edited by Christine Alexander and David Owen. Sydney, Australia: Juvenilia Press, 2005.

——— and Juliet McMaster, eds. *The Child Writer from Austen to Woolf*. Cambridge: Cambridge University Press, 2005. [Contains Rachel M. Brownstein's "Endless Imitation: Austen's and Byron's Juvenilia": 122–137; Margaret Anne Doody's "Jane Austen, that disconcerting 'child'": 101–121.]

Austen, Jane. *Catharine and Other Writings*. Edited by Margaret Anne Doody and Douglas Murray. Oxford: Oxford University Press [World's Classics], 1993.

———. *Juvenilia*. Edited by Peter Sabor. Cambridge: Cambridge University Press, 2006.

———. *Minor Works*. Edited by R. W. Chapman. *The Works of Jane Austen*, Vol. 6. London: Oxford University Press, 1963.

———. '*Sir Charles Grandison*'. Transcribed and edited by Brian Southam, foreword by Lord David Cecil. Oxford, U.K.: Clarendon Press, 1980.

Grey, J. David, ed. *Jane Austen's Beginnings: The Juvenilia and Lady Susan*. Ann Arbor, Mich., and London: UMI Research Press, 1989.

Southam, Brian C. *Jane Austen's Literary Manuscripts: A Study of the Novelist's Development through the Surviving Papers*. New Edition. London and New York: Athlone Press, 2001.

L

language and style There are various ways to approach the subject of language in Jane Austen and to isolate the ingredients of her style. One way is through computation or computer-generated word counts. These can be comparative, that is, comparing, for instance, the instances of dialogue usage in, say, *Northanger Abbey* with *Persuasion* or *Sanditon* or with a specific work of another writer such as Virginia Woolf and one of her novels such as *The Waves*. Alternatively, the distribution of dialogue between characters in a specific novel can be computed. Again, incidences of common words in the dialogue of major characters or the "correlation of the relative frequencies of the thirty most common words in Jane Austen's dialogue" can be given in tabulated form (Burrows, *Computation into Criticism* 86).

Another approach would be narrative rather than statistical analysis of conversation and dialogue in Jane Austen's work through, for instance, comparative generalization relating to the varieties of speech of various characters. These matters can be viewed historically, also using other writers, her contemporaries and predecessors, to reveal what is special about Jane Austen's use of dialogue, what is representative, and what is learned from others. Illuminating, also, is to examine comprehensively her vocabulary, instances of slang and vulgarity, specific nouns, verbs, adjectives, and adverbs, and so on. This approach (found, for instance, in Phillipps) is then followed by descriptive analysis of sentence structures, including tenses, auxiliaries such as "do," "will, and shall," the use of infinitives, the present and past participle, the passive voice, different kinds of verbs, nouns, personal and relative pronouns, adjectives, adverbs, prepositions, conjunctions and direct and indirect speech. Phillipps, in his *Jane Austen's English,* follows this with an analysis of differing "Modes of address" (208–216) such as surnames, or last names. Page in his *The Language of Jane Austen* covers similar territory and also has an illuminating chapter on the use of letters in the novels ([168]–186).

Looking at specific word patterns in individual novels can be yet another way of examining language and style in Jane Austen. To take two instances, Mark Schorer, in his "Fiction and the Matrix of Analogy," notes that *Persuasion* has a "stylistic base derived from commerce and property, the counting house and the inherited estate" (cited Phillipps, 65). Schorer usefully focuses attention on the frequency of financial metaphors in Jane Austen's work. David Lodge's "The Vocabulary of 'Mansfield Park,'" draws attention to the frequency of such words as "manners," "conduct," and "those indicating an order of social or secular values" such as "appropriate, becoming, ceremony, correct, decorum," and others. Lodge writes that "such words cluster together thickly in the comparisons between Portsmouth and Mansfield" (100–101).

To return to computation analysis, Burrow's tables reveal that the "Incidences of Six Common Words in the Dialogue of Major Characters," the words being "we," "us," "very," "quite," "of," and "in," the word "we" is used the most by Lydia and the least by Darcy in *Pride and Prejudice.* In *Persuasion,* Admiral Croft uses "we" the most and Mrs. Smith the least (see Burrows, 76–77). In terms of dialogue and the distribution of words spoken in *Pride and Prejudice,* Elizabeth Bennet has 13,597 instances and Wickham (2,040) the least. In *Persuasion,* Anne has the most, 4,336 instances, Admiral Croft (2,034), the least (see Burrows xiv–xv).

Another interesting facet "of Jane Austen's narrative is that there is so little of it. It comprises only about three-fifths of her words used in her six novels, and in *Emma,* only a trifle over half" (Burrows "Style," 178). Her descriptive passages such as that depicting the "immediate environs" of Lyme Regis in *Persuasion* do not reflect mid–18th-century or Johnsonian patterns but romantic early 19th-century ones. The Johnsonian qualities of argument and didacticism are replaced by feeling and self-expression found, for instance, in phrases such as "unwearied contemplation" or "green chasms between romantic rocks" (95). Jane Austen's indebtedness, however, to Dr. Johnson and the Augustan period is reflected in her use of "the great abstract nouns of the classical and English moralists" (C. S. Lewis, 363), in words such as "handsome," "elegance," "candour," or to take one other instance, "prudent."

A movement from controlled "Johnsonian balance and symmetry towards a much freer form" (Page, "Language," 267) may be noted in Jane Austen's work. In *Sense and Sensibility,* Elinor tells Willoughby, "If their praise is censure, your censure may be praise, for they are not more undiscerning, than you are prejudiced and unjust" (50). The first half of the sentence to the second comma consists of *chiasmus,* or "a sequence of two phrases or clauses which are parallel in syntax." The second half, a parallelism, or "a similar word-order and structure" (Abrams, 281, 12). However, also in *Sense and Sensibility,* Jane Austen is capable of conveying her "character's thoughts and feelings, from moment to moment" (Page, "Language," 267). "The figure of a man on horseback drew her eyes to the window. He stopt at their gate. It was a gentleman, it was Colonel Brandon himself. Now she should hear more; and she trembled in expectation

of it. But—it was *not* Colonel Brandon—neither his air—nor his height . . . He had just dismounted;—she could not be mistaken;—it *was* Edward" (Jane Austen's emphasis, 358). The short sentences, the italics and punctuation, the lack of order, serve to depict Elinor's confusion. They also illustrate Jane Austen's use of interior monologue and ability to convey her characters' thought processes (see Page, "Language," 267–268).

Jane Austen's style and language is characterized by its tremendous variety. The use of dialogue, interior monologue, varied sentence structures, and varying vocabulary are just a few of the devices Jane Austen uses. Language, words are a signpost to character and value. In the "Juvenilia," for instance, the heroine's mother warns her daughter in "Love and Freindship": "Beware of the unmeaning Luxuries of Bath and of the stinking fish of Southampton" (79)—it is difficult to be more direct and colloquial. At other times, Jane Austen can play tricks on her readers' expectations. For instance, in *Emma,* a reply is expected from the heroine to Knightley's proposal. Instead, Jane Austen writes, "What did she say?—Just what she ought of course. A lady always does" (431).

BIBLIOGRAPHY

Abrams, M. H. *A Glossary of Literary Terms,* 8th ed. Boston: Thomson, 2005: 27–29.

Austen, Jane. *Emma.* Edited by R. W. Chapman. *The Novels of Jane Austen,* Vol. 4. 3d ed. Oxford: Oxford University Press, 1986.

———. "Love and Freindship." In *Minor Works,* edited by R. W. Chapman. *The Works of Jane Austen,* Vol. 6. London: Oxford University Press, 1963.

———. *Mansfield Park.* Edited by R. W. Chapman. *The Novels of Jane Austen,* Vol. 3. 3d ed. Oxford: Oxford University Press, 1988 reprint.

———. *Northanger Abbey and Persuasion.* Edited by R. W. Chapman. *The Novels of Jane Austen,* Vol. 2. 3d ed. Oxford: Oxford University Press, 1965.

———. *Pride and Prejudice.* Edited by R. W. Chapman. *The Novels of Jane Austen,* Vol. 2. 3d ed. Oxford: Oxford University Press, 1932.

———. *Sense and Sensibility.* Edited by R. W. Chapman. *The Novels of Jane Austen,* Vol. 1. 3d ed. Oxford: Clarendon Press, 1943.

Burrows, J. F. *Computation Into Criticism: A Study of Jane Austen's Novels and an Experiment in Method.* Oxford, U.K.: Clarendon Press, 1987.

———. "Style." In *The Cambridge Companion to Jane Austen,* edited by Edward Copeland and Juliet McMaster, 170–188. Cambridge: Cambridge University Press, 1997.

Lewis, C. S. "A Note on Jane Austen," *Essays in Criticism* 4 (1954): 359–371.

Lodge, David. "The Vocabulary of *Mansfield Park.*" In *Language of Fiction: Essays in Criticism and Verbal Analysis of the English Novel.* London and New York: Routledge and Kegan Paul, Columbia University Press, 1966, 94–113.

Mandal, Anthony. "Language." In *Jane Austen in Context,* edited by Janet Todd. Cambridge: Cambridge University Press, 2005, 23–32.

Page, Norman. *The Language of Jane Austen.* Oxford, U.K.: Basil Blackwell, 1972.

———. "Jane Austen's Language." In *The Jane Austen Companion,* edited by J. David Grey, A. Walton Litz, and Brian Southam, 261–270. New York: Macmillan, 1986.

Phillipps, K. C. *Jane Austen's English.* London: Andre Deutsch, 1970.

Schorer, Mark. "Fiction and the Matrix of Analogy," *Kenyon Review,* 40 (1949): 539–560.

Tandon, Bharat. *Jane Austen and the Morality of Conversation.* London: Anthem Press, 2003.

law and lawyers Somewhat surprisingly, the words "lawyer," "lawyers," and "attorney" occur on only nine, one, and seven occasions, respectively, in Jane Austen's novels. In English law, the attorney merged with the solicitor in 1873 and the title was abolished. Previously, an attorney had more limited functions than a solicitor. They largely drew up contracts arbitrating disputes, dealing with mortgages, and so on. Mrs. Bennet's "father had been an attorney" and left a not inconsiderable amount (28). Lawyers are also mentioned in *Sanditon* (401), *Northanger Abbey* (205), *Sense and Sensibility* (269), and *Persuasion* (9–11, 20), and in *Emma* there are two: Mr. John Knightley (79), and William Coxe is "a pert young lawyer" (137). Barristers who could argue in most courts of the land, and used the legal training as an entrée into politics and a training

ground for judges, rarely appear in Jane Austen's work. There is in *Sanditon* a reference in the "List of Subscribers" to the local lending library a "Mr Beard—Solicitor, Grays Inn" (389). Grays Inn was in the London Inns of Court, where barristers were trained.

Lawyers do not play prominent roles in her novels, nor do legal disputes. None of Jane Austen's brothers became lawyers, although the family was involved in legal disputes. Francis Austen II (1698–1791), an ancestor on her father's side, became a prosperous attorney (see *FR,* 2–3). The most prominent legal cases involving her family were the dispute concerning the Stoneleigh estate inheritance and the arrest and trial on a shoplifting charge of her aunt Jane Leigh Perrot (née Cholmeley) (*FR,* 156, 120–124).

BIBLIOGRAPHY

Austen, Jane. *Emma.* Edited by R. W. Chapman. *The Novels of Jane Austen,* Vol. 4. 3d ed. Oxford: Oxford University Press, 1986.

———. *Northanger Abbey and Persuasion.* Edited by R. W. Chapman. *The Novels of Jane Austen,* Vol. 2. 3d ed. Oxford: Oxford University Press, 1965.

———. *Pride and Prejudice.* Edited by R. W. Chapman. *The Novels of Jane Austen,* Vol. 2. 3d ed. II. Oxford: Oxford University Press, 1932.

———. "Sanditon." In *Minor Works,* edited by R. W. Chapman. *The Works of Jane Austen,* Vol. 6. London: Oxford University Press, 1963, 363–427.

———. *Sense and Sensibility.* Edited by R. W. Chapman. *The Novels of Jane Austen,* Vol. 1. 3d ed. I. Oxford, U.K.: Clarendon Press, 1943.

Le Faye, Deirdre. *Jane Austen: A Family Record.* 2d ed. Cambridge: Cambridge University Press, 2004.

Olsen, Kirstin. "Law." In *All Things Austen: An Encyclopedia of Austen's World.* 2 vols. Westport, Conn., and London: Greenwood Press, I: 406–408.

Lewes, George Henry (1817–1878) An accomplished journalist, literary critic, editor, publisher's adviser, dramatist, philosopher, novelist, in short, an eminent literary jack-of-all-trades, Lewes is probably best remembered today for his relationship with George Eliot (1819–80), with whom he lived from 1854–55 until his death in 1878.

Lewes was probably the foremost Victorian exponent of Jane Austen's greatness. His championing of her achievements is found in three main essays: "Recent Novels: French and English," *Fraser's Magazine* (December 1847); "The Lady Novelists," *Westminster Review* (July 1852); and at its most sustained in his "The Novels of Jane Austen," *Blackwood's Edinburgh Magazine* (July 1859).

For Lewes, the novel above all must contain "a correct representation of life." The main lines of Lewes's views of Jane Austen are found in his December 1847 essay, in which he places fiction as a genre in "the first rank of literature" and among its practitioners "Fielding and Miss Austen are the greatest novelists in our language." On the other hand, "Scott has greater invention, more varied powers, a more poetical and pictorial imagination, but although his delineation of character is generally true, as far as it goes, it is never deep." Lewes went even further, calling Jane Austen "a prose Shakespeare" and praising "her marvellous dramatic power [which] seems more than any thing in Scott akin to the greatest quality in Shakespeare."

Lewes reinforced this comparison in an unsigned review of an anonymous novel *The Fair Carew.* Writing in a weekly journal that he helped edit, *The Leader,* on November 22, 1851, Lewes observes that Jane Austen, in common with Shakespeare, possesses "a central power of dramatic creation, the power of constructing and animating character" and that "in place of [Shakespeare's] poetry we must put her daring prose—daring from its humble truthfulness."

The notion of Jane Austen as a "prose Shakespeare" and her artistic achievement are the hub of Lewes's tribute to her in his "The Lady Novelists," published in the *Westminster Review* in July 1852. Her character portraits are noted for their "marvellous reality and subtle distinctive traits." She is a genius. "First and foremost let Jane Austen be named," Lewes writes, "the greatest artist that has ever written, using the term to signify the most perfect mastery over the means to her end."

Lewes's most sustained appraisal is found in his "The Novels of Jane Austen," published in *Blackwood's Magazine* in July 1859. He praises her characterization and aesthetic skill, while at the same time finds her wanting in the areas of the "picturesque and passionate," too prosaic in her authorial observation and somewhat lacking in "culture, reach of mind, depth of emotional sympathy"—unlike, for instance, a writer such as George Eliot (with whom he was living)! Lewes's lengthy account, written at the height of his critical powers, is replete with subtle critical distinctions: "all her power is dramatic power; she loses her hold on us directly she ceases to speak through the *personae*; she is then like a great actor *off* the stage." It is Jane Austen's "dramatic instinct which makes the construction of her stories so admirable." However, Lewes admits that "the absence of breadth, picturesqueness and passion, will . . . limit the appreciating audience of" her work "to the small circle of cultivated minds." She is again favorably compared with Shakespeare; however, "her place is among great artists, but it is not high among them." Yet unlike most of her contemporaries, her work "must endure. Such art as hers can never grow old, never be superseded." Lewes emphasizes her realism, and concludes, "Her place is among the Immortals; but the pedestal is erected in a quiet niche of the great temple" (Southam 7, 124–125, 130, 140–141, 159, 156–157, 160, 166). Essentially, his is the most sustained, subtle, and important critical assessment of Jane Austen's achievement published between Sir Walter Scott's 1815–16 *Quarterly Review* essay, Richard Whately's January 1821 essay in the same journal, and the reassessments of Jane Austen following the 1870 publication of Austen-Leigh's *Memoir.*

See also Charlotte Brontë.

BIBLIOGRAPHY

Duffy, Joseph. "Criticism, 1814–1870." In *The Jane Austen Companion,* edited by J. David Grey, A. Walton Litz, and Brian Southam, 93–101. New York: Macmillan, 1986.

Jane Austen Volume I, 1811–1870, The Critical Heritage. Edited by B. C. Southam. London and New York: Routledge, 1979.

libraries   On December 18, 1798, Jane Austen wrote to her sister, Cassandra, that she had received an invitation "requesting my name as a Subscriber to [a] Library" shortly to open, and that Cassandra's name "is accordingly given. My Mother finds the money." Jane tells her sister that as "an inducement to subscribe," the librarian or proprietor, a "Mrs. Martin tells us that her Collection is not to consist only of Novels, but of every kind of Literature . . . She might have spared this pretension to *our* family, who are great Novel-readers & not ashamed of being so" (Jane Austen's emphasis, *Letters,* 26). As David Gilson demonstrates in his "Books Owned by Jane Austen," section "K" of Gilson's A *Bibliography of Jane Austen,* Jane Austen owned many books, and her father had an extensive private library (431–446). The importance of a "family library" is discussed in *Pride and Prejudice,* and Darcy's library at Pemberley is the "work of many generations" (38); the subject serves as an initial point of contact between Elizabeth and Darcy.

The reference in the December 18, 1798, letter is to a Subscribers or Circulation Library. These sprouted up in provincial towns during the late 18th century and the first half of the 19th. Some operated as auxiliaries to other businesses. In Bath, William Frederick's circulating library in 1770 had 9,000 books, and by the time of Jane Austen's initial visit to Bath during the 1790s, there were nine such libraries. The subscribers paid an annual or quarterly fee and could then take out as many books as they wished. Some regarded circulating libraries as potential sources of immorality. Mr. Collins is horrified to discover that he has been asked to read aloud from a work of fiction "from a circulating library" (68). Provided a basic fee could be found, the circulating library and its potentially pernicious content were open to all. In Portsmouth, Fanny Price "became a subscriber, amazed at being any thing in *propria persona* . . . to be a renter, a chuser of books!" (Jane Austen's emphasis, 398). Libraries were also places of social contact and meeting, and in *Sanditon* the list of subscribers provides an advertising source of information on the local inhabitants (389).

BIBLIOGRAPHY

Austen, Jane. *Jane Austen's Letters.* Collected and edited by Deirdre Le Faye. Oxford: Oxford University Press, 1995.

———. *Mansfield Park.* Edited by R. W. Chapman. *The Novels of Jane Austen,* Vol. 3. 3d ed. Oxford: Oxford University Press, 1988 reprint.

———. *Pride and Prejudice.* Edited by R. W. Chapman. *The Novels of Jane Austen,* Vol. 2. 3d ed. Oxford: Oxford University Press, 1932.

———. "Sanditon." In *Minor Works,* edited by R. W. Chapman. *The Works of Jane Austen,* Vol. 6. London: Oxford University Press, 1963.

Gilson, David. A *Bibliography of Jane Austen.* Winchester, Hampshire, U.K., and New Castle, Del.: St. Paul's Bibliographies, Oak Knoll Press, 1997, 431–436.

Olsen, Kirstin. "Circulating Libraries." In *All Things Austen: An Encyclopedia of Austen's World.* 2 vols. Westport, Conn., and London: Greenwood Press, II: 593–595.

Richardson, Alan. "Reading Practices." In *Jane Austen in Context,* edited by Janet Todd, 401–402. Cambridge: Cambridge University Press, 2005.

London Jane Austen frequently visited London. Her first visit was probably in 1788, when with her parents she visited her father's sister Philadelphia, who lived in Marylebone, at that time on the north side of the city. She frequently stayed with her brother Henry, whose bank was in Covent Garden, a center of commerce. Jane Austen's letters reveal that she stayed with Henry when he lived in Brompton (1808), the more upscale Sloane Street (1811 and 1813), over his bank in Henrietta Street (1813 and 1814), and for several months at Hans Place (1814 and 1815). She made other visits, especially for a very short time, say, a night, when she traveled to and from visiting her relatives in Kent. The third extant letter she writes is to her sister, Cassandra, dated August 23, 1796. She is on her way to visit her brother Edward in Kent. She comments, "Here I am once more in this Scene of Dissipation & vice, and I begin already to find my Morals corrupted." In the evenings, she is "to be at Astley's," a horse circus opened in 1770, near Westminster Bridge (*Letters,* 5).

Other letters reveal that Jane Austen took full advantage of what London offered, the capital city, with the largest population by far in the country—in 1808 it had 900,000 of the population of England, the total for the country being 8,500,000. The city was growing rapidly in population and in the areas it occupied. Jane enjoyed its variety and diversity, its busy thoroughfares and shops, the art galleries, exhibitions, and concerts. She writes to Cassandra, September 15, 1813, from her brother Henry's Henrietta Street address, where she has stopped on her way to Godmersham Park in Kent, about theater visits: "Fanny & the two little girls are gone to take Places for tonight at Covent Garden; Clandestine Marriage & *Midas*"—plays by George Colman the elder (1732–94) and Kane O'Hara (1714?–82). London is the fashion center of the kingdom. Jane Austen learns about the latest fashion: "I learnt from Mrs. Tickars's young Lady, to my high amusement, that the stays now are not made to force the Bosom up at all; *that* was a very unbecoming unnatural fashion" (Jane Austen's emphasis, *Letters*, 219–220).

London was also a publishing center, and all of Jane Austen's novels were initially published there. It was also the center of advertising and newspapers. John Murray charged Jane Austen £50 for advertising *Emma* in 1816. Just before his business collapsed, her brother Henry went to live at the fashionable Hans Place. In 1814, from this address, Jane Austen prepared the second edition of *Mansfield Park*, corrected proofs of *Emma*, and continued working on *Persuasion*. Henry then fell ill, and one of his surgeons had royal contracts with the prince regent, resulting eventually in Jane Austen's dedicating *Emma* to him. London was, in other words, the place where important contacts were established.

There is a plethora of references to the capital city throughout Jane Austen's work, and they reflect her complicated, mixed attitude toward London. In her juvenilia, it is a "hot house of Vice" ("Catharine," 239), the home of "insipid Vanities and idle Dissipations" ("Love and Freindship," 78), and "favourite haunts of Dissipation" ("Lesley Castle," 121). In *Sense and Sensibility*, Mrs. Dashwood feels it appropriate as part of Marianne's education, that she "*should* go to town; I would have every young woman of your condition in life, acquainted with the manners and amusements of London." Moreover, she will be suitably accompanied (Jane Austen's emphasis,

156). London also is a place to hide in. Lydia and Wickham travel there in *Pride and Prejudice* for "concealment," and Darcy is able to track them down only through the services of a servant—the equivalent of a private detective (282). The vain Robert Ferrars is introduced in *Sense and Sensibility* as an anonymous shopper fastidiously selecting a pearled toothpick case (220–221). In *Emma*, Frank Churchill mysteriously disappears for a time—he has gone to London to buy a piano, a surprise for Jane Fairfax (205).

In *Mansfield Park*, Fanny Price is "disposed to think the influence of London very much at war with all respectable attachments" (433). Edward Bertram's assessment of London is a balanced one: "We do not look in great cities for our best morality. It is not there, that respectable people of my denomination [beliefs] can do most good" (93). On the other hand, London and specifically Gracechurch Street, at the heart of the commercial area, is the home of the Gardiners. They have grown wealthy on trade, and clearly in *Pride and Prejudice* are positive elements, indeed highly regarded by the exceedingly aristocratic Darcy.

In short, London represented life, to quote Boswell's *Life of Dr. Johnson*: "he who is tired of London is tired of Life because London has all Life has to offer." Johnson subsequently said, "I think the full tide of human existence is at Charing Cross." London had the best shops, society, art, fashion, and culture. It was the political, administrative, and transportation capital, and its press controlled the news, its schools were perceived as the best—Jane Fairfax, for instance, in *Emma* lived in London with the Campbells "and had been given an excellent education" (164). On the other hand, it was associated with a lack of morality and vice, a challenge to the old, stable values based on rural existence. Such a paradox lies at the center of a novel such as *Mansfield Park*. The only one of Jane Austen's novels in which the action actually takes place in London is *Sense and Sensibility*. Elinor Dashwood and Mrs. Jennings, on a fine March Sunday, walk in Kensington Gardens (271). In a letter dated April 25, 1811, to her sister Cassandra, Jane Austen writes, "I had a pleasant walk in Kensington G[ardens] on Sunday . . . everything was fresh & beautiful" (*Letters*, 184). In fact, winter was the best time to be in London: Parliament was in session and the most influential were then in town. Consequently, the best parties and balls were arranged and the main theaters such as Covent Garden and Drury Lane were open. The season extended into spring, but by Easter most of the well connected went back to their country estates (*Mansfield Park*, 295; *Pride and Prejudice,*: 117, 238; *Emma*, 259, 308).

BIBLIOGRAPHY

Austen, Jane. *Jane Austen's Letters.* Collected and edited by Deirdre Le Faye. Oxford: Oxford University Press, 1995.

———. "Catharine," "Lesley Castle," and "Love and Freindship." In *Minor Works,* edited by R. W. Chapman. *The Works of Jane Austen.* London: Oxford University Press, 1963.

———. *Emma.* Edited by R. W. Chapman. *The Novels of Jane Austen,* Vol. 4. 3d ed. Oxford: Oxford University Press, 1986.

———. *Mansfield Park.* Edited by R. W. Chapman. *The Novels of Jane Austen,* Vol. 3. 3d ed. Oxford: Oxford University Press, 1988 reprint.

———. *Northanger Abbey and Persuasion.* Edited by R. W. Chapman. *The Novels of Jane Austen,* Vol. 2. 3d ed. Oxford: Oxford University Press, 1965.

———. *Pride and Prejudice.* Edited by R. W. Chapman. *The Novels of Jane Austen,* Vol. 2. 3d ed. Oxford: Oxford University Press, 1932.

———. *Sense and Sensibility.* Edited by R. W. Chapman. *The Novels of Jane Austen,* Vol. 1. 3d ed. Oxford, U.K.: Clarendon Press, 1943.

Edwards, Anne Marie. "Jane Austen in London." In *The Jane Austen Companion,* edited by J. David Grey, A. Walton Litz, and Brian Southam, 283–285. New York: Macmillan, 1986.

Olsen, Kirstin. *All Things Austen: An Encyclopedia of Austen's World.* 2 vols. Westport, Conn., and London: Greenwood Press, I: 413–418.

Pinion, F. B. *A Jane Austen Companion.* London and New York: Macmillan, St. Martin's Press, 1973.

Stabler, Jane. "Cities." In *Jane Austen in Context.* Cambridge: Cambridge University Press, 2005, 204–214.

***Lovers Vows* (*The Child of Love*)** (1790) An important role in *Mansfield Park* is taken by a performance of Elizabeth Inchbald's (1753–1821) adaptation of the German dramatist August von Kotzebue's (1761–1819) *Das Kind der Liebe* (*The Child of Love*) (1790). Elizabeth Inchbald's adaptation, *Lovers Vows*, was initially performed at the Theatre Royal, Covent Garden, on October 11, 1798. It received 42 performances, was very popular, and was printed 12 times by the end of 1799 before becoming anthologized. *Lovers Vows* was performed on at least 17 occasions at the Theatre Royal Bath during the period in which Jane Austen was in Bath—between 1801 and 1806.

Lovers Vows was a controversial play for the times, especially for its presentation of lower-class characters such as the cottagers and Anhalt as being more virtuous in their behavior than the aristocratic seducers of impoverished women, Count Cassel and Baron Wildenhaim. In *Mansfield Park*, Edmund's immediate objection to the choice of play is a reflection of its reputation for being risqué. Jane Austen seems to take some knowledge of the play for granted among her readers. In book 1, chapter 13, Yates talks of the play's rehearsals at Ecclesford and scatters the characters' names around as if they are familiar to others apart from himself. Three chapters later, discussion of the allotment of parts, and what they demand, also assumes familiarity with the text. The argument between the Bertram sisters over who should play the part of Agatha is highlighted by knowing the extent of the physical contact or proximity Agatha has with Frederic, performed by Henry. There also are parallels between Baron Wildenhaim in Inchbald's adaptation and Sir Thomas Bertram—both encourage mercenary marriages. Maria, who performs Agatha, the deserted fallen woman, certainly anticipates plot developments in *Mansfield Park,* as do Mary and Edmund intensely performing together their scene witnessed by Fanny Price. Sir Thomas, on his unexpected return to *Mansfield Park,* immediately cancels the theatrical performances. This is partly due to the reputation of the play, to the manner of its performance, its implicit threat to his authority and wishes, plus the chaos it has caused in his home.

BIBLIOGRAPHY

Austen, Jane. *Mansfield Park.* Edited by John Wiltshire. Cambridge: Cambridge University Press, 2005. [The Cambridge edition of the Works of Jane Austen: Wiltshire's edition contains the complete text of *Lovers Vows,* 557–629.]

Butler, Marilyn. *Jane Austen and the War of Ideas.* Oxford, U.K.: Clarendon Press, 1975, 232–236.

Gay, Penny. *Jane Austen and the Theatre.* Cambridge: Cambridge University Press, 2002, 103–110.

M

marginalia Two books known to be in Jane Austen's possession contain her marginalia. Her four-volume copy of OLIVER GOLDSMITH's *The History of England, from the Earliest Times to the Death of George II,* published by T. Davies and others in 1771, contains her annotations. These are largely focused in the last two volumes. The first volume contains her summary of events, but without marginal comments. Jane Austen's observations begin approximately halfway through the third volume, with the start of the English Civil War in 1642. They continue till the end of the fourth volume and the death of George II in 1760. The annotations have been attributed to the period of Jane Austen's youth and related to her *The History of England,* in which she drew on Goldsmith's *History.*

The second book with her annotations is Vicesimus Knox's (1752–1821) *Elegant Extracts: or useful and entertaining Passages in Prose Selected for the Improvement of Scholars,* published in London, with no date of publication but first published around 1770, with frequent new editions. The annotations again belong to Jane Austen's youth, as in 1801 she gave the volume to Anna, her eight-year-old niece. Jane Austen's notes relate to Knox's extracts from William Robertson's *The History of Scotland during the reigns of Queen Mary and of King James VI* (London, 2d ed., 1759) concerning Mary, Queen of Scots, and extracts from David Hume's *The History of England, from the Invasion of Julius Caesar to the Revolution in 1688* (London, 1763). She makes notes on "The Character of Queen Elizabeth." Her annotations to Goldsmith and Knox are published in Peter Sabor's "New Cambridge Edition of the Works of Jane Austen," volume of her *Juvenilia,* (316–355) (Cambridge: Cambridge University Press, 2006).

See also GOLDSMITH, OLIVER.

BIBLIOGRAPHY

Gilson, David. *A Bibliography of Jane Austen.* Winchester and New Castle, Del.: St. Paul's Bibliographies, Oak Knoll Press, 1997.

Le Faye, Deirdre. "New Marginalia in Jane Austen's Books," *Book Collector* 49 (2000): 222–226.

marriage The attempt to find a suitable marriage partner is at the heart of Jane Austen's plots. According to the opening paragraph of *Pride and Prejudice,* "It is a truth universally acknowledged, that a single man in possession of a good fortune, must be in want of a wife" (1). Although Jane Austen did not marry, "she did not indeed pass through life without being the object of warm affection" (*Memoir,* 29). At the age of 20, she was attracted to Tom Lefroy (1776–1869), who did not propose to her, subsequently married, and spent his life in Ireland. In 1798, she was courted by Samuel Blackall (1770–1842), a fellow of Emmanuel College, Cambridge, who took his time in proposing. Jane wrote to her sister, Cassandra, on November 17, 1798: "This is rational enough; there is less love and more sense in it than sometimes appeared before, and I am very well satisfied. It will all go on exceedingly well, and decline away in a very reasonable manner." On July 3, 1813, after hearing of his marriage, she hoped that his bride will "be of a silent turn & rather ignorant" (*Letters*, 19, 216). Cassandra revealed after Jane's death that on a family holiday in Devon she met someone; "I never heard" her "speak of anyone else with such admiration." Cassandra "had no doubt that a mutual attachment was in progress between" them. "They parted—but he made it plain that he should seek them out again—& shortly afterward he died!" At the age of almost 27 in December 1801, Jane Austen did receive a proposal from the brother of close friends, a Harris Bigg Wither (1781–1833). She accepted him one evening, and then the next morning turned him down (*Memoir*, 187–188).

On occasion in her letters, Jane Austen reveals an awareness that frequently there is little if any love in marriage. She writes to Cassandra on October 27, 1798: "Mrs. Hall of Sherbourn was brought to bed yesterday of a dead child, some weeks before she expected, oweing [sic] to a fright.—I suppose she happened unawares to look at her husband" (*Letters*, 17). Her fictional Elinor in *Sense and Sensibility* wonders "at the strange unsuitableness which often existed between husband and wife" (118).

Marriage, however, in the world of her novels is a necessity primarily for economic and social reasons. Love, however, has a place in Jane Austen's world. Her niece Fanny Knight was in doubt over her feelings toward the man courting her. Her aunt wrote to her on November 18, 1814: "I thought you really very much in love.—But you certainly are not at all—there is no concealing it." She continues: "His situation in life, family, friends, & above all his Character—his uncommonly amiable mind, strict principles, just notions, good habits—*all* that *you* know so well how to value, *All* that really is of the first importance." Jane Austen adds that in spite of all this, of paramount importance is "the desirableness of your growing in love with him. I recommend this most thoroughly." Above all, "Anything is to be preferred or endured rather than marrying without Affection."

Fanny did not marry until six years later, when she became the second wife of the much older Sir Edward Knatchbull, a wealthy local landowner with six children. She did not pay attention in November 1814 to her aunt Jane's advice in favor of her then suitor, John Plumptre (1761–1864): "the eldest son of a Man of Fortune, the Brother of your particular friend, & belonging to your own Country.—Think of all this Fanny" (*Letters*, 279–280). Jane Austen's work shows her to be wary of those who do not take such factors into consideration. For instance, in the early "Love and Freindship", people who disdain "the false glare of Fortune" have "gracefully purloined" others' money (81, 88). The most obvious instance of a seemingly mercenary marriage occurs in *Pride and Prejudice*, where the heroine's close friend Charlotte Lucas knows that Collins does not love her. He has proposed to Elizabeth and been refused. Charlotte is from a large family, and if she does not marry, she has only a life of dependence before her in the role of the unmarried aunt in her brother's home. She tells Elizabeth: "I am not romantic you know," and explains, "I never was. I ask only a comfortable home; and considering Mr. Collins's character, connections, and situation in life, I am convinced that my chance of happiness with him is as fair, as most people can boast on entering the married state." Charlotte quickly becomes pregnant and manages her husband brilliantly, encouraging, for instance, his gardening activities. She does not appear unhappy and is not condemned by the narrator, although initially Elizabeth is shocked: "she could not have supposed it possible that . . . [Charlotte] would have sacrificed every better feeling to worldly advantage" (125).

There are overt fortune seekers in Jane Austen's novels. Lucy Steele in *Sense and Sensibility* manages to catch a wealthy, well-connected husband. Mary Crawford, a much more complex character, in *Mansfield Park* finds herself growing more attracted to the younger son, Edmund, than to Tom, the elder son, who will inherit the estate. Ultimately, she appears to end up alone but has an inheritance to fall back on. There are other reasons for marriage in Jane Austen's world apart from money. Lady Catherine de Bourgh considers the dynastic one to be of prime importance. In *Persuasion*, Elizabeth Elliot is fortunate, although she may not be aware of it, not to marry her cousin William Elliot, heir to her father's title. Class factors are closely related to dynastic ones. Lady Catherine, for instance, accuses Elizabeth Bennet of being "a young woman without family, connections or fortune" and of having "upstart pretensions" in her designs on Darcy. Elizabeth's reply reflects her own sense of intrinsic worth and a shift in the class system: "He is a gentleman; I am a gentleman's daughter; so far we are equal" (356). However, in *Emma*, the illegitimate Harriet Smith is unsuitable as a wife for Frank Churchill, Elton, and certainly Mr. Knightley.

Human relationships are complex, but there are formal rituals. Marianne's visit to Willoughby at his home is considered inappropriate and perceived as a sign that they are formally engaged. Catherine Morland should not have driven alone in an open carriage with Thorpe. Dances are important, as couples can snatch brief conversations alone with one each other—Bingley with Jane, for instance. Parental approval must formally be sought. Lady Russell considers Wentworth unsuitable and persuades the 19-year-old Anne Elliot to give him up.

There are a number of offstage liaisons: Willoughby with Miss Williams, which produces a daughter; Wickham with Lydia—they are forced to marry by Darcy; Henry Crawford with Maria Rushworth. In *Lady Susan*, from the "Juvenilia," Lady Susan carries on various affairs. Those who are married, such as the Bennets, play on each others' nerves; the Palmers in *Sense and Sensibility* have not been married long, and the husband clearly mistreats the wife. There are widows and widowers. Miss Bates's single fate is not to be envied. In *Persuasion*, however, the Crofts and the Harvilles are clearly happy.

At the conclusion of *Emma*, Knightley's proposal is followed by the narrator's "What did she say?—Just what she ought of course" (431). When he read this, Anthony Trollope scribbled on the flyleaf of his copy that the comment "robs the reader of much of the charm which he has promised himself." Jane Austen's depiction of the sexual passions has been found wanting: "You are talking of Jane Austen and sex, gentlemen? . . . The subjects are mutually exclusive. That dried-up lady snob lived behind lace curtains all her life" (cited McMaster, 287–288).

In essence, Jane Austen, possibly like her heroine Anne Elliot, "had been forced into prudence in her youth, she learned romance as she grew older" (30). In her letter to her niece Fanny Knight of November 18, 1814, Jane Austen cautioned Fanny that her admirer's "expressions then would not do for one who had rather more Acuteness, Penetration & Taste, than Love, which was your case" (*Letters*, 279). The consequences of passion in her novels are great. Perhaps the best summation of her depiction of love and marriage is left to the poet W. H. Auden (1907–73), who writes in his "Letters to Lord Byron" (1937) of Jane Austen: "It makes me most uncomfortable to see / An English spinster of the middle class / Describe the amorous effects of 'brass' [money]." Auden adds: "Reveal so frankly and with such sobriety / The economic basis of society" (cited Southam, II, 299).

BIBLIOGRAPHY

Auden, W. H. "Letters to Lord Byron." In *Jane Austen Volume 2, 1870–1940: The Critical Heritage*, edited by B. C. Southam. London and New York: Routledge: 1987, 11, 299.

Austen, Jane. *Jane Austen's Letters*. Collected and edited by Deirdre Le Faye. Oxford: Oxford University Press, 1995.

———. "Love and Freindship." In *Minor Works*, edited by R. W. Chapman. *The Works of Jane Austen*. Vol. 6. London: Oxford University Press, 1963.

———. *Pride and Prejudice*. Edited by R. W. Chapman. *The Novels of Jane Austen*, Vol. 2. 3d ed. Oxford: Oxford University Press, 1932.

———. *Sense and Sensibility*. Edited by R. W. Chapman. *The Novels of Jane Austen*, Vol. 1. 3d ed. Oxford, U.K.: Clarendon Press, 1943.

Austen-Leigh, James Edward. *A Memoir of Jane Austen and Other Family Recollections*. Edited by K. Sutherland. Oxford, U.K.: Oxford University Press [World's Classics], 2002.

McMaster, Juliet. "Love and Marriage." In *The Jane Austen Companion*, edited by J. David Grey, A. Walton Litz, and Brian Southam, 286–296. New York: Macmillan, 1986. [An excellent account.]

military The last years of the 18th century and the first decade and a half of the 19th century saw

Britain involved in one kind of military conflict after another overseas. The wars in a sense were a continuation of earlier conflicts. The Seven Years' War, waged between 1756 and 1763, was fought on the European continent and on land and sea in North America, India, the West Indies, and West Africa. Ireland always needed a military presence. The American Revolution, the French Revolution, and the long struggle with Napoleon on land and sea (see NAPOLEONIC WARS) led to an increase in the size of the military.

The French wars between 1793 and 1795 witnessed a fourfold increase in the navy, from around 30,000 men in the early 1790s to around 140,000 in 1810. Those involved with the army increased over a similar period from approximately 45,000 to 250,000 by 1812. In 1792, there were 3,100 army officers, and in 1814 around 10,600. Jane Austen's novels are primarily concerned with officers as opposed to the non-commissioned ranks; her immediate family had direct naval rather than army involvement. However, the army does enter into her fiction. General Tilney in *Northanger Abbey* is the highest-ranking army officer, and there are various colonels. Nothing is said of their military activities: Colonel Brandon's regiment served in the West Indies, and the less senior Frederick Tilney was captain in an actual regiment, the 12th Light Dragoons, and there is mention of heavy drinking (153).

The militia figures more prominently in the novels. Service in the militia offered advantages. Enlistment was for five years rather than life or much longer periods; parish help for dependents was provided; service was guaranteed close to home, rarely overseas; and bounties in the form of relatively large signing-on sums were offered. Jane Austen's brother HENRY joined the Oxfordshire Militia as a lieutenant in 1793. Four years later, he was a captain and adjutant, and in 1801 he became an army agent and banker. Weston in *Emma* as a young man joined the county militia, became Captain Weston, and was a "general favourite." His motives were not patriotic but hedonistic, to satisfy an "active, cheerful mind and social temper" (15).

Emma is the Jane Austen novel in which there is an actual war orphan. Lieutenant Fairfax, of the infantry, had married Jane Bates. Their union had "its day of fame and pleasure, hope and interest." Sadly, Fairfax died in action overseas and his wife three years later of consumption. The upbringing of their daughter, Jane, was left to Colonel Campbell, whose life Fairfax had saved when he nearly died of camp fever. Colonel Campbell's income "by pay and appointments was handsome" (163–164) but insufficient to provide for Jane in addition to his own daughter. Consequently, Jane, a war orphan, goes to Highbury to her aunt and grandmother to regain her spirits and prepare for the life of a governess. In this way, Jane Austen's fiction introduces the sensitive subject of the victims of military service and the inadequate provision, if any, provided for them. Captain Harville, too, in *Persuasion* is a victim of the war, as is Captain Benwick. The former, while sustaining actual physical wounds, remains cheerful. Benwick, on the other hand, is deeply affected by the loss of his fiancée and melancholic (96–97).

Wickham also claims in *Pride and Prejudice* that his "chief inducement" in becoming a lieutenant in the militia "was the prospect of constant society, and good society" (79). Following his marriage, he transfers to the regular army, is moved up to the north of England, and a higher rank than ensign is purchased for him by Darcy. *Pride and Prejudice* contains an important structured role involving the militia. In chapter 7 of the novel, there is "news and happiness [of] the recent arrival of a militia regiment in the neighbourhood" with Meryton as its headquarters. This is greeted by Mrs. Bennet with affectionate reminiscences. She "liked a red coat," and she dreams of the possibility of "a smart young colonel, with five or six thousand a year" for one of her eligible daughters (28–29). So the presence of the militia locally provides a source of eligible wealthy bachelors—in this instance, Wickham, although with characteristic Jane Austen irony, he is not wealthy and not an appropriate catch for one of Mrs. Bennet's daughters. Once the winter is over, the regiment moves to Brighton, on the south coast, and Kitty and Lydia Bennet are distressed by such a move and the removal of their fun. Lydia manages to obtain an invitation from Colonel Forster and his wife to visit and see "all the glories of camp" (232). The consequences are Lydia's elopement with Wickham.

The navy figures much more prominently than the army in Jane Austen's own life and her work. Two of her brothers, Francis and Charles, went into the navy at a very young age, went to sea, and eventually rose to prominent ranks. She wrote to her brother Francis, then a captain, on July 3, 1813, and on active service: "Your Profession has its douceurs to recompense for some of its' [sic] Privations" (*Letters*, 214). The negatives included high mortality rates and accidents at sea, the fever (Jane Austen and Francis's sister Cassandra's fiancé contracted a fever in the West Indies and died), drunkenness, sexual abuse, shipboard discipline, which was brutal, lengthy absences from home and family, and a promotion system depending on contacts and money (fictionally treated in *Mansfield Park* and *Persuasion*). The positives included the possibilities of enormous prize money, as in the case of Wentworth in *Persuasion*, and other financial inducements.

Mary Crawford, in chapter 11 of the first book of *Mansfield Park*, tells Fanny, "the profession, either navy or army, is its own justification. It has everything in its favour; heroism, danger, bustle, fashion. Soldiers and sailors are always acceptable in society. Nobody can wonder that men are soldiers and sailors" (109). She neglects to mention the seamier side of military life depicted, for instance, in the Portsmouth scenes in *Mansfield Park*, the depiction of Fanny's unemployed father—a former naval man—and the dockyards. The surroundings, the Ramparts, where Henry Crawford walks with Fanny on one arm and Susan, her sister, on the other, with "the ever-varying hues of the sea . . . dancing in its glee and dashing against the ramparts," contrast noticeably with the "bad air" and "bad smells" of Fanny's father's house. All the reader is given of the actual ships is "the effects of the shadows pursuing each other, on the ship at Spithead and the island beyond," where the naval vessels congregate to sail away to battle (409, 432, 409).

Persuasion is the novel in which the navy plays a crucial role. Admiral Croft served at the decisive Battle of Trafalgar (1805) and then in the East Indies. His wife exercised her right to be with him and had a "reddened and weather-beaten complexion" (48). She had crossed the Atlantic four times during the 15 years they had been married. Her brother Wentworth became a captain following action off St. Domingo in February 1806—an action in which Francis Austen participated. Wentworth "had been lucky in his profession, but spending freely, what had come freely, had realized nothing" (27).

Jane Austen's detailed knowledge of the navy is exhibited in her final novel and in *Mansfield Park*. She is aware of the navy lists, obtained by the Musgrove girls in order to find details confirming Wentworth's first command, of the sloop *Asp* (64–65). The sloop was wrecked by a gale shortly following Wentworth's bringing in of a French frigate in 1808. This was the start of his prize money, which, six years later, amounted to a fortune. In a letter to her sister, Cassandra, written on May 27, 1801, she refers to her sailor brother Charles involved in similar action. "He has received 30£ for his share of the privateer & expects 10£ more—but of what avail is it to take prizes if he lays out the produce in presents to his Sisters. He has been buying Gold chains & Topaze Crosses for us" (*Letters*, 91). These reappear in fictional form in *Mansfield Park*.

Dick Musgrove, "troublesome, hopeless," was sent to sea to get rid of him. His family literally press-ganged him to sea, where he died. The family had "the good fortune to lose [him] before he reached his twentieth year" (*Persuasion*,: 50). Anne Elliot's words to the melancholic Captain Harville at the White Hart in Bath are overheard by Wentworth and provide the climax and resolution of the story. Anne tells Harville, "You are always labouring and toiling, exposed to every risk and hardship. Your home, country, friends, all quitted. Neither time nor health, nor life, to be called your own. It would be too hard indeed . . . if woman's feelings were to be added to all this" (233).

BIBLIOGRAPHY

Austen, Jane. *Jane Austen's Letters*. Collected and edited by Deirdre Le Faye. Oxford: Oxford University Press, 1995.

———. *Emma*. Edited by R. W. Chapman. *The Novels of Jane Austen*, Vol. 4. 3d ed. Oxford: Oxford University Press, 1986.

―――. *Mansfield Park*. Edited by R. W. Chapman. *The Novels of Jane Austen*, Vol. 3. 3d ed. Oxford: Oxford University Press, 1988 reprint.

―――. *Northanger Abbey and Persuasion*. Edited by R. W. Chapman. *The Novels of Jane Austen*, Vol. 2. 3d ed. Oxford: Oxford University Press, 1965.

―――. *Pride and Prejudice*. Edited by R. W. Chapman. *The Novels of Jane Austen*, Vol. 2. 3d ed. Oxford: Oxford University Press, 1932.

―――. *Sense and Sensibility*. Edited by R. W. Chapman. *The Novels of Jane Austen*, Vol. 1. 3d ed. Oxford, U.K.: Clarendon Press, 1943.

Grey, J. David. "Military (Army and Navy)." *The Jane Austen Companion*, edited by J. David Grey, A. Walton Litz, and Brian Southam, 307–313. New York: Macmillan, 1986.

Southam, Brian. *Jane Austen and the Navy*. London and New York: Hambledon, 2000. [The most detailed informative account published.]

―――. "Professions." In *Jane Austen in Context*, edited by Janet Todd, 366–367. Cambridge: Cambridge University Press, 2005.

Milton, John (1608–1674) Extracts from the work of the great writer John Milton are mentioned in the fifth chapter of the opening volume of *Northanger Abbey*. Its narrator refers to "the abilities of the nine hundredth abridger of the History of England, or of the man who collects and publishes in a volume some dozen lines of Milton, Pope and Prior" (37). Milton's early poem "L'Allegro" (1632) is cited in the second volume, chapter 18 of *Emma*. The insensitive Mrs. Elton tells Mr. Weston: "at this rate it would be *May* before Hymen's saffron robe would be put on for us!" (Jane Austen's emphasis 308). This allusion is to "L'Allegro" lines 125–126: "There let Hymen oft appear / In saffron robe, with taper clear." Parallels have been drawn between the description of Robert Martin, the yeoman farmer, and his courtship of Harriet Smith, with passages in Milton's *Paradise Lost* (1667: *Emma*, 28–33). Similarly in *Sense and Sensibility*, Willoughby has been compared with Milton's Adam and Satan in his great poem and the Miltonic *motif* of "disobedience, temptation, lying, loyalty to a fallen partner, fall, and punish-

ment, is re-enacted in the Edward Ferrars and Lucy Steele subplot" (Harris, 76).

In *Persuasion*, Anne Elliot visits her old school friend living in impoverished circumstances in Bath. She observes that Mrs. Smith has not been defeated by poverty or embittered: "here was that elasticity of mind, that disposition to be comforted, that power of turning readily from evil to good, and of finding employment which carried her out of herself, which was from Nature alone. It was the choicest gift of Heaven" (154). Here Anne has as her subtext *Paradise Lost*, book 5, line 18.

Perhaps the most sustained use of Milton in Jane Austen's work is found in *Mansfield Park*. Again, she draws on the poet's *Paradise Lost* and the same text she uses in *Persuasion*. At the conclusion of the fourth chapter of the opening volume of *Mansfield Park*, Henry Crawford tells his sister Mary that he considers "the blessing of a wife as most justly described in those discreet lines of the poet, 'Heaven's *last* best gift'." There is irony here especially as the tempter Henry Crawford speaks the line. "Heaven's *last* best gift" (Jane Austen's emphasis 43) follows the creation of animals and birds in Genesis, 2:18–23, and is recalled in the fifth book of *Paradise Lost*. Adam wakes up to find Eve still asleep besides him. He "[hung] over her enamour'd" and "Her hand soft touching, whisper'd thus: 'Awake, / My fairest, my espous'd, my latest found, / Heaven's last best gift, my ever new delight, / Awake; the morning shines" (lines 17–20: Wiltshire, 649–650).

In addition to this use of Milton, characteristics of the description of Sotherton grounds in the first volume, chapters 9 and 10 of *Mansfield Park* resemble the description of Milton's Paradise in the fourth book of *Paradise Lost*. At Sotherton, "the lawn, bounded on each side by a high wall . . . contained beyond the first planted ærea . . . and beyond the bowling-green a long terrace walk . . . commanding a view . . . into the tops of the trees of the wilderness immediately adjoining" (90). So, too, in Milton, "a verdurous wall," an "enclosure green," "a steep wilderness . . . With thicket overgrown, grottesque and wilde / Access deni'd" (IV, 133–137). In Milton's classic poem and Jane Austen's novel, paradise, imprisonment, and temptation are closely interwoven.

BIBLIOGRAPHY

Jane Austen. *Emma.* Edited by R. W. Chapman. *The Novels of Jane Austen,* Vol. 4. 3d ed. Oxford: Oxford University Press, 1986.

―――. *Mansfield Park.* Edited by R. W. Chapman. *The Novels of Jane Austen,* Vol. 3. 3d ed. Oxford: Oxford University Press, 1988 reprint.

―――. *Northanger Abbey and Persuasion.* Edited by R. W. Chapman. *The Novels of Jane Austen,* Vol. 2. 3d ed. Oxford: Oxford University Press, 1965.

Harris, Jocelyn. *Jane Austen's Art of Memory.* Cambridge: Cambridge University Press, 1989.

money and trade Jane Austen wrote during a time of tremendous economic transition. She died two years after the conclusion of the NAPOLEONIC WARS. These led to unemployment among many of those who had fought the wars. Her life coincided with the transformation of the British economy and social structure from a largely rural and agricultural foundation to an increasingly urban and industrial base. Such a change was accompanied by population growth. Between 1790 and 1820, there was a yearly economic growth of between 2 and 3 percent. Her novels on the whole do not depict the growth of large urban cities such as Birmingham, Manchester, or Liverpool. However, a naval base such as Portsmouth, a spa town such as Bath, and the capital city London do enter the world of her novels. These works are pervaded with rank and snobbery. Lady Catherine de Bourgh, for instance, in *Pride and Prejudice,* would not be seen with people such as the Gardiners, who had grown wealthy through trade carried out in London.

The richest male characters in her novels are associated with land and their estates: Darcy with Pemberley, Knightley with Donwell Abbey, Rushworth with Sotherton. The landed estates make them "independent" (a word used 36 times in Jane Austen's novels) and obviously, if unmarried, targets for mothers such as Mrs. Bennet wishing to marry off one of her daughters to the most eligible, or wealthiest, bachelor. Merchants, or those in trade, on the other hand, were dependant on others and credit rather than real wealth. Trade was perceived as urban, as a town-based activity as opposed to the "independent," land-based wealth. Trade appears in various forms from the milliner's shop or the circulating library in *Pride and Prejudice,* or, to give one other instance, commercial exploitation of the environment as in *Sanditon.* Lawyers traded on both the country estates and the urban world. Mr. Bennet is engaged in the law, although he does not seem ever to act as an attorney.

Jane Austen personally experienced the consequences of economic fluctuations related to the Napoleonic Wars. Her brother Henry was a banker and ran an army agency—he acted financially for the families of army officers overseas. He lived in the style befitting a banker in London, and Jane Austen frequently visited him. As the war with France came to an end in 1815 and the economy reverted to a peacetime one, his business began to collapse. Many small banks collapsed, and in 1816, he became bankrupt, his family lost heavily, and even Jane Austen was not exempt. She lost her saving of just over £13 made from the profits of *Mansfield Park.* Fortunately, "the £600 she had already received as profits on her novels had been safely invested in Navy 5 per cent stock" (*FR,* 234). Before this, she also felt the consequences of not having some kind of regular income. Her sister's fiancé, Tom Fowle, died in the West Indies in 1797. His will provided a small but regular income for Cassandra, his fiancée. Jane Austen's father died in 1805. His will provided for his widow but not for his daughters. Cassandra was covered by Tom Fowle's legacy. Jane Austen was not. Her economic insecurity may well be the underlying cause for the creative spurt evident in her publication efforts during the last decade or so of her life.

Attitudes to trade were not totally hostile. In *Pride and Prejudice,* for instance, Sir William Lucas, who has made a reasonable fortune in trade in Meryton, serves as mayor of the town and has been knighted. He has, however, "a disgust to his business and to his residence in a small market town" and purchases a house in the country that he renames Lucas Lodge (18). Charles Bingley, a highly eligible bachelor, inherits £100,000 from his father, who "acquired by trade" his fortune in the north of England. Bingley's aim is to acquire "a good house and the liberty of a manor" to become a gentleman with a landed estate (15).

More significantly, in *Mansfield Park,* the Bertram family depends for its economic well-being on a "West Indian Property" (5). The Bertrams find themselves in financial difficulties: "some recent losses on" Sir Thomas Bertram's "West India Estate, in addition to his eldest son's extravagance" (24). The "Antigua estate is to make such poor returns," and in consequence the family is left "rather straitened" (30). It is unclear what the problem is. The sugar cane crop could have collapsed. There is the possibility that the estate is involved with "the slave trade"—Fanny asks Sir Thomas about it (198). The immorality of this trade and the implication of the entire Antigua visit by Sir Thomas has engendered a fierce critical debate (see entry on *Mansfield Park* in part II).

Incomes and wealth are in the world of Jane Austen's novels the measure by which a bachelor is judged. There are heiresses also. In *Pride and Prejudice,* Miss Bingley has a fortune of "twenty thousand pounds" (15) and Miss King has "ten thousand pounds" (149). On the other hand, Elizabeth Bennet has only £1,000 to invest. The highest annual income in the novels is Mr. Rushworth's in *Mansfield Park* with £12,000; Darcy has 2,000 less, not to mention his magnificent estate. Bingley has half that amount. Much lower down on the scale is the £100 per year the foolish, headstrong Lydia Bennet receives from her dowry. She would also receive part of her father's inheritance when he dies. Clergymen, on the whole, received £200 per year plus, of course, the accommodation. Edward Ferrars in *Sense and Sensibility* has £300 a year. This "cannot enable him to marry" (284). Such an income brings two servants. An income over about £4,000 per year means many servants and retainers and at least two houses, including one in London.

It is very difficult to provide modern equivalents of such sums except to repeat that in Jane Austen's world an income of above £4,000 per annum with an accompanying estate and property constituted real wealth. Anything below £100 per annum meant the bread line, and £1,000 per annum with property

ensured a reasonable status. Money in Jane Austen's work plays a crucial role. There is a distinction between its role in the first three novels and the last three, and in *Sanditon* it is the generating focus. In the early novels, the unmarried woman is in a perilous position and must marry for financial security and well-being. In *Mansfield Park, Emma,* and *Persuasion,* Fanny Price, Jane Fairfax, and Anne Elliot, respectively, are the playthings of chance. Emma observes of Jane Fairfax and her situation with Frank Churchill: "'The world is not theirs, nor the world's law'" (400)—a misquotation from *Romeo and Juliet,* 5, i, 71. Fanny Price economically has nothing and Anne Elliot only "advice is good or bad only as the event decides" (*Persuasion,* 246). In the end, there are satisfactory, presumably happy resolutions, but before that Jane, Fanny, and Anne can do little to influence their fate and economic well-being.

BIBLIOGRAPHY

Austen, Jane. *Emma.* Edited by R. W. Chapman. *The Novels of Jane Austen,* Vol. 4. 3d ed. Oxford: Oxford University Press, 1986.

———. *Mansfield Park.* Edited by R. W. Chapman. *The Novels of Jane Austen,* Vol. 3. 3d ed. Oxford: Oxford University Press, 1988 reprint.

———. *Northanger Abbey and Persuasion.* Edited by R. W. Chapman. *The Novels of Jane Austen,* Vol. 2. 3d ed. Oxford: Oxford University Press, 1965.

———. *Pride and Prejudice.* Edited by R. W. Chapman. *The Novels of Jane Austen,* Vol. 2. 3d ed. Oxford: Oxford University Press, 1932.

———. *Sense and Sensibility.* Edited by R. W. Chapman. *The Novels of Jane Austen,* Vol. 1. 3d ed. Oxford, U.K.: Clarendon Press, 1943.

Copeland, Edward. "Money." In *The Cambridge Companion to Jane Austen,* edited by Edward Copeland and Juliet McMaster, 131–148. Cambridge: Cambridge University Press, 1997.

Ellis, Markman. "Trade." In *Jane Austen in Context,* edited by Janet Todd, 415–424. Cambridge: Cambridge University Press, 2005.

Le Faye, Deirdre. *Jane Austen: A Family Record.* 2d ed. Cambridge: Cambridge University Press, 2004.

Montgomery, James (1771–1854)   Sir Edward Denham asserts in *Sanditon* that "Montgomery has all the Fire of Poetry" (397). Born in Ayrshire in Scotland, the son of a Moravian minister, Montgomery, after a rather checkered career, settled in Sheffield in Yorkshire, where he became a noted journalist and newspaper editor. Imprisoned for apparently pro-French Revolutionary sympathies, and a keen supporter of the abolition of the slave trade, Montgomery was a prolific hymn writer, reviewer, and poet. He achieved national fame with the 1806 publication of *The Wanderer of Switzerland and Other Poems.* A political poem, it spoke out against Napoleon and for Britain's freedom endangered by Napoleon. His poems "The Grave" (1806) and "The Peak Mountains" (1812) were highly regarded for their strength of feeling.

See also ROBERT BURNS, THOMAS CAMPBELL, and WILLIAM WORDSWORTH.

BIBLIOGRAPHY

Austen, Jane. *Sanditon.* In *Minor Works,* edited by R. W. Chapman. *The Works of Jane Austen.* Vol. 6. London: Oxford University Press, 1963, 363–427.

Tolley, G. "Montgomery, James (1771–1854)." In *Oxford Dictionary of National Biography.* 60 vols., edited by H. C. G. Matthew and Brian Harrison, 38: 856–858. Oxford: Oxford University Press, 2004.

Murray, John (1778–1843) John Murray, the publisher of Albermarle Street, London, published Byron and the *Quarterly Review,* among other literary and philosophical works. He moved to the 50 Albemarle Street premises in June 1812, placing the firm at the center of London literary activity. Murray published, in February 1816, the second edition of *Mansfield Park,* of which 750 copies were printed and sold in three volumes for 18 shillings. In January 1820, 498 copies were remaindered at 2 shillings 6d. William Gifford (1756–1826), editor of the *Quarterly Review* and Murray's regular reader, read *Emma* for Murray, and Gifford reported on September 29, 1815, in its favor. Murray offered £450 for the copyright and also the copyrights of *Mansfield Park* and *Sense and Sensibility. Emma* was published at the author's expense, the publisher receiving 10 percent commission, and then she received profits and held the copyright. Dedicated to the prince regent, 2,000 copies of *Emma* were printed by Murray in three volumes and sold at £1.1s. By October 1816, 1,248 copies were sold. The canny Murray took his loss for the second edition of *Mansfield Park* against this, and Jane Austen received only £38.10s for her initial payment in February 1817. In 1820, 534 copies remained unsold and were remaindered at 2s.

Jane Austen referred to Murray in a letter to Cassandra dated October 17, 1815, as "a Rogue of course, but a civil one" (*Letters,* 291). Henry Austen had Murray publish posthumously *Northanger Abbey* and *Persuasion* in December 1817. Murray published them together in four volumes, with a "Biographical Notice of the Author" by her brother Henry. Murray printed 1,750 copies, priced at 24 shillings; the title page was dated 1818. Cassandra's profit was almost £519 by 1821, when 283 copies were remaindered.

BIBLIOGRAPHY

Austen, Jane. *Jane Austen's Letters.* Edited by Deirdre Le Faye. 3d ed. Oxford: Oxford University Press, 1995.

Gilson, David. *A Bibliography of Jane Austen.* Winchester and New Castle, Del.: St. Paul's Bibliographies and Oak Knoll Press, 1997.

music Caroline Bingley in *Pride and Prejudice* expects that the accomplished young lady should "have a thorough knowledge of music, singing, drawing, dancing, and the modern languages" (39). Elizabeth Bennet sings and plays, as does Anne Elliot in *Persuasion.* Marianne Dashwood and Jane Fairfax also play the piano, and Mary Crawford is a fairly accomplished harpist. Musical accomplishment in addition to practicing an instrument, usually the piano or harp, included the copying out of music from printed sources. Among Jane Austen's possessions at Chawton are volumes of music copied in her hand. She practiced the pianoforte every morning before breakfast and accompanied herself on occasions, singing "simple old songs" in the evenings. Caroline Austen in "My Aunt Jane Austen: A Memoir" writes that her aunt "began her day with music—for which I conclude she had a natural taste; as she thus kept it up . . . was never induced . . . to play in company; and none of her family cared much for it." Caroline adds, "I suppose that she might not trouble *them*, she chose her practising time right before breakfast—when she could have the room to herself—She practised regularly every morning—She played very pretty tunes *I* thought." Also "Much that she played from was manuscript, copied out by herself—and so neatly and correctly, that it was as easy to read as print" (Caroline's emphasis: *Memoirs*, 170–171).

Somewhat in the manner of Anne Elliot, Jane Austen played to give "pleasure only to herself" (47). Mary Bennet's lengthy hours of practice at the pianoforte and study are perceived as efforts to make up for social inadequacy and lack of physical attractiveness, rather than a real love of music. Marianne Dashwood is able to perform "a very magnificent concerto" (149), and her delight in singing is silenced by grief. Mary Crawford uses her harp, "as elegant as herself" (65), to charm Edmund. The mystery of the Broadwood pianoforte propels the plot of *Emma*. Its sudden arrival at Highbury embarrasses Jane Fairfax and stimulates gossip. At the Coles' dinner party following speculation concerning the pianoforte, attention focuses on the Coles' new grand piano. None of the family is able to play it, but Mr. Cole, who loves music, purchased it anyway. Structural analysis of chapter 8 of the second book of *Emma* displays a musical A-B-C-D//A-B-C-D form: the chapter "is presided over by two pianofortes, one square and one grand, one absent and one present." Its motifs are those of "food (dinner), sex (piano), property (the Coles' opulent house), and freedom of movement (arrivals and departures). But the emphasis is on sex, love, and what often attends them, jealousy." Indeed, "the piano is coded feminine and associated with women's emotional life," offering opportunities for personal emotional expression and to attract the opposite sex (Wiesenfarth, 156).

The harp, too, appears in the novels as having a similar function as the pianoforte. Mary Crawford is not the sole practitioner. The Musgrove girls, too, attempt to play the harp; Georgina Darcy plays the harp and the pianoforte superbly well. In *Sanditon*, the harp is mentioned twice (383, 421) and once in *Sense and Sensibility* (250). At the time, the popularity of the harp rivaled that of the pianoforte. Jane Austen's cousin Eliza Feuillide (née Hancock) played it and so did Fanny Knight, her niece. At a London musical party, Jane Austen heard the leading harp virtuoso, Johann Wiepart, "whose name," she told Cassandra, "seems famous tho' new to me" (*Letters*, 183: April 25, 1811). Sometimes Jane Austen objected to the music she heard. She writes to Cassandra in a letter from Bath on June 2, 1799: "There is to be a grand gala on tuesday [sic] evening in Sydney Gardens;—a Concert, with Illuminations & fireworks." She adds somewhat ambiguously, "even the Concert will have more than its' [sic] usual charm with me, as the Gardens are large enough for me to get pretty well beyond the reach of its sounds." In a later letter to Cassandra dated March 5–8, 1814, she anticipates that, despite the performance of a celebrated singer, Thomas Arne's opera "Artaxerxes will be very tiresome!" (*Letters*, 43, 260).

The only composer named in Jane Austen's novels is Johann Baptist Cramer (1771–1858), who came to England from Germany at the age of three. In addition to being an infant prodigy and a virtuoso pianist, he was a prolific composer of works for the pianoforte. Frank Churchill sends Jane Fairfax some of his pianoforte work with the Broadwood gift (242). In a letter to Cassandra of September 16, 1813, she refers to "Hook's Lessons for Beginners," that is James Hook's (1746–1827) *Guida di Musica, being a completed book of instruction for the Harpsichord or the Pianoforte* (1790; new edition, 1810) (*Letters*, 224, 420). There appears to be no other direct mention of specific composers.

BIBLIOGRAPHY

Austen, Jane. *Jane Austen's Letters*. Collected and edited by Deirdre Le Faye. Oxford: Oxford University Press, 1995.

———. *Emma*. Edited by R. W. Chapman. *The Novels of Jane Austen*, Vol. 4. 3d ed. Oxford: Oxford University Press, 1986.

———. *Mansfield Park*. Edited by R. W. Chapman. *The Novels of Jane Austen*, Vol. 3. 3d ed. Oxford: Oxford University Press, 1988 reprint.

———. *Northanger Abbey and Persuasion.* Edited by R. W. Chapman. *The Novels of Jane Austen,* Vol. 2. 3d ed. Oxford: Oxford University Press, 1965.

———. *Pride and Prejudice.* Edited by R. W. Chapman. *The Novels of Jane Austen,* Vol. 2. 3d ed. Oxford: Oxford University Press, 1932.

———. "Sanditon." In *Minor Works,* edited by R. W. Chapman. *The Works of Jane Austen,* Vol. 6. London: Oxford University Press, 1963, 363–427.

———. *Sense and Sensibility.* Edited by R. W. Chapman. *The Novels of Jane Austen,* Vol. 1. 3d ed. Oxford, U.K.: Clarendon Press, 1943.

Austen-Leigh, James Edward. *A Memoir of Jane Austen and Other Family Recollections.* Edited by Kathryn Sutherland. Oxford: Oxford University Press [World's Classics], 2002.

Piggott, Patrick. *The Innocent Diversion: A Study of Music in the Life and Writings of Jane Austen.* London: Douglas Cleverdon, 1979.

———. "Music." In *The Jane Austen Companion,* edited by J. David Grey, A. Walton Litz, and Brian Southam, 314–316. New York: Macmillan, 1986.

Wiesenfarth, Joseph. "A Likely Story: The Coles' Dinner Party." In *Approaches to Teaching Austen's Emma,* edited by Marcia McClintock Folsom, [151]–158. New York: MLA, 2004.

N

Napoleonic Wars For most of Jane Austen's life, England was at war with France and its allies. The main conflicts were the American Revolution (1778–83), the French Revolutionary Wars (1793–1802), and the lengthy Napoleonic War period, extending from 1803 until 1815. These conflicts were on a global scale, and Jane Austen's own family was involved directly. Her brothers Charles and Francis served in the navy and were engaged in active naval conflicts. Her relative Eliza's first husband, Jean-François Capot, the comte de Feuillide, was guillotined during the French Revolution.

Napoleon achieved control of France in 1799, and following his victory at the Battle of Marengo in 1800, became a direct threat to Britain. The subsequent Treaty of Amiens (1801) returned captured colonial territory to France; however, in May 1803, war broke out again. There were threats of an imminent invasion—reflected in *Northanger Abbey* with its talk of whispering and gossip concerning external threats. Francis Austen was involved in the naval defense of the southern coastline. For two years, Napoleon's navy played cat-and-mouse games with the Royal Navy, tempting it to follow French ships to the West Indies and back (see *Mansfield Park*, 236). Francis was again involved in this and also in the 1804 attack on the French fleet at Boulogne. As the captain of the *Canopus*, he was part of a chasing party to the West Indies and then, in 1805, was associated with the defeat of the French at Trafalgar (*Sanditon*, 380), at which Admiral Nelson died in battle.

The action following Trafalgar then moved to land warfare, including the bloody conflict in the Iberian peninsula conducted under the leadership of the Duke of Wellington. In 1814 Napoleon's armies were defeated at Leipzig. In March 1814, the British army reached Paris, and by autumn Napoleon was exiled to Elba. Demobilization took place; however, Napoleon escaped and was finally defeated at Waterloo and then exiled to the remote South Atlantic outpost of St. Helena.

These wars clearly had an economic impact. For instance, the prices of food and other basic commodities increased (*Sanditon*, 380, 392–393) due to a sequence of indifferent harvests and an attempt by Napoleon to block continental ports to British shipping. Domestically, taxes were increased to offset the cost of war. There was a tax on luxury goods, and in the 1790s income tax was introduced. Those who had profited by the war, such as Jane's brother Henry in the immediate post-1815 period, saw their businesses collapse. Naval personnel such as Wentworth, for instance, profited considerably through the acquisition of French booty. Napoleon's harassment of shipping had stimulated British farmers to focus on improved agricultural methods (Robert Martin in *Emma* is a fine example of this). The years 1813 to 1816 witnessed excellent harvests, and the coming of peace led to a fall in agricultural prices, after which farmers' and landlords' profits dropped drastically. In such a fluctuating economy, Admiral Croft in *Persuasion* is able, for instance, to afford to rent Kellynch Hall. The Admiral clearly has far more assets than Sir Walter Elliot: He is a "wealthy naval commander" (18), whereas Sir Walter is singularly unproductive.

See also MILITARY.

BIBLIOGRAPHY

Austen, Jane. *Emma.* Edited by R. W. Chapman. *The Novels of Jane Austen,* Vol. 4. 3d ed. Oxford: Oxford University Press, 1986.

———. *Mansfield Park,* Edited by R. W. Chapman. *The Novels of Jane Austen,* Vol. 3. 3d ed. Oxford: Oxford University Press, 1988 reprint.

———. *Northanger Abbey and Persuasion.* Edited by R. W. Chapman. *The Novels of Jane Austen,* Vol. 2. 3d ed. Oxford: Oxford University Press, 1965.

———. *Pride and Prejudice.* Edited by R. W. Chapman. *The Novels of Jane Austen,* Vol. 2. 3d ed. Oxford: Oxford University Press, 1932.

———. "Sanditon" and "The Watsons." In *Minor Works,* edited by R. W. Chapman. *The Works of Jane Austen,* Vol. 6. London: Oxford University Press, 1963.

Olsen, Kirstin. "Napoleonic Wars." In *All Things Austen: An Encyclopedia of Austen's World.* 2 vols. Westport, Conn., and London: Greenwood Press, II: 463–466.

Roberts, Warren. "Nationalism and Empire." In *Jane Austen in Context,* edited by Janet Todd, 327–336. Cambridge: Cambridge University Press, 2005.

Southam, Brian. *Jane Austen and the Navy.* London and New York: Hambledon, 2000. [Replete with details of the naval battles Jane Austen's brothers were engaged in.]

P

Pope, Alexander (1688–1744) There are various references to the work of the poet and satirist Alexander Pope throughout Jane Austen's writing. In *Sense and Sensibility,* at their second meeting, apparently Marianne "received every assurance of" Willoughby's "admiring Pope no more than is proper" (47). This alludes to the risqué nature of Pope's material found, for instance, in *The Rape of the Lock* (1712). Pope's satirical poem, in which Lord Petrie snips a lock of Arabella Fermor's hair, while she sips her coffee during a card game of ombre, underpins elements in *Sense and Sensibility, Mansfield Park,* and *Persuasion.* In *Sense and Sensibility,* Elinor perceives that the hair in the ring Edward is wearing, Lucy's, "must have been procured by some theft or contrivance unknown to herself" (98). Foolishly, Marianne "so obligingly bestowed on" Willoughby, a lock from her hair (183). In *Persuasion,* the vain, egocentric Sir Walter marks time with an "elegant little clock" that "had 'struck eleven with its silver sounds'" (144), a line from *The Rape of the Lock,* also indicating vanity and narcissism.

In *Mansfield Park,* Henry Crawford notices that Fanny's "hair [is] arranged as neatly as it always is, and one curl falling forward" (296), the implication being that, as in *The Rape of the Lock,* she is ready for sexual experience. Like Arabella Fermor in Pope's poem, Fanny, too, is preoccupied with which cross she should wear around her neck at a ball (254). Fanny's conversation with Mary Crawford on what she should wear is full of erotic suggestions in a similar manner to Pope's poem. Mary Crawford speaks of her brother: "Do you think Henry will claim the necklace as mine . . . or are you imagining he would be too much flattered by seeing round your lovely throat an ornament?" (259). Mary Crawford, in assisting her brother Henry in his attempt to seduce Fanny, is playing the role of Pope's Clarissa in his poem who assists the Baron in his seduction of Arabella. However, Fanny resists and Mary ends up with her own locks unplucked.

Other references to Pope in Jane Austen include, in *Northanger Abbey,* a citation from his "Elegy to the Memory of an Unfortunate Lady" (1712). In the first chapter "From Pope," Catherine Morland "learnt to censure those who 'bear about the mockery of woe'" (line 15: 15). Pope's "Essay on Man" is slightly misquoted in a letter Jane Austen writes to her sister Cassandra, dated October 26, 1813: "There has been one infallible Pope in the World," probably thinking of Pope's line in his poem, "One truth is clear, Whatever is, is right" (line 284: *Letters,* 245, 425). In her juvenile "A Collection of Letters," the line "Ride where you may, be Candid where you can" is a parody of the opening epistle line 15 in Pope's "Essay": "Laugh where we must, be candid where we can" (154).

BIBLIOGRAPHY

Austen, Jane. *Jane Austen's Letters.* Collected and edited by Deirdre Le Faye. Oxford: Oxford University Press, 1995.

———. "A Collection of Letters." In *Minor Works,* edited by R. W. Chapman. *The Works of Jane Austen,* Vol. 6. London: Oxford University Press, 1963 Reprint, 150–170.

———. *Mansfield Park.* Edited by R. W. Chapman. *The Novels of Jane Austen,* Vol. 3. 3d ed. Oxford: Oxford University Press, 1988 reprint.

———. *Northanger Abbey and Persuasion.* Edited by R. W. Chapman. *The Novels of Jane Austen,* Vol. 2. 3d ed. Oxford: Oxford University Press, 1965.

———. *Sense and Sensibility.* Edited by R. W. Chapman. *The Novels of Jane Austen,* Vol. 1. 3d ed. Oxford, U.K.: Clarendon Press, 1943.

Harris, Jocelyn. *Jane Austen's Art of Memory.* Cambridge: Cambridge University Press, 1989.

Prince Regent (King Geroge IV) George-Augustus-Frederick (1762–1830) was the eldest son of George III (1738–1820). Prince of Wales since birth, on February 6, 1811, following his father's inability to conduct state affairs, he became prince regent and succeeded in 1820 as King George IV. Known for an extravagant lifestyle and as a patron of the arts, in 1785 he secretly had married Mrs. Maria Fitzherbert, older than he was, twice widowed, and a Roman Catholic. She was unacceptable as the wife of the heir to the throne. In 1795, bigamously but in order to pay off debts and to please his increasingly ill father, he married his cousin Princess Caroline of Brunswick. The marriage was doomed from the start and became increasingly acrimonious. Jane Austen wrote on February 16, 1813, to her friend Martha Lloyd: "if I must give up the Princess, I am resolved to at least always to think that she would have been respectable, if the Prince had behaved only tolerably by her at first" (*Letters,* 208).

The prince's behavior set a tone for licentiousness in high society. He built in Brighton a residence, the Pavilion, where he resided with Mrs. Fitzherbert. Wickham's attitude in *Pride and Prejudice* and the Crawfords' behavior in *Mansfield Park* reflect something of the irresponsible, hedonistic, rakish attitudes from the prince's circle. Under pressure from the prince's librarian, the Reverend James Stanier Clarke, Jane Austen dedicated *Emma* to the prince regent. Clarke claimed that the prince was an adamant admirer of Jane Austen's novels, and sometime afterward she sent him a presentation copy. The prince's thanks "for the handsome Copy you sent him of your last excellent Novel" were sent to her by Clarke (March 27, 1816: *Letters,* 311) from the Royal Pavilion. The copy is now at Windsor Castle (Gilson, 74). There is no real evidence that the prince actually read *Emma* or any other of Jane Austen's work.

BIBLIOGRAPHY

Austen, Jane. *Jane Austen's Letters.* Collected and edited by Deirdre Le Faye. 3d ed. Oxford: Oxford University Press, 1995.

Gilson, David. *A Bibliography of Jane Austen.* Winchester, Hampshire, U.K. and New Castle, Del.: St. Paul's Bibliographies, Oak Knoll Press, 1997.

Le Faye, Deirdre. *Jane Austen: The World of her Novels.* New York: Harry N. Abrams, 2002.

R

Radcliffe, Mrs. Ann (1764–1823)   At least four works by the writer of gothic fiction influenced Jane Austen. Mrs. Radcliffe's first novel, *The Castles of Athlin and Dunbayne* (1789), is reflected in "Love and Freindship." In both, the heroes fall in love with the heroines during their initial encounter. Faintings frequently occur in both, and the hero also raves in delirium. In letter eight of Jane Austen's juvenile work, Sophia is described as "rather above the middle size, most elegantly formed. A soft languor spread over her lovely features, but increased their Beauty" (85). In Mrs. Radcliffe's novel, Laura is "about twenty, her person was of middle stature . . . and very elegantly formed. The bloom of her youth was shaded by a soft and passive melancholy" (Pinion, 173).

In chapter 4 of *Emma*, Harriet Smith tells Emma that Mr. Martin "never read the Romance of the Forest, nor the Children of the Abbey" (29). This is a reference to Mrs. Radcliffe's novel published in 1791. This novel, Radcliffe's *A Sicilian Romance* (1790), and *The Mysteries of Udolpho* (1794) are reflected in *Northanger Abbey*. Incidents in *A Sicilian Romance* are seen in the fantasy that General Tilney's wife was still "shut up for causes unknown, and receiving from the pitiless hands of her husband a nightly supply of coarse food" (188). *The Romance of the Forest* provides the subtext for Henry Tilney's tale and the happenings during the first night of Catherine Morland's stay at the Abbey. In *The Romance*, the heroine, Adeline, stays at a ruined abbey and soon discovers a secret room in which

there is a rusty dagger and a roll of paper—on this is the tale of a man who was kept prisoner there.

The language and events of *The Mysteries of Udolpho*, as has been pointed out (see Pinion and Gaull's introduction to the edition, for instance), pervade *Northanger Abbey*. To indicate a few instances: the black veil and Laurentina, Montoni, St. Aubin, and Dorothy are overt allusions to Mrs. Radcliffe's novel. In *Udolpho*, Emily persuades Dorothée, the aging housekeeper, to display the rooms where the marchioness was poisoned. In *Northanger Abbey*, Catherine's obsession to explore Mrs. Tilney's rooms is fueled by her reading of *Udolpho*. Catherine spends too much time alone reading, indulging in fantasies, induced partly by her reading of Mrs. Radcliffe's novels. Emily, the heroine of *Udolpho*, is an orphan, alone in a large, frightening house. There are clearly parallels with the situation of Fanny in *Mansfield Park*.

There are curious parallels, too, between Jane Austen's *Northanger Abbey* and Mrs. Radcliffe's own life. The wife of a lawyer and editor of newspapers, she "occupied her long evenings alone, writing stories that reflected her own fantasy life." Furthermore "so reclusive was" Mrs. Radcliffe "that for the last thirteen years of her life, she was reputed to be dead or driven mad by an excess of imagination." She apparently stopped writing after her last novel, centered on the Inquisition, *The Italian* (1797). In this novel, its villain, an evil monk, is a victim of his past and the "conflict between his instincts and his actions, and by his superhuman ambitions and his mortal limitations" (Gaull, 224, 228). The emphasis in Radcliffe's novels of the fantasy world of the inner imagination; exaggeration; foreign settings and characters; women as the victims of ruthless, apparently larger than life villains preying on them; and ancient, haunted mysterious surroundings all constitute what became known as the gothic novel. The language and incidents are clearly parodied in *Northanger Abbey.*

BIBLIOGRAPHY

Austen, Jane. "Love and Freindship." In *Minor Works,* edited by R. W. Chapman. *The Works of Jane Austen,* Vol. 6. London: Oxford University Press, 1963, [76]–109.

———. *Emma.* Edited by R. W. Chapman. *The Novels of Jane Austen,* Vol. 4. 3d ed. Oxford: Oxford University Press, 1986 reprint.

———. *Northanger Abbey and Persuasion.* Edited by R. W. Chapman. *The Novels of Jane Austen,* Vol. 5. 3d ed. London: Oxford University Press, 1965 reprint.

———. *Northanger Abbey.* Edited by Marilyn Gaull. New York, London: Pearson, Longman, 2005. [Longman Cultural Editions.]

Pinion, F. B. *A Jane Austen Companion.* London: Macmillan; New York: St. Martin's Press, 1973.

Repton, Humphry (1752–1818) Humphry Repton was a very fashionable estate improver. The author of *Observations on the Theory and Practice of Landscape Gardening* (1803), in which he advocated estate improvements, his later *Fragments on the Theory and Practice of Landscape Gardening* (1816) was more conservative, defending older ways of landscaping. Jane Austen had direct experience and knowledge of Repton's work. Her mother's cousin, the Reverend Thomas Leigh, called on Repton to improve his property at Aldestrop, Gloucestershire, in 1799. Jane Austen and her mother visited Aldestrop in 1806 and witnessed Repton's improvements. The rectory gardens were merged with the estate to create the effect of a house standing in a park. Thomas Leigh then inherited the larger estate of Stoneleigh Abbey in Warwickshire and again hired Repton to transform the landscape.

Repton is directly referred to in *Mansfield Park.* In the sixth chapter of the first book, Rushworth tells the garrulous Mrs. Norris that Sotherton Court "wants improvement . . . beyond any thing." Maria Bertram supports her fiancée: "Your best friend on such an occasion . . . would be Mr. Repton, I imagine" (53). In this instance, Mrs. Norris, and subsequently Edmund and Fanny, oppose improvements. Repton and improvements are advocated by a dubious character such as Henry Crawford, who wishes to change Thornton Lacey. His plans involving the moving of "the farm-yard" are a parody of a passage in Repton's *Observations* (241, Duckworth, "Landscape," 283). Radical improvements such as those advocated in Repton's 1803 volumes are not viewed positively in other novels. For instance, in *Sense and Sensibility,* Mrs. Dashwood's ideas for changes at Barton Cottage reveal her extravagance and selfishness (29–30), and John Dashwood's enclosing of Norland commons and the cutting down of old walnut trees to construct a greenhouse and a flower garden are frowned upon (225–226). In *Pride and Prejudice,* Lady Catherine de Bourgh attempts to compete with the elegance of Pemberley, her estate has been improved, through gaudy additions. In *Northanger Abbey,* General Tilney has obsessively furnished Northanger Abbey with modern, fashionable furniture, and the kitchen has the latest appliances. All this deflates the expectations of the heroine, Catherine Morland. In *Sanditon,* the old village undergoes transformation as a resort for the aging. Capitalist acquisitiveness benefits from the transformation.

Jane Austen's attitude toward Repton's ideas is somewhat ambivalent. Donwell Abbey in *Emma,* with its "abundance of timber in rows and avenues, which neither fashion nor extravagance had rooted up" (358,) is associated with the sturdy, positive reliable values found in her hero, Knightley. Yet although improvements are not allowed in his house, in his fields he applies the findings of the latest agricultural reports, drainage, and crop-rotation developments. In short, Jane Austen draws on Repton. She appears critical, yet seems aware that transformation is inevitable, to be viewed in the manner of Charlotte Heywood, the heroine of *Sanditon,* "with the calmness of amused Curiosity" (384).

BIBLIOGRAPHY

Austen, Jane. *Mansfield Park*. Edited by R. W. Chapman. *The Novels of Jane Austen*, Vol. 3. 3d ed. Oxford: Oxford University Press, 1988.

———. *Northanger Abbey and Persuasion*. Edited by R. W. Chapman. *The Novels of Jane Austen*, Vol. 2. 3d ed. Oxford: Oxford University Press, 1965.

———. *Pride and Prejudice*. Edited by R. W. Chapman. *The Novels of Jane Austen*, Vol. 2. 3d ed. Oxford: Oxford University Press, 1932.

———. "Sanditon." In *Minor Works*, edited by R. W. Chapman. *The Works of Jane Austen*, 363–427. London: Oxford University Press, 1963.

Duckworth, Alistair. "Improvements." In *The Jane Austen Companion*, edited by J. David Grey, A. Walton Litz, and Brian Southam, 223–227. New York: Macmillan, 1986.

———. "Landscape." In *Jane Austen in Context*, edited by Janet Todd, 278–288. Cambridge: Cambridge University Press, 2005.

———. *The Improvement of the Estate: A Study of Jane Austen's Novels*. New edition. Baltimore and London: Johns Hopkins University Press, 1994.

Richardson, Samuel (1689–1761) J. E. Austen-Leigh writes in his *Memoir* that Jane Austen's "knowledge of Richardson's works was such as no one is likely again to acquire." He adds, "Every circumstance narrated in Sir Charles Grandison, all that was ever said or done in the cedar parlour, was familiar to her; and the wedding days of Lady L. and Lady G. were as well remembered as if they had been living friends." In his "Biographical Notice," her brother Henry recorded that "Richardson, and particularly his last novel *Sir Charles Grandison*, ranked highest with her for fiction" (*Memoir*,: 71, 231).

Jane Austen's juvenilia and later work contain numerous references to the work of Richardson, regarded as the father of the novel form. In 1977, a manuscript play, "Sir Charles Grandison," was attributed to Jane Austen and reveals its author's close knowledge of the seven-volume novel. Her youthful dramatic compression of the novel exhibits its admiration for and parody of Richardson's plot. In this, a heroine, Harriet, is plunged onto the London marriage market. She attempts to avoid the designs on her of the villain, the well-connected Sir

Hargrave Pollexfen. She falls in love with the kind Sir Charles, who is socially far above her. He, however, is in love with a foreigner and struggling with his principles and desires—motifs that resurface in Jane Austen's novels.

Jane Austen's juvenilia, her elaborate puns and jokes, the emphasis on the drama's subtitle, "Sir Charles Grandison, or the happy man," draw attention to a repetitive phrase in Richardson's novel. The hero's happy state will be his marriage and married life—if this state is obtainable. "Scholars have traced multiple resemblances between *Sir Charles Grandison* and Austen's later works." There is, for instance, the development of Fanny Price's love for Edmund in *Mansfield Park* or the occurrence at Pemberley in *Pride and Prejudice*, when Elizabeth Bennet is much impressed by Mrs. Reynolds, the housekeeper's, high esteem for Darcy as a landlord—in this she mirrors a character and attitude in *Grandison* (Stabler, 45).

Austen's knowledge and admiration of Richardson is not limited to *Grandison*. In *Sanditon*, Sir Edward's "fancy had been early caught by all the impassioned, & most exceptionable parts of Richardsons; & such Authors as have since appeared to tread in Richardson's steps, so far as Man's determined pursuit of Woman in defiance of every opposition of feeling & convenience is concerned" (404). Writing to her sister, Cassandra, on September 15, 1813, she again displays intimate knowledge of textual detail found in *Sir Charles Grandison*, when referring to "Harriot Byron's feather"—in other words, to letter 22 of Richardson's novel— "A white Paris sort of cap, glittering with spangles, and encircled by a chaplet of artificial flowers, with a little white feather perking from the left ear."

In another letter to Cassandra written shortly afterward, on October 12, 1813, Jane Austen writes, "Like Harriot Byron I ask, what am I to do with my Gratitude?" This refers to letter 33 of Richardson's novel: "What shall I do with my gratitude! Oh my dear, I am *overwhelmed* with my gratitude" (Richardson's emphasis, *Letters*, 220, 419, 234, 423). Richardson's Harriot is also gently mocked in the juvenilia, in, for instance, chapter 5 of "Frederic & Elfrida," when Elfrida too succumbs to "a succession of fainting fits" (11). Also in the manner of Richardson's Harriot Byron, the heroine in "Love and Freindship" (Letter 8), "fainted alternately on a sofa" (86).

In her *Jane Austen's Art of Memory* (1989), Jocelyn Harris demonstrates Jane Austen's knowledge, and use of Richardson's *Pamela* (1740–41), in, for instance, *Emma, Northanger Abbey, Pride and Prejudice*, and *Sense and Sensibility*. For instance, Darcy follows the precedent set in *Pamela* by proposing to the same woman, socially below him, not once but twice. According to Austen family tradition, one of the author's nieces remembered seeing in the Steventon sitting room a bill for *Clarissa* (1747–48). As Harris observes, "Jane Austen adopted the stories of Eliza Brandon and her daughter Eliza Williams in *Sense and Sensibility*, with very little change from *Clarissa*." She also comments that in the third chapter of *Northanger Abbey*, Jane Austen notes "a letter from Mr. Richardson, No. 97, vol. II Rambler," after citing "as a celebrated writer has maintained, that no young lady can be justified in falling in love before the gentleman's love is declared" (Harris, 57, 132; *Northanger Abbey*, 29–30).

BIBLIOGRAPHY

Austen, Jane. *Jane Austen's Letters*. Collected and edited by Deirdre Le Faye. Oxford: Oxford University Press, 1995.

———. *Jane Austen's 'Sir Charles Grandison.'* Transcribed and edited by Brian Southam. Oxford, U.K.: Clarendon Press, 1980.

———. "Frederic & Elfrida." In *Minor Works*, edited by R. W. Chapman. *The Works of Jane Austen*. London: Oxford University Press, 1963.

———. *Northanger Abbey and Persuasion*. Edited by R. W. Chapman. *The Novels of Jane Austen*, Vol. 2. 3d ed. Oxford: Oxford University Press, 1965.

Austen-Leigh, J. E. *A Memoir of Jane Austen and Other Family Recollections*. Edited by Kathryn Sutherland. Oxford: Oxford University Press [World's Classics], 2002.

Harris, Jocelyn. *Jane Austen's Art of Memory*. Cambridge: Cambridge University Press, 1989.

Stabler, Jane. "Literary Influence." In *Jane Austen in Context*, edited by Janet Todd, 41–50. Cambridge: Cambridge University Press, 2005.

S

Scott, Sir Walter (1771–1832) Jane Austen wrote to her niece ANNA AUSTEN on September 28, 1814: "Walter Scott has no business to write novels, especially good ones.—It is not fair." She adds, "He has Fame & Profit enough as a Poet, and should not be taking the bread out of other people's mouths.—I do not like him, & do not mean to like Waverley [Scott's novel published in 1814] if I can help it—but I fear I must" (*Letters*, 277). In 1813, Scott was known to the reading public as a poet. *Waverley* and the novels establishing his reputation as a great novelist were published after 1814 and anonymously. A reviewer of *Waverley* asked, "Why a poet of established fame, should dwindle into a scribbler of novels, we cannot tell" (Todd and Bowden, 310).

Scott partly answered such a question in his unsigned review of *Emma*, dated October 1815, published in the March 1816 issue of the *Quarterly Review*. Scott's was the first major critical review of Austen's work and was the result of an invitation from JOHN MURRAY, the publisher and founding proprietor of the *Quarterly*. The great Sir Walter Scott, whose novels within the next decade or so would receive tremendous praise from Europe and North America and provide the inspiration for many operas, in his assessment of *Emma* "draws attention to detail—to the neatness, and point of the prose style, to the precision and finish of the character-drawing." Furthermore, as if he is justifying his own fiction, Scott "sees the relationship between these aspects of technique and the cre-ation of a fictional world which remains faithful to the events and situations in 'the current of ordinary life.'" In Jane Austen's *Emma*, there is "the modern novel." Southam writes, "the significance of this review, in the history of criticism as well as in Jane Austen studies, is the breadth of its perspective" (Southam, 1: 13).

Jane Austen did not view it with such hindsight. She wrote to John Murray on April 1, 1816, thanking him for the copy of the *Quarterly Review* he had sent her. She comments on the review: "The Authoress of *Emma* has no reason I think to complain of her treatment in it—except in the total omission of Mansfield Park." She added, "I cannot but be sorry that so clever a Man [the review was published anonymously] as the Reveiwer [*sic*] of *Emma*, should consider it as unworthy of being noticed" (*Letters*, 313).

Scott's commendation of Austen's *Emma* in the *Quarterly Review* does not constitute his only remarks on Jane Austen. Others are found in more private venues, such as his letters and journals. In a letter to his friend the Scottish dramatist and poet Joanna Baillie (1762–1851), dated February 10, 1822, he writes that Jane Austen is the "Authoress of some novels which have a great deal of nature in them—nature in ordinary and middle life to be sure but valuable from its strong resemblance and correct drawing" (Southam, 1: 106).

In a journal entry of March 14, 1826, Scott relates that he has reread for the third time the "very finely written" *Pride and Prejudice*. For Scott,

Jane Austen "had a talent for describing the involvement and feelings and characters of ordinary life which is to me the most wonderful I ever met with." He adds: "The Big Bow-wow strain I can do myself like any now going, but the exquisite touch which renders ordinary commonplace things and characters interesting from the truth of the description and the sentiment is denied me"—an enormous tribute from one great narrative writer to a fellow artist. Scott observes, "What a pity such a gifted creature died so early!"

Other journal entries and remarks attributed to Scott reinforce his great admiration for Jane Austen. In a journal entry for March 28, 1826, Scott writes that "the women do this better—Edgeworth, Ferrier, Austen have all had their portraits of real society, far superior to any thing Man, vain Man, has produced of the like nature" (Southam, 1: 106).

Jane Austen in her work did not ignore Sir Walter Scott's own achievement. His work is mentioned more than six times, twice in *Sense and Sensibility*, twice in *Persuasion*, and on three occasions in *Sanditon* and in *Mansfield Park*. In *Sense and Sensibility*, Elinor tells Marianne that Willoughby appreciates the "beauties" of "Cowper and Scott" (47). According to Edward Ferrars, Marianne, if she were very wealthy, would purchase "books!—Thomson, Cowper, Scott—she would buy them all over and over again; she would buy up every copy, I believe, to prevent their falling into unworthy hands" (92). A similar identification of Scott as a poet is found in *Persuasion*. Anne Elliot and Captain Benwick talk of "Scott and Lord Byron" (107). An alliance of Benwick with Louisa Musgrove, Anne considers, would lead to Louisa learning "to be an enthusiast for Scott and Lord Byron" (167).

In *Sanditon*, the references are also to Scott as a poet. His "beautiful Lines on the Sea," and lines from *Marmion* and *The Lady of the Lake* are cited. However, Scott is unfavorably compared with ROB-ERT BURNS: "If Scott *has* a fault, it is the want of Passion—Tender, Elegant, Descriptive—but *Tame*" (Jane Austen's emphasis, 396–397). In *Mansfield Park*, Scott's *Marmion* (1808) is alluded to in chapter 7 with the arrival of the harp (64). Jane Austen sent a copy of *Marmion*, of which she herself had

mixed feelings, to her brother Charles when he was serving in the navy in Bermuda (Knox-Shaw, 223). In chapter 9 of *Mansfield Park*, Fanny cites from the description of Melrose Abbey in the second canto of Scott's best-selling poem *The Lay of the Last Minstrel*: "blown by the night wind of Heaven . . . [a] Scottish monarch sleeps below" (86). Jane Austen's fictional references are all tributes to Scott's poetic achievements: His greatness as a novelist did not fully emerge until after Jane Austen's death.

BIBLIOGRAPHY

Austen, Jane. *Jane Austen's Letters*. Collected and edited by Deirdre Le Faye. 3d ed. Oxford: Oxford University Press, 1995.

———. *Mansfield Park*. Edited by R. W. Chapman. *The Novels of Jane Austen*, Vol. 3. 3d ed. Oxford, U.K.: Clarendon Press, 1988 reprint.

———. *Northanger Abbey and Persuasion*. Edited by R. W. Chapman. *The Novels of Jane Austen*, Vol. 5. 3d ed. London: Oxford University Press, 1965.

———. *Sanditon*. In *Minor Works*, edited by R. W. Chapman. *The Novels of Jane Austen*, Vol. 6. London: Oxford University Press, 1963.

———. *Sense and Sensibility*. Edited by R. W. Chapman. *The Novels of Jane Austen*, Vol. 5. 3d ed. London: Oxford University Press, 1943 impression.

Knox-Shaw, Peter. *Jane Austen and the Enlightenment*. Cambridge: Cambridge University Press, 2004.

Southam, Brian C. *Jane Austen: Volume 1, 1811–1870: The Critical Heritage*. London and New York: Routledge, 1979.

Todd, William B., and Ann Bowden. *Sir Walter Scott: a bibliographical history*. New Castle, Del.: Oak Knoll Press, 1998.

Shakespeare, William (1564–1616) GEORGE HENRY LEWES, writing in *Fraser's Magazine* in December 1847, accords Jane Austen a very high accolade. She is "a prose Shakespeare" (687). Richard Simpson, reviewing Austen-Leigh's *Memoir* in the *North British Review* in April 1870, observes, "Within her range her characterization is truly Shakespearian; but she has scarcely a spark of poetry" (131). Such comparisons form a lengthy tradition in response to Jane Austen.

Shakespeare's comedies, histories, and tragedies are cited in her novels and other work. In her juvenile "History of England," she relies heavily on, for example, *Henry IV*. For instance, "Henry the 4th . . . falling ill, his son the Prince of Wales came and took away the crown; whereon the King made a long speech, for which I must refer the Reader to Shakespear's [sic] Plays, & the Prince made a still longer" (139)—in other words, *2 Henry IV*. In the final letter of "Love and Freindship," Laura tells Marianne: "One of our most admired Performances was *Macbeth*, in which we were truly great. The Manager always played *Banquo* himself, his Wife my *Lady Macbeth*. I did the *Three Witches* and Philander acted *all the rest*" (Jane Austen's emphasis, 108).

Northanger Abbey contains three Shakespearean quotations. The first is from *Othello*, the second from *Measure for Measure*, and the third from *Twelfth Night*. They follow one another in the first chapter of the novel. Jane Austen's heroine "from Shakespeare . . . gained a great store of information—among the rest, that" and Iago, Isabella, and Viola are then cited (16). All three provide signals to the reader of what is to happen in *Northanger Abbey*. In the first, Iago plots to use a handkerchief to frame Desdemona: Jane Austen's heroine must learn to recognize and to deal with human deceit, dishonesty, and duplicity. In *Measure for Measure*, Isabella is pleading with her brother Claudius to accept his fate, to die, rather than that she should sacrifice her honor by sleeping with Angelo. These lines should serve as a warning to Catherine when she meets the seemingly virtuous Isabella Thorpe. Her morality, it emerges, is to gain a wealthy and well-connected husband, and Isabella encourages her brother to behave in exactly the same manner. In *Twelfth Night*, Viola disguised as a man, describes the fidelity of a woman to Duke Orsino: "She never told her love, / But let her concealment . . . / Feed on her damask cheek." She, in the lines cited in *Northanger Abbey*, "sat," a word not cited by Jane Austen, "like Patience on a monument / Smiling at Grief" (*Twelfth Night*, 2.4.110–112, 114–115). Viola speaks these lines in disguise; Jane Austen is counseling fidelity and discretion in love to Catherine—advice she does not always follow.

Emma contains fewer Shakespearian citations, although Jocelyn Harris argues that the allusions of being in love found in the novel are based on *A Midsummer Night's Dream*. In the ninth chapter of the first book of *Emma*, Harriet Smith tells Emma, "The course of true love never did run smooth" (75). She is quoting Lysander's words to Hermia in the first act and first scene of *Dream* (line 134). Shakespeare's comedy "is a play about the imagination." Emma imagines matchmaking relationships for various characters; she indulges in schemes: "True love runs smooth in neither *A Midsummer Night's Dream* nor in *Emma* because of the blind self-delusion of love" (Harris, 169, 174).

General Shakespearean references are scattered throughout *Mansfield Park*. For instance, in the 13th chapter of the first book, Henry Crawford comments, "I could be fool enough at this moment to undertake any character, from Shylock or Richard III" (123). Both were perceived as villainous parts, very popular onstage, and should serve as signals as to Henry Crawford's character. Observations on Shakespeare are found in the final volume of the novel. In the third chapter, Henry Crawford confesses to having not "had a volume of Shakespeare in [his] hand before, since I was fifteen." He then remembers that he "once saw Henry the 8th acted" (338)—a play frequently performed in the late 18th century and early years of the 19th century, but less common on the stage today. Fanny has been reading passages aloud, the "'many fine speeches' by male characters, together with the absence of bawdy passages, probably also contributed to its popularity and its choice by [Jane Austen] for Fanny's reading aloud" (Wiltshire, ed., 714). Crawford's subsequently reading aloud from the play fascinates Fanny. The play contains, among its characters, Wolsey, the cardinal who found justification for condoning adultery; Henry VIII, whose lusts must receive religious sanction; and the wronged Queen. Each character has their reflection in *Emma*: Henry Crawford represents the lustful, Maria Bertram elements of the wronged Queen.

Crawford and Edmund discuss reading aloud and Shakespeare. For the former, "Shakespeare one gets acquainted with without knowing how.

It is a part of an Englishman's constitution." He continues reflecting that Shakespeare's "thoughts and beauties are so spread abroad that one touches them every where, one is intimate with him by instinct." Edmund, on the other hand, responds: "We all talk Shakespeare, use his similes, and describe with his descriptions," which sums up Jane Austen's use of Shakespeare. Edmund (a name for a righteous character echoing that of the "bastard son" of the Duke of Gloucester in *King Lear*) then accords his rival Crawford rare praise: "To know him [Shakespeare] in bits and scraps, is common enough; to know him pretty thoroughly is, perhaps, not uncommon; but to read him well aloud is no every-day talent" (338).

These are not the only references to Shakespeare in Jane Austen's work. For instance, in the first book of *Sense and Sensibility*, chapter 15, Mrs. Dashwood reminds Marianne that they have not concluded their reading of *Hamlet* (85). It is somewhat curious, given the extent that Shakespeare pervades her writing, that quotations from him are very difficult to locate in Jane Austen's letters.

BIBLIOGRAPHY

Austen, Jane. *Emma*. Edited by R. W. Chapman. *The Novels of Jane Austen*, Vol. 4. 3d ed. Oxford: Oxford University Press, 1986.

———. "History of England" and "Love and Friendship." In *Minor Works*, edited by R. W. Chapman. *The Works of Jane Austen*, Vol. 6. London: Oxford University Press, 1963, 139–150, [76]–109.

———. *Mansfield Park*. Edited by R. W. Chapman. *The Novels of Jane Austen,* Vol. 3. 3d ed. Oxford: Oxford University Press, 1988.

———. *Mansfield Park*. Edited by John Wiltshire. The Cambridge Edition of the Works of Jane Austen. Cambridge: Cambridge University Press, 2005.

———. *Northanger Abbey and Persuasion*. Edited by R. W. Chapman. *The Novels of Jane Austen*, Vol. 5. London: Oxford University Press, 1965.

———. *Sense and Sensibility*. Edited by R. W. Chapman. *The Novels of Jane Austen*, Vol. 1. 3d ed. Oxford, U.K.: Clarendon Press, 1943.

Harris, Jocelyn. *Jane Austen's Art of Memory*. Cambridge: Cambridge University Press, 1989.

Lewes, George Henry. [Jane Austen], *Fraser's Magazine* 36 (December 1847): 687.

Simpson, Richard. [Review of *Memoir*], *North British Review* 52 (April 1870): 131.

Wiltshire, John, "'The Hartfield Edition': Jane Austen and Shakespeare." *Persuasions* 21 (1991): 212–223.

Sheridan, Richard Brinsley (1751–1816)   Jane Austen knew the dramatic work of Sheridan from an early age. His well-known comedy *The Rivals* was performed at Steventon in July 1794. Jane Austen also probably played the role of Mrs. Candour in an 1808 reading performance or staging of *The School for Scandal* (1777) at Manydown Park (Wiltshire, 683). In her "History of England," she tells her readers to consult Sheridan's *The Critic* (1779) for further details of the life of Sir Walter Raleigh. In *The Critic*, "they will find many interesting anecdotes as well of him as of his friend Sir Christopher Hatton" (148). The line "We fainted alternately on a sofa" in "Love and Freindship" (86), has striking similarities with the stage direction in *The Critic*: "They faint alternately in each other's arms" (Pinion, 54).

The Rivals and *The School for Scandal* are two of the plays proposed for Mansfield performance in *Mansfield Park* (131). The choice is Inchbald's version of Kotzebue's drama, retitled *Lovers' Vows*. Sheridan himself adapted a Kotzebue drama, *The Spaniards*, under the title *Pizarro* (1794). At a dinner party, Sheridan is cited as remarking that *Pride and Prejudice* was "one of the cleverest things he ever read," and he recommended to a neighbor that she immediately purchase the new novel (Gilson, 26).

BIBLIOGRAPHY

Austen, Jane. *Mansfield Park*. Edited by R. W. Chapman. *The Novels of Jane Austen*, Vol. 3. Oxford: Oxford University Press, 1988.

———. *Mansfield Park*. Edited by John Wiltshire. *The Cambridge Edition of the Works of Jane Austen*. Cambridge: Cambridge University Press, 2005.

———. "History of England" and "Love and Friendship." In *Minor Works*, Edited by R. W. Chapman.

The Works of Jane Austen, Vol. 6. London: Oxford University Press, 1963.

Gilson, David. *A Bibliography of Jane Austen.* Winchester, Hampshire, U.K. and New Castle, Del.: St. Paul's Bibliographies and Oak Knoll Press, 1997.

Pinion, F. B. *A Jane Austen Companion.* London: Macmillan; New York: St. Martin's Press, 1973.

slave trade   There are two references to the slave trade in *Emma,* occurring close to each other. In conversation with Mrs. Elton concerning her own future, Jane Fairfax comments, "There are places in town, offices, where inquiry would soon produce something—Offices for the sale—not quite of human flesh—but of human intellect." Mrs. Elton replies, "Oh! my dear, human flesh! You quite shock me," and adds, "if you mean a fling at the slave-trade, I assure you Mr. Suckling [her wealthy Bristol-based brother-in-law] was always a friend to the abolition." Jane replies, "I did not mean, I was not thinking of the slave-trade" (300). In *Mansfield Park,* on the other hand, somewhat surprisingly, given the ambiguous nature of the source of Sir Thomas Bertram's family wealth, based on plantations in Antigua, there is only one overt reference. Fanny tells Edmund, "Did not you hear me ask him [Sir Thomas] about the slave trade last night?" (198).

The slave trade was topical. Through the work of Thomas Clarkson, William Wilberforce, and others, many of whom were Evangelicals (see CLERGY), the British slave trade was abolished in 1807. Slavery, however, was still practiced in the West Indies, including the Antigua sugar plantations. Bristol, referred to in *Emma,* had been a center for slave transportation to and from the West Indies.

The questions as to the foundations of the Bertram family fortunes have produced a lively critical debate. Claudia L. Johnson, in her *Jane Austen: Women, Politics and the Novel* (1998), asserts, for instance, that "the family fortunes [Sir Thomas] rescues" on his overseas trip "depend on slave labor in the West Indies" (96). Edward Said in his *Culture and Imperialism* (1993) argues that Fanny Price is a "transported commodity" and in a sense a slave. Sir Thomas's return from his West Indian possessions and the burning of the bound copies of *Lovers'*

Vows equates with the behavior of the slave master (106). Brian Southam in his "The Silence of the Bertrams" (1995) vigorously debates Said's contention "that the Bertram estate is 'sustained' by the West Indian plantations" (Wiltshire, lxxv). There is little doubt that the last has not been heard of readings focusing on the slave trade and feminism associating Sir Thomas's apparent imperialist treatment of women with the treatment of slaves on his plantations.

BIBLIOGRAPHY

Austen, Jane. *Emma.* Edited by R. W. Chapman. *The Novels of Jane Austen,* Vol. 4. 3d ed. Oxford: Oxford University Press, 1986.

———. *Mansfield Park.* Edited by R. W. Chapman. *The Novels of Jane Austen,* Vol. 3. 3d ed. Oxford: Oxford University Press, 1988 reprint.

———. *Mansfield Park.* Edited by John Wiltshire. *The Cambridge Edition of the Works of Jane Austen.* Cambridge: Cambridge University Press, 2005. [Wiltshire's introduction provides a succinct account of the critical debates concerning the novel.]

Johnson, Claudia L. *Jane Austen: Women, Politics and the Novel.* Chicago: University of Chicago Press, 1988.

Said, Edward W. *Culture and Imperialism.* London and New York: Vintage, 1994.

Southam, Brian C. "The Silence of the Bertrams: Slavery and the Chronology of *Mansfield Park.*" *Times Literary Supplement,* February 17, 1995, 13–14.

Southey, Robert (1774–1843)   The poet and writer Robert Southey (1774–1843) was the nephew of the Reverend Herbert Hill (1749–1828), who in 1808 married Jane Austen's childhood friend Catherine Bigg (1775–1848). Jane Austen visited her friend and the Reverend Hill after 1810 when he became a rector at Streatham, south of London. Southey visited the Hill family in 1813 and wrote subsequently to Sir Egerton Brydges (1762–1837): "You mention Miss Austen; her novels are more true to nature, and have (for my sympathies) passages of finer feeling than any other of this age." He adds, evidently aware of her relationship with his uncle, "She was a person of whom I have heard so well, and think so highly, that I regret not having seen her, nor ever having had an opportunity of testifying to her the respect which I felt for her" (*Letters*, 575).

Jane Austen evidently knew Southey's work but does not cite him in her novels. She writes to her sister, Cassandra, on October 1, 1808: "We have got the 2ᵈ vol. of Espriella's Letters, & I read it aloud by candlelight. The Man describes well, but is horribly anti-English. He deserves to be the foreigner he assumes" (*Letters*, 141). She refers to *Letters from England; by Dom Manuel Alvarez Espriella*, published in 1807 and regarded as the work of a Spaniard. It was in fact by Robert Southey, who uses the narrative device of the "imaginary foreign traveler as a way of challenging the English to face their own defects." Parallels have been drawn between a passage in Southey's letters: "the tribes of wealth and fashion swarm down to the sea coast. . . . The price they pay for . . . lodgings is exorbitant" and *Sanditon* (Doody, 352–353).

Writing to Cassandra on October 12, 1813, Jane Austen comments, "Southey's Life of Nelson;—I am tired of Lives of Nelson being that I never read any. I will read this however if" her brother Frank is mentioned in it. Frank is not mentioned in Southey's 1813 *Life of Nelson*. In a letter to her friend Alethea Bigg, written on January 24, 1817, Jane Austen comments: "We have been reading the 'Poet's Pilgrimage to Waterloo,' & generally with much approbation." She continues, "Nothing will please all the world, you know; but parts of it suit me better than much that he [Southey] has written before. The opening—the *Proem* I believe he calls it—is very beautiful." Jane Austen then comments to Alethea, whose sister Catherine is married to Southey's uncle: "Poor Man! One cannot but grieve for the loss of the Son so fondly described. Has he at all recovered it? What do Mʳ and Mʳˢ Hill know of his present state?" Southey's poems were published in 1816. Jane Austen's concern is not with his poems celebrating national victory over the French but with his *proem*. This contains a moving description of Southey's only (at this date) son, Herbert, who died in April 1816 (*Letters*, 235, 423, 327–328, 462).

BIBLIOGRAPHY

Austen, Jane. *Jane Austen's Letters*. Collected and edited by Deirdre Le Faye. 3d ed. Oxford: Oxford University Press, 1995.

Doody, Margaret Anne. "Jane Austen's Reading." In *The Jane Austen Companion*, edited by J. David Grey, A. Walton Litz, and Brian Southam, 347–363. New York: Macmillan, 1986.

Sterne, Laurence (1713–1768) There are at least two identifiable references to Sterne, Jane Austen's idiosyncratic fictional predecessor, in her work. In the fifth chapter of the first book of *Northanger Abbey*, Sterne's nonfictional achievements are included among those writers and works who are praised: "While the abilities of the nine-hundredth abridger of the History of England, or of the man who collects and publishes in a volume some dozen lines of Milton, Pope, and Prior . . . and a chapter from Sterne, are eulogized by a thousand pens," in contrast with a "general wish of decrying the capacity and undervaluing the labour of the novelist" (37).

Jane Austen's knowledge of *The Life and Opinions of Tristram Shandy* (1760–1767), the work for which Sterne is probably best known today, is demonstrated in a letter. She writes to her sister, Cassandra, on September 14, 1804, and refers to James, who "is the delight of our lives; he is quite an uncle Toby's annuity to us"—a reference to book 3, chapter 20 of *Tristram Shandy* (*Letters*, 93, 380). The most important allusion to Sterne, however, in Jane Austen's work is to his *A Sentimental Journey through France and Italy*, an account of the author's visit to France in 1765–66, published in 1768. In the first volume of *Mansfield Park*, chapter 10, Maria Bertram's frustration erupts: "I cannot get out, as the starling said" (99), as she faces the locked Sotherton gate. Her words echo those in the chapter named "The Passport, The Hotel at Paris" in *A Sentimental Journey*. Sterne's narrator Yorick has risked his life during wartime by going to Paris without a passport. As he reflects on the consequences if he is caught, he encounters and frees an entrapped starling. These words and Maria's are a plea for freedom. Subsequently in *Mansfield Park*, her behavior with Henry Crawford, who appears to release her from imprisonment, in fact banishes her from society.

BIBLIOGRAPHY

Austen, Jane. *Mansfield Park*. Edited by R. W. Chapman. *The Novels of Jane Austen,* Vol. 3. 3d ed. Oxford: Oxford University Press, 1988.

———. *Mansfield Park*. Edited by John Wiltshire. Cambridge: Cambridge University Press, 2005. *[The Cambridge Edition of the Works of Jane Austen],* lv–ivii, 670–671.

T

theater Amateur theatricals were popular in middle-class and upper-class homes during the latter half of 18th- and early 19th-century England. At Steventon, Jane Austen as a girl witnessed from 1782 to 1790 on a regular basis productions and plays that were read aloud in the family circle. The school Jane and her sister Cassandra attended from 1785 to 1786 at Reading was directed by a Mrs. La Tournelle, who was noted for her enthusiasm for the theater. In *Mansfield Park*, Jane Austen writes, "A love of the theatre is so general, an itch for acting so strong among young people" (121). Her taste, however, was not for the tragic: "One of Edward's Mistresses was Jane Shore, who has had a play written about her [a reference to Nicholas Rowe's 1714 drama], but it is a tragedy & therefore not worth reading" ("History of England," 141).

Among the plays performed at Steventon were Sheridan's *The Rivals* and Susannah Centlivre's comedy *The Wonder! A Woman Keeps a Secret* (1714), performed in 1785, for which Jane's father's "barn is fitting up quite like a theatre, & all the young folks are to take part" (cited Gay, 4). Another comedy performed was David Garrick's 1773 revision of the reworking of the Jacobean dramatists Beaumont and Fletcher's *The Chances*. In this, a philanderer is ultimately converted into constancy by a highly intelligent young woman. To mention one other drama performed during this period at Steventon, Henry Fielding's *Tom Thumb* was put on in 1788. It "is a rollicking farce with a cast of giants and midgets." There is also drunkenness and "large breasts" (Gay, 5).

Outside Sotherton, Jane Austen definitely saw performances in Bath in 1799 of Kotzebue's *The Birth-Day* in Thomas Dibdin's adaptation and a comedy by George Colman the younger, *Blue Beard, or Female Comedy!* There are parallels between Kotzebue's play and themes in *Emma*. The heroine is also named Emma, she is without a mother, and she spends much of her time looking after her ill father. Jane Austen lived in Bath between 1801 and 1806. Bath had an active theatrical life, and there is a detailed description of the Orchard Street Theatre in chapter 12 of *Northanger Abbey* (92). Generally, theater visits required a male escort; following the death of her father, Jane Austen would probably have visited the theater less than previously. It was in London, where she usually stayed with her brother Henry, that Jane Austen went to the theater. Her letters reveal that she saw Edmund Kean as Shylock in *The Merchant of Venice* at Drury Lane in 1814, and also went to Covent Garden on a regular basis. She wished to see the greater actress Sarah Siddons (1775–1831) but was unable to. She wrote to Cassandra on April 25, 1811: "I should particularly have liked seeing her in Constance [*King John*], & could swear at her with little effort for disappointing me." She and Henry went instead "to the Lyceum & saw the Hypocrite, an old play taken from Moliere's *Tartuffe*, & were well entertained" (*Letters*, 184).

In addition to her letters, there are also many references to the theater and plays in Jane Austen's works. The best-known example is in *Mansfield Park*, where preparations and rehearsals of Kotzebue's LOVERS' VOWS and its consequences play a formative role in the novel. Most of Jane Austen's fictional references are to SHAKESPEARE. There are, however, allusions to plays such as Colman's *The Heir at Law*, Susanna Centrelivre's *The Gamester*, and Richard Cumberland's *Wheel of Fortune* (*Mansfield Park*, 131). There are references in her works to 40 plays, and she must have been aware of many more.

Negative attitudes to the theater are found in the responses of Sir Thomas and Edmund Bertram in *Mansfield Park* (124–127). *Sir Charles Grandison*, a dramatic reduction in five short acts of Samuel Richardson's enormous novel, probably written when young, is the sole known example of Jane Austen's actual experimentation with the genre of dramatic composition. Dramatic metaphors, themes, and motifs are common in her juvenilia and novels, whether in the form of misunderstandings, disguises, duplicity, or allusion.

BIBLIOGRAPHY

Austen, Jane. *Jane Austen's Letters.* Collected and edited by Deirdre Le Faye. 3d ed. Oxford: Oxford University Press, 1995.

———. *Mansfield Park.* Edited by R. W. Chapman. *The Novels of Jane Austen*, Vol. 3. 3d ed. Oxford: Oxford University Press, 1988 reprint.

———. "History of England." In *Minor Works*, edited by R. W. Chapman. *The Works of Jane Austen*, Vol. 6. London: Oxford University Press, 1963.

———. *Northanger Abbey and Persuasion.* Edited by R. W. Chapman. *The Novels of Jane Austen*, Vol. 2. 3d ed. Oxford: Oxford University Press, 1965.

Gay, Penny. *Jane Austen and the Theatre.* Cambridge: Cambridge University Press, 2002.

travel and transportation   As her life and letters reveal, Jane Austen was a frequent traveler. She visited friends and relatives in various parts of Gloucestershire, Berkshire, Surrey, and especially Kent. She lived for extensive periods of time in BATH, Southampton, and LONDON. The creation of turnpike organizations and private acts of Parliament during the latter half of the 18th century for the creation and maintenance of turnpike gates and roads, especially along busy intercity roads, made traveling easier. Travelers, animals, carts, wagons, and other means of transportation were subject to a toll. The military and mail services did not have to pay. These improved roads are mentioned, for instance, in *The Watsons* (321), *Sanditon* (367), *Sense and Sensibility* (197), and *Pride and Prejudice* (275).

Travel, however, was still subject to all kinds of inconveniences. Many of these appear in Jane Austen's works: disgraceful inns (*Emma*, 193, 206); unwashed, smelly, or snoring passengers and bad weather (*Northanger Abbey*, 19). Parcels and trunks created difficulties, and passengers had to park and load them more often themselves. They were also a considerable problem to load onto the back of the coach (see, for instance, *Pride and Prejudice*, 213–214; *Mansfield Park*, 444). In spite of the tolls levied, even the main roads were not in good condition, and the side roads were even worse. A coach could lose a wheel, or overturn, as happens in *Sanditon* (364), and is feared in *Northanger Abbey* (19). In *Emma*, Mr. Woodhouse's anxiety concerning "the corner into Vicarage-Lane" is that fear of being overturned (280). Highwaymen were not uncommon, and their number became magnified in the imagination of frightened travelers (*Northanger Abbey*, 19). Travel took place mostly during the day. At night, the coachmen had limited vision and travel was undertaken in emergencies, during the full moon and at the time of balls or other social events (see, for instance, *Sense and Sensibility*, 33, and *Emma*, 128).

Inn trade along the major roads depended on the coach trade. The coachman rested or changed horses, and passengers needed somewhere to eat, wash, or relieve themselves, and exercise. Inns frequently served as stopping places for meals between destinations and often luggage became mislaid (see, for instance, *Northanger Abbey* 232, 235).

The main forms or means of travel were walking, horse, and various apparatuses dependent on the horse. Elizabeth Bennet enjoys walking, although her mother objects to her going to visit her sick sister on the grounds that Elizabeth "will not be fit to be seen" when she reaches Netherfield Park, and the snobs and the lazy who inhabit the pages of *Pride and Prejudice* also do not approve: "That she should have walked three miles so early in the day in such dirty weather, and by herself, was almost incredible to Mrs. Hurst and Miss Bingley" (32). The spoiled, self-indulgent Emma Woodhouse enjoys walking, telling her anxious father that she can "change [her] shoes, you know, the moment I got home; and it is not the sort of thing that gives me cold" (*Emma*, 127). Walking is by no means confined to the country. Jane Austen, when she lived in Bath, comments in a letter to Cassandra, written on April 8, 1805: "we do nothing but walk about" (*Letters*, 99).

Horses exist as a necessity in Jane Austen's work. They are ever present and in the singular and plural are mentioned 159 times. The crude John Thorpe claims to horse trade in *Northanger Abbey*. In *Emma*, the Box Hill trip is delayed owing to the lameness of a carriage horse (357). In *Mansfield Park*, Fanny Price is saddened by the loss of "her valued friend the old grey poney" (35). In *Sense and Sensibility*, Marianne accepts Willoughby's gift of a horse without considering the propriety of taking something from him, or the consequent expenses needed for stabling, grooming, and feeding the horse (58).

Water was another means of travel, and during Jane Austen's life span the canal system was extending throughout the British Isles, especially for carrying commercial goods, but it was too slow to attract passengers. If inland water travel was not really an option, sea travel was frequently used. The navy was an important factor in Jane Austen's life, and her brothers were engaged in naval duties. Sea journeys were a necessity for travel, for instance, to the Caribbean. Jane Austen's sister, Cassandra, lost her fiancé from disease contracted in the Caribbean, and in *Mansfield Park*, favorable trade winds bring Sir Thomas Bertram home earlier than anticipated. The sea and the navy form the background of *Persuasion*.

Travel on land, whether between or within towns, was carried out by various means, depending of course, on the horse. The various kinds of appliances or carriages used reflected social status,

wealth, and, in some instances, etiquette. A woman had to be accompanied. Jane Austen's letters reveal that she was joined by a sister, brother, or other relative on her journeys. In *Mansfield Park*, Fanny's lowly social status is reflected in the fact that she as a "little girl performed her long journey in safety" and alone from Portsmouth to Northampton (12). After she has encountered the wrath of the General, Catherine in *Northanger Abbey* is unceremoniously evicted from Northanger Abbey and sent home alone (225).

There was a hierarchy of vehicles based on rank, wealth, and fashion. At least seven are mentioned in Jane Austen's work. The most popular two-wheeled vehicle was the gig. This was drawn by a single horse and is all that the impoverished John Thorpe, Mr. Collins, and Sir Edward Denham in *The Watsons* can afford. Admiral Croft, on the other hand, in *Persuasion* uses one not for economic reasons but because he is uncertain on land and the gig was not difficult to drive. A more expensive version was one drawn by a pair of horses, the curricle. Willoughby drives Marianne to Allenham in his curricle, and Catherine Morland, finding herself in one with Henry Tilney, is "as happy a being as ever existed" (156).

Four-wheeled vehicles were more expensive and designated higher social status. The lightest, mostly drawn by two horses, was the phaeton. In *Pride and Prejudice*, Mrs. Gardiner considers the pleasures of driving around Pemberley in "a low phaeton, with a nice little pair of ponies" after Darcy and Elizabeth have married. Lady Catherine de Bourgh has her pale, sickly daughter Anne driven in one (168). A *landau* was heavier and with more refinements. It had a hood, or covering, at the front and the back, and it was totally open or closed, or half-open at the front or back. Its variant, the landaulet, or demi-landau, has one hood that folded at the back. At the end of *Persuasion*, Anne becomes "The mistress of a very pretty landaulette," (250), appropriate to her new position as the wife of the very wealthy Captain Wentworth.

Even larger and more accommodating of a greater number of passengers was the barouche. This carried six people, four of them inside and two on its box. The barouche is frequently used in

Mansfield Park (see, 77, 222). Even heavier, with a box and double hood, is a barouche-landau, much prized by the snobbish, status-conscious Mrs. Elton in *Emma* (see 274, 343). Other forms of transportation include the chaise, designed for three passengers and pulled by a number of horses (see *Pride and Prejudice,* 3, 30, 155). There is also the chariot; in *Mansfield Park,* one is owned by the aging Mrs. Rushworth and is associated "with true dowager propriety" (202–203)—it had a driver's box and could take a maximum of six passengers. There were many private vehicles around. General Tilney drives in a chaise-and-four, with liveried postilions, and "numerous outriders, properly mounted" (*Northanger Abbey,* 156).

Inside large towns such as Bath and London, those with money used either sedan chairs, the hack chaise, or the hackney coach. Urban travel had its own special problems. Streets frequently were narrow and dirty, and various objects including dirty water and the contents of chamber pots were flung from upstairs windows onto the street below. The absence of lighting was an additional hazard (*Northanger Abbey,*: 44, 91, 82; *Pride and Prejudice,* 72).

A phaeton, the kind of carriage most favored by high society.

A landaulet with Birch's, patent Roof, and Ackermann's patent Moveable Axles. *Ackermann Print, March 1818*

Speeds differed, depending on the conveyance. The slower vehicles probably averaged approximately four to six miles an hour. On the other hand, Darcy, who can command the best horses and carriages, travels "fifty miles of good road" and slightly more than "half a day's journey," which suggests that he is traveling at around eight miles per hour (178). A journey from Sotherton to Mansfield Park, a distance of 10 miles, takes around two hours. Probably the fastest time recorded in the novels is that of Willoughby in *Sense and Sensibility.* He makes the trip from London to Cleveland, near Bristol in Somerset, a journey of approximately 125 miles in 12 hours. Willoughby is anxious to see Marianne before her anticipated death, and he leaves his chaise only for a 10-minute "nuncheon," or snack, at Marlborough (318).

Improved roads and quicker forms of transportation allowed people to travel farther for leisure. In *Pride and Prejudice,* for instance, the Gardiners, who have prospered in trade, make a fateful visit to Derbyshire and visit stately homes, including Darcy's Pemberley. Tourist exploitation is a major thematic preoccupation in *Sanditon.* Bath prospered from its gift shops and tourist sites. London remained the great mecca, however, for a visit, tourism, and travel.

BIBLIOGRAPHY

Austen, Jane. *Jane Austen's Letters.* Collected and edited by Deirdre Le Faye. Oxford: Oxford University Press, 1995.

————. *Emma.* Edited by R. W. Chapman. *The Novels of Jane Austen,* Vol. 4. 3d ed. Oxford: Oxford University Press, 1986.

————. *Mansfield Park.* Edited by R. W. Chapman. *The Novels of Jane Austen,* Vol. 3. 3d ed. Oxford: Oxford University Press, 1988 reprint.

————. *Northanger Abbey and Persuasion.* Edited by R. W. Chapman. *The Novels of Jane Austen,* Vol. 2. 3d ed. Oxford: Oxford University Press, 1965.

————. *Pride and Prejudice.* Edited by R. W. Chapman. *The Novels of Jane Austen,* Vol. 2. 3d ed. Oxford: Oxford University Press, 1932.

————. *Sense and Sensibility.* Edited by R. W. Chapman. *The Novels of Jane Austen,* Vol. 1. 3d ed. Oxford: Clarendon Press, 1943.

————. "Sanditon" and "The Watsons." In *Minor Works,* edited by R. W. Chapman. *The Works of Jane Austen,* Vol. 6. London: Oxford University Press, 1963.

Hanaway, Lorraine. "Travel and Transportation." In *The Jane Austen Companion,* edited by J. David Grey, A. Walton Litz, and Brian Southam, 388–391. New York: Macmillan, 1986.

Olsen, Kirstin. "Carriages and Coaches" and "Travel." In *All Things Austen: An Encyclopedia of Austen's World.* 2 vols. Westport, Conn., and London: Greenwood Press, I: 107–137; II: 683–688.

Pinion, F. B. *A Jane Austen Companion.* London: Macmillan, 1973.

Rogers, Pat. "Transport." In *Jane Austen in Context,* edited by Janet Todd, 425–433. Cambridge: Cambridge University Press, 2005.

W

Whately, Richard (1787–1863) Richard Whately was one of the most important early commentators on Jane Austen and among the first to recognize her importance as a serious writer whose moral values are conveyed in fiction. A clergyman and theologian, he became in 1831 the archbishop of Dublin. Whately wrote many reviews and articles for the leading early 19th-century heavyweight journals. His unsigned, extensive sympathetic review of *Northanger Abbey* and *Persuasion* appeared in the *Quarterly Review* in January 1821, xxiv, 352–376. His extensive analysis and description of Jane Austen's technique, her facility in handling her plots, brilliance of characterization, and "moral lessons" are frequently found in subsequent writing on her work. Whately is also perhaps the first to praise Jane Austen's "vivid distinctness of description," and "minute fidelity of detail" (Southam, 95–96).

BIBLIOGRAPHY

Jane Austen Volume I, 1811–1870 The Critical Heritage. Edited by B. C. Southam. London and New York: Routledge, 1979, 19–20, 87–105.

Wollstonecraft, Mary (1759–1797) There is no evidence that Jane Austen read the work of Mary Wollstonecraft (1759–97). Wollstonecraft's *A Vindication of the Rights of Men* (1790), *A Vindication of the Rights of Women* (1792), *Letters Written During a Short Residence in Sweden, Norway and Denmark* (1796), and *Maria; or The Wrongs of Woman* (1798) are important documents in feminist history and the advocacy of women's rights. Wollstonecraft exposed double standards, of "Fundamentally different codes of morality for men and women" (Johnson, 14). Her husband, William Godwin (1756–1836), in his *Memoirs of the Author of the Vindication of the Rights of Women* (1798), exposed her child's illegitimacy, sensibility, and attempts at suicide. Late 20th-century feminist critics contend that Mary Wollstonecraft's life and work play an important role in understanding the background of Jane Austen's novels and place them in "the context of feminist ideas" (Kirkham, 157).

BIBLIOGRAPHY

Butler, Marilyn. *Jane Austen and the War of Ideas.* Oxford, U.K.: Clarendon Press, 1975.

Johnson, Claudia L. *Jane Austen: Women, Politics and the Novel.* Chicago and London: University of Chicago Press, 1988.

Kirkham, Margaret. "Jane Austen and Contemporary Feminism." In *The Jane Austen Companion,* edited by J. David Grey, A. Walton Litz, and Brian Southam, 154–159. New York: Macmillan, 1986.

Wordsworth, William (1770–1850) Somewhat surprisingly, there is only one reference to the work of the romantic poet William Wordsworth in Jane Austen's writing. In *Sanditon,* a specific Wordsworth poem is not mentioned, but his work receives Sir Edward Denham's highest praise. He comments, "Montgomery has all the Fire of Poetry, Wordsworth has the true soul of it." Robert Burns, however, has "Pre-eminence," and Wordsworth is not mentioned again in the conversation that follows with Charlotte (397–398).

Parallels have been drawn between *Persuasion* and Wordsworth's "Tintern Abbey" (1798). Both draw on concern with the past, memory, and change, with "the power of time and circumstance to transform our stories and ourselves." Similarly, the use of nature and its relationship to human destiny and psychology are found in *Northanger Abbey* and Wordsworth (Morgan, 367).

See also ROBERT BURNS, THOMAS CAMPBELL, and JAMES MONTGOMERY.

BIBLIOGRAPHY

Austen, Jane. *Sanditon.* In *Minor Works,* edited by R. W. Chapman. *The Works of Jane Austen,* Vol. 6. London: Oxford University Press, 1963, 363–427.

Morgan, Susan. "Jane Austen and Romanticism." In *The Jane Austen Companion,* edited by J. David Grey, A. Walton Litz, and Brian Southam, 364–368. New York: Macmillan, 1986.

PART IV

Appendixes

CHRONOLOGY OF AUSTEN'S LIFE AND WORKS

This chronology is indebted to Deirdre Le Faye, *A Chronology of Jane Austen and Her Family* (2006). The following abbreviations have been used: "*Chronology*" refers to Deirdre Le Faye, *A Chronology of Jane Austen and Her Family,* and *Letters* is for Deirdre Le Faye, *Jane Austen's Letters.* 3rd ed. (1995).

1775

December 16. Jane Austen born at Steventon, Hampshire, seventh child of Rev. George Austen (1731–1805), rector of Steventon and Deane, and Cassandra Austen, née Leigh (1739–1827).

1779

July 3. Jane Austen's eldest brother, James Austen (1765–1819), enters St. John's College, Oxford.

1781

Spring. A distant cousin, Thomas Knight II (d. 1794), and his wife, Catherine (1753–1812), of Godmersham in Kent visit Steventon and take a great interest in Edward Austen (1767–1852), Jane Austen's third brother.

December? Jane Austen's cousin Eliza Hancock (1761–1813) marries Jean-François Capot, comte de Feuillide (c. 1751–94).

1782

Summer? First mention of Jane Austen in Austen family tradition.

December. Austen children assist with family amateur theatrical production at Sotherton of Thomas Francklin's tragedy *Matilda.* This is the first of various plays performed over the next six years in the Austen home.

1783

Edward Austen is adopted by Mr. and Mrs. Thomas Knight II and begins to spend time with them at their estate at Godmersham, Kent.

March. Jane Austen, her sister Cassandra Austen (1773–1845), and cousin Jane Cooper (1771–98) attend Mrs. Cawley's boarding school in Oxford, and then in Southampton, until they succumb to a typhoid epidemic and return to Steventon in early September.

May 3. Rev. I. P. George Lefroy (1745–1806) moves into the neighboring parish of Ashe. His wife, Anne Brydges (1749–1804), known as "Madame Lefroy," becomes a close friend and mentor of the young Jane Austen.

1784

July. Austen family perform R. B. Sheridan's *The Rivals* at Steventon.

1785

Late spring. Jane Austen and Cassandra Austen attend Mrs. La Tournelle's Ladies Boarding School at the Abbey House, Reading, Berkshire.

1786

Edward Austen sets off on a European grand tour. He does not return home for two years.

April 15. Jane Austen's fifth brother, Francis (1774–1865), enters the Royal Naval Academy at Portsmouth.

Mid-December. Jane Austen and Cassandra Austen leave school to be educated at home.

December 21. Philadelphia Hancock (1730–92), Jane Austen's father's younger sister, visits the

Austens with her daughter Eliza and her son Hastings (1785–1801). The Austens and "older" visitors participate in Steventon theatrical performances.

1787–1788

Jane Austen starts writing "Juvenilia."

November. James Austen returns from France.

December 26–December 29. Susannah Centlivre's *The Wonder* is performed at Steventon.

1788

January. *The Chances* performed at Steventon.

March 22. *The Tragedy of Tom Thumb* performed. Jane Austen's eldest brother, James Austen, writes the prologue.

July 1. Henry Austen (1771–1850), Jane Austen's fourth brother, enters St. John's College, Oxford.

Mid-July–end July. Jane Austen and Cassandra Austen accompany their parents on a visit to the home of the girls' great uncle Francis Austen (1698–1791) at Sevenoaks, Kent.

Early August? The Austens return to Hampshire via London. This is probably Jane Austen's first visit to the city.

September 1. Jane Austen's "Sir William Montague" is dedicated to Cassandra Austen.

Mid-September. Eliza, her mother, and Hastings return to France.

December 22. Francis leaves the Royal Naval Academy and the following day leaves for the East Indies on the frigate HMS *Perseverance*.

December–January 1789. Performance of two farces at Steventon: Isaac Bickerstaff's *The Sultan, or a Peep into the Seraglio* and James Townley's *High Life Below Stairs*.

1789

January 31. James Austen and Henry Austen at Oxford begin to publish a weekly magazine, *The Loiterer* (until March 1790).

Spring? Jane Austen begins a lifelong friendship with Martha Lloyd (1765–1843) and her sister Mary (1771–1843) after their mother rents Deane parsonage.

June 7. James Austen is ordained at Oxford as a priest.

July 14. Mob storms the Bastille; French Revolution begins in earnest.

December 22. Frank is promoted to midshipman of the *Perseverance*.

1790

During the year, Eliza, her mother, and Hastings return from revolutionary France.

June 13. Jane Austen completes "Love and Freindship," which she dedicates to Eliza.

1791

March–April. Eliza's mother becomes ill with breast cancer.

July 20. Jane Austen's sixth and youngest brother, Charles (1779–1852), enters the Royal Naval Academy at Portsmouth.

November 6. Frank transfers from HMS *Perseverance* to HMS *Crown* and then, four days later, still in the East Indies, to HMS *Minerva*.

November 26. Jane Austen completes "The History of England," which she dedicates to Cassandra Austen.

December 27. Edward Austen marries Elizabeth Bridges (1773–1808) at Godmersham Park, about seven miles east of Canterbury, Kent, at a double wedding ceremony. At the same time, William Deedes (1761–1834) marries Sophia Bridges (1772–1844). They will have 19 children.

1792

January. Jane Austen writes "Verses with a Needlework Bag" for Mary Lloyd as the Lloyds leave Deane for Ibthorpe.

January 3. Jane Austen uses this date at the start of "Lesley Castle"—dedicated to her brother Henry.

February 26. Mrs. Philadelphia Hancock dies in London.

March 27. James marries Anne Mathew (1759–95), daughter of a general. Couple moves to Deane Parsonage in June.

April 26. Jane Austen in London and goes to the theater.

May 6. Jane Austen compiling "Volume the Third," copying into it "Evelyn" and "Catharine, or the Bower."

August. Jane Austen, back at Steventon, dedicates "Catharine, or the Bower" to Cassandra.

September–early December. Jane Cooper, Jane Austen's cousin (1771–98) stays at Steventon. Jane Austen probably writes "A Collection of Letters," dedicated to Jane Cooper.

September 21. French monarchy is abolished.

September 22. New French Republic is declared.

October 4. Jane Austen and Cassandra Austen attend a ball at Basingstoke, Hampshire.

Mid-October. Jane Austen and Cassandra Austen visit the Lloyds at Ibthorpe and attend a ball where they encounter the Misses Cox, an event recalled in Jane's letter of November 20, 1800 (*Letters,* 61).

December. Cassandra Austen possibly becomes engaged to Rev. Tom Fowle (1765–97), her father's former pupil.

December 11. At Steventon, Jane Cooper marries Capt. Thomas Williams (1761–1841). Rev. Tom Fowle conducts the service.

December 27. Frank, on promotion to lieutenant, leaves HMS *Minerva* and the next day, still in the East Indies, joins the HMS *Dispatch.*

1793

January 23. Birth of Frances Catherine Austen (Fanny Knight: 1793–1882) to Edward Austen and his wife, Elizabeth, at Rowling, Kent. Soon after, Jane writes "Scraps," dedicated to Fanny.

February 1. French Republican government declares war on Great Britain and Holland.

March–July 1794. Reign of Terror in France.

April 8. Henry Austen becomes a lieutenant in the Oxfordshire militia.

April 15. Birth of James Austen and Anne's first child, June Anna Elizabeth, known as Anna and subsequently Anna Lefroy (1793–1872).

June 2. Jane Austen dedicates "A Fragment" and "The Generous Curate" to Anna.

June 3. Jane Austen writes the final item of "Juvenilia," "Ode to Pity," and dedicates it to Cassandra Austen.

November. Jane possibly begins "Lady Susan," writing until 1795.

November 13. Frank returns to England from the East Indies.

December. Jane Austen and Cassandra Austen, probably with Frank, visit relations in Southampton and attend balls.

1794

February 22. Comte de Feuillide is guillotined in Paris.

May 10. Birth at Rowling, Kent, of second of Edward Austen and Elizabeth's 11 children, Edward (1794–1879), later known as Edward Knight II.

July. Jane Austen and Cassandra Austen, staying with their uncle and aunt, Rev. Thomas Leigh (1734–1813) and Mary (1731–97), at Adlestrop, Gloucestershire.

August? Jane Austen and Cassandra Austen visit Kent.

September 14. Charles leaves the Royal Naval Academy and goes to sea as a midshipman on HMS *Daedalus.*

October 23. Death of Edward's adoptive father, Thomas Knight II; estates are left to his widow, and, after her death, to be inherited by Edward Austen.

December 5. Jane Austen's father buys a small mahogany writing desk—her writing desk?

End of December. Henry Austen appointed Acting Paymaster of the Oxfordshires—retains this position until he finishes his military service early in 1801.

1795

Jane Austen probably writes "Elinor and Marianne," epistolary version of what became *Sense and Sensibility.*

May 3. James's wife Anne dies suddenly at Deane. Subsequently, James Austen takes the infant Anna to Steventon to be looked after by her grandparents and young aunts.

Early September. Tom Fowle, Cassandra's fiancé, becomes domestic chaplain to Lord Craven, whose regiment is shortly to leave for the West Indies.

Autumn. Jane Austen attending balls.

October 10. Tom Fowle makes will leaving £1,000 to Cassandra Austen.

December–January 1796. Cassandra Austen, probably staying with the Fowle family at Kintbury,

Berkshire, to take leave of her fiancé before he departs for the West Indies. Tom Lefroy (1776–1869), on his way to study law in London, stays with his uncle Rev. George Lefroy (1745–1806) at Ashe in Hampshire. He and Jane become romantically involved.

1796

Jane Austen subscribes to Fanny Burney's new fiction *Camilla* (5 vols) and annotates her copy.

January 9–10. Jane Austen's first extant letter, to Cassandra Austen, who is staying with the Fowles. She mentions Tom Lefroy and balls she's been attending.

After January 15. Tom Lefroy leaves for London.

January 19. Rev. Tom Fowle sails for the West Indies.

April 20. Jane and Cassandra visit their cousin Edward Cooper (1770–1835) and family at Harpsden, Oxfordshire.

June. Charles as midshipman under Capt. Thomas Williams (1761–1841) on the HMS *Unicorn* engaged in naval battles with the French off the Scilly Isles.

August 22. Jane Austen and others leave for London and then to Rowling, Kent, where she stays with her brother Edward Austen.

Mid-September. Jane Austen leaves Rowling for London.

October. Jane Austen begins writing "First Impressions" *(Pride and Prejudice)*.

November. James Austen proposes to Mary Lloyd (1771–1843) and is accepted.

1797

Napoleon becomes commander of the French army.

January 17. James Austen marries Mary Lloyd.

February 13. Rev. Tom Fowle dies off San Domingo, West Indies, and is buried at sea. News does not reach Cassandra Austen and the Fowle family until April.

August. Jane Austen finishes "First Impressions."

November. Jane Austen begins transforming "Elinor and Marianne" into *Sense and Sensibility.*

November 1. Jane Austen's father offers "First Impressions" to the London publisher Thomas

Cadell; the offer is rejected by return post, sight unseen.

Mid-November. Catherine Knight relinquishes Godmersham to Edward Austen and his family.

November–December. Jane Austen's first recorded visit to Bath. She, Cassandra Austen, and their mother stay with her mother's brother James Leigh Perrot (1735–1817) and his wife, Jane Cholmeley (1744–1836), at 1 Paragon Buildings.

December 13. Charles is promoted to rank of lieutenant.

December 31. Henry Austen marries Eliza de Feuillide in London.

December 1797–January 1798. Jane Austen introduced to Rev. Samuel Blackall (1770–1842) of Emmanuel College, Cambridge.

1798

April. Defense of the Realm Act passed: "information to be collected regarding the U.K.'s resources in terms of manpower, weapons, equipment and stores" *(Chronology:* 209).

May 2–4. Irish Rebellion begins.

Summer. Jane Austen probably begins "Susan" (posthumously published and titled *Northanger Abbey* by Henry).

Early August. Mrs. Knight leaves Godmersham, and Edward Austen and his family take over.

August 1–2. Decisive Battle of the Nile, at which Admiral Nelson is victorious over the French fleet. News of victory does not reach general British public until early October.

August 7. Jane's cousin Jane Cooper (Lady Williams) dies in a driving accident—her carriage overturns—on the Isle of Wight.

Late August. Rev. Austen, Jane Austen's mother, Jane Austen, and Cassandra Austen come to stay at Godmersham.

October 10. Fourth son, William (1798–1843), of Edward and Elizabeth born at Godmersham.

October 12. French army lands in Ireland.

October 24. Cassandra Austen remains at Godmersham; Jane Austen and her parents return to Steventon via Dartford, Kent.

November 17. Birth of James Edward Austen (1798–1874), first son of James Austen and Mary Lloyd.

James Edward, in 1869, writes the *Memoir* of his aunt Jane Austen.

1799

January 3. Frank promoted to commander and appointed to the HMS *Peterel* at Gibraltar.

January 14. Jane Austen and Cassandra Austen subscribe to Mrs. Martin's Basingstoke subscription library.

April. Rev. Thomas Leigh pays Humphrey Repton consultation fee regarding improvements at Adlestrop.

May 17–late June. Jane Austen and her mother visit Bath with Edward Austen and his wife. Stay at 13 Queen Square.

From June 19 till October 25, 1800, no extant Jane Austen letters.

Summer. Jane Austen probably completes "Susan."

August 8. Jane Austen's aunt Mrs. Leigh-Perrot charged with theft of white lace.

August 14. Mrs. Leigh-Perrot arrested and committed to jail at Ilchester in Somerset.

1800

Jane Austen probably completes burlesque play *Sir Charles Grandison.*

March 21. Frank captures two French ships in naval engagements near Marseille and is subsequently promoted to post captain.

March 29. Taunton Assizes trial of Mrs. Leigh-Perrot; jury unanimously acquits her.

October 23. Jane Austen walks to Deane, extant letters.

November 27. Jane Austen staying at Ibthorpe, Hampshire, with Mrs. Lloyd and unmarried daughters.

Late November–early December. Rev. Austen decides to retire and move to Bath. Jane Austen said to be very upset by the decision heard on return from Ibthorpe.

1801

January 14. Decision taken to sell Rev. Austen's library of about 500 volumes.

January 24. Henry Austen resigns his commission to become a banker and army agent in London.

January–February. Jane visits old friends Catherine and Althea Bigg (1775–1848, 1777–1847) at Manydown, near Basingstoke.

May. Mrs. Austen, Jane Austen, and Cassandra Austen leave Steventon for Bath. On the way they visit the Lloyds at Ibthorpe. They later stay with Leigh-Perrots at 1 Paragon Buildings prior to leasing 4 Sydney Place. James and family move into Steventon rectory.

May 27. Charles John writes that he has bought topaz crosses and gold chains for Jane Austen and Cassandra Austen.

Mid-summer June–September. Jane Austen and family holiday in the West Country, where tradition has it that Jane Austen had a romance between now and autumn 1804.

August 29. Frank appointed flag-captain of HMS *Neptune.*

End September. Jane Austen visits James Austen and family at Steventon.

October 5. Jane Austen returns to Bath.

October 9. Hastings de Feuillide dies at age 15.

1802

Most of first half of the year Jane Austen spends in Bath.

March 27. Peace of Amiens with France.

Midsummer. Jane Austen and family, with Charles, go to Dawlish, and probably Teignmouth, on holiday, also probably to Wales.

September 1. Jane Austen and Cassandra Austen visit Steventon.

September 3–October 28. Jane Austen, Cassandra Austen, and Charles stay at Godmersham with Edward Austen and his family.

November 25–3 December. Jane Austen and Cassandra Austen visit Manydown and the Bigg sisters.

December 2. Harris Bigg-Wither (1781–1833), proposes marriage to Jane Austen and she accepts him.

December 3. The following morning Jane Austen withdraws her consent. She and Cassandra Austen return immediately to Steventon.

December 4. Jane Austen and Cassandra Austen return to Bath.

Late in 1802 or early in 1803 Jane Austen revises "Susan" (*Northanger Abbey*).

1803

Spring. Via Henry, Jane Austen sells the copyright of "Susan" for £10 to the London publisher Crosby & Co., who promise immediate publication but in fact do not publish the novel.

April. Charles rejoins HMS *Endymion* as first lieutenant.

May 16. Napoleon breaks the Peace of Amiens.

May 18. Resumption of war between Britain and France.

July 4. Frank ordered to Ramsgate to command a troop defending the coast.

Summer. Troops of volunteers and militia rounded up to counter possible French invasion.

September 17?—mid-October. Jane Austen and Cassandra Austen stay at Godmersham.

October 17–18. Jane Austen and Cassandra Austen are at Ashe Rectory, where they stay with the Lefroys.

October 24. Jane Austen and Cassandra Austen return to Bath.

November 5. Jane Austen and family in Lyme Regis, Dorset; large fire breaks out in the town on the previous day.

1804

Probably in Bath, writes *The Watsons*, leaves unfinished.

May 2. Frank is back at sea as captain of HMS *Leopard* from May 22 until end of September, taking part in the blockade of Napoleon's fleet off Boulogne.

August–October 25. Jane Austen and family away from Bath.

August/Early September. At Lyme Regis. Jane slightly unwell early in September.

September 13. Jane Austen walks on the Cobb in the morning.

September 14. Jane Austen bathed again in the sea.

October 10. Charles promoted to command HMS *Indian* and to patrol American Atlantic seaboard.

October 25. Austen family returns to Bath and rents 3 Green Park Buildings.

November 2. Harris Bigg Wither marries Anne Howe Frith.

November 13. Birth of Edward's fourth daughter Louisa (1804–89) Jane Austen's god-daughter, at Godmersham.

December 16. Madame Lefroy dies after a fall from her horse.

1805

Jane Austen makes copy of "Lady Susan."

January 21. Jane Austen's father dies in the morning, at the age of 73.

January 26. Rev. George Austen is buried in the crypt of St. Swithin's Walcot, Bath. Father's death leaves Jane Austen's mother with some income, and Cassandra Austen has a small legacy from her late fiancé; Jane Austen, however, is dependent on others.

March 25. Mrs. Austen and daughters move to temporary lodgings at 25 Gay Street, Bath, beginning of a period of uncertainty.

March 29. Frank takes command of HMS *Canopus*, Admiral Louis's flagship, and until August is part of fleet chasing French admiral de Villeneuve in the West Indies and back.

April 16. Mrs. Lloyd dies at Ibthorpe.

April 21. It is decided that Martha Lloyd should live with the Austens from now on.

June 18. Caroline Mary Craven (1805–80), daughter of James, born at Steventon.

June 19. Jane Austen and family arrive at Godmersham and remain in Kent until September 17.

September 18. Jane Austen and family arrive at Worthing in Sussex, after spending a few hours in Brighton. They remain in Worthing until at least early November.

October 21. Battle of Trafalgar, defeat of French fleet, death of Nelson: Frank, on escort duties near Malta, just misses the battle.

1806

January 3. Jane Austen arrives at Steventon, where she spends most of January.

January 30. Jane Austen and Cassandra Austen go to Manydown to stay with the Bigg sisters.

February 24. Jane and Cassandra Austen return to Steventon.

March 13. Jane and Cassandra leave for Bath to join their mother in temporary lodgings in Trim Street.

July 2. The sisters finally leave Bath with relief and go to Clifton, Bristol, where Jane Austen writes "Lines to Martha Lloyd."

End of July. Jane and Cassandra Austen go to Adlestrop to visit the Leighs.

July 24. Frank marries Mary Gibson (d. 1823, following the birth of 11th child) and in 1828 marries Martha Lloyd. On or about July 24, Jane Austen writes verses on her brother's marriage.

August 5–14. Jane Austen and family stay at Stoneleigh Abbey in Warwickshire with distant relatives.

August 14–late September. Austens stay with the Coopers at Hamstall Ridware, Staffordshire, where Edward, Jane Austen's cousin, has been rector since 1799.

October 4. Mrs. Austen and daughters join Frank and Mary at Steventon.

October 10. They take temporary lodgings in Southampton until March 1807.

End of October? Jane Austen has whooping cough.

November 16. Edward's sixth daughter, Cassandra Jane (1806–34), born at Godmersham.

1807

January. Cassandra Austen spends more time at Godmersham helping Edward's growing family. Returns to Southampton in March.

March 10–March 11? Jane Austen, her mother, Cassandra Austen (later), Frank, and Frank's wife move into a house in Castle Square, Southampton.

March 23. Frank becomes commander of HMS *St. Albans* on convoy duty to the East Indies and China.

April 27. Southampton. The birth of Mary Jane (1807–36), the eldest daughter of Frank and Mary Gibson. Around this time, Jane Austen writes the verse "On Sir Home Popham's Sentence, April 1807."

May 18. Charles Austen marries Fanny Palmer (1790–1814) in Bermuda.

June 22. Frank and *St. Albans* leave Portsmouth for the Cape of Good Hope.

September 1–September 11. Jane Austen and Cassandra Austen with Mrs. Austen at Chawton,

Hampshire, for a family gathering organized by Edward Austen at Chawton Great House.

September 12. They return to Southampton.

Late December 1807?–early 1808. Jane Austen and Cassandra Austen stay at Manydown.

1808

January 1. Frank and *St. Albans* at Spithead, Portsmouth, till early February, when they leave for St. Helena.

January 23. Jane Austen, Cassandra Austen, and Alethea Bigg due at Steventon.

February 4. At Steventon.

February 25. Jane Austen and Cassandra Austen are staying at Kintbury with the Fowles.

May 15. Jane Austen is at Steventon with Henry.

May 16. Jane Austen goes to 16 Michael's Place, Brompton, London, with Henry.

June 14. Jane Austen goes to Godmersham.

June 18. Jane Austen visits Canterbury.

June 19. Charles, aboard HMS *Indian,* captures a French privateer in the West Indies.

June 23. Jane Austen goes to stay in Canterbury.

June 25. Jane Austen back at Godmersham.

July 8. Edward Austen and Jane Austen set off for Southampton, spending the night in Guildford.

July 9. Arrive back in Southampton, where Jane Austen remains until April 1809.

August 12. Frank and *St. Albans* to carry supplies and officers to Portugal at the start of the Peninsular War.

August 26. Jane Austen writes verses "To Miss Bigg . . ." and "On the same occasion—but not sent—."

September 2. Frank back at Spithead and Portsmouth Harbor.

September 28. Cassandra Austen arrives at Godmersham for a lengthy visit. Birth of Edward's sixth son and 11th child, Brook John (1808–78).

October 10. Mrs. Edward Austen, Elizabeth, dies suddenly at Godmersham.

Late October. Edward Austen offers his mother and sisters a house either near Godmersham or at Chawton; they choose Chawton Cottage.

October 25. At Manydown, Jane Austen's friend Catherine Bigg marries Rev. Herbert Hill (1749–1828).

December 16. Fourth anniversary of Mrs. Lefroy's death and Jane Austen's 33rd birthday. She writes the verses "To the Memory of Mrs. Lefroy."

1809

Early part of the year, Jane Austen remains at Southampton.

April 5. Using the name "Mrs. Ashton Dennis," Jane Austen writes unsuccessfully to Crosby & Co. in an attempt to get them to publish "Susan." They have had the ms. since spring 1803. Jane Austen offers to send another copy if they have mislaid it.

April 8. Richard Crosby replies that he will sell the ms. back for £10 but will prevent anyone else from publishing it.

May 15–June 30. Jane Austen at Godmersham.

July 7. Mrs. Austen, Jane Austen, and Cassandra Austen move from Southampton to Chawton, where during her "first year of residence" Jane Austen "revises *Sense and Sensibility* with a view to publication and possibly works on 'First Impressions' as well, converting it into *Pride and Prejudice*" (*Chronology:* 370).

July 26. Jane Austen composes a verse letter to Frank congratulating him on the birth on July 12 of his first son (Francis-William, 1809–1858).

July 26, 1809–April 18, 1811. Absence of extant letters from Jane Austen.

1810

Jane Austen continues to revise *Sense and Sensibility.*

May 10. Charles is promoted to the rank of post-captain and receives command of HMS *Swiftsure.*

July–August. Jane Austen and Cassandra Austen visit Manydown and Steventon.

August 1. Frank returns on HMS *St. Albans* from the China seas.

1811

"Probably during the early months" of the year "*Sense and Sensibility* is accepted for publication on commission by Thomas Egerton" (*Chronology:* 395).

February. Jane Austen is at Chawton. She writes brief verses "Lines on Maria Beckford" and probably begins *Mansfield Park.*

Late March/Early April. Edward Austen takes Jane Austen to London to stay with Henry Austen at 64 Sloane Street, Knightsbridge.

April 16. Jane Austen sees Benjamin West's picture *Christ Healing the Sick* at the British Gallery (Pall Mall).

April 25. Jane Austen writes to Cassandra at Godmersham that she is busy correcting proofs for *Sense and Sensibility,* which she can "no more forget . . . than a mother can forget her sucking child" (*Letters,* 182).

End of April. Jane Austen writes the verse "On the Weald of Kent Canal Bill."

May 2. Jane Austen probably leaves Sloane Street, London, to visit her friend Catherine Bigg and her husband, Rev. Herbert Hill, at Streatham (south of London).

May 9. Jane Austen probably collected by James Austen and returns to Chawton.

July 9. Frank takes command of HMS *Elephant,* part of the British North Sea fleet.

August 1. Eliza Austen (1761–1813), Henry's wife, comes to stay.

August 3. Frank and HMS *Elephant* are off Portsmouth until early October.

August 8. Charles with his wife, Fanny, and two daughters come to stay at Chawton Cottage. Jane Austen hasn't seen him in almost seven years and has never seen the children.

August 15. Charles and family leave Chawton with Eliza, Henry's wife.

October 27. Jane Austen writes verses "On a Headache."

October 30. First advertisements for *Sense and Sensibility* published by Thomas Egerton in three volumes. Egerton prints 750 or 1,000 copies, and Jane Austen retains copyright for 28 years.

November 20. Charles appointed flag-captain and commands HMS *Namur,* a guardship.

November 26. Jane Austen and Edward Austen are at Steventon.

November 30. Jane Austen leaves Steventon to return to Chawton.

Winter. Jane Austen probably starts revising "First Impressions" (*Pride and Prejudice*).

1812

February. Anonymous review of *Sense and Sensibility* in *The Critical Review.*

May. Anonymous review of the novel in *The British Critic.*

June 9. Jane Austen and her mother visit Steventon.

June 17. The United States declares war on Britain.

June 25. Jane and her mother go to Basingstoke and then to Chawton.

October 14. Death of Mrs. Knight at White Friars, Canterbury.

October–early November. Henry Austen negotiates on Jane Austen's behalf with Thomas Egerton for the sale of the copyright of *Pride and Prejudice.* Henry's lawyer William Seymour considers proposing to Jane Austen.

November. Jane Austen writes verse "A Middle-Aged Flirt."

November 10. Official confirmation of Edward's change of name from Austen to Knight.

November 29. Jane Austen confirms in a letter to Martha Lloyd that Egerton has purchased the copyright of *Pride and Prejudice* (*Letters*, 197).

November–December–January 1813. Jane Austen correcting proofs of *Pride and Prejudice.*

1813

January 27. Jane Austen receives her first copy of *Pride and Prejudice.*

January 28. Official publication date, 3 vols., price 18s, possibly 1,500 copies printed.

January 29. Jane Austen working on *Mansfield Park.*

Early February. Anonymous review of *Pride and Prejudice* in *The British Critic*; the novel is a great success.

February 6. Jane Austen walks to Alton in a high wind that makes her cold worse.

February 14. Severe weather at Chawton.

April 22. Edward Austen takes Jane Austen to London after receiving a report of the deteriorating health of Eliza, Henry's wife.

April 24. Eliza dies.

May 1. Jane Austen returns to Chawton Cottage.

May 16. Jane Austen dines with family at Chawton Great House.

May 19. Henry Austen and Jane Austen return to London, stopping at Guildford, Esher, and Kingston before reaching Sloane Street.

May 21. Henry Austen takes Jane Austen to the exhibition of watercolors at the Spring Gardens.

May 24. Henry Austen and Jane Austen go to Somerset House Art Exhibition and to the Reynolds exhibition in Pall Mall.

May 26. They return to Chawton, via Windsor, Henley, Reading, and Steventon.

May 28. At Steventon.

June–September. Henry Austen leaves Sloane Street to live over his bank at 10 Henrietta Street.

June 1. Jane Austen returns to Chawton Cottage, probably to finish *Mansfield Park.*

June 5. Jane Austen reads *Pride and Prejudice* to her niece Fanny Catherine Knight.

July. Jane Austen probably completes *Mansfield Park* at Chawton Cottage.

July 6. In a letter to Frank, Jane Austen tells him that every copy of *Sense and Sensibility* has been sold, with a profit of £140 to her and that she is working on another book. She has used the names of two of his ships and will remove them if he objects—he does not (*Letters*, 214–217).

September 14. Jane Austen and family leave Chawton for a London theater visit. Jane Austen stays with Henry Austen at 10 Henrietta Street. Henry Austen breaks confidence about Jane Austen's authorship.

September 15. Jane Austen shops, visits the dentist, and goes to Covent Garden Theater.

September 16. Shopping and another visit to the dentist.

September 17. To Godmersham: Jane Austen's first visit since 1809.

September 23. Jane Austen has suffered from facial pain but apparently is better.

September 25. *Sense and Sensibility* to receive a second edition.

September 30. Jane Austen with her niece Fanny Catherine visits the local poor.

Early October. In London, Jane Austen's publisher Egerton prints a second edition of *Pride and Prejudice*, priced at 18s in three vols.

October 22. Jane Austen visits Canterbury.

November? Mansfield Park is accepted for publication by Egerton.

November 2. Jane Austen again visits Canterbury.

November 15. James Austen is back in London.

December 21. Jane Austen returns to Chawton.

1814

January 21. Jane Austen starts writing *Emma* at Chawton.

February. Jane Austen probably is correcting proofs for *Mansfield Park.*

March 1. Henry Austen takes Jane Austen to London, going via Farnham and Guildford to Cobham, where they spend the night. "En route [Henry] starts to read *Mansfield Park*" (*Chronology*: 473).

March 2. Following breakfast at Kingston, they reach Henrietta Street.

March 5. They see Edmund Kean as Shylock in *The Merchant of Venice* at Drury Lane "& were delighted!" (*Chronology*, 474).

March 9. Jane Austen writes to Cassandra, "Henry has finished Mansfield Park & his approbation has not lessened" (*Letters*, 261).

Early April. Jane Austen leaves London with Cassandra, breaks off return journey to Chawton to visit Catherine (Bigg) Hill at Streatham.

April 11. Napoleon officially abdicates and is then exiled to Elba.

April 25. Cold and showery day, Jane Austen, Cassandra, and others dine at Chawton Great House.

May 7. Frank signs off from HMS *Elephant*, now on half pay, does not go to sea again until January 1845.

May 9. Publication of *Mansfield Park* by Egerton, at 18s for three vols., possibly 1,250 copies printed. Jane Austen's profit eventually is at least £320. At Chawton, Jane Austen starts keeping list of "Opinions of *Mansfield Park.*"

June 24. Jane Austen leaves Chawton for Great Bookham, near Leatherhead and Box Hill in Surrey, to stay with her cousins the Cookes, Rev. Samuel Cooke (1741–1820), and his wife, Cassandra Leigh Cooke (1743/4–1826), a novelist. Rev. Cooke calls *Mansfield Park* "the most sensible Novel he ever read" (*Letters*, 263).

June 25. Henry Austen moves to a new London address, 23 Hans Place, off Sloane Street, Chelsea.

July 8. Jane Austen probably returns to Chawton.

August 10. Jane Austen is at Chawton Cottage.

August 17. Still at Chawton.

August 22. Jane Austen goes to stay with Henry Austen at his new house in Chelsea.

September 2. Jane Austen drives from Chelsea to see the Hills at Streatham, also has viewed Benjamin West's painting *Christ Rejected,* which she prefers to his *Christ Healing the Sick.*

September 3. Henry Austen takes Jane Austen back to Chawton.

September 4. Jane Austen is probably back at Chawton Cottage.

September 6. Charles's wife, Fanny Palmer, dies aboard HMS *Namur.*

November 18. First edition of *Mansfield Park* sold out.

November 25. Jane Austen goes to London to stay with Henry Austen at 23 Hans Place.

November 30. Jane Austen and Henry Austen call on Egerton to discuss a second edition of *Mansfield Park*: Egerton refuses to publish one.

December 5. Jane Austen returns to Chawton.

December 24. The Treaty of Ghent officially ends war with the United States.

December 26. Jane Austen and Cassandra Austen go to Winchester to stay with Mrs. Heathcote (1773–1855) and her sister, Jane Austen's oldest friend Alethea Bigg.

1815

In Paris, Mme. Isabelle de Montolieu publishes her translation of *Sense and Sensibility.*

January 2. Jane Austen and Cassandra Austen stay with James Austen at Steventon.

January 11. Jane Austen and Cassandra Austen visit Ashe Rectory to stay with Rev. George Lefroy (1782–1823) and his family. The eldest son of Mme. Lefroy became the rector of Ashe, near Basingstoke, in 1806.

January 14. Jane Austen and Cassandra Austen return to Steventon.

January 16. They return to Chawton, Jane Austen writing *Emma.*

March. Napoleon escapes and resumes power in France; war breaks out again.

March 29. Jane Austen finishes *Emma*.

June 18. Defeat of Napoleon at Waterloo finally ends war with France.

July 30. Jane Austen copies out untitled poem by Lord Byron, calling it "Lines of Lord Byron, in the Character of Buonaparte."

August 8. Jane Austen starts *Persuasion* at Chawton Cottage.

August 21. Jane Austen probably goes to London with Henry Austen to negotiate the publication of *Emma*.

September 3. Jane Austen and Henry Austen back at Steventon.

September 5. Leaves Steventon.

September 8. Jane Austen at Chawton.

September 29. William Gifford, influential editor of the *Quarterly Review*, sends most favorable review of *Emma* to John Murray, the London publisher.

October 4. Jane Austen leaves Chawton for London with Henry, she intends to stay for a week or so.

October 15. Murray writes to Henry Austen "offering £450 for the copyrights of *Sense and Sensibility, Mansfield Park,* and *Emma* combined" (*Chronology*: 517).

October 16. Henry Austen falls ill.

October 20. Henry Austen is seriously ill; Jane Austen remains in London.

October 27. Henry Austen is recovering.

Early November. Prince regent sends his librarian, Rev. James Stanier Clarke (1764–1834), to call upon Jane Austen and invite her to visit Carlton House, his London residence.

November 3. Jane Austen replies to Murray's letter, saying that Henry Austen is too ill to reply and asks him to call at Hans Place.

Mid-November. Emma is included in Murray's list of publications "in the press": Jane Austen and Henry Austen reach agreement with him to publish an edition of 2,000 copies on commission, and a second edition of *Mansfield Park* (750 copies). Jane Austen spends the next few weeks correcting copy and proofs of *Emma*.

November 13. Jane Austen goes to Carlton House and is shown around by Rev. Clarke.

November 16. Clarke responds to Jane Austen's letter of the previous day and assures her that the prince regent expects *Emma* to be dedicated to him, also hopes she will write a novel with a clergyman as a hero.

November 24. Jane Austen correcting proof sheets of *Emma*.

December 11. Jane Austen sends Murray list of people who should receive dedication copies of *Emma* and details of the dedication page.

December 16. Jane Austen leaves Hans Place to return to Chawton. *Emma* advertised to be published this day but fails to appear.

December 21. Rev. Clarke thanks Jane Austen for the presentation copy of *Emma*.

December 23. Emma announced as published: 2,000 copies printed in three vols., price 1 guinea, title page dated 1816. At Chawton, Jane Austen starts compiling "Opinions of *Emma*."

December 25. Henry Austen is borrowing large sums from Edward Austen and others in the wake of bank closures and bankruptcy following the conclusion of the Napoleonic Wars and is desperately trying to stave off financial ruin.

1816

General post–Napoleonic Wars slump, social and political unrest, many bank failures. Publication of a first U.S. edition of *Emma* by Mathew Carey in Philadelphia. Early in 1816, Henry Austen purchases back the ms. plus the copyright of *Susan/Northanger Abbey* from Richard Crosby, paying £10, the original sum paid. Jane Austen changes the title to "Catherine" and makes other changes plus writing an advertisement explaining the delays in publication.

February 19. Second edition of *Mansfield Park* published by John Murray in a print run of 750 copies of three vols., priced at 18s.

February 20. Charles's ship HMS *Phoenix* totally wrecked off Asia Minor coast; he and the crew survive.

March. Review establishing Jane Austen's reputation as a major writer published in the *Quarterly Review*, 14, no. 27, dated October 1815; the anonymous author is Sir Walter Scott.

March 2. Henry's bank collapses. He is now bankrupt, and some family members experience substantial losses, especially Edward Austen (£20,000). Jane Austen's loss is relatively minimal (£25.7s), Cassandra's loss is £132.6s.6d.

March 27. Rev. Clarke writes to thank Jane Austen for the prince regent's presentation copy and tries to get her to write a historically based romance dealing with the House of Coburg.

April 1. Jane Austen replies to Rev. Clarke expressing her inability to write a historical romance.

April 22. Charles, at a court-martial for losing HMS *Phoenix*, is honorably acquitted.

May 2. Jane Austen probably writes "Plan of a Novel."

May 23. Jane Austen, who had not been feeling well for some time, accompanied by Cassandra, goes to Cheltenham Spa to take the waters. On the way there and back, they visit Steventon.

Early June. Jane and Cassandra Austen stay with the Fowles at Kintbury on returning from Cheltenham Spa.

June 11. At Steventon.

June 15. Jane Austen returns to Chawton.

July 8. Jane Austen is at Chawton, working on the original chapter 10 of *Persuasion*.

July 18. Jane Austen dates the canceled chapter of *Persuasion*.

August 6. Jane Austen finishes *Persuasion*.

August 28. Jane Austen is ill with back pains.

September 6. Jane Austen leaves Chawton Cottage after a brief stay; she probably works on "Evelyn" and "Catherine."

October 19. Murray records profit on *Emma* but a loss on the second edition of *Mansfield Park*, so all Jane Austen receives is £38.18s.1d.

December 17. Jane Austen feels too weak to accept an invitation to dine; Cassandra Austen, too, declines in order to be with Jane Austen.

December 20. Henry Austen is ordained at Salisbury and becomes curate of Chawton.

1817

Mid-January. Jane Austen visits Francis and his family in Alton.

January 27. At Chawton Cottage, Jane Austen begins writing *Sanditon*.

February 21. John Murray pays Jane Austen £38.18s.1d from profit on *Emma*.

Beginning of March. Terms of James Leigh-Perrot's will are a disappointment to Jane Austen's family.

March 13. Jane Austen writes Fanny Knight from Chawton: "Miss Catherine [*Northanger Abbey*] is put on the Shelve for the present . . . but I have a something [*Persuasion*] ready for Publication" (*Letters*, 333).

March 18. Jane Austen is too unwell to continue writing *Sanditon*.

April 6. Jane Austen tells Charles that she has been ill for some weeks and is made worse by the news of James Leigh's will.

April 13. Illness now confines Jane Austen to her bedroom; the local apothecary, Mr. Curtis, is unable to help, and Mr. Lyford from Winchester is called in.

April 27. Jane Austen makes her will, leaving £50 to Henry, £50 to Mme Bigeon (Henry's faithful French servant), and the remainder to Cassandra, the executrix.

May 24. Jane Austen leaves Chawton Cottage, accompanied by Cassandra, for Winchester, where they take lodgings in College Street.

May 27. Jane Austen writes to James Edward at Exeter College, Oxford, saying she feels better and not totally confined to bed.

May 28?–May 29? Jane Austen's last known letter, written from Mrs. David's at College Street, probably to her friend Mrs. Frances Tilson (1777–1823) in London (*Letters*, 343).

June 9. Jane Austen is gravely ill and in a hopeless condition.

June 19. Charles sees Jane Austen for what he believes to be the last time.

July 15. Jane Austen, feeling better, writes the poem "When Winchester races first took their beginning"; however, in the evening, she takes a turn for the worse and spends most of the time sleeping.

July 17. Jane Austen is taken for dead around 5:30 P.M.

July 18. Jane Austen dies in the early morning.

July 22. Public revelation in the *Hampshire Courier* obituary of Jane Austen that she is the author of her novels.

July 24. Jane Austen is buried in Winchester Cathedral; Cassandra Austen and Mary Lloyd remain at home.

September 10. Jane Austen's will is proved. Her earnings from her novels amount to £630. Adding the sale price of the five remaining copyrights in 1832 to the publisher Richard Bentley, her total literary earnings are more than £1,625.

December 20. Probable publication date of *Northanger Abbey* and *Persuasion* by John Murray, who prints 1,750 copies at 24 shillings for four vols. The title page is dated 1817: Henry's "Biographical Notice" of Jane Austen, dated 13 December, is included.

BIBLIOGRAPHY OF
JANE AUSTEN'S WORKS

This bibliography is arranged by genre and, within a genre, by date of publication.

A. Bibliography

Gilson, David. *A Bibliography of Jane Austen.* 1982. Reprint, with a new introduction and corrections by the author. Winchester, Hants., England: St. Paul's Bibliographies; New Castle, Del.: Oak Knoll Press, 1997.

B. Letters

Austen-Leigh, J. E. *A Memoir of Jane Austen and Other Family Recollections.* Edited by Kathryn Sutherland. Oxford: Oxford University Press, 2002.

Brabourne, Edward, Lord, ed. *Letters of Jane Austen edited with an introduction and critical remarks by Edward, Lord Brabourne.* 2 vols. London: Richard Bentley and Son, 1884.

Chapman, R. W., ed. *Jane Austen's Letters to Her Sister Cassandra and Others.* 2 vols. Oxford: Clarendon Press, 1932.

Le Faye, Deirdre, ed. *Jane Austen's Letters.* 3rd ed. Oxford: Oxford University Press, 1995.

Modert, Jo, ed. *Jane Austen's Manuscript Letters in Facsimile . . .* Carbondale: Southern Illinois University Press, 1990.

C. Novels

Emma. Edited by R. W. Chapman. The Oxford Illustrated Jane Austen. Vol. 4. Oxford: Oxford University Press, 1986.

———. Edited by James Kinsley. With introduction and notes by Adela Pinch and Vivien Jones. Oxford: Oxford University Press, 2003.

———. Edited by Richard Cronin and Dorothy McMillan. The Cambridge Edition of the Works of Jane Austen. Cambridge: Cambridge University Press, 2005.

Lady Susan. Edited by R. W. Chapman. Oxford, U.K.: Clarendon Press, 1925.

———. Edited by R. W. Chapman. In The Works of Jane Austen. Vol. 4, *Minor Works.* Oxford: Oxford University Press, 1986.

———. Edited by Christine Alexander and David Own. With illustrations by Juliet McMaster. Sydney, Australia: Juvenilia Press [University of New South Wales], 2005.

Mansfield Park. Edited by R. W. Chapman. The Oxford Illustrated Jane Austen. Vol. 3. London: Oxford University Press, 1988.

———. Edited by Claudia L. Johnson. New York: W. W. Norton, 1998.

———. Edited by James Kinsley. With an introduction and notes by Jane Stabler. Oxford World Classics. Oxford University Press, 2003.

———. Edited by Kathryn Sutherland. London: Penguin Books, 2003.

———. Edited by John Wiltshire. The Cambridge Edition of the Works of Jane Austen. Cambridge: Cambridge University Press, 2005.

Northanger Abbey and Persuasion, edited by R. W. Chapman. *The Novels of Jane Austen.* Vol. 5. London: Oxford University Press, 1965.

———. Edited by Claire Grogan. Broadview Literary Texts: Peterborough, Ontario, Canada: Broadview Press, 1998.

———. Edited by James Kinsley and John Davie. With an introduction and notes by Claudia L.

Johnson. Oxford World's Classics. Oxford: Oxford University Press, 2003.

———. Edited by Marilyn Gaul. A Longman Cultural Edition. New York and London: Pearson, Longman, 2005.

———. Edited by Barbara M. Benedict, and Deirdre Le Faye. The Cambridge Edition of the Works of Jane Austen. Cambridge: Cambridge University Press, 2006.

Persuasion. Introduction by David Daiches. The Norton Library: New York: W. W. Norton & Co., 1958.

———. Edited by Patricia Meyer Spacks. A Norton Critical Edition. New York: W. W. Norton & Co., 1995.

———. Edited by Linda Bree. Broadview Literary Texts. Peterborough, Ontario, Canada: Broadview Press, 1998.

———. Edited by John Davie. With introduction and notes by Claude Rawson. Oxford World's Classics. Oxford: Oxford University Press, 1998.

———. Edited by Antje Blank, and Janet Todd. Cambridge Edition of the Works of Jane Austen. Cambridge: Cambridge University Press, 2006.

Pride and Prejudice. Introduction by Tony Tanner. Harmondsworth, Middlesex, England: Penguin Books, 1975.

———. Edited by R. W. Chapman. *The Novels of Jane Austen.* Vol. 2 Reprint. Oxford: Oxford University Press, 1998.

———. Edited by Donald Gray. 3rd ed. A Norton Critical Edition. New York: W. W. Norton, 2000.

———. Edited by James Kinsley. With introduction and notes by Fiona Stafford. Oxford: Oxford University Press, 2004.

———. Edited by Pat Rogers. The Cambridge Edition of the Works of Jane Austen. Cambridge: Cambridge University Press, 2006.

[*Sanditon*] *Fragment of a Novel Written by Jane Austen January–March 1817.* Edited by R. W. Chapman. Oxford, U.K.: Clarendon Press, 1925.

———. *Somehow lengthened, by Alice Cobbett: a development of "Sanditon" (Jane Austen's fragmentary last novel).* London: Ernest Benn, 1932.

———. *An Unfinished Novel. Reproduced in Facsimile from the Manuscript in the Possession of King's College, Cambridge.* Introduction by B. C. Southam. Oxford: The Clarendon Press; London: The Scholar Press, 1975.

———. *[by] Jane Austen and another lady [Marie Dobbs].* Boston: Houghton Mifflin, 1975.

——— In *The Works of Jane Austen.* Vol. 6, *Minor Works.* Edited by R. W. Chapman. Reprint. Oxford: Oxford University Press, 1986, 363–427.

Sense and Sensibility. Edited by R. W. Chapman. The Novels of Jane Austen. Vol. 1. Reprint. Oxford: Oxford University Press, 1943.

———. Edited by James Kinsley. With introduction and notes by Margaret Anne Doody and Claire Lamont. Oxford: Oxford University Press, 2004.

———. Edited by Edward Copeland. Cambridge Edition of the Works of Jane Austen. Cambridge: Cambridge University Press, 2006.

The Watsons. Completed in accordance with her intentions by Edith [Jane Austen's great grand-niece] and Francis Brown. London: Elkin Mathews, 1928.

Sense and Sensibility with Lady Susan and the Watsons. Introduction by Q. D. Leavis. Illustrations by Philip Gough. London: Macdonald, 1958.

The Watsons. Completed by David Hopkinson. London: Peter Davies, 1977.

———. In *The Works of Jane Austen.* Vol. 6, *Minor Works.* Edited by R. W. Chapman. Reprint. Oxford: Oxford University Press. 1986, 314–363.

D. Juvenilia, Poetry and Other Works

Charades &c Written a Hundred Years Ago by Jane Austen and her family. London: Spottiswoode & Co., [1895].

Minor Works. Edited by R. W. Chapman. The Works of Jane Austen. Vol. 6. London: Oxford University Press, 1963.

'*Sir Charles Grandison.*' Transcribed and edited by Brian Southam. Foreword by Lord David Cecil. Oxford, U.K.: Clarendon Press, 1980.

"Verses." In *The Works of Jane Austen. Minor Works.* Vol. 6. Edited by R. W. Chapman. Reprint. Oxford: Oxford University Press. 1986. [440]–452.

Austen, Jane. *Catharine and Other Writings.* World's Classics. Edited by Margaret Anne Doody and Douglas Murray. Oxford: Oxford University Press, 1993.

"Verses." In *Jane Austen's Catherine and Other Writings.* Edited by Margaret Anne Doody and Douglas Murray. Oxford: Oxford University Press, 1993, 234–246.

Collected Poems and Verse of the Austen Family. Edited and with an introduction and notes by David Selwyn. Manchester, U.K.: Carcanet Press, 1996.

"The Juvenilia Press Editions" [facing title page]. *Lady Susan by Jane Austen.* Edited by Christine Alexander and David Owen. Sydney: Juvenilia Press, 2005.

Juvenilia. Edited by Peter Sabor. Cambridge Edition of the Works of Jane Austen. Cambridge: Cambridge University Press, 2006.

BIBLIOGRAPHY OF SECONDARY SOURCES

This bibliography is alphabetically arranged by author's or editor's surname.

Amis, Kingsley. "What Became of Jane Austen?" *Spectator,* October 4, 1957, 339–340. [Reprinted in *Jane Austen: A Collection of Critical Essays.* Edited by Ian Watt. Englewood Cliffs, N.J.: Prentice Hall Inc., 1963, 141–144.]

Auerbach, Emily. *Searching for Jane Austen.* Madison: University of Wisconsin Press, 2004.

Auerbach, Nina Joan. *Communities of Women: An Idea in Fiction.* Cambridge: Harvard University Press, 1978.

———. "'O Brave New World': Evolution and Resolution in *Persuasion,*" *ELH* 39 (1972): 112–128.

Babb, Howard. *Jane Austen's Novels: The Fabric of Dialogue.* Columbus: Ohio State University Press, 1962.

Beer, Frances, "Introduction," *The Juvenilia of Jane Austen and Charlotte Brontë.* Harmondsworth, Middlesex, England: Penguin Books, 1986, 7–19.

Bradbury, Malcolm. "Jane Austen's *Emma,*" *Critical Quarterly* 4 (1962): 335–346.

Bradley, A. C. "On Jane Austen." 1911. Reprinted in B. C. Southam. *Jane Austen: The Critical Heritage.* Vol. 2. London: Routledge and Kegan Paul, 233–239.

Burrows, J. F. *Computation into Criticism: A Study of Jane Austen's Novels and an Experiment in Method.* Oxford, U.K.: Clarendon Press, 1987.

———. *Jane Austen's* Emma. Sydney: Sydney University Press, 1968.

Butler, Marilyn. "History, Politics and Religion." In *The Jane Austen Companion,* edited by J. David Grey, A. Walton Litz, and Brian Southam, 190–208. New York: Macmillan, 1986.

———. *Jane Austen and the War of Ideas.* Oxford, U.K.: Clarendon Press, 1975.

Castle, Terry. Introduction to *Jane Austen. Northanger Abbey, Lady Susan, The Watsons, and Sanditon.* Oxford World's Classics. Edited by John Davie. Oxford: Oxford University Press, 1990, vii–xxxii.

Chapman, Robert W. *Jane Austen: Facts and Problems.* Oxford, U.K.: Clarendon Press, 1948.

Copeland, Edward, and Juliet McMaster, eds. *The Cambridge Companion to Jane Austen.* Cambridge: Cambridge University Press, 1997.

Cornish, Francis Warre. *Jane Austen.* English Men of Letters. London: Macmillan, 1913.

De Rose, Peter L., and S. W. McGuire. *A Concordance to the Works of Jane Austen.* 3 vols., New York and London: Garland, 1982.

Doody, Margaret Anne. "Jane Austen, that disconcerting 'child.'" In *The Child Writer from Austen to Woolf,* edited by Christine Alexander and Juliet McMaster. Cambridge: Cambridge University Press, 2005, [101]–121.

Drabble, Margaret. Foreword to *Jane Austen's Beginnings: The Juvenilia and* Lady Susan. Edited by J. David Grey. Ann Arbor, Mich., and London: UMI Research Press, 1989, [xii]–xiv.

Duckworth, Alistair M., *The Improvement of the Estate: A Study of Jane Austen's Novels.* Baltimore and London: Johns Hopkins University Press, 1971.

Emden, Cecil S. "The Composition of *Northanger Abbey,*" *Review of English Studies* NS. 19, no. 75 (August 1968): 279–287.

Emsley, Sarah. *Jane Austen's Philosophy of the Virtues.* New York: Palgrave Macmillan, 2005.

Farrer, Reginald, "Jane Austen, ob. July 18, 1817." *Quarterly Review,* July 1917. Reprinted in B. C. Southam, *Heritage.* Vol. 2, 245–272.

Fergus, Jan. "'My sore-throats, you know, are always worse than anybody's': Mary Musgrove and Jane Austen's Art of Whining." In *Jane Austen's Business: Her World and Her Profession,* edited by Juliet McMaster and Bruce Stovel, 69–80. London and New York: Macmillan Press and St. Martin's Press, 1996.

Fleishman, Avrom. *A Reading of Mansfield Park: An Essay in Critical Synthesis.* Minneapolis: University of Minnesota Press, 1967.

Folsom, Marcia McClintock. *Approaches to Teaching Austen's Emma.* New York: MLA, 2004.

Gay, Penny. *Jane Austen and the Theatre.* Cambridge: Cambridge University Press, 2002.

Giardetti, Melora. *Personal and Political Transformation in the Texts of Jane Austen.* Lampeter, Wales, and Lewiston, N.Y.: Edwin Mellon Press, 2003.

Gilbert, Sandra M., and Susan Gubar, *The Madwoman in the Attic: The Woman Writer and the Nineteenth Century Literary Imagination.* New Haven, Conn., and London: Yale University Press, 1979, 107–145.

Gilson, David, and J. David Grey. "Jane Austen's Juvenilia and Lady Susan: An Annotated Bibliography." In *Jane Austen's Beginnings: The Juvenilia and* Lady Susan, edited by J. David Grey, 243–260. Ann Arbor, Mich., and London: UMI Research Press, 1989.

Gilson, David. "Jane Austen's Verses," *Book Collector* 33, no. 1 (Spring 1984): 25–37; 34; no. 3 (Autumn 1985): 384–385.

Goetsch, Paul. "Laughter in *Pride and Prejudice.*" In *Redefining the Modern: Essays on Literature and Society in Honour of Joseph Wiesenfarth,* edited by William Baker and Ira B. Nadel, 29–43. Cranbury, N.J.: Associated University Presses, 2004.

Greene, Donald, "New Verses by Jane Austen," *Nineteenth Century Fiction* 30 (1975): 257–260.

Grey, David J., A. Walton Litz, and Brian Southam, eds. *The Jane Austen Companion.* New York: Macmillan, 1986.

Griffin, Cynthia, "The Development of Realism in Jane Austen's Early Novels," *English Literary History* 30 (1963): 36–52.

Halperin, John. "Unengaged Laughter: Jane Austen's Juvenilia." In *Jane Austen's Beginnings: The Juvenilia and* Lady Susan, edited by J. David Grey, [29]–44. Ann Arbor, Mich., and London: UMI Research Press, 1989.

Harding, D. W. *Regulated Hatred and Other Essays on Jane Austen.* Edited by Monica Lawlor. London Atlantic Highlands, N.J.: Athlone Press, 1998.

Hardy, Barbara. *A Reading of Jane Austen.* London: Peter Owen, 1975.

Harper, Heather. Introduction to *A Collection of Letters.* Edited by Juliet McMaster et al. Edmonton, Alberta, Canada: Juvenilia Press [Department of English, University of Alberta], 1998, ix–xviii.

Harris, Jocelyn. *Jane Austen's Art of Memory.* Cambridge: Cambridge University Press, 1989.

Herrle, Jeffrey. Introduction to *Jane Austen's Catharine or the Bower.* Edited by Juliet McMaster et al. 1999. Reprint, Edmonton, Alberta, Canada: Juvenilia Press [Department of English, University of Alberta], 2005.

Honan, Park. *Jane Austen: Her Life.* London: Weiderfeld and Nicolson, 1987.

Hubback, John Henry, and Edith Charlotte Hubback. *Jane Austen's sailor brothers, being the adventures of Sir Frances Austen, G.C.B., Admiral of the Fleet, and Rear-Admiral Charles Austen.* London: John Lane. The Bodley Head, 1906.

Hutton, Richard Holt. "Miss Austen's Posthumous Pieces," *Spectator,* 22 July 1871, 891–892.

Johnson, Claudia L. *Jane Austen: Women, Politics, and the Novel.* Chicago and London: University of Chicago Press, 1988.

———. "'The Kingdom at Sixes and Sevens': Politeness and the Juvenilia." In *Jane Austen's Beginnings: The Juvenilia and* Lady Susan, edited by J. David Grey, [45]–58. Ann Arbor, Mich., and London: UMI Research Press, 1989.

Jones, Darryl. *Jane Austen.* Houndmills, Basingstoke, Hamps., England: Palgrave Macmillan, 2004.

Jones, Vivien. *How to Study a Jane Austen Novel.* Houndmills, Basingstoke, Hamps., England: Macmillan, 1987.

Kaplan, Deborah. *Jane Austen among Women*. Baltimore, Md.: Johns Hopkins University Press, 1992.

Kelly, Gary. "Jane Austen, Romantic Feminism, and Civil Society." In *Jane Austen and the Discourse of Feminism,* edited by Devoney Looser, 19–33. New York: St. Martin's Press, 1995.

Kent, Christopher. "Learning History with, and from, Jane Austen." In *Jane Austen's Beginnings: The Juvenilia and* Lady Susan, edited by J. David Grey, [59]–72. Ann Arbor, Mich., and London: UMI Research Press.

Kettle, Arnold. *An Introduction to the English Novel*. London: Hutchinson's University Library, 1951.

Knox-Shaw, Peter. *Jane Austen and the Enlightenment*. Cambridge: Cambridge University Press, 2004.

Knuth, Deborah J., "'You, Who I Know will enter into all my feelings': Friendship in Jane Austen's Juvenilia and *Lady Susan*." In *Jane Austen's Beginnings: The Juvenilia and* Lady Susan, edited by J. David Grey, 95–106. Ann Arbor, Mich., and London: UMI Research Press, 1989.

Lambdin, Laura Cooner, and Robert Thomas Lambdin, "Humor and Wit in Jane Austen's Poems and Charades." In *A Companion to Jane Austen Studies,* edited by Laura Cooner Lambdin and Robert Thomas Lambdin, [275]–281. Westport, Conn.: Greenwood Press, 2000.

Lane, Maggie. *Jane Austen and Food*. London and Rio Grande, Ohio: The Hambledon Press, 1995.

Langland, Elizabeth. "*Pride and Prejudice*: Jane Austen and Her Readers." In *A Companion to Jane Austen Studies,* edited by Laura Cooner Lambdin and Robert Thomas Lambdin, 41–56. Westport, Conn.: Greenwood Press, 2000.

Lascelles, Mary. *Jane Austen and Her Art*. Oxford: Oxford University Press, 1939.

Leavis, Q. D., "A Critical Theory of Jane Austen's Writings," *Scrutiny* 10 and 12 (1941–1945). Reprinted in *Collected Essays,* Vol. 1, *The Englishness of the English Novel,* edited by G. Singh. Cambridge: Cambridge University Press, 1983.

Lewes, George Henry. "The Novels of Jane Austen," *Blackwood's Edinburgh Magazine* (July 1859): 99–113. In Southam, *Heritage*: I: 148–166.

Le Faye, Deirdre. *A Chronology of Jane Austen and Her Family*. Cambridge: Cambridge University Press, 2006.

———. *Jane Austen: A Family Record*. 2nd ed. Cambridge: Cambridge University Press, 2004.

———. *Jane Austen: The World of Her Novels*. New York: Harry N. Abrams, Inc. 2002.

Lewis, C. S. "A Note on Jane Austen," *Essays in Criticism* 4 (1954): 359–371.

———. "A Note on Jane Austen." In *Selected Literary Essays by C. S. Lewis,* edited by Walter Hooper. Cambridge: Cambridge University Press, 1969.

Litz, A. Walton. *Jane Austen: A Study of Her Artistic Development*. New York: Oxford University Press, 1965.

Lodge, David, ed. *Jane Austen's Emma: A Casebook*. Nashville, Tenn., and London: Aurora Publishers Inc., 1970.

———. "The Vocabulary of *Mansfield Park*." In *Language of Fiction. Essays in Criticism and Verbal Analysis of the English Novel,* edited by David Lodge, 94–113. London: Routledge, 1966.

Londry, Michael. "Amelia Webster." In Amelia Webster *and* The Three Sisters *epistolary "novels" by Jane Austen*. Edited by Juliet McMaster et al. Edmonton, Alberta, Canada. Juvenilia Press [Department of English, University of Alberta], 1993, 4–6.

MacDonagh, Oliver. *Jane Austen: Real and Imagined Worlds*. New Haven, Conn.: Yale University Press, 1991.

MacDonald, Gina, and Andrew F. MacDonald, eds. *Jane Austen on Screen*. Cambridge: Cambridge University Press, 2003.

Marsh, Nicholas, *Jane Austen: The Novels*. New York: St. Martin's Press, 1998.

Martin, Ellen E. "The Madness of Jane Austen: Metonymic Style and Literature's Resistance to Interpretation." In *Jane Austen's Beginnings: The Juvenilia and* Lady Susan, edited by J. David Grey, [83]–94. Ann Arbor, Mich., and London: UMI Research Press, 1989.

McAleer, John. "What a Biographer Can Learn about Jane Austen from Her Juvenilia." In *Jane Austen's Beginnings: The Juvenilia and Lady Susan,* edited by J. David Grey, [7]–25. Ann Arbor, Mich., and London: UMI Research Press, 1989.

McMaster, Juliet, "The Juvenilia: Energy versus Sympathy." In *A Companion to Jane Austen Studies,* edited by Laura Cooner Lambdin and Robert

Thomas Lambdin, [173]–189. Westport, Conn: Greenwood Press, 2000.

———. "Talking about Talking in *Pride and Prejudice.*" In *Jane Austen's Business; Her World and Her Profession.* London: Macmillan; New York: St. Martin's Press, 1996, 81–94.

———. "Teaching 'Love and Freindship.'" In *Jane Austen's Beginnings: The Juvenilia and* Lady Susan, edited by J. David Grey, [135]–151. Ann Arbor, Mich., and London: UMI Research Press, 1989.

———, and Bruce Stovel, eds. *Jane Austen's Business; Her World and Her Profession.* London: Macmillan; New York: St. Martin's Press, 1996.

Miller, D. A., *Jane Austen, or The Secret of Style.* Princeton, N.J., and Oxford: Princeton University Press, 2003.

Mooneyham, Laura G. *Romance, Language, and Education in Jane Austen's Novels.* London and New York: Macmillan and St. Martin's Press, 1988.

Mudrick, Marvin. *Jane Austen: Irony as Defence and Discovery.* Princeton, N.J.: Princeton University Press, 1952.

Nabokov, Vladimir. "*Mansfield Park* (1814)." In *Lectures on Literature,* edited by Fredson Bowers. New York and London: Harcourt Brace Jovanovich, Bruccoli Clark, 1980, 9–60.

Neill, Edward. *The Politics of Jane Austen.* London and New York: Macmillan and St. Martin's Press, 1999.

Olsen, Kirstin. *All Things Austen: An Encyclopedia of Austen's World.* 2 vols. Westport, Conn.: Greenwood Press, 2005.

Page, Norman. *The Language of Jane Austen:* Oxford, U.K.: Basil Blackwell, 1972.

Paglia, Camille. *Sexual Personae: Art and Decadence from Nefertiti to Emily Dickinson.* New Haven, Conn.: Yale University Press, 1990.

Palmer, Sally B. "Slipping the Leash: Lady Bertram's Lapdog." *Persuasion On-Line* 25, no. 1 (Winter 2004). Available online. URL: www.jasna.org/pesuasions/online/vol25no1/palmer.html.

Perkins, Moreland. *Reshaping the Sexes in* Sense and Sensibility. Charlottesville and London: University Press of Virginia, 1998.

Phillipps, K. C. *Jane Austen's English.* London: Andre Deutsch, 1970.

Pinion, F. B. *A Jane Austen Companion: A Critical Survey and Reference Book.* London: Macmillan and St. Martin's Press, 1973.

Poplawski, Paul. *A Jane Austen Encyclopaedia.* Westport, Conn: Greenwood Press, 1998.

Robbins, Susan Pepper. "Jane Austen's Epistolary Fiction." In *Jane Austen's Beginnings: The Juvenilia and* Lady Susan, edited by J. David Grey, [215]–224. Ann Arbor and London: UMI Research Press, 1989.

Rogers, J. Pat, "The Critical History of *Mansfield Park.*" In *A Companion to Jane Austen Studies,* edited by Laura Cooner Lambdin and Robert Thomas Lambdin, [71]–86. Westport, Conn.: Greenwood Press, 2000.

Rosenblum, Barbara, and Pamela White. *Index of English Literary Manuscripts.* Vol. 6, *1800–1900. Part I: Arnold–Gissing.* London and New York: Mansell, 1982.

Said, Edward W. "Jane Austen and Empire," In *Raymond Williams: Critical Perspectives,* edited by Terry Eagleton. Boston: Northeastern University Press, 1989, 150–164. Reprinted in Said, *Culture and Imperialism.* New York: Knopf, 1993, 80–97.

Schama, Simon. *A History of Britain.* Vol. 3, *The Fate of Empire, 1776–2000.* London: BBC, 2002.

Selwyn, David. *Jane Austen and Leisure.* London: Humbledon Press, 1999.

———. "Poetry." In *Jane Austen in Context,* edited by Janet Todd. The Cambridge Edition of the Works of Jane Austen. Cambridge: Cambridge University Press, 59–67.

Shannon, Edgar F. Jr. "*Emma*: Character and Construction." *PMLA* 71 (1956): 637–650.

Showalter, Elaine. "Retrenchments." In *Jane Austen's Business,* edited by J. McMaster and Bruce Stovel, 181–191. London and New York: St. Martin's Press, 1996.

Smith, Elton E. "Jane Austen's Prayers; Deism Becoming Theism." In *A Companion to Jane Austen Studies,* edited by Laura Cooner Lambdin and Robert Thomas Lambdin, [283]–289. Westport, Conn.: Greenwood Press, 2000.

Sodeman, Melissa. "Domestic Mobility in *Persuasion* and *Sanditon.*" *Studies in English Literature* 45, no. 4 (Autumn 2005): 787–812.

Southam, B. C., ed. *Jane Austen: The Critical Heritage.* 2 vols. London: Routledge and Kegan Paul. 1979, 1987.

———. *Jane Austen: Northanger Abbey and Persuasion: A Case Book.* London: Macmillan, 1976.

————. *Jane Austen and the Navy*. London: Hambledon and London, 2000.

————. *Jane Austen's Literary Manuscripts: A Study of the Novelist's Development Through the Surviving Papers*. New edition. London: The Athlone Press, 2001.

Spacks, Patricia Meyer. *The Female Imagination: A Literary and Psychological Investigation of Women's Writing*. New York: Knopf, 1975.

Speirs, Logan. "Sir Charles Grandison or the Happy Man. A Comedy," *English Studies*, 66 (February 1985): 25–35.

Spence, Jon. *Becoming Jane Austen: A Life*. London and New York: Hambledon and London, 2003.

Stokes, Myra. *The Language of Jane Austen*. Basingstoke, Hants., England: Macmillan, 1991.

Sulloway, Alison G. *Jane Austen and the Province of Womanhood*. Philadelphia: University of Pennsylvania Press, 1989.

Sutherland, Kathryn. [Explanatory Note.] *A Memoir of Jane Austen and Other Family Recollections*. Oxford: Oxford University Press, 2002.

————. *Jane Austen's Textual Lives: From Aeschylus to Bollywood*. Oxford: Oxford University Press, 2005.

Tandon, Bharat. *Jane Austen and the Morality of Conversation*. London: Anthem Press, 2003.

Tanner, Tony. Introduction to *Mansfield Park*. Penguin Classics Edition. Harmondsworth, Middlesex, England: Penguin Books, 1966. [Reprinted as an appendix to Kathryn Sutherland, ed. *Mansfield Park*, 2003.]

————. *Jane Austen*. London: Macmillan, 1986.

Trilling, Lionel. "Jane Austen and *Mansfield Park*." In *The Pelican Guide to English Literature*. Vol. 5, *From Blake to Byron*, edited by Boris Ford, 112–129. Harmondsworth, Middlesex, England: Penguin, 1957.

————. "*Emma* and the Legend of Jane Austen" [Introduction]. *Emma*. Boston: Houghton-Riverside, 1956, v–xxvi.

Vorachek, Laura. "'The Instrument of the Century:' The Piano as an Icon of Female Sexuality in the Nineteenth Century." *George Eliot–George Henry Lewes Studies* 38–39 (2000): 26–43.

Waldron, Mary. *Jane Austen and the Fiction of Her Times*. Cambridge: Cambridge University Press, 1999.

Watt, Ian P., ed. *Jane Austen: A Collection of Critical Essays*. Englewood Cliffs, N.J.. Prentice Hall, 1963.

Wiesenfarth, Joseph. *The Errand of Form: An Assay of Jane Austen's Art*. New York: Fordham University Press, 1967.

————. "A Likely Story: The Coles' Dinner Party." In *Approaches to Teaching Austen's Emma*, edited by Marcia McClintock Folsom, 151–158. New York: MLA, 2004.

————. "Austen and Apollo." In *Jane Austen Today*, edited by Joel Weinsheimer, 46–63. Athens: University of Georgia Press, 1975.

————. *Gothic Manners and the Classic English Novel*. Madison: University of Wisconsin Press, 1988.

————. "*The Watsons* as Pretext," *Persuasions* 8 (1986): 101–111.

Wilson, Edmund. "A Long Talk about Jane Austen." *New Yorker*, October 13, 1940.

Wiltshire, John. "Health, Comfort and Creativity: A Reading of Emma." In *Approaches to Teaching Austen's Emma*, edited by Marcia McClintock Folsom, 169–178. New York: MLA, 2004.

————. *Jane Austen and the Body*: "The Picture of Health." Cambridge: Cambridge University Press, 1992.

————. *Recreating Jane Austen*. Cambridge: Cambridge University Press, 2001.

Woolf, Virginia. *The Common Reader*. New York: Harcourt, Brace and World, 1925.

INDEX